Dynamic HTML Reference and Software Development Kit

PUBLISHED BY
Microsoft Press
A Division of Microsoft Corporation
One Microsoft Way
Redmond, Washington 98052-6399

Library of Congress Cataloging-in-Publication Data.
Dynamic HTML Reference and Software Development Kit / Microsoft
    Corporation.
        p. cm.
    ISBN 0-7356-0638-2
    1. DHTML (Document markup language) I. Microsoft Corporation.
QA76.76.H94D96   1999
005.7'2--dc21   98-55331
                                                                CIP

Printed and bound in the United States of America.

3 4 5 6 7 8 9   QMQM   4 3 2 1 0 9

Distributed in Canada by Penguin Books Canada Limited.

A CIP catalogue record for this book is available from the British Library.

Microsoft Press books are available through booksellers and distributors worldwide. For further information about international editions, contact your local Microsoft Corporation office or contact Microsoft Press International directly at fax (425) 936-7329. Visit our Web site at mspress.microsoft.com.

Acquisitions Editor: Eric Stroo
Project Editor: Wendy Zucker

Project Leads: Jacqueline Sowell, Lanie Kurata
Principal Compositor: Kristine Haugseth
Project Designer: Gwen Gray
Indexer: Laura Pinter
Group Manager: Marilyn Johnstone
Contributing Writers: Stephen Cote, Jeff Kirkham, Lanie Kurata, Matt Oshry, Peter Siegel, Jacqueline Sowell, Scot Vidican
Contributing Editors: Leslie Wilder, Sharon Neill
Reviewers: Lance Silver, Judy Nessen, Guy Smith, Steve Smith, Waudean Thomas, Bradley Yamauchi

Preface

This book, the *Dynamic HTML Reference and Software Development Kit*, is an indispensable tool for designing and developing compelling Web solutions using Microsoft® Internet Explorer. Although the book contains information applicable to all versions of Internet Explorer, its focus is on Internet Explorer 5 and the added benefits Dynamic HTML (DHTML) and related technologies provide for Web designers and developers.

You can use this book as a comprehensive reference for creating Web-based applications and content using Internet Explorer 5 features. The numerous samples in the book illustrate clearly how to incorporate these features quickly and easily into your Web site.

Note To get the most out of this book, you should already be comfortable with coding DHTML and Microsoft® JScript® (compatible with ECMA 262 language specification) or Microsoft® Visual Basic® Scripting Edition (VBScript).

What This Book Contains

This book contains three parts. The first part discusses the development of Internet Explorer and describes its latest application development features. The second and largest part presents detailed reference material, and the third part provides supplementary information in the form of appendixes.

Part I: The Power of DHTML

Chapter 1 outlines the development of Internet Explorer from version 1.0 to 5. Chapter 2 focuses on application development solutions made possible by the new technologies in Internet Explorer 5.

Part II: DHTML and Default Behaviors Reference

Chapter 3 contains object model references for Internet Explorer objects, properties, methods, events, and collections. These references include information about HTML, the Document Object Model (DOM), Cascading Style Sheets (CSS), and Cascading Style Sheets – Positioning (CSS-P). Each reference contains an Applies To section, which presents detailed information about object availability for different versions of Internet Explorer (3.0 through 5) and platforms (Win16, Microsoft® Win32®, Macintosh, and UNIX). Chapter 4 contains the HTML Component References, and Chapter 5 is dedicated to Default Behaviors references. Chapters 4 and 5 are relevant only to Internet Explorer 5.

Part III: Appendixes

The appendixes provide supplementary information that is useful for HTML and script authoring. The information ranges from general authoring tools, such as a list of color names and a table organizing CSS and CSS-P properties by property type, to a reference of Internet Explorer-specific command identifiers.

Book Conventions

A number of different conventions are used in this book.

Typological Conventions

Convention	Meaning
Bold	Indicates keywords, such as objects, properties, methods, and events, that must be typed as written—for example, the **alert** method. This formatting is also used with monospace to indicate a default possible value, such as `false`.
Italic	Specifies a placeholder for which you must supply a value or string. For example, if a syntax block contains *iHeight*, you need to replace *iHeight* with an integer representing the screen height, in pixels.
ALL UPPERCASE	Indicates an HTML attribute or element. For example, in `<IMG SRC="mygraphic.bmp">`, IMG is the element, and SRC is the attribute providing the file name for the associated image.
MiXed Case	Represents the case sensitivity of JScript (compatible with ECMA 262 language specification). For example, mixed case is a requirement for the **clearAttributes** method in *object*.**clearAttributes( )**.
`monospace`	Represents possible values, such as `center`; Boolean values, such as `true` or `false`; string values for method parameters, such as `ScrollbarDown`; or literal settings, such as `event.returnValue = false`. Example blocks illustrating code are also in this font.
...(ellipsis)	Stands for values that can be repeated. For example, more than one *sURN* string can be listed in <A URN = *sURN* ... >.
' '	Used for values already within double quotation marks as shown for the style color in: <P **onmouseout** = "this.style.color = 'black' ">.
" "	Used to specify a string with spaces, such as src.**title** = "this is bold text". Double quotation marks can also appear in HTML elements. For an example, see the preceding convention.

Convention	Meaning
I	Separates values, one of which can apply to a CSS attribute—for example, { **background-attachment**: `scroll I fixed` }.
I I	Separates composite values, one or more of which can apply to a CSS attribute—for example, { **background**: *sColor* II *sImage* II *sRepeat* II *sAttachment* II *sPosition* }.

Hungarian Notation

This book uses Hungarian notation to mark the data types of variable names. These data types have the following form: *s* for string, *b* for Boolean, *i* for integer, *o* for object, and *coll* for collection. In practice, this convention looks like this for each of the types: *sVariable*, *bVariable*, *iVariable*, *oVariable*, and *collVariable*.

Applies To Lists

Most reference pages contain an Applies To section, which specifies the objects that each referenced property, method, event, or collection supports. Each object is listed only once for each reference, under the version of Internet Explorer for which the object support first appeared. In addition, the lists provide platform information that notes whether the object support applies to Win16, Win32, Macintosh, and/or UNIX versions of Internet Explorer.

Note Because Internet Explorer 1.0 and 2.0 have no programmable object model for Web developers, they do not appear in any Applies To section. Also, UNIX does not appear in any Internet Explorer 3.0 Applies To section. Version 4.0 was the first version of Internet Explorer developed for the UNIX platform.

Event Syntax Tables

Each event reference page has a syntax table that illustrates each type of event binding syntax. These types include binding in a script tag with **FOR** and **EVENT** attributes, in a script reference as properties, and in object tags as inline attributes.

Sample Code and Web Site Documentation

The majority of reference pages in this book include sample code. To see these examples in action, simply access the same reference page on the enclosed Web Workshop CD-ROM, one of two CD-ROMs included with this book.

The Web Workshop CD-ROM contains a snapshot of the Web site posted at http://msdn.microsoft.com/workshop. The snapshot includes feature articles, technical overviews, tutorials, reference material, sample code, and demo applications that pull multiple Internet technologies together. Both the Web Workshop CD-ROM and the Web site provide Extensible Markup Language (XML), C++, Component Object Model (COM), and browser extensibility documentation that goes beyond the scope of this reference. For the latest information about developing and designing for

Internet Explorer, periodically check the Web Workshop site for updates to the information contained here.

For best results, use Internet Explorer 5 to run the interactive samples provided on the Web Workshop CD-ROM and Web site. The second CD-ROM included with this book contains the Internet Explorer 5 program.

Power of Dynamic HTML

Through Dynamic HTML (DHTML), Web content comes
alive, and every element on a page becomes truly interactive.
The chapters in this part of the book provide the background
for understanding the functionality of DHTML. They contain
an introduction to the development of Internet Explorer and
outline the major features of the latest release, Internet
Explorer 5.

Introduction

Evolution of Microsoft Internet Explorer

Over the course of just a few short years, Internet Explorer has become the premier tool for Internet, intranet, and—on Win32 systems—desktop browsing. The browser has developed over that time from a simple HTML rendering engine to a stable, fast, and efficient Web authoring platform.

This chapter outlines the major innovations introduced by each release of Internet Explorer, with an emphasis on Web authoring features. The description of each feature set becomes more detailed for each succeeding version of the browser.

Internet Explorer 1.0

In 1995, Microsoft released its initial offering in the browser market, Internet Explorer 1.0. This version, based on NCSA Mosaic, supported World Wide Web Consortium (W3C) Hypertext Markup Language (HTML) standards and earned a market share of several percentage points within weeks of its introduction.

Internet Explorer 1.0 could be most aptly described as a basic browser. However, it represented a first step in the process of supporting the standards that would allow a browser to display a wide variety of content with predictable results.

Internet Explorer 2.0

Internet Explorer 2.0, released in late 1995, aimed at improving the browsing experience for end users. Version 2.0 extended the browser's support of the latest open Internet standards, such as the now ubiquitous HTML and Hypertext Transfer Protocol (HTTP). In general, browsing the Web still meant viewing static pages, yet Internet Explorer 2.0 did that job well. Its market share inched up a few percentage points into the teens.

Despite these improvements, the browser still had a long way to go. It lacked backward compatibility and easy extensibility. Customizations required proprietary COM interfaces, not to mention some creative workarounds.

Internet Explorer 3.0

Premiering in August 1996, Internet Explorer 3.0 represented a more versatile browser. It provided a much better vehicle for browsing dynamic content on the Web because of its support of standards and its component architecture. Also, it contained a security infrastructure that reflected the Web's growing role in exchanging information and applications. Version 3.0 delivered functionality that Web developers and C++/COM programmers had been waiting for. Despite significant architectural changes, it still managed to maintain backward compatibility with version 2.0.

Version 3.0 was the first Internet Explorer release to provide active content authoring for Web developers. Two pivotal innovations supported the development of active content in this version:

- **Scripting languages.** These languages included VBScript and JScript (compatible with ECMA language specification).

- **Microsoft® ActiveX® Controls and Java applets.** Internet Explorer 3.0 hosted a scripting environment, the ActiveX Layout Control Pad, which simplified scripting to the object models of embedded Java applets and ActiveX Controls.

Web authors were able to combine these innovations to bring static HTML to life. Most importantly, they could do so because COM interfaces were no longer the only way to customize and extend browser behavior.

Internet Explorer 3.0 featured enhanced support of W3C standards. For example, Internet Explorer was among the first browsers to adopt the HTML 3.2 standard. In addition, Version 3.0 pioneered support for W3C cascading style sheets (CSS). For the first time, Web authors could separate content from style information. Combined with the introduction of client-side scripting, this advance made it easier to create interactive effects, such as rollover highlights.

Internet Explorer 3.0 also delivered a host of features for more secure communication and safer software downloading. The Cryptography Application Programming Interface (CryptoAPI) provided basic secure communication using public and private keys; applications no longer needed to develop and maintain their own cryptography mechanisms. The Microsoft® Authenticode® technology certified not only the origin of downloaded code, but also its integrity. Secure channel protocols, such as Secure Socket Layer (SSL) version 1.0, provided secure communications over a TCP/IP connection.

Total cost of ownership became a theme beginning with version 3.0. An improved Software Development Kit (SDK) enhanced the process of customization. Multi-platform support—Win16, Win32, and Macintosh—increased the reach of the product. In addition, the Internet Explorer Administration Kit (IEAK) facilitated large-scale deployment and ongoing management on the Internet and corporate intranets. The IEAK allowed companies to create and update customized installations of the Internet Explorer browser with relative ease.

Before year's end in 1996, versions of Internet Explorer for the Macintosh, UNIX, and Microsoft® Windows® 3.1 operating systems joined those for Windows 95 and Microsoft® Windows NT® on the market. By June 1997, many top sites, as measured by PC-Meter and others, reported that use of Internet Explorer averaged more than 20 percent of their audience. By the end of the year, its depth and breadth had won Internet Explorer 3.0 a market share of more than 30 percent, making it one of the two most popular browsers on the Web.

Internet Explorer 4.0

Building on innovations in version 3.0, Internet Explorer 4.0 went even further toward making Web pages truly dynamic. Dynamic HTML (DHTML), a complete object model, and extensive open standards support made version 4.0 the most flexible Web authoring platform yet. Introduced in August 1997, Internet Explorer 4.0 included powerful and dynamic visual effects and enhanced programmability.

Internet Explorer 4.0 implemented the latest Internet standards recommendations, including:

- HTML 4.0
- CSS1 and CSS – Positioning (CSS-P)
- Document Object Model (DOM)
- ECMA-262 compatible scripting
- Pioneering support for XML, a markup language that separates data from content. Support includes parser, object model, and data source object model
- HTTP 1.1
- Platform for Internet Content Selection (PICS)
- Portable Network Graphics (PNG), for image compression

The term DHTML applies to the capability to alter content, style settings, and position values on the client machine. This approach meant the end for `document.write` and Common Gateway Interface (CGI) scripts as the preferred techniques for programming interactivity into Web pages.

Before the adoption of DHTML, Web pages would interface with the server to create an illusion of interactivity. On the client side, the user could only interact with a Web page through HTML Forms, but even HTML Forms required roundtrips to the server each time the content needed verification or updating. Plug-ins provided some level of interactivity and programmability in version 3.0. However, downloading delays, security concerns, and platform limitations slowed their adoption.

DHTML provided the application program interface (API) for HTML. This API allowed the Web developer to use the processing power of the client when modifying a page. With the advent of DHTML, the browser reflowed a page to render content changes rather than initiating another download of the page. DHTML preserved rendering speed while minimizing server traffic. For the first time, Web developers could build in dynamic responses to user actions, without the delays caused by server interactions.

DHTML provided HTML and script access to dynamic content, styles, and positioning, summarized as follows:

Dynamic content

Enabled manipulation of actual elements on a Web page and provided these four key innovations:

- Access to all HTML elements as script objects with full object models for the document, style, and table objects.

- Collections, which provided easy scripting of the objects.

- Access to a full event model, which supported multiple ways to bind objects to events and introduced event bubbling, a way to trap events at any container level in the document hierarchy.

- Dynamic changes to text and HTML on an HTML page.

Dynamic styles

Allowed Web designers to change Web document style and formatting at any time, without another visit to the server. Dynamic styles, which were based on CSS1, ushered in instant page updates of object size, color, and positioning.

Dynamic positioning

Incorporated pixel-precise placement of HTML elements into Web page design. Dynamic positioning, which was based on the W3C CSS-P, enabled images to be layered over one another and text to flow around an image. The sluggish performance of pages using table-based positioning became a thing of the past.

Internet Explorer 4.0 made it easier to build Internet and intranet solutions using HTML and scripting technologies. In addition to DHTML, version 4.0 supported data binding and script encapsulation. Data binding allowed Web developers to disseminate rich data from almost any data source to HTML elements on their Web pages. Script encapsulation into scriptlets, or .sct files, separated HTML content from scripting code. This feature allowed designers and developers to work side by side on the same project. Scriptlets formed the foundation for DHTML behaviors in Internet Explorer 5.

Internet Explorer 4.0 enhanced cross-platform support. A Web author could easily create pages that would run on all of the popular platforms. In addition to broad platform support, core DHTML and Channel Definition Format (CDF) files were among the new features.

As one of the most secure browsers to date, Internet Explorer 4.0 supported a variety of security features:

- **Server and client authentication.** X.509 v3 standards-based digital identification or digital certificates identified the user to Web servers, and server authentication with server certificates verified valid Web sites.

- **Secure sockets layer (SSL) 2.0/3.0.** The SSL protocol provided secure communications over a TCP/IP connection.

- **Security zones.** Security zones allowed users to set restrictive security options for Internet content, while at the same time giving reasonable trust to local intranet content.

- **Certificate management.** Using certificates, network administrators could control which Java applets, ActiveX Controls, or other software could be accessed and run on their intranets, based on the publisher's identity.

- **Authenticode technology.** Authenticode technology ensured accountability and integrity of Web executables, including Java applets, plug-ins, and ActiveX Controls.

The following privacy safeguards and content ratings were also made available in this release:

- **PICS.** Platform for Internet Content Selection (PICS) services ratings were provided to users so that they could set these ratings to allow or disallow viewing of any content that they might deem inappropriate.

- **Profile Assistant.** Internet Explorer 4.0 provided the first implementation of privacy capabilities developed by the emerging W3C Platform for Privacy Preferences (P3) standards. This put control over the disclosure of any and all information into users' hands.

In a release as ambitious as Version 4.0, it's difficult to describe all of the end-user, enterprise, and Web scripting and COM programming features. However, its many innovative features helped elevate Internet Explorer 4.0 to the most popular Web browser available. It won a market share of more than 50 percent by late 1997. More than 100 of the top Internet service providers in 20 countries provided Internet Explorer and Microsoft® Outlook® Express to their customers, representing more than 6.5 million users worldwide. By early 1998, Internet Explorer became the most popular browsing software in 19 countries, including Brazil, Greece, Korea, Mexico, Russia, and the United Kingdom, based on statistics from Internet service providers and Web traffic to top sites.

Internet Explorer 5

Released in March 1999, Internet Explorer 5 has streamlined and enhanced many of the dynamic features of Internet Explorer 4.0. Internet Explorer 5, however, is much more than flashy effects. Its fundamental architectures, such as data transfer, mouse capture, and enhanced data handling, enable Web designers and developers to create truly compelling Web content and applications.

Internet Explorer 5 provides the following benefits:

- **Control.** Its pixel-perfect text and graphic positioning bring desktop publishing techniques to the Web.

- **Interactivity**. Its flexible object model provides the ability to script all objects and change most properties on the fly.

- **Componentization.** Its components allow content markup, style and formatting markup, and script to be separated to make development and maintenance easy.

Internet Explorer 5 delivers a simpler, faster, more reliable Web browser to end users through the following improvements:

- Manipulating and loading documents is quicker and easier than before. For example, databound pages in Internet Explorer 5 render up to 100 times faster than they did in Internet Explorer 4.0.

- Installing Internet Explorer 5 requires only 6.5 MB of disk space compared with 40 MB needed for version 4.0.

- The AutoComplete feature relieves the end user from typing repetitively. After the user has typed a few letters in the address box, a drop-down list appears with suggested addresses. These suggestions are previously visited addresses that have been stored in an encrypted file.

- Windows Search Assistant, located inside the Search bar, provides a common query interface for end users when they are starting a search. Now end users can use a task-based approach to find information on the Web; they no longer need to be familiar with the various common and specialty search engines.

Version 5 provides enhanced support of version 4.0 standards-based technologies as well as support for these new standards:

- CSS2, the combined CSS style and positioning specification

- DOM, Level 1

- Extensible Stylesheet Language (XSL)

- Dynamic properties (recently submitted to the W3C)

- DHTML behaviors (recently submitted to the W3C)

Internet Explorer 5 elevates the browser to a full-fledged application development platform. Its enhanced DHTML includes a rich set of features that enable developers to mimic the functionality of Windows applications with ease in a Web application. Internet Explorer 5 is the ideal platform for building applications for the Web through its support of the following features:

- **DHTML behaviors.** DHTML behaviors are simple, lightweight components that, when applied to standard HTML elements on a page through CSS, can enhance the element's default behavior. Behaviors provide a method to separate script from content on a page, making it easy to reuse code across multiple pages while improving overall manageability of the page. Internet Explorer 5 comes bundled with a number of default behaviors, including a way to expose client capabilities information and persist browser state information.

- **Persistence.** The ability to persist data on the client eliminates the need to use cookies to maintain designated settings for documents stored on a remote server.

- **Dynamic properties.** Similar to formulas on a spreadsheet, dynamic properties make the behavior of one object on the page contingent upon that of another. For example, Web developers can make font size on a page dependent on screen size by adding this simple line of code on a page:
  ```
  <BODY STYLE="font-size:expression(this.clientWidth/20)">
  ```

- **Client capabilities.** Through the introduction of client capabilities, Internet Explorer 5 makes it easier than ever for Web developers to customize content based on the capabilities that the client browser supports.

- **Application architectures.** Internet Explorer 5 comes bundled with a set of features that enable the Web developer to incorporate the look and feel of Windows and Macintosh applications in a Web application. Data transfer, for one, enables drag-and-drop functionality and custom cut, copy, and paste editing through the standard context menu. Mouse capture gives Web developers complete control over all mouse activity on a page when implementing menus and custom context menus.

- **HTML Applications.** HTAs make Internet Explorer 5 a part of the Windows development platform. HTAs are trusted and display only the menus, icons, toolbars, and title information created by the Web designer or author.

Internet Explorer 5 also offers the following improvements in layout and style:

- **Table rendering.** Internet Explorer 5 finally solves the problem of slow table rendering by supporting fixed-layout tables. To take advantage of this functionality, Web developers just need to set the new CSS attribute **table-layout** to `fixed` when specifying table column sizes. In many cases, the use of fixed-layout tables improves performance from 100 seconds to 1. Fixed-layout tables improve rendering speed because the browser renders each table row as it downloads rather than simultaneously.

- **Display sizes for text.** Web developers using Internet Explorer 5 can benefit greatly from improvements in style control. The new **currentStyle** object, which contains the current values for all the elements' CSS properties, makes it easy to produce accurate display sizes. Developers no longer have to guess the effects of CSS rules when developing styles for Web pages.

Further enhancements have been added to Internet Explorer 5 based on feature requests. The ability to override the default context menu is one enhancement. Web developers can now use the **oncontextmenu** event to create a custom context menu that appears when the user right-clicks on a page. Another enhancement is improved printing support. The **print** method enables a Web developer to print a page through script. In addition, two related events, **onbeforeprint** and **onafterprint**, provide better control over the printed document, such as making all information on the page visible before printing and then reverting back to the original state after printing.

Conclusion

Internet Explorer has played a major role in the evolution of Web applications and presentation of content. Its support of Internet standards, browser security, technology platforms, and application development has successively evolved over the past three versions to include the following features.

Type of support	Internet Explorer 3	Internet Explorer 4	Internet Explorer 5
Internet standards	W3C HTML 3.2 standard W3C CSS1	W3C XML standard W3C P3	W3C CSS2 XSL DOM, Level 1
Browser security	Signed Certificates Authenticode CryptoAPI SSL	x509 digital certificates SSL 2.0 and 3.0 Security zones PICS ratings	x509 v3 digital certificates
Technology platforms	Windows 95 Windows 98 Windows NT Windows 3.1 Macintosh	Windows 95 Windows 98 Windows NT Windows 3.1 Macintosh UNIX	Windows 95 Windows 98 Windows NT Windows 3.1 Macintosh UNIX
Application development	Java Applets ActiveX Components IEAK JScript and VBScript	DHTML Object Model Dynamic styles Data binding Dynamic positioning Scriptlets	DHTML behaviors Dynamic properties Persistence Client capabilities HTAs

The remainder of this book describes DHTML and related technologies. Through its references and samples, the book offers powerful solutions for Web designers and authors who want to create dynamic content and applications for the Internet and intranet.

CHAPTER 2

Application Development Solutions in Internet Explorer 5

The new features in Internet Explorer 5 have elevated this browser to a rich application development platform. Whether you develop Web or HTML applications, you can use these features to customize the end-user experience and reduce production time. The new features in Internet Explorer 5 include:

- Dynamic HTML (DHTML) behaviors
- Persistence
- Client capabilities
- Application architectures, such as data transfer, mouse capture, dynamic properties, and the document object model
- HTML Applications

This chapter introduces each of these powerful features. For more information about them and sample code illustrating their use, see the Web Workshop CD-ROM included with this book or visit the Web Workshop site at http://www.microsoft.com/msdnonline/.

DHTML Behaviors

DHTML behaviors, a new Internet Explorer 5 feature, represent a major advance in Web authoring. They're flexible, lightweight components that can encapsulate specific functionality for use on a single HTML page or across an entire site. When applied to an HTML element, a DHTML behavior extends that element's default functionality.

The use of behaviors allows you—the Web developer or designer— to separate script from content. Such a division makes each page shorter and more manageable. Moreover, it allows the browser to download code once and use it multiple times. By using behaviors, designers can easily attach interactive effects to otherwise static content, and authors can radically cut production time by scripting an entire library of reusable behaviors for designers to choose from.

Through the proposed cascading style sheets (CSS) **behavior** attribute, Internet Explorer 5 makes applying a behavior to an element no different from attaching a style to an HTML element on a page. Adding a rollover highlight to a list, for example, is as easy as adding a CSS style to an element, as the following example demonstrates.

```
<HEAD>
/* applies highlighting behavior to all LI elements on the page */
<STYLE>
.LI { behavior:url (hilite.htc) }
</STYLE>
</HEAD>
:
:
<UL>
    <LI>HTML Authoring</LI>
    <LI>HTML Help Authoring</LI>
    <LI>HTML References</LI>
</UL>
```

To harness the power of behaviors, all you have to do is define the behavior as a style on each page. As a CSS style, the behavior can be defined inline using the **STYLE** attribute or in the style block using the **CLASS** or **ID** of the object. Because Internet Explorer 5 supports multiple values for a **CLASS** on an object, attaching a behavior through the **CLASS** does not limit your other style options.

You can create a behavior that toggles the **display** property of an element's children when the user clicks the mouse. The following example shows how you can implement that behavior as an HTML Component.

```
<PUBLIC:COMPONENT>
<PUBLIC:PROPERTY NAME="child" />
<PUBLIC:ATTACH EVENT="onclick" ONEVENT="ExpandCollapse()" />
<SCRIPT LANGUAGE="JScript">
function ExpandCollapse()
{
var i;
var sDisplay;

// Determine current state of the list (expanded or collapsed).
bCollapsed = (element.document.all(child).runtimeStyle.display == "none");
// Toggle the display and listStyleImage properties depending
// on the expanded or collapsed state of the list.
if (bCollapsed)
{
    runtimeStyle.listStyleImage = "url(minus.gif)";
    element.document.all(child).runtimeStyle.display = "";
}
```

```
else
{
   runtimeStyle.listStyleImage = "url(plus.gif)";
   element.document.all(child).runtimeStyle.display = "none";
}
}
</SCRIPT>
</PUBLIC:COMPONENT>
```

You can use this behavior within HTML as shown in the following example.

```
<HEAD>
<STYLE>
.Collapsing {behavior:url(collapsing.htc)}
</STYLE>
</HEAD>

<UL>
<LI CLASS="Collapsing" CHILD="Topics1">HTML Authoring</LI>
<UL ID="Topics1">
<LI><A HREF="file1.asp">Beginner's Guide</A></LI>
<LI><A HREF="file2.asp">Authoring Tips</A></LI>
<LI><A HREF="file3.asp">HTML Coding Tips</A></LI>
</UL>
<LI CLASS="Collapsing" CHILD="Topics2">HTML References</LI>
<UL ID="Topics2">
<LI><A HREF="file4.htm">Elements</A></LI>
<LI><A HREF="file5.htm">Character Sets</A></LI>
</UL>
<LI CLASS="Collapsing" CHILD="Topics3">HTML Applications (HTA)</LI>
<UL ID="Topics3">
<LI><A HREF="file6.htm">Overview</A></LI>
<LI><A HREF="file7.htm">Reference</A></LI>
</UL>
</UL>
```

This generic behavior, when applied to a **UL** element, enables the static list to expand and collapse as the user clicks the list. Another way to use a behavior is to set the position of an object incrementally from any start or end point on the screen. When applied to an **IMG** element, the behavior can move an otherwise statically positioned image across the screen.

Note Microsoft support of DHTML behaviors is limited to systems running Internet Explorer 5 or later on Win32 and UNIX. Browsers that do not support DHTML behaviors ignore the **behavior** attribute on a Web page; instead, the browsers render the element as usual, but the behavior does not apply.

HTML Components

As of Internet Explorer 5, you can use either HTML Components (HTCs) or scriptlets, which have been renamed Windows Scripting Components (WSC), to implement your own DHTML behaviors in script. You can write HTCs and scriptlets using VBScript, JScript, or any third-party scripting language that supports the ActiveX scripting interfaces.

HTCs provide a simple way to implement DHTML behaviors in script. An HTC file is an HTML file, saved with a .htc extension, that contains scripts and a set of HTC-specific elements that expose properties, methods, and events that define the component.

As an HTML file, an HTC provides the same access as DHTML to all elements on the page. You can access all elements within an HTC from script as objects using their **ID**. This access enables you to dynamically manipulate all attributes and methods of HTC elements through script by calling them as properties and methods of these objects.

The following example shows how you can implement a simple rollover highlighting behavior as an HTML Component:

```
<PUBLIC:COMPONENT>
<PUBLIC:ATTACH EVENT="onmouseover" ONEVENT="Hilite()" />
<PUBLIC:ATTACH EVENT="onmouseout"  ONEVENT="Restore()" />
<SCRIPT LANGUAGE="JScript">
    var normalColor;
    function Hilite()
    {
      normalColor  = runtimeStyle.color;  // save original values
      runtimeStyle.color  = "red";
    }

    function Restore()
    {
      runtimeStyle.color  = normalColor;  // restore original values
    }
</SCRIPT>
</PUBLIC:COMPONENT>
```

For more information about HTCs, see Chapter 4, "HTML Components Reference."

Default Behaviors

Internet Explorer 5 introduces a number of behaviors built into the browser. Known as default behaviors, they deliver an improved browsing experience by enabling end users to customize how they view Web pages. The pretested code provided by default behaviors allows you to optimize content for client machines. Default behaviors also create a consistent user interface, whether browsing takes place on the Windows desktop or an HTTP server. Because they are part of the browser, these behaviors require no extra download time. For more information about default behaviors, see Chapter 5, "Default Behaviors Reference."

Persistence

Introduced in Internet Explorer 5, persistence enables you to specify the type of information about an object that is saved to the client machine during current and future sessions. Persistence offers several advantages. It speeds Web-page navigation by eliminating trips to the server and avoiding limitations imposed by the use of cookies. It also streamlines authoring by enabling you to store persistence information on the client.

Internet Explorer 5 implements persistence as a set of DHTML default behaviors. The new persistence behaviors include **saveSnapshot**, **saveHistory**, **saveFavorite**, and **userData**. Simply define each of these behaviors as a style for the objects that should persist. The style definition indicates whether you are linking to a default behavior through the presence of #default.

You can use persistence to maintain state information about a Web page. For example, a collapsible list of links within a table of contents can retain state information by remaining expanded to the user's last selection—even if the user leaves and then navigates back to the page. Similarly, you can repopulate form elements with the last-used values, as shown in the following example for the **saveSnapShot** behavior.

```
<FORM ID="oPersistForm" STYLE="behavior:url(#default#saveSnapshot)">
First Name: <INPUT TYPE=text>
Last Name: <INPUT TYPE=text>
Exemptions: <INPUT TYPE=text>
</FORM>
```

Persistence behaviors allow maximum flexibility for how much of the page you persist. They can be attached to individual objects, such as a text box, or they can be attached to entire containers, such as a **FORM** or a **DIV**. When defined for a container, these behaviors automatically persist information for every object the container holds.

Client Capabilities

Client capabilities provide information about the browsing environment, including screen resolution, screen dimensions, color depth, CPU type, or connection type (whether LAN or modem). By making this information available on the client, you can cache pages, minimize server roundtrips, and free up server resources as content generation shifts back to the client. In addition, if a client-side script detects a low-bandwidth modem connection to the server, it can expedite the download process by requesting low-resolution images from the server. In these ways, using client capabilities helps improve overall performance.

Internet Explorer 4.0 only exposed client capabilities as properties through the
DHTML Object Model. Beginning with Internet Explorer 5, however, all of this
functionality has been encapsulated into one default DHTML behavior, the
clientCaps behavior. For information and examples, see the **clientCaps** behavior in
Chapter 5, "Default Behaviors."

Application Architectures

DHTML behaviors, persistence, and client capabilities are just part of what makes
Internet Explorer 5 a robust development platform. New architectural features for
application development include data transfer, mouse capture, dynamic properties, and
the Document Object Model (DOM).

Data Transfer

Internet Explorer 5 introduces extensive data transfer functionality. Data transfer
involves writing information to and reading information from a clipboard through a
data transfer object. The information that is transferred includes the data format and
the data. Data transfer allows you to circumvent the browser defaults and implement
custom editing code.

In Internet Explorer 4.0, programmatic control over data transfer operations was very
limited. Internet Explorer 5 provides data transfer objects, methods, and properties.
Internet Explorer 5 supplies data transfer control in the form of two objects,
dataTransfer and **clipboardData**. Each provides a gateway through which
information is set on source objects and retrieved by data objects. Methods, events,
and properties provide functionality for cut, copy, and paste operations.

Data transfer now provides programmatic control over which data formats get
transferred from data source to data target through the Clipboard. The following two
processes use data transfer:

- **Cut, copy, and paste editing.** The Edit and shortcut menus in the browser
  facilitate repeated editing tasks, such as copy, cut, and paste, by persisting
  information in the Clipboard. One example of this capability is pasting the same
  data multiple times through the use of the **clipboardData** object, as shown in the
  following example.

```
<SCRIPT> // Enable the Copy shortcut menu.
function fnBeforeCopy () { window.event.returnValue = false; }

// Copy text to the clipboard when the user selects Copy.
function fnCopy () {
window.event.returnValue = false;
window.clipboardData.setData("Text",window.event.srcElement.innerText)
;
}
```

```
// Enable the Paste shortcut menu.
function fnBeforePaste() { window.event.returnValue = false; }
}

// Copy text from the clipboard when the user selects Paste.
 fnPaste() {
window.event.returnValue = false; window.event.srcElement.innerText =
window.clipboardData.getData("Text");
}
</SCRIPT>

Home Phone: <DIV oncopy="fnCopy()"
onbeforeCopy="fnBeforeCopy()">(425)555-1212</DIV>
Spouse's Phone: <DIV onbeforepaste="fnBeforePaste()"
onpaste="fnPaste()">Enter phone here</DIV>
```

- **Drag-and-drop operations.** The drag-and-drop functionality available through the **dataTransfer** object adds the advantages of immediacy and intuitiveness to the user's interaction, because the user can simply select an HTML element and drag it to a new location. This functionality only works for one-time operations, because once the drag operation ends, the data being transferred disappears.

Mouse Capture

Internet Explorer 5 introduces mouse capture to Web-based applications. This capability is suited for building drop-down menus, shortcut menus, spreadsheets, and more.

Previously, Web authors relied solely on event bubbling to capture events. Event bubbling still has its place as a technique for handling events at any level in the containership hierarchy. However, monitoring events using event bubbling entails tedious tracking, because multiple objects in a spreadsheet—for example, table cells, table rows, table heads, and so on— can fire many events, all of which bubble. In contrast, mouse capture monitors only mouse events. Moreover, mouse capture operates regardless of an object's location in the containership hierarchy. An object can capture either all events for the document or only events for those objects the document contains.

An object with mouse capture receives all mouse events. The new **oncontextmenu** event enables you to cancel the default behavior of the browser's context menu, capture the right-click on an object, and display a custom context menu for the object. Once the menu appears, it has capture, which means it can programmatically track all mouse events affecting it. The **onmouseover** event can highlight a menu item, the **onmouseout** event can return the item to normal, and the **onclick** event can trigger the action associated with the menu option. For more information about creating custom drop-down menus using mouse capture, see the Web Workshop CD-ROM included with this book.

Dynamic Properties

Internet Explorer 4.0, with its support for CSS positioning, made incredible visual effects possible, which previously only ActiveX Controls or Java applets had delivered. The only problem was the time needed to code the visual effect and to anticipate all of the possible conditions that might impact it. Through dynamic properties, Internet Explorer 5 makes creating dynamic effects quick and easy. Dynamic properties allow you to declare property values as formulas. These formulas, moreover, can reference property values from other elements, enabling the behavior of one object to be contingent on that of another.

Dynamic properties are easy to implement using four new methods: **getExpression**, **recalc**, **removeExpression**, and **setExpression**. Dynamic property formulas are assigned in script with the **setExpression** method. They also can be assigned inline in the **STYLE** block or in the **STYLE** attribute, using the **expression** notation in CSS.

Dynamic properties enable you to describe relationships between objects, properties, and variables as functions rather than as an explicit sequence of steps to follow. Thus, dynamic properties minimize the amount of code required in a document. In fact, you can use dynamic properties to implement some effects formerly possible only with scripting. Using dynamic properties, you can perform the following kinds of tasks:

- Recalculate totals in a table when a user enters a change into a cell.

- Animate elements to move across the page at a pace set by a timer.

- Position elements relative to a moving mouse pointer, or relative to the size of the window, as shown in the following example using the **setExpression** method.

```
<STYLE>
BODY {font-family: arial; font-size: 18pt; font-weight: bold;}
DIV { width: 80px; height: 80px; text-align: center; position:
absolute; }
</STYLE>

// Create 5 differently colored rectangles, labeling them
// according to their designated positioning in the window.
<DIV ID=Blue style="background: blue;">Top Left</DIV>
<DIV ID=Red style="background: red;">Bottom Left</DIV>
<DIV ID=Green style="background: green;">Top Right</DIV>
<DIV ID=Yellow style="background: yellow;">Bottom Right</DIV>
<DIV ID=Purple style="background: purple">Center</DIV>
```

```
<SCRIPT>
// Place the blue rectangle on the top left corner.
Blue.style.setExpression("posLeft", "document.body.clientLeft + 10");
Blue.style.setExpression("posTop", "document.body.clientTop + 10");

// Place the yellow rectangle on the bottom right corner.
Yellow.style.setExpression("posLeft", "document.body.clientWidth -
90");
Yellow.style.setExpression("posTop", "document.body.clientHeight -
                                  document.body.style.border - 90");
// Place the red rectangle on the bottom left corner.
Red.style.setExpression("posLeft", "document.body.clientLeft + 10");
Red.style.setExpression("posTop", "document.body.clientHeight -
                                  document.body.style.border - 90");
// Place the green rectangle on the top right corner.
Green.style.setExpression("posLeft", "document.body.clientWidth -
90");
Green.style.setExpression("posTop", "document.body.clientTop + 10");

// Place the purple rectangle in the center of the window.
Purple.style.setExpression("posLeft", "(document.body.clientWidth -
80)/2");
Purple.style.setExpression("posTop", "(document.body.clientHeight -
80)/2");
</SCRIPT>
```

This code, when executed, puts a rectangle in each corner of the window, and one in the center.

Document Object Model

New to Internet Explorer 5, the DOM interface allows authors to access different nodes of a document tree. A node is a reference to an element, an attribute, or a string of text. The DOM does not implement all of the DHTML Object Model. As a result, the DOM is best applied to building and managing complex documents and data used with the DHTML Object Model.

Internet Explorer 5 seamlessly integrates into the DHTML Object Model those properties, methods, and collections that the DOM interface exposes. Internet Explorer 5 also enforces the same security restrictions for the DOM as for the DHTML Object Model.

The DOM interface is platform and language neutral, enabling full script access to HTML and XML documents. The DOM, in fact, is the object model for XML, which means you can programmatically manipulate the content, structure, and style of a document.

The DOM is often the most efficient way to manipulate the HTML document structure for two reasons:

- You can use the DOM to move one part of the document tree to another without destroying and re-creating the content. This capability makes for shorter, more efficient code.

  For tables, swapping rows is as easy as invoking the DOM **swapNode** method on the table row, as shown in the following example:

```
<SCRIPT>

var oShuffle=oTable.rows(2);
function fnShuffle() {
    oShuffle.swapNode(oShuffle.previousSibling);
}
</SCRIPT>
<TABLE ID="oTable">
<TR><TD>This is cell 1, row 1</TD><TD>This is cell 2, row 1</TD></TR>
<TR><TD>This is cell 1, row 2</TD><TD>This is cell 2, row 2</TD></TR>
<TR STYLE="background-color: #CFCFCF;">
<TD>Shuffle This Row</TD>
<TD>Shuffle This Row</TD>
</TR>
</TABLE>
```

  In DHTML, this process would require destroying and re-creating the bottom table row and the two cells—a slower, much less efficient process.

- You can create nodes and attach them to any point in the document tree. There are different types of nodes: document nodes, element nodes, attribute nodes, and text nodes, listed in the order of increasing granularity.

The DOM provides ways to query a specified node to determine its location in the document hierarchy and its relationship to other nodes. For example, given reference to a node in a list, the DOM members can be used to identify the adjacent, parent, and child nodes.

The ability to manipulate nodes allows authors to perform complex operations on the document without rewriting the content. Your script can work directly with element and text nodes in the document tree to identify nodes, create new nodes, and manipulate existing nodes with the speed and efficiency that only the DOM can provide.

HTML Applications

HTML Applications (HTAs) are a new vehicle for distributing HTML and script-based applications. HTAs are trusted applications that display only the menus, icons, toolbars, and title information that you include. HTAs use the power of Internet Explorer—its object model, performance, rendering power, protocol support, and channel-download technology—without enforcing the browser's strict security model and user interface.

HTAs not only support everything a Web page does—namely, HTML, CSS, scripting languages, and behaviors—HTAs also feature HTA-specific functionality. This added functionality provides control over user interface design and access to the client system. Run as trusted applications, HTAs are not subject to the same security constraints as Web pages. As with any executable file, the user is asked once, before the HTA is downloaded, whether to save or run the application. If the HTA is saved to the client machine, it simply runs on demand thereafter. The end result is that HTAs run like any executable (.exe) file written in C++ or Visual Basic.

HTAs are suited to many uses, whether you are prototyping, making wizards, or building full-scale applications. Whatever DHTML and script deliver now—forms, multimedia, Web applications, HTML editors, and browsers—so can HTAs. HTAs also make some tasks easier. The simplicity of generating prototypes using HTAs makes it possible for Web authors to script dialog boxes and alerts while C++ or Visual Basic authors program the underlying functionality.

You can create an HTA by writing an HTML page and saving it with the .hta file extension. To write a simple HTA, save the phrase "Hello, World!" in a file with the .hta file extension but without the beginning **HTML** and **BODY** tags. Internet Explorer is so forgiving that the missing tags do not cause an error.

After an HTA has been created, users can launch it by double-clicking its program icon, running it from the Start menu, opening it through a URL, or starting it from the command line. Once running, the HTA renders everything within the paired **BODY** tags and displays the value set in the **TITLE** tag as the window caption.

Conclusion

Internet Explorer 5 includes a number of new features that facilitate application development, including DHTML behaviors, persistence, client capabilities, architectures, and HTAs. These features enable Web authors and designers to create powerful, compelling, and efficient Web applications quickly and easily.

DHTML, HTC, and Default Behaviors References

Features in Internet Explorer, such as Dynamic HTML, HTML Components, and Default Behaviors, make it easy to author Web pages that are engaging and interactive. The following chapters outline the elements, objects, behaviors, properties, methods, events, and collections that make these features so adaptable.

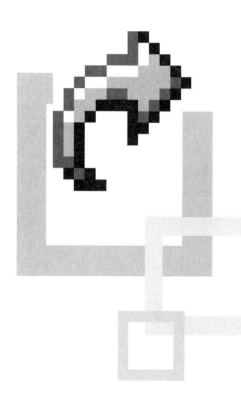

DHTML References

This chapter is a complete reference to all the objects, properties, methods, events, and collections supported in Dynamic HTML (DHTML) as of Internet Explorer 5.

Objects

The following section provides an alphabetical list of objects defined by DHTML. Each object definition contains a list of attributes/properties, methods, events, collections, behaviors, and cascading style sheets (CSS) attributes for the object. It also identifies the version of Internet Explorer in which the object was first introduced.

A Element | A Object

Designates the start or destination of a hypertext link.

Remarks

The **A** (anchor) element requires the **href** or the **name** property to be specified.

Both text and images can be included within an anchor. An image that is an anchor has a border whose color indicates whether the link has been visited.

The **A** element is an inline element and requires a closing tag.

This element is available in HTML and script as of Internet Explorer 3.0.

Attributes/Properties

		CLASS	
accessKey	**canHaveChildren**[*]	**className**	**clientHeight**[*]
clientLeft[*]	**clientTop**[*]	**clientWidth**[*]	**currentStyle**[*]
dataFld	**dataSrc**	**dir**	**firstChild**[*]

[*]   This property has no corresponding attribute.

Attributes/Properties *(continued)*

hash*	host*	hostname*	href
id	innerHTML*	innerText*	isTextEdit*
lang	language	lastChild*	Methods
name	nextSibling*	nodeName*	nodeType*
nodeValue*	offsetHeight*	offsetLeft*	offsetParent*
offsetTop*	offsetWidth*	outerHTML*	outerText*
parentElement*	parentNode*	parentTextEdit*	pathname*
port*	previousSibling*	protocol*	readyState*
recordNumber*	rel	rev	runtimeStyle*
scopeName*	scrollHeight*	scrollLeft*	scrollTop*
scrollWidth*	search*	sourceIndex*	style
tabIndex	tagName*	tagUrn*	target
title	uniqueID*	urn	

*   This property has no corresponding attribute.

Methods

addBehavior	appendChild	applyElement
attachEvent	blur	clearAttributes
click	cloneNode	componentFromPoint
contains	detachEvent	focus
getAdjacentText	getAttribute	getBoundingClientRect
getClientRects	getElementsByTagName	getExpression
hasChildNodes	insertAdjacentElement	insertAdjacentHTML
insertAdjacentText	insertBefore	mergeAttributes
releaseCapture	removeAttribute	removeBehavior
removeChild	removeExpression	removeNode
replaceAdjacentText	replaceChild	replaceNode
scrollIntoView	setAttribute	setCapture
setExpression	swapNode	

DHTML Objects

Events

onbeforecopy	onbeforecut	onbeforeeditfocus	onbeforepaste
onblur	onclick	oncopy	oncut
ondblclick	ondrag	ondragend	ondragenter
ondragleave	ondragover	ondragstart	ondrop
onfocus	onhelp	onkeydown	onkeypress
onkeyup	onlosecapture	onmousedown	onmousemove
onmouseout	onmouseover	onmouseup	onpaste
onpropertychange	onreadystatechange	onresize	onselectstart

Collections

all	attributes	behaviorUrns	childNodes	children

Default Behaviors

anchor	clientCaps	download	homePage	httpFolder
saveFavorite	saveHistory	saveSnapshot	time	userData

CSS Properties

Note For a list of corresponding attributes, see Appendix C.

active†	background	backgroundColor
backgroundImage	backgroundPosition	backgroundPositionX*
backgroundPositionY*	backgroundRepeat	behavior
bottom	clear	color
cursor	direction	font
fontFamily	fontSize	fontStyle
fontVariant	fontWeight	hover†
layoutGridMode	left	letterSpacing
lineHeight	link†	overflow
overflowX	overflowY	pixelBottom*
pixelHeight*	pixelLeft*	pixelRight*

*   This property has no corresponding attribute.

$\dagger$ This attribute has no corresponding property.

CSS Properties *(continued)*

Note For a list of corresponding attributes, see Appendix C.

pixelTop[*]	**pixelWidth**[*]	**posBottom**[*]
posHeight[*]	**position**	**posLeft**[*]
posRight[*]	**posTop**[*]	**posWidth**[*]
right	**styleFloat**	**textAutospace**
textDecoration	**textDecorationBlink**[*]	**textDecorationLineThrough**[*]
textDecorationNone[*]	**textDecorationOverline**[*]	**textDecorationUnderline**[*]
textTransform	**top**	**unicodeBidi**
visibility	**visited**[†]	**width**
wordSpacing	**zIndex**	

*   This property has no corresponding attribute.

†   This attribute has no corresponding property.

Example

The following examples show how to use the **A** element.

```
<-- Link to a server. -->
<A HREF="http://www.microsoft.com">Microsoft home page.</A>

<-- Link to a file in the same directory. -->
<A HREF="home.htm">home.htm</A>

<-- Open a file in the window specified by TARGET. -->
<A TARGET="viewer" HREF="sample.htm">Open in window</A>

<-- Include an IMG element as a part of the link. -->
<A HREF="http://www.microsoft.com"><IMG SRC="images/bullet.gif">link</A>

<-- Link to an anchor. -->
<A HREF="#anchor">anchor</A>

<-- Define an anchor. -->
<A NAME="anchor">

<-- Invoke a JScript function. -->
<A HREF="javascript:window.open()">link</A>
```

ACRONYM Element | ACRONYM Object

Indicates an acronym abbreviation.

Remarks

The **ACRONYM** element is an inline element and requires a closing tag.

This element is available in HTML and script as of Internet Explorer 4.0.

Attributes/Properties

	CLASS		
canHaveChildren[*]	**className**	**currentStyle**[*]	**dir**
firstChild[*]	**id**	**innerHTML**[*]	**innerText**[*]
isTextEdit[*]	**lang**	**language**	**lastChild**[*]
nextSibling[*]	**nodeName**[*]	**nodeType**[*]	**nodeValue**[*]
offsetHeight[*]	**offsetLeft**[*]	**offsetParent**[*]	**offsetTop**[*]
offsetWidth[*]	**outerHTML**[*]	**outerText**[*]	**parentElement**[*]
parentNode[*]	**parentTextEdit**[*]	**previousSibling**[*]	**readyState**[*]
recordNumber[*]	**runtimeStyle**[*]	**scopeName**[*]	**sourceIndex**[*]
style	**tabIndex**	**tagName**[*]	**tagUrn**[*]
title	**uniqueID**[*]		

[*]   This property has no corresponding attribute.

Methods

addBehavior	**appendChild**	**applyElement**
attachEvent	**blur**	**clearAttributes**
cloneNode	**componentFromPoint**	**detachEvent**
focus	**getAdjacentText**	**getBoundingClientRect**
getClientRects	**getElementsByTagName**	**getExpression**
hasChildNodes	**insertAdjacentElement**	**insertBefore**

Methods *(continued)*

mergeAttributes	**removeBehavior**	**removeChild**
removeExpression	**removeNode**	**replaceAdjacentText**
replaceChild	**replaceNode**	**setExpression**
swapNode		

Events

onblur	**ondrag**	**ondragend**	**ondragenter**
ondragleave	**ondragover**	**ondragstart**	**ondrop**
onfocus	**onkeydown**	**onkeypress**	**onkeyup**
onreadystatechange	**onselectstart**		

Collections

all	**attributes**	**behaviorUrns**	**childNodes**	**children**

Default Behaviors

clientCaps	**download**	**homePage**	**httpFolder**	**saveFavorite**
saveHistory	**saveSnapshot**	**time**	**userData**	

CSS Properties

Note For a list of corresponding attributes, see Appendix C.

backgroundPositionX[*]	**backgroundPositionY**[*]	**behavior**	**direction**
layoutGridMode	**overflow**	**overflowX**	**overflowY**
pixelBottom[*]	**pixelHeight**[*]	**pixelLeft**[*]	**pixelRight**[*]
pixelTop[*]	**pixelWidth**[*]	**posBottom**[*]	**posHeight**[*]
posLeft[*]	**posRight**[*]	**posTop**[*]	**posWidth**[*]
textAutospace	**unicodeBidi**	**width**	

[*]   This property has no corresponding attribute.

Example

The following example shows how to use the **ACRONYM** element.

```
<ACRONYM>MSN</ACRONYM>
```

ADDRESS Element | ADDRESS Object

Specifies information, such as address, signature, and authorship, of the current document.

DHTML Objects

Remarks

The **ADDRESS** element is a block element and requires a closing tag.

This element is available in HTML as of Internet Explorer 3.0 and in script as of Internet Explorer 4.0.

Attributes/Properties

	CLASS		
canHaveChildren*	className	clientHeight*	clientLeft*
clientTop*	clientWidth*	currentStyle*	dir
firstChild*	id	innerHTML*	innerText*
isTextEdit*	lang	language	lastChild*
nextSibling*	nodeName*	nodeType*	nodeValue*
offsetHeight*	offsetLeft*	offsetParent*	offsetTop*
offsetWidth*	outerHTML*	outerText*	parentElement*
parentNode*	parentTextEdit*	previousSibling*	readyState*
recordNumber*	runtimeStyle*	scopeName*	scrollHeight*
scrollLeft*	scrollTop*	scrollWidth*	sourceIndex*
style	tabIndex	tagName*	tagUrn*
title	uniqueID*		

* This property has no corresponding attribute.

Methods

addBehavior	appendChild	applyElement
attachEvent	blur	clearAttributes
click	cloneNode	componentFromPoint
contains	detachEvent	focus
getAdjacentText	getAttribute	getBoundingClientRect

Methods *(continued)*

getClientRects	getElementsByTagName	getExpression
hasChildNodes	insertAdjacentElement	insertAdjacentHTML
insertAdjacentText	insertBefore	mergeAttributes
releaseCapture	removeAttribute	removeBehavior
removeChild	removeExpression	removeNode
replaceAdjacentText	replaceChild	replaceNode
scrollIntoView	setAttribute	setCapture
setExpression	swapNode	

Events

onbeforecopy	onbeforecut	onbeforepaste	onblur
onclick	oncopy	oncut	ondblclick
ondrag	ondragend	ondragenter	ondragleave
ondragover	ondragstart	ondrop	onfocus
onhelp	onkeydown	onkeypress	onkeyup
onlosecapture	onmousedown	onmousemove	onmouseout
onmouseover	onmouseup	onpaste	onpropertychange
onreadystatechange	onresize	onselectstart	

Collections

all	attributes	behaviorUrns	childNodes	children

Default Behaviors

clientCaps	download	homePage	httpFolder	saveFavorite
saveHistory	saveSnapshot	time	userData	

CSS Properties

Note For a list of corresponding attributes, see Appendix C.

background	backgroundColor	backgroundImage
backgroundPosition	backgroundPositionX[*]	backgroundPositionY[*]
backgroundRepeat	behavior	bottom
clear	color	cursor
direction	font	fontFamily
fontSize	fontStyle	fontVariant
fontWeight	layoutGridMode	left
letterSpacing	lineBreak	lineHeight
overflow	overflowX	overflowY
pixelBottom[*]	pixelHeight[*]	pixelLeft[*]
pixelRight[*]	pixelTop[*]	pixelWidth[*]
posBottom[*]	posHeight[*]	position
posLeft[*]	posRight[*]	posTop[*]
posWidth[*]	right	styleFloat
textAutospace	textDecoration	textDecorationBlink[*]
textDecorationLineThrough[*]	textDecorationNone[*]	textDecorationOverline[*]
textDecorationUnderline[*]	textJustify	textTransform
top	unicodeBidi	visibility
width	wordBreak	wordSpacing
zIndex		

[*]   This property has no corresponding attribute.

Example

The following example shows how to use the **ADDRESS** element.

```
<ADDRESS>This text will be italic.</ADDRESS>
```

APPLET Element | APPLET Object

Places executable content on the page.

Remarks

The **APPLET** element is a block element and requires a closing tag.

This element is available in HTML as of Internet Explorer 3.0 and in script as of Internet Explorer 4.0.

Attributes/Properties

			CLASS
accessKey	align	altHTML[*]	className
clientHeight[*]	clientLeft[*]	clientTop[*]	clientWidth[*]
codeBase	currentStyle[*]	dataFld	dataSrc
disabled	firstChild[*]	form[*]	hspace
id	isTextEdit[*]	lang	language
lastChild[*]	name	nextSibling[*]	nodeName[*]
nodeType[*]	nodeValue[*]	offsetHeight[*]	offsetLeft[*]
offsetParent[*]	offsetTop[*]	offsetWidth[*]	outerHTML[*]
outerText[*]	parentElement[*]	parentNode[*]	parentTextEdit[*]
previousSibling[*]	readyState[*]	recordNumber[*]	runtimeStyle[*]
scopeName[*]	scrollHeight[*]	scrollLeft[*]	scrollTop[*]
scrollWidth[*]	sourceIndex[*]	src	style
tabIndex	tagName[*]	tagUrn[*]	title
uniqueID[*]	vspace		

[*] This property has no corresponding attribute.

Methods

addBehavior	applyElement	attachEvent
blur	clearAttributes	click
cloneNode	componentFromPoint	contains
detachEvent	focus	getAdjacentText

Methods *(continued)*

getAttribute	getBoundingClientRect	getClientRects
getElementsByTagName	hasChildNodes	insertAdjacentElement
mergeAttributes	releaseCapture	removeAttribute
removeBehavior	removeExpression	replaceAdjacentText
scrollIntoView	setAttribute	setCapture
setExpression	swapNode	

Events

onbeforeeditfocus	onblur	oncellchange	onclick
ondataavailable	ondatasetchanged	ondatasetcomplete	ondblclick
onfocus	onhelp	onkeydown	onkeypress
onkeyup	onload	onlosecapture	onmousedown
onmousemove	onmouseout	onmouseover	onmouseup
onpropertychange	onreadystatechange	onresize	onrowenter
onrowexit	onrowsdelete	onrowsinserted	onscroll

Collections

all	attributes	behaviorUrns	childNodes	children

Default Behaviors

clientCaps	download	homePage

CSS Properties

Note For a list of corresponding attributes, see Appendix C.

backgroundPositionX[*]	backgroundPositionY[*]	behavior	bottom
clear	color	cursor	fontSize
height	layoutGridMode	left	overflow
overflowX	overflowY	pixelBottom[*]	pixelHeight[*]
pixelLeft[*]	pixelRight[*]	pixelTop[*]	pixelWidth[*]
posBottom[*]	posHeight[*]	position	posLeft[*]

[*] This property has no corresponding attribute.

CSS Properties *(continued)*

Note For a list of corresponding attributes, see Appendix C.

posRight[*]	**posTop**[*]	**posWidth**[*]	**right**
styleFloat	**textAutospace**	**top**	**visibility**
width	**zIndex**		

* This property has no corresponding attribute.

AREA Element | AREA Object

Defines the shape, coordinates, and associated URL of one hyperlink region within a client-side image **MAP**.

Remarks

Any number of **AREA** elements can be contained within the same **MAP** element.

The format of the **COORDS** value depends on the value of the **SHAPE** attribute.

The **AREA** element is not rendered, and it requires a closing tag.

This element is available in HTML as of Internet Explorer 3.0 and in script as of Internet Explorer 4.0.

Attributes/Properties

		CLASS	
accessKey	**alt**	**className**	**coords**
currentStyle[*]	**dir**	**firstChild**[*]	**hash**[*]
host[*]	**hostname**[*]	**href**	**id**
isTextEdit[*]	**lang**	**language**	**lastChild**[*]
nextSibling[*]	**nodeName**[*]	**nodeType**[*]	**nodeValue**[*]
noHref	**offsetHeight**[*]	**offsetLeft**[*]	**offsetParent**[*]
offsetTop[*]	**offsetWidth**[*]	**outerHTML**[*]	**outerText**[*]
parentElement[*]	**parentNode**[*]	**parentTextEdit**[*]	**pathname**[*]
port[*]	**previousSibling**[*]	**protocol**[*]	**readyState**[*]
recordNumber[*]	**runtimeStyle**[*]	**scopeName**[*]	**search**[*]

Attributes/Properties *(continued)*

shape	**sourceIndex**[*]	**style**	**tabIndex**
tagName[*]	**tagUrn**[*]	**target**	**title**
uniqueID[*]			

[*] This property has no corresponding attribute.

Methods

addBehavior	**applyElement**	**attachEvent**
blur	**clearAttributes**	**click**
cloneNode	**componentFromPoint**	**contains**
detachEvent	**focus**	**getAdjacentText**
getAttribute	**getBoundingClientRect**	**getClientRects**
getElementsByTagName	**getExpression**	**hasChildNodes**
insertAdjacentElement	**insertAdjacentHTML**	**insertAdjacentText**
mergeAttributes	**releaseCapture**	**removeAttribute**
removeBehavior	**removeExpression**	**replaceAdjacentText**
scrollIntoView	**setAttribute**	**setCapture**
setExpression	**swapNode**	

Events

onbeforecopy	**onbeforecut**	**onbeforeeditfocus**	**onbeforepaste**
onblur	**onclick**	**oncopy**	**oncut**
ondblclick	**ondrag**	**ondragend**	**ondragenter**
ondragleave	**ondragover**	**ondragstart**	**ondrop**
onfocus	**onhelp**	**onkeydown**	**onkeypress**
onkeyup	**onlosecapture**	**onmousedown**	**onmousemove**
onmouseout	**onmouseover**	**onmouseup**	**onpaste**
onpropertychange	**onreadystatechange**	**onselectstart**	

Collections

all	**attributes**	**behaviorUrns**	**childNodes**	**children**

Default Behaviors

clientCaps	download	homePage	httpFolder	saveFavorite
saveHistory	saveSnapshot	time	userData	

CSS Properties

Note For a list of corresponding attributes, see Appendix C.

backgroundPositionX[*]	backgroundPositionY[*]	behavior	direction
layoutGridMode	pixelBottom[*]	pixelHeight[*]	pixelLeft[*]
pixelRight[*]	pixelTop[*]	pixelWidth[*]	posBottom[*]
posHeight[*]	posLeft[*]	posRight[*]	posTop[*]
posWidth[*]	textAutospace	unicodeBidi	width

* This property has no corresponding attribute.

Example

The following example shows how to use an **AREA** element to create an image map of the solar system. Clicking the sun or any planet links to an individual image. The user can click the Back button from the image to return to the solar system image map.

```
<P><IMG SRC="solarsys.gif" WIDTH=504 HEIGHT=126 BORDER=0
    ALT="Solar System" USEMAP="#SystemMap">

<MAP NAME="SystemMap">
    <AREA SHAPE="rect" COORDS="0,0,82,126"
        HREF="/workshop/graphics/sun.gif">
    <AREA SHAPE="circle" COORDS="90,58,3"
        HREF="/workshop/graphics/merglobe.gif">
    <AREA SHAPE="circle" COORDS="124,58,8"
        HREF="/workshop/graphics/venglobe.gif">
    <AREA SHAPE="circle" COORDS="162,58,10"
        HREF="/workshop/graphics/earglobe.gif">
    <AREA SHAPE="circle" COORDS="203,58,8"
        HREF="/workshop/graphics/marglobe.gif">
    <AREA SHAPE="poly" COORDS="221,34,238,37,257,32,278,44,284,
        60,281,75,288,91,267,87,253,89,237,81,229,64,228,54"
        HREF="/workshop/graphics/jupglobe.gif">
    <AREA SHAPE="poly" COORDS="288,19,316,39,330,37,348,47,351,66,
        349,74,367,105,337,85,324,85,307,77,303,60,307,50"
        HREF="/workshop/graphics/satglobe.gif">
    <AREA SHAPE="poly" COORDS="405,39,408,50,411,57,410,71,404,78,
        393,80,383,86,381,75,376,69,376,56,380,48,393,44"
        HREF="/workshop/graphics/uraglobe.gif">
```

```
      <AREA SHAPE="poly" COORDS="445,38,434,49,431,53,427,62,430,72,
          435,77,445,92,456,77,463,72,463,62,462,53,455,47"
          HREF="/workshop/graphics/nepglobe.gif">
      <AREA SHAPE="circle" COORDS="479,66,3"
          HREF="/workshop/graphics/pluglobe.gif">
  </MAP>
```

To see this code in action, refer to the Web Workshop CD-ROM.

Attribute Object

Represents an attribute or property of an HTML element as an object.

Remarks

The **Attribute** object is accessible through the **attributes** collection.

A valid attribute or property can be any DHTML property or event that applies to the object, or an **expando**.

This object is available in script as of Internet Explorer 5.

Attributes/Properties

nodeName[*]   **nodeType**[*]   **nodeValue**[*]   **specified**[*]

*   This property has no corresponding attribute.

Example

The following example shows how to use the **Attribute** object to create a list of attributes that are specified.

```
<SCRIPT>
function fnFind(){
    for(var i=0;i<oList.attributes.length;i++){
        if(oList.attributes[i].specified){
            alert(oList.attributes[i].nodeName + " = "
            + oList.attributes[i].nodeValue);
        }
    }
}
</SCRIPT>

<UL onclick="fnFind()">
<LI ID = "oItem1" ACCESSKEY = "L">List Item 1
</UL>
```

B Element | B Object

Specifies that the text should be rendered in bold.

Remarks

The **B** element is an inline element and requires a closing tag.

This element is available in HTML as of Internet Explorer 3.0 and in script as of Internet Explorer 4.0.

Attributes/Properties

	CLASS		
canHaveChildren[*]	className	clientHeight[*]	clientLeft[*]
clientTop[*]	clientWidth[*]	currentStyle[*]	dir
firstChild[*]	id	innerHTML[*]	innerText[*]
isTextEdit[*]	lang	language	lastChild[*]
nextSibling[*]	nodeName[*]	nodeType[*]	nodeValue[*]
offsetHeight[*]	offsetLeft[*]	offsetParent[*]	offsetTop[*]
offsetWidth[*]	outerHTML[*]	outerText[*]	parentElement[*]
parentNode[*]	parentTextEdit[*]	previousSibling[*]	readyState[*]
recordNumber[*]	runtimeStyle[*]	scopeName[*]	scrollHeight[*]
scrollLeft[*]	scrollTop[*]	scrollWidth[*]	sourceIndex[*]
style	tabIndex	tagName	tagUrn
title	uniqueID		

[*] This property has no corresponding attribute.

Methods

addBehavior	appendChild	applyElement
attachEvent	blur	clearAttributes
click	cloneNode	componentFromPoint
contains	detachEvent	focus
getAdjacentText	getAttribute	getBoundingClientRect
getClientRects	getElementsByTagName	getExpression
hasChildNodes	insertAdjacentElement	insertAdjacentHTML

Methods *(continued)*

insertAdjacentText	insertBefore	mergeAttributes
releaseCapture	removeAttribute	removeBehavior
removeChild	removeExpression	removeNode
replaceAdjacentText	replaceChild	replaceNode
scrollIntoView	setAttribute	setCapture
setExpression	swapNode	

Events

onbeforecopy	onbeforecut	onbeforepaste	onblur
onclick	oncopy	oncut	ondblclick
ondrag	ondragend	ondragenter	ondragleave
ondragover	ondragstart	ondrop	onfocus
onhelp	onkeydown	onkeypress	onkeyup
onlosecapture	onmousedown	onmousemove	onmouseout
onmouseover	onmouseup	onpaste	onpropertychange
onreadystatechange	onresize	onselectstart	

Collections

all	attributes	behaviorUrns	childNodes	children

Default Behaviors

clientCaps	download	homePage	httpFolder	saveFavorite
saveHistory	saveSnapshot	time	userData	

CSS Properties

Note For a list of corresponding attributes, see Appendix C.

background	backgroundColor	backgroundImage
backgroundPosition	backgroundPositionX[*]	backgroundPositionY[*]
backgroundRepeat	behavior	bottom
clear	color	cursor

* This property has no corresponding attribute.

CSS Properties *(continued)*

> **Note** For a list of corresponding attributes, see Appendix C.

direction	font	fontFamily
fontSize	fontStyle	fontVariant
fontWeight	layoutGridMode	left
letterSpacing	lineHeight	overflow
overflowX	overflowY	pixelBottom*
pixelHeight*	pixelLeft*	pixelRight*
pixelTop*	pixelWidth*	posBottom*
posHeight*	position	posLeft*
posRight*	posTop*	posWidth*
right	styleFloat	textAutospace
textDecoration	textDecorationBlink*	textDecorationLineThrough*
textDecorationNone*	textDecorationOverline*	textDecorationUnderline*
textTransform	top	unicodeBidi
visibility	width	wordSpacing
zIndex		

* This property has no corresponding attribute.

Example

The following example shows how to use the **B** element.

```
<B>This text will be displayed bold.</B>
```

BASE Element | BASE Object

Specifies an explicit URL used to resolve links and references to external sources, such as images and style sheets.

Remarks

When used, the **BASE** element must appear within the **HEAD** of the document before any elements that refer to an external source. A closing tag is not required.

This element is available in HTML as of Internet Explorer 3.0 and in script as of Internet Explorer 4.0.

Attributes/Properties

currentStyle[*]	firstChild[*]	href	id
isTextEdit[*]	lastChild[*]	nextSibling[*]	nodeName[*]
nodeType[*]	nodeValue[*]	parentElement[*]	parentNode[*]
parentTextEdit[*]	previousSibling[*]	readyState[*]	runtimeStyle[*]
scopeName[*]	sourceIndex[*]	style[*]	tagName[*]
tagUrn[*]	target	uniqueID[*]	

   [*]   This property has no corresponding attribute.

Methods

addBehavior	applyElement	attachEvent
clearAttributes	cloneNode	componentFromPoint
contains	detachEvent	getAdjacentText
getAttribute	getBoundingClientRect	getClientRects
getElementsByTagName	hasChildNodes	insertAdjacentElement
mergeAttributes	removeAttribute	removeBehavior
replaceAdjacentText	setAttribute	swapNode

Events

onreadystatechange

Collections

all	attributes	behaviorUrns	childNodes	children

Default Behaviors

clientCaps	download	homePage

Example

The following example shows how to set the base URL of the document to a reference folder. Internet Explorer uses the **BASE** element to resolve the link to http://www.microsoft.com/workshop/author/dhtml/reference/properties/href_2.asp.

```
<HEAD>
<BASE HREF="http://www.microsoft.com/workshop/author/dhtml/reference">
</HEAD>
```

```
<BODY>
Click <A HREF="properties/href_2.asp">here</A> to learn about the
href property.
</BODY>
```

The following example shows how to use script to retrieve the base URL from the document if a valid **BASE** element has been specified in the document. Otherwise, it returns null.

```
<SCRIPT>
function GetBase()
{
    var oBaseColl = document.all.tags('BASE');
    return ( (oBaseColl && oBaseColl.length) ? oBaseColl[0].href :
        null );
}
</SCRIPT>
```

BASEFONT Element | BASEFONT Object

Sets a base font value to be used as the default font when rendering text.

Remarks

This element can be used only within the **BODY** element or the **HEAD** element. **BASEFONT** should appear before any displayed text in the **BODY** of the document.

A closing tag is not required.

This element is available in HTML as of Internet Explorer 3.0 and in script as of Internet Explorer 4.0.

Attributes/Properties

color	**currentStyle**[*]	**face**	**firstChild**[*]
id	**isTextEdit**[*]	**lastChild**[*]	**nextSibling**[*]
nodeName[*]	**nodeType**[*]	**nodeValue**[*]	**parentElement**[*]
parentNode[*]	**parentTextEdit**[*]	**previousSibling**[*]	**readyState**[*]
runtimeStyle[*]	**scopeName**[*]	**size**	**sourceIndex**[*]
style[*]	**tagName**[*]	**tagUrn**[*]	**uniqueID**[*]

[*] This property has no corresponding attribute.

Methods

addBehavior	applyElement	attachEvent
clearAttributes	cloneNode	componentFromPoint
contains	detachEvent	getAdjacentText
getAttribute	getBoundingClientRect	getClientRects
getElementsByTagName	hasChildNodes	insertAdjacentElement
insertAdjacentHTML	insertAdjacentText	mergeAttributes
removeAttribute	removeBehavior	replaceAdjacentText
setAttribute	swapNode	

Events

onreadystatechange

Collections

all	attributes	behaviorUrns	childNodes	children

Default Behaviors

clientCaps	download	homePage

Example

The following example shows how to use the **BASEFONT** element to set the base font size and then temporarily override that size using a **FONT** element.

```
No BASEFONT size specified yet.
<BASEFONT SIZE=4> Set the BASEFONT size.
<FONT SIZE=2> Temporarily override the BASEFONT size.</FONT>
Resume the BASEFONT size.
```

BDO Element | BDO Object

Allows authors to disable the bidirectional algorithm for selected fragments of text.

Remarks

The **BDO** element is an inline element and requires a closing tag.

This element is used to control the reading order of a block of text.

The Unicode bidirectional algorithm automatically reverses embedded character sequences according to their inherent direction. For example, the base direction of an English document is left-to-right (ltr). If portions of a paragraph within this document contain a language with the right-to-left (rtl) reading order, the direction of that language is reversed correctly by the user agent applying the bidirectional algorithm.

The bidirectional algorithm and the **DIR** attribute generally suffice for embedded direction changes. However, incorrect results can occur if you expose formatted text to the bidirectional algorithm. For example, the bidirectional algorithm may incorrectly invert a paragraph containing English and Hebrew that is formatted for e-mail. Because the reading order of the Hebrew text has been inverted once for the e-mail, exposing it to the bidirectional algorithm inverts the words a second time.

The **BDO** element can be used to turn off the algorithm and control the reading order. The **DIR** attribute is mandatory when you use the **BDO** element.

This element is available in HTML and script as of Internet Explorer 5.

Attributes/Properties

		CLASS	
accessKey	**canHaveChildren**[*]	**className**	**clientHeight**[*]
clientLeft[*]	**clientTop**[*]	**clientWidth**[*]	**currentStyle**[*]
dir	**firstChild**[*]	**id**	**innerHTML**[*]
innerText[*]	**isTextEdit**[*]	**lang**	**language**
lastChild[*]	**nextSibling**[*]	**nodeName**[*]	**nodeType**[*]
nodeValue[*]	**offsetHeight**[*]	**offsetLeft**[*]	**offsetParent**[*]
offsetTop[*]	**offsetWidth**[*]	**outerHTML**[*]	**outerText**[*]
parentElement[*]	**parentNode**[*]	**parentTextEdit**[*]	**previousSibling**[*]
readyState[*]	**scopeName**[*]	**scrollHeight**[*]	**scrollLeft**[*]
scrollTop[*]	**scrollWidth**[*]	**sourceIndex**[*]	**tabIndex**
tagName[*]	**tagUrn**[*]	**title**	

[*] This property has no corresponding attribute.

Methods

addBehavior	**appendChild**	**applyElement**
blur	**clearAttributes**	**cloneNode**
componentFromPoint	**focus**	**getAdjacentText**

DHTML Objects

Methods *(continued)*

getElementsByTagName	getExpression	hasChildNodes
insertAdjacentElement	insertBefore	mergeAttributes
removeBehavior	removeChild	removeExpression
removeNode	replaceAdjacentText	replaceChild
replaceNode	setExpression	swapNode

Events

onafterupdate	onbeforecopy	onbeforecut	onbeforepaste
onbeforeupdate	onblur	oncellchange	onclick
oncopy	oncut	ondblclick	ondrag
ondragend	ondragenter	ondragleave	ondragover
ondragstart	ondrop	onerrorupdate	onfilterchange
onfocus	onhelp	onkeydown	onkeypress
onkeyup	onlosecapture	onmousedown	onmousemove
onmouseout	onmouseover	onmouseup	onpaste
onpropertychange	onreadystatechange	onscroll	onselectstart

Collections

all	attributes	behaviorUrns	childNodes	children	filters

Default Behaviors

clientCaps	download	homePage

Example

The following string has text in the left-to-right order of English and in the right-to-left order of Hebrew: This fragment is in English, WERBEH NI SI TNEMGARF SIHT.

Assume that the right-to left text (WERBEH NI SI TNEMGARF SIHT) has already been inverted so that it displays in the correct direction. If the Unicode bidirectional algorithm is subsequently applied to the text, the text inverts a second time and displays incorrectly left-to-right instead of right-to-left.

The solution is to override the bidirectional algorithm and put the block of text in the correct reading order inside a **BDO** element, whose **DIR** attribute is set to ltr:

```
<BDO DIR="ltr">This fragment is in English, WERBEH NI SI TNEMGARF SIHT.</BDO>
```

BGSOUND Element | BGSOUND Object

Enables pages with background sounds or soundtracks to be created.

Remarks

The **BGSOUND** element can be used only within the **HEAD** element. A closing tag is not required.

This element is available in HTML as of Internet Explorer 3.0 and in script as of Internet Explorer 4.0.

Attributes/Properties

balance	currentStyle*	id	loop
nextSibling*	nodeName*	nodeType*	nodeValue*
outerHTML*	outerText*	parentElement*	parentNode*
parentTextEdit*	previousSibling*	readyState*	recordNumber*
runtimeStyle*	scopeName*	sourceIndex*	src
style*	tagName*	tagUrn*	uniqueID*
volume			

* This property has no corresponding attribute.

Methods

addBehavior	applyElement	attachEvent
clearAttributes	cloneNode	componentFromPoint
detachEvent	getAttribute	getElementsByTagName
insertAdjacentElement	mergeAttributes	removeAttribute
removeBehavior	setAttribute	swapNode

Events

onreadystatechange

Collections

all	**attributes**	**behaviorUrns**

Default Behaviors

clientCaps	**download**	**homePage**

CSS Properties

Note For a list of corresponding attributes, see Appendix C.

behavior	**textAutospace**

BIG Element | BIG Object

Specifies that the enclosed text should be displayed in a larger font than the current font.

Remarks

The **BIG** element is an inline element and requires a closing tag.

This element is available in HTML as of Internet Explorer 3.0 and in script as of Internet Explorer 4.0.

Attributes/Properties

	CLASS		
canHaveChildren[*]	**className**	**clientHeight**[*]	**clientLeft**[*]
clientTop[*]	**clientWidth**[*]	**currentStyle**[*]	**dir**
firstChild[*]	**id**	**innerHTML**[*]	**innerText**[*]
isTextEdit[*]	**lang**	**language**	**lastChild**[*]
nextSibling[*]	**nodeName**[*]	**nodeType**[*]	**nodeValue**[*]
offsetHeight[*]	**offsetLeft**[*]	**offsetParent**[*]	**offsetTop**[*]
offsetWidth[*]	**outerHTML**[*]	**outerText**[*]	**parentElement**[*]
parentNode[*]	**parentTextEdit**[*]	**previousSibling**[*]	**readyState**[*]
recordNumber[*]	**runtimeStyle**[*]	**scopeName**[*]	**scrollHeight**[*]
scrollLeft[*]	**scrollTop**[*]	**scrollWidth**[*]	**sourceIndex**[*]
style	**tabIndex**	**tagName**[*]	**tagUrn**[*]
title	**uniqueID**[*]		

[*]   This property has no corresponding attribute.

Methods

addBehavior	appendChild	applyElement
attachEvent	blur	clearAttributes
click	cloneNode	componentFromPoint
contains	detachEvent	focus
getAdjacentText	getAttribute	getBoundingClientRect
getClientRects	getElementsByTagName	getExpression
hasChildNodes	insertAdjacentElement	insertAdjacentHTML
insertAdjacentText	insertBefore	mergeAttributes
releaseCapture	removeAttribute	removeBehavior
removeChild	removeExpression	removeNode
replaceAdjacentText	replaceChild	replaceNode
scrollIntoView	setAttribute	setCapture
setExpression	swapNode	

Events

onbeforecopy	onbeforecut	onbeforepaste	onblur
onclick	oncopy	oncut	ondblclick
ondrag	ondragend	ondragenter	ondragleave
ondragover	ondragstart	ondrop	onfocus
onhelp	onkeydown	onkeypress	onkeyup
onlosecapture	onmousedown	onmousemove	onmouseout
onmouseover	onmouseup	onpaste	onpropertychange
onreadystatechange	onresize	onselectstart	

Collections

all	attributes	behaviorUrns	childNodes	children

Default Behaviors

clientCaps	download	homePage	httpFolder	saveFavorite
saveHistory	saveSnapshot	time	userData	

CSS Properties

Note For a list of corresponding attributes, see Appendix C.

background	backgroundColor	backgroundImage
backgroundPosition	backgroundPositionX[*]	backgroundPositionY[*]
backgroundRepeat	behavior	bottom
clear	color	cursor
direction	font	fontFamily
fontSize	fontStyle	fontVariant
fontWeight	layoutGridMode	left
letterSpacing	lineHeight	overflow
overflowX	overflowY	pixelBottom[*]
pixelHeight[*]	pixelLeft[*]	pixelRight[*]
pixelTop[*]	pixelWidth[*]	posBottom[*]
posHeight[*]	position	posLeft[*]
posRight[*]	posTop[*]	posWidth[*]
right	styleFloat	textAutospace
textDecoration	textDecorationBlink[*]	textDecorationLineThrough[*]
textDecorationNone[*]	textDecorationOverline[*]	textDecorationUnderline[*]
textTransform	top	unicodeBidi
visibility	width	wordSpacing
zIndex		

* This property has no corresponding attribute.

Example

The following example shows how to use the **BIG** element.

```
<BIG>This text is larger</BIG> than this text.
```

BLOCKQUOTE Element | BLOCKQUOTE Object

Sets a quotation apart from adjacent text.

Remarks

The **BLOCKQUOTE** element is a block element and requires a closing tag.

This element is available in HTML as of Internet Explorer 3.0 and in script as of Internet Explorer 4.0.

Attributes/Properties

canHaveChildren[*]	CLASS className	clientHeight[*]	clientLeft[*]
clientTop[*]	clientWidth[*]	currentStyle[*]	dir
firstChild[*]	id	innerHTML[*]	innerText[*]
isTextEdit[*]	lang	language	lastChild[*]
nextSibling[*]	nodeName[*]	nodeType[*]	nodeValue[*]
offsetHeight[*]	offsetLeft[*]	offsetParent[*]	offsetTop[*]
offsetWidth[*]	outerHTML[*]	outerText[*]	parentElement[*]
parentNode[*]	parentTextEdit[*]	previousSibling[*]	readyState[*]
recordNumber[*]	runtimeStyle[*]	scopeName[*]	scrollHeight[*]
scrollLeft[*]	scrollTop[*]	scrollWidth[*]	sourceIndex[*]
style	tabIndex	tagName[*]	tagUrn[*]
title	uniqueID[*]		

[*] This property has no corresponding attribute.

Methods

addBehavior	appendChild	applyElement
attachEvent	blur	clearAttributes
click	cloneNode	componentFromPoint
contains	detachEvent	focus
getAdjacentText	getAttribute	getBoundingClientRect
getClientRects	getElementsByTagName	getExpression
hasChildNodes	insertAdjacentElement	insertAdjacentHTML

Methods *(continued)*

insertAdjacentText	insertBefore	mergeAttributes
releaseCapture	removeAttribute	removeBehavior
removeChild	removeExpression	removeNode
replaceAdjacentText	replaceChild	replaceNode
scrollIntoView	setAttribute	setCapture
setExpression	swapNode	

Events

onbeforecopy	onbeforecut	onbeforepaste	onblur
onclick	oncopy	oncut	ondblclick
ondrag	ondragend	ondragenter	ondragleave
ondragover	ondragstart	ondrop	onfocus
onhelp	onkeydown	onkeypress	onkeyup
onlosecapture	onmousedown	onmousemove	onmouseout
onmouseover	onmouseup	onpaste	onpropertychange
onreadystatechange	onresize	onselectstart	

Collections

all	attributes	behaviorUrns	childNodes	children

Default Behaviors

clientCaps	download	homePage	httpFolder	saveFavorite
saveHistory	saveSnapshot	time	userData	

CSS Properties

Note For a list of corresponding attributes, see Appendix C.

background	backgroundColor	backgroundImage
backgroundPosition	backgroundPositionX[*]	backgroundPositionY[*]
backgroundRepeat	behavior	border
borderBottom	borderBottomColor	borderBottomStyle

* This property has no corresponding attribute.

CSS Properties *(continued)*

Note For a list of corresponding attributes, see Appendix C.

borderBottomWidth	borderColor	borderLeft
borderLeftColor	borderLeftStyle	borderLeftWidth
borderRight	borderRightColor	borderRightStyle
borderRightWidth	borderStyle	borderTop
borderTopColor	borderTopStyle	borderTopWidth
borderWidth	bottom	clear
color	cursor	direction
font	fontFamily	fontSize
fontStyle	fontVariant	fontWeight
layoutGrid	layoutGridChar	layoutGridCharSpacing
layoutGridLine	layoutGridMode	layoutGridType
left	letterSpacing	lineBreak
lineHeight	margin	marginBottom
marginLeft	marginRight	marginTop
overflow	overflowX	overflowY
pageBreakAfter	pageBreakBefore	pixelBottom[*]
pixelHeight[*]	pixelLeft[*]	pixelRight[*]
pixelTop[*]	pixelWidth[*]	posBottom[*]
posHeight[*]	position	posLeft[*]
posRight[*]	posTop[*]	posWidth[*]
right	styleFloat	textAlign
textAutospace	textDecoration	textDecorationBlink[*]
textDecorationLineThrough[*]	textDecorationNone[*]	textDecorationOverline[*]
textDecorationUnderline[*]	textIndent	textJustify
textTransform	top	unicodeBidi
visibility	width	wordBreak
wordSpacing	zIndex	

[*]   This property has no corresponding attribute.

Example

The following example shows how to use the **BLOCKQUOTE** element.

```
<P>He said,
<BLOCKQUOTE>"Hi there!"</BLOCKQUOTE>
```

BODY Element | body Object

Specifies the beginning and end of the document body.

Remarks

The **BODY** element can be accessed from script through the **document** object.

Event handlers for the **onblur**, **onfocus**, **onload**, or **onunload** event can be hosted on the **window** object for the **BODY** element.

The **BODY** element is a block element and requires a closing tag.

This element is available in HTML as of Internet Explorer 3.0 and in script as of Internet Explorer 4.0.

Attributes/Properties

aLink	**background**	**bgColor**	**bgProperties**
bottomMargin	**canHaveChildren**[*]	**CLASS** **className**	**clientHeight**[*]
clientLeft[*]	**clientTop**[*]	**clientWidth**[*]	**currentStyle**[*]
dataFld	**dataFormatAs**	**dataSrc**	**dir**
firstChild[*]	**id**	**innerHTML**[*]	**innerText**[*]
isTextEdit[*]	**lang**	**language**	**lastChild**[*]
leftMargin	**link**	**nextSibling**[*]	**nodeName**[*]
nodeType[*]	**nodeValue**[*]	**noWrap**	**offsetHeight**[*]
offsetLeft[*]	**offsetParent**[*]	**offsetTop**[*]	**offsetWidth**[*]
parentElement[*]	**parentNode**[*]	**parentTextEdit**[*]	**previousSibling**[*]
readyState[*]	**rightMargin**	**runtimeStyle**[*]	**scopeName**[*]
scroll	**scrollHeight**[*]	**scrollLeft**[*]	**scrollTop**[*]

*   This property has no corresponding attribute.

Attributes/Properties *(continued)*

scrollWidth*	sourceIndex*	style	tabIndex
tagName*	tagUrn*	text	title
topMargin	uniqueID*	vLink	

* This property has no corresponding attribute.

Methods

addBehavior	appendChild	applyElement
attachEvent	blur	clearAttributes
click	cloneNode	componentFromPoint
contains	createControlRange	createTextRange
detachEvent	doScroll	focus
getAdjacentText	getAttribute	getBoundingClientRect
getClientRects	getElementsByTagName	getExpression
hasChildNodes	insertAdjacentElement	insertAdjacentHTML
insertAdjacentText	insertBefore	mergeAttributes
releaseCapture	removeAttribute	removeBehavior
removeChild	removeExpression	removeNode
replaceAdjacentText	replaceChild	replaceNode
setAttribute	setCapture	setExpression
swapNode		

Events

onafterprint	onbeforeprint	onclick	ondblclick
ondrag	ondragend	ondragenter	ondragleave
ondragover	ondragstart	ondrop	onfilterchange
onkeydown	onkeypress	onkeyup	onlosecapture
onmousedown	onmousemove	onmouseout	onmouseover
onmouseup	onpropertychange	onreadystatechange	onscroll
onselectstart			

Collections

all   attributes   behaviorUrns   childNodes   children   filters

Default Behaviors

clientCaps   download   homePage   httpFolder

CSS Properties

Note For a list of corresponding attributes, see Appendix C.

background	backgroundAttachment	backgroundColor
backgroundImage	backgroundPosition	backgroundPositionX[*]
backgroundPositionY[*]	backgroundRepeat	behavior
border	borderBottom	borderBottomColor
borderBottomStyle	borderBottomWidth	borderColor
borderLeft	borderLeftColor	borderLeftStyle
borderLeftWidth	borderRight	borderRightColor
borderRightStyle	borderRightWidth	borderStyle
borderTop	borderTopColor	borderTopStyle
borderTopWidth	borderWidth	color
cursor	direction	display
filter	font	fontFamily
fontSize	fontStyle	fontVariant
fontWeight	layoutGrid	layoutGridChar
layoutGridCharSpacing	layoutGridLine	layoutGridMode
layoutGridType	letterSpacing	lineBreak
lineHeight	margin	marginBottom
marginLeft	marginRight	marginTop
overflow	overflowX	overflowY
padding	paddingBottom	paddingLeft
paddingRight	paddingTop	pageBreakAfter
pageBreakBefore	pixelBottom[*]	pixelHeight[*]

*   This property has no corresponding attribute.

CSS Properties *(continued)*

Note For a list of corresponding attributes, see Appendix C.

pixelLeft[*]	**pixelRight**[*]	**pixelTop**[*]
pixelWidth[*]	**posBottom**[*]	**posHeight**[*]
posLeft[*]	**posRight**[*]	**posTop**[*]
posWidth[*]	**textAlign**	**textAutospace**
textDecoration	**textDecorationBlink**[*]	**textDecorationLineThrough**[*]
textDecorationNone[*]	**textDecorationOverline**[*]	**textDecorationUnderline**[*]
textIndent	**textJustify**	**textTransform**
unicodeBidi	**visibility**	**width**
wordBreak	**wordSpacing**	**zIndex**

* This property has no corresponding attribute.

Example

The following example shows how to use the **BODY** element in script.

```
var oBody = document.body;
```

Applies To

WIN16	WIN32	MAC

document

UNIX

document

BR Element | BR Object

Inserts a line break.

Remarks

The **BR** element does not require a closing tag.

This element is available in HTML as of Internet Explorer 3.0 and in script as of Internet Explorer 4.0.

Attributes/Properties

CLASS

className	clear	currentStyle[*]	id
isTextEdit[*]	nextSibling[*]	nodeName[*]	nodeType[*]
nodeValue[*]	offsetHeight[*]	offsetLeft[*]	offsetParent[*]
offsetTop[*]	offsetWidth[*]	outerHTML[*]	outerText[*]
parentElement[*]	parentNode[*]	parentTextEdit[*]	previousSibling[*]
readyState[*]	recordNumber[*]	runtimeStyle[*]	scopeName[*]
sourceIndex[*]	style	tagName[*]	tagUrn[*]
uniqueID[*]			

[*] This property has no corresponding attribute.

Methods

addBehavior	applyElement	attachEvent
clearAttributes	cloneNode	componentFromPoint
detachEvent	getAdjacentText	getAttribute
getElementsByTagName	getExpression	hasChildNodes
insertAdjacentElement	mergeAttributes	releaseCapture
removeAttribute	removeBehavior	removeExpression
replaceAdjacentText	scrollIntoView	setAttribute
setCapture	setExpression	swapNode

Events

onlosecapture   onreadystatechange

Collections

attributes   behaviorUrns

Default Behaviors

clientCaps   download   homePage

CSS Properties

Note For a list of corresponding attributes, see Appendix C.

backgroundPositionX*	backgroundPositionY*	behavior	layoutGridMode
pixelBottom*	pixelHeight*	pixelLeft*	pixelRight*
pixelTop*	pixelWidth*	posBottom*	posHeight*
posLeft*	posRight*	posTop*	posWidth*
textAutospace	width		

*   This property has no corresponding attribute.

BUTTON Element | BUTTON Object

Specifies a container for rich HTML that is rendered as a button.

Remarks

When the **BUTTON** element is submitted in a form, Internet Explorer 5 and later submits the **VALUE** attribute, if it exists. Otherwise, the **innerText** property is submitted. In Internet Explorer 4.0, only the **innerText** value is submitted.

The **BUTTON** element is an inline element and requires a closing tag.

This element is available in HTML and script as of Internet Explorer 4.0.

Attributes/Properties

		CLASS	
accessKey	canHaveChildren*	className	clientHeight*
clientLeft*	clientTop*	clientWidth*	currentStyle*
dataFld	dataFormatAs	dataSrc	dir
disabled	firstChild*	form*	id
innerHTML*	innerText*	isTextEdit*	lang
language	lastChild*	name	nextSibling*
nodeName*	nodeType*	nodeValue*	offsetHeight*
offsetLeft*	offsetParent*	offsetTop*	offsetWidth*
outerHTML*	outerText*	parentElement*	parentNode*
parentTextEdit*	previousSibling*	readyState*	recordNumber*

Attributes/Properties *(continued)*

runtimeStyle*	scopeName*	scrollHeight*	scrollLeft*
scrollTop*	scrollWidth*	sourceIndex*	style
tabIndex	tagName*	tagUrn*	title
type	uniqueID*	value	

*   This property has no corresponding attribute.

Methods

addBehavior	appendChild	applyElement
attachEvent	blur	clearAttributes
click	cloneNode	componentFromPoint
contains	createTextRange	detachEvent
focus	getAdjacentText	getAttribute
getBoundingClientRect	getClientRects	getElementsByTagName
getExpression	hasChildNodes	insertAdjacentElement
insertAdjacentHTML	insertAdjacentText	insertBefore
mergeAttributes	releaseCapture	removeAttribute
removeBehavior	removeChild	removeExpression
removeNode	replaceAdjacentText	replaceChild
replaceNode	scrollIntoView	setAttribute
setCapture	setExpression	swapNode

Events

onbeforeeditfocus	onblur	onclick	ondblclick
ondragenter	ondragleave	ondragover	ondrop
onfilterchange	onfocus	onhelp	onkeydown
onkeypress	onkeyup	onlosecapture	onmousedown
onmousemove	onmouseout	onmouseover	onmouseup
onpropertychange	onreadystatechange	onresize	onselectstart

Collections

| all | attributes | behaviorUrns | childNodes | children | filters |

Default Behaviors

| clientCaps | download | homePage | httpFolder | saveFavorite |
| saveHistory | saveSnapshot | time | userData | |

CSS Properties

Note For a list of corresponding attributes, see Appendix C.

background	backgroundColor	backgroundImage
backgroundPosition	backgroundPositionX[*]	backgroundPositionY[*]
backgroundRepeat	behavior	border
borderBottom	borderBottomColor	borderBottomStyle
borderBottomWidth	borderColor	borderLeft
borderLeftColor	borderLeftStyle	borderLeftWidth
borderRight	borderRightColor	borderRightStyle
borderRightWidth	borderStyle	borderTop
borderTopColor	borderTopStyle	borderTopWidth
borderWidth	bottom	clear
color	direction	display
filter	font	fontFamily
fontSize	fontStyle	fontVariant
fontWeight	height	layoutGridMode
left	letterSpacing	lineHeight
margin	marginBottom	marginLeft
marginRight	marginTop	padding
paddingBottom	paddingLeft	paddingRight
paddingTop	pageBreakAfter	pageBreakBefore
pixelBottom[*]	pixelHeight[*]	pixelLeft[*]

[*]   This property has no corresponding attribute.

CSS Properties *(continued)*

Note For a list of corresponding attributes, see Appendix C.

pixelRight*	pixelTop*	pixelWidth*
posBottom*	posHeight*	position
posLeft*	posRight*	posTop*
posWidth*	right	styleFloat
textAutospace	textDecoration	textDecorationBlink*
textDecorationLineThrough*	textDecorationNone*	textDecorationOverline*
textDecorationUnderline*	textIndent	textTransform
top	unicodeBidi	visibility
width	wordSpacing	zIndex

* This property has no corresponding attribute.

CAPTION Element | CAPTION Object

Specifies a caption for a **TABLE**.

Remarks

The **CAPTION** element is a block element and requires a closing tag.

This element is available in HTML as of Internet Explorer 3.0 and in script as of Internet Explorer 4.0.

Attributes/Properties

align	canHaveChildren*	CLASS className	clientHeight*
clientLeft*	clientTop*	clientWidth*	currentStyle*
dir	firstChild*	id	innerHTML*
innerText*	isTextEdit*	lang	language
lastChild*	nextSibling*	nodeName*	nodeType*
nodeValue*	offsetHeight*	offsetLeft*	offsetParent*
offsetTop*	offsetWidth*	parentElement*	parentNode*
parentTextEdit*	previousSibling*	readyState*	recordNumber*

* This property has no corresponding attribute.

Attributes/Properties *(continued)*

runtimeStyle*	scopeName*	scrollHeight*	scrollLeft*
scrollTop*	scrollWidth*	sourceIndex*	style
tabIndex	tagName*	tagUrn*	title
uniqueID*	vAlign		

* This property has no corresponding attribute.

Methods

addBehavior	appendChild	applyElement
attachEvent	blur	clearAttributes
click	cloneNode	componentFromPoint
contains	detachEvent	focus
getAdjacentText	getAttribute	getBoundingClientRect
getClientRects	getElementsByTagName	getExpression
hasChildNodes	insertAdjacentElement	insertAdjacentHTML
insertAdjacentText	insertBefore	mergeAttributes
releaseCapture	removeAttribute	removeBehavior
removeChild	removeExpression	removeNode
replaceAdjacentText	replaceChild	replaceNode
scrollIntoView	setAttribute	setCapture
setExpression	swapNode	

Events

onbeforecopy	onbeforecut	onbeforepaste	onblur
onclick	oncopy	oncut	ondblclick
ondrag	ondragend	ondragenter	ondragleave
ondragover	ondragstart	ondrop	onfocus
onhelp	onkeydown	onkeypress	onkeyup
onlosecapture	onmousedown	onmousemove	onmouseout
onmouseover	onmouseup	onpaste	onpropertychange
onreadystatechange	onselectstart		

Collections

all	attributes	behaviorUrns	childNodes	children

Default Behaviors

clientCaps	download	homePage	httpFolder	saveFavorite
saveHistory	time	userData		

CSS Properties

Note For a list of corresponding attributes, see Appendix C.

background	backgroundColor	backgroundImage
backgroundPosition	backgroundPositionX*	backgroundPositionY*
backgroundRepeat	behavior	border
borderBottom	borderBottomColor	borderBottomStyle
borderBottomWidth	borderColor	borderLeft
borderLeftColor	borderLeftStyle	borderLeftWidth
borderRight	borderRightColor	borderRightStyle
borderRightWidth	borderStyle	borderTop
borderTopColor	borderTopStyle	borderTopWidth
borderWidth	clear	color
cursor	direction	font
fontFamily	fontSize	fontStyle
fontVariant	fontWeight	layoutGridMode
letterSpacing	lineHeight	margin
marginBottom	marginLeft	marginRight
marginTop	padding	paddingBottom
paddingLeft	paddingRight	paddingTop
pixelBottom*	pixelHeight*	pixelLeft*
pixelRight*	pixelTop*	pixelWidth*
posBottom*	posHeight*	posLeft*
posRight*	posTop*	posWidth*

* This property has no corresponding attribute.

CSS Properties *(continued)*

Note For a list of corresponding attributes, see Appendix C.

textAutospace	**textDecoration**	**textDecorationBlink**[*]
textDecorationLineThrough[*]	**textDecorationNone**[*]	**textDecorationOverline**[*]
textDecorationUnderline[*]	**textTransform**	**unicodeBidi**
visibility	**width**	**wordSpacing**
zIndex		

[*] This property has no corresponding attribute.

Example

The following example shows how to use the **CAPTION** element.

```
<TABLE>
<CAPTION VALIGN=BOTTOM>
This caption will appear below the table.
</CAPTION>
<TR>
<TD>
This text is inside the table.
</TD>
</TR>
</TABLE>
```

CENTER Element | CENTER Object

Centers subsequent text and images.

Remarks

The **CENTER** element is a block element and requires a closing tag.

This element is available in HTML as of Internet Explorer 3.0 and in script as of Internet Explorer 4.0.

Attributes/Properties

canHaveChildren[*]	**CLASS** **className**	**clientHeight**[*]	**clientLeft**[*]
clientTop[*]	**clientWidth**[*]	**currentStyle**[*]	**dir**
firstChild[*]	**id**	**innerHTML**[*]	**innerText**[*]
isTextEdit[*]	**lang**	**language**	**lastChild**[*]
nextSibling[*]	**nodeName**[*]	**nodeType**[*]	**nodeValue**[*]

Attributes/Properties *(continued)*

offsetHeight*	offsetLeft*	offsetParent*	offsetTop*
offsetWidth*	outerHTML*	outerText*	parentElement*
parentNode*	parentTextEdit*	previousSibling*	readyState*
recordNumber*	runtimeStyle*	scopeName*	scrollHeight*
scrollLeft*	scrollTop*	scrollWidth*	sourceIndex*
style	tabIndex	tagName*	tagUrn*
uniqueID*			

* This property has no corresponding attribute.

Methods

addBehavior	appendChild	applyElement
attachEvent	blur	clearAttributes
click	cloneNode	componentFromPoint
contains	detachEvent	focus
getAdjacentText	getAttribute	getBoundingClientRect
getClientRects	getElementsByTagName	getExpression
hasChildNodes	insertAdjacentElement	insertAdjacentHTML
insertAdjacentText	insertBefore	mergeAttributes
releaseCapture	removeAttribute	removeBehavior
removeChild	removeExpression	removeNode
replaceAdjacentText	replaceChild	replaceNode
scrollIntoView	setAttribute	setCapture
setExpression	swapNode	

Events

onbeforecopy	onbeforecut	onbeforepaste	onblur
onclick	oncopy	oncut	ondblclick
ondrag	ondragend	ondragenter	ondragleave
ondragover	ondragstart	ondrop	onfocus
onhelp	onkeydown	onkeypress	onkeyup

Events *(continued)*

onlosecapture	onmousedown	onmousemove	onmouseout
onmouseover	onmouseup	onpaste	onpropertychange
onreadystatechange	onresize	onselectstart	

Collections

all	attributes	behaviorUrns	childNodes	children

Default Behaviors

clientCaps	download	homePage	httpFolder	saveFavorite
saveHistory	saveSnapshot	time	userData	

CSS Properties

Note For a list of corresponding attributes, see Appendix C.

background	backgroundColor	backgroundImage
backgroundPosition	backgroundPositionX*	backgroundPositionY*
backgroundRepeat	behavior	border
borderBottom	borderBottomColor	borderBottomStyle
borderBottomWidth	borderColor	borderLeft
borderLeftColor	borderLeftStyle	borderLeftWidth
borderRight	borderRightColor	borderRightStyle
borderRightWidth	borderStyle	borderTop
borderTopColor	borderTopStyle	borderTopWidth
borderWidth	bottom	clear
color	cursor	direction
font	fontFamily	fontSize
fontStyle	fontVariant	fontWeight
layoutGrid	layoutGridChar	layoutGridCharSpacing
layoutGridLine	layoutGridMode	layoutGridType
left	letterSpacing	lineBreak

CSS Properties *(continued)*

lineHeight	margin	marginBottom
marginLeft	marginRight	marginTop
overflow	overflowX	overflowY
pageBreakAfter	pageBreakBefore	pixelBottom*
pixelHeight*	pixelLeft*	pixelRight*
pixelTop*	pixelWidth*	posBottom*
posHeight*	position	posLeft*
posRight*	posTop*	posWidth*
right	styleFloat	textAlign
textAutospace	textDecoration	textDecorationBlink*
textDecorationLineThrough*	textDecorationNone*	textDecorationOverline*
textDecorationUnderline*	textIndent	textJustify
textTransform	top	unicodeBidi
visibility	width	wordBreak
wordSpacing	zIndex	

* This property has no corresponding attribute.

Example

The following example shows how to use the **CENTER** element.

```
<CENTER>This text appears centered on the page.</CENTER>
```

CITE Element | CITE Object

Indicates a citation (a reference to a book, paper, or other published source material). Text renders in italic.

Remarks

The **CITE** element is an inline element and requires a closing tag.

This element is available in HTML as of Internet Explorer 3.0 and in script as of Internet Explorer 4.0.

Attributes/Properties

	CLASS		
canHaveChildren*	className	clientHeight*	clientLeft*
clientTop*	clientWidth*	currentStyle*	dir
firstChild*	id	innerHTML*	innerText*
isTextEdit*	lang	language	lastChild*
nextSibling*	nodeName*	nodeType*	nodeValue*
offsetHeight*	offsetLeft*	offsetParent*	offsetTop*
offsetWidth*	outerHTML*	outerText*	parentElement*
parentNode*	parentTextEdit*	previousSibling*	readyState*
recordNumber*	runtimeStyle*	scopeName*	scrollHeight*
scrollLeft*	scrollTop*	scrollWidth*	sourceIndex*
style	tabIndex	tagName*	tagUrn*
title	uniqueID*		

* This property has no corresponding attribute.

Methods

addBehavior	appendChild	applyElement
attachEvent	blur	clearAttributes
click	cloneNode	componentFromPoint
contains	detachEvent	focus
getAdjacentText	getAttribute	getBoundingClientRect
getClientRects	getElementsByTagName	getExpression
hasChildNodes	insertAdjacentElement	insertAdjacentHTML
insertAdjacentText	insertBefore	mergeAttributes
releaseCapture	removeAttribute	removeBehavior
removeChild	removeExpression	removeNode
replaceAdjacentText	replaceChild	replaceNode
scrollIntoView	setAttribute	setCapture
setExpression	swapNode	

Events

onbeforecopy	onbeforecut	onbeforepaste	onblur
onclick	oncopy	oncut	ondblclick
ondrag	ondragend	ondragenter	ondragleave
ondragover	ondragstart	ondrop	onfocus
onhelp	onkeydown	onkeypress	onkeyup
onlosecapture	onmousedown	onmousemove	onmouseout
onmouseover	onmouseup	onpaste	onpropertychange
onreadystatechange	onresize	onselectstart	

Collections

all	attributes	behaviorUrns	childNodes	children

Default Behaviors

clientCaps	download	homePage	httpFolder	saveFavorite
saveHistory	saveSnapshot	time	userData	

CSS Properties

Note For a list of corresponding attributes, see Appendix C.

background	backgroundColor	backgroundImage
backgroundPosition	backgroundPositionX*	backgroundPositionY*
backgroundRepeat	behavior	bottom
clear	color	cursor
direction	font	fontFamily
fontSize	fontStyle	fontVariant
fontWeight	layoutGridMode	left
letterSpacing	lineHeight	overflow
overflowX	overflowY	pixelBottom*
pixelHeight*	pixelLeft*	pixelRight*
pixelTop*	pixelWidth*	posBottom*

* This property has no corresponding attribute.

CSS Properties *(continued)*

Note For a list of corresponding attributes, see Appendix C.

posHeight[*]	**position**	**posLeft**[*]
posRight[*]	**posTop**[*]	**posWidth**[*]
right	**styleFloat**	**textAutospace**
textDecoration	**textDecorationBlink**[*]	**textDecorationLineThrough**[*]
textDecorationNone[*]	**textDecorationOverline**[*]	**textDecorationUnderline**[*]
textTransform	**top**	**unicodeBidi**
visibility	**width**	**wordSpacing**
zIndex		

*   This property has no corresponding attribute.

Example

The following example shows how to use the **CITE** element.

```
<CITE>Book Title.</CITE>
```

clipboardData Object

Provides access to predefined clipboard formats for use in editing operations.

Remarks

The **clipboardData** object is reserved for editing actions performed through the Edit menu, shortcut menu, and shortcut keys. It transfers information using the system clipboard and retains it until data from the next editing operation supplants it. This form of data transfer is particularly suited to multiple pastes of the same data.

This object is available in script as of Internet Explorer 5.

Methods

clearData   **getData**   **setData**

Example

The following example shows how to use the **setData** and **getData** methods with the **clipboardData** object to perform a cut-and-paste operation through the shortcut menu.

```
<SCRIPT>
var sNewString = "new content associated with this object";
var sSave = "";

// Selects the text that is to be cut.

function fnLoad() {
    var r = document.body.createTextRange();
    r.findText(oSource.innerText);
    r.select();
}

// Stores the text of the SPAN in a variable that is set
// to an empty string in the variable declaration above.

function fnBeforeCut() {
    sSave = oSource.innerText;
    event.returnValue = false;
}

// Associates the variable sNewString with the text being cut.

function fnCut() {
    event.returnValue = false;
    window.clipboardData.setData("Text", sNewString);
}

function fnBeforePaste() {
    event.returnValue = false;
}

// The second parameter set in getData causes sNewString
// to be pasted into the text input. Passing no second
// parameter causes the text in the SPAN to be pasted.

function fnPaste() {
    event.returnValue = false;
    oTarget.value = window.clipboardData.getData("Text", sNewString);
}

</SCRIPT>
</HEAD>
<BODY>

<SPAN ID="oSource" onbeforecut="fnBeforeCut()" oncut="fnCut()">
    Cut this Text
</SPAN>

<INPUT ID="oTarget" TYPE="text" VALUE="Paste the Text Here"
        onbeforepaste="fnBeforePaste()" onpaste="fnPaste()">
</BODY>
```

To see this code in action, refer to the Web Workshop CD-ROM.

Applies To

 WIN16   WIN32   MAC   UNIX

window

CODE Element | CODE Object

Specifies a code sample.

Remarks

The **CODE** element is an inline element and requires a closing tag.

This element is available in HTML as of Internet Explorer 3.0 and in script as of Internet Explorer 4.0.

Attributes/Properties

	CLASS		
canHaveChildren*	className	clientHeight*	clientLeft*
clientTop*	clientWidth*	currentStyle*	dir
firstChild*	id	innerHTML*	innerText*
isTextEdit*	lang	language	lastChild*
nextSibling*	nodeName*	nodeType*	nodeValue*
offsetHeight*	offsetLeft*	offsetParent*	offsetTop*
offsetWidth*	outerHTML*	outerText*	parentElement*
parentNode*	parentTextEdit*	previousSibling*	readyState*
recordNumber*	runtimeStyle*	scopeName*	scrollHeight*
scrollLeft*	scrollTop*	scrollWidth*	sourceIndex*
style	tagName*	tagUrn*	title
uniqueID*			

*   This property has no corresponding attribute.

Methods

addBehavior	appendChild	applyElement
attachEvent	clearAttributes	click
cloneNode	componentFromPoint	contains
detachEvent	getAdjacentText	getAttribute

DHTML Objects

Methods *(continued)*

getBoundingClientRect	getClientRects	getElementsByTagName
getExpression	hasChildNodes	insertAdjacentElement
insertAdjacentHTML	insertAdjacentText	insertBefore
mergeAttributes	releaseCapture	removeAttribute
removeBehavior	removeChild	removeExpression
removeNode	replaceAdjacentText	replaceChild
replaceNode	scrollIntoView	setAttribute
setCapture	setExpression	swapNode

Events

onbeforecopy	onbeforecut	onbeforepaste	onclick
oncopy	oncut	ondblclick	ondrag
ondragend	ondragenter	ondragleave	ondragover
ondragstart	ondrop	onhelp	onkeydown
onkeypress	onkeyup	onlosecapture	onmousedown
onmousemove	onmouseout	onmouseover	onmouseup
onpaste	onpropertychange	onreadystatechange	onresize
onselectstart			

Collections

all	attributes	behaviorUrns	childNodes	children

Default Behaviors

clientCaps	download	homePage	httpFolder	saveFavorite
saveHistory	saveSnapshot	time	userData	

CSS Properties

Note For a list of corresponding attributes, see Appendix C.

background	**backgroundColor**	**backgroundImage**
backgroundPosition	**backgroundPositionX**[*]	**backgroundPositionY**[*]
backgroundRepeat	**behavior**	**bottom**
clear	**color**	**cursor**
direction	**font**	**fontFamily**
fontSize	**fontStyle**	**fontVariant**
fontWeight	**layoutGridMode**	**left**
letterSpacing	**lineHeight**	**overflow**
overflowX	**overflowY**	**pixelBottom**[*]
pixelHeight[*]	**pixelLeft**[*]	**pixelRight**[*]
pixelTop[*]	**pixelWidth**[*]	**posBottom**[*]
posHeight[*]	**position**	**posLeft**[*]
posRight[*]	**posTop**[*]	**posWidth**[*]
right	**styleFloat**	**textAutospace**
textDecoration	**textDecorationBlink**[*]	**textDecorationLineThrough**[*]
textDecorationNone[*]	**textDecorationOverline**[*]	**textDecorationUnderline**[*]
textTransform	**top**	**unicodeBidi**
visibility	**width**	**wordSpacing**
zIndex		

[*] This property has no corresponding attribute.

Example

The following example shows how to use the **CODE** element.

```
<CODE>Here is some text in a small, fixed-width font.</CODE>
```

COL Element | COL Object

Specifies column-based defaults for the table properties.

Remarks

The **COL** element is a block element and requires a closing tag.

This element is available in HTML as of Internet Explorer 3.0 and in script as of Internet Explorer 4.0.

Attributes/Properties

	BGCOLOR[†]		CLASS
align		canHaveChildren[*]	className
clientHeight[*]	clientLeft[*]	clientTop[*]	clientWidth[*]
currentStyle[*]	dir	firstChild[*]	id
isTextEdit[*]	lang	lastChild[*]	nextSibling[*]
nodeName[*]	nodeType[*]	nodeValue[*]	offsetHeight[*]
offsetLeft[*]	offsetParent[*]	offsetTop[*]	offsetWidth[*]
parentElement[*]	parentNode[*]	parentTextEdit[*]	previousSibling[*]
readyState[*]	recordNumber[*]	runtimeStyle[*]	scopeName[*]
scrollHeight[*]	scrollLeft[*]	scrollTop[*]	scrollWidth[*]
sourceIndex[*]	span	style	tagName[*]
tagUrn[*]	uniqueID[*]	vAlign	width

[*] This property has no corresponding attribute.

[†] This attribute has no corresponding property.

Methods

addBehavior	appendChild	applyElement
attachEvent	clearAttributes	cloneNode
componentFromPoint	contains	detachEvent
getAdjacentText	getAttribute	getBoundingClientRect
getClientRects	getElementsByTagName	getExpression
hasChildNodes	insertAdjacentElement	insertBefore
mergeAttributes	removeAttribute	removeBehavior

Methods *(continued)*

removeChild	removeExpression	removeNode
replaceAdjacentText	replaceChild	replaceNode
scrollIntoView	setAttribute	setExpression
swapNode		

Events

onreadystatechange

Collections

all	attributes	behaviorUrns	childNodes	children

Default Behaviors

clientCaps	download	homePage

CSS Properties

Note For a list of corresponding attributes, see Appendix C.

background	backgroundColor	backgroundImage
backgroundPosition	backgroundPositionX*	backgroundPositionY*
backgroundRepeat	behavior	clear
color	cursor	direction
font	fontFamily	fontSize
fontStyle	fontVariant	fontWeight
layoutGridMode	letterSpacing	lineHeight
pixelBottom*	pixelHeight*	pixelLeft*
pixelRight*	pixelTop*	pixelWidth*
posBottom*	posHeight*	posLeft*
posRight*	posTop*	posWidth*
textAutospace	textDecoration	textDecorationBlink*

CSS Properties *(continued)*

textDecorationLineThrough[*]	**textDecorationNone**[*]	**textDecorationOverline**[*]
textDecorationUnderline[*]	**textTransform**	**unicodeBidi**
verticalAlign	**visibility**	**width**
wordSpacing	**zIndex**	

*   This property has no corresponding attribute.

Example

The following example shows how to use the **COL** element with the **ALIGN** attribute to specify the alignment of columns.

```
<TABLE>
<COLGROUP><COL ALIGN=RIGHT><COL ALIGN=LEFT></COLGROUP>
<COLGROUP><COL ALIGN=CENTER></COLGROUP>
<TBODY>
<TR>
<TD>This is the first column in the group and it is right-aligned.</TD>
<TD>This is the second column in the group and it is left-aligned.</TD>
<TD>This column is in a new group and it is centered.</TD>
</TR>
</TABLE>
```

COLGROUP Element | COLGROUP Object

Contains a group of columns.

Remarks

The **COLGROUP** element is a block element and requires a closing tag.

This element is available in HTML as of Internet Explorer 3.0 and in script as of Internet Explorer 4.0.

Attributes/Properties

	BGCOLOR[†]		CLASS
align		**canHaveChildren**[*]	**className**
clientHeight[*]	**clientLeft**[*]	**clientTop**[*]	**clientWidth**[*]
currentStyle[*]	**dir**	**firstChild**[*]	**id**
isTextEdit[*]	**lang**	**lastChild**[*]	**nextSibling**[*]
nodeName[*]	**nodeType**[*]	**nodeValue**[*]	**offsetHeight**[*]

*   This property has no corresponding attribute.

†   This attribute has no corresponding property.

Attributes/Properties *(continued)*

offsetLeft[*]	offsetParent[*]	offsetTop[*]	offsetWidth[*]
parentElement[*]	parentNode[*]	parentTextEdit[*]	previousSibling[*]
readyState[*]	recordNumber[*]	runtimeStyle[*]	scopeName[*]
scrollHeight[*]	scrollLeft[*]	scrollTop[*]	scrollWidth[*]
sourceIndex[*]	span	style[*]	tagName[*]
tagUrn[*]	title	uniqueID[*]	vAlign
width			

[*]   This property has no corresponding attribute.

[†]   This attribute has no corresponding property.

Methods

addBehavior	appendChild	applyElement
attachEvent	clearAttributes	cloneNode
componentFromPoint	contains	detachEvent
getAdjacentText	getAttribute	getBoundingClientRect
getClientRects	getElementsByTagName	getExpression
hasChildNodes	insertAdjacentElement	insertBefore
mergeAttributes	removeAttribute	removeBehavior
removeChild	removeExpression	removeNode
replaceAdjacentText	replaceChild	replaceNode
scrollIntoView	setAttribute	setExpression
swapNode		

Events

onreadystatechange

Collections

all	attributes	behaviorUrns	childNodes	children

Default Behaviors

clientCaps	download	homePage

CSS Properties

Note For a list of corresponding attributes, see Appendix C.

background	**backgroundColor**	**backgroundImage**
backgroundPosition	**backgroundPositionX**[*]	**backgroundPositionY**[*]
backgroundRepeat	**behavior**	**clear**
color	**cursor**	**direction**
font	**fontFamily**	**fontSize**
fontStyle	**fontVariant**	**fontWeight**
layoutGridMode	**letterSpacing**	**lineHeight**
pixelBottom[*]	**pixelHeight**[*]	**pixelLeft**[*]
pixelRight[*]	**pixelTop**[*]	**pixelWidth**[*]
posBottom[*]	**posHeight**[*]	**posLeft**[*]
posRight[*]	**posTop**[*]	**posWidth**[*]
textAutospace	**textDecoration**	**textDecorationBlink**[*]
textDecorationLineThrough[*]	**textDecorationNone**[*]	**textDecorationOverline**[*]
textDecorationUnderline[*]	**textTransform**	**unicodeBidi**
visibility	**width**	**wordSpacing**
zIndex		

[*] This property has no corresponding attribute.

Example

The following example shows how to use the **COLGROUP** element.

```
<TABLE>
<COLGROUP ALIGN="RIGHT"></COLGROUP>
<COLGROUP SPAN="2" ALIGN="LEFT"></COLGROUP>
<TBODY>
<TR>
<TD>This column is in the first group and is right-aligned.</TD>
<TD>This column is in the second group and is left-aligned.</TD>
<TD>This column is in the second group and is left-aligned.</TD>
</TR>
</TABLE>
```

COMMENT Element | COMMENT Object

Indicates a comment that is not displayed.

Remarks

The **COMMENT** element requires a closing tag.

This element is treated as a no-scope element and does not expose any **children**.

This element is available in HTML as of Internet Explorer 3.0 and in script as of Internet Explorer 4.0.

Attributes/Properties

canHaveChildren*	currentStyle*	firstChild*	id
isTextEdit*	lang	lastChild*	nextSibling*
nodeName*	nodeType*	nodeValue*	offsetParent*
outerHTML*	outerText*	parentElement*	parentNode*
parentTextEdit*	previousSibling*	readyState*	recordNumber*
runtimeStyle*	scopeName*	sourceIndex*	style*
tagName*	tagUrn*	uniqueID*	

* This property has no corresponding attribute.

Methods

addBehavior	appendChild	applyElement
attachEvent	clearAttributes	cloneNode
componentFromPoint	detachEvent	getAdjacentText
getAttribute	getBoundingClientRect	getClientRects
hasChildNodes	insertAdjacentElement	insertAdjacentHTML
insertAdjacentText	insertBefore	mergeAttributes
removeAttribute	removeBehavior	removeChild
removeNode	replaceAdjacentText	replaceChild
replaceNode	scrollIntoView	setAttribute
swapNode		

Events

> onpropertychange   onreadystatechange

Collections

> attributes   behaviorUrns   childNodes

Default Behaviors

> clientCaps   download   homePage

currentStyle Object

Represents the cascaded format and style of the object as specified by global style sheets, inline styles, and HTML attributes.

Remarks

The **currentStyle** object returns the cascaded styles on an element, but the **style** object returns only the styles that have been applied inline on an element through the **STYLE** attribute. Thus, the style values retrieved through the **currentStyle** object may differ from the style values retrieved through the **style** object. For example, if the **color** property is set on a paragraph only through a linked or embedded style sheet, and not inline, then *object*.**currentStyle**.**color** returns the color, whereas *object*.**style**.**color** does not return a value. If, however, the author specifies <P STYLE="color:'red'">, the **currentStyle** and **style** objects return the value red.

The object reflects the order of style precedence in cascading style sheets (CSS). The CSS order of precedence for the presentation of HTML is:

1. Inline styles
2. Style sheet rules
3. Attributes on HTML tags
4. Intrinsic definition of the HTML tag

Accordingly, the **currentStyle** object returns the **fontWeight** value normal on a bold tag if normal is specified in a style sheet.

The **currentStyle** object returns values that reflect the applied style settings for the page and might not reflect what is rendering at the time a value is retrieved. For example, an object that has "color:red; display:none" returns **currentStyle**.**color** as red even though the object is not being rendered on the page. The **currentStyle** object, then, is not affected by the rendering constraints. The third example demonstrates this behavior. Disabled style sheets also do not affect **currentStyle** values.

The returned value is in the same units as those used to set the object. For example, if the color of an object is set inline using `STYLE="color:'green'"`, *object*.**currentStyle**.**color** returns `green` and not `#00FF00` (the RGB hexadecimal equivalent to green). However, capitalization and redundant white space that appear in the object values set by the author are lost when the **currentStyle** object returns the object values.

The object supports user-defined properties in style rules. See the second example below.

The **currentStyle** object is asynchronous. This means that a style cannot be set and then immediately queried—the old value is returned. Thus, for a script to obtain the expected behavior of **currentStyle** with methods such as **addImport**, the script needs to include a function that calls the method and a function to check **currentStyle**. For a script to check the current style when a page is loading, the script must wait until the **BODY** element is loaded and the page has been rendered, or the value of **currentStyle** might not reflect what is being displayed.

This element is available in script as of Internet Explorer 5.

Properties/Attributes

Note These properties have no corresponding attributes.

backgroundAttachment	**backgroundColor**	**backgroundImage**
backgroundPositionX	**backgroundPositionY**	**backgroundRepeat**
borderBottomColor	**borderBottomStyle**	**borderBottomWidth**
borderColor	**borderLeftColor**	**borderLeftStyle**
borderLeftWidth	**borderRightColor**	**borderRightStyle**
borderRightWidth	**borderStyle**	**borderTopColor**
borderTopStyle	**borderTopWidth**	**borderWidth**
bottom	**clear**	**clipBottom**
clipLeft	**clipRight**	**clipTop**
color	**cursor**	**direction**
display	**fontFamily**	**fontSize**
fontStyle	**fontVariant**	**fontWeight**
height	**layoutGridChar**	**layoutGridCharSpacing**

Properties/Attributes *(continued)*

Note These properties have no corresponding attributes.

layoutGridLine	layoutGridMode	layoutGridType
left	letterSpacing	lineHeight
listStyleImage	listStylePosition	listStyleType
margin	marginBottom	marginLeft
marginRight	marginTop	overflow
overflowX	overflowY	padding
paddingBottom	paddingLeft	paddingRight
paddingTop	pageBreakAfter	pageBreakBefore
position	right	styleFloat
tableLayout	textAlign	textDecoration
textIndent	textTransform	top
unicodeBidi	verticalAlign	visibility
width	zIndex	

Example

In this example, the text color has been set to brown. If you click a colored area and the background color is the same as the text color, the checkColor function changes the background color, so the text can be read. Otherwise, the function takes no action.

```
<SCRIPT>
function checkColor(oObj)
{
  if (oObj.currentStyle.backgroundColor == 'brown')
    {
        oObj.style.backgroundColor = 'white';
    }
  else
    :
}
</SCRIPT>
</HEAD>
:
<P STYLE="background-color: 'brown'"
    onclick="checkColor(this)">
```

To see this code in action, refer to the Web Workshop CD-ROM.

Note This example works only if the body and text colors are set using either color names or RGB hexadecimal values, but not a mix of the two.

The following example uses the **currentStyle** object to retrieve values of the user-defined property created in the style rule. The alert returns the value `myvalue`.

```
<STYLE>
    P { myproperty:myvalue }
</STYLE>
<BODY>
<P ID=oPrgrph>
:
<SCRIPT>
alert(oPrgrph.currentStyle.myproperty)
</SCRIPT>
```

To see this code in action, refer to the Web Workshop CD-ROM.

The following example shows that the **TD** object width returned by the **currentStyle** object is its cascaded width value rather than the width rendered on the screen.

```
<BODY ID=oBdy>
:
<TABLE BORDER>
<TR><TD WIDTH=1100 ID=oTblD>text</TD></TR>
</TABLE>
:
<SCRIPT>
alert("The TD object currentStyle.width is " + oTblD.currentStyle.width +
    ".\nThe width of the window is " + oBdy.clientWidth +
    "px.\nThe width of the screen is " + screen.width + "px." )
</SCRIPT>
```

To see this code in action, refer to the Web Workshop CD-ROM.

Applies To

WIN16   **WIN32**   **MAC**   **UNIX**

A, ACRONYM, ADDRESS, APPLET, AREA, B, BASE, BASEFONT, BDO, BGSOUND, BIG, BLOCKQUOTE, BODY, BR, BUTTON, CAPTION, CENTER, CITE, CODE, COL, COLGROUP, COMMENT, DD, DEL, DFN, DIR, DIV, DL, DT, EM, EMBED, FIELDSET, FONT, FORM, HEAD, Hn, HTML, I, IMG, INPUT type=button, INPUT type=checkbox, INPUT type=file, INPUT type=image, INPUT type=password, INPUT type=radio, INPUT type=reset, INPUT type=submit, INPUT type=text, INS, ISINDEX, KBD, LABEL, LEGEND, LI, LINK, LISTING, MAP, MARQUEE, MENU, META, NEXTID, NOBR, OBJECT, OL, OPTION, P, PLAINTEXT, PRE, Q, S, SAMP, SELECT, SMALL, SPAN, STRIKE, STRONG, STYLE, SUB, SUP, TABLE, TBODY, TD, TEXTAREA, TFOOT, TH, THEAD, TITLE, TR, TT, U, UL, VAR, WBR, XMP

dataTransfer Object

Provides access to predefined clipboard formats for use in drag-and-drop operations.

Remarks

The **dataTransfer** object makes it possible to customize the handling of drag-and-drop operations. It is available through the **event** object.

The **dataTransfer** object is used in source and target events. Typically, the **setData** method is used with source events to provide information about the data being transferred. In contrast, the **getData** method is used with target events to stipulate which data and data formats to retrieve.

This object is available in script as of Internet Explorer 5.

Attributes/Properties

dropEffect[*]   **effectAllowed**[*]

* This property has no corresponding attribute.

Methods

clearData   **getData**   **setData**

Example

The following example shows how to use the **setData** and **getData** methods of the **dataTransfer** object.

```
<HEAD>
<SCRIPT>
var sAnchorURL;

function InitiateDrag()
/*  The setData parameters tell the source object
    to transfer data as a URL and provide the path.  */
{
    event.dataTransfer.setData("URL", oSource.href);
}

function FinishDrag()
/*  The parameter passed to getData tells the target
    object what data format to expect.  */
{
    sAnchorURL = event.dataTransfer.getData("URL")
    oTarget.innerText = sAnchorURL;
}
</SCRIPT>
</HEAD>
```

```
<BODY>
<A ID=oSource HREF="about:Example_Complete" onclick="return(false)"
    ondragstart="InitiateDrag()">Test Anchor</A>
<SPAN ID=oTarget ondragenter="FinishDrag()">Drop the Link Here</SPAN>
</BODY>
```

To see this code in action, refer to the Web Workshop CD-ROM.

Applies To

 WIN16   WIN32   MAC   UNIX

event

DD Element | DD Object

Indicates the definition in a definition list. The definition is usually indented in the definition list.

Remarks

The **DD** element is a block element and does not require a closing tag.

This element is available in HTML as of Internet Explorer 3.0 and in script as of Internet Explorer 4.0.

Properties/Attributes

Note With the exception of **className**, these properties have no corresponding attributes.

	CLASS		
canHaveChildren	**className**	**clientHeight**	**clientLeft**
clientTop	**clientWidth**	**currentStyle**	**dir**
firstChild	**id**	**innerHTML**	**innerText**
isTextEdit	**lang**	**language**	**lastChild**
nextSibling	**nodeName**	**nodeType**	**nodeValue**
noWrap	**offsetHeight**	**offsetLeft**	**offsetParent**
offsetTop	**offsetWidth**	**outerHTML**	**outerText**
parentElement	**parentNode**	**parentTextEdit**	**previousSibling**
readyState	**recordNumber**	**runtimeStyle**	**scopeName**
scrollHeight	**scrollLeft**	**scrollTop**	**scrollWidth**
sourceIndex	**style**	**tabIndex**	**tagName**
tagUrn	**title**	**uniqueID**	

DHTML Objects

Methods

addBehavior	appendChild	applyElement
attachEvent	blur	clearAttributes
click	cloneNode	componentFromPoint
contains	detachEvent	focus
getAdjacentText	getAttribute	getBoundingClientRect
getClientRects	getElementsByTagName	getExpression
hasChildNodes	insertAdjacentElement	insertAdjacentHTML
insertAdjacentText	insertBefore	mergeAttributes
releaseCapture	removeAttribute	removeBehavior
removeChild	removeExpression	removeNode
replaceAdjacentText	replaceChild	replaceNode
scrollIntoView	setAttribute	setCapture
setExpression	swapNode	

Events

onbeforecopy	onbeforecut	onbeforepaste	onblur
onclick	oncopy	oncut	ondblclick
ondrag	ondragend	ondragenter	ondragleave
ondragover	ondragstart	ondrop	onfocus
onhelp	onkeydown	onkeypress	onkeyup
onlosecapture	onmousedown	onmousemove	onmouseout
onmouseover	onmouseup	onpaste	onpropertychange
onreadystatechange	onresize	onselectstart	

Collections

all	attributes	behaviorUrns	childNodes	children

Default Behaviors

clientCaps	download	homePage	httpFolder	saveFavorite
saveHistory	saveSnapshot	time	userData	

CSS Properties

Note For a list of corresponding attributes, see Appendix C.

background	backgroundColor	backgroundImage
backgroundPosition	backgroundPositionX[*]	backgroundPositionY[*]
backgroundRepeat	behavior	border
borderBottom	borderBottomColor	borderBottomStyle
borderBottomWidth	borderColor	borderLeft
borderLeftColor	borderLeftStyle	borderLeftWidth
borderRight	borderRightColor	borderRightStyle
borderRightWidth	borderStyle	borderTop
borderTopColor	borderTopStyle	borderTopWidth
borderWidth	bottom	clear
color	cursor	direction
font	fontFamily	fontSize
fontStyle	fontVariant	fontWeight
layoutGrid	layoutGridChar	layoutGridCharSpacing
layoutGridLine	layoutGridMode	layoutGridType
left	letterSpacing	lineBreak
lineHeight	margin	marginBottom
marginLeft	marginRight	marginTop
overflow	overflowX	overflowY
pageBreakAfter	pageBreakBefore	pixelBottom[*]
pixelHeight[*]	pixelLeft[*]	pixelRight[*]
pixelTop[*]	pixelWidth[*]	posBottom[*]
posHeight[*]	position	posLeft[*]
posRight[*]	posTop[*]	posWidth[*]
right	styleFloat	textAlign
textAutospace	textDecoration	textDecorationBlink[*]
textDecorationLineThrough[*]	textDecorationNone[*]	textDecorationOverline[*]
textDecorationUnderline[*]	textIndent	textJustify

CSS Properties *(continued)*

textTransform	top	unicodeBidi
visibility	width	wordBreak
wordSpacing	zIndex	

*   This property has no corresponding attribute.

Example

The following example shows how to use the **DD** element in a definition list.

```
<DL>
<DT>Cat
<DD>A small domesticated mammal.
<DT>Lizard
<DD>A reptile generally found in dry areas.
</DL>
```

DEL Element | DEL Object

Indicates text that has been deleted from the document.

Remarks

The **DEL** element is an inline element and requires a closing tag.

This element is available in HTML and script as of Internet Explorer 4.0.

Attributes/Properties

	CLASS		
canHaveChildren[*]	className	currentStyle[*]	dir
firstChild[*]	id	innerHTML[*]	innerText[*]
isTextEdit[*]	lang	language	lastChild[*]
nextSibling[*]	nodeName[*]	nodeType[*]	nodeValue[*]
offsetHeight[*]	offsetLeft[*]	offsetParent[*]	offsetTop[*]
offsetWidth[*]	outerHTML[*]	outerText[*]	parentElement[*]
parentNode[*]	parentTextEdit[*]	previousSibling[*]	readyState[*]
recordNumber[*]	runtimeStyle[*]	scopeName[*]	sourceIndex[*]
style	tabIndex	tagName[*]	tagUrn[*]
title	uniqueID[*]		

*   This property has no corresponding attribute.

Methods

addBehavior	**appendChild**	**applyElement**
attachEvent	**blur**	**clearAttributes**
cloneNode	**componentFromPoint**	**detachEvent**
focus	**getAdjacentText**	**getBoundingClientRect**
getClientRects	**getElementsByTagName**	**getExpression**
hasChildNodes	**insertAdjacentElement**	**insertBefore**
mergeAttributes	**removeBehavior**	**removeChild**
removeExpression	**removeNode**	**replaceAdjacentText**
replaceChild	**replaceNode**	**setExpression**
swapNode		

Events

onblur	**ondrag**	**ondragend**	**ondragenter**
ondragleave	**ondragover**	**ondragstart**	**ondrop**
onfocus	**onkeydown**	**onkeypress**	**onkeyup**
onreadystatechange	**onselectstart**		

Collections

all	**attributes**	**behaviorUrns**	**childNodes**	**children**

Default Behaviors

clientCaps	**download**	**homePage**	**httpFolder**	**saveFavorite**
saveHistory	**saveSnapshot**	**time**	**userData**	

CSS Properties

Note For a list of corresponding attributes, see Appendix C.

backgroundPositionX[*]	**backgroundPositionY**[*]	**behavior**	**direction**
layoutGridMode	**overflow**	**overflowX**	**overflowY**
pixelBottom[*]	**pixelHeight**[*]	**pixelLeft**[*]	**pixelRight**[*]

CSS Properties *(continued)*

pixelTop[*]	pixelWidth[*]	posBottom[*]	posHeight[*]
posLeft[*]	posRight[*]	posTop[*]	posWidth[*]
textAutospace	unicodeBidi	width	

* This property has no corresponding attribute.

Example

The following example shows how to use the **DEL** element to mark deleted text.

```
<DEL>This text has been revised.</DEL>
```

DFN Element | DFN Object

Indicates the defining instance of a term.

Remarks

The **DFN** element is an inline element and requires a closing tag.

This element is available in HTML as of Internet Explorer 3.0 and in script as of Internet Explorer 4.0.

Properties/Attributes

Note With the exception of **className**, these properties have no corresponding attributes.

	CLASS		
canHaveChildren	className	clientHeight	clientLeft
clientTop	clientWidth	currentStyle	dir
firstChild	id	innerHTML	innerText
isTextEdit	lang	language	lastChild
nextSibling	nodeName	nodeType	nodeValue
offsetHeight	offsetLeft	offsetParent	offsetTop
offsetWidth	outerHTML	outerText	parentElement
parentNode	parentTextEdit	previousSibling	readyState
recordNumber	runtimeStyle	scopeName	scrollHeight
scrollLeft	scrollTop	scrollWidth	sourceIndex
style	tabIndex	tagName	tagUrn
title	uniqueID		

Methods

addBehavior	appendChild	applyElement
attachEvent	blur	clearAttributes
click	cloneNode	componentFromPoint
contains	detachEvent	focus
getAdjacentText	getAttribute	getBoundingClientRect
getClientRects	getElementsByTagName	getExpression
hasChildNodes	insertAdjacentElement	insertAdjacentHTML
insertAdjacentText	insertBefore	mergeAttributes
releaseCapture	removeAttribute	removeBehavior
removeChild	removeExpression	removeNode
replaceAdjacentText	replaceChild	replaceNode
scrollIntoView	setAttribute	setCapture
setExpression	swapNode	

Events

onbeforecopy	onbeforecut	onbeforepaste	onblur
onclick	oncopy	oncut	ondblclick
ondrag	ondragend	ondragenter	ondragleave
ondragover	ondragstart	ondrop	onfocus
onhelp	onkeydown	onkeypress	onkeyup
onlosecapture	onmousedown	onmousemove	onmouseout
onmouseover	onmouseup	onpaste	onpropertychange
onreadystatechange	onresize	onselectstart	

Collections

all	attributes	behaviorUrns	childNodes	children

Default Behaviors

clientCaps	download	homePage	httpFolder	saveFavorite
saveHistory	saveSnapshot	userData		

CSS Properties

Note For a list of corresponding attributes, see Appendix C.

background	backgroundColor	backgroundImage
backgroundPosition	backgroundPositionX[*]	backgroundPositionY[*]
backgroundRepeat	behavior	bottom
clear	color	cursor
direction	font	fontFamily
fontSize	fontStyle	fontVariant
fontWeight	layoutGridMode	left
letterSpacing	lineHeight	overflow
overflowX	overflowY	pixelBottom[*]
pixelHeight[*]	pixelLeft[*]	pixelRight[*]
pixelTop[*]	pixelWidth[*]	posBottom[*]
posHeight[*]	position	posLeft[*]
posRight[*]	posTop[*]	posWidth[*]
right	styleFloat	textAutospace
textDecoration	textDecorationBlink[*]	textDecorationLineThrough[*]
textDecorationNone[*]	textDecorationOverline[*]	textDecorationUnderline[*]
textIndent	textTransform	top
unicodeBidi	visibility	width
wordSpacing	zIndex	

* This property has no corresponding attribute.

Example

The following example shows how to use the **DFN** element with a term definition.

```
<DFN>HTML stands for hypertext markup language.</DFN>
```

DIR Element | DIR Object

Denotes a directory list.

Remarks

The **DIR** element is a block element and requires a closing tag.

This element is available in HTML as of Internet Explorer 3.0 and in script as of Internet Explorer 4.0.

Attributes/Properties

canHaveChildren[*]	CLASS className	clientHeight[*]	clientLeft[*]
clientTop[*]	clientWidth[*]	currentStyle[*]	dir
firstChild[*]	id	innerHTML[*]	innerText[*]
isTextEdit[*]	lang	language	lastChild[*]
nextSibling[*]	nodeName[*]	nodeType[*]	nodeValue[*]
offsetHeight[*]	offsetLeft[*]	offsetParent[*]	offsetTop[*]
offsetWidth[*]	outerHTML[*]	outerText[*]	parentElement[*]
parentNode[*]	parentTextEdit[*]	previousSibling[*]	readyState[*]
recordNumber[*]	runtimeStyle[*]	scopeName[*]	scrollHeight[*]
scrollLeft[*]	scrollTop[*]	scrollWidth[*]	sourceIndex[*]
style	tabIndex	tagName[*]	tagUrn[*]
title	uniqueID[*]		

[*] This property has no corresponding attribute.

Methods

addBehavior	appendChild	applyElement
attachEvent	blur	clearAttributes
click	cloneNode	componentFromPoint
contains	detachEvent	focus
getAdjacentText	getAttribute	getBoundingClientRect
getClientRects	getElementsByTagName	getExpression
hasChildNodes	insertAdjacentElement	insertAdjacentHTML

DHTML Objects

Methods *(continued)*

insertAdjacentText	insertBefore	mergeAttributes
releaseCapture	removeAttribute	removeBehavior
removeChild	removeExpression	removeNode
replaceAdjacentText	replaceChild	replaceNode
scrollIntoView	setAttribute	setCapture
setExpression	swapNode	

Events

onbeforecopy	onbeforecut	onbeforepaste	onblur
onclick	oncopy	oncut	ondblclick
ondrag	ondragend	ondragenter	ondragleave
ondragover	ondragstart	ondrop	onfocus
onhelp	onkeydown	onkeypress	onkeyup
onlosecapture	onmousedown	onmousemove	onmouseout
onmouseover	onmouseup	onpaste	onpropertychange
onreadystatechange	onresize	onselectstart	

Collections

all	attributes	behaviorUrns	childNodes	children

Default Behaviors

clientCaps	download	homePage	httpFolder	saveFavorite
saveHistory	saveSnapshot	time	userData	

CSS Properties

Note For a list of corresponding attributes, see Appendix C.

background	backgroundColor	backgroundImage
backgroundPosition	backgroundPositionX[*]	backgroundPositionY[*]
backgroundRepeat	behavior	border
borderBottom	borderBottomColor	borderBottomStyle

* This property has no corresponding attribute.

CSS Properties *(continued)*

Note For a list of corresponding attributes, see Appendix C.

borderBottomWidth	borderColor	borderLeft
borderLeftColor	borderLeftStyle	borderLeftWidth
borderRight	borderRightColor	borderRightStyle
borderRightWidth	borderStyle	borderTop
borderTopColor	borderTopStyle	borderTopWidth
borderWidth	bottom	clear
color	cursor	direction
font	fontFamily	fontSize
fontStyle	fontVariant	fontWeight
layoutGrid	layoutGridChar	layoutGridCharSpacing
layoutGridLine	layoutGridMode	layoutGridType
left	letterSpacing	lineBreak
lineHeight	margin	marginBottom
marginLeft	marginRight	marginTop
overflow	overflowX	overflowY
pageBreakAfter	pageBreakBefore	pixelBottom[*]
pixelHeight[*]	pixelLeft[*]	pixelRight[*]
pixelTop[*]	pixelWidth[*]	posBottom[*]
posHeight[*]	position	posLeft[*]
posRight[*]	posTop[*]	posWidth[*]
right	styleFloat	textAlign
textAutospace	textDecoration	textDecorationBlink[*]
textDecorationLineThrough[*]	textDecorationNone[*]	textDecorationOverline[*]
textDecorationUnderline[*]	textIndent	textJustify
textTransform	top	unicodeBidi
visibility	width	wordBreak
wordSpacing	zIndex	

[*] This property has no corresponding attribute.

DHTML Objects

Example

The following example shows how to use the **DIR** element to create a directory list.

```
<DIR>
<LI>Art
<LI>History
<LI>Literature
<LI>Sports
<LI>Entertainment
<LI>Science
</DIR>
```

DIV Element | DIV Object

Specifies a container that renders HTML.

Remarks

The **DIV** element is a block element and requires a closing tag.

This element is available in HTML as of Internet Explorer 3.0 and in script as of Internet Explorer 4.0.

Attributes/Properties

align	canHaveChildren[*]	**CLASS** className	clientHeight[*]
clientLeft[*]	clientTop[*]	clientWidth[*]	currentStyle[*]
dataFld	dataFormatAs	dataSrc	dir
firstChild[*]	id	innerHTML[*]	isTextEdit[*]
lang	language	lastChild[*]	nextSibling[*]
nodeName[*]	nodeType[*]	nodeValue[*]	noWrap
offsetHeight[*]	offsetLeft[*]	offsetParent[*]	offsetTop[*]
offsetWidth[*]	outerHTML[*]	outerText[*]	parentElement[*]
parentNode[*]	parentTextEdit[*]	previousSibling[*]	readyState[*]
recordNumber[*]	runtimeStyle[*]	scopeName[*]	scrollHeight[*]
scrollLeft[*]	scrollTop[*]	scrollWidth[*]	sourceIndex[*]
style	tabIndex	tagName[*]	tagUrn[*]
title	uniqueID[*]		

*   This property has no corresponding attribute.

Methods

addBehavior	appendChild	applyElement
attachEvent	blur	clearAttributes
click	cloneNode	componentFromPoint
contains	detachEvent	doScroll
getAdjacentText	getAttribute	getBoundingClientRect
getClientRects	getElementsByTagName	getExpression
hasChildNodes	insertAdjacentElement	insertAdjacentHTML
insertAdjacentText	insertBefore	mergeAttributes
releaseCapture	removeAttribute	removeBehavior
removeChild	removeExpression	removeNode
replaceAdjacentText	replaceChild	replaceNode
scrollIntoView	setAttribute	setCapture
setExpression	swapNode	

Events

onbeforecopy	onbeforecut	onbeforeeditfocus	onbeforepaste
onblur	onclick	oncopy	oncut
ondblclick	ondrag	ondragend	ondragenter
ondragleave	ondragover	ondragstart	ondrop
onfilterchange	onfocus	onhelp	onkeydown
onkeypress	onkeyup	onlosecapture	onmousedown
onmousemove	onmouseout	onmouseover	onmouseup
onpaste	onpropertychange	onreadystatechange	onresize
onscroll	onselectstart		

Collections

all	attributes	behaviorUrns	childNodes	children	filters

Default Behaviors

clientCaps	download	homePage	httpFolder	saveFavorite
saveHistory	saveSnapshot	time	userData	

CSS Properties

Note For a list of corresponding attributes, see Appendix C.

background	backgroundColor	backgroundImage
backgroundPosition	backgroundPositionX*	backgroundPositionY*
backgroundRepeat	behavior	border
borderBottom	borderBottomColor	borderBottomStyle
borderBottomWidth	borderColor	borderLeft
borderLeftColor	borderLeftStyle	borderLeftWidth
borderRight	borderRightColor	borderRightStyle
borderRightWidth	borderStyle	borderTop
borderTopColor	borderTopStyle	borderTopWidth
borderWidth	bottom	clear
clip	color	cursor
direction	display	filter
font	fontFamily	fontSize
fontStyle	fontVariant	fontWeight
height	layoutGrid	layoutGridChar
layoutGridCharSpacing	layoutGridLine	layoutGridMode
layoutGridType	left	letterSpacing
lineBreak	lineHeight	margin
marginBottom	marginLeft	marginRight
marginTop	overflow	overflowX
overflowY	padding	paddingBottom
paddingLeft	paddingRight	paddingTop
pageBreakAfter	pageBreakBefore	pixelBottom*

*   This property has no corresponding attribute.

CSS Properties *(continued)*

Note For a list of corresponding attributes, see Appendix C.

pixelHeight*	pixelLeft*	pixelRight*
pixelTop*	pixelWidth*	posBottom*
posHeight*	position	posLeft*
posRight*	posTop*	posWidth*
right	styleFloat	textAlign
textAutospace	textDecoration	textDecorationBlink*
textDecorationLineThrough*	textDecorationNone*	textDecorationOverline*
textDecorationUnderline*	textIndent	textJustify
textTransform	top	unicodeBidi
visibility	width	wordBreak
wordSpacing	zIndex	

*   This property has no corresponding attribute.

Example

The following example shows how to create a **DIV** container.

```
<DIV>
This text represents a section.
</DIV>

<DIV ALIGN=CENTER>
This text represents another section, and its text is centered.
</DIV>
```

DL Element | DL Object

Denotes a definition list.

Remarks

The **DL** element is a block element and does not require a closing tag.

This element is available in HTML as of Internet Explorer 3.0 and in script as of Internet Explorer 4.0.

Attributes/Properties

	CLASS		
canHaveChildren[*]	className	clientHeight[*]	clientLeft[*]
clientTop[*]	clientWidth[*]	compact	currentStyle[*]
dir	firstChild[*]	id	innerHTML[*]
isTextEdit[*]	lang	language	lastChild[*]
nextSibling[*]	nodeName[*]	nodeType[*]	nodeValue[*]
offsetHeight[*]	offsetLeft[*]	offsetParent[*]	offsetTop[*]
offsetWidth[*]	outerHTML[*]	outerText[*]	parentElement[*]
parentNode[*]	parentTextEdit[*]	previousSibling[*]	readyState[*]
recordNumber[*]	runtimeStyle[*]	scopeName[*]	scrollHeight[*]
scrollLeft[*]	scrollTop[*]	scrollWidth[*]	sourceIndex[*]
style	tabIndex	tagName[*]	tagUrn[*]
title	uniqueID[*]		

[*] This property has no corresponding attribute.

Methods

addBehavior	appendChild	applyElement
attachEvent	blur	clearAttributes
click	cloneNode	componentFromPoint
contains	detachEvent	focus
getAdjacentText	getAttribute	getBoundingClientRect
getClientRects	getElementsByTagName	getExpression
hasChildNodes	insertAdjacentElement	insertAdjacentHTML
insertAdjacentText	insertBefore	mergeAttributes
releaseCapture	removeAttribute	removeBehavior
removeChild	removeExpression	removeNode
replaceAdjacentText	replaceChild	replaceNode
scrollIntoView	setAttribute	setCapture
setExpression	swapNode	

Events

onbeforecopy	onbeforecut	onbeforepaste	onblur
onclick	oncopy	oncut	ondblclick
ondrag	ondragend	ondragenter	ondragleave
ondragover	ondragstart	ondrop	onfocus
onhelp	onlosecapture	onmousedown	onmousemove
onmouseout	onmouseover	onmouseup	onpaste
onpropertychange	onreadystatechange	onresize	onselectstart

Collections

all	attributes	behaviorUrns	childNodes	children

Default Behaviors

clientCaps	download	homePage	httpFolder	saveFavorite
saveHistory	saveSnapshot	time	userData	

CSS Properties

Note For a list of corresponding attributes, see Appendix C.

background	backgroundColor	backgroundImage
backgroundPosition	backgroundPositionX*	backgroundPositionY*
backgroundRepeat	behavior	border
borderBottom	borderBottomColor	borderBottomStyle
borderBottomWidth	borderColor	borderLeft
borderLeftColor	borderLeftStyle	borderLeftWidth
borderRight	borderRightColor	borderRightStyle
borderRightWidth	borderStyle	borderTop
borderTopColor	borderTopStyle	borderTopWidth
borderWidth	bottom	clear
color	cursor	direction

CSS Properties *(continued)*

Note For a list of corresponding attributes, see Appendix C.

font	**fontFamily**	**fontSize**
fontStyle	**fontVariant**	**fontWeight**
layoutGrid	**layoutGridChar**	**layoutGridCharSpacing**
layoutGridLine	**layoutGridMode**	**layoutGridType**
left	**letterSpacing**	**lineBreak**
lineHeight	**margin**	**marginBottom**
marginLeft	**marginRight**	**marginTop**
overflow	**overflowX**	**overflowY**
pageBreakAfter	**pageBreakBefore**	**pixelBottom**[*]
pixelHeight[*]	**pixelLeft**[*]	**pixelRight**[*]
pixelTop[*]	**pixelWidth**[*]	**posBottom**[*]
posHeight[*]	**position**	**posLeft**[*]
posRight[*]	**posTop**[*]	**posWidth**[*]
right	**styleFloat**	**textAlign**
textAutospace	**textDecoration**	**textDecorationBlink**[*]
textDecorationLineThrough[*]	**textDecorationNone**[*]	**textDecorationOverline**[*]
textDecorationUnderline[*]	**textIndent**	**textJustify**
textTransform	**top**	**unicodeBidi**
visibility	**width**	**wordBreak**
wordSpacing	**zIndex**	

[*]   This property has no corresponding attribute.

Example

The following example shows how to use the **DL** element to create a definition list.

```
<DL>
<DT>Cat
<DD>A small domesticated mammal.
<DT>Lizard
<DD>A reptile generally found in dry areas.
</DL>
```

!DOCTYPE Element

Specifies the HTML document type definition (DTD) to which the document corresponds.

Remarks

Different versions of the DTD can be used depending on the level of compatibility the author wants to indicate.

The **!DOCTYPE** element does not require a closing tag.

This element is available in HTML as of Internet Explorer 3.0.

Example

The following examples show how to use the **!DOCTYPE** element to specify compatibility with the HTML 3.2 DTD and strict adherence to the HTML 4.0 DTD.

```
<!DOCTYPE HTML PUBLIC "-//W3C//DTD HTML 3.2//EN">
<!DOCTYPE HTML PUBLIC "-//W3C//DTD HTML 4.0 Strict//EN">
```

document Object

Represents the HTML document in a given browser window.

Remarks

Use the **document** object to retrieve information about the document, to examine and modify the HTML elements and text within the document, and to process events.

The **document** object is available at all times. Retrieve the object by applying the **document** property to a **window** or an element object. When used by itself, the **document** object represents the document in the current window.

This object is available in script as of Internet Explorer 3.0.

Attributes/Properties

activeElement*	aLinkColor*	bgColor*	body*
charset*	cookie*	defaultCharset*	designMode*
documentElement*	domain*	expando*	fgColor*
fileCreatedDate*	fileModifiedDate*	fileSize*	lastModified*

DHTML Objects

Attributes/Properties *(continued)*

linkColor[*]	location[*]	parentWindow[*]	protocol[*]
readyState[*]	referrer[*]	selection[*]	title[*]
uniqueID[*]	URL[*]	vlinkColor[*]	

* This property has no corresponding attribute.

Methods

attachEvent	clear	clearAttributes
close	createElement	createStyleSheet
createTextNode	detachEvent	elementFromPoint
execCommand	getElementById	getElementsByName
getElementsByTagName	mergeAttributes	open
queryCommandEnabled	queryCommandIndeterm	queryCommandState
queryCommandSupported	queryCommandValue	recalc
releaseCapture	write	writeln

Events

onbeforeeditfocus	onclick	oncontextmenu	ondblclick
ondrag	ondragend	ondragenter	ondragleave
ondragover	ondragstart	ondrop	onhelp
onkeydown	onkeypress	onkeyup	onmousedown
onmousemove	onmouseout	onmouseover	onmouseup
onpropertychange	onreadystatechange	onstop	

Collections

all	anchors	applets	childNodes	children
embeds	forms	frames	images	links
scripts	styleSheets			

Examples

The following example shows how to check for a document title and display the title (if not null) in an alert.

```
if (document.title!="")
    alert("The title is " + document.title)
```

The following example shows how to create an event handler function that displays the current position of the mouse (relative to the upper-left corner of the document) in the browser's status window.

```
<HTML>
<HEAD><TITLE>Report mouse moves</TITLE>
<SCRIPT LANGUAGE="JScript">
function reportMove() {
    window.status = "X=" + window.event.x + " Y=" + window.event.y;
}
</SCRIPT>
<BODY onmousemove="reportMove()">
<H1>Welcome!</H1>
</BODY>
</HTML>
```

Applies To

 WIN16   WIN32   MAC

window

 UNIX

window

DT Element | DT Object

Indicates a definition term within a definition list.

Remarks

The **DT** element is a block element and does not require a closing tag.

This element is available in HTML as of Internet Explorer 3.0 and in script as of Internet Explorer 4.0.

Attributes/Properties

	CLASS		
canHaveChildren[*]	className	clientHeight[*]	clientLeft[*]
clientTop[*]	clientWidth[*]	currentStyle[*]	dir
firstChild[*]	id	innerHTML[*]	isTextEdit[*]
lang	language	lastChild[*]	nextSibling[*]
nodeName[*]	nodeType[*]	nodeValue[*]	noWrap
offsetHeight[*]	offsetLeft[*]	offsetParent[*]	offsetTop[*]
offsetWidth[*]	outerHTML[*]	outerText[*]	parentElement[*]
parentNode[*]	parentTextEdit[*]	previousSibling[*]	readyState[*]
recordNumber[*]	runtimeStyle[*]	scopeName[*]	scrollHeight[*]
scrollLeft[*]	scrollTop[*]	scrollWidth[*]	sourceIndex[*]
style	tabIndex	tagName[*]	tagUrn[*]
title	uniqueID[*]		

[*] This property has no corresponding attribute.

Methods

addBehavior	appendChild	applyElement
attachEvent	blur	clearAttributes
click	cloneNode	componentFromPoint
contains	detachEvent	focus
getAdjacentText	getAttribute	getBoundingClientRect
getClientRects	getElementsByTagName	getExpression
hasChildNodes	insertAdjacentElement	insertAdjacentHTML
insertAdjacentText	insertBefore	mergeAttributes
releaseCapture	removeAttribute	removeBehavior
removeChild	removeExpression	removeNode
replaceAdjacentText	replaceChild	replaceNode
scrollIntoView	setAttribute	setCapture
setExpression	swapNode	

Events

onbeforecopy	onbeforecut	onbeforepaste	onblur
onclick	oncopy	oncut	ondblclick
ondrag	ondragend	ondragenter	ondragleave
ondragover	ondragstart	ondrop	onfocus
onhelp	onkeydown	onkeypress	onkeyup
onlosecapture	onmousedown	onmousemove	onmouseout
onmouseover	onmouseup	onpaste	onpropertychange
onreadystatechange	onresize	onselectstart	

Collections

all	attributes	behaviorUrns	childNodes	children

Default Behaviors

clientCaps	download	homePage	httpFolder	saveFavorite
saveHistory	saveSnapshot	time	userData	

CSS Properties

Note For a list of corresponding attributes, see Appendix C.

background	backgroundColor	backgroundImage
backgroundPosition	backgroundPositionX*	backgroundPositionY*
backgroundRepeat	behavior	border
borderBottom	borderBottomColor	borderBottomStyle
borderBottomWidth	borderColor	borderLeft
borderLeftColor	borderLeftStyle	borderLeftWidth
borderRight	borderRightColor	borderRightStyle
borderRightWidth	borderStyle	borderTop
borderTopColor	borderTopStyle	borderTopWidth
borderWidth	clear	color

CSS Properties *(continued)*

Note For a list of corresponding attributes, see Appendix C.

cursor	**direction**	**font**
fontFamily	**fontSize**	**fontStyle**
fontVariant	**fontWeight**	**layoutGrid**
layoutGridChar	**layoutGridCharSpacing**	**layoutGridLine**
layoutGridMode	**layoutGridType**	**left**
letterSpacing	**lineBreak**	**lineHeight**
margin	**marginBottom**	**marginLeft**
marginRight	**marginTop**	**overflow**
overflowX	**overflowY**	**pageBreakAfter**
pageBreakBefore	**pixelBottom**[*]	**pixelHeight**[*]
pixelLeft[*]	**pixelRight**[*]	**pixelTop**[*]
pixelWidth[*]	**posBottom**[*]	**posHeight**[*]
position	**posLeft**[*]	**posRight**[*]
posTop[*]	**posWidth**[*]	**styleFloat**
textAlign	**textAutospace**	**textDecoration**
textDecorationBlink[*]	**textDecorationLineThrough**[*]	**textDecorationNone**[*]
textDecorationOverline[*]	**textDecorationUnderline**[*]	**textIndent**
textJustify	**textTransform**	**top**
unicodeBidi	**visibility**	**width**
wordBreak	**wordSpacing**	**zIndex**

[*]   This property has no corresponding attribute.

Example

The following example shows how to use the **DT** element with terms in a definition list.

```
<DL>
<DT>Cat
<DD>A small domesticated mammal.
<DT>Lizard
<DD>A reptile generally found in dry areas.
</DL>
```

EM Element | EM Object

Emphasizes text, usually by rendering it in italic.

Remarks

The **EM** element is an inline element and requires a closing tag.

This element is available in HTML as of Internet Explorer 3.0 and in script as of Internet Explorer 4.0.

Attributes/Properties

canHaveChildren[*]	**CLASS** className	clientHeight[*]	clientLeft[*]
clientTop[*]	clientWidth[*]	currentStyle[*]	dir
firstChild[*]	id	innerHTML[*]	innerText[*]
isTextEdit[*]	lang	language	lastChild[*]
nextSibling[*]	nodeName[*]	nodeType[*]	nodeValue[*]
offsetHeight[*]	offsetLeft[*]	offsetParent[*]	offsetTop[*]
offsetWidth[*]	outerHTML[*]	outerText[*]	parentElement[*]
parentNode[*]	parentTextEdit[*]	previousSibling[*]	readyState[*]
recordNumber[*]	runtimeStyle[*]	scopeName[*]	scrollHeight[*]
scrollLeft[*]	scrollTop[*]	scrollWidth[*]	sourceIndex[*]
style	tabIndex	tagName[*]	tagUrn[*]
title	uniqueID[*]		

[*] This property has no corresponding attribute.

Methods

addBehavior	appendChild	applyElement
attachEvent	blur	clearAttributes
click	cloneNode	componentFromPoint
contains	detachEvent	focus
getAdjacentText	getAttribute	getBoundingClientRect
getClientRects	getElementsByTagName	getExpression
hasChildNodes	insertAdjacentElement	insertAdjacentHTML

Methods *(continued)*

insertAdjacentText	insertBefore	mergeAttributes
releaseCapture	removeAttribute	removeBehavior
removeChild	removeExpression	removeNode
replaceAdjacentText	replaceChild	replaceNode
scrollIntoView	setAttribute	setCapture
setExpression	swapNode	

Events

onbeforecopy	onbeforecut	onbeforepaste	onblur
onclick	oncopy	oncut	ondblclick
ondrag	ondragend	ondragenter	ondragleave
ondragover	ondragstart	ondrop	onfocus
onhelp	onkeydown	onkeypress	onkeyup
onlosecapture	onmousedown	onmousemove	onmouseout
onmouseover	onmouseup	onpaste	onpropertychange
onreadystatechange	onresize	onselectstart	

Collections

all	attributes	behaviorUrns	childNodes	children

Default Behaviors

clientCaps	download	homePage	httpFolder	saveFavorite
saveHistory	saveSnapshot	time	userData	

CSS Properties

Note For a list of corresponding attributes, see Appendix C.

background	backgroundColor	backgroundImage
backgroundPosition	backgroundPositionX[*]	backgroundPositionY[*]
backgroundRepeat	behavior	clear
color	cursor	direction

* This property has no corresponding attribute.

CSS Properties *(continued)*

> **Note** For a list of corresponding attributes, see Appendix C.
>
> | | | |
> |---|---|---|
> | **font** | **fontFamily** | **fontSize** |
> | **fontStyle** | **fontVariant** | **fontWeight** |
> | **layoutGridMode** | **left** | **letterSpacing** |
> | **lineHeight** | **overflow** | **overflowX** |
> | **overflowY** | **pixelBottom**[*] | **pixelHeight**[*] |
> | **pixelLeft**[*] | **pixelRight**[*] | **pixelTop**[*] |
> | **pixelWidth**[*] | **posBottom**[*] | **posHeight**[*] |
> | **position** | **posLeft**[*] | **posRight**[*] |
> | **posTop**[*] | **posWidth**[*] | **styleFloat** |
> | **textAutospace** | **textDecoration** | **textDecorationBlink**[*] |
> | **textDecorationLineThrough**[*] | **textDecorationNone**[*] | **textDecorationOverline**[*] |
> | **textDecorationUnderline**[*] | **textTransform** | **top** |
> | **unicodeBidi** | **visibility** | **width** |
> | **wordSpacing** | **zIndex** | |

> [*] This property has no corresponding attribute.

Example

The following example shows how to use the **EM** element to emphasize text.

```
<EM>This text will be emphasized in some way (most likely with italics).</EM>
```

EMBED Element | EMBED Object

Allows documents of any type to be embedded.

Remarks

The **EMBED** element must appear inside the **BODY** element of the document.

Users need to have an appropriate application for viewing the data installed on their computer.

The **EMBED** element is a block element and does not require a closing tag.

This element is available in HTML as of Internet Explorer 3.0 and in script as of Internet Explorer 4.0.

Properties/Attributes

		CLASS	
accessKey	align	className	clientHeight*
clientLeft*	clientTop*	clientWidth*	currentStyle*
dir	firstChild*	height	hidden*
id	isTextEdit*	lang	language
lastChild*	nextSibling*	nodeName*	nodeType*
nodeValue*	offsetHeight*	offsetLeft*	offsetParent*
offsetTop*	offsetWidth*	outerHTML*	outerText*
palette*	parentElement*	parentNode*	parentTextEdit*
pluginspage	previousSibling*	readyState*	recordNumber*
runtimeStyle*	scopeName*	scrollHeight*	scrollLeft*
scrollTop*	scrollWidth*	sourceIndex*	src
style	tabIndex	tagName*	tagUrn*
title	uniqueID*	units	width

* This property has no corresponding attribute.

Methods

addBehavior	applyElement	attachEvent
blur	clearAttributes	click
cloneNode	componentFromPoint	contains
detachEvent	focus	getAdjacentText
getAttribute	getBoundingClientRect	getClientRects
getElementsByTagName	hasChildNodes	insertAdjacentElement
mergeAttributes	releaseCapture	removeAttribute
removeBehavior	removeExpression	replaceAdjacentText
scrollIntoView	setAttribute	setCapture
setExpression	swapNode	

Events

onblur	onclick	ondblclick	onfocus
onhelp	onload	onlosecapture	onmousedown
onmousemove	onmouseout	onmouseover	onmouseup
onpropertychange	onreadystatechange	onresize	onscroll

Collections

all	attributes	behaviorUrns	childNodes	children

Default Behaviors

clientCaps	download	homePage

CSS Properties

Note For a list of corresponding attributes, see Appendix C.

backgroundPositionX*	backgroundPositionY*	behavior
border	borderBottom	borderBottomColor
borderBottomStyle	borderBottomWidth	borderColor
borderLeft	borderLeftColor	borderLeftStyle
borderLeftWidth	borderRight	borderRightColor
borderRightStyle	borderRightWidth	borderStyle
borderTop	borderTopColor	borderTopStyle
borderTopWidth	borderWidth	clear
cursor	direction	height
layoutGridMode	left	margin
marginBottom	marginLeft	marginRight
marginTop	overflow	overflowX
overflowY	pixelBottom*	pixelHeight*
pixelLeft*	pixelRight*	pixelTop*

CSS Properties *(continued)*

pixelWidth[*]	posBottom[*]	posHeight[*]
position	posLeft[*]	posRight[*]
posTop[*]	posWidth[*]	styleFloat
textAutospace	top	unicodeBidi
visibility	width	

* This property has no corresponding attribute.

event Object

Represents the state of an event, such as the element in which the event occurred, the state of the keyboard keys, the location of the mouse, and the state of the mouse buttons.

Remarks

The **event** object is available only during an event. That is, you can use it in event handlers but not in other code.

Although all **event** properties are available to all **event** objects, some properties might not have meaningful values during some events. For example, the **fromElement** and **toElement** properties are meaningful only when processing the **onmouseover** and **onmouseout** events.

For VBScript, you must access the **event** object through the **window** object.

This object is available in script as of Internet Explorer 4.0.

Attributes/Properties

altKey[*]	button[*]	cancelBubble[*]	clientX[*]
clientY[*]	ctrlKey[*]	dataFld[*]	dataTransfer[*]
fromElement[*]	keyCode[*]	offsetX[*]	offsetY[*]
propertyName[*]	reason[*]	recordset[*]	repeat[*]
returnValue[*]	screenX[*]	screenY[*]	shiftKey[*]
srcElement[*]	srcFilter[*]	srcUrn[*]	toElement[*]
type[*]	x[*]	y[*]	

* This property has no corresponding attribute.

Collections

bookmarks   **boundElements**

Examples

The following example shows how to check whether the user clicked the mouse within a link, and to prevent the link from being navigated if the SHIFT key is down.

```
<HTML>
<HEAD><TITLE>Cancels Links</TITLE>
<SCRIPT LANGUAGE="JScript">
function cancelLink() {
    if (window.event.srcElement.tagName == "A" && window.event.shiftKey)
        window.event.returnValue = false;
}
</SCRIPT>
<BODY onclick="cancelLink()">
```

The following example shows how to display the current mouse position in the browser's status window.

```
<BODY onmousemove="window.status = 'X=' + window.event.x + ' Y='
    + window.event.y">
```

Applies To

 WIN16   WIN32   MAC   UNIX

window

external Object

Allows access to an additional object model provided by host applications of the Internet Explorer browser components.

Remarks

In a hosting scenario, the object model is defined by the application hosting the Internet Explorer components. For more information, see the documentation that comes with the hosting application.

This object is available in script as of Internet Explorer 4.0.

This object is not supported in HTML Applications (HTAs).

Attributes/Properties

menuArguments*

*   This property has no corresponding attribute.

Methods

AddChannel	**AddDesktopComponent**	**AddFavorite**
AutoCompleteSaveForm	**AutoScan**	**ImportExportFavorites**
IsSubscribed	**NavigateAndFind**	**ShowBrowserUI**

Applies To

IE 4   **WIN16**   **WIN32**   **MAC**   **UNIX**

window

FIELDSET Element | FIELDSET Object

Draws a box around the text and other elements that the field set contains.

Remarks

The **FIELDSET** element is a block element and requires a closing tag.

This element is useful for grouping elements in a form and for distinctively marking text in a document.

The **FIELDSET** element has the same behavior as a window frame. Because window frames do not have scroll bars, assigning the **overflow** property a value of scroll renders the window as if the value were hidden.

This element is available in HTML and script as of Internet Explorer 4.0.

Attributes/Properties

			CLASS
accessKey	**align**	**canHaveChildren**[*]	**className**
clientHeight[*]	**clientLeft**[*]	**clientTop**[*]	**clientWidth**[*]
currentStyle[*]	**dir**	**firstChild**[*]	**id**
innerHTML[*]	**innerText**[*]	**isTextEdit**[*]	**lang**
language	**lastChild**[*]	**nextSibling**[*]	**nodeName**[*]
nodeType[*]	**nodeValue**[*]	**offsetHeight**[*]	**offsetLeft**[*]
offsetParent[*]	**offsetTop**[*]	**offsetWidth**[*]	**outerHTML**[*]
outerText[*]	**parentElement**[*]	**parentNode**[*]	**parentTextEdit**[*]
previousSibling[*]	**readyState**[*]	**recordNumber**[*]	**runtimeStyle**[*]

[*]   This property has no corresponding attribute.

Attributes/Properties *(continued)*

scopeName*	scrollHeight*	scrollLeft*	scrollTop*
scrollWidth*	sourceIndex*	style	tabIndex
tagName*	tagUrn*	title	uniqueID*

* This property has no corresponding attribute.

Methods

addBehavior	appendChild	applyElement
attachEvent	blur	clearAttributes
click	cloneNode	componentFromPoint
contains	detachEvent	focus
getAdjacentText	getAttribute	getBoundingClientRect
getClientRects	getElementsByTagName	getExpression
hasChildNodes	insertAdjacentElement	insertAdjacentHTML
insertAdjacentText	insertBefore	mergeAttributes
releaseCapture	removeAttribute	removeBehavior
removeChild	removeExpression	removeNode
replaceAdjacentText	replaceChild	replaceNode
scrollIntoView	setAttribute	setCapture
setExpression	swapNode	

Events

onbeforecopy	onbeforecut	onbeforeeditfocus	onbeforepaste
onblur	onclick	oncopy	oncut
ondblclick	ondrag	ondragend	ondragenter
ondragleave	ondragover	ondragstart	ondrop
onfilterchange	onfocus	onhelp	onkeydown
onkeypress	onkeyup	onlosecapture	onmousedown
onmousemove	onmouseout	onmouseover	onmouseup
onpaste	onpropertychange	onreadystatechange	onresize
onselectstart			

DHTML Objects

Collections

all   attributes   behaviorUrns   childNodes   children   filters

Default Behaviors

clientCaps   download   homePage   time

CSS Properties

Note For a list of corresponding attributes, see Appendix C.

background	backgroundColor	backgroundImage
backgroundPosition	backgroundPositionX*	backgroundPositionY*
backgroundRepeat	behavior	border
borderBottom	borderBottomColor	borderBottomStyle
borderBottomWidth	borderColor	borderLeft
borderLeftColor	borderLeftStyle	borderLeftWidth
borderRight	borderRightColor	borderRightStyle
borderRightWidth	borderStyle	borderTop
borderTopColor	borderTopStyle	borderTopWidth
borderWidth	bottom	clear
color	cursor	direction
font	fontFamily	fontSize
fontStyle	fontVariant	fontWeight
height	layoutGrid	layoutGridChar
layoutGridCharSpacing	layoutGridLine	layoutGridMode
layoutGridType	left	letterSpacing
lineBreak	lineHeight	margin
marginBottom	marginLeft	marginRight
marginTop	overflow	overflowX
overflowY	pageBreakAfter	pageBreakBefore
pixelBottom*	pixelHeight*	pixelLeft*

* This property has no corresponding attribute.

CSS Properties *(continued)*

Note For a list of corresponding attributes, see Appendix C.

pixelRight*	pixelTop*	pixelWidth*
posBottom*	posHeight*	position
posLeft*	posRight*	posTop*
posWidth*	right	styleFloat
textAlign	textAutospace	textDecoration
textDecorationBlink*	textDecorationLineThrough*	textDecorationNone*
textDecorationOverline*	textDecorationUnderline*	textIndent
textJustify	textTransform	top
unicodeBidi	visibility	width
wordBreak	wordSpacing	zIndex

* This property has no corresponding attribute.

FONT Element | FONT Object

Specifies a new font, size, and color to be used for rendering the enclosed text.

Remarks

The **FONT** element requires a closing tag.

This element is available in HTML as of Internet Explorer 3.0 and in script as of Internet Explorer 4.0.

Attributes/Properties

	CLASS		
canHaveChildren*	className	color	currentStyle*
dir	face	firstChild*	id
innerHTML*	innerText*	isTextEdit*	lang
language	lastChild*	nextSibling*	nodeName*
nodeType*	nodeValue*	offsetHeight*	offsetLeft*
offsetParent*	offsetTop*	offsetWidth*	outerHTML*
outerText*	parentElement*	parentNode*	parentTextEdit*

DHTML Objects

Attributes/Properties *(continued)*

previousSibling[*]	**readyState**[*]	**recordNumber**[*]	**runtimeStyle**[*]
scopeName[*]	**size**	**sourceIndex**[*]	**style**
tabIndex	**tagName**[*]	**tagUrn**[*]	**uniqueID**[*]

* This property has no corresponding attribute.

Methods

addBehavior	**appendChild**	**applyElement**
attachEvent	**blur**	**clearAttributes**
click	**cloneNode**	**componentFromPoint**
contains	**detachEvent**	**focus**
getAdjacentText	**getAttribute**	**getBoundingClientRect**
getClientRects	**getElementsByTagName**	**getExpression**
hasChildNodes	**insertAdjacentElement**	**insertAdjacentHTML**
insertAdjacentText	**insertBefore**	**mergeAttributes**
releaseCapture	**removeAttribute**	**removeBehavior**
removeChild	**removeExpression**	**removeNode**
replaceAdjacentText	**replaceChild**	**replaceNode**
scrollIntoView	**setAttribute**	**setCapture**
setExpression	**swapNode**	

Events

onblur	**onclick**	**ondblclick**	**ondrag**
ondragend	**ondragenter**	**ondragleave**	**ondragover**
ondragstart	**ondrop**	**onfocus**	**onhelp**
onkeydown	**onkeypress**	**onkeyup**	**onlosecapture**
onmousedown	**onmousemove**	**onmouseout**	**onmouseover**
onmouseup	**onpropertychange**	**onreadystatechange**	**onselectstart**

Collections

all	**attributes**	**behaviorUrns**	**childNodes**	**children**

Default Behaviors

clientCaps	download	homePage	httpFolder	saveFavorite
saveHistory	saveSnapshot	time	userData	

CSS Properties

Note For a list of corresponding attributes, see Appendix C.

backgroundPositionX*	backgroundPositionY*	behavior	direction
layoutGridMode	overflow	overflowX	overflowY
pixelBottom*	pixelHeight*	pixelLeft*	pixelRight*
pixelTop*	pixelWidth*	posBottom*	posHeight*
posLeft*	posRight*	posTop*	posWidth*
textAutospace	unicodeBidi	width	

*   This property has no corresponding attribute.

FORM Element | FORM Object

Specifies that the contained controls are part of a form.

Remarks

Forms enable client-side users to submit data to a server in a standardized format. The creator of a form designs the form to collect the required data using a variety of controls, such as **INPUT** or **SELECT**. Users viewing the form can fill in the data and then click the Submit button to send it to the server. A script on the server can then process the data.

Each control element's **NAME** attribute must be defined for its data to be submitted with the form. An element in a form can be referenced by the **NAME** or **ID** property, or through the **elements** collection.

When the focus is on a control in a form and the user presses ESC, the value of the control reverts to the last value. When the user presses the key again, the form is reset. If the focus is on the form but not on a particular control and the user presses ESC once, the form is reset.

If the form has only one text box and the user presses ENTER, the **onsubmit** event fires. If the form has a **Submit** button, the button has a dark border, which indicates that the user can press ENTER to submit the form.

The **FORM** element is a block element and requires a closing tag.

This element is available in HTML and script as of Internet Explorer 3.0.

Attributes/Properties

	AUTOCOMPLETE		CLASS
action		canHaveChildren[*]	className
clientHeight[*]	clientLeft[*]	clientTop[*]	clientWidth[*]
		ENCTYPE	
currentStyle[*]	dir	encoding	firstChild[*]
id	innerHTML[*]	innerText[*]	isTextEdit[*]
lang	language	lastChild[*]	method
name	nextSibling[*]	nodeName[*]	nodeType[*]
nodeValue[*]	offsetHeight[*]	offsetLeft[*]	offsetParent[*]
offsetTop[*]	offsetWidth[*]	outerHTML[*]	outerText[*]
parentElement[*]	parentNode[*]	parentTextEdit[*]	previousSibling[*]
readyState[*]	recordNumber[*]	runtimeStyle[*]	scopeName[*]
scrollHeight[*]	scrollLeft[*]	scrollTop[*]	scrollWidth[*]
sourceIndex[*]	style	tabIndex	tagName[*]
tagUrn[*]	target	title	uniqueID[*]

[*]   This property has no corresponding attribute.

Methods

addBehavior	appendChild	applyElement
attachEvent	blur	clearAttributes
click	cloneNode	componentFromPoint
contains	detachEvent	focus
getAdjacentText	getAttribute	getBoundingClientRect
getClientRects	getElementsByTagName	getExpression
hasChildNodes	insertAdjacentElement	insertAdjacentHTML
insertAdjacentText	insertBefore	mergeAttributes

Methods *(continued)*

releaseCapture	removeAttribute	removeBehavior
removeChild	removeExpression	removeNode
replaceAdjacentText	replaceChild	replaceNode
reset	scrollIntoView	setAttribute
setCapture	setExpression	submit
swapNode	urns	

Events

onbeforecopy	onbeforecut	onbeforepaste	onblur
onclick	oncopy	oncut	ondblclick
ondrag	ondragend	ondragenter	ondragleave
ondragover	ondragstart	ondrop	onfocus
onhelp	onkeydown	onkeypress	onkeyup
onlosecapture	onmousedown	onmousemove	onmouseout
onmouseover	onmouseup	onpaste	onpropertychange
onreadystatechange	onreset	onresize	onselectstart
onsubmit			

Collections

all	attributes	behaviorUrns	childNodes	children	elements

Default Behaviors

clientCaps	download	homePage	httpFolder	saveFavorite
saveHistory	saveSnapshot	time	userData	

CSS Properties

Note For a list of corresponding attributes, see Appendix C.

background	backgroundColor	backgroundImage
backgroundPosition	backgroundPositionX*	backgroundPositionY*
backgroundRepeat	behavior	border
borderBottom	borderBottomColor	borderBottomStyle

CSS Properties *(continued)*

borderBottomWidth	borderColor	borderLeft
borderLeftColor	borderLeftStyle	borderLeftWidth
borderRight	borderRightColor	borderRightStyle
borderRightWidth	borderStyle	borderTop
borderTopColor	borderTopStyle	borderTopWidth
borderWidth	bottom	clear
color	cursor	direction
font	fontFamily	fontSize
fontStyle	fontVariant	fontWeight
layoutGrid	layoutGridChar	layoutGridCharSpacing
layoutGridLine	layoutGridMode	layoutGridType
left	letterSpacing	lineBreak
lineHeight	margin	marginBottom
marginLeft	marginRight	marginTop
overflow	overflowX	overflowY
pageBreakAfter	pageBreakBefore	pixelBottom[*]
pixelHeight[*]	pixelLeft[*]	pixelRight[*]
pixelTop[*]	pixelWidth[*]	posBottom[*]
posHeight[*]	position	posLeft[*]
posRight[*]	posTop[*]	posWidth[*]
right	styleFloat	textAlign
textAutospace	textDecoration	textDecorationBlink[*]
textDecorationLineThrough[*]	textDecorationNone[*]	textDecorationOverline[*]
textDecorationUnderline[*]	textIndent	textJustify
textTransform	top	unicodeBidi
visibility	width	wordBreak
wordSpacing	zIndex	

* This property has no corresponding attribute.

Example

This example shows how to create a basic form containing a text entry box for the user's name and a select control for choosing a favorite ice cream flavor. When the user clicks the Submit button, the form sends the form data to the URL listed in the **ACTION** property. The value of the **METHOD** property determines how the data is sent to the server.

```
<HTML>
    <FORM ACTION="http://example.microsoft.com/sample.asp" METHOD="POST">
        Enter your name: <INPUT NAME="FName"><BR>
        Favorite Ice Cream Flavor:
        <SELECT NAME="Flavor">
            <OPTION VALUE="Chocolate">Chocolate
            <OPTION VALUE="Strawberry">Strawberry
            <OPTION VALUE="Vanilla" SELECTED>Vanilla
        </SELECT>
        <P><INPUT TYPE=SUBMIT>
    </FORM>
</HTML>
```

FRAME Element | FRAME Object

Specifies an individual frame within a **FRAMESET** element.

Remarks

The **FRAME** element is a block element and does not require a closing tag.

If a user opens a Web folder inside a frame and then clicks on something in the Web folder, the file or folder that the user clicks takes over the entire window. For example, suppose that a page contains two frames, one frame pointing to http://www.microsoft.com and the second frame pointing to a network drive. If the user clicks a file or folder in the second frame, that frame takes control of the entire window, including the first frame.

A Web folder is a part of the file system hierarchy, but it does not necessarily represent anything in the file system. An example is Network Neighborhood.

This element is available in HTML and script as of Internet Explorer 3.0.

Attributes/Properties

APPLICATION†		CLASS	
	borderColor	className	dataFld
dataSrc	firstChild*	frameBorder	height
id	isTextEdit*	lang	language
lastChild*	marginHeight	marginWidth	name
nextSibling*	nodeName*	nodeType*	nodeValue*
noResize	offsetHeight*	offsetLeft*	offsetParent*
offsetTop*	offsetWidth*	parentElement*	parentNode*
parentTextEdit*	previousSibling*	readyState*	runtimeStyle*
scopeName*	scrolling	self*	sourceIndex*
src	style*	tagName*	tagUrn*
title	uniqueID*	width	

*   This property has no corresponding attribute.

†   This attribute has no corresponding property.

Methods

addBehavior	applyElement	attachEvent
blur	clearAttributes	cloneNode
componentFromPoint	contains	detachEvent
focus	getAdjacentText	getAttribute
getElementsByTagName	hasChildNodes	insertAdjacentElement
mergeAttributes	removeAttribute	removeBehavior
replaceAdjacentText	setAttribute	swapNode

Events

onblur   onfocus   onresize

Collections

all   attributes   behaviorUrns   childNodes   children

Default Behaviors

clientCaps   download   homePage

CSS Properties

Note For a list of corresponding attributes, see Appendix C.

backgroundPositionX[*]	**backgroundPositionY**[*]	**behavior**	**layoutGridMode**
pixelBottom[*]	**pixelHeight**[*]	**pixelLeft**[*]	**pixelRight**[*]
pixelTop[*]	**pixelWidth**[*]	**posBottom**[*]	**posHeight**[*]
posLeft[*]	**posRight**[*]	**posTop**[*]	**posWidth**[*]
textAutospace	**width**		

* This property has no corresponding attribute.

Example

The following example shows how to use the **FRAME** element.

```
<FRAME FRAMEBORDER=0 SCROLLING=NO SRC="sample.htm">
```

If your page is in a frame (FRAME1), the following example shows how to reference an object with ID=sID in a different frame (FRAME2) of the same frame set.

```
parent.frames.FRAME2.sID.innertext
```

FRAMESET Element | FRAMESET Object

Specifies a frame set, which is used to organize multiple frames and nested frame sets.

Remarks

The **FRAMESET** element is a block element and requires a closing tag.

If a user opens a Web folder inside a frame and then clicks something in the Web folder, the file or folder that the user clicks takes over the entire window. For example, suppose that a page contains two frames, one frame pointing to http://www.microsoft.com and the second frame pointing to a network drive. If the user clicks a file or folder in the second frame, that frame takes control of the entire window. For file types that the browser cannot host, such as .txt files, a separate window in the appropriate host application is opened.

A Web folder is a part of the file system hierarchy, but it does not necessarily represent anything in the file system. An example is Network Neighborhood.

This element is available in HTML as of Internet Explorer 3.0 and in script as of Internet Explorer 4.0.

Attributes/Properties

			CLASS
border	borderColor	canHaveChildren[*]	className
cols	firstChild[*]	frameBorder	frameSpacing
id	isTextEdit[*]	lang	language
lastChild[*]	nextSibling[*]	nodeName[*]	nodeType[*]
nodeValue[*]	parentElement[*]	parentNode[*]	parentTextEdit[*]
previousSibling[*]	readyState[*]	rows	runtimeStyle[*]
scopeName[*]	sourceIndex[*]	style[*]	tabIndex
tagName[*]	tagUrn[*]	title	uniqueID[*]

[*] This property has no corresponding attribute.

Methods

addBehavior	appendChild	applyElement
attachEvent	blur	clearAttributes
cloneNode	componentFromPoint	contains
detachEvent	focus	getAdjacentText
getAttribute	getElementsByTagName	hasChildNodes
insertAdjacentElement	insertAdjacentHTML	insertAdjacentText
insertBefore	mergeAttributes	removeAttribute
removeBehavior	removeChild	removeNode
replaceAdjacentText	replaceChild	replaceNode
setAttribute	swapNode	

Events

onafterprint	onbeforeprint	onbeforeunload	onblur
onfocus	onload	onunload	

Collections

all	attributes	behaviorUrns	childNodes	children

Default Behaviors

clientCaps   **download**   **homePage**

CSS Properties

Note For a list of corresponding attributes, see Appendix C.

backgroundPositionX[*]   **backgroundPositionY**[*]   **behavior**   **layoutGridMode**

pixelBottom[*]   **pixelHeight**[*]   **pixelLeft**[*]   **pixelRight**[*]

pixelTop[*]   **pixelWidth**[*]   **posBottom**[*]   **posHeight**[*]

posLeft[*]   **posRight**[*]   **posTop**[*]   **posWidth**[*]

textAutospace   **width**

[*]   This property has no corresponding attribute.

Example

The following example shows how to use the **FRAMESET** element to load frames into three columns.

```
<FRAMESET COLS="25%, 50%, *">
<FRAME SRC="contents.htm">
<FRAME SRC="info.htm">
<FRAME SCROLLING="NO" SRC="graphic.htm">
</FRAMESET>
```

HEAD Element | HEAD Object

Provides an unordered collection of information about the document.

Remarks

The **HEAD** element requires a closing tag.

The **HEAD** element provides information that does not affect the rendering of the document but that might be useful to the browser. The following tags are valid in this element: **BASE, BASEFONT, BGSOUND, LINK, META, NEXTID, SCRIPT, STYLE,** and **TITLE**.

This element is available in HTML as of Internet Explorer 3.0 and in script as of Internet Explorer 4.0.

Attributes/Properties

canHaveChildren*	**CLASS** className	clientHeight*	clientLeft*
clientTop*	clientWidth*	currentStyle*	firstChild*
id	innerHTML*	innerText*	isTextEdit*
lang	lastChild*	nextSibling*	nodeName*
nodeType*	nodeValue*	parentElement*	parentNode*
parentTextEdit*	previousSibling*	readyState*	runtimeStyle*
scopeName*	scrollHeight*	scrollLeft*	scrollTop*
scrollWidth*	sourceIndex*	style*	tagName*
tagUrn*	uniqueID*		

* This property has no corresponding attribute.

Methods

addBehavior	appendChild	applyElement
attachEvent	clearAttributes	cloneNode
componentFromPoint	contains	detachEvent
getAdjacentText	getAttribute	getElementsByTagName
hasChildNodes	insertAdjacentElement	insertBefore
mergeAttributes	removeAttribute	removeBehavior
removeChild	removeNode	replaceAdjacentText
replaceChild	replaceNode	setAttribute
swapNode		

Events

onreadystatechange

Collections

all	attributes	behaviorUrns	childNodes	children

Default Behaviors

clientCaps	download	homePage

Example

The following example shows how to use the **HEAD** element to create a document title.

```
<HEAD>
<TITLE>A Simple Document</TITLE>
</HEAD>
```

history Object

Contains information about the URLs the visited by the client.

Remarks

For security reasons, the **history** object does not expose the actual URLs in the browser history. It does allow navigation through the browser history by exposing the **back**, **forward**, and **go** methods. A particular document in the browser history can be identified as an index relative to the current page. For example, specifying -1 as a parameter for the **go** method is the equivalent of clicking the Back button.

This object is available in script as of Internet Explorer 3.0.

Attributes/Properties

length[*]

* This property has no corresponding attribute.

Methods

back	forward	go

Applies To

 WIN16   WIN32   MAC

window

 UNIX

window

Hn Element | Hn Object

Renders text in heading style.

Remarks

The **Hn** element is a block element and requires a closing tag to restore the formatting to normal.

Use H1 through H6 to specify different sizes and styles of headings.

This element is available in HTML as of Internet Explorer 3.0 and in script as of Internet Explorer 4.0.

Attributes/Properties

		CLASS	
align	canHaveChildren*	className	clientHeight*
clientLeft*	clientTop*	clientWidth*	currentStyle*
dir	firstChild*	id	innerHTML*
innerText*	isTextEdit*	lang	language
lastChild*	nextSibling*	nodeName*	nodeType*
nodeValue*	offsetHeight*	offsetLeft*	offsetParent*
offsetTop*	offsetWidth*	outerHTML*	outerText*
parentElement*	parentNode*	parentTextEdit*	previousSibling*
readyState*	recordNumber*	runtimeStyle*	scopeName*
scrollHeight*	scrollLeft*	scrollTop*	scrollWidth*
sourceIndex*	style	tabIndex	tagName*
tagUrn*	title	uniqueID*	

* This property has no corresponding attribute.

Methods

addBehavior	appendChild	applyElement
attachEvent	blur	clearAttributes
click	cloneNode	componentFromPoint
contains	detachEvent	focus
getAdjacentText	getAttribute	getBoundingClientRect

Methods *(continued)*

getClientRects	**getElementsByTagName**	**getExpression**
hasChildNodes	**insertAdjacentElement**	**insertAdjacentHTML**
insertAdjacentText	**insertBefore**	**mergeAttributes**
releaseCapture	**removeAttribute**	**removeBehavior**
removeChild	**removeExpression**	**removeNode**
replaceAdjacentText	**replaceChild**	**replaceNode**
scrollIntoView	**setAttribute**	**setCapture**
setExpression	**swapNode**	

Events

onbeforecopy	**onbeforecut**	**onbeforepaste**	**onblur**
onclick	**oncopy**	**oncut**	**ondblclick**
ondrag	**ondragend**	**ondragenter**	**ondragleave**
ondragover	**ondragstart**	**ondrop**	**onfocus**
onhelp	**onkeydown**	**onkeypress**	**onkeyup**
onlosecapture	**onmousedown**	**onmousemove**	**onmouseout**
onmouseover	**onmouseup**	**onpaste**	**onpropertychange**
onreadystatechange	**onresize**	**onselectstart**	

Collections

all	**attributes**	**behaviorUrns**	**childNodes**	**children**

Default Behaviors

clientCaps	**download**	**homePage**	**httpFolder**	**saveFavorite**
saveHistory	**saveSnapshot**	**time**	**userData**	

CSS Properties

Note For a list of corresponding attributes, see Appendix C.

background	**backgroundColor**	**backgroundImage**
backgroundPosition	**backgroundPositionX**[*]	**backgroundPositionY**[*]
backgroundRepeat	**behavior**	**border**

DHTML Objects

CSS Properties *(continued)*

borderBottom	borderBottomColor	borderBottomStyle
borderBottomWidth	borderColor	borderLeft
borderLeftColor	borderLeftStyle	borderLeftWidth
borderRight	borderRightColor	borderRightStyle
borderRightWidth	borderStyle	borderTop
borderTopColor	borderTopStyle	borderTopWidth
borderWidth	bottom	clear
color	cursor	direction
font	fontFamily	fontSize
fontStyle	fontVariant	fontWeight
layoutGrid	layoutGridChar	layoutGridCharSpacing
layoutGridLine	layoutGridMode	layoutGridType
left	letterSpacing	lineBreak
lineHeight	margin	marginBottom
marginLeft	marginRight	marginTop
overflow	overflowX	overflowY
pageBreakAfter	pageBreakBefore	pixelBottom[*]
pixelHeight[*]	pixelLeft[*]	pixelRight[*]
pixelTop[*]	pixelWidth[*]	posBottom[*]
posHeight[*]	position	posLeft[*]
posRight[*]	posTop[*]	posWidth[*]
right	styleFloat	textAlign
textAutospace	textDecoration	textDecorationBlink[*]
textDecorationLineThrough[*]	textDecorationNone[*]	textDecorationOverline[*]
textDecorationUnderline[*]	textIndent	textJustify
textTransform	top	unicodeBidi
visibility	width	wordBreak
wordSpacing		

[*]   This property has no corresponding attribute.

Example

The following example shows how to use a **H1** heading.

```
<H1>Welcome to Internet Explorer!</H1>
```

HR Element | HR Object

Draws a horizontal rule.

Remarks

The **HR** element is a block element and requires a closing tag.

This element is available in HTML as of Internet Explorer 3.0 and in script as of Internet Explorer 4.0.

Attributes/Properties

	CLASS		
align	className	color	firstChild[*]
id	isTextEdit[*]	language	lastChild[*]
nextSibling[*]	nodeName[*]	nodeType[*]	nodeValue[*]
noShade	offsetHeight[*]	offsetLeft[*]	offsetParent[*]
offsetTop[*]	offsetWidth[*]	outerHTML[*]	outerText[*]
parentElement[*]	parentNode[*]	parentTextEdit[*]	previousSibling[*]
readyState[*]	recordNumber[*]	runtimeStyle[*]	scopeName[*]
size[*]	sourceIndex[*]	style	tabIndex
tagName[*]	tagUrn[*]	title	uniqueID[*]
width			

[*]   This property has no corresponding attribute.

Methods

addBehavior	applyElement	attachEvent
blur	clearAttributes	click
cloneNode	componentFromPoint	contains
detachEvent	focus	getAdjacentText
getAttribute	getElementsByTagName	getExpression

Methods *(continued)*

hasChildNodes	**insertAdjacentElement**	**insertAdjacentHTML**
insertAdjacentText	**mergeAttributes**	**releaseCapture**
removeAttribute	**removeBehavior**	**removeExpression**
replaceAdjacentText	**scrollIntoView**	**setAttribute**
setCapture	**setExpression**	**swapNode**

Events

onblur	**onclick**	**oncopy**	**ondblclick**
ondrag	**ondragend**	**ondragenter**	**ondragleave**
ondragover	**ondragstart**	**ondrop**	**onfocus**
onhelp	**onkeydown**	**onkeypress**	**onkeyup**
onlosecapture	**onmousedown**	**onmousemove**	**onmouseout**
onmouseover	**onmouseup**	**onpropertychange**	**onreadystatechange**
onresize	**onselectstart**		

Collections

all	**attributes**	**behaviorUrns**	**childNodes**	**children**

Default Behaviors

clientCaps	**download**	**homePage**	**httpFolder**	**saveFavorite**
saveHistory	**saveSnapshot**	**time**	**userData**	

CSS Properties

Note For a list of corresponding attributes, see Appendix C.

backgroundPositionX[*]	**backgroundPositionY**[*]	**behavior**
borderBottom	**borderBottomColor**	**borderBottomStyle**
borderBottomWidth	**borderColor**	**borderLeft**
borderLeftColor	**borderLeftStyle**	**borderLeftWidth**
borderRight	**borderRightColor**	**borderRightStyle**

[*] This property has no corresponding attribute.

CSS Properties *(continued)*

Note For a list of corresponding attributes, see Appendix C.

borderRightWidth	**borderStyle**	**borderTop**
borderTopColor	**borderTopStyle**	**borderTopWidth**
borderWidth	**bottom**	**clear**
cursor	**height**	**layoutGrid**
layoutGridChar	**layoutGridCharSpacing**	**layoutGridLine**
layoutGridMode	**layoutGridType**	**left**
lineBreak	**margin**	**marginBottom**
marginLeft	**marginRight**	**marginTop**
pixelBottom[*]	**pixelHeight**[*]	**pixelLeft**[*]
pixelRight[*]	**pixelTop**[*]	**pixelWidth**[*]
posBottom[*]	**posHeight**[*]	**position**
posLeft[*]	**posRight**[*]	**posTop**[*]
posWidth[*]	**right**	**styleFloat**
textAlign	**textAutospace**	**textIndent**
textJustify	**top**	**visibility**
width	**wordBreak**	

[*] This property has no corresponding attribute.

HTML Element | HTML Object

Identifies the document as containing HTML elements.

Remarks

By default, the **document** object is the parent of the **HTML** element.

The **HTML** element requires a closing tag.

This element is available in HTML as of Internet Explorer 3.0 and in script as of Internet Explorer 4.0.

Attributes/Properties

	CLASS		
canHaveChildren*	className	clientHeight*	clientLeft*
clientTop*	clientWidth*	currentStyle*	firstChild*
id	innerHTML*	innerText*	isTextEdit*
lastChild*	nextSibling*	nodeName*	nodeType*
nodeValue*	parentElement*	parentNode*	parentTextEdit*
previousSibling*	readyState*	runtimeStyle*	scopeName*
scrollHeight*	scrollLeft*	scrollTop*	scrollWidth*
sourceIndex*	style*	tagName*	tagUrn*
uniqueID*	XMLNS†		

* This property has no corresponding attribute.

† This attribute has no corresponding property.

Methods

addBehavior	appendChild	applyElement
attachEvent	clearAttributes	cloneNode
componentFromPoint	contains	detachEvent
getAdjacentText	getAttribute	getElementsByTagName
hasChildNodes	insertAdjacentElement	insertBefore
mergeAttributes	removeAttribute	removeBehavior
removeChild	removeNode	replaceAdjacentText
replaceChild	replaceNode	setAttribute
swapNode		

Events

onreadystatechange

Collections

all	attributes	behaviorUrns	childNodes	children

Default Behaviors

clientCaps	download	homePage

CSS Properties

Note For a list of corresponding attributes, see Appendix C.

background	**backgroundAttachment**	**backgroundColor**
backgroundImage	**backgroundPosition**	**backgroundRepeat**
behavior	**color**	**cursor**
font	**fontFamily**	**fontSize**
fontStyle	**fontVariant**	**fontWeight**
letterSpacing	**lineHeight**	**textAutospace**
textDecoration	**textDecorationBlink**[*]	**textDecorationLineThrough**[*]
textDecorationNone[*]	**textDecorationOverline**[*]	**textDecorationUnderline**[*]
textTransform	**visibility**	**wordSpacing**

[*] This property has no corresponding attribute.

Example

The following example shows how to use an **HTML** element.

```
<HTML>
<BODY>
<P>This is an HTML document.</P>
</BODY>
</HTML>
```

HTML Comment Element

Prevents any enclosed text or HTML source code from being parsed and displayed in the browser window.

Remarks

Comments can contain other HTML elements. Comments do not nest.

The start and end tags are required.

Example

The following example shows how to insert a comment into HTML code.

```
<!-- This text will not appear in the browser window. -->
```

I Element | I Object

Specifies that the text should be rendered in italic, where available.

Remarks

The **I** element is an inline element and requires a closing tag.

This element is available in HTML as of Internet Explorer 3.0 and in script as of Internet Explorer 4.0.

Attributes/Properties

canHaveChildren[*]	CLASS className	clientHeight[*]	clientLeft[*]
clientTop[*]	clientWidth[*]	currentStyle[*]	dir
firstChild[*]	id	innerHTML[*]	innerText[*]
isTextEdit[*]	lang	language	lastChild[*]
nextSibling[*]	nodeName[*]	nodeType[*]	nodeValue[*]
offsetHeight[*]	offsetLeft[*]	offsetParent[*]	offsetTop[*]
offsetWidth[*]	outerHTML[*]	outerText[*]	parentElement[*]
parentNode[*]	parentTextEdit[*]	previousSibling[*]	readyState[*]
recordNumber[*]	runtimeStyle[*]	scopeName[*]	scrollHeight[*]
scrollLeft[*]	scrollTop[*]	scrollWidth[*]	sourceIndex[*]
style	tabIndex	tagName[*]	tagUrn[*]
title	uniqueID[*]		

[*]   This property has no corresponding attribute.

Methods

addBehavior	appendChild	applyElement
attachEvent	blur	clearAttributes
click	cloneNode	componentFromPoint
contains	detachEvent	focus
getAdjacentText	getAttribute	getBoundingClientRect
getClientRects	getElementsByTagName	getExpression
hasChildNodes	insertAdjacentElement	insertAdjacentHTML

DHTML Objects

Methods *(continued)*

insertAdjacentText	**insertBefore**	**mergeAttributes**
releaseCapture	**removeAttribute**	**removeBehavior**
removeChild	**removeExpression**	**removeNode**
replaceAdjacentText	**replaceChild**	**replaceNode**
scrollIntoView	**setAttribute**	**setCapture**
setExpression	**swapNode**	

Events

onbeforecopy	**onbeforecut**	**onbeforepaste**
onblur	**onclick**	**oncopy**
oncut	**ondblclick**	**ondrag**
ondragend	**ondragenter**	**ondragleave**
ondragover	**ondragstart**	**ondrop**
onfocus	**onhelp**	**onkeydown**
onkeypress	**onkeyup**	**onlosecapture**
onmousedown	**onmousemove**	**onmouseout**
onmouseover	**onmouseup**	**onpaste**
onpropertychange	**onreadystatechange**	**onresize**
onselectstart		

Collections

all	**attributes**	**behaviorUrns**	**childNodes**	**children**

Default Behaviors

clientCaps	**download**	**homePage**	**httpFolder**	**saveFavorite**
saveHistory	**saveSnapshot**	**time**	**userData**	

CSS Properties

Note For a list of corresponding attributes, see Appendix C.

background	**backgroundColor**	**backgroundImage**
backgroundPosition	**backgroundPositionX**[*]	**backgroundPositionY**[*]
backgroundRepeat	**behavior**	**bottom**
clear	**color**	**cursor**
direction	**font**	**fontFamily**
fontSize	**fontStyle**	**fontVariant**
fontWeight	**layoutGridMode**	**left**
letterSpacing	**lineHeight**	**overflow**
overflowX	**overflowY**	**pixelBottom**[*]
pixelHeight[*]	**pixelLeft**[*]	**pixelRight**[*]
pixelTop[*]	**pixelWidth**[*]	**posBottom**[*]
posHeight[*]	**position**	**posLeft**[*]
posRight[*]	**posTop**[*]	**posWidth**[*]
right	**styleFloat**	**textAutospace**
textDecoration	**textDecorationBlink**[*]	**textDecorationLineThrough**[*]
textDecorationNone[*]	**textDecorationOverline**[*]	**textDecorationUnderline**[*]
textTransform	**top**	**unicodeBidi**
visibility	**width**	**wordSpacing**
zIndex		

[*] This property has no corresponding attribute.

Example

The following example shows how to use the **I** element to make text italic.

```
<I>This text will be in italic.</I>
```

IFRAME Element | IFRAME Object

Creates inline floating frames.

Remarks

The **IFRAME** element is a block element and requires a closing tag.

IFRAME functions as a document within a document, or like a floating **FRAME**. The **frames** collection provides access to the contents of an **IFRAME** object. Use the **frames** collection to read or write to elements contained in an **IFRAME**. For example, the syntax for accessing the **backgroundColor** style of the **BODY** object in an **IFRAME** is:

```
sColor = document.frames("sFrameName").document.body.style.backgroundColor;
```

Properties of the **IFRAME** object, but not the contents of the **IFRAME**, can be accessed through the object model of the page where the **IFRAME** object resides. For example, the syntax for accessing the **border** style of the **IFRAME** object is:

```
sBorderValue = document.all.oFrame.style.border;
```

This element is available in HTML and script as of Internet Explorer 4.0.

Attributes/Properties

		APPLICATION[†]
accessKey	align	
	CLASS	
canHaveChildren[*]	className	dataFld
dataSrc	firstChild[*]	frameBorder
hspace	id	innerHTML[*]
innerText[*]	isTextEdit[*]	lang
language	lastChild[*]	marginHeight
marginWidth	name	nextSibling[*]
nodeName[*]	nodeType[*]	nodeValue[*]
offsetHeight[*]	offsetLeft[*]	offsetParent[*]
offsetTop[*]	offsetWidth[*]	outerHTML[*]
outerText[*]	parentElement[*]	parentNode[*]

DHTML Objects

Attributes/Properties *(continued)*

parentTextEdit*	previousSibling*	readyState*
recordNumber*	runtimeStyle*	scopeName*
scrolling	sourceIndex*	src
style	tabIndex	tagName*
tagUrn*	title	uniqueID*
vspace		

* This property has no corresponding attribute.

† This attribute has no corresponding property.

Methods

addBehavior	appendChild	applyElement
attachEvent	blur	clearAttributes
cloneNode	componentFromPoint	contains
detachEvent	focus	getAdjacentText
getAttribute	getElementsByTagName	getExpression
hasChildNodes	insertAdjacentElement	insertAdjacentHTML
insertAdjacentText	insertBefore	mergeAttributes
removeAttribute	removeBehavior	removeChild
removeExpression	removeNode	replaceAdjacentText
replaceChild	replaceNode	scrollIntoView
setAttribute	setExpression	swapNode

Events

onblur	onfocus

Collections

all	attributes	behaviorUrns	childNodes	children

Default Behaviors

clientCaps	download	homePage	time

CSS Properties

Note For a list of corresponding attributes, see Appendix C.

backgroundPositionX[*]	**backgroundPositionY**[*]	**behavior**
border	**borderBottom**	**borderBottomColor**
borderBottomStyle	**borderBottomWidth**	**borderColor**
borderLeft	**borderLeftColor**	**borderLeftStyle**
borderLeftWidth	**borderRight**	**borderRightColor**
borderRightStyle	**borderRightWidth**	**borderStyle**
borderTop	**borderTopColor**	**borderTopStyle**
borderTopWidth	**borderWidth**	**bottom**
clear	**cursor**	**display**
height	**layoutGridMode**	**left**
margin	**marginBottom**	**marginLeft**
marginRight	**marginTop**	**overflow**
overflowX	**overflowY**	**pixelBottom**[*]
pixelHeight[*]	**pixelLeft**[*]	**pixelRight**[*]
pixelTop[*]	**pixelWidth**[*]	**posBottom**[*]
posHeight[*]	**position**	**posLeft**[*]
posRight[*]	**posTop**[*]	**posWidth**[*]
right	**styleFloat**	**textAutospace**
top	**visibility**	**width**

[*] This property has no corresponding attribute.

Example

The following example shows how to create a frame containing the page sample.htm.

```
<IFRAME ID=IFrame1 FRAMEBORDER=0 SCROLLING=NO SRC="sample.htm"></IFRAME>
```

The following example shows how to return a reference to the **all** collection of the document contained by the **IFRAME**.

```
var collAll = document.frames("IFrame1").document.all
```

IMG Element | IMG Object

Embeds an image or a video clip in the document.

Remarks

The **IMG** element is an inline element and does not require a closing tag.

This element does not fire the **onfocus** event when it receives the input focus, unless it has been associated with a **MAP** element.

This element is available in HTML as of Internet Explorer 3.0 and in script as of Internet Explorer 4.0.

Attributes/Properties

			CLASS
align	**alt**	**border**	**className**
clientHeight[*]	**clientLeft**[*]	**clientTop**[*]	**clientWidth**[*]
complete[*]	**currentStyle**[*]	**dataFld**	**dataSrc**
dir	**dynsrc**	**fileCreatedDate**[*]	**fileModifiedDate**[*]
fileSize[*]	**fileUpdatedDate**[*]	**firstChild**[*]	**height**
hspace	**id**	**isMap**	**isTextEdit**[*]
lang	**language**	**lastChild**[*]	**loop**
lowsrc	**name**	**nextSibling**[*]	**nodeName**[*]
nodeType[*]	**nodeValue**[*]	**offsetHeight**[*]	**offsetLeft**[*]
offsetParent[*]	**offsetTop**[*]	**offsetWidth**[*]	**outerHTML**[*]
outerText[*]	**parentElement**[*]	**parentNode**[*]	**parentTextEdit**[*]
previousSibling[*]	**protocol**[*]	**readyState**[*]	**recordNumber**[*]
runtimeStyle[*]	**scopeName**[*]	**scrollHeight**[*]	**scrollLeft**[*]
scrollTop[*]	**scrollWidth**[*]	**sourceIndex**[*]	**src**
start[*]	**style**	**tabIndex**	**tagName**[*]
tagUrn[*]	**title**	**uniqueID**[*]	**useMap**
vspace	**width**		

[*] This property has no corresponding attribute.

Methods

addBehavior	applyElement	attachEvent
blur	clearAttributes	click
cloneNode	componentFromPoint	contains
detachEvent	focus	getAdjacentText
getAttribute	getBoundingClientRect	getClientRects
getElementsByTagName	getExpression	hasChildNodes
insertAdjacentElement	insertAdjacentHTML	insertAdjacentText
mergeAttributes	releaseCapture	removeAttribute
removeBehavior	removeExpression	replaceAdjacentText
scrollIntoView	setAttribute	setCapture
setExpression	swapNode	

Events

onabort	onbeforecopy	onbeforecut	onbeforepaste
onblur	onclick	oncopy	oncut
ondblclick	ondrag	ondragend	ondragenter
ondragleave	ondragover	ondragstart	ondrop
onerror	onfilterchange	onfocus	onhelp
onload	onlosecapture	onmousedown	onmousemove
onmouseout	onmouseover	onmouseup	onpaste
onpropertychange	onreadystatechange	onresize	onselectstart

Collections

all	attributes	behaviorUrns	childNodes	children	filters

Default Behaviors

clientCaps	download	homePage	httpFolder	saveFavorite
saveHistory	saveSnapshot	time	userData	

CSS Properties

Note For a list of corresponding attributes, see Appendix C.

background	backgroundColor	backgroundImage
backgroundPosition	backgroundPositionX[*]	backgroundPositionY[*]
backgroundRepeat	behavior	border
borderBottom	borderBottomColor	borderBottomStyle
borderBottomWidth	borderColor	borderLeft
borderLeftColor	borderLeftStyle	borderLeftWidth
borderRight	borderRightColor	borderRightStyle
borderRightWidth	borderStyle	borderTop
borderTopColor	borderTopStyle	borderTopWidth
borderWidth	bottom	clear
cursor	direction	display
filter	font	fontFamily
fontStyle	fontVariant	fontWeight
height	layoutGridMode	left
letterSpacing	lineHeight	margin
marginBottom	marginLeft	marginRight
marginTop	padding	paddingBottom
paddingLeft	paddingRight	paddingTop
pixelBottom[*]	pixelHeight[*]	pixelLeft[*]
pixelRight[*]	pixelTop[*]	pixelWidth[*]
posBottom[*]	posHeight[*]	position
posLeft[*]	posRight[*]	posTop[*]
posWidth[*]	right	styleFloat
textAutospace	top	unicodeBidi
verticalAlign	visibility	width
wordSpacing		

[*] This property has no corresponding attribute.

Example

The following example shows how to use the **IMG** element to embed an bitmap image (.bmp file) on a page.

```
<IMG SRC=mygraphic.bmp>
```

INPUT Element | INPUT Object

Creates a variety of form input controls.

Remarks

The **INPUT** element controls are inline elements. They specify one of these form input controls:

button	checkbox	file	hidden	image
password	radio	reset	submit	text

Example

The following example shows how to use the different input tag types.

```
<FORM ACTION="http://intranet/survey" METHOD=POST>
<P>Name</P>
<BR><INPUT NAME="CONTROL1" TYPE=TEXT VALUE="Your Name">
<P>Password</P>
<BR><INPUT TYPE="PASSWORD" NAME="CONTROL2">
<P>Color</P>
<BR><INPUT TYPE="RADIO" NAME="CONTROL3" VALUE="0" CHECKED>Red
<INPUT TYPE="RADIO" NAME="CONTROL3" VALUE="1">Green
<INPUT TYPE="RADIO" NAME="CONTROL3" VALUE="2">Blue
<P>Comments</P>
<BR><INPUT TYPE="TEXT" NAME="CONTROL4" SIZE="20,5" MAXLENGTH="250">
<P><INPUT NAME="CONTROL5" TYPE=CHECKBOX CHECKED>Send receipt</P>
<P><INPUT TYPE="SUBMIT" VALUE="OK"><INPUT TYPE="RESET" VALUE="Reset"></P>
</FORM>
```

INPUT type=button Element | INPUT type=button Object

Creates a button control.

Remarks

The **button** element is an inline element and does not require a closing tag.

This element is available in HTML and script as of Internet Explorer 3.0.

DHTML Objects

Attributes/Properties

		CLASS	
accessKey	canHaveChildren[*]	className	clientHeight[*]
clientLeft[*]	clientTop[*]	clientWidth[*]	currentStyle[*]
dataFld	dataFormatAs	dataSrc	defaultValue[*]
dir	disabled	firstChild[*]	form[*]
id	isTextEdit[*]	lang	language
lastChild[*]	name	nextSibling[*]	nodeName[*]
nodeType[*]	nodeValue[*]	offsetHeight[*]	offsetLeft[*]
offsetParent[*]	offsetTop[*]	offsetWidth[*]	outerHTML[*]
outerText[*]	parentElement[*]	parentNode[*]	parentTextEdit[*]
previousSibling[*]	readyState[*]	recordNumber[*]	runtimeStyle[*]
scopeName[*]	scrollHeight[*]	scrollLeft[*]	scrollTop[*]
scrollWidth[*]	size	sourceIndex[*]	style
tabIndex	tagName[*]	tagUrn[*]	title
type	uniqueID[*]	value	

[*]   This property has no corresponding attribute.

Methods

addBehavior	appendChild	applyElement
attachEvent	blur	clearAttributes
click	cloneNode	componentFromPoint
contains	createTextRange	detachEvent
focus	getAdjacentText	getAttribute
getBoundingClientRect	getClientRects	getExpression
hasChildNodes	insertAdjacentElement	insertAdjacentHTML
insertAdjacentText	insertBefore	mergeAttributes
releaseCapture	removeAttribute	removeBehavior
removeChild	removeExpression	removeNode

Methods *(continued)*

replaceAdjacentText	replaceChild	replaceNode
scrollIntoView	select	setAttribute
setCapture	setExpression	swapNode

Events

onbeforeeditfocus	onblur	onclick	ondblclick
ondrag	ondragend	ondragenter	ondragleave
ondragover	ondragstart	ondrop	onfilterchange
onfocus	onhelp	onkeydown	onkeypress
onkeyup	onlosecapture	onmousedown	onmousemove
onmouseout	onmouseover	onmouseup	onpropertychange
onreadystatechange	onresize	onselectstart	

Collections

attributes	behaviorUrns	filters

Default Behaviors

clientCaps	download	homePage	httpFolder	saveFavorite
saveHistory	saveSnapshot	time	userData	

CSS Properties

Note For a list of corresponding attributes, see Appendix C.

background	backgroundColor	backgroundImage
backgroundPosition	backgroundPositionX*	backgroundPositionY*
backgroundRepeat	behavior	border
borderBottom	borderBottomColor	borderBottomStyle
borderBottomWidth	borderColor	borderLeft
borderLeftColor	borderLeftStyle	borderLeftWidth
borderRight	borderRightColor	borderRightStyle
borderRightWidth	borderStyle	borderTop

CSS Properties *(continued)*

borderTopColor	**borderTopStyle**	**borderTopWidth**
borderWidth	**bottom**	**clear**
color	**cursor**	**direction**
display	**filter**	**font**
fontFamily	**fontSize**	**fontStyle**
fontVariant	**fontWeight**	**height**
layoutGridMode	**left**	**letterSpacing**
lineHeight	**margin**	**marginBottom**
marginLeft	**marginRight**	**marginTop**
pixelBottom[*]	**pixelHeight**[*]	**pixelLeft**[*]
pixelRight[*]	**pixelTop**[*]	**pixelWidth**[*]
posBottom[*]	**posHeight**[*]	**position**
posLeft[*]	**posRight**[*]	**posTop**[*]
posWidth[*]	**right**	**styleFloat**
textAutospace	**textDecoration**	**textDecorationBlink**[*]
textDecorationLineThrough[*]	**textDecorationNone**[*]	**textDecorationOverline**[*]
textDecorationUnderline[*]	**textTransform**	**top**
unicodeBidi	**visibility**	**width**
wordSpacing	**zIndex**	

[*]   This property has no corresponding attribute.

Example

The following example shows how to define a button that responds appropriately
when clicked.

```
<INPUT TYPE=button ID=btnEmergency VALUE="In case of emergency,
push this button!"
    onClick="alert('Aaaaaaaggggghh!!!!')">
```

INPUT type=checkbox Element | INPUT type=checkbox Object

Creates a check box control.

Remarks

The **checkbox** element is an inline element and does not require a closing tag. When a **checkbox** element is selected, a **NAME/VALUE** pair is submitted with the **FORM**. The default value of **checkbox** is on.

The **height** and **width** styles are exposed to the **checkbox** element as of Internet Explorer 5. The size of the element is set based on the values provided by the author, except when a given size is below a particular minimum. The size is calculated as follows:

1. If the **height** or **width** is greater than 20 pixels, the padding around the check box is set to 4 pixels, and the inner height or width is set to 8 pixels.

2. If the **height** or **width** is less than 20 pixels but greater than 13 pixels, the padding around the check box is equal to one half the specified **height** or **width** minus 13. For example, if the specified **width** of the check box is 17, the equation would be: (17-13)/2.

3. If the **height** or **width** is less than 12 pixels, the padding around the check box is set to 0 and the inner width is set to the value specified by the author.

This element is available in HTML and script as of Internet Explorer 3.0.

Attributes/Properties

			CLASS
accessKey	canHaveChildren[*]	checked	className
clientHeight[*]	clientLeft[*]	clientTop[*]	clientWidth[*]
currentStyle[*]	dataFld	dataSrc	defaultChecked[*]
defaultValue[*]	dir	disabled	firstChild[*]
form[*]	id	indeterminate[*]	isTextEdit[*]
lang	language	lastChild[*]	name
nextSibling[*]	nodeName[*]	nodeType[*]	nodeValue[*]
offsetHeight[*]	offsetLeft[*]	offsetParent[*]	offsetTop[*]
offsetWidth[*]	outerHTML[*]	outerText[*]	parentElement[*]

Attributes/Properties *(continued)*

parentNode[*]	parentTextEdit[*]	previousSibling[*]	readyState[*]
recordNumber[*]	runtimeStyle[*]	scopeName[*]	scrollHeight[*]
scrollLeft[*]	scrollTop[*]	scrollWidth[*]	size
sourceIndex[*]	status[*]	style	tabIndex
tagName[*]	tagUrn[*]	title	type
uniqueID[*]	value		

[*] This property has no corresponding attribute.

Methods

addBehavior	appendChild	applyElement
attachEvent	blur	clearAttributes
click	cloneNode	componentFromPoint
contains	detachEvent	focus
getAdjacentText	getAttribute	getBoundingClientRect
getClientRects	getExpression	hasChildNodes
insertAdjacentElement	insertAdjacentHTML	insertAdjacentText
insertBefore	mergeAttributes	releaseCapture
removeAttribute	removeBehavior	removeChild
removeExpression	removeNode	replaceAdjacentText
replaceChild	replaceNode	scrollIntoView
select	setAttribute	setCapture
setExpression	swapNode	

Events

onbeforeeditfocus	onblur	onclick	ondblclick
ondrag	ondragend	ondragenter	ondragleave
ondragover	ondragstart	ondrop	onfilterchange
onfocus	onhelp	onkeydown	onkeypress

Events *(continued)*

onkeyup	onlosecapture	onmousedown	onmousemove
onmouseout	onmouseover	onmouseup	onpropertychange
onreadystatechange	onselectstart		

Collections

attributes   behaviorUrns   filters

Default Behaviors

clientCaps	download	homePage	httpFolder	saveFavorite
saveHistory	saveSnapshot	time	userData	

CSS Properties

Note For a list of corresponding attributes, see Appendix C.

background	backgroundColor	backgroundImage
backgroundPosition	backgroundPositionX*	backgroundPositionY*
backgroundRepeat	behavior	border
borderBottom	borderBottomColor	borderBottomStyle
borderBottomWidth	borderColor	borderLeft
borderLeftColor	borderLeftStyle	borderLeftWidth
borderRight	borderRightColor	borderRightStyle
borderRightWidth	borderStyle	borderTop
borderTopColor	borderTopStyle	borderTopWidth
borderWidth	bottom	clear
color	cursor	direction
display	filter	font
fontFamily	fontSize	fontStyle
fontVariant	fontWeight	height
layoutGridMode	left	letterSpacing

CSS Properties *(continued)*

lineHeight	**margin**	**marginBottom**
marginLeft	**marginRight**	**marginTop**
pixelBottom[*]	**pixelHeight**[*]	**pixelLeft**[*]
pixelRight[*]	**pixelTop**[*]	**pixelWidth**[*]
posBottom[*]	**posHeight**[*]	**position**
posLeft[*]	**posRight**[*]	**posTop**[*]
posWidth[*]	**right**	**styleFloat**
textAutospace	**textDecoration**	**textDecorationBlink**[*]
textDecorationLineThrough[*]	**textDecorationNone**[*]	**textDecorationOverline**[*]
textDecorationUnderline[*]	**textTransform**	**top**
unicodeBidi	**visibility**	**width**
wordSpacing	**zIndex**	

[*] This property has no corresponding attribute.

Example

The following example shows how to define two check boxes with explanatory text. The **onclick** events call two script functions. The first check box is checked.

```
<INPUT TYPE=checkbox CHECKED ID=chk1 onclick="choosebox1()">Uncheck
    this check box for some free advice.
<p><INPUT TYPE=checkbox ID=chk2 onclick="choosebox2()">Or check
    this check box for a message from our sponsors.
<p ID=SampText>
```

The following script is implemented when the user clicks the check boxes.

```
<SCRIPT>
function choosebox1(){
        alert("Never play leapfrog with a unicorn!")
}
function choosebox2(){
    SampText.insertAdjacentHTML("AfterBegin","Buy WonderWidgets! ");
}
</SCRIPT>
```

INPUT type=file Element | INPUT type=file Object

Creates a file upload object with a text box and Browse button.

Remarks

For a file upload to take place:

- The file element must be enclosed within a **FORM** element.
- A value must be specified for the **NAME** attribute of the **file** element.
- The **METHOD** attribute of the **FORM** element must be set to `post`.
- The **ENCTYPE** attribute of the **FORM** element must be set to `multipart/formdata`.

To handle a file upload to the server, a server-side process that can handle multipart/form-data submissions must be running. For example, the Microsoft Posting Acceptor allows Microsoft Internet Information Server to accept file uploads. Additional Common Gateway Interface (CGI) scripts that can handle multipart/form-data submissions are available on the Web.

The **file** element is an inline element and does not require a closing tag.

This element is available in HTML and script as of Internet Explorer 4.0. The file upload add-on is required to use the **file** element in Internet Explorer 3.02. Users can enter a file path in the text box or click the Browse button to browse the file system.

Attributes/Properties

		CLASS	
accessKey	canHaveChildren[*]	className	clientHeight[*]
clientLeft[*]	clientTop[*]	clientWidth[*]	currentStyle[*]
dataFld	dataSrc	defaultValue[*]	dir
disabled	firstChild[*]	form[*]	id
isTextEdit[*]	lang	language	lastChild[*]
name	nextSibling[*]	nodeName[*]	nodeType[*]
nodeValue[*]	offsetHeight[*]	offsetLeft[*]	offsetParent[*]
offsetTop[*]	offsetWidth[*]	outerHTML[*]	outerText[*]
parentElement[*]	parentNode[*]	parentTextEdit[*]	previousSibling[*]

Attributes/Properties *(continued)*

readyState*	recordNumber*	runtimeStyle*	scopeName*
scrollHeight*	scrollLeft*	scrollTop*	scrollWidth*
size	sourceIndex*	style	tabIndex
tagName*	tagUrn*	title	type
uniqueID*	value		

* This property has no corresponding attribute.

Methods

addBehavior	appendChild	applyElement
attachEvent	blur	clearAttributes
click	cloneNode	componentFromPoint
contains	detachEvent	focus
getAdjacentText	getAttribute	getBoundingClientRect
getClientRects	getExpression	hasChildNodes
insertAdjacentElement	insertAdjacentHTML	insertAdjacentText
insertBefore	mergeAttributes	releaseCapture
removeAttribute	removeBehavior	removeChild
removeExpression	removeNode	replaceAdjacentText
replaceChild	replaceNode	scrollIntoView
select	setAttribute	setCapture
setExpression	swapNode	

Events

onbeforeeditfocus	onblur	onclick	ondblclick
ondrag	ondragend	ondragenter	ondragleave
ondragover	ondragstart	ondrop	onfilterchange
onfocus	onhelp	onkeydown	onkeypress
onkeyup	onlosecapture	onmousedown	onmousemove
onmouseout	onmouseover	onmouseup	onpropertychange
onreadystatechange	onresize	onselectstart	

Collections

attributes   behaviorUrns   filters

Default Behaviors

clientCaps   download   homePage   httpFolder   saveFavorite

saveHistory   saveSnapshot   time   userData

CSS Properties

Note For a list of corresponding attributes, see Appendix C.

background	backgroundColor	backgroundImage
backgroundPosition	backgroundPositionX[*]	backgroundPositionY[*]
backgroundRepeat	behavior	border
borderBottom	borderBottomColor	borderBottomStyle
borderBottomWidth	borderColor	borderLeft
borderLeftColor	borderLeftStyle	borderLeftWidth
borderRight	borderRightColor	borderRightStyle
borderRightWidth	borderStyle	borderTop
borderTopColor	borderTopStyle	borderTopWidth
borderWidth	bottom	clear
color	cursor	direction
display	filter	font
fontFamily	fontSize	fontStyle
fontVariant	fontWeight	height
layoutGridMode	left	letterSpacing
lineHeight	margin	marginBottom
marginLeft	marginRight	marginTop
pixelBottom[*]	pixelHeight[*]	pixelLeft[*]
pixelRight[*]	pixelTop[*]	pixelWidth[*]
posBottom[*]	posHeight[*]	position
posLeft[*]	posRight[*]	posTop[*]
posWidth[*]	right	styleFloat

CSS Properties *(continued)*

textAutospace	textDecoration	textDecorationBlink[*]
textDecorationLineThrough[*]	textDecorationNone[*]	textDecorationOverline[*]
textDecorationUnderline[*]	textTransform	top
unicodeBidi	visibility	width
wordSpacing	zIndex	

* This property has no corresponding attribute.

Example

This example shows how to use the **file** element to upload a file to a server. This sample code requires the Microsoft Posting Acceptor, which can be used with Internet Information Server or Personal Web Server.

The following HTML submits a file selected by the user to Cpshost.dll, which is installed with Posting Acceptor.

```
<FORM NAME="oForm"
   ACTION="/scripts/cpshost.dll?PUBLISH?/scripts/repost.asp"
   ENCTYPE="multipart/form-data"
   METHOD="post">
<INPUT TYPE="file" NAME="oFile1">
<INPUT TYPE="text"
   NAME="TargetURL"
   VALUE="/users/">
<INPUT TYPE="submit" VALUE="Upload File">
</FORM>
```

The following example shows the Active Server Page (ASP) content of Repost.asp. Notice that the properties of the uploaded file are accessible from the submitted form.

```
<%@ LANGUAGE = JScript %>
<% Response.buffer=true; %>
<HTML>
<TITLE>Repost Example</TITLE>
<BODY>
<H1>Upload Status</H1>
<P>
Destination: <B><% Response.Write(Request.Form("TargetURL")) %></B>
</P>
<%
   Response.write("<P>Name: " + Request.Form("FileName") + "</P>");
   Response.write("<P>Size: " + Request.Form("FileSize") + "</P>");
   Response.write("<P>Path: " + Request.Form("FilePath") + "</P>");
%>
</BODY>
</HTML>
```

INPUT type=hidden Element | INPUT type=hidden Object

Transmits state information about client/server interaction.

Remarks

The **hidden** element does not require a closing tag.

This input type presents no control to the user, but sends the value of the **value** property with the submitted form.

This element is available in HTML and script as of Internet Explorer 3.0.

Attributes/Properties

CLASS

className	dataFld	dataSrc	defaultValue*
form*	id	isTextEdit*	lang
language	name	nextSibling*	nodeName*
nodeType*	nodeValue*	offsetParent*	outerHTML*
outerText*	parentElement*	parentNode*	parentTextEdit*
previousSibling*	readyState*	recordNumber*	runtimeStyle*
scopeName*	sourceIndex*	style	tagName*
tagUrn*	type	uniqueID*	value

* This property has no corresponding attribute.

Methods

addBehavior	applyElement	attachEvent
clearAttributes	cloneNode	componentFromPoint
createTextRange	detachEvent	getAdjacentText
getAttribute	getExpression	insertAdjacentElement
insertAdjacentHTML	insertAdjacentText	mergeAttributes
releaseCapture	removeAttribute	removeBehavior

DHTML Objects

Methods *(continued)*

removeChild	removeExpression	replaceAdjacentText
replaceChild	setAttribute	setCapture
setExpression	swapNode	

Events

onbeforeeditfocus	onfocus	onlosecapture
onpropertychange	onreadystatechange	

Collections

attributes	behaviorUrns

Default Behaviors

clientCaps	download	homePage	httpFolder	saveFavorite
saveHistory	saveSnapshot	time	userData	

CSS Properties

Note For a list of corresponding attributes, see Appendix C.

behavior	textAutospace

INPUT type=image Element | INPUT type=image Object

Creates an image control that, when clicked, causes the form to be immediately submitted.

Remarks

The **image** element is an inline element and does not require a closing tag.

The x-coordinate is submitted under the name of the control with *.x* appended, and the y-coordinate is submitted under the name of the control with *.y* appended. Any **value** property is ignored. The image is specified by the **src** property, exactly as for the **IMG** element.

This element is available in HTML and script as of Internet Explorer 3.0.

Attributes/Properties

			CLASS
accessKey	align	canHaveChildren*	className
clientHeight*	clientLeft*	clientTop*	clientWidth*
complete*	currentStyle*	dataFld	dataSrc
defaultValue*	dir	disabled	firstChild*
form*	id	isTextEdit*	lang
language	lastChild*	name	nextSibling*
nodeName*	nodeType*	nodeValue*	offsetHeight*
offsetLeft*	offsetParent*	offsetTop*	offsetWidth*
outerHTML*	outerText*	parentElement*	parentNode*
parentTextEdit*	previousSibling*	readyState*	recordNumber*
runtimeStyle*	scopeName*	scrollHeight*	scrollLeft*
scrollTop*	scrollWidth*	size	sourceIndex*
src	style	tabIndex	tagName*
tagUrn*	title	type	uniqueID*
value			

* This property has no corresponding attribute.

Methods

addBehavior	appendChild	applyElement
attachEvent	blur	clearAttributes
click	cloneNode	componentFromPoint
contains	detachEvent	focus
getAdjacentText	getAttribute	getBoundingClientRect
getClientRects	getExpression	hasChildNodes
insertAdjacentElement	insertAdjacentHTML	insertAdjacentText
insertBefore	mergeAttributes	releaseCapture
removeAttribute	removeBehavior	removeChild
removeExpression	removeNode	replaceAdjacentText

Methods *(continued)*

replaceChild	replaceNode	scrollIntoView
select	setAttribute	setCapture
setExpression	swapNode	

Events

onbeforeeditfocus	onblur	onclick	ondblclick
ondrag	ondragend	ondragenter	ondragleave
ondragover	ondragstart	ondrop	onfilterchange
onfocus	onhelp	onkeydown	onkeypress
onkeyup	onlosecapture	onmousedown	onmousemove
onmouseout	onmouseover	onmouseup	onpropertychange
onreadystatechange	onresize	onselectstart	

Collections

attributes	behaviorUrns	filters

Default Behaviors

clientCaps	download	homePage	httpFolder	saveFavorite
saveHistory	saveSnapshot	time	userData	

CSS Properties

Note For a list of corresponding attributes, see Appendix C.

background	backgroundColor	backgroundImage
backgroundPosition	backgroundPositionX[*]	backgroundPositionY[*]
backgroundRepeat	behavior	border
borderBottom	borderBottomColor	borderBottomStyle
borderBottomWidth	borderColor	borderLeft
borderLeftColor	borderLeftStyle	borderLeftWidth
borderRight	borderRightColor	borderRightStyle
borderRightWidth	borderStyle	borderTop

* This property has no corresponding attribute.

CSS Properties *(continued)*

> **Note** For a list of corresponding attributes, see Appendix C.

borderTopColor	**borderTopStyle**	**borderTopWidth**
borderWidth	**bottom**	**clear**
color	**cursor**	**direction**
display	**filter**	**font**
fontFamily	**fontSize**	**fontStyle**
fontVariant	**fontWeight**	**height**
layoutGridMode	**left**	**letterSpacing**
lineHeight	**margin**	**marginBottom**
marginLeft	**marginRight**	**marginTop**
pixelBottom[*]	**pixelHeight**[*]	**pixelLeft**[*]
pixelRight[*]	**pixelTop**[*]	**pixelWidth**[*]
posBottom[*]	**posHeight**[*]	**position**
posLeft[*]	**posRight**[*]	**posTop**[*]
posWidth[*]	**right**	**styleFloat**
textAutospace	**textDecoration**	**textDecorationBlink**[*]
textDecorationLineThrough[*]	**textDecorationNone**[*]	**textDecorationOverline**[*]
textDecorationUnderline[*]	**textTransform**	**top**
unicodeBidi	**visibility**	**width**
wordSpacing	**zIndex**	

[*]   This property has no corresponding attribute.

INPUT type=password Element | INPUT type=password Object

Creates a single-line text entry control similar to the **text** control, except that text is not displayed as the user enters it.

Remarks

The **password** element is an inline element and does not require a closing tag.

This element is available in HTML and script as of Internet Explorer 3.0.

Attributes/Properties

	AUTOCOMPLETE		CLASS
accessKey		canHaveChildren*	className
clientHeight*	clientLeft*	clientTop*	clientWidth*
currentStyle*	dataFld	dataSrc	defaultValue*
dir	disabled	firstChild*	form*
id	isTextEdit*	lang	language
lastChild*	maxLength	name	nextSibling*
nodeName*	nodeType*	nodeValue*	offsetHeight*
offsetLeft*	offsetParent*	offsetTop*	offsetWidth*
outerHTML*	outerText*	parentElement*	parentNode*
parentTextEdit*	previousSibling*	readOnly	readyState*
recordNumber*	runtimeStyle*	scopeName*	scrollHeight*
scrollLeft*	scrollTop*	scrollWidth*	size
sourceIndex*	style	tabIndex	tagName*
tagUrn*	title	type	uniqueID*
value	vcard_name		

*   This property has no corresponding attribute.

Methods

addBehavior	appendChild	applyElement
attachEvent	blur	clearAttributes
click	cloneNode	componentFromPoint
contains	createTextRange	detachEvent
focus	getAdjacentText	getAttribute
getBoundingClientRect	getClientRects	getExpression
hasChildNodes	insertAdjacentElement	insertAdjacentHTML
insertAdjacentText	insertBefore	mergeAttributes
releaseCapture	removeAttribute	removeBehavior
removeChild	removeExpression	removeNode

Methods *(continued)*

replaceAdjacentText	replaceChild	replaceNode
scrollIntoView	select	setAttribute
setCapture	setExpression	swapNode

Events

onbeforeeditfocus	onblur	onclick	ondblclick
ondrag	ondragend	ondragenter	ondragleave
ondragover	ondragstart	ondrop	onfilterchange
onfocus	onhelp	onkeydown	onkeypress
onkeyup	onlosecapture	onmousedown	onmousemove
onmouseout	onmouseover	onmouseup	onpropertychange
onreadystatechange	onresize	onselectstart	

Collections

attributes	behaviorUrns	filters

Default Behaviors

clientCaps	download	homePage	httpFolder	saveFavorite
saveHistory	saveSnapshot	time	userData	

CSS Properties

Note For a list of corresponding attributes, see Appendix C.

background	backgroundColor	backgroundImage
backgroundPosition	backgroundPositionX*	backgroundPositionY*
backgroundRepeat	behavior	border
borderBottom	borderBottomColor	borderBottomStyle
borderBottomWidth	borderColor	borderLeft
borderLeftColor	borderLeftStyle	borderLeftWidth
borderRight	borderRightColor	borderRightStyle
borderRightWidth	borderStyle	borderTop
borderTopColor	borderTopStyle	borderTopWidth

CSS Properties *(continued)*

borderWidth	bottom	clear
color	cursor	direction
display	filter	font
fontFamily	fontSize	fontStyle
fontVariant	fontWeight	height
layoutGridMode	left	letterSpacing
lineHeight	margin	marginBottom
marginLeft	marginRight	marginTop
pixelBottom*	pixelHeight*	pixelLeft*
pixelRight*	pixelTop*	pixelWidth*
posBottom*	posHeight*	position
posLeft*	posRight*	posTop*
posWidth*	right	styleFloat
textAlign	textAutospace	textDecoration
textDecorationBlink*	textDecorationLineThrough*	textDecorationNone*
textDecorationOverline*	textDecorationUnderline*	textTransform
top	unicodeBidi	visibility
width	wordSpacing	zIndex

* This property has no corresponding attribute.

Example

The following example shows how to define a password field.

```
Username <INPUT TYPE=button ID=txtUser>
Password <INPUT TYPE=password ID=txtPassword>
```

The following script shows how to check whether the password is valid for the specified user.

```
<SCRIPT>
if (txtUser.value == "Paul")
   if (txtPassword.value == "2ifbysea")
   {
      alert("Password accepted.  Enjoy your ride.");
      return true;
   }
</SCRIPT>
```

DHTML Objects

INPUT type=radio Element | INPUT type=radio Object

Creates a radio button control.

Remarks

The **radio** element is an inline element and does not require a closing tag.

A radio button control is used for mutually exclusive sets of values. Each radio button control in a group should be given the same name. Only one radio button in the group can be selected at any given time. Only the selected radio button in the group generates a **NAME/VALUE** pair in the submitted data. Radio buttons require an explicit **value** property.

This element is available in HTML and script as of Internet Explorer 3.0.

Attributes/Properties

			CLASS
accessKey	canHaveChildren*	checked	className
clientHeight*	clientLeft*	clientTop*	clientWidth*
currentStyle*	dataFld	dataSrc	defaultChecked*
defaultValue*	dir	disabled	firstChild*
form*	id	isTextEdit*	lang
language	lastChild*	name	nextSibling*
nodeName*	nodeType*	nodeValue*	offsetHeight*
offsetLeft*	offsetParent*	offsetTop*	offsetWidth*
outerHTML*	outerText*	parentElement*	parentNode*
parentTextEdit*	previousSibling*	readyState*	recordNumber*
runtimeStyle*	scopeName*	scrollHeight*	scrollLeft*
scrollTop*	scrollWidth*	size	sourceIndex*
status*	style	tabIndex	tagName*
tagUrn*	title	type	uniqueID*
value			

* This property has no corresponding attribute.

DHTML Objects

Methods

addBehavior	appendChild	applyElement
attachEvent	blur	clearAttributes
click	cloneNode	componentFromPoint
contains	detachEvent	focus
getAdjacentText	getAttribute	getBoundingClientRect
getClientRects	getExpression	hasChildNodes
insertAdjacentElement	insertAdjacentHTML	insertAdjacentText
insertBefore	mergeAttributes	releaseCapture
removeAttribute	removeBehavior	removeChild
removeExpression	removeNode	replaceAdjacentText
replaceChild	replaceNode	scrollIntoView
select	setAttribute	setCapture
setExpression	swapNode	

Events

onbeforeeditfocus	onblur	onclick	ondblclick
ondrag	ondragend	ondragenter	ondragleave
ondragover	ondragstart	ondrop	onfilterchange
onfocus	onhelp	onkeydown	onkeypress
onkeyup	onlosecapture	onmousedown	onmousemove
onmouseout	onmouseover	onmouseup	onpropertychange
onreadystatechange	onselectstart		

Collections

attributes   behaviorUrns   filters

Default Behaviors

clientCaps	download	homePage	httpFolder	saveFavorite
saveHistory	saveSnapshot	time	userData	

CSS Properties

Note For a list of corresponding attributes, see Appendix C.

background	backgroundColor	backgroundImage
backgroundPosition	backgroundPositionX*	backgroundPositionY*
backgroundRepeat	behavior	border
borderBottom	borderBottomColor	borderBottomStyle
borderBottomWidth	borderColor	borderLeft
borderLeftColor	borderLeftStyle	borderLeftWidth
borderRight	borderRightColor	borderRightStyle
borderRightWidth	borderStyle	borderTop
borderTopColor	borderTopStyle	borderTopWidth
borderWidth	bottom	clear
color	cursor	direction
display	filter	font
fontFamily	fontSize	fontStyle
fontVariant	fontWeight	height
layoutGridMode	left	letterSpacing
lineHeight	margin	marginBottom
marginLeft	marginRight	marginTop
pixelBottom*	pixelHeight*	pixelLeft*
pixelRight*	pixelTop*	pixelWidth*
posBottom*	posHeight*	position
posLeft*	posRight*	posTop*
posWidth*	right	styleFloat
textAutospace	textDecoration	textDecorationBlink*

CSS Properties *(continued)*

textDecorationLineThrough[*]	textDecorationNone[*]	textDecorationOverline[*]
textDecorationUnderline[*]	textTransform	top
unicodeBidi	visibility	width
wordSpacing	zIndex	

[*] This property has no corresponding attribute.

Example

The following example shows how to create three radio buttons.

```
<INPUT type=radio name="radio" CHECKED>1-10 years old
<INPUT type=radio name="radio">11 years old
<INPUT type=radio name="radio">12-120 years old
```

The following example shows how to use script to detect which radio button has been chosen.

```
<SCRIPT>
function detect()
{
    if (radio[0].checked)
        alert("You're between 1 and 10 years old.")
    else if (radio[1].checked)
        alert("You're 11 years old.")
    else
        alert("You're between 12 and 120 years old.")
}
</SCRIPT>
```

INPUT type=reset Element | INPUT type=reset Object

Creates a button that, when clicked, resets the form's controls to their initial values.

Remarks

The **reset** element is an inline element and does not require a closing tag.

You can specify the label to be displayed on the button just as for the **submit** button.

This element is available in HTML and script as of Internet Explorer 3.0.

Attributes/Properties

		CLASS	
accessKey	canHaveChildren[*]	className	clientHeight[*]
clientLeft[*]	clientTop[*]	clientWidth[*]	currentStyle[*]
dataFld	dataSrc	defaultValue[*]	dir
disabled	firstChild[*]	form[*]	id
isTextEdit[*]	lang	language	lastChild[*]
name	nextSibling[*]	nodeName[*]	nodeType[*]
nodeValue[*]	offsetHeight[*]	offsetLeft[*]	offsetParent[*]
offsetTop[*]	offsetWidth[*]	outerHTML[*]	outerText[*]
parentElement[*]	parentNode[*]	parentTextEdit[*]	previousSibling[*]
readyState[*]	recordNumber[*]	runtimeStyle[*]	scopeName[*]
scrollHeight[*]	scrollLeft[*]	scrollTop[*]	scrollWidth[*]
size	sourceIndex[*]	style	tabIndex
tagName[*]	tagUrn[*]	title	type
uniqueID[*]	value		

[*] This property has no corresponding attribute.

Methods

addBehavior	appendChild	applyElement
attachEvent	blur	clearAttributes
click	cloneNode	componentFromPoint
contains	createTextRange	detachEvent
focus	getAdjacentText	getAttribute
getBoundingClientRect	getClientRects	getExpression
hasChildNodes	insertAdjacentElement	insertAdjacentHTML
insertAdjacentText	insertBefore	mergeAttributes
releaseCapture	removeAttribute	removeBehavior
removeChild	removeExpression	removeNode

DHTML Objects

Methods *(continued)*

replaceAdjacentText	**replaceChild**	**replaceNode**
scrollIntoView	**select**	**setAttribute**
setCapture	**setExpression**	**swapNode**

Events

onbeforeeditfocus	**onblur**	**onclick**	**ondblclick**
ondrag	**ondragend**	**ondragenter**	**ondragleave**
ondragover	**ondragstart**	**ondrop**	**onfilterchange**
onfocus	**onhelp**	**onkeydown**	**onkeypress**
onkeyup	**onlosecapture**	**onmousedown**	**onmousemove**
onmouseout	**onmouseover**	**onmouseup**	**onpropertychange**
onreadystatechange	**onresize**	**onselectstart**	

Collections

attributes	**behaviorUrns**	**filters**

Default Behaviors

clientCaps	**download**	**homePage**	**httpFolder**	**saveFavorite**
saveHistory	**saveSnapshot**	**time**	**userData**	

CSS Properties

Note For a list of corresponding attributes, see Appendix C.

background	**backgroundColor**	**backgroundImage**
backgroundPosition	**backgroundPositionX**[*]	**backgroundPositionY**[*]
backgroundRepeat	**behavior**	**border**
borderBottom	**borderBottomColor**	**borderBottomStyle**
borderBottomWidth	**borderColor**	**borderLeft**
borderLeftColor	**borderLeftStyle**	**borderLeftWidth**
borderRight	**borderRightColor**	**borderRightStyle**
borderRightWidth	**borderStyle**	**borderTop**

* This property has no corresponding attribute.

CSS Properties *(continued)*

Note For a list of corresponding attributes, see Appendix C.

borderTopColor	**borderTopStyle**	**borderTopWidth**
borderWidth	**bottom**	**clear**
color	**cursor**	**direction**
display	**filter**	**font**
fontFamily	**fontSize**	**fontStyle**
fontVariant	**fontWeight**	**height**
layoutGridMode	**left**	**letterSpacing**
lineHeight	**margin**	**marginBottom**
marginLeft	**marginRight**	**marginTop**
pixelBottom[*]	**pixelHeight**[*]	**pixelLeft**[*]
pixelRight[*]	**pixelTop**[*]	**pixelWidth**[*]
posBottom[*]	**posHeight**[*]	**position**
posLeft[*]	**posRight**[*]	**posTop**[*]
posWidth[*]	**right**	**styleFloat**
textAutospace	**textDecoration**	**textDecorationBlink**[*]
textDecorationLineThrough[*]	**textDecorationNone**[*]	**textDecorationOverline**[*]
textDecorationUnderline[*]	**textTransform**	**top**
unicodeBidi	**visibility**	**width**
wordSpacing	**zIndex**	

[*] This property has no corresponding attribute.

INPUT type=submit Element | INPUT type=submit Object

Creates a button that, when clicked, submits the form.

Remarks

The **submit** element is an inline element and does not require a closing tag.

You can use the **value** attribute to provide a noneditable label to be displayed on the button. The default label is application-specific. If the user clicks a Submit button to submit the form and the button has a **name** attribute specified, the button contributes a name/value pair to the submitted data.

This element is available in HTML and script as of Internet Explorer 3.0.

Attributes/Properties

		CLASS	
accessKey	canHaveChildren*	className	clientHeight*
clientLeft*	clientTop*	clientWidth*	currentStyle*
dataFld	dataSrc	defaultValue*	dir
disabled	firstChild*	form*	id
isTextEdit*	lang	language	lastChild*
name	nextSibling*	nodeName*	nodeType*
nodeValue*	offsetHeight*	offsetLeft*	offsetParent*
offsetTop*	offsetWidth*	outerHTML*	outerText*
parentElement*	parentNode*	parentTextEdit*	previousSibling*
readyState*	recordNumber*	runtimeStyle*	scopeName*
scrollHeight*	scrollLeft*	scrollTop*	scrollWidth*
size	sourceIndex*	style	tabIndex
tagName*	tagUrn*	title	type
uniqueID*	value		

*   This property has no corresponding attribute.

Methods

addBehavior	appendChild	applyElement
attachEvent	blur	clearAttributes
click	cloneNode	componentFromPoint
contains	createTextRange	detachEvent
focus	getAdjacentText	getAttribute
getBoundingClientRect	getClientRects	getExpression
hasChildNodes	insertAdjacentElement	insertAdjacentHTML
insertAdjacentText	insertBefore	mergeAttributes
releaseCapture	removeAttribute	removeBehavior

Methods *(continued)*

removeChild	removeExpression	removeNode
replaceAdjacentText	replaceChild	replaceNode
scrollIntoView	select	setAttribute
setCapture	setExpression	swapNode

Events

onbeforeeditfocus	onblur	onclick	ondblclick
ondrag	ondragend	ondragenter	ondragleave
ondragover	ondragstart	ondrop	onfilterchange
onfocus	onhelp	onkeydown	onkeypress
onkeyup	onlosecapture	onmousedown	onmousemove
onmouseout	onmouseover	onmouseup	onpropertychange
onreadystatechange	onresize	onselectstart	

Collections

attributes	behaviorUrns	filters

Default Behaviors

clientCaps	download	homePage	httpFolder	saveFavorite
saveHistory	saveSnapshot	time	userData	

CSS Properties

Note For a list of corresponding attributes, see Appendix C.

background	backgroundColor	backgroundImage
backgroundPosition	backgroundPositionX*	backgroundPositionY*
backgroundRepeat	behavior	border
borderBottom	borderBottomColor	borderBottomStyle
borderBottomWidth	borderColor	borderLeft
borderLeftColor	borderLeftStyle	borderLeftWidth
borderRight	borderRightColor	borderRightStyle

CSS Properties *(continued)*

borderRightWidth	**borderStyle**	**borderTop**
borderTopColor	**borderTopStyle**	**borderTopWidth**
borderWidth	**bottom**	**clear**
color	**cursor**	**direction**
display	**filter**	**font**
fontFamily	**fontSize**	**fontStyle**
fontVariant	**fontWeight**	**height**
layoutGridMode	**left**	**letterSpacing**
lineHeight	**margin**	**marginBottom**
marginLeft	**marginRight**	**marginTop**
pixelBottom[*]	**pixelHeight**[*]	**pixelLeft**[*]
pixelRight[*]	**pixelTop**[*]	**pixelWidth**[*]
posBottom[*]	**posHeight**[*]	**position**
posLeft[*]	**posRight**[*]	**posTop**[*]
posWidth[*]	**right**	**styleFloat**
textAutospace	**textDecoration**	**textDecorationBlink**[*]
textDecorationLineThrough[*]	**textDecorationNone**[*]	**textDecorationOverline**[*]
textDecorationUnderline[*]	**textTransform**	**top**
unicodeBidi	**visibility**	**width**
wordSpacing	**zIndex**	

* This property has no corresponding attribute.

INPUT type=text Element | INPUT type=text Object

Creates a single-line text entry control.

Remarks

The **text** element is an inline element and does not require a closing tag.

The **SIZE** attribute sets the number of visible characters in the **text** element. The **MAXLENGTH** attribute sets the maximum number of characters that the user can enter.

This element is available in HTML and script as of Internet Explorer 3.0.

Attributes/Properties

accessKey	AUTOCOMPLETE	canHaveChildren*	CLASS className
clientHeight*	clientLeft*	clientTop*	clientWidth*
currentStyle*	dataFld	dataSrc	defaultValue*
dir	disabled	firstChild*	form*
id	isTextEdit*	lang	language
lastChild*	maxLength	name	nextSibling*
nodeName*	nodeType*	nodeValue*	offsetHeight*
offsetLeft*	offsetParent*	offsetTop*	offsetWidth*
outerHTML*	outerText*	parentElement*	parentNode*
parentTextEdit*	previousSibling*	readOnly	readyState*
recordNumber*	runtimeStyle*	scopeName*	scrollHeight*
scrollLeft*	scrollTop*	scrollWidth*	size
sourceIndex*	style	tabIndex	tagName*
tagUrn*	title	type	uniqueID*
value	vcard_name		

*   This property has no corresponding attribute.

Methods

addBehavior	appendChild	applyElement
attachEvent	blur	clearAttributes
click	cloneNode	componentFromPoint
contains	createTextRange	detachEvent
focus	getAdjacentText	getAttribute
getBoundingClientRect	getClientRects	getExpression
hasChildNodes	insertAdjacentElement	insertAdjacentHTML
insertAdjacentText	insertBefore	mergeAttributes
releaseCapture	removeAttribute	removeBehavior
removeChild	removeExpression	removeNode
replaceAdjacentText	replaceChild	replaceNode
scrollIntoView	select	setAttribute
setCapture	setExpression	swapNode

Events

onafterupdate	onbeforeeditfocus	onbeforeupdate	onblur
onchange	onclick	ondblclick	ondrag
ondragend	ondragenter	ondragleave	ondragover
ondragstart	ondrop	onerrorupdate	onfilterchange
onfocus	onhelp	onkeydown	onkeypress
onkeyup	onlosecapture	onmousedown	onmousemove
onmouseout	onmouseover	onmouseup	onpropertychange
onreadystatechange	onresize	onselect	onselectstart

Collections

attributes	behaviorUrns	filters

Default Behaviors

clientCaps	download	homePage	httpFolder	saveFavorite
saveHistory	saveSnapshot	time	userData	

CSS Properties

Note For a list of corresponding attributes, see Appendix C.

background	**backgroundColor**	**backgroundImage**
backgroundPosition	**backgroundPositionX***	**backgroundPositionY***
backgroundRepeat	**behavior**	**border**
borderBottom	**borderBottomColor**	**borderBottomStyle**
borderBottomWidth	**borderColor**	**borderLeft**
borderLeftColor	**borderLeftStyle**	**borderLeftWidth**
borderRight	**borderRightColor**	**borderRightStyle**
borderRightWidth	**borderStyle**	**borderTop**
borderTopColor	**borderTopStyle**	**borderTopWidth**
borderWidth	**bottom**	**clear**
color	**cursor**	**direction**
display	**filter**	**font**
fontFamily	**fontSize**	**fontStyle**
fontVariant	**fontWeight**	**height**
imeMode	**layoutGridMode**	**left**
letterSpacing	**lineHeight**	**margin**
marginBottom	**marginLeft**	**marginRight**
marginTop	**pixelBottom***	**pixelHeight***
pixelLeft*	**pixelRight***	**pixelTop***
pixelWidth*	**posBottom***	**posHeight***
position	**posLeft***	**posRight***
posTop*	**posWidth***	**right**
styleFloat	**textAlign**	**textAutospace**
textDecoration	**textDecorationBlink***	**textDecorationLineThrough***
textDecorationNone*	**textDecorationOverline***	**textDecorationUnderline***
textTransform	**top**	**unicodeBidi**
visibility	**width**	**wordSpacing**
zIndex		

*   This property has no corresponding attribute.

Example

The following example shows how to display an empty text entry control that can contain 15 characters without scrolling.

```
<INPUT TYPE=text VALUE="" NAME="textbox" SIZE=15>
```

The following example shows how to use script to detect the contents of the text entry control and display it in a dialog box.

```
<SCRIPT>
function detectEntry()
{
    alert("Your name is " + textbox.value)
}
</SCRIPT>
```

INS Element | INS Object

Indicates text that has been inserted into the document.

Remarks

The **INS** element is an inline element and does not require a closing tag.

This element is available in HTML and script as of Internet Explorer 4.0.

Attributes/Properties

	CLASS		
canHaveChildren[*]	className	currentStyle[*]	dir
firstChild[*]	id	innerHTML[*]	innerText[*]
isTextEdit[*]	lang	language	lastChild[*]
nextSibling[*]	nodeName[*]	nodeType[*]	nodeValue[*]
offsetHeight[*]	offsetLeft[*]	offsetParent[*]	offsetTop[*]
offsetWidth[*]	outerHTML[*]	outerText[*]	parentElement[*]
parentNode[*]	parentTextEdit[*]	previousSibling[*]	readyState[*]
recordNumber[*]	runtimeStyle[*]	scopeName[*]	sourceIndex[*]
style	tabIndex	tagName[*]	tagUrn[*]
title	uniqueID[*]		

[*]   This property has no corresponding attribute.

Methods

addBehavior	appendChild	applyElement
attachEvent	blur	clearAttributes
cloneNode	componentFromPoint	detachEvent
focus	getAdjacentText	getBoundingClientRect
getClientRects	getElementsByTagName	getExpression
hasChildNodes	insertAdjacentElement	insertBefore
mergeAttributes	removeBehavior	removeChild
removeExpression	removeNode	replaceAdjacentText
replaceChild	replaceNode	setExpression
swapNode		

Events

onblur	onfocus	onreadystatechange

Collections

all	attributes	behaviorUrns	childNodes	children

Default Behaviors

clientCaps	download	homePage	time

CSS Properties

Note For a list of corresponding attributes, see Appendix C.

backgroundPositionX*	backgroundPositionY*	behavior	direction
layoutGridMode	overflow	overflowX	overflowY
pixelBottom*	pixelHeight*	pixelLeft*	pixelRight*
pixelTop*	pixelWidth*	posBottom*	posHeight*
posLeft*	posRight*	posTop*	posWidth*
textAutospace	unicodeBidi	width	

*   This property has no corresponding attribute.

Example

The following example shows how to use the **INS** element for inserted text.

```
<INS datetime="1997-10-01T12:15:30-05:00">This text has been inserted.</INS>
```

ISINDEX Element | ISINDEX Object

Causes the browser to display a dialog box that prompts the user for a single line of input.

Remarks

The **ISINDEX** element is an inline element and does not require a closing tag.

In HTML 4, this element is deprecated, and **INPUT** is recommended for use instead. The **tagName** property for **ISINDEX** returns **INPUT**.

The **ISINDEX** element belongs in the **body** of the document.

This element is available in HTML as of Internet Explorer 3.0 and in script as of Internet Explorer 4.0.

Attributes/Properties

CLASS

className	**clientHeight***	**clientLeft***	**clientTop***	**clientWidth***
currentStyle*	**id**	**lang**	**language**	**readyState***
scopeName*	**scrollHeight***	**scrollLeft***	**scrollTop***	**scrollWidth***
STYLE†				
	tabIndex	**tagUrn***		

*   This property has no corresponding attribute.

†   This attribute has no corresponding property.

Methods

addBehavior	**blur**	**componentFromPoint**	**focus**
getBoundingClientRect	**getClientRects**	**removeBehavior**	

Events

onblur	**onfocus**	**onreadystatechange**	**onresize**

Collections

behaviorUrns

Default Behaviors

clientCaps   download   homePage

CSS Properties

Note For a list of corresponding attributes, see Appendix C.

background	backgroundColor	backgroundImage
backgroundPosition	backgroundRepeat	behavior
border	borderBottom	borderBottomColor
borderBottomStyle	borderBottomWidth	borderColor
borderLeft	borderLeftColor	borderLeftStyle
borderLeftWidth	borderRight	borderRightColor
borderRightStyle	borderRightWidth	borderStyle
borderTop	borderTopColor	borderTopStyle
borderTopWidth	borderWidth	bottom
clear	color	display
font	fontFamily	fontSize
fontStyle	fontVariant	fontWeight
height	left	letterSpacing
lineHeight	margin	marginBottom
marginLeft	marginRight	marginTop
padding	paddingBottom	paddingLeft
paddingRight	paddingTop	pageBreakAfter
pageBreakBefore	position	right
styleFloat	textAutospace	textDecoration
textDecorationBlink[*]	textDecorationLineThrough[*]	textDecorationNone[*]
textDecorationOverline[*]	textDecorationUnderline[*]	textIndent
textTransform	top	visibility
wordSpacing	zIndex	

* This property has no corresponding attribute.

Example

The following example shows how to replace the **ISINDEX** default prompt.

```
<ISINDEX PROMPT="Enter a keyword to search for in the index">
```

KBD Element | KBD Object

Displays text in a fixed-width font.

Remarks

The **KBD** element is an inline element and requires a closing tag.

This element is available in HTML as of Internet Explorer 3.0 and in script as of Internet Explorer 4.0.

Attributes/Properties

	CLASS		
canHaveChildren[*]	className	clientHeight[*]	clientLeft[*]
clientTop[*]	clientWidth[*]	currentStyle[*]	dir
firstChild[*]	id	innerHTML[*]	innerText[*]
isTextEdit[*]	lang	language	lastChild[*]
nextSibling[*]	nodeName[*]	nodeType[*]	nodeValue[*]
offsetHeight[*]	offsetLeft[*]	offsetParent[*]	offsetTop[*]
offsetWidth[*]	outerHTML[*]	outerText[*]	parentElement[*]
parentNode[*]	parentTextEdit[*]	previousSibling[*]	readyState[*]
recordNumber[*]	runtimeStyle[*]	scopeName[*]	scrollHeight[*]
scrollLeft[*]	scrollTop[*]	scrollWidth[*]	sourceIndex[*]
style	tabIndex	tagName[*]	tagUrn[*]
title	uniqueID[*]		

[*]   This property has no corresponding attribute.

Methods

addBehavior	appendChild	applyElement
attachEvent	blur	clearAttributes
click	cloneNode	componentFromPoint
contains	detachEvent	focus

Methods *(continued)*

getAdjacentText	getAttribute	getBoundingClientRect
getClientRects	getElementsByTagName	getExpression
hasChildNodes	insertAdjacentElement	insertAdjacentHTML
insertAdjacentText	insertBefore	mergeAttributes
releaseCapture	removeAttribute	removeBehavior
removeChild	removeExpression	removeNode
replaceAdjacentText	replaceChild	replaceNode
scrollIntoView	setAttribute	setCapture
setExpression	swapNode	

Events

onblur	onclick	ondblclick	ondrag
ondragend	ondragenter	ondragleave	ondragover
ondragstart	ondrop	onfocus	onhelp
onkeydown	onkeypress	onkeyup	onlosecapture
onmousedown	onmousemove	onmouseout	onmouseover
onmouseup	onpropertychange	onreadystatechange	onresize
onselectstart			

Collections

all	attributes	behaviorUrns	childNodes	children

Default Behaviors

clientCaps	download	homePage	httpFolder	saveFavorite
saveHistory	saveSnapshot	time	userData	

CSS Properties

Note For a list of corresponding attributes, see Appendix C.

background	backgroundColor	backgroundImage
backgroundPosition	backgroundPositionX[*]	backgroundPositionY[*]
backgroundRepeat	behavior	bottom

CSS Properties *(continued)*

clear	color	cursor
direction	font	fontFamily
fontSize	fontStyle	fontVariant
fontWeight	layoutGridMode	left
letterSpacing	lineHeight	overflow
overflowX	overflowY	pixelBottom[*]
pixelHeight[*]	pixelLeft[*]	pixelRight[*]
pixelTop[*]	pixelWidth[*]	posBottom[*]
posHeight[*]	position	posLeft[*]
posRight[*]	posTop[*]	posWidth[*]
right	styleFloat	textAutospace
textDecoration	textDecorationBlink[*]	textDecorationLineThrough[*]
textDecorationNone[*]	textDecorationOverline[*]	textDecorationUnderline[*]
textTransform	top	unicodeBidi
visibility	width	wordSpacing
zIndex		

* This property has no corresponding attribute.

Example

The following example shows how to use the **KBD** element.

```
<KBD>This text is rendered in a fixed-width font.</KBD>
```

LABEL Element | LABEL Object

Specifies a label for another element on the page.

Remarks

The **LABEL** element is an inline element and requires a closing tag. Labels cannot be nested.

To bind **LABEL** to another control, set the **FOR** attribute of the **LABEL** element equal to the **ID** of the control. Binding **LABEL** to the **NAME** attribute of the control has no effect. However, to submit a form, you must specify a **NAME** on the control to which the **LABEL** element is being bound.

There are two ways to underline the designated access key. The rich text support in the **LABEL** object makes it possible to wrap the **U** element around the character in the label text that is specified by the **accessKey** property. If you prefer applying style formatting through a Cascading Style Sheet (CSS), enclose the designated character in a **SPAN** and set the style to `"text-decoration: underline"`.

If the user clicks the label, the **onclick** event goes to the label and then bubbles to the control specified by the **htmlFor** property. Pressing the access key for the label is the same as clicking the label.

This element is available in HTML and script as of Internet Explorer 4.0.

Attributes/Properties

		CLASS	
accessKey	**canHaveChildren**[*]	**className**	**clientHeight**[*]
clientLeft[*]	**clientTop**[*]	**clientWidth**[*]	**currentStyle**[*]
dataFld	**dataFormatAs**	**dataSrc**	**dir**
	FOR		
firstChild[*]	**htmlFor**	**id**	**innerHTML**[*]
innerText[*]	**isTextEdit**[*]	**lang**	**language**
lastChild[*]	**nextSibling**[*]	**nodeName**[*]	**nodeType**[*]
nodeValue[*]	**offsetHeight**[*]	**offsetLeft**[*]	**offsetParent**[*]
offsetTop[*]	**offsetWidth**[*]	**outerHTML**[*]	**outerText**[*]
parentElement[*]	**parentNode**[*]	**parentTextEdit**[*]	**previousSibling**[*]
readyState[*]	**recordNumber**[*]	**runtimeStyle**[*]	**scopeName**[*]
scrollHeight[*]	**scrollLeft**[*]	**scrollTop**[*]	**scrollWidth**[*]
sourceIndex[*]	**style**	**tabIndex**	**tagName**[*]
tagUrn[*]	**title**	**uniqueID**[*]	

[*] This property has no corresponding attribute.

Methods

addBehavior	**appendChild**	**applyElement**
attachEvent	**blur**	**clearAttributes**
click	**cloneNode**	**componentFromPoint**
contains	**detachEvent**	**focus**
getAdjacentText	**getAttribute**	**getBoundingClientRect**

DHTML Objects

Methods *(continued)*

getClientRects	**getElementsByTagName**	**getExpression**
hasChildNodes	**insertAdjacentElement**	**insertAdjacentHTML**
insertAdjacentText	**insertBefore**	**mergeAttributes**
releaseCapture	**removeAttribute**	**removeBehavior**
removeChild	**removeExpression**	**removeNode**
replaceAdjacentText	**replaceChild**	**replaceNode**
scrollIntoView	**setAttribute**	**setCapture**
setExpression	**swapNode**	

Events

onbeforecopy	**onbeforecut**	**onbeforepaste**	**onblur**
onclick	**ondblclick**	**ondrag**	**ondragend**
ondragenter	**ondragleave**	**ondragover**	**ondragstart**
ondrop	**onfocus**	**onhelp**	**onkeydown**
onkeypress	**onkeyup**	**onlosecapture**	**onmousedown**
onmousemove	**onmouseout**	**onmouseover**	**onmouseup**
onpropertychange	**onreadystatechange**	**onresize**	**onselectstart**

Collections

all	**attributes**	**behaviorUrns**	**childNodes**	**children**

Default Behaviors

clientCaps	**download**	**homePage**	**httpFolder**	**saveFavorite**
saveHistory	**saveSnapshot**	**userData**		

CSS Properties

Note For a list of corresponding attributes, see Appendix C.

background	**backgroundColor**	**backgroundImage**
backgroundPosition	**backgroundPositionX**[*]	**backgroundPositionY**[*]
backgroundRepeat	**behavior**	**bottom**

[*] This property has no corresponding attribute.

CSS Properties *(continued)*

Note For a list of corresponding attributes, see Appendix C.

clear	**color**	**cursor**
direction	**font**	**fontFamily**
fontSize	**fontStyle**	**fontVariant**
fontWeight	**layoutGridMode**	**left**
letterSpacing	**lineHeight**	**overflow**
overflowX	**overflowY**	**pixelBottom**[*]
pixelHeight[*]	**pixelLeft**[*]	**pixelRight**[*]
pixelTop[*]	**pixelWidth**[*]	**posBottom**[*]
posHeight[*]	**position**	**posLeft**[*]
posRight[*]	**posTop**[*]	**posWidth**[*]
right	**styleFloat**	**textAutospace**
textDecoration	**textDecorationBlink**[*]	**textDecorationLineThrough**[*]
textDecorationNone[*]	**textDecorationOverline**[*]	**textDecorationUnderline**[*]
textTransform	**top**	**unicodeBidi**
visibility	**width**	**wordSpacing**
zIndex		

[*]   This property has no corresponding attribute.

Example

The following example shows how to use a combination of the **LABEL** object and the **accessKey** property to set focus on a text box.

```
<LABEL FOR="oCtrlID" ACCESSKEY="1">
    #<U>1</U>: Press Alt+1 to set focus to textbox
</LABEL>
<INPUT TYPE="text" NAME="TXT1" VALUE="binding sample 1"
       SIZE="20" TABINDEX="1" ID="oCtrlID">
```

To see this code in action, refer to the Web Workshop CD-ROM.

LEGEND Element | LEGEND Object

Inserts a caption into the box drawn by the **FIELDSET** object.

Remarks

The **LEGEND** element is a block element and requires a closing tag.

This element must be the first element in **FIELDSET**.

This element is available in HTML and script as of Internet Explorer 4.0.

Attributes/Properties

			CLASS
accessKey	**align**	**canHaveChildren**[*]	**className**
clientHeight[*]	**clientLeft**[*]	**clientTop**[*]	**clientWidth**[*]
currentStyle[*]	**dir**	**firstChild**[*]	**id**
innerHTML[*]	**innerText**[*]	**isTextEdit**[*]	**lang**
language	**lastChild**[*]	**nextSibling**[*]	**nodeName**[*]
nodeType[*]	**nodeValue**[*]	**offsetHeight**[*]	**offsetLeft**[*]
offsetParent[*]	**offsetTop**[*]	**offsetWidth**[*]	**outerHTML**[*]
outerText[*]	**parentElement**[*]	**parentNode**[*]	**parentTextEdit**[*]
previousSibling[*]	**readyState**[*]	**runtimeStyle**[*]	**scopeName**[*]
scrollHeight[*]	**scrollLeft**[*]	**scrollTop**[*]	**scrollWidth**[*]
style	**tabIndex**	**tagName**[*]	**tagUrn**[*]
title	**uniqueID**[*]		

[*] This property has no corresponding attribute.

Methods

addBehavior	**appendChild**	**applyElement**
attachEvent	**blur**	**clearAttributes**
click	**cloneNode**	**componentFromPoint**
contains	**detachEvent**	**focus**
getAdjacentText	**getAttribute**	**getBoundingClientRect**
getClientRects	**getElementsByTagName**	**getExpression**

Methods *(continued)*

hasChildNodes	insertAdjacentElement	insertAdjacentHTML
insertAdjacentText	insertBefore	mergeAttributes
releaseCapture	removeAttribute	removeBehavior
removeChild	removeExpression	removeNode
replaceAdjacentText	replaceChild	replaceNode
scrollIntoView	setAttribute	setCapture
setExpression	swapNode	

Events

onbeforecopy	onbeforecut	onbeforepaste	onblur
onclick	oncopy	oncut	ondblclick
onfocus	onhelp	onkeydown	onkeypress
onkeyup	onlosecapture	onmousedown	onmousemove
onmouseout	onmouseover	onmouseup	onpaste
onpropertychange	onreadystatechange	onresize	

Collections

all	attributes	behaviorUrns	childNodes	children

Default Behaviors

clientCaps	download	homePage	time

CSS Properties

Note For a list of corresponding attributes, see Appendix C.

background	backgroundColor	backgroundImage
backgroundPosition	backgroundPositionX*	backgroundPositionY*
backgroundRepeat	behavior	bottom
clear	color	cursor
direction	font	fontFamily
fontSize	fontStyle	fontVariant

CSS Properties *(continued)*

fontWeight	layoutGridMode	left
letterSpacing	lineBreak	lineHeight
overflow	overflowX	overflowY
pixelBottom[*]	pixelHeight[*]	pixelLeft[*]
pixelRight[*]	pixelTop[*]	pixelWidth[*]
posBottom[*]	posHeight[*]	position
posLeft[*]	posRight[*]	posTop[*]
posWidth[*]	right	styleFloat
textAutospace	textDecoration	textDecorationBlink[*]
textDecorationLineThrough[*]	textDecorationNone[*]	textDecorationOverline[*]
textDecorationUnderline[*]	textJustify	textTransform
top	unicodeBidi	visibility
width	wordBreak	wordSpacing
zIndex		

* This property has no corresponding attribute.

LI Element | LI Object

Denotes one item in a list.

Remarks

The **LI** element is an inline element and does not require a closing tag.

The **TYPE** attribute values disc, circle, and square apply to unordered lists; the values 1, a, A, i, and I apply to ordered lists.

This element is available in HTML as of Internet Explorer 3.0 and in script as of Internet Explorer 4.0.

Attributes/Properties

	CLASS		
canHaveChildren[*]	**className**	**clientHeight**[*]	**clientLeft**[*]
clientTop[*]	**clientWidth**[*]	**currentStyle**[*]	**dir**
firstChild[*]	**id**	**innerHTML**[*]	**innerText**[*]
isTextEdit[*]	**lang**	**language**	**lastChild**[*]
nextSibling[*]	**nodeName**[*]	**nodeType**[*]	**nodeValue**[*]
offsetHeight[*]	**offsetLeft**[*]	**offsetParent**[*]	**offsetTop**[*]
offsetWidth[*]	**outerHTML**[*]	**outerText**[*]	**parentElement**[*]
parentNode[*]	**parentTextEdit**[*]	**previousSibling**[*]	**readyState**[*]
recordNumber[*]	**runtimeStyle**[*]	**scopeName**[*]	**scrollHeight**[*]
scrollLeft[*]	**scrollTop**[*]	**scrollWidth**[*]	**sourceIndex**[*]
style	**tabIndex**	**tagName**[*]	**tagUrn**[*]
title	**type**	**uniqueID**[*]	**value**

[*] This property has no corresponding attribute.

Methods

addBehavior	**appendChild**	**applyElement**
attachEvent	**blur**	**clearAttributes**
click	**cloneNode**	**componentFromPoint**
contains	**detachEvent**	**focus**
getAdjacentText	**getAttribute**	**getBoundingClientRect**
getClientRects	**getElementsByTagName**	**getExpression**
hasChildNodes	**insertAdjacentElement**	**insertAdjacentHTML**
insertAdjacentText	**insertBefore**	**mergeAttributes**
releaseCapture	**removeAttribute**	**removeBehavior**
removeChild	**removeExpression**	**removeNode**
replaceAdjacentText	**replaceChild**	**replaceNode**
scrollIntoView	**setAttribute**	**setCapture**
setExpression	**swapNode**	

Events

onbeforecopy	onbeforecut	onbeforepaste	onblur
onclick	oncopy	oncut	ondblclick
ondrag	ondragend	ondragenter	ondragleave
ondragover	ondragstart	ondrop	onfocus
onhelp	onkeydown	onkeypress	onkeyup
onlosecapture	onmousedown	onmousemove	onmouseout
onmouseover	onmouseup	onpaste	onpropertychange
onreadystatechange	onresize	onselectstart	

Collections

all	attributes	behaviorUrns	childNodes	children

Default Behaviors

clientCaps	download	homePage	httpFolder	saveFavorite
saveHistory	saveSnapshot	time	userData	

CSS Properties

Note For a list of corresponding attributes, see Appendix C.

background	backgroundColor	backgroundImage
backgroundPosition	backgroundPositionX*	backgroundPositionY*
backgroundRepeat	behavior	border
borderBottom	borderBottomColor	borderBottomStyle
borderBottomWidth	borderColor	borderLeft
borderLeftColor	borderLeftStyle	borderLeftWidth
borderRight	borderRightColor	borderRightStyle
borderRightWidth	borderStyle	borderTop
borderTopColor	borderTopStyle	borderTopWidth
borderWidth	bottom	clear
color	cursor	direction

* This property has no corresponding attribute.

CSS Properties *(continued)*

Note For a list of corresponding attributes, see Appendix C.

font	fontFamily	fontSize
fontStyle	fontVariant	fontWeight
layoutGrid	layoutGridChar	layoutGridCharSpacing
layoutGridLine	layoutGridMode	layoutGridType
left	letterSpacing	lineBreak
lineHeight	listStyle	listStyleImage
listStylePosition	listStyleType	margin
marginBottom	marginLeft	marginRight
marginTop	overflow	overflowX
overflowY	pageBreakAfter	pageBreakBefore
pixelBottom*	pixelHeight*	pixelLeft*
pixelRight*	pixelTop*	pixelWidth*
posBottom*	posHeight*	position
posLeft*	posRight*	posTop*
posWidth*	right	styleFloat
textAlign	textAutospace	textDecoration
textDecorationBlink*	textDecorationLineThrough*	textDecorationNone*
textDecorationOverline*	textDecorationUnderline*	textIndent
textJustify	textTransform	top
unicodeBidi	visibility	width
wordBreak	wordSpacing	zIndex

*   This property has no corresponding attribute.

Example

The following example shows how to use the **LI** element with the individual items of a directory list.

```
<DIR>
<LI>Art
<LI>History
<LI>Literature
<LI>Sports
<LI>Entertainment
<LI>Science
</DIR>
```

LINK Element | LINK Object

Enables the current document to use styles defined in an external style sheet.

Remarks

The **LINK** element does not require a closing tag.

This element can be used only within the **HEAD** tag.

This element is available in HTML as of Internet Explorer 3.0 and in script as of Internet Explorer 4.0.

Attributes/Properties

currentStyle[*]	disabled	firstChild[*]	href
id	isTextEdit[*]	lastChild[*]	media
name	nextSibling[*]	nodeName[*]	nodeType[*]
nodeValue[*]	parentElement[*]	parentNode[*]	parentTextEdit[*]
previousSibling[*]	readyState[*]	rel	rev
runtimeStyle[*]	scopeName[*]	sourceIndex[*]	style[*]
tagName[*]	tagUrn[*]	title	uniqueID[*]

[*]   This property has no corresponding attribute.

Methods

addBehavior	applyElement	attachEvent
clearAttributes	cloneNode	componentFromPoint
contains	detachEvent	getAdjacentText
getAttribute	getBoundingClientRect	getClientRects
getElementsByTagName	hasChildNodes	insertAdjacentElement
mergeAttributes	removeAttribute	removeBehavior
replaceAdjacentText	setAttribute	swapNode

Events

onerror	onload	onreadystatechange

Collections

all	attributes	behaviorUrns	childNodes	children

Default Behaviors

clientCaps	download	homePage

Example

The following example shows how to apply the styles.css style sheet to a page.

```
<LINK REL=stylesheet HREF="styles.css" >
```

LISTING Element | LISTING Object

Renders text in a fixed-width font.

Remarks

This tag is no longer recommended. Use the **PRE** or **SAMP** tag instead.

Attributes/Properties

	CLASS		
canHaveChildren[*]	className	clientHeight[*]	clientLeft[*]
clientTop[*]	clientWidth[*]	currentStyle[*]	dir
firstChild[*]	id	innerHTML[*]	innerText[*]
isTextEdit[*]	lang	language	lastChild[*]
nextSibling[*]	nodeName[*]	nodeType[*]	nodeValue[*]
offsetHeight[*]	offsetLeft[*]	offsetParent[*]	offsetTop[*]
offsetWidth[*]	outerHTML[*]	outerText[*]	parentElement[*]
parentNode[*]	parentTextEdit[*]	previousSibling[*]	readyState[*]
recordNumber[*]	runtimeStyle[*]	scopeName[*]	scrollHeight[*]
scrollLeft[*]	scrollTop[*]	scrollWidth[*]	sourceIndex[*]
style	tabIndex	tagName[*]	tagUrn[*]
title	uniqueID[*]		

[*] This property has no corresponding attribute.

Methods

addBehavior	appendChild	applyElement
attachEvent	blur	clearAttributes
click	cloneNode	componentFromPoint
contains	detachEvent	focus
getAdjacentText	getAttribute	getBoundingClientRect
getClientRects	getElementsByTagName	getExpression
hasChildNodes	insertAdjacentElement	insertAdjacentHTML
insertAdjacentText	insertBefore	mergeAttributes
releaseCapture	removeAttribute	removeBehavior
removeChild	removeExpression	removeNode
replaceAdjacentText	replaceChild	replaceNode
scrollIntoView	setAttribute	setCapture
setExpression	swapNode	

Events

onbeforecopy	onbeforecut	onbeforepaste	onblur
onclick	oncopy	oncut	ondblclick
ondrag	ondragend	ondragenter	ondragleave
ondragover	ondragstart	ondrop	onfocus
onhelp	onkeydown	onkeypress	onkeyup
onlosecapture	onmousedown	onmousemove	onmouseout
onmouseover	onmouseup	onpaste	onpropertychange
onreadystatechange	onresize	onselectstart	

Collections

all	attributes	behaviorUrns	childNodes	children

Default Behaviors

clientCaps	download	homePage	httpFolder	saveFavorite
saveHistory	saveSnapshot	time	userData	

CSS Properties

Note For a list of corresponding attributes, see Appendix C.

background	backgroundColor	backgroundImage
backgroundPosition	backgroundPositionX[*]	backgroundPositionY[*]
backgroundRepeat	behavior	border
borderBottom	borderBottomColor	borderBottomStyle
borderBottomWidth	borderColor	borderLeft
borderLeftColor	borderLeftStyle	borderLeftWidth
borderRight	borderRightColor	borderRightStyle
borderRightWidth	borderStyle	borderTop
borderTopColor	borderTopStyle	borderTopWidth
borderWidth	bottom	clear
color	cursor	direction
font	fontFamily	fontSize
fontStyle	fontVariant	fontWeight
layoutGrid	layoutGridChar	layoutGridCharSpacing
layoutGridLine	layoutGridMode	layoutGridType
left	letterSpacing	lineBreak
lineHeight	margin	marginBottom
marginLeft	marginRight	marginTop
overflow	overflowX	overflowY
pageBreakAfter	pageBreakBefore	pixelBottom[*]
pixelHeight[*]	pixelLeft[*]	pixelRight[*]
pixelTop[*]	pixelWidth[*]	posBottom[*]
posHeight[*]	position	posLeft[*]
posRight[*]	posTop[*]	posWidth[*]
right	styleFloat	textAlign
textAutospace	textDecoration	textDecorationBlink[*]
textDecorationLineThrough[*]	textDecorationNone[*]	textDecorationOverline[*]

CSS Properties *(continued)*

textDecorationUnderline[*]	textIndent	textJustify
textTransform	top	unicodeBidi
visibility	wordBreak	wordSpacing
zIndex		

*   This property has no corresponding attribute.

location Object

Contains information about the current URL.

Remarks

The **href** property contains the entire URL, and the other properties contain portions of the URL. The default property for the **location** object is **location.href**. For example, setting `location='http://microsoft.com'` is equivalent to setting `location.href='http://microsoft.com'`.

By setting any of the following properties, the browser immediately navigates to the specified URL.

This object is available in script as of Internet Explorer 3.0.

Attributes/Properties

Note   These properties have no corresponding attributes.

hash	host	hostname	href	pathname
port	protocol	search		

Methods

assign	reload	replace

Applies To

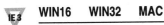

WIN16   WIN32   MAC

document, window

UNIX

document, window

MAP Element | MAP Object

Contains coordinate data for client-side image maps.

Remarks

An image map is a graphic image, with predefined regions, that contains links to other documents or anchors. For example, you could create an image of the solar system containing links that the user can click to navigate to pages for the individual planets.

The **MAP** object is referenced with the **USEMAP** attribute in an **IMG** element, as follows:

```
<IMG SRC="solarsys.gif" USEMAP="#SystemMap">
```

A **MAP** element contains a set of **AREA** elements defining the linking regions in the image.

The **MAP** element requires a closing tag.

This element is available in HTML as of Internet Explorer 3.0 and in script as of Internet Explorer 4.0.

Attributes/Properties

	CLASS		
canHaveChildren[*]	className	currentStyle[*]	dir
firstChild[*]	id	innerHTML[*]	innerText[*]
isTextEdit[*]	lang	language	lastChild[*]
name	nextSibling[*]	nodeName[*]	nodeType[*]
nodeValue[*]	offsetHeight[*]	offsetLeft[*]	offsetParent[*]
offsetTop[*]	offsetWidth[*]	outerHTML[*]	outerText[*]
parentElement[*]	parentNode[*]	parentTextEdit[*]	previousSibling[*]
readyState[*]	recordNumber[*]	runtimeStyle[*]	scopeName[*]
sourceIndex[*]	style	tagName[*]	tagUrn[*]
title	uniqueID[*]		

[*] This property has no corresponding attribute.

Methods

addBehavior	appendChild	applyElement
attachEvent	clearAttributes	click
cloneNode	componentFromPoint	contains
detachEvent	getAdjacentText	getAttribute
getBoundingClientRect	getClientRects	getElementsByTagName
hasChildNodes	insertAdjacentElement	insertAdjacentHTML
insertAdjacentText	insertBefore	mergeAttributes
releaseCapture	removeAttribute	removeBehavior
removeChild	removeNode	replaceAdjacentText
replaceChild	replaceNode	scrollIntoView
setAttribute	setCapture	swapNode

Events

onclick	ondblclick	ondrag	ondragend
ondragenter	ondragleave	ondragover	ondragstart
ondrop	onhelp	onkeydown	onkeypress
onkeyup	onlosecapture	onmousedown	onmousemove
onmouseout	onmouseover	onmouseup	onpropertychange
onreadystatechange	onscroll	onselectstart	

Collections

all	areas	attributes	behaviorUrns	childNodes	children

Default Behaviors

clientCaps	download	homePage	httpFolder	saveFavorite
saveHistory	saveSnapshot	userData		

CSS Properties

Note For a list of corresponding attributes, see Appendix C.

backgroundPositionX[*]	**backgroundPositionY**[*]	**behavior**	**direction**
layoutGridMode	**pixelBottom**[*]	**pixelHeight**[*]	**pixelLeft**[*]
pixelRight[*]	**pixelTop**[*]	**pixelWidth**[*]	**posBottom**[*]
posHeight[*]	**posLeft**[*]	**posRight**[*]	**posTop**[*]
posWidth[*]	**textAutospace**	**unicodeBidi**	**width**

*   This property has no corresponding attribute.

Example

The following example shows how to create an image map of the solar system. The user can click the sun or any planet in the image map to see a larger version of the image. The user can click the Back button from the image to return to the solar system image map.

```
<P><IMG SRC="solarsys.gif" WIDTH=504 HEIGHT=126 BORDER=0
    ALT="Solar System" USEMAP="#SystemMap">

<MAP NAME="SystemMap">
    <AREA SHAPE="rect" COORDS="0,0,82,126"
        HREF="/workshop/graphics/sun.gif">
    <AREA SHAPE="circle" COORDS="90,58,3"
        HREF="/workshop/graphics/merglobe.gif">
    <AREA SHAPE="circle" COORDS="124,58,8"
        HREF="/workshop/graphics/venglobe.gif">
    <AREA SHAPE="circle" COORDS="162,58,10"
        HREF="/workshop/graphics/earglobe.gif">
    <AREA SHAPE="circle" COORDS="203,58,8"
        HREF="/workshop/graphics/marglobe.gif">
    <AREA SHAPE="poly" COORDS="221,34,238,37,257,32,278,44,284,60,
        281,75,288,91,267,87,253,89,237,81,229,64,228,54"
        HREF="/workshop/graphics/jupglobe.gif">
    <AREA SHAPE="poly" COORDS="288,19,316,39,330,37,348,47,351,66,
        349,74,367,105,337,85,324,85,307,77,303,60,307,50"
        HREF="/workshop/graphics/satglobe.gif">
    <AREA SHAPE="poly" COORDS="405,39,408,50,411,57,410,71,
        404,78,393,80,383,86,381,75,376,69,376,56,380,48,393,44"
        HREF="/workshop/graphics/uraglobe.gif">
    <AREA SHAPE="poly" COORDS="445,38,434,49,431,53,427,62,430,72,
        435,77,445,92,456,77,463,72,463,62,462,53,455,47"
        HREF="/workshop/graphics/nepglobe.gif">
    <AREA SHAPE="circle" COORDS="479,66,3"
        HREF="/workshop/graphics/pluglobe.gif">
</MAP>
```

To see this code in action, refer to the Web Workshop CD-ROM.

MARQUEE Element | MARQUEE Object

Creates a scrolling text marquee.

Remarks

The **MARQUEE** element is a block element and requires a closing tag.

The width of the **MARQUEE** element defaults to 100 percent. When a **MARQUEE** is in a **TD** that does not specify a width, you should explicitly set the width of **MARQUEE**. If neither the **MARQUEE** nor the **TD** has a width specified, the marquee is collapsed to a 1-pixel width.

To create a vertically scrolling **MARQUEE**, set its **scrollLeft** property to 0. To create a horizontally scrolling marquee, set its **scrollTop** property to 0, overriding any script setting.

This element is available in HTML as of Internet Explorer 3.0 and in script as of Internet Explorer 4.0.

Attributes/Properties

			CLASS
behavior	**bgColor**	**canHaveChildren**[*]	**className**
clientHeight[*]	**clientLeft**[*]	**clientTop**[*]	**clientWidth**[*]
currentStyle[*]	**dataFld**	**dataFormatAs**	**dataSrc**
dir	**direction**	**firstChild**[*]	**height**
hspace	**id**	**innerHTML**[*]	**innerText**[*]
isTextEdit[*]	**lang**	**language**	**lastChild**[*]
loop	**nextSibling**[*]	**nodeName**[*]	**nodeType**[*]
nodeValue[*]	**offsetHeight**[*]	**offsetLeft**[*]	**offsetParent**[*]
offsetTop[*]	**offsetWidth**[*]	**outerHTML**[*]	**outerText**[*]
parentElement[*]	**parentNode**[*]	**parentTextEdit**[*]	**previousSibling**[*]
readyState[*]	**recordNumber**[*]	**runtimeStyle**[*]	**scopeName**[*]
scrollAmount	**scrollDelay**	**scrollHeight**[*]	**scrollLeft**[*]
scrollTop[*]	**sourceIndex**[*]	**style**	**tabIndex**
tagName[*]	**tagUrn**[*]	**title**	**trueSpeed**
uniqueID[*]	**vspace**	**width**	

* This property has no corresponding attribute.

Methods

addBehavior	appendChild	applyElement
attachEvent	blur	clearAttributes
click	cloneNode	componentFromPoint
contains	detachEvent	focus
getAdjacentText	getAttribute	getBoundingClientRect
getClientRects	getElementsByTagName	getExpression
hasChildNodes	insertAdjacentElement	insertAdjacentHTML
insertAdjacentText	insertBefore	mergeAttributes
releaseCapture	removeAttribute	removeBehavior
removeChild	removeExpression	removeNode
replaceAdjacentText	replaceChild	replaceNode
scrollIntoView	setAttribute	setCapture
setExpression	start	stop
swapNode		

Events

onbeforeeditfocus	onblur	onbounce	onclick
ondblclick	ondrag	ondragend	ondragenter
ondragleave	ondragover	ondragstart	ondrop
onfilterchange	onfinish	onfocus	onhelp
onkeydown	onkeypress	onkeyup	onlosecapture
onmousedown	onmousemove	onmouseout	onmouseover
onmouseup	onpropertychange	onreadystatechange	onresize
onscroll	onselectstart	onstart	

Collections

all	attributes	behaviorUrns	childNodes
children	filters		

Default Behaviors

clientCaps	download	homePage	httpFolder	saveFavorite
saveHistory	saveSnapshot	time	userData	

CSS Properties

Note For a list of corresponding attributes, see Appendix C.

background	backgroundColor	backgroundImage
backgroundPosition	backgroundPositionX*	backgroundPositionY*
backgroundRepeat	behavior	border
borderBottom	borderBottomColor	borderBottomStyle
borderBottomWidth	borderColor	borderLeft
borderLeftColor	borderLeftStyle	borderLeftWidth
borderRight	borderRightColor	borderRightStyle
borderRightWidth	borderStyle	borderTop
borderTopColor	borderTopStyle	borderTopWidth
borderWidth	bottom	clear
color	cursor	direction
display	filter	font
fontFamily	fontSize	fontStyle
fontVariant	fontWeight	height
layoutGrid	layoutGridChar	layoutGridCharSpacing
layoutGridLine	layoutGridMode	layoutGridType
left	letterSpacing	lineBreak
lineHeight	margin	marginBottom
marginLeft	marginRight	marginTop
padding	paddingBottom	paddingLeft
paddingRight	paddingTop	pageBreakAfter
pageBreakBefore	pixelBottom*	pixelHeight*
pixelLeft*	pixelRight*	pixelTop*

* This property has no corresponding attribute.

CSS Properties *(continued)*

> **Note** For a list of corresponding attributes, see Appendix C.

pixelWidth[*]	**posBottom**[*]	**posHeight**[*]
position	**posLeft**[*]	**posRight**[*]
posTop[*]	**posWidth**[*]	**right**
styleFloat	**textAlign**	**textAutospace**
textDecoration	**textDecorationBlink**[*]	**textDecorationLineThrough**[*]
textDecorationNone[*]	**textDecorationOverline**[*]	**textDecorationUnderline**[*]
textIndent	**textJustify**	**textTransform**
top	**unicodeBidi**	**visibility**
width	**wordBreak**	**wordSpacing**
zIndex		

[*] This property has no corresponding attribute.

Example

The following example shows how to create a marquee that scrolls from left to right across the screen and moves 10 pixels every 200 milliseconds.

```
<MARQUEE DIRECTION=RIGHT BEHAVIOR=SCROLL SCROLLAMOUNT=10 SCROLLDELAY=200>
This is a scrolling marquee.
</MARQUEE>
```

MENU Element | MENU Object

Specifies that the following block consists of individual menu items.

Remarks

The **MENU** element is a block element.

This element is available in HTML as of Internet Explorer 3.0 and in script as of Internet Explorer 4.0.

Attributes/Properties

	CLASS		
canHaveChildren[*]	**className**	**clientHeight**[*]	**clientLeft**[*]
clientTop[*]	**clientWidth**[*]	**currentStyle**[*]	**dir**
firstChild[*]	**id**	**innerHTML**[*]	**innerText**[*]

DHTML Objects

Attributes/Properties *(continued)*

isTextEdit[*]	lang	lastChild[*]	nextSibling[*]
nodeName[*]	nodeType[*]	nodeValue[*]	offsetHeight[*]
offsetLeft[*]	offsetParent[*]	offsetTop[*]	offsetWidth[*]
outerHTML[*]	outerText[*]	parentElement[*]	parentNode[*]
parentTextEdit[*]	previousSibling[*]	readyState[*]	recordNumber[*]
runtimeStyle[*]	scopeName[*]	scrollHeight[*]	scrollLeft[*]
scrollTop[*]	scrollWidth[*]	sourceIndex[*]	style
tabIndex	tagName[*]	tagUrn[*]	title
uniqueID[*]			

[*] This property has no corresponding attribute.

Methods

addBehavior	appendChild	applyElement
attachEvent	blur	clearAttributes
click	cloneNode	componentFromPoint
contains	detachEvent	focus
getAdjacentText	getAttribute	getBoundingClientRect
getClientRects	getElementsByTagName	getExpression
hasChildNodes	insertAdjacentElement	insertAdjacentHTML
insertAdjacentText	insertBefore	mergeAttributes
releaseCapture	removeAttribute	removeBehavior
removeChild	removeExpression	removeNode
replaceAdjacentText	replaceChild	replaceNode
scrollIntoView	setAttribute	setCapture
setExpression	swapNode	

Events

onbeforecopy	onbeforecut	onbeforepaste	onblur
onclick	oncopy	oncut	ondblclick
ondrag	ondragend	ondragenter	ondragleave

Events (*continued*)

ondragover	ondragstart	ondrop	onfocus
onhelp	onkeydown	onkeypress	onkeyup
onlosecapture	onmousedown	onmousemove	onmouseout
onmouseover	onmouseup	onpaste	onpropertychange
onreadystatechange	onresize	onselectstart	

Collections

all	attributes	behaviorUrns	childNodes	children

Default Behaviors

clientCaps	download	homePage	httpFolder	saveFavorite
saveHistory	saveSnapshot	time	userData	

CSS Properties

Note For a list of corresponding attributes, see Appendix C.

background	backgroundColor	backgroundImage
backgroundPosition	backgroundPositionX[*]	backgroundPositionY[*]
backgroundRepeat	behavior	border
borderBottom	borderBottomColor	borderBottomStyle
borderBottomWidth	borderColor	borderLeft
borderLeftColor	borderLeftStyle	borderLeftWidth
borderRight	borderRightColor	borderRightStyle
borderRightWidth	borderStyle	borderTop
borderTopColor	borderTopStyle	borderTopWidth
borderWidth	bottom	clear
color	cursor	direction
font	fontFamily	fontSize
fontStyle	fontVariant	fontWeight
layoutGrid	layoutGridChar	layoutGridCharSpacing
layoutGridLine	layoutGridMode	layoutGridType

CSS Properties *(continued)*

left	letterSpacing	lineBreak
lineHeight	margin	marginBottom
marginLeft	marginRight	marginTop
overflow	overflowX	overflowY
pageBreakAfter	pageBreakBefore	pixelBottom[*]
pixelHeight[*]	pixelLeft[*]	pixelRight[*]
pixelTop[*]	pixelWidth[*]	posBottom[*]
posHeight[*]	position	posLeft[*]
posRight[*]	posTop[*]	posWidth[*]
right	styleFloat	textAlign
textAutospace	textDecoration	textDecorationBlink[*]
textDecorationLineThrough[*]	textDecorationNone[*]	textDecorationOverline[*]
textDecorationUnderline[*]	textIndent	textJustify
textTransform	top	unicodeBidi
visibility	width	wordBreak
wordSpacing	zIndex	

[*]   This property has no corresponding attribute.

Example

The following example shows how to use the **MENU** element to create a menu with two items.

```
<MENU>
<LI>This is the first item in the menu.
<LI>And this is the second item in the menu.
</MENU>
```

META Element | META Object

Conveys hidden information about the document to the server and the client. The element also embeds document information that some search engines use for indexing and categorizing documents on the World Wide Web.

Remarks

The **META** element does not require a closing tag.

This element can be used only within the **HEAD** element.

This element is available in HTML as of Internet Explorer 3.0 and in script as of Internet Explorer 4.0.

Attributes/Properties

charset	clientHeight*	clientLeft*	clientTop*
clientWidth*	content	currentStyle*	defaultCharset*
HTTP-EQUIV httpEquiv	isTextEdit*	name	parentElement*
parentTextEdit*	runtimeStyle*	scrollHeight*	scrollLeft*
scrollTop*	scrollWidth*	sourceIndex*	style*
tagName*	url		

* This property has no corresponding attribute.

Methods

contains	getAttribute	removeAttribute	setAttrIbute

navigator Object

Contains information about the Web browser.

Remarks

This object is available in script as of Internet Explorer 3.0.

Attributes/Properties

Note These properties have no corresponding attributes.

appCodeName	appMinorVersion	appName	appVersion
browserLanguage	cookieEnabled	cpuClass	onLine
platform	systemLanguage	userAgent	userLanguage
userProfile			

Methods

javaEnabled	taintEnabled

Collections

> **plugins**

Applies To

 WIN16   WIN32   MAC

window

 UNIX

window

NEXTID Object

Creates unique identifiers that text editing software can read.

Remarks

The **NEXTID** element does not require a closing tag.

This element can be used only within the **HEAD** tag.

This element is available in HTML and script as of Internet Explorer 4.0.

Attributes/Properties

canHaveChildren[*]	**className**[*]	**currentStyle**[*]	**firstChild**[*]
id[*]	**innerHTML**[*]	**innerText**[*]	**isTextEdit**[*]
lang[*]	**language**[*]	**lastChild**[*]	**nextSibling**[*]
nodeName[*]	**nodeType**[*]	**nodeValue**[*]	**offsetHeight**[*]
offsetLeft[*]	**offsetParent**[*]	**offsetTop**[*]	**offsetWidth**[*]
outerHTML[*]	**outerText**[*]	**parentElement**[*]	**parentNode**[*]
parentTextEdit[*]	**previousSibling**[*]	**readyState**[*]	**recordNumber**[*]
runtimeStyle[*]	**scopeName**[*]	**sourceIndex**[*]	**style**[*]
tagName[*]	**tagUrn**[*]		

*   This property has no corresponding attribute.

Methods

addBehavior	appendChild	applyElement
clearAttributes	cloneNode	componentFromPoint
contains	getAdjacentText	getAttribute
getBoundingClientRect	getClientRects	hasChildNodes
insertAdjacentElement	insertBefore	mergeAttributes
removeAttribute	removeBehavior	removeChild
removeNode	replaceAdjacentText	replaceChild
replaceNode	setAttribute	swapNode

Events

onclick	ondblclick	ondragstart	onfilterchange
onhelp	onkeydown	onkeypress	onkeyup
onmousemove	onmouseover	onmouseup	onreadystatechange
onselectstart			

Collections

attributes	behaviorUrns	childNodes	children	filters

Default Behaviors

clientCaps	download	homePage

NOBR Element | NOBR Object

Renders text without line breaks.

Remarks

The **NOBR** element does not require a closing tag.

This element is available in HTML and script as of Internet Explorer 4.0.

Attributes/Properties

CLASS

className	clientHeight*	clientLeft*	clientTop*
clientWidth*	currentStyle*	dir	id
innerHTML*	innerText*	isTextEdit*	lang
language	offsetHeight*	offsetLeft*	offsetParent*
offsetTop*	offsetWidth*	outerHTML*	outerText*
parentElement*	parentTextEdit*	readyState*	recordNumber*
runtimeStyle*	scopeName*	scrollHeight*	scrollLeft*
scrollTop*	scrollWidth*	sourceIndex*	style*
tagName*	tagUrn*	uniqueID*	

* This property has no corresponding attribute.

Methods

addBehavior	attachEvent	click
componentFromPoint	contains	detachEvent
getAttribute	getBoundingClientRect	getClientRects
getExpression	insertAdjacentHTML	insertAdjacentText
releaseCapture	removeAttribute	removeBehavior
removeExpression	scrollIntoView	setAttribute
setCapture	setExpression	

Events

onbeforecopy	onbeforecut	onbeforepaste	onclick
oncopy	oncut	ondblclick	ondrag
ondragend	ondragenter	ondragleave	ondragover
ondragstart	ondrop	onhelp	onkeydown
onkeypress	onkeyup	onlosecapture	onmousemove
onmouseover	onmouseup	onpaste	onpropertychange
onreadystatechange	onselectstart		

Collections

behaviorUrns

Default Behaviors

clientCaps   **download**   **homePage**

Example

The following example shows how to use the **NOBR** element to prevent text lines from being broken.

```
<NOBR>Here's a line of text I don't want to be broken . . .
here's the end of the line.</NOBR>
```

NOFRAMES Element | NOFRAMES Object

Contains HTML for browsers that do not support **FRAMESET** elements.

Remarks

The **NOFRAMES** element is a block element and requires a closing tag.

This element is available in HTML as of Internet Explorer 3.0 and in script as of Internet Explorer 4.0.

Attributes/Properties

id   **readyState**[*]   **scopeName**[*]   **tagUrn**[*]

[*] This property has no corresponding attribute.

Methods

addBehavior   **componentFromPoint**   **removeBehavior**

Events

onreadystatechange

Collections

behaviorUrns

Default Behaviors

clientCaps   **download**   **homePage**

CSS Properties

Note For a list of corresponding attributes, see Appendix C.

behavior   **textAutospace**

Example

The following example shows how to use the **NOFRAMES** element.

```
<FRAMESET>
<NOFRAMES>You need Internet Explorer version 3.0 or later to view
frames!</NOFRAMES>
</FRAMESET>
```

NOSCRIPT Element | NOSCRIPT Object

Specifies HTML to be displayed in browsers that do not support scripting.

Remarks

The **NOSCRIPT** element is a block element and requires a closing tag.

This element is available in HTML and script as of Internet Explorer 4.0.

Attributes/Properties

id   **readyState**[*]   **scopeName**[*]   **tagUrn**[*]

*   This property has no corresponding attribute.

Methods

addBehavior   **componentFromPoint**   **removeBehavior**

Events

onreadystatechange

Collections

behaviorUrns

Default Behaviors

clientCaps   **download**   **homePage**

CSS Properties

Note For a list of corresponding attributes, see Appendix C.

behavior   **textAutospace**

OBJECT Element | OBJECT Object

Inserts an object into the HTML page.

Remarks

The **OBJECT** element is a block element and requires a closing tag.

An object can appear in the **HEAD** or the **BODY** of a document.

Possible return values (those generated by DHTML Object Model properties) on the **OBJECT** element depend on the implementation of the **OBJECT**. For example, the **readyState** property returns null or error if the **OBJECT** does not implement a **readyState** property. DHTML Object Model properties available for an **OBJECT** depend on the contents of the **OBJECT**. For supported properties, see the documentation for the individual object.

Events are sent directly to the **OBJECT** element. If the event is returned by the embedded object, it bubbles accordingly. If the event is not returned, it does not bubble.

The following example shows how **OBJECT** event handlers can be defined in script.

```
<SCRIPT FOR=oObject EVENT=eEvent>
:
</SCRIPT>

<OBJECT ID=oObject CLASSID="xyz.abc">
</OBJECT>
```

Note The **object** property for the **OBJECT** element is a way of reconciling DHTML Object Model members that are duplicated by the **OBJECT** element's implementation and DHTML. For instance, if the **OBJECT** implements an item method, and DHTML implements an item method, use `document.all.objectID.object.item()` to access the one defined for the **OBJECT**.

This element is available in HTML as of Internet Explorer 3.0 and in script as of Internet Explorer 4.0.

Attributes/Properties

accessKey	align	altHTML[*]	canHaveChildren[*]
classid	CLASS className	clientHeight[*]	clientLeft[*]
clientTop[*]	clientWidth[*]	code	codeBase
codeType	currentStyle[*]	data	dataFld
dataSrc	dir	form[*]	height
hspace	id	isTextEdit[*]	lang
language	name	nextSibling[*]	nodeName[*]
nodeType[*]	nodeValue[*]	object[*]	offsetHeight[*]
offsetLeft[*]	offsetParent[*]	offsetTop[*]	offsetWidth[*]
outerHTML[*]	outerText[*]	parentElement[*]	parentNode[*]
parentTextEdit[*]	previousSibling[*]	readyState[*]	recordNumber[*]
recordset[*]	runtimeStyle[*]	scopeName[*]	scrollHeight[*]
scrollLeft[*]	scrollTop[*]	scrollWidth[*]	sourceIndex[*]
style	tabIndex	tagName[*]	tagUrn[*]
title	type	uniqueID[*]	vspace
width			

* This property has no corresponding attribute.

Methods

addBehavior	applyElement	attachEvent
blur	clearAttributes	click
cloneNode	componentFromPoint	detachEvent
focus	getAdjacentText	getAttribute
getBoundingClientRect	getClientRects	insertAdjacentElement
insertBefore	mergeAttributes	releaseCapture
removeAttribute	removeBehavior	removeExpression
removeNode	replaceAdjacentText	replaceNode
scrollIntoView	setAttribute	setCapture
setExpression	swapNode	

Events

onbeforeeditfocus	onblur	oncellchange	onclick
ondataavailable	ondatasetchanged	ondatasetcomplete	ondblclick
ondrag	ondragend	ondragenter	ondragleave
ondragover	ondragstart	ondrop	onerror
onfocus	onkeydown	onkeypress	onkeyup
onlosecapture	onpropertychange	onreadystatechange	onresize
onrowenter	onrowexit	onrowsdelete	onrowsinserted
onscroll	onselectstart		

Collections

all	attributes	behaviorUrns

Default Behaviors

clientCaps	download	homePage	httpFolder	saveFavorite
saveHistory	saveSnapshot	userData		

DHTML Objects

CSS Properties

Note For a list of corresponding attributes, see Appendix C.

backgroundPositionX[*]	backgroundPositionY[*]	behavior
border	borderBottom	borderBottomColor
borderBottomStyle	borderBottomWidth	borderColor
borderLeft	borderLeftColor	borderLeftStyle
borderLeftWidth	borderRight	borderRightColor
borderRightStyle	borderRightWidth	borderStyle
borderTop	borderTopColor	borderTopStyle
borderTopWidth	borderWidth	bottom
clear	cursor	direction
height	layoutGridMode	left
margin	marginBottom	marginLeft
marginRight	marginTop	pixelBottom[*]
pixelHeight[*]	pixelLeft[*]	pixelRight[*]
pixelTop[*]	pixelWidth[*]	posBottom[*]
posHeight[*]	position	posLeft[*]
posRight[*]	posTop[*]	posWidth[*]
right	styleFloat	textAutospace
top	unicodeBidi	visibility
width		

* This property has no corresponding attribute.

OL Element | OL Object

Draws lines of text as a numbered list.

Remarks

The **OL** element is a block element and requires a closing tag.

The **TYPE** attribute sets the list type for all ensuing lists unless a different type value is set.

This element is available in HTML as of Internet Explorer 3.0 and in script as of Internet Explorer 4.0.

Attributes/Properties

	CLASS		
canHaveChildren*	className	clientHeight*	clientLeft*
clientTop*	clientWidth*	currentStyle*	dir
firstChild*	id	innerHTML*	innerText*
isTextEdit*	lang	language	lastChild*
nextSibling*	nodeName*	nodeType*	nodeValue*
offsetHeight*	offsetLeft*	offsetParent*	offsetTop*
offsetWidth*	outerHTML*	outerText*	parentElement*
parentNode*	parentTextEdit*	previousSibling*	readyState*
recordNumber*	runtimeStyle*	scopeName*	scrollHeight*
scrollLeft*	scrollTop*	scrollWidth*	sourceIndex*
start	style	tabIndex	tagName*
tagUrn*	title	type	uniqueID*

* This property has no corresponding attribute.

Methods

addBehavior	appendChild	applyElement
attachEvent	blur	clearAttributes
click	cloneNode	componentFromPoint
contains	detachEvent	focus
getAdjacentText	getAttribute	getBoundingClientRect
getClientRects	getElementsByTagName	getExpression
hasChildNodes	insertAdjacentElement	insertAdjacentHTML
insertAdjacentText	insertBefore	mergeAttributes
releaseCapture	removeAttribute	removeBehavior
removeChild	removeExpression	removeNode
replaceAdjacentText	replaceChild	replaceNode
scrollIntoView	setAttribute	setCapture
setExpression	swapNode	

Events

onbeforecopy	onbeforecut	onbeforepaste	onblur
onclick	oncopy	oncut	ondblclick
ondrag	ondragend	ondragenter	ondragleave
ondragover	ondragstart	ondrop	onfocus
onhelp	onkeydown	onkeypress	onkeyup
onlosecapture	onmousedown	onmousemove	onmouseout
onmouseover	onmouseup	onpaste	onpropertychange
onreadystatechange	onresize	onselectstart	

Collections

all	attributes	behaviorUrns	childNodes	children

Default Behaviors

clientCaps	download	homePage	httpFolder	saveFavorite
saveHistory	saveSnapshot	time	userData	

CSS Properties

Note For a list of corresponding attributes, see Appendix C.

background	backgroundColor	backgroundImage
backgroundPosition	backgroundPositionX[*]	backgroundPositionY[*]
backgroundRepeat	behavior	border
borderBottom	borderBottomColor	borderBottomStyle
borderBottomWidth	borderColor	borderLeft
borderLeftColor	borderLeftStyle	borderLeftWidth
borderRight	borderRightColor	borderRightStyle
borderRightWidth	borderStyle	borderTop
borderTopColor	borderTopStyle	borderTopWidth
borderWidth	bottom	clear
color	cursor	direction

CSS Properties *(continued)*

font	fontFamily	fontSize
fontStyle	fontVariant	fontWeight
layoutGrid	layoutGridChar	layoutGridCharSpacing
layoutGridLine	layoutGridMode	layoutGridType
left	letterSpacing	lineBreak
lineHeight	listStyle	listStyleImage
listStylePosition	listStyleType	margin
marginBottom	marginLeft	marginRight
marginTop	overflow	overflowX
overflowY	pageBreakAfter	pageBreakBefore
pixelBottom[*]	pixelHeight[*]	pixelLeft[*]
pixelRight[*]	pixelTop[*]	pixelWidth[*]
posBottom[*]	posHeight[*]	position
posLeft[*]	posRight[*]	posTop[*]
posWidth[*]	right	styleFloat
textAlign	textAutospace	textDecoration
textDecorationBlink[*]	textDecorationLineThrough[*]	textDecorationNone[*]
textDecorationOverline[*]	textDecorationUnderline[*]	textIndent
textJustify	textTransform	top
unicodeBidi	visibility	width
wordBreak	wordSpacing	zIndex

*   This property has no corresponding attribute.

Example

The following example shows how to use the **OL** element to create a numbered list.

```
<OL>
<LI>This is the first item in the list.
<LI>And this is the second item in the list.
</OL>

<OL START=3>
<LI>This is item number 3.
</OL>
```

```
<OL TYPE=A>
<LI>This is item A.
</OL>
```

OPTION Element | OPTION Object

Denotes one choice in a **SELECT** element.

Remarks

The **OPTION** element is a block element and does not require a closing tag.

Although **OPTION** elements do not appear in the **all** collection, you can gain access to these elements by applying the **options** collection to the **SELECT** element.

Except for **background-color** and **color**, style settings applied through the **style** object for the **OPTION** element are ignored. In addition, style settings applied directly to individual **options** override those applied to the containing **SELECT** element as a whole.

This element is available in HTML and script as of Internet Explorer 3.0.

Attributes/Properties

canHaveChildren*	CLASS className	clientHeight*	clientLeft*
clientTop*	clientWidth*	currentStyle*	defaultSelected*
dir	firstChild*	form*	id
index*	innerHTML*	innerText*	isTextEdit*
lang	language	lastChild*	nextSibling*
nodeName*	nodeType*	nodeValue*	offsetHeight*
offsetLeft*	offsetParent*	offsetTop*	offsetWidth*
parentElement*	parentNode*	parentTextEdit*	previousSibling*
readyState*	recordNumber*	runtimeStyle*	scopeName*
scrollHeight*	scrollLeft*	scrollTop*	scrollWidth*
selected	style*	tagName*	tagUrn*
text*	uniqueID*	value	

*   This property has no corresponding attribute.

Methods

addBehavior	**appendChild**	**applyElement**
attachEvent	**clearAttributes**	**click**
cloneNode	**componentFromPoint**	**contains**
detachEvent	**getAdjacentText**	**getAttribute**
getBoundingClientRect	**getClientRects**	**getExpression**
hasChildNodes	**insertAdjacentElement**	**insertAdjacentHTML**
insertAdjacentText	**insertBefore**	**mergeAttributes**
releaseCapture	**removeAttribute**	**removeBehavior**
removeChild	**removeExpression**	**removeNode**
replaceAdjacentText	**replaceChild**	**replaceNode**
setAttribute	**setCapture**	**setExpression**
swapNode		

Events

onlosecapture   **onpropertychange**   **onreadystatechange**   **onselectstart**

Collections

attributes   **behaviorUrns**   **childNodes**   **children**

Default Behaviors

clientCaps	**download**	**homePage**	**httpFolder**	**saveFavorite**
saveHistory	**saveSnapshot**	**time**	**userData**	

CSS Properties

Note For a list of corresponding attributes, see Appendix C.

backgroundColor	**backgroundPositionX**[*]	**backgroundPositionY**[*]
behavior	**clear**	**color**
direction	**layoutGridMode**	**pixelBottom**[*]
pixelHeight[*]	**pixelLeft**[*]	**pixelRight**[*]
pixelTop[*]	**pixelWidth**[*]	**posBottom**[*]

[*]   This property has no corresponding attribute.

CSS Properties *(continued)*

Note For a list of corresponding attributes, see Appendix C

posHeight[*]   posLeft[*]   posRight[*]

posTop[*]   posWidth[*]   textAutospace

unicodeBidi   width

* This property has no corresponding attribute.

Example

The following example shows how to create a drop-down list box with the names of different cars that the user can select.

```
<SELECT NAME="Cars" SIZE="1">
<OPTION VALUE="1">BMW
<OPTION VALUE="2">PORSCHE
<OPTION VALUE="3" SELECTED>MERCEDES
</SELECT>
```

The following example in JScript (compatible with ECMA 262 language specification) shows how to display the text for all options in the first **SELECT** list in the document.

```
var oElement = document.all.tags("SELECT").item(0);
if ( oElement != null )
{
    for ( i = 0; i<el.options.length; i++ )
    {
        alert("Option " + i + " is " + oElement.options(i).text);
    }
}
```

P Element | P Object

Denotes a paragraph.

Remarks

The **P** element is a block element and does not require a closing tag.

This element is available in HTML as of Internet Explorer 3.0 and in script as of Internet Explorer 4.0.

Attributes/Properties

		CLASS	
align	canHaveChildren[*]	className	clientHeight[*]
clientLeft[*]	clientTop[*]	clientWidth[*]	currentStyle[*]
dir	firstChild[*]	id	innerHTML[*]
innerText[*]	isTextEdit[*]	lang	language
lastChild[*]	nextSibling[*]	nodeName[*]	nodeType[*]
nodeValue[*]	offsetHeight[*]	offsetLeft[*]	offsetParent[*]
offsetTop[*]	offsetWidth[*]	outerHTML[*]	outerText[*]
parentElement[*]	parentNode[*]	parentTextEdit[*]	previousSibling[*]
readyState[*]	recordNumber[*]	runtimeStyle[*]	scopeName[*]
scrollHeight[*]	scrollLeft[*]	scrollTop[*]	scrollWidth[*]
sourceIndex[*]	style	tabIndex	tagName[*]
tagUrn[*]	title	uniqueID[*]	

[*] This property has no corresponding attribute.

Methods

addBehavior	appendChild	applyElement
attachEvent	blur	clearAttributes
click	cloneNode	componentFromPoint
contains	detachEvent	focus
getAdjacentText	getAttribute	getBoundingClientRect
getClientRects	getElementsByTagName	getExpression
hasChildNodes	insertAdjacentElement	insertAdjacentHTML
insertAdjacentText	insertBefore	mergeAttributes
releaseCapture	removeAttribute	removeBehavior
removeChild	removeExpression	removeNode
replaceAdjacentText	replaceChild	replaceNode
scrollIntoView	setAttribute	setCapture
setExpression	swapNode	

Events

onbeforecopy	onbeforecut	onbeforepaste	onblur
onclick	oncopy	oncut	ondblclick
ondrag	ondragend	ondragenter	ondragleave
ondragover	ondragstart	ondrop	onfocus
onhelp	onkeydown	onkeypress	onkeyup
onlosecapture	onmousedown	onmousemove	onmouseout
onmouseover	onmouseup	onpaste	onpropertychange
onreadystatechange	onresize	onselectstart	

Collections

all	attributes	behaviorUrns	childNodes	children

Default Behaviors

clientCaps	download	homePage	httpFolder	saveFavorite
saveHistory	saveSnapshot	time	userData	

CSS Properties

Note For a list of corresponding attributes, see Appendix C.

background	backgroundColor	backgroundImage
backgroundPosition	backgroundPositionX[*]	backgroundPositionY[*]
backgroundRepeat	behavior	border
borderBottom	borderBottomColor	borderBottomStyle
borderBottomWidth	borderColor	borderLeft
borderLeftColor	borderLeftStyle	borderLeftWidth
borderRight	borderRightColor	borderRightStyle
borderRightWidth	borderStyle	borderTop
borderTopColor	borderTopStyle	borderTopWidth
borderWidth	bottom	clear
color	cursor	direction

CSS Properties *(continued)*

font	**fontFamily**	**fontSize**
fontStyle	**fontVariant**	**fontWeight**
layoutGrid	**layoutGridChar**	**layoutGridCharSpacing**
layoutGridLine	**layoutGridMode**	**layoutGridType**
left	**letterSpacing**	**lineBreak**
lineHeight	**margin**	**marginBottom**
marginLeft	**marginRight**	**marginTop**
overflow	**overflowX**	**overflowY**
pageBreakAfter	**pageBreakBefore**	**pixelBottom**[*]
pixelHeight[*]	**pixelLeft**[*]	**pixelRight**[*]
pixelTop[*]	**pixelWidth**[*]	**posBottom**[*]
posHeight[*]	**position**	**posLeft**[*]
posRight[*]	**posTop**[*]	**posWidth**[*]
right	**styleFloat**	**textAlign**
textAutospace	**textDecoration**	**textDecorationBlink**[*]
textDecorationLineThrough[*]	**textDecorationNone**[*]	**textDecorationOverline**[*]
textDecorationUnderline[*]	**textIndent**	**textJustify**
textTransform	**top**	**unicodeBidi**
visibility	**width**	**wordBreak**
wordSpacing	**zIndex**	

* This property has no corresponding attribute.

Example

The following example shows how to use the **P** element to create a paragraph.

```
<P>This is a paragraph.</P>
```

PARAM Element | PARAM Object

Sets the property value for a given object.

Remarks

The **PARAM** element does not require a closing tag.

The **PARAM** element is valid within the **APPLET**, **EMBED**, and **OBJECT** elements.

This element is available in HTML as of Internet Explorer 3.0.

Attributes/Properties

dataFld	dataFormatAs	dataSrc	name	value

Methods

removeExpression	setExpression

PLAINTEXT Element | PLAINTEXT Object

Renders text in a fixed-width font without processing tags.

Remarks

The **PLAINTEXT** element is a block element. The closing tag is optional.

This element is available in HTML as of Internet Explorer 3.0 and in script as of Internet Explorer 4.0.

Attributes/Properties

	CLASS		
canHaveChildren*	className	clientHeight*	clientLeft*
clientTop*	clientWidth*	currentStyle*	dir
firstChild*	id	innerText*	isTextEdit*
lang	language	lastChild*	nextSibling*
nodeName*	nodeType*	nodeValue*	offsetHeight*
offsetLeft*	offsetParent*	offsetTop*	offsetWidth*
outerHTML*	outerText*	parentElement*	parentNode*

Attributes/Properties *(continued)*

parentTextEdit[*]	previousSibling[*]	readyState[*]	recordNumber[*]
runtimeStyle[*]	scopeName[*]	scrollHeight[*]	scrollLeft[*]
scrollTop[*]	scrollWidth[*]	sourceIndex[*]	style
tabIndex	tagName[*]	tagUrn[*]	title
uniqueID[*]			

[*] This property has no corresponding attribute.

Methods

addBehavior	appendChild	applyElement
attachEvent	blur	clearAttributes
click	cloneNode	componentFromPoint
contains	detachEvent	focus
getAdjacentText	getAttribute	getElementsByTagName
hasChildNodes	insertAdjacentElement	insertAdjacentHTML
insertBefore	mergeAttributes	releaseCapture
removeAttribute	removeBehavior	removeChild
removeNode	replaceAdjacentText	replaceChild
replaceNode	scrollIntoView	setAttribute
setCapture	swapNode	

Events

onbeforecopy	onbeforecut	onbeforepaste	onblur
onclick	oncopy	oncut	ondblclick
ondrag	ondragend	ondragenter	ondragleave
ondragover	ondragstart	ondrop	onfocus
onhelp	onkeydown	onkeypress	onkeyup
onlosecapture	onmousedown	onmousemove	onmouseout
onmouseover	onmouseup	onpaste	onpropertychange
onreadystatechange	onselectstart		

Collections

all	attributes	behaviorUrns	childNodes	children

Default Behaviors

clientCaps	download	homePage	httpFolder	saveFavorite
saveHistory	saveSnapshot	time	userData	

CSS Properties

Note For a list of corresponding attributes, see Appendix C.

background	backgroundColor	backgroundImage
backgroundPosition	backgroundPositionX[*]	backgroundPositionY[*]
backgroundRepeat	behavior	border
borderBottom	borderBottomColor	borderBottomStyle
borderBottomWidth	borderColor	borderLeft
borderLeftColor	borderLeftStyle	borderLeftWidth
borderRight	borderRightColor	borderRightStyle
borderRightWidth	borderStyle	borderTop
borderTopColor	borderTopStyle	borderTopWidth
borderWidth	clear	color
cursor	direction	font
fontFamily	fontSize	fontStyle
fontVariant	fontWeight	layoutGrid
layoutGridChar	layoutGridCharSpacing	layoutGridLine
layoutGridMode	layoutGridType	letterSpacing
lineBreak	lineHeight	margin
marginBottom	marginLeft	marginRight
marginTop	overflow	overflowX
overflowY	pageBreakAfter	pageBreakBefore
pixelBottom[*]	pixelHeight[*]	pixelLeft[*]
pixelRight[*]	pixelTop[*]	pixelWidth[*]
posBottom[*]	posHeight[*]	posLeft[*]

CSS Properties *(continued)*

posRight[*]	posTop[*]	posWidth[*]
textAlign	textAutospace	textDecoration
textDecorationBlink[*]	textDecorationLineThrough[*]	textDecorationNone[*]
textDecorationOverline[*]	textDecorationUnderline[*]	textIndent
textJustify	textTransform	unicodeBidi
width	wordBreak	wordSpacing
zIndex		

[*]   This property has no corresponding attribute.

PRE Element | PRE Object

Renders text in a fixed-width font.

Remarks

The **PRE** element is a block element and requires a closing tag.

This element is available in HTML as of Internet Explorer 3.0 and in script as of Internet Explorer 4.0.

Attributes/Properties

	CLASS		
canHaveChildren[*]	className	clientHeight[*]	clientLeft[*]
clientTop[*]	clientWidth[*]	currentStyle[*]	dir
firstChild[*]	id	innerHTML[*]	innerText[*]
isTextEdit[*]	lang	language	lastChild[*]
nextSibling[*]	nodeName[*]	nodeType[*]	nodeValue[*]
offsetHeight[*]	offsetLeft[*]	offsetParent[*]	offsetTop[*]
offsetWidth[*]	outerHTML[*]	outerText[*]	parentElement[*]
parentNode[*]	parentTextEdit[*]	previousSibling[*]	readyState[*]
recordNumber[*]	runtimeStyle[*]	scopeName[*]	scrollHeight[*]
scrollLeft[*]	scrollTop[*]	scrollWidth[*]	sourceIndex[*]
style	tabIndex	tagName[*]	tagUrn[*]
title	uniqueID[*]		

[*]   This property has no corresponding attribute.

Methods

addBehavior	appendChild	applyElement
attachEvent	blur	clearAttributes
click	cloneNode	componentFromPoint
contains	detachEvent	focus
getAdjacentText	getAttribute	getBoundingClientRect
getClientRects	getElementsByTagName	getExpression
hasChildNodes	insertAdjacentElement	insertAdjacentHTML
insertAdjacentText	insertBefore	mergeAttributes
releaseCapture	removeAttribute	removeBehavior
removeChild	removeExpression	removeNode
replaceAdjacentText	replaceChild	replaceNode
scrollIntoView	setAttribute	setCapture
setExpression	swapNode	

Events

onbeforecopy	onbeforecut	onbeforepaste	onblur
onclick	oncopy	oncut	ondblclick
ondrag	ondragend	ondragenter	ondragleave
ondragover	ondragstart	ondrop	onfocus
onhelp	onkeydown	onkeypress	onkeyup
onlosecapture	onmousedown	onmousemove	onmouseout
onmouseover	onmouseup	onpaste	onpropertychange
onreadystatechange	onresize	onselectstart	

Collections

all	attributes	behaviorUrns	childNodes	children

Default Behaviors

clientCaps	download	homePage	httpFolder	saveFavorite
saveHistory	saveSnapshot	time	userData	

CSS Properties

Note For a list of corresponding attributes, see Appendix C.

background	backgroundColor	backgroundImage
backgroundPosition	backgroundPositionX[*]	backgroundPositionY[*]
backgroundRepeat	behavior	border
borderBottom	borderBottomColor	borderBottomStyle
borderBottomWidth	borderColor	borderLeft
borderLeftColor	borderLeftStyle	borderLeftWidth
borderRight	borderRightColor	borderRightStyle
borderRightWidth	borderStyle	borderTop
borderTopColor	borderTopStyle	borderTopWidth
borderWidth	bottom	clear
color	cursor	direction
font	fontFamily	fontSize
fontStyle	fontVariant	fontWeight
layoutGrid	layoutGridChar	layoutGridCharSpacing
layoutGridLine	layoutGridMode	layoutGridType
left	letterSpacing	lineBreak
lineHeight	margin	marginBottom
marginLeft	marginRight	marginTop
overflow	overflowX	overflowY
pageBreakAfter	pageBreakBefore	pixelBottom[*]
pixelHeight[*]	pixelLeft[*]	pixelRight[*]
pixelTop[*]	pixelWidth[*]	posBottom[*]
posHeight[*]	position	posLeft[*]
posRight[*]	posTop[*]	posWidth[*]
right	styleFloat	textAlign
textAutospace	textDecoration	textDecorationBlink[*]
textDecorationLineThrough[*]	textDecorationNone[*]	textDecorationOverline[*]

[*]   This property has no corresponding attribute

CSS Properties *(continued)*

Note For a list of corresponding attributes, see Appendix C.

textDecorationUnderline[*]	textIndent	textJustify
textTransform	top	unicodeBidi
visibility	width	wordBreak
wordSpacing	zIndex	

* This property has no corresponding attribute.

Example

The following example shows how to use the **PRE** element.

```
<PRE>Here's some plain text.</PRE>
```

Q Element | Q Object

Sets apart a quotation in text.

Remarks

The **Q** element is an inline element and requires a closing tag.

This element is available in HTML and script as of Internet Explorer 4.0.

Attributes/Properties

	CLASS		
canHaveChildren[*]	className	currentStyle[*]	dir
firstChild[*]	id	innerHTML[*]	innerText[*]
isTextEdit[*]	lang	language	lastChild[*]
nextSibling[*]	nodeName[*]	nodeType[*]	nodeValue[*]
offsetHeight[*]	offsetLeft[*]	offsetParent[*]	offsetTop[*]
offsetWidth[*]	outerHTML[*]	outerText[*]	parentElement[*]
parentNode[*]	parentTextEdit[*]	previousSibling[*]	readyState[*]
recordNumber[*]	runtimeStyle[*]	scopeName[*]	sourceIndex[*]
style	tabIndex	tagName[*]	tagUrn[*]
title	uniqueID[*]		

* This property has no corresponding attribute.

Methods

addBehavior	**appendChild**	**applyElement**
attachEvent	**blur**	**clearAttributes**
cloneNode	**componentFromPoint**	**detachEvent**
focus	**getAdjacentText**	**getBoundingClientRect**
getClientRects	**getElementsByTagName**	**getExpression**
hasChildNodes	**insertAdjacentElement**	**insertBefore**
mergeAttributes	**removeBehavior**	**removeChild**
removeExpression	**removeNode**	**replaceAdjacentText**
replaceChild	**replaceNode**	**setExpression**
swapNode		

Events

onblur	**ondrag**	**ondragend**	**ondragenter**
ondragleave	**ondragover**	**ondragstart**	**ondrop**
onfocus	**onkeydown**	**onkeypress**	**onkeyup**
onreadystatechange	**onselectstart**		

Collections

all	**attributes**	**behaviorUrns**	**childNodes**	**children**

Default Behaviors

clientCaps	**download**	**homePage**	**httpFolder**	**saveFavorite**
saveHistory	**saveSnapshot**	**time**	**userData**	

CSS Properties

Note For a list of corresponding attributes, see Appendix C.

backgroundPositionX*	**backgroundPositionY***	**behavior**	**direction**
layoutGridMode	**overflow**	**overflowX**	**overflowY**
pixelBottom*	**pixelHeight***	**pixelLeft***	**pixelRight***
pixelTop*	**pixelWidth***	**posBottom***	**posHeight***
posLeft*	**posRight***	**posTop***	**posWidth***
textAutospace	**unicodeBidi**	**width**	

* This property has no corresponding attribute.

Example

The following example shows how to use the **Q** element to set a quotation apart in text.

```
<P>He said,
<Q>"Hi there!"</Q>
```

RT Element | RT Object

Designates the ruby text for the **RUBY** element.

Remarks

The **RT** element is an inline element and does not require a closing tag.

The ruby text specified by the **RT** element is positioned above or inline with the **rubyPosition** property. Browsers that do not support the **RT** element render the ruby text inline with the base text.

This element is available in HTML and script as of Internet Explorer 5.

Attributes/Properties

CLASS

className	**dir**	**id**	**innerHTML**[*]	**innerText**[*]
lang	**language**	**name**	**offsetHeight**[*]	**offsetLeft**[*]
offsetParent[*]	**offsetTop**[*]	**offsetWidth**[*]	**outerHTML**[*]	**outerText**[*]
		STYLE[†]		
readyState[*]	**scopeName**[*]		**tabIndex**	**tagName**[*]
tagUrn[*]	**title**			

*   This property has no corresponding attribute.

†   This attribute has no corresponding property.

Methods

addBehavior	**blur**	**componentFromPoint**	**focus**
getExpression	**removeBehavior**	**removeExpression**	**setExpression**

Events

onafterupdate	onbeforeupdate	onblur	onclick
ondblclick	ondragstart	onerrorupdate	onfilterchange
onfocus	onhelp	onkeydown	onkeypress
onkeyup	onmousedown	onmousemove	onmouseout
onmouseover	onmouseup	onreadystatechange	onselectstart

Collections

behaviorUrns	children	filters

Default Behaviors

clientCaps	download	homePage

CSS Properties

Note For a list of corresponding attributes, see Appendix C.

backgroundPositionX[*]	backgroundPositionY[*]	behavior	direction
layoutGridMode	overflow	overflowX	overflowY
pixelBottom[*]	pixelHeight[*]	pixelLeft[*]	pixelRight[*]
pixelTop[*]	pixelWidth[*]	posBottom[*]	posHeight[*]
posLeft[*]	posRight[*]	posTop[*]	posWidth[*]
styleFloat	textAutospace	unicodeBidi	width

[*]   This property has no corresponding attribute.

Example

The following example shows how to use the **RT** element.

```
<RUBY>
   Base Text
   <RT>Ruby Text
</RUBY>
```

To see this code in action, refer to the Web Workshop CD-ROM.

RUBY Element | RUBY Object

Designates an annotation or pronunciation guide to be placed above or inline with a string of text.

Remarks

The **RUBY** element is an inline element and requires a closing tag.

A *ruby* is an annotation or pronunciation guide for a string of text. The string of text annotated with a ruby is referred to as the *base*.

The only valid object within the **RUBY** element is the **RT** element. Text not contained within the ruby text object, **RT**, is assumed to be a part of the base.

This element is available in HTML and script as of Internet Explorer 5.

Attributes/Properties

CLASS

className	dir	id	innerHTML[*]
innerText[*]	lang	language	name
offsetHeight[*]	offsetLeft[*]	offsetParent[*]	offsetTop[*]
offsetWidth[*]	outerHTML[*]	outerText[*]	readyState[*]
		STYLE[†]	
recordNumber[*]	scopeName[*]		tabIndex
tagName[*]	tagUrn[*]	title	

* This property has no corresponding attribute.

† This attribute has no corresponding property.

Methods

addBehavior	blur	componentFromPoint	focus
getExpression	removeBehavior	removeExpression	setExpression

Events

onafterupdate	onbeforeupdate	onblur	onclick
ondblclick	ondragstart	onerrorupdate	onfilterchange
onfocus	onhelp	onkeydown	onkeypress
onkeyup	onmousedown	onmousemove	onmouseout
onmouseover	onmouseup	onreadystatechange	onselectstart

Collections

behaviorUrns   children   filters

Default Behaviors

clientCaps   download   homePage

CSS Properties

Note For a list of corresponding attributes, see Appendix C.

backgroundPositionX*	backgroundPositionY*	behavior	direction
layoutGridMode	overflow	overflowX	overflowY
pixelBottom*	pixelHeight*	pixelLeft*	pixelRight*
pixelTop*	pixelWidth*	posBottom*	posHeight*
position	posLeft*	posRight*	posTop*
posWidth*	rubyAlign	rubyOverhang	rubyPosition
styleFloat	textAutospace	unicodeBidi	width

* This property has no corresponding attribute.

Example

The following example shows how to use the **RUBY** element to specify one string of text as the base and a second string of text as the ruby.

```
<RUBY>
   Base Text
   <RT>Ruby Text
</RUBY>
```

To see this code in action, refer to the Web Workshop CD-ROM.

rule Object

Represents a style within a cascading style sheet (CSS) that consists of a selector and one or more declarations.

Remarks

The **rule** object defines a set of CSS attributes applied to a set of HTML elements. For example, a rule consisting of the selector **H1** and the declaration `font-family:Arial` defines all **H1** elements to render in the default font.

This object is available in script as of Internet Explorer 5.

Attributes/Properties

Note These properties have no corresponding attributes.

readOnly	**runtimeStyle**	**selectorText**	**style**

Example

The following example shows how to define a single rule.

```
<STYLE>
    H1 { color: red; }
</STYLE>
```

If the style sheet containing this rule is the first style sheet in the document, the code in the following example returns the **rule** object associated with the rule.

```
oRule=document.styleSheets(0).rules(0)
```

runtimeStyle Object

Represents the cascaded format and style of the object that overrides the format and style specified in global style sheets, inline styles, and HTML attributes.

Remarks

The **runtimeStyle** object sets and retrieves the format and style of an object, and overrides existing formats and styles in the process. Other than having precedence over the **style** object and not persisting, the **runtimeStyle** object is equivalent to the **style** object.

Attributes/Properties

Note These properties have no corresponding attributes.

background	backgroundAttachment	backgroundColor
backgroundImage	backgroundPosition	backgroundPositionX
backgroundPositionY	backgroundRepeat	border
borderBottom	borderBottomColor	borderBottomStyle
borderBottomWidth	borderColor	borderLeft
borderLeftColor	borderLeftStyle	borderLeftWidth
borderRight	borderRightColor	borderRightStyle
borderRightWidth	borderStyle	borderTop
borderTopColor	borderTopStyle	borderTopWidth
borderWidth	bottom	clear
clip	color	cssText
cursor	direction	display
filter	font	fontFamily
fontSize	fontStyle	fontVariant
fontWeight	height	layoutGrid
layoutGridChar	layoutGridCharSpacing	layoutGridLine
layoutGridMode	layoutGridType	left
letterSpacing	lineHeight	listStyle
listStyleImage	listStylePosition	listStyleType
margin	marginBottom	marginLeft
marginRight	marginTop	overflow
overflowX	overflowY	padding
paddingBottom	paddingLeft	paddingRight
paddingTop	pageBreakAfter	pageBreakBefore
pixelBottom	pixelHeight	pixelLeft
pixelRight	pixelTop	pixelWidth
posBottom	posHeight	position

DHTML Objects

Attributes/Properties *(continued)*

Note These properties have no corresponding attributes.

posLeft	**posRight**	**posTop**
posWidth	**right**	**styleFloat**
tableLayout	**textAlign**	**textDecoration**
textDecorationBlink	**textDecorationLineThrough**	**textDecorationNone**
textDecorationOverline	**textDecorationUnderline**	**textIndent**
textTransform	**top**	**unicodeBidi**
verticalAlign	**visibility**	**width**
zIndex		

Example

The following example shows how setting a value on the **runtimeStyle** object affects the **currentStyle** object, but not the **style** object.

```
<STYLE>
function fnChangeValue(sValue){
   if(oDIV.runtimeStyle.backgroundColor == oDIV.style.backgroundColor){
      sValue="";
   }
   oDIV.runtimeStyle.backgroundColor = sValue;
   alert(oDIV.style.backgroundColor +
      "\n" + oDIV.currentStyle.backgroundColor +
      "\n" + oDIV.runtimeStyle.backgroundColor);
}
</SCRIPT>

<DIV ID = "oDIV">
This is a demonstration DIV.
</DIV>

<INPUT TYPE = "button" VALUE = "Change Color" onclick="fnChangeValue('blue')">
```

To see this code in action, refer to the Web Workshop CD-ROM.

Applies To

  WIN16   WIN32   MAC   UNIX

A, ACRONYM, ADDRESS, APPLET, AREA, B, BASE, BASEFONT, BGSOUND, BIG, BLOCKQUOTE, BODY, BR, BUTTON, CAPTION, CENTER, CITE, CODE, COL, COLGROUP, COMMENT, DD, DEL, DFN, DIR, DIV, DL, DT, EM, EMBED, FIELDSET, FONT, FORM, FRAME, FRAMESET, HEAD, Hn, HR, HTML, I,

Applies To *(continued)*

 WIN16   WIN32   MAC   UNIX

IFRAME, IMG, INPUT type=button, INPUT type=checkbox, INPUT type=file, INPUT type=hidden, INPUT type=image, INPUT type=password, INPUT type=radio, INPUT type=reset, INPUT type=submit, INPUT type=text, INS, KBD, LABEL, LEGEND, LI, LINK, LISTING, MAP, MARQUEE, MENU, META, NEXTID, NOBR, OBJECT, OL, OPTION, P, PLAINTEXT, PRE, Q, rule, S, SAMP, SCRIPT, SELECT, SMALL, SPAN, STRIKE, STRONG, SUB, SUP, TABLE, TBODY, TD, TEXTAREA, TFOOT, TH, THEAD, TITLE, TR, TT, U, UL, VAR, XMP

S Element | S Object

Renders text in strike-through type.

Remarks

The **S** element is an inline element and requires a closing tag.

This element is available in HTML as of Internet Explorer 3.0 and in script as of Internet Explorer 4.0.

Attributes/Properties

canHaveChildren[*]	CLASS className	clientHeight[*]	clientLeft[*]
clientTop[*]	clientWidth[*]	currentStyle[*]	dir
firstChild[*]	id	innerHTML[*]	innerText[*]
isTextEdit[*]	lang	language	lastChild[*]
nextSibling[*]	nodeName[*]	nodeType[*]	nodeValue[*]
offsetHeight[*]	offsetLeft[*]	offsetParent[*]	offsetTop[*]
offsetWidth[*]	outerHTML[*]	outerText[*]	parentElement[*]
parentNode[*]	parentTextEdit[*]	previousSibling[*]	readyState[*]
recordNumber[*]	runtimeStyle[*]	scopeName[*]	scrollHeight[*]
scrollLeft[*]	scrollTop[*]	scrollWidth[*]	sourceIndex[*]
style	tabIndex	tagName[*]	tagUrn[*]
title	uniqueID[*]		

[*]   This property has no corresponding attribute.

Methods

addBehavior	appendChild	applyElement
attachEvent	blur	clearAttributes
click	cloneNode	componentFromPoint
contains	detachEvent	focus
getAdjacentText	getAttribute	getBoundingClientRect
getClientRects	getElementsByTagName	getExpression
hasChildNodes	insertAdjacentElement	insertAdjacentHTML
insertAdjacentText	insertBefore	mergeAttributes
releaseCapture	removeAttribute	removeBehavior
removeChild	removeExpression	removeNode
replaceAdjacentText	replaceChild	replaceNode
scrollIntoView	setAttribute	setCapture
setExpression	swapNode	

Events

onbeforecopy	onbeforecut	onbeforepaste	onblur
onclick	oncopy	oncut	ondblclick
ondrag	ondragend	ondragenter	ondragleave
ondragover	ondragstart	ondrop	onfocus
onhelp	onkeydown	onkeypress	onkeyup
onlosecapture	onmousedown	onmousemove	onmouseout
onmouseover	onmouseup	onpaste	onpropertychange
onreadystatechange	onresize	onselectstart	

Collections

all	attributes	behaviorUrns	childNodes	children

Default Behaviors

clientCaps	download	homePage	httpFolder	saveFavorite
saveHistory	saveSnapshot	time	userData	

CSS Properties

Note For a list of corresponding attributes, see Appendix C.

background	**backgroundColor**	**backgroundImage**
backgroundPosition	**backgroundPositionX**[*]	**backgroundPositionY**[*]
backgroundRepeat	**behavior**	**bottom**
clear	**color**	**cursor**
direction	**font**	**fontFamily**
fontSize	**fontStyle**	**fontVariant**
fontWeight	**layoutGridMode**	**left**
letterSpacing	**lineHeight**	**overflow**
overflowX	**overflowY**	**pixelBottom**[*]
pixelHeight[*]	**pixelLeft**[*]	**pixelRight**[*]
pixelTop[*]	**pixelWidth**[*]	**posBottom**[*]
posHeight[*]	**position**	**posLeft**[*]
posRight[*]	**posTop**[*]	**posWidth**[*]
right	**styleFloat**	**textAutospace**
textDecoration	**textDecorationBlink**[*]	**textDecorationLineThrough**[*]
textDecorationNone[*]	**textDecorationOverline**[*]	**textDecorationUnderline**[*]
textTransform	**top**	**unicodeBidi**
visibility	**width**	**wordSpacing**
zIndex		

[*] This property has no corresponding attribute.

Example

The following example shows how to use the **S** element to create strike-through type.

```
<S>This text has a line through it.</S>
```

SAMP Element | SAMP Object

Specifies a code sample.

Remarks

The **SAMP** element is an inline element and requires a closing tag.

This element is available in HTML as of Internet Explorer 3.0 and in script as of Internet Explorer 4.0.

Attributes/Properties

	CLASS		
canHaveChildren[*]	className	clientHeight[*]	clientLeft[*]
clientTop[*]	clientWidth[*]	currentStyle[*]	dir
firstChild[*]	id	innerHTML[*]	innerText[*]
isTextEdit[*]	lang	language	lastChild[*]
nextSibling[*]	nodeName[*]	nodeType[*]	nodeValue[*]
offsetHeight[*]	offsetLeft[*]	offsetParent[*]	offsetTop[*]
offsetWidth[*]	outerHTML[*]	outerText[*]	parentElement[*]
parentNode[*]	parentTextEdit[*]	previousSibling[*]	readyState[*]
recordNumber[*]	runtimeStyle[*]	scopeName[*]	scrollHeight[*]
scrollLeft[*]	scrollTop[*]	scrollWidth[*]	sourceIndex[*]
style	tabIndex	tagName[*]	tagUrn[*]
title	uniqueID[*]		

[*] This property has no corresponding attribute.

Methods

addBehavior	appendChild	applyElement
attachEvent	blur	clearAttributes
click	cloneNode	componentFromPoint
contains	detachEvent	focus
getAdjacentText	getAttribute	getBoundingClientRect
getClientRects	getElementsByTagName	getExpression
hasChildNodes	insertAdjacentElement	insertAdjacentHTML

Methods *(continued)*

InsertAdjacentText	insertBefore	mergeAttributes
releaseCapture	removeAttribute	removeBehavior
removeChild	removeExpression	removeNode
replaceAdjacentText	replaceChild	replaceNode
scrollIntoView	setAttribute	setCapture
setExpression	swapNode	

Events

onbeforecopy	onbeforecut	onbeforepaste	onblur
onclick	oncopy	oncut	ondblclick
ondrag	ondragend	ondragenter	ondragleave
ondragover	ondragstart	ondrop	onfocus
onhelp	onkeydown	onkeypress	onkeyup
onlosecapture	onmousedown	onmousemove	onmouseout
onmouseover	onmouseup	onpaste	onpropertychange
onreadystatechange	onresize	onselectstart	

Collections

all	attributes	behaviorUrns	childNodes	children

Default Behaviors

clientCaps	download	homePage	httpFolder	saveFavorite
saveHistory	saveSnapshot	time	userData	

CSS Properties

Note For a list of corresponding attributes, see Appendix C.

background	backgroundColor	backgroundImage
backgroundPosition	backgroundPositionX*	backgroundPositionY*
backgroundRepeat	behavior	bottom
clear	color	cursor

*   This property has no corresponding attribute.

CSS Properties *(continued)*

Note For a list of corresponding attributes, see Appendix C.

direction	**font**	**fontFamily**
fontSize	**fontStyle**	**fontVariant**
fontWeight	**layoutGridMode**	**left**
letterSpacing	**lineHeight**	**overflow**
overflowX	**overflowY**	**pixelBottom**[*]
pixelHeight[*]	**pixelLeft**[*]	**pixelRight**[*]
pixelTop[*]	**pixelWidth**[*]	**posBottom**[*]
posHeight[*]	**position**	**posLeft**[*]
posRight[*]	**posTop**[*]	**posWidth**[*]
right	**styleFloat**	**textAutospace**
textDecoration	**textDecorationBlink**[*]	**textDecorationLineThrough**[*]
textDecorationNone[*]	**textDecorationOverline**[*]	**textDecorationUnderline**[*]
textTransform	**top**	**unicodeBidi**
visibility	**width**	**wordSpacing**
zIndex		

[*] This property has no corresponding attribute.

Example

The following example shows how to use **SAMP** to create a code sample.

```
<SAMP>Here is some text in a small fixed-width font.</SAMP>
```

screen Object

Contains information about the client's screen and rendering capabilities.

Remarks

This object is available in script as of Internet Explorer 4.0.

Attributes/Properties

Note These properties have no corresponding attributes.

availHeight	**availWidth**	**bufferDepth**	**colorDepth**
fontSmoothingEnabled	**height**	**updateInterval**	**width**

Applies To

 WIN16   WIN32   MAC   UNIX

window

SCRIPT Element | SCRIPT Object

Specifies a script for the page that is interpreted by a script engine.

Remarks

The **SCRIPT** element is a block element and requires a closing tag.

Code within the **SCRIPT** block that is not contained within a function is executed immediately as the page is loaded. To keep scripts from being displayed on down-level browsers, nest the **SCRIPT** block within a **COMMENT** block.

Script appearing after a **FRAMESET** element is ignored.

This element is available in HTML as of Internet Explorer 3.0 and in script as of Internet Explorer 4.0.

Attributes/Properties

clientHeight[*]	**clientLeft**[*]	**clientTop**[*]	**clientWidth**[*]
defer	**event**	**firstChild**[*]	**FOR** **htmlFor**
id	**innerHTML**[*]	**innerText**[*]	**isTextEdit**[*]
lang	**language**	**lastChild**[*]	**nextSibling**[*]
nodeName[*]	**nodeType**[*]	**nodeValue**[*]	**parentElement**[*]
parentNode[*]	**parentTextEdit**[*]	**previousSibling**[*]	**readyState**[*]
recordNumber[*]	**runtimeStyle**[*]	**scopeName**[*]	**scrollHeight**[*]
scrollLeft[*]	**scrollTop**[*]	**scrollWidth**[*]	**sourceIndex**[*]
src	**style**[*]	**tagName**[*]	**tagUrn**[*]
text[*]	**type**	**uniqueID**[*]	

[*]   This property has no corresponding attribute.

Methods

addBehavior	**applyElement**	**attachEvent**
clearAttributes	**cloneNode**	**componentFromPoint**
contains	**detachEvent**	**getAdjacentText**
getAttribute	**getElementsByTagName**	**hasChildNodes**
insertAdjacentElement	**mergeAttributes**	**removeAttribute**
removeBehavior	**replaceAdjacentText**	**setAttribute**
swapNode		

Events

onerror	**onload**	**onpropertychange**	**onreadystatechange**

Collections

all	**attributes**	**behaviorUrns**	**childNodes**	**children**

Default Behaviors

clientCaps	**download**	**homePage**	**saveSnapshot**

CSS Properties

Note For a list of corresponding attributes, see Appendix C.

backgroundPositionX[*]	**backgroundPositionY**[*]	**behavior**
layoutGridMode	**pixelBottom**[*]	**pixelHeight**[*]
pixelLeft[*]	**pixelRight**[*]	**pixelTop**[*]
pixelWidth[*]	**posBottom**[*]	**posHeight**[*]
posLeft[*]	**posRight**[*]	**posTop**[*]
posWidth[*]	**textAutospace**	**width**

[*] This property has no corresponding attribute.

SELECT Element | SELECT Object

Denotes a list box or drop-down list.

Remarks

The **SELECT** element is an inline element and requires a closing tag.

This element is available in HTML and script as of Internet Explorer 3.0.

Attributes/Properties

			CLASS
accessKey	**align**	**canHaveChildren**[*]	**className**
clientHeight[*]	**clientLeft**[*]	**clientTop**[*]	**clientWidth**[*]
currentStyle[*]	**dataFld**	**dataSrc**	**dir**
disabled	**firstChild**[*]	**form**[*]	**id**
innerHTML[*]	**innerText**[*]	**isTextEdit**[*]	**lang**
language	**lastChild**[*]	**length**[*]	**multiple**
name	**nextSibling**[*]	**nodeName**[*]	**nodeType**[*]
nodeValue[*]	**offsetHeight**[*]	**offsetLeft**[*]	**offsetParent**[*]
offsetTop[*]	**offsetWidth**[*]	**outerHTML**[*]	**outerText**[*]
parentElement[*]	**parentNode**[*]	**parentTextEdit**[*]	**previousSibling**[*]
readyState[*]	**recordNumber**[*]	**runtimeStyle**[*]	**scopeName**[*]
scrollHeight[*]	**scrollLeft**[*]	**scrollTop**[*]	**scrollWidth**[*]
selectedIndex[*]	**size**	**sourceIndex**[*]	**style**
tabIndex	**tagName**[*]	**tagUrn**[*]	**title**
type	**uniqueID**[*]		

[*]   This property has no corresponding attribute.

Methods

addBehavior	**appendChild**	**applyElement**
attachEvent	**blur**	**clearAttributes**
click	**cloneNode**	**componentFromPoint**

Methods *(continued)*

contains	detachEvent	focus
getAdjacentText	getAttribute	getBoundingClientRect
getClientRects	getElementsByTagName	getExpression
hasChildNodes	insertAdjacentElement	insertAdjacentHTML
insertAdjacentText	insertBefore	mergeAttributes
releaseCapture	removeAttribute	removeBehavior
removeChild	removeExpression	removeNode
replaceAdjacentText	replaceChild	replaceNode
scrollIntoView	setAttribute	setCapture
setExpression	swapNode	urns

Events

onbeforeeditfocus	onblur	onchange	onclick
ondblclick	ondragenter	ondragleave	ondragover
ondrop	onfocus	onhelp	onkeydown
onkeypress	onkeyup	onlosecapture	onmousedown
onmousemove	onmouseout	onmouseover	onmouseup
onpropertychange	onreadystatechange	onresize	onscroll
onselectstart			

Collections

all	attributes	behaviorUrns	childNodes	children	options

Default Behaviors

clientCaps	download	homePage	httpFolder	saveFavorite
saveHistory	saveSnapshot	time	userData	

CSS Properties

Note For a list of corresponding attributes, see Appendix C.

background	**backgroundColor**	**backgroundImage**
backgroundPosition	**backgroundPositionX**[*]	**backgroundPositionY**[*]
backgroundRepeat	**behavior**	**bottom**
clear	**color**	**direction**
display	**font**	**fontFamily**
fontSize	**fontStyle**	**fontVariant**
fontWeight	**layoutGridMode**	**left**
letterSpacing	**lineHeight**	**overflow**
overflowX	**overflowY**	**pixelBottom**[*]
pixelHeight[*]	**pixelLeft**[*]	**pixelRight**[*]
pixelTop[*]	**pixelWidth**[*]	**posBottom**[*]
posHeight[*]	**position**	**posLeft**[*]
posRight[*]	**posTop**[*]	**posWidth**[*]
right	**styleFloat**	**textAutospace**
textDecoration	**textDecorationBlink**[*]	**textDecorationLineThrough**[*]
textDecorationNone[*]	**textDecorationOverline**[*]	**textDecorationUnderline**[*]
textTransform	**top**	**unicodeBidi**
visibility	**width**	**wordSpacing**

[*] This property has no corresponding attribute.

Example

The following example shows how to create a drop-down list box. The **SIZE** attribute defaults to 1, so it could be omitted here.

```
<SELECT NAME="Cats" SIZE="1">
<OPTION VALUE="1">Calico
<OPTION VALUE="2">Tortie
<OPTION VALUE="3" SELECTED>Siamese
</SELECT>
```

The next example shows how to create a multi-select list box by setting the **SIZE** and **MULTIPLE** attributes. To retrieve the selected options for a multi-select list box, iterate through the **options** collection and check for **SELECTED** set to `true`.

```
<SELECT NAME="Cars" SIZE="3" MULTIPLE>
<OPTION VALUE="1" SELECTED>BMW
<OPTION VALUE="2">PORSCHE
<OPTION VALUE="3" SELECTED>MERCEDES
</SELECT>
```

The following example shows how to add a new option to the end of an existing **SELECT** list. In JScript (compatible with ECMA 262 language specification) and Javascript, the new **Option** constructor can also be used.

```
var oOption = document.createElement("OPTION");
oOption.text="Apples";
oOption.value="5";
document.all.oMyList.add(oOption);
```

selection Object

Represents the active selection, which is a highlighted block of text, and/or other elements in the document on which a user or a script can carry out some action.

Remarks

You typically use the **selection** object as input from the user to identify what portion of the document to act on, or as output to the user showing the results of an action.

Users and scripts can create selections. Users create selections by dragging the mouse over a portion of the document. Scripts create selections by calling the **select** method on a text range or similar object. To retrieve the active selection, apply the **selection** keyword to the document object. To carry out work on a selection, create a text range object from the selection using the **createRange** method.

A document can have only one selection at a time. The selection has a type that determines whether it is empty or contains a block of text and/or elements. Although an empty selection contains nothing, you can use it to mark a position in the document.

This object is available in script as of Internet Explorer 4.0.

Attributes/Properties

type[*]

[*] This property has no corresponding attribute.

Methods

clear   **createRange**   **empty**

Applies To

 WIN16   WIN32   MAC   UNIX

document

SMALL Element | SMALL Object

Specifies that the enclosed text should be displayed in a smaller font.

Remarks

The **SMALL** element is an inline element and requires a closing tag.

This element is available in HTML as of Internet Explorer 3.0 and in script as of Internet Explorer 4.0.

Attributes/Properties

	CLASS		
canHaveChildren*	className	clientHeight*	clientLeft*
clientTop*	clientWidth*	currentStyle*	dir
firstChild*	id	innerHTML*	innerText*
isTextEdit*	lang	language	lastChild*
nextSibling*	nodeName*	nodeType*	nodeValue*
offsetHeight*	offsetLeft*	offsetParent*	offsetTop*
offsetWidth*	outerHTML*	outerText*	parentElement*
parentNode*	parentTextEdit*	previousSibling*	readyState*
recordNumber*	runtimeStyle*	scopeName*	scrollHeight*
scrollLeft*	scrollTop*	scrollWidth*	sourceIndex*
style	tabIndex	tagName*	tagUrn*
title	uniqueID*		

*   This property has no corresponding attribute.

Methods

addBehavior	appendChild	applyElement
attachEvent	blur	clearAttributes
click	cloneNode	componentFromPoint

Methods *(continued)*

contains	detachEvent	focus
getAdjacentText	getAttribute	getBoundingClientRect
getClientRects	getElementsByTagName	getExpression
hasChildNodes	insertAdjacentElement	insertAdjacentHTML
insertAdjacentText	insertBefore	mergeAttributes
releaseCapture	removeAttribute	removeBehavior
removeChild	removeExpression	removeNode
replaceAdjacentText	replaceChild	replaceNode
scrollIntoView	setAttribute	setCapture
setExpression	swapNode	

Events

onbeforecopy	onbeforecut	onbeforepaste	onblur
onclick	oncopy	oncut	ondblclick
ondrag	ondragend	ondragenter	ondragleave
ondragover	ondragstart	ondrop	onfocus
onhelp	onkeydown	onkeypress	onkeyup
onlosecapture	onmousedown	onmousemove	onmouseout
onmouseover	onmouseup	onpaste	onpropertychange
onreadystatechange	onresize	onselectstart	

Collections

all	attributes	behaviorUrns	childNodes	children

Default Behaviors

clientCaps	download	homePage	httpFolder	saveFavorite
saveHistory	saveSnapshot	time	userData	

CSS Properties

Note For a list of corresponding attributes, see Appendix C.

background	**backgroundColor**	**backgroundImage**
backgroundPosition	**backgroundPositionX**[*]	**backgroundPositionY**[*]
backgroundRepeat	**behavior**	**bottom**
clear	**color**	**cursor**
direction	**font**	**fontFamily**
fontSize	**fontStyle**	**fontVariant**
fontWeight	**layoutGridMode**	**left**
letterSpacing	**lineHeight**	**overflow**
overflowX	**overflowY**	**pixelBottom**[*]
pixelHeight[*]	**pixelLeft**[*]	**pixelRight**[*]
pixelTop[*]	**pixelWidth**[*]	**posBottom**[*]
posHeight[*]	**position**	**posLeft**[*]
posRight[*]	**posTop**[*]	**posWidth**[*]
right	**styleFloat**	**textAutospace**
textDecoration	**textDecorationBlink**[*]	**textDecorationLineThrough**[*]
textDecorationNone[*]	**textDecorationOverline**[*]	**textDecorationUnderline**[*]
textTransform	**top**	**unicodeBidi**
visibility	**width**	**wordSpacing**
zIndex		

[*] This property has no corresponding attribute.

Example

The following example shows how to use the **SMALL** element to display text in a smaller font.

```
<SMALL>This text is smaller</SMALL> than this text.
```

SPAN Element | SPAN Object

Specifies an inline text container.

Remarks

The **SPAN** element is an inline element and requires a closing tag.

This element is especially useful for applying cascading style sheets (CSS) styles.

This element is available in HTML as of Internet Explorer 3.0 and in script as of Internet Explorer 4.0.

Attributes/Properties

	CLASS		
canHaveChildren[*]	className	clientHeight[*]	clientLeft[*]
clientTop[*]	clientWidth[*]	currentStyle[*]	dataFld
dataFormatAs	dataSrc	dir	firstChild[*]
id	innerHTML[*]	innerText[*]	isTextEdit[*]
lang	language	lastChild[*]	nextSibling[*]
nodeName[*]	nodeType[*]	nodeValue[*]	offsetHeight[*]
offsetLeft[*]	offsetParent[*]	offsetTop[*]	offsetWidth[*]
outerHTML[*]	outerText[*]	parentElement[*]	parentNode[*]
parentTextEdit[*]	previousSibling[*]	readyState[*]	recordNumber[*]
runtimeStyle[*]	scopeName[*]	scrollHeight[*]	scrollLeft[*]
scrollTop[*]	scrollWidth[*]	sourceIndex[*]	style
tabIndex	tagName[*]	tagUrn[*]	title
uniqueID[*]			

[*]   This property has no corresponding attribute.

Methods

addBehavior	appendChild	applyElement
attachEvent	blur	clearAttributes
click	cloneNode	componentFromPoint
contains	detachEvent	doScroll
focus	getAdjacentText	getAttribute

Methods *(continued)*

getBoundingClientRect	getClientRects	getElementsByTagName
getExpression	hasChildNodes	insertAdjacentElement
insertAdjacentHTML	insertAdjacentText	insertBefore
mergeAttributes	releaseCapture	removeAttribute
removeBehavior	removeChild	removeExpression
removeNode	replaceAdjacentText	replaceChild
replaceNode	scrollIntoView	setAttribute
setCapture	setExpression	swapNode

Events

onbeforecopy	onbeforecut	onbeforeeditfocus	onbeforepaste
onblur	onclick	oncopy	oncut
ondblclick	ondrag	ondragend	ondragenter
ondragleave	ondragover	ondragstart	ondrop
onfilterchange	onfocus	onhelp	onkeydown
onkeypress	onkeyup	onlosecapture	onmousedown
onmousemove	onmouseout	onmouseover	onmouseup
onpaste	onpropertychange	onreadystatechange	onresize
onselectstart			

Collections

all	attributes	behaviorUrns	childNodes	children	filters

Default Behaviors

clientCaps	download	homePage	httpFolder	saveFavorite
saveHistory	saveSnapshot	time	userData	

CSS Properties

Note For a list of corresponding attributes, see Appendix C.

background	**backgroundColor**	**backgroundImage**
backgroundPosition	**backgroundPositionX**[*]	**backgroundPositionY**[*]
backgroundRepeat	**behavior**	**border**
borderBottom	**borderBottomColor**	**borderBottomStyle**
borderBottomWidth	**borderColor**	**borderLeft**
borderLeftColor	**borderLeftStyle**	**borderLeftWidth**
borderRight	**borderRightColor**	**borderRightStyle**
borderRightWidth	**borderStyle**	**borderTop**
borderTopColor	**borderTopStyle**	**borderTopWidth**
borderWidth	**bottom**	**clear**
color	**cursor**	**direction**
display	**filter**	**font**
fontFamily	**fontSize**	**fontStyle**
fontVariant	**fontWeight**	**height**
layoutGridMode	**left**	**letterSpacing**
lineHeight	**margin**	**marginBottom**
marginLeft	**marginRight**	**marginTop**
overflow	**overflowX**	**overflowY**
pixelBottom[*]	**pixelHeight**[*]	**pixelLeft**[*]
pixelRight[*]	**pixelTop**[*]	**pixelWidth**[*]
posBottom[*]	**posHeight**[*]	**position**
posLeft[*]	**posRight**[*]	**posTop**[*]
posWidth[*]	**right**	**styleFloat**
textAutospace	**textDecoration**	**textDecorationBlink**[*]
textDecorationLineThrough[*]	**textDecorationNone**[*]	**textDecorationOverline**[*]
textDecorationUnderline[*]	**textTransform**	**top**
unicodeBidi	**verticalAlign**	**visibility**
width	**wordSpacing**	**zIndex**

* This property has no corresponding attribute.

Example

The following example shows how to use the **SPAN** element to create an inline text container.

```
<P>This paragraph contains a single <SPAN STYLE="color: blue">blue</SPAN> word.
```

STRIKE Element | STRIKE Object

Renders text in strike-through type.

Remarks

The **STRIKE** element is an inline element and requires a closing tag.

This element is available in HTML as of Internet Explorer 3.0 and in script as of Internet Explorer 4.0.

Attributes/Properties

	CLASS		
canHaveChildren[*]	className	clientHeight[*]	clientLeft[*]
clientTop[*]	clientWidth[*]	currentStyle[*]	dir
firstChild[*]	id	innerHTML[*]	innerText[*]
isTextEdit[*]	lang	language	lastChild[*]
nextSibling[*]	nodeName[*]	nodeType[*]	nodeValue[*]
offsetHeight[*]	offsetLeft[*]	offsetParent[*]	offsetTop[*]
offsetWidth[*]	outerHTML[*]	outerText[*]	parentElement[*]
parentNode[*]	parentTextEdit[*]	previousSibling[*]	readyState[*]
recordNumber[*]	runtimeStyle[*]	scopeName[*]	scrollHeight[*]
scrollLeft[*]	scrollTop[*]	scrollWidth[*]	sourceIndex[*]
style	tabIndex	tagName[*]	tagUrn[*]
title	uniqueID[*]		

[*] This property has no corresponding attribute.

Methods

addBehavior	appendChild	applyElement
attachEvent	blur	clearAttributes
click	cloneNode	componentFromPoint

Methods *(continued)*

contains	detachEvent	focus
getAdjacentText	getAttribute	getBoundingClientRect
getClientRects	getElementsByTagName	getExpression
hasChildNodes	insertAdjacentElement	insertAdjacentHTML
insertAdjacentText	insertBefore	mergeAttributes
releaseCapture	removeAttribute	removeBehavior
removeChild	removeExpression	removeNode
replaceAdjacentText	replaceChild	replaceNode
scrollIntoView	setAttribute	setCapture
setExpression	swapNode	

Events

onbeforecopy	onbeforecut	onbeforepaste	onblur
onclick	oncopy	oncut	ondblclick
ondrag	ondragend	ondragenter	ondragleave
ondragover	ondragstart	ondrop	onfocus
onhelp	onkeydown	onkeypress	onkeyup
onlosecapture	onmousedown	onmousemove	onmouseout
onmouseover	onmouseup	onpaste	onpropertychange
onreadystatechange	onresize	onselectstart	

Collections

all	attributes	behaviorUrns	childNodes	children

Default Behaviors

clientCaps	download	homePage	httpFolder	saveFavorite
saveHistory	saveSnapshot	time	userData	

CSS Properties

Note For a list of corresponding attributes, see Appendix C.

background	backgroundColor	backgroundImage
backgroundPosition	backgroundPositionX[*]	backgroundPositionY[*]
backgroundRepeat	behavior	bottom
clear	color	cursor
direction	font	fontFamily
fontSize	fontStyle	fontVariant
fontWeight	layoutGridMode	left
letterSpacing	lineHeight	overflow
overflowX	overflowY	pixelBottom[*]
pixelHeight[*]	pixelLeft[*]	pixelRight[*]
pixelTop[*]	pixelWidth[*]	posBottom[*]
posHeight[*]	position	posLeft[*]
posRight[*]	posTop[*]	posWidth[*]
right	styleFloat	textAutospace
textDecoration	textDecorationBlink[*]	textDecorationLineThrough[*]
textDecorationNone[*]	textDecorationOverline[*]	textDecorationUnderline[*]
textTransform	top	unicodeBidi
visibility	width	wordSpacing
zIndex		

[*] This property has no corresponding attribute.

Example

The following example shows how to use the **STRIKE** element to create strike-through type.

```
<STRIKE>This text has a line through it.</STRIKE>
```

STRONG Element | STRONG Object

Renders text in bold.

Remarks

The **STRONG** element is an inline element and requires a closing tag.

This element is available in HTML as of Internet Explorer 3.0 and in script as of Internet Explorer 4.0.

Attributes/Properties

	CLASS		
canHaveChildren[*]	className	clientHeight[*]	clientLeft[*]
clientTop[*]	clientWidth[*]	currentStyle[*]	dir
firstChild[*]	id	innerHTML[*]	innerText[*]
isTextEdit[*]	lang	language	lastChild[*]
nextSibling[*]	nodeName[*]	nodeType[*]	nodeValue[*]
offsetHeight[*]	offsetLeft[*]	offsetParent[*]	offsetTop[*]
offsetWidth[*]	outerHTML[*]	outerText[*]	parentElement[*]
parentNode[*]	parentTextEdit[*]	previousSibling[*]	readyState[*]
recordNumber[*]	runtimeStyle[*]	scopeName[*]	scrollHeight[*]
scrollLeft[*]	scrollTop[*]	scrollWidth[*]	sourceIndex[*]
style	tabIndex	tagName[*]	tagUrn[*]
title	uniqueID[*]		

[*] This property has no corresponding attribute.

Methods

addBehavior	appendChild	applyElement
attachEvent	blur	clearAttributes
click	cloneNode	componentFromPoint
contains	detachEvent	focus
getAdjacentText	getAttribute	getBoundingClientRect
getClientRects	getElementsByTagName	getExpression
hasChildNodes	insertAdjacentElement	insertAdjacentHTML

Methods *(continued)*

insertAdjacentText	insertBefore	mergeAttributes
releaseCapture	removeAttribute	removeBehavior
removeChild	removeExpression	removeNode
replaceAdjacentText	replaceChild	replaceNode
scrollIntoView	setAttribute	setCapture
setExpression	swapNode	

Events

onbeforecopy	onbeforecut	onbeforepaste	onblur
onclick	oncopy	oncut	ondblclick
ondrag	ondragend	ondragenter	ondragleave
ondragover	ondragstart	ondrop	onfocus
onhelp	onkeydown	onkeypress	onkeyup
onlosecapture	onmousedown	onmousemove	onmouseout
onmouseover	onmouseup	onpaste	onpropertychange
onreadystatechange	onresize	onselectstart	

Collections

all	attributes	behaviorUrns	childNodes	children

Default Behaviors

clientCaps	download	homePage	httpFolder	saveFavorite
saveHistory	saveSnapshot	time	userData	

CSS Properties

Note For a list of corresponding attributes, see Appendix C.

background	backgroundColor	backgroundImage
backgroundPosition	backgroundPositionX[*]	backgroundPositionY[*]
backgroundRepeat	behavior	bottom
clear	color	cursor
direction	font	fontFamily

[*] This property has no corresponding attribute.

CSS Properties *(continued)*

> **Note** For a list of corresponding attributes, see Appendix C.

fontSize	**fontStyle**	**fontVariant**
fontWeight	**layoutGridMode**	**left**
letterSpacing	**lineHeight**	**overflow**
overflowX	**overflowY**	**pixelBottom**[*]
pixelHeight[*]	**pixelLeft**[*]	**pixelRight**[*]
pixelTop[*]	**pixelWidth**[*]	**posBottom**[*]
posHeight[*]	**position**	**posLeft**[*]
posRight[*]	**posTop**[*]	**posWidth**[*]
right	**styleFloat**	**textAutospace**
textDecoration	**textDecorationBlink**[*]	**textDecorationLineThrough**[*]
textDecorationNone[*]	**textDecorationOverline**[*]	**textDecorationUnderline**[*]
textTransform	**top**	**unicodeBidi**
visibility	**width**	**wordSpacing**
zIndex		

*   This property has no corresponding attribute.

Example

> The following example shows how to use the **STRONG** element to emphasize text in bold.
>
> ```
> <STRONG>This text is strongly emphasized (shown as bold).</STRONG>
> ```

STYLE Element | style Object

> Specifies a style sheet for the page.

Remarks

> The **STYLE** element is a block element and requires a closing tag.
>
> The **STYLE** element should appear in the **HEAD** section of an HTML document. Internet Explorer 4.0 and later permit multiple style blocks.
>
> This element is available in HTML as of Internet Explorer 3.0 and in script as of Internet Explorer 4.0.

Attributes/Properties

behavior	**currentStyle**[*]	**innerHTML**[*]	**innerText**[*]
media	**parentElement**[*]	**type**	

[*] This property has no corresponding attribute.

Methods

addBehavior   **removeBehavior**

Events

onerror

Collections

behaviorUrns

Example

The following example shows how to enclose style declarations in the **STYLE** tag and change one of those settings using the **style** object.

```
<HEAD>
<STYLE>
   BODY {  background-color: white; color: black;  }
   H1 {  font: 8pt Arial bold;  }
   P  {  font: 10pt Arial; text-indent: 0.5in;  }
   A  {  text-decoration: none; color: blue;  }
</STYLE>
<SCRIPT>
    oParagraph.style.fontSize = 14;
</SCRIPT>
</HEAD>
<BODY>
<P>Sample Paragraph Text</P>
</BODY>
```

style Object

Represents the current settings of all possible inline styles for a given element.

Remarks

Inline styles are cascading style sheets (CSS) style assignments that you apply directly to individual HTML elements using the **STYLE=** attribute. Use the **style** object to examine these assignments and either make new assignments or change existing ones.

To retrieve the **style** object, apply the **style** keyword to an **element** object. To retrieve the current setting for an inline style, apply the corresponding style property to the **style** object.

The **style** object does not give access to the style assignments in style sheets. To obtain information about styles in style sheets, use the **styleSheets** collection to gain access to the individual style sheets defined in the document.

The following properties are not available when the **style** object is accessed from the **rule** object: **posHeight**, **posWidth**, **posTop**, **posLeft**, **pixelHeight**, **pixelWidth**, **pixelTop**, and **pixelLeft**.

This object is available in script as of Internet Explorer 4.0.

Attributes/Properties

background[*]	**backgroundAttachment**[*]	**backgroundColor**[*]
backgroundImage[*]	**backgroundPosition**[*]	**backgroundPositionX**[*]
backgroundPositionY[*]	**backgroundRepeat**[*]	**border**[*]
borderBottom[*]	**borderBottomColor**[*]	**borderBottomStyle**[*]
borderBottomWidth[*]	**borderColor**[*]	**borderLeft**[*]
borderLeftColor[*]	**borderLeftStyle**[*]	**borderLeftWidth**[*]
borderRight[*]	**borderRightColor**[*]	**borderRightStyle**[*]
borderRightWidth[*]	**borderStyle**[*]	**borderTop**[*]
borderTopColor[*]	**borderTopStyle**[*]	**borderTopWidth**[*]
borderWidth[*]	**bottom**[*]	**clear**[*]
clip[*]	**color**[*]	**cssText**[*]
cursor[*]	**direction**[*]	**display**[*]
filter[*]	**font**[*]	**fontFamily**[*]
fontSize[*]	**fontStyle**[*]	**fontVariant**[*]
fontWeight[*]	**height**[*]	**layoutGrid**[*]
layoutGridChar[*]	**layoutGridCharSpacing**[*]	**layoutGridLine**[*]
layoutGridMode[*]	**layoutGridType**[*]	**left**[*]
letterSpacing[*]	**lineHeight**[*]	**listStyle**[*]
listStyleImage[*]	**listStylePosition**[*]	**listStyleType**[*]

[*] This property has no corresponding attribute.

Attributes/Properties *(continued)*

margin*	marginBottom*	marginLeft*
marginRight*	marginTop*	overflow*
overflowX*	overflowY*	padding*
paddingBottom*	paddingLeft*	paddingRight*
paddingTop*	pageBreakAfter*	pageBreakBefore*
pixelBottom*	pixelHeight*	pixelLeft*
pixelRight*	pixelTop*	pixelWidth*
posBottom*	posHeight*	position*
posLeft*	posRight*	posTop*
posWidth*	right*	styleFloat*
tableLayout*	textAlign*	textDecoration*
textDecorationBlink*	textDecorationLineThrough*	textDecorationNone*
textDecorationOverline*	textDecorationUnderline*	textIndent*
textTransform*	top*	unicodeBidi*
verticalAlign*	visibility*	width*
zIndex*		

* This property has no corresponding attribute.

Methods

getExpression   removeExpression   setExpression

Examples

The following example shows how to set the document body text font to Verdana.

```
document.body.style.fontFamily = "Verdana"
```

The following example shows how to position all absolutely positioned images in the given document at the top of the document.

```
var oImages = document.all.tags("IMG");
if (oImages.length) {
    for (var iImg = 0; iImg < oImages.length; iImg++) {
        var oImg = oImages(iImg);
        if (oImg.style.position == "absolute") {
            oImg.style.top = 0;
        }
    }
}
```

Applies To

WIN16   WIN32   MAC   UNIX

A, ACRONYM, ADDRESS, APPLET, AREA, B, BASE, BASEFONT, BGSOUND,
BIG, BLOCKQUOTE, BODY, BR, BUTTON, CAPTION, CENTER, CITE, CODE,
COL, COLGROUP, COMMENT, DD, DEL, DFN, DIR, DIV, DL, DT, EM, EMBED,
FIELDSET, FONT, FORM, FRAME, FRAMESET, HEAD, Hn, HR, HTML, I,
IFRAME, IMG, INPUT type=button, INPUT type=checkbox, INPUT type=file,
INPUT type=hidden, INPUT type=image, INPUT type=password, INPUT type=radio,
INPUT type=reset, INPUT type=submit, INPUT type=text, INS, KBD, LABEL,
LEGEND, LI, LINK, LISTING, MAP, MARQUEE, MENU, META, NEXTID,
NOBR, OBJECT, OL, OPTION, P, PLAINTEXT, PRE, Q, rule, S, SAMP, SCRIPT,
SELECT, SMALL, SPAN, STRIKE, STRONG, SUB, SUP, TABLE, TBODY, TD,
TEXTAREA, TFOOT, TH, THEAD, TITLE, TR, TT, U, UL, VAR, XMP

styleSheet Object

Represents a single style sheet in the document.

Remarks

This object retrieves information about the style sheet, such as the URL of the source
file for the style sheet and the element in the document that owns (defines) the style
sheet. The object is also used to modify the style sheet.

You retrieve a style sheet object from the **styleSheets** collection or from the **imports**
collection. Each item in these collections is a style sheet. A **styleSheet** object is
available for a style sheet only if it is included in a document with a **STYLE** or **LINK**
element, or with an **@import** statement in a **STYLE** element.

This object is available in script as of Internet Explorer 4.0.

Attributes/Properties

Note These properties have no corresponding attributes.

disabled	id	owningElement	parentStyleSheet
readOnly	type		

Methods

addImport	addRule	removeRule

Collections

imports   **rules**

Default Behaviors

clientCaps   **download**   **homePage**

Example

The following example shows how to use the **styleSheet** object to change cascading style sheets (CSS) values from inline and imported styles.

```
<STYLE>
BODY {background-color: #CFCFCF;}
@import url("otherStyleSheet.css");
</STYLE>
<SCRIPT>
window.onload=fnInit;
function fnInit(){
    // Access a rule in styleSheet, change backgroundColor to blue.
    var oStyleSheet=document.styleSheets[0];
    var oRule=oStyleSheet.rules[0];
    oRule.backgroundColor="#0000FF";
    // Add a rule for P elements to have yellow backgrounds.
    oStyleSheet.addRule("P","background-color: #FFFF00;");
    // Change and imported rule:
    oStyleSheet.imports[0].color="#000000";
}
</SCRIPt>
```

Applies To

 WIN16   **WIN32**   **MAC**   **UNIX**

styleSheets

SUB Element | SUB Object

Specifies that the enclosed text should be displayed in subscript, using a smaller font than the current font.

Remarks

The **SUB** element is an inline element and requires a closing tag.

This element is available in HTML as of Internet Explorer 3.0 and in script as of Internet Explorer 4.0.

Attributes/Properties

	CLASS		
canHaveChildren[*]	className	clientHeight[*]	clientLeft[*]
clientTop[*]	clientWidth[*]	currentStyle[*]	dir
firstChild[*]	id	innerHTML[*]	innerText[*]
isTextEdit[*]	lang	language	lastChild[*]
nextSibling[*]	nodeName[*]	nodeType[*]	nodeValue[*]
offsetHeight[*]	offsetLeft[*]	offsetParent[*]	offsetTop[*]
offsetWidth[*]	outerHTML[*]	outerText[*]	parentElement[*]
parentNode[*]	parentTextEdit[*]	previousSibling[*]	readyState[*]
recordNumber[*]	runtimeStyle[*]	scopeName[*]	scrollHeight[*]
scrollLeft[*]	scrollTop[*]	scrollWidth[*]	sourceIndex[*]
style	tabIndex	tagName[*]	tagUrn[*]
title	uniqueID[*]		

[*] This property has no corresponding attribute.

Methods

addBehavior	appendChild	applyElement
attachEvent	blur	clearAttributes
click	cloneNode	componentFromPoint
contains	detachEvent	focus
getAdjacentText	getAttribute	getBoundingClientRect
getClientRects	getElementsByTagName	getExpression
hasChildNodes	insertAdjacentElement	insertAdjacentHTML
insertAdjacentText	insertBefore	mergeAttributes
releaseCapture	removeAttribute	removeBehavior
removeChild	removeExpression	removeNode
replaceAdjacentText	replaceChild	replaceNode
scrollIntoView	setAttribute	setCapture
setExpression	swapNode	

DHTML Objects

Events

onbeforecopy	onbeforecut	onbeforepaste	onblur
onclick	oncopy	oncut	ondblclick
ondrag	ondragend	ondragenter	ondragleave
ondragover	ondragstart	ondrop	onfocus
onhelp	onkeydown	onkeypress	onkeyup
onlosecapture	onmousedown	onmousemove	onmouseout
onmouseover	onmouseup	onpaste	onpropertychange
onreadystatechange	onresize	onselectstart	

Collections

all	attributes	behaviorUrns	childNodes	children

Default Behaviors

clientCaps	download	homePage	httpFolder	saveFavorite
saveHistory	saveSnapshot	time	userData	

CSS Properties

Note For a list of corresponding attributes, see Appendix C.

background	backgroundColor	backgroundImage
backgroundPosition	backgroundPositionX*	backgroundPositionY*
backgroundRepeat	behavior	bottom
clear	color	cursor
direction	font	fontFamily
fontSize	fontStyle	fontVariant
fontWeight	layoutGridMode	left
letterSpacing	lineHeight	overflow
overflowX	overflowY	pixelBottom*
pixelHeight*	pixelLeft*	pixelRight*
pixelTop*	pixelWidth*	posBottom*

* This property has no corresponding attribute.

CSS Properties *(continued)*

> **Note** For a list of corresponding attributes, see Appendix C.

posHeight[*]	position	posLeft[*]
posRight[*]	posTop[*]	posWidth[*]
right	styleFloat	textAutospace
textDecoration	textDecorationBlink[*]	textDecorationLineThrough[*]
textDecorationNone[*]	textDecorationOverline[*]	textDecorationUnderline[*]
textTransform	top	unicodeBidi
visibility	width	wordSpacing
zIndex		

* This property has no corresponding attribute.

Example

The following example shows how to use **SUB** to create (X_1, Y_1).

```
(X<SUB>1</SUB>,Y<SUB>1</SUB>)
```

SUP Element | SUP Object

Specifies that the enclosed text should be displayed in superscript, using a smaller font than the current font.

Remarks

The **SUP** element is an inline element and requires a closing tag.

This element is available in HTML as of Internet Explorer 3.0 and in script as of Internet Explorer 4.0.

Attributes/Properties

canHaveChildren[*]	CLASS className	clientHeight[*]	clientLeft[*]
clientTop[*]	clientWidth[*]	currentStyle[*]	dir
firstChild[*]	id	innerHTML[*]	innerText[*]
isTextEdit[*]	lang	language	lastChild[*]
nextSibling[*]	nodeName[*]	nodeType[*]	nodeValue[*]

* This property has no corresponding attribute.

Attributes/Properties *(continued)*

offsetHeight*	offsetLeft*	offsetParent*	offsetTop*
offsetWidth*	outerHTML*	outerText*	parentElement*
parentNode*	parentTextEdit*	previousSibling*	readyState*
recordNumber*	runtimeStyle*	scopeName*	scrollHeight*
scrollLeft*	scrollTop*	scrollWidth*	sourceIndex*
style	tabIndex	tagName*	tagUrn*
title	uniqueID*		

*   This property has no corresponding attribute.

Methods

addBehavior	appendChild	applyElement
attachEvent	blur	clearAttributes
click	cloneNode	componentFromPoint
contains	detachEvent	focus
getAdjacentText	getAttribute	getBoundingClientRect
getClientRects	getElementsByTagName	getExpression
hasChildNodes	insertAdjacentElement	insertAdjacentHTML
insertAdjacentText	insertBefore	mergeAttributes
releaseCapture	removeAttribute	removeBehavior
removeChild	removeExpression	removeNode
replaceAdjacentText	replaceChild	replaceNode
scrollIntoView	setAttribute	setCapture
setExpression	swapNode	

Events

onbeforecopy	onbeforecut	onbeforepaste	onblur
onclick	oncopy	oncut	ondblclick
ondrag	ondragend	ondragenter	ondragleave
ondragover	ondragstart	ondrop	onfocus
onhelp	onkeydown	onkeypress	onkeyup

Events (*continued*)

onlosecapture	onmousedown	onmousemove	onmouseout
onmouseover	onmouseup	onpaste	onpropertychange
onreadystatechange	onresize	onselectstart	

Collections

all	attributes	behaviorUrns	childNodes	children

Default Behaviors

clientCaps	download	homePage	httpFolder	saveFavorite
saveHistory	saveSnapshot	time	userData	

CSS Properties

Note For a list of corresponding attributes, see Appendix C.

background	backgroundColor	backgroundImage
backgroundPosition	backgroundPositionX[*]	backgroundPositionY[*]
backgroundRepeat	behavior	bottom
clear	color	cursor
direction	font	fontFamily
fontSize	fontStyle	fontVariant
fontWeight	layoutGridMode	left
letterSpacing	lineHeight	overflow
overflowX	overflowY	pixelBottom[*]
pixelHeight[*]	pixelLeft[*]	pixelRight[*]
pixelTop[*]	pixelWidth[*]	posBottom[*]
posHeight[*]	position	posLeft[*]
posRight[*]	posTop[*]	posWidth[*]
right	styleFloat	textAutospace
textDecoration	textDecorationBlink[*]	textDecorationLineThrough[*]
textDecorationNone[*]	textDecorationOverline[*]	textDecorationUnderline[*]
textTransform	top	unicodeBidi
visibility	width	wordSpacing
zIndex		

* This property has no corresponding attribute.

Example

The following example shows how to use **SUP** to create $X^2 + Y^2$.

```
X<SUP>2</SUP> + Y<SUP>2</SUP>
```

TABLE Element | TABLE Object

Specifies that the contained content is organized into a table with rows and columns.

Remarks

The following tags are valid within a table: **CAPTION, COL, COLGROUP, TBODY, TD, TFOOT, TH, THEAD,** and **TR.**

The **TABLE** element is a block element and requires a closing tag.

When a document is loading, modifications to a table are restricted until the **window.onload** event occurs. Read-only access is allowed at any time.

The **TABLE** object model is read-only for databound tables. For example, a script to remove a table row works correctly on an unbound table, but does not work on a databound table. The properties of a table object are still available, but changes to the bound data in a table have to be made to the data source.

This element is available in HTML as of Internet Explorer 3.0 and in script as of Internet Explorer 4.0.

Attributes/Properties

accessKey	align	background	bgColor
border	borderColor	borderColorDark[*]	borderColorLight[*]
canHaveChildren[*]	caption[*]	cellPadding	cellSpacing
CLASS			
className	clientHeight[*]	clientLeft[*]	clientTop[*]
clientWidth[*]	cols	currentStyle[*]	dataPageSize
dataSrc	dir	firstChild[*]	frame
height	id	innerHTML[*]	innerText[*]
isTextEdit[*]	lang	language	lastChild[*]
nextSibling[*]	nodeName[*]	nodeType[*]	nodeValue[*]
offsetHeight[*]	offsetLeft[*]	offsetParent[*]	offsetTop[*]

* This property has no corresponding attribute.

Attributes/Properties *(continued)*

offsetWidth[*]	outerHTML[*]	outerText[*]	parentElement[*]
parentNode[*]	parentTextEdit[*]	previousSibling[*]	readyState[*]
recordNumber[*]	rules	runtimeStyle[*]	scopeName[*]
scrollHeight[*]	scrollLeft[*]	scrollTop[*]	scrollWidth[*]
sourceIndex[*]	style	tabIndex	tagName[*]
tagUrn[*]	tFoot[*]	tHead[*]	title
uniqueID[*]	width		

[*]   This property has no corresponding attribute.

Methods

addBehavior	appendChild	applyElement
attachEvent	blur	clearAttributes
click	cloneNode	componentFromPoint
contains	createCaption	createTFoot
createTHead	deleteCaption	detachEvent
firstPage	focus	getAdjacentText
getAttribute	getBoundingClientRect	getClientRects
getElementsByTagName	getExpression	hasChildNodes
insertAdjacentElement	insertBefore	insertRow
lastPage	mergeAttributes	nextPage
previousPage	refresh	releaseCapture
removeAttribute	removeBehavior	removeChild
removeExpression	removeNode	replaceAdjacentText
replaceChild	replaceNode	scrollIntoView
setAttribute	setCapture	setExpression
swapNode		

Events

onbeforeeditfocus	onblur	onclick	ondblclick
ondrag	ondragend	ondragenter	ondragleave
ondragover	ondragstart	ondrop	onfilterchange

DHTML Objects

Events *(continued)*

onfocus	onhelp	onkeydown	onkeypress
onkeyup	onlosecapture	onmousedown	onmousemove
onmouseout	onmouseover	onmouseup	onpropertychange
onreadystatechange	onresize	onscroll	onselectstart

Collections

all	attributes	behaviorUrns	cells	childNodes
children	filters	rows	tBodies	

Default Behaviors

clientCaps	download	homePage	httpFolder	saveFavorite
saveHistory	saveSnapshot	time	userData	

CSS Properties

Note For a list of corresponding attributes, see Appendix C.

background	backgroundColor	backgroundImage
backgroundPosition	backgroundPositionX*	backgroundPositionY*
backgroundRepeat	behavior	border
borderBottom	borderBottomColor	borderBottomStyle
borderBottomWidth	borderCollapse	borderColor
borderLeft	borderLeftColor	borderLeftStyle
borderLeftWidth	borderRight	borderRightColor
borderRightStyle	borderRightWidth	borderStyle
borderTop	borderTopColor	borderTopStyle
borderTopWidth	borderWidth	bottom
clear	color	cursor
direction	display	filter
font	fontFamily	fontSize
fontStyle	fontVariant	fontWeight

*   This property has no corresponding attribute.

CSS Properties *(continued)*

Note For a list of corresponding attributes, see Appendix C.

height	**layoutGrid**	**layoutGridChar**
layoutGridCharSpacing	**layoutGridLine**	**layoutGridMode**
layoutGridType	**left**	**letterSpacing**
lineBreak	**lineHeight**	**margin**
marginBottom	**marginLeft**	**marginRight**
marginTop	**overflow**	**overflowX**
overflowY	**padding**	**paddingBottom**
paddingLeft	**paddingRight**	**paddingTop**
pageBreakAfter	**pageBreakBefore**	**pixelBottom**[*]
pixelHeight[*]	**pixelLeft**[*]	**pixelRight**[*]
pixelTop[*]	**pixelWidth**[*]	**posBottom**[*]
posHeight[*]	**position**	**posLeft**[*]
posRight[*]	**posTop**[*]	**posWidth**[*]
right	**styleFloat**	**tableLayout**
textAlign	**textAutospace**	**textDecoration**
textDecorationBlink[*]	**textDecorationLineThrough**[*]	**textDecorationNone**[*]
textDecorationOverline[*]	**textDecorationUnderline**[*]	**textIndent**
textJustify	**textTransform**	**top**
unicodeBidi	**visibility**	**width**
wordBreak	**wordSpacing**	**zIndex**

[*] This property has no corresponding attribute.

Example

The following example shows how to use the **TABLE** element to create a table with two rows and two columns.

```
<TABLE BORDER=1 WIDTH=80%>
<THEAD>
<TR>
<TH>Heading 1</TH>
<TH>Heading 2</TH>
</TR>
```

```
<TBODY>
<TR>
<TD>Row 1, Column 1 text.</TD>
<TD>Row 1, Column 2 text.</TD>
</TR>
<TR>
<TD>Row 2, Column 1 text.</TD>
<TD>Row 2, Column 2 text.</TD>
</TR>
</TABLE>
```

TBODY Element | TBODY Object

Designates rows as the body of the table.

Remarks

The **TBODY** element is a block element and requires a closing tag.

This element is exposed for all tables, even if the table did not explicitly define a **TBODY** element.

This element is available in HTML as of Internet Explorer 3.0 and in script as of Internet Explorer 4.0.

Attributes/Properties

			CLASS
align	bgColor	canHaveChildren*	className
clientHeight*	clientLeft*	clientTop*	clientWidth*
currentStyle*	dir	firstChild*	id
innerHTML*	innerText*	isTextEdit*	lang
language	lastChild*	nextSibling*	nodeName*
nodeType*	nodeValue*	offsetHeight*	offsetLeft*
offsetParent*	offsetTop*	offsetWidth*	outerHTML*
outerText*	parentElement*	parentNode*	parentTextEdit*
previousSibling*	readyState*	recordNumber*	runtimeStyle*
scopeName*	scrollHeight*	scrollLeft*	scrollTop*
scrollWidth*	sourceIndex*	style	tabIndex
tagName*	tagUrn*	title	uniqueID*
vAlign			

*   This property has no corresponding attribute.

DHTML Objects

Methods

addBehavior	appendChild	applyElement
attachEvent	blur	clearAttributes
click	cloneNode	componentFromPoint
contains	deleteRow	deleteTFoot
deleteTHead	detachEvent	focus
getAdjacentText	getAttribute	getBoundingClientRect
getClientRects	getElementsByTagName	getExpression
hasChildNodes	insertAdjacentElement	insertBefore
insertRow	mergeAttributes	releaseCapture
removeAttribute	removeBehavior	removeChild
removeExpression	removeNode	replaceAdjacentText
replaceChild	replaceNode	scrollIntoView
setAttribute	setCapture	setExpression
swapNode		

Events

onblur	onclick	ondblclick	ondrag
ondragend	ondragenter	ondragleave	ondragover
ondragstart	ondrop	onfocus	onhelp
onkeydown	onkeypress	onkeyup	onlosecapture
onmousedown	onmousemove	onmouseout	onmouseover
onmouseup	onpropertychange	onreadystatechange	onselectstart

Collections

all	attributes	behaviorUrns	childNodes	children	rows

Default Behaviors

clientCaps	download	homePage	time

CSS Properties

Note For a list of corresponding attributes, see Appendix C.

background	backgroundColor	backgroundImage
backgroundPosition	backgroundPositionX[*]	backgroundPositionY[*]
backgroundRepeat	behavior	clear
color	cursor	direction
font	fontFamily	fontSize
fontStyle	fontVariant	fontWeight
layoutGridMode	letterSpacing	lineHeight
pixelBottom[*]	pixelHeight[*]	pixelLeft[*]
pixelRight[*]	pixelTop[*]	pixelWidth[*]
posBottom[*]	posHeight[*]	posLeft[*]
posRight[*]	posTop[*]	posWidth[*]
textAutospace	textDecoration	textDecorationBlink[*]
textDecorationLineThrough[*]	textDecorationNone[*]	textDecorationOverline[*]
textDecorationUnderline[*]	textTransform	unicodeBidi
verticalAlign	visibility	width
wordSpacing	zIndex	

* This property has no corresponding attribute.

Example

This example shows how to create a table with two rows. The first row is in the table head. The second row is in the table body.

```
<TABLE>
<THEAD>
<TR>
<TD>
This text is in the THEAD
</TD>
</TR>
</THEAD>
<TBODY>
<TR>
<TD>
This text is in the TBODY
</TD>
</TR>
</TBODY>
</TABLE>
```

TD Element | TD Object

Specifies a cell in a table.

Remarks

The **TD** element is a block element and requires a closing tag.

This element is available in HTML as of Internet Explorer 3.0 and in script as of Internet Explorer 4.0.

Attributes/Properties

align	background	bgColor	borderColor
borderColorDark*	borderColorLight*	canHaveChildren*	cellIndex*
CLASS className	clientHeight*	clientLeft*	clientTop*
clientWidth*	colSpan	currentStyle*	dir
firstChild*	id	innerHTML*	innerText*
isTextEdit*	lang	language	lastChild*
nextSibling*	nodeName*	nodeType*	nodeValue*
noWrap	offsetHeight*	offsetLeft*	offsetParent*
offsetTop*	offsetWidth*	outerHTML*	outerText*
parentElement*	parentNode*	parentTextEdit*	previousSibling*
readyState*	recordNumber*	rowSpan	runtimeStyle*
scopeName*	scrollHeight*	scrollLeft*	scrollTop*
scrollWidth*	sourceIndex*	style	tabIndex
tagName*	tagUrn*	title	uniqueID*
vAlign			

* This property has no corresponding attribute.

Methods

addBehavior	appendChild	applyElement
attachEvent	blur	clearAttributes
click	cloneNode	componentFromPoint
contains	detachEvent	focus

Methods *(continued)*

getAdjacentText	getAttribute	getBoundingClientRect
getClientRects	getElementsByTagName	getExpression
hasChildNodes	insertAdjacentElement	insertAdjacentHTML
insertAdjacentText	insertBefore	mergeAttributes
releaseCapture	removeAttribute	removeBehavior
removeChild	removeExpression	removeNode
replaceAdjacentText	replaceChild	replaceNode
scrollIntoView	setAttribute	setCapture
setExpression	swapNode	

Events

onbeforecopy	onbeforecut	onbeforeeditfocus	onbeforepaste
onblur	onclick	oncopy	oncut
ondblclick	ondrag	ondragend	ondragenter
ondragleave	ondragover	ondragstart	ondrop
onfilterchange	onfocus	onhelp	onkeydown
onkeypress	onkeyup	onlosecapture	onmousedown
onmousemove	onmouseout	onmouseover	onmouseup
onpaste	onpropertychange	onreadystatechange	onselectstart

Collections

all	attributes	behaviorUrns	childNodes	children	filters

Default Behaviors

clientCaps	download	homePage	time

CSS Properties

Note For a list of corresponding attributes, see Appendix C.

background	backgroundColor	backgroundImage
backgroundPosition	backgroundPositionX[*]	backgroundPositionY[*]
backgroundRepeat	behavior	border

DHTML Objects

CSS Properties *(continued)*

borderBottom	borderBottomColor	borderBottomStyle
borderBottomWidth	borderColor	borderLeft
borderLeftColor	borderLeftStyle	borderLeftWidth
borderRight	borderRightColor	borderRightStyle
borderRightWidth	borderStyle	borderTop
borderTopColor	borderTopStyle	borderTopWidth
borderWidth	clear	color
cursor	direction	display
filter	font	fontFamily
fontSize	fontStyle	fontVariant
fontWeight	layoutGrid	layoutGridChar
layoutGridCharSpacing	layoutGridLine	layoutGridMode
layoutGridType	letterSpacing	lineBreak
lineHeight	margin	marginBottom
marginLeft	marginRight	marginTop
overflow	padding	paddingBottom
paddingLeft	paddingRight	paddingTop
pageBreakAfter	pageBreakBefore	pixelBottom[*]
pixelHeight[*]	pixelLeft[*]	pixelRight[*]
pixelTop[*]	pixelWidth[*]	posBottom[*]
posHeight[*]	posLeft[*]	posRight[*]
posTop[*]	posWidth[*]	textAlign
textAutospace	textDecoration	textDecorationBlink[*]
textDecorationLineThrough[*]	textDecorationNone[*]	textDecorationOverline[*]
textDecorationUnderline[*]	textIndent	textJustify
textTransform	unicodeBidi	verticalAlign
visibility	width	wordBreak
wordSpacing	zIndex	

[*]   This property has no corresponding attribute.

TEXTAREA Element | TEXTAREA Object

Specifies a multiline text input control.

Remarks

The **TEXTAREA** element is an inline element and requires a closing tag.

The default font is fixed pitch.

This element is available in HTML and script as of Internet Explorer 3.0.

Attributes/Properties

		CLASS	
accessKey	canHaveChildren[*]	className	clientHeight[*]
clientLeft[*]	clientTop[*]	clientWidth[*]	cols
currentStyle[*]	dataFld	dataSrc	defaultValue[*]
dir	disabled	firstChild[*]	form[*]
id	innerText[*]	isTextEdit[*]	lang
language	lastChild[*]	name	nextSibling[*]
nodeName[*]	nodeType[*]	nodeValue[*]	offsetHeight[*]
offsetLeft[*]	offsetParent[*]	offsetTop[*]	offsetWidth[*]
outerHTML[*]	outerText[*]	parentElement[*]	parentNode[*]
parentTextEdit[*]	previousSibling[*]	readOnly	readyState[*]
recordNumber[*]	rows	runtimeStyle[*]	scopeName[*]
scrollHeight[*]	scrollLeft[*]	scrollTop[*]	scrollWidth[*]
sourceIndex[*]	style	tabIndex	tagName[*]
tagUrn[*]	title	type	uniqueID[*]
value[*]	wrap		

[*] This property has no corresponding attribute.

Methods

addBehavior	appendChild	applyElement
attachEvent	blur	clearAttributes
click	cloneNode	componentFromPoint

Methods *(continued)*

contains	createTextRange	detachEvent
doScroll	focus	getAdjacentText
getAttribute	getBoundingClientRect	getClientRects
getElementsByTagName	getExpression	hasChildNodes
insertAdjacentElement	insertAdjacentHTML	insertAdjacentText
insertBefore	mergeAttributes	releaseCapture
removeAttribute	removeBehavior	removeChild
removeExpression	removeNode	replaceAdjacentText
replaceChild	replaceNode	scrollIntoView
select	setAttribute	setCapture
setExpression	swapNode	

Events

onafterupdate	onbeforecopy	onbeforecut	onbeforeeditfocus
onbeforepaste	onbeforeupdate	onblur	onchange
onclick	ondblclick	ondrag	ondragend
ondragenter	ondragleave	ondragover	ondragstart
ondrop	onerrorupdate	onfilterchange	onfocus
onhelp	onkeydown	onkeypress	onkeyup
onlosecapture	onmousedown	onmousemove	onmouseout
onmouseover	onmouseup	onpropertychange	onreadystatechange
onresize	onscroll	onselect	onselectstart

Collections

all	attributes	behaviorUrns	childNodes	children	filters

Default Behaviors

clientCaps	download	homePage	httpFolder	saveFavorite
saveHistory	saveSnapshot	time	userData	

CSS Properties

Note For a list of corresponding attributes, see Appendix C.

background	backgroundColor	backgroundImage
backgroundPosition	backgroundPositionX[*]	backgroundPositionY[*]
backgroundRepeat	behavior	border
borderBottom	borderBottomColor	borderBottomStyle
borderBottomWidth	borderColor	borderLeft
borderLeftColor	borderLeftStyle	borderLeftWidth
borderRight	borderRightColor	borderRightStyle
borderRightWidth	borderStyle	borderTop
borderTopColor	borderTopStyle	borderTopWidth
borderWidth	bottom	clear
color	cursor	direction
display	filter	font
fontFamily	fontSize	fontStyle
fontVariant	fontWeight	height
imeMode	layoutGridMode	left
letterSpacing	lineHeight	margin
marginBottom	marginLeft	marginRight
marginTop	overflow	overflowX
overflowY	padding	paddingBottom
paddingLeft	paddingRight	paddingTop
pixelBottom[*]	pixelHeight[*]	pixelLeft[*]
pixelRight[*]	pixelTop[*]	pixelWidth[*]
posBottom[*]	posHeight[*]	position
posLeft[*]	posRight[*]	posTop[*]
posWidth[*]	right	styleFloat

CSS Properties *(continued)*

textAlign	**textAutospace**	**textDecoration**
textDecorationBlink[*]	**textDecorationLineThrough**[*]	**textDecorationNone**[*]
textDecorationOverline[*]	**textDecorationUnderline**[*]	**textTransform**
top	**unicodeBidi**	**visibility**
width	**wordSpacing**	**zIndex**

* This property has no corresponding attribute.

Example

The following example shows how to set the cascading style sheets (CSS) **overflow** attribute to hidden to remove the scroll bars from the **TEXTAREA**.

```
<TEXTAREA STYLE="overflow:hidden" ID=txtComments>
    The patient is in stable condition after suffering an attack of
    the insatiable munchies.
</TEXTAREA>
```

TextNode Object

Represents a string of text as a node in the document hierarchy.

Remarks

Use the **createTextNode** method to create a **TextNode** object. Once you create the **TextNode** object, you can add it to the document using the **appendChild**, **replaceNode**, or **insertBefore** method.

This object is available in script as of Internet Explorer 5.

Attributes/Properties

Note These properties have no corresponding attributes.

data	**length**	**nextSibling**	**nodeName**
nodeType	**nodeValue**	**previousSibling**	

Methods

splitText

Example

The following example shows how to use the **TextNode** object to change the text of an **LI** object.

```
<SCRIPT>
function fnChangeText(){
    var oTextNode = document.createTextNode("New List Item 1");
    var oReplaceNode = oItem1.firstChild.replaceNode(oTextNode);
}
</SCRIPT>

<UL onclick = "fnChangeText()">
<LI ID = oItem1>List Item 1
</UL>
```

TextRange Object

Represents text in an HTML element.

Remarks

Use this object to retrieve and modify text in an element, to locate specific strings in the text, and to carry out commands that affect the appearance of the text.

To retrieve a text range object, apply the **createTextRange** method to a **BODY**, **BUTTON**, or **TEXTAREA** element or an **INPUT** element that has **text** type. Modify the extent of the text range by moving its start and end positions with methods such as **move**, **moveToElementText**, and **findText**. Within the text range, you can retrieve and modify plain text or HTML text. These forms of text are identical except that HTML text includes HTML tags and plain text does not.

This feature might not be available on non-Win32 platforms. For the latest information on Internet Explorer cross-platform compatibility, see article Q172976 in the Microsoft Knowledge Base on the Web Workshop CD-ROM.

This object is available in script as of Internet Explorer 4.0.

Attributes/Properties

Note These properties have no corresponding attributes.

boundingHeight	**boundingLeft**	**boundingTop**	**boundingWidth**
htmlText	**offsetLeft**	**offsetTop**	**text**

Methods

collapse	**compareEndPoints**	**duplicate**
execCommand	**expand**	**findText**
getBookmark	**getBoundingClientRect**	**getClientRects**
inRange	**isEqual**	**move**
moveEnd	**moveStart**	**moveToBookmark**
moveToElementText	**moveToPoint**	**parentElement**
pasteHTML	**queryCommandEnabled**	**queryCommandIndeterm**
queryCommandState	**queryCommandSupported**	**queryCommandValue**
scrollIntoView	**select**	**setEndPoint**

Example

The following example in JScript (compatible with ECMA 262 language specification) changes the text of a **BUTTON** element to Clicked.

```
var b = document.all.tags("BUTTON");
if (b!=null) {
    var r = b[0].createTextRange();
    if (r != null) {
        r.text = "Clicked";
    }
}
```

TextRectangle Object

Specifies a rectangle that contains a line of text in an element or a **TextRange** object.

Remarks

A collection of **TextRectangle** objects is retrieved by applying the **getClientRects** method to an element or text range object. The **getClientRects** method returns a collection of rectangles, exposing for each rectangle the left, top, right, and bottom coordinates relative to the client.

In the Gettysburg Address below, four **TextRectangle** objects can be created for the **B** element (bold text).

Four score and seven years ago **our fathers brought forth . . . a new nation, conceived in liberty and dedicated to the proposition that all men are created equal.** Now we are engaged in a great civil war . . .

The **TextRectangle** objects are:

- The rectangle around "our fathers"
- The rectangle around "brought forth . . . a new nation, conceived in liberty"
- The rectangle around "and dedicated to the proposition that all men are"
- The rectangle around "created equal"

If the window is resized, the **TextRectangle** objects are not updated. Because the objects are a snapshot of the layout, the objects should be updated following an **onresize** event.

This object is available in script as of Internet Explorer 5.

Attributes/Properties

Note These properties have no corresponding attributes.

bottom	left	right	top

Example

The following example shows how to use the **getClientRects** and **getBoundingClientRect** methods to highlight text lines in an object.

```
<HEAD>
<SCRIPT>
var rcts;
var keyCount=0;

function Highlight(obj) {
    rcts = obj.getClientRects();
    rctLength= rcts.length;

    if (keyCount > rctLength-1) {
        idBeige.style.display="none";
        keyCount = 0
}

    // Set the rendering properties for the yellow DIV.
    cdRight = rcts[keyCount].right + idBody.scrollLeft;
    cdLeft = rcts[keyCount].left + idBody.scrollLeft;
    cdTop = rcts[keyCount].top + idBody.scrollTop;
    cdBottom = rcts[keyCount].bottom + idBody.scrollTop;
    idYellow.style.top = cdTop;
    idYellow.style.width = (cdRight-cdLeft) - 5;
    idYellow.style.display = 'inline';
```

```
      // Set the rendering properties for the beige DIV.
      bndRight = obj.getBoundingClientRect().right + idBody.scrollLeft;
      bndLeft = obj.getBoundingClientRect().left + idBody.scrollLeft;
      bndTop = obj.getBoundingClientRect().top + idBody.scrollTop;
      idBeige.style.top = bndTop;
      idBeige.style.width = (bndRight-bndLeft) - 5;
      idBeige.style.height = cdTop - bndTop;
      if (keyCount>0){ idBeige.style.display = 'inline';
      }
      keyCount++;
}
</SCRIPT>
</HEAD>

<BODY ID="idBody">
<DIV ID="oID_1" onclick="Highlight(this)"
    onkeydown="Highlight(this)">
A large block of text should go here. Click on this
block of text multiple times to see each line
highlight with every click of the mouse button.
Once each line has been highlighted, the process
begins again starting with the first line.
</DIV>
<DIV STYLE="position:absolute; left:5; top:400;z-index:-1; background-color:yellow;
display:none" ID="idYellow"></DIV>
<DIV STYLE="position:absolute; left:5; top:400;z-index:-1; background-color:beige;
display:none" ID="idBeige"></DIV>
</BODY>
```

To see this code in action, refer to the Web Workshop CD-ROM.

The next example shows how to use the **TextRectangle** collection and
getBoundingClientRect method to determine position within an element. In each
line, the left-justified text does not extend to the right margin of the box that contains
the text. Using this collection, you can determine the coordinates of the rectangle that
surrounds only the content in each line. By reading these rectangles and then
comparing the coordinates against the rectangle around the ball image, the sample
instructs the ball to move over the text only and not to the end of the line.

```
<HEAD>
<SCRIPT>
var timid = -1;
var timoID_2 = -1;
var nLine;
var nPosInLine;
var oRcts;
var nDivLen;
var nEraser;
```

```
function LoadDone() {
    oTextRange = document.body.createTextRange();
    // Get bounding rect of the range.
    oRcts = oTextRange.getClientRects();
    nLine = 0;
    oBndRct = obj.getBoundingClientRect();
    nDivLen = oBndRct.right - oBndRct.left + 1;
    MoveTo();
}

function MoveTo() {
    if (nLine >= oRcts.length) {
        nLine = 0;
    }
    obj.style.top = oRcts[nLine].top;
    nPosInLine = oRcts[nLine].left;
    nEraser = 0;
    timoID_2 = setInterval("MoveToInLine()",60);
}

function MoveToInLine() {
    if (nPosInLine >= oRcts[nLine].right - nDivLen) {
        clearInterval(timoID_2);
        timoID_2 = -1;
        obj.style.left = oRcts[nLine].right - nDivLen;
        nLine++;
        timid = setTimeout("MoveTo()", 100);
        return;
    }
    if (nEraser == 0) {
        nEraser = 1;
    }
    else {
        nEraser = 0;
    }
    im.src = "/workshop/graphics/dot.gif";
    obj.style.left = nPosInLine;
    nPosInLine += 3;
}

function End() {
    if(timid != -1) {
        clearInterval(timid);
        timid = -1;
    }
    if(timoID_2 != -1) {
        clearInterval(timoID_2);
        timoID_2 = -1;
    }
}
</SCRIPT>
</HEAD>
```

```
<BODY ID="bodyid" onload="LoadDone()"
    onresize="End();LoadDone();" onunload="End()">
<P STYLE="text-align:center">
<B>The quick brown fox jumps over the lazy dog.</B>
</P>
<DIV ID="obj" STYLE="position:absolute">
<IMG ID="im" SRC="/workshop/graphics/dot.gif"
    BORDER=0 HEIGHT=16 WIDTH=16>
</DIV>
</BODY>
```

To see this code in action, refer to the Web Workshop CD-ROM.

TFOOT Element | TFOOT Object

Designates rows as the table's footer.

Remarks

The **TFOOT** element is a block element and requires a closing tag.

This element is available in HTML as of Internet Explorer 3.0 and in script as of Internet Explorer 4.0.

Attributes/Properties

			CLASS
align	bgColor	canHaveChildren*	className
clientHeight*	clientLeft*	clientTop*	clientWidth*
currentStyle*	dir	firstChild*	id
innerHTML*	innerText*	isTextEdit*	lang
language	lastChild*	nextSibling*	nodeName*
nodeType*	nodeValue*	offsetHeight*	offsetLeft*
offsetParent*	offsetTop*	offsetWidth*	outerHTML*
outerText*	parentElement*	parentNode*	parentTextEdit*
previousSibling*	readyState*	recordNumber*	runtimeStyle*
scopeName*	scrollHeight*	scrollLeft*	scrollTop*
scrollWidth*	sourceIndex*	style*	tabIndex
tagName*	tagUrn*	title	uniqueID*
vAlign			

* This property has no corresponding attribute.

Methods

addBehavior	appendChild	applyElement
attachEvent	blur	clearAttributes
click	cloneNode	componentFromPoint
contains	deleteRow	detachEvent
focus	getAdjacentText	getAttribute
getBoundingClientRect	getClientRects	getElementsByTagName
getExpression	hasChildNodes	insertAdjacentElement
insertBefore	insertRow	mergeAttributes
releaseCapture	removeAttribute	removeBehavior
removeChild	removeExpression	removeNode
replaceAdjacentText	replaceChild	replaceNode
scrollIntoView	setAttribute	setCapture
setExpression	swapNode	

Events

onblur	onclick	ondblclick	ondragenter
ondragstart	onfocus	onhelp	onkeydown
onkeypress	onkeyup	onlosecapture	onmousedown
onmousemove	onmouseout	onmouseover	onmouseup
onpropertychange	onreadystatechange	onselectstart	

Collections

all   attributes   behaviorUrns   childNodes   children   rows

Default Behaviors

clientCaps   download   homePage   time

CSS Properties

Note For a list of corresponding attributes, see Appendix C.

background	**backgroundColor**	**backgroundImage**
backgroundPosition	**backgroundPositionX**[*]	**backgroundPositionY**[*]
backgroundRepeat	**behavior**	**clear**
color	**cursor**	**direction**
display	**font**	**fontFamily**
fontSize	**fontStyle**	**fontVariant**
fontWeight	**layoutGridMode**	**letterSpacing**
lineHeight	**pixelBottom**[*]	**pixelHeight**[*]
pixelLeft[*]	**pixelRight**[*]	**pixelTop**[*]
pixelWidth[*]	**posBottom**[*]	**posHeight**[*]
posLeft[*]	**posRight**[*]	**posTop**[*]
posWidth[*]	**textAutospace**	**textDecoration**
textDecorationBlink[*]	**textDecorationLineThrough**[*]	**textDecorationNone**[*]
textDecorationOverline[*]	**textDecorationUnderline**[*]	**textTransform**
unicodeBidi	**verticalAlign**	**visibility**
width	**wordSpacing**	**zIndex**

[*] This property has no corresponding attribute.

Example

The following example shows a table with two rows. The first row is in the table body. The second row is in the table footer.

```
<TABLE>
<TBODY>
<TR>
<TD>
This text is in the table body.
</TD>
</TR>
</TBODY>
<TFOOT>
<TR>
<TD>
This text is in the table footer.
</TD>
</TR>
</TFOOT>
</TABLE>
```

TH Element | TH Object

Specifies a header column. Header columns are centered within the cell and are bold.

Remarks

The **TH** element is a block element and requires a closing tag.

This element is available in HTML as of Internet Explorer 3.0 and in script as of Internet Explorer 4.0.

Attributes/Properties

align	**background**	**bgColor**	**borderColor**
borderColorDark[*]	**borderColorLight**[*]	**canHaveChildren**[*]	**CLASS** **className**
clientHeight[*]	**clientLeft**[*]	**clientTop**[*]	**clientWidth**[*]
colSpan	**currentStyle**[*]	**dir**	**firstChild**[*]
id	**innerHTML**[*]	**innerText**[*]	**isTextEdit**[*]
lang	**language**	**lastChild**[*]	**nextSibling**[*]
nodeName[*]	**nodeType**[*]	**nodeValue**[*]	**noWrap**
offsetHeight[*]	**offsetLeft**[*]	**offsetParent**[*]	**offsetTop**[*]
offsetWidth[*]	**outerHTML**[*]	**outerText**[*]	**parentElement**[*]
parentNode[*]	**parentTextEdit**[*]	**previousSibling**[*]	**readyState**[*]
recordNumber[*]	**rowSpan**	**runtimeStyle**[*]	**scopeName**[*]
scrollHeight[*]	**scrollLeft**[*]	**scrollTop**[*]	**scrollWidth**[*]
sourceIndex[*]	**style**[*]	**tabIndex**	**tagName**[*]
tagUrn[*]	**title**	**uniqueID**[*]	**vAlign**

[*] This property has no corresponding attribute.

Methods

addBehavior	**appendChild**	**applyElement**
attachEvent	**blur**	**clearAttributes**
click	**cloneNode**	**componentFromPoint**
contains	**detachEvent**	**focus**
getAdjacentText	**getAttribute**	**getBoundingClientRect**

DHTML Objects

Methods *(continued)*

getClientRects	getElementsByTagName	getExpression
hasChildNodes	insertAdjacentElement	insertAdjacentHTML
insertAdjacentText	insertBefore	mergeAttributes
releaseCapture	removeAttribute	removeBehavior
removeChild	removeExpression	removeNode
replaceAdjacentText	replaceChild	replaceNode
scrollIntoView	setAttribute	setCapture
setExpression	swapNode	

Events

onbeforecopy	onbeforecut	onbeforepaste	onblur
onclick	oncopy	oncut	ondblclick
ondragenter	ondragstart	onfilterchange	onfocus
onhelp	onkeydown	onkeypress	onkeyup
onlosecapture	onmousedown	onmousemove	onmouseout
onmouseover	onmouseup	onpaste	onpropertychange
onreadystatechange	onselectstart		

Collections

all	attributes	behaviorUrns	childNodes	filters

Default Behaviors

clientCaps	download	homePage	time

CSS Properties

Note For a list of corresponding attributes, see Appendix C.

background	backgroundColor	backgroundImage
backgroundPosition	backgroundPositionX*	backgroundPositionY*
backgroundRepeat	behavior	border
borderBottom	borderBottomColor	borderBottomStyle

* This property has no corresponding attribute.

CSS Properties *(continued)*

Note For a list of corresponding attributes, see Appendix C.

borderBottomWidth	borderColor	borderLeft
borderLeftColor	borderLeftStyle	borderLeftWidth
borderRight	borderRightColor	borderRightStyle
borderRightWidth	borderStyle	borderTop
borderTopColor	borderTopStyle	borderTopWidth
borderWidth	clear	color
cursor	direction	filter
font	fontFamily	fontSize
fontStyle	fontVariant	fontWeight
layoutGrid	layoutGridChar	layoutGridCharSpacing
layoutGridLine	layoutGridMode	layoutGridType
letterSpacing	lineBreak	lineHeight
margin	marginBottom	marginLeft
marginRight	marginTop	pixelBottom[*]
pixelHeight[*]	pixelLeft[*]	pixelRight[*]
pixelTop[*]	pixelWidth[*]	posBottom[*]
posHeight[*]	posLeft[*]	posRight[*]
posTop[*]	posWidth[*]	textAlign
textAutospace	textDecoration	textDecorationBlink[*]
textDecorationLineThrough[*]	textDecorationNone[*]	textDecorationOverline[*]
textDecorationUnderline[*]	textIndent	textJustify
textTransform	unicodeBidi	verticalAlign
visibility	width	wordBreak
wordSpacing	zIndex	

[*]   This property has no corresponding attribute.

THEAD Element | THEAD Object

Designates rows as the table's header.

Remarks

The **THEAD** element is a block element and requires a closing tag.

This element is available in HTML as of Internet Explorer 3.0 and in script as of Internet Explorer 4.0.

Attributes/Properties

			CLASS
align	bgColor	canHaveChildren*	className
clientHeight*	clientLeft*	clientTop*	clientWidth*
currentStyle*	dir	firstChild*	id
innerHTML*	innerText*	isTextEdit*	lang
language	lastChild*	nextSibling*	nodeName*
nodeType*	nodeValue*	offsetHeight*	offsetLeft*
offsetParent*	offsetTop*	offsetWidth*	outerHTML*
outerText*	parentElement*	parentNode*	parentTextEdit*
previousSibling*	readyState*	recordNumber*	runtimeStyle*
scopeName*	scrollHeight*	scrollLeft*	scrollTop*
scrollWidth*	sourceIndex*	style*	tabIndex
tagName*	tagUrn*	title	uniqueID*
vAlign			

* This property has no corresponding attribute.

Methods

addBehavior	appendChild	applyElement
attachEvent	blur	clearAttributes
click	cloneNode	componentFromPoint
contains	deleteRow	detachEvent
focus	getAdjacentText	getAttribute
getBoundingClientRect	getClientRects	getElementsByTagName

Methods *(continued)*

getExpression	hasChildNodes	insertAdjacentElement
insertBefore	insertRow	mergeAttributes
releaseCapture	removeAttribute	removeBehavior
removeChild	removeExpression	removeNode
replaceAdjacentText	replaceChild	replaceNode
scrollIntoView	setAttribute	setCapture
setExpression	swapNode	

Events

onblur	onclick	ondblclick	ondragenter
ondragstart	onfocus	onhelp	onkeydown
onkeypress	onkeyup	onlosecapture	onmousedown
onmousemove	onmouseout	onmouseover	onmouseup
onpropertychange	onreadystatechange	onselectstart	

Collections

all	attributes	behaviorUrns	childNodes	children	rows

Default Behaviors

clientCaps	download	homePage	time

CSS Properties

Note For a list of corresponding attributes, see Appendix C.

background	backgroundColor	backgroundImage
backgroundPosition	backgroundPositionX*	backgroundPositionY*
backgroundRepeat	behavior	clear
color	cursor	direction
display	font	fontFamily
fontSize	fontStyle	fontVariant
fontWeight	layoutGridMode	letterSpacing
lineHeight	pixelBottom*	pixelHeight*

CSS Properties *(continued)*

pixelLeft[*]	**pixelRight**[*]	**pixelTop**[*]
pixelWidth[*]	**posBottom**[*]	**posHeight**[*]
posLeft[*]	**posRight**[*]	**posTop**[*]
posWidth[*]	**textAutospace**	**textDecoration**
textDecorationBlink[*]	**textDecorationLineThrough**[*]	**textDecorationNone**[*]
textDecorationOverline[*]	**textDecorationUnderline**[*]	**textTransform**
unicodeBidi	**verticalAlign**	**visibility**
width	**wordSpacing**	**zIndex**

[*]   This property has no corresponding attribute.

DHTML Objects

Example

The following example shows a table with two rows. The first row is in the table header. The second row is in the table body.

```
<TABLE>
<THEAD>
<TR>
<TD>
This text is in the table header.
</TD>
</TR>
</THEAD>
<TBODY>
<TR>
<TD>
This text is in the table body.
</TD>
</TR>
</TBODY>
</TABLE>
```

TITLE Element | title Object

Contains the title of the document.

Remarks

The **TITLE** element is a block element and requires a closing tag.

This element can be used only within the **HEAD** element. Any text between the opening and closing **TITLE** tags displays in the browser title bar and in the Microsoft

Windows taskbar. In Web pages, "Microsoft Internet Explorer" is added to the title. In HTML Applications, by contrast, only the specified title appears.

This element is available in HTML as of Internet Explorer 3.0 and in script as of Internet Explorer 4.0.

Attributes/Properties

currentStyle[*]	firstChild[*]	id	innerText[*]
isTextEdit[*]	lang	lastChild[*]	nextSibling[*]
nodeName[*]	nodeType[*]	nodeValue[*]	parentElement[*]
parentNode[*]	parentTextEdit[*]	previousSibling[*]	readyState[*]
runtimeStyle[*]	scopeName[*]	sourceIndex[*]	style[*]
tagName[*]	tagUrn[*]	text[*]	uniqueID[*]

[*]   This property has no corresponding attribute.

Methods

addBehavior	applyElement	attachEvent
clearAttributes	cloneNode	componentFromPoint
contains	detachEvent	getAdjacentText
getAttribute	getElementsByTagName	hasChildNodes
insertAdjacentElement	mergeAttributes	removeAttribute
removeBehavior	replaceAdjacentText	setAttribute
swapNode		

Events

onreadystatechange

Collections

all	attributes	behaviorUrns	childNodes	children

Default Behaviors

clientCaps	download	homePage

CSS Properties

Note For a list of corresponding attributes, see Appendix C.

backgroundPositionX[*]	**backgroundPositionY**[*]	**behavior**	**pixelBottom**[*]
pixelHeight[*]	**pixelLeft**[*]	**pixelRight**[*]	**pixelTop**[*]
pixelWidth[*]	**posBottom**[*]	**posHeight**[*]	**posLeft**[*]
posRight[*]	**posTop**[*]	**posWidth**[*]	**textAutospace**
width			

[*]   This property has no corresponding attribute.

Example

The following example shows how to add a title to a **HEAD** element.

```
<HEAD>
<TITLE>"Welcome to Internet Explorer!"</TITLE>
</HEAD>
```

Applies To

WIN16	**WIN32**	**MAC**	
document			

UNIX	
document	

TR Element | TR Object

Specifies a row in a table.

Remarks

The **TR** element is a block element and requires a closing tag.

Within a row, the following tags are valid: **TD** and **TH**.

This element is available in HTML as of Internet Explorer 3.0 and in script as of Internet Explorer 4.0.

The **TR** element does not explicitly support the **HEIGHT** attribute. You can use the cascading style sheets (CSS) **height** attribute to achieve the same effect.

Attributes/Properties

align	bgColor	borderColor	borderColorLight[*]
	CLASS		
canHaveChildren[*]	className	clientHeight[*]	clientLeft[*]
clientTop[*]	clientWidth[*]	currentStyle[*]	dir
firstChild[*]	id	innerHTML[*]	innerText[*]
isTextEdit[*]	lang	language	lastChild[*]
nextSibling[*]	nodeName[*]	nodeType[*]	nodeValue[*]
offsetHeight[*]	offsetLeft[*]	offsetParent[*]	offsetTop[*]
offsetWidth[*]	outerHTML[*]	outerText[*]	parentElement[*]
parentNode[*]	parentTextEdit[*]	previousSibling[*]	readyState[*]
recordNumber[*]	rowIndex[*]	runtimeStyle[*]	scopeName[*]
scrollHeight[*]	scrollLeft[*]	scrollTop[*]	scrollWidth[*]
sectionRowIndex[*]	sourceIndex[*]	style	tabIndex
tagName[*]	tagUrn[*]	title	uniqueID[*]
vAlign			

[*]   This property has no corresponding attribute.

Methods

addBehavior	appendChild	applyElement
attachEvent	blur	clearAttributes
click	cloneNode	componentFromPoint
contains	deleteCell	detachEvent
focus	getAdjacentText	getAttribute
getBoundingClientRect	getClientRects	getElementsByTagName
getExpression	hasChildNodes	insertAdjacentElement
insertBefore	insertCell	mergeAttributes
releaseCapture	removeAttribute	removeBehavior
removeChild	removeExpression	removeNode
replaceAdjacentText	replaceChild	replaceNode
scrollIntoView	setAttribute	setCapture
setExpression	swapNode	

DHTML Objects

Events

onbeforecopy	onbeforecut	onbeforeeditfocus	onbeforepaste
onblur	onclick	oncopy	oncut
ondblclick	ondrag	ondragend	ondragenter
ondragleave	ondragover	ondragstart	ondrop
onfilterchange	onfocus	onhelp	onkeydown
onkeypress	onkeyup	onlosecapture	onmousedown
onmousemove	onmouseout	onmouseover	onmouseup
onpaste	onpropertychange	onreadystatechange	onselectstart

Collections

all	attributes	behaviorUrns	cells	childNodes	children

Default Behaviors

clientCaps	download	homePage	time

CSS Properties

Note For a list of corresponding attributes, see Appendix C.

background	backgroundColor	backgroundImage
backgroundPosition	backgroundPositionX*	backgroundPositionY*
backgroundRepeat	behavior	clear
color	cursor	direction
display	font	fontFamily
fontSize	fontStyle	fontVariant
fontWeight	height	layoutGrid
layoutGridChar	layoutGridCharSpacing	layoutGridLine
layoutGridMode	layoutGridType	letterSpacing
lineBreak	lineHeight	margin
marginBottom	marginLeft	marginRight
marginTop	padding	paddingBottom

* This property has no corresponding attribute.

CSS Properties *(continued)*

Note For a list of corresponding attributes, see Appendix C.

paddingLeft	paddingRight	paddingTop
pageBreakAfter	pageBreakBefore	pixelBottom[*]
pixelHeight[*]	pixelLeft[*]	pixelRight[*]
pixelTop[*]	pixelWidth[*]	posBottom[*]
posHeight[*]	posLeft[*]	posRight[*]
posTop[*]	posWidth[*]	textAlign
textAutospace	textDecoration	textDecorationBlink[*]
textDecorationLineThrough[*]	textDecorationNone[*]	textDecorationOverline[*]
textDecorationUnderline[*]	textIndent	textJustify
textTransform	unicodeBidi	verticalAlign
visibility	width	wordBreak
wordSpacing	zIndex	

[*] This property has no corresponding attribute.

Example

The following example shows how to create a table with two rows.

```
<TABLE>
<TR>
<TD>
This is the first row.
</TD>
</TR>
<TR>
<TD>
This is the second row.
</TD>
</TR>
</TABLE>
```

TT Element | TT Object

Renders text in a fixed-width font.

Remarks

The **TT** element is an inline element and requires a closing tag.

This element is available in HTML as of Internet Explorer 3.0 and in script as of Internet Explorer 4.0.

Attributes/Properties

canHaveChildren[*]	**CLASS** className	clientHeight[*]	clientLeft[*]
clientTop[*]	clientWidth[*]	currentStyle[*]	dir
firstChild[*]	id	innerHTML[*]	innerText[*]
isTextEdit[*]	lang	language	lastChild[*]
nextSibling[*]	nodeName[*]	nodeType[*]	nodeValue[*]
offsetHeight[*]	offsetLeft[*]	offsetParent[*]	offsetTop[*]
offsetWidth[*]	outerHTML[*]	outerText[*]	parentElement[*]
parentNode[*]	parentTextEdit[*]	previousSibling[*]	readyState[*]
recordNumber[*]	runtimeStyle[*]	scopeName[*]	scrollHeight[*]
scrollLeft[*]	scrollTop[*]	scrollWidth[*]	sourceIndex[*]
style	tabIndex	tagName[*]	tagUrn[*]
title	uniqueID[*]		

[*] This property has no corresponding attribute.

Methods

addBehavior	appendChild	applyElement
attachEvent	blur	clearAttributes
click	cloneNode	componentFromPoint
contains	detachEvent	focus
getAdjacentText	getAttribute	getBoundingClientRect
getClientRects	getElementsByTagName	getExpression
hasChildNodes	insertAdjacentElement	insertAdjacentHTML

Methods *(continued)*

insertAdjacentText	insertBefore	mergeAttributes
releaseCapture	removeAttribute	removeBehavior
removeChild	removeExpression	removeNode
replaceAdjacentText	replaceChild	replaceNode
scrollIntoView	setAttribute	setCapture
setExpression	swapNode	

Events

onbeforecopy	onbeforecut	onbeforepaste	onblur
onclick	oncopy	oncut	ondblclick
ondrag	ondragend	ondragenter	ondragleave
ondragover	ondragstart	ondrop	onfocus
onhelp	onkeydown	onkeypress	onkeyup
onlosecapture	onmousedown	onmousemove	onmouseout
onmouseover	onmouseup	onpaste	onpropertychange
onreadystatechange	onresize	onselectstart	

Collections

all	attributes	behaviorUrns	childNodes	children

Default Behaviors

clientCaps	download	homePage	httpFolder	saveFavorite
saveHistory	saveSnapshot	time	userData	

CSS Properties

Note For a list of corresponding attributes, see Appendix C.

background	backgroundColor	backgroundImage
backgroundPosition	backgroundPositionX[*]	backgroundPositionY[*]
backgroundRepeat	behavior	bottom
clear	color	cursor
direction	font	fontFamily

CSS Properties *(continued)*

fontSize	fontStyle	fontVariant
fontWeight	layoutGridMode	left
letterSpacing	lineHeight	overflow
overflowX	overflowY	pixelBottom*
pixelHeight*	pixelLeft*	pixelRight*
pixelTop*	pixelWidth*	posBottom*
posHeight*	position	posLeft*
posRight*	posTop*	posWidth*
right	styleFloat	textAutospace
textDecoration	textDecorationBlink*	textDecorationLineThrough*
textDecorationNone*	textDecorationOverline*	textDecorationUnderline*
textTransform	top	unicodeBidi
visibility	width	wordSpacing
zIndex		

* This property has no corresponding attribute.

Example

The following example shows how to use the TT element to render text in a fix-width font.

```
<TT>Here's some plain text.</TT>
```

U Element | U Object

Renders text that is underlined.

Remarks

The **U** element is an inline element and requires a closing tag.

This element is available in HTML as of Internet Explorer 3.0 and in script as of Internet Explorer 4.0.

Attributes/Properties

	CLASS		
canHaveChildren[*]	className	clientHeight[*]	clientLeft[*]
clientTop[*]	clientWidth[*]	currentStyle[*]	dir
firstChild[*]	id	innerHTML[*]	innerText[*]
isTextEdit[*]	lang	language	lastChild[*]
nextSibling[*]	nodeName[*]	nodeType[*]	nodeValue[*]
offsetHeight[*]	offsetLeft[*]	offsetParent[*]	offsetTop[*]
offsetWidth[*]	outerHTML[*]	outerText[*]	parentElement[*]
parentNode[*]	parentTextEdit[*]	previousSibling[*]	readyState[*]
recordNumber[*]	runtimeStyle[*]	scopeName[*]	scrollHeight[*]
scrollLeft[*]	scrollTop[*]	scrollWidth[*]	sourceIndex[*]
style	tabIndex	tagName[*]	tagUrn[*]
title	uniqueID[*]		

* This property has no corresponding attribute.

Methods

addBehavior	appendChild	applyElement
attachEvent	blur	clearAttributes
click	cloneNode	componentFromPoint
contains	detachEvent	focus
getAdjacentText	getAttribute	getBoundingClientRect
getClientRects	getElementsByTagName	getExpression
hasChildNodes	insertAdjacentElement	insertAdjacentHTML
insertAdjacentText	insertBefore	mergeAttributes
releaseCapture	removeAttribute	removeBehavior
removeChild	removeExpression	removeNode
replaceAdjacentText	replaceChild	replaceNode
scrollIntoView	setAttribute	setCapture
setExpression	swapNode	

Events

onbeforecopy	onbeforecut	onbeforepaste	onblur
onclick	oncopy	oncut	ondblclick
ondrag	ondragend	ondragenter	ondragleave
ondragover	ondragstart	ondrop	onfocus
onhelp	onkeydown	onkeypress	onkeyup
onlosecapture	onmousedown	onmousemove	onmouseout
onmouseover	onmouseup	onpaste	onpropertychange
onreadystatechange	onresize	onselectstart	

Collections

all	attributes	behaviorUrns	childNodes	children

Default Behaviors

clientCaps	download	homePage	httpFolder	saveFavorite
saveHistory	saveSnapshot	time	userData	

CSS Properties

Note For a list of corresponding attributes, see Appendix C.

background	backgroundColor	backgroundImage
backgroundPosition	backgroundPositionX[*]	backgroundPositionY[*]
backgroundRepeat	behavior	bottom
clear	color	cursor
direction	font	fontFamily
fontSize	fontStyle	fontVariant
fontWeight	layoutGridMode	left
letterSpacing	lineHeight	overflow
overflowX	overflowY	pixelBottom[*]
pixelHeight[*]	pixelLeft[*]	pixelRight[*]
pixelTop[*]	pixelWidth[*]	posBottom[*]

[*] This property has no corresponding attribute.

CSS Properties *(continued)*

> **Note** For a list of corresponding attributes, see Appendix C.

posHeight[*]	**position**	**posLeft**[*]
posRight[*]	**posTop**[*]	**posWidth**[*]
right	**styleFloat**	**textAutospace**
textDecoration	**textDecorationBlink**[*]	**textDecorationLineThrough**[*]
textDecorationNone[*]	**textDecorationOverline**[*]	**textDecorationUnderline**[*]
textTransform	**top**	**unicodeBidi**
visibility	**width**	**wordSpacing**
zIndex		

*   This property has no corresponding attribute.

Example

The following example shows how use the **U** element to underline text.

```
<U>This text is underlined.</U>
```

UL Element | UL Object

Draws lines of text as a bulleted list.

Remarks

The **UL** element is a block element and requires a closing tag.

The **TYPE** attribute determines the list type for all ensuing lists unless a different type value is set.

This element is available in HTML as of Internet Explorer 3.0 and in script as of Internet Explorer 4.0.

Attributes/Properties

	CLASS		
canHaveChildren[*]	**className**	**clientHeight**[*]	**clientLeft**[*]
clientTop[*]	**clientWidth**[*]	**currentStyle**[*]	**dir**
firstChild[*]	**id**	**innerHTML**[*]	**innerText**[*]
isTextEdit[*]	**lang**	**language**	**lastChild**[*]
nextSibling[*]	**nodeName**[*]	**nodeType**[*]	**nodeValue**[*]

Attributes/Properties *(continued)*

offsetHeight*	offsetLeft*	offsetParent*	offsetTop*
offsetWidth*	outerHTML*	outerText*	parentElement*
parentNode*	parentTextEdit*	previousSibling*	readyState*
recordNumber*	runtimeStyle*	scopeName*	scrollHeight*
scrollLeft*	scrollTop*	scrollWidth*	sourceIndex*
style	tabIndex	tagName*	tagUrn*
title	type	uniqueID*	

*   This property has no corresponding attribute.

Methods

addBehavior	appendChild	applyElement
attachEvent	blur	clearAttributes
click	cloneNode	componentFromPoint
contains	detachEvent	focus
getAdjacentText	getAttribute	getBoundingClientRect
getClientRects	getElementsByTagName	getExpression
hasChildNodes	insertAdjacentElement	insertAdjacentHTML
insertAdjacentText	insertBefore	mergeAttributes
releaseCapture	removeAttribute	removeBehavior
removeChild	removeExpression	removeNode
replaceAdjacentText	replaceChild	replaceNode
scrollIntoView	setAttribute	setCapture
setExpression	swapNode	

Events

onbeforecopy	onbeforecut	onbeforepaste	onblur
onclick	oncopy	oncut	ondblclick
ondrag	ondragend	ondragenter	ondragleave
ondragover	ondragstart	ondrop	onfocus
onhelp	onkeydown	onkeypress	onkeyup

Events *(continued)*

onlosecapture	onmousedown	onmousemove	onmouseout
onmouseover	onmouseup	onpaste	onpropertychange
onreadystatechange	onresize	onselectstart	

Collections

all	attributes	behaviorUrns	childNodes	children

Default Behaviors

clientCaps	download	homePage	httpFolder	saveFavorite
saveHistory	saveSnapshot	time	userData	

CSS Properties

Note For a list of corresponding attributes, see Appendix C.

background	backgroundColor	backgroundImage
backgroundPosition	backgroundPositionX*	backgroundPositionY*
backgroundRepeat	behavior	border
borderBottom	borderBottomColor	borderBottomStyle
borderBottomWidth	borderColor	borderLeft
borderLeftColor	borderLeftStyle	borderLeftWidth
borderRight	borderRightColor	borderRightStyle
borderRightWidth	borderStyle	borderTop
borderTopColor	borderTopStyle	borderTopWidth
borderWidth	bottom	clear
color	cursor	direction
font	fontFamily	fontSize
fontStyle	fontVariant	fontWeight
layoutGrid	layoutGridChar	layoutGridCharSpacing
layoutGridLine	layoutGridMode	layoutGridType
left	letterSpacing	lineBreak
lineHeight	listStyle	listStyleImage

CSS Properties *(continued)*

listStylePosition	listStyleType	margin
marginBottom	marginLeft	marginRight
marginTop	overflow	overflowX
overflowY	pageBreakAfter	pageBreakBefore
pixelBottom*	pixelHeight*	pixelLeft*
pixelRight*	pixelTop*	pixelWidth*
posBottom*	posHeight*	position
posLeft*	posRight*	posTop*
posWidth*	right	styleFloat
textAlign	textAutospace	textDecoration
textDecorationBlink*	textDecorationLineThrough*	textDecorationNone*
textDecorationOverline*	textDecorationUnderline*	textIndent
textJustify	textTransform	top
unicodeBidi	visibility	width
wordBreak	wordSpacing	zIndex

*   This property has no corresponding attribute.

Example

The following example shows how to use the **UL** element to create a bulleted list.

```
<UL>
<LI>This is the first bulleted item in the list.
<LI>And this is the second bulleted item in the list.
</UL>
```

userProfile Object

Provides methods that allow a script to request read access to and perform read actions on a user's profile information.

Remarks

The request is queued up before reading or writing is performed. This simplifies the user experience because users are only prompted once for profile release permissions for a batch of requests.

This object is available in script as of Internet Explorer 4.0.

Methods

addReadRequest   **clearRequest**   **doReadRequest**   **getAttribute**

Example

The following is an example of a script that can be run on the client to read various values from the profile information.

```
// Queue up a request for read access to multiple profile attributes.
navigator.userProfile.addReadRequest("vcard.displayname");
navigator.userProfile.addReadRequest("vcard.gender");

// Request access to the information.
navigator.userProfile.doReadRequest(usage-code, "Acme Corporation");

// Now perform read operations to access the information.
name = navigator.userProfile.getAttribute("vcard.displayname");
gender = navigator.userProfile.getAttribute("vcard.gender");

// The script can now use the 'name' and 'gender' variables
// to personalize content or to send information back to the server.

// Clear the request queue to prepare for future information requests.
navigator.userProfile.clearRequest();
```

Applies To

 WIN16   WIN32   MAC   UNIX

navigator

VAR Element | VAR Object

Renders text in a small fixed-width font.

Remarks

The **VAR** element is an inline element and requires a closing tag.

This element is available in HTML as of Internet Explorer 3.0 and in script as of Internet Explorer 4.0.

Attributes/Properties

	CLASS		
canHaveChildren[*]	className	clientHeight[*]	clientLeft[*]
clientTop[*]	clientWidth[*]	currentStyle[*]	dir
firstChild[*]	id	innerHTML[*]	innerText[*]

Attributes/Properties *(continued)*

isTextEdit[*]	lang	language	lastChild[*]
nextSibling[*]	nodeName[*]	nodeType[*]	nodeValue[*]
offsetHeight[*]	offsetLeft[*]	offsetParent[*]	offsetTop[*]
offsetWidth[*]	outerHTML[*]	outerText[*]	parentElement[*]
parentNode[*]	parentTextEdit[*]	previousSibling[*]	readyState[*]
recordNumber[*]	runtimeStyle[*]	scopeName[*]	scrollHeight[*]
scrollLeft[*]	scrollTop[*]	scrollWidth[*]	sourceIndex[*]
style	tabIndex	tagName[*]	tagUrn[*]
title	uniqueID[*]		

[*] This property has no corresponding attribute.

Methods

addBehavior	appendChild	applyElement
attachEvent	blur	clearAttributes
click	cloneNode	componentFromPoint
contains	detachEvent	focus
getAdjacentText	getAttribute	getBoundingClientRect
getClientRects	getElementsByTagName	getExpression
hasChildNodes	insertAdjacentElement	insertAdjacentHTML
insertAdjacentText	insertBefore	mergeAttributes
releaseCapture	removeAttribute	removeBehavior
removeChild	removeExpression	removeNode
replaceAdjacentText	replaceChild	replaceNode
scrollIntoView	setAttribute	setCapture
setExpression	swapNode	

Events

onblur	onclick	ondblclick	ondrag
ondragend	ondragenter	ondragleave	ondragover
ondragstart	ondrop	onfocus	onhelp

Events *(continued)*

onkeydown	onkeypress	onkeyup	onlosecapture
onmousedown	onmousemove	onmouseout	onmouseover
onmouseup	onpropertychange	onreadystatechange	onresize
onselectstart			

Collections

all	attributes	behaviorUrns	childNodes	children

Default Behaviors

clientCaps	download	homePage	httpFolder	saveFavorite
saveHistory	saveSnapshot	time	userData	

CSS Properties

Note For a list of corresponding attributes, see Appendix C.

background	backgroundColor	backgroundImage
backgroundPosition	backgroundPositionX[*]	backgroundPositionY[*]
backgroundRepeat	behavior	bottom
clear	color	cursor
direction	font	fontFamily
fontSize	fontStyle	fontVariant
fontWeight	layoutGridMode	left
letterSpacing	lineHeight	overflow
overflowX	overflowY	pixelBottom[*]
pixelHeight[*]	pixelLeft[*]	pixelRight[*]
pixelTop[*]	pixelWidth[*]	posBottom[*]
posHeight[*]	position	posLeft[*]
posRight[*]	posTop[*]	posWidth[*]
right	styleFloat	textAutospace
textDecoration	textDecorationBlink[*]	textDecorationLineThrough[*]
textDecorationNone[*]	textDecorationOverline[*]	textDecorationUnderline[*]

CSS Properties *(continued)*

textTransform	**top**	**unicodeBidi**
visibility	**width**	**wordSpacing**
zIndex		

* This property has no corresponding attribute.

Example

The following example shows how to use the **VAR** element.

```
Enter the <VAR>filename</VAR> in the dialog box.
```

WBR Element | WBR Object

Inserts a soft line break into a block of **NOBR** text.

Remarks

The **WBR** element does not require a closing tag.

This element is available in HTML as of Internet Explorer 3.0 and in script as of Internet Explorer 4.0.

Attributes/Properties

Note These properties have no corresponding attributes.

currentStyle	**id**	**outerHTML**	**outerText**
scopeName	**tagUrn**		

Methods

addBehavior	**componentFromPoint**	**getAttribute**	**removeAttribute**
removeBehavior	**scrollIntoView**	**setAttribute**	

Collections

behaviorUrns

Default Behaviors

clientCaps	**download**	**homePage**

CSS Properties

> **Note** For a list of corresponding attributes, see Appendix C.

behavior   **textAutospace**

Example

The following example shows how to use the **WBR** element to create line breaks. In contrast, the **NOBR** elements does not break lines.

```
<NOBR>This line of text does not break, no matter how narrow the window gets.</NOBR>
<NOBR>This one, however,<WBR> breaks after the word "however,"
if the window gets small enough.</NOBR>
```

window Object

Represents an open window in the browser.

Remarks

You can use the **window** object to retrieve information about the state of the window. You can also use this object to gain access to the document in the window, to the events that occur in the window, and to features of the browser that affect the window.

Typically, the browser creates one **window** object when it opens an HTML document. However, if a document defines one or more frames (that is, contains one or more **FRAME** or **IFRAME** tags), the browser creates one **window** object for the original document and one additional **window** object for each frame. These additional objects are child windows of the original window and can be affected by actions that occur in the original. For example, closing the original window causes all child windows to close. You can also create new windows (and corresponding **window** objects) using methods such as **open**, **showModalDialog**, and **showModelessDialog**.

You can apply any window property, method, or collection to any variable or expression that evaluates to a **window** object, regardless of how that window was created. Additionally, you can access all window properties, methods, and collections in the current window by using the property, method, or collection name directly— that is, without prefixing it with an expression that evaluates to the current **window** object. However, to help make more readable code and to avoid potential ambiguities, many authors use the **window** keyword when accessing window properties, methods, and collections for the current window. This keyword always refers to the current window.

> **Note** Window property, method, and collection names are reserved keywords and cannot be used as the names of variables and routines.

The **dialogArguments**, **dialogHeight**, **dialogLeft**, **dialogTop**, **dialogWidth**, and **returnValue** properties are available only for windows created using the **showModalDialog** and **showModelessDialog** methods.

This object is available in script as of Internet Explorer 3.0.

Attributes/Properties

Note These properties have no corresponding attributes.

clientInformation	closed	defaultStatus	dialogArguments
dialogHeight	dialogLeft	dialogTop	dialogWidth
document	event	external	history
length	location	name	navigator
offscreenBuffering	opener	parent	returnValue
screen	screenLeft	screenTop	self
status	top		

Methods

alert	attachEvent	blur	clearInterval
clearTimeout	close	confirm	detachEvent
execScript	focus	moveBy	moveTo
navigate	open	print	prompt
resizeBy	resizeTo	scroll	scrollBy
scrollTo	setInterval	setTimeout	showHelp
showModalDialog	showModelessDialog		

Events

onafterprint	onbeforeprint	onbeforeunload	onblur	onerror
onfocus	onhelp	onload	onresize	onunload

Collections

frames

Examples

The following example shows how to display an alert for the current window.

```
alert("A simple message.")
```

The following example shows how to check whether the current window contains child windows and, if it does, display the names of those child windows.

```
if ( window.frames != null ) {
    for ( i = 0; i< window.frames.length; i++ )
        window.alert ("Child window " +i+ " is named "+window.frames(i).name);
}
```

The following example shows how to create a simple event handler function for the window's **onload** event. In the absence of a "window" element, the **BODY** element hosts the following **window** object events: **onblur**, **onbeforeunload**, **onfocus**, **onload**, and **onunload**.

```
<BODY onload="window.status='Page is loaded!'">
```

XML Element | XML Object

Defines an XML data island on an HTML page.

Remarks

The **XML** element requires a closing tag.

This element is available in HTML and script as of Internet Explorer 5.

Note The **readyState** property of the **XML** element, available as a string value, corresponds to the **readyState** property of the **XMLDOMDocument** object, which is available as a long value. The string values correspond to the long values of the XML document object's property as follows:

0   uninitialized

1   loading

2   loaded

3   interactive

4   complete

For example, consider the following **xmldoc** data island:

```
<xml id=xmldoc src="123.xml"></xml>
```

Use one of the following two methods to check the value of the **readyState** property to determine if the XML data island has been completely downloaded.

- Using the **readyState** property of the **XML** element:

```
if (xmldoc.readyState == "complete")
    window.alert ("The XML document is ready.");
```

- Using the **readyState** property of the **XMLDOMDocument** object:

```
if (xmldoc.XMLDocument.readyState == 4)
    window.alert ("The XML document is ready.");
```

Attributes/Properties

id	**readyState**[*]	**scopeName**[*]	**src**
tagUrn[*]	**XMLDocument**[*]		

[*]   This property has no corresponding attribute.

Methods

addBehavior	**componentFromPoint**	**removeBehavior**

Events

ondataavailable	**ondatasetchanged**	**ondatasetcomplete**	**onreadystatechange**
onrowenter	**onrowexit**	**onrowsdelete**	**onrowsinserted**

Collections

behaviorUrns

Default Behaviors

clientCaps	**download**	**homePage**

CSS Properties

Note For a list of corresponding attributes, see Appendix C.

behavior	**textAutospace**

Example

The following example shows how to define a simple XML data island that can be embedded directly in an HTML page.

```
<XML ID="oMetaData">
  <METADATA>
     <AUTHOR>John Smith</AUTHOR>
     <GENERATOR>Visual Notepad</GENERATOR>
     <PAGETYPE>Reference</PAGETYPE>
     <ABSTRACT>Specifies a data island</ABSTRACT>
  </METADATA>
</XML>
```

The following example shows how to use script to retrieve the text contained within the **ABSTRACT** field of the data island.

```
var oNode = oMetaData.XMLDocument.selectSingleNode("METADATA/ABSTRACT");
alert(oNode.text);
```

XMP Element | XMP Object

Renders text in a fixed-width font used for examples.

Remarks

Use of this element is no longer recommended. Use the **PRE** or **SAMP** element instead.

Attributes/Properties

	CLASS		
canHaveChildren[*]	className	clientHeight[*]	clientLeft[*]
clientTop[*]	clientWidth[*]	currentStyle[*]	dir
firstChild[*]	id	innerHTML[*]	innerText[*]
isTextEdit[*]	lang	language	lastChild[*]
nextSibling[*]	nodeName[*]	nodeType[*]	nodeValue[*]
offsetHeight[*]	offsetLeft[*]	offsetParent[*]	offsetTop[*]
offsetWidth[*]	outerHTML[*]	outerText[*]	parentElement[*]
parentNode[*]	parentTextEdit[*]	previousSibling[*]	readyState[*]
recordNumber[*]	runtimeStyle[*]	scopeName[*]	scrollHeight[*]

Attributes/Properties *(continued)*

scrollLeft[*]	scrollTop[*]	scrollWidth[*]	sourceIndex[*]
style	tabIndex	tagName[*]	tagUrn[*]
title	uniqueID[*]		

*   This property has no corresponding attribute.

Methods

addBehavior	appendChild	applyElement
attachEvent	blur	clearAttributes
click	cloneNode	componentFromPoint
contains	detachEvent	focus
getAdjacentText	getAttribute	getBoundingClientRect
getClientRects	getElementsByTagName	hasChildNodes
insertAdjacentElement	insertAdjacentHTML	insertBefore
mergeAttributes	releaseCapture	removeAttribute
removeBehavior	removeChild	removeNode
replaceAdjacentText	replaceChild	replaceNode
scrollIntoView	setAttribute	setCapture
swapNode		

Events

onblur	onclick	ondblclick	ondrag
ondragend	ondragenter	ondragleave	ondragover
ondragstart	ondrop	onfocus	onhelp
onkeydown	onkeypress	onkeyup	onlosecapture
onmousedown	onmousemove	onmouseout	onmouseover
onmouseup	onpropertychange	onreadystatechange	onresize
onselectstart			

Collections

all	attributes	behaviorUrns	childNodes	children

Default Behaviors

clientCaps	download	homePage	httpFolder	saveFavorite
saveHistory	saveSnapshot	time	userData	

CSS Properties

Note For a list of corresponding attributes, see Appendix C.

background	backgroundColor	backgroundImage
backgroundPosition	backgroundPositionX*	backgroundPositionY*
backgroundRepeat	behavior	border
borderBottom	borderBottomColor	borderBottomStyle
borderBottomWidth	borderColor	borderLeft
borderLeftColor	borderLeftStyle	borderLeftWidth
borderRight	borderRightColor	borderRightStyle
borderRightWidth	borderStyle	borderTop
borderTopColor	borderTopStyle	borderTopWidth
borderWidth	bottom	clear
color	cursor	direction
font	fontFamily	fontSize
fontStyle	fontVariant	fontWeight
layoutGrid	layoutGridChar	layoutGridCharSpacing
layoutGridLine	layoutGridMode	layoutGridType
left	letterSpacing	lineBreak
lineHeight	margin	marginBottom
marginLeft	marginRight	marginTop
overflow	overflowX	overflowY
pageBreakAfter	pageBreakBefore	pixelBottom*
pixelHeight*	pixelLeft*	pixelRight*
pixelTop*	pixelWidth*	posBottom*
posHeight*	position	posLeft*

CSS Properties *(continued)*

posRight[*]	posTop[*]	posWidth[*]
right	styleFloat	textAlign
textAutospace	textDecoration	textDecorationBlink[*]
textDecorationLineThrough[*]	textDecorationNone[*]	textDecorationOverline[*]
textDecorationUnderline[*]	textIndent	textJustify
textTransform	top	unicodeBidi
visibility	wordBreak	wordSpacing
zIndex		

* This property has no corresponding attribute.

Properties

The following section provides a complete list of properties, including cascading style sheets (CSS) properties, exposed by the Dynamic HTML (DHTML) Object Model. Entries are arranged in alphabetical order.

As of Internet Explorer 5, you can use an **expression** in the **STYLE** block or **STYLE** attribute in place of the specified value for CSS properties. For more information, see the documentation for Dynamic Properties on the Web Workshop CD-ROM.

ACCESSKEY Attribute | accessKey Property

Sets or retrieves the accelerator key for the object.

Syntax

HTML   *<ELEMENT* **ACCESSKEY** = *sAccessKey ... >*

Scripting   *object*.**accessKey** [= *sAccessKey*]

Possible Values

sAccessKey   Character string specifying an alphanumeric keyboard key.

The property is read/write with no default value.

Remarks

When the user simultaneously presses the ALT key and the accelerator key assigned to an object, the object receives focus.

By default, the **accessKey** property sets focus to the object. In addition, some controls perform an action after receiving focus. For example, using **accessKey** on a button fires the **onclick** event, whereas using **accessKey** on a radio button fires the **onclick** event and toggles the **checked** property, visibly selecting or deselecting the control.

As of Internet Explorer 5, scoped elements that do not implicitly expose the **accessKey** property support the property by setting the **TABINDEX** attribute to any valid negative or positive integer.

DHTML Properties

Example

The following example shows how to use the **LABEL** object and the **accessKey** property to set focus on a text box. The rich text support in the **LABEL** object makes it possible to underline the designated **accessKey**.

```
<LABEL FOR="fp1" ACCESSKEY="1">#<U>1</U>:
    Press Alt+1 to set focus to textbox</LABEL>
<INPUT TYPE="text" NAME="T1" VALUE=text1 SIZE="20"
    TABINDEX="1" ID="fp1">
```

To see this code in action, refer to the Web Workshop CD-ROM.

Applies To

 WIN16   WIN32   MAC   UNIX

A, APPLET, AREA, BUTTON, EMBED, FIELDSET, IFRAME, INPUT type=button, INPUT type=checkbox, INPUT type=file, INPUT type=image, INPUT type=password, INPUT type=radio, INPUT type=reset, INPUT type=submit, INPUT type=text, LABEL, LEGEND, OBJECT, SELECT, TABLE, TEXTAREA

 WIN16   WIN32   MAC   UNIX

BDO

ACTION Attribute | action Property

Sets or retrieves the URL to which the **FORM** content is to be sent for processing.

Syntax

HTML   <FORM **ACTION** = *sURL* ... >

Scripting *form*.**action** [= *sURL*]

Possible Values

sURL   String specifying the URL to be used. If a relative path is specified, the base URL of the document is assumed.

The property is read/write with no default value.

Remarks

The way the data is submitted depends on the value of the **method** and **encoding** properties.

Example

The following example shows how to specify a URL for posting a form by using the **ACTION** attribute.

```
<HTML>
    <FORM ACTION="http://example.microsoft.com/sample.asp"
        METHOD="POST">
        Enter your name: <INPUT NAME="FName"><BR>
        Favorite IceCream Flavor:
        <SELECT NAME="Flavor">
            <OPTION VALUE="Chocolate">Chocolate
            <OPTION VALUE="Strawberry">Strawberry
            <OPTION VALUE="Vanilla" SELECTED>Vanilla
        </SELECT>
        <P><INPUT TYPE=SUBMIT>
    </FORM>
</HTML>
```

The next example shows how to specify a URL for the MailTo protocol by using the **ACTION** attribute.

```
<form ACTION="mailto:sales@widgets.com" method=GET>
    <input name=subject type=hidden
        value="Widget%20Product%20Information%20Request">
    Enter your full mailing address<BR>
    <TextArea name=body cols=40></textarea>
    <input type=submit value="Send Request"
</form>
```

Applies To

 WIN16   WIN32   MAC

FORM

 UNIX

FORM

active Pseudo-class

Sets the style of anchor when the link is engaged or active.

Syntax

HTML   [A]:**active** { *attribute1:parameter1* [; *attribute2:parameter2* [; . . .]] }

Scripting N/A

Possible Values

attribute   Any attribute applicable to text.

parameter Any of the range of values available to the corresponding attribute.

The default value of the pseudo-class is browser specific.

Remarks

Active means that the user is currently navigating the link. The **active** pseudo-class is often used to set specific styles for the other states of a link: **link**, **visited**, and **hover**. Using pseudo-classes on objects other than the **A** object has no effect.

Example

The following example shows how to use the active pseudo-class to set the attributes of the active link.

```
A:active { font-weight:bold; color:purple }
```

Applies To

 WIN16   WIN32   MAC   UNIX

A

activeElement Property

Retrieves the object that has the focus.

Syntax

HTML   N/A

Scripting   [*oActive* =] *document*.**activeElement**

Possible Values

oActive   Object representing the element that has the focus.

The property is read-only with no default value.

Applies To

 WIN16   WIN32   MAC   UNIX

document

ALIGN Attribute | align Property

Sets or retrieves how the object is aligned with adjacent text.

Syntax

HTML   *<ELEMENT* **ALIGN =** "absbottom" | "absmiddle" | "baseline" | "bottom" | "left" | "middle" | "right" | "texttop" | "top">

Scripting *object*.**align** [= *sAlign*]

DHTML Properties

Possible Values

absbottom   Aligns the bottom of the object with the absolute bottom of the surrounding text. The absolute bottom is equal to the baseline of the text minus the height of the largest descender in the text.

absmiddle   Aligns the middle of the object with the middle of the surrounding text. The absolute middle is the midpoint between the absolute bottom and text top of the surrounding text.

baseline   Aligns the bottom of the object with the baseline of the surrounding text.

bottom   Aligns the bottom of the object with the bottom of the surrounding text. The bottom is equal to the baseline minus the standard height of a descender in the text.

left   Aligns the object to the left of the surrounding text. All preceding and subsequent text flows to the right of the object. This is the default value.

middle   Aligns the middle of the object with the surrounding text.

right   Aligns the object to the right of the surrounding text. All subsequent text flows to the left of the object.

texttop   Aligns the top of the object with the absolute top of the surrounding text. The absolute top is the baseline plus the height of the largest ascender in the text.

top   Aligns the top of the object with the top of the text. The top of the text is the baseline plus the standard height of an ascender in the text.

Remarks

For the **INPUT** object, this attribute applies only to the **image** type. It is undefined for all other types.

Applies To

 WIN16   WIN32   MAC

APPLET, IFRAME, IMG, INPUT type=image, OBJECT

 UNIX   WIN16   WIN32   MAC

APPLET, EMBED, FIELDSET, IFRAME, IMG, INPUT type=image, OBJECT, SELECT

ALIGN Attribute | align Property

Sets or retrieves the alignment of the caption or legend.

Syntax

HTML   *<ELEMENT* **ALIGN** = `"bottom"` | `"center"` | `"left"` | `"right"` | `"top"` ... *>*

Scripting   *object*.**align** [= *sAlign*]

Possible Values

bottom   Aligns bottom-center.

center   Aligns center.

left   Aligns left.

right   Aligns right.

top   Aligns top-center.

The property is read/write with no default value.

Remarks

The **LEGEND** tag is used only within a **FIELDSET** tag. The contents of the **LEGEND** tag are displayed by overwriting the information in the top border of the **FIELDSET**.

The **CAPTION** tag is used only within a **TABLE** tag. Its contents are displayed centered above the table and do not interact at all with the table border.

Applies To

 WIN16   WIN32   MAC

CAPTION

UNIX   WIN16   WIN32   MAC

CAPTION, LEGEND

ALIGN Attribute | align Property

Sets or retrieves the table alignment.

Syntax

HTML   <TABLE **ALIGN** = "left" | "center" | "right"... >

Scripting *table*.**align** [= *sAlign*]

Possible Values

left   Aligns to the left edge.

center   Aligns to the center.

right   Aligns to the right edge.

The property is read/write with a default value of left.

Applies To

 WIN16   WIN32   MAC

TABLE

 UNIX

TABLE

ALIGN Attribute | align Property

Sets or retrieves the alignment of the object relative to the display or table.

Syntax

HTML   <*ELEMENT* **ALIGN** = "center" | "justify" | "left" | "right" ... >

Scripting *object*.**align** [= *sAlign*]

DHTML Properties

Possible Values

center   Aligns to the center.

justify   Aligns to the left and right edge.

left   Aligns to the left edge.

right   Aligns to the right edge.

The property is read/write with a default value of left, except for the TH element.

Remarks

The default value for the **TH** element is center.

Applies To

 WIN16   WIN32   MAC

COL, COLGROUP, DIV, HR, P, TD, TH, TR

 UNIX   WIN16   WIN32   MAC

COL, COLGROUP, DIV, Hn, HR, P, TBODY, TD, TFOOT, TH, THEAD, TR

ALINK Attribute | aLink Property

Sets or retrieves the color of all active links in the element.

Syntax

HTML   <BODY **ALINK** = *sColor* ... >

Scripting   *body*.**aLink** [= *sColor*]

Possible Values

sColor   String specifying one of the color names or hexadecimal color values in the "Color Table" in Appendix C.

The property is read/write with no default value.

Remarks

Some browsers do not recognize color names, but all browsers should recognize red-green-blue (RGB) color values and display them correctly.

Applies To

 WIN16   WIN32   MAC   UNIX

BODY

aLinkColor Property

Sets or retrieves the color of all active links in the document.

Syntax

HTML   N/A

Scripting   *document*.**aLinkColor** [= *sColor*]

Possible Values

sColor   String specifying one of the color names or red-green-blue (RGB) values
in the "Color Table" in Appendix C.

The property is read/write with a default value of #0000ff.

Remarks

Some browsers do not recognize color names, but all browsers should recognize RGB
color values and display them correctly.

Applies To

 WIN16   WIN32   MAC

document

 UNIX

document

ALT Attribute | alt Property

Sets or retrieves a text alternative to the graphic.

Syntax

HTML   *<ELEMENT* **ALT** = *sTxt* ... *>*

Scripting *object*.**alt** [= *sTxt*]

DHTML Properties

Possible Values

sTxt   String specifying the text to display as an alternative to the graphic.

The property is read/write with no default value.

Remarks

The text is used to replace the graphic for text-only browsers, to display in the window before the graphic has loaded, and to act as a ToolTip when the user hovers the mouse over the graphic.

Example

The following example uses the **ALT** attribute to indicate that the icon displayed denotes a read/write property.

```
<IMG SRC="http://example.microsoft.com/rw.gif" ALT="Read/Write Property">
```

Applies To

 WIN16   WIN32   MAC

IMG

 WIN16   WIN32   MAC   UNIX

AREA, IMG

altHTML Property

Sets or retrieves the optional alternative HTML script to execute if the object fails to load.

Syntax

HTML   N/A

Scripting *object*.**altHTML** [= *sHTMLCode*]

Possible Values

sHTMLCode   String specifying alternative HTML code to execute.

The property is read/write with no default value.

Applies To

 WIN16   WIN32   MAC   UNIX

APPLET, OBJECT

altKey Property

Retrieves the current state of the ALT key.

Syntax

HTML   N/A

Scripting   [*bAltKeyDown* =] *event*.**altKey**

Possible Values

false   ALT key is not down.

true   ALT key is down.

The property is read-only with no default value.

Applies To

 WIN16   WIN32   MAC   UNIX

event

appCodeName Property

Retrieves the code name of the browser.

Syntax

HTML   N/A

Scripting   [*sCodeName* =] *navigator*.**appCodeName**

Possible Values

Mozilla   String returned by Internet Explorer and Netscape Navigator.

sCodeName   String specifying the browser's code name.

The property is read-only with a default value of Mozilla.

Applies To

 WIN16   WIN32   MAC

navigator

 UNIX

navigator

appMinorVersion Property

Retrieves the application's minor version value.

Syntax

HTML   N/A

Scripting   [*sMinorVersion* =] *navigator*.**appMinorVersion**

Possible Values

0   String returned by Internet Explorer 4.0 and 5, specifying a minor
                       version of zero.

sMinorVersion   String specifying the browser's minor version.

The property is read-only with a default value of 0.

Applies To

 WIN16   WIN32   MAC   UNIX

navigator

appName Property

Retrieves the name of the browser.

Syntax

HTML   N/A

Scripting   [*sAppName* =] *navigator*.**appName**

Possible Values

`Microsoft Internet Explorer`	String returned by Internet Explorer.
`Netscape`	String returned by Netscape Navigator.
sAppName	String specifying the browser's name.

The property is read-only with a default value of `Microsoft Internet Explorer`, or as specified by other browsers.

Applies To

 WIN16   WIN32   MAC

navigator

 UNIX

navigator

appVersion Property

Retrieves the platform and version of the browser.

Syntax

HTML   N/A

Scripting   [*sVersion* =] *navigator*.**appVersion**

Possible Values

sVersion   String specifying the platform and version information for the browser.

The property is read-only with a default value specified by the browser.

Remarks

The **appVersion** property returns a value based on the browser name and browser version. The following example shows the format of the returned value.

```
4.0 (compatible; MSIE 4.01; Windows 95)
```

Applies To

 WIN16   WIN32   MAC

navigator

UNIX

navigator

AUTOCOMPLETE Attribute

Sets or retrieves whether AutoComplete is enabled for the object.

Syntax

HTML   <ELEMENT **AUTOCOMPLETE** = "off" ... >

Scripting   N/A

Possible Values

off   AutoComplete is disabled.

The attribute has no default value.

Remarks

When AutoComplete is enabled, suggestions are provided for the **VALUE** of a text field. Suggestion values are mapped values based on the **NAME** attribute or vCard schema specified by the **VCARD_NAME** attribute.

If AutoComplete is disabled, values are not stored and suggested values are not presented.

Although **PASSWORD** values can be mapped for AutoComplete, the ability to store this information can be disabled in the browser, and the user is prompted for a confirmation before the value is stored.

Information provided by the AutoComplete feature is not exposed to the object model, and is not visible to a Web page until the user selects one of the suggestions as a value for the text field.

This attribute is not supported in HTML Applications.

Example

The following example shows how to use the **AUTOCOMPLETE** attribute to disable the AutoComplete feature.

```
<INPUT TYPE="password" AUTOCOMPLETE="off">
```

Applies To

 WIN16   WIN32   MAC   UNIX

INPUT type=password, INPUT type=text, FORM

availHeight Property

Retrieves the height of the working area of the system's screen, excluding the Windows taskbar.

Syntax

HTML   N/A

Scripting   [*iHeight* =] *screen*.**availHeight**

Possible Values

iHeight   Integer specifying the available screen height, in pixels.

The property is read-only with no default value.

Applies To

 WIN16   WIN32   MAC   UNIX

screen

availWidth Property

Retrieves the width of the working area of the system's screen, excluding the Windows taskbar.

Syntax

HTML   N/A

Scripting   [*iWidth* =] *screen*.**availWidth**

Possible Values

iWidth   Integer specifying the available screen width, in pixels.

The property is read-only with no default value.

Applies To

 WIN16   WIN32   MAC   UNIX

screen

background Attribute | background Property

Sets or retrieves the separate background properties for the object at once.

Syntax

HTML   { **background:** *sColor* || *sImage* || *sRepeat* || *sAttachment* || *sPosition* }

Scripting   *object*.**style.background** [= [*sColor*] [*sImage*] [*sRepeat*] [*sAttachment*]
[*sPosition*]]

Possible Values

sColor   Any of the range of values available to the **backgroundColor** property.

sImage   Any of the range of values available to the **backgroundImage**
property.

sRepeat   Any of the range of values available to the **backgroundRepeat**
property.

sAttachment   Any of the range of values available to the **backgroundAttachment**
property.

sPosition   Any of the range of values available to the **backgroundPosition**
property.

The property is read/write with a default value of `transparent none repeat scroll`
`0% 0%`. The cascading style sheets (CSS) attribute is not inherited.

Remarks

The **background** property is a composite property. Separate properties can be used to
specify each of the individual properties, but in many cases it is more convenient to
set them in one place using this composite property.

Individual background properties not set by the composite background property are set to their default values. For example, the default value for *sImage* is none. Setting **background**: white is equivalent to setting **background**: white none repeat scroll 0% 0%. So, in addition to setting the background color to white, setting **background**: white clears any *sImage*, *sRepeat*, *sAttachment*, or *sPosition* values previously set.

The background properties render in the object's content and padding; however, borders are set using the **border** properties.

In Internet Explorer 3.0, elements that expose the **background** property only support the *sColor* and *sImage* values; the *sAttachment* value is only supported by the **BODY**, **TABLE**, and **TD** elements. In block elements, such as **P** and **DIV**, background images and colors appear only behind text in Internet Explorer 3.0; in Internet Explorer 4.0 and later, the background stretches from margin to margin when used with block elements.

Although objects do not inherit the **background** property, the background image or color of an object's parent appears behind an object if a background is not specified.

For more information about supported colors, see the "Color Table" in Appendix C.

Example

The following examples demonstrate how to use the **background** property and the **background** attribute to set the background values at once.

The sample below uses inline event handlers to modify the **background-color** and **background-position** attributes of an image. These attributes are specified in an embedded style sheet using the **background** attribute.

```
<STYLE>
.style1{background: beige url(sphere.jpg) no-repeat top center }
.style2{background: ivory url(sphere.jpeg) no-repeat bottom right }
</STYLE>
</HEAD>
<BODY>
<SPAN onmouseover="this.className='style1'"
    onmouseout="this.className='style2'">
. . . </SPAN>
```

To see this code in action, refer to the Web Workshop CD-ROM.

The sample below shows how to use inline scripting to modify the **backgroundColor** and **backgroundPosition** properties of an image.

```
<SPAN onclick="this.style.background='beige url(sphere.jpeg)
  no-repeat top center'">
. . . </SPAN>
```

To see this code in action, refer to the Web Workshop CD-ROM.

DHTML Properties

Applies To

 WIN16   WIN32   MAC

A, ADDRESS, B, BIG, BLOCKQUOTE, BODY, CAPTION, CENTER, CITE, CODE, DD, DIV, DT, EM, FORM, I, IMG, INPUT type=button, INPUT type=checkbox, INPUT type=image, INPUT type=password, INPUT type=radio, INPUT type=reset, INPUT type=submit, INPUT type=text, KBD, LI, LISTING, MARQUEE, P, PLAINTEXT, PRE, S, SAMP, SELECT, SMALL, SPAN, STRIKE, STRONG, SUB, SUP, TABLE, TD, TEXTAREA, TH, TT, U, VAR, XMP

 UNIX   WIN16   WIN32   MAC

A, ADDRESS, B, BIG, BLOCKQUOTE, BODY, BUTTON, CAPTION, CENTER, CITE, CODE, COL, COLGROUP, DD, DFN, DIR, DIV, DL, DT, EM, FIELDSET, FORM, Hn, HTML, I, IMG, INPUT type=button, INPUT type=checkbox, INPUT type=file, INPUT type=image, INPUT type=password, INPUT type=radio, INPUT type=reset, INPUT type=submit, INPUT type=text, ISINDEX, KBD, LABEL, LEGEND, LI, LISTING, MARQUEE, MENU, OL, P, PLAINTEXT, PRE, S, SAMP, SELECT, SMALL, SPAN, STRIKE, STRONG, style, SUB, SUP, TABLE, TBODY, TD, TEXTAREA, TFOOT, TH, THEAD, TR, TT, U, UL, VAR, XMP

 WIN16   WIN32   MAC   UNIX

runtimeStyle

BACKGROUND Attribute | background Property

Sets or retrieves the background picture tiled behind the text and graphics on the page.

Syntax

HTML   <BODY **BACKGROUND** = *sURL* ... >

Scripting *body*.**background** [= *sURL*]

Possible Values

sURL   String specifying the URL of the file to be used as the background picture for the page.

The property is read/write with no default value.

Applies To

 WIN16   WIN32   MAC

BODY

 UNIX

BODY

BACKGROUND Attribute | background Property

Sets or retrieves the background picture tiled behind the text and graphics in the object.

Syntax

HTML   *<ELEMENT* **BACKGROUND** *= sURL ... >*

Scripting   *object.***background** [*= sURL*]

Possible Values

sURL   String specifying the URL of the file to be used as the background picture.

The property is read/write with no default value.

Applies To

 WIN16   WIN32   MAC

TABLE, TD, TH

 UNIX

TABLE, TD, TH

DHTML Properties

background-attachment Attribute | backgroundAttachment Property

Sets or retrieves whether the background image scrolls with the content of the object or is fixed.

Syntax

HTML   { **background-attachment:** `scroll` | `fixed` }

Scripting *object*.**style.backgroundAttachment** [= *sAttachment*]

Possible Values

`scroll`   Background image scrolls with the content.

`fixed`   Background image does not scroll with the content.

The property is read/write with a default value of `scroll`; the cascading style sheets (CSS) attribute is not inherited.

Remarks

This property can be set with the other background properties by using the **background** composite property.

Internet Explorer 3.0 supports the **background-attachment** attribute, but only when it's set by using the **background** attribute.

Example

The following examples show how to use the **background-attachment** attribute and the **backgroundAttachment** property to fix the background.

The sample below uses an inline style sheet to fix the background so that it does not scroll with the text.

```
<STYLE >
    BODY { background-attachment: fixed }
</STYLE>
</HEAD>
<BODY background="some.jpg">
```

To see this code in action, refer to the Web Workshop CD-ROM.

The sample below uses inline scripting to fix the background so that it does not scroll with the content.

```
<BODY ID="oBdy" background="marble05.jpg"
onload="oBdy.style.backgroundAttachment = 'fixed'">
```

To see this code in action, refer to the Web Workshop CD-ROM.

Applies To

 WIN16   WIN32   MAC   UNIX

BODY, HTML, style

 WIN16   WIN32   MAC   UNIX

currentStyle, runtimeStyle

background-color Attribute | backgroundColor Property

Sets or retrieves the color behind the content of the object.

Syntax

HTML   { **background-color:** transparent | *sColor* }

Scripting   *object*.**style.backgroundColor** [= *sColor*]

Possible Values

transparent   Color of the next parent the background shines through.

sColor   Any of the range of values specified in the "Color Table" in Appendix C.

The property is read/write with a default value of transparent; the cascading style sheets (CSS) attribute is not inherited.

Remarks

This property can be set with the other background properties by using the **background** composite property.

Internet Explorer 3.0 supports the **background-color** attribute, but only when it's set by using the **background** attribute.

Example

The following examples show how to use the **background-color** attribute and the **backgroundColor** property to specify the background color.

The sample below uses an inline style sheet to set the background color to beige.

```
<SPAN STYLE="font-size:14; background-color:beige">
. . . </SPAN>
```

To see this code in action, refer to the Web Workshop CD-ROM.

The sample below uses inline scripting to set the background color to beige.

```
<SPAN onmouseover="this.style.backgroundColor='beige'">
. . . </SPAN>
```

To see this code in action, refer to the Web Workshop CD-ROM.

Applies To

 WIN16   WIN32   MAC

OPTION

 WIN16   WIN32   MAC   UNIX

A, ADDRESS, B, BIG, BLOCKQUOTE, BODY, BUTTON, CAPTION, CENTER, CITE, CODE, COL, COLGROUP, DD, DFN, DIR, DIV, DL, DT, EM, FIELDSET, FORM, Hn, HTML, I, IMG, INPUT type=button, INPUT type=checkbox, INPUT type=file, INPUT type=image, INPUT type=password, INPUT type=radio, INPUT type=reset, INPUT type=submit, INPUT type=text, ISINDEX, KBD, LABEL, LEGEND, LI, LISTING, MARQUEE, MENU, OL, OPTION, P, PLAINTEXT, PRE, S, SAMP, SELECT, SMALL, SPAN, STRIKE, STRONG, style, SUB, SUP, TABLE, TBODY, TD, TEXTAREA, TFOOT, TH, THEAD, TR, TT, U, UL, VAR, XMP

 WIN16   WIN32   MAC   UNIX

currentStyle, runtimeStyle

background-image Attribute | backgroundImage Property

Sets or retrieves the background image of the object.

DHTML Properties

Syntax

HTML   { **background-image:** url(*sUrl*) | none }

Scripting *object*.**style.backgroundImage** [= *sLocation*]

Possible Values

none   Color of the next parent through which the background shines through.

url(*sUrl*) Location of the image file, where *sURL* is an absolute or relative URL.

The property is read/write with a default value of none; the cascading style sheets (CSS) attribute is not inherited.

Remarks

The URL identifies the image file. When setting a background image, you can set a background color to be used when the image is unavailable. When the image is available, it overlays the background color.

This property can be set with the other background properties by using the **background** composite property.

Internet Explorer 3.0 supports the **background-image** attribute only when it's set by using the **background** attribute.

Example

The following examples show how to use the **background-image** attribute and the **backgroundImage** property to specify the background image.

The sample below uses a call to an embedded (global) style sheet to show and hide the background image.

```
<STYLE>
    .setUrl  { background-image: url(sphere.jpg) }
    .loseUrl { background-image: url(none) }
</STYLE>
</HEAD>
<BODY>
<SPAN STYLE="font-size:14" onmouseover="this.className='setUrl'"
    onmouseout="this.className='loseUrl'"> . . . </SPAN>
```

To see this code in action, refer to the Web Workshop CD-ROM.

The sample below uses inline scripting to show and hide the background image.

```
<SPAN onmouseover="this.style.backgroundImage='url(sphere.jpeg)'">
. . . </SPAN>
```

To see this code in action, refer to the Web Workshop CD-ROM.

Applies To

WIN16   WIN32   MAC   UNIX

A, ADDRESS, B, BIG, BLOCKQUOTE, BODY, BUTTON, CAPTION, CENTER, CITE, CODE, COL, COLGROUP, DD, DFN, DIR, DIV, DL, DT, EM, FIELDSET, FORM, Hn, HTML, I, IMG, INPUT type=button, INPUT type=checkbox, INPUT type=file, INPUT type=image, INPUT type=password, INPUT type=radio, INPUT type=reset, INPUT type=submit, INPUT type=text, ISINDEX, KBD, LABEL, LEGEND, LI, LISTING, MARQUEE, MENU, OL, P, PLAINTEXT, PRE, S, SAMP, SELECT, SMALL, SPAN, STRIKE, STRONG, style, SUB, SUP, TABLE, TBODY, TD, TEXTAREA, TFOOT, TH, THEAD, TR, TT, U, UL, VAR, XMP

WIN16   WIN32   MAC   UNIX

currentStyle, runtimeStyle

background-position Attribute | backgroundPosition Property

Sets or retrieves the position of the background of the element.

Syntax

HTML   { **background-position:** [*percentage* | *length*]{1,2} | [top | center | bottom] || [left | center | right] }

Scripting *object*.**style.backgroundPosition** [= *sPosition*]

Possible Values

percentage One or two percentage values consisting of a number, followed by a %.

length One or two length values consisting of a floating-point number, followed by an absolute units designators (cm, mm, in, pt, pc, or px) or a relative units designator (em or ex). For more information about the supported length units for CSS attributes, see "CSS Length Units" in Appendix C.

top Vertical alignment is at the top.

center Vertical alignment is centered.

bottom Vertical alignment is at the bottom.

left Horizontal alignment is to the left.

center Horizontal alignment is centered.

right Horizontal alignment is to the right.

The property is read/write with a default value of 0% 0%; the cascading style sheets (CSS) attribute is not inherited.

Remarks

The {1,2} indicates that one or two values may be specified. If only one value is set, that value applies to the horizontal coordinate, and the vertical is set to 50%. If both are set, the first value applies to the horizontal coordinate and the second value applies to the vertical.

Setting the values to 0% 0% positions the **background-image** to the upper-left corner of the element's content excluding the padding.

Specifying right center has the following effect: Because right is assumed to be an x-coordinate direction, right overwrites the center value and the background shifts right accordingly.

This property can be set with the other background properties by using the **background** composite property.

DHTML Properties

Example

The following examples show how to use the **background-position** attribute and the **backgroundPosition** property to specify the position of a background image.

The sample below uses a call to an embedded style sheet to move the sphere.

```
<STYLE>
    .style1 { background-image:"url(sphere.jpg)";
        background-repeat:"no-repeat";
        background-position:"top center"; }
    .style2 {background-image:"url(sphere.jpeg)";
        background-repeat:"no-repeat";
        background-position:"bottom right"; }
</STYLE>
</HEAD>
<BODY onload="oSpan.className='style1'">
<SPAN STYLE="font-size:14" ID="oSpan" onclick="this.className='style2'"
ondblclick="this.className='style1'">
. . . </SPAN>
```

To see this code in action, refer to the Web Workshop CD-ROM.

The sample below uses an inline style sheet to move the sphere.

```
<SPAN onmouseover="this.style.backgroundImage='url(sphere.jpeg)';
this.style.backgroundRepeat='no-repeat'; this.style.backgroundPosition=
'top center'">
```

To see this code in action, refer to the Web Workshop CD-ROM.

Applies To

 WIN16   WIN32   MAC   UNIX

A, ADDRESS, B, BIG, BLOCKQUOTE, BODY, BUTTON, CAPTION, CENTER, CITE, CODE, COL, COLGROUP, DD, DFN, DIR, DIV, DL, DT, EM, FIELDSET, FORM, Hn, HTML, I, IMG, INPUT type=button, INPUT type=checkbox, INPUT type=file, INPUT type=image, INPUT type=password, INPUT type=radio, INPUT type=reset, INPUT type=submit, INPUT type=text, ISINDEX, KBD, LABEL, LEGEND, LI, LISTING, MARQUEE, MENU, OL, P, PLAINTEXT, PRE, S, SAMP, SELECT, SMALL, SPAN, STRIKE, STRONG, style, SUB, SUP, TABLE, TBODY, TD, TEXTAREA, TFOOT, TH, THEAD, TR, TT, U, UL, VAR, XMP

 WIN16   WIN32   MAC   UNIX

runtimeStyle

backgroundPositionX Property

Sets or retrieves the x-coordinate of the **backgroundPosition** property.

Syntax

HTML   N/A

Scripting   *object*.**style.backgroundPositionX** [= *iPositionX*]

Possible Values

iPositionX   Integer specifying the x-coordinate of the **backgroundPosition** property.

The property is read/write with no default value.

Applies To

 WIN16   WIN32   MAC   UNIX

A, ACRONYM, ADDRESS, APPLET, AREA, B, BASE, BASEFONT, BIG,
BLOCKQUOTE, BODY, BR, BUTTON, CAPTION, CENTER, CITE, CODE, COL,
COLGROUP, COMMENT, DD, DEL, DFN, DIR, DIV, DL, DT, EM, EMBED,
FIELDSET, FONT, FORM, FRAME, FRAMESET, HEAD, Hn, HR, I, IFRAME,
IMG, INPUT type=button, INPUT type=checkbox, INPUT type=file, INPUT
type=image, INPUT type=password, INPUT type=radio, INPUT type=reset, INPUT
type=submit, INPUT type=text, INS, KBD, LABEL, LEGEND, LI, LINK, LISTING,
MAP, MARQUEE, MENU, META, NEXTID, NOBR, OBJECT, OL, OPTION, P,
PLAINTEXT, PRE, Q, S, SAMP, SCRIPT, SELECT, SMALL, SPAN, STRIKE,
STRONG, style, SUB, SUP, TABLE, TBODY, TD, TEXTAREA, TFOOT, TH,
THEAD, TITLE, TR, TT, U, UL, VAR, XMP

 WIN16   WIN32   MAC   UNIX

currentStyle, RT, RUBY, runtimeStyle

DHTML Properties

backgroundPositionY Property

Sets or retrieves the y-coordinate of the **backgroundPosition** property.

Syntax

HTML   N/A

Scripting   *object*.**style.backgroundPositionY** [= *iPositionY*]

Possible Values

iPositionY   Integer specifying the y-coordinate of the **backgroundPosition** property.

The property is read/write with no default value.

Applies To

 WIN16   WIN32   MAC   UNIX

A, ACRONYM, ADDRESS, APPLET, AREA, B, BASE, BASEFONT, BIG, BLOCKQUOTE, BODY, BR, BUTTON, CAPTION, CENTER, CITE, CODE, COL, COLGROUP, COMMENT, DD, DEL, DFN, DIR, DIV, DL, DT, EM, EMBED, FIELDSET, FONT, FORM, FRAME, FRAMESET, HEAD, Hn, HR, I, IFRAME, IMG, INPUT type=button, INPUT type=checkbox, INPUT type=file, INPUT type=image, INPUT type=password, INPUT type=radio, INPUT type=reset, INPUT type=submit, INPUT type=text, INS, KBD, LABEL, LEGEND, LI, LINK, LISTING, MAP, MARQUEE, MENU, META, NEXTID, NOBR, OBJECT, OL, OPTION, P, PLAINTEXT, PRE, Q, S, SAMP, SCRIPT, SELECT, SMALL, SPAN, STRIKE, STRONG, style, SUB, SUP, TABLE, TBODY, TD, TEXTAREA, TFOOT, TH, THEAD, TITLE, TR, TT, U, UL, VAR, XMP

 WIN16   WIN32   MAC   UNIX

currentStyle, RT, RUBY, runtimeStyle

background-repeat Attribute | backgroundRepeat Property

Sets or retrieves whether the **backgroundImage** property of the object is repeated.

Syntax

HTML   { **background-repeat:** repeat I no-repeat I repeat-x I repeat-y }

Scripting   *object*.**style.backgroundRepeat** [= *sRepeat*]

Possible Values

repeat   Image is repeated horizontally and vertically.

no-repeat Image is not repeated.

repeat-x Image is repeated horizontally.

repeat-y Image is repeated vertically.

The property is read/write with a default value of repeat; the cascading style sheets (CSS) attribute is not inherited.

Remarks

The repeat-x and repeat-y values make the image repeat horizontally and vertically, respectively, creating a single band of images from one side to the other.

This property can be set with the other background properties by using the **background** composite property.

Example

The following examples show how to use the **background-repeat** attribute and the **backgroundRepeat** property to specify whether the background image repeats.

The sample below uses a call to an embedded (global) style sheet to change whether the image repeats.

```
<STYLE>
    .style1 { background-image: url( sphere.jpg ) ;
        background-repeat: repeat ;}
    .style2 { background-image: url( sphere.jpeg ) ;
        background-repeat: no-repeat ; }
</STYLE>
</HEAD>
<BODY>
```

```
<SPAN onmouseover="this.className='style1'"
onmouseout="this.className='style2'" onclick="this.className=''">
. . . </SPAN>
```

To see this code in action, refer to the Web Workshop CD-ROM.

The sample below uses inline scripting to change whether the image repeats.

```
<SPAN onmouseover="this.style.backgroundImage='url(sphere.jpeg)';
this.style.backgroundRepeat='repeat'">
:
</SPAN>
```

To see this code in action, refer to the Web Workshop CD-ROM.

Applies To

WIN16   WIN32   MAC   UNIX

A, ADDRESS, B, BIG, BLOCKQUOTE, BODY, BUTTON, CAPTION, CENTER,
CITE, CODE, COL, COLGROUP, DD, DFN, DIR, DIV, DL, DT, EM, FIELDSET,
FORM, Hn, HTML, I, IMG, INPUT type=button, INPUT type=checkbox, INPUT
type=file, INPUT type=image, INPUT type=password, INPUT type=radio, INPUT
type=reset, INPUT type=submit, INPUT type=text, ISINDEX, KBD, LABEL,
LEGEND, LI, LISTING, MARQUEE, MENU, OL, P, PLAINTEXT, PRE, S, SAMP,
SELECT, SMALL, SPAN, STRIKE, STRONG, style, SUB, SUP, TABLE, TBODY,
TD, TEXTAREA, TFOOT, TH, THEAD, TR, TT, U, UL, VAR, XMP

WIN16   WIN32   MAC   UNIX

currentStyle, runtimeStyle

BALANCE Attribute | balance Property

Retrieves the value indicating how the volume of the background sound is divided
between the left and right speakers.

Syntax

HTML   <BGSOUND **BALANCE** = *iBalance* ... >

Scripting   [*iBalance* =] *bgsound*.**balance**

Possible Values

iBalance   Integer value within the -10,000 to +10,000 range. A -10,000 value indicates that all sound is directed to the left speaker. A +10,000 value indicates that all sound is directed to the right speaker. A 0 value indicates that the sound is balanced between the left and right speakers.

The property is read-only with a default value of 0.

Applies To

 WIN16   WIN32   MAC   UNIX

BGSOUND

BEHAVIOR Attribute | behavior Property

Sets or retrieves how the text scrolls in the marquee.

Syntax

HTML   <MARQUEE **BEHAVIOR** = "scroll" | "alternate" | "slide" ... >

Scripting *marquee*.**behavior** [= *sScroll*]

Possible Values

scroll   Marquee scrolls in the direction specified by the **direction** property. The text scrolls off the end and starts over.

alternate Marquee's scroll direction reverses when its content reaches the edge of the container.

slide   Marquee scrolls in the direction specified by the **direction** property. The text scrolls to the end and stops.

The property is read/write with a default value of scroll.

Example

The following example moves a piece of text down the page using a **MARQUEE** object.

```
<MARQUEE loop=1 height=200  width=740
        style="position:absolute; top:0; left:10"
        SCROLLAMOUNT=10 SCROLLDELAY=20 BEHAVIOR="SLIDE" DIRECTION="DOWN">
```

```
<UL>
  Use Dynamic HTML to differentiate your content and create
  compelling Web sites.
</UL>
</MARQUEE>
```

To see this code in action, refer to the Web Workshop CD-ROM.

Applies To

WIN16	WIN32	MAC

MARQUEE

UNIX

MARQUEE

behavior Attribute | behavior Property

Sets or retrieves the location of the DHTML behavior.

Syntax

HTML   { **behavior :** url(*sLocation*) | url(*#objID*) | url(*#default#behaviorName*)

Scripting *object*.**style.behavior** [= *sURL*]

Possible Values

url(*sLocation*)	Script implementation of a DHTML behavior, where *sLocation* is an absolute or relative URL.
url(*#objID*)	Binary implementation of a behavior, where *objID* is the **ID** attribute specified in an **OBJECT** tag.
Url(*#default#behaviorName*)	One of Internet Explorer's default behaviors, identified by *behaviorName*.

The property is read/write with no default value; the proposed cascading style sheets (CSS) extension attribute is not inherited.

Remarks

You can apply multiple behaviors to an element by specifying a space-delimited list of URLs for the **behavior** attribute, as shown in the following syntax.

```
<ELEMENT STYLE="behavior:url( a1.htc ) url( a2.htc ) ..." >
```

In the Example section, one example demonstrates how two behaviors can be applied to an element to achieve a combination of effects. Conflicts resulting from applying multiple behaviors to an element are resolved based on the order in which the behavior was applied to the element. Each succeeding behavior takes precedence over the previous behavior in the order. For example, if multiple behaviors set the element's color, the color set by the behavior that was last applied to the element prevails. The same rule applies in resolving name conflicts, such as with property, method, or event names exposed by multiple behaviors.

Once the **behavior** property has been defined for the element, the **addBehavior** method can be used to dynamically attach additional behaviors to the element.

Note A behavior that is attached to an element by using the **addBehavior** method or by applying the proposed CSS **behavior** attribute inline is not automatically detached from the element when the element is removed from the document hierarchy. However, a behavior attached using a style rule defined in the document is detached automatically as the element is removed from the document tree.

Example

The following examples show how to use the **behavior** property on a page.

The sample below implements an expanding/collapsing table of contents by applying the behavior as an inline style to the **LI** element. In this particular case, two behaviors implemented as HTML Components (HTC) have been applied to the element to achieve a combination of mouseover highlighting and expanding/collapsing effects.

```
<UL>
  <LI STYLE="behavior:url(ul.htc) url(hilite.htc)">HTML</LI>
  <UL>
      <LI>IE 4.0 authoring tips</LI>
      :
  </UL>
</UL>
```

The same sample could be rewritten to define the **behavior** attribute in a separate **<STYLE>** block, as follows:

```
<style>
   .CollapsingAndHiliting {behavior:url(ul.htc) url(hilite.htc)}
</style>

<UL>
  <LI CLASS="CollapsingAndHiliting">HTML</LI>
  <UL>
      <LI>IE 4.0 authoring tips</LI>
      :
  </UL>
</UL>
```

Or the **behavior** property could be set in script in the following manner:

```
<SCRIPT>
   function window.onload()
   {
      idTopic1.style.behavior = "url(ul.htc) url(hilite.htc)";
   }
</SCRIPT>
 :
<UL>
  <LI ID=idTopic1>HTML Authoring</LI>
  <UL>
      <LI>IE 4.0 authoring tips</LI>
      :
  </UL>
</UL>
```

To see this code in action, refer to the Web Workshop CD-ROM.

If the same expanding/collapsing example were to use a DHTML behavior implemented in C++ as an ActiveX® control, the code would look slightly different. In the sample below, the **behavior** attribute points to the **ID** property of the object specified in the **OBJECT** tag.

```
<STYLE>
   .Collapsing { behavior:url(#myObject) }
</STYLE>

<OBJECT ID=myObject ... ></OBJECT>
<UL>
  <LI CLASS="Collapsing">HTML Authoring</LI>
  <UL>
      <LI>IE 4.0 authoring tips</LI>
      :
  </UL>
</UL>
```

Applies To

| WIN16 | WIN32 | MAC | UNIX |

A, ACRONYM, ADDRESS, APPLET, AREA, B, BASE, BASEFONT, BGSOUND, BIG, BLOCKQUOTE, BODY, BR, BUTTON, CAPTION, CENTER, CITE, CODE, COL, COLGROUP, COMMENT, DD, DEL, DFN, DIR, DIV, DL, DT, EM, EMBED, FIELDSET, FONT, FORM, FRAME, FRAMESET, HEAD, Hn, HR, HTML, I, IFRAME, IMG, INPUT type=button, INPUT type=checkbox, INPUT type=file, INPUT type=hidden, INPUT type=image, INPUT type=password, INPUT type=radio, INPUT type=reset, INPUT type=submit, INPUT type=text, INS, ISINDEX, KBD, LABEL, LEGEND, LI, LINK, LISTING, MAP, MARQUEE, MENU, NEXTID, NOBR, NOFRAMES, NOSCRIPT, OBJECT, OL, OPTION, P, PLAINTEXT, PRE, Q, RT, RUBY, S, SAMP, SCRIPT, SELECT, SMALL, SPAN, STRIKE, STRONG, STYLE, SUB, SUP, TABLE, TBODY, TD, TEXTAREA, TFOOT, TH, THEAD, TITLE, TR, TT, U, UL, VAR, WBR, XML, XMP

DHTML Properties

BGCOLOR Attribute | bgColor Property

Sets or retrieves the background color behind the object.

Syntax

HTML   *<ELEMENT **BGCOLOR** = sColor ... >*

Scripting   *object*.**bgColor** [= *sColor*]

Possible Values

sColor String specifying one of the color names or red-green-blue (RGB) values in the "Color Table" in Appendix C.

The property is read/write. The default value is determined by the browser.

Remarks

Some browsers do not recognize color names, but all browsers should recognize RGB color values and display them correctly.

Applies To

 WIN16   WIN32   MAC

BODY, document, MARQUEE, TABLE, TBODY, TD, TFOOT, TH, THEAD, TR

 UNIX

BODY, document, MARQUEE, TABLE, TBODY, TD, TFOOT, TH, THEAD, TR

BGCOLOR Attribute

Sets or retrieves the background color behind the element.

Syntax

HTML   *<ELEMENT BGCOLOR = sColor ... >*

Scripting N/A

Possible Values

sColor String specifying one of the color names or red-green-blue (RGB) values in the "Color Table" in Appendix C.

The default value is determined by the browser.

Remarks

JScript® (compatible with ECMA 262 language specification) supports the entire set of colors as color names and as their corresponding RGB values. However, JScript always returns the property as a string specifying the RGB color value, regardless of the format the value was set to.

Some browsers do not recognize color names, but all browsers should recognize RGB color values and display them correctly.

Applies To

 WIN16   WIN32   MAC

COL, COLGROUP

 UNIX

COL, COLGROUP

BGPROPERTIES Attribute | bgProperties Property

Sets or retrieves the properties for the background picture.

Syntax

HTML	<BODY **BGPROPERTIES** = "fixed" ... >
Scripting	*body*.**bgProperties** [= *sProperties*]

Possible Values

""	Scrolling background.
fixed	Fixed (nonscrolling) background.

The property is read/write with a default value of an empty string ("").

Remarks

The property, for example, specifies whether the picture is a fixed watermark or scrolls with the page. This attribute/property is supported only by Internet Explorer.

Example

The following example uses a fixed background image for the page.

```
<BODY BACKGROUND="/ie/images/watermrk.gif" BGPROPERTIES="fixed"
BGCOLOR=#FFFFFF TEXT=#000000 LINK=#ff6600 VLINK=#330099>
```

Applies To

 WIN16   WIN32   MAC

BODY

 UNIX

BODY

border Attribute | border Property

Sets or retrieves the properties to be drawn around the object.

Syntax

HTML   { **border:** *sWidth* || *sStyle* || *sColor* }

Scripting   *object*.**style.border** [= [*sWidth*] [*sStyle*] [*sColor*]]

Possible Values

sWidth   Any of the range of values available to the **borderWidth** property.

sStyle   Any of the range of values available to the **borderStyle** property.

sColor   Any of the range of values available to the **borderColor** property.

The property is read/write with a default value of medium none; the cascading style sheets (CSS) attribute is not inherited.

Remarks

The **border** property is composite property for setting the *sWidth*, *sStyle*, and *sColor* values for all four sides of an object.

All individual border properties not set by the composite border property are set to their default values. For example, the default value for *sWidth* is medium.

The setting **border**=thin is identical to **border**=thin none; the default value for color picks up the text color if one is not initially set. So, in addition to setting the *sWidth* to thin, the property clears any *sStyle* or *sColor* that has been previously set.

Setting a border to 0 or omitting the attribute causes no border to be displayed. Supplying the border attribute without a value defaults to a single border.

To use this property, inline elements must have an absolute **position** or layout. Element layout is set by providing a value for the **height** property or the **width** property.

If an *sColor* is not specified, the text color is used.

For more information about supported colors, see the "Color Table" in Appendix C.

Example

The following examples show how to use the **border** attribute and the **border** property to specify the composite border properties.

The sample below uses a call to an embedded style sheet to modify the border attributes.

```
<STYLE>
    .applyBorder { border: 0.2cm groove orange }
    .removeBorder { border: none }
</STYLE>
</HEAD>
<BODY>
<TABLE BORDER>
<TR>
    <TD onmouseover="this.className='applyBorder'"
        onmouseout="this.className='removeBorder'">
    <IMG src="sphere.jpg"></TD>
</TR>
</TABLE>
```

To see this code in action, refer to the Web Workshop CD-ROM.

The sample below uses inline scripting to modify the border properties.

```
<TD onmouseover="this.style.border='0.2cm groove pink'">
```

To see this code in action, refer to the Web Workshop CD-ROM.

Applies To

 WIN16   WIN32   MAC   UNIX

BLOCKQUOTE, BODY, BUTTON, CAPTION, CENTER, DD, DIR, DIV, DL, DT, EMBED, FIELDSET, FORM, Hn, IFRAME, IMG, INPUT type=button, INPUT type=checkbox, INPUT type=file, INPUT type=image, INPUT type=password, INPUT type=radio, INPUT type=reset, INPUT type=submit, INPUT type=text, ISINDEX, LI, LISTING, MARQUEE, MENU, OBJECT, OL, P, PLAINTEXT, PRE, SPAN, style, TABLE, TD, TEXTAREA, TH, UL, XMP

 WIN16   WIN32   MAC   UNIX

runtimeStyle

BORDER Attribute | border Property

Sets or retrieves the space between the frames, including the 3-D border.

Syntax

HTML   <FRAMESET **BORDER** = *iSpace* ... >

Scripting *frameset*.**border** [= *iSpace*]

Possible Values

iSpace Integer specifying the number of pixels to reserve as space between frames.

The property is read/write with no default value.

Remarks

The border can be set only on an outermost **FRAMESET** tag. Setting a border for an inner **FRAMESET** is ignored, even if a border is not defined on the outermost **FRAMESET**.

Applies To

 WIN16   WIN32   MAC   UNIX

FRAMESET

BORDER Attribute | border Property

Sets or retrieves the width of the border to be drawn around the object.

Syntax

HTML   <*ELEMENT* **BORDER** = *iBorder* ... >

Scripting *object*.**border** [= *iBorder*]

Possible Values

iBorder Integer specifying the number of pixels in the object's border.

The property is read/write with no default value.

Remarks

Setting a border to 0 or omitting the attribute causes no border to be displayed. Supplying the **BORDER** attribute without a value defaults to a single border.

Applies To

 WIN16   WIN32   MAC

IMG, TABLE

 UNIX

IMG, TABLE

border-bottom Attribute | borderBottom Property

Sets or retrieves the properties of the bottom border of the object.

Syntax

HTML   { **border-bottom:** *sWidth* | *sStyle* | *sColor* }

Scripting *object*.**style.borderBottom** [= [*sWidth*] [*sStyle*] [*sColor*]]

Possible Values

sWidth   Any of the range of values available to the **borderBottomWidth** property.

sStyle   Any of the range of values available to the **borderBottomStyle** property.

sColor   Any of the range of values available to the **borderBottomColor** property.

The property is read/write with a default value of medium none; the cascading style sheets (CSS) attribute is not inherited.

Remarks

The **borderBottom** property is composite property for setting the *sWidth*, *sColor*, and *sStyle* values for the bottom border of an object.

All individual border properties not set by the composite **borderBottom** property are set to their default values. For example, the default value for *sWidth* is medium.

To use this property, inline elements must have an `absolute` **position** or layout. Element layout is set by providing a value for the **height** property or the **width** property.

If an *sColor* is not specified, the text color is used.

For more information about supported colors, see the "Color Table" in Appendix C.

Example

The following examples show how to use the **borderBottom** property and the **border-bottom** attribute to specify the various properties for the bottom border.

The sample below uses a call to an embedded (global) style sheet to change the attributes of the bottom border.

```
<STYLE>
    TD   { border-bottom: 0.5cm solid yellow; }
    .change { border-bottom: 0.5cm groove pink; }
</STYLE>
</HEAD>
<BODY>
<TABLE>
<TR>
<TD onmouseover="this.className='change'"
    onmouseout="this.className=''"><IMG src="sphere.jpg"></TD>
</TR>
</TABLE>
```

To see this code in action, refer to the Web Workshop CD-ROM.

The sample below uses inline scripting to change the bottom border.

```
<TD onmouseover="this.style.borderBottom='0.3cm groove yellow'">
```

To see this code in action, refer to the Web Workshop CD-ROM.

Applies To

 WIN16   WIN32   MAC   UNIX

BLOCKQUOTE, BODY, BUTTON, CAPTION, CENTER, DD, DIR, DIV, DL, DT, EMBED, FIELDSET, FORM, Hn, HR, IFRAME, IMG, INPUT type=button, INPUT type=checkbox, INPUT type=file, INPUT type=image, INPUT type=password, INPUT type=radio, INPUT type=reset, INPUT type=submit, INPUT type=text, ISINDEX, LI, LISTING, MARQUEE, MENU, OBJECT, OL, P, PLAINTEXT, PRE, SPAN, style, TABLE, TD, TEXTAREA, TH, UL, XMP

WIN16 WIN32 MAC UNIX

runtimeStyle

border-bottom-color Attribute | borderBottomColor Property

Sets or retrieves the color of the bottom border of the object.

Syntax

HTML   { **border-bottom-color:** *sColor* }

Scripting *object*.**style.borderBottomColor** [= *sColor*]

Possible Values

sColor String specifying one of the color names or red-green-blue (RGB) values in the "Color Table" in Appendix C.

The property is read/write with a default value equal to the value of the **color** property; the cascading style sheets (CSS) attribute is not inherited.

Remarks

To use this property, inline elements must have an `absolute` **position** or layout. Element layout is set by providing a value for the **height** property or the **width** property.

Some browsers do not recognize color names, but all browsers should recognize RGB color values and display them correctly.

Example

The following examples show how to use the **border-bottom-color** attribute and the **borderBottomColor** property to specify the border color.

The sample below uses a call to an embedded style sheet to change the color of the bottom border.

```
<STYLE>
    TD { border-bottom-color: red;
        border-width: 0.5cm; border-style: groove }
    .blue { border-bottom-color: blue }
</STYLE>
</HEAD>
<BODY>
```

```
<TABLE BORDER>
<TR>
    <TD onmouseover="this.className='blue'"
        onmouseout="this.className=''">
        <IMG src="sphere.jpg">
    </TD>
</TR>
</TABLE>
```

To see this code in action, refer to the Web Workshop CD-ROM.

The sample below uses inline scripting to change the color of the bottom border.

```
<TD onmouseover="this.style.borderWidth='0.5cm';
    this.style.borderBottomColor='blue'">
```

To see this code in action, refer to the Web Workshop CD-ROM.

Applies To

 WIN16   WIN32   MAC

HR

 WIN16   WIN32   MAC   UNIX

BLOCKQUOTE, BODY, BUTTON, CAPTION, CENTER, DD, DIR, DIV, DL, DT, EMBED, FIELDSET, FORM, Hn, HR, IFRAME, IMG, INPUT type=button, INPUT type=checkbox, INPUT type=file, INPUT type=image, INPUT type=password, INPUT type=radio, INPUT type=reset, INPUT type=submit, INPUT type=text, ISINDEX, LI, LISTING, MARQUEE, MENU, OBJECT, OL, P, PLAINTEXT, PRE, SPAN, style, TABLE, TD, TEXTAREA, TH, UL, XMP

IE 5 **WIN16   WIN32   MAC   UNIX**

currentStyle, runtimeStyle

border-bottom-style Attribute | borderBottomStyle Property

Sets or retrieves the style of the bottom border of the object.

Syntax

HTML   { **border-bottom-style:** none | dotted | dashed | solid | double | groove | ridge | inset | outset }

Scripting   *object*.**style.borderBottomStyle** [= *sStyle*]

Possible Values

none   No border is drawn, regardless of any specified **border-width** value.

dotted   Border is a dotted line on the Macintosh platform as of Internet Explorer 4.01, and a solid line on the Windows and UNIX platforms.

dashed   Border is a dashed line on the Macintosh platform as of Internet Explorer 4.01, and a solid line on the Windows and UNIX platforms.

solid   Border is a solid line.

double   Border is a double line drawn on top of the background of the object. The sum of the two single lines and the space between equals the **border-width** value. The border width must be at least 3 pixels wide to draw a double border.

groove   3-D groove is drawn in colors based on the value.

ridge   3-D ridge is drawn in colors based on the value.

inset   3-D inset is drawn in colors based on the value.

outset   3-D outset is drawn in colors based on the value.

The property is read/write with a default value of none; the cascading style sheets (CSS) attribute is not inherited.

Remarks

A **border-width** greater than 0 must be set for the **border-bottom-style** attribute to render.

To use this property, inline elements must have an absolute **position** or layout. Element layout is set by providing a value for the **height** property or the **width** property.

DHTML Properties

Example

The following examples show how to use the **border-bottom-style** attribute and the **borderBottomStyle** property to specify the border style.

The sample below uses a call to an embedded style sheet to change the style of the bottom border to groove.

```
<STYLE>
    TD { border-bottom-style: solid;
        border-width= 0.3cm }
    .change { border-bottom-style: groove }
</STYLE>
</HEAD>
<BODY>
<TABLE BORDER>
<TR>
  <TD onmouseover="this.className='change'"
      onmouseout="this.className=''">
    <IMG src="sphere.jpg">
  </TD>
</TR>
</TABLE>
```

To see this code in action, refer to the Web Workshop CD-ROM.

The sample below uses inline scripting to change the style of the bottom border to groove.

```
<TD onmouseover="this.style.borderWidth='0.5cm';
                 this.style.borderBottomStyle='groove'">
```

To see this code in action, refer to the Web Workshop CD-ROM.

Applies To

 WIN16   WIN32   MAC   UNIX

BLOCKQUOTE, BODY, BUTTON, CAPTION, CENTER, DD, DIR, DIV, DL, DT, EMBED, FIELDSET, FORM, Hn, HR, IFRAME, IMG, INPUT type=button, INPUT type=checkbox, INPUT type=file, INPUT type=image, INPUT type=password, INPUT type=radio, INPUT type=reset, INPUT type=submit, INPUT type=text, ISINDEX, LI, LISTING, MARQUEE, MENU, OBJECT, OL, P, PLAINTEXT, PRE, SPAN, style, TABLE, TD, TEXTAREA, TH, UL, XMP

 WIN16   WIN32   MAC   UNIX

currentStyle, runtimeStyle

border-bottom-width Attribute | borderBottomWidth Property

Sets or retrieves the width of the bottom border of the object.

Syntax

HTML   { **border-bottom-width:** `medium` | `thin` | `thick` | *width*}

Scripting   *object*.**style.borderBottomWidth** [= *sWidth*]

Possible Values

`medium`   Default width.

`thin`   Width less than the default.

`thick`   Width greater than the default.

width   Width value consisting of a floating-point number, followed by an absolute units designator (`cm`, `mm`, `in`, `pt`, `pc`, or `px`) or a relative units designator (`em` or `ex`). For more information about supported length units for CSS attributes, see "CSS Length Units" in Appendix C.

The property is read/write with a default value of `medium`; the cascading style sheets (CSS) attribute is not inherited.

Remarks

To use this property, inline elements must have an `absolute` **position** or layout. Element layout is set by providing a value for the **height** property or the **width** property.

The property is supported on block and replaced objects only.

Example

The following examples show how to use the **border-bottom-width** attribute and the **borderBottomWidth** property to specify the border width.

The sample below uses a call to an embedded (global) style sheet to change the width of the bottom border to 1 centimeter when a mouse click occurs.

```
<STYLE>
    TD { border-bottom-width: 3mm }
    .changeborder1 { border-bottom-width: 1cm }
</STYLE>
</HEAD>
<BODY>
```

```
<TABLE BORDER>
<TR>
    <TD onclick="this.className='changeborder1'"
        ondblclick="this.className=''">
        <IMG src="sphere.jpg">
    </TD>
</TR>
</TABLE>
```

To see this code in action, refer to the Web Workshop CD-ROM.

The sample below uses inline scripting to change the width of the bottom border to 1 centimeter when a mouse click occurs.

```
<TD onclick="this.style.borderBottomWidth='1cm'">
```

To see this code in action, refer to the Web Workshop CD-ROM.

Applies To

 WIN16   WIN32   MAC   UNIX

BLOCKQUOTE, BODY, BUTTON, CAPTION, CENTER, DD, DIR, DIV, DL, DT, EMBED, FIELDSET, FORM, Hn, HR, IFRAME, IMG, INPUT type=button, INPUT type=checkbox, INPUT type=file, INPUT type=image, INPUT type=password, INPUT type=radio, INPUT type=reset, INPUT type=submit, INPUT type=text, ISINDEX, LI, LISTING, MARQUEE, MENU, OBJECT, OL, P, PLAINTEXT, PRE, SPAN, style, TABLE, TD, TEXTAREA, TH, UL, XMP

 WIN16   WIN32   MAC   UNIX

currentStyle, runtimeStyle

border-collapse Attribute | borderCollapse Property

Sets or retrieves whether the row and cell borders of a table are joined into a single border or detached as in standard HTML.

Syntax

HTML   { **border-collapse :** separate I collapse }

Scripting   *table*.**style.borderCollapse** [= *sCollapse*]

Possible Values

separate Borders are detached (standard HTML).

collapse Borders are collapsed, where adjacent, into a single border.

The property is read/write with a default value of separate; the cascading style sheets (CSS) attribute is not inherited.

Example

The following example shows how to use the **border-collapse** attribute and the **borderCollapse** property to manipulate the border on a table.

```
<TABLE ID=oTable STYLE="border-collapse:collapse">
<TR><TD>EST</TD><TD>9:00 a.m.</TD></TR>
<TR><TD>CST</TD><TD>8:00 a.m.</TD></TR>
<TR><TD>PST</TD><TD>6:00 a.m.</TD></TR>
</TABLE>

<P>
<INPUT TYPE=button
    onclick="oTable.style.borderCollapse='separate'"
    VALUE="separate">
<INPUT TYPE=button
    onclick="oTable.style.borderCollapse='collapse'"
    VALUE="collapse">
```

To see this code in action, refer to the Web Workshop CD-ROM.

Applies To

WIN16	WIN32	MAC	UNIX

TABLE

border-color Attribute | borderColor Property

Sets or retrieves the border color of the object.

Syntax

HTML   { **border-color:** *sColor* {1,4} }

Scripting   *object*.**style.borderColor** [= *sColor*]

Possible Values

sColor   String specifying one of the color names or red-green-blue (RGB) values in
the "Color Table" in Appendix C.

The property is read/write with a default value equal to the value of the **color**
property; the cascading style sheets (CSS) attribute is not inherited.

Remarks

Some browsers do not recognize color names, but all browsers should recognize RGB
color values and display them correctly.

In HTML syntax, {1,4} indicates that up to four different colors can be specified in
this order: top, right, bottom, left. If one color is supplied, it is used for all four sides.
If two colors are supplied, the first is used for the top and bottom, and the second is
used for left and right. If three colors are supplied, they are used for top, right and left,
and bottom, respectively.

To use this property, inline elements must have an absolute **position** or layout.
Element layout is set by providing a value for the **height** property or the **width**
property.

The property is supported on block and replaced objects only.

Example

The following examples show how to use the **border-color** attribute and the
borderColor property to specify the color of the border.

The sample below uses a call to an embedded (global) style sheet to change the color
of the border to blue from an initial value of red when the user moves the mouse over
the image.

```
<STYLE>
    TD { border-color: red; border-width: 0.5cm }
    .blue  { border-color: blue }
</STYLE>
</HEAD>
<BODY>
<TABLE BORDER>
<TR>
    <TD onmouseover="this.className='blue'"
        onmouseout="this.className=''">
        <IMG src="sphere.jpg">
    </TD>
</TR>
</TABLE>
```

To see this code in action, refer to the Web Workshop CD-ROM.

The sample below uses inline scripting to change the border color to `blue` when the mouse is moved over the image.

```
<TD onmouseover="this.style.borderWidth='0.5cm';
                 this.style.borderColor='blue';
                 this.style.borderStyle='solid'">
```

To see this code in action, refer to the Web Workshop CD-ROM.

Applies To

 WIN16   WIN32   MAC   UNIX

BLOCKQUOTE, BODY, BUTTON, CAPTION, CENTER, DD, DIR, DIV, DL, DT, EMBED, FIELDSET, FORM, Hn, HR, IFRAME, IMG, INPUT type=button, INPUT type=checkbox, INPUT type=file, INPUT type=image, INPUT type=password, INPUT type=radio, INPUT type=reset, INPUT type=submit, INPUT type=text, ISINDEX, LI, LISTING, MARQUEE, MENU, OBJECT, OL, P, PLAINTEXT, PRE, SPAN, style, TABLE, TD, TEXTAREA, TH, UL, XMP

 WIN16   WIN32   MAC   UNIX

currentStyle, runtimeStyle

BORDERCOLOR Attribute | borderColor Property

Sets or retrieves the border color of the object.

Syntax

HTML   *<ELEMENT* **BORDERCOLOR** = *sColor ... >*

Scripting   *object.***borderColor** [= *sColor*]

Possible Values

sColor   String specifying one of the color names or red-green-blue (RGB) values in the "Color Table" in Appendix C.

The property is read/write with no default value.

Remarks

You must set the **borderColor** property for the object, except when using this attribute/property with frames.

Some browsers do not recognize color names, but all browsers should recognize RGB color values and display them correctly.

Applies To

WIN16   WIN32   MAC

TABLE, TD, TH, TR

WIN16   WIN32   MAC   UNIX

FRAME, FRAMESET, TABLE, TD, TH, TR

borderColorDark Property

Sets or retrieves the color for one of the two colors used to draw the 3-D border of the object.

Syntax

HTML   N/A

Scripting *object*.**borderColorDark** [= *sColor*]

Possible Values

sColor String specifying one of the color names or red-green-blue (RGB) values in the "Color Table" in Appendix C.

The property is read/write with no default value.

Remarks

The property is the opposite of **borderColorLight** and must be used with the **border** property corresponding to the **BORDER** attribute. This property does not affect the cascading style sheets (CSS) **border** composite properties.

Some browsers do not recognize color names, but all browsers should recognize RGB color values and display them correctly.

Applies To

 WIN16   WIN32   MAC

TABLE, TD, TH

 UNIX

TABLE, TD, TH

borderColorLight Property

Sets or retrieves the color for one of the two colors used to draw the 3-D border of the object.

Syntax

HTML   N/A

Scripting *object*.**borderColorLight** [= *sColor*]

Possible Values

sColor String specifying one of the color names or red-green-blue (RGB) values in the "Color Table" in Appendix C.

The property is read/write with no default value.

Remarks

The property is the opposite of **borderColorDark** and must be used with the **border** property corresponding to the **BORDER** attribute. This property does not affect the cascading style sheets (CSS) **border** composite properties.

Some browsers do not recognize color names, but all browsers should recognize RGB color values and display them correctly.

Applies To

 WIN16   WIN32   MAC

TABLE, TD, TH, TR

 UNIX

TABLE, TD, TH, TR

border-left Attribute | borderLeft Property

Sets or retrieves the properties of the left border of the object.

Syntax

HTML	{ **border-left:** *sWidth* ‖ *sStyle* ‖ *sColor* }
Scripting	*object*.**style.borderLeft** [= [*sWidth*] [*sStyle*] [*sColor*]]

Possible Values

sWidth   Any of the range of values available to the **borderLeftWidth** property.

sStyle   Any of the range of values available to the **borderLeftStyle** property.

sColor   Any of the range of values available to the **borderLeftColor** property.

The property is read/write with a default value of medium none; the cascading style sheets (CSS) attribute is not inherited.

Remarks

The **borderLeft** property is composite property for setting the *sWidth*, *sColor*, and *sStyle* values for the left border of an object.

All individual border properties not set by the composite **borderLeft** property are set to their default values. For example, the default value for *sWidth* is medium.

If *sColor* is not specified, the text color is used. For more information about supported colors, see the "Color Table" in Appendix C.

To use this property, inline elements must have an absolute **position** or layout. Element layout is set by providing a value for the **height** property or the **width** property.

Example

The following examples show how to use the **borderLeft** property and the **border-left** attribute to specify the composite **border-left** properties.

The sample below uses a call to an embedded (global) style sheet to modify the attributes of the left border.

```
<STYLE>
    TD { border-left: 0.5cm solid yellow ; }
    .change { border-left: 0.5cm groove pink ; }
</STYLE>
</HEAD>
<BODY>
```

```
<TABLE>
<TR>
    <TD onmouseover="this.className='change'"
        onmouseout="this.className=''">
        <IMG src="sphere.jpg">
    </TD>
</TR>
</TABLE>
```

To see this code in action, refer to the Web Workshop CD-ROM.

The sample below uses inline scripting to change the properties of the left border.

```
<TD onmouseover="this.style.borderLeft='0.3cm groove yellow'">
```

To see this code in action, refer to the Web Workshop CD-ROM.

Applies To

 WIN16   WIN32   MAC   UNIX

BLOCKQUOTE, BODY, BUTTON, CAPTION, CENTER, DD, DIR, DIV, DL, DT, EMBED, FIELDSET, FORM, Hn, HR, IFRAME, IMG, INPUT type=button, INPUT type=checkbox, INPUT type=file, INPUT type=image, INPUT type=password, INPUT type=radio, INPUT type=reset, INPUT type=submit, INPUT type=text, ISINDEX, LI, LISTING, MARQUEE, MENU, OBJECT, OL, P, PLAINTEXT, PRE, SPAN, style, TABLE, TD, TEXTAREA, TH, UL, XMP

 WIN16   WIN32   MAC   UNIX

runtimeStyle

border-left-color Attribute | borderLeftColor Property

Sets or retrieves the color of the left border of the object.

Syntax

HTML   { **border-left-color:** *sColor* }

Scripting *object*.**style.borderLeftColor** [= *sColor*]

Possible Values

sColor String specifying one of the color names or red-green-blue (RGB) values in the "Color Table" in Appendix C.

The property is read/write with a default value equal to the value of the **color** property; the cascading style sheets (CSS) attribute is not inherited.

Remarks

To use this property, inline elements must have an `absolute` **position** or layout. Element layout is set by providing a value for the **height** property or the **width** property.

Some browsers do not recognize color names, but all browsers should recognize RGB color values and display them correctly.

Example

The following examples show how to use the **border-left-color** attribute and the **borderLeftColor** property to specify the color of the left border.

The sample below uses a call to an embedded style sheet to change the color of the left border from a value of `red` to `blue` when an **onmouseover** event occurs.

```
<STYLE>
    TD { border-left-color: red;
        border-width: 0.5cm; border-style: groove }
    .blue { border-left-color: blue }
</STYLE>
</HEAD>
<BODY>
<TABLE BORDER>
<TR>
    <TD onmouseover="this.className='blue'"
        onmouseout="this.className=''">
        <IMG src="sphere.jpg">
    </TD>
</TR>
</TABLE>
```

To see this code in action, refer to the Web Workshop CD-ROM.

The sample below uses inline scripting to change the color of the left border to `blue` when an **onmouseover** event occurs.

```
<TD onmouseover="this.style.borderWidth='0.5cm';
    this.style.borderLeftColor='blue'">
```

To see this code in action, refer to the Web Workshop CD-ROM.

Applies To

WIN16	WIN32	MAC	UNIX

BLOCKQUOTE, BODY, BUTTON, CAPTION, CENTER, DD, DIR, DIV, DL, DT, EMBED, FIELDSET, FORM, Hn, HR, IFRAME, IMG, INPUT type=button, INPUT type=checkbox, INPUT type=file, INPUT type=image, INPUT type=password, INPUT type=radio, INPUT type=reset, INPUT type=submit, INPUT type=text, ISINDEX, LI, LISTING, MARQUEE, MENU, OBJECT, OL, P, PLAINTEXT, PRE, SPAN, style, TABLE, TD, TEXTAREA, TH, UL, XMP

WIN16	WIN32	MAC	UNIX

currentStyle, runtimeStyle

border-left-style Attribute | borderLeftStyle Property

Sets or retrieves the style of the left border of the object.

Syntax

HTML   { **border-left-style:** none I dotted I dashed I solid I double I groove I ridge I inset I outset }

Scripting *object*.**style.borderLeftStyle** [= *sStyle*]

Possible Values

none   No border is drawn, regardless of any specified **border-width** value.

dotted Border is a dotted line on the Macintosh platform as of Internet Explorer 4.01, and a solid line on the Windows and UNIX platforms.

dashed Border is a dashed line on the Macintosh platform as of Internet Explorer 4.01, and a solid line on the Windows and UNIX platforms.

solid   Border is a solid line.

double Border is a double line drawn on top of the background of the object. The sum of the two single lines and the space between equals the **border-width** value. The border width must be at least 3 pixels wide to draw a double border.

groove 3-D groove is drawn in colors based on the value.

Possible Values *(continued)*

ridge   3-D ridge is drawn in colors based on the value.

inset   3-D inset is drawn in colors based on the value.

outset   3-D outset is drawn in colors based on the value.

The property is read/write with a default value of none; the cascading style sheets (CSS) attribute is not inherited.

Remarks

A **border-width** greater than 0 must be set for the **border-left-style** attribute to render.

To use this property, inline elements must have an absolute **position** or layout. Element layout is set by providing a value for the **height** property or the **width** property.

Example

The following examples show how to use the **border-left-style** attribute and the **borderLeftStyle** property to specify the style of the left border.

The sample below uses a call to an embedded (global) style sheet to change the style of the left border from solid to groove when an **onmouseover** event occurs.

```
<STYLE>
    TD { border-left-style: solid; border-width= 0.3cm }
    .change { border-left-style: groove  }
</STYLE>
</HEAD>
<BODY>
<TABLE BORDER>
<TR>
    <TD onmouseover="this.className='change'"
        onmouseout="this.className=''">
        <IMG src="sphere.jpg">
    </TD>
</TR>
</TABLE>
```

To see this code in action, refer to the Web Workshop CD-ROM.

The sample below uses inline scripting to change the style of the left border to groove on an **onmouseover** event.

```
<TD onmouseover="this.style.borderWidth='0.5cm';
                 this.style.borderLeftStyle='groove'">
```

To see this code in action, refer to the Web Workshop CD-ROM.

Applies To

 WIN16   WIN32   MAC   UNIX

BLOCKQUOTE, BODY, BUTTON, CAPTION, CENTER, DD, DIR, DIV, DL, DT, EMBED, FIELDSET, FORM, Hn, HR, IFRAME, IMG, INPUT type=button, INPUT type=checkbox, INPUT type=file, INPUT type=image, INPUT type=password, INPUT type=radio, INPUT type=reset, INPUT type=submit, INPUT type=text, ISINDEX, LI, LISTING, MARQUEE, MENU, OBJECT, OL, P, PLAINTEXT, PRE, SPAN, style, TABLE, TD, TEXTAREA, TH, UL, XMP

IE 5   **WIN16   WIN32   MAC   UNIX**

currentStyle, runtimeStyle

border-left-width Attribute | borderLeftWidth Property

Sets or retrieves the width of the left border of the object.

Syntax

HTML   { **border-left-width:** medium |thin | thick |*width* }

Scripting *object*.**style.borderLeftWidth** [= *sWidth*]

Possible Values

medium Default width.

thin Width less than the default.

thick Width greater than the default.

width Width value consisting of a floating-point number, followed by an absolute units designator (cm, mm, in, pt, pc, or px) or a relative units designator (em or ex). For more information about the supported length units for CSS attributes, see "CSS Length Units" in Appendix C.

The property is read/write with a default value of medium; the cascading style sheets (CSS) attribute is not inherited.

Remarks

To use this property, inline elements must have an `absolute` **position** or layout. Element layout is set by providing a value for the **height** property or the **width** property.

The property is supported on block and replaced objects only.

Example

The following examples show how to use the **border-left-width** attribute and the **borderLeftWidth** property to specify the border width.

The sample below uses a call to an embedded (global) style sheet to change the width of the left border to 1 centimeter when a mouse click occurs.

```
<STYLE>
    TD { border-left-width: 3mm }
    .changeborder1 { border-left-width: 1cm }
</STYLE>
</HEAD>
<BODY>
<TABLE BORDER>
<TR>
    <TD onclick="this.className='changeborder1'"
        ondblclick="this.className=''">
        <IMG src="sphere.jpg">
    </TD>
</TR></TABLE>
```

To see this code in action, refer to the Web Workshop CD-ROM.

The sample below uses inline scripting to change the width of the left border to 1 centimeter when a mouse click occurs.

```
<TD onclick="this.style.borderLeftWidth='1cm'">
```

To see this code in action, refer to the Web Workshop CD-ROM.

Applies To

 WIN16   WIN32   MAC   UNIX

BLOCKQUOTE, BODY, BUTTON, CAPTION, CENTER, DD, DIR, DIV, DL, DT, EMBED, FIELDSET, FORM, Hn, HR, IFRAME, IMG, INPUT type=button, INPUT type=checkbox, INPUT type=file, INPUT type=image, INPUT type=password, INPUT type=radio, INPUT type=reset, INPUT type=submit, INPUT type=text, ISINDEX, LI, LISTING, MARQUEE, MENU, OBJECT, OL, P, PLAINTEXT, PRE, SPAN, style, TABLE, TD, TEXTAREA, TH, UL, XMP

currentStyle, runtimeStyle

border-right Attribute | borderRight Property

Sets or retrieves the properties of the right border of the object.

Syntax

HTML   { **border-right:** *sWidth* ‖ *sStyle* ‖ *sColor* }

Scripting   *object*.**style.borderRight** [= [*sWidth*] [*sStyle*] [*sColor*]]

Possible Values

sWidth   Any of the range of values available to the **borderRightWidth** property.

sStyle   Any of the range of values available to the **borderRightStyle** property.

sColor   Any of the range of values available to the **borderRightColor** property.

The property is read/write with a default value of medium none; the cascading style sheets (CSS) attribute is not inherited.

Remarks

The **borderRight** property is a composite property for setting the *sWidth*, *sColor*, and *sStyle* values for the right border of an object.

All individual border properties not set by the composite **borderRight** property are set to their default values. For example, the default value for *sWidth* is medium.

If *sColor* is not specified, the text color is used. For more information about supported colors, see the "Color Table" in Appendix C.

To use this property, inline elements must have an absolute **position** or layout. Element layout is set by providing a value for the **height** property or the **width** property.

Example

The following examples show how to use the **borderRight** property and the **border-right** attribute to specify the composite properties.

The sample below uses a call to an embedded (global) style sheet to change the attributes of the right border when an **onmouseover** event occurs.

```
<STYLE>
    TD { border-right: 0.5cm solid yellow; }
    .change { border-right: 0.5cm groove pink; }
</STYLE>
</HEAD>
<BODY>
<TABLE>
<TR>
    <TD onmouseover="this.className='change'"
        onmouseout="this.className=''">
        <IMG src="sphere.jpg"></TD>
</TR>
</TABLE>
```

To see this code in action, refer to the Web Workshop CD-ROM.

The sample below uses inline scripting to change the attributes of the right border when an **onmouseover** event occurs.

```
<TD onmouseover="this.style.borderRight='0.3cm groove yellow'">
```

To see this code in action, refer to the Web Workshop CD-ROM.

Applies To

 WIN16   WIN32   MAC   UNIX

BLOCKQUOTE, BODY, BUTTON, CAPTION, CENTER, DD, DIR, DIV, DL, DT, EMBED, FIELDSET, FORM, Hn, HR, IFRAME, IMG, INPUT type=button, INPUT type=checkbox, INPUT type=file, INPUT type=image, INPUT type=password, INPUT type=radio, INPUT type=reset, INPUT type=submit, INPUT type=text, ISINDEX, LI, LISTING, MARQUEE, MENU, OBJECT, OL, P, PLAINTEXT, PRE, SPAN, style, TABLE, TD, TEXTAREA, TH, UL, XMP

 WIN16   WIN32   MAC   UNIX

runtimeStyle

border-right-color Attribute | borderRightColor Property

Sets or retrieves the color of the right border of the object.

Syntax

| HTML | { **border-right-color:** *sColor* } |
| Scripting | *object*.**style.borderRightColor** [= *sColor*] |

Possible Values

sColor String specifying one of the color names or red-green-blue (RGB) values in the "Color Table" in Appendix C.

The property is read/write with a default value equal to the value of the **color** property; the cascading style sheets (CSS) attribute is not inherited.

Remarks

To use this property, inline elements must have an `absolute` **position** or layout. Element layout is set by providing a value for the **height** property or the **width** property.

Some browsers do not recognize color names, but all browsers should recognize RGB color values and display them correctly.

Example

The following examples show how to use the **border-right-color** attribute and the **borderRightColor** property to specify the color of the right border.

The sample below uses a call to an embedded (global) style sheet to change the color of the right border from red to blue when an **onmouseover** event occurs.

```
<STYLE>
    TD { border-right-color: red;
        border-width: 0.5cm; border-style: groove }
    .blue { border-right-color: blue }
</STYLE>
</HEAD>
<BODY>
```

```
<TABLE BORDER>
<TR>
    <TD onmouseover="this.className='blue'"
        onmouseout="this.className=''">
        <IMG src="sphere.jpg">
    </TD>
</TR>
</TABLE>
```

To see this code in action, refer to the Web Workshop CD-ROM.

The sample below uses inline scripting to change the color of the right border to blue when an **onmouseover** event occurs.

```
<TD onmouseover="this.style.borderWidth='0.5cm';
    this.style.borderRightColor='blue';>
```

To see this code in action, refer to the Web Workshop CD-ROM.

Applies To

 WIN16   WIN32   MAC   UNIX

BLOCKQUOTE, BODY, BUTTON, CAPTION, CENTER, DD, DIR, DIV, DL, DT, EMBED, FIELDSET, FORM, Hn, HR, IFRAME, IMG, INPUT type=button, INPUT type=checkbox, INPUT type=file, INPUT type=image, INPUT type=password, INPUT type=radio, INPUT type=reset, INPUT type=submit, INPUT type=text, ISINDEX, LI, LISTING, MARQUEE, MENU, OBJECT, OL, P, PLAINTEXT, PRE, SPAN, style, TABLE, TD, TEXTAREA, TH, UL, XMP

 WIN16   WIN32   MAC   UNIX

currentStyle, runtimeStyle

border-right-style Attribute | borderRightStyle Property

Sets or retrieves the style of the right border of the object.

Syntax

HTML   { **border-right-style:** none | dotted | dashed | solid | double | groove | ridge | inset | outset }

Scripting *object*.**style.borderRightStyle** [= *sStyle*]

Possible Values

none No border is drawn, regardless of any specified **border-width** value.

dotted Border is a dotted line on the Macintosh platform as of Internet Explorer 4.01, and a solid line on the Windows and UNIX platforms.

dashed Border is a dashed line on the Macintosh platform as of Internet Explorer 4.01, and a solid line on the Windows and UNIX platforms.

solid Border is a solid line.

double Border is a double line drawn on top of the background of the object. The sum of the two single lines and the space between equals the **border-width** value. The border width must be at least 3 pixels wide to draw a double border.

groove 3-D groove is drawn in colors based on the value.

ridge 3-D ridge is drawn in colors based on the value.

inset 3-D inset is drawn in colors based on the value.

outset 3-D outset is drawn in colors based on the value.

The property is read/write with a default value of none; the cascading style sheets (CSS) attribute is not inherited.

Remarks

To use this property, inline elements must have an absolute **position** or layout. Element layout is set by providing a value for the **height** property or the **width** property.

A **border-width** greater than 0 must be set for the **border-right-style** attribute to render.

Example

The following examples show how to use the **border-right-style** attribute and the **borderRightStyle** property to specify the border style.

The sample below uses a call to an embedded (global) style sheet to change the style of the right border from solid to groove when an **onmouseover** event occurs.

```
<STYLE>
    TD { border-right-style: solid; border-width= 0.3cm }
    .change { border-right-style:  groove }
</STYLE>
</HEAD>
<BODY>
```

```
<TABLE BORDER>
<TR>
    <TD onmouseover="this.className='change'"
        onmouseout="this.className=''">
        <IMG src="sphere.jpg">
    </TD>
</TR>
</TABLE>
```

To see this code in action, refer to the Web Workshop CD-ROM.

The sample below uses inline scripting to change the style of the right border to groove when an **onmouseover** event occurs.

```
<TD onmouseover="this.style.borderWidth='0.5cm';
                 this.style.borderRightStyle='groove'">
```

To see this code in action, refer to the Web Workshop CD-ROM.

Applies To

 WIN16   WIN32   MAC   UNIX

BLOCKQUOTE, BODY, BUTTON, CAPTION, CENTER, DD, DIR, DIV, DL, DT, EMBED, FIELDSET, FORM, Hn, HR, IFRAME, IMG, INPUT type=button, INPUT type=checkbox, INPUT type=file, INPUT type=image, INPUT type=password, INPUT type=radio, INPUT type=reset, INPUT type=submit, INPUT type=text, ISINDEX, LI, LISTING, MARQUEE, MENU, OBJECT, OL, P, PLAINTEXT, PRE, SPAN, style, TABLE, TD, TEXTAREA, TH, UL, XMP

 WIN16   WIN32   MAC   UNIX

currentStyle, runtimeStyle

border-right-width Attribute | borderRightWidth Property

Sets or retrieves the width of the right border of the object.

Syntax

HTML   { **border-right-width:** medium | thin | thick | *width* }

Scripting *object*.**style.borderRightWidth** [= *sWidth*]

Possible Values

`medium` Default width.

`thin` Width less than the default.

`thick` Width greater than the default.

width Width value consisting of a floating-point number, followed by an absolute units designator (`cm`, `mm`, `in`, `pt`, `pc`, or `px`) or a relative units designator (`em` or `ex`). For more information about the supported length units for CSS attributes, see "CSS Length Units" in Appendix C.

The property is read/write with a default value of `medium`; the cascading style sheets (CSS) attribute is not inherited.

Remarks

To use this property, inline elements must have an `absolute` **position** or layout. Element layout is set by providing a value for the **height** property or the **width** property.

The property is supported on block and replaced objects only.

Example

The following examples show how to use the **border-right-width** attribute and the **borderRightWidth** property to specify the width of the right border.

The sample below uses a call to an embedded (global) style sheet to change the width of the right border to 1 centimeter when a mouse click occurs.

```
<STYLE>
    TD { border-right-width: 3mm }
    .changeborder1 { border-right-width: 1cm }
</STYLE>
</HEAD>
<BODY>
<TABLE BORDER>
<TR>
    <TD onclick="this.className='changeborder1'"
        ondblclick="this.className=''">
        <IMG src="sphere.jpg">
    </TD>
</TR></TABLE>
```

To see this code in action, refer to the Web Workshop CD-ROM.

The sample below uses inline script to change the width of the right border to 1 centimeter when a mouse click occurs.

```
<TD onclick="this.style.borderRightWidth='1cm'">
```

To see this code in action, refer to the Web Workshop CD-ROM.

Applies To

 WIN16   WIN32   MAC   UNIX

BLOCKQUOTE, BODY, BUTTON, CAPTION, CENTER, DD, DIR, DIV, DL, DT, EMBED, FIELDSET, FORM, Hn, HR, IFRAME, IMG, INPUT type=button, INPUT type=checkbox, INPUT type=file, INPUT type=image, INPUT type=password, INPUT type=radio, INPUT type=reset, INPUT type=submit, INPUT type=text, ISINDEX, LI, LISTING, MARQUEE, MENU, OBJECT, OL, P, PLAINTEXT, PRE, SPAN, style, TABLE, TD, TEXTAREA, TH, UL, XMP

 WIN16   WIN32   MAC   UNIX

currentStyle, runtimeStyle

border-style Attribute | borderStyle Property

Sets or retrieves the style of the left, right, top, and bottom borders of the object.

Syntax

HTML   { **border-style:** none | dotted | dashed| solid |double |groove | ridge |inset | outset }

Scripting *object*.**style.borderStyle** [= *sStyle*]

Possible Values

none   No border is drawn, regardless of any specified **border-width** value.

dotted   Border is a dotted line on the Macintosh platform as of Internet Explorer 4.01, and a solid line on the Windows and UNIX platforms.

dashed   Border is a dashed line on the Macintosh platform as of Internet Explorer 4.01, and a solid line on the Windows and UNIX platforms.

solid   Border is a solid line.

Possible Values *(continued)*

double   Border is a double line drawn on top of the background of the object. The sum of the two single lines and the space between equals the **border-width** value. The border width must be at least 3 pixels wide to draw a double border.

groove   3-D groove is drawn in colors based on the value.

ridge   3-D ridge is drawn in colors based on the value.

inset   3-D inset is drawn in colors based on the value.

outset   3-D outset is drawn in colors based on the value.

The property is read/write with a default value of none; the cascading style sheets (CSS) attribute is not inherited.

Remarks

To use this property, inline elements must have an absolute **position** or layout. Element layout is set by providing a value for the **height** property or the **width** property.

A **border-width** greater than 0 must be set for the **border-style** attribute to render.

Example

The following examples show how to use the **border-style** attribute and the **borderStyle** property to specify the border style.

The sample below uses a call to an embedded (global) style sheet to change the border style to groove when an **onmouseover** event occurs.

```
<STYLE>
    TD   { border-style: solid; border-width= 0.5cm }
    .change { border-style: groove }
</STYLE>
</HEAD>
<BODY>
<TABLE BORDER>
<TR>
    <TD onmouseover="this.className='change'"
        onmouseout="this.className=''">
        <IMG src="sphere.jpg">
    </TD>
</TR>
</TABLE>
```

To see this code in action, refer to the Web Workshop CD-ROM.

DHTML Properties

The sample below uses inline scripting to change the border style to `groove` when an **onmouseover** event occurs.

```
<TD onmouseover="this.style.borderWidth='0.5cm';
    this.style.borderStyle='groove'">
```

To see this code in action, refer to the Web Workshop CD-ROM.

Applies To

WIN16   WIN32   MAC   UNIX

BLOCKQUOTE, BODY, BUTTON, CAPTION, CENTER, DD, DIR, DIV, DL, DT, EMBED, FIELDSET, FORM, Hn, HR, IFRAME, IMG, INPUT type=button, INPUT type=checkbox, INPUT type=file, INPUT type=image, INPUT type=password, INPUT type=radio, INPUT type=reset, INPUT type=submit, INPUT type=text, ISINDEX, LI, LISTING, MARQUEE, MENU, OBJECT, OL, P, PLAINTEXT, PRE, SPAN, style, TABLE, TD, TEXTAREA, TH, UL, XMP

WIN16   WIN32   MAC   UNIX

currentStyle, runtimeStyle

border-top Attribute | borderTop Property

Sets or retrieves the properties of the top border of the object.

Syntax

HTML   { **border-top:** *sWidth* | *sStyle* | *sColor* }

Scripting   *object*.**style.borderTop** [= [*sWidth*] [*sStyle*] [*sColor*]]

Possible Values

sWidth   Any of the range of values available to the **borderTopWidth** property.

sStyle   Any of the range of values available to the **borderTopStyle** property.

sColor   Any of the range of values available to the **borderTopColor** property.

The property is read/write with a default value of `medium none`; the cascading style sheets (CSS) attribute is not inherited.

Remarks

The **borderTop** property is a composite property for setting the *sWidth*, *sColor*, and *sStyle* values for the top border of an object.

All individual border properties not set by the composite **borderTop** property are set to their default values. For example, the default value for *sWidth* is `medium`.

If an *sColor* is not specified, the text color is used. For more information about supported colors, see the "Color Table" in Appendix C.

To use this property, inline elements must have an `absolute` **position** or layout. Element layout is set by providing a value for the **height** property or the **width** property.

Example

The following examples show how to use the **border-top** attribute and the **borderTop** property to specify the composite properties.

The sample below uses a call to an embedded style sheet to change the attributes of the top border when an **onmouseover** event occurs.

```
<STYLE>
    TD   { border-top: 0.5cm solid yellow; }
    .change { border-top: 0.5cm groove pink; }
</STYLE>
</HEAD>
<BODY>
<TABLE>
<TR>
    <TD onmouseover="this.className='change'"
        onmouseout="this.className=''">
        <IMG src="sphere.jpg">
    </TD>
</TR>
</TABLE>
```

To see this code in action, refer to the Web Workshop CD-ROM.

The sample below uses inline scripting to change the top border when an **onmouseover** event occurs.

```
<TD onmouseover="this.style.borderTop='0.3cm groove yellow'">
```

To see this code in action, refer to the Web Workshop CD-ROM.

Applies To

WIN16   WIN32   MAC   UNIX

BLOCKQUOTE, BODY, BUTTON, CAPTION, CENTER, DD, DIR, DIV, DL, DT, EMBED, FIELDSET, FORM, Hn, HR, IFRAME, IMG, INPUT type=button, INPUT type=checkbox, INPUT type=file, INPUT type=image, INPUT type=password, INPUT type=radio, INPUT type=reset, INPUT type=submit, INPUT type=text, ISINDEX, LI, LISTING, MARQUEE, MENU, OBJECT, OL, P, PLAINTEXT, PRE, SPAN, style, TABLE, TD, TEXTAREA, TH, UL, XMP

WIN16   WIN32   MAC   UNIX

runtimeStyle

border-top-color Attribute | borderTopColor Property

Sets or retrieves the color of the top border of the object.

Syntax

HTML   { **border-top-color:** *sColor* }

Scripting *object*.**style.borderTopColor** [= *sColor*]

Possible Values

sColor   String specifying one of the color names or red-green-blue (RGB) values in the "Color Table" in Appendix C.

The property is read/write with a default value equal to the value of the **color** property; the cascading style sheets (CSS) attribute is not inherited.

Remarks

To use this property, inline elements must have an `absolute` **position** or layout. Element layout is set by providing a value for the **height** property or the **width** property.

Some browsers do not recognize color names, but all browsers should recognize RGB color values and display them correctly.

Example

The following examples demonstrate use of both the **border-top-color** attribute and the **borderTopColor** property to specify the color of the top border.

The sample below uses a call to an embedded (global) style sheet to change the color of the top border to blue when an **onmouseover** event occurs.

```
<STYLE>
    TD { border-top-color: red;
        border-width: 0.5cm; border-style: groove }
    .blue { border-top-color: blue }
</STYLE>
</HEAD>
<BODY>
<TABLE BORDER>
<TR>
    <TD onmouseover="this.className='blue'"
        onmouseout="this.className=''">
    </TD>
</TR>
</TABLE>
```

To see this code in action, refer to the Web Workshop CD-ROM.

The sample below uses inline scripting to change the color of the top border to blue when an **onmouseover** event occurs.

```
<TD onmouseover="this.style.borderWidth='0.5cm';
    this.style.borderTopColor='blue'">
```

To see this code in action, refer to the Web Workshop CD-ROM.

Applies To

 WIN16   WIN32   MAC   UNIX

BLOCKQUOTE, BODY, BUTTON, CAPTION, CENTER, DD, DIR, DIV, DL, DT, EMBED, FIELDSET, FORM, Hn, HR, IFRAME, IMG, INPUT type=button, INPUT type=checkbox, INPUT type=file, INPUT type=image, INPUT type=password, INPUT type=radio, INPUT type=reset, INPUT type=submit, INPUT type=text, ISINDEX, LI, LISTING, MARQUEE, MENU, OBJECT, OL, P, PLAINTEXT, PRE, SPAN, style, TABLE, TD, TEXTAREA, TH, UL, XMP

 WIN16   WIN32   MAC   UNIX

currentStyle, runtimeStyle

border-top-style Attribute | borderTopStyle Property

Sets or retrieves the style of the top border of the object.

Syntax

HTML   { **border-top-style:** none | dotted | dashed | solid |double | groove | ridge | inset | outset }

Scripting *object*.**style.borderTopStyle** [= *sStyle*]

Possible Values

none   No border is drawn, regardless of any specified **border-width** value.

dotted   Border is a dotted line on the Macintosh platform as of Internet Explorer 4.01, and a solid line on the Windows and UNIX platforms.

dashed   Border is a dashed line on the Macintosh platform as of Internet Explorer 4.01, and a solid line on the Windows and UNIX platforms.

solid   Border is a solid line.

double   Border is a double line drawn on top of the background of the object. The sum of the two single lines and the space between equals the **border-width** value. The border width must be at least 3 pixels wide to draw a double border.

groove   3-D groove is drawn in colors based on the value.

ridge   3-D ridge is drawn in colors based on the value.

inset   3-D inset is drawn in colors based on the value.

outset   3-D outset is drawn in colors based on the value.

The property is read/write with a default value of none; the cascading style sheets (CSS) attribute is not inherited.

Remarks

To use this property, inline elements must have an absolute **position** or layout. Element layout is set by providing a value for the **height** property or the **width** property.

A **border-width** greater than 0 must be set for the **border-top-style** attribute to render.

Example

The following examples show how to use the **border-top-style** attribute and the **borderTopStyle** property to specify the top border's style.

The sample below uses a call to an embedded (global) style sheet to change the style of the top border from `solid` to `groove` when an **onmouseover** event occurs.

```
<STYLE>
    TD { border-top-style: solid;
        border-width= 0.3cm }
    .change { border-top-style: groove }
</STYLE>
</HEAD>
<BODY>
<TABLE BORDER>
<TR>
    <TD onmouseover="this.className='change'"
        onmouseout="this.className=''">
        <IMG src="sphere.jpg">
    </TD>
</TR>
</TABLE>
```

To see this code in action, refer to the Web Workshop CD-ROM.

The sample below uses inline scripting to change the style of the top border to `groove` when an **onmouseover** event occurs.

```
<TD onmouseover="this.style.borderWidth='0.5cm';
    this.style.borderTopStyle='groove'">
```

To see this code in action, refer to the Web Workshop CD-ROM.

Applies To

 WIN16   WIN32   MAC   UNIX

BLOCKQUOTE, BODY, BUTTON, CAPTION, CENTER, DD, DIR, DIV, DL, DT, EMBED, FIELDSET, FORM, Hn, HR, IFRAME, IMG, INPUT type=button, INPUT type=checkbox, INPUT type=file, INPUT type=image, INPUT type=password, INPUT type=radio, INPUT type=reset, INPUT type=submit, INPUT type=text, ISINDEX, LI, LISTING, MARQUEE, MENU, OBJECT, OL, P, PLAINTEXT, PRE, SPAN, style, TABLE, TD, TEXTAREA, TH, UL, XMP

 WIN16   WIN32   MAC   UNIX

currentStyle, runtimeStyle

border-top-width Attribute | borderTopWidth Property

Sets or retrieves the width of the top border of the object.

Syntax

HTML	{ **border-top-width:** medium	thin	thick	*width* }
Scripting	*object*.**style.borderTopWidth** [= *sWidth*]

Possible Values

medium	Default width.
thin	Width less than the default.
thick	Width greater than the default.
width	Width value consisting of a floating-point number, followed by an absolute units designator (cm, mm, in, pt, pc, or px) or a relative units designator (em or ex). For more information about the supported length units for CSS attributes, see "CSS Length Units" in Appendix C.

The property is read/write with a default value of medium; the cascading style sheets (CSS) attribute is not inherited.

Remarks

To use this property, inline elements must have an absolute **position** or layout. Element layout is set by providing a value for the **height** property or the **width** property.

The property is supported on block and replaced objects only.

Example

The following examples show how to use the **border-top-width** attribute and the **borderTopWidth** property to specify the width of the top border.

The sample below uses a call to an embedded (global) style sheet to change the width to 1 centimeter when a mouse click occurs.

```
<STYLE>
    TD { border-top-width: 3mm }
    .changeborder1 { border-top-width: 1cm }
</STYLE>
</HEAD>
<BODY>
```

DHTML Properties

```
<TABLE BORDER>
<TR>
    <TD onclick="this.className='changeborder1'"
        ondblclick="this.className=''">
        <IMG src="sphere.jpg">
    </TD>
</TR>
</TABLE>
```

To see this code in action, refer to the Web Workshop CD-ROM.

The sample below uses inline script to change the width to 1 centimeter when a mouse click occurs.

```
<TD onclick="this.style.borderTopWidth='1cm'">
```

To see this code in action, refer to the Web Workshop CD-ROM.

Applies To

 WIN16   WIN32   MAC   UNIX

BLOCKQUOTE, BODY, BUTTON, CAPTION, CENTER, DD, DIR, DIV, DL, DT, EMBED, FIELDSET, FORM, Hn, HR, IFRAME, IMG, INPUT type=button, INPUT type=checkbox, INPUT type=file, INPUT type=image, INPUT type=password, INPUT type=radio, INPUT type=reset, INPUT type=submit, INPUT type=text, ISINDEX, LI, LISTING, MARQUEE, MENU, OBJECT, OL, P, PLAINTEXT, PRE, SPAN, style, TABLE, TD, TEXTAREA, TH, UL, XMP

 WIN16   WIN32   MAC   UNIX

currentStyle, runtimeStyle

border-width Attribute | borderWidth Property

Sets or retrieves the width of the left, right, top, and bottom borders of the object.

Syntax

HTML   { **border-width:** [medium | thin | thick | *width*] {1,4} }

Scripting   *object*.**style.borderWidth** [= *sWidth*]

Possible Values

`medium`   Default width.

`thin`   Width less than the default.

`thick`   Width greater than the default.

width   String consisting of a floating-point number, followed by an absolute units designator (`cm`, `mm`, `in`, `pt`, `pc`, or `px`) or a relative units designator (`em` or `ex`). For more information about the supported length units for CSS attributes, see "CSS Length Units" in Appendix C.

The property is read/write with a default value of `medium`; the cascading style sheets (CSS) attribute is not inherited.

Remarks

In HTML syntax, {1,4} indicates that up to four different widths may be specified in this order: top, right, bottom, left. If one width is supplied, it is used for all four sides. If two widths are supplied, the first is used for the top and bottom borders, and the second is used for left and right borders. If three widths are supplied, they are used for top, right and left, and bottom borders, respectively.

To use this property, inline elements must have an `absolute` **position** or layout. Element layout is set by providing a value for the **height** property or the **width** property.

The **borderWidth** property is not rendered if the **borderStyle** property is set to `none`.

Example

The following examples show how to use the **border-width** attribute and the **borderWidth** property to specify the border width.

The sample below uses a call to an embedded (global) style sheet to change the border width to 1 centimeter when a mouse click occurs.

```
<STYLE>
    TD { border-width: 3mm }
    .changeborder1 { border-width: 1cm }
</STYLE>
</HEAD>
<BODY>
<TABLE BORDER>
<TR>
    <TD onclick="this.className='changeborder1'"
        ondblclick="this.className=''">
        <IMG src="sphere.jpg"></TD>
</TR>
</TABLE>
```

To see this code in action, refer to the Web Workshop CD-ROM.

The sample below uses inline script to change the border width to 1 centimeter when a mouse click occurs.

```
<TD onclick="this.style.borderWidth='1cm'">
```

To see this code in action, refer to the Web Workshop CD-ROM.

Applies To

 WIN16   WIN32   MAC   UNIX

BLOCKQUOTE, BODY, BUTTON, CAPTION, CENTER, DD, DIR, DIV, DL, DT, EMBED, FIELDSET, FORM, Hn, HR, IFRAME, IMG, INPUT type=button, INPUT type=checkbox, INPUT type=file, INPUT type=image, INPUT type=password, INPUT type=radio, INPUT type=reset, INPUT type=submit, INPUT type=text, ISINDEX, LI, LISTING, MARQUEE, MENU, OBJECT, OL, P, PLAINTEXT, PRE, SPAN, style, TABLE, TD, TEXTAREA, TH, UL, XMP

 WIN16   WIN32   MAC   UNIX

currentStyle, runtimeStyle

bottom Property

Retrieves the bottom coordinate of the rectangle surrounding the object content.

Syntax

HTML   N/A

Scripting [*iCoord* =] *oTextRectangle*.**bottom**

Possible Values

iCoord Integer specifying the bottom coordinate of the rectangle, in pixels.

The property is read-only with no default value.

Remarks

Use the following syntax to access the bottom coordinate of the second text rectangle of a **TextRange** object:

```
oRct = oTextRange.getClientRects();
oRct[1].bottom;
```

Note The collection index starts at 0, so the second item index is 1.

Use the following syntax to access the bottom coordinate of the bounding rectangle of an element object:

```
oBndRct = oElement.getBoundingClientRect();
oBndRct.bottom;
```

Example

The following example shows how to use the **getBoundingClientRect** method to retrieve the coordinates of the bounds of the text rectangles within the element.

```
<SCRIPT>
function getCoords(oObject) {
    oBndRct=oObject.getBoundingClientRect();
    alert("Bounding rectangle = \nUpper left coordinates: "
        + oBndRct.left + " " + oBndRct.top +
        "\nLower right coordinates: "
        + oBndRct.right + " " + oBndRct.bottom);
}
</SCRIPT>
</HEAD>
<BODY>
<P ID=oPara onclick="getCoords(this)">
```

To see this code in action, refer to the Web Workshop CD-ROM.

Applies To

 WIN16   **WIN32**   **MAC**   **UNIX**

TextRectangle Object

bottom Attribute | bottom Property

Sets or retrieves the bottom position of the object in relation to the bottom of the next positioned object in the document hierarchy.

Syntax

HTML   { **bottom:** auto | *length* | *percentage* }

Scripting   *object*.**style.bottom** [= *sBottom*]

Possible Values

auto Default position according to the regular HTML layout of the page.

length String consisting of a floating-point number, followed by an absolute units designator (cm, mm, in, pt, pc, or px) or a relative units designator (em or ex). For more information about the supported length units for CSS attributes, see "CSS Length Units" in Appendix C.

percentage String value expressed as a percentage of the height of the parent object. Percentage values are specified as a number followed by a %.

The property is read/write with a default value of auto; the cascading style sheets (CSS) attribute is not inherited.

Remarks

The **bottom** attribute should only be used when the **position** attribute is set; otherwise, the value of the **bottom** attribute is ignored.

Because the value of the **bottom** property is a string, the property cannot be used in script to calculate the position of the object in the document; instead, the **pixelBottom** or **posBottom** property should be used.

Example

The following example shows how to use the **bottom** attribute to set a **DIV** object 50 pixels from the bottom of the client area.

```
<DIV STYLE = "position:absolute; bottom:50px">
. . .
</DIV>
```

Applies To

 WIN16   WIN32   MAC   UNIX   WIN16   WIN32

A, ADDRESS, APPLET, B, BIG, BLOCKQUOTE, BUTTON, CENTER, CITE, CODE, DD, DFN, DIR, DIV, DL, FIELDSET, FORM, Hn, HR, I, IFRAME, IMG, INPUT type=button, INPUT type=checkbox, INPUT type=file, INPUT type=image, INPUT type=password, INPUT type=radio, INPUT type=reset, INPUT type=submit, INPUT type=text, ISINDEX, KBD, LABEL, LEGEND, LI, LISTING, MARQUEE, MENU, OBJECT, OL, P, PRE, S, SAMP, SELECT, SMALL, SPAN, STRIKE, STRONG, style, SUB, SUP, TABLE, TEXTAREA, TT, U, UL, VAR, XMP

 WIN16   WIN32   MAC   UNIX

currentStyle, runtimeStyle

DHTML Properties

BOTTOMMARGIN Attribute | bottomMargin Property

Sets or retrieves the bottom margin for the entire body of the page.

Syntax

HTML   <BODY **BOTTOMMARGIN** = *sPixels* ... >

Scripting   *body*.**bottomMargin** [= *sPixels*]

Possible Values

sPixels   String specifying the number of pixels for the bottom margin.

The property is read/write with a default value of 15.

Remarks

If the value is set to "", the bottom margin is set exactly on the bottom edge. The value specified overrides the default margin.

Applies To

 WIN16   WIN32   MAC   UNIX

BODY

boundingHeight Property

Retrieves the height of the rectangle that bounds the **TextRange** object.

Syntax

HTML   N/A

Scripting [*iHeight* =] *TextRange*.**boundingHeight**

Possible Values

iHeight   Integer specifying the height of the bounding rectangle.

The property is read-only with no default value.

Example

The following example shows how to retrieve the value of the **boundingHeight** property for the given text area.

```
<SCRIPT>
function boundDim(oObject)
{
    var collTextarea = document.all.tags("TEXTAREA");
    if (collTextarea != null) {
        var oTextRange = oObject.createTextRange();
        if (oTextRange != null) {
            alert("The bounding height is \n" +
                oTextRange.boundingHeight);
        }
    }
}
</SCRIPT>
</HEAD>
<BODY>
<TEXTAREA COLS=100 ROWS=2 ID=oElmnt1
    onclick="boundDim(this)"> . . . </TEXTAREA>
```

To see this code in action, refer to the Web Workshop CD-ROM.

Applies To

 WIN16   WIN32   MAC   UNIX

TextRange

boundingLeft Property

Retrieves the left coordinate of the rectangle that bounds the **TextRange** object.

Syntax

HTML   N/A

Scripting   [*iLeft* =] *TextRange*.**boundingLeft**

Possible Values

iLeft   Integer specifying the left coordinate of the bounding rectangle.

The property is read-only with no default value.

Example

The following example shows how to retrieve the value of the **boundingLeft** property for the given text area.

```
<SCRIPT>
function boundDim(oObject)
{
    var collTextarea = document.all.tags("TEXTAREA");
    if (collTextarea != null) {
        var oTextRage = oObject.createTextRange();
        if (oTextRange != null) {
            alert("The bounding left is \n" +
                oTextRange.boundingLeft);
        }
    }
}
</SCRIPT>
</HEAD>
<BODY>
<TEXTAREA COLS=100 ROWS=2 ID=oTextarea
    onclick="boundDim(this)"> . . . </TEXTAREA>
```

To see this code in action, refer to the Web Workshop CD-ROM.

Applies To

 WIN16   WIN32   MAC   UNIX

TextRange

boundingTop Property

Retrieves the top coordinate of the rectangle that bounds the **TextRange** object.

Syntax

HTML   N/A

Scripting [*iTop* =] *TextRange*.**boundingTop**

Possible Values

iTop   Integer specifying the top coordinate of the bounding rectangle.

The property is read-only with no default value.

Example

The following example shows how to retrieve the value of the **boundingTop** property for the given text area.

```
<SCRIPT>
function boundDim(oObject)
{
    var collTextarea = document.all.tags("TEXTAREA");
    if (collTextarea != null) {
        var oTextRange = oObject.createTextRange();
        if (oTextRange != null) {
            alert("The bounding top is \n" +
                oTextRange.boundingTop);
        }
    }
}
</SCRIPT>
</HEAD>
<BODY>
<TEXTAREA COLS=100 ROWS=2 ID=oTextarea
    onclick="boundDim(this)"> . . . </TEXTAREA>
```

To see this code in action, refer to the Web Workshop CD-ROM.

Applies To

 WIN16   WIN32   MAC   UNIX

TextRange

boundingWidth Property

Retrieves the width of the rectangle that bounds the **TextRange** object.

Syntax

HTML   N/A

Scripting [*iWidth* =] *TextRange*.**boundingWidth**

Possible Values

iWidth   Integer specifying the width of the bounding rectangle.

The property is read-only with no default value.

Example

The following example shows how to retrieve the value of the **boundingWidth** property for the given text area.

```
<SCRIPT>
function boundDim(oObject)
{
    var collTextarea = document.all.tags("TEXTAREA");
    if (collTextarea != null) {
        var oTextRange = oObject.createTextRange();
        if (oTextRange != null) {
            alert("The bounding width is \n" +
                oTextRange.boundingWidth);
        }
    }
}
</SCRIPT>
</HEAD>
<BODY>
<TEXTAREA COLS=100 ROWS=2 ID=oTextarea
    onclick="boundDim(this)"> . . . </TEXTAREA>
```

To see this code in action, refer to the Web Workshop CD-ROM.

Applies To

  WIN16 WIN32 MAC UNIX

TextRange

browserLanguage Property

Retrieves the current browser language.

Syntax

HTML   N/A

Scripting   [*sLanguage* =] *navigator*.**browserLanguage**

Possible Values

sLanguage   String specifying one of the language code values. For more information about the codes, see the enclosed Web Workshop CD.

The property is read-only with a default value of en-us.

Applies To

 WIN16   WIN32   MAC   UNIX

navigator

bufferDepth Property

Sets or retrieves the number of bits per pixel used for colors in the off-screen bitmap buffer.

Syntax

HTML   N/A

Scripting   *screen*.**bufferDepth** [= *iBitsPerPixel*]

Possible Values

0	Integer specifying no explicit buffering. The **colorDepth** property is set to the screen depth.
-1	Integer specifying buffering at the screen depth. The **colorDepth** property is set to the screen depth.
1, 4, 8, 15, 16, 24, 32	Integer specifying the number of bits per pixel to use for the off-screen buffer. The **colorDepth** property is also set to this value. The value 15 specifies 16 bits per pixel, in which only 15 bits are used in a 5-5-5 layout of red-green-blue (RGB) values.

The property is read/write with a default value of 0.

Remarks

Nonsupported values cause **bufferDepth** to be set to -1.

When **bufferDepth** is -1 and the user changes system settings that affect the screen depth, the buffer depth is automatically updated to the new depth. This is not the case if **bufferDepth** is set to a specific value.

Applies To

 WIN16   WIN32   MAC   UNIX

screen

button Property

Retrieves the mouse button pressed by the user.

Syntax

HTML N/A

Scripting [*sWhichButton* =] *event*.**button**

Possible Values

0   No button is pressed.

1   Left button is pressed.

2   Right button is pressed.

3   Both left and right buttons are pressed.

4   Middle button is pressed.

5   Both left and middle buttons are pressed.

6   Both right and middle buttons are pressed.

7   All three buttons are pressed.

The property is read-only with a default value of 0.

Remarks

This property is used with the **onmousedown**, **onmouseup**, and **onmousemove** events. For other events, it defaults to 0 regardless of the state of the mouse buttons.

Applies To

 WIN16   WIN32   MAC   UNIX

event

cancelBubble Property

Sets or retrieves whether the current event should bubble up the hierarchy of event handlers.

Syntax

HTML   N/A

Scripting *event*.**cancelBubble** [= *bCancel*]

Possible Values

`false` Enables bubbling.

`true` Cancels bubbling for this event, preventing the next event handler in the hierarchy from receiving the event.

The property is read/write with a default value of `false`.

Remarks

Using this property to cancel bubbling for an event does not affect subsequent events.

Example

The following example shows how to use the **cancelBubble** property. The document fragment cancels bubbling of the **onclick** event if it occurs in the **IMG** object when the user presses the SHIFT key. This prevents the event from bubbling up to the **onclick** event handler for the document.

```
<SCRIPT LANGUAGE="JScript">
function checkCancel()
{
    if (window.event.shiftKey)
        window.event.cancelBubble = true;
}
function showSrc()
{
    if (window.event.srcElement.tagName == "IMG")
        alert(window.event.srcElement.src);
}
</SCRIPT>

<BODY onclick="showSrc()">
<IMG onclick="checkCancel()" SRC="sample.gif">
```

Applies To

 WIN16   WIN32   MAC   UNIX

event

canHaveChildren Property

Retrieves a Boolean value indicating whether the object can contain other objects.

Syntax

HTML   N/A

Scripting [*bChildren* =] *object*.**canHaveChildren**

Possible Values

bChildren   Boolean value indicating whether the object can be a parent to child objects.

The property is read-only with no default value.

Remarks

Objects do not have to contain children for the **canHaveChildren** property to return `true`. This property is useful in determining whether objects can be appended as children.

Example

The following example shows how to use the **canHaveChildren** property to add a new object to the first element in a Web page that can contain children.

```
<SCRIPT>
window.onload=fnInit;
function fnInit(){
   var oNewObject=document.createElement("SPAN");
   var oNewText=document.createTextNode("Test");
   oNewObject.appendChild(oNewText);
   for(var i=0;i<document.all.length;i++){
      if(document.all[i].canHaveChildren==true){
         document.all[i].appendChild(oNewObject);
         break;
      }
   }
}
</SCRIPT>
```

```
<INPUT TYPE=button VALUE="Add Child" onclick="fnAddChild()">
<DIV ID=oGrandParent STYLE="background-color: #CFCFCF;">
<WBR>WBR - </WBR>
<BR>
<NOBR>NOBR - </NOBR>
<P>P - <s/P>
</DIV>
```

To see this code in action, refer to the Web Workshop CD-ROM.

Applies To

WIN16   WIN32   MAC   UNIX

A, ACRONYM, ADDRESS, B, BDO, BIG, BLOCKQUOTE, BODY, BUTTON, CAPTION, CENTER, CITE, CODE, COL, COLGROUP, COMMENT, DD, DEL, DFN, DIR, DIV, DL, DT, EM, FIELDSET, FONT, FORM, FRAMESET, HEAD, Hn, HTML, I, IFRAME, INPUT type=button, INPUT type=checkbox, INPUT type=file, INPUT type=image, INPUT type=password, INPUT type=radio, INPUT type=reset, INPUT type=submit, INPUT type=text, INS, KBD, LABEL, LEGEND, LI, LISTING, MAP, MARQUEE, MENU, NEXTID, OBJECT, OL, OPTION, P, PLAINTEXT, PRE, Q, S, SAMP, SELECT, SMALL, SPAN, STRIKE, STRONG, SUB, SUP, TABLE, TBODY, TD, TEXTAREA, TFOOT, TH, THEAD, TR, TT, U, UL, VAR, XMP

caption Property

Retrieves the **CAPTION** object of the **TABLE**.

Syntax

HTML   N/A

Scripting   [*oCaption* =] *table*.**caption**

Possible Values

null   No caption exists for the table.

oCaption   Object that represents the table caption.

The property is read-only with a default value of null.

Example

The following example shows how to set the inline style for the **caption** property.

```
document.all.myTable.caption.style.color = "blue"
```

Applies To

 WIN16   WIN32   MAC   UNIX

table

cellIndex Property

Retrieves the position of the object in the **cells** collection of a given row.

Syntax

HTML   N/A

Scripting   [*iIndex* =] *td*.**cellIndex**

Possible Values

iIndex   Integer specifying the position of the object.

The property is read-only with no default value.

Remarks

Collection indexes are in the source order of the HTML document. When a cell spans multiple rows, that cell only appears in the **cells** collection for the first row that the cell spans.

Applies To

 WIN16   WIN32   MAC   UNIX

TD

CELLPADDING Attribute | cellPadding Property

Sets or retrieves the amount of space between the border of the cell and the content of the cell.

Syntax

HTML   <TABLE **CELLPADDING** = *iPadding*[%] ... >

Scripting *table*.**cellPadding** [= *iPadding*]

Possible Values

iPadding   Integer specifying the amount of space, in pixels, between the border and the content.

iPadding%   Integer followed by a percent sign (%). This indicates the amount of space between the border and the content as a percentage of the available space.

The property is read/write with no default value.

Applies To

 WIN16   WIN32   MAC

TABLE

 UNIX

TABLE

CELLSPACING Attribute | cellSpacing Property

Sets or retrieves the amount of space between cells in a table.

Syntax

HTML   <TABLE **CELLSPACING** = *iSpacing*[%] ... >

Scripting *table*.**cellSpacing** [= *iSpacing*]

DHTML Properties

Possible Values

> *iSpacing*   Integer specifying the amount of space, in pixels, between the border and the content.
>
> *iSpacing%*   Integer followed by a percent sign (%). This indicates the amount of space between the border and the content as a percentage of the available space.

> The property is read/write with no default value.

Example

> The following example shows how to use the **CELLSPACING** attribute and the **cellSpacing** property.

```
<TABLE ID=oTable BORDER CELLSPACING=10>
    <TR>
        <TD>Cell 1</TD>
        <TD>Cell 2</TD>
    </TR>
</TABLE>
:
<BUTTON onclick="oTable.cellSpacing=20">Larger spacing</BUTTON>
<BUTTON onclick="oTable.cellSpacing=5">Smaller spacing</BUTTON>
```

> To see this code in action, refer to the Web Workshop CD-ROM.

Applies To

 WIN16   WIN32   MAC

TABLE

 UNIX

TABLE

CHARSET Attribute | charset Property

> Sets or retrieves the character set of the document.

Syntax

> **HTML**   <META **CHARSET** = *sCharSet* ... >
>
> **Scripting** *object*.**charset** [= *sCharSet*]

Possible Values

sCharSet String specifying the character set.

The property is read/write with no default value.

Example

The following example shows how to set the character set for the document.

```
<META HTTP-EQUIV="Content-Type"
    CONTENT="text/html; CHARSET=Windows-1251">
```

Applies To

 WIN16   WIN32   MAC   UNIX

document, META

@charset Rule

Retrieves the character set for an external style sheet.

Syntax

HTML   **@charset** *sCharacterSet*

Scripting N/A

Possible Values

sCharacterSet String specifying the character set.

The rule has no default value.

Remarks

At most, you can use one **@charset** in an external style sheet, and it must appear at the top of the file, not preceded by any characters. The **@charset** rule cannot be in an embedded style sheet.

Example

The following example shows how the @**charset** rule is implemented.

```
@charset "Windows-1251";
```

CHECKED Attribute | checked Property

Sets or retrieves a value indicating whether the given check box or radio button is selected.

Syntax

HTML   *<ELEMENT* **CHECKED** ... *>*

Scripting *input*.**checked** [*= bChecked*]

Possible Values

false Control is not selected.

true   Control is selected.

The property is read/write with a default value of false.

Remarks

Check boxes that are not selected do not return their values when the form is submitted.

Example

The following example shows how to retrieve the **checked** property to fire an event.

```
<HEAD>
<SCRIPT>
function checkthis()
{
    if (oCheckbox.checked == true)
    {
        alert("It's got a check; now off to Microsoft!");
        window.open("http://www.microsoft.com");
    }
}
</SCRIPT>
</HEAD>
<BODY>
Check here if you wish to go to Microsoft:
<INPUT ID=oCheckbox TYPE=checkbox onclick=checkthis()>
</BODY>
```

To see this code in action, refer to the Web Workshop CD-ROM.

Applies To

 WIN16   WIN32   MAC

INPUT TYPE=checkbox, INPUT TYPE=radio

 UNIX

INPUT TYPE=checkbox, INPUT TYPE=radio

CLASSID Attribute | classid Property

Retrieves the class identifier for the object.

Syntax

HTML   <OBJECT **CLASSID** = *sID* ... >

Scripting [*sID* =] *object*.**classid**

Possible Values

sID String specifying the class identifier for the object. The format is
"clsid:XXXXXXXX-XXXX-XXXX-XXXX-XXXXXXXXXXXX" for
registered ActiveX Controls.

The property is read-only with no default value.

Applies To

 WIN16   WIN32   MAC

OBJECT

 UNIX

OBJECT

CLASS Attribute | className Property

Sets or retrieves the class of the object.

Syntax

HTML   *<ELEMENT* **CLASS** = *sClass ... >*

Scripting *object.***className** [= *sClass*]

Possible Values

sClass String specifying the class or style rule.

The property is read/write.

Remarks

The class is typically used to associate a particular style rule in a style sheet with the element.

As of Internet Explorer 5, you can apply multiple styles to an element by specifying more than one style for the **CLASS** attribute. To apply multiple styles to a single element, use the following syntax:

```
<ELEMENT CLASS = sClass [ sClass2 [ sClass3 ... ] ] ... >
```

When multiple styles are specified for an element, it is possible for a conflict to develop if two or more styles define the same attribute differently. In this case, the conflict is resolved by applying styles to the element in the following order, according to the CSS selector used to define the style:

1. Element
2. **CLASS**
3. **ID**
4. Inline styles

When two or more selectors pertain to an element, a style defined later takes precedence over a style defined earlier.

Example

The following example shows how to apply one or more styles to an HTML element.

```
<HEAD>
    <STYLE TYPE="text/css">
        P {font-size: 24pt;}
        .redText {color: red;}
```

```
        .blueText {color: blue;}
        .italicText {font-style: italic;}
    </STYLE>
</HEAD>

<BODY>
    <P>
        Large text, no class specified, one implied.
    </P>
    <P CLASS="redText">
        Large text, .redText class specified.
    </P>
    <P CLASS="blueText italicText">
        Large text, .blueText and .italicText classes specified.
    </P>
</BODY>
```

To see this code in action, refer to the Web Workshop CD-ROM.

Applies To

 WIN16   WIN32   MAC   UNIX

A, ACRONYM, ADDRESS, APPLET, AREA, B, BIG, BLOCKQUOTE, BODY,
BR, BUTTON, CAPTION, CENTER, CITE, CODE, COL, COLGROUP, DD, DEL,
DFN, DIR, DIV, DL, DT, EM, EMBED, FIELDSET, FONT, FORM, FRAME,
FRAMESET, HEAD, Hn, HR, HTML, I, IFRAME, IMG, INPUT type=button,
INPUT type=checkbox, INPUT type=file, INPUT type=hidden, INPUT type=image,
INPUT type=password, INPUT type=radio, INPUT type=reset, INPUT type=submit,
INPUT type=text, INS, ISINDEX, KBD, LABEL, LEGEND, LI, LISTING, MAP,
MARQUEE, MENU, NEXTID, NOBR, OBJECT, OL, OPTION, P, PLAINTEXT,
PRE, Q, S, SAMP, SELECT, SMALL, SPAN, STRIKE, STRONG, SUB, SUP,
TABLE, TBODY, TD, TEXTAREA, TFOOT, TH, THEAD, TR, TT, U, UL, VAR,
XMP

IE 5 **WIN16   WIN32   MAC   UNIX**

BDO, RT, RUBY

clear Attribute | clear Property

Sets or retrieves whether the object allows floating objects on its left and/or right sides, so that the next text displays past the floating objects.

Syntax

HTML   { **clear:** none | left | right | both }

Scripting *object*.**style.clear** [= *sClear*]

Possible Values

none Floating objects are allowed on both sides.

left Object is moved below any floating object on the left side.

right Object is moved below any floating object on the right side.

both Object is moved below any floating object.

The property is read/write with a default value of none; the cascading style sheets (CSS) attribute is not inherited.

Remarks

The value of this property lists the sides where floating objects are not accepted.

Example

The following examples show how to use both the **clear** attribute and the **clear** property to specify placement of text relative to floating objects.

The sample below uses a call to an embedded style sheet to move the text below the floating objects when italic text is encountered.

```
<STYLE>
    I { clear:"left"}
</STYLE>
```

To see this code in action, refer to the Web Workshop CD-ROM.

The sample below changes the position of the paragraph relative to the floating object on its left side.

```
<HEAD>
<SCRIPT>
function fnClear(){
    oClear.style.clear=left;
}
function fnClear2(){
    oClear.style.clear="none";
}
</SCRIPT>
</HEAD>

<BODY>
    <img src="/workshop/graphics/sphere.jpg" style="float:left">
    <SPAN ID="oClear">
        <P>This is an example of the clear attribute.<P>
    </span>

    <P>
        <INPUT TYPE=button value="clear = left " onclick="fnClear()">
        <INPUT TYPE=button value="clear = none " onclick="fnClear2()">
    </P>
</BODY>
```

To see this code in action, refer to the Web Workshop CD-ROM.

Applies To

 WIN16   WIN32   MAC   UNIX

A, ADDRESS, APPLET, B, BIG, BLOCKQUOTE, BUTTON, CAPTION, CENTER, CITE, CODE, COL, COLGROUP, DD, DFN, DIR, DIV, DL, DT, EM, EMBED, FIELDSET, FORM, Hn, HR, I, IFRAME, IMG, INPUT type=button, INPUT type=checkbox, INPUT type=file, INPUT type=image, INPUT type=password, INPUT type=radio, INPUT type=reset, INPUT type=submit, INPUT type=text, ISINDEX, KBD, LABEL, LEGEND, LI, LISTING, MARQUEE, MENU, OBJECT, OL, OPTION, P, PLAINTEXT, PRE, S, SAMP, SELECT, SMALL, SPAN, STRIKE, STRONG, style, SUB, SUP, TABLE, TBODY, TD, TEXTAREA, TFOOT, TH, THEAD, TR, TT, U, UL, VAR, XMP

 WIN16   WIN32   MAC   UNIX

currentStyle, runtimeStyle

CLEAR Attribute | clear Property

Sets or retrieves the side on which floating objects are not to be positioned when a line break is inserted into the document.

Syntax

HTML   <BR **CLEAR** = "all" | "left" | "right" | "none" ... >

Scripting *br*.**clear** [= *sValue*]

Possible Values

all   Object is moved below any floating object.

left   Object is moved below any floating object on the left side.

right Object is moved below any floating object on the right side.

none   Floating objects are allowed on all sides.

The property is read/write with no default value.

Applies To

WIN16   WIN32   MAC

BR

UNIX

BR

clientHeight Property

Retrieves the height of the object without taking into account any margin, border, scroll bar, or padding that might have been applied to the object.

Syntax

HTML   N/A

Scripting [*iHeight* =] *object*.**clientHeight**

Possible Values

iHeight   Integer specifying the height of the object, in pixels.

The property is read-only with no default value.

Example

The following example shows how the **clientHeight** property and the **offsetHeight** property measure document width differently.

Note The height of the **DIV** is set to 100, and this is the value retrieved by the **offsetHeight** property, not the **clientHeight** property.

```
<DIV ID=oDiv STYLE="overflow:scroll; width:200; height:100"> . . . </DIV>
<BUTTON onclick="alert(oDiv.clientHeight)">client height</BUTTON>
<BUTTON onclick="alert(oDiv.offsetHeight)">offset heightY</BUTTON>
```

To see this code in action, refer to the Web Workshop CD-ROM.

Applies To

 WIN16   WIN32   MAC   UNIX

APPLET, BODY, BUTTON, CAPTION, DIV, EMBED, FIELDSET, IMG, INPUT type=button, INPUT type=checkbox, INPUT type=file, INPUT type=image, INPUT type=password, INPUT type=radio, INPUT type=reset, INPUT type=submit, INPUT type=text, LEGEND, MARQUEE, OBJECT, SPAN, TABLE, TD, TEXTAREA, TR

IE 5   **WIN16   WIN32   MAC   UNIX**

A, ADDRESS, B, BDO, BIG, BLOCKQUOTE, CENTER, CITE, CODE, COL, COLGROUP, DD, DFN, DIR, DL, DT, EM, FORM, HEAD, Hn, HTML, I, ISINDEX, KBD, LABEL, LI, LISTING, MENU, META, NOBR, OL, OPTION, P, PLAINTEXT, PRE, S, SAMP, SCRIPT, SELECT, SMALL, STRIKE, STRONG, SUB, SUP, TBODY, TFOOT, TH, THEAD, TT, U, UL, VAR, XMP

clientInformation Property

Retrieves the **navigator** object.

Syntax

HTML   N/A

Scripting   [*oNavigator* =] *window*.**clientInformation**

Possible Values

oNavigator **navigator** object containing information about the browser.

The property is read-only.

Remarks

Generally, this property is used to obtain information about the browser, such as version and name, as well as whether certain features are enabled.

Example

The following JScript® (compatible with ECMA 262 language specification) example checks whether the user agent name of the browser contains "MSIE". If it does, the browser is Microsoft Internet Explorer.

```
if (window.clientInformation.userAgent.indexOf( "MSIE " ) > 0)
    // The browser is Microsoft Internet Explorer.
```

The following JScript example checks whether Java applets can be run.

```
if (window.clientInformation.javaEnabled() == true )
    // Java is enabled; applets can run.
```

Applies To

WIN16	WIN32	MAC	UNIX

Window

clientLeft Property

Retrieves the distance between the **offsetLeft** property and the true left side of the client area.

Syntax

HTML   N/A

Scripting [*iDistance* =] *object*.**clientLeft**

Possible Values

iDistance Integer specifying the described distance, in pixels.

The property is read-only with no default value.

Remarks

The difference between the **offsetLeft** and **clientLeft** properties is the border of the object.

Applies To

WIN16   WIN32   MAC   UNIX

APPLET, BODY, BUTTON, CAPTION, DIV, EMBED, FIELDSET, IMG, INPUT type=button, INPUT type=checkbox, INPUT type=file, INPUT type=image, INPUT type=password, INPUT type=radio, INPUT type=reset, INPUT type=submit, INPUT type=text, LEGEND, MARQUEE, OBJECT, SPAN, TABLE, TD, TEXTAREA, TR

IE 5

WIN16   WIN32   MAC   UNIX

A, ADDRESS, B, BDO, BIG, BLOCKQUOTE, CENTER, CITE, CODE, COL, COLGROUP, DD, DFN, DIR, DL, DT, EM, FORM, HEAD, Hn, HTML, I, ISINDEX, KBD, LABEL, LI, LISTING, MENU, META, NOBR, OL, OPTION, P, PLAINTEXT, PRE, S, SAMP, SCRIPT, SELECT, SMALL, STRIKE, STRONG, SUB, SUP, TBODY, TFOOT, TH, THEAD, TT, U, UL, VAR, XMP

clientTop Property

Retrieves the distance between the **offsetTop** property and the true top of the client area.

Syntax

HTML   N/A

Scripting [*iDistance* =] *object*.**clientTop**

Possible Values

iDistance   Integer specifying the described distance.

The property is read-only with no default value.

Remarks

The difference between the **offsetTop** and the **clientTop** properties is the border area of the object.

DHTML Properties

Applies To

 WIN16   WIN32   MAC   UNIX

APPLET, BODY, BUTTON, CAPTION, DIV, EMBED, FIELDSET, IMG, INPUT
type=button, INPUT type=checkbox, INPUT type=file, INPUT type=image, INPUT
type=password, INPUT type=radio, INPUT type=reset, INPUT type=submit, INPUT
type=text, LEGEND, MARQUEE, OBJECT, SPAN, TABLE, TD, TEXTAREA, TR

IE 5   **WIN16   WIN32   MAC   UNIX**

A, ADDRESS, B, BDO, BIG, BLOCKQUOTE, CENTER, CITE, CODE, COL,
COLGROUP, DD, DFN, DIR, DL, DT, EM, FORM, HEAD, Hn, HTML, I,
ISINDEX, KBD, LABEL, LI, LISTING, MENU, META, NOBR, OL, OPTION, P,
PLAINTEXT, PRE, S, SAMP, SCRIPT, SELECT, SMALL, STRIKE, STRONG,
SUB, SUP, TBODY, TFOOT, TH, THEAD, TT, U, UL, VAR, XMP

clientWidth Property

Retrieves the width of the object without taking into account any margin, border,
scroll bar, or padding that might have been applied to the object.

Syntax

HTML   N/A

Scripting   [*iWidth* =] *object*.**clientWidth**

Possible Values

iWidth   Integer specifying the width of the object, in pixels.

The property is read-only with no default value.

Example

The following example shows how the **clientWidth** property and the **offsetWidth**
property measure document width differently.

Note The width of the **DIV** is set to 200, and this is the value retrieved by the **offsetWidth**
property, not the **clientWidth** property.

```
<DIV ID=oDiv STYLE="overflow:scroll; width:200; height:100"> . . . </DIV>
<BUTTON onclick="alert(oDiv.clientWidth)">client width</BUTTON>
<BUTTON onclick="alert(oDiv.offsetWidth)">offset widthY</BUTTON>
```

To see this code in action, refer to the Web Workshop CD-ROM.

Applies To

WIN16   WIN32   MAC   UNIX

APPLET, BODY, BUTTON, CAPTION, DIV, EMBED, FIELDSET, IMG, INPUT
type=button, INPUT type=checkbox, INPUT type=file, INPUT type=image, INPUT
type=password, INPUT type=radio, INPUT type=reset, INPUT type=submit, INPUT
type=text, LEGEND, MARQUEE, OBJECT, SPAN, TABLE, TD, TEXTAREA, TR

WIN16   WIN32   MAC   UNIX

A, ADDRESS, B, BDO, BIG, BLOCKQUOTE, CENTER, CITE, CODE, COL,
COLGROUP, DD, DFN, DIR, DL, DT, EM, FORM, HEAD, Hn, HTML, I,
ISINDEX, KBD, LABEL, LI, LISTING, MENU, META, NOBR, OL, OPTION, P,
PLAINTEXT, PRE, S, SAMP, SCRIPT, SELECT, SMALL, STRIKE, STRONG,
SUB, SUP, TBODY, TFOOT, TH, THEAD, TT, U, UL, VAR, XMP

DHTML Properties

clientX Property

Retrieves the x-coordinate of the position of the mouse cursor relative to the client
area of the window, excluding window decorations or scroll bars.

Syntax

HTML   N/A

Scripting   [*iXPos* =] *event*.**clientX**

Possible Values

iXPos   Integer specifying the x-coordinate of the mouse hit position, in pixels.

The property is read-only with no default value.

Example

The following example shows how to use the **clientX** property to determine the mouse
position relative to the window. The status window shows the mouse position.

```
<SCRIPT>
function clientCoords()
{
    var offsetInfo = ""
    clientInfo = "The x coordinate is: " + window.event.clientX + "\r"
    clientInfo += "The y coordinate is: " + window.event.clientY + "\r"
    alert(clientInfo);
}
</SCRIPT>
```

```
</HEAD>
<BODY onmousemove="window.status = 'X=' + window.event.clientX +
    ' Y=' + window.event.clientY"
    ondblclick="clientCoords()">
```

To see this code in action, refer to the Web Workshop CD-ROM.

Applies To

 WIN16   WIN32   MAC   UNIX

event

clientY Property

Retrieves the y-coordinate of the position of the mouse cursor relative to the client area of the window, excluding window decorations or scroll bars.

Syntax

HTML   N/A

Scripting [*iYPos* =] *event*.**clientY**

Possible Values

iYPos   Integer specifying the y-coordinate of the mouse hit position, in pixels.

The property is read-only with no default value.

Example

The following example shows how to use the **clientY** property to determine the mouse position relative to the window. The status window shows the mouse position.

```
<SCRIPT>
function clientCoords()
{
    var offsetInfo = ""
    clientInfo = "The x coordinate is: " + window.event.clientX + "\r"
    clientInfo += "The y coordinate is: " + window.event.clientY + "\r"
    alert(clientInfo);
}
</SCRIPT>
</HEAD>
<BODY onmousemove="window.status = 'X=' + this.clientX + ' Y=' +
        this.clientY"
    ondblclick="clientCoords()">
```

To see this code in action, refer to the Web Workshop CD-ROM.

Applies To

 WIN16   WIN32   MAC   UNIX

event

clip Attribute | clip Property

Sets or retrieves which part of a positioned object is visible.

Syntax

HTML   { **clip:** auto | rect (*top* | *right* | *bottom* | *left*) }

Scripting *object*.**style.clip** [= *sClip*]

Possible Values

auto	Clip to expose entire object.
rect (*top right bottom left*)	*Top*, *right*, *bottom*, and *left* specify length values, any of which may be replaced by auto, leaving that side not clipped.

The property is read/write with a default value of auto; the cascading style sheets (CSS) attribute is not inherited.

Remarks

This property defines the shape and size of the positioned object that is visible. The **position** must be set to absolute. Any part of the object that is outside the clipping region is transparent. Any coordinate can be replaced by the value auto, which exposes the respective side (meaning the side is not clipped).

The order of the values **clip**:rect(0 0 50 50) renders the object invisible, as it sets the top and right positions of the clipping region to 0. To achieve a 50-by-50 view port, use **clip**:rect(0 50 50 0).

The **clip** attribute and property are available on the Macintosh platform, as of Internet Explorer 5.

Example

The following examples show how to use the **clip** attribute and the **clip** property to modify the appearance of an image.

The sample below uses a call to an embedded (global) style sheet to clip the image.

```
<DIV Style="position:absolute;top:0;left:200;
    clip:rect(0.6cm 3cm 2cm 0.5cm)">
<IMG SRC="sphere.jpg">
</DIV>
```

To see this code in action, refer to the Web Workshop CD-ROM.

The sample below uses inline scripting to clip the image.

```
<IMG ID="sphere" SRC="sphere.jpeg"
    STYLE="position:absolute;top:0cm;left:0cm;">
<BUTTON
    onclick="sphere.style.clip='rect(0.2cm 0.6cm 1cm 0.1cm)'">
    Clip Image</BUTTON>
```

To see this code in action, refer to the Web Workshop CD-ROM.

Applies To

 WIN16   WIN32   UNIX   MAC

DIV, style

 MAC   WIN16   WIN32   UNIX

DIV, runtimeStyle

clipBottom Property

Retrieves the bottom coordinate of the object clipping region.

Syntax

HTML   N/A

Scripting   [*sBottom* =] *currentStyle*.**clipBottom**

Possible Values

auto   Clip to expose the entire object.

sBottom Length value, which may have a units designator (px, pt, em, cm, mm, or in) appended. For more information about the supported length units, see "CSS Length Units" in Appendix C.

The property is read-only with no default value.

Remarks

Setting the value to auto exposes the bottom side, meaning the side is not clipped.

Example

The following example shows how to read the **clipBottom** property from the **currentStyle** object of an image.

```
<SCRIPT>
function setClip(sOptionValue) {
    oImage.style.clip="rect(0,100,"+sOptionValue+",0)";
    if (oImage.currentStyle.clipBottom == "60px") {
        alert("The image has been clipped to 60px.");
        }
:
}
</SCRIPT>
:
<IMG ID=oImage SRC="/workshop/graphics/sphere.jpg">
:
Pick an amount to clip the bottom:
    // The option value is sent as an argument:
<SELECT onchange="setClip(value)">
<OPTION VALUE=100>reset </OPTION>
<OPTION VALUE=40>40px </OPTION>
<OPTION VALUE=50>50px </OPTION>
<OPTION VALUE=60>60px </OPTION>
</SELECT>
```

To see this code in action, refer to the Web Workshop CD-ROM.

Applies To

 WIN16   WIN32   MAC   UNIX

currentStyle

DHTML Properties

clipLeft Property

Retrieves the left coordinate of the object clipping region.

Syntax

HTML   N/A

Scripting [*sLeft* =] *currentStyle*.**clipLeft**

Possible Values

auto   Clip to expose the entire object.

sLeft   Length value, which may have a units designator (px, pt, em, cm, mm, or in) appended. For more information about the supported length units, see "CSS Length Units" in Appendix C.

The property is read-only with no default value.

Remarks

Setting the value to auto exposes the left side, meaning the side is not clipped.

Example

The following example shows how to read the **clipLeft** property from the **currentStyle** object of an image.

```
<SCRIPT>
function setClip(sOptionValue) {
    oImage.style.clip="rect(0,100,100,"+sOptionValue+")";
    if (oImage.currentStyle.clipLeft == "60px") {
        alert("The image has been clipped to 60 px.");
        }
    :
}
</SCRIPT>
:
<IMG ID=oImage SRC="/workshop/graphics/sphere.jpg">
:
Pick an amount to clip the left:
    // The option value is sent as an argument:
<SELECT onchange="setClip(value)">
<OPTION VALUE=100>reset </OPTION>
<OPTION VALUE=40>40px </OPTION>
<OPTION VALUE=50>50px </OPTION>
<OPTION VALUE=60>60px </OPTION>
</SELECT>
```

To see this code in action, refer to the Web Workshop CD-ROM.

Applies To

 WIN16   WIN32   MAC   UNIX

currentStyle

clipRight Property

Retrieves the right coordinate of the object clipping region.

Syntax

HTML   N/A

Scripting   [*sRight* =] *currentStyle*.**clipRight**

Possible Values

auto   Clip to expose the entire object.

sRight   Length value, which may have a units designator (px, pt, em, cm, mm, or in)
          appended. For more information about the supported length units, see "CSS
          Length Units" in Appendix C.

The property is read-only with no default value.

Remarks

Setting the value to auto exposes the right side, meaning the side is not clipped.

Example

The following example shows how to read the **clipRight** property from the
currentStyle object of an image.

```
<SCRIPT>
function setClip(sOptionValue) {
    oImage.style.clip="rect(0,"+sOptionValue+",100,0)";
    if (oElmnt1.currentStyle.clipRight == "60px") {
        alert("The image has been clipped to 60 px.");
        }
:
}
</SCRIPT>
:
<IMG ID=oImage SRC="/workshop/graphics/sphere.jpg">
:
```

```
Pick an amount to clip the right:
    // The option value is sent as an argument:
<SELECT onchange="setClip(value)">
<OPTION VALUE=100>reset </OPTION>
<OPTION VALUE=40>40px </OPTION>
<OPTION VALUE=50>50px </OPTION>
<OPTION VALUE=60>60px </OPTION>
</SELECT>
```

To see this code in action, refer to the Web Workshop CD-ROM.

Applies To

 WIN16   WIN32   MAC   UNIX

currentStyle

clipTop Property

Retrieves the top coordinate of the object clipping region.

Syntax

HTML   N/A

Scripting   [*sTop* =] *currentStyle*.**clipTop**

Possible Values

auto   Clip to expose the entire object.

sTop   Length value, which may have a units designator (px, pt, em, cm, mm, or in) appended. For more information about the supported length units, see "CSS Length Units" in Appendix C.

The property is read-only with no default value.

Remarks

Setting the value to auto exposes the top side, meaning the side is not clipped.

Example

The following example shows how to read the **clipTop** property from the **currentStyle** object of an image.

```
<SCRIPT>
function setClip(sOptionValue) {
    oImage.style.clip="rect("+sOptionValue+",100,100,0)";
```

```
        if (oImage.currentStyle.clipTop == "60px") {
            alert("The image has been clipped to 60px.");
            }
    :
    }
</SCRIPT>
    :
<IMG ID=oImage SRC="/workshop/graphics/sphere.jpg">
    :
Pick an amount to clip the top:
    // The option value is sent as an argument:
<SELECT onchange="setClip(value)">
<OPTION VALUE=100>reset </OPTION>
<OPTION VALUE=40>40px </OPTION>
<OPTION VALUE=50>50px </OPTION>
<OPTION VALUE=60>60px </OPTION>
</SELECT>
```

To see this code in action, refer to the Web Workshop CD-ROM.

Applies To

 WIN16   WIN32   MAC   UNIX

currentStyle

closed Property

Retrieves whether the referenced window is closed.

Syntax

HTML   N/A

Scripting [*bClosed* =] *window*.**closed**

Possible Values

false Window is open.

true Window is closed.

The property is read-only with a default value of false.

Applies To

 WIN16   WIN32   MAC   UNIX

window

CODE Attribute | code Property

Sets or retrieves the URL of the file containing the compiled Java class.

Syntax

HTML   <OBJECT **CODE** = *sURL* ... >

Scripting *object*.**code** [= *sURL*]

Possible Values

sURL   URL of the file.

The property is read/write with no default value.

Applies To

 WIN16   WIN32   MAC   UNIX

OBJECT

CODEBASE Attribute | codeBase Property

Sets or retrieves the URL referencing where to find the implementation of the object.

Syntax

HTML   <*ELEMENT* **CODEBASE** = *sURL*[**#version**=*a,b,c,d*] ... >

Scripting *object*.**codeBase** [= *sURL*]

Possible Values

sUrl   URL from which the component should be downloaded.

a   High-order word of the major version of the component available at the specified URL.

b   Low-order word of the major version of the component available at the specified URL.

c   High-order word of the minor version of the component available at the specified URL.

d   Low-order word of the minor version of the component available at the specified URL.

Possible Values *(continued)*

-1,-1,-1,-1   Values for *a,b,c,d* indicating that the component should be downloaded from the server if the release date is later than the installation date on the client machine. If the component is installed on the client machine, and the release date is the same or earlier than the installation date, only an HTTP header transaction occurs.

The property is read/write with no default value.

Remarks

Applets do not support versioning information supplied as part of the URL.

Example

The following example shows how to specify the download location for the Common Dialog control using the **CODEBASE** attribute.

```
<OBJECT ID="CommonDialog1" WIDTH=32 HEIGHT=32
    CLASSID="CLSID:F9043C85-F6F2-101A-A3C9-08002B2F49FB"
    CODEBASE="http://activex.microsoft.com/controls/vb5/comdlg32.cab
    #version=1,0,0,0">
</OBJECT>
```

Applies To

 WIN16   WIN32   MAC

APPLET, OBJECT

 UNIX

APPLET, OBJECT

CODETYPE Attribute | codeType Property

Sets or retrieves the Internet media type for the code associated with the object.

Syntax

HTML   <OBJECT **CODETYPE** = *sType* ... >

Scripting *object*.**codeType** [= *sType*]

Possible Values

>   *sType*   String specifying the media type.

>   The property is read/write with no default value.

Applies To

WIN16   WIN32   MAC

OBJECT

UNIX

OBJECT

COLOR Attribute | color Property

>   Sets or retrieves the color to be used by the object.

Syntax

>   **HTML**   *<ELEMENT* **COLOR** = *sColor* ... >
>
>   **Scripting** *object*.**color** [= *sColor*]

Possible Values

>   *sColor*   String specifying one of the color names or red-green-blue (RGB) values in
>   the "Color Table" in Appendix C.

>   The property is read/write with no default value.

Remarks

>   Specifying the color as a color name may not be recognized by some browsers,
>   whereas the RGB color value should always be displayed accurately.

Applies To

WIN16   WIN32   MAC

BASEFONT, FONT, HR

UNIX

BASEFONT, FONT, HR

color Attribute | color Property

Sets or retrieves the color of the text of the object.

DHTML Properties

Syntax

HTML   { **color** : *sColor* }

Scripting *object*.**style.color** [= *sColor*]

Possible Values

sColor String specifying one of the color names or red-green-blue (RGB) values in
the "Color Table" in Appendix C.

The property is read/write with no default value; the cascading style sheets (CSS)
attribute is inherited.

Remarks

The following different ways can be used to specify a color—in this example, red.

```
EM { color: red }           /* natural language / CNS */
EM { color: #F00 }          /* #RGB */
EM { color: #FF0000 }       /* #RRGGBB */
EM { color: rgb 1.0 0.0 0.0 }  /* float range: 0.0 - 1.0 */
```

Specifying the color as a color name may not be recognized by some browsers,
whereas the RGB color value should always be displayed accurately.

Example

The following examples show how to use the **color** attribute and the **color** property to
change an object's text color.

The sample below uses a call to an embedded (global) style sheet to change the text
color to red on an **onmouseover** event.

```
<STYLE>
    .color1 { color: red }
    .color2 { color: }
</STYLE>
</HEAD>
<BODY>
<SPAN STYLE="font-size:14" onmouseover="this.className='color1'"
    onmouseout="this.className='color2'"> . . .
```

To see this code in action, refer to the Web Workshop CD-ROM.

The sample below uses inline scripting to change the text color to red on an **onmouseover** event.

```
<SPAN STYLE="font-size:14" onmouseover="this.style.color='red'">
:
</SPAN>
```

To see this code in action, refer to the Web Workshop CD-ROM.

Applies To

 WIN16   WIN32   MAC

A, ADDRESS, B, BIG, BLOCKQUOTE, BODY, CAPTION, CENTER, CITE, CODE, DD, DFN, DIR, DIV, DL, DT, EM, FORM, Hn, I, ISINDEX, KBD, LI, LISTING, MENU, OL, OPTION, P, PLAINTEXT, PRE, S, SAMP, SMALL, SPAN, STRIKE, STRONG, SUB, SUP, TABLE, TH, TR, TT, U, UL, VAR, XMP

 UNIX   WIN16   WIN32   MAC

A, ADDRESS, APPLET, B, BIG, BLOCKQUOTE, BODY, BUTTON, CAPTION, CENTER, CITE, CODE, COL, COLGROUP, DD, DFN, DIR, DIV, DL, DT, EM, FIELDSET, FORM, Hn, HTML, I, INPUT type=button, INPUT type=checkbox, INPUT type=file, INPUT type=image, INPUT type=password, INPUT type=radio, INPUT type=reset, INPUT type=submit, INPUT type=text, ISINDEX, KBD, LABEL, LEGEND, LI, LISTING, MARQUEE, MENU, OL, OPTION, P, PLAINTEXT, PRE, S, SAMP, SELECT, SMALL, SPAN, STRIKE, STRONG, style, SUB, SUP, TABLE, TBODY, TD, TEXTAREA, TFOOT, TH, THEAD, TR, TT, U, UL, VAR, XMP

IE 5 **WIN16   WIN32   MAC   UNIX**

currentStyle, runtimeStyle

colorDepth Property

Retrieves the number of bits per pixel used for colors on the destination device or buffer.

Syntax

HTML   N/A

Scripting [*iBitsPerPixel =*] *screen*.**colorDepth**

Possible Values

`1, 4, 8,` `15, 16,` `24, 32` Integer specifying the number of bits per pixel to use for the off-screen buffer. The value 15 specifies 16 bits per pixel, in which only 15 bits are used in a 5-5-5 layout of red-green-blue (RGB) values.

The property is read-only with no default value.

Remarks

Retrieving the property's value through script enables you to select an appropriate color to return to the browser.

If **bufferDepth** is 0 or -1, **colorDepth** is equal to the bits-per-pixel value for the screen or printer. If **bufferDepth** is nonzero, **colorDepth** is equal to **bufferDepth**.

Applies To

 WIN16   WIN32   MAC   UNIX

screen

COLS Attribute | cols Property

Retrieves the width of the object.

Syntax

HTML   <ELEMENT **COLS** = *iCount* ... >

Scripting   [*iCount* =] *object*.**cols**

Possible Values

iCount Integer specifying the number of characters.

The property is read-only with a default value of `20`.

Applies To

 WIN16   WIN32   MAC

TEXTAREA

 UNIX

TEXTAREA

COLS Attribute | cols Property

Sets or retrieves the number of columns in the table.

Syntax

HTML   <TABLE **COLS** = *iCount* ... >

Scripting *table*.**cols** [= *iCount*]

Possible Values

iCount Integer specifying the number of columns.

The property is read/write with no default value.

Remarks

Specifying this number can speed up the processing of the table.

Example

The following example shows how to use the **COLS** attribute and the **cols** property.

```
<SCRIPT>
function checkCols(oObject)
{
    var iColumns = oObject.cols;
    alert (iColumns);
}
</SCRIPT>
</HEAD>
<BODY>
<TABLE ID=oTable BORDER COLS=3 onclick="checkCols(this)">
<TR><TD>Column 1</TD><TD>Column 2</TD><TD>Column 3</TD></TR>
</TABLE>
```

To see this code in action, refer to the Web Workshop CD-ROM.

Applies To

 WIN16   **WIN32**   **MAC**

TABLE

 UNIX

TABLE

COLS Attribute | cols Property

Sets or retrieves a comma-delimited string of frame widths.

Syntax

HTML   <FRAMESET **COLS** = *iWidth* "[% | *]" [, *iWidth* "[% | *]" ...] ... >

Scripting *frameset*.**cols** [= *iWidth* "[% | *]" [, *iWidth* "[% | *]" ...]]

Possible Values

iWidth	Integer specifying the frame width, in pixels.
iWidth%	Integer specifying the frame width as a percentage of total available width.
*iWidth**	Integer specifying the frame width as a relative value. After allocating pixel or percentage values, the remaining space is divided among all relative-sized frames.

The property is read/write with no default value.

Remarks

The number of comma-separated items is equal to the number of frames contained within the **FRAMESET**, and the value of each item determines the frame width.

Example

The following example defines a two-column frame, with the first occupying 40 percent of the available width and the second occupying the remaining 60 percent.

```
<FRAMESET COLS="40%, 60%">
```

The next example defines a four-column frame. The first is 50 pixels wide, and the fourth is 80 pixels wide. The second occupies two-thirds of the remaining width, and the third occupies the final third of the remaining width.

```
<FRAMESET COLS="50, 2*, *, 80">
```

Applies To

 WIN16   WIN32   MAC

FRAMESET

 UNIX

FRAMESET

COLSPAN Attribute | colSpan Property

Sets or retrieves the number of columns in the **TABLE** that the object should span.

Syntax

    HTML   <ELEMENT **COLSPAN** = *iCount* ... >

    Scripting *object*.**colSpan** [= *iCount*]

Possible Values

    iCount Integer specifying the number of columns to span.

    The property is read/write with no default value.

Remarks

    This property can only be changed after the page has been loaded.

Applies To

 WIN16   WIN32   MAC

    TD, TH

 UNIX

    TD, TH

COMPACT Attribute | compact Property

Sets or retrieves whether the list should be compacted to remove extra space between list objects.

Syntax

    HTML   <DL **COMPACT** ... >

    Scripting *dl*.**compact** [= *bCompactList*]

Possible Values

    `false` Removes extra space between objects.

    `true` Does not remove extra space between objects.

    The property is read/write with a default value of `false`.

Applies To

 WIN16   WIN32   MAC   UNIX

DL

complete Property

Retrieves whether the object is fully loaded.

Syntax

HTML   N/A

Scripting   [*bComplete* =] *object*.**complete**

Possible Values

false Object has not been loaded.

true   Object has been loaded.

The property is read-only with a default value of false.

Applies To

 WIN16   WIN32   MAC   UNIX

IMG, INPUT type=image

CONTENT Attribute | content Property

Sets or retrieves meta-information to be associated with **HTTP-EQUIV** or **NAME**.

Syntax

HTML   <META **CONTENT** = *sDescription* ... >

Scripting *meta*.**content** [= *sDescription*]

Possible Values

sDescription   String specifying the meta-information.

The property is read/write with no default value.

Example

The following example shows how to make the browser reload the document every two seconds.

```
<META HTTP-EQUIV="REFRESH" CONTENT=2>
```

The next example shows how to specify the character set for the document.

```
<META HTTP-EQUIV="Content-Type"
    CONTENT="text/html; CHARSET=Windows-1251">
```

Applies To

 WIN16   WIN32   MAC

META

 UNIX

META

cookie Property

Sets or retrieves the string value of a cookie, which is a small piece of information stored by the browser.

Syntax

HTML   N/A

Scripting   *document*.**cookie** [= "name"=*value;* ["expires"=*date;* "domain"=
domainname; "path"=*path;* "secure";]]

Possible Values

name=*value;*	Each cookie is stored in a name=value pair called a crumb— that is, if the cookie name is "id" and you want to save id's value as "this", the cookie would be saved as id=this. You can save as many name=value pairs in the cookie as you want, but the cookie is always returned as a string of all the cookies that apply to the page. So the string that is returned has to be parsed to find the values of individual cookies.

Possible Values *(continued)*

expires=*date;* If no expiration date is set on a cookie, it expires when the browser is closed. Setting an expiration date in the future causes the cookie to be saved across browser sessions. Setting an expiration date in the past deletes a cookie. Specify the date using GMT format.

domain=*domainname;* The domain of the cookie can be set, which allows pages on a domain made up of more than one server to share cookie information.

path=*path;* Setting a path for the cookie allows the current document to share cookie information with other pages within the same domain—that is, if the path is set to /thispathname, all pages in /thispathname and all pages in subfolders of /thispathname can access the same cookie information.

secure; Specifying a cookie as secure means that the stored cookie information can be accessed only from a secure environment.

The property is read/write with no default value.

Remarks

Use the JScript (compatible with ECMA 262 language specification) **split** method to extract a value stored in a cookie.

Example

The following example shows how to create a cookie with a specified name and value. The value is passed to the JScript **escape** function to ensure that the value contains only valid characters. When the cookie is retrieved, the JScript **unescape** function should be used to translate the value back to its original form.

```
<SCRIPT>
// Create a cookie with the specified name and value.
// The cookie expires at the end of the 20th century.
function SetCookie(sName, sValue)
{
  document.cookie = sName + "=" + escape(sValue) + ";
  expires=Mon, 31 Dec 1999 23:59:59 UTC;";
}
</SCRIPT>
```

The next example shows how to retrieve the value of the portion of the **cookie** specified by the *sName* parameter.

```
<SCRIPT>
// Retrieve the value of the cookie with the specified name.
function GetCookie(sName)
{
  // Cookies are separated by semicolons.
  var aCookie = document.cookie.split(";");
  for (var i=0; i < aCookie.length; i++)
  {
    // A name/value pair (a crumb) is separated by an equal sign.
    var aCrumb = aCookie[i].split("=");
    if (sName == aCrumb[0])
      return unescape(aCrumb[1]);
  }

  // A cookie with the requested name does not exist.
  return null;
}
</SCRIPT>
```

Applies To

 WIN16   WIN32   MAC

document

 UNIX

document

cookieEnabled Property

Retrieves whether client-side cookies are enabled in the browser.

Syntax

HTML   N/A

Scripting   [*bEnabled* =] *navigator*.**cookieEnabled**

Possible Values

false	The browser does not support cookies.
true	The browser supports cookies.

The property is read-only with no default value.

Applies To

 WIN16   WIN32   MAC   UNIX

navigator

COORDS Attribute | coords Property

Sets or retrieves the coordinates of a hyperlink **AREA** within an image **MAP**.

Syntax

HTML   <AREA **COORDS** = *sCoords* ... >

Scripting *object*.**coords** [= *sCoords*]

Possible Values

sCoords String specifying the coordinates. The format of this string depends on the value of the **SHAPE** attribute of the **AREA** element. For more information, see Remarks.

The property is read/write with no default value.

Remarks

The format of the *sCoords* string depends on the value of the **SHAPE** attribute as follows:

SHAPE= "circ" or "circle"	**COORDS**= "*x1,y1,r*" – Where *x1,y2* are the coordinates of the center of the circle, and *r* is the radius of the circle.
SHAPE= "poly" or "polygon"	**COORDS**= "*x1,y1,x2,y2...xn,yn*" – Where each *x,y* pair contains the coordinates of one vertex of the polygon.
SHAPE= "rect" or "rectangle"	**COORDS**= "*x1,y1,x2,y2*" – Where *x1,y1* are the coordinates of the upper-left corner of the rectangle and *x2,y2* are the coordinates of the upper-right coordinates of the rectangle.

Example

The following example provides the full code for an image map of the solar system. Clicking on the sun or any planet links to an individual image. The user can click the Back button from the image to return to the solar system image map.

```
<P><IMG SRC="solarsys.gif" WIDTH=504 HEIGHT=126
    BORDER=0 ALT="Solar System" USEMAP="#SystemMap">
```

```
<MAP NAME="SystemMap">
    <AREA SHAPE="rect" COORDS="0,0,82,126"
        HREF="/workshop/graphics/sun.gif">
    <AREA SHAPE="circle" COORDS="90,58,3"
        HREF="/workshop/graphics/merglobe.gif">
    <AREA SHAPE="circle" COORDS="124,58,8"
        HREF="/workshop/graphics/venglobe.gif">
    <AREA SHAPE="circle" COORDS="162,58,10"
        HREF="/workshop/graphics/earglobe.gif">
    <AREA SHAPE="circle" COORDS="203,58,8"
        HREF="/workshop/graphics/marglobe.gif">
    <AREA SHAPE="poly"
        COORDS="221,34,238,37,257,32,278,44,284,60,281,75,
            288,91,267,87,253,89,237,81,229,64,228,54"
        HREF="/workshop/graphics/jupglobe.gif">
    <AREA SHAPE="poly"
        COORDS="288,19,316,39,330,37,348,47,351,66,349,74,
            367,105,337,85,324,85,307,77,303,60,307,50"
        HREF="/workshop/graphics/satglobe.gif">
    <AREA SHAPE="poly"
        COORDS="405,39,408,50,411,57,410,71,404,78,393,80,
            383,86,381,75,376,69,376,56,380,48,393,44"
        HREF="/workshop/graphics/uraglobe.gif">
    <AREA SHAPE="poly"
        COORDS="445,38,434,49,431,53,427,62,430,72,435,77,
            445,92,456,77,463,72,463,62,462,53,455,47"
        HREF="/workshop/graphics/nepglobe.gif">
    <AREA SHAPE="circle" COORDS="479,66,3"
        HREF="/workshop/graphics/pluglobe.gif">
</MAP>
```

To see this code in action, refer to the Web Workshop CD-ROM.

Applies To

 WIN16   WIN32   MAC

AREA

 UNIX

AREA

cpuClass Property

Retrieves a string denoting the CPU class.

Syntax

HTML   N/A

Scripting   [*sCPU* =] *navigator*.**cpuClass**

Possible Values

x86   Intel processor.

68K   Motorola processor.

Alpha   Digital processor.

PPC   Motorola/IBM processor.

Other   Other CPU classes, including Sun SPARC.

The property is read-only with no default value.

Applies To

 WIN16   WIN32   MAC   UNIX

navigator

cssText Property

Sets or retrieves the persisted representation of the style rule.

Syntax

HTML   N/A

Scripting   *object*.**style.cssText** [= *sTxt*]

Possible Values

sTxt   String specifying the text.

The property is read/write with no default value.

Example

The following example shows how to use the **cssText** property to retrieve the cascading style sheets (CSS) style set on an object.

```
<P ID=oPara STYLE="color:'green'; font-weight:bold">
This is the test paragraph.</P>
:
<BUTTON onclick="alert(oPara.style.cssText)">
Get CSS attributes</BUTTON>
```

To see this code in action, refer to the Web Workshop CD-ROM.

Applies To

 WIN16   WIN32   MAC   UNIX

runtimeStyle, style

ctrlKey Property

Retrieves the state of the CTRL key.

Syntax

HTML   N/A

Scripting   [*bEvent* =] *event*.**ctrlKey**

Possible Values

false CTRL key is not down.

true   CTRL key is down.

The property is read-only with no default value.

Applies To

 WIN16   WIN32   MAC   UNIX

event

cursor Attribute | cursor Property

Sets or retrieves the type of cursor to display as the mouse pointer moves over the object.

DHTML Properties

Syntax

HTML   { **cursor:** auto | crosshair | default | hand | move | e-resize | ne-resize | nw-resize | n-resize | se-resize | sw-resize | s-resize | w-resize | text | wait | help }

Scripting   *object*.**style.cursor** [= *sCursor*]

Possible Values

auto	Browser determines which cursor to display based on the current context.
crosshair	Simple cross hair.
default	Platform-dependent default cursor (usually an arrow).
hand	Hand.
move	Crossed arrows indicating something is to be moved.
*-resize	Arrow indicating edge is to be moved (* may be n, ne, nw, s, se, sw, e, or w—each representing a compass direction).
text	Editable text (usually an I-bar).
wait	Hourglass or watch indicating that the program is busy and the user should wait.
help	Arrow with question mark indicating Help is available.

The property is read/write with a default value of auto; the cascading style sheets (CSS) attribute is inherited.

Example

The following examples show how to use the **cursor** attribute and the **cursor** property to change the cursor as it passes over an object.

The sample below uses a call to an embedded (global) style sheet to set the cursor to hand as the cursor passes over all paragraphs.

```
<STYLE>
    P { cursor:hand }
</STYLE>
```

To see this code in action, refer to the Web Workshop CD-ROM.

The sample below uses inline scripting to set the cursor to hand as the cursor passes over the paragraph.

```
<P onmouseover="this.style.cursor='hand'">
```

To see this code in action, refer to the Web Workshop CD-ROM.

Applies To

 WIN16   WIN32   MAC   UNIX

A, ADDRESS, APPLET, B, BIG, BLOCKQUOTE, BODY, CAPTION, CENTER, CITE, CODE, COL, COLGROUP, DD, DFN, DIR, DIV, DL, DT, EM, EMBED, FIELDSET, FORM, Hn, HR, HTML, I, IFRAME, IMG, INPUT type=button, INPUT type=checkbox, INPUT type=file, INPUT type=image, INPUT type=password, INPUT type=radio, INPUT type=reset, INPUT type=submit, INPUT type=text, KBD, LABEL, LEGEND, LI, LISTING, MARQUEE, MENU, OBJECT, OL, P, PLAINTEXT, PRE, S, SAMP, SMALL, SPAN, STRIKE, STRONG, style, SUB, SUP, TABLE, TBODY, TD, TEXTAREA, TFOOT, TH, THEAD, TR, TT, U, UL, VAR, XMP

 WIN16   WIN32   MAC   UNIX

currentStyle, runtimeStyle

DATA Attribute | data Property

Retrieves the URL that references the data of the object.

Syntax

HTML   <OBJECT **DATA** = *sURL* ... >

Scripting [*sURL* =] *object*.**data**

Possible Values

sURL   String specifying the URL of the data.

The property is read-only with no default value.

Applies To

 WIN16   WIN32   MAC

OBJECT

UNIX

OBJECT

data Property

Sets or retrieves the value of a **TextNode** object.

Syntax

HTML   N/A

Scripting   *object*.**data** [= *sData*]

Possible Values

sData   Value of the **TextNode**.

The property is read/write with no default value.

Example

The following example shows how to use the **data** property to change the value of a text node.

```
<SCRIPT>
function fnChangeValue(){
    var oNode = oList.firstChild.childNodes(0);
    var oNewText = document.createTextNode();
    oNewText.data="Create Data";
    oNode.replaceNode(oNewText);
    oNode.  = "New Node Value";

}
</SCRIPT>

<UL ID = oList onclick = "fnChangeValue()">
<LI>Start Here
</UL>
```

Applies To

 WIN16   WIN32   MAC   UNIX

TextNode

DATAFLD Attribute | dataFld Property

Sets or retrieves which field of a given data source (as specified by the **dataSrc** property) to bind to the given object.

Syntax

HTML   <ELEMENT **DATAFLD** = *sField* ... >

Scripting *object*.**dataFld** [= *sField*]

Possible Values

sField String specifying the field name.

The property is read/write with no default value.

Example

The following example shows how to bind a text box to the flavor field supplied by a data source object with an ID of ice_cream. Because the text box is contained within a table, the text box is repeated and all values in the flavor column are displayed.

```
<TABLE DATASRC="#ice_cream">
   <TR><TD><INPUT TYPE=TEXTBOX DATAFLD=flavor></TD></TR>
</TABLE>
```

The next example shows how the **SELECT** object is bound to the card_type column of a data source control with an ID of "order". The value of the field in the data set determines the option that is initially selected. In addition, when the user selects a different option from **SELECT**, the value of the card_type field in the current record of the data set is updated.

```
<SELECT DATASRC="#order" DATAFLD="card_type">
   <OPTION>Visa
   <OPTION>Mastercard
   <OPTION>American Express
   <OPTION>Diner's Club
   <OPTION>Discover
</SELECT>
```

DHTML Properties

Applies To

| **WIN16** | **WIN32** | **MAC** | **UNIX** |

A, APPLET, BODY, BUTTON, DIV, FRAME, IFRAME, IMG, INPUT type=button,
INPUT type=checkbox, INPUT type=file, INPUT type=hidden, INPUT type=image,
INPUT type=password, INPUT type=radio, INPUT type=reset, INPUT type=submit,
INPUT type=text, LABEL, MARQUEE, OBJECT, PARAM, SELECT, SPAN,
TEXTAREA

dataFld Property

Retrieves the data column affected by the **oncellchange** event.

Syntax

HTML   N/A

Scripting   [*sDataFld* =] *event*.**dataFld**

Possible Values

sDataFld   String specifying a data column in the current record set.

The property is read-only.

Applies To

| **WIN16** | **WIN32** | **MAC** | **UNIX** |

event

DATAFORMATAS Attribute | dataFormatAs Property

Sets or retrieves how to render the data supplied to the object .

Syntax

HTML   <ELEMENT **DATAFORMATAS** = "text" | "html" ... >

Scripting   *object*.**dataFormatAs** [= *sFormat*]

Possible Values

>text Data rendered as text.
>
>html Data rendered as HTML.

>The property is read/write with a default value of text.

Example

>The following **DIV** and **SPAN** examples show how to supply data in HTML format.
>
>```
><DIV DATAFLD="Column2" DATAFORMATAS="html"></DIV>
>```
>
>```
><SPAN DATASRC="#bank_acct" DATAFLD="balance" DATAFORMATAS="html"></SPAN>
>```
>
>The following **TEXTAREA** example shows how to supply data in text format.
>
>```
><TEXTAREA DATASRC="#customer" DATAFLD="address" DATAFORMATAS="text"
>    ROWS=6 COLS=60>
></TEXTAREA>
>```

Applies To

 WIN16   WIN32   MAC   UNIX

>BODY, BUTTON, DIV, INPUT type=button, LABEL, MARQUEE, PARAM, SPAN

DATAPAGESIZE Attribute | dataPageSize Property

>Sets or retrieves the number of records displayed in a table bound to a data source.

Syntax

>**HTML**   <TABLE **DATAPAGESIZE** = *iSize* ... >
>
>**Scripting** *table*.**dataPageSize** [= *iSize*]

Possible Values

>*iSize* Integer specifying the number of records in the table.

>The property is read/write with no default value.

Remarks

Use the **nextPage** and **previousPage** methods to display the subsequent and previous pages of records in the table.

Example

The following example shows how a text box is bound to the customer_name field supplied by a data source object with an ID of "customer". Because the text box is located within a data-bound **TABLE**, the text box is repeated to display each of the records in the data source. The **DATAPAGESIZE** attribute on the **TABLE** limits the display to 10 records.

```
<TABLE DATASRC="#customer" DATAPAGESIZE=10>
   <TR><TD><INPUT TYPE=TEXTBOX DATAFLD="customer_name"></TD></TR>
</TABLE>
```

Applies To

 WIN16   WIN32   MAC   UNIX

TABLE

DATASRC Attribute | dataSrc Property

Sets or retrieves the source of the data for data binding.

Syntax

HTML   <ELEMENT **DATASRC** = *sID* ... >

Scripting *object*.**dataSrc** [= *sID*]

Possible Values

sID String specifying the identifier of the data source.

The property is read/write with no default value.

Remarks

Tabular and single-valued data consumers use the **dataSrc** property to specify a binding. The property takes a string that corresponds to the unique identifier of a data source object (DSO) on the page. The string should be prefixed by a hash (#) mark.

When the **dataSrc** property is applied to a tabular data consumer, the entire data set is repeated by the consuming elements.

When the **dataSrc** property is applied to a **TABLE**, any contained single-valued consumer objects that specify a **dataFld** property are repeated for each record in the supplied data set. To complete the binding, the binding agent interrogates the enclosing **TABLE** for its data source. A tabular data consumer contained within another tabular data consumer (**TABLE**) must specify an explicit **dataSrc**.

Example

In the following example, a text box is bound to the customer_name field of a data source object with an ID of "customer". Because the text box is located within a data-bound **TABLE**, the text box is repeated to display each of the records provided by the data source.

```
<TABLE DATASRC="#customer">
  <TR><TD><INPUT TYPE=TEXTBOX DATAFLD="customer_name"><TD><TR>
</TABLE>
```

Applies To

 WIN16   WIN32   MAC   UNIX

A, APPLET, BODY, BUTTON, DIV, FRAME, IFRAME, IMG, INPUT type=button, INPUT type=checkbox, INPUT type=file, INPUT type=hidden, INPUT type=image, INPUT type=password, INPUT type=radio, INPUT type=reset, INPUT type=submit, INPUT type=text, LABEL, MARQUEE, OBJECT, PARAM, SELECT, SPAN, TABLE, TEXTAREA

defaultCharset Property

Sets or retrieves the default character set of the document.

Syntax

HTML   N/A

Scripting   *object*.**defaultCharset** [= *sCharset*]

Possible Values

sCharset   String specifying the default character set.

The property is read/write with a default value of iso-8859-1.

Applies To

 WIN16   WIN32   MAC   UNIX

META, document

defaultChecked Property

Sets or retrieves whether the check box or radio button is selected by default.

Syntax

HTML   N/A

Scripting   *input*.**defaultChecked** [= *bChecked*]

Possible Values

true   Check box or radio button is selected by default.

false   Check box or radio button is not selected by default.

The property is read/write with a default value of true.

Remarks

The property can be changed programmatically, but doing so has no effect on the appearance of the check box or radio button or on how forms are submitted.

Applies To

 WIN16   WIN32   MAC

INPUT TYPE=checkbox, INPUT TYPE=radio

 UNIX

INPUT TYPE=checkbox, INPUT TYPE=radio

defaultSelected Property

Sets or retrieves whether the option is selected by default.

Syntax

HTML   N/A

Scripting   *option*.**defaultSelected** [= *bSelected*]

Possible Values

true   Option is selected by default.

false   Option is not selected by default.

The property is read/write with a default value of true.

Remarks

The property can be changed programmatically, but doing so has no effect on the appearance of the option or on how forms are submitted. The property does change the appearance of the selected option if the form is reset.

Applies To

 WIN16   WIN32   MAC

OPTION

 UNIX

OPTION

defaultStatus Property

Sets or retrieves the default message displayed in the status bar at the bottom of the window.

Syntax

HTML   N/A

Scripting   *window*.**defaultStatus** [= *sMessage*]

Possible Values

sMessage   String specifying the message for the status bar.

The property is read/write with no default value.

Remarks

Do not confuse **defaultStatus** with **status**. The **status** property reflects a priority or transient message in the status bar, such as the message that appears when an **onmouseover** event occurs over an anchor.

Applies To

 WIN16   WIN32   MAC

window

 UNIX

window

defaultValue Property

Sets or retrieves the initial contents of the object.

Syntax

HTML   N/A

Scripting   *object*.**defaultValue** [= *sValue*]

Possible Values

sValue   String specifying the initial value of the object.

The property is read/write with no default value.

Remarks

The value of the property can be changed programmatically, but doing so has no effect on the appearance of the object or on how forms are submitted. It does, however, change the initial value of the control when the form is reset.

Applies To

 WIN16   WIN32   MAC

INPUT type=button, INPUT type=checkbox, INPUT type=file, INPUT type=hidden, INPUT type=image, INPUT type=password, INPUT type=radio, INPUT type=reset, INPUT type=submit, INPUT type=text, TEXTAREA

 UNIX

INPUT type=button, INPUT type=checkbox, INPUT type=file, INPUT type=hidden, INPUT type=image, INPUT type=password, INPUT type=radio, INPUT type=reset, INPUT type=submit, INPUT type=text, TEXTAREA

DHTML Properties

DEFER Attribute | defer Property

Sets or retrieves whether the script contains an inline executable function.

Syntax

HTML	<SCRIPT **DEFER** ... >
Scripting	*script*.**defer** [= *bDefer*]

Possible Values

false	Execution is not deferred.
true	Execution is deferred.

The property is read/write with a default value of false.

Remarks

Using the attribute at design time can improve the download performance of a page because the browser does not need to parse and execute the script and can continue downloading and parsing the page instead.

Applies To

 WIN16   WIN32   MAC   UNIX

SCRIPT

designMode Property

Toggles between browsing and editing the document.

Syntax

HTML	N/A
Scripting	*document*.**designMode** [= *sMode*]

Possible Values

On	Document can be edited by the user.
Off	Inherit	Document can only be viewed by the user.

The property is read/write with a default value of Inherit.

Remarks

When **designMode**=On, script execution is suspended.

Applies To

 WIN16   WIN32   MAC   UNIX

document

dialogArguments Property

Retrieves the variable or array of variables passed into the modal dialog window.

Syntax

HTML   N/A

Scripting   [*vVariables* =] *window*.**dialogArguments**

Possible Values

vVariables   String, numeric, object, or array value containing arguments.

The property is read-only with no default value.

Remarks

This property applies only to windows created using the **showModalDialog** method.

Applies To

 WIN16   WIN32   MAC   UNIX

window

dialogHeight Property

Sets or retrieves the height of the modal dialog window.

Syntax

HTML   N/A

Scripting   *window*.**dialogHeight** [= *iHeight*]

Possible Values

iHeight   Integer specifying the height, in ems.

The property is read/write with no default value.

Remarks

This property applies only to windows created using the **showModalDialog** method.

Example

The following example shows how to create a dialog window using the **dialogHeight** property to set the new window's height.

```
<SCRIPT>
function someMessage()
{
    event.srcElement.blur();
    window.showModalDialog("message.htm", "",
        "dialogWidth:5cm; dialogHeight:10cm")
}
</SCRIPT>
</HEAD>
<BODY>
<SELECT onchange="someMessage()">
    <OPTION>Item 1</OPTION>
    <OPTION>Item 2</OPTION>
    <OPTION>Item 3</OPTION>
</SELECT>
```

To see this code in action, refer to the Web Workshop CD-ROM.

Applies To

 WIN16   WIN32   MAC   UNIX

window

dialogLeft Property

Sets or retrieves the left coordinate of the modal dialog window.

Syntax

HTML   N/A

Scripting *window*.**dialogLeft** [= *iLeft*]

Possible Values

iLeft Integer specifying the left coordinate, in ems.

The property is read/write with no default value.

Remarks

This property applies only to windows created using the **showModalDialog** method.

Example

The following example shows how to create a dialog window using the **dialogLeft** property to set the position relative to the left side of the screen.

Note Do not break the script code into two lines as in the fourth line of the example. This was done for readability only.

```
<SCRIPT>
function someMessage()
{
    event.srcElement.blur();
    window.showModalDialog("message.htm", "",
        "dialogWidth:5cm; dialogHeight:10cm;
        dialogTop:0cm; dialogLeft:0cm")
}
</SCRIPT>
</HEAD>
<BODY>
<SELECT onchange="someMessage()">
    <OPTION>Item 1</OPTION>
    <OPTION>Item 2</OPTION>
    <OPTION>Item 3</OPTION>
</SELECT>
```

To see this code in action, refer to the Web Workshop CD-ROM.

Applies To

WIN16	WIN32	MAC	UNIX

window

dialogTop Property

Sets or retrieves the top coordinate of the dialog window.

Syntax

HTML   N/A

Scripting *window*.**dialogTop** [= *iTop*]

Possible Values

iTop   Integer specifying the top coordinate, in ems.

The property is read/write with no default value.

Remarks

This property applies only to windows created using the **showModalDialog** method.

Example

The following example shows how to create a dialog window using the **dialogTop** property to set the position relative to the top of the screen.

Note Do not break the script code into two lines as in the fourth line of the example. This was done for readability only.

```
<SCRIPT>
function someMessage()
{
    event.srcElement.blur();
    window.showModalDialog("message.htm", "",
        "dialogWidth:5cm; dialogHeight:10cm;
        dialogTop:0cm; dialogLeft:0cm")
}
</SCRIPT>
</HEAD>
<BODY>
<SELECT onchange="someMessage()">
    <OPTION>Item 1</OPTION>
    <OPTION>Item 2</OPTION>
    <OPTION>Item 3</OPTION>
</SELECT>
```

To see this code in action, refer to the Web Workshop CD-ROM.

Applies To

 WIN16   WIN32   MAC   UNIX

window

dialogWidth Property

Sets or retrieves the width of the modal dialog window.

Syntax

HTML   N/A

Scripting *window*.**dialogWidth** [= *iWidth*]

Possible Values

iWidth   Integer specifying the width, in ems.

The property is read/write with no default value.

Remarks

This property applies only to dialog windows created using the **showModalDialog** method.

Example

The following example shows how to create a dialog window using the **dialogWidth** property to set the new window's width.

```
<SCRIPT>
function someMessage()
{
    event.srcElement.blur();
    window.showModalDialog("message.htm", "",
    "dialogWidth:5cm; dialogHeight:10cm")
}
</SCRIPT>
</HEAD>
<BODY>
<SELECT onchange="someMessage()">
    <OPTION>Item 1</OPTION>
    <OPTION>Item 2</OPTION>
    <OPTION>Item 3</OPTION>
</SELECT>
```

To see this code in action, refer to the Web Workshop CD-ROM.

DHTML Properties

Applies To

 WIN16   WIN32   MAC   UNIX

window

DIR Attribute | dir Property

Sets or retrieves the reading order of the object.

Syntax

HTML   <ELEMENT **DIR** = "ltr" | "rtl">

Scripting   *object*.**dir** [= *sDir*]

Possible Values

ltr Text flow is left-to-right.

rtl Text flow is right-to-left.

The property is read/write with a default value of ltr.

Applies To

 WIN16   WIN32   MAC   UNIX

A, ACRONYM, ADDRESS, AREA, B, BDO, BIG, BLOCKQUOTE, BODY,
BUTTON, CAPTION, CENTER, CITE, CODE, COL, COLGROUP, DD, DEL,
DFN, DIR, DIV, DL, DT, EM, EMBED, FIELDSET, FONT, FORM, Hn, I, IMG,
INPUT type=button, INPUT type=checkbox, INPUT type=file, INPUT type=image,
INPUT type=password, INPUT type=radio, INPUT type=reset, INPUT type=submit,
INPUT type=text, INS, KBD, LABEL, LEGEND, LI, LISTING, MAP, MARQUEE,
MENU, NOBR, OBJECT, OL, OPTION, P, PLAINTEXT, PRE, Q, RT, RUBY, S,
SAMP, SELECT, SMALL, SPAN, STRIKE, STRONG, SUB, SUP, TABLE, TBODY,
TD, TEXTAREA, TFOOT, TH, THEAD, TR, TT, U, UL, VAR, XMP

DIRECTION Attribute | direction Property

Sets or retrieves which direction the text should scroll.

Syntax

HTML   <MARQUEE **DIRECTION** = "left" | "right" | "down" | "up" ... >

Scripting *marquee*.**direction** [= *sDirection*]

Possible Values

left   Marquee scrolls left.

right   Marquee scrolls right.

down   Marquee scrolls down.

up   Marquee scrolls up.

The property is read/write with a default value of left.

Applies To

 WIN16   WIN32   MAC

MARQUEE

 UNIX

MARQUEE

direction Attribute | direction Property

Sets or retrieves the reading order of the specified object.

Syntax

HTML   { **direction:** [ltr | rtl | inherit] }

Scripting *object*.**style.direction** [= *sDirection*]

Possible Values

ltr   Text flow is left-to-right.

rtl   Text flow is right-to-left.

inherit Text flow value is inherited.

The property is read/write with a default value of ltr.

Applies To

 WIN16   **WIN32**   **MAC**   **UNIX**

A, ACRONYM, ADDRESS, AREA, B, BDO, BIG, BLOCKQUOTE, BODY, BUTTON, CAPTION, CENTER, CITE, CODE, COL, COLGROUP, currentStyle, DD, DEL, DFN, DIR, DIV, DL, DT, EM, EMBED, FIELDSET, FONT, FORM, Hn, I, IMG, INPUT type=button, INPUT type=checkbox, INPUT type=file, INPUT type=image, INPUT type=password, INPUT type=radio, INPUT type=reset, INPUT type=submit, INPUT type=text, INS, KBD, LABEL, LEGEND, LI, LISTING, MAP, MARQUEE, MENU, NOBR, OBJECT, OL, OPTION, P, PLAINTEXT, PRE, Q, RT, RUBY, runtimeStyle, S, SAMP, SELECT, SMALL, SPAN, STRIKE, STRONG, style, SUB, SUP, TABLE, TBODY, TD, TEXTAREA, TFOOT, TH, THEAD, TR, TT, U, UL, VAR, XMP

DISABLED Attribute | disabled Property

Sets or retrieves whether a control or style is disabled.

Syntax

HTML   <ELEMENT **DISABLED** ... >

Scripting   *object*.**disabled** [= *bDisabled*]

Possible Values

false   Control is not disabled.

true   Control is disabled.

The property is read/write with a default value of false.

Remarks

When a control is disabled, it appears dimmed and does not respond to user input.
When a style is disabled, all of the **rules** cease to be rendered.

The **disabled** property applies to the **STYLE** object, not the **style** property.

Example

The following example shows how to use the **disabled** property to enable or disable a
STYLE object and a control.

```
<STYLE ID=oStyle>
.styletest{background-color: black; color: white;}
.styletest2{background-color: black; color: red;}
</STYLE>

<SCRIPT>
function fnSwitch(){
   if(oParagraph.enablement == "enabled"){
      // Use an arbitrary attribute to track the status.
      oParagraph.enablement = "disabled";
      oButton.value = "Set disabled to false";
      oStyle.disabled = true;
      oDisableMe.disabled = true;
   }
   else{
      oButton.value = "Set disabled to true";
      oParagraph.enablement = "enabled";
      oStyle.disabled = false;
      oDisableMe.disabled = false;
    }
}
</SCRIPT>

:

<P enablement = "enabled" ID = oParagraph CLASS = "styletest">
A paragraph of text.

<INPUT TYPE = button ID = oDisableMe
CLASS = "styletest"
VALUE = "Demonstration Button"
onclick = "alert('Demonstration button')">
</P>

<INPUT TYPE=button
ID=oButton
VALUE="Set disabled to true"
onclick="fnSwitch()">
```

To see this code in action, refer to the Web Workshop CD-ROM.

DHTML Properties

Applies To

 WIN16   WIN32   MAC   UNIX

APPLET, BUTTON, INPUT type=button, INPUT type=checkbox, INPUT type=file, INPUT type=image, INPUT type=password, INPUT type=radio, INPUT type=reset, INPUT type=submit, INPUT type=text, LINK, SELECT, TEXTAREA

disabled Property

Sets or retrieves whether a style sheet is applied to an object.

Syntax

HTML   N/A

Scripting   *styleSheet*.**disabled** [= *bDisabled*]

Possible Values

false   Style sheet is selected.

true   Style sheet is not selected.

The property is read/write with a default value of false.

Remarks

The value of this property can also change per media-dependent style sheets.

Example

The following example shows how to use the **disabled** property to toggle whether a style sheet is applied to the **BODY** element.

```
<STYLE>
BODY {background-color: #000000; color: #FFFF00;}
</STYLE>
<SCRIPT>
function fnToggle(){
    var oStyle=document.styleSheets[0];
    if (oStyle.disabled==true){
        oStyle.disabled=flase;
    }
    else{
        oStyle.disabled=true;
    }
}
</SCRIPT>
<BODY>
```

```
<P>
Click Toggle Style Sheet to enable/disable
styles applied to the BODY element.
</P>
<P>
<INPUT TYPE="button"
    VALUE="Toggle Style Sheet"
    onclick="fnToggle()">
</P>
</BODY>
```

Applies To

WIN16	WIN32	MAC	UNIX

styleSheet

display Attribute | display Property

Sets or retrieves whether the object is rendered.

Syntax

HTML   { **display:** block | none | inline | list-item | table-header-group | table-footer-group }

Scripting *object*.**style.display** [= *sDisplay*]

Possible Values

block	Object is rendered as a block element.
none	Object is not rendered.
inline	Object is rendered as an inline element sized by the dimensions of the content.
list-item	Object is rendered as a block element, and a list-item marker is added.
table-header-group	Table header is always displayed before all other rows and row groups, and after any top captions. The header is displayed on each page spanned by a table.
table-footer-group	Table footer is always displayed after all other rows and row groups, and before any bottom captions. The footer is displayed on each page spanned by a table.

The property is read/write with a default value of block for block elements and inline for inline elements; the cascading style sheets (CSS) attribute is not inherited.

DHTML Properties

Remarks

In Internet Explorer 4.0, the `block`, `inline`, and `list-item` values are not supported explicitly, but do render the element.

The `block` and `inline` values are supported explicitly as of Internet Explorer 5.

All visible HTML **objects** are block or inline. For example, a **DIV** object is a block element, and a **SPAN** object is an inline element. Block elements typically start a new line and can contain other block elements and inline elements. Inline elements do not typically start a new line and can contain other inline elements or data. Changing the values for the **display** property affects the layout of the surrounding content by:

- Adding a new line after the element with the value `block`.
- Removing a line from the element with the value `inline`.
- Hiding the data for the element with the value `none`.

In contrast to the **visibility** property, **display**=none reserves no space for the object on the screen.

The `table-header-group` and `table-footer-group` values can be used to specify that the contents of the **THEAD** and **TFOOT** objects are displayed on every page for a table that spans multiple pages.

Example

The following sample shows the effect of changing the values for the **display** property between `inline`, `block`, and `none`.

```
<SPAN ID=oSpan>
This is a SPAN
</SPAN>
in a sentence.
<P>
<INPUT TYPE=button VALUE="Block"
    onclick="oSpan.style.display='block'">
:
```

To see this code in action, refer to the Web Workshop CD-ROM.

The next example shows how to use function calls to hide and show table rows and cells.

```
<SCRIPT>
function getPets()
{
    oRow1Cell2.style.display="none";
    oRow2Cell2.style.display="block";
    oRow3Cell2.style.display="none";
}
</SCRIPT>
```

```
:
<TABLE>
<TR ID="oRow1"><TD>Horses</TD>
<TD ID="oRow1Cell2">Thoroughbreds</TD>
<TD>Fast</TD></TR>
<TR ID="oRow2"><TD>Dogs</TD>
<TD ID="oRow2Cell2">Greyhounds</TD>
<TD>Fast</TD></TR>
<TR ID="oRow3"><TD>Marsupials</TD>
<TD ID="oRow3Cell2">Opossums</TD>
<TD>Slow</TD></TR>
</TABLE>
:
<INPUT TYPE=button onclick="getPets()"
    VALUE="Show household pets">
```

To see this code in action, refer to the Web Workshop CD-ROM.

Applies To

 WIN16   WIN32   MAC   UNIX

BODY, BUTTON, DIV, IFRAME, IMG, INPUT type=button, INPUT
type=checkbox, INPUT type=file, INPUT type=image, INPUT type=password,
INPUT type=radio, INPUT type=reset, INPUT type=submit, INPUT type=text,
ISINDEX, MARQUEE, SELECT, SPAN, style, TABLE, TEXTAREA

 WIN16   WIN32   MAC   UNIX

currentStyle, runtimeStyle, TD, TFOOT, THEAD, TR

documentElement Property

Retrieves a reference to the root node of the document.

Syntax

HTML   N/A

Scripting   [*oElement* =] *document*.**documentElement**

Possible Values

oElement   Reference to the document element.

The property is read-only with no default value.

Remarks

The root node of a typical HTML document is the **HTML** object.

Example

The following example shows how to use the **documentElement** property to retrieve the **innerHTML** property of the entire document.

```
<SCRIPT>
function fnGetHTML(){
    var sData = document.documentElement.innerHTML;
    oResults.value=sData;
}
</SCRIPT>

<TEXTAREA ID = oResults COLS = 50 ROWS = 10>
</TEXTAREA>
```

Applies To

 WIN16   WIN32   MAC   UNIX

document

domain Property

Sets or retrieves the security domain of the document.

Syntax

HTML   N/A

Scripting *document*.**domain** [= *sDomain*]

Possible Values

sDomain String specifying the domain suffix.

The property is read/write with no default value.

Remarks

The property initially returns the host name of the server the page is served from. The property can be assigned the domain suffix to allow sharing of pages across frames. For example, a page in one frame from home.microsoft.com and a page from www.microsoft.com would initially not be able to communicate with each other. However, by setting the domain property of both pages to the suffix, microsoft.com, both pages are considered secure and communication between the pages is allowed.

Applies To

 WIN16   WIN32   MAC   UNIX

document

dropEffect Property

Sets or retrieves, on the target element, which cursor to display during a drag-and-drop operation.

Syntax

HTML   N/A

Scripting   *event.dataTransfer*.**dropEffect**[*= sCursorStyle*]

Possible Values

copy   String specifying the copy cursor.

link   String specifying the link cursor.

move   String specifying the move cursor.

none   String indicating no cursor is specified. The no-drop cursor displays instead.

The property is read/write with a default value of none.

Remarks

The target object can set the **dropEffect** during the **ondragenter**, **ondragover**, and **ondrop** events. To display the desired cursor until the final drop, the default action of the **ondragenter**, **ondragover**, and **ondrop** events must be canceled and the **dropEffect** must be set. Otherwise, the copy cursor, move cursor, or link cursor set by this property displays only until the first valid drop target is intersected, at which point the cursor is replaced by the drop/no-drop cursor for the duration of the drag operation.

The drag-and-drop behaviors implemented in Internet Explorer 4.0 and supported by Internet Explorer 5 can affect **dropEffect** behavior in certain situations. Internet Explorer delivers default drag-and-drop functionality for **anchor**, **image**, **TEXTAREA**, and **text box**. When one of these objects comprises the source element, the default drop effect cannot be overridden by setting the **dropEffect** of the target element. The source object's default behavior must be canceled.

For **dropEffect** to work, it must be used with the **effectAllowed** property of the source object. The actual value—whether copy, move, or link—must match that set in **effectAllowed**. If **effectAllowed** is not explicitly set, **dropEffect** must be set to the default value of **effectAllowed** for that particular source object.

The **dropEffect** property applies standard system cursors.

Example

The following example shows how to set the **dropEffect** and **effectAllowed** properties of the **dataTransfer** object.

```
<HEAD>
<SCRIPT>
var sMoveText;
var sSaveDiv = "";
var sSaveSpan = "";

// Changes to text of target and source objects must be manually coded.
function fnSetInfo()
{
  sSaveDiv = oTarget.innerText;    // Updates text in target object.
  sSaveSpan = oSource.innerText;   // Updates text in source object.
  event.dataTransfer.effectAllowed = "move";  // Moves text.
}

/* This function is called by the target object in the ondrop event.
   It cancels the default actions, sets the cursor to the system
   move icon, specifies which data format to retrieve, and then
   sets the innerText property of oTarget object to the information
   from getData.
*/
function fnGetInfo()
{
  event.returnValue = false;
  event.dataTransfer.dropEffect = "move";
  sMoveText = event.dataTransfer.getData("Text");
  oTarget.innerText = sMoveText;
}

/* This function cancels the default action in ondragenter and
   ondragover so that the copy cursor displays until
   the selection is dropped.
*/
function fnCancelDefault()
{
  event.returnValue = false;
  event.dataTransfer.dropEffect = "copy";
}

</SCRIPT>
</HEAD>
```

```
<BODY>
<B>
  [not this text]
<SPAN ID=oSource ondragstart="fnSetInfo()">
  [ select and drag this text ]
</SPAN>
  [not this text]
</B>
<DIV ID=oTarget ondrop="fnGetInfo()"
                ondragover="fnCancelDefault()"
                ondragenter="fnCancelDefault()">[ drop text here ]
</DIV>
</BODY>
```

To see this code in action, refer to the Web Workshop CD-ROM.

Applies To

WIN16	WIN32	MAC	UNIX

dataTransfer

DYNSRC Attribute | dynsrc Property

Sets or retrieves the address of a video clip or VRML world to be displayed in the window.

Syntax

HTML   <IMG **DYNSRC** = *sURL* ... >

Scripting *img*.**dynsrc** [= *sURL*]

Possible Values

sURL   String specifying the URL of the video source.

The property is read/write with no default value.

Applies To

WIN32	MAC

IMG

UNIX

IMG

effectAllowed Property

Sets or retrieves, on the source element, which data transfer operations are allowed for the object.

Syntax

HTML   N/A

Scripting   *event.dataTransfer*.**effectAllowed**[= *sEffect*]

Possible Values

copy	String specifying that the selection is to be copied.
link	String specifying that the data transfer operation links the selection to the drop target.
move	String specifying that the selection is moved to the target location when dropped.
copyLink	String specifying that the selection is copied or linked, depending on the target default.
copyMove	String specifying that the selection is copied or moved, depending on the target default.
linkMove	String specifying that the selection is linked or moved, depending on the target default.
all	String specifying that all drop effects are supported.
none	String specifying that dropping is disabled and that the no-drop cursor displays.
uninitialized	String specifying that no value has been set through the **effectAllowed** property. In this case, the default effect still works, though it cannot be queried through this property.

The property is read/write with a default value of copy.

Remarks

Set the **effectAllowed** property in the **ondragstart** event. This property is used most effectively with the **dropEffect** property.

This property can be used to override the default behavior in other applications. For example, the browser script can set the **effectAllowed** property to copy and thereby override the Microsoft® Word default of move. Within the browser, copy is the default **effectAllowed** behavior, except for anchors, which are set to link by default.

Setting **effectAllowed** to none disables dropping, but still displays the no-drop cursor.
To avoid displaying the no-drop cursor, cancel the **returnValue** of the **ondragstart**
window.

Example

The following example shows how to move text in a drag-and-drop operation.

```
<HEAD>
<SCRIPT>
var sMoveText;
var sSaveDiv = "";
var sSaveSpan = "";

/* This function updates the text in the target and source objects
   and then moves the text.
*/
function Initiate_Drag()
{
  sSaveDiv = oTarget.innerText;
  sSaveSpan = oSource.innerText;
  event.dataTransfer.effectAllowed = "move";
}

/* This function cancels the default action, sets the cursor to the
   move icon, and then specifies the data format to retrieve.
*/
function Finish_Drag()
{
  event.returnValue = false;
  event.dataTransfer.dropEffect = "move";
  sMoveText = event.dataTransfer.getData("Text");
  oTarget.innerText = sMoveText;
}

/* This function cancels the default action in ondragover and ondrop
   so that the move cursor displays until the selection is dropped.
*/
function Over()
{
  event.returnValue = false;
}

function Drop()
{
  event.returnValue = false;        // Cancels the default action.
}
</SCRIPT>
</HEAD>
```

```
<BODY>
<B>
  [not this text]
<SPAN ID=oSource ondragstart="Initiate_Drag()">
  [ select and drag this text ]
</SPAN>
  [not this text]
</B>
<DIV ID=oTarget ondragenter="Finish_Drag()"
                ondragover="Over()"
                ondrop="Drop()">[ drop text here ]</DIV>
</BODY>
```

To see this code in action, refer to the Web Workshop CD-ROM.

Applies To

 WIN16   WIN32   MAC   UNIX

dataTransfer

ENCTYPE Attribute | encoding Property

Sets or retrieves the MIME encoding for the form.

Syntax

HTML   <FORM **ENCTYPE** = *sType* ... >

Scripting   *object*.**encoding** [= *sType*]

Possible Values

sType   String specifying the format of the data being submitted by the form.

The property is read/write with a default value of `application/x-www-form-urlencoded`.

Remarks

Internet Explorer 4.0 also recognizes multipart/form-data, which, along with a POST method, is required to submit a file upload to the server.

Applies To

 WIN16   WIN32   MAC

FORM

 UNIX

FORM

EVENT Attribute | event Property

Retrieves the event for which the script is written.

Syntax

HTML   <SCRIPT **EVENT** = *sEvent* ... >

Scripting   [*sEvent* =] *script*.**event**

Possible Values

sEvent   String specifying the event. The value for an **onmouseover** event, for example, is "onmouseover()".

The property is read-only with no default value.

Example

The following example shows how to use the **EVENT** attribute and the **event** property.

```
<SCRIPT ID=oButtonScript FOR="oButton" EVENT="onclick()">
    var sMessage1 = "Flip"
    var sMessage2 = "Flop"
    if (oButton.innerText == sMessage1) {
        oButton.innerText = sMessage2;
        }
    else {
    if (oButton.innerText == sMessage2) {
        oButton.innerText = sMessage1;
        }
</SCRIPT>
</HEAD>
<BODY>
:
<BUTTON ID="oButton" onmouseout="alert(oButtonScript.event)">Flip</BUTTON>
```

To see this code in action, refer to the Web Workshop CD-ROM.

Applies To

WIN16   WIN32   MAC

SCRIPT

UNIX

SCRIPT

expando Property

Sets or retrieves whether arbitrary variables can be created within an object.

Syntax

HTML   N/A

Scripting *document*.**expando** [= *bExpand*]

Possible Values

true   Creation of arbitrary variables is allowed.

false   Creation of arbitrary variables is not allowed.

The property is read/write with a default value of true.

Remarks

You can extend the properties on an object by creating arbitrary properties with values. You need to take care, however, because you can unintentionally set a property value when scripting in a case-sensitive language such as JScript (compatible with ECMA 262 language specification). For example, if the property value is "borderColor" and you type the value "bordercolor = 'blue'", you have, in fact, created another property on the style object called "bordercolor" with the value 'blue'. If you query the value of the property, the value "blue" is returned. However, the borders for the element do not turn blue.

Visual Basic® Scripting Edition (VBScript) does not support **expando** properties on its native language objects, nor does it cause Internet Explorer to create **expando** properties on its objects. Internet Explorer supports creation of **expando** properties on its objects, in any language, through **setAttribute**.

DHTML Properties

Applies To

 WIN16   WIN32   MAC   UNIX

document

FACE Attribute | face Property

Sets or retrieves the current fonts family.

Syntax

HTML   <ELEMENT **FACE** = *sTypeface* ... >

Scripting *object*.**face** [= *sTypeface*]

Possible Values

sTypeface   String specifying the font family.

The property is read/write with no default value.

Example

The following example shows how to set the font family using the **FACE** attribute and the **face** property.

```
<FONT FACE="Arial" ID=oFont>
:
<SCRIPT>
    alert(oFont.face + "\n" + "When you click this, the font will change.");
    oFont.face = 'Courier';
    alert(oFont.face + "\n" + "The font has changed.");
</SCRIPT>
```

To see this code in action, refer to the Web Workshop CD-ROM.

Applies To

 WIN16   WIN32   MAC

FONT

 WIN16   WIN32   MAC   UNIX

BASEFONT, FONT

fgColor Property

Sets or retrieves the foreground (text) color of the document.

Syntax

HTML   N/A

Scripting *document*.**fgColor** [= *sColor*]

Possible Values

sColor String value set to any one of the color names or values given in the "Color Table" in Appendix C.

The property is read/write with a default value of #000000.

Applies To

  WIN16   WIN32   MAC

document

  UNIX

document

fileCreatedDate Property

Retrieves the date the file was created.

Syntax

HTML   N/A

Scripting [*sDate* =] *object*.**fileCreatedDate**

Possible Values

sDate String specifying the date the file was created (for example, Monday, December 08, 1997).

The property is read-only with no default value.

Example

The following example shows how to use the **fileCreatedDate** property to count the number of days since the document was created.

```
<SCRIPT>
window.onload=fnInit;
function fnInit(){
   // Date that the document was created:
   var oCreated=new Date(document.fileCreatedDate);
   // Today's Date:
   var oToday=new Date();
   var iSeconds=1000;
   var iMinutes=60;
   var iHours=24;
   // Divisor to convert milliseconds into days:
   var iDays=iSeconds * iMinutes * iHours;
   var iDaysBetween=(oToday.getTime() - oCreated.getTime()) / iDays;

   alert("Created: " + oCreated
      + "\nDays since created: " + iDaysBetween
   );

}
</SCRIPT>
```

Applies To

 WIN16   WIN32   MAC   UNIX

document, IMG

fileModifiedDate Property

Retrieves the date the file was last modified.

Syntax

HTML   N/A

Scripting   [*sDate* =] *object*.**fileModifiedDate**

Possible Values

sDate   String specifying the date of the last file modification (for example, Monday, December 08, 1997).

The property is read-only with no default value.

Applies To

 WIN16   WIN32   MAC   UNIX

document, IMG

fileSize Property

Retrieves the file size.

Syntax

HTML   N/A

Scripting [*iSize* =] *object*.**fileSize**

Possible Values

iSize   Integer specifying the file size.

The property is read-only with no default value.

Applies To

 WIN16   WIN32   MAC   UNIX

document, IMG

fileUpdatedDate Property

Retrieves the date the file was last updated.

Syntax

HTML   N/A

Scripting [*sDate* =] *img*.**fileUpdatedDate**

Possible Values

sDate   String specifying the date of the last update (for example, Monday, December 08, 1997).

The property is read-only with no default value.

Applies To

 WIN16   WIN32   MAC   UNIX

IMG

filter Attribute | filter Property

Sets or retrieves the filter or collection of filters applied to the object.

Syntax

| HTML | { **filter:** *filtertype1(parameter1, parameter2,...)* [*filtertype2(parameter1, parameter2,...)*]... } |

Scripting   *object*.**style.filter** [= *sFilter*]

Possible Values

| *filtertype1(parameter1, parameter2,...)* | Any of the following types and their associated parameters: Visual Filter, Reveal Transition Filter, or Blend Transition Filter. |

The property is read/write with no default value; the proposed cascading style sheets (CSS) extension attribute is not inherited.

Remarks

When using a **SPAN** or **DIV** object, be sure to specify at least one of the three required CSS attributes: **height**, **width**, or **position** (absolute or relative).

The shadow filter can be applied to the **IMG** object by setting the filter on the image's parent container.

The filter mechanism is extensible and allows you to develop and add additional filters later.

This property is not available on the Macintosh platform.

Example

The following examples show how to use the **filter** attribute and the **filter** property to apply filters.

The sample below uses an inline style sheet to set the filter on an image.

```
<IMG STYLE="filter:blur(strength=50) flipv()"
    SRC="cone.jpg">
```

To see this code in action, refer to the Web Workshop CD-ROM.

The sample below uses inline scripting to set the filter on an image.

```
<SCRIPT>
function doFilter ()
{
    filterFrom.filters.item(0).Apply();
    // 12 is the dissolve filter.
    filterFrom.filters.item(0).Transition=12;
    imageFrom.style.visibility = "hidden";
    filterTo.style.visibility = "";
    filterFrom.filters.item(0).play(14);
}
</SCRIPT>
</HEAD>
<BODY>
Click on the image to start the filter.<BR>
// Call the function.
<DIV ID="filterFrom" onClick="doFilter()"
    STYLE="position:absolute;
        width:200;
        height:250;
        background-color:white;
        filter:revealTrans()">
<IMG ID="imageFrom"
    STYLE="position:absolute;
        top:20;
        left:20;"
    SRC="sphere.jpg">
<DIV ID="filterTo"
    STYLE="position:absolute;
        width:200;
        height:250;
        top:20;
        left:20;
        background:white;
        visibility:hidden;">
</DIV>
</DIV>
```

To see this code in action, refer to the Web Workshop CD-ROM.

Applies To

WIN32   UNIX   WIN16

BODY, BUTTON, DIV, IMG, INPUT type=button, INPUT type=checkbox, INPUT type=file, INPUT type=image, INPUT type=password, INPUT type=radio, INPUT type=reset, INPUT type=submit, INPUT type=text, MARQUEE, SPAN, style, TABLE, TD, TEXTAREA, TH

WIN16   WIN32   MAC   UNIX

runtimeStyle

firstChild Property

Retrieves a reference to the first child in the **childNodes** collection of the object.

Syntax

HTML   N/A

Scripting   [*oElement* =] *object*.**firstChild**

Possible Values

oElement   First child object.

The property is read-only with no default value.

Example

The following example shows how to use the **firstChild** attribute to obtain the first child element of an object.

```
<SCRIPT>
var oFirstChild = oList.firstChild;
</SCRIPT>

<BODY>
<UL ID = oList>
<LI>List Item 1
<LI>List Item 2
<LI>List Item 3
</UL>
<BODY>
```

Applies To

 WIN16   WIN32   MAC   UNIX

A, ACRONYM, ADDRESS, APPLET, AREA, B, BASE, BASEFONT, BDO, BIG, BLOCKQUOTE, BODY, BUTTON, CAPTION, CENTER, CITE, CODE, COL, COLGROUP, COMMENT, DD, DEL, DFN, DIR, DIV, DL, DT, EM, EMBED, FIELDSET, FONT, FORM, FRAME, FRAMESET, HEAD, Hn, HR, HTML, I, IFRAME, IMG, INPUT type=button, INPUT type=checkbox, INPUT type=file, INPUT type=image, INPUT type=password, INPUT type=radio, INPUT type=reset, INPUT type=submit, INPUT type=text, INS, KBD, LABEL, LEGEND, LI, LINK, LISTING, MAP, MARQUEE, MENU, NEXTID, OL, OPTION, P, PLAINTEXT, PRE, Q, S, SAMP, SCRIPT, SELECT, SMALL, SPAN, STRIKE, STRONG, SUB, SUP, TABLE, TBODY, TD, TEXTAREA, TFOOT, TH, THEAD, TITLE, TR, TT, U, UL, VAR, XMP

float Attribute | styleFloat Property

Sets or retrieves whether the object floats, causing text to flow around it.

Syntax

HTML   { **float:** none | left | right }

Scripting *object.style*.**styleFloat** [= *sFloat*]

Possible Values

none   Object is displayed where it appears in the text.

left   Text flows to the right of the object.

right Text flows to the left of the object.

The property is read/write with a default value of none; the cascading style sheets (CSS) attribute has a default value of none and is not inherited.

Remarks

With a value of left or right, the object is treated as block-level (that is, the **display** property is ignored). For example, floating paragraphs allow the paragraphs to appear side-by-side on a page.

Objects following a floating object move in relation to the position of the floating object.

The floating object is moved left or right until it reaches the border, padding, or margin of another block-level object.

DIV and **SPAN** objects must have a width set for the **float** attribute to render; in Internet Explorer 5, **DIV** and **SPAN** objects are assigned a width by default and render if a width is not specified.

Example

The following example shows the **float** attribute affecting the flow of the text. The sphere image floats to the left of the text, and the cone floats to the right.

```
<img src="sphere.jpg" style="float:left">
<img src="cone.jpg" style="float:right">
```

To see this code in action, refer to the Web Workshop CD-ROM.

The next example shows how to use the **styleFloat** property. When the user mouses over the button, the images are swapped using inline scripting and the **styleFloat** property.

```
<IMG ID=oSphere SRC="sphere.jpeg" STYLE="float:left">
<IMG ID=oCone SRC="cone.jpeg" STYLE="float:right">
:
<BUTTON onmouseover="oSphere.style.styleFloat='right'; oCone.style.styleFloat='left'"
    onmouseout="oSphere.style.styleFloat='left'; oCone.style.styleFloat='right'">
    Flip-flop images.
</BUTTON>
```

To see this code in action, refer to the Web Workshop CD-ROM.

Applies To

 IE 4 **WIN16** **WIN32** **MAC** **UNIX**

APPLET, BUTTON, DIV, EMBED, Hn, HR, IFRAME, INPUT type=button, INPUT type=reset, INPUT type=submit, MARQUEE, OBJECT, SELECT, SPAN, style, TABLE, TEXTAREA

IE 5 **WIN16** **WIN32** **MAC** **UNIX**

A, ADDRESS, B, BIG, BLOCKQUOTE, CENTER, CITE, CODE, currentStyle, DD, DFN, DIR, DL, DT, EM, FIELDSET, FORM, I, IMG, INPUT type=checkbox, INPUT type=file, INPUT type=image, INPUT type=password, INPUT type=radio, INPUT type=text, ISINDEX, KBD, LABEL, LEGEND, LI, LISTING, MENU, OL, P, PRE, RT, RUBY, runtimeStyle, S, SAMP, SMALL, STRIKE, STRONG, SUB, SUP, TT, U, UL, VAR, XMP

font Attribute | font Property

Sets or retrieves the separate font properties (**fontWeight**, **fontVariant**, **fontSize**, and **fontFamily**) for text in the object.

Syntax

HTML   { **font:** caption | icon | menu | messagebox | smallcaption | statusbar | [*font-style* || *font-variant* || *font-weight*] *font-size* [*line-height*] *font-family* }

Scripting   *object*.**style.font** [= *sFont*]

Possible Values

caption	Font of the text in objects that have captions (buttons, labels, and so on).
icon	Font of the text in icon labels.
menu	Font of the text in menus.
messagebox	Font of the text in dialog boxes.
smallcaption	Font of the text in small controls.
statusbar	Font of the text in window status bars.
font-style	String having any of the range of values available to the **fontStyle** property.
font-variant	String having any of the range of values available to the **fontVariant** property.
font-weight	String having any of the range of values available to the **fontWeight** property.
font-size	String having any of the range of values available to the **fontSize** property.
line-height	String having any of the range of values available to the **lineHeight** property.
font-family	String having any of the range of values available to the **fontFamily** property.

The property is read/write with the default value set by the browser; the cascading style sheets (CSS) attribute is inherited.

Remarks

Setting the **font** property also sets the component properties. In this case, the string must be a combination of valid values for the component properties, with no more than one value per property. If the string does not contain a value for a component property, that property is set to its default. The font properties must be defined in this order: **font-style**, **font-variant**, **font-weight**, **font-size**, **line-height**, and **font-family**.

Internet Explorer 4.0 and later supports length values specified as a relative measurement, using the height of the element's font (em) or the height of the letter "x" (ex).

Internet Explorer 3.0 only supports bold for the *sWeight* value.

Example

The following examples show how to use the **font** attribute and the **font** property to change font characteristics.

The sample below uses an inline style sheet to set the font attributes.

```
<SPAN STYLE="font:italic normal bolder 12pt Arial">
:
</SPAN>
```

To see this code in action, refer to the Web Workshop CD-ROM.

The sample below uses inline scripting to set the font properties.

```
<DIV onmouseover="this.style.font = 'italic small-caps bold 12pt serif'">
:
</DIV>
```

To see this code in action, refer to the Web Workshop CD-ROM.

Applies To

 WIN16   WIN32   MAC   UNIX

A, ADDRESS, B, BIG, BLOCKQUOTE, BODY, BUTTON, CAPTION, CENTER, CITE, CODE, COL, COLGROUP, DD, DFN, DIR, DIV, DL, DT, EM, FIELDSET, FORM, Hn, HTML, I, IMG, INPUT type=button, INPUT type=checkbox, INPUT type=file, INPUT type=image, INPUT type=password, INPUT type=radio, INPUT type=reset, INPUT type=submit, INPUT type=text, ISINDEX, KBD, LABEL, LEGEND, LI, LISTING, MARQUEE, MENU, OL, P, PLAINTEXT, PRE, S, SAMP, SELECT, SMALL, SPAN, STRIKE, STRONG, style, SUB, SUP, TABLE, TBODY, TD, TEXTAREA, TFOOT, TH, THEAD, TR, TT, U, UL, VAR, XMP

WIN16   WIN32   MAC   UNIX

runtimeStyle

@font-face Rule

Retrieves a font to embed in the HTML document.

Syntax

HTML   **@font-face** {font-family:*fontFamilyName*; src:url(*sURL*);}

Scripting N/A

Possible Values

fontFamilyName Any of the range of values available to the **fontFamily** property.

src:url(*sURL*) Location of the font file, where *sURL* is an absolute or relative URL.

The rule has no default value.

Remarks

This feature allows you to use specific fonts that might not be available on your local system. The URL should point to an embedded OpenType file (.eot or .ote format). The file contains compressed font data that is converted to a TrueType font.

Example

The following example shows how to embed a font in an HTML document by referencing its source from another site.

```
<HTML>
<HEAD>
<STYLE>
   @font-face {
       font-family:comic;
       src:url( http://valid_url/some_font_file.eot );
   }
</STYLE>
</HEAD>
<BODY>
<P STYLE="font-family:comic;font-size:18pt">
This paragraph uses the font-face rule defined
in the above style element.  The rule embeds
an OpenType file for the Comic Sans font.
</P>
</BODY>
</HTML>
```

font-family Attribute | fontFamily Property

Sets or retrieves the name of the font used for text in the object.

Syntax

HTML { **font-family:** *family-name* | *generic-name* [, *family-name* | *generic-name*] }

Scripting *object*.**style.fontFamily** [= *sFamily*]

Possible Values

family-name String specifying any of the available font families supported by the browser (for example, Times, Helvetica, Zapf-Chancery, Western, or Courier).

generic-name String specifying any of the following font families: serif, sans-serif, cursive, fantasy, or monospace.

The property is read/write with the default value set by the browser; the cascading style sheets (CSS) attribute is inherited.

Remarks

The value is a prioritized list of font family names and/or generic family names. List items are separated by commas to minimize confusion between multiple-word font family names. If the font family name contains white space, it should be quoted with single or double quotation marks; generic font family names are values and, accordingly, no quotes should be used.

Because you don't know which fonts users have installed, you should provide a list of alternatives with a generic font family at the end of the list. This list can include embedded fonts. For more information about embedding fonts, see the **@font-face** rule.

If fantasy is specified for *generic-name,* the text renders in the default font.

DHTML Properties

Example

The following examples show how to use the **font-family** attribute and the **fontFamily** property to change font characteristics.

The sample below uses a call to an embedded style sheet to set the font family.

```
<STYLE>
    P { font-family: Arial }
    .other { font-family: Courier }
</STYLE>
```

To see this code in action, refer to the Web Workshop CD-ROM.

The sample below uses inline scripting to change the font family on an **onmousedown** event.

```
<DIV onmousedown="this.style.fontFamily='Courier'">
```

To see this code in action, refer to the Web Workshop CD-ROM.

Applies To

 IE 3   **WIN16**   **WIN32**   **MAC**

A, ADDRESS, B, BASEFONT, BIG, BLOCKQUOTE, BODY, CAPTION, CENTER, CITE, CODE, DD, DFN, DIR, DIV, DL, DT, FORM, Hn, I, ISINDEX, KBD, LI, LISTING, MARQUEE, MENU, OL, P, PLAINTEXT, PRE, S, SAMP, SMALL, SPAN, STRIKE, STRONG, SUB, SUP, TABLE, TD, TH, TR, TT, U, UL, VAR, XMP

 IE 4   **UNIX**   **WIN16**   **WIN32**   **MAC**

A, ADDRESS, B, BASEFONT, BIG, BLOCKQUOTE, BODY, BUTTON, CAPTION, CENTER, CITE, CODE, COL, COLGROUP, DD, DFN, DIR, DIV, DL, DT, EM, FIELDSET, FORM, Hn, HTML, I, IMG, INPUT type=button, INPUT type=checkbox, INPUT type=file, INPUT type=image, INPUT type=password, INPUT type=radio, INPUT type=reset, INPUT type=submit, INPUT type=text, ISINDEX, KBD, LABEL, LEGEND, LI, LISTING, MARQUEE, MENU, OL, P, PLAINTEXT, PRE, S, SAMP, SELECT, SMALL, SPAN, STRIKE, STRONG, style, SUB, SUP, TABLE, TBODY, TD, TEXTAREA, TFOOT, TH, THEAD, TR, TT, U, UL, VAR, XMP

 IE 5   **WIN16**   **WIN32**   **MAC**   **UNIX**

currentStyle, runtimeStyle

font-size Attribute | fontSize Property

Sets or retrieves the size of the font used for text in the object.

Syntax

HTML   { **font-size:** *absolute-size* | *relative-size* | *length* | *percentage* }

Scripting *object*.**style.fontSize** [= *sSize*]

Possible Values

absolute-size Set of keywords that indicate predefined font sizes. Possible keywords include [xx-small | x-small | small | medium | large | x-large | xx-large]. Named font sizes scale according to the user's font setting preferences.

relative-size Set of keywords that are interpreted as relative to the font size of the parent object. Possible values include [larger | smaller].

length Value expressed as an absolute measure (cm, mm, in, pt, pc, or px) or as a relative measure (em or ex).

percentage Percentage value of the parent object's font size. In Internet Explorer 3.0, the value is calculated as a percentage of the default font size.

The property is read/write with a default value of medium; the cascading style sheets (CSS) attribute is inherited.

Remarks

Negative values are not allowed. Font sizes using the proportional "em" measure are computed based on the font size of the parent object.

Internet Explorer 4.0 and later supports length values specified as a relative measurement, using the height of the element's font (em) or the height of the letter "x" (ex).

Example

The following examples show how to use the **font-size** attribute and the **fontSize** property to change font characteristics.

The sample below sets the font size on several paragraphs using different size values.

```
<STYLE>
   BODY{font-size: 10pt }
   .P1 {font-size: 14pt }
   .P2 {font-size: 75% }
```

```
        .P3 {font-size: xx-large }
        .P4 {font-size: larger }
</STYLE>
```

To see this code in action, refer to the Web Workshop CD-ROM.

The sample below uses inline scripting to set the font size to 14pt on an **onmouseover** event.

```
<DIV STYLE="font-size:12pt" onmouseover="this.style.fontSize='14pt'">
:
</DIV>
```

To see this code in action, refer to the Web Workshop CD-ROM.

Applies To

 WIN16   WIN32   MAC

A, ADDRESS, B, BIG, BLOCKQUOTE, BODY, CAPTION, CENTER, CITE, DD, DFN, DIR, DIV, DL, DT, EM, FORM, Hn, I, ISINDEX, KBD, LI, MARQUEE, MENU, OL, P, S, SMALL, SPAN, STRIKE, STRONG, SUB, SUP, TABLE, TD, TH, TR, U, UL

 UNIX   WIN16   WIN32   MAC

A, ADDRESS, APPLET, B, BIG, BLOCKQUOTE, BODY, BUTTON, CAPTION, CENTER, CITE, CODE, COL, COLGROUP, DD, DFN, DIR, DIV, DL, DT, EM, FIELDSET, FORM, Hn, HTML, I, INPUT type=button, INPUT type=checkbox, INPUT type=file, INPUT type=image, INPUT type=password, INPUT type=radio, INPUT type=reset, INPUT type=submit, INPUT type=text, ISINDEX, KBD, LABEL, LEGEND, LI, LISTING, MARQUEE, MENU, OL, P, PLAINTEXT, PRE, S, SAMP, SELECT, SMALL, SPAN, STRIKE, STRONG, style, SUB, SUP, TABLE, TBODY, TD, TEXTAREA, TFOOT, TH, THEAD, TR, TT, U, UL, VAR, XMP

 WIN16   WIN32   MAC   UNIX

currentStyle, runtimeStyle

fontSmoothingEnabled Property

Retrieves whether the user has enabled font smoothing in the Display control panel.

Syntax

HTML	N/A
Scripting	[*bEnabled* =] *screen*.**fontSmoothingEnabled**

Possible Values

false	Smoothing is disabled.
true	Smoothing is enabled.

The property is read-only with a default value of false.

Remarks

Font smoothing can be enabled by checking the Smooth Edges of the Screen Fonts option in the Display control panel. In Windows 98 and Windows 2000, this option is located on the control panel's Effects tab. In Windows NT 4.0 and Windows 95, this option is located on the Plus! tab.

Note In Windows 95, the Plus! tab is available only if Microsoft Plus! is installed.

Applies To

 WIN16   WIN32   MAC   UNIX

screen

font-style Attribute | fontStyle Property

Sets or retrieves whether the font style of the object is italic, normal, or oblique.

Syntax

HTML	{ **font-style:** normal	italic	oblique }
Scripting	*object*.**style.fontStyle** [= *sStyle*]

Possible Values

> `normal` Font is normal.
>
> `italic` Font is italicized.
>
> `oblique` Font is italicized.

> The property is read/write with a default value of `normal`; the cascading style sheets (CSS) attribute is inherited.

Remarks

> The possible value `oblique` is available as of Internet Explorer 4.0. Internet Explorer 4.0 renders italic and oblique fonts identically.

Example

> The following examples show how to use the **font-style** attribute and the **fontStyle** property to change font characteristics.

> The sample below uses **H3** as a selector to set the font's style in H3 headings to `italic`.

```
<STYLE>
    H3 { font-style: italic }
</STYLE>
```

> To see this code in action, refer to the Web Workshop CD-ROM.

> The sample below uses inline scripting to set the font style to `italic` on an **onmousedown** event.

```
<DIV onmousedown="this.style.fontStyle='italic'">
```

> To see this code in action, refer to the Web Workshop CD-ROM.

Applies To

 WIN16   WIN32   MAC

A, ADDRESS, B, BIG, BLOCKQUOTE, BODY, CAPTION, CENTER, CITE, CODE, DD, DFN, DIR, DIV, DL, DT, EM, FORM, Hn, I, ISINDEX, KBD, LI, LISTING, MARQUEE, MENU, OL, P, PLAINTEXT, PRE, S, SAMP, SMALL, SPAN, STRIKE, STRONG, SUB, SUP, TABLE, TD, TH, TR, TT, U, UL, VAR, XMP

IE 4 | **UNIX** | **WIN16** | **WIN32** | **MAC**

A, ADDRESS, B, BIG, BLOCKQUOTE, BODY, BUTTON, CAPTION, CENTER, CITE, CODE, COL, COLGROUP, DD, DFN, DIR, DIV, DL, DT, EM, FIELDSET, FORM, Hn, HTML, I, IMG, INPUT type=button, INPUT type=checkbox, INPUT type=file, INPUT type=image, INPUT type=password, INPUT type=radio, INPUT type=reset, INPUT type=submit, INPUT type=text, ISINDEX, KBD, LABEL, LEGEND, LI, LISTING, MARQUEE, MENU, OL, P, PLAINTEXT, PRE, S, SAMP, SELECT, SMALL, SPAN, STRIKE, STRONG, style, SUB, SUP, TABLE, TBODY, TD, TEXTAREA, TFOOT, TH, THEAD, TR, TT, U, UL, VAR, XMP

IE 5 | **WIN16** | **WIN32** | **MAC** | **UNIX**

currentStyle, runtimeStyle

font-variant Attribute | fontVariant Property

Sets or retrieves whether the text of the object is in small capital letters.

Syntax

HTML	{ **font-variant:** normal	small-caps }
Scripting	*object*.**style.fontVariant** [= *sVariant*]

Possible Values

normal   Font is normal.

small-caps   Font is set in small capitals.

The property is read/write with a default value of normal; the cascading style sheets (CSS) attribute is inherited.

Remarks

Internet Explorer 4.0 renders small-caps as uppercase letters in a smaller size.

DHTML Properties

Example

The following examples show how to use the **font-variant** attribute and the **fontVariant** property to change the font to small capitals.

The sample below uses **P** as a selector in an embedded (global) style sheet to set the font style to small-caps in all paragraphs.

```
<P STYLE="font-variant: small-caps">
```

To see this code in action, refer to the Web Workshop CD-ROM.

The sample below uses inline scripting to set the font style to small-caps on an **onmousedown** event.

```
<DIV onmousedown="this.style.fontVariant='small-caps'">
```

To see this code in action, refer to the Web Workshop CD-ROM.

Applies To

 WIN16   WIN32   MAC   UNIX

A, ADDRESS, B, BIG, BLOCKQUOTE, BODY, BUTTON, CAPTION, CENTER, CITE, CODE, COL, COLGROUP, DD, DFN, DIR, DIV, DL, DT, EM, FIELDSET, FORM, Hn, HTML, I, IMG, INPUT type=button, INPUT type=checkbox, INPUT type=file, INPUT type=image, INPUT type=password, INPUT type=radio, INPUT type=reset, INPUT type=submit, INPUT type=text, ISINDEX, KBD, LABEL, LEGEND, LI, LISTING, MARQUEE, MENU, OL, P, PLAINTEXT, PRE, S, SAMP, SELECT, SMALL, SPAN, STRIKE, STRONG, style, SUB, SUP, TABLE, TBODY, TD, TEXTAREA, TFOOT, TH, THEAD, TR, TT, U, UL, VAR, XMP

 WIN16   WIN32   MAC   UNIX

currentStyle, runtimeStyle

font-weight Attribute | fontWeight Property

Sets or retrieves the weight of the bold text of the object.

Syntax

HTML   { **font-weight:** `normal` | `bold` | `bolder` | `lighter` | `100` | `200` | `300` | `400` | `500` | `600` | `700` | `800` | `900` }

Scripting *object*.**style.fontWeight** [= *sWeight*]

Possible Values

normal	Font is normal.
bold	Font is bold.
bolder	Font is heavier than regular bold.
lighter	Font is lighter than normal.
100	Font is at least as light as the 200 weight.
200	Font is at least as bold as the 100 weight and at least as light as the 300 weight.
300	Font is at least as bold as the 200 weight and at least as light as the 400 weight.
400	Font is normal.
500	Font is at least as bold as the 400 weight and at least as light as the 600 weight.
600	Font is at least as bold as the 500 weight and at least as light as the 700 weight.
700	Font is bold.
800	Font is at least as bold as the 700 weight and at least as light as the 900 weight.
900	Font is at least as bold as the 800 weight.

The property is read/write with a default value of normal; the cascading style sheets (CSS) attribute is inherited.

Remarks

The key words for **font-weight** values are mapped to specific font variations depending on the fonts that are installed on the user's computer. In many cases, the user cannot see the difference between different **font-weight** settings because the system chooses the closest match.

Setting the **font-weight** to 400 is equivalent to normal, and 700 is equivalent to bold. A **font-weight** of bolder or lighter is interpreted relative to the parent object's weight. A value of bolder for text whose parent is normal would set the text to bold.

Internet Explorer 4.0 supports only normal and bold.

Internet Explorer 3.0 supports the **font-weight** attribute through the **font** attribute.

Example

The following examples show how to use the **font-weight** attribute and the **fontWeight** property to change the font weight.

The sample below uses **LI** as a selector in an embedded (global) style sheet to set the font weight to `bolder`.

```
<STYLE>
LI { font-weight:bolder }
</STYLE>
```

To see this code in action, refer to the Web Workshop CD-ROM.

The sample below uses inline scripting to set the font weight to `bolder` on an **onmouseover** event.

```
<P STYLE="font-size:14" onmouseover="this.style.fontWeight='bolder'">
```

To see this code in action, refer to the Web Workshop CD-ROM.

Applies To

 WIN16   WIN32   MAC

A, ADDRESS, B, BIG, BLOCKQUOTE, BODY, CAPTION, CENTER, CITE, CODE, DD, DFN, DIR, DIV, DL, DT, EM, FORM, Hn, I, ISINDEX, KBD, LI, MARQUEE, MENU, OL, P, PLAINTEXT, PRE, S, SAMP, SMALL, SPAN, STRIKE, STRONG, SUB, SUP, TABLE, TD, TH, TR, TT, U, UL, VAR, XMP

 UNIX   WIN16   WIN32   MAC

A, ADDRESS, B, BIG, BLOCKQUOTE, BODY, BUTTON, CAPTION, CENTER, CITE, CODE, COL, COLGROUP, DD, DFN, DIR, DIV, DL, DT, EM, FIELDSET, FORM, Hn, HTML, I, IMG, INPUT type=button, INPUT type=checkbox, INPUT type=file, INPUT type=image, INPUT type=password, INPUT type=radio, INPUT type=reset, INPUT type=submit, INPUT type=text, ISINDEX, KBD, LABEL, LEGEND, LI, LISTING, MARQUEE, MENU, OL, P, PLAINTEXT, PRE, S, SAMP, SELECT, SMALL, SPAN, STRIKE, STRONG, style, SUB, SUP, TABLE, TBODY, TD, TEXTAREA, TFOOT, TH, THEAD, TR, TT, U, UL, VAR, XMP

 WIN16   WIN32   MAC   UNIX

currentStyle, runtimeStyle

form Property

Retrieves a reference to the form on which the object is embedded.

Syntax

HTML   N/A

Scripting   [*oForm* =] *object*.**form**

Possible Values

oForm   Form containing the object.

The property is read-only with no default value.

Remarks

Null is returned if the object is not on a form.

Applies To

 WIN16   **WIN32**   **MAC**

INPUT type=button, INPUT type=checkbox, INPUT type=file, INPUT type=hidden, INPUT type=image, INPUT type=password, INPUT type=radio, INPUT type=reset, INPUT type=submit, INPUT type=text, OPTION, SELECT, TEXTAREA

 WIN16   **WIN32**   **MAC**   **UNIX**

APPLET, BUTTON, EMBED, INPUT type=button, INPUT type=checkbox, INPUT type=file, INPUT type=hidden, INPUT type=image, INPUT type=password, INPUT type=radio, INPUT type=reset, INPUT type=submit, INPUT type=text, OBJECT, OPTION, SELECT, TEXTAREA

FRAME Attribute | frame Property

Sets or retrieves the way the border frame around the table is displayed.

Syntax

HTML   <TABLE **FRAME** = "void" | "above" | "below" | "border" | "box" | "hsides" | "lhs" | "rhs" | "vsides" ... >

Scripting   *table*.**frame** [= *sFrame*]

Possible Values

void	All outside table borders are removed.
above	Border on the top side of the border frame is displayed.
below	Border on the bottom side of the table frame is displayed.
border	Borders on all sides of the table frame are displayed.
box	Borders on all sides of the table frame are displayed.
hsides	Borders on the top and bottom sides of the table frame are displayed.
lhs	Border on the left side of the table frame is displayed.
rhs	Border on the right side of the table frame is displayed.
vsides	Borders on the left and right sides of the table frame are displayed.

The property is read/write with a default value of void.

Example

The following example shows how to use the **FRAME** attribute.

```
<TABLE FRAME="above">
<TR><TD>A table with</TD><TD>the value of frame set to "above"</TD></TR>
<TR><TD>cell</TD><TD>cell</TD></TR>
</TABLE>
```

To see this code in action, refer to the Web Workshop CD-ROM.

Applies To

 WIN16   WIN32   MAC

TABLE

 UNIX

TABLE

FRAMEBORDER Attribute | frameBorder Property

Sets or retrieves whether to display a border for the frame.

Syntax

HTML   *<ELEMENT* **FRAMEBORDER** = "1" | "0" | "no" | "yes" ... >

Scripting *object*.**frameBorder** [= *sBorder*]

Possible Values

1   Inset border is drawn.

0   No border is drawn.

no   No border is drawn.

yes Inset border is drawn.

The property is read/write with a default value of 1.

Remarks

Invalid settings default to displaying borders.

Applies To

 WIN16   WIN32   MAC

FRAME, FRAMESET, IFRAME

 UNIX

FRAME, FRAMESET, IFRAME

FRAMESPACING Attribute | frameSpacing Property

Sets or retrieves the amount of additional space between the frames.

Syntax

HTML   <ELEMENT **FRAMESPACING** = *sPixels* ... >

Scripting   *object*.**frameSpacing** [= *sPixels*]

Possible Values

sPixels   String specifying the spacing, in pixels.

The property is read/write with a default value of 2 pixels.

Remarks

The amount defined for **frameSpacing** does not include the width of the frame border. Frame spacing can be set on one or more **FRAMESET** objects and applies to all contained **FRAMESET** objects, unless the contained object defines a different frame spacing.

Applies To

WIN16	WIN32	MAC

FRAMESET

UNIX

FRAMESET

fromElement Property

Retrieves the object the cursor is exiting during the **onmouseover** and **onmouseout** events.

Syntax

HTML   N/A

Scripting   [*oObject* =] *event*.**fromElement**

Possible Values

oObject Element being moved over.

The property is read-only with no default value.

Example

The following example shows how the alert returns "mouse arrived" when the cursor is moved over the button.

```
<SCRIPT>
function testMouse(oObject) {
    if(!oObject.contains(event.fromElement)) {
        alert("mouse arrived");
    }
}
</SCRIPT>
:
<BUTTON ID=oButton onmouseover="testMouse(this)">Mouse Over This.</BUTTON>
```

To see this code in action, refer to the Web Workshop CD-ROM.

Applies To

WIN16	WIN32	MAC	UNIX

event

hash Property

Sets or retrieves the subsection of the **href** property that follows the hash (#) mark.

Syntax

HTML   N/A

Scripting *object*.**hash** [= *sHash*]

Possible Values

sHash String specifying the part of the URL following the hash (#) mark.

The property is read/write with no default value.

Remarks

If there is no hash, this property returns an empty string.

This property is useful for moving to a bookmark within a document. Assigning an invalid value does not cause an error.

Applies To

 WIN16   WIN32   MAC

A, location

 UNIX   WIN16   WIN32   MAC

A, AREA, location

height Property

Retrieves the vertical resolution of the screen.

Syntax

HTML   N/A

Scripting   [*iHeight* =] *screen*.**height**

Possible Values

iHeight   Screen height, in pixels.

The property is read-only with no default value.

Applies To

 WIN16   WIN32   MAC   UNIX

screen

height Attribute | height Property

Sets or retrieves the height of the object.

Syntax

HTML   { **height:**   auto | *height* | *percentage* }

Scripting   *object*.**style.height** [= *sHeight*]

Possible Values

auto   Default height.

height String consisting of a floating-point number, followed by an absolute units designator (cm, mm, in, pt, pc, or px) or a relative units designator (em or ex). For more information about the supported length units for CSS attributes, see "CSS Length Units" in Appendix C.

percentage String value expressed as a percentage of the height of the parent object. Percentage values are specified as a number, followed by %.

The property is read/write with a default value of auto; the CSS attribute is not inherited.

Remarks

If the **height** property of an **IMG** is specified, but the **width** property is not specified, the resulting width of the **IMG** is sized proportionally according to the specified **height** property and the actual width, in pixels, of the image in the source file.

Consider the following example:

Dimensions of image in source file, in pixels: 100 X 50 (W X H)

Specified image height:	2in
Specified image width:	*not specified*
Resulting image height:	2in
Resulting image width:	4in ((100 / 50) * 2 inches)

If the **height** property of an **IMG** is specified, and the height and width of the image in the source file are identical, the width of the image matches the height.

If the **height** property and **width** property of an **IMG** are specified, the resulting image dimensions match those specified.

The height of a block object encompasses **border-top**, **border-bottom**, **padding-top**, **padding-bottom**, **margin-top**, **margin-bottom**, and **height**. The sum of the values of each of the attributes equals the height of the parent object's content.

Percentage values refer to the parent object's height. Negative values are not allowed.

To carry out operations on the numeric value of this property, use **pixelHeight** or **posHeight**.

DHTML Properties

Example

The following examples show how to use the **height** attribute and the **height** property to change the height of the object.

The sample below uses an inline style sheet to set an image's height to 4 centimeters.

```
<IMG SRC="sphere.jpg" STYLE="height:4cm">
```

To see this code in action, refer to the Web Workshop CD-ROM.

The sample below uses inline scripting to change the image's height when an **onclick** event occurs.

```
<BUTTON onclick="height1.style.height='1cm'">Shrink sphere</BUTTON>
```

To see this code in action, refer to the Web Workshop CD-ROM.

Applies To

 WIN16   WIN32   MAC   UNIX

APPLET, BUTTON, DIV, EMBED, FIELDSET, HR, IFRAME, IMG, INPUT type=button, INPUT type=file, INPUT type=image, INPUT type=password, INPUT type=radio, INPUT type=reset, INPUT type=submit, INPUT type=text, ISINDEX, MARQUEE, OBJECT, SPAN, style, TABLE, TEXTAREA

 WIN16   WIN32   MAC   UNIX

currentStyle, INPUT type=checkbox, runtimeStyle, TR

HEIGHT Attribute | height Property

Sets or retrieves the height of the object.

Syntax

HTML   <ELEMENT **HEIGHT** = *sHeight* ["**%**"] ... >

Scripting *object*.**height** [= *sHeight*]

Possible Values

sHeight   Integer specifying the height, in pixels.

sHeight%   Value expressed as a percentage of the parent object's height.

The property is read/write with no default value.

Remarks

If the **height** property of an **IMG** is specified, but the **width** property is not specified, the resulting width of the **IMG** is sized proportionally according to the specified **height** property and the actual width , in pixels, of the image in the source file.

Consider the following example:

Dimensions of image in source file, in pixels:	100 X 50 (W X H)
Specified image height:	2in
Specified image width:	*not specified*
Resulting image height:	2in
Resulting image width:	4in ((100 / 50) * 2 inches)

If the **height** property of an **IMG** is specified, and the height and width of the image in the source file are identical, the width of the image matches the height.

If both the **height** property and the **width** property of an **IMG** are specified, the resulting image dimensions match those specified.

Percentage values are based on the height of the parent object.

When scripting the height property, use either the **pixelHeight** or **posHeight** property to numerically manipulate the height value.

This property specifies the calculated height of the object, in pixels. For table rows and table cells, this property has a range of 0 to 32,750 pixels.

If the value of the corresponding HTML attribute was set using a percentage, this property specifies the height, in pixels, represented by that percentage.

The scripting property is read/write for the **IMG** object, but read-only for other objects.

Applies To

 WIN16   WIN32   MAC

EMBED, IMG, MARQUEE, OBJECT

 UNIX   WIN16   WIN32   MAC

EMBED, FRAME, IMG, MARQUEE, OBJECT, TABLE

hidden Property

Sets or retrieves whether the embedded object is invisible.

Syntax

HTML   N/A

Scripting   *embed*.**hidden** [= *bHidden*]

Possible Values

false   The object is not hidden.

true   The object is hidden.

The property is read/write with a default value of false.

Applies To

 WIN16   **WIN32**   **MAC**   **UNIX**

EMBED

host Property

Sets or retrieves the host name and port number for the location or URL.

Syntax

HTML   N/A

Scripting   *object*.**host** [= *sHost*]

Possible Values

sHost String specifying the host name and port number.

The property is read/write with no default value.

Remarks

The property is the concatenation of the **hostname** and **port** properties, separated by a colon (hostname:port). When the **port** property is null, the **host** property is the same as the **hostname** property.

The **host** property may be set at any time, although it is safer to set the **href** property to change a location. If the specified host cannot be found, an error is returned.

Applies To

 WIN16   WIN32   MAC

A, location

 UNIX   WIN16   WIN32   MAC

A, AREA, location

hostname Property

Sets or retrieves the host name part of the location or URL.

Syntax

HTML   N/A

Scripting   *object*.**hostname** [= *sHostname*]

Possible Values

sHostname   String specifying the host and domain name, or the numerical IP address.

The property is read/write with no default value.

Remarks

If no host name is available, this property returns an empty string.

Applies To

 WIN16   WIN32   MAC

A, location

 UNIX   WIN16   WIN32   MAC

A, AREA, location

hover Pseudo-class

Sets the style of the anchor when the user hovers the mouse over the links.

Syntax

HTML   [A]:hover { *attribute1:parameter1* [; *attribute2:parameter2* [; . . .]] }

Scripting N/A

Possible Values

attribute   Any attribute applicable to text.

parameter Any of the range of values available to the corresponding attribute.

The default value is browser-specific.

Remarks

"Hover" means that the user has the mouse positioned over the link and has hesitated. The style does not change if the user simply passes the mouse over the link. The hover pseudo-class is often used with specific styles for the other states of a link: **active**, **link**, and **visited**.

Using pseudo-classes on objects other than the **A** object has no effect.

The syntax in the example below uses a colon (:) to specify a pseudo-class.

Example

The following example shows how to set the style of an anchor. When the user hovers the mouse over a hyperlink in the document to which the style sheet has been applied, the text is displayed in red, converted to uppercase, and spaced 1 centimeter apart.

```
<STYLE>
    A:hover { color:red; text-transform:uppercase; letter-spacing:1cm }
</STYLE>
```

Applies To

	WIN16	WIN32	MAC	UNIX
A				

href Property

Sets or retrieves the URL of the linked style sheet.

Syntax

> **HTML**   N/A
>
> **Scripting** *object*.**style.href** [= *sURL*]

Possible Values

> *sURL* String specifying the URL.
>
> The property is read/write with no default value.

Remarks

> The property returns the URL if the style sheet is a **LINK**. If the style sheet is a **STYLE**, the property returns NULL.

Applies To

 WIN16   WIN32   MAC   UNIX

> styleSheet

HREF Attribute | href Property

Sets or retrieves the destination URL or anchor point.

Syntax

> **HTML**   <ELEMENT **HREF** = *sURL* ... >
>
> **Scripting** *object*.**href** [= *sURL*]

Possible Values

> *sURL* String specifying the URL or anchor point.
>
> The property is read/write with no default value.

Remarks

HREF attributes on anchors can be used to jump to bookmarks or any object's identification attribute.

When an anchor is specified, the text between the opening and closing anchor tags represents the link to that address.

Applies To

WIN16	WIN32	MAC

A, AREA, LINK

UNIX

A, AREA, LINK

HREF Attribute | href Property

Sets or retrieves the baseline URL on which relative links are based.

Syntax

HTML   <BASE **HREF** = *sURL* ... >

Scripting *base*.**href** [= *sURL*]

Possible Values

sURL   String specifying the URL.

The property is read/write with no default value.

Applies To

WIN16	WIN32	MAC

BASE

UNIX

BASE

href Property

Sets or retrieves the entire URL as a string.

Syntax

HTML N/A

Scripting *location*.**href** [= *sURL*]

Possible Values

sURL String specifying the URL.

The property is read/write with no default value.

Example

The following example shows a select list of URLs. The user is taken to the URL
selected from the options if the selection is a change from the default value of the
select list.

```
<SELECT onchange="window.location.href=this.options[this.selectedIndex].value">
<OPTION VALUE="http://www.microsoft.com/ie">Internet Explorer</OPTION>
<OPTION VALUE="http://www.microsoft.com">Microsoft Home</OPTION>
<OPTION VALUE="http://www.microsoft.com/msdn">Developer Network</OPTION>
</SELECT>
```

Applies To

 WIN16   WIN32   MAC

location

 UNIX

location

HSPACE Attribute | hspace Property

Sets or retrieves the horizontal margin for the object.

Syntax

HTML <ELEMENT **HSPACE** = *iMargin* ... >

Scripting *object*.**hspace** [= *iMargin*]

Possible Values

iMargin Integer specifying the horizontal margin, in pixels.

The property is read/write with a default value of 0.

Remarks

This property is similar to **border**, except the margins don't have color when the element is a link.

Applies To

 WIN16   WIN32   MAC

APPLET, IMG, MARQUEE, OBJECT

 UNIX   WIN16   WIN32   MAC

APPLET, IFRAME, IMG, MARQUEE, OBJECT

FOR Attribute | htmlFor Property

Retrieves the object that is being bound to the event script.

Syntax

HTML   <SCRIPT **FOR** = *oObject* ... >

Scripting [*oObject* =] *script*.**htmlFor**

Possible Values

oObject Scripting object or object identifier.

The property is read-only with no default value.

Applies To

 WIN16   WIN32   MAC

SCRIPT

 UNIX

SCRIPT

FOR Attribute | htmlFor Property

Sets or retrieves the object to which the given label object is assigned.

Syntax

HTML   <LABEL **FOR** = *sID* ... >

Scripting *label*.**htmlFor** [= *sID*]

Possible Values

sID String specifying the identifier of the element to which the label element is assigned.

The property is read/write with no default value.

Applies To

 WIN16   WIN32   MAC   UNIX

LABEL

htmlText Property

Retrieves the HTML source as a valid HTML fragment.

Syntax

HTML   N/A

Scripting [*sTxt* =] *TextRange*.**htmlText**

Possible Values

sTxt String specifying the HTML source.

The property is read-only with no default value.

Remarks

The property corresponds to the fragment portion of the CF_HTML clipboard format.

This feature may not be available on non-Win32® platforms. For the latest information on Microsoft Internet Explorer cross-platform compatibility, see article Q172976 in the Microsoft Knowledge Base.

Applies To

 WIN16   WIN32   MAC   UNIX

TextRange

HTTP-EQUIV Attribute | httpEquiv Property

Sets or retrieves whether the content of the **META** tag is bound to an HTTP response header.

Syntax

HTML   <META **HTTP-EQUIV** = *sInformation* ... >

Scripting *meta*.**httpEquiv** [= *sInformation*]

Possible Values

sInformation String specifying information used in the response header.

The property is read/write with no default value.

Remarks

If the property is omitted, the **name** property should be used to identify the meta-information. The **httpEquiv** property is not case sensitive.

Example

The following example shows how to reload a document every two seconds.

```
<META HTTP-EQUIV="REFRESH" CONTENT=2>
```

Applies To

 WIN16   WIN32   MAC

META

 UNIX

META

ID Attribute | id Property

Retrieves the string identifying the object.

Syntax

HTML   *<ELEMENT* **ID** = *sID* ... >

Scripting   [*sID* =] *object*.**id**

Possible Values

sID   Any alphanumeric string that begins with a letter. The underscore can also be used.

The property is read-only with no default value.

Remarks

The **id** should be unique throughout the scope of the current document. If a document contains more than one object with the same identifier, the objects are exposed as a collection that can be referenced only by ordinal position.

Example

The following example shows how to set the **ID** attribute and then pass this property to a function to manipulate the object to which it is attached.

```
<SCRIPT>
function checkCols(oObject)
{
    var iColumns = oObject.cols;
    alert (iColumns);
}
</SCRIPT>
</HEAD>
<BODY>
<TABLE ID=oTable BORDER COLS=3 onclick="checkCols(this)">
<TR><TD>Column 1</TD><TD>Column 2</TD><TD>Column 3</TD></TR>
</TABLE>
```

To see this code in action, refer to the Web Workshop CD-ROM.

DHTML Properties

Applies To

 WIN16   WIN32   MAC   UNIX

A, ACRONYM, ADDRESS, APPLET, AREA, B, BASE, BASEFONT, BGSOUND, BIG, BLOCKQUOTE, BODY, BR, BUTTON, CAPTION, CENTER, CITE, CODE, COL, COLGROUP, COMMENT, DD, DEL, DFN, DIR, DIV, DL, DT, EM, EMBED, FIELDSET, FONT, FORM, FRAME, FRAMESET, HEAD, Hn, HR, HTML, I, IFRAME, IMG, INPUT type=button, INPUT type=checkbox, INPUT type=file, INPUT type=hidden, INPUT type=image, INPUT type=password, INPUT type=radio, INPUT type=reset, INPUT type=submit, INPUT type=text, INS, ISINDEX, KBD, LABEL, LEGEND, LI, LINK, LISTING, MAP, MARQUEE, MENU, NEXTID, NOBR, NOFRAMES, NOSCRIPT, OBJECT, OL, OPTION, P, PLAINTEXT, PRE, Q, S, SAMP, SCRIPT, SELECT, SMALL, SPAN, STRIKE, STRONG, styleSheet, SUB, SUP, TABLE, TBODY, TD, TEXTAREA, TFOOT, TH, THEAD, TR, TT, U, UL, VAR, WBR, XMP

IE 5   **WIN16   WIN32   MAC   UNIX**

BDO, RT, RUBY, TITLE, XML

ime-mode Attribute | imeMode Property

Sets or retrieves the state of an Input Method Editor (IME) that allows a user to enter Chinese, Japanese, and Korean characters.

Syntax

HTML   { **ime-mode:** auto | *active* | *inactive* | *disabled* }

Scripting *object*.**style.imeMode** [= *sMode*]

Possible Values

auto	Does not affect the status of the IME mode. This is the same as not specifying the **ime-mode** attribute.
active	Specifies that all characters are entered using the IME. Users can still deactivate the IME.
inactive	Specifies that all characters are entered without the IME. Users can still activate the IME.
deactivated	Specifies that the IME is completely disabled. Users cannot activate the IME if the control has focus.

The property is read/write with a default value of `auto`; the proposed cascading style sheets (CSS) extension attribute is inherited.

Remarks

An Input Method Editor (IME) allows users to enter and edit Chinese, Japanese, and Korean characters. The IME is an essential component for writing Chinese, Japanese, and Korean scripts. These writing systems have many more characters than can be encoded for a regular keyboard. The IMEs for these languages use sequences of base characters that describe an individual or group of characters to enter a larger set of characters. Base characters can be component letters from Hangul syllables, phonetic components for Japanese Kanji characters, or various combinations for Chinese characters.

To compose text with an IME, the user generally uses dictionary lookup and a contextual analysis, especially when homonyms are frequent, as in Japanese. A user typically starts by entering a few component characters, optionally selecting from various choices, and a confirmation command.

Input Method Editors have two principle states:

- Inactive mode. The keyboard acts like a regular keyboard and input is limited to a small set of characters.

- Active mode. The IME accepts component characters or other processing commands.

HTML authors can provide some control to users by specifying an IME mode for a specific text entry. For example, if Japanese users enter information in a registration form, they might be required to enter their names in Kanji and Roman characters. By default, the users would have to make sure that the IME is inactive when entering their names in the Latin alphabet. The user would activate the IME to enter Kanji letters, then deactivate the IME to complete the form in the Latin alphabet. By controlling the IME mode, you can prevent the user from having to activate and deactivate the IME.

Example

The following sample illustrates the use of the **ime-mode** attribute.

```
<INPUT TYPE = text STYLE = "ime-mode:active">
```

Applies To

 WIN16   WIN32   MAC   UNIX

INPUT_text, TEXTAREA

@import Rule

Imports an external style sheet.

Syntax

HTML   @**import** url(*sUrl*);

Scripting N/A

Possible Values

sUrl String specifying the URL referencing a cascading style sheet.

The rule has no default value.

Remarks

The semicolon shown in the preceding Syntax section is required; if the semicolon is omitted, the style sheet does not import properly and an error message is generated.

The **@import** rule, like the **LINK** element, links an external style sheet to a document. This rule can help you establish a consistent "look" across multiple HTML pages. Whereas the **LINK** element specifies the name of the style sheet to import using its **HREF** attribute, the **@import** rule specifies the style sheet definition inside a **LINK** object or a **STYLE** tag. In the scripting model, this means the **owningElement** property of the style sheet defined through the **@import** rule is either a **LINK** object or a **STYLE** tag.

The **@import** rule should occur at the start of a style sheet, before any declarations. Although Internet Explorer 4.0 allows **@import** statements to appear anywhere within the style sheet definition, the rules contained within the **@import** style sheet are applied to the document before any other rules defined for the containing style sheet. This rule ordering affects rendering.

Rules in the style sheet override rules in the imported style sheet.

Example

The following example shows how to import a style sheet located at "http://anotherStyleSheet.css".

```
<STYLE type="css/text">
    @import url(http://anotherStyleSheet.css);
    P {color:blue}
</STYLE>
```

!important Declaration

Increases the weight or importance of a particular rule.

Syntax

HTML	{ *sAttribute:sValue***!important** }
Scripting	N/A

Possible Values

sAttribute	Any cascading style sheets (CSS) attribute.
sValue	Any of the range of values available to the corresponding attribute.

The declaration has no default value.

Example

The following example shows how to use the **!important** declaration on a style rule. The color of the text would normally be green because inline styles overrule the rules set in a **STYLE** tag. The **!important** declaration in the following style rule, however, sets the paragraph contents to red.

```
<STYLE>
    P {color:red!important}
</STYLE>
<P STYLE="color:green">This will be red.</P>
```

Applies To

 WIN16   WIN32   MAC   UNIX

A, ADDRESS, B, BIG, BLOCKQUOTE, BODY, CAPTION, CENTER, CITE, CODE, COL, COLGROUP, DD, DFN, DIR, DIV, DL, DT, EM, FIELDSET, FORM, Hn, HTML, I, IMG, INPUT type=button, INPUT type=checkbox, INPUT type=file, INPUT type=hidden, INPUT type=image, INPUT type=password, INPUT type=radio, INPUT type=reset, INPUT type=submit, INPUT type=text, KBD, LABEL, LEGEND, LI, LISTING, MARQUEE, MENU, OL, P, PLAINTEXT, PRE, S, SAMP, SELECT, SMALL, SPAN, STRIKE, STRONG, SUB, SUP, TABLE, TBODY, TD, TEXTAREA, TFOOT, TH, THEAD, TR, TT, U, UL, VAR, XMP

indeterminate Property

Sets or retrieves whether the user has changed the status of a check box.

Syntax

HTML   N/A

Scripting   *checkbox*.**indeterminate** [= *bDim*]

Possible Values

false   The check box is not dimmed.

true   The check box is checked and dimmed.

The property is read/write with a default value of false.

Remarks

When **indeterminate** is set to true, the check box appears checked, but dimmed, indicating an indeterminate state. The **indeterminate** property can be used to indicate that the user has not acted on the control.

The value of **indeterminate** is independent of the values for the **checked** and **status** properties. Creating an indeterminate state is different from disabling the control. Consequently, a check box in the indeterminate state can still receive the focus. When the user clicks an indeterminate control, the indeterminate state is turned off and the checked state of the check box is toggled.

Applies To

 WIN16   WIN32   MAC   UNIX

INPUT type=checkbox

index Property

Sets or retrieves the ordinal position of the option in the list box.

Syntax

HTML   N/A

Scripting   *option*.**index**[= *iIndex*]

Possible Values

iIndex Integer specifying the ordinal position.

The property is read/write with no default value.

Applies To

WIN16   WIN32   MAC

OPTION

UNIX

OPTION

DHTML Properties

innerHTML Property

Sets or retrieves the HTML between the start and end tags of the object.

Syntax

HTML   N/A

Scripting *object*.**innerHTML** [= *sHTML*]

Possible Values

sHTML String specifying the contents between the start and end tags.

The property is read/write with no default value.

Remarks

The property takes a string specifying a valid combination of text and elements, except for the **HTML**, **HEAD**, **FRAME**, and **TITLE** elements.

When the **innerHTML** property is set, the given string completely replaces the existing content of the object. If the string contains HTML tags, the string is parsed and formatted as it is placed into the document.

This property is accessible at run time as of Internet Explorer 5. Removing elements at run time before the closing tag has been parsed could prevent other areas of the document from rendering.

When inserting script using **innerHTML**, you must include the **DEFER** attribute in the **SCRIPT** element.

The **innerHTML** property is read-only on the **HTML**, **TABLE**, **TBODY**, **TFOOT**, **THEAD**, and **TR** objects.

Example

The following example shows how to use the **innerHTML** property. The affected text and any tags within it are changed by the events.

```
<P onmouseover="this.innerHTML='<B>Mouse out
    to change back.</B>'"
    onmouseout="this.innerHTML='<I>
    Mouse over again to change.</I>'">
    <I>Mouse over this text to change it.</I></P>
```

To see this code in action, refer to the Web Workshop CD-ROM.

The next example shows how to use the **innerHTML** property to insert script into the page.

```
var sHTML="<input type=button onclick=" + "
    go2()" + " value='Click Me'><BR>"
var sScript='<SCRIPT DEFER>'
    sScript = sScript + 'function go2()
    { alert("Hello from inserted script.") }'
sScript = sScript + '</script' + '>';
ScriptDiv.innerHTML=sHTML + sScript;
```

To see this code in action, refer to the Web Workshop CD-ROM.

Applies To

 WIN16   WIN32   MAC   UNIX

A, ACRONYM, ADDRESS, B, BIG, BLOCKQUOTE, BODY, BUTTON, CAPTION, CENTER, CITE, CODE, DD, DEL, DFN, DIR, DIV, DL, DT, EM, FIELDSET, FONT, FORM, Hn, I, IFRAME, INS, KBD, LABEL, LEGEND, LI, LISTING, MAP, MARQUEE, MENU, NEXTID, NOBR, OL, P, PRE, Q, S, SAMP, SMALL, SPAN, STRIKE, STRONG, SUB, SUP, TABLE, TBODY, TD, TFOOT, TH, TT, U, UL, VAR

 WIN16   WIN32   MAC   UNIX

BDO, HEAD, HTML, OPTION, RT, RUBY, SCRIPT, SELECT, STYLE, THEAD, TR, XMP

innerText Property

Sets or retrieves the text between the start and end tags of the object.

Syntax

HTML   N/A

Scripting *object*.**innerText** [= *sTxt*]

Possible Values

sTxt String of text.

The property is read/write with no default value.

Remarks

When the property is set, the given string completely replaces the existing content of the object, except for **HTML**, **HEAD**, and **TITLE** tags.

You cannot set this property while the document is loading. Wait for the **onload** event before attempting to set the property. When dynamically creating a tag using the **TextRange**, **innerHTML**, or **outerHTML** properties, use JScript (compatible with ECMA 262 language specification) to create new events to handle the newly formed tags. Visual Basic Scripting Edition (VBScript) is not supported.

The **innerText** property is read-only on the **HTML**, **TABLE**, **TBODY**, **TFOOT**, **THEAD**, and **TR** objects.

Example

The following example shows how to use the **innerText** property to replace an object's contents. The object surrounding the text is not replaced.

```
<P ID=oPara>Here's the text that will change.</P>
:
<BUTTON onclick="oPara.innerText='WOW! It changed!'">Change text</BUTTON>
<BUTTON onclick="oPara.innerText='And back again'">Reset</BUTTON>
```

To see this code in action, refer to the Web Workshop CD-ROM.

Applies To

 WIN16　WIN32　MAC　UNIX

A, ACRONYM, ADDRESS, B, BIG, BLOCKQUOTE, BODY, BUTTON, CAPTION, CENTER, CITE, CODE, DD, DEL, DFN, DIR, EM, FIELDSET, FONT, FORM, Hn, I, IFRAME, INS, KBD, LABEL, LEGEND, LI, LISTING, MAP, MARQUEE, MENU, OL, P, PLAINTEXT, PRE, Q, S, SAMP, SMALL, SPAN, STRIKE, STRONG, SUB, SUP, TD, TEXTAREA, TH, TITLE, TT, U, UL, VAR, XMP

IE 5 **WIN16　WIN32　MAC　UNIX**

BDO, HEAD, HTML, NEXTID, NOBR, OPTION, RT, RUBY, SCRIPT, SELECT, STYLE, TABLE, TBODY, TEXTAREA, TFOOT, THEAD, TR, XMP

ISMAP Attribute | isMap Property

Retrieves whether the image is a server-side image map.

Syntax

HTML　　<IMG **ISMAP** ... >

Scripting　[*bMap* =] *img*.**isMap**

Possible Values

false	The image is not a server-side map.
true	The image is a server-side map.

The property is read-only with a default value of false.

Applies To

 WIN16　WIN32　MAC

IMG

 UNIX

IMG

isTextEdit Property

Retrieves whether a **TextRange** object can be created using the given object.

Syntax

HTML	N/A
Scripting	[*bEdit* =] *object*.**isTextEdit**

Possible Values

false	A **TextRange** object cannot be created.
true	A **TextRange** object can be created.

The property is read-only with no default value.

Remarks

Only the **BODY**, **BUTTON**, and **TEXTAREA** objects, and an **INPUT** object having a **button**, **hidden**, **password**, **reset**, **submit**, or **text** type, can be used to create a **TextRange** object.

Applies To

WIN16   WIN32   MAC

OPTION

WIN16   WIN32   MAC   UNIX

A, ACRONYM, ADDRESS, APPLET, AREA, B, BASE, BASEFONT, BIG, BLOCKQUOTE, BODY, BR, BUTTON, CAPTION, CENTER, CITE, CODE, COL, COLGROUP, COMMENT, DD, DEL, DFN, DIR, DIV, DL, DT, EM, EMBED, FIELDSET, FONT, FORM, FRAME, FRAMESET, HEAD, Hn, HR, HTML, I, IFRAME, IMG, INPUT type=button, INPUT type=checkbox, INPUT type=file, INPUT type=hidden, INPUT type=image, INPUT type=password, INPUT type=radio, INPUT type=reset, INPUT type=submit, INPUT type=text, INS, KBD, LABEL, LEGEND, LI, LINK, LISTING, MAP, MARQUEE, MENU, META, NEXTID, NOBR, OBJECT, OL, OPTION, P, PLAINTEXT, PRE, Q, S, SAMP, SCRIPT, SELECT, SMALL, SPAN, STRIKE, STRONG, SUB, SUP, TABLE, TBODY, TD, TEXTAREA, TFOOT, TH, THEAD, TITLE, TR, TT, U, UL, VAR, XMP

Text along right margin: **DHTML Properties**

IE 5 **WIN16**   **WIN32**   **MAC**   **UNIX**

BDO

keyCode Property

Sets or retrieves the Unicode key code associated with the key that caused the event.

Syntax

HTML   N/A

Scripting *event*.**keyCode** [= *sKeyCode*]

Possible Values

sKeyCode   String specifying the Unicode key code.

The property is read/write with no default value.

Remarks

The property is used with the **onkeydown**, **onkeyup**, and **onkeypress** events.

The property's value is 0 if no key caused the event.

Applies To

IE 4 **WIN16**   **WIN32**   **MAC**   **UNIX**

event

LANG Attribute | lang Property

Sets or retrieves the language to use.

Syntax

HTML   *<ELEMENT* **LANG** = *sLanguage* ... >

Scripting *object*.**lang** [= *sLanguage*]

Possible Values

sLanguage   String specifying an ISO standard language abbreviation.

The property is read/write with no default value.

Remarks

The parser can use this property to determine how to display language-specific choices for quotations, numbers, and so on.

Applies To

WIN16   WIN32   MAC   UNIX

A, ACRONYM, ADDRESS, APPLET, AREA, B, BIG, BLOCKQUOTE, BODY, BUTTON, CAPTION, CENTER, CITE, CODE, COL, COLGROUP, COMMENT, DD, DEL, DFN, DIR, DIV, DL, DT, EM, EMBED, FIELDSET, FONT, FORM, FRAME, FRAMESET, HEAD, Hn, I, IFRAME, IMG, INPUT type=button, INPUT type=checkbox, INPUT type=file, INPUT type=hidden, INPUT type=image, INPUT type=password, INPUT type=radio, INPUT type=reset, INPUT type=submit, INPUT type=text, INS, ISINDEX, KBD, LABEL, LEGEND, LI, LISTING, MAP, MARQUEE, MENU, NEXTID, NOBR, OBJECT, OL, OPTION, P, PLAINTEXT, PRE, Q, S, SAMP, SCRIPT, SELECT, SMALL, SPAN, STRIKE, STRONG, SUB, SUP, TABLE, TBODY, TD, TEXTAREA, TFOOT, TH, THEAD, TITLE, TR, TT, U, UL, VAR, XMP

WIN16   WIN32   MAC   UNIX

BDO, RT, RUBY

LANGUAGE Attribute | language Property

Sets or retrieves the language in which the current script is written.

Syntax

HTML   **LANGUAGE** = "JScript" | "javascript" | "vbs" | "vbscript" | "XML"| *sLanguage*

Scripting   *object*.**language** [= *sLanguage*]

Possible Values

JScript   Specifies that the language is JScript (compatible with ECMA 262 language specification).

javascript Specifies that the script is JavaScript.

vbs   Specifies that the language is Visual Basic Scripting Edition (VBScript).

Possible Values *(continued)*

vbscript   Specifies that the script is VBScript.

XML   Specifies that the script is XML.

sLanguage String specifying a browser-supported language.

The property is read/write with no default value.

Remarks

The property can refer to any scripting language. Internet Explorer 4.0 ships with JScript and VBScript scripting engines.

In Internet Explorer, the default scripting engine is JScript.

In Internet Explorer 5, the **LANGUAGE** attribute of the **SCRIPT** element can be set to XML.

Applies To

 WIN16   WIN32   MAC   UNIX

A, ACRONYM, ADDRESS, APPLET, AREA, B, BIG, BLOCKQUOTE, BODY, BUTTON, CAPTION, CENTER, CITE, CODE, DD, DEL, DFN, DIR, DIV, DL, DT, EM, EMBED, FIELDSET, FONT, FORM, FRAME, FRAMESET, Hn, HR, I, IFRAME, IMG, INPUT type=button, INPUT type=checkbox, INPUT type=file, INPUT type=hidden, INPUT type=image, INPUT type=password, INPUT type=radio, INPUT type=reset, INPUT type=submit, INPUT type=text, INS, ISINDEX, KBD, LABEL, LEGEND, LI, LISTING, MAP, MARQUEE, NEXTID, NOBR, OBJECT, OL, OPTION, P, PLAINTEXT, PRE, Q, S, SAMP, SCRIPT, SELECT, SMALL, SPAN, STRIKE, STRONG, SUB, SUP, TABLE, TBODY, TD, TEXTAREA, TFOOT, TH, THEAD, TR, TT, U, UL, VAR, XMP

 WIN16   WIN32   MAC   UNIX

BDO, RT, RUBY

lastChild Property

Retrieves a reference to the last child in the **childNodes** collection of an object.

Syntax

HTML	N/A

Scripting [*oElement* =] *object*.**lastChild**

Possible Values

oElement   Last child object.

The property is read-only with no default value.

Example

The following example shows how to use the **lastChild** property to obtain a reference to the last child element of an object.

```
<SCRIPT>
var olastChild = oList.lastChild;
</SCRIPT>

<BODY>
<UL ID = oList>
<LI>List Item 1
<LI>List Item 2
<LI>List Item 3
</UL>
<BODY>
```

Applies To

WIN16	WIN32	MAC	UNIX

A, ACRONYM, ADDRESS, APPLET, AREA, B, BASE, BASEFONT, BDO, BIG, BLOCKQUOTE, BODY, BUTTON, CAPTION, CENTER, CITE, CODE, COL, COLGROUP, COMMENT, DD, DEL, DFN, DIR, DIV, DL, DT, EM, EMBED, FIELDSET, FONT, FORM, FRAME, FRAMESET, HEAD, Hn, HR, HTML, I, IFRAME, IMG, INPUT type=button, INPUT type=checkbox, INPUT type=file, INPUT type=image, INPUT type=password, INPUT type=radio, INPUT type=reset, INPUT type=submit, INPUT type=text, INS, KBD, LABEL, LEGEND, LI, LINK, LISTING, MAP, MARQUEE, MENU, NEXTID, OL, OPTION, P, PLAINTEXT,

Applies To *(continued)*

WIN16   WIN32   MAC   UNIX

PRE, Q, S, SAMP, SCRIPT, SELECT, SMALL, SPAN, STRIKE, STRONG, SUB, SUP, TABLE, TBODY, TD, TEXTAREA, TFOOT, TH, THEAD, TITLE, TR, TT, U, UL, VAR, XMP

lastModified Property

Retrieves the date the page was last modified if the page supplies one.

Syntax

HTML   N/A

Scripting   [*sModified* =] *document*.**lastModified**

Possible Values

sModified   String specifying the most recent date the page was modified, in the form "MM/DD/YY hh:mm:ss".

The property is read-only with no default value.

Applies To

WIN16   WIN32   MAC

document

UNIX

document

layout-grid Attribute | layoutGrid Property

Sets or retrieves the composite document grid properties that specify the layout of text characters.

Syntax

HTML   { **layout-grid:** *sMode* ‖ *sType* ‖ *sLine* ‖ *sChar* ‖ *sSpace* }

Scripting   *oObject*.**style.layoutGrid** [= [*sMode*] [*sType*] [*sLine*] [*sChar*] [*sSpace*]]

Possible Values

sMode Any of the range of values available to the **layoutGridMode** property.

sType Any of the range of values available to the **layoutGridType** property.

sLine Any of the range of values available to the **layoutGridLine** property.

sChar Any of the range of values available to the **layoutGridChar** property.

sSpace Any of the range of values available to the **layoutGridCharSpacing** property.

The property is read/write with no default value; the proposed cascading style sheets (CSS) extension attribute is inherited.

Remarks

Web documents in East Asian languages, such as Chinese or Japanese, commonly use page layout for characters according to a one- or two-dimensional grid. You can use the **layout-grid** attribute to incorporate this layout in Web documents.

Example

The following example shows how to use the **layout-grid** attribute to specify character layout for a block of text.

```
<STYLE>
DIV.layout { layout-grid: char line 12px 12px .5in }
</STYLE>

<DIV CLASS = "layout">
This is a block element containing a sentence of sample text.
</DIV>
```

Applies To

WIN16	WIN32	MAC	UNIX

style

WIN16	WIN32	MAC	UNIX

BLOCKQUOTE, BODY, CENTER, DD, DIR, DIV, DL, DT, FIELDSET, FORM, Hn, HR, LI, LISTING, MARQUEE, MENU, OL, P, PLAINTEXT, PRE, runtimeStyle, TABLE, TD, TH, TR, UL, XMP

layout-grid-char Attribute | layoutGridChar Property

Sets or retrieves the size of the character grid used for rendering the text contents of an element.

Syntax

HTML	{ **layout-grid-char:** none	auto	*length*	*percentage* }
Scripting	*oObject*.**style.layoutGridChar** [= *vCharSize*]

Possible Values

none	String specifying that no character grid is set.
auto	String specifying that the grid is determined by the largest character in the font of the element.
length	String consisting of a floating-point number, followed by an absolute units designator (cm, mm, in, pt, pc, or px) or a relative units designator (em or ex). For more information about the supported length units for CSS attributes, see "CSS Length Units" in Appendix C.
percentage	String value expressed as a percentage derived from the dimensions of the parent object. Percentage values are specified as a number, followed by a %.

The property is read/write with a default value of none; the proposed cascading style sheets (CSS) extension attribute is inherited.

Remarks

The visual effects of the **layout-grid-char** attribute are similar to the **lineHeight** property.

Web documents in East Asian languages, such as Chinese or Japanese, commonly use page layout for characters according to a one- or two-dimensional grid.

The **layout-grid-char** attribute only applies to block-level elements.

Note For this property to have an effect, the **layout-grid-mode** attribute must be set to line or both.

Example

The following example shows how to use the **layout-grid-char** attribute to specify character layout for a block of text.

```
<STYLE>
DIV.layout { layout-grid-char: auto }
</STYLE>

<DIV CLASS = "layout">
This is a block element containing a sentence of sample text.
</DIV>
```

Applies To

	WIN16	WIN32	MAC	UNIX

style

	WIN16	WIN32	MAC	UNIX

BLOCKQUOTE, BODY, CENTER, currentStyle, DD, DIR, DIV, DL, DT, FIELDSET, FORM, Hn, HR, LI, LISTING, MARQUEE, MENU, OL, P, PLAINTEXT, PRE, runtimeStyle, TABLE, TD, TH, TR, UL, XMP

layout-grid-char-spacing Attribute | layoutGridCharSpacing Property

Sets or retrieves the character spacing to use for rendering the text contents of an element with the **layout-grid-type** attribute set to loose.

Syntax

HTML   { **layout-grid-char-spacing:** auto | *iLength* | *iPercent* }

Scripting *oObject*.**style.layoutGridCharSpacing** [= *vCharSpace*]

Possible Values

auto   String specifying that the grid is determined by the largest character in the font of the element.

iLength Floating-point number and an absolute units designator (cm, mm, in, pt, pc, or px) or a relative units designator (em or ex).

iPercent Percentage derived from the dimensions of the parent.

The property is read/write with a default value of `auto`; the proposed cascading style sheets (CSS) extension attribute is inherited.

Remarks

The visual effects of the **layout-grid-char-spacing** attribute are similar to the **lineHeight** property.

Web documents in East Asian languages, such as Chinese or Japanese, commonly use page layout for characters according to a one- or two-dimensional grid.

The **layout-grid-char-spacing** attribute only applies to block-level elements.

Note For this property to have an effect, the **layout-grid-mode** attribute must be set to `char` or `both`, and the **layout-grid-type** attribute must be set to `loose`.

Example

The following example shows how to use the **layout-grid-char-spacing** attribute to specify character layout for a block of text.

```
<STYLE>
DIV.layout { layout-grid-char-spacing: auto }
</STYLE>

<DIV CLASS = "layout">
This is a block element containing a sentence of sample text.
</DIV>
```

Applies To

WIN16	WIN32	MAC	UNIX

style

WIN16	WIN32	MAC	UNIX

BLOCKQUOTE, BODY, CENTER, currentStyle, DD, DIR, DIV, DL, DT, FIELDSET, FORM, Hn, HR, LI, LISTING, MARQUEE, MENU, OL, P, PLAINTEXT, PRE, runtimeStyle, TABLE, TD, TH, TR, UL, XMP

layout-grid-line Attribute | layoutGridLine Property

Sets or retrieves the line grid value to use for rendering the text contents of an element.

DHTML Properties

Syntax

HTML	{ **layout-grid-line:** none	auto	*Length*	*Percentage* }
Scripting	*oObject*.**style.layoutGridLine** [= *vLineSpace*]

Possible Values

none	String indicating that no line grid is specified.
auto	String specifying the grid is determined by the largest character in the font of the element.
Length	String consisting of a floating-point number, followed by an absolute units designator (cm, mm, in, pt, pc, or px) or a relative units designator (em or ex). For more information about the supported length units for CSS attributes, see "CSS Length Units" in Appendix C.
Percentage	String value expressed as a percentage derived from the dimensions of the parent object. Percentage values are specified as a number, followed by a %.

The property is read/write with a default value of none; the proposed cascading style sheets (CSS) extension attribute is inherited.

Remarks

The visual effects of the **layout-grid-line** attribute are similar to the **lineHeight** property.

Web documents in East Asian languages, such as Chinese or Japanese, commonly use page layout for characters according to a one- or two-dimensional grid.

The **layout-grid-line** attribute only applies to block-level elements.

Note For this property to have an effect, the **layout-grid-mode** attribute must be set to line or both.

Example

The following example shows how to use the **layout-grid-line** attribute to specify character layout for a block of text.

```
<STYLE>
DIV.layout { layout-grid-line: auto }
</STYLE>

<DIV CLASS = "layout">
This is a block element containing a sentence of sample text.
</DIV>
```

Applies To

WIN16	**WIN32**	**MAC**	**UNIX**

style

WIN16	**WIN32**	**MAC**	**UNIX**

BLOCKQUOTE, BODY, CENTER, currentStyle, DD, DIR, DIV, DL, DT, FIELDSET, FORM, Hn, HR, LI, LISTING, MARQUEE, MENU, OL, P, PLAINTEXT, PRE, runtimeStyle, TABLE, TD, TH, TR, UL, XMP

layout-grid-mode Attribute | layoutGridMode Property

Sets or retrieves whether the text layout grid uses two dimensions.

Syntax

HTML   { **layout-grid-mode:** none I line I char I both }

Scripting *oObject*.**style.layoutGridMode** [= *sMode*]

Possible Values

both String specifying that both char and line grid modes are enabled. This setting is necessary to fully enable layout grid on an element.

none String specifying that no grid is used.

line String specifying that only a line grid is used. This is recommended for use with inline elements, such as a **SPAN**, to disable the horizontal grid on runs of text that act as a single entity in the grid layout.

Possible Values *(continued)*

char String specifying that only a character grid is used. This is recommended for use with block-level elements, such as a **BLOCKQUOTE**, where the line grid is intended to be disabled.

The property is read/write with a default value of both; the proposed cascading style sheets (CSS) extension attribute is inherited.

Remarks

Web documents in East Asian languages, such as Chinese or Japanese, commonly use page layout for characters according to a one- or two-dimensional grid.

Example

The following example shows how to use the **layout-grid-mode** attribute to specify character layout for a block of text.

```
<STYLE>
DIV.layout {  layout-grid-mode: line }
</STYLE>

<DIV CLASS = "layout">
This is a block element containing a sentence of sample text.
</DIV>
```

Applies To

 WIN16   WIN32   MAC   UNIX

style

IE 5 **WIN16   WIN32   MAC   UNIX**

A, ACRONYM, ADDRESS, APPLET, AREA, B, BASE, BASEFONT, BDO, BIG, BLOCKQUOTE, BODY, BR, BUTTON, CAPTION, CENTER, CITE, CODE, COL, COLGROUP, currentStyle, DD, DEL, DFN, DIR, DIV, DL, DT, EM, EMBED, FIELDSET, FONT, FORM, FRAME, FRAMESET, HEAD, Hn, HR, I, IFRAME, IMG, INPUT type=button, INPUT type=checkbox, INPUT type=file, INPUT type=image, INPUT type=password, INPUT type=radio, INPUT type=reset, INPUT type=submit, INPUT type=text, INS, KBD, LABEL, LEGEND, LI, LISTING, MAP, MARQUEE, MENU, META, NEXTID, NOBR, OBJECT, OL, OPTION, P, PLAINTEXT, PRE, Q, RT, RUBY, runtimeStyle, S, SAMP, SCRIPT, SELECT, SMALL, SPAN, STRIKE, STRONG, SUB, SUP, TABLE, TBODY, TD, TEXTAREA, TFOOT, TH, THEAD, TR, TT, U, UL, VAR, XMP

DHTML Properties

layout-grid-type Attribute | layoutGridType Property

Sets or retrieves the type of grid to use for rendering the text contents of an element.

Syntax

HTML { **layout-grid-type:** `loose` | `strict` | `fixed` }

Scripting *oObject*.**style.layoutGridType** [= *sType*]

Possible Values

`loose` String indicating the grid used in Chinese (Genko) and Korean. Only the ideographs, kanas, and wide characters are snapped to the grid. Other characters are rendered as usual as though the **layout-grid-mode** attribute was set to `none` or `line` for text spans containing those characters. This mode also disables special text justification and character width adjustments normally applied to the element. Finally, if a line break opportunity cannot be found in a text span that goes over the line boundary, the text is pushed to the next line and the last part of the previous line is left blank.

`strict` String indicating the grid used in Japanese. In this mode, a constant width increment is applied to characters as follows:

- The wide characters are incremented to obtain an exact grid fit if no other width adjustment effect is applied.

- Narrow characters (except cursive scripts and cursive fonts) are incremented by half the increment applied to wide characters.

`fixed` String indicating the grid used for monospaced layout. The layout rules are:

- All noncursive characters are treated as equal; every character is centered within a single grid space by default.

- Runs of cursive characters are treated as strips the same way as in a `strict` grid.

- Justification or any other character-width changing behaviors are disabled.

The property is read/write with a default value of `loose`; the proposed cascading style sheets (CSS) extension attribute is inherited.

Remarks

Web documents in East Asian languages, such as Chinese or Japanese, commonly use page layout for characters according to a one- or two-dimensional grid.

The **layout-grid-type** attribute only applies to block-level elements.

Example

The following example shows how to use the **layout-grid-type** attribute to specify character layout for a block of text.

```
<STYLE>
DIV.layout { layout-grid-type: strict }
</STYLE>

<DIV CLASS = "layout">
This is a block element containing a sentence of sample text.
</DIV>
```

Applies To

WIN16	WIN32	MAC	UNIX

style

WIN16	WIN32	MAC	UNIX

BLOCKQUOTE, BODY, CENTER, currentStyle, DD, DIR, DIV, DL, DT, FIELDSET, FORM, Hn, HR, LI, LISTING, MARQUEE, MENU, OL, P, PLAINTEXT, PRE, runtimeStyle, TABLE, TD, TH, TR, UL, XMP

left Attribute | left Property

Sets or retrieves the position of the object relative to the left edge of the next positioned object in the document hierarchy.

Syntax

HTML   { **left:** auto | *length* | *percentage* }

Scripting *object*.**style.left** [= *sLeft*]

Possible Values

> auto   Default position according to the regular HTML layout of the page.
>
> *length*   Floating-point number and an absolute units designator (cm, mm, in, pt, pc, or px) or a relative units designator (em or ex).
>
> *percentage* Value expressed as a percentage of the height of the parent object.

> The property is read/write with a default value of auto; the cascading style sheets (CSS) attribute is not inherited.

Remarks

> This property is used with the **position** attribute. This value corresponds to the **offsetLeft** property of the object and does not include the border of the parent object.
>
> When scripting the **left** property, use either the **pixelLeft** or **posLeft** property for numeric manipulation of a **left** value.

Example

> The following examples show how to use the **left** attribute and the **left** property to change the position of the object.
>
> The sample below uses an inline style sheet to set the position of an image 100 pixels to the right of the parent object's left edge.

```
<DIV STYLE="position:absolute;left:100px">
<IMG SRC="cone.jpg"></DIV>
```

> To see this code in action, refer to the Web Workshop CD-ROM.
>
> The sample below uses inline scripting to change the images' position on an **onclick** event.

```
<BUTTON onclick="cone.style.left='100px'; sphere.style.left='200px'">
. . .</BUTTON>
```

> To see this code in action, refer to the Web Workshop CD-ROM.

Applies To

 WIN16   **WIN32**   **MAC**

> HR

WIN16 WIN32 MAC UNIX

A, ADDRESS, APPLET, B, BIG, BLOCKQUOTE, BUTTON, CENTER, CITE, CODE, DD, DFN, DIR, DIV, DL, DT, EM, EMBED, FIELDSET, FORM, Hn, HR, I, IFRAME, IMG, INPUT type=button, INPUT type=checkbox, INPUT type=file, INPUT type=image, INPUT type=password, INPUT type=radio, INPUT type=reset, INPUT type=submit, INPUT type=text, ISINDEX, KBD, LABEL, LEGEND, LI, LISTING, MARQUEE, MENU, OBJECT, OL, P, PRE, S, SAMP, SELECT, SMALL, SPAN, STRIKE, STRONG, style, SUB, SUP, TABLE, TEXTAREA, TT, U, UL, VAR, XMP

 WIN16 WIN32 MAC UNIX

currentStyle, runtimeStyle

left Property

Retrieves the left coordinate of the rectangle surrounding the object content.

Syntax

HTML   N/A

Scripting [*iCoord =*] *oTextRectangle*.**left**

Possible Values

iCoord   Integer specifying the left coordinate of the rectangle, in pixels.

The property is read-only with no default value.

Remarks

Use the following syntax to access the left coordinate of the second text rectangle of a **TextRange** object:

```
oRct = oTextRange.getClientRects();
oRct[1].left;
```

The collection index starts at 0, so the second item index is 1.

Use the following syntax to access the left coordinate of the bounding rectangle of an element object:

```
oBndRct = oElement.getBoundingClientRect();
oBndRct.left;
```

Example

The following example shows how to retrieve the coordinates of the bounds of the text rectangles within the element.

```
<SCRIPT>
function getCoords(oObject) {
    oBndRct=oObject.getBoundingClientRect();
    alert("Bounding rectangle = \nUpperleft coordinates: "
        + oBndRct.left + " " + oBndRct.top +
        "\nLowerright coordinates: "
        + oBndRct.right + " " + oBndRct.bottom);
}
</SCRIPT>
</HEAD>
<BODY>
<P ID=oPara onclick="getCoords(this)">
```

To see this code in action, refer to the Web Workshop CD-ROM.

Applies To

 WIN16   WIN32   MAC   UNIX

TextRectangle

LEFTMARGIN Attribute | leftMargin Property

Sets or retrieves the left margin for the entire body of the page, overriding the default margin.

Syntax

HTML   <BODY **LEFTMARGIN** = *sMargin* ... >

Scripting   *body*.**leftMargin** [= *sMargin*]

Possible Values

sMargin   String specifying the left margin, in pixels.

The property is read/write with a default value of 10.

Remarks

If the value is set to "", the left margin is exactly on the left edge.

Applies To

 WIN16   WIN32   MAC   UNIX

BODY

length Property

Retrieves the number of objects in a collection.

Syntax

HTML   N/A

Scripting [*iLength* =] *object*.**length**

Possible Values

iLength   Integer specifying the number of objects.

The property is read-only with no default value (see Remarks section).

Remarks

The **window.length** property returns the number of frames contained in a window.

Although this property is read-only for most of the objects listed in Applies To, it is read/write for the **areas** collection (image maps), **options** collection (select boxes), and the **SELECT** object.

In all other cases, this property has read-only permission, which means that you can retrieve, but not change, its current value.

Applies To

 WIN16   WIN32   MAC

anchors, elements, forms, history, links, options, SELECT

 WIN16   WIN32   MAC   UNIX

all, anchors, applets, areas, bookmarks, cells, children, elements, embeds, filters, forms, frames, history, images, imports, links, options, plugins, rows, rules, scripts, SELECT, styleSheets, tbodies, window

WIN16   WIN32   MAC   UNIX

attributes, behaviorUrns, boundElements, childNodes, controlRange, TextRectangle

length Property

Retrieves the number of characters in a **TextNode** object.

Syntax

HTML   N/A

Scripting [*iLength* =] *object*.**length**

Possible Values

iLength   Integer specifying the number of characters in a **TextNode** object.

The property is read-only with no default value.

Example

The following example shows how to use the **length** property to specify where a **TextNode** is split using the **splitText** method.

```
<SCRIPT>
function fnChangeValue(){
    var oListItem = document.createElement("LI");
    oList.appendChild(oListItem);
    var oNode = oList.firstChild.childNodes(0);
    var oTextNode = oList.firstChild.childNodes(0);
    var oSplit = oTextNode.splitText(oTextNode.length/2);
    oListItem.appendChild(oSplit);

}
</SCRIPT>

<UL ID = oList onclick = "fnChangeValue()">
<LI>Start Here
</UL>
```

Applies To

 WIN16   WIN32   MAC   UNIX

TextNode

letter-spacing Attribute | letterSpacing Property

Sets or retrieves the amount of additional space between letters in the object.

Syntax

HTML   { **letter-spacing:**   normal | *length* }

Scripting   *object*.**style.letterSpacing** [= *sSpacing*]

Possible Values

normal   Default spacing.

length   Floating-point number and an absolute units designator (cm, mm, in, pt, pc, or px) or a relative units designator (em or ex).

The property is read/write with a default value of normal; the cascading style sheets (CSS) attribute is inherited.

Remarks

The attribute adds the specified letter spacing after each character. To avoid affecting the spacing at the end of a word, place the last character outside the closing tag. Letter spacing can be influenced by justification. To add the length value to the default space between characters, you can use negative values.

Example

The following examples show how to use the **letter-spacing** attribute and the **letterSpacing** property to change the space between letters.

The sample below uses **BLOCKQUOTE** as a selector to change the spacing to -0.2 millimeters for all **BLOCKQUOTE** objects on the page.

```
<STYLE>
    BLOCKQUOTE { letter-spacing: -0.2mm }
</STYLE>
```

To see this code in action, refer to the Web Workshop CD-ROM.

DHTML Properties

The sample below uses inline scripting to set the spacing to 1 millimeter on an **onmouseover** event.

```
<DIV STYLE="font-size:14" onmouseover="this.style.letterSpacing='1mm'">
:
</DIV>
```

To see this code in action, refer to the Web Workshop CD-ROM.

Applies To

 WIN16   WIN32   MAC   UNIX

A, ADDRESS, B, BIG, BLOCKQUOTE, BODY, BUTTON, CAPTION, CENTER, CITE, CODE, COL, COLGROUP, DD, DFN, DIR, DIV, DL, DT, EM, FIELDSET, FORM, Hn, HTML, I, IMG, INPUT type=button, INPUT type=checkbox, INPUT type=file, INPUT type=image, INPUT type=password, INPUT type=radio, INPUT type=reset, INPUT type=submit, INPUT type=text, ISINDEX, KBD, LABEL, LEGEND, LI, LISTING, MARQUEE, MENU, OL, P, PLAINTEXT, PRE, S, SAMP, SELECT, SMALL, SPAN, STRIKE, STRONG, style, SUB, SUP, TABLE, TBODY, TD, TEXTAREA, TFOOT, TH, THEAD, TR, TT, U, UL, VAR, XMP

 WIN16   WIN32   MAC   UNIX

currentStyle, runtimeStyle

line-break Attribute | lineBreak Property

Sets or retrieves line-breaking rules for Japanese text.

Syntax

HTML   { **line-break :** normal | strict }

Scripting *object*.**style.lineBreak** [= *sBreak*]

Possible Values

normal   Applies the normal line-breaking rules for Japanese text.

strict   Enforces stricter line-breaking rules for Japanese text.

The property is read/write with a default value of normal; the proposed cascading style sheets (CSS) extension property is inherited.

Applies To

| WIN16 | WIN32 | MAC | UNIX |

ADDRESS, BLOCKQUOTE, BODY, CENTER, DD, DIR, DIV, DL, DT, FIELDSET, FORM, Hn, HR, LEGEND, LI, LISTING, MARQUEE, MENU, OL, P, PLAINTEXT, PRE, TABLE, TD, TH, TR, UL, XMP

line-height Attribute | lineHeight Property

Sets or retrieves the distance between lines in the object.

Syntax

HTML   { **line-height:** normal | *height* | *percentage* }

Scripting   *object*.**style.lineHeight** [= *sHeight*]

Possible Values

normal   Default height.

height   String consisting of a floating-point number, followed by an absolute units designator (cm, mm, in, pt, pc, or px) or a relative units designator (em or ex). For more information about the supported length units for CSS attributes, see "CSS Length Units" in Appendix C.

percentage   String value expressed as a percentage of the height of the parent object. Percentage values are specified as a number, followed by %.

The property is read/write with a default value of normal; the cascading style sheets (CSS) attribute is inherited.

Remarks

Line height is the distance between the descender of the font to the top of the internal leading of the font. A negative line height is allowed to achieve various shadowing effects.

If a formatted line contains more than one object, the maximum line height applies. In this case, negative values are not allowed.

Internet Explorer 3.0 supports the **line-height** attribute through the **font** attribute.

Example

The following examples show how to use the **line-height** attribute and the **lineHeight** property to control the height of paragraph lines.

The sample below uses **P** and **BLOCKQUOTE** as selectors in an embedded (global) style sheet to change the distance between the lines in all **P** and **BLOCKQUOTE** objects.

```
<STYLE>
    P { line-height: 8mm}
    BLOCKQUOTE { line-height: 4mm }
</STYLE>
```

To see this code in action, refer to the Web Workshop CD-ROM.

The sample below uses inline scripting to set the distance between lines on an **onmouseover** event.

```
<DIV STYLE="font-size:14" onmouseover="this.style.lineHeight='6mm'">
:
</DIV>
```

To see this code in action, refer to the Web Workshop CD-ROM.

Applies To

 WIN16   WIN32   MAC   UNIX

A, ADDRESS, B, BIG, BLOCKQUOTE, BODY, BUTTON, CAPTION, CENTER, CITE, CODE, COL, COLGROUP, DD, DFN, DIR, DIV, DL, DT, EM, FIELDSET, FORM, Hn, HTML, I, IMG, INPUT type=button, INPUT type=checkbox, INPUT type=file, INPUT type=image, INPUT type=password, INPUT type=radio, INPUT type=reset, INPUT type=submit, INPUT type=text, ISINDEX, KBD, LABEL, LEGEND, LI, LISTING, MARQUEE, MENU, OL, P, PLAINTEXT, PRE, S, SAMP, SELECT, SMALL, SPAN, STRIKE, STRONG, style, SUB, SUP, TABLE, TBODY, TD, TEXTAREA, TFOOT, TH, THEAD, TR, TT, U, UL, VAR, XMP

 WIN16   WIN32   MAC   UNIX

currentStyle, runtimeStyle

link Pseudo-class

Sets or retrieves the style of the **A** element for the default state of the link.

Syntax

HTML   [A]:link { *attribute1:parameter1* [; *attribute2:parameter2* [; . . .]] }

Scripting N/A

Possible Values

attribute   Any attribute applicable to text.

parameter Any of the range of values available to the corresponding attribute.

The pseudo-class is read/write with a browser-specific default.

Remarks

The **link** pseudo-class is often set with specific styles for the other states of a link: **active**, **visited**, and **hover**.

Internet Explorer 3.0 applies the **link** pseudo-class value to the **visited** pseudo-class.

Example

The following example shows how to use the **link** pseudo-class.

```
<STYLE>
    A:link{ color: #FF0000 }          // unvisited link
    A:visited { color: #CFCFCF }      // visited links
</STYLE>
```

Applies To

 WIN16   WIN32   MAC

A

 UNIX

A

LINK Attribute | link Property

Sets or retrieves the color of the document links for the object.

Syntax

HTML   <BODY **LINK** = *sColor* ... >

Scripting *body*.**link** [= *sColor*]

Possible Values

sColor String specifying one of the color names or red-green-blue (RGB) values in the "Color Table" in Appendix C.

The property is read/write with no default value.

Remarks

The **link** property cannot be set through the **BODY** object's **onload** event, but the **linkColor** property can.

Some browsers do not recognize color names, but all browsers should recognize RGB color values and display them correctly.

Applies To

IE 3	WIN16	WIN32	MAC
	BODY		

IE 4	UNIX
	BODY

linkColor Property

Sets or retrieves the color of the document links.

Syntax

HTML   N/A

Scripting *document*.**linkColor** [= *sColor*]

Possible Values

sColor String specifying one of the color names or values given in the "Color Table" in Appendix C.

The property is read/write with a default value of #0000ff.

Remarks

The **linkColor** property can be set through the **BODY** object's **onload** event, but the **link** property cannot.

Applies To

 WIN16   **WIN32**   **MAC**

document

 UNIX

document

list-style attribute | listStyle Property

Sets or retrieves the **listStyleType**, **listStylePosition**, and **listStyleImage** object properties simultaneously.

Syntax

HTML   { **list-style:** *sType* | *sPosition* | *sImage* }

Scripting *object*.**style.listStyle** [= *sStyle*]

Possible Values

sType   Any of the range of values available to the **listStyleType** property.

sPosition Any of the range of values available to the **listStylePosition** property.

sImage   Any of the range of values available to the **listStyleImage** property.

The property is read/write with a default value set by the browser; the cascading style sheets (CSS) attribute is inherited.

Remarks

This composite property can specify both a URL and a **list-style-type** attribute, which is used if the URL is not found.

When the left margin of a list item is set to 0 using one of the **margin** properties, the list item markers do not show. The margin should be set to a minimum of 30 points.

Example

The following examples show how to use the **list-style** attribute and the **listStyle** property to set the style of lists.

The sample below uses **UL** and **UL.compact** as selectors in an embedded style sheet to define the styles of two different unordered lists. For **UL.compact** to override the image set with the **UL** selector, the **list-style-image** attribute must explicitly be set to none.

```
<STYLE>
    UL { list-style: outside url(dot.gif) }
    UL.compact { list-style-image: none; list-style: inside circle }
</STYLE>
</HEAD>
<BODY>
<UL>
    <LI>...
    <LI>...
</UL>
<UL CLASS=compact>
    <LI>...
    <LI>...
</UL>
```

To see this code in action, refer to the Web Workshop CD-ROM.

The sample below uses inline scripting to change the style for the list. The circle is used if the image cannot be found.

```
<UL onmouseover="this.style.listStyle='url(dot.gif) circle'">
```

To see this code in action, refer to the Web Workshop CD-ROM.

Applies To

WIN16	**WIN32**	**MAC**	**UNIX**

LI, OL, style, UL

WIN16	**WIN32**	**MAC**	**UNIX**

runtimeStyle

list-style-image Attribute | listStyleImage Property

Sets or retrieves which image to use as a list-item marker for the object.

Syntax

HTML   { **list-style-image:** none | url(*sURL*) }

Scripting *object*.**style.listStyleImage** [= *sLocation*]

Possible Values

none   No image specified.

url(*sURL*) Location of the image where *sURL* is an absolute or relative URL.

The property is read/write with a default value of none; the cascading style sheets (CSS) attribute is inherited.

Remarks

When the image is available, it replaces the marker set with the **listStyleType** marker.

If the left margin of the list item is set to 0 using one of the **margin** properties, the list-item markers do not show. The margin should be set to a minimum of 30 points.

Example

The following examples show how to use the **list-style-image** attribute and the **listStyleImage** property to set the image for markers.

The sample below uses **UL** as a selector in an embedded style sheet to set the marker to an image (dot.gif).

```
<STYLE>
    UL { list-style-image: url(dot.gif) }
</STYLE>
```

To see this code in action, refer to the Web Workshop CD-ROM.

The sample below uses inline scripting to change the list-item marker's style to an image on an **onmouseover** event.

```
<UL onmouseover="this.style.listStyleImage='url(dot.gif)'">
```

To see this code in action, refer to the Web Workshop CD-ROM.

Applies To

 WIN16   WIN32   MAC   UNIX

LI, OL, style, UL

 WIN16   WIN32   MAC   UNIX

currentStyle, runtimeStyle

list-style-position Attribute | listStylePosition Property

Sets or retrieves how the list-item marker is drawn relative to the content of the object.

Syntax

HTML   { **list-style-position:** outside | inside }

Scripting *object*.**style.listStylePosition** [= *sPosition*]

Possible Values

outside Marker is placed outside the text, and any wrapping text is not aligned under the marker.

inside Marker is placed inside the text, and any wrapping text is aligned under the marker.

The property is read/write with a default value of outside; the cascading style sheets (CSS) attribute is inherited.

Remarks

This property applies only to objects with a **display** value of list-item.

If the left margin of a list item is set to 0 using one of the **margin** properties, the list-item markers do not show. The margin should be set to a minimum of 30 points.

Example

The following examples show how to use the **list-style-position** attribute and the **listStylePosition** property to set the position for markers.

The sample below uses **UL** and **UL.compact** as selectors in an embedded (global) style sheet to set the position of the list-item markers.

```
<STYLE>
    UL   { list-style-position: inside }
    UL.compact { list-style-position: outside }
</STYLE>
</HEAD>
<BODY>
<UL>
    <LI>...
    <LI>...
</UL>
<UL CLASS=compact>
    <LI>...
    <LI>...
</UL>
```

To see this code in action, refer to the Web Workshop CD-ROM.

The sample below uses inline scripting to change the marker position on mouse events.

```
<SPAN STYLE="width:3cm" onmouseover="this.style.listStylePosition='inside'"
    onmouseout="this.style.listStylePosition='outside'">
```

To see this code in action, refer to the Web Workshop CD-ROM.

Applies To

WIN16	WIN32	MAC	UNIX

LI, OL, style, UL

WIN16	WIN32	MAC	UNIX

currentStyle, runtimeStyle

list-style-type Attribute | listStyleType Property

Sets or retrieves the predefined type of the line-item marker for the object.

Syntax

HTML   { **list-style-type:** disc | circle | square | decimal
| lower-roman | upper-roman | lower-alpha | upper-alpha | none }

Scripting *object*.**style.listStyleType** [= *sType*]

Possible Values

`disc`	Solid circles.
`circle`	Outlined circles.
`square`	Solid squares.
`decimal`	1, 2, 3, 4, and so on.
`lower-roman`	i, ii, iii, iv, and so on.
`upper-roman`	I, II, III, IV, and so on.
`lower-alpha`	a, b, c, d, and so on.
`upper-alpha`	A, B, C, D, and so on.
`none`	No marker is shown.

The property is read/write with a default value of `disc`; the cascading style sheets (CSS) attribute is inherited.

Remarks

The property determines the appearance of the list-item marker if **list-style-image** is `none` or if the image pointed to by the URL cannot be displayed.

If the left margin of a line item is set to 0 using one of the **margin** properties, the list-item markers do not show. The margin should be set to a minimum of 30 points.

Example

The following examples show how to use the **list-style-type** attribute and the **listStyleType** property to set the markers.

The sample below uses **UL** as a selector in an embedded (global) style sheet to change the marker type to `circle`.

```
<STYLE>
    UL { list-style-type: circle }
</STYLE>
```

To see this code in action, refer to the Web Workshop CD-ROM.

The sample below uses inline scripting to change the marker type on an **onmouseover** event.

```
<UL onmouseover="this.style.listStyleType='circle'">
```

To see this code in action, refer to the Web Workshop CD-ROM.

Applies To

 WIN16   WIN32   MAC   UNIX

LI, OL, style, UL

 WIN16   WIN32   MAC   UNIX

currentStyle, runtimeStyle

LOOP Attribute | loop Property

Sets or retrieves how many times a sound or video loops when activated.

Syntax

HTML   *<ELEMENT* **LOOP** = *iLoop* ... >

Scripting *object*.**loop** [= *iLoop*]

Possible Values

iLoop Positive integer specifying the number of loops, or -1, which causes the sound or video to loop infinitely.

The property is read/write with a default value of 1.

Remarks

To restart a video or sound after changing its **loop** property, set the **dynsrc** property or **src** property, respectively, to itself, as demonstrated in the example below. In Internet Explorer 4.0, when you restart a video by changing its **loop** property, the video opens and plays in a new window.

Following are descriptions of how **loop** works for some boundary cases.

```
<BGSOUND src="file:///c:\win95\system\msremind.wav">          Loops one time.

<BGSOUND src="file:///c:\win95\system\msremind.wav" LOOP=0>   Loops one time.

<BGSOUND src="file:///c:\win95\system\msremind.wav" LOOP=-1>  Loops infinitely.
```

Example

The following example shows how to use the **loop** property to change the number of times a background sound loops.

```
<SCRIPT>
function loopOnce() {
    oBGSound.loop = 1;
    oBGSound.src = oBGSound.src; // reload sound
}
function loopContinuously() {
    oBGSound.loop = -1;
    oBGSound.src = oBGSound.src; // reload sound
}
</SCRIPT>
:
<BGSOUND id="oBGSound" src="sound.wav">
<BUTTON onclick="loopOnce()">Loop Sound Once</BUTTON>
<BUTTON onclick="loopContinuously()">Loop Sound Continuously</BUTTON>
```

To see this code in action, refer to the Web Workshop CD-ROM.

Applies To

 WIN16   WIN32   MAC

BGSOUND, IMG

 UNIX

BGSOUND, IMG

LOOP Attribute | loop Property

Sets or retrieves how many times a **MARQUEE** plays.

Syntax

HTML   *<ELEMENT* **LOOP** *= iLoop ... >*

Scripting *object*.**loop** [*= iLoop*]

Possible Values

iLoop Positive integer specifying the number of loops, or -1, which causes the **MARQUEE** to loop infinitely.

The property is read/write with a default value of -1.

Remarks

In each of the following boundary cases, the **MARQUEE** loops infinitely.

```
<MARQUEE SCROLLAMOUNT=30>
This is some scrolling text.</MARQUEE>

<MARQUEE SCROLLAMOUNT=30 LOOP=-1>
This is some scrolling text.</MARQUEE>
```

If the **loop** property is set to NULL or 0 in script, a script error occurs.

Applies To

 WIN16   WIN32   MAC   UNIX

MARQUEE

LOWSRC Attribute | lowsrc Property

Sets or retrieves a lower resolution image to display.

Syntax

HTML   <IMG **LOWSRC** = *sURL* ... >

Scripting   *object*.**lowsrc** [= *sURL*]

Possible Values

sURL   String specifying the URL of the lower resolution image.

The property is read/write with no default value.

Remarks

If the **src** property is set in code, the new URL starts loading into the image area and aborts the transfer of any image data that is already loading into the same area. So, you should alter the **lowsrc** property before setting the **src** property. If the URL in the **src** property references an image that is not the same size as the image cell it is loaded into, the source image is scaled to fit.

Applies To

 WIN16   WIN32   MAC   UNIX

IMG

margin Attribute | margin Property

Sets or retrieves the width of the left and right margins and the height of the top and bottom margins of the object.

Syntax

HTML   { **margin:** [*length* | *percentage* | `auto`]{1,4} }

Scripting   *object*.**style.margin** [= *sMargin*]

Possible Values

length	String consisting of a floating-point number, followed by an absolute units designator (`cm`, `mm`, `in`, `pt`, `pc`, or `px`) or a relative units designator (`em` or `ex`). For more information about the supported length units for CSS attributes, see "CSS Length Units" in Appendix C.
percentage	String value expressed as a percentage of the height of the parent object. Percentage values are specified as a number, followed by a %.
`auto`	Value set to be equal to the value of the opposite side.

The property is read/write with a default value of `0`; the cascading style sheets (CSS) attribute is not inherited.

Remarks

This is a composite property. In the HTML syntax, the {1,4} means that up to four values can be specified in this order: top, right, bottom, and left. If one width is supplied, it is used for all four sides. If two widths are supplied, the first is used for the top and bottom borders, and the second is used for left and right borders. If three widths are supplied, they are used for top, right and left, and bottom borders, respectively. Negative margins are supported except for top and bottom margins on inline objects.

Margins are always transparent.

Inline elements must have an `absolute` position or layout to use this property. Element layout is set by providing a value for the **height** property or the **width** property.

In Internet Explorer 3.0, the margin value is added to the default value for the object. In Internet Explorer 4.0 and later, the margin value is absolute. The margin properties do not work with the **TD** and **TR** objects in Internet Explorer 4.0, although they work in Internet Explorer 3.0. Apply the margin to an object within the **TD**, such as **DIV** or **P**, to set margins in the cell for Internet Explorer 4.0 and later.

Possible length values specified relative to the height of the element's font (em) or the height of the letter "x" (ex) are supported as of Internet Explorer 4.0.

Example

The following examples show how to use the **margin** attribute and the **margin** property to change the margin of the object.

The sample below uses **IMG** as a selector to set the margin of images to 1 centimeter.

```
<STYLE>
    IMG { margin: 1cm }
</STYLE>
```

To see this code in action, refer to the Web Workshop CD-ROM.

The sample below uses inline scripting to set the margin of the image to 5 millimeters on an **onmouseover** event.

```
<IMG src="sphere.jpg" onmouseover="this.style.margin='5mm'">
```

To see this code in action, refer to the Web Workshop CD-ROM.

Applies To

 WIN16   WIN32   MAC

BLOCKQUOTE, BODY, CAPTION, CENTER, DD, DIR, DIV, DL, DT, FORM, Hn, HR, INPUT type=button, INPUT type=checkbox, INPUT type=file, INPUT type=image, INPUT type=password, INPUT type=radio, INPUT type=reset, INPUT type=submit, INPUT type=text, ISINDEX, LI, LISTING, MARQUEE, MENU, OL, P, PLAINTEXT, PRE, TABLE, UL, XMP

 UNIX   WIN16   WIN32   MAC

BLOCKQUOTE, BODY, BUTTON, CAPTION, CENTER, DD, DIR, DIV, DL, DT, EMBED, FIELDSET, FORM, Hn, HR, IFRAME, IMG, INPUT type=button, INPUT type=checkbox, INPUT type=file, INPUT type=image, INPUT type=password, INPUT type=radio, INPUT type=reset, INPUT type=submit, INPUT type=text, ISINDEX, LI, LISTING, MARQUEE, MENU, OBJECT, OL, P, PLAINTEXT, PRE, SPAN, style, TABLE, TD, TEXTAREA, TH, TR, UL, XMP

 WIN16   WIN32   MAC   UNIX

currentStyle, runtimeStyle

margin-bottom Attribute | marginBottom Property

Sets or retrieves the height of the bottom margin of the object.

Syntax

HTML	{ **margin-bottom:** [*height* | *percentage* | auto] }
Scripting	*object*.**style.marginBottom** [= *sHeight*]

Possible Values

auto	Value set to equal the value of the opposite side.
height	String consisting of a floating-point number, followed by an absolute units designator (cm, mm, in, pt, pc, or px) or a relative units designator (em or ex). For more information about the supported length units for CSS attributes, see "CSS Length Attributes" in Appendix C.
percentage	String value expressed as a percentage of the height of the parent object. Percentage values are specified as a number, followed by a %.

The property is read/write with a default value of 0; the cascading style sheets (CSS) attribute is not inherited.

Remarks

Negative margins are supported, except for top and bottom margins on inline objects.

Inline elements must have an absolute position or layout to use this property. Element layout is set by providing a value for the **height** property or the **width** property.

In Internet Explorer 3.0, the margin value is added to the default value for the object. In Internet Explorer 4.0 and later, the margin value is absolute. The margin properties do not work with the **TD** and **TR** objects in Internet Explorer 4.0, although they work in Internet Explorer 3.0. Apply the margin to an object within the **TD**, such as **DIV** or **P**, to set margins in the cell for Internet Explorer 4.0 and later.

Specifying possible length values relative to the height of the element's font (em) or the height of the letter "x" (ex) is supported as of Internet Explorer 4.0.

Example

The following examples show how to use the **margin-bottom** attribute and the **marginBottom** property to change the margin of the object.

The sample below uses **IMG** as a selector to set the bottom margin on images to 2 centimeters.

```
<STYLE>
    IMG { margin-bottom: 2cm }
</STYLE>
```

To see this code in action, refer to the Web Workshop CD-ROM.

The sample below uses inline scripting to set the image's bottom margin to 1 centimeter on an **onmouseover** event.

```
<IMG src="sphere.jpg"onmouseover="this.style.marginBottom='1cm'">
```

To see this code in action, refer to the Web Workshop CD-ROM.

Applies To

 WIN16   WIN32   MAC

BLOCKQUOTE, BODY, CAPTION, CENTER, DD, DIR, DIV, DL, DT, FORM, Hn, HR, ISINDEX, LI, MARQUEE, MENU, OL, P, PLAINTEXT, PRE, TABLE, TD, TH, UL, XMP

 UNIX   WIN16   WIN32   MAC

BLOCKQUOTE, BODY, BUTTON, CAPTION, CENTER, DD, DIR, DIV, DL, DT, EMBED, FIELDSET, FORM, Hn, HR, IFRAME, IMG, INPUT type=button, INPUT type=checkbox, INPUT type=file, INPUT type=image, INPUT type=password, INPUT type=radio, INPUT type=reset, INPUT type=submit, INPUT type=text, ISINDEX, LI, LISTING, MARQUEE, MENU, OBJECT, OL, P, PLAINTEXT, PRE, SPAN, style, TABLE, TD, TEXTAREA, TH, TR, UL, XMP

 WIN16   WIN32   MAC   UNIX

currentStyle, runtimeStyle

MARGINHEIGHT Attribute | marginHeight Property

Sets or retrieves the top and bottom margin height before displaying the text in a frame.

Syntax

HTML   *<ELEMENT* **MARGINHEIGHT** = *iHeight ... >*

Scripting *object*.**marginHeight** [= *iHeight*]

Possible Values

iHeight   Integer specifying the height, in pixels.

The property is read/write with no default value.

Remarks

Margins cannot be less than 1 pixel, or so large that the text cannot be displayed.

If **marginHeight** is specified but **marginWidth** is not, **marginWidth** is set to 0.

Applies To

 WIN16   WIN32   MAC

FRAME, IFRAME

 UNIX

FRAME, IFRAME

margin-left Attribute | marginLeft Property

Sets or retrieves the width of the left margin of the object.

Syntax

HTML   { **margin-left:** [*width* | *percentage* | `auto`] }

Scripting *object*.**style.marginLeft** [= *sWidth*]

Possible Values

width   String consisting of a floating-point number, followed by an absolute units designator (cm, mm, in, pt, pc, or px) or a relative units designator (em or ex). For more information about the supported length units for CSS attributes, see "CSS Length Units" in Appendix C.

percentage Value expressed as a percentage of the height of the parent object.

auto   String value equal to the value of the opposite side.

The property is read/write with a default value of 0; the cascading style sheets (CSS) attribute is not inherited.

Remarks

Negative margins are supported except for top and bottom margins on inline objects.

Inline elements must have an absolute position or layout to use this property. Element layout is set by providing a value for the **height** property or the **width** property.

In Internet Explorer 3.0, the margin value is added to the default value for the object. In Internet Explorer 4.0 and later, the margin value is absolute. The margin properties do not work with the **TD** and **TR** objects in Internet Explorer 4.0, although they work in Internet Explorer 3.0. Apply the margin to an object within the **TD**, such as **DIV** or **P**, to set margins in the cell for Internet Explorer 4.0 and later.

Possible length values relative to the height of the element's font (em) or the height of the letter "x" (ex) are supported as of Internet Explorer 4.0.

Example

The following examples show how to use the **margin-left** attribute and the **marginLeft** property to change the margin of the object.

The sample below uses **IMG** as a selector to set the left margin to 2 centimeters for all images.

```
<STYLE>
    IMG { margin-left:2cm }
</STYLE>
```

To see this code in action, refer to the Web Workshop CD-ROM.

The sample below uses inline scripting to set the image's left margin to 1 centimeter on an **onmouseover** event.

```
<IMG src="sphere.jpg" onclick="this.style.marginLeft='1cm'">
```

To see this code in action, refer to the Web Workshop CD-ROM.

DHTML Properties

Applies To

 WIN16   WIN32   MAC

BLOCKQUOTE, BODY, CAPTION, CENTER, DD, DIR, DIV, DL, DT, FORM, Hn, HR, ISINDEX, LI, MARQUEE, MENU, OL, P, PLAINTEXT, PRE, TABLE, TD, TH, UL, XMP

 UNIX   WIN16   WIN32   MAC

BLOCKQUOTE, BODY, BUTTON, CAPTION, CENTER, DD, DIR, DIV, DL, DT, EMBED, FIELDSET, FORM, Hn, HR, IFRAME, IMG, INPUT type=button, INPUT type=checkbox, INPUT type=file, INPUT type=image, INPUT type=password, INPUT type=radio, INPUT type=reset, INPUT type=submit, INPUT type=text, ISINDEX, LI, LISTING, MARQUEE, MENU, OBJECT, OL, P, PLAINTEXT, PRE, SPAN, style, TABLE, TD, TEXTAREA, TH, TR, UL, XMP

 WIN16   WIN32   MAC   UNIX

currentStyle, runtimeStyle

margin-right Attribute | marginRight Property

Sets or retrieves the width of the right margin of the object.

Syntax

HTML   { **margin-right:** [*width* | *percentage* | auto] }

Scripting *object*.**style.marginRight** [= *sWidth*]

Possible Values

width   String consisting of a floating-point number, followed by an absolute units designator (cm, mm, in, pt, pc, or px) or a relative units designator (em or ex). For more information about the supported length units for CSS attributes, see "CSS Length Units" in Appendix C.

percentage String value expressed as a percentage of the width of the parent object. Percentage values are specified as a number, followed by a %.

auto   Value set equal to that of the opposite side.

The property is read/write with a default value of 0; the cascading style sheets (CSS) attribute is not inherited.

DHTML Properties

Remarks

Negative margins are supported, except for top and bottom margins on inline objects.

Inline elements must have an `absolute` position or layout to use this property. Element layout is set by providing a value for the **height** property or the **width** property.

In Internet Explorer 3.0, the margin value is added to the default value for the object. In Internet Explorer 4.0 and later, the margin value is absolute. The margin properties do not work with the **TD** and **TR** objects in Internet Explorer 4.0, although they work in Internet Explorer 3.0. Apply the margin to an object within the **TD**, such as **DIV** or **P**, to set margins in the cell for Internet Explorer 4.0 and later.

Possible length values relative to the height of the element's font (`em`) or the height of the letter "x" (`ex`) are supported as of Internet Explorer 4.0.

Example

The following examples show how to use the **margin-right** attribute and the **marginRight** property to change the margin of the object.

The sample below uses **IMG** as a selector and `margin1` as a class in an embedded style sheet to set the right margin of an event as a result of an **onclick** or **ondblclick** event.

```
<STYLE>
    IMG { margin-right:1cm }
    .margin1 { margin-right:2cm }
</STYLE>
</HEAD>
<BODY>
<IMG src="sphere.jpg" onclick="this.className='margin1'"
    ondblclick="this.className=''">
```

To see this code in action, refer to the Web Workshop CD-ROM.

The sample below uses inline scripting to set the image's right margin to 1 centimeter on a mouse click.

```
<IMG src="sphere.jpeg" onclick="this.style.marginRight='1cm'">
```

To see this code in action, refer to the Web Workshop CD-ROM.

Applies To

WIN16   WIN32   MAC

BLOCKQUOTE, BODY, CAPTION, CENTER, DD, DIR, DIV, DL, DT, FORM, Hn, HR, ISINDEX, LI, MARQUEE, MENU, OL, P, PLAINTEXT, PRE, TABLE, TD,

TH, UL, XMP

 UNIX   WIN16   WIN32   MAC

BLOCKQUOTE, BODY, BUTTON, CAPTION, CENTER, DD, DIR, DIV, DL, DT, EMBED, FIELDSET, FORM, Hn, HR, IFRAME, IMG, INPUT type=button, INPUT type=checkbox, INPUT type=file, INPUT type=image, INPUT type=password, INPUT type=radio, INPUT type=reset, INPUT type=submit, INPUT type=text, ISINDEX, LI, LISTING, MARQUEE, MENU, OBJECT, OL, P, PLAINTEXT, PRE, SPAN, style, TABLE, TD, TEXTAREA, TH, TR, UL, XMP

 WIN16   WIN32   MAC   UNIX

currentStyle, runtimeStyle

margin-top Attribute | marginTop Property

Sets or retrieves the height of the top margin of the object.

Syntax

HTML	{ **margin-top:** [*height*	*percentage*	auto] }
Scripting	*object*.**style.marginTop** [= *sHeight*]

Possible Values

height	String consisting of a floating-point number, followed by an absolute units designator (cm, mm, in, pt, pc, or px) or a relative units designator (em or ex). For more information about the supported length units for CSS attributes, see "CSS Length Units" in Appendix C.
percentage	Value expressed as a percentage of the height of the parent object.
auto	Value set equal to that of the opposite side.

The property is read/write with a default value of 0; the cascading style sheets (CSS) attribute is not inherited.

Remarks

Negative margins are supported except for top and bottom margins on inline objects.

Inline elements must have an absolute **position** or layout to use this property. Element layout is set by providing a value for the **height** property or the **width** property.

In Internet Explorer 3.0, the margin value is added to the default value for the object. In Internet Explorer 4.0 and later, the margin value is absolute. The margin properties do not work with the **TD** and **TR** objects in Internet Explorer 4.0, although they work in Internet Explorer 3.0. Apply the margin to an object within the **TD**, such as **DIV** or **P**, to set margins in the cell for Internet Explorer 4.0 and later.

Possible length values relative to the height of the element's font (em) or the height of the letter "x" (ex) are supported as of Internet Explorer 4.0.

Example

The following examples show how to use the **margin-top** attribute and the **marginTop** property to change the margin of the object.

The sample below uses **HR** as a selector and margin1 as a class in an embedded style sheet to set the top margin, and then change the margin on an **onclick** event.

```
<STYLE>
    HR { margin-top: 2cm }
    .margin1 { margin-top: 4cm }
</STYLE>
</HEAD>
<BODY>
<HR onclick="this.className='margin1'" ondblclick="this.className=''">
</STYLE>
```

To see this code in action, refer to the Web Workshop CD-ROM.

The sample below uses inline scripting to change the margin on an **onclick** event.

```
<HR onclick="this.style.marginTop='2cm'"
ondblclick="this.style.marginTop=''">
```

To see this code in action, refer to the Web Workshop CD-ROM.

Applies To

 WIN16   WIN32   MAC

BLOCKQUOTE, BODY, CAPTION, CENTER, DD, DIR, DIV, DL, DT, FORM, Hn, HR, ISINDEX, LI, MARQUEE, MENU, OL, P, PLAINTEXT, PRE, TABLE, TD, TH, UL, XMP

 UNIX   WIN16   WIN32   MAC

BLOCKQUOTE, BODY, BUTTON, CAPTION, CENTER, DD, DIR, DIV, DL, DT, EMBED, FIELDSET, FORM, Hn, HR, IFRAME, IMG, INPUT type=button, INPUT type=checkbox, INPUT type=file, INPUT type=image, INPUT type=password,

Applies To *(continued)*

UNIX	WIN16	WIN32	MAC

INPUT type=radio, INPUT type=reset, INPUT type=submit, INPUT type=text, ISINDEX, LI, LISTING, MARQUEE, MENU, OBJECT, OL, P, PLAINTEXT, PRE, SPAN, style, TABLE, TD, TEXTAREA, TH, TR, UL, XMP

WIN16	WIN32	MAC	UNIX

currentStyle, runtimeStyle

MARGINWIDTH Attribute | marginWidth Property

Sets or retrieves the left and right margin setting before displaying the text in a frame.

Syntax

HTML *<ELEMENT* **MARGINWIDTH** = *iWidth ... >*

Scripting *object*.**marginWidth** [= *iWidth*]

Possible Values

iWidth Integer specifying the width, in pixels.

The property is read/write with no default value.

Remarks

Margins cannot be less than 1 pixel, or so large that the text cannot be displayed.

If **marginWidth** is specified but **marginHeight** is not, **marginHeight** is set to 0.

Applies To

WIN16	WIN32	MAC

FRAME, IFRAME

UNIX

FRAME, IFRAME

MAXLENGTH Attribute | maxLength Property

Sets or retrieves the maximum number of characters that the user can enter into a text control.

Syntax

HTML   <INPUT TYPE="text" **MAXLENGTH** = *iLength* ... >

Scripting *object*.**maxLength** [= *iLength*]

Possible Values

iLength   Integer specifying the maximum length of the input.

The property is read/write with a default of no limit.

Remarks

The property limits the number of characters the user can enter. The property does not limit programmatic assignments to the **value** property. The property's value can be larger than the **size** of the text box, in which case the text box scrolls as necessary as the user types.

Applies To

 WIN16   WIN32   MAC   UNIX

INPUT type=text, INPUT type=password

MEDIA Attribute | media Property

Sets or retrieves the media type.

Syntax

HTML   <*ELEMENT* **MEDIA** = "screen" | "print" | "all" ... >

Scripting *object*.**media** [= *sMedia*]

Possible Values

screen Output is intended for computer screens.

print   Output is intended for printed material and for documents on screen viewed in Print Preview mode.

all   Applies to all devices.

(margin tab: DHTML Properties)

The property is read/write with no default value.

Applies To

WIN16	WIN32	MAC	UNIX

LINK

WIN16	WIN32	MAC	UNIX

STYLE

@media Rule

Sets the media types for a set of **styleSheet** rules.

Syntax

HTML   @**media** *sMediaType* { *sRules* }

Scripting N/A

Possible Values

sMediaType	screen	Output is intended for computer screens.
	print	Output is intended for printed material and for documents on screen viewed in Print Preview mode.
	all	Applies to all devices.
sRules		One or more rules in a **styleSheet** object.

The rule has no default value.

Example

The following example shows how to use the @**media** rule.

```
// For computer screens, the font size is 12pt.

@media screen {
    BODY {font-size: 12pt;}
}
// When printed, the font size is 8pt.
@media print {
    BODY {font-size: 8pt;}
}
```

Applies To

 WIN16   WIN32   MAC   UNIX

STYLE

menuArguments Property

Returns the window object where the context menu item was executed.

Syntax

HTML   N/A

Scripting   [*oWindow* =] *window.external*.**menuArguments**

Possible Values

oWindow   Reference to the window object where the context menu was opened.

The property is read-only with no default value.

Remarks

This property is accessible only through script specified in the registry for a new context menu entry.

The **menuArguments** property returns an object reference of the window where the context menu was opened. The **event** object is exposed through this object reference, allowing you to query the **srcElement**, **clientX**, and **clientY** properties.

This property is not supported in HTML Applications (HTAs).

Example

The following example shows how to use the **menuArguments** property. This sample changes selected text to uppercase, or inserts text if nothing was selected.

```
<SCRIPT LANGUAGE = "JavaScript">

// Get the window object where the context menu was opened.
var oWindow = window.external.menuArguments;

// Get the document object exposed through oWindow.
var oDocument = oWindow.document;

// Get the selection from oDocument.
// in oDocument.
var oSelect = oDocument.selection;
```

```
    // Create a TextRange from oSelect.
    var oSelectRange = oSelect.createRange();

    // Get the text of the selection.
    var sNewText = oSelectRange.text;

    // If nothing was selected, insert some text.
    if (sNewText.length == 0){
        oSelectRange.text = "INSERT TEXT";
    }

    // Otherwise, convert the selection to uppercase.
    else{
        oSelectRange.text = sNewText.toUpperCase();
    }
</SCRIPT>
```

Applies To

 WIN16   WIN32   MAC   UNIX

external

METHOD Attribute | method Property

Sets or retrieves how the form data is sent to the server.

Syntax

HTML	<FORM **METHOD** = "get" | "post" ... >
Scripting	*form*.**method** [= *sMethod*]

Possible Values

get Append the arguments to the action URL and open it as if it were an anchor.

post Send the data through an HTTP post transaction.

The property is read/write with no default value.

Applies To

 WIN16   WIN32   MAC

FORM

UNIX

FORM

METHODS Attribute | Methods Property

Sets or returns the list of HTTP methods supported by the object.

Syntax

HTML   <A **METHODS** = *sMethod* ... >

Scripting *a*.**Methods** [= *sMethod*]

Possible Values

sMethod   Comma-separated list of HTTP methods supported by the object for public
use.

The property is read/write.

Remarks

These methods are more accurately given by the HTTP protocol when it is used.
However, for reasons similar to those for the **title** property, it can be useful to include
the information in advance in the link. The HTML user agent can choose a different
rendering as a function of the methods allowed; for example, if an object has a method
that supports searching, an icon denoting this can be rendered.

Applies To

 WIN16   WIN32   MAC   UNIX

A

MULTIPLE Attribute | multiple Property

Sets or retrieves whether multiple items in the list can be selected.

Syntax

HTML   <SELECT **MULTIPLE** ... >

Scripting *select*.**multiple** [= *bMultiple*]

Possible Values

false   Multiple items cannot be selected.

true   Multiple items can be selected.

The property is read/write with a default value of false.

Example

The following example shows how to use the **MULTIPLE** attribute and the **multiple** property to set the ability to choose multiple items in a list.

```
<SELECT ID=oSelect MULTIPLE>
<OPTION>Item 1</OPTION>
<OPTION>Item 2</OPTION>
<OPTION>Item 3</OPTION>
</SELECT>
:
<BUTTON onclick="oSelect.multiple=false">One</BUTTON>
<BUTTON onclick="oSelect.multiple=true">Many</BUTTON>
```

To see this code in action, refer to the Web Workshop CD-ROM.

Applies To

WIN16	WIN32	MAC

SELECT

UNIX

SELECT

NAME Attribute | name Property

Sets or retrieves the name of a window or the frame, so it can be targeted from links in other documents.

Syntax

HTML   *<ELEMENT* **NAME** *= sName ... >*

Scripting *object.***name** [*= sName*]

Possible Values

sName   String specifying a frame.

_blank   Link is loaded into a new, unnamed window.

_parent Link is loaded over the parent. If the frame has no parent, this value refers to _self.

_self   Page is replaced with the specified link.

_top   Link is loaded at the topmost level.

The property is read/write with no default value.

Remarks

To access a window's **name** property, use the **window** keyword.

Example

The following example shows how to assign the **name** property to the window object.

```
window.name="MyWindow";
```

The **name** property on the **window** frequently comes from the **FRAME** definition.

```
parent.frames[0].name="Left";
```

The **NAME** attribute for a window can only be persisted in HTML when defined in a frame within a frame set.

```
<FRAMESET>
    <FRAME NAME="Left" SRC="blank.htm">
    <FRAME NAME="Right" SRC="contents.htm">
</FRAMESET>
```

The **name** property can be assigned using the window's **open** method.

```
window.open("file.htm","Frame1");
```

Applies To

 WIN16   WIN32   MAC

FRAME, IFRAME, window

 UNIX

FRAME, IFRAME, window

NAME Attribute | name Property

Sets or retrieves the name of the **META** object.

Syntax

HTML   <META **NAME** = *sName* ... >

Scripting   *object*.**name** [= *sName*]

Possible Values

sName   String specifying an arbitrary name or one of the following values:

Description   String. The associated **CONTENT** attribute describes the containing document. Some search engines use this to provide the user with a document summary in the result of a search.

Generator   String. The associated **CONTENT** attribute identifies the name of the application used to create the document.

Keywords   String. The associated **CONTENT** attribute consists of comma-delimited words describing the document. Some search engines use this to allow the user to perform a keyword search.

ProgID   String. The associated **CONTENT** attribute contains the programmatic identifier of the document's default editor.

Robots   String. The associated **CONTENT** attribute indicates whether the containing document can be indexed by search engines that recognize the **META** object.

    all   Search engines can index the containing document.

    noindex   Search engines cannot index the containing document.

Template   String. The associated **CONTENT** attribute specifies the location of the template used to edit the document. Use this with the ProgID **META** object if the editor supports document templates.

The property is read/write with no default value.

Remarks

The **NAME** attribute is typically assigned one of the well-defined values above, but any arbitrary value can be specified. Custom tools can be developed to perform special actions on documents containing arbitrary **META** tags.

To enable the smart edit features in Internet Explorer 5 or later, add a **META** tag to the **HEAD** of the document. Associate `ProgID` with the **NAME** attribute, and associate the programmatic identifier of the desired editor with the **CONTENT** attribute. If the specified editor is not installed or properly registered on the user's system, the edit button is not displayed. To determine the programmatic identifier of your editor, see the documentation for the editor.

Example

The following example shows how **META** tags can be used to display a smart edit button on the toolbar. Because the ProgID **META** tag is associated with the programmatic identifier of Microsoft Word, the button displays the Microsoft Word icon. In addition, when the button is clicked, Internet Explorer loads the document into Microsoft Word using the specified document template.

```
<META NAME="ProgID" CONTENT="word.document">
<META NAME="Template" CONTENT="C:\Program Files\Microsoft Office\Office\html.dot">
```

Applies To

 WIN16   WIN32   MAC

META

 UNIX

META

NAME Attribute | name Property

Sets or retrieves the name of the control, bookmark, or application.

Syntax

HTML   *<ELEMENT* **NAME** = *sName* ... >

Scripting *object*.**name** [= *sName*]

Possible Values

sName String specifying the name.

The property is read/write with no default value.

Remarks

The **name** property is used to bind the value of the control when a **FORM** object is submitted. The name is not the value that is displayed for the **button**, **reset**, and **submit** input types. Submitting the form submits the internally stored value, not the value displayed.

JScript (compatible with ECMA 262 language specification) allows the name to be changed at run time. This does not cause the name in the programming model to change in the collection of elements, but it changes the name used for submitting elements.

In Internet Explorer 5, the **name** property cannot be set at run time on **anchor** objects dynamically created with the **createElement** method. To create an **anchor** with a **NAME** attribute, include the attribute and value when using the **createElement** method, or use the **innerHTML** property.

Example

The following example shows how to set the **NAME** attribute on a dynamically created **anchor** object.

```
var oAnchor = document.createElement("<A NAME='AnchorName'></A>");
```

Applies To

 WIN16   WIN32   MAC

A, APPLET, FORM, IMG, INPUT type=button, INPUT type=checkbox, INPUT type=hidden, INPUT type=image, INPUT type=password, INPUT type=radio, INPUT type=reset, INPUT type=submit, INPUT type=text, LINK, MAP, OBJECT, PARAM, SELECT, TEXTAREA

 UNIX   WIN16   WIN32   MAC

A, APPLET, BUTTON, FORM, IMG, INPUT type=button, INPUT type=checkbox, INPUT type=file, INPUT type=hidden, INPUT type=image, INPUT type=password, INPUT type=radio, INPUT type=reset, INPUT type=submit, INPUT type=text, LINK, MAP, OBJECT, PARAM, SELECT, TEXTAREA

nameProp Property

Retrieves the file name specified in the **href** or **src** property of the object.

Syntax

HTML   N/A

Scripting [= *sFileName*=] *object*.**nameProp**

Possible Values

sFileName String specifying the name of a file specified by the object, not including the path or protocol.

The property is read-only with no default value.

Example

The following example shows how to use the **nameProp** property to set the **innerText** property of a link to the file name specified by an **A** element.

```
<SCRIPT>
window.onload=fnInit;
function fnInit(){
   oLink.innerText=oLink.nameProp;
}
</SCRIPT>
<A ID="oLink"
   HREF="http://www.microsoft.com/workshop/author/dhtml/dhtmlrefs.asp">
</A>
```

Applies To

 WIN16   WIN32   MAC   UNIX

A, IMG

nextSibling Property

Retrieves a reference to the next sibling for the specified object.

Syntax

HTML   N/A

Scripting [*oElement* =] *object*.**nextSibling**

Possible Values

oElement   Reference to the next sibling of an object.

The property is read-only with no default value.

Example

The following example shows how to use the **nextSibling** property to obtain the next sibling of a list item.

```
<SCRIPT>
// Returns the list item labeled 'List Item 2'.
var oSibling = oList.childNodes(0).nextSibling;
</SCRIPT>

<BODY>
<UL ID = oList>
<LI>List Item 1
<LI>List Item 2
<LI>List Item 3
</UL>
<BODY>
```

Applies To

 WIN16   WIN32   MAC   UNIX

A, ACRONYM, ADDRESS, APPLET, AREA, B, BASE, BASEFONT, BDO, BGSOUND, BIG, BLOCKQUOTE, BODY, BR, BUTTON, CAPTION, CENTER, CITE, CODE, COL, COLGROUP, COMMENT, DD, DEL, DFN, DIR, DIV, DL, DT, EM, EMBED, FIELDSET, FONT, FORM, FRAME, FRAMESET, HEAD, Hn, HR, HTML, I, IFRAME, IMG, INPUT type=button, INPUT type=checkbox, INPUT type=file, INPUT type=hidden, INPUT type=image, INPUT type=password, INPUT type=radio, INPUT type=reset, INPUT type=submit, INPUT type=text, INS, KBD, LABEL, LEGEND, LI, LINK, LISTING, MAP, MARQUEE, MENU, NEXTID, OBJECT, OL, OPTION, P, PLAINTEXT, PRE, Q, S, SAMP, SCRIPT, SELECT, SMALL, SPAN, STRIKE, STRONG, SUB, SUP, TABLE, TBODY, TD, TEXTAREA, TextNode, TFOOT, TH, THEAD, TITLE, TR, TT, U, UL, VAR, XMP

nodeName Property

Retrieves the name of a particular type of node.

Syntax

HTML　　N/A

Scripting　[*sTagName* | *sAttrName* | #text=] *object*.**nodeName**

Possible Values

sTagName　　Name of the element, also available through the **tagName** property.

sAttrName　　Name of the attribute, where the node is an **Attribute** object.

#text　　　　Node that is a **TextNode**.

The property is read-only with no default value.

Example

The following example shows how to use the **nodeName** property to obtain the name of an element.

```
<SCRIPT>
// Returns the element name 'LI' of the list item labeled 'List Item 2'.
var sName = oList.childNodes(1).nodeName;
</SCRIPT>

<BODY>
<UL ID = oList>
<LI>List Item 1
<LI>List Item 2
<LI>List Item 3
</UL>
<BODY>
```

Applies To

 WIN16　　WIN32　　MAC　　UNIX

A, ACRONYM, ADDRESS, APPLET, AREA, Attribute, B, BASE, BASEFONT, BDO, BGSOUND, BIG, BLOCKQUOTE, BODY, BR, BUTTON, CAPTION, CENTER, CITE, CODE, COL, COLGROUP, COMMENT, DD, DEL, DFN, DIR, DIV, DL, DT, EM, EMBED, FIELDSET, FONT, FORM, FRAME, FRAMESET, HEAD, Hn, HR, HTML, I, IFRAME, IMG, INPUT type=button, INPUT type=checkbox, INPUT type=file, INPUT type=hidden, INPUT type=image,

Applies To *(continued)*

 WIN16   WIN32   MAC   UNIX

INPUT type=password, INPUT type=radio, INPUT type=reset, INPUT type=submit, INPUT type=text, INS, KBD, LABEL, LEGEND, LI, LINK, LISTING, MAP, MARQUEE, MENU, NEXTID, OBJECT, OL, OPTION, P, PLAINTEXT, PRE, Q, S, SAMP, SCRIPT, SELECT, SMALL, SPAN, STRIKE, STRONG, SUB, SUP, TABLE, TBODY, TD, TEXTAREA, TextNode, TFOOT, TH, THEAD, TITLE, TR, TT, U, UL, VAR, XMP

nodeType Property

Retrieves the type of the requested node.

Syntax

HTML   N/A

Scripting [*iType* =] *oNode*.**nodeType**

Possible Values

1   Element node.

3   Text node.

The property is read-only with no default value.

Remarks

If the node represents an attribute retrieved from the **attributes** collection, the **nodeType** returns null.

Example

The following example shows how to assign the **nodeType** value of the **BODY** object to a variable.

```
var iType = document.body.nodeType;
```

The next example shows how to assign the **nodeType** value of a node created with the **createElement** method to a variable.

```
var oNode = document.createElement("B");
document.body.insertBefore(oNode);
var iType = oNode.nodeType;
```

Applies To

WIN16   WIN32   MAC   UNIX

A, ACRONYM, ADDRESS, APPLET, AREA, Attribute, B, BASE, BASEFONT, BDO, BGSOUND, BIG, BLOCKQUOTE, BODY, BR, BUTTON, CAPTION, CENTER, CITE, CODE, COL, COLGROUP, COMMENT, DD, DEL, DFN, DIR, DIV, DL, DT, EM, EMBED, FIELDSET, FONT, FORM, FRAME, FRAMESET, HEAD, Hn, HR, HTML, I, IFRAME, IMG, INPUT type=button, INPUT type=checkbox, INPUT type=file, INPUT type=hidden, INPUT type=image, INPUT type=password, INPUT type=radio, INPUT type=reset, INPUT type=submit, INPUT type=text, INS, KBD, LABEL, LEGEND, LI, LINK, LISTING, MAP, MARQUEE, MENU, NEXTID, OBJECT, OL, OPTION, P, PLAINTEXT, PRE, Q, S, SAMP, SCRIPT, SELECT, SMALL, SPAN, STRIKE, STRONG, SUB, SUP, TABLE, TBODY, TD, TEXTAREA, TextNode, TFOOT, TH, THEAD, TITLE, TR, TT, U, UL, VAR, XMP

nodeValue Property

Sets or retrieves the value of a node.

Syntax

HTML   N/A

Scripting *object*.**nodeValue** [= *sValue*]

Possible Values

sValue   String value or null.

The property is read/write with no default value.

Remarks

If the object is a text node, the **nodeValue** property returns a string specifying the text contained by the node.

If the object is an attribute retrieved from the **attributes** collection, the **nodeValue** property returns the value of the attribute if it has been specified, or null otherwise.

If the object is an element, the **nodeValue** property returns null. Use the **nodeName** property to determine the element name.

Example

The following example shows how to alter the text of the specified list item by setting the **nodeValue** property of the text node contained by that list item.

```
<SCRIPT>
function fnChangeValue(oList, iItem, sValue){
    // Only perform the operation on lists.
    if (oList.nodeName != "UL" && oList.nodeName != "OL")
        return false;

    // Only perform the operation if the specified index is
    // within the acceptable range of available list items.
    if (iItem > oList.childNodes.length -1)
        return false;

    // Get a reference to the specified list item.
    var oLI = oList.childNodes(i);
    if (!oLI)
        return false;

    // Get a reference to the text node contained by the list item.
    var oText = oLI.childNodes(0);
    // Ensure that the node is a text node.
    if (oText.nodeType != 3)
        return false;

    oText.nodeValue = sValue;
    return true;
}
</SCRIPT>

<UL ID="oList" onclick="fnChangeValue(this, 0, 'New Node value')">
<LI>Old Node Value
</UL>
```

Applies To

 WIN16   WIN32   MAC   UNIX

A, ACRONYM, ADDRESS, APPLET, AREA, Attribute, B, BASE, BASEFONT, BDO, BGSOUND, BIG, BLOCKQUOTE, BODY, BR, BUTTON, CAPTION, CENTER, CITE, CODE, COL, COLGROUP, COMMENT, DD, DEL, DFN, DIR, DIV, DL, DT, EM, EMBED, FIELDSET, FONT, FORM, FRAME, FRAMESET, HEAD, Hn, HR, HTML, I, IFRAME, IMG, INPUT type=button, INPUT type=checkbox, INPUT type=file, INPUT type=hidden, INPUT type=image, INPUT type=password, INPUT type=radio, INPUT type=reset, INPUT type=submit, INPUT type=text, INS, KBD, LABEL, LEGEND, LI, LINK, LISTING, MAP, MARQUEE,

Applies To *(continued)*

 WIN16   WIN32   MAC   UNIX

MENU, NEXTID, OBJECT, OL, OPTION, P, PLAINTEXT, PRE, Q, S, SAMP,
SCRIPT, SELECT, SMALL, SPAN, STRIKE, STRONG, SUB, SUP, TABLE,
TBODY, TD, TEXTAREA, TextNode, TFOOT, TH, THEAD, TITLE, TR, TT, U, UL,
VAR, XMP

NOHREF Attribute | noHref Property

Sets or retrieves whether clicks in this region cause action.

Syntax

HTML   <AREA **NOHREF** ... >

Scripting   *area*.**noHref** [= *bHref*]

Possible Values

false   Clicks cause action.

true   Clicks do not cause action.

The property is read/write with a default value of false.

Applies To

 WIN16   WIN32   MAC

AREA

 UNIX

AREA

NORESIZE Attribute | noResize Property

Sets or retrieves whether the user can resize the frame.

Syntax

HTML   <*ELEMENT* **NORESIZE** ... >

Scripting *object*.**noResize** [= *bResize*]

Possible Values

> `false` User can resize the frame.
>
> `true` User cannot resize the frame.
>
> The property is read/write with a default value of `false`.

Applies To

 WIN16   WIN32   MAC   UNIX

> FRAME

NOSHADE Attribute | noShade Property

Sets or retrieves whether the horizontal rule is drawn with 3-D shading.

Syntax

> **HTML**   <HR **NOSHADE** ... >
>
> **Scripting**   *hr*.**noShade** [= *bShade*]

Possible Values

> `false`   Horizontal rule is drawn with 3-D shading.
>
> `true`   Horizontal rule is drawn without 3-D shading.
>
> The property is read/write with a default value of `false`.

Applies To

 WIN16   WIN32   MAC

> HR

 UNIX

> HR

NOWRAP Attribute | noWrap Property

Sets or retrieves whether the browser automatically performs wordwrap.

Syntax

HTML	*<ELEMENT* **NOWRAP** ... *>*
Scripting	*object*.**noWrap** [= *bWrap*]

Possible Values

false	Browser automatically wraps the text.
true	Browser does not wrap the text.

The property is read/write with a default value of false.

Applies To

WIN16	WIN32	MAC	

TD, TH

WIN16	WIN32	MAC	UNIX

BODY, DD, DIV, DT, TD, TH

object Property

Retrieves the contained object.

Syntax

HTML	N/A
Scripting	[*oObject* =] *object*.**object**

Possible Values

oObject Contained object.

The property is read-only with no default value.

Remarks

If the control's object model uses a conflicting namespace, precede the control's property with **object** to resolve the conflict.

Applies To

 WIN16 WIN32 MAC UNIX

OBJECT

offscreenBuffering Property

Sets or retrieves whether objects are drawn offscreen before being made visible to the user.

Syntax

HTML   N/A

Scripting   *window*.**offscreenBuffering** [= *vBuffering*]

Possible Values

auto   String value that allows Internet Explorer to decide when offscreen buffering is used.

true   Boolean value that enables offscreen buffering.

false   Boolean value that disables offscreen buffering.

The property is read/write with a default value of auto.

Remarks

The value of the **offscreenBuffering** property determines how the current page is drawn. When the property is set to true, objects are added to an offscreen buffer. Once all objects are drawn, the contents of the offscreen buffer are made visible to the user. When the property is set to false, objects are rendered directly to the screen.

By default, Internet Explorer decides when to buffer objects offscreen. In addition, Internet Explorer automatically enables offscreen buffering when Microsoft DirectX®-based components are used on the page.

Applies To

 WIN16 WIN32 MAC UNIX

window

offsetHeight Property

Retrieves the height of the object relative to the layout or coordinate parent, as given by the **offsetParent** property.

Syntax

HTML   N/A

Scripting   [*iHeight* =] *object*.**offsetHeight**

Possible Values

iHeight   Integer specifying the height, in pixels.

The property is read-only with no default value.

Remarks

You can determine the location, width, and height of an object by using a combination of the **offsetLeft**, **offsetTop**, **offsetHeight**, and **offsetWidth** properties. These numeric properties specify the physical coordinates and dimensions of the object relative to the object's offset parent.

Example

The following example shows how to adjust the size of a clock's readout to fit the current width and height of the document body.

```
<HTML>
<HEAD><TITLE>A Simple Clock</TITLE>
<SCRIPT LANGUAGE="JScript">
function startClock()
{
    window.setInterval("Clock_Tick()", 1000);
    Clock_Tick();
}

var iRatio = 4;
function Clock_Tick()
{
    var dToday = Date();
    var sTime = s.substring(11,19);
    var iDocHeight = document.body.offsetHeight;
    var iDocWidth = document.body.offsetWidth;

    if ((iDocHeight*iRatio)>iDocWidth)
        iDocHeight = iDocWidth / iRatio;
    document.all.MyTime.innerText = sTime;
    document.all.MyTime.style.fontSize = iDocHeight;
}
```

```
</SCRIPT>
<BODY onload="startClock()">
<P ID="MyTime"> </P>
</BODY>
</HTML>
```

The next example shows the difference between using the **offsetHeight** property and the **clientHeight** property to measure the object size.

```
<DIV ID=oDiv STYLE="overflow:scroll; width:200; height:100"> . . . </DIV>
<BUTTON onclick="alert(oDiv.clientHeight)">client height</BUTTON>
<BUTTON onclick="alert(oDiv.offsetHeight)">offset height</BUTTON>
```

To see this code in action, refer to the Web Workshop CD-ROM.

Applies To

 WIN16   WIN32   MAC   UNIX

A, ACRONYM, ADDRESS, APPLET, AREA, B, BIG, BLOCKQUOTE, BODY, BR, BUTTON, CAPTION, CENTER, CITE, CODE, COL, COLGROUP, DD, DEL, DFN, DIR, DIV, DL, DT, EM, EMBED, FIELDSET, FONT, FORM, FRAME, Hn, HR, I, IFRAME, IMG, INPUT type=button, INPUT type=checkbox, INPUT type=file, INPUT type=image, INPUT type=password, INPUT type=radio, INPUT type=reset, INPUT type=submit, INPUT type=text, INS, KBD, LABEL, LEGEND, LI, LISTING, MAP, MARQUEE, MENU, NEXTID, NOBR, OBJECT, OL, OPTION, P, PLAINTEXT, PRE, Q, S, SAMP, SELECT, SMALL, SPAN, STRIKE, STRONG, SUB, SUP, TABLE, TBODY, TD, TEXTAREA, TFOOT, TH, THEAD, TR, TT, U, UL, VAR, XMP

 WIN16   WIN32   MAC   UNIX

BDO, RT, RUBY

offsetLeft Property

Retrieves the calculated left position of the object relative to the layout or coordinate parent, as given by the **offsetParent** property.

Syntax

HTML   N/A

Scripting   [*iCoord* =] *object*.**offsetLeft**

Possible Values

iCoord Integer specifying the left position, in pixels.

The property is read-only with no default value.

Remarks

You can determine the location, width, and height of an object by using a combination of the **offsetLeft**, **offsetTop**, **offsetHeight**, and **offsetWidth** properties. These numeric properties specify the physical coordinates and dimensions of the object relative to the object's offset parent.

Example

The following example shows how to use the **offsetLeft** property to determine whether an object is in the user's view.

```
<SCRIPT>
function isinView(oObject)
{
    var oParent = oObject.offsetParent;
    var iOffsetLeft = oDiv.offsetLeft;
    var iClientWidth = oParent.clientWidth;
    if (iOffsetLeft > iClientWidth) {
        alert("Scroll right for the message.");
        }
}
</SCRIPT>
:
<BUTTON onclick="isinView(this)">Click here</BUTTON>
:
<DIV ID=oDiv STYLE="position:absolute; top:200; left:1200;">
:
</DIV>
```

To see this code in action, refer to the Web Workshop CD-ROM.

Applies To

 WIN16   WIN32   MAC   UNIX

A, ACRONYM, ADDRESS, APPLET, AREA, B, BIG, BLOCKQUOTE, BODY, BR, BUTTON, CAPTION, CENTER, CITE, CODE, COL, COLGROUP, DD, DEL, DFN, DIR, DIV, DL, DT, EM, EMBED, FIELDSET, FONT, FORM, FRAME, Hn, HR, I, IFRAME, IMG, INPUT type=button, INPUT type=checkbox, INPUT type=file, INPUT type=image, INPUT type=password, INPUT type=radio, INPUT type=reset, INPUT type=submit, INPUT type=text, INS, KBD, LABEL, LEGEND, LI, LISTING, MAP, MARQUEE, MENU, NEXTID, NOBR, OBJECT, OL,

DHTML Properties

Applies To *(continued)*

 WIN16   WIN32   MAC   UNIX

OPTION, P, PLAINTEXT, PRE, Q, S, SAMP, SELECT, SMALL, SPAN, STRIKE, STRONG, SUB, SUP, TABLE, TBODY, TD, TEXTAREA, TextRange, TFOOT, TH, THEAD, TR, TT, U, UL, VAR, XMP

 WIN16   WIN32   MAC   UNIX

BDO, RT, RUBY

offsetParent Property

Retrieves a reference to the container object that defines the top and left offsets for the object.

Syntax

HTML   N/A

Scripting [*oElement* =] *object*.**offsetParent**

Possible Values

oElement   Container object.

The property is read-only with no default value.

Remarks

The **offsetLeft** and **offsetTop** property values are relative to the object specified by the **offsetParent** property for the object. Most of the time the property returns the **BODY** object.

Note For **TD**, the **offsetParent** property returns **TABLE** in Internet Explorer 5. In Internet Explorer 4.0, it returns **TR**. Use the **parentElement** property if it is important to retrieve the immediate container of the table cell.

Example

The following example shows how to determine the position of a **TD** object. Although the **TD** object appears to the far right in the document, its position is close to the x- and y-axis because its offset parent is a **TABLE** object rather than the document body.

Note For Internet Explorer 4.0, this same sample returns a position of 0,0 because the offset parent is the table row.

```
<HTML>
<HEAD>
  <TITLE>Elements: Positions</TITLE>
  <SCRIPT LANGUAGE="JScript">

  function showPosition()
  {
    var oElement = document.all.oCell;

    alert("The TD element is at (" + oElement.offsetLeft +
          "," + oElement.offsetTop + ")\n" + "The offset parent is "
          + oElement.offsetParent.tagName );
  }
  </SCRIPT>
</HEAD>
<BODY onload="showPosition()">
<P>This document contains a right-aligned table.
<TABLE BORDER=1 ALIGN=right>
  <TR>
    <TD ID=oCell>This is a small table.</TD>
  </TR>
</TABLE>
</BODY>
</HTML>
```

Applies To

WIN16   WIN32   MAC   UNIX

A, ACRONYM, ADDRESS, APPLET, AREA, B, BIG, BLOCKQUOTE, BODY, BR, BUTTON, CAPTION, CENTER, CITE, CODE, COL, COLGROUP, COMMENT, DD, DEL, DFN, DIR, DIV, DL, DT, EM, EMBED, FIELDSET, FONT, FORM, FRAME, Hn, HR, I, IFRAME, IMG, INPUT type=button, INPUT type=checkbox, INPUT type=file, INPUT type=hidden, INPUT type=image, INPUT type=password, INPUT type=radio, INPUT type=reset, INPUT type=submit, INPUT type=text, INS, KBD, LABEL, LEGEND, LI, LISTING, MAP, MARQUEE, MENU, NEXTID, NOBR, OBJECT, OL, OPTION, P, PLAINTEXT, PRE, Q, S, SAMP, SELECT, SMALL, SPAN, STRIKE, STRONG, SUB, SUP, TABLE, TBODY, TD, TEXTAREA, TFOOT, TH, THEAD, TR, TT, U, UL, VAR, XMP

IE 5 | **WIN16   WIN32   MAC   UNIX**

BDO, RT, RUBY

offsetTop Property

Retrieves the calculated top position of the object relative to the layout or coordinate parent, as given by the **offsetParent** property.

Syntax

HTML   N/A

Scripting [*iCoord* =] *object*.**offsetTop**

Possible Values

iCoord Integer specifying the top position, in pixels.

The property is read-only with no default value.

Remarks

You can determine the location, width, and height of an object by using a combination of the **offsetLeft**, **offsetTop**, **offsetHeight**, and **offsetWidth** properties. These numeric properties specify the physical coordinates and dimensions of the object relative to the object's offset parent.

Example

The following example shows how to use the **offsetTop** property to determine whether an object is in view.

```
<SCRIPT>
function isinView(oObject)
{
    var oParent = oObject.offsetParent;
    var iOffsetTop = oObject.offsetTop;
    var iClientHeight = oParent.clientHeight;
    if (iOffsetHeight > iClientHeight) {
        alert("Scroll down for the message.");
    }
}
</SCRIPT>
:
<BUTTON onclick="isinView(this)">Click here</BUTTON>
:
<DIV ID=oDiv STYLE="position:absolute; top:900; left:0;">
:
</DIV>
```

To see this code in action, refer to the Web Workshop CD-ROM.

Applies To

 IE 4

WIN16   WIN32   MAC   UNIX

A, ACRONYM, ADDRESS, APPLET, AREA, B, BIG, BLOCKQUOTE, BODY,
BR, BUTTON, CAPTION, CENTER, CITE, CODE, COL, COLGROUP, DD, DEL,
DFN, DIR, DIV, DL, DT, EM, EMBED, FIELDSET, FONT, FORM, FRAME, Hn,
HR, I, IFRAME, IMG, INPUT type=button, INPUT type=checkbox, INPUT
type=file, INPUT type=image, INPUT type=password, INPUT type=radio, INPUT
type=reset, INPUT type=submit, INPUT type=text, INS, KBD, LABEL, LEGEND,
LI, LISTING, MAP, MARQUEE, MENU, NEXTID, NOBR, OBJECT, OL,
OPTION, P, PLAINTEXT, PRE, Q, S, SAMP, SELECT, SMALL, SPAN, STRIKE,
STRONG, SUB, SUP, TABLE, TBODY, TD, TEXTAREA, TextRange, TFOOT, TH,
THEAD, TR, TT, U, UL, VAR, XMP

IE 5

WIN16   WIN32   MAC   UNIX

BDO, RT, RUBY

offsetWidth Property

Retrieves the width of the object relative to the layout or coordinate parent, as given
by the **offsetParent** property.

Syntax

HTML   N/A

Scripting   [*iWidth* =] *object*.**offsetWidth**

Possible Values

iWidth   Integer specifying the width, in pixels.

The property is read-only with no default value.

Remarks

You can determine the location, width, and height of an object by using a combination
of the **offsetLeft**, **offsetTop**, **offsetHeight**, and **offsetWidth** properties. These
numeric properties specify the physical coordinates and dimensions of the object
relative to the object's offset parent.

Example

The following example shows how to adjust the size of a clock's readout to fit the current width and height of the document body.

```
<HTML>
<HEAD><TITLE>A Simple Clock</TITLE>
<SCRIPT LANGUAGE="JScript">
function startClock()
{
    window.setInterval("Clock_Tick()", 1000);
    Clock_Tick();
}

var ratio = 4;
function Clock_Tick()
{
    var s = Date();
    var t = s.substring(11,19);
    var doc_height = document.body.offsetHeight;
    var doc_width = document.body.offsetWidth;

    if ((doc_height*ratio)>doc_width)
        doc_height = doc_width / ratio;
        document.all.MyTime.innerText = t;
        document.all.MyTime.style.fontSize = doc_height;
}
</SCRIPT>
<BODY onload="startClock()">
<P ID="MyTime"> </P>
</BODY>
</HTML>
```

The next example shows the difference between using the **offsetWidth** property and the **clientWidth** property to measure the document size.

```
<DIV ID=oDiv STYLE="overflow:scroll; width:200; height:100"> . . . </DIV>
<BUTTON onclick="alert(oDiv.clientWidth)">client width</BUTTON>
<BUTTON onclick="alert(oDiv.offsetWidth)">offset width</BUTTON>
```

To see this code in action, refer to the Web Workshop CD-ROM.

Applies To

 WIN16   WIN32   MAC   UNIX

A, ACRONYM, ADDRESS, APPLET, AREA, B, BIG, BLOCKQUOTE, BODY, BR, BUTTON, CAPTION, CENTER, CITE, CODE, COL, COLGROUP, DD, DEL, DFN, DIR, DIV, DL, DT, EM, EMBED, FIELDSET, FONT, FORM, FRAME, Hn, HR, I, IFRAME, IMG, INPUT type=button, INPUT type=checkbox, INPUT type=file, INPUT type=image, INPUT type=password, INPUT type=radio,

Applies To *(continued)*

 WIN16   WIN32   MAC   UNIX

INPUT type=reset, INPUT type=submit, INPUT type=text, INS, KBD, LABEL, LEGEND, LI, LISTING, MAP, MARQUEE, MENU, NEXTID, NOBR, OBJECT, OL, OPTION, P, PLAINTEXT, PRE, Q, S, SAMP, SELECT, SMALL, SPAN, STRIKE, STRONG, SUB, SUP, TABLE, TBODY, TD, TEXTAREA, TFOOT, TH, THEAD, TR, TT, U, UL, VAR, XMP

 WIN16   WIN32   MAC   UNIX

BDO, RT, RUBY

offsetX Property

Retrieves the horizontal coordinate of the mouse's position relative to the object firing the event.

Syntax

HTML   N/A

Scripting   [*iCoord* =] *event*.**offsetX**

Possible Values

iCoord   Integer specifying the horizontal coordinate, in pixels.

The property is read-only with no default value.

Remarks

The coordinates match the **offsetLeft** and **offsetTop** properties of the object. Use **offsetParent** to find the container object that defines this coordinate system.

Example

The following example shows how to use the **offsetX** property to determine the mouse position relative to the container that fired the event. The status bar at the bottom of the window shows the mouse position relative to the **BODY**.

```
<SCRIPT>
function offsetCoords()
{
    var offsetInfo = ""
    offsetInfo = "The x coordinate is: " + window.event.offsetX + "\r"
    offsetInfo += "The y coordinate is: " + window.event.offsetY + "\r"
```

```
        alert(offsetInfo);
}
</SCRIPT>
</HEAD>
<BODY onmousemove="window.status = 'X=' + window.event.offsetX +
    ' Y=' + window.event.offsetY" ondblclick="offsetCoords()">
:
<DIV onclick="offsetCoords();" . . . position:absolute; top:200;
    left:300;">
:
</DIV>
```

To see this code in action, refer to the Web Workshop CD-ROM.

Applies To

 WIN16   WIN32   MAC   UNIX

event

offsetY Property

Retrieves the vertical coordinate of the mouse's position relative to the object firing the event.

Syntax

HTML   N/A

Scripting [*iCoord* =] *event*.**offsetY**

Possible Values

iCoord Integer specifying the vertical coordinate, in pixels.

The property is read-only with no default value.

Remarks

The coordinates match the **offsetLeft** and **offsetTop** properties of the object. Use **offsetParent** to find the container object that defines this coordinate system.

Example

The following example shows how to use the **offsetY** property to determine the mouse position relative to the container that fired the event. The status bar at the bottom of the window shows the mouse position relative to the **BODY**.

```
<SCRIPT>
function offsetCoords()
{
    var offsetInfo = ""
    offsetInfo = "The x coordinate is: " + window.event.offsetX + "\r"
    offsetInfo += "The y coordinate is: " + window.event.offsetY + "\r"
    alert(offsetInfo);
}
</SCRIPT>
</HEAD>
<BODY onmousemove="window.status = 'X=' + window.event.offsetX +
    ' Y=' + window.event.offsetY"
    ondblclick="offsetCoords()">
:
<DIV onclick="offsetCoords();" . . . position:absolute; top:200;
    left:300;">
:
</DIV>
```

To see this code in action, refer to the Web Workshop CD-ROM.

Applies To

 WIN16   WIN32   MAC   UNIX

event

onLine Property

Retrieves whether the system is in global offline mode.

Syntax

HTML   N/A

Scripting   [*bOnLine* =] *navigator*.**onLine**

Possible Values

true   System is not in global offline mode.

false   System is in global offline mode.

The property is read-only with no default value.

Remarks

The user can modify the global offline state by selecting the Work Offline item from
the Internet Explorer (version 4.0 and later) File menu. This property does not indicate
whether the system is connected to the network.

Applies To

 WIN16   WIN32   MAC   UNIX

navigator

opener Property

Sets or retrieves a reference to the window that created the current window.

Syntax

HTML   N/A

Scripting   *window*.**opener** [= *sWindow*]

Possible Values

sWindow   String specifying the window reference.

The property is read/write with no default value.

Applies To

 WIN16   WIN32   MAC   UNIX

window

outerHTML Property

Sets or retrieves the object and its content in HTML.

Syntax

HTML   N/A

Scripting   *object*.**outerHTML** [= *sHTML*]

Possible Values

sHTML   String specifying content and HTML tags.

The property is read/write with no default value.

Remarks

The property can be any valid string specifying a combination of text and tags, except for the **HTML**, **HEAD**, **FRAMESET**, and **TITLE** elements.

When the property is set, the given string completely replaces the object, including its start and end tags. If the string contains HTML tags, the string is parsed and formatted as it is placed into the document.

This property is accessible at run time as of Internet Explorer 5. Removing elements at run time before the closing tag has been parsed can prevent other areas of the document from rendering.

You cannot set this property while the document is loading. Wait for the **onload** event before attempting to set the property. When dynamically creating a tag using the **TextRange**, **innerHTML**, or **outerHTML** properties, use JScript (compatible with ECMA 262 language specification) to create new events to handle the newly formed tags. Visual Basic Scripting Edition (VBScript) is not supported.

The **outerHTML** property is read-only on the **BODY**, **TBODY**, **TD**, **TFOOT**, **TH**, **THEAD**, and **TR** objects.

Example

The following example shows how to use the **outerHTML** property to copy an object, accompanying attributes, and children to a list when a user clicks one of the objects.

```
<SCRIPT>
function fnCopyHTML(){
    var oWorkItem = event.srcElement;
    if((oWorkItem.tagName != "UL") && (oWorkItem.tagName != "LI")){
        alert("Adding " + oWorkItem.outerHTML + " to the list.");
        oScratch.innerHTML += oWorkItem.outerHTML + "<BR>";
    }
}
</SCRIPT>

<UL onclick = "fnCopyHTML()">
<LI><B>Bold text</b>
<LI><I>Italic text</I>
<LI><U>Underlined text</i>
<LI><STRIKE>Strikeout text</STRIKE>
</UL>
<P>
<DIV ID = "oScratch" >
</DIV>
```

To see this code in action, refer to the Web Workshop CD-ROM.

Applies To

 WIN16   WIN32   MAC   UNIX

A, ACRONYM, ADDRESS, APPLET, AREA, B, BGSOUND, BIG, BLOCKQUOTE, BR, BUTTON, CENTER, CITE, CODE, COMMENT, DD, DEL, DFN, DIR, DIV, DL, DT, EM, EMBED, FIELDSET, FONT, FORM, Hn, HR, I, IFRAME, IMG, INPUT type=button, INPUT type=checkbox, INPUT type=file, INPUT type=hidden, INPUT type=image, INPUT type=password, INPUT type=radio, INPUT type=reset, INPUT type=submit, INPUT type=text, INS, KBD, LABEL, LEGEND, LI, LISTING, MAP, MARQUEE, MENU, NEXTID, NOBR, OBJECT, OL, P, PLAINTEXT, PRE, Q, S, SAMP, SELECT, SMALL, SPAN, STRIKE, STRONG, SUB, SUP, TABLE, TBODY, TD, TEXTAREA, TFOOT, TH, THEAD, TR, TT, U, UL, VAR, XMP

 WIN16   WIN32   MAC   UNIX

BDO, RT, RUBY, WBR

outerText Property

Sets or retrieves the text of the object.

Syntax

HTML   N/A

Scripting *object*.**outerText** [= *sTxt*]

Possible Values

sTxt   String of text.

The property is read/write with no default value.

Remarks

When the property is set, the given string completely replaces the original text in the object, except in **HTML**, **HEAD**, and **TITLE** objects.

You cannot set this property while the document is loading. Wait for the **onload** event before attempting to set the property. If a tag is dynamically created using **TextRange**, **innerHTML**, or **outerHTML**, use JScript (compatible with ECMA 262 language specification) to create new events to handle the newly formed tags. Visual Basic Scripting Edition (VBScript) is not supported.

The **outerText** property is read-only on the **TBODY**, **TD**, **TFOOT**, **TH**, **THEAD**, and **TR** objects.

Example

The following example shows how to use the **outerText** property to replace an object's contents. The object itself is also replaced.

```
<DIV ID=oDiv>
<P ID=oPara>Here's the text that will change.</P>
</DIV>
:
<BUTTON onclick="oPara.outerText='WOW!
    It changed!'">Change text</BUTTON>
<BUTTON onclick="oDiv.innerHTML='<P ID=oPara>
    And back again</P>'">Reset</BUTTON>
```

To see this code in action, refer to the Web Workshop CD-ROM.

Applies To

 WIN16   WIN32   MAC   UNIX

A, ACRONYM, ADDRESS, APPLET, AREA, B, BGSOUND, BIG, BLOCKQUOTE, BR, BUTTON, CENTER, CITE, CODE, COMMENT, DD, DEL, DFN, DIR, DIV, DL, DT, EM, EMBED, FIELDSET, FONT, FORM, Hn, HR, I, IFRAME, IMG, INPUT type=button, INPUT type=checkbox, INPUT type=file, INPUT type=hidden, INPUT type=image, INPUT type=password, INPUT type=radio, INPUT type=reset, INPUT type=submit, INPUT type=text, INS, KBD, LABEL, LEGEND, LI, LISTING, MAP, MARQUEE, MENU, NEXTID, NOBR, OBJECT, OL, P, PLAINTEXT, PRE, Q, S, SAMP, SELECT, SMALL, SPAN, STRIKE, STRONG, SUB, SUP, TABLE, TBODY, TD, TEXTAREA, TFOOT, TH, THEAD, TR, TT, U, UL, VAR, XMP

 WIN16   WIN32   MAC   UNIX

BDO, RT, RUBY, WBR

overflow Attribute | overflow Property

Sets or retrieves how to manage the content of the object when the content exceeds the height and/or width of the object.

Syntax

HTML   { **overflow:** visible | scroll | hidden | auto }

Scripting *object*.**style.overflow** [= *sOverflow*]

Possible Values

visible   Content is not clipped, and scroll bars are not added.

scroll   Content is clipped, and scroll bars are added even if the content does not exceed the dimensions of the objects.

hidden   Content exceeding the dimensions of the object is not shown.

auto   Content is clipped, and scrolling is added only when necessary.

The property is read/write with a default value of visible; the cascading style sheets (CSS) attribute is not inherited.

Remarks

For the **TEXTAREA** object, only the hidden value is valid. Setting the overflow to hidden on a **TEXTAREA** object hides its scroll bars.

As of Internet Explorer 5, the **TD** element supports the **overflow** property, with a default value of hidden, if the **tableLayout** property for the parent **TABLE** is set to fixed. In a fixed table layout, content that exceeds the dimensions of the cell is clipped if the **overflow** property is set to either hidden, scroll, or auto. Otherwise, setting the value of the **overflow** property to visible causes the extra text to overflow into the right neighboring cell (or left if the **direction** property is set to rtl), continuing until the end of the row.

The default value for the **BODY** element is auto.

Setting the **overflow** property to visible causes the object to clip to the size of window or frame that contains the object.

This property is available on the Macintosh platform as of Internet Explorer 5.

Example

The following examples show how to use the **overflow** attribute and the **overflow** property to manage content of the object.

The sample below uses an inline style to automatically adjust itself to overflowing content when the page is loaded.

```
<DIV ID=oTxt STYLE="width: 200px; height: 200px; overflow: auto;">
:
</DIV>
```

This sample below provides scripting to cycle through the different overflow values when a button is clicked.

```
<SCRIPT>
function fnSwitchFlow(){
    if(oTxt.style.overflow=="auto"){
        oTxt.style.overflow="scroll";
    }
    :
}
</SCRIPT>
:
<INPUT onclick="fnSwitchFlow()" value="Switch overflow">
```

To see this code in action, refer to the Web Workshop CD-ROM.

Applies To

 WIN16   WIN32   UNIX   MAC

ADDRESS, APPLET, B, BIG, BLOCKQUOTE, CENTER, CITE, CODE, DD, DFN, DIR, DIV, DL, DT, EM, EMBED, FIELDSET, FORM, Hn, I, IFRAME, KBD, LABEL, LEGEND, LI, LISTING, MENU, OL, P, PRE, S, SAMP, SELECT, SMALL, SPAN, STRIKE, STRONG, style, SUB, SUP, TABLE, TEXTAREA, TT, U, UL, VAR, XMP

IE 5   **WIN16   WIN32   MAC   UNIX**

A, ACRONYM, ADDRESS, APPLET, B, BDO, BIG, BLOCKQUOTE, BODY, CENTER, CITE, CODE, currentStyle, DD, DEL, DFN, DIR, DIV, DL, DT, EM, EMBED, FIELDSET, FONT, FORM, Hn, I, IFRAME, INS, KBD, LABEL, LEGEND, LI, LISTING, MENU, OL, P, PLAINTEXT, PRE, Q, RT, RUBY, runtimeStyle, S, SAMP, SELECT, SMALL, SPAN, STRIKE, STRONG, SUB, SUP, TABLE, TD, TEXTAREA, TT, U, UL, VAR, XMP

overflow-x Attribute | overflowX Property

Sets or retrieves how to manage the content of the object when the content exceeds the width of the object.

Syntax

HTML   { **overflow-x:** visible | scroll | hidden | auto }

Scripting   *object*.**style.overflowX** [= *sOverflow*]

Possible Values

visible   Content is not clipped, and scroll bars are not added. Elements are clipped to the size of the containing window or frame.

scroll   Content is clipped. Scroll bars are added even if the content does not exceed the dimensions of the object

hidden   Content that exceeds the dimensions of the object is not shown.

auto   Content is clipped, and scrolling is added only when necessary.

The property is read/write with a default value of visible; the proposed cascading style sheets (CSS) extension attribute is not inherited.

Remarks

For the **TEXTAREA** object, only the hidden value is valid. Setting the property to hidden on a **TEXTAREA** object hides its scroll bars.

Applies To

 WIN16   WIN32   UNIX   MAC

ADDRESS, APPLET, B, BIG, BLOCKQUOTE, CENTER, CITE, CODE, DD, DFN, DIR, DIV, DL, DT, EM, EMBED, FIELDSET, FORM, Hn, I, IFRAME, KBD, LABEL, LEGEND, LI, LISTING, MENU, OL, P, PRE, S, SAMP, SELECT, SMALL, SPAN, STRIKE, STRONG, style, SUB, SUP, TABLE, TEXTAREA, TT, U, UL, VAR, XMP

 WIN16   WIN32   MAC   UNIX

A, ACRONYM, ADDRESS, APPLET, B, BDO, BIG, BLOCKQUOTE, BODY, CENTER, CITE, CODE, currentStyle, DD, DEL, DFN, DIR, DIV, DL, DT, EM, EMBED, FIELDSET, FONT, FORM, Hn, I, IFRAME, INS, KBD, LABEL,

Applies To *(continued)*

 WIN16   WIN32   MAC   UNIX

LEGEND, LI, LISTING, MENU, OL, P, PLAINTEXT, PRE, Q, RT, RUBY, runtimeStyle, S, SAMP, SELECT, SMALL, SPAN, STRIKE, STRONG, SUB, SUP, TABLE, TEXTAREA, TT, U, UL, VAR, XMP

overflow-y Attribute | overflowY Property

Sets or retrieves how to manage the content of the object when the content exceeds the height of the object.

Syntax

HTML   { **overflow-y:** `visible` | `scroll` | `hidden` | `auto` }

Scripting *object*.**style.overflowY** [= *sOverflow*]

Possible Values

`visible`   Content is not clipped, and scroll bars are not added. Elements are clipped to the size of the containing window or frame.

`scroll`   Content is clipped. Scroll bars are added even if the content does not exceed the dimensions of the object.

`hidden`   Content that exceeds the dimensions of the object is not shown.

`auto`   Content is clipped, and scrolling is added only when necessary.

The property is read/write with a default value of `visible`; the proposed cascading style sheets (CSS) extension attribute is not inherited.

Remarks

For the **TEXTAREA** object, only the `hidden` value is valid. Setting the property to `hidden` on a **TEXTAREA** object hides its scroll bars.

Applies To

 WIN16   WIN32   UNIX   MAC

ADDRESS, APPLET, B, BIG, BLOCKQUOTE, CENTER, CITE, CODE, DD, DFN, DIR, DIV, DL, DT, EM, EMBED, FIELDSET, FORM, Hn, I, IFRAME, KBD, LABEL, LEGEND, LI, LISTING, MENU, OL, P, PRE, S, SAMP, SELECT,

Applies To *(continued)*

WIN16	**WIN32**	**UNIX**	**MAC**

SMALL, SPAN, STRIKE, STRONG, style, SUB, SUP, TABLE, TEXTAREA, TT, U, UL, VAR, XMP

WIN16	**WIN32**	**MAC**	**UNIX**

A, ACRONYM, ADDRESS, APPLET, B, BDO, BIG, BLOCKQUOTE, BODY, CENTER, CITE, CODE, currentStyle, DD, DEL, DFN, DIR, DIV, DL, DT, EM, EMBED, FIELDSET, FONT, FORM, Hn, I, IFRAME, INS, KBD, LABEL, LEGEND, LI, LISTING, MENU, OL, P, PLAINTEXT, PRE, Q, RT, RUBY, runtimeStyle, S, SAMP, SELECT, SMALL, SPAN, STRIKE, STRONG, SUB, SUP, TABLE, TEXTAREA, TT, U, UL, VAR, XMP

owningElement Property

Retrieves the next object that is in the HTML hierarchy.

Syntax

HTML   N/A

Scripting   [*oElement* =] *styleSheet*.**owningElement**

Possible Values

oElement   Next element in the hierarchy.

The property is read-only with no default value.

Remarks

The **owningElement** property usually returns the **STYLE** or **LINK** object that defined the style sheet.

Applies To

WIN16	**WIN32**	**MAC**	**UNIX**

styleSheet

padding Attribute | padding Property

Sets or retrieves how much space to insert between the object and its margin or, if there is a border, between the object and its border.

Syntax

HTML   { **padding:** [*length* I *percentage*]{1,4} }

Scripting *object*.**style.padding** [= *sPadding*]

Possible Values

length	String consisting of a floating-point number, followed by an absolute units designator (cm, mm, in, pt, pc, or px) or a relative units designator (em or ex). For more information about the supported length units for CSS attributes, see "CSS Length Units" in Appendix C.
percentage	String value expressed as a percentage of the width of the parent object. Percentage values are specified as a number, followed by a %.

The property is read/write with a default value of 0; the cascading style sheets (CSS) attribute is not inherited.

Remarks

Padding describes how much space to insert between the object and its margin or, if there is a border, between the object and its border.

Inline elements must have an absolute position or layout to use this property. Set the element layout by providing a value for the **height** property or the **width** property.

This is a composite property. In the HTML syntax, the {1,4} means that up to four padding values can be specified in this order: top, right, bottom, left. If one width is supplied, it is used for all four sides. If two widths are supplied, the first is used for the top and bottom borders, and the second is used for left and right borders. If three widths are supplied, they are used for top, right and left, and bottom borders, respectively. Negative values are not allowed.

Example

The following examples show how to use both the **padding** attribute and the **padding** property.

The sample below uses **TD** as a selector and `padding1` as a class in an embedded style sheet to set the padding for the **TD** object.

```
<STYLE>
    TD { padding: 3mm 8mm }
    .padding1  { padding: 1cm }
</STYLE>
</HEAD>
<BODY>
<TABLE BORDER>
<TR>
    <TD onmouseover="this.className='padding1'"
    onmouseout="this.className=''" ALIGN=middle>
    <IMG src="sphere.jpg">
    </TD>
</TR>
</TABLE>
```

To see this code in action, refer to the Web Workshop CD-ROM.

This sample below uses inline scripting to set the cell's top and bottom padding to 0.5 centimeters and its left and right padding to 0.2 centimeters on an **onmouseover** event.

```
<TD onmouseover="this.style.padding='0.5cm 0.2cm'"
    onmouseout="this.style.padding=''" ALIGN=middle>
    <IMG src="sphere.jpeg">
</TD>
```

To see this code in action, refer to the Web Workshop CD-ROM.

Applies To

 **WIN16   WIN32   MAC   UNIX**

BODY, BUTTON, CAPTION, DIV, ISINDEX, MARQUEE, style, TABLE, TD, TEXTAREA

 MAC

IMG, TR

IE 5 **WIN16   WIN32   MAC   UNIX**

currentStyle, runtimeStyle

padding-bottom Attribute | paddingBottom Property

Sets or retrieves how much space to insert between the bottom border of the object and the content.

Syntax

HTML	{ **padding-bottom:** *length*	*percentage* }
Scripting	*object*.**style.paddingBottom** [= *sPadding*]

Possible Values

length	String consisting of a floating-point number, followed by an absolute units designator (cm, mm, in, pt, pc, or px) or a relative units designator (em or ex). For more information about the supported length units for CSS attributes, see "CSS Length Units" in Appendix C.
percentage	String value expressed as a percentage of the width of the parent object. Percentage values are specified as a number, followed by a %.

The property is read/write with a default value of 0; the cascading style sheets (CSS) attribute is not inherited.

Remarks

Inline elements must have an absolute position or layout to use this property. Element layout is set by providing a value for the **height** property or the **width** property.

Negative values are not allowed.

Example

The following examples show how to use the **padding-bottom** attribute and the **paddingBottom** property.

The sample below uses **TD** as a selector in an embedded style sheet to set the bottom padding for all cells to 1 centimeter.

```
<STYLE>
    TD { padding-bottom: 1cm }
</STYLE>
```

To see this code in action, refer to the Web Workshop CD-ROM.

The sample below uses inline scripting to set the cell's bottom padding to 1 centimeter on an **onmouseover** event.

```
<TD onmouseover="this.style.paddingBottom='1cm'"
    onmouseout="this.style.paddingBottom=''">
    <IMG src="sphere.jpg">
</TD>
```

To see this code in action, refer to the Web Workshop CD-ROM.

Applies To

 WIN16   WIN32   MAC   UNIX

BODY, BUTTON, CAPTION, DIV, ISINDEX, MARQUEE, style, TABLE, TD, TEXTAREA

 MAC

IMG, TR

 WIN16   WIN32   MAC   UNIX

currentStyle, runtimeStyle

padding-left Attribute | paddingLeft Property

Sets or retrieves how much space to insert between the left border of the object and the content.

Syntax

HTML   { **padding-left:** *length* | *percentage* }

Scripting *object*.**style.paddingLeft** [= *sPadding*]

Possible Values

length   String consisting of a floating-point number, followed by an absolute units designator (cm, mm, in, pt, pc, or px) or a relative units designator (em or ex). For more information about the supported length units for CSS attributes, see "CSS Length Units" in Appendix C.

percentage Value expressed as a percentage of the width of the parent object. Percentage values are specified as a number, followed by a %.

The property is read/write with a default value of 0; the cascading style sheets (CSS) attribute is not inherited.

Remarks

Inline elements must have an `absolute` position or layout to use this property. Set the element layout by providing a value for the **height** property or the **width** property.

Negative values are not allowed.

Example

The following examples show how to use the **padding-left** attribute and the **paddingLeft** property.

The sample below uses **TD** as a selector in an embedded style sheet to set the left padding for all table cells to 1 centimeter.

```
<STYLE>
    TD { padding-left: 1cm }
</STYLE>
```

To see this code in action, refer to the Web Workshop CD-ROM.

The sample below uses inline scripting to set the cell's left padding to 1 centimeter on an **onmouseover** event.

```
<TD onmouseover="this.style.paddingLeft='1cm'"
    onmouseout="this.style.paddingLeft=''">
    <IMG src="sphere.jpg">
</TD>
```

To see this code in action, refer to the Web Workshop CD-ROM.

Applies To

IE 4   **WIN16   WIN32   MAC   UNIX**

BODY, BUTTON, CAPTION, DIV, ISINDEX, MARQUEE, style, TABLE, TD, TEXTAREA

IE 4   **MAC**

IMG, TR

IE 5   **WIN16   WIN32   MAC   UNIX**

currentStyle, runtimeStyle

padding-right Attribute | paddingRight Property

Sets or retrieves how much space to insert between the right border of the object and the content.

Syntax

HTML	{ **padding-right:** *length* | *percentage* }
Scripting	*object*.**style.paddingRight** [= *sPadding*]

Possible Values

length String consisting of a floating-point number, followed by an absolute units designator (cm, mm, in, pt, pc, or px) or a relative units designator (em or ex). For more information about the supported length units for CSS attributes, see "CSS Length Units" in Appendix C.

percentage String value expressed as a percentage of the width of the parent object. Percentage values are specified as a number, followed by a %.

The property is read/write with a default value of 0; the cascading style sheets (CSS) attribute is not inherited.

Remarks

Inline elements must have an absolute position or layout to use this property. Element layout is set by providing a value for the **height** property or the **width** property.

Negative values are not allowed.

Example

The following examples show how to use the **padding-right** attribute and the **paddingRight** property.

The sample below uses **TD** as a selector in an embedded style sheet to set the right padding for all table cells to 1 centimeter.

```
<STYLE>
    TD { padding-right: 1cm }
</STYLE>
```

To see this code in action, refer to the Web Workshop CD-ROM.

The sample below uses inline scripting to set the cell's right padding to 1 centimeter on an **onmouseover** event.

```
<TD onmouseover="this.style.paddingRight='1cm'"
    onmouseout="this.style.paddingRight=''">
    <IMG src="sphere.jpg">
</TD>
```

To see this code in action, refer to the Web Workshop CD-ROM.

Applies To

IE 4	WIN16	WIN32	MAC	UNIX

BODY, BUTTON, CAPTION, DIV, ISINDEX, MARQUEE, style, TABLE, TD, TEXTAREA

IE 4	MAC

IMG, TR

IE 5	WIN16	WIN32	MAC	UNIX

currentStyle, runtimeStyle

padding-top Attribute | paddingTop Property

Sets or retrieves the amount of space to insert between the top border of the object and the content.

Syntax

HTML   { **padding-top:** *length | percentage* }

Scripting *object*.**style.paddingTop** [*= sPadding*]

Possible Values

length   String consisting of a floating-point number, followed by an absolute units designator (cm, mm, in, pt, pc, or px) or a relative units designator (em or ex). For more information about the supported length units for CSS attributes, see "CSS Length Units" in Appendix C.

percentage String value expressed as a percentage of the width of the parent object. Percentage values are specified as a number, followed by a %.

The property is read/write with a default value of 0; the cascading style sheets (CSS) attribute is not inherited.

Remarks

Inline elements must have an `absolute` position or layout to use this property. Element layout is set by providing a value for the **height** property or the **width** property.

Negative values are not allowed.

Example

The following examples show how to use the **padding-top** attribute and the **paddingTop** property.

The sample below uses **TD** as a selector in an embedded style sheet to set the top padding for all table cells to 1 centimeter.

```
<STYLE>
    TD { padding-top: 1cm }
</STYLE>
```

To see this code in action, refer to the Web Workshop CD-ROM.

The sample below uses inline scripting to set the cell's top padding to 1 centimeter on an **onmouseover** event.

```
<TD onmouseover="this.style.paddingTop='1cm'"
    onmouseout="this.style.paddingTop=''">
    <IMG src="sphere.jpg">
</TD>
```

To see this code in action, refer to the Web Workshop CD-ROM.

Applies To

 WIN16   WIN32   MAC   UNIX

BODY, BUTTON, CAPTION, DIV, ISINDEX, MARQUEE, style, TABLE, TD, TEXTAREA

 MAC

IMG, TR

 WIN16   WIN32   MAC   UNIX

currentStyle, runtimeStyle

page-break-after Attribute | pageBreakAfter Property

DHTML Properties

Sets or retrieves whether a page break occurs after the object.

Syntax

HTML   { **page-break-after:** always }

Scripting *object*.**style.pageBreakAfter** [= *sBreak*]

Possible Values

always Always insert a page break after the object.

The property is read/write with no default value; the cascading style sheets (CSS) attribute is not inherited.

Remarks

If there are conflicts between this property and the **pageBreakBefore** value on the object previously displayed in the browser, the value that results in the largest number of page breaks is used.

Example

The following examples show how to use the **page-break-after** attribute and the **pageBreakAfter** property to start printing on a new page.

The sample below uses the **P** element as a selector in an embedded style sheet to break the page at the end of all paragraphs.

```
<STYLE>
    P { page-break-after: always }
</STYLE>
</HEAD>
<BODY>
<P>
:
</P>
```

To see this code in action, refer to the Web Workshop CD-ROM.

The sample below uses a call to a function to turn off the page break after the object having an **id** value of idParagraph.

```
<SCRIPT>
function offBreak()
{
    idParagraph.style.pageBreakAfter="";
}
</SCRIPT>
</HEAD>
<BODY>
<BUTTON onClick="offBreak()">Turn off break</BUTTON>
```

To see this code in action, refer to the Web Workshop CD-ROM.

Applies To

 WIN16   WIN32   MAC   UNIX

BLOCKQUOTE, BODY, BUTTON, CENTER, DD, DIR, DIV, DL, DT, FIELDSET, FORM, Hn, ISINDEX, LI, LISTING, MARQUEE, MENU, OL, P, PLAINTEXT, PRE, UL, XMP

 WIN16   WIN32   MAC   UNIX

currentStyle, runtimeStyle, style, TABLE, TD, TR

page-break-before Attribute | pageBreakBefore Property

Sets or retrieves whether a page break occurs before the object.

Syntax

> **HTML**   { **page-break-before:** always }
>
> **Scripting** *object*.**style.pageBreakBefore** [= *sBreak*]

Possible Values

always   Always insert a page break before the object.

The property is read/write with no default value; the cascading style sheets (CSS) attribute is not inherited.

DHTML Properties

Remarks

This property applies when a document gets printed.

If there are conflicts between this property and the **pageBreakAfter** value on the next object to be displayed in the browser , the value that results in the largest number of page breaks is used.

Page breaks are not permitted inside positioned objects.

Example

The following examples show how to use the **page-break-before** attribute and the **pageBreakBefore** property to start printing on a new page.

The sample below uses the **H3** element as a selector in an embedded style sheet to break the page before all **H3** headings.

```
<STYLE>
    H3 { page-break-before: always }
</STYLE>
</HEAD>
<BODY>
<H3>Start New Section on New Page</H3>
```

To see this code in action, refer to the Web Workshop CD-ROM.

The sample below turns off the page break before the object having an **id** value of idParagraph. When the page is printed, a page break occurs before the first paragraph, unless the user clicks the Turn Off Break button.

```
<SCRIPT>
function offBreak()
{
    idParagraph.style.pageBreakBefore="";
}
</SCRIPT>
</HEAD>
<BODY>
<BUTTON onClick="offBreak()">Turn off break</BUTTON>
<P ID="Paragraph" STYLE="page-break-before: always">
:
</P>
```

To see this code in action, refer to the Web Workshop CD-ROM.

Applies To

 WIN16   WIN32   MAC   UNIX

BLOCKQUOTE, BODY, BUTTON, CENTER, DD, DIR, DIV, DL, DT, FIELDSET, FORM, Hn, ISINDEX, LI, LISTING, MARQUEE, MENU, OL, P, PLAINTEXT, PRE, UL, XMP

 WIN16   WIN32   MAC   UNIX

currentStyle, runtimeStyle, style, TABLE, TD, TR

palette Property

Sets or retrieves the palette used for the embedded document.

Syntax

HTML   N/A

Scripting *embed*.**palette** [= *sPalette*]

Possible Values

sPalette String specifying the palette.

The property is read/write with no default value.

Applies To

 WIN16   WIN32   MAC

EMBED

 UNIX

EMBED

parent Property

Retrieves the parent of the window in the object hierarchy.

Syntax

HTML   N/A

Scripting [*oElement* =] *window*.**parent**

Possible Values

oElement   Parent object.

The property is read-only with no default value.

Remarks

For a document, the parent is the containing window. For a window defined using **FRAME**, the parent is the window that contains the corresponding **FRAMESET** definition.

Applies To

 WIN16   WIN32   MAC

window

 UNIX

window

parentElement Property

Retrieves the parent object in the object hierarchy.

Syntax

HTML   N/A

Scripting   [*oElement* =] *object*.**parentElement**

Possible Values

oElement   Parent object.

The property is read-only with no default value.

Remarks

The topmost object returns NULL as its parent.

Applies To

 WIN16   WIN32   MAC   UNIX

TextRange

parentNode Property

Retrieves the parent object in the document hierarchy.

Syntax

HTML   N/A

Scripting   [*oElement* =] *object*.**parentNode**

Possible Values

oElement   Parent object.

The property is read-only with no default value.

Remarks

The topmost object returns NULL as its parent.

Example

The following examples show how to implement the **parentNode** attribute.

The sample below shows how to assign the **parentNode** value of a **SPAN** object to a variable.

```
<SCRIPT>
var oParent = oSpan.parentNode;
</SCRIPt>
:
<BODY>
<SPAN ID=oSpan>A Span</SPAN>
<BODY>
```

The sample below shows how to assign the **parentNode** value of a node created with the **createElement** method to a variable.

```
var oNode = document.createElement("B");
document.body.insertBefore(oNode);
var sType = oNode.parentNode;
```

Applies To

 | **WIN16**   **WIN32**   **MAC**   **UNIX**

A, ACRONYM, ADDRESS, APPLET, AREA, B, BASE, BASEFONT, BDO, BGSOUND, BIG, BLOCKQUOTE, BODY, BR, BUTTON, CAPTION, CENTER, CITE, CODE, COL, COLGROUP, COMMENT, DD, DEL, DFN, DIR, DIV, DL,

Applies To *(continued)*

 WIN16   WIN32   MAC   UNIX

DT, EM, EMBED, FIELDSET, FONT, FORM, FRAME, FRAMESET, HEAD, Hn,
HR, HTML, I, IFRAME, IMG, INPUT type=button, INPUT type=checkbox, INPUT
type=file, INPUT type=hidden, INPUT type=image, INPUT type=password, INPUT
type=radio, INPUT type=reset, INPUT type=submit, INPUT type=text, INS, KBD,
LABEL, LEGEND, LI, LINK, LISTING, MAP, MARQUEE, MENU, NEXTID,
OBJECT, OL, OPTION, P, PLAINTEXT, PRE, Q, S, SAMP, SCRIPT, SELECT,
SMALL, SPAN, STRIKE, STRONG, SUB, SUP, TABLE, TBODY, TD,
TEXTAREA, TFOOT, TH, THEAD, TITLE, TR, TT, U, UL, VAR, XMP

parentStyleSheet Property

Retrieves the style sheet that was used for importing style sheets.

Syntax

HTML   N/A

Scripting   [*sStyleSheet* =] *styleSheet*.**parentStyleSheet**

Possible Values

sStyleSheet   File name of the style sheet.

The property is read-only with no default value.

Applies To

 WIN16   WIN32   MAC   UNIX

styleSheet

parentTextEdit Property

Retrieves the object in the document hierarchy that can be used to create a text range
that contains the original object.

Syntax

HTML   N/A

Scripting   [*oObject* =] *object*.**parentTextEdit**

Possible Values

oObject   Container object that supports text ranges.

The property is read-only with no default value.

Remarks

The property is an object if the parent exists; otherwise, it is null. For example, the **parentTextEdit** property of the **BODY** is null.

Example

The following example shows how to retrieve the parent object (if needed), create the text range, move to the original object, and select the first word in the object.

```
<SCRIPT LANGUAGE="JScript">
function selectWord()
{
    var oSource = window.event.srcElement ;
    if (!oSource.isTextEdit)
        oSource = window.event.srcElement.parentTextEdit;
    if (oSource != null) {
        var oTextRange = oSource.createTextRange();
        oTextRange.moveToElementText(window.event.srcElement);
        oTextRange.collapse();
        oTextRange.expand("word");
        oTextRange.select();
    }
}
</SCRIPT>
```

Applies To

 WIN16   WIN32   MAC   UNIX

A, ACRONYM, ADDRESS, APPLET, AREA, B, BASE, BASEFONT, BGSOUND, BIG, BLOCKQUOTE, BODY, BR, BUTTON, CAPTION, CENTER, CITE, CODE, COL, COLGROUP, COMMENT, DD, DEL, DFN, DIR, DIV, DL, DT, EM, EMBED, FIELDSET, FONT, FORM, FRAME, FRAMESET, HEAD, Hn, HR, HTML, I, IFRAME, IMG, INPUT type=button, INPUT type=checkbox, INPUT type=file, INPUT type=hidden, INPUT type=image, INPUT type=password, INPUT type=radio, INPUT type=reset, INPUT type=submit, INPUT type=text, INS, KBD, LABEL, LEGEND, LI, LINK, LISTING, MAP, MARQUEE, MENU, META, NEXTID, NOBR, OBJECT, OL, OPTION, P, PLAINTEXT, PRE, Q, S, SAMP, SCRIPT, SELECT, SMALL, SPAN, STRIKE, STRONG, SUB, SUP, TABLE, TBODY, TD, TEXTAREA, TFOOT, TH, THEAD, TITLE, TR, TT, U, UL, VAR, XMP

IE 5   WIN16   WIN32   MAC   UNIX

BDO

parentWindow Property

Retrieves a reference to the container object of the window.

Syntax

> **HTML**   N/A
>
> **Scripting** [*sParent* =] *document*.**parentWindow**

Possible Values

> *sParent* String specifying the name of the parent window.
>
> The property is read-only with no default value.

Applies To

 IE 4   WIN16   WIN32   MAC   UNIX

document

pathname Property

Sets or retrieves the file name or path specified by the object.

Syntax

> **HTML**   N/A
>
> **Scripting** *object*.**pathname** [= *sName*]

Possible Values

> *sName* String specifying the file name or object path.
>
> The property is read/write with no default value.

Applies To

IE 3   WIN16   WIN32   MAC

A, AREA, location

UNIX

A, AREA, location

pixelBottom Property

Sets or retrieves the bottom position of the object.

Syntax

HTML   N/A

Scripting   *object*.**style.pixelBottom** [= *iBottom*]

Possible Values

iBottom   Integer specifying the bottom position, in pixels.

The property is read/write with no default value.

Remarks

The **pixelBottom** property reflects the value of the cascading style sheets (CSS) **bottom** attribute for positioned items. The property always returns 0 for nonpositioned items because "bottom" has meaning only when the object is positioned.

Unlike the **bottom** property whose value is a string, the **pixelBottom** value is an integer and is always interpreted in pixels.

Example

The following example shows how to use the **pixelBottom** property to set a positioned **DIV** at the bottom of the client area.

```
oDiv.style.pixelBottom = 0;
```

Applies To

 WIN16   WIN32   MAC   UNIX

A, ACRONYM, ADDRESS, APPLET, AREA, B, BASE, BASEFONT, BIG, BLOCKQUOTE, BODY, BR, BUTTON, CAPTION, CENTER, CITE, CODE, COL, COLGROUP, COMMENT, DD, DEL, DFN, DIR, DIV, DL, DT, EM, EMBED, FIELDSET, FONT, FORM, FRAME, FRAMESET, HEAD, Hn, HR, I, IFRAME, IMG, INPUT type=button, INPUT type=checkbox, INPUT type=file, INPUT type=image, INPUT type=password, INPUT type=radio, INPUT type=reset,

Applies To *(continued)*

 WIN16   WIN32   MAC   UNIX

INPUT type=submit, INPUT type=text, INS, KBD, LABEL, LEGEND, LI, LINK,
LISTING, MAP, MARQUEE, MENU, META, NEXTID, NOBR, OBJECT, OL,
OPTION, P, PLAINTEXT, PRE, Q, S, SAMP, SCRIPT, SELECT, SMALL, SPAN,
STRIKE, STRONG, style, SUB, SUP, TABLE, TBODY, TD, TEXTAREA, TFOOT,
TH, THEAD, TITLE, TR, TT, U, UL, VAR, XMP

 WIN16   WIN32   MAC   UNIX

RT, RUBY, runtimeStyle

DHTML Properties

pixelHeight Property

Sets or retrieves the height of the object.

Syntax

HTML   N/A

Scripting *object*.**style.pixelHeight** [= *iHeight*]

Possible Values

iHeight Integer specifying the height, in pixels.

The property is read/write with no default value.

Remarks

Set this property to change the value of the height without changing the units
designator. Unlike the **height** property whose value is a string, this property's value is
an integer and is always interpreted in pixels.

Example

The following example shows how to increment **pixelHeight** using a timer.

```
<SCRIPT>
function scaleThis()
{
    if (sphere.style.pixelWidth <900) {
        sphere.style.pixelWidth += 4;
        sphere.style.pixelHeight +=4;
        window.setTimeout("scaleThis();", 1);
    }
}
```

```
    :
</SCRIPT>
```

To see this code in action, refer to the Web Workshop CD-ROM.

Applies To

 WIN16   WIN32   MAC   UNIX

A, ACRONYM, ADDRESS, APPLET, AREA, B, BASE, BASEFONT, BIG,
BLOCKQUOTE, BODY, BR, BUTTON, CAPTION, CENTER, CITE, CODE, COL,
COLGROUP, COMMENT, DD, DEL, DFN, DIR, DIV, DL, DT, EM, EMBED,
FIELDSET, FONT, FORM, FRAME, FRAMESET, HEAD, Hn, HR, I, IFRAME,
IMG, INPUT type=button, INPUT type=checkbox, INPUT type=file, INPUT
type=image, INPUT type=password, INPUT type=radio, INPUT type=reset, INPUT
type=submit, INPUT type=text, INS, KBD, LABEL, LEGEND, LI, LINK, LISTING,
MAP, MARQUEE, MENU, META, NEXTID, NOBR, OBJECT, OL, OPTION, P,
PLAINTEXT, PRE, Q, S, SAMP, SCRIPT, SELECT, SMALL, SPAN, STRIKE,
STRONG, style, SUB, SUP, TABLE, TBODY, TD, TEXTAREA, TFOOT, TH,
THEAD, TITLE, TR, TT, U, UL, VAR, XMP

IE 5   **WIN16   WIN32   MAC   UNIX**

RT, RUBY, runtimeStyle

pixelLeft Property

Sets or retrieves the left position of the object.

Syntax

HTML   N/A

Scripting *object*.**style.pixelLeft** [= *iLeft*]

Possible Values

iLeft   Integer specifying the left position, in pixels.

The property is read/write with no default value.

Remarks

The **pixelLeft** property reflects the value of the CSS **left** attribute for positioned items. The property always returns 0 for nonpositioned items because "left" has meaning only when the object is positioned. Use the **offsetLeft** property to calculate actual positions within the document area.

Unlike the **left** property, the **pixelLeft** value is an integer, not a string, and is always interpreted in pixels.

Applies To

 WIN16   WIN32   MAC   UNIX

A, ACRONYM, ADDRESS, APPLET, AREA, B, BASE, BASEFONT, BIG, BLOCKQUOTE, BODY, BR, BUTTON, CAPTION, CENTER, CITE, CODE, COL, COLGROUP, COMMENT, DD, DEL, DFN, DIR, DIV, DL, DT, EM, EMBED, FIELDSET, FONT, FORM, FRAME, FRAMESET, HEAD, Hn, HR, I, IFRAME, IMG, INPUT type=button, INPUT type=checkbox, INPUT type=file, INPUT type=image, INPUT type=password, INPUT type=radio, INPUT type=reset, INPUT type=submit, INPUT type=text, INS, KBD, LABEL, LEGEND, LI, LINK, LISTING, MAP, MARQUEE, MENU, META, NEXTID, NOBR, OBJECT, OL, OPTION, P, PLAINTEXT, PRE, Q, S, SAMP, SCRIPT, SELECT, SMALL, SPAN, STRIKE, STRONG, style, SUB, SUP, TABLE, TBODY, TD, TEXTAREA, TFOOT, TH, THEAD, TITLE, TR, TT, U, UL, VAR, XMP

 WIN16   WIN32   MAC   UNIX

RT, RUBY, runtimeStyle

pixelRight Property

Sets or retrieves the right position of the object.

Syntax

HTML   N/A

Scripting   *object*.**style.pixelRight** [= *iRight*]

Possible Values

iRight   Integer specifying the right position, in pixels.

The property is read/write with no default value.

Remarks

The **pixelRight** property reflects the value of the cascading style sheets (CSS) **right** attribute for positioned items. The property always returns 0 for nonpositioned items because "right" has meaning only when the object is positioned.

Unlike the **right** property whose value is a string, the **pixelRight** value is an integer and is always interpreted in pixels.

Applies To

WIN16	WIN32	MAC	UNIX

A, ACRONYM, ADDRESS, APPLET, AREA, B, BASE, BASEFONT, BIG, BLOCKQUOTE, BODY, BR, BUTTON, CAPTION, CENTER, CITE, CODE, COL, COLGROUP, COMMENT, DD, DEL, DFN, DIR, DIV, DL, DT, EM, EMBED, FIELDSET, FONT, FORM, FRAME, FRAMESET, HEAD, Hn, HR, I, IFRAME, IMG, INPUT type=button, INPUT type=checkbox, INPUT type=file, INPUT type=image, INPUT type=password, INPUT type=radio, INPUT type=reset, INPUT type=submit, INPUT type=text, INS, KBD, LABEL, LEGEND, LI, LINK, LISTING, MAP, MARQUEE, MENU, META, NEXTID, NOBR, OBJECT, OL, OPTION, P, PLAINTEXT, PRE, Q, S, SAMP, SCRIPT, SELECT, SMALL, SPAN, STRIKE, STRONG, style, SUB, SUP, TABLE, TBODY, TD, TEXTAREA, TFOOT, TH, THEAD, TITLE, TR, TT, U, UL, VAR, XMP

WIN16	WIN32	MAC	UNIX

RT, RUBY, runtimeStyle

pixelTop Property

Sets or retrieves the top position of the object.

Syntax

HTML   N/A

Scripting *object*.**style.pixelTop** [= *iTop*]

Possible Values

iTop   Integer specifying the top position, in pixels.

The property is read/write with no default value.

Remarks

The **pixelTop** property reflects the value of the CSS **top** attribute for positioned items. The property always returns 0 for nonpositioned items because "top" has meaning only when the object is positioned. Use the **offsetTop** property to calculate actual positions within the document area.

Unlike the **top** property whose value is a string, the **pixelTop** value is an integer and is always interpreted in pixels.

Applies To

 WIN16   WIN32   MAC   UNIX

A, ACRONYM, ADDRESS, APPLET, AREA, B, BASE, BASEFONT, BIG, BLOCKQUOTE, BODY, BR, BUTTON, CAPTION, CENTER, CITE, CODE, COL, COLGROUP, COMMENT, DD, DEL, DFN, DIR, DIV, DL, DT, EM, EMBED, FIELDSET, FONT, FORM, FRAME, FRAMESET, HEAD, Hn, HR, I, IFRAME, IMG, INPUT type=button, INPUT type=checkbox, INPUT type=file, INPUT type=image, INPUT type=password, INPUT type=radio, INPUT type=reset, INPUT type=submit, INPUT type=text, INS, KBD, LABEL, LEGEND, LI, LINK, LISTING, MAP, MARQUEE, MENU, META, NEXTID, NOBR, OBJECT, OL, OPTION, P, PLAINTEXT, PRE, Q, S, SAMP, SCRIPT, SELECT, SMALL, SPAN, STRIKE, STRONG, style, SUB, SUP, TABLE, TBODY, TD, TEXTAREA, TFOOT, TH, THEAD, TITLE, TR, TT, U, UL, VAR, XMP

 WIN16   WIN32   MAC   UNIX

RT, RUBY, runtimeStyle

pixelWidth Property

Sets or retrieves the width of the object.

Syntax

HTML   N/A

Scripting *object*.**style.pixelWidth** [= *iWidth*]

Possible Values

iWidth   Integer specifying the width, in pixels.

The property is read/write with no default value.

Remarks

Set this property to change the value of the width without changing the units designator. Unlike the **width** property whose value is a string, the **pixelWidth** value is an integer and is always interpreted in pixels.

Example

The following example shows how to increment the **pixelWidth** using a timer.

```
<SCRIPT>
function scaleThis()
{
    if (sphere.style.pixelWidth <900) {
        sphere.style.pixelWidth += 4;
        sphere.style.pixelHeight +=4;
        window.setTimeout("scaleThis();", 1);
    }
}
:
</SCRIPT>
```

To see this code in action, refer to the Web Workshop CD-ROM.

Applies To

 WIN16   WIN32   MAC   UNIX

A, ACRONYM, ADDRESS, APPLET, AREA, B, BASE, BASEFONT, BIG, BLOCKQUOTE, BODY, BR, BUTTON, CAPTION, CENTER, CITE, CODE, COL, COLGROUP, COMMENT, DD, DEL, DFN, DIR, DIV, DL, DT, EM, EMBED, FIELDSET, FONT, FORM, FRAME, FRAMESET, HEAD, Hn, HR, I, IFRAME, IMG, INPUT type=button, INPUT type=checkbox, INPUT type=file, INPUT type=image, INPUT type=password, INPUT type=radio, INPUT type=reset, INPUT type=submit, INPUT type=text, INS, KBD, LABEL, LEGEND, LI, LINK, LISTING, MAP, MARQUEE, MENU, META, NEXTID, NOBR, OBJECT, OL, OPTION, P, PLAINTEXT, PRE, Q, S, SAMP, SCRIPT, SELECT, SMALL, SPAN, STRIKE, STRONG, style, SUB, SUP, TABLE, TBODY, TD, TEXTAREA, TFOOT, TH, THEAD, TITLE, TR, TT, U, UL, VAR, XMP

IE 5 **WIN16   WIN32   MAC   UNIX**

RT, RUBY, runtimeStyle

platform Property

Retrieves the name of the user's operating system.

Syntax

HTML   N/A

Scripting [*sPlatform* =] *navigator*.**platform**

Possible Values

HP-UX	HP UNIX-based machines.
MacPPC	Macintosh PowerPC-based machines.
Mac68K	Macintosh 68K-based machines.
SunOS	Solaris-based machines.
Win32	Windows 32-bit platform.
Win16	Windows 16-bit platform.
WinCE	Windows CE platform.

The property is read-only with no default value.

Applies To

 WIN16   WIN32   MAC   UNIX

navigator

PLUGINSPAGE Attribute | pluginspage Property

Sets or retrieves the URL of the plug-in used to view an embedded document.

Syntax

HTML   <EMBED **PLUGINSPAGE** = *sURL* ... >

Scripting [*sURL* =] *embed*.**pluginspage**

Possible Values

sURL String specifying the URL of the plug-in(s).

The property is read-only with no default value.

DHTML Properties

Applies To

 WIN16   WIN32   MAC   UNIX

EMBED

port Property

Sets or retrieves the port number in a URL.

Syntax

HTML   N/A

Scripting *object*.**port** [= *sPort*]

Possible Values

sPort String specifying the port number associated with the URL.

The property is read/write with a default value of 21 for the FTP protocol, 70 for the gopher protocol, 80 for the HTTP protocol, and 443 for the HTTPS protocol.

Remarks

Proprietary protocols that do not require a port return 0 or an empty string.

Applies To

 WIN16   WIN32   MAC

A, AREA, location

 UNIX

A, AREA, location

posBottom Property

Sets or retrieves the bottom position of the object in the units specified by the cascading style sheets (CSS) **bottom** attribute.

Syntax

HTML   N/A

Scripting *object*.**style.posBottom** [= *fBottom*]

Possible Values

fBottom   Any valid floating-point number that uses the same length units as the
bottom attribute.

The property is read/write with no default value.

Remarks

This property reflects the value of the CSS **bottom** attribute for positioned items. This
property always returns 0 for nonpositioned items because "bottom" has meaning only
when the object is positioned.

Setting this property changes the value of the bottom position, but leaves the length
units designator for the property unchanged.

Unlike the **bottom** property whose value is a string, the value of the **posBottom**
property is a floating-point number.

Example

The following example shows how to use the **posBottom** property to set a positioned
DIV to the bottom of the client area.

```
oDiv.style.posBottom = 0;
```

Applies To

 WIN16   WIN32   MAC   UNIX

A, ACRONYM, ADDRESS, APPLET, AREA, B, BASE, BASEFONT, BIG,
BLOCKQUOTE, BODY, BR, BUTTON, CAPTION, CENTER, CITE, CODE, COL,
COLGROUP, COMMENT, DD, DEL, DFN, DIR, DIV, DL, DT, EM, EMBED,
FIELDSET, FONT, FORM, FRAME, FRAMESET, HEAD, Hn, HR, I, IFRAME,
IMG, INPUT type=button, INPUT type=checkbox, INPUT type=file, INPUT
type=image, INPUT type=password, INPUT type=radio, INPUT type=reset, INPUT
type=submit, INPUT type=text, INS, KBD, LABEL, LEGEND, LI, LINK, LISTING,
MAP, MARQUEE, MENU, META, NEXTID, NOBR, OBJECT, OL, OPTION, P,
PLAINTEXT, PRE, Q, S, SAMP, SCRIPT, SELECT, SMALL, SPAN, STRIKE,
STRONG, style, SUB, SUP, TABLE, TBODY, TD, TEXTAREA, TFOOT, TH,
THEAD, TITLE, TR, TT, U, UL, VAR, XMP

IE 5   **WIN16   WIN32   MAC   UNIX**

RT, RUBY, runtimeStyle

DHTML Properties

posHeight Property

Sets or retrieves the height of the object in the units specified by the cascading style sheets (CSS) **height** attribute.

Syntax

HTML   N/A

Scripting   *object*.**style.posHeight** [= *fHeight*]

Possible Values

fHeight   Any valid floating-point number that uses the same length units as the **height** attribute.

The property is read/write with no default value.

Remarks

Unlike the **height** property whose value is a string, the value of the **posHeight** property is a floating-point number. Setting the **posHeight** property changes the value of the height, but leaves the units designator for the property unchanged.

Example

The following example shows how to use JScript (compatible with ECMA 262 language specification) to increase the height of the first **IMG** element by 10 units.

```
document.all.tags("IMG").item(0).style.posHeight += 10;
```

Applies To

WIN16	WIN32	MAC	UNIX

A, ACRONYM, ADDRESS, APPLET, AREA, B, BASE, BASEFONT, BIG, BLOCKQUOTE, BODY, BR, BUTTON, CAPTION, CENTER, CITE, CODE, COL, COLGROUP, COMMENT, DD, DEL, DFN, DIR, DIV, DL, DT, EM, EMBED, FIELDSET, FONT, FORM, FRAME, FRAMESET, HEAD, Hn, HR, I, IFRAME, IMG, INPUT type=button, INPUT type=checkbox, INPUT type=file, INPUT type=image, INPUT type=password, INPUT type=radio, INPUT type=reset, INPUT type=submit, INPUT type=text, INS, KBD, LABEL, LEGEND, LI, LINK, LISTING, MAP, MARQUEE, MENU, META, NEXTID, NOBR, OBJECT, OL, OPTION, P, PLAINTEXT, PRE, Q, S, SAMP, SCRIPT, SELECT, SMALL, SPAN, STRIKE, STRONG, style, SUB, SUP, TABLE, TBODY, TD, TEXTAREA, TFOOT, TH, THEAD, TITLE, TR, TT, U, UL, VAR, XMP

DHTML Properties

IE 5	**WIN16**	**WIN32**	**MAC**	**UNIX**

RT, RUBY, runtimeStyle

position Attribute | position Property

Retrieves the type of positioning used for the object.

Syntax

HTML   { **position:** static | absolute | relative }

Scripting [*sPosition* =] *object*.**style.position**

Possible Values

static   No special positioning; the object obeys the layout rules of HTML.

absolute   Object is positioned relative to the next positioned parent—or to the **BODY** if there isn't one—using the **top** and **left** properties.

relative   Object is positioned according to the normal flow, then offset by the **top** and **left** properties.

This read-only property has a default value of static; the cascading style sheets (CSS) attribute is not inherited.

Remarks

Setting the property to absolute pulls the object out of the "flow" of the document and positions it regardless of the layout of surrounding objects. If other objects already occupy the given position, they do not affect the positioned object, nor does the positioned object affect them. Instead, all objects are drawn at the same place, causing the objects to overlap. This overlap is controlled by using the **z-index** attribute or property. Absolutely positioned objects do not have margins, but they do have borders and padding.

Setting the property to relative places the object in the natural HTML flow of the document, but offsets the position of the object based on the preceding content. For example, you can create superscript text by placing the text in a **SPAN** that is positioned relative to the remaining text in the paragraph:

```
<P>The superscript in this name
    <SPAN STYLE="position:relative;
    top:-3px">xyz </SPAN> is "xyz".</P>
```

Text and objects that follow a relatively positioned object occupy their own space and do not overlap the natural space for the positioned object. Contrast this with an absolutely positioned object, where subsequent text and objects occupy what would have been the natural space for the positioned object before it was pulled out of the flow.

The size of content determines the size of objects with layout. For example, setting the **height** and **position** properties on a **DIV** object gives it layout. The contents of the **DIV** determine the size of the **width**.

See the Applies To listings for elements that can be relatively and absolutely positioned.

Example

The following examples show how to use the absolute, static, and relative values of the **position** property.

```
<STYLE>
.pitem { position: static }
</STYLE>

<SCRIPT>
function fnAbsolute(){
    oSpan.style.position="absolute";
}
function fnRelative(){
    oSpan.style.position="relative";
}
function fnStatic(){
    oSpan.style.position="static";
}
</SCRIPT>
<P>
<SPAN ID=oSpan CLASS="pitem">
This is a SPAN in a paragraph of text.
</SPAN>

This is a paragraph of text.</P>

<INPUT onclick="fnRelative()" TYPE=button VALUE="Relative">
<INPUT onclick="fnAbsolute()" TYPE=button VALUE="Absolute">
<INPUT onclick="fnStatic()" TYPE=button VALUE="Static">
```

To see this code in action, refer to the Web Workshop CD-ROM.

Applies To

WIN16	WIN32	MAC	UNIX

A, ADDRESS, APPLET, B, BDO, BIG, BLOCKQUOTE, BUTTON, CENTER, CITE, CODE, DD, DFN, DIR, DIV, DL, DT, EM, EMBED, FIELDSET, FORM, Hn, HR, I, IFRAME, IMG, INPUT type=button, INPUT type=checkbox, INPUT type=file, INPUT type=image, INPUT type=password, INPUT type=radio, INPUT type=reset, INPUT type=submit, INPUT type=text, ISINDEX, KBD, LABEL, LEGEND, LI, LISTING, MARQUEE, MENU, OBJECT, OL, P, PRE, RUBY, S, SAMP, SELECT, SMALL, SPAN, STRIKE, STRONG, style, SUB, SUP, TABLE, TEXTAREA, TT, U, UL, VAR, XMP

WIN16	WIN32	MAC	UNIX

currentStyle, runtimeStyle

posLeft Property

Sets or retrieves the left position of the object in the units specified by the cascading style sheets (CSS) **left** attribute.

Syntax

HTML   N/A

Scripting   *object*.**style.posLeft** [= *fLeft*]

Possible Values

fLeft   Any valid floating-point number that uses the same length units as the **left** attribute.

The property is read/write with no default value.

Remarks

This property reflects the value of the CSS **left** attribute for positioned items. This property always returns 0 for nonpositioned items because "left" has meaning only when the object is positioned. Use the **offsetLeft** property to calculate actual positions within the document area.

Setting this property changes the value of the left position, but leaves the units designator for the property unchanged.

Unlike the **left** property whose value is a string, the value of the **posLeft** property is a floating-point number.

Example

The following example shows how to use JScript (compatible with ECMA 262 language specification) to move the first **IMG** object left by 10 units.

```
document.all.tags("IMG").item(0).style.posLeft -= 10;
```

The next example shows how increment **posLeft** using a timer.

```
<SCRIPT>
function moveThis()
{
:

    if (sphere.style.posLeft<900) {
        sphere.style.posTop += 2;
        sphere.style.posLeft += 2;
        window.setTimeout("moveThis();", 1);
        }
}
:
</SCRIPT>
```

To see this code in action, refer to the Web Workshop CD-ROM.

Applies To

 WIN16   WIN32   MAC   UNIX

A, ACRONYM, ADDRESS, APPLET, AREA, B, BASE, BASEFONT, BIG, BLOCKQUOTE, BODY, BR, BUTTON, CAPTION, CENTER, CITE, CODE, COL, COLGROUP, COMMENT, DD, DEL, DFN, DIR, DIV, DL, DT, EM, EMBED, FIELDSET, FONT, FORM, FRAME, FRAMESET, HEAD, Hn, HR, I, IFRAME, IMG, INPUT type=button, INPUT type=checkbox, INPUT type=file, INPUT type=image, INPUT type=password, INPUT type=radio, INPUT type=reset, INPUT type=submit, INPUT type=text, INS, KBD, LABEL, LEGEND, LI, LINK, LISTING, MAP, MARQUEE, MENU, META, NEXTID, NOBR, OBJECT, OL, OPTION, P, PLAINTEXT, PRE, Q, S, SAMP, SCRIPT, SELECT, SMALL, SPAN, STRIKE, STRONG, style, SUB, SUP, TABLE, TBODY, TD, TEXTAREA, TFOOT, TH, THEAD, TITLE, TR, TT, U, UL, VAR, XMP

IE 5 **WIN16   WIN32   MAC   UNIX**

RT, RUBY, runtimeStyle

posRight Property

Sets or retrieves the right position of the object in the units specified by the cascading style sheets (CSS) **right** attribute.

Syntax

HTML   N/A

Scripting   *object*.**style.posRight** [= *fRight*]

Possible Values

fRight   Any valid floating-point number that uses the same length units as the **right** attribute.

The property is read/write with no default value.

Remarks

This property reflects the value of the CSS **right** attribute for positioned items. This property always returns 0 for nonpositioned items because "right" has meaning only when the object is positioned.

Setting this property changes the value of the right position, but leaves the units designator for the property unchanged.

Unlike the **right** property whose value is a string, the value of the **posRight** property is a floating-point number.

Example

The following example shows how to use the **posRight** property to set a positioned **DIV** 10 pixels from the right of the client area.

```
oDiv.style.posRight = 10;
```

Applies To

 WIN16   WIN32   MAC   UNIX

A, ACRONYM, ADDRESS, APPLET, AREA, B, BASE, BASEFONT, BIG, BLOCKQUOTE, BODY, BR, BUTTON, CAPTION, CENTER, CITE, CODE, COL, COLGROUP, COMMENT, DD, DEL, DFN, DIR, DIV, DL, DT, EM, EMBED, FIELDSET, FONT, FORM, FRAME, FRAMESET, HEAD, Hn, HR, I, IFRAME, IMG, INPUT type=button, INPUT type=checkbox, INPUT type=file,

DHTML Properties

Applies To *(continued)*

 WIN16   WIN32   MAC   UNIX

INPUT type=image, INPUT type=password, INPUT type=radio, INPUT type=reset, INPUT type=submit, INPUT type=text, INS, KBD, LABEL, LEGEND, LI, LINK, LISTING, MAP, MARQUEE, MENU, META, NEXTID, NOBR, OBJECT, OL, OPTION, P, PLAINTEXT, PRE, Q, S, SAMP, SCRIPT, SELECT, SMALL, SPAN, STRIKE, STRONG, style, SUB, SUP, TABLE, TBODY, TD, TEXTAREA, TFOOT, TH, THEAD, TITLE, TR, TT, U, UL, VAR, XMP

 WIN16   WIN32   MAC   UNIX

RT, RUBY, runtimeStyle

posTop Property

Sets or retrieves the top position of the object in the units specified by the cascading style sheets (CSS) **top** attribute.

Syntax

HTML   N/A

Scripting   *object*.**style.posTop** [= *fTop*]

Possible Values

fTop   Any valid floating-point number that uses the same length units as the **top** attribute.

The property is read/write with no default value.

Remarks

This property reflects the value of the CSS **top** attribute for positioned items. This property always returns 0 for nonpositioned items because "top" has meaning only when the object is positioned. Use the **offsetTop** property to calculate actual positions within the document area.

Setting this property changes the value of the top position, but leaves the units designator for the property unchanged.

Unlike the **top** property whose value is a string, the value of the **posTop** property is a floating-point number.

Example

The following example shows how to use JScript (compatible with ECMA 262 language specification) to move the first **IMG** object up by 10 units.

```
document.all.tags("IMG").item(0).style.posTop -= 10;
```

To see this code in action, refer to the Web Workshop CD-ROM.

The next example shows how to increment **posTop** using a timer.

```
<SCRIPT>
function moveThis()
{
:
    if (sphere.style.posLeft<900) {
        sphere.style.posTop += 2;
        sphere.style.posLeft += 2;
        window.setTimeout("moveThis();", 1);
        }
}
:
</SCRIPT>
```

To see this code in action, refer to the Web Workshop CD-ROM.

Applies To

 WIN16   WIN32   MAC   UNIX

A, ACRONYM, ADDRESS, APPLET, AREA, B, BASE, BASEFONT, BIG, BLOCKQUOTE, BODY, BR, BUTTON, CAPTION, CENTER, CITE, CODE, COL, COLGROUP, COMMENT, DD, DEL, DFN, DIR, DIV, DL, DT, EM, EMBED, FIELDSET, FONT, FORM, FRAME, FRAMESET, HEAD, Hn, HR, I, IFRAME, IMG, INPUT type=button, INPUT type=checkbox, INPUT type=file, INPUT type=image, INPUT type=password, INPUT type=radio, INPUT type=reset, INPUT type=submit, INPUT type=text, INS, KBD, LABEL, LEGEND, LI, LINK, LISTING, MAP, MARQUEE, MENU, META, NEXTID, NOBR, OBJECT, OL, OPTION, P, PLAINTEXT, PRE, Q, S, SAMP, SCRIPT, SELECT, SMALL, SPAN, STRIKE, STRONG, style, SUB, SUP, TABLE, TBODY, TD, TEXTAREA, TFOOT, TH, THEAD, TITLE, TR, TT, U, UL, VAR, XMP

IE 5 **WIN16   WIN32   MAC   UNIX**

RT, RUBY, runtimeStyle

posWidth Property

Sets or retrieves the width of the object in the units specified by the cascading style sheets (CSS) **width** attribute.

Syntax

HTML   N/A

Scripting   *object*.**style.posWidth** [= *fWidth*]

Possible Values

fWidth   Any valid floating-point number that uses the same length units as the **width** attribute.

The property is read/write with no default value.

Remarks

Setting the **posWidth** property changes the value of the width, but leaves the units designator for the property unchanged.

Unlike the **width** property whose value is a string, this property's value is a floating-point number.

Example

The following example shows how to use JScript (compatible with ECMA 262 language specification) to increase the width of the first **IMG** object by 10 units.

```
document.all.tags("IMG").item(0).style.posWidth += 10;
```

Applies To

 WIN16   WIN32   MAC   UNIX

A, ACRONYM, ADDRESS, APPLET, AREA, B, BASE, BASEFONT, BIG, BLOCKQUOTE, BODY, BR, BUTTON, CAPTION, CENTER, CITE, CODE, COL, COLGROUP, COMMENT, DD, DEL, DFN, DIR, DIV, DL, DT, EM, EMBED, FIELDSET, FONT, FORM, FRAME, FRAMESET, HEAD, Hn, HR, I, IFRAME, IMG, INPUT type=button, INPUT type=checkbox, INPUT type=file, INPUT type=image, INPUT type=password, INPUT type=radio, INPUT type=reset, INPUT type=submit, INPUT type=text, INS, KBD, LABEL, LEGEND, LI, LINK, LISTING, MAP, MARQUEE, MENU, META, NEXTID, NOBR, OBJECT, OL, OPTION, P,

Applies To *(continued)*

 WIN16   WIN32   MAC   UNIX

PLAINTEXT, PRE, Q, S, SAMP, SCRIPT, SELECT, SMALL, SPAN, STRIKE, STRONG, style, SUB, SUP, TABLE, TBODY, TD, TEXTAREA, TFOOT, TH, THEAD, TITLE, TR, TT, U, UL, VAR, XMP

 WIN16   WIN32   MAC   UNIX

RT, RUBY, runtimeStyle

previousSibling Property

Retrieves a reference to the previous sibling for the specified object.

Syntax

HTML   N/A

Scripting   [*oElement* =] *object*.**previousSibling**

Possible Values

oElement   Reference to the previous sibling of an object.

The property is read-only with no default value.

Example

The following example shows how to use the **previousSibling** property to obtain the previous sibling of a list item.

```
<SCRIPT>
// Returns the list item labeled 'List Item 1'.
var oSibling = oList.childNodes(1).previousSibling;
</SCRIPT>
:
<BODY>
<UL ID = oList>
<LI>List Item 1
<LI>List Item 2
<LI>List Item 3
</UL>
</BODY>
```

Applies To

 WIN16   WIN32   MAC   UNIX

A, ACRONYM, ADDRESS, APPLET, AREA, B, BASE, BASEFONT, BDO,
BGSOUND, BIG, BLOCKQUOTE, BODY, BR, BUTTON, CAPTION, CENTER,
CITE, CODE, COL, COLGROUP, COMMENT, DD, DEL, DFN, DIR, DIV, DL, DT,
EM, EMBED, FIELDSET, FONT, FORM, FRAME, FRAMESET, HEAD, Hn, HR,
HTML, I, IFRAME, IMG, INPUT type=button, INPUT type=checkbox, INPUT
type=file, INPUT type=hidden, INPUT type=image, INPUT type=password, INPUT
type=radio, INPUT type=reset, INPUT type=submit, INPUT type=text, INS, KBD,
LABEL, LEGEND, LI, LINK, LISTING, MAP, MARQUEE, MENU, NEXTID,
OBJECT, OL, OPTION, P, PLAINTEXT, PRE, Q, S, SAMP, SCRIPT, SELECT,
SMALL, SPAN, STRIKE, STRONG, SUB, SUP, TABLE, TBODY, TD,
TEXTAREA, TextNode, TFOOT, TH, THEAD, TITLE, TR, TT, U, UL, VAR, XMP

propertyName Property

Retrieves the name of the property that has changed on the object.

Syntax

HTML   N/A

Scripting [*sProperty* =] *event*.**propertyName**

Possible Values

sProperty Name of the property whose value changed during the event.

The property is read-only with no default value.

Remarks

This property of the **event** object is used with the **onpropertychange** event.

Example

The following example shows how to use the **propertyName** property with the
onpropertychange event.

```
<HEAD>
<SCRIPT>
function changeProp()
{
    btnProp.value = "This is the new VALUE";
}
```

```
function changeCSSProp()
{
    btnStyleProp.style.backgroundColor = "aqua";
}
</SCRIPT>
</HEAD>
<BODY>
<P>The event object property propertyName is
    used here to return which property has been
    altered.</P>

<INPUT TYPE=button ID=btnProp onclick="changeProp()"
       VALUE="Click to change the VALUE property
       of this button"
       onpropertychange='alert(event.propertyName + "
       property has changed value")'>
<INPUT TYPE=button ID=btnStyleProp
       onclick="changeCSSProp()"
       VALUE="Click to change the CSS backgroundColor
       property of this button"
       onpropertychange='alert(event.propertyName + "
       property has changed value")'>
</BODY>
```

To see this code in action, refer to the Web Workshop CD-ROM.

Applies To

 WIN16   WIN32   MAC   UNIX

event

protocol Property

Sets or retrieves the protocol portion of a URL.

Syntax

HTML   N/A

Scripting   *object*.**protocol** [= *sProtocol*]

Possible Values

sProtocol   Protocol used to transfer information.

The property is read/write with no default value.

Remarks

The **protocol** property specifies how information is transferred from the host to the client. Internet Explorer supports several predefined protocols, including HTTP and FTP.

The **protocol** property returns the initial substring of a URL, including the first colon (for example, http:). The **document** and **location** objects expose the **protocol** property as read-only. The property returns the expanded text of the protocol acronym. For example, the HTTP protocol is returned as Hypertext Transfer Protocol.

Applies To

 WIN16   WIN32   MAC

A, AREA, document, location

 UNIX   WIN16   WIN32   MAC

A, AREA, document, IMG, location

qualifier Property

Retrieves the name of the data member provided by a data source object.

Syntax

HTML	N/A
Scripting	[*sQualifier* =] *event*.**qualifier**

Possible Values

sQualifier   String specifying the name of the data member or an empty string, which indicates the default data member.

The property is read-only with no default value.

Remarks

Check the **qualifier** property in the event handlers of a data source object (DSO) if:

- The DSO supports multiple, named data members.

- You have specified a qualifier in association with the **DATASRC** attribute of an element bound to that DSO.

Valid qualifiers are specific to the DSO implementation. Check the documentation of the DSO to determine if it supports named data members and to determine the valid names for those data members.

Example

The following example demonstrates the typical handling of the **ondatasetcomplete** event fired by a DSO that supports named data members. The hypothetical spreadsheet control defines the name of its data members to match the ranges that can be specified within a typical spreadsheet environment, such as Microsoft® Excel. In the example, the named data member is restricted to the first seven cells of the first column.

```
<SCRIPT>
// Fired when all the data is available.
function handle_dscomplete()
{
    var oEvent = window.event;
    // Ignore the notification for the default data member.
    if (oEvent.qualifier != "")
    {
        // Get a recordset corresponding to the named data member as indicated
        // by the qualifier property.
        var oNamedRS = oEvent.srcElement.namedRecordset(oEvent.qualifier);

        // Now walk the recordset.
        oNamedRS.MoveFirst();
        for (int i = 0; i < oNamedRS.RecordCount; i++)
        {
            var vValue = oNamedRS.Fields(0).value;
            oNamedRS.MoveNext();
        }
    }
}
</SCRIPT>

<!-- The CLASSID below does not correspond to a valid object. -->
<OBJECT CLASSID="clsid:00000000-0000-0000-0000-000000000000" ID="dsoSpreadSheet"
    ondatasetcomplete="handle_dscomplete()">

<!-- Bind the TABLE to the named recordset "A1:A7" provided by the spreadsheet control.
-->
<TABLE DATASRC="#dsoSpreadsheet.A1:A7">
    <TR><TD><SPAN DATAFLD="A"></SPAN></TD></TR>
</TABLE>
```

Applies To

| IE 5 | WIN16 | WIN32 | MAC | UNIX |

event

readOnly Property

Retrieves whether the rule or style sheet is defined on the page or is imported.

Syntax

HTML	N/A
Scripting	[*bReadOnly* =] *object*.**readOnly**

Possible Values

false	Rule or style sheet is obtained through a **LINK** object or the **@import** rule.
true	Rule or style sheet is defined on the page.

The property is read-only with a default value of false.

Remarks

Style sheets obtained through a **LINK** object or the **@import** rule cannot be modified while in edit mode.

Applies To

 WIN16   WIN32   MAC   UNIX

styleSheet, rule

READONLY Attribute | readOnly Property

Sets or retrieves whether the content of the object is read-only.

Syntax

HTML	*<ELEMENT* **READONLY** ... *>*
Scripting	*object*.**readOnly** [= *bRead*]

Possible Values

false	Property is not set on the object.
true	Object is set to read-only.

The property is read/write with a default value of false.

Remarks

If the **readOnly** property is set, the user cannot enter or edit text in the control. The **readOnly** property allows the object to receive the focus, whereas the **disabled** property does not.

Applies To

 WIN16   WIN32   MAC   UNIX

INPUT type=text, INPUT type=password, TEXTAREA

readyState Property

Retrieves the current state of the object being downloaded.

Syntax

HTML   N/A

Scripting   [*sState* =] *object*.**readyState**

Possible Values

uninitialized	Object is not initialized with data.
loading	Object is loading its data.
loaded	Object has finished loading its data.
interactive	User can interact with the object even though it is not fully loaded.
complete	Object is completely initialized.

The property is read-only with no default value.

Remarks

Each object can determine which of the five states it exposes.

All objects, except the **OBJECT** tag, that expose the **readyState** property return the value as a string. The **OBJECT** tag returns an integer in the range of 0 (uninitialized) through 4 (complete).

Applies To

 WIN16   WIN32   MAC

Hn

WIN16   WIN32   MAC   UNIX

document, IMG, LINK, OBJECT, SCRIPT

IE 5 **WIN16   WIN32   MAC   UNIX**

A, ACRONYM, ADDRESS, APPLET, AREA, B, BASE, BASEFONT, BDO,
BGSOUND, BIG, BLOCKQUOTE, BODY, BR, BUTTON, CAPTION, CENTER,
CITE, CODE, COL, COLGROUP, COMMENT, DD, DEL, DFN, DIR, DIV, DL, DT,
EM, EMBED, FIELDSET, FONT, FORM, FRAME, FRAMESET, HEAD, Hn, HR,
HTML, I, IFRAME, INPUT type=button, INPUT type=checkbox, INPUT type=file,
INPUT type=hidden, INPUT type=image, INPUT type=password, INPUT
type=radio, INPUT type=reset, INPUT type=submit, INPUT type=text, INS,
ISINDEX, KBD, LABEL, LEGEND, LI, LISTING, MAP, MARQUEE, MENU,
NEXTID, NOBR, NOFRAMES, NOSCRIPT, OL, OPTION, P, PLAINTEXT, PRE,
Q, RT, RUBY, S, SAMP, SELECT, SMALL, SPAN, STRIKE, STRONG, SUB, SUP,
TABLE, TBODY, TD, TEXTAREA, TFOOT, TH, THEAD, TITLE, TR, TT, U, UL,
VAR, XML, XMP

reason Property

Retrieves the result of data transfer for a data source object.

Syntax

HTML   N/A

Scripting   [*iReason* =] *event*.**reason**

Possible Values

0   Data transmitted successfully.

1   Data transfer aborted.

2   Data transferred in error.

The property is read-only with no default value.

Remarks

The property specifies the state of completion.

Applies To

 WIN16   WIN32   MAC   UNIX

event

recordNumber Property

Retrieves the ordinal record from the data set that generated the object.

Syntax

HTML   N/A

Scripting   [*iNumber* =] *object*.**recordNumber**

Possible Values

iNumber   Integer specifying the record number.

The property is read-only with no default value.

Remarks

The property applies to elements contained within a bound, repeated table.

You can use this property with ADO recordset available from every data source object through the object's **recordset** property.

Applies To

 WIN16   WIN32   MAC   UNIX

A, ACRONYM, ADDRESS, APPLET, AREA, B, BIG, BLOCKQUOTE, BR, BUTTON, CAPTION, CENTER, CITE, CODE, COL, COLGROUP, COMMENT, DD, DEL, DFN, DIR, DIV, DL, DT, EM, EMBED, FIELDSET, FONT, FORM, Hn, HR, I, IFRAME, IMG, INPUT type=button, INPUT type=checkbox, INPUT type=file, INPUT type=hidden, INPUT type=image, INPUT type=password, INPUT type=radio, INPUT type=reset, INPUT type=submit, INPUT type=text, INS, KBD, LABEL, LI, LISTING, MAP, MARQUEE, MENU, NEXTID, NOBR, OBJECT, OL, OPTION, P, PLAINTEXT, PRE, Q, S, SAMP, SCRIPT, SELECT, SMALL, SPAN, STRIKE, STRONG, SUB, SUP, TABLE, TBODY, TD, TEXTAREA, TFOOT, TH, THEAD, TR, TT, U, UL, VAR, XMP

WIN16   WIN32   MAC   UNIX

RUBY

recordset Property

Retrieves a reference to the default recordset from a data source object.

Syntax

HTML   N/A

Scripting   [*oRecordset* =] *object*.**recordset**

Possible Values

oRecordset   Object specifying the recordset.

The property is read-only with no default value.

To retrieve a named recordset from a data source object, use the **namedRecordset** method.

Applies To

 WIN16   WIN32   MAC   UNIX

event, OBJECT

referrer Property

Retrieves the URL of the previous location.

Syntax

HTML   N/A

Scripting   [*sUrl* =] *document*.**referrer**

Possible Values

sUrl   String specifying the URL of the referring page.

The property is read-only with no default value.

Remarks

The property returns a value only when the current page has been reached through a link from the previous page. Otherwise, **document.referrer** returns an empty string; it also returns an empty string when the link is from a secure site.

For example, if PageA.htm has a link to PageB.htm, and the user clicks that link, the **document.referrer** on PageB.htm returns PageA.htm. However, if the user is on PageA.htm and types PageB.htm into the address line or uses Open in the File menu to navigate to PageB.htm, **document.referrer** returns an empty string.

Applies To

 WIN16   WIN32   MAC

document

 UNIX

document

REL Attribute | rel Property

Sets or retrieves the relationship(s) described by the hypertext link from the anchor to the target.

Syntax

HTML   *<ELEMENT* **REL** = *sRelation ...>*

Scripting *object.***rel** [= *sRelation*]

Possible Values

sRelation   String specifying the relationship between the anchor and the target.

Alternate	Substitute version of the file containing the link.
Stylesheet	Style sheet.
Start	First document of a set.
Next	Next document in a sequence.
Prev	Previous document in a sequence.
Contents	Table of contents document.
Index	Index document for the current page.
Glossary	Glossary for the current page.

DHTML Properties

Possible Values (*continued*)

Copyright	Copyright notice for the current page.
Chapter	Page that is a chapter for a set of pages.
Section	Page that is a section for a set of pages.
Shortcut Icon	**href** containing a path to an icon file to be used for the favorite or link.
Subsection	Page that is a subsection for a set of pages.
Appendix	Page that is an appendix for the set of pages.
Help	Help document.
Bookmark	Bookmark.
Offline	**href** containing a path to the CDF file to be used for an offline favorite.

The property is read/write with no default value.

Remarks

The value is a comma-separated list of one or more of the preceding values. The default relationship is void. The **rel** property is used only when the **href** property is present.

Shortcut Icon and Offline apply only to the **LINK** object.

The Offline possible value is available in Internet Explorer 5 and later.

Applies To

WIN16	WIN32	MAC	
A			

UNIX	WIN16	WIN32	MAC
A, LINK			

repeat Property

Retrieves whether an event is being repeated.

Syntax

HTML   N/A

Scripting   [*bRepeat* =] *event*.**repeat**

Possible Values

bRepeat   Boolean specifying whether the event was repeated.

The property is read-only with no default value.

Remarks

The **repeat** property returns `true` only if the **onkeydown** event is repeated.

Applies To

 | **WIN16** | **WIN32** | **MAC** | **UNIX**
---

event

returnValue Property

Sets or retrieves the return value from the modal dialog window.

Syntax

HTML   N/A

Scripting   *window*.**returnValue** [= *vValue*]

Possible Values

vValue   Return value from the window.

The property is read/write with no default value.

Remarks

This property applies only to windows created using the **showModalDialog** method.

Applies To

 WIN16   WIN32   MAC   UNIX

window

returnValue Property

Sets or retrieves the return value from the event.

Syntax

HTML   N/A

Scripting   *event*.**returnValue** [= *bValue*]

Possible Values

true   Value from the event is returned.

false   Default action of the event on the source object is canceled.

The property is read/write with a default value of true.

Remarks

The value of this property takes precedence over values returned by the function, such as through a JScript (compatible with ECMA 262 language specification) **return** statement.

Applies To

 WIN16   WIN32   MAC   UNIX

event

REV Attribute | rev Property

Sets or retrieves the relationship(s) described by the hypertext link from the anchor to the target.

Syntax

HTML   *<ELEMENT* **REV** = *sRelation* ...>

Scripting *object*.**rev** [= *sRelation*]

Possible Values

sRelation String specifying the relationship between the anchor and the target.

Alternate	Substitute version of the file containing the link.
Stylesheet	Style sheet.
Start	First document of a set.
Next	Next document in a sequence.
Prev	Previous document in a sequence.
Contents	Table of contents document.
Index	Index document for the current page.
Glossary	Glossary for the current page.
Copyright	Copyright notice for the current page.
Chapter	Page that is a chapter for a set of pages.
Section	Page that is a section for a set of pages.
Subsection	Page that is a subsection for a set of pages.
Appendix	Page that is an appendix for the set of pages.
Help	Help document.
Bookmark	Bookmark.

The property is read/write with no default value.

Remarks

This property is similar to the **rel** property, but the semantics of their link type are in the reverse direction. A link from A to B with REL="X" expresses the same relationship as a link from B to A with REV="X". An anchor can have **rel** and **rev** properties.

Applies To

WIN16	WIN32	MAC	
A			

UNIX	WIN16	WIN32	MAC	
A, LINK				

right Property

Retrieves the right coordinate of the rectangle surrounding the object content.

Syntax

HTML   N/A

Scripting [*iCoord* =] *oTextRectangle*.**right**

Possible Values

iCoord Integer specifying the right coordinate of the rectangle, in pixels.

The property is read-only with no default value.

Remarks

Use the following syntax to access the right coordinate of the second text rectangle of a **TextRange** object.

```
oRct = oTextRange.getClientRects();
oRct[1].right;
```

Note The collection index starts at 0, so the second item index is 1.

Use the following syntax to access the right coordinate of the bounding rectangle of an element object.

```
oBndRct = oElement.getBoundingClientRect();
oBndRct.right;
```

Example

The following example shows how to use the **getBoundingClientRect** method to retrieve the coordinates of the bounds of the text rectangles within the element.

```
<SCRIPT>
function getCoords(oObject) {
    oBndRct=oObject.getBoundingClientRect();
    alert("Bounding rectangle = \nUpper left coordinates: "
        + oBndRct.left + " " + oBndRct.top +
        "\nLower right coordinates: "
        + oBndRct.right + " " + oBndRct.bottom);
}
</SCRIPT>
</HEAD>
<BODY>
<P ID=oPara onclick="getCoords(this)">
```

To see this code in action, refer to the Web Workshop CD-ROM.

Applies To

 WIN16   WIN32   MAC   UNIX

TextRectangle Object

right Attribute | right Property

Sets or retrieves the position of the object relative to the right edge of the next positioned object in the document hierarchy.

Syntax

HTML	{ **right:** auto I *length* I *percentage* }
Scripting	*object*.**style.right** [= *sRight*]

Possible Values

auto	Default position according to the regular HTML layout of the page.
length	String consisting of a floating-point number, followed by an absolute units designator (cm, mm, in, pt, pc, or px) or a relative units designator (em or ex). For more information about the supported length units for Cascading Style Sheet attributes, see "CSS Length Units" in Appendix C.
percentage	String value expressed as a percentage of the height of the parent object. Percentage values are specified as a number, followed by a %.

The property is read/write with a default value of auto; the CSS attribute is not inherited.

Remarks

The **right** attribute should only be used when the position attribute is set; otherwise, the value of the **right** attribute is ignored.

Because the value of the **right** property is a string, the property cannot be used in script to calculate the position of the object in the document; instead, the **pixelRight** or **posRight** property should be used.

Example

The following example shows how to use the **right** attribute to set a **DIV** object 50 pixels from the right of the client area.

```
<DIV STYLE = "position:absolute; right:50px">
. . .
</DIV>
```

DHTML Properties

Applies To

IE 4	WIN16	WIN32	MAC	UNIX	WIN16	WIN32

A, ADDRESS, APPLET, B, BIG, BLOCKQUOTE, BUTTON, CENTER, CITE, CODE, DD, DFN, DIR, DIV, DL, FIELDSET, FORM, Hn, HR, I, IFRAME, IMG, INPUT type=button, INPUT type=checkbox, INPUT type=file, INPUT type=image, INPUT type=password, INPUT type=radio, INPUT type=reset, INPUT type=submit, INPUT type=text, ISINDEX, KBD, LABEL, LEGEND, LI, LISTING, MARQUEE, MENU, OBJECT, OL, P, PRE, S, SAMP, SELECT, SMALL, SPAN, STRIKE, STRONG, style, SUB, SUP, TABLE, TEXTAREA, TT, U, UL, VAR, XMP

IE 5	WIN16	WIN32	MAC	UNIX

currentStyle, runtimeStyle

RIGHTMARGIN Attribute | rightMargin Property

Sets or retrieves the right margin for the entire body of the page.

Syntax

HTML   <BODY **RIGHTMARGIN** = *sMargin* ... >

Scripting *object*.**rightMargin** [= *sMargin*]

Possible Values

sMargin String specifying the margin, in pixels.

The property is read/write with a default value of 10.

Remarks

If the value is an empty string, the right margin is on the right edge.

The value set on the property overrides the default margin.

Applies To

IE 4	WIN16	WIN32	MAC	UNIX

BODY

rowIndex Property

Retrieves the position of the object in the **rows** collection for the **TABLE**.

Syntax

HTML N/A

Scripting [*iIndex* =] *oTR*.**rowIndex**

Possible Values

iIndex Integer specifying the index number.

The property is read-only with no default value.

Remarks

This property is different from **sectionRowIndex**, which indicates the object's position in the **TBODY**, **THEAD**, or **TFOOT rows** collection. These sections are mutually exclusive, so the **TR** is always contained in one of these sections and in the **TABLE**. The **rowIndex** property of an object is determined by the order in which the object appears in the HTML source.

Applies To

 WIN16 WIN32 MAC UNIX

TR

ROWS Attribute | rows Property

Sets or retrieves the number of horizontal rows the object should contain.

Syntax

HTML <ELEMENT **ROWS** = *iRows* ... >

Scripting *object*.**rows** [= *iRows*]

Possible Values

iRows Integer specifying the number of rows.

The property is read/write with a default value of 2.

Applies To

 WIN16   WIN32   MAC

TEXTAREA

 UNIX

TEXTAREA

ROWS Attribute | rows Property

Sets or retrieves a comma-delimited string of frame heights.

Syntax

HTML   <FRAMESET **ROWS** = *iHeight* [, *iHeight*...]

Scripting *object*.**rows** [= *iHeight* [, *iHeight*...]]

Possible Values

iHeight	Integer specifying the frame height, in pixels.
iHeight%	Integer specifying the frame height as a percentage of total available width.
iHeight*	Integer specifying the frame height as a relative value. After allocating pixel or percentage values, the remaining space is divided among all relative-sized frames.

The property is read/write with no default value.

Remarks

The number of comma-separated items is equal to the number of frames contained within the **FRAMESET**, and the value of each item determines the frame height.

Example

The following example shows how to define a two-row frame, with the first occupying 40 percent of the available height and the second occupying the remaining 60 percent.

```
<FRAMESET ROWS="40%, 60%">
```

The next example shows how to define a four-row frame. The first is 50 pixels high and the fourth is 80 pixels high. The second occupies two-thirds of the remaining height, and the third occupies the final one-third of the remaining height.

```
<FRAMESET ROWS="50, 2*, *, 80">
```

Applies To

 WIN16   WIN32   MAC   UNIX

FRAMESET

ROWSPAN Attribute | rowSpan Property

Sets or retrieves how many rows in a **TABLE** the cell should span.

Syntax

HTML   *<ELEMENT* **ROWSPAN** = *iRows* ... *>*

Scripting *object*.**rowSpan** [= *iRows*]

Possible Values

iRows   Integer specifying the number of spanned rows.

The property is read/write with no default value.

Remarks

This property can be changed only after the page has been loaded.

Applies To

 WIN16   WIN32   MAC

TD, TH

 UNIX

TD, TH

ruby-align Attribute | rubyAlign Property

Sets or retrieves the position of the ruby text specified by the **RT** object.

Syntax

HTML   { **ruby-align:** auto | left | center | right | distribute-letter | distribute-space | line-edge }

Scripting *object*.**style.rubyAlign** [= *sRubyAlign*]

DHTML Properties

Possible Values

auto	Browser determines how the ruby text is aligned. The recommended behavior for an ideographic (East Asian character) ruby is to be aligned in the distribute-space mode. The recommended behavior for a Latin character ruby is to be aligned in the center mode.
left	Ruby text is left-aligned with the base.
center	Ruby text is centered within the width of the base. If the length of the base is smaller than the length of the ruby text, the base is centered within the width of the ruby text.
right	Ruby text is right-aligned with the base.
distribute-letter	Ruby text is evenly distributed across the width of the base if the width of the ruby text is smaller than the width of the base. If the width of the ruby text is at least the width of the base, the ruby text is center-aligned.
distribute-space	Ruby text is evenly distributed across the width of the base if the width of the ruby text is smaller than the width of the base. White space precedes the first and follows the last character in the ruby text, equal to half the kerning of the ruby text. If the width of the ruby text is at least the width of the base, the ruby text is centered.
line-edge	Ruby text is centered if it is not adjacent to a line edge. If it is adjacent to a line edge, the side of the ruby lines up with the side of the base text.

The property is read/write with a default value of auto; the proposed cascading style sheets (CSS) extension attribute is not inherited.

Remarks

The **rubyAlign** property specifies the alignment of the ruby text defined by the **RT** object and is set on the **RUBY** object.

Example

The following shows how to use the **ruby-align** attribute and the **rubyAlign** property to set the alignment of the ruby text. It uses an inline style sheet to set the **ruby-align** attribute to right.

```
<RUBY ID=oRuby STYLE = "ruby-align: right">
Ruby base.
<RT>Ruby text.
</RUBY>
<INPUT TYPE=button VALUE="Center"onclick="oRuby.style.rubyAlign='center';">
```

To see this code in action, refer to the Web Workshop CD-ROM.

Applies To

 WIN16   WIN32   MAC   UNIX

RUBY

ruby-overhang Attribute | rubyOverhang Property

Sets or retrieves the position of the ruby text specified by the **RT** object.

Syntax

HTML   { **ruby-overhang:** auto | whitespace | none }

Scripting   *object*.**style.rubyOverhang** [= *sRubyOverhang*]

Possible Values

auto   Ruby text overhangs any other text adjacent to the base text.

whitespace Ruby text overhangs only white-space characters.

none   Ruby text overhangs only text adjacent to its base.

The property is read/write with a default value of auto; the proposed cascading style sheets (CSS) extension attribute is not inherited.

Remarks

The **rubyOverhang** property specifies the overhang of the ruby text defined by the **RT** object, and is set on the **RUBY** object.

Example

The following example shows how to use the **ruby-overhang** attribute and the **rubyOverhang** property to set the overhang of the ruby text. It uses an inline style sheet to set the **ruby-overhang** attribute to none.

```
<RUBY ID=oRuby STYLE = "ruby-overhang: none">
Ruby base.
<RT>Ruby text.
</RUBY>
<INPUT TYPE=button VALUE="Whitespace"onclick="oRuby.style.rubyOverhang='whitespace';">
```

To see this code in action, refer to the Web Workshop CD-ROM.

Applies To

 WIN16 WIN32 MAC UNIX

RUBY

ruby-position Attribute | rubyPosition Property

Sets or retrieves the position of the ruby text specified by the **RT** object.

Syntax

HTML   { **ruby-position:** above | inline }

Scripting *object*.**style.rubyPosition** [= *sRubyPlacement*]

Possible Values

above   Ruby text is positioned above the base text.

inline Ruby text is positioned inline with the base text.

The property is read/write with a default value of above; the proposed cascading style sheets (CSS) extension attribute is not inherited.

Remarks

The **rubyPosition** property specifies the position of the ruby text defined by the **RT** object, and is set on the **RUBY** object.

Example

The following example shows how to use the **ruby-position** attribute and the **rubyPosition** property to set the position of the ruby text. It uses an inline style sheet to set the **ruby-position** attribute to inline.

```
<RUBY ID=oRuby STYLE = "ruby-position: inline">
Ruby base.
<RT>Ruby text.
</RUBY>
<P>
<INPUT TYPE=button VALUE="Above"onclick="oRuby.style.rubyPosition='above';">
```

To see this code in action, refer to the Web Workshop CD-ROM.

Applies To

 WIN16 WIN32 MAC UNIX

RUBY

RULES Attribute | rules Property

Sets or retrieves which dividing lines (inner borders) are displayed.

Syntax

HTML   <TABLE **RULES** = "all" | "cols" | "groups" | "none" | "rows" ... >

Scripting *table*.**rules** [= *sRule*]

Possible Values

all   Border is displayed on all rows and columns.

cols   Borders are displayed between all table columns.

groups Horizontal borders are displayed between all table groups. Groups are specified by the **THEAD**, **TBODY**, **TFOOT**, and **COLGROUP** objects.

none   All interior table borders are removed.

rows   Horizontal borders are displayed between all table rows.

The property is read/write with no default value.

Remarks

The value none turns off the interior borders only. To turn off table borders, set the **rules** property to empty, or do not add the **RULES** attribute to the **TABLE** object.

Example

The following example shows how to set the table **RULES** attribute and then change the table borders using the **rules** property.

```
<TABLE ID=oTable RULES="cols">
<TR>
<TD>EST</TD><TD>1am</TD><TD>8pm</TD>
</TR>
<TR>
<TD>CST</TD><TD>2am</TD><TD>9pm</TD>
</TR>
<TR>
<TD>MST</TD><TD>3am</TD><TD>10pm</TD>
</TR>
</TABLE>
:
<BUTTON onclick="oTable.rules=''">No borders</BUTTON>
<BUTTON onclick="oTable.rules='all'">All borders</BUTTON>
```

To see this code in action, refer to the Web Workshop CD-ROM.

Applies To

 WIN16   WIN32   MAC   UNIX

styleSheet

scopeName Property

Retrieves the namespace defined for the element.

Syntax

HTML   N/A

Scripting   [*sScope* =] *object*.**scopeName**

Possible Values

sScope   For custom tags, specifies the namespace prefix used with the tag. This namespace is declared in the document using the **XMLNS** attribute of the **HTML** element.

HTML   For all standard HTML tags in a document, specifies the default value.

The property is read-only with a default value of HTML.

Example

The following example shows how to use values returned by the **scopeName** and **tagUrn** properties to for a simple *HelloWorld* custom tag. The property values are displayed in the browser's status bar.

```
<HTML XMLNS:InetSDK='http://www.microsoft.com/workshop'>

<STYLE>
@media all {
    InetSDK\:HelloWorld { behavior:url (simple.htc) }
}
</STYLE>
<SCRIPT>
    function window.onload()
    {
        window.status = 'scopeName = ' + hello.scopeName +
                        '; tagUrn = '  + hello.tagUrn;
    }
</SCRIPT>
<BODY>
    <InetSDK:HelloWorld ID='hello'></InetSDK:HelloWorld>

</BODY>
</HTML>
```

To see this code in action, refer to the Web Workshop CD-ROM.

Applies To

WIN16   WIN32   MAC

Hn, ISINDEX

WIN16   WIN32   MAC   UNIX

A, ACRONYM, ADDRESS, APPLET, AREA, B, BASE, BASEFONT, BDO,
BGSOUND, BIG, BLOCKQUOTE, BODY, BR, BUTTON, CAPTION, CENTER,
CITE, CODE, COL, COLGROUP, COMMENT, DD, DEL, DFN, DIR, DIV, DL, DT,
EM, EMBED, FIELDSET, FONT, FORM, FRAME, FRAMESET, HEAD, Hn, HR,
HTML, I, IFRAME, IMG, INPUT type=button, INPUT type=checkbox, INPUT
type=file, INPUT type=hidden, INPUT type=image, INPUT type=password, INPUT
type=radio, INPUT type=reset, INPUT type=submit, INPUT type=text, INS,
ISINDEX, KBD, LABEL, LEGEND, LI, LINK, LISTING, MAP, MARQUEE,
MENU, NEXTID, NOBR, NOFRAMES, NOSCRIPT, OBJECT, OL, OPTION, P,
PLAINTEXT, PRE, Q, RT, RUBY, S, SAMP, SCRIPT, SELECT, SMALL, SPAN,
STRIKE, STRONG, SUB, SUP, TABLE, TBODY, TD, TEXTAREA, TFOOT, TH,
THEAD, TITLE, TR, TT, U, UL, VAR, WBR, XML, XMP

screenLeft Property

Retrieves the left edge of the client's position.

Syntax

HTML   N/A

Scripting   [*iPos* =] *object*.**screenLeft**

Possible Values

iPos Integer specifying the screen coordinates, in pixels, of the client's left edge.

The property is read-only with no default value.

Applies To

 WIN16 WIN32 MAC UNIX

window

screenTop Property

Retrieves the top edge of the client's position in screen coordinates.

Syntax

HTML N/A

Scripting [*iPos* =] *object*.**screenTop**

Possible Values

iPos Integer specifying the screen coordinates, in pixels, of the client's top edge.

The property is read-only with no default value.

Applies To

 WIN16 WIN32 MAC UNIX

window

screenX Property

Retrieves the horizontal position of the mouse relative to the user's screen.

Syntax

HTML N/A

Scripting [*iSize* =] *event*.**screenX**

Possible Values

iSize Integer specifying the horizontal position of the mouse, in pixels.

The property is read-only with no default value.

Applies To

WIN16	WIN32	MAC	UNIX

event

screenY Property

Retrieves the vertical position of the mouse relative to the user's screen.

Syntax

HTML   N/A

Scripting   [*iSize* =] *event*.**screenY**

Possible Values

iSize   Integer specifying the vertical position of the mouse, in pixels.

The property is read-only, with no default value.

Applies To

WIN16	WIN32	MAC	UNIX

event

SCROLL Attribute | scroll Property

Sets or retrieves whether the scroll bars are turned on or off.

Syntax

HTML   <BODY **SCROLL** = "yes" | "no" ... >

Scripting   *body*.**scroll** [= *sScroll*]

Possible Values

yes   Turns on the scroll bars.

no   Turns off the scroll bars.

The property is read/write with a default value of yes.

Applies To

 WIN16   WIN32   MAC   UNIX

BODY

SCROLLAMOUNT Attribute | scrollAmount Property

Sets or retrieves the number of pixels the text scrolls between each subsequent drawing of the **MARQUEE**.

Syntax

HTML   **<MARQUEE SCROLLAMOUNT** = *iAmount* ... >

Scripting *marquee*.**scrollAmount** [= *iAmount*]

Possible Values

iAmount   Integer specifying the number of pixels.

The property is read/write with a default value of 6.

Applies To

 WIN16   WIN32   MAC

MARQUEE

 UNIX

MARQUEE

SCROLLDELAY Attribute | scrollDelay Property

Sets or retrieves the speed of the **MARQUEE** scroll, in milliseconds.

Syntax

HTML   **<MARQUEE SCROLLDELAY** = *iDelay* ... >

Scripting *marquee*.**scrollDelay** [= *iDelay*]

Possible Values

> *iDelay* Integer specifying the delay, in milliseconds.

> The property is read/write with a default value of 85.

Applies To

 WIN16   WIN32   MAC

MARQUEE

 UNIX

MARQUEE

scrollHeight Property

> Retrieves the scrolling height of the object.

Syntax

> **HTML**   N/A
>
> **Scripting** [*iHeight* =] *object*.**scrollHeight**

Possible Values

> *iHeight* Nonnegative integer representing the height, in pixels.

> The property is read-only with no default value.

Remarks

> The height is the distance between the top and bottom edges of the object's content.

Example

> The following example shows how to use the **scrollHeight** property.

```
<SCRIPT>
function fnCheckScroll(){
    var iNewHeight = oDiv.scrollHeight;
    alert("The value of the scrollHeight property is: "
        + iNewHeight);
}
</SCRIPT>
:
```

```
<DIV ID=oDiv STYLE="overflow:scroll; height=200;
    width=250; text-align:left">
:
</DIV>
<INPUT TYPE=button VALUE="Check scrollHeight"
    onclick="fnCheckScroll()">
```

To see this code in action, refer to the Web Workshop CD-ROM.

Applies To

 WIN16   WIN32   MAC   UNIX

APPLET, BODY, BUTTON, CAPTION, DIV, EMBED, FIELDSET, IMG, INPUT
type=button, INPUT type=checkbox, INPUT type=file, INPUT type=image, INPUT
type=password, INPUT type=radio, INPUT type=reset, INPUT type=submit, INPUT
type=text, LEGEND, MARQUEE, OBJECT, SPAN, TABLE, TD, TEXTAREA, TR

 WIN16   WIN32   MAC   UNIX

A, ADDRESS, B, BDO, BIG, BLOCKQUOTE, CENTER, CITE, CODE, COL,
COLGROUP, DD, DFN, DIR, DL, DT, EM, FORM, HEAD, Hn, HTML, I,
ISINDEX, KBD, LABEL, LI, LISTING, MENU, META, NOBR, OL, OPTION, P,
PLAINTEXT, PRE, S, SAMP, SCRIPT, SELECT, SMALL, STRIKE, STRONG,
SUB, SUP, TBODY, TFOOT, TH, THEAD, TT, U, UL, VAR, XMP

SCROLLING Attribute | scrolling Property

Sets or retrieves whether the frame can be scrolled.

Syntax

HTML   *<ELEMENT* **SCROLLING** = "auto" | "no" | "yes" ... >

Scripting *object*.**scrolling** [= *sScrolling*]

Possible Values

auto The browser determines whether the scroll bars are necessary.

no   The frame cannot be scrolled.

yes   The frame can be scrolled.

The property is read/write with a default value of auto.

Applies To

 WIN16   WIN32   MAC

FRAME, IFRAME

 UNIX

FRAME, IFRAME

scrollLeft Property

Sets or retrieves the distance between the left edge of the object and the leftmost portion of the content currently visible in the window.

Syntax

HTML   N/A

Scripting   *object*.**scrollLeft** [= *iDistance*]

Possible Values

iDistance   Integer specifying the distance, in pixels.

The property is read/write with a default value of 0.

Remarks

The property's value is equal to the horizontal distance that the content of the object has been scrolled. Although the value can be set to any positive or negative value, if the assigned value is less than 0, the property is set to 0. If the assigned value is greater than the maximum possible, the property is set to the maximum possible.

This property can be set inline, but the results may not be consistent while the page is loading.

This property is always 0 for objects that do not have scroll bars. For these objects, setting the property has no effect.

When a **MARQUEE** object is scrolling vertically its **scrollLeft** property is set to 0, overriding any script setting.

Example

The following example shows how to use the **scrollLeft** property to determine the amount of scrolling done by an object.

```
<DIV ID=oDiv STYLE="position:absolute; width:200px;
    height:100px; overflow:scroll"
    onclick=alert(this.scrollLeft)>
<SPAN STYLE="width:250px"> . . . </SPAN></DIV>
```

To see this code in action, refer to the Web Workshop CD-ROM.

Applies To

 WIN16   WIN32   MAC   UNIX

APPLET, BODY, BUTTON, CAPTION, DIV, EMBED, FIELDSET, IMG, INPUT type=button, INPUT type=checkbox, INPUT type=file, INPUT type=image, INPUT type=password, INPUT type=radio, INPUT type=reset, INPUT type=submit, INPUT type=text, LEGEND, MARQUEE, OBJECT, SPAN, TABLE, TD, TEXTAREA, TR

 WIN16   WIN32   MAC   UNIX

A, ADDRESS, B, BDO, BIG, BLOCKQUOTE, CENTER, CITE, CODE, COL, COLGROUP, DD, DFN, DIR, DL, DT, EM, FORM, HEAD, Hn, HTML, I, ISINDEX, KBD, LABEL, LI, LISTING, MENU, META, NOBR, OL, OPTION, P, PLAINTEXT, PRE, S, SAMP, SCRIPT, SELECT, SMALL, STRIKE, STRONG, SUB, SUP, TBODY, TFOOT, TH, THEAD, TT, U, UL, VAR, XMP

scrollTop Property

Sets or retrieves the distance between the top of the object and the topmost portion of the content currently visible in the window.

Syntax

HTML   N/A

Scripting *object*.**scrollTop** [= *iDistance*]

Possible Values

iDistance Integer specifying the distance, in pixels.

The property is read/write with a default value of 0.

Remarks

The property's value is equal to the vertical distance that the content of the object has been scrolled. Although the value can be set to any positive or negative value, if the assigned value is less than 0, the property is set to 0. If the assigned value is greater than the maximum possible, the property is set to the maximum possible value.

This property can be set inline, but the results may not be consistent while the page is loading.

This property is always 0 for objects that do not have scroll bars. For these objects, setting the property has no effect.

When a **MARQUEE** object is scrolling horizontally, its **scrollTop** property is set to 0, overriding any script setting.

Example

The following example shows how to use the **scrollTop** property to determine the amount of scrolling done by an object.

```
<DIV ID=oDiv STYLE="position:absolute; width:200px;
    height:100px; overflow:scroll"
    onclick=alert(this.scrollTop)>
<SPAN STYLE="width:250px"> . . . </SPAN></DIV>
```

To see this code in action, refer to the Web Workshop CD-ROM.

Applies To

 WIN16   WIN32   MAC   UNIX

APPLET, BODY, BUTTON, CAPTION, DIV, EMBED, FIELDSET, IMG, INPUT type=button, INPUT type=checkbox, INPUT type=file, INPUT type=image, INPUT type=password, INPUT type=radio, INPUT type=reset, INPUT type=submit, INPUT type=text, LEGEND, MARQUEE, OBJECT, SPAN, TABLE, TD, TEXTAREA, TR

IE 5 | **WIN16   WIN32   MAC   UNIX**

A, ADDRESS, B, BDO, BIG, BLOCKQUOTE, CENTER, CITE, CODE, COL, COLGROUP, DD, DFN, DIR, DL, DT, EM, FORM, HEAD, Hn, HTML, I, ISINDEX, KBD, LABEL, LI, LISTING, MENU, META, NOBR, OL, OPTION, P, PLAINTEXT, PRE, S, SAMP, SCRIPT, SELECT, SMALL, STRIKE, STRONG, SUB, SUP, TBODY, TFOOT, TH, THEAD, TT, U, UL, VAR, XMP

scrollWidth Property

Retrieves the scrolling width of the object.

Syntax

HTML   N/A

Scripting   [*iWidth* =] *object*.**scrollWidth**

Possible Values

iWidth   Positive integer specifying the width, in pixels.

The property is read-only with no default value.

Remarks

The width is the distance between the left and right edges of the object's visible content.

Example

The following example shows how to use the **scrollWidth** property to compare the rendered width of a **DIV** element with the width of the content. The width of the element, as rendered on the page, is exposed through the **offsetWidth** property. When using the **overflow** property set to auto, the content can exceed the dimensions of an element, and scroll bars appear. The **scrollWidth** property is used to retrieve the width of the content within the element.

```
<SCRIPT>
function fnCheckScroll(){
    var iScrollWidth = oDiv.scrollWidth;
    var iOffsetWidth = oDiv.offsetWidth;
    var iDifference = iScrollWidth - iOffsetWidth;
    alert("Width: " + iOffsetWidth
        + "\nContent Width: " + iScrollWidth
        + "\nDifference: " + iDifference);
}
</SCRIPT>
:
<DIV ID=oDiv STYLE="overflow:scroll; height=200; width=250;
    text-align:left">
:
</DIV>
<INPUT TYPE=button VALUE="Check scrollWidth"
    onclick="fnCheckScroll()">
```

To see this code in action, refer to the Web Workshop CD-ROM.

Applies To

 WIN32   MAC   UNIX

APPLET, BODY, BUTTON, CAPTION, DIV, EMBED, FIELDSET, IMG, INPUT
type=button, INPUT type=checkbox, INPUT type=file, INPUT type=image, INPUT
type=password, INPUT type=radio, INPUT type=reset, INPUT type=submit, INPUT
type=text, LEGEND, OBJECT, SPAN, TABLE, TD, TEXTAREA, TR

IE 5 **WIN32   MAC   UNIX**

A, ADDRESS, B, BDO, BIG, BLOCKQUOTE, CENTER, CITE, CODE, COL,
COLGROUP, DD, DFN, DIR, DL, DT, EM, FORM, HEAD, Hn, HTML, I,
ISINDEX, KBD, LABEL, LI, LISTING, MENU, META, NOBR, OL, OPTION, P,
PLAINTEXT, PRE, S, SAMP, SCRIPT, SELECT, SMALL, STRIKE, STRONG,
SUB, SUP, TBODY, TFOOT, TH, THEAD, TT, U, UL, VAR, XMP

search Property

Sets or retrieves the substring of the **href** property that follows the question mark.

Syntax

HTML   N/A

Scripting *object*.**search** [= *sSearch*]

Possible Values

sSearch Substring of the **href** property.

The property is read/write with no default value.

Remarks

The substring that follows the question mark is the query string or form data.

Applies To

 WIN16   WIN32   MAC

A, AREA, location

 UNIX

A, AREA, location

sectionRowIndex Property

Retrieves the position of the object in the **TBODY, THEAD, TFOOT,** or **rows** collection.

Syntax

HTML   N/A

Scripting [*iIndex* =] *oTR*.**sectionRowIndex**

Possible Values

iIndex Integer specifying the index position of the object.

The property is read-only with no default value.

Remarks

The **TBODY, THEAD,** and **TFOOT** sections are mutually exclusive, so a **TR** is always contained in one of these sections and in the **TABLE**. The **rowIndex** property indicates the position of the object in the **rows** collection for the **TABLE**. The **rowIndex** property of an object is determined by the order in which the object appears in the HTML source.

Applies To

WIN16	WIN32	MAC	UNIX

TR

SELECTED Attribute | selected Property

Sets or retrieves whether the option in the list box is the default item.

Syntax

HTML   <OPTION **SELECTED** ... >

Scripting *select*.options[*iIndex*].**selected** [=*bSelected*]

Possible Values

false	The item is not selected as the default.
true	The item is selected as the default.

The property is read/write with a default value of false.

Remarks

If the property is not set, the first item is selected by default.

The property is used to determine whether a value is submitted with the form. If the value of the control matches the default value, the control's value is not submitted. The value is only submitted when the control's value does not match the default value.

Applies To

 WIN16   WIN32   MAC

OPTION

 UNIX

OPTION

selectedIndex Property

Sets or retrieves an integer specifying the index of the selected option in a **SELECT** object.

Syntax

HTML   N/A

Scripting *select*.**selectedIndex** [= *iIndex*]

Possible Values

iIndex Integer specifying the index.

The property is read/write with no default value.

Remarks

Options in a **SELECT** object are indexed in the order in which they are defined, starting with an index of 0. You can set the **selectedIndex** property at any time. The display of the **SELECT** object updates immediately when you set the **selectedIndex** property. Both forms of the syntax specify the same value.

The **selectedIndex** property returns -1 if a **SELECT** object does not contain any selected items.

Setting the **selectedIndex** property clears any existing selected items.

The **selectedIndex** property is most useful when used with **SELECT** objects that support selecting only one item at a time—that is, those in which the **MULTIPLE** property is not specified. If the **MULTIPLE** property is specified for a **SELECT** object, the **selectedIndex** property returns only the index of the first selected item, if any.

The **selected** property is most useful when used with **SELECT** objects that support selecting more than one item at a time—that is, those in which the **MULTIPLE** property is specified. You can use the **selected** property to determine whether an individual item in a **SELECT** object is selected. In addition, selected items are not cleared when the **selected** property is set. This allows multiple items in the list to be selected at the same time.

Example

The following example shows how to use the **selectedIndex** property to retrieve individual values from a **SELECT** object. When a site is selected from the list, the browser displays the associated page.

```
<SELECT onchange="window.location.href=this.options
    [this.selectedIndex].value">
<OPTION>Select a site to visit from this list.</OPTION>
<OPTION VALUE="http://www.microsoft.com/ie">
    Internet Explorer</OPTION>
<OPTION VALUE="http://www.microsoft.com">
    Microsoft Home</OPTION>
<OPTION VALUE="http://www.microsoft.com/msdn">
    Developer Network</OPTION>
</SELECT>
```

Applies To

 WIN16   WIN32   MAC

SELECT

UNIX

SELECT

selectorText Property

Retrieves a string that identifies which elements the corresponding rule applies to.

Syntax

HTML   N/A

Scripting [*sSelectorText* =] *rule*.**selectorText**

Possible Values

sSelectorText   String specifying the element that the rule applies to.

The property is read-only.

Remarks

A selector can be either a simple selector (such as 'H1') or a contextual selector (such as 'H1 B'), which consists of several simple selectors.

Applies To

 WIN16   WIN32   MAC   UNIX

rule

self Property

Retrieves a reference to the current window or frame.

Syntax

HTML   N/A

Scripting [*oSelf* =] *object*.**self**

Possible Values

oSelf Current window or frame.

The property is read-only with no default value.

Remarks

The property provides a way to explicitly refer to the current window or frame.

Use the **self** property to distinguish a window from a frame with the same name. You can also use the **self** property to make implicit window references explicit. This improves scripting efficiency.

Applies To

 WIN16   WIN32   MAC

window

 WIN16   WIN32   MAC   UNIX

FRAME, window

SHAPE Attribute | shape Property

Sets or retrieves the shape of a hyperlink **AREA** in an image **MAP**.

Syntax

HTML   <AREA **SHAPE** = "circ" | "circle" | "poly" | "polygon" | "rect" | "rectangle" ... >

Scripting *area*.**shape** [= *sShape*]

Possible Values

circ	Circle.
circle	Circle.
poly	Polygon.
polygon	Polygon.
rect	Rectangle.
rectangle	Rectangle.

The property is read/write with no default value.

The value of the **SHAPE** attribute determines the format of the **COORDS** attribute.

Example

The following example provides the full code for an image map of the solar system. When a user clicks on the sun or any planet, the user is taken to a link to the image associated with the x,y coordinate. The user can click the Back button from the image to return to the solar system image map.

```
<P><IMG SRC="solarsys.gif" WIDTH=504 HEIGHT=126
    BORDER=0 ALT="Solar System" USEMAP="#SystemMap">

<MAP NAME="SystemMap">
    <AREA SHAPE="rect" COORDS="0,0,82,126"
        HREF="/workshop/graphics/sun.gif">
    <AREA SHAPE="circle" COORDS="90,58,3"
        HREF="/workshop/graphics/merglobe.gif">
    <AREA SHAPE="circle" COORDS="124,58,8"
        HREF="/workshop/graphics/venglobe.gif">
    <AREA SHAPE="circle" COORDS="162,58,10"
        HREF="/workshop/graphics/earglobe.gif">
    <AREA SHAPE="circle" COORDS="203,58,8"
        HREF="/workshop/graphics/marglobe.gif">
    <AREA SHAPE="poly" COORDS="221,34,238,37,257,32,278,
        44,284,60,281,75,288,91,267,87,253,89,237,81,229,
        64,228,54" HREF="/workshop/graphics/jupglobe.gif">
    <AREA SHAPE="poly" COORDS="288,19,316,39,330,37,348,
        47,351,66,349,74,367,105,337,85,324,85,307,77,303,
        60,307,50" HREF="/workshop/graphics/satglobe.gif">
    <AREA SHAPE="poly" COORDS="405,39,408,50,411,57,410,
        71,404,78,393,80,383,86,381,75,376,69,376,56,380,
        48,393,44" HREF="/workshop/graphics/uraglobe.gif">
    <AREA SHAPE="poly" COORDS="445,38,434,49,431,53,427,62,
        430,72,435,77,445,92,456,77,463,72,463,62,462,53,
        455,47" HREF="/workshop/graphics/nepglobe.gif">
    <AREA SHAPE="circle" COORDS="479,66,3"
        HREF="/workshop/graphics/pluglobe.gif">
</MAP>
```

To see this code in action, refer to the Web Workshop CD-ROM.

Applies To

 WIN16   WIN32   MAC

AREA

 UNIX

AREA

shiftKey Property

Retrieves the state of the SHIFT key.

Syntax

HTML	N/A
Scripting	[*bKey* =] *event*.**shiftKey**

Possible Values

false	The SHIFT key is not down.
true	The SHIFT key is down.

The property is read-only with no default value.

Applies To

 WIN16   WIN32   MAC   UNIX

event

SIZE Attribute | size Property

Sets or retrieves the font size of the object.

Syntax

HTML	*<ELEMENT* **SIZE** = *iSize* ... >
Scripting	*object*.**size** [= *iSize*]

Possible Values

iSize   Integer in the range of 1 through 7, with 7 representing the largest font.

The property is read/write with no default value.

Applies To

 WIN16   WIN32   MAC

BASEFONT, FONT

UNIX

BASEFONT, FONT

size Property

Sets or retrieves the height of the **HR** object.

Syntax

HTML   N/A

Scripting *hr*.**size** [= *iSize*]

Possible Values

iSize   Integer specifying the height of the horizontal rule, in pixels.

The property is read/write with no default value.

Applies To

 WIN16   WIN32   MAC

HR

 UNIX

HR

SIZE Attribute | size Property

Sets or retrieves the size of the control.

Syntax

HTML   <*ELEMENT* **SIZE** = *iSize* ... >

Scripting *object*.**size** [= *iSize*]

Possible Values

iSize   Integer specifying the size.

The property is read/write with no default value.

DHTML Properties

Remarks

Although this property is read/write, no change is visible when you set the size of the **INPUT type=reset**, **INPUT type=submit**, and **INPUT type=image** objects; however, you can detect a change to the **size** property for these objects in code.

For the **INPUT type=text** object, the size is in characters and represents the width of the text box. When the size is specified, the **SELECT** object represents a list box with the specified number of rows.

Applies To

WIN16   WIN32   MAC

INPUT type=button, INPUT type=checkbox, INPUT type=file, INPUT type=image, INPUT type=password, INPUT type=radio, INPUT type=reset, INPUT type=submit, INPUT type=text, SELECT

UNIX

INPUT type=button, INPUT type=checkbox, INPUT type=file, INPUT type=image, INPUT type=password, INPUT type=radio, INPUT type=reset, INPUT type=submit, INPUT type=text, SELECT

sourceIndex Property

Retrieves the ordinal position of the object in the source order in which the object appears in the **all** collection.

Syntax

HTML   N/A

Scripting   [*iIndex* =] *object*.**sourceIndex**

Possible Values

iIndex Ordinal position of the object.

The property is read-only with no default value.

Example

The following example shows how to use the **sourceIndex** property to identify the previous and next elements in the **all** collection.

```
<SCRIPT>
function fnHandler(){
    var oElement=event.srcElement;
    var iIndex=oElement.sourceIndex;
    oNumber.innerText=iIndex;
    oNext.innerText=document.all[iIndex+1].tagName;
    oPrev.innerText=document.all[iIndex-1].tagName;
}
</SCRIPT>

<BODY onmousemove="fnHandler()">
<TABLE>
<TR><TD>Element Name</TD><TD ID=oName></TD></TR>
<TR><TD>Next Element</TD><TD ID=oNext></TD></TR>
<TR><TD>Previous Element</TD><TD ID=oPrev></TD></TR>

</TABLE>
</BODY>
```

To see this code in action, refer to the Web Workshop CD-ROM.

Applies To

 IE 4   **WIN16**   **WIN32**   **MAC**   **UNIX**

A, ACRONYM, ADDRESS, APPLET, AREA, B, BASE, BASEFONT, BGSOUND, BIG, BLOCKQUOTE, BODY, BR, BUTTON, CAPTION, CENTER, CITE, CODE, COL, COLGROUP, COMMENT, DD, DEL, DFN, DIR, DIV, DL, DT, EM, EMBED, FIELDSET, FONT, FORM, FRAME, FRAMESET, HEAD, Hn, HR, HTML, I, IFRAME, IMG, INPUT type=button, INPUT type=checkbox, INPUT type=file, INPUT type=hidden, INPUT type=image, INPUT type=password, INPUT type=radio, INPUT type=reset, INPUT type=submit, INPUT type=text, INS, KBD, LABEL, LI, LINK, LISTING, MAP, MARQUEE, MENU, META, NEXTID, NOBR, OBJECT, OL, P, PLAINTEXT, PRE, Q, S, SAMP, SCRIPT, SELECT, SMALL, SPAN, STRIKE, STRONG, SUB, SUP, TABLE, TBODY, TD, TEXTAREA, TFOOT, TH, THEAD, TITLE, TR, TT, U, UL, VAR, XMP

IE 5   **WIN16**   **WIN32**   **MAC**   **UNIX**

BDO

SPAN Attribute | span Property

Sets or retrieves the number of columns in the group.

Syntax

HTML   *<ELEMENT* **SPAN** *= iSpan ... >*

Scripting *object*.**span** [*= iSpan*]

Possible Values

iSpan Integer specifying the number of spanned columns.

The property is read/write with no default value.

Remarks

The **span** property should be ignored if the **COLGROUP** object contains one or more **COL** objects. The **span** property provides a more convenient way of grouping columns without having to specify **COL** objects.

Example

The following example shows how to set the **COL** object to SPAN=2 so that the **COL** object spans two columns. The text is right-aligned in those two columns.

```
<TABLE BORDER>
<COLGROUP>
<COL SPAN=2 ALIGN=RIGHT>
<COL ALIGN=LEFT>
<TBODY>
<TR>
<TD>This is the first column in the group and it is
    right-aligned.</TD>
<TD>This is the second column in the group and it is
    right-aligned.</TD>
<TD>This is the third column in the group and it is
    left-aligned.</TD>
</TR>
</TABLE>
```

To see this code in action, refer to the Web Workshop CD-ROM.

Applies To

 WIN16   WIN32   MAC

COL, COLGROUP

UNIX

COL, COLGROUP

specified Property

Retrieves whether an attribute has been specified.

Syntax

HTML	N/A
Scripting	[*bSpecified* =] *object*.**specified**

Possible Values

true	The attribute is specified.
false	The attribute is not specified.

The property is read-only with no default value.

Remarks

An attribute is specified if it is set through HTML or script.

Example

The following example shows how to use the **specified** property to determine whether an attribute has been specified. The steps include using the **createElement** method to create a new **LI** object, the **createTextNode** method to create a new text node, and the **appendChild** method to add the new elements to the list.

```
<SCRIPT>
function fnFindSpecified(){
   var oAttributes=oList.attributes;
   alert(oAttributes(0).nodeName);
   for(var i=0;i<oAttributes.length;i++){
      var oNode=document.createElement("LI");
      var oNodeValue=document.createTextNode(i + " "
                     + oAttributes(i).nodeName + " = "
                     + oAttributes(i).nodeValue);
      oList.appendChild(oNode);
      oNode.appendChild(oNodeValue);
      if(oAttributes(i).nodeValue!=null){
         alert(oAttributes(i).nodeName
         + " specified: " + oAttributes(i).specified);
      }
   }
}
</SCRIPT>
```

```
<UL ID = oList onclick = "fnFindSpecified()">
<LI>Click to Find Specified Attributes
</UL>
```

Applies To

 WIN16   WIN32   MAC   UNIX

Attribute

SRC Attribute | src Property

Retrieves the URL of a sound to be played.

Syntax

HTML   <BGSOUND **SRC** = *sURL* ... >

Scripting   [*sURL* =] *object*.**src**

Possible Values

sURL   String specifying the URL of the sound.

The property is read-only with no default value.

Applies To

 WIN16   WIN32   MAC

BGSOUND

 UNIX

BGSOUND

SRC Attribute | src Property

Retrieves the URL to an external file that contains the source code or data.

Syntax

HTML   <SCRIPT **SRC** = *sURL* ... >

Scripting   [*sURL* =] *oScript*.**src**

Possible Values

> *sURL*   String specifying the URL of the source code or data.

> The property is read-only with no default value.

Remarks

> The **SRC** attribute was first available in Internet Explorer 3.02. The **src** property is exposed through the object model as of Internet Explorer 4.0.

> In Internet Explorer 5, the **SRC** attribute of the **SCRIPT** element can refer to an XML data set if the **LANGUAGE** attribute is set to XML.

Applies To

 WIN16   WIN32   MAC   UNIX

SCRIPT

SRC Attribute | src Property

> Sets or retrieves a URL to be loaded by the object.

Syntax

> **HTML**   *<ELEMENT* **SRC** *= sURL ... >*
>
> **Scripting**   *object*.**src** [*= sURL*]

Possible Values

> *sURL*   String specifying the URL to be loaded.

> The property is read/write with no default value.

Example

> The following example uses the **src** property to change the **SRC** attribute for the image.
>
> ```
> <BODY onmousedown="oImage.src='sphere.jpg'"
>     onmouseup="oImage.src='cone.jpg'">
> :
> <IMG ID=oImage SRC="cone.jpeg">
> ```
>
> To see this code in action, refer to the Web Workshop CD-ROM.

Applies To

 WIN16   WIN32   MAC

EMBED, FRAME, IFRAME, IMG

 WIN16   WIN32   MAC   UNIX

APPLET, EMBED, FRAME, IFRAME, IMG, INPUT type=image

 WIN16   WIN32   MAC   UNIX

XML

srcElement Property

Retrieves the object that fired the event.

Syntax

HTML   N/A

Scripting [*oObject* =] *event*.**srcElement**

Possible Values

oObject Object that fired the event.

The property is read-only with no default value.

Example

The following example shows how to retrieve the parent object (if needed), create the text range, move to the original object, and select the first word in the object.

```
<SCRIPT LANGUAGE="JScript">
function selectWord() {
    var oSource = window.event.srcElement ;
    if (!oSource.isTextEdit)
        oSource = window.event.srcElement.parentTextEdit;
    if (oSource != null) {
        var oTextRange = oSource.createTextRange();
        oTextRange.moveToElementText(window.event.srcElement);
        oTextRange.collapse();
        oTextRange.expand("word");
        oTextRange.select();
    }
}
</SCRIPT>
```

Applies To

 WIN16   WIN32   MAC   UNIX

event

srcFilter Property

Retrieves the filter object that caused the **onfilterchange** event to fire.

Syntax

HTML   N/A

Scripting   [*sSrcFilter* =] *event*.**srcFilter**

Possible Values

sSrcFilter Filter object firing the event.

The property is read-only with no default value.

Applies To

 WIN16   WIN32   MAC   UNIX

event

srcUrn Property

Retrieves the Uniform Resource Name (URN) of the behavior that fired the event.

Syntax

HTML   N/A

Scripting   [*sUrn* =] *event*.**srcUrn**

Possible Values

sUrn Specifies the URN identifier of the behavior that fired the event.

The property is read-only with a default value of null.

Remarks

This property is set to null, unless both of the following conditions are true:

- A behavior is attached to the element on which the event is fired.
- The behavior defined in the preceding bullet has specified a URN identifier and fired the event.

Applies To

 WIN16   WIN32   MAC   UNIX

event

START Attribute | start Property

Sets or retrieves the starting number for an ordered list.

Syntax

HTML   <OL **START** = *iStart* ... >

Scripting   *object*.**start** [= *iStart*]

Possible Values

iStart Integer specifying the starting number.

The property is read/write with a default value of 1.

Applies To

 WIN16   WIN32   MAC

OL

 UNIX

OL

start Property

Sets or retrieves when a video clip file should start playing.

Syntax

HTML <IMG **START** = "fileopen" | "mouseover" ...>

Scripting *img*.**start** [= *sStart*]

Possible Values

fileopen   The video starts as soon as it is finished loading.

mouseover   The video starts when the user moves the mouse over the animation.

The property is read/write with a default value of fileopen.

Remarks

The **start** property applies only to **IMG** objects with the **DYNSRC** attribute specified.

Applies To

WIN16	**WIN32**	**MAC**	
IMG			

UNIX	
IMG	

status Property

Sets or retrieves the message in the status bar at the bottom of the window.

Syntax

HTML N/A

Scripting *window*.**status** [= *sStatus*]

Possible Values

sStatus String specifying the message.

The property is read/write with no default value.

Remarks

Do not confuse **status** with **defaultStatus**. The **defaultStatus** property specifies the default message displayed in the status bar.

Applies To

 WIN16   WIN32   MAC

window

 UNIX

window

status Property

Sets or retrieves whether the check box or radio button is selected.

Syntax

HTML   N/A

Scripting   *object*.**status** [= *bStatus*]

Possible Values

false   Indicates that the control is not selected.

true   Indicates that the control is selected.

The property is read/write with a default value of false.

Example

The following example shows how to use the **status** property to control a disabled check box.

```
<INPUT ID=oCheckbox TYPE=checkbox CHECKED DISABLED>
    :
<SPAN onclick="oCheckbox.status=false"
    STYLE="font-weight:bold">I disagree</SPAN>.
<SPAN onclick="oCheckbox.status=true"
    STYLE="font-weight:bold">I agree</SPAN>.
```

To see this code in action, refer to the Web Workshop CD-ROM.

Applies To

 WIN16   WIN32   MAC   UNIX

INPUT TYPE=checkbox, INPUT TYPE=radio

STYLE Attribute

Sets an inline style for the element.

Syntax

HTML *<ELEMENT* **STYLE** = *sStyle ... >*

Possible Values

sStyle   String specifying the inline style.

Remarks

This attribute is not accessible through scripting. To access styles using scripting, use the **style** object.

Applies To

 WIN16   WIN32   MAC

A, ADDRESS, B, BIG, BLOCKQUOTE, BODY, CAPTION, CENTER, CITE, CODE, DD, DFN, DIR, DIV, DL, DT, EM, EMBED, FORM, HR, I, INPUT type=button, INPUT type=checkbox, INPUT type=file, INPUT type=hidden, INPUT type=image, INPUT type=password, INPUT type=radio, INPUT type=reset, INPUT type=submit, INPUT type=text, KBD, LI, LISTING, MARQUEE, MENU, OL, P, PLAINTEXT, PRE, S, SAMP, SMALL, SPAN, STRIKE, STRONG, SUB, SUP, TABLE, TR, TT, U, UL, VAR, XMP

 UNIX   WIN16   WIN32   MAC

A, ACRONYM, ADDRESS, APPLET, AREA, B, BIG, BLOCKQUOTE, BODY, BR, BUTTON, CAPTION, CENTER, CITE, CODE, COL, COLGROUP, DD, DEL, DFN, DIR, DIV, DL, DT, EM, EMBED, FIELDSET, FONT, FORM, Hn, HR, I, IFRAME, IMG, INPUT type=button, INPUT type=checkbox, INPUT type=file, INPUT type=hidden, INPUT type=image, INPUT type=password, INPUT type=radio, INPUT type=reset, INPUT type=submit, INPUT type=text, INS, ISINDEX, KBD,

DHTML Properties

Applies To *(continued)*

 UNIX   WIN16   WIN32   MAC

LABEL, LEGEND, LI, LISTING, MAP, MARQUEE, MENU, OBJECT, OL, P,
PLAINTEXT, PRE, Q, S, SAMP, SELECT, SMALL, SPAN, STRIKE, STRONG,
SUB, SUP, TABLE, TBODY, TD, TEXTAREA, TR, TT, U, UL, VAR, XMP

IE 5   **WIN16   WIN32   MAC   UNIX**

RT, RUBY

systemLanguage Property

Retrieves the default language that the system is using.

Syntax

HTML   N/A

Scripting   [*sLanguage* =] *navigator*.**systemLanguage**

Possible Values

sLanguage   String specifying any of the appropriate language code values.

The property is read-only with a system-specific default.

Applies To

IE 4   **WIN16   WIN32   MAC   UNIX**

navigator

TABINDEX Attribute | tabIndex Property

Sets or retrieves the tab index for the object.

Syntax

HTML   *<ELEMENT* **TABINDEX** = *iIndex* ... >

Scripting   *object*.**tabIndex** [= *iIndex*]

Possible Values

iIndex Nonnegative integer specifying the tab index. To remove the object from the order, use -1.

The property is read/write with no default value.

Remarks

Tab selection order is determined by the value of **tabIndex** as follows:

1. All objects with a **tabIndex** greater than 0 are selected in increasing tab index order, or in source order for duplicate tab index values.

2. All objects with a **tabIndex** equal to 0, or without **tabIndex** set, are selected next, in source order.

3. Elements with a negative **tabIndex** are omitted from tabbing order.

The valid range for the **tabIndex** property value is -32767 to 32767.

The following elements are tab stops by default and can have focus: **A**, **BODY**, **BUTTON**, **EMBED**, **FRAME**, **IFRAME**, **IMG**, **INPUT**, **ISINDEX**, **OBJECT**, **SELECT**, and **TEXTAREA**.

The following elements can have focus by default but are not tab stops; however, they can be set as tab stops: **APPLET**, **DIV**, **FRAMESET**, **SPAN**, **TABLE**, and **TD**.

The **THEAD** and **TFOOT** elements can be set to participate in the tabbing sequence, yet they do not highlight when they receive focus.

As of Internet Explorer 5, scoped elements support the **tabIndex** property and can have focus. These elements are not tab stops and do not have focus by default. Setting the **tabIndex** property to a valid positive integer makes the element a tab stop. The element can have focus if the **tabIndex** property is set to any valid negative or positive integer.

Elements that can have focus fire the **onblur** and **onfocus** events as of Internet Explorer 4.0, and the **onkeydown**, **onkeypress**, and **onkeyup** events as of Internet Explorer 5.

Example

The following examples show how to use the **tabIndex** property.

The sample below specifies the tab order for three text fields, and removes the Submit button from the tab order by specifying a negative value.

```
<INPUT TYPE="text" TABINDEX="1">
<INPUT TYPE="text" TABINDEX="3">
<INPUT TYPE="text" TABINDEX="2">
<INPUT TYPE="submit" TABINDEX="-1">
```

To see this code in action, refer to the Web Workshop CD-ROM.

The sample below assigns a tab order to an unordered list for Internet Explorer 5 and later. To cycle through the tab order of the list, the user presses the TAB key. Because the list items can have focus, the focus rectangle is visible when the user selects an item from the list.

```
<UL>
  <LI TABINDEX="1">Item 1
  <LI TABINDEX="2">Item 1
  <LI TABINDEX="3">Item 1
  <LI TABINDEX="4">Item 1
  <LI TABINDEX="5">Item 1
</UL>
```

To see this code in action, refer to the Web Workshop CD-ROM.

Applies To

 WIN16   WIN32   MAC   UNIX

A, APPLET, AREA, BODY, BUTTON, DIV, EMBED, FIELDSET, FRAMESET, IFRAME, INPUT type=button, INPUT type=checkbox, INPUT type=file, INPUT type=image, INPUT type=password, INPUT type=radio, INPUT type=reset, INPUT type=submit, INPUT type=text, ISINDEX, MARQUEE, OBJECT, SELECT, SPAN, TABLE, TD, TEXTAREA

 WIN16   WIN32   MAC   UNIX

ACRONYM, ADDRESS, B, BDO, BIG, BLOCKQUOTE, CAPTION, CENTER, CITE, DD, DEL, DFN, DIR, DL, DT, EM, FIELDSET, FONT, FORM, Hn, HR, I, IMG, INS, KBD, LABEL, LEGEND, LI, LISTING, MARQUEE, MENU, OL, P, PLAINTEXT, PRE, Q, RT, RUBY, S, SAMP, SMALL, STRIKE, STRONG, SUB, SUP, TBODY, TFOOT, TH, THEAD, TR, TT, U, UL, VAR, XMP

table-layout Attribute | tableLayout Property

Sets or retrieves whether the table layout is fixed.

Syntax

HTML	{ **table-layout :** auto I fixed }
Scripting	*table*.**style.tableLayout** [= *sLayout*]

Possible Values

auto   Column width is determined by the widest unbreakable content in the column cells.

fixed Table and column widths are set either by the sum of the widths on the **COL** objects or, if these are not specified, by the contents in the first row of cells.

The property is read/write with a default value of auto; the cascading style sheets (CSS) attribute is not inherited.

Remarks

You can optimize table rendering performance by specifying the **tableLayout** property. This property causes Internet Explorer to incrementally render the table, thus providing users with information at a faster pace. The **tableLayout** property determines the layout of a table in the following order.

1. By using information in the width property for the **COL** or **COLGROUP** element.

2. By analyzing the formatting of the first table row.

3. By an equal division of the columns.

If the content of a cell exceeds the fixed width of the column, the content is wrapped or, if wrapping is not possible, it is clipped. If the row height is specified, wrapped text is clipped when it exceeds the set height.

Setting the property to fixed significantly improves table rendering speed, particularly for longer tables.

Setting row height further improves rendering speed, again enabling the browser's parser to begin rendering the row without having to examine the content of each cell in the row to determine row height.

DHTML Properties

Example

The following example shows how to use the CSS attribute to set the table layout to fixed.

```
<TABLE STYLE="table-layout:fixed" WIDTH=600>
<COL WIDTH=100><COL WIDTH=300><COL WIDTH=200>
<TR HEIGHT=20>
<TD>...</TD><TD>...</TD><TD>...</TD>
</TR>
:
</TABLE>
```

To see this code in action, refer to the Web Workshop CD-ROM.

Applies To

WIN16	WIN32	MAC	UNIX

style

WIN16	WIN32	MAC	UNIX

currentStyle, runtimeStyle, TABLE

tagName Property

Retrieves the tag name for the object.

Syntax

HTML   N/A

Scripting   [*sName* =] *object*.**tagName**

Possible Values

sName   String specifying the object's tag name.

The property is read-only with no default value.

Example

The following example shows how to retrieve the tag name for an object having the identifier that was specified in the prompt window.

```
<SCRIPT>
var idValue = window.prompt("Get the tag with this ID:;
if (idValue != null) {
    alert(document.all[idValue].tagName)
}
</SCRIPT>
```

Applies To

 WIN16　WIN32　MAC　UNIX

A, ACRONYM, ADDRESS, APPLET, AREA, B, BASE, BASEFONT, BGSOUND, BIG, BLOCKQUOTE, BODY, BR, BUTTON, CAPTION, CENTER, CITE, CODE, COL, COLGROUP, COMMENT, DD, DEL, DFN, DIR, DIV, DL, DT, EM, EMBED, FIELDSET, FONT, FORM, FRAME, FRAMESET, HEAD, Hn, HR, HTML, I, IFRAME, IMG, INPUT type=button, INPUT type=checkbox, INPUT type=file, INPUT type=hidden, INPUT type=image, INPUT type=password, INPUT type=radio, INPUT type=reset, INPUT type=submit, INPUT type=text, INS, KBD, LABEL, LEGEND, LI, LINK, LISTING, MAP, MARQUEE, MENU, META, NEXTID, NOBR, OBJECT, OL, OPTION, P, PLAINTEXT, PRE, Q, S, SAMP, SCRIPT, SELECT, SMALL, SPAN, STRIKE, STRONG, SUB, SUP, TABLE, TBODY, TD, TEXTAREA, TFOOT, TH, THEAD, TITLE, TR, TT, U, UL, VAR, XMP

IE 5　**WIN16　WIN32　MAC　UNIX**

BDO, RT, RUBY

tagUrn Property

Retrieves the longer Uniform Resource Name (URN) specified in the namespace declaration.

Syntax

HTML　N/A

Scripting　[*sUrn* =] *object*.**tagUrn**

Possible Values

sUrn　For custom tags, returns the long URN specified in the namespace declaration. This namespace is declared in the document using the **XMLNS** attribute of the **HTML** element.

null　Returned for standard HTML tags, or for custom tags that omit the namespace declaration.

The property is read-only with a default value of null.

Example

The following example shows how to create a simple *HelloWorld* custom tag using the values returned by the **scopeName** and **tagUrn** properties. The property values are displayed in the browser's status bar.

```
<HTML XMLNS:InetSDK='http://www.microsoft.com/workshop'>

<STYLE>
@media all {
    InetSDK\:HelloWorld { behavior:url (simple.htc) }
}
</STYLE>
<SCRIPT>
    function window.onload()
    {
        window.status = 'scopeName = ' + hello.scopeName +
                        '; tagUrn = '  + hello.tagUrn;
    }
</SCRIPT>
<BODY>
    <InetSDK:HelloWorld ID='hello'></InetSDK:HelloWorld>

</BODY>
</HTML>
```

To see this code in action, refer to the Web Workshop CD-ROM.

Applies To

 WIN16   WIN32   MAC

Hn, ISINDEX

 WIN16   WIN32   MAC   UNIX

A, ACRONYM, ADDRESS, APPLET, AREA, B, BASE, BASEFONT, BDO, BGSOUND, BIG, BLOCKQUOTE, BODY, BR, BUTTON, CAPTION, CENTER, CITE, CODE, COL, COLGROUP, COMMENT, DD, DEL, DFN, DIR, DIV, DL, DT, EM, EMBED, FIELDSET, FONT, FORM, FRAME, FRAMESET, HEAD, Hn, HR, HTML, I, IFRAME, IMG, INPUT type=button, INPUT type=checkbox, INPUT type=file, INPUT type=hidden, INPUT type=image, INPUT type=password, INPUT type=radio, INPUT type=reset, INPUT type=submit, INPUT type=text, INS, ISINDEX, KBD, LABEL, LEGEND, LI, LINK, LISTING, MAP, MARQUEE, MENU, NEXTID, NOBR, NOFRAMES, NOSCRIPT, OBJECT, OL, OPTION, P, PLAINTEXT, PRE, Q, RT, RUBY, S, SAMP, SCRIPT, SELECT, SMALL, SPAN, STRIKE, STRONG, SUB, SUP, TABLE, TBODY, TD, TEXTAREA, TFOOT, TH, THEAD, TITLE, TR, TT, U, UL, VAR, WBR, XML, XMP

TARGET Attribute | target Property

Sets or retrieves the window or frame at which to target the contents.

Syntax

HTML   *<ELEMENT* **TARGET** *= sTarget* | "_blank" | "_parent" | "_search" | "_self" | "_top" ... >

Scripting *object*.**target** [*= sTarget*]

Possible Values

_blank   Load the linked document into a new blank window. This window is not named.

_parent   Load the linked document into the immediate parent of the document that the link is in.

_search   Load the linked document into the browser's search pane. This value is available in Internet Explorer 5 or later.

_self   Load the linked document into the same window the link was clicked in (the active window).

_top   Load the linked document into the topmost window.

The property is read/write with no default value.

Remarks

If there is no frame or window that matches the specified target, a new window is opened for the link.

The default value for **target** depends on the URL and site. If the user does not leave the site, the default is _self, but if the user exits to a new site, the default is _top.

Example

The following example shows how to use a link to load the page into the top frame of the current frameset.

```
<A HREF="newpage.htm" TARGET="_top">Go to New Page.</A>
```

Applies To

 WIN16   WIN32   MAC

A, AREA, BASE, FORM

UNIX

A, AREA, BASE, FORM

text-autospace Attribute | textAutospace Property

Sets or retrieves the autospacing and narrow space width adjustment of text.

Syntax

HTML   { **text-autospace :** none | ideograph-alpha | ideograph-numeric | ideograph-parenthesis | ideograph-space }

Scripting object.**textAutospace** [= *sIdeograph*]

Possible Values

none   No adjustment takes place.

sIdeograph ideograph-alpha   Creates extra spacing between runs of ideographic and non-ideographic text, such as Latin-based, Cyrillic, Greek, Arabic, or Hebrew text.

ideograph-numeric   Creates extra spacing between runs of ideographic text and numeric characters.

ideograph-parenthesis Creates extra spacing between a normal (non-wide) parenthesis and an ideograph.

ideograph-space   Extends the width of the space character when it is adjacent to ideographs.

The property is read/write with a default value of none; the cascading style sheets (CSS) attribute is inherited.

Remarks

An ideograph is a character in the East Asian writing system that represents a concept or an idea, but not a particular word or phrase.

Applies To

WIN16	WIN32	MAC	UNIX

A, ACRONYM, ADDRESS, APPLET, AREA, B, BASE, BASEFONT, BDO, BGSOUND, BIG, BLOCKQUOTE, BODY, BR, BUTTON, CAPTION, CENTER, CITE, CODE, COL, COLGROUP, COMMENT, DD, DEL, DFN, DIR, DIV, DL, DT, EM, EMBED, FIELDSET, FONT, FORM, FRAME, FRAMESET, HEAD, Hn, HR, HTML, I, IFRAME, IMG, INPUT type=button, INPUT type=checkbox, INPUT type=file, INPUT type=hidden, INPUT type=image, INPUT type=password, INPUT type=radio, INPUT type=reset, INPUT type=submit, INPUT type=text, INS, ISINDEX, KBD, LABEL, LEGEND, LI, LINK, LISTING, MAP, MARQUEE, MENU, NEXTID, NOBR, NOFRAMES, NOSCRIPT, OBJECT, OL, OPTION, P, PLAINTEXT, PRE, Q, RT, RUBY, S, SAMP, SCRIPT, SELECT, SMALL, SPAN, STRIKE, STRONG, styleSheet, SUB, SUP, TABLE, TBODY, TD, TEXTAREA, TFOOT, TH, THEAD, TITLE, TR, TT, U, UL, VAR, WBR, XML, XMP

text Property

Sets or retrieves the text contained within the range.

Syntax

HTML   N/A

Scripting *TextRange*.**text** [= *sTxt*]

Possible Values

sTxt   String specifying the contained text.

The property is read/write with no default value.

Remarks

The text is formatted within the current context of the document. You cannot set the property while the document is loading. Wait for the **onload** event before attempting to set the property.

This feature might not be available on non-Win32 platforms. For the latest information about Internet Explorer cross-platform compatibility, see article Q172976 in the Microsoft Knowledge Base article found on the Web Workshop CD-ROM.

Applies To

 WIN16   WIN32   MAC   UNIX

TextRange

TEXT Attribute | text Property

Sets or retrieves the text (foreground) color for the document body.

Syntax

HTML   <BODY **TEXT** = *sColor* ... >

Scripting *body*.**text** [= *sColor*]

Possible Values

sColor String specifying any of the color names or values given in "Color Table" in
Appendix C.

The property is read/write with no default value.

Remarks

Some browsers do not recognize color names, but all browsers should recognize RGB
color values and display them correctly.

Example

The following example shows how to use the **text** property to change the text color of
the document body.

```
<BODY ID="oBody">
:
<BUTTON onmouseover="oBody.text='green'">GREEN</BUTTON>
<BUTTON onmouseover="oBody.text='red'">RED</BUTTON>
<BUTTON onmouseover="oBody.text='blue'">BLUE</BUTTON>
```

To see this code in action, refer to the Web Workshop CD-ROM.

Applies To

 WIN16   WIN32   MAC

BODY

 UNIX

BODY

text Property

Retrieves the text of the block object as a string.

Syntax

> **HTML**   N/A
>
> **Scripting** [*sTxt* =] *object*.**text**

Possible Values

> *sTxt* String specifying the block object's text.
>
> The property is read-only with no default value.

Applies To

 WIN16   WIN32   MAC   UNIX

> SCRIPT, TITLE

text Property

Sets or retrieves the text string specified by the **OPTION** tag.

Syntax

> **HTML**   N/A
>
> **Scripting** *object*.**text** [= *sTxt*]

Possible Values

> *sTxt* Text string of the **OPTION** tag.
>
> The property is read/write with no default value.

Remarks

> The **text** property controls which text appears. The **text** and **value** properties are distinct from one another. Changing the **text** property does not alter an existing value, which is set within the **OPTION** tag.

Example

The following example shows how to make the text string specified after each
OPTION available through the **text** property.

```
<SCRIPT>
function fnShow(){
    for(var i=0;i<oSel.options.length;i++){
        oSel.options[i].text+=" (slugs)";
    }
}
function fnFlash(){
    var sQuery="";
    for(var i=0;i<oSel.options.length;i++){
        sQuery+=i + " - Value=" + oSel.options[i].value +
        " - Text=" + oSel.options[i].text + "\n";
    }
    alert(sQuery);
}
</SCRIPT>

<SELECT ID=oSel onchange="fnFlash()">
    <OPTION VALUE="US">Seattle
    <OPTION VALUE="FRANCE">Paris
    <OPTION VALUE="MEXICO">Cabo San Lucas
</SELECT>
<INPUT TYPE=button VALUE="Show Attractions" onclick="fnShow()">
```

To see this code in action, refer to the Web Workshop CD-ROM.

Applies To

 WIN16　　WIN32　　MAC

OPTION

 UNIX

OPTION

text-align Attribute | textAlign Property

Sets or retrieves whether the text in the object is left-aligned, right-aligned, centered,
or justified.

Syntax

HTML　　{ **text-align:** left | right | center | justify }

Scripting　*object*.**style.textAlign** [= *sAlign*]

DHTML Properties

Possible Values

left   Text is aligned to the left.

right   Text is aligned to the right.

center   Text is centered.

Justify   Text is justified.

The property is read/write with a default value of left; the cascading style sheets
(CSS) attribute is inherited.

Remarks

The justify possible value is available as of Internet Explorer 4.0.

Because this property is inherited, all block-level objects inside a **DIV** object having
textAlign=center are centered.

Example

The following examples show how to use the **text-align** attribute and the **textAlign**
property to align text within the object.

The sample below uses **P** as a selector and two classes to call an embedded style sheet
that aligns the text according to the respective rule.

```
<STYLE>
    P { text-align: center  }
    .align1 { text-align: right  }
    .align2 { text-align: justify }
</STYLE>
</HEAD>
<BODY>
<P onclick= "this.className='align1'"
    ondblclick="this.className='align2'">
. . . </P>
```

To see this code in action, refer to the Web Workshop CD-ROM.

The sample below uses inline scripting to change the alignment of the text when an
onmouseover event occurs.

```
<P STYLE="font-size:14"
    onmouseover="this.style.textAlign='center'">
. . . </P>
```

To see this code in action, refer to the Web Workshop CD-ROM.

Applies To

 WIN16   WIN32   MAC

BLOCKQUOTE, BODY, DD, DIR, DIV, DL, DT, FORM, HR, LI, LISTING, MARQUEE, MENU, OL, P, PLAINTEXT, PRE, TABLE

 UNIX   WIN16   WIN32   MAC

BLOCKQUOTE, BODY, CENTER, DD, DIR, DIV, DL, DT, FIELDSET, FORM, Hn, HR, LI, LISTING, MARQUEE, MENU, OL, P, PLAINTEXT, PRE, style, TABLE, TD, TH, TR, UL, XMP

 WIN16   WIN32   MAC   UNIX

currentStyle, INPUT type=password, INPUT type=text, runtimeStyle, TEXTAREA

text-decoration Attribute | textDecoration Property

Sets or retrieves whether the text in the object has blink, line-through, overline, or underline decorations.

Syntax

HTML   { **text-decoration:** none ‖ underline ‖ overline ‖ line-through ‖ blink }

Scripting *object*.**style.textDecoration** [= *sDecoration*]

Possible Values

none	Text has no decoration.
underline	Text is underlined.
overline	Text has a line over it.
line-through	Text has a line drawn through it.
blink	Not implemented.

The property is read/write with a default value of none (see the Remarks section); the cascading style sheets (CSS) attribute is not inherited.

Remarks

The default value is none, with these exceptions:

1. The following tags have a default value of underline: **A** with **href**, **U**, and **INS**.
2. The following tags have a default value of line-through: **STRIKE**, **S**, and **DEL**.

If the value none is placed at the end of the values, all values are cleared. For example, setting {**text-decoration**: underline overline blink none} causes none of the decorations to render.

If the object has no text (for example, the **IMG** object in HTML) or is an empty object (for example, "<EM> </EM>"), this property has no effect.

If you set the **text-decoration** attribute to none on the **BODY** object, **A** objects are still underlined. To remove the underline on **A** objects, either set the style inline or use **A** as a selector in the global style sheet.

Specifying the **textDecoration** property for block elements affects all inline children. If it is specified for, or affects, an inline element, it affects all boxes generated by the element.

The overline and blink possible values are available as of Internet Explorer 4.0. Although blink is exposed, it is not rendered.

Example

The following examples show how to use the **text-decoration** attribute and the **textDecoration** property to decorate text within the object.

The sample below uses an inline style sheet to draw a line through the text within the object.

```
<DIV STYLE="text-decoration: line-through">
:
</DIV>
```

To see this code in action, refer to the Web Workshop CD-ROM.

The sample below uses inline scripting to underline the text within the **SPAN** object when an **onmouseover** event occurs.

```
<SPAN STYLE="font-size:14"
onmouseover=this.style.textDecoration="underline"
:
</SPAN>
```

To see this code in action, refer to the Web Workshop CD-ROM.

DHTML Properties

Applies To

 WIN16   WIN32   MAC

A, ADDRESS, B, BIG, BLOCKQUOTE, BODY, CAPTION, CENTER, CITE, CODE, DD, DFN, DIR, DIV, DL, DT, EM, FORM, I, KBD, LI, LISTING, MARQUEE, MENU, OL, P, PLAINTEXT, PRE, S, SAMP, SMALL, SPAN, STRIKE, STRONG, SUB, SUP, TABLE, TD, TH, TR, TT, U, UL, VAR, XMP

 UNIX   WIN16   WIN32   MAC

A, ADDRESS, B, BIG, BLOCKQUOTE, BODY, BUTTON, CAPTION, CENTER, CITE, CODE, COL, COLGROUP, DD, DFN, DIR, DIV, DL, DT, EM, FIELDSET, FORM, Hn, HTML, I, INPUT type=button, INPUT type=checkbox, INPUT type=file, INPUT type=image, INPUT type=password, INPUT type=radio, INPUT type=reset, INPUT type=submit, INPUT type=text, ISINDEX, KBD, LABEL, LEGEND, LI, LISTING, MARQUEE, MENU, OL, P, PLAINTEXT, PRE, S, SAMP, SELECT, SMALL, SPAN, STRIKE, STRONG, style, SUB, SUP, TABLE, TBODY, TD, TEXTAREA, TFOOT, TH, THEAD, TR, TT, U, UL, VAR, XMP

 WIN16   WIN32   MAC   UNIX

currentStyle, runtimeStyle

textDecorationBlink Property

Property not implemented.

textDecorationLineThrough Property

Sets or retrieves whether the text in the object has a line drawn through it.

Syntax

HTML   N/A

Scripting   *object.style*.**textDecorationLineThrough** [= *bLineThrough*]

Possible Values

true   Apply the line-through.

false   Prevent the line-through.

The property is read/write with no default value.

Example

The following example shows how to apply line-through to cross out text when the user clicks it with a mouse.

```
<P onclick="this.style.textDecorationLineThrough=true;">
Click this if you think it's unimportant.
</P>
```

Applies To

 WIN16   WIN32   MAC

A, ADDRESS, B, BIG, BLOCKQUOTE, BODY, CAPTION, CENTER, CITE, CODE, DD, DFN, DIR, DIV, DL, DT, EM, FORM, I, KBD, LI, LISTING, MARQUEE, MENU, OL, P, PLAINTEXT, PRE, S, SAMP, SMALL, SPAN, STRIKE, STRONG, SUB, SUP, TABLE, TD, TH, TR, TT, U, UL, VAR, XMP

 UNIX   WIN16   WIN32   MAC

A, ADDRESS, B, BIG, BLOCKQUOTE, BODY, BUTTON, CAPTION, CENTER, CITE, CODE, COL, COLGROUP, DD, DFN, DIR, DIV, DL, DT, EM, FIELDSET, FORM, Hn, HTML, I, INPUT type=button, INPUT type=checkbox, INPUT type=file, INPUT type=image, INPUT type=password, INPUT type=radio, INPUT type=reset, INPUT type=submit, INPUT type=text, ISINDEX, KBD, LABEL, LEGEND, LI, LISTING, MARQUEE, MENU, OL, P, PLAINTEXT, PRE, S, SAMP, SELECT, SMALL, SPAN, STRIKE, STRONG, style, SUB, SUP, TABLE, TBODY, TD, TEXTAREA, TFOOT, TH, THEAD, TR, TT, U, UL, VAR, XMP

 WIN16   WIN32   MAC   UNIX

runtimeStyle

textDecorationNone Property

Sets or retrieves whether the **textDecoration** property for the object has been set to none.

Syntax

HTML   N/A

Scripting   *object.style*.**textDecorationNone** [= *bDecoration*]

Possible Values

> true Property is set to none.
>
> false Property is not set to none.

The property is read/write with no default value.

Applies To

 WIN16 WIN32 MAC

A, ADDRESS, B, BIG, BLOCKQUOTE, BODY, CAPTION, CENTER, CITE, CODE, DD, DFN, DIR, DIV, DL, DT, EM, FORM, I, KBD, LI, LISTING, MARQUEE, MENU, OL, P, PLAINTEXT, PRE, S, SAMP, SMALL, SPAN, STRIKE, STRONG, SUB, SUP, TABLE, TD, TH, TR, TT, U, UL, VAR, XMP

 UNIX WIN16 WIN32 MAC

A, ADDRESS, B, BIG, BLOCKQUOTE, BODY, BUTTON, CAPTION, CENTER, CITE, CODE, COL, COLGROUP, DD, DFN, DIR, DIV, DL, DT, EM, FIELDSET, FORM, Hn, HTML, I, INPUT type=button, INPUT type=checkbox, INPUT type=file, INPUT type=image, INPUT type=password, INPUT type=radio, INPUT type=reset, INPUT type=submit, INPUT type=text, ISINDEX, KBD, LABEL, LEGEND, LI, LISTING, MARQUEE, MENU, OL, P, PLAINTEXT, PRE, S, SAMP, SELECT, SMALL, SPAN, STRIKE, STRONG, style, SUB, SUP, TABLE, TBODY, TD, TEXTAREA, TFOOT, TH, THEAD, TR, TT, U, UL, VAR, XMP

 WIN16 WIN32 MAC UNIX

runtimeStyle

textDecorationOverline Property

Sets or retrieves whether the text in the object has a line drawn over it.

Syntax

HTML N/A

Scripting *object.style*.**textDecorationOverline** [= *bOverline*]

Possible Values

true   A line is drawn over the text.

false   A line is not drawn over the text.

The property is read/write with no default value.

Example

The following example shows how to draw a line over text when the user moves the mouse over the text.

```
<P onmouseover="this.style.textDecorationOverline=true;">
Mouse over this text for an overline.
</P>
```

Applies To

 WIN16   WIN32   MAC

A, ADDRESS, B, BIG, BLOCKQUOTE, BODY, CAPTION, CENTER, CITE, CODE, DD, DFN, DIR, DIV, DL, DT, EM, FORM, I, KBD, LI, LISTING, MARQUEE, MENU, OL, P, PLAINTEXT, PRE, S, SAMP, SMALL, SPAN, STRIKE, STRONG, SUB, SUP, TABLE, TD, TH, TR, TT, U, UL, VAR, XMP

 UNIX   WIN16   WIN32   MAC

A, ADDRESS, B, BIG, BLOCKQUOTE, BODY, BUTTON, CAPTION, CENTER, CITE, CODE, COL, COLGROUP, DD, DFN, DIR, DIV, DL, DT, EM, FIELDSET, FORM, Hn, HTML, I, INPUT type=button, INPUT type=checkbox, INPUT type=file, INPUT type=image, INPUT type=password, INPUT type=radio, INPUT type=reset, INPUT type=submit, INPUT type=text, ISINDEX, KBD, LABEL, LEGEND, LI, LISTING, MARQUEE, MENU, OL, P, PLAINTEXT, PRE, S, SAMP, SELECT, SMALL, SPAN, STRIKE, STRONG, style, SUB, SUP, TABLE, TBODY, TD, TEXTAREA, TFOOT, TH, THEAD, TR, TT, U, UL, VAR, XMP

 WIN16   WIN32   MAC   UNIX

runtimeStyle

textDecorationUnderline Property

Sets or retrieves whether the text in the object is underlined.

Syntax

HTML   N/A

Scripting   *object*.**style.textDecorationUnderline** [= *bUnderline*]

Possible Values

true   Apply the underline.

false   Prevent the underline.

The property is read/write with no default value.

Example

The following example shows how to underline the text when the user clicks it with the mouse.

```
<P onclick="this.style.textDecorationUnderline=true;">
Click this if you think it's important.
</P>
```

Applies To

 WIN16   WIN32   MAC

A, ADDRESS, B, BIG, BLOCKQUOTE, BODY, CAPTION, CENTER, CITE,
CODE, DD, DFN, DIR, DIV, DL, DT, EM, FORM, I, KBD, LI, LISTING,
MARQUEE, MENU, OL, P, PLAINTEXT, PRE, S, SAMP, SMALL, SPAN,
STRIKE, STRONG, SUB, SUP, TABLE, TD, TH, TR, TT, U, UL, VAR, XMP

 UNIX   WIN16   WIN32   MAC

A, ADDRESS, B, BIG, BLOCKQUOTE, BODY, BUTTON, CAPTION, CENTER,
CITE, CODE, COL, COLGROUP, DD, DFN, DIR, DIV, DL, DT, EM, FIELDSET,
FORM, Hn, HTML, I, INPUT type=button, INPUT type=checkbox, INPUT
type=file, INPUT type=image, INPUT type=password, INPUT type=radio, INPUT
type=reset, INPUT type=submit, INPUT type=text, ISINDEX, KBD, LABEL,
LEGEND, LI, LISTING, MARQUEE, MENU, OL, P, PLAINTEXT, PRE, S, SAMP,
SELECT, SMALL, SPAN, STRIKE, STRONG, style, SUB, SUP, TABLE, TBODY,
TD, TEXTAREA, TFOOT, TH, THEAD, TR, TT, U, UL, VAR, XMP

IE 5	WIN16	WIN32	MAC	UNIX

runtimeStyle

text-indent Attribute | textIndent Property

Sets or retrieves the indentation of the text in the object.

Syntax

HTML   { **text-indent:** *length* | *percentage* }

Scripting   *object*.**style.textIndent** [= *sIndent*]

Possible Values

length   String consisting of a floating-point number, followed by an absolute units designator (cm, mm, in, pt, pc, or px) or a relative units designator (em or ex). For more information about the supported length units for Cascading Style Sheet (CSS) attributes, see "CSS Length Units" in Appendix C.

percentage   String value expressed as a percentage of length of the parent object. Percentage values are specified as a number, followed by a %.

The property is read/write with a default value of 0; the CSS attribute is inherited.

Remarks

The property can be negative. An indent is not inserted in the middle of an object that is broken by another object (such as **BR** in HTML).

Example

The following examples show how to use the **text-indent** attribute and the **textIndent** property to indent the object's text.

The sample below uses calls to an embedded style sheet to change the indent on the text when an **onclick** event occurs. The text was originally indented 2 centimeters using **DIV** as a selector in the style sheet.

```
<STYLE>
    DIV { text-indent: 2cm }
    .click1 { text-indent: 50% }
    .click2 { text-indent: }
</STYLE>
</HEAD>
```

```
<BODY>
<DIV onclick="this.className='click1'"
    ondblclick="this.className='click2'">
. . . </DIV>
```

To see this code in action, refer to the Web Workshop CD-ROM.

The sample below uses inline scripting to indent the text within the **DIV** when an **onmouseover** event occurs.

```
<DIV onmouseover=this.style.textIndent="2cm"
:
</DIV>
```

To see this code in action, refer to the Web Workshop CD-ROM.

Applies To

 WIN16   WIN32   MAC   UNIX

BLOCKQUOTE, BUTTON, CENTER, DD, DIR, DIV, DL, DT, FORM, Hn, ISINDEX, LI, LISTING, MENU, OL, P, PLAINTEXT, PRE, style, UL, XMP

 WIN16   WIN32   MAC   UNIX

BODY, currentStyle, DFN, FIELDSET, HR, MARQUEE, runtimeStyle, TABLE, TD, TH, TR

text-justify Attribute | textJustify Property

Determines the type of alignment used to justify text in the object.

Syntax

HTML   { **text-justify :** inter-word | newspaper | distribute | distribute-all-lines | inter-ideograph | auto }

Scripting   *object.style*.**textJustify** [= *sAlign*]

Possible Values

inter-word Aligns text by increasing spacing between words. This value's spacing behavior is the fastest way to make all lines of text equal in length. Its justification behavior does not affect the last line of the paragraph.

newspaper Increases or decreases spacing between letters and between words. It is the most sophisticated form of justification for Latin alphabets.

Possible Values *(continued)*

distribute	Handles spacing much like newspaper value. This form of justification is optimized for East Asian documents, particularly Thai.
distribute-all-lines	Justifies lines in the same way as the distribute value, except that it justifies the last line of the paragraph too. This form of justification is intended for ideographic text.
inter-ideograph	Provides full justification for ideographic text. It increases or decreases both inter-ideograph and inter-word spacing.
auto	Allows the browser user agent to determine which justification algorithm to apply.

The property is read/write with a default value of auto; the proposed cascading style sheets (CSS) extension attribute is not inherited.

Remarks

For this property to affect text layout, the **text-align** property must be set to justify.

Applies To

WIN16	WIN32	MAC	UNIX

ADDRESS, BLOCKQUOTE, BODY, CENTER, DD, DIR, DIV, DL, DT, FIELDSET, FORM, Hn, HR, LEGEND, LI, LISTING, MARQUEE, MENU, OL, P, PLAINTEXT, PRE, TABLE, TD, TH, TR, UL, XMP

text-transform Attribute | textTransform Property

Sets or retrieves the rendering of the text in the object.

Syntax

HTML { **text-transform:** none I capitalize I uppercase I lowercase }

Scripting *object*.**style.textTransform** [= *sTransform*]

DHTML Properties

Possible Values

none	Text is not transformed.
capitalize	Transforms the first character of each word to uppercase.
uppercase	Transforms all the characters to uppercase.
lowercase	Transforms all the characters to lowercase.

The property is read/write with a default value of none; the cascading style sheets (CSS) attribute is inherited.

Example

The following examples show how to use the **text-transform** attribute and the **textTransform** property to transform text within the object.

The sample below uses three calls to an embedded (global) style sheet to transform the text.

```
<STYLE>
    .transform1 { text-transform: uppercase }
    .transform2 { text-transform: lowercase }
    .transform3 { text-transform: none }
</STYLE>
</HEAD>
<BODY>
<DIV STYLE="font-size:14"
    onmouseover="this.className='transform1'"
    onclick= "this.className='transform2'"
    ondblclick="this.className='transform3'">
:
</DIV>
```

To see this code in action, refer to the Web Workshop CD-ROM.

The sample below uses inline scripting to transform the text on different mouse events.

```
<DIV STYLE="font-size:14"
    onmouseover="this.style.textTransform='uppercase'"
    onmouseout="this.style.textTransform='lowercase'"
    onclick="this.style.textTransform='none'">
:
</DIV>
```

To see this code in action, refer to the Web Workshop CD-ROM.

Applies To

 WIN16   WIN32   MAC   UNIX

A, ADDRESS, B, BIG, BLOCKQUOTE, BODY, BUTTON, CAPTION, CENTER, CITE, CODE, COL, COLGROUP, DD, DFN, DIR, DIV, DL, DT, EM, FIELDSET, FORM, Hn, HTML, I, INPUT type=button, INPUT type=checkbox, INPUT type=file, INPUT type=image, INPUT type=password, INPUT type=radio, INPUT type=reset, INPUT type=submit, INPUT type=text, ISINDEX, KBD, LABEL, LEGEND, LI, LISTING, MARQUEE, MENU, OL, P, PLAINTEXT, PRE, S, SAMP, SELECT, SMALL, SPAN, STRIKE, STRONG, style, SUB, SUP, TABLE, TBODY, TD, TEXTAREA, TFOOT, TH, THEAD, TR, TT, U, UL, VAR, XMP

IE 5   **WIN16   WIN32   MAC   UNIX**

currentStyle, runtimeStyle

tFoot Property

Retrieves the table footer of the **TABLE**.

Syntax

HTML   N/A

Scripting   [*sTFoot* =] *table*.**tFoot**

Possible Values

sTFoot   Value of the **TFOOT** object.

The property is read-only with no default value.

Remarks

If no **TFOOT** exists, the value of the property is `null`.

Example

The following example shows how to set the inline style for the **TFOOT** object to blue.

```
document.all.myTable.tFoot.style.color = "blue"
```

Applies To

 WIN16   WIN32   MAC   UNIX

TABLE

tHead Property

Retrieves the table header of the **TABLE**.

Syntax

HTML   N/A

Scripting [*sTHead* =] *table*.**tHead**

Possible Values

sTHead   Value of the **THEAD** object.

The property is read-only with no default value.

Remarks

If no **THEAD** exists, the value for the property is `null`.

Example

The following example shows how to set the inline style for the **THEAD** object to blue.

```
document.all.myTable.tHead.style.color = "blue"
```

Applies To

 WIN16   WIN32   MAC   UNIX

TABLE

TITLE Attribute | title Property

Sets or retrieves the title of the style sheet.

Syntax

HTML   <LINK **TITLE** = *sTitle* ... >

Scripting *link*.**title** [= *sTitle*]

Possible Values

>   *sTitle*   Title of the style sheet.

>   The property is read/write with no default value.

Remarks

>   The **title** is a string used to identify a style sheet.

Applies To

WIN16	WIN32	MAC	UNIX

LINK

TITLE Attribute | title Property

>   Sets or retrieves advisory information (a ToolTip) for the object.

Syntax

>   **HTML**   *<ELEMENT* **TITLE** = *sTitle ... >*

>   **Scripting**   *object.***title** [= *sTitle*]

Possible Values

>   *sTitle*   String of advisory text for the object.

>   The property is read/write with no default value.

Remarks

>   Internet Explorer renders the title as a ToolTip when the user hovers the mouse over
>   the object.

Example

>   The following example shows how to create a function to retrieve advisory text set
>   with the **title** property.

```
<SCRIPT>
function boldAdvise(src) {
    src.title="this is bold text";
    return;
    }
</SCRIPT>
:
<SPAN onmouseover="boldAdvise(this)">bold section</SPAN>
```

To see this code in action, refer to the Web Workshop CD-ROM.

Applies To

WIN16   WIN32   MAC   UNIX

A, ACRONYM, ADDRESS, APPLET, AREA, B, BIG, BLOCKQUOTE, BODY, BUTTON, CAPTION, CITE, CODE, COLGROUP, DD, DEL, DFN, DIR, DIV, DL, DT, EM, EMBED, FIELDSET, FORM, FRAME, FRAMESET, Hn, HR, I, IFRAME, IMG, INPUT type=button, INPUT type=checkbox, INPUT type=file, INPUT type=image, INPUT type=password, INPUT type=radio, INPUT type=reset, INPUT type=submit, INPUT type=text, INS, KBD, LABEL, LEGEND, LI, LISTING, MAP, MARQUEE, MENU, OBJECT, OL, P, PLAINTEXT, PRE, Q, S, SAMP, SELECT, SMALL, SPAN, STRIKE, STRONG, SUB, SUP, TABLE, TBODY, TD, TEXTAREA, TFOOT, TH, THEAD, TR, TT, U, UL, VAR, XMP

WIN16   WIN32   MAC   UNIX

BDO, RT, RUBY

toElement Property

Retrieves the object being moved to as a result of an **onmouseover** or **onmouseout** event.

Syntax

HTML   N/A

Scripting [*oObject* =] *event*.**toElement**

Possible Values

oObject   Object being moved to.

The property is read-only with no default value.

Example

The following example shows how to create a function to return "mouse gone" when the user moves the mouse away from the button.

```
<SCRIPT>
function fnGetTo(){
    var oWorkItem=event.srcElement;
    oData.innerHTML=oWorkItem.TagName;
}
```

```
</SCRIPT>
:
<SPAN onmouseout="fnGetTo()">
    <P>Mouse Over This.</P>
    <P>toElement: <SPAN ID="oData"></SPAN></P>
</SPAN>
```

To see this code in action, refer to the Web Workshop CD-ROM.

Applies To

 WIN16   WIN32   MAC   UNIX

event

top Attribute | top Property

Sets or retrieves the position of the object relative to the top of the next positioned object in the document hierarchy.

Syntax

HTML   { **top:** auto | *length* | *percentage* }

Scripting *object*.**style.top** [= *sTop*]

Possible Values

auto   Default position according to the regular HTML layout of the page.

length   String consisting of a floating-point number, followed by an absolute units designator (cm, mm, in, pt, pc, or px) or a relative units designator (em or ex). For more information about the supported length units for cascading style sheets (CSS) attributes, see "CSS Length Units" in Appendix C.

percentage String value expressed as a percentage of the height of the parent object. Percentage values are specified as a number, followed by a %.

The property is read/write with a default value of auto; the CSS attribute is not inherited.

Remarks

The **top** attribute should only be used when the position attribute is set; otherwise, the value of the **top** attribute is ignored.

Because the value of the **top** property is a string, the property cannot be used in scripting to calculate the position of the object in the document; instead, the **pixelTop** or **posTop** property should be used.

Example

The following examples show how to use the **top** attribute and the **top** property to change the position of the object.

The sample below uses an inline style sheet to set an image's position.

```
<DIV STYLE="position:absolute;top:100px">
. . . </DIV>
```

To see this code in action, refer to the Web Workshop CD-ROM.

The sample below uses inline scripting to change (on mouse events) the image's position from the position set by an inline style sheet.

```
<IMG SRC="cone.jpg" STYLE="position:absolute;
    top:'80px';" onmouseover="this.style.top='100px'"
    onmouseout="this.style.top='80px'" >
```

To see this code in action, refer to the Web Workshop CD-ROM.

Applies To

 WIN16   WIN32   MAC   UNIX

A, ADDRESS, APPLET, B, BIG, BLOCKQUOTE, BUTTON, CENTER, CITE, CODE, DD, DFN, DIR, DIV, DL, DT, EM, EMBED, FIELDSET, FORM, Hn, HR, I, IFRAME, IMG, INPUT type=button, INPUT type=checkbox, INPUT type=file, INPUT type=image, INPUT type=password, INPUT type=radio, INPUT type=reset, INPUT type=submit, INPUT type=text, ISINDEX, KBD, LABEL, LEGEND, LI, LISTING, MARQUEE, MENU, OBJECT, OL, P, PRE, S, SAMP, SELECT, SMALL, SPAN, STRIKE, STRONG, style, SUB, SUP, TABLE, TEXTAREA, TT, U, UL, VAR, XMP

 WIN16   WIN32   MAC   UNIX

currentStyle, runtimeStyle

top Property

Retrieves the topmost ancestor window, which is its own parent.

Syntax

HTML   N/A

Scripting   [*oTop* =] *window*.**top**

Possible Values

oTop   Topmost parent window.

The property is read-only with no default value.

Applies To

 WIN16   WIN32   MAC

window

 UNIX

window

top Property

Retrieves the top coordinate of the rectangle surrounding the object content.

Syntax

HTML   N/A

Scripting   [*iCoord* =] *oTextRectangle*.**top**

Possible Values

iCoord   Integer specifying the top coordinate of the rectangle, in pixels.

The property is read-only with no default value.

Remarks

Use the following syntax to access the top coordinate of the second text rectangle of a **TextRange** object:

```
oRct = oTextRange.getClientRects();
oRct[1].top;
```

Note The collection index starts at 0, so the second item index is 1.

Use the following syntax to access the top coordinate of the bounding rectangle of an object:

```
oBndRct = oElement.getBoundingClientRect();
oBndRct.top;
```

Example

The following example shows how to use the **getBoundingClientRect** method to retrieve the coordinates of the bounds of the text rectangles within the element.

```
<SCRIPT>
function getCoords(oObject) {
    oBndRct=oObject.getBoundingClientRect();
    alert("Bounding rectangle = \nUpper left coordinates: "
        + oBndRct.left + " " + oBndRct.top +
        "\nLower right coordinates: "
        + oBndRct.right + " " + oBndRct.bottom);
}
</SCRIPT>
</HEAD>
<BODY>
<P ID=oPara onclick="getCoords(this)">
```

To see this code in action, refer to the Web Workshop CD-ROM.

Applies To

 | **WIN16** | **WIN32** | **MAC** | **UNIX**

TextRectangle

TOPMARGIN Attribute | topMargin Property

Sets or retrieves the margin for the top of the page.

Syntax

HTML   <BODY **TOPMARGIN** = *iMargin* ... >

Scripting *body*.**topMargin** [= *iMargin*]

Possible Values

> *iMargin*   Integer specifying the top margin of the body, in pixels.

> The property is read/write with a default value of 15.

Remarks

> If the value is set to "0" or "", the top margin is on the top edge of the window or frame.

Applies To

WIN16   WIN32   MAC

BODY

UNIX

BODY

TRUESPEED Attribute | trueSpeed Property

> Sets or retrieves whether the position of the marquee is calculated using the **scrollDelay** and **scrollAmount** properties and the actual time elapsed from the last clock tick.

Syntax

> **HTML**   <MARQUEE **TRUESPEED** ... >

> **Scripting** *marquee*.**trueSpeed** [= *bSpeed*]

Possible Values

> false   The marquee computes movement based on 60-millisecond ticks of the clock. This means every **scrollDelay** value under 60 is ignored, and the marquee advances the amount of **scrollAmount** each 60 milliseconds. For example, if **scrollDelay** is 6 and **scrollAmount** is 10, the marquee advances 10 pixels every 60 milliseconds.

> true   The marquee advances the pixel value of **scrollAmount** by the number of milliseconds set for **scrollDelay**. For example, the marquee would advance 10 pixels for every 6 milliseconds if **scrollDelay** is 6, **scrollAmount** is 10, and the value of **trueSpeed** is true.

> The property is read/write with a default value of false.

Remarks

When the **HTML** attribute is present, the specified **scrollDelay** value is used to move the marquee text. Without this attribute, all **scrollDelay** values of 59 milliseconds or less are rounded to 60.

Applies To

 WIN16   WIN32   MAC   UNIX

MARQUEE

TYPE Attribute | type Property

Sets or retrieves the style of the list.

Syntax

HTML   *<ELEMENT* **TYPE** = "1" | "a" | "A" | "i" | "I" | "disc" | "circle" | "square" ... >

Scripting *object*.**type** [= *sType*]

Possible Values

1	Associate numbers with each item in an ordered list.
a	Associate lowercase letters with each item in an ordered list.
A	Associate uppercase letters with each item in an ordered list.
i	Associate Roman numerals with each item in an ordered list.
I	Associate Roman numerals with each item in an ordered list.
disc	Associate a solid disc with each item in an unordered list.
circle	Associate a hollow circle with each item in an unordered list.
square	Associate a solid square with each item in an unordered list.

The property is read/write with a default value of 1 for an ordered list and a default value of disc for an unordered list.

Example

The following example shows how to set the line item markers to lowercase Roman numerals.

```
<OL TYPE="i">
<LI>First Item
<LI>Second Item
<LI>Third Item
</OL>
```

To see this code in action, refer to the Web Workshop CD-ROM.

Applies To

 WIN16   WIN32   MAC

LI, OL

 UNIX   WIN16   WIN32   MAC

LI, OL, UL

type Property

Retrieves the type of selection.

Syntax

HTML   N/A

Scripting   [*sType* =] *selection*.**type**

Possible Values

none	No selection/insertion point.
text	Text selection.
control	Control selection.

The property is read-only with no default value.

Remarks

The **selection** object is off the **document** object.

Example

The following example shows how to create an alert to give the type of selection for any selection in the body. If the user drags the mouse over the text ("Some text"), the alert reads Text. If the user drags the mouse over the space to the right of the text, the alert reads None.

```
<BODY onclick="alert(document.selection.type)">
Some text.
```

Applies To

 WIN16   WIN32   MAC   UNIX

selection

TYPE Attribute | type Property

Retrieves the cascading style sheets (CSS) language in which the style sheet is written.

Syntax

HTML   <STYLE **TYPE** = *sType* ... >

Scripting [*sType* =] *object*.**type**

Possible Values

sType   String specifying the CSS language of the style sheet.

The property is read-only with no default value.

Remarks

The property can be any string, including an empty string. Valid style sheets for Internet Explorer 4.0 are set to "text/css".

Applies To

 WIN16   WIN32   MAC   UNIX

STYLE

TYPE Attribute | type Property

Retrieves the appearance and default behavior of the button.

Syntax

HTML	<BUTTON **TYPE** = "button"	"reset"	"submit" ... >

Scripting [*sType* =] *button*.**type**

Possible Values

button   Creates a Command button.

reset   Creates a Reset button. If it's in a form, this button resets the fields in the form to their initial values.

submit   Creates a Submit button. If it's in a form, this button submits the form.

The property is read-only with a default value of button.

Remarks

A Submit button has the same default behavior as a button created by using the **submit** type with the **INPUT** object. If a user presses the ENTER key while viewing a form that contains a Submit button, the form is submitted. This default behavior of a Submit button is indicated by a border surrounding the button. The border appears when any control within the form receives the focus, other than another button. If the Submit button has a **name** property, the button contributes a name/value pair to the submitted data.

Applies To

 WIN16   WIN32   MAC   UNIX

BUTTON

type Property

Retrieves the event name from the event object.

Syntax

HTML	N/A

Scripting [*sType* =] *event*.**type**

Possible Values

> *sType* String specifying the event name.
>
> The property is read-only with no default value.

Remarks

> Events are returned without the "on" prefix. For example, the **onclick** event is returned as "click".

Applies To

WIN16	WIN32	MAC	UNIX

event

TYPE Attribute | type Property

> Sets or retrieves the MIME type of the object.

Syntax

> **HTML**   <OBJECT **TYPE** = *sType* ... >
>
> **Scripting** *object*.**type** [= *sType*]

Possible Values

> *sType* String specifying the MIME type of the object.
>
> The property is read/write with no default value.

Remarks

> MIME stands for Multipurpose Internet Mail Extension. MIME is a set of enhancements to Simple Mail Transfer Protocol (SMTP) allowing an Internet message to include a mixture of audio, images, video, and text components, and to accommodate a variety of international character sets.
>
> The property is used to retrieve a class identifier for the object when no **CLASSID=** attribute is given.

Applies To

WIN16	WIN32	MAC

OBJECT

UNIX

OBJECT

type Property

Retrieves the cascading style sheets (CSS) language in which the style sheet is written.

Syntax

HTML   N/A

Scripting [*sType* =] *styleSheet*.**type**

Possible Values

sType   String specifying the CSS language of the style sheet.

The property is read-only with no default value.

Remarks

The property can be any string, including an empty string. Style sheets having any
type other than "text/css" are not supported for Internet Explorer 4.0.

Applies To

 WIN16   WIN32   MAC   UNIX

styleSheet

TYPE Attribute | type Property

Retrieves the type of intrinsic control represented by the object.

Syntax

HTML   *<ELEMENT* **TYPE** = *sType* ... *>*

Scripting [*sType* =] *object*.**type**

DHTML Properties

Possible Values

INPUT

button   Creates a button control.

checkbox   Creates a checkbox for simple Boolean attributes or for attributes that
            can take multiple values at the same time. The input consists of a
            number of check box controls, each of which has the same name. Each
            selected check box generates a separate name/value pair in the
            submitted data, even if this results in duplicate names. The default
            value for check boxes is on.

file   Creates a file upload object.

hidden   Creates a control hidden from the user, but the value of the **value**
            property is sent with the submitted form.

image   Creates an image control that can be clicked, causing the form to be
            immediately submitted. The coordinates of the selected point are
            measured in pixels from the upper-left corner of the image and are
            submitted with the form as two name/value pairs. The x-coordinate is
            submitted under the name of the control with .x appended, and the y-
            coordinate is submitted under the name of the control with .y
            appended. Any **value** property is ignored. The image is specified by
            the **src** property, exactly as for the **IMG** object.

password   Creates a control similar to the text control. The password control,
            however, does not display the text that the user enters.

radio   Creates radio buttons used for mutually exclusive sets of values. Each
            radio button control in the group should be given the same name. Only
            the selected radio button in the group generates a name/value pair in
            the submitted data. Radio buttons require an explicit **value** property.

reset   Creates a button that resets the form's controls to their specified initial
            values when the user clicks the button. You can specify the label to be
            displayed on the button just as for the Submit button.

submit   Creates a button that submits the form. You can use the **value** attribute
            to provide a label that cannot be edited, which is displayed on the
            button. The default label is application-specific. If the user clicks a
            Submit button to submit the form, and that button has a **name** attribute
            specified, that button contributes a name/value pair to the submitted
            data.

text   Creates a single-line text-entry control. Use the value with the **size** and
            maxLength properties.

Possible Values *(continued)*

SELECT

select-multiple Creates a multiple-select list box.

select-one Specifies a single-select list box.

TEXTAREA

textarea Creates a multiple-line text-entry control. Use the value with the **size** and **maxLength** properties.

The property is read-only with no default value.

Applies To

INPUT type=button, INPUT type=checkbox, INPUT type=file, INPUT type=hidden, INPUT type=image, INPUT type=password, INPUT type=radio, INPUT type=reset, INPUT type=submit, INPUT type=text

INPUT type=button, INPUT type=checkbox, INPUT type=file, INPUT type=hidden, INPUT type=image, INPUT type=password, INPUT type=radio, INPUT type=reset, INPUT type=submit, INPUT type=text, SELECT, TEXTAREA

TYPE Attribute | type Property

Retrieves the MIME type for the associated scripting engine.

Syntax

HTML <SCRIPT **TYPE** = "text/ecmascript" | "text/Jscript" | "text/javascript" | "text/vbs" | "text/vbscript" | "text/xml"... >

Scripting [*sType* =] *script*.**type**

Possible Values

text/ecmascript ECMAScript.

text/Jscript JScript (compatible with ECMA 262 language specification).

text/javascript JScript.

Possible Values *(continued)*

text/vbs	VBScript.
text/vbscript	VBScript (same as text/vbs).
text/xml	XML.

The property is read-only with no default value.

Remarks

The property can refer to any browser-supported scripting language specified in Possible Values.

To avoid conflict, match the **type** with the language type specified in the **language** property.

Applies To

WIN16	**WIN32**	**MAC**	**UNIX**

SCRIPT

unicode-bidi Attribute | unicodeBidi Property

Sets or retrieves the level of embedding with respect to the bidirectional algorithm.

Syntax

HTML   { **unicode-bidi :** normal | embed | bidi-override }

Scripting object.**unicodeBidi** [= *sEmbedLevel*]

Possible Values

normal	Element does not open an additional level of embedding. For inline elements, implicit reordering works across element boundaries.
embed	Element opens an additional level of embedding. The value of the **direction** property specifies the embedding level. Inside the element, reordering is implicit.
bidi-override	Same as the embed possible value, except inside the element, reordering is strictly in sequence according to the **direction** property. This value overrides the implicit bidirectional algorithm.

The property is read/write with a default value of normal; the cascading style sheets (CSS) attribute is inherited.

Remarks

The **unicodeBidi** property is used with the **direction** property.

The Unicode bidirectional algorithm automatically reverses embedded character sequences according to their inherent direction. For example, the base direction of an English document is left-to-right. If portions of a paragraph within the document contain a language with a right-to-left reading order, the direction of that language displays correctly right-to-left. The user agent applying the bidirectional algorithm correctly reverses the language direction.

Applies To

 WIN16   WIN32   MAC   UNIX

A, ACRONYM, ADDRESS, AREA, B, BDO, BIG, BLOCKQUOTE, BODY, BUTTON, CAPTION, CENTER, CITE, CODE, COL, COLGROUP, currentStyle, DD, DEL, DFN, DIR, DIV, DL, DT, EM, EMBED, FIELDSET, FONT, FORM, Hn, I, IMG, INPUT type=button, INPUT type=checkbox, INPUT type=file, INPUT type=image, INPUT type=password, INPUT type=radio, INPUT type=reset, INPUT type=submit, INPUT type=text, INS, KBD, LABEL, LEGEND, LI, LISTING, MAP, MARQUEE, MENU, NOBR, OBJECT, OL, OPTION, P, PLAINTEXT, PRE, Q, RT, RUBY, runtimeStyle, S, SAMP, SELECT, SMALL, SPAN, STRIKE, STRONG, style, SUB, SUP, TABLE, TBODY, TD, TEXTAREA, TFOOT, TH, THEAD, TR, TT, U, UL, VAR, XMP

uniqueID Property

Retrieves an auto-generated unique identifier for the object.

Syntax

HTML   N/A

Scripting   [*sID* =] *object*.**uniqueID**

Possible Values

sID   Unique identifier for the object.

The property is read-only with no default value.

Remarks

When you apply this property to the **document** object, the browser automatically generates a new identifier that you can assign to an element's **ID** property.

A new ID is generated and assigned to the element the first time the property is retrieved. Every subsequent access to the property on the same element returns the same ID.

Note The unique identifier generated is not guaranteed to be the same every time the page is loaded.

Example

The following examples show how to use the **uniqueID** property.

The sample below shows how to use the **uniqueID** property to hook up an element to a function defined within a behavior. From a behavior, the sample sets up a timer to fire every second. The sample defines two tick functions: one on the scriptlet, and one on the page. Every time the timer fires, the behavior-defined tick function is called. To ensure that the correct tick function gets called, the sample uses the **uniqueID** property to hook up the element to the tick function defined in the behavior's namespace.

```
<PUBLIC:METHOD NAME="tick" />
<PUBLIC:METHOD NAME="startFly" />
<PUBLIC:PROPERTY NAME="from" />
<PUBLIC:PROPERTY NAME="fromX" />
<PUBLIC:PROPERTY NAME="fromY" />
<PUBLIC:PROPERTY NAME="delay" />
:
<SCRIPT LANGUAGE="jscript">
var currCount;
var flyCount;
var flying;
var msecs;
var oTop, oLeft;

msecs = 50;
flyCount = 20;
flying = false;

runtimeStyle.position = "relative";
runtimeStyle.visibility = "hidden";

window.attachEvent("onload", onload);
```

```
function onload()
{
  // Delay commences from the window.onLoad event.
  if (delay != "none")
  {
     window.setTimeout(uniqueID+".tick()", delay);
  }
}

function tick()
{
   if (flying == false)
   {
      startFly();
   }
   else
   {
      doFly();
   }
}
:
</SCRIPT>
```

To see this code in action, refer to the Web Workshop CD-ROM.

The sample below shows how to create a property that causes the browser to auto-generate a unique ID for an element that is inserted into the page by a behavior.

```
<PUBLIC:ATTACH EVENT="onload" FOR="window" ONEVENT="init()" />
<SCRIPT LANGUAGE="JScript">

function init()
{
   // Specifying an ID=document.uniqueID ensures that a unique identifier
   // is assigned to the element being inserted into the page by
   // the behavior.
   newTextAreaID = element.document.uniqueID;
   element.document.body.insertAdjacentHTML ("beforeEnd",
   "<P><TEXTAREA STYLE='height: 200 ;
      width: 350' ID= " + newTextAreaID + "></TEXTAREA></P>");
}
</SCRIPT>
```

Applies To

WIN16   WIN32   MAC   UNIX

A, ACRONYM, ADDRESS, APPLET, AREA, B, BASE, BASEFONT, BGSOUND, BIG, BLOCKQUOTE, BODY, BR, BUTTON, CAPTION, CENTER, CITE, CODE, COL, COLGROUP, COMMENT, DD, DEL, DFN, DIR, DIV, DL, document, DT, EM, EMBED, FIELDSET, FONT, FORM, FRAME, FRAMESET, HEAD, Hn, HR, HTML, I, IFRAME, IMG, INPUT type=button, INPUT type=checkbox,

Side tab: **DHTML Properties**

Applies To (*continued*)

 WIN16   WIN32   MAC   UNIX

INPUT type=file, INPUT type=hidden, INPUT type=image, INPUT type=password, INPUT type=radio, INPUT type=reset, INPUT type=submit, INPUT type=text, INS, KBD, LABEL, LEGEND, LI, LINK, LISTING, MAP, MARQUEE, MENU, NOBR, OBJECT, OL, OPTION, P, PLAINTEXT, PRE, Q, S, SAMP, SCRIPT, SELECT, SMALL, SPAN, STRIKE, STRONG, SUB, SUP, TABLE, TBODY, TD, TEXTAREA, TFOOT, TH, THEAD, TITLE, TR, TT, U, UL, VAR, XMP

UNITS Attribute | units Property

Sets or retrieves the units for the height and width of the **EMBED** object.

Syntax

HTML   <EMBED **UNITS** = *sUnits* ... >

Scripting *embed*.**units** [= *sUnits*]

Possible Values

sUnits   String specifying the measure units for the **EMBED** object—for example, pixels (px) or ems (em). For more information about the supported length units, see "CSS Length Units" in Appendix C.

The property is read/write with no default value.

Applies To

IE 4 **WIN16   WIN32   MAC   UNIX**

EMBED

updateInterval Property

Sets or retrieves the update interval for the screen.

Syntax

HTML   N/A

Scripting *screen*.**updateInterval** [= *iInterval*]

Possible Values

iInterval Integer specifying milliseconds.

The property is read/write with a default value of 0.

Remarks

The property can be set to an integer value specifying the number of milliseconds between updates to the screen. A value of 0 disables the update interval.

The interval causes invalidations to the window to be buffered and then drawn in the specified millisecond intervals. The purpose is to limit excessive invalidations that reduce the overall painting performance, which can happen if there are too many flipbook-style animations occurring at once.

Use this property judiciously; a value too small or too large adversely affects the page rendering response.

Applies To

 WIN16   WIN32   MAC   UNIX

screen

URL Property

Sets or retrieves the URL for the current document.

Syntax

HTML   N/A

Scripting *document*.**URL** [= *sURL*]

Possible Values

sURL String specifying the URL.

The property is read/write with no default value.

Remarks

The URL property is case sensitive.

This property is an alias for the **location.href** property on the window.

Applies To

 WIN16   WIN32   MAC   UNIX

document

URL Attribute | url Property

Sets or retrieves the URL to reload after the time specified by the **CONTENT** attribute of the **META** object has elapsed.

Syntax

> **HTML**   <META **URL** = *sURL* ... >
>
> **Scripting**   *meta*.**url** [= *sURL*]

Possible Values

> *sURL*   String specifying a URL.

> The property is read/write with no default value.

Applies To

 WIN16   WIN32   MAC   UNIX

META

URN Attribute | urn Property

Sets or retrieves a Uniform Resource Name (URN) for a target document.

Syntax

> **HTML**   <A **URN** = *sURN* ... >
>
> **Scripting**   *a*.**urn** [= *sURN*]

Possible Values

> *sURN*   String specifying a URN.

> The property is read/write with no default value.

Remarks

URNs are an adjunct to Uniform Resource Locators (URLs). URLs, the addresses used on the World Wide Web, usually specify a particular file on a particular machine, whereas URNs specify the identity of a resource, rather than its location.

Applies To

 WIN16   WIN32   MAC   UNIX

A

USEMAP Attribute | useMap Property

Sets or retrieves the URL, often with a bookmark extension (#name), to use as a client-side image map.

Syntax

HTML   <IMG **USEMAP =** *sURL* ... >

Scripting *img*.**useMap** [= *sURL*]

Possible Values

sURL   String specifying the URL of the image map.

The property is read/write with no default value.

Remarks

The **useMap** property identifies the image as a client-side image map by associating a **MAP** object with the image. This **MAP** object contains **AREA** objects that define regions within the image that the user can click to navigate to a designated URL.

You can dynamically assign the maps to the image through the **useMap** property.

Example

The following example specifies "map1" as the image map underlying image.gif. The map can be changed to "map2" by clicking the button.

```
<MAP NAME="map1">
<AREA NAME="area1" COORDS="0,0,40,40" HREF="doc1.htm"
    TARGET="frame1">
<AREA NAME="area2" COORDS="40,0,80,40" HREF="doc2.htm"
    TARGET="frame1">
<AREA NAME="area3" COORDS="10,40,40,80" HREF="doc3.htm"
    TARGET="frame1">
```

DHTML Properties

```
<AREA NAME="area4" COORDS="40,40,80,80" HREF="doc4.htm"
    TARGET="frame1">
</MAP>
    :
<IMG USEMAP="#map1" ID=idImg SRC="image.gif">
    :
<BUTTON onclick="idImg.useMap='#map2'">
    Change Maps</BUTTON>
```

Applies To

 WIN16   WIN32   MAC

IMG

 UNIX

IMG

userAgent Property

Retrieves a string equivalent to the HTTP user-agent request header.

Syntax

HTML   N/A

Scripting [*sUserAgent* =] *navigator*.**userAgent**

Possible Values

sUserAgent   String specifying a valid HTTP user agent.

The property is read-only with a browser-specific default value.

Remarks

The HTTP user-agent request header contains information about compatibility, the browser, and the platform name. Additional information about the browser is available from the **appName** property, and additional information about the platform is available from the **appVersion** property. The value returned by the **userAgent** property is different depending on the browser and platform versions. For example, Internet Explorer 4.01 returns the following string for Windows 95.

```
Mozilla/4.0 (compatible; MSIE 4.01; Windows 95)
```

Example

The following example shows how to use the **userAgent** property to specify a required platform before additional script is executed. For example, if Windows 95 is a requirement for the document, you can use a variable to determine whether the user is running the necessary operating system. The variable "bIs95" is set to `true` if Windows 95 is found in the **userAgent** value, and the additional script is processed.

```
<SCRIPT>
var bIs95=false;
window.onload=fnInit;
function fnInit(){
    if(navigator.userAgent.indexOf("Windows 95")>-1){
        bIs95=true;
    }
    if(bIs95==true){
        // Process additional script.
    }
}
</SCRIPT>
```

Applies To

 WIN16   WIN32   MAC

navigator

 UNIX

navigator

userLanguage Property

Retrieves the current user language.

Syntax

HTML   N/A

Scripting   [*sLanguage* =] *navigator*.**userLanguage**

Possible Values

sLanguage   String consisting of any of the possible return values listed for language codes.

The property is read-only with a browser-specific default value.

Applies To

 WIN16   WIN32   MAC   UNIX

navigator

VALIGN Attribute | vAlign Property

Sets or retrieves whether the caption appears at the top or bottom of the **TABLE**.

Syntax

HTML   <CAPTION **VALIGN** = "top" | "bottom" ... >

Scripting *caption*.**vAlign** [= *sAlign*]

Possible Values

top   Places the caption at the top of the table.

bottom Places the caption at the bottom of the table.

The property is read/write with a default value of top.

Applies To

 WIN16   WIN32   MAC   UNIX

CAPTION

VALIGN Attribute | vAlign Property

Sets or retrieves how text and other content are vertically aligned within the object that contains them.

Syntax

HTML   <*ELEMENT* **VALIGN** = "middle" | "center" | "baseline" | "bottom" | "top" ... >

Scripting *object*.**vAlign** [= *sAlign*]

Possible Values

middle   Aligns the text in the middle of the object.

center   Aligns the text in the middle of the object.

Possible Values *(continued)*

baseline   Aligns the base line of the first line of text with the base lines in adjacent objects.

bottom   Aligns the text at the bottom of the object.

top   Aligns the text at the top of the object.

The property is read/write with a default value of middle.

Applies To

WIN16	WIN32	MAC	

TD, TR

WIN16	WIN32	MAC	UNIX

COL, COLGROUP, TBODY, TD, TFOOT, TH, THEAD, TR

value Property

Sets or retrieves the value of the object.

Syntax

HTML   N/A

Scripting   *object*.**value** [= *sValue*]

Possible Values

sValue   String specifying the value of the object.

The property is read/write with no default value.

Example

In the following example, when you click the text area, the alert displays "This is the **value** of a TEXTAREA."

```
<TEXTAREA onclick="alert(this.value)">
This is the value of a TEXTAREA.
</TEXTAREA>
```

Applies To

 WIN16   WIN32   MAC

TEXTAREA

 UNIX

TEXTAREA

VALUE Attribute | value Property

Sets or retrieves the value of the object.

Syntax

HTML   *<ELEMENT* **VALUE** = *sValue ... >*

Scripting *object.***value** [= *sValue*]

Possible Values

sValue   String specifying the value of an object or a **FORM** control. The purpose of
the string depends on the type of control, as follows:

checkbox The selected value. The control submits this value only if the user
has selected the control. Otherwise, the control submits no value.

file   The value, a file name, typed by the user into the control. Unlike
other controls, this value is read-only.

hidden   The control submits this value when the form is submitted.

OPTION   The selected value. The containing list box control submits this
value only if the user has selected this option.

password The default value. The control displays this value when it is first
created and when the user clicks the reset button.

radio   The button label. If not set, the label defaults to "Reset".

reset   The selected value. The control submits this value only if the user
has selected the control. Otherwise, the control submits no value.

submit   The button label. If not set, the label defaults to "Submit Query".

text   The default value. The control displays this value when it is first
created and when the user clicks the reset button.

This property is read/write with a default value of on for the **checkbox** and **radio** objects, Submit Query for the **submit** object, and Reset for the **reset** object. All other objects have no default value.

Remarks

The purpose of the string depends on the type of control.

The **VALUE** attribute of the **PARAM** object specifies a value passed to an **APPLET**, **EMBED**, or **OBJECT** object.

Example

The following example shows how to set the value for each option to an integer string (for example, a part number).

```
<SELECT>
<OPTION VALUE="123">Item One
<OPTION VALUE="456">Item Two
<OPTION VALUE="789">Item Three
</SELECT>
```

Applies To

 WIN16   WIN32   MAC

INPUT type=button, INPUT type=checkbox, INPUT type=hidden, INPUT type=image, INPUT type=password, INPUT type=radio, INPUT type=reset, INPUT type=submit, INPUT type=text, OPTION, PARAM

 WIN16   WIN32   MAC   UNIX

BUTTON, INPUT type=button, INPUT type=checkbox, INPUT type=file, INPUT type=hidden, INPUT type=image, INPUT type=password, INPUT type=radio, INPUT type=reset, INPUT type=submit, INPUT type=text, OPTION, PARAM

VALUE Attribute | value Property

Sets or retrieves the count of ordered lists as they progress.

Syntax

HTML   <LI **VALUE** = *sValue* ... >

Scripting *li*.**value** [= *sValue*]

Possible Values

sValue   String specifying the count.

The property is read/write with no default value.

Example

The following example shows how to set the value to an integer string for each line item.

```
<OL>
<LI VALUE="1">One
<LI VALUE="2">Two
<LI VALUE="3">Three
</OL>
```

Applies To

 WIN16   WIN32   MAC

LI

 UNIX

LI

VCARD_NAME Attribute | vcard_name Property

Sets or retrieves the vCard value of the object to use for the AutoComplete box.

Syntax

HTML   <ELEMENT**VCARD_NAME** = *sVCard*... >

Scripting object.**vcard_name** [= *sVCard*]

Possible Values

vCard.Business.City	Business city mapped to the vCard.Business.City schema.
vCard.Business.Country	Business country mapped to the vCard.Business.Country schema.
vCard.Business.Fax	Business fax number mapped to the vCard.Business.Fax schema.
vCard.Business.Phone	Business telephone number mapped to the vCard.Business.Phone schema.

Possible Values *(continued)*

vCard.Business.State	Business state, province, or territory mapped to the vCard.Business.State schema.
vCard.Business.StreetAddress	Business street address mapped to the vCard.Business.StreetAddress schema.
vCard.Business.URL	Business Web site address mapped to the vCard.Business.URL schema.
vCard.Business.Zipcode	Business postal code number mapped to the vCard.Business.Zipcode schema.
vCard.Cellular	Cellular phone number mapped to the vCard.Cellular schema.
vCard.Company	Company name mapped to the vCard.Company schema.
vCard.Department	Company or agency department name mapped to the vCard.Department schema.
vCard.DisplayName	User-selected display name mapped to the vCard.DisplayName schema.
vCard.Email	E-mail address mapped to the vCard.Email schema.
vCard.FirstName	First name mapped to the vCard.FirstName schema.
vCard.Gender	Gender mapped to the vCard.Gender schema.
vCard.Home.City	Home city mapped to the vCard.Home.City schema.
vCard.Home.Country	Home country mapped to the vCard.Home.Country schema.
vCard.Home.Fax	Home fax number mapped to the vCard.Home.FAX schema.
vCard.Home.Phone	Home phone number mapped to the vCard.Home.Phone schema.
vCard.Home.State	Home state, province, or territory mapped to the vCard.Home.State schema.
vCard.Home.StreetAddress	Home street address mapped to the vCard.Home.StreetAddress schema.
vCard.Home.Zipcode	Home postal code number mapped to the vCard.Home.Zipcode schema.

DHTML Properties

Possible Values *(continued)*

`vCard.Homepage`	Web page address mapped to the vCard.Homepage schema.
`vCard.JobTitle`	Company or agency job title mapped to the vCard.JobTitle schema.
`vCard.LastName`	Last name mapped to the vCard.LastName schema.
`vCard.MiddleName`	Middle name mapped to the vCard.MiddleName schema.
`vCard.Notes`	Additional notes mapped to the vCard.Notes schema.
`vCard.Office`	Office location mapped to the vCard.Office schema.
`vCard.Pager`	Pager number mapped to the vCard.Pager schema.

The property is read/write with no default value.

Remarks

The **VCARD_NAME** attribute is used for the AutoComplete box.

When a **VCARD_NAME** attribute and possible value is specified, the AutoComplete box is populated with mapped values from the Profile Assistant and any other submitted values stored for that domain. For example, if a user enters an e-mail address into a text field that exposes a **VCARD_NAME** attribute with the possible value `vCard.Email`, AutoComplete suggests any e-mail information provided in the Profile Assistant. If the user submits a different e-mail address, the new information becomes available on that domain for other text fields with the same **VCARD_NAME** value.

If the **VCARD_NAME** attribute is not specified, the name of the text field is used to map the submitted information. However, information from the Profile Assistant is not used.

You can disable the AutoComplete feature by specifying the no possible value for the **AUTOCOMPLETE** attribute.

Although you cannot map **PASSWORD** values for AutoComplete, the browser can disable the ability to store this information and prompt the user for a confirmation before storing the value.

The object model and a Web page do not have access to information provided by the AutoComplete feature until the user selects one of the suggestions for the text field.

This property is not supported in HTML Applications.

Example

The following sample shows how to use the **VCARD_NAME** attribute. A **NAME** attribute is provided with a value `CustomerEmail`, and a **VCARD_NAME** attribute is provided with a value of `vCard.Email`. Information supplied to this text field is mapped to the vCard schema rather than the **NAME** of the text field. If the **VCARD_NAME** attribute was omitted, the supplied information would be mapped to the specified **NAME**.

```
<INPUT
TYPE = text NAME= "CustomerEmail"
VCARD_NAME = "vCard.Email"
>
```

Applies To

 WIN16   WIN32   MAC   UNIX

INPUT_text, INPUT_password

vertical-align Attribute | verticalAlign Property

Sets or retrieves the vertical positioning of the object.

Syntax

HTML   { **vertical-align:** `baseline` | `sub` | `super` | `top` | `middle` | `bottom` | `text-top` | `text-bottom` }

Scripting   *object*.**style.verticalAlign** [= *sAlign*]

Possible Values

baseline	Aligns the contents of an object supporting **VALIGN** to the baseline.
sub	Vertically aligns the text to subscript.
super	Vertically aligns the text to superscript.
top	Vertically aligns the contents of an object supporting **VALIGN** to the top of the object.
middle	Vertically aligns the contents of an object supporting **VALIGN** to the middle of the object.

Possible Values *(continued)*

bottom   Vertically aligns the contents of an object supporting **VALIGN** to the bottom of the object.

text-top   Vertically aligns the text of an object supporting **VALIGN** to the top of the object.

text-bottom   Vertically aligns the text of an object supporting **VALIGN** to the bottom of the object.

The property is read/write with a default value of baseline; the cascading style sheets (CSS) attribute is not inherited.

Remarks

The values sub and super are supported on text. The other values are supported for objects that support **VALIGN**.

Example

The following example shows how to use the **verticalAlign** property to align text within a table cell.

```
 <TABLE BORDER width=100>
<TR>
    <TD onmouseover="this.style.verticalAlign='bottom'"
    onmouseout="this.style.verticalAlign=''">
    text to align</TD>
</TR>
</TABLE>
```

To see this code in action, refer to the Web Workshop CD-ROM.

Applies To

WIN16	WIN32	MAC	UNIX

COL, IMG, SPAN, style, TBODY, TD, TFOOT, TH, THEAD, TR

WIN16	WIN32	MAC	UNIX

currentStyle, runtimeStyle

visibility Attribute | visibility Property

Sets or retrieves whether the content of the object is displayed.

Syntax

| **HTML** | { **visibility:** inherit | visible | hidden } |

Scripting *object*.**style.visibility** [= *sVisibility*]

Possible Values

inherit   Object inherits the visibility of the next parent object.

visible   Object is visible.

hidden   Object is hidden.

The property is read/write with a default value of inherit; the cascading style sheets (CSS) attribute is not inherited unless the value is set to inherit.

Remarks

Unlike **display:none**, objects that are not visible still reserve the same physical space in the content layout as they would if they were visible. You can change the visibility through scripting to show and hide overlapping content based on user interaction. For a child object to be visible, the parent object must also be visible.

Example

The following examples show how to use the **visibility** attribute and the **visibility** property to determine whether the object is visible.

The sample below uses two calls to an embedded (global) style sheet to hide and then show the image when the user moves the mouse over and off the text.

```
<STYLE>
    .vis1 { visibility: visible }
    .vis2 { visibility: hidden }
</STYLE>
</HEAD>
<BODY>
<IMG ID="oSphere" SRC="sphere.jpg">
<P onmouseover="oSphere.className='vis2'"
   onmouseout="oSphere.className='vis1'">
   Move the mouse over this text to make the sphere
   disappear.</P>
```

To see this code in action, refer to the Web Workshop CD-ROM.

The sample below uses a call to a function to hide the image.

```
<SCRIPT>
function disappear()
{
    oSphere.style.visibility="hidden";
    }
function reappear()
{
    oSphere.style.visibility="visible";
    }
</SCRIPT>
</HEAD>
<BODY>
<IMG SRC="sphere.jpeg" ID="oSphere">
Move the mouse over <SPAN ID="oTxt" onmouseover="disappear()"
    onmouseout="reappear()"> this text</SPAN>
    to see the sphere disappear.
```

To see this code in action, refer to the Web Workshop CD-ROM.

Applies To

 WIN16   WIN32   MAC   UNIX

A, ADDRESS, APPLET, B, BIG, BLOCKQUOTE, BODY, BUTTON, CAPTION, CENTER, CITE, CODE, COL, COLGROUP, DD, DFN, DIR, DIV, DL, DT, EM, EMBED, FIELDSET, FORM, Hn, HR, HTML, I, IFRAME, IMG, INPUT type=button, INPUT type=checkbox, INPUT type=file, INPUT type=image, INPUT type=password, INPUT type=radio, INPUT type=reset, INPUT type=submit, INPUT type=text, ISINDEX, KBD, LABEL, LEGEND, LI, LISTING, MARQUEE, MENU, OBJECT, OL, P, PRE, S, SAMP, SELECT, SMALL, SPAN, STRIKE, STRONG, style, SUB, SUP, TABLE, TBODY, TEXTAREA, TFOOT, TH, THEAD, TT, U, UL, VAR, XMP

 WIN16   WIN32   MAC   UNIX

currentStyle, runtimeStyle, TD, TR

visited Pseudo-class

Sets the style of the anchor for previously visited links.

Syntax

HTML   [A]:visited { *attribute1:parameter1* [; *attribute2:parameter2* [; . . .]] }

Scripting N/A

Possible Values

attribute   Any attribute applicable to text.

parameter   Any of the range of values available to the corresponding attribute.

The default value is browser-specific.

Remarks

The **visited** pseudo-class is often used with the following pseudo-elements to define the various states of a link: **active**, **link**, and **hover**.

Using pseudo-classes on elements other than the **A** element has no effect.

Example

The following example shows how to set unvisited links to red and visited links to blue. The example below uses a colon to specify a pseudo-class.

```
:link     { color: red }        // unvisited link
:visited  { color: blue }       // visited links
```

Applies To

WIN16	WIN32	MAC
A		

UNIX
A

VLINK ATTRIBUTE | vLink Property

Sets or retrieves the color of links in the object that have already been visited.

Syntax

HTML   <BODY **VLINK** = *sColor* ... >

Scripting *body*.**vlink** [= *sColor*]

Possible Values

sColor One of the color names or values in "Color Table" in Appendix C.

The property is read/write with no default value.

Remarks

Some browsers do not recognize color names, but all browsers should recognize RGB color values and display them correctly.

Applies To

 WIN16   WIN32   MAC

BODY

 UNIX

BODY

vlinkColor Property

Sets or retrieves the color of links that the user has visited.

Syntax

HTML   N/A

Scripting *document*.**vlinkColor** [= *sColor*]

Possible Values

sColor One of the color names or values in "Color Table" in Appendix C.

The property is read/write with a default value of *#800080*.

Applies To

 WIN16   WIN32   MAC

document

 UNIX

document

VOLUME Attribute | volume Property

Retrieves the volume setting for the sound.

Syntax

HTML   <BGSOUND **VOLUME** = *iVolume* ... >

Scripting [*iVolume* =] *bgsound*.**volume**

Possible Values

iVolume   Integer ranging from -10,000 to 0, with 0 being full Wave Output volume.

The property is read-only with no default value.

Remarks

The higher the setting, the louder the sound is.

Applies To

 WIN16   WIN32   MAC   UNIX
_____

BGSOUND

VSPACE Attribute | vspace Property

Sets or retrieves the vertical margin for the object.

Syntax

HTML   <*ELEMENT* **VSPACE** = *iMargin* ... >

Scripting *object*.**vspace** [= *iMargin*]

Possible Values

iMargin   Integer specifying the vertical margin, in pixels.

The property is read/write with no default value.

Remarks

This property is similar to **border**, except the margins don't have color when the object is a link.

Applies To

 WIN16   WIN32   MAC

APPLET, IMG, MARQUEE, OBJECT

 UNIX   WIN16   WIN32   MAC

APPLET, IFRAME, IMG, MARQUEE, OBJECT

WHITESPACE Attribute | whiteSpace Property

Property not implemented.

width Property

Retrieves the horizontal resolution of the screen.

Syntax

HTML   N/A

Scripting   [*iWidth* =] *screen*.**width**

Possible Values

iWidth   Integer specifying the width, in pixels.

The property is read-only with no default value.

Applies To

 WIN16   WIN32   MAC   UNIX

screen

WIDTH Attribute | width Property

Sets or retrieves the calculated width of the object.

Syntax

HTML   <*ELEMENT* **WIDTH** = *sWidth* [**%**] ... >

Scripting   *object*.**width** [= *sWidth*]

Possible Values

sWidth   Integer specifying the width, in pixels.

sWidth%   Value expressed as a percentage of the width of the parent object.

This property is read/write for the **IMG** object and read-only for other objects. There is no default value.

Remarks

If you specify the **width** property of an **IMG**, but not the **height** property, the resulting height of the **IMG** is sized proportionally according to the specified **width** property and the actual height, in pixels, of the source image file. Consider the following example:

Dimensions of image in source file (pixels):	100 X 50 (W X H)
Specified image width:	2in
Specified image height:	*not specified*
Resulting image width:	2in
Resulting image height:	1in ((50/100) * 2 inches)

If you specify the **width** property of an **IMG**, and the height and width of the image in the source file are identical, the height of the image matches the width.

If you specify the **height** property and the **width** property of an **IMG**, the resulting image dimensions match those specified.

Although you can specify the width as a percentage, this property always retrieves the width, in pixels.

Percentage values refer to the parent object's width. Negative values are not allowed.

To perform operations on the numeric value of this property, use **pixelWidth** or **posWidth**.

Example

The following example shows how to set the image's width to 20 pixels, regardless of the original size of the image.

```
<IMG SRC="large.gif" WIDTH="20">
```

Applies To

 WIN16   WIN32   MAC   UNIX

EMBED, HR, IMG, MARQUEE, OBJECT, TABLE

 WIN16   WIN32   MAC   UNIX

COL, COLGROUP, EMBED, FRAME, IMG, MARQUEE, OBJECT, TABLE

width Attribute | width Property

Sets or retrieves the width of the object.

Syntax

HTML   { **width:** auto | *width* | *percentage* }

Scripting *object*.**style.width** [= *sWidth*]

Possible Values

auto   Default width of the object.

width   String consisting of a floating-point number, followed by an absolute units designator (cm, mm, in, pt, pc, or px) or a relative units designator (em or ex). For more information about the supported length units for cascading style sheets (CSS) attributes, see "CSS Length Units" in Appendix C.

percentage String value expressed as a percentage of the width of parent object. Percentage values are specified as a number, followed by a %.

The property is read/write with a default value of auto; the CSS attribute is not inherited.

Remarks

If you specify the **width** property of an **IMG**, but not the **height** property, the resulting height of the **IMG** is sized proportionally according to the specified **width** property and the actual height, in pixels, of the source image file. Consider the following example:

Dimensions of image in source file, in pixels:	100 X 50 (W X H)
Specified image width:	2in
Specified image height:	*not specified*
Resulting image width:	2in
Resulting image height:	1in ((50/100) * 2 inches)

If you specify the **width** property of an **IMG**, and the height and width of the image in the source file are identical, the height of the image matches the width.

If you specify the **height** property and the **width** property of an **IMG**, the resulting image dimensions match those specified.

The width of a block object encompasses **borderLeft**, **borderRight**, **paddingLeft**, **paddingRight**, **marginLeft**, **marginRight**, and **width**—the sum of which equals the width of the parent's content.

Percentage values refer to the parent object's width. Negative values are not allowed.

To carry out operations on the numeric value of this property, use **pixelWidth** or **posWidth**.

Example

The following examples show how to use the **width** attribute and the **width** property to change the width of the object.

The sample below uses an inline style sheet to set the width of an image.

```
<DIV STYLE="position:absolute;top:10px;left:10px;width=1in">
. . . </DIV>
```

To see this code in action, refer to the Web Workshop CD-ROM.

The sample below uses inline scripting to set the width of an image when an **onclick** event occurs.

```
<IMG SRC="sphere.jpg" onclick="this.style.width='1cm'"
    ondblclick="this.style.width=''">
```

To see this code in action, refer to the Web Workshop CD-ROM.

Applies To

 WIN16   WIN32   MAC   UNIX

A, ACRONYM, ADDRESS, APPLET, AREA, B, BASE, BASEFONT, BIG,
BLOCKQUOTE, BODY, BR, BUTTON, CAPTION, CENTER, CITE, CODE, COL,
COLGROUP, COMMENT, DD, DEL, DFN, DIR, DIV, DL, DT, EM, EMBED,
FIELDSET, FONT, FORM, FRAME, FRAMESET, HEAD, Hn, HR, I, IFRAME,
IMG, INPUT type=button, INPUT type=checkbox, INPUT type=file, INPUT
type=image, INPUT type=password, INPUT type=radio, INPUT type=reset, INPUT
type=submit, INPUT type=text, INS, KBD, LABEL, LEGEND, LI, LINK, MAP,
MARQUEE, MENU, META, NEXTID, NOBR, OBJECT, OL, OPTION, P,
PLAINTEXT, PRE, Q, S, SAMP, SCRIPT, SELECT, SMALL, SPAN, STRIKE,
STRONG, style, SUB, SUP, TABLE, TBODY, TD, TEXTAREA, TFOOT, TH,
THEAD, TITLE, TR, TT, U, UL, VAR

IE 5   **WIN16   WIN32   MAC   UNIX**

currentStyle, RT, RUBY, runtimeStyle

word-break Attribute | wordBreak Property

Sets or retrieves line-breaking behavior within words, particularly where multiple
languages appear in the object.

Syntax

HTML   { **word-break :** normal | break-all | keep-all }

Scripting object.style.**wordBreak** [= *sBreak*]

Possible Values

normal   Allows line breaking within words according to the rules of the language
for Asian and non-Asian text.

break-all Behaves the same as normal for Asian text, yet allows the line to break
arbitrarily for non-Asian text. This value is suited to Asian text that
contains some excerpts of non-Asian text.

keep-all   Does not allow word breaking for Chinese, Japanese, and Korean.
Functions the same way as normal for all non-Asian languages. This
value is optimized for text that includes small amounts of Chinese,
Japanese, or Korean.

The property is read/write with a default value of `normal`; the proposed cascading style sheets (CSS) extension attribute is inherited.

Applies To

 WIN16   WIN32   MAC   UNIX

ADDRESS, BLOCKQUOTE, BODY, CENTER, DD, DIR, DIV, DL, DT, FIELDSET, FORM, Hn, HR, LEGEND, LI, LISTING, MARQUEE, MENU, OL, P, PLAINTEXT, PRE, TABLE, TD, TH, TR, UL, XMP

word-spacing Attribute | wordSpacing Property

Sets or retrieves the amount of additional space between words in the object.

Syntax

HTML   { **word-spacing:** `normal` | *length* }

Scripting *object*.**style.wordSpacing** [= *sSpacing*]

Possible Values

`normal`   Default spacing.

length   String consisting of a floating-point number, followed by an absolute units designator (`cm`, `mm`, `in`, `pt`, `pc`, or `px`) or a relative units designator (`em` or `ex`). For more information about the supported length units for cascading style sheets (CSS) attributes, see "CSS Length Units" in Appendix C.

The property is read/write with a default value of `normal`; the CSS attribute is inherited.

Remarks

The **word-spacing** attribute is available only on the Macintosh, as of Internet Explorer 4.01.

The attribute adds the specified spacing after each word. Justification can influence word spacing.

The *length* value indicates an addition to the default space between words. Negative values are permitted.

DHTML Properties

Example

The following sample shows how to use the **word-spacing** attribute.

```
<STYLE>
SPAN.spacing{word-spacing: 10;}
</STYLE>
<SCRIPT>
function fnChangeSpace(){
    oSpan.style.wordSpacing =
        oSelSpace.options[oSelSpace.selectedIndex].text;
}
</SCRIPT>
<SELECT ID = "oSelSpace" onchange =
        "fnChangeSpace()">
<OPTION>10
<OPTION>15
<OPTION>20
</SELECT>
<SPAN ID = "oSpan" CLASS = "spacing">
The quick brown fox jumped over the lazy dog.
</SPAN>
```

Applies To

 WIN16   WIN32   MAC   UNIX

BUTTON, Hn, ISINDEX

MAC

A, ADDRESS, B, BIG, BLOCKQUOTE, BODY, CAPTION, CENTER, CITE, CODE, COL, COLGROUP, DD, DFN, DIR, DIV, DL, DT, EM, FIELDSET, FORM, HTML, I, IMG, INPUT type=button, INPUT type=checkbox, INPUT type=file, INPUT type=image, INPUT type=password, INPUT type=radio, INPUT type=reset, INPUT type=submit, INPUT type=text, KBD, LABEL, LEGEND, LI, LISTING, MARQUEE, MENU, OL, P, PLAINTEXT, PRE, S, SAMP, SELECT, SMALL, SPAN, STRIKE, STRONG, SUB, SUP, TABLE, TBODY, TD, TEXTAREA, TFOOT, TH, THEAD, TR, TT, U, UL, VAR, XMP

WRAP Attribute | wrap Property

Sets or retrieves how to handle wordwrapping in the object.

Syntax

HTML   <TEXTAREA **WRAP** = "soft" | "hard" | "off" ... >

Scripting   *object*.**wrap** [= *sWrap*]

Possible Values

soft   Text is displayed with wordwrapping and submitted without carriage returns and line feeds.

hard   Text is displayed with wordwrapping and submitted with soft returns and line feeds.

off   Wordwrapping is disabled. The lines appear exactly as the user types them.

The property is read/write with a default value of soft.

Remarks

To detect the difference between soft and hard, you must submit the content within the **TEXTAREA** to an HTTP server.

Example

The following example shows how to dynamically set the **wrap** property of a **TEXTAREA** to one of its possible values.

```
<SCRIPT>
function ChangeWrap(oSelect, oTA)
{
    cValue = oSelect.options(oSelect.selectedIndex).value;
    oTA.wrap = cValue;
}
</SCRIPT>
...
<SELECT ID=cboWrap onchange="ChangeWrap(this, txt1)">
<OPTION VALUE=soft>soft
<OPTION VALUE=hard>hard
<OPTION VALUE=off>off
</SELECT>
<P>
<TEXTAREA ID=txt1 STYLE="height:200;width:200"></TEXTAREA>
```

To see this code in action, refer to the Web Workshop CD-ROM.

Applies To

 WIN16   **WIN32**   **MAC**   **UNIX**

TEXTAREA

Sidebar: **DHTML Properties**

x Property

Retrieves the x-coordinate of the mouse cursor relative to the parent element.

Syntax

HTML N/A

Scripting [*iX* =] *event*.**x**

Possible Values

iX   Integer specifying the horizontal coordinate of the mouse, in pixels.

The property is read-only with no default value.

Remarks

In browser versions earlier than Internet Explorer 5, the **x** property retrieves a coordinate relative to the client.

If the mouse is outside the window when the event is called, this property returns -1. If an element is absolutely positioned and fires a mouse event, or is not the child of an absolutely positioned element, the **x** property returns a coordinate relative to the **BODY** element.

Example

The following example shows how to display the current mouse position in the browser's status window.

```
<BODY onmousemove="window.status = 'X=' + window.event.x +
    ' Y=' + window.event.y">
```

Applies To

WIN16	WIN32	MAC	UNIX

event

XMLDocument Property

Retrieves a reference to the XML Document Object Model (DOM) exposed by the object.

Syntax

HTML   N/A

Scripting [*oXMLObject* =] *object*.**XMLDocument**

Possible Values

oXMLObject   Reference to the XML DOM exposed by the object.

The property is read-only with no default value.

Remarks

For a complete description of the XML DOM exposed by the **XMLDocument** property, see the XML DOM Reference on the Web Workshop CD-ROM.

Example

The following example shows how to use the **XMLDocument** property to access the object model of an **XML** data island.

```
<SCRIPT>
function fnCheck(){
    var oNode = oMetaData.XMLDocument.selectSingleNode
        ("METADATA/ABSTRACT");
    alert(oNode.text);
}
</SCRIPT>

<XML ID="oMetaData">
  <METADATA>
     <AUTHOR>John Smith</AUTHOR>
     <GENERATOR>Visual Notepad</GENERATOR>
     <PAGETYPE>Reference</PAGETYPE>
     <ABSTRACT>Specifies a data island</ABSTRACT>
  </METADATA>
</XML>

<INPUT TYPE=button VALUE="Test" onclick="fnCheck()">
```

Applies To

 WIN16   WIN32   MAC   UNIX

XML

XMLNS Attribute

Declares a namespace for custom tags in an HTML document.

Syntax

HTML   <HTML **XMLNS:***sNamespace* [= *sUrn*] ... >

Script   N/A

Possible Values

sNamespace   Namespace that is used as a prefix for custom tags in a document.

sUrn   Optional. Uniform Resource Name (URN) string that uniquely identifies the namespace.

Remarks

The syntax for **XMLNS** is based on the W3C Namespace Specification for XML. Although the W3C draft allows you to declare namespaces on all tags, Internet Explorer supports namespace declaration only on the **HTML** tag.

You can declare multiple namespaces on the **HTML** tag, as shown in the following syntax:

```
<HTML XMLNS:Prefix1 XMLNS:Prefix2="www.microsoft.com">
```

Example

The following example shows how to declare a namespace when one of the default behaviors in Internet Explorer, **clientCaps**, is used as a custom tag in an HTML document. The declared *MSIE* namespace is used as a prefix to reference the **clientCaps** behavior.

The example shows how the **clientCaps** behavior can be used to install the Internet Explorer Data Binding component, if the component does not already exist in the user's system.

```
<HTML XMLNS:MSIE>
<HEAD>
<STYLE>
@media all {
    MSIE\:clientCaps {behavior:url(#default#clientcaps);}
```

```
}
</STYLE>

<SCRIPT>
function window.onload()
{
   var bDataBindingAvailable  = false;
   var sDataBindingVersion = '';
   var sDataBindingID =
       "{333C7BC4-460F-11D0-BC04-0080C7055A83}";
   bDataBindingAvailable =
       oClientCaps.isComponentInstalled(sDataBindingID,"clsid");

   // If data binding is unavailable, install it.
   if (!bDataBindingAvailable)
   {
      oClientCaps.addComponentRequest (sDataBindingID,
          "componentid");
      bDataBindingAvailable = oClientCaps.doComponentRequest();
   }
   :
}
</SCRIPT>
</HEAD>

<BODY BGCOLOR="#FFFFFF">
   :
   <MSIE:CLIENTCAPS ID="oClientCaps" />

   :
</BODY>
```

To see this code in action, refer to the Web Workshop CD-ROM.

Applies To

 WIN16   WIN32   MAC   UNIX

HTML

y Property

Retrieves the y-coordinate of the mouse cursor relative to the parent element.

Syntax

HTML   N/A

Scripting [*iY* =] *event*.**y**

Possible Values

iY   Integer specifying the vertical coordinate of the mouse, in pixels.

The property is read-only with no default value.

Remarks

In browser versions earlier than Internet Explorer 5, the **y** property retrieves a coordinate relative to the client.

If the mouse is outside the window at the time the event fires, this property returns -1. If an element is absolutely positioned and fires a mouse event, or is not the child of an absolutely positioned element, the **y** property returns a coordinate relative to the **BODY** element.

Example

The following example shows how to display the current mouse position in the browser's status window.

```
<BODY onmousemove="window.status = 'X=' + window.event.x +
    ' Y=' + window.event.y">
```

Applies To

 WIN16   WIN32   MAC   UNIX

z-index Attribute | zIndex Property

Sets or retrieves the stacking order of positioned objects.

Syntax

HTML   { **z-index:** auto | *sOrder* }

Scripting *object*.**style.zIndex** [= *sOrder*]

Possible Values

auto   Bottom-to-top stacking in the order that the objects for which **z-index** is set appear in the HTML source.

sOrder String specifying the order as an integer.

The property is read/write with a default value of auto; the cascading style sheets (CSS) attribute is not inherited.

Remarks

Positive **z-index** values are positioned above a negative (or lesser value) **z-index**. Two objects with the same **z-index** are stacked according to source order.

Example

The following examples show how to use the **z-index** attribute and the **zIndex** property to change the stacking order of objects.

The sample below uses an inline style sheet to set the stacking order.

```
<IMG SRC="cone.jpg" STYLE="position:absolute;
    top:100; left:100; z-index:4">
<DIV STYLE="position:absolute; top:100; left:100;
    color:red; background-color:beige; font-weight:bold;
    z-index:1">
. . . </DIV>
```

To see this code in action, refer to the Web Workshop CD-ROM.

The sample below uses inline scripting to set the stacking order.

```
<IMG ID="cone" SRC="cone.jpeg"
    STYLE="position:absolute;top:10px;left:10px;"
    onclick="cone.style.zIndex=1; sphere.style.zIndex=2">
<IMG ID="sphere" SRC="sphere.jpg"
    STYLE="position:absolute;top:1px;left:1px;"
    onclick="cone.style.zIndex=2; sphere.style.zIndex=1">
```

To see this code in action, refer to the Web Workshop CD-ROM.

Applies To

 WIN16   WIN32   MAC   UNIX

A, ADDRESS, APPLET, B, BIG, BLOCKQUOTE, BODY, BUTTON, CAPTION, CENTER, CITE, CODE, COL, COLGROUP, DD, DFN, DIR, DIV, DL, DT, EM, FIELDSET, FORM, I, INPUT type=button, INPUT type=checkbox, INPUT type=file, INPUT type=image, INPUT type=password, INPUT type=radio, INPUT type=reset, INPUT type=submit, INPUT type=text, ISINDEX, KBD, LABEL, LEGEND, LI, LISTING, MARQUEE, MENU, OL, P, PLAINTEXT, PRE, S, SAMP, SMALL, SPAN, STRIKE, STRONG, style, SUB, SUP, TABLE, TBODY, TD, TEXTAREA, TFOOT, TH, THEAD, TR, TT, U, UL, VAR, XMP

 WIN16   WIN32   MAC   UNIX

currentStyle, runtimeStyle

Methods

The following section provides a complete list of methods exposed by the DHTML Object Model. Entries are arranged in alphabetical order.

add Method

Adds an element to the collection.

Syntax

object.add(*oElement* [, *iIndex*])

Parameters

oElement Required. Element object to add.

iIndex Optional. Integer indicating the index position in the collection where the element is placed. If no value is given, the method places the element at the end of the collection.

Return Value

No return value.

Remarks

Before you can add an element to a collection, you must create it first by using the **createElement** method.

The **add** method can be used on the **AREA** object only after the page has been loaded. If the method is applied inline, a run-time error occurs.

Applies To

WIN16	**WIN32**	**MAC**	**UNIX**

areas, options

WIN16	**WIN32**	**MAC**	**UNIX**

controlRange

addBehavior Method

Attaches a behavior to the element.

Syntax

iID = *object*.addBehavior(*sUrl*)

Parameters

sUrl   Required. String specifying any one of the following values:

sValue	Location of the behavior, in URL format.
"#default#*behaviorName*"	One of Internet Explorer's default behaviors, identified by *behaviorName*.
"#*objID*"	Binary implementation of a behavior, where *objID* is the **ID** attribute specified in an **OBJECT** tag.

Return Value

Integer. Returns an identifier that can later be used to detach the behavior from the element.

Remarks

This method lets you attach a behavior without having to use cascading style sheets (CSS).

Unless the behavior specified in the **addBehavior** call is one of the default behaviors built into Internet Explorer, the **addBehavior** call causes Internet Explorer to download the behavior asynchronously, before the behavior is attached to the element.

Because of the asynchronous nature of the **addBehavior** method, its return value cannot be relied on to determine whether the behavior was successfully applied to the element. Waiting for the **onreadystatechange** event to fire and verifying that the **readyState** property of the element is set to complete ensures that the behavior is completely attached to the element, and that all the behavior's members are available for scripting. Otherwise, attempting to use any of the behavior-defined members before the behavior is attached to the element results in a scripting error, indicating that the object does not support that particular member.

Note A behavior attached to an element by using the **addBehavior** method, or by applying the proposed CSS **behavior** attribute inline, is not automatically detached from the element when the element is removed from the document hierarchy. However, a behavior attached using a style rule defined in the document is detached automatically as the element is removed from the document tree.

Example

The following example shows how to dynamically attach a behavior that implements a mouseover highlighting effect to all **LI** elements on a page.

```
<SCRIPT LANGUAGE="JScript">
var collBehaviorID = new Array();
var collLI = new Array ();
var countLI = 0;

function attachBehavior()
{
    collLI = document.all.tags ("LI");
    countLI = collLI.length;
     for (i=0; i < countLI; i++)
     {
        var iID = collLI[i].addBehavior ("hilite.htc");

        if (iID)
            collBehaviorID[i] = iID;
     }
}

</SCRIPT>

:
// Click <A HREF="javascript:attachBehavior()">here</A>
// to add a highlighting effect as you hover over each item below.
:
```

To see this code in action, refer to the Web Workshop CD-ROM.

Applies To

 WIN16 WIN32   MAC   UNIX

A, ACRONYM, ADDRESS, APPLET, AREA, B, BASE, BASEFONT, BGSOUND, BIG, BLOCKQUOTE, BODY, BR, BUTTON, CAPTION, CENTER, CITE, CODE, COL, COLGROUP, COMMENT, DD, DEL, DFN, DIR, DIV, DL, DT, EM, EMBED, FIELDSET, FONT, FORM, FRAME, FRAMESET, HEAD, Hn, HR, HTML, I, IFRAME, IMG, INPUT type=button, INPUT type=checkbox, INPUT type=file, INPUT type=hidden, INPUT type=image, INPUT type=password, INPUT type=radio, INPUT type=reset, INPUT type=submit, INPUT type=text, INS, ISINDEX, KBD, LABEL, LEGEND, LI, LINK, LISTING, MAP, MARQUEE, MENU, NEXTID, NOBR, NOFRAMES, NOSCRIPT, OBJECT, OL, OPTION, P, PLAINTEXT, PRE, Q, RT, RUBY, S, SAMP, SCRIPT, SELECT, SMALL, SPAN, STRIKE, STRONG, STYLE, SUB, SUP, TABLE, TBODY, TD, TEXTAREA, TFOOT, TH, THEAD, TITLE, TR, TT, U, UL, VAR, WBR, XML, XMP

AddChannel Method

Presents a dialog box that allows the user either to add the specified channel or change the channel URL if it already is installed.

Syntax

window.external.AddChannel(*sURLToCDF*)

Parameters

sURLToCDF   Required. URL of a Channel Definition Format (CDF) file to be installed.

Return Value

No return value.

Remarks

If the call fails, an error dialog box appears. You can suppress the dialog box by using the **onerror** event.

Note This method is for use by publishers shipping Active Channel™ content. Active Channel technology is available as of Internet Explorer 4.0.

This method is not supported in HTML Applications (HTAs).

Example

The following example shows how to present a dialog box that allows the user to add the channel described in the specified CDF file.

```
window.external.AddChannel("http://domain/folder/file.cdf");
```

Applies To

 WIN16   WIN32   MAC   UNIX

external

AddDesktopComponent Method

Adds a Web site or image to the Active Desktop™.

Syntax

*window.external.*AddDesktopComponent(*sURL, sType* [, *iLeft, iTop, iWidth, iHeight*])

Parameters

sURL   Required. Location of the Web site or image to be added to the Active Desktop.

sType   Required. Type of item being added. The value `image` specifies the component is an image. The value `website` specifies the component is a Web site.

iLeft   Optional. Position of the left edge, in screen coordinates.

iTop   Optional. Position of the top edge, in screen coordinates.

iWidth Optional. Width, in screen units.

iHeight Optional. Height, in screen units.

Return Value

No return value.

Remarks

The user must have Active Desktop installed for the **AddDesktopComponent** method to work. If Active Desktop is not installed, the method is not invoked.

This method is not supported in HTML Applications (HTAs).

Example

The following example shows how to add the Microsoft Web site as an Active Desktop component.

```
window.external.AddDesktopComponent(
    "http://www.microsoft.com",
    "website",
    100,100,200,200
);
```

DHTML Methods

Applies To

WIN16   WIN32   MAC   UNIX

external

AddFavorite Method

Prompts the user with a dialog box to add the specified URL to the Favorites list.

Syntax

external.AddFavorite(*sURL* [, *sTitle*])

Parameters

sURL   Required. URL of the favorite to be added to the Favorites list.

sTitle   Optional. Suggested title to be used in the Favorites list. The user is given the opportunity to change the title in the Add Favorite dialog box.

Return Value

No return value.

Remarks

Calling the **AddFavorite** method in a script produces the same dialog box that appears when the user selects Add to Favorites from the Favorites menu.

This method is not supported in HTML Applications (HTAs).

Example

The following example shows script that prompts the user to add the current page to the Favorites list.

```
window.external.AddFavorite(location.href, document.title);
```

To see this code in action, refer to the Web Workshop CD-ROM.

Applies To

WIN32   MAC   UNIX

external

addImport Method

Adds a style sheet to the **imports** collection for the specified style sheet.

Syntax

iIndex = *stylesheet*.addImport(*sURL* [, *iIndex*])

Parameters

sURL   Required. Location of the source file for the style sheet.

iIndex   Optional. Requested position for the style sheet in the collection. If this value is not given, the style sheet is added to the end of the collection.

Return Value

Integer. Returns an integer index value specifying the position of the imported style sheet in the **imports** collection.

Remarks

The return value is a zero-based index value.

Applies To

WIN16	WIN32	MAC	UNIX

styleSheet

addReadRequest Method

Adds an entry to the queue for read requests.

Syntax

bSuccess = *userProfile*.addReadRequest(*sAttributeName* [, *vReserved*])

Parameters

sAttributeName   Required. One of the standard vCard names. (For more information, see the **getAttribute** method.) If anything else is used, the request is ignored and nothing is added to the read requests queue.

vReserved   Optional. Internet Explorer currently ignores this parameter.

Return Value

Boolean. Returns `true` if the request has been added to the queue successfully, or `false` otherwise. A return value of `false` means that either the attribute name was not recognized or the attribute already appeared in the request queue.

Remarks

This method appends a vCard name to the read requests queue. The read requests queue is a list of read requests waiting to be initiated. To initiate the accumulated, or compound, read requests in the queue, call **doReadRequest**. To clear the queue, call **clearRequest**.

Applies To

 WIN32   MAC   UNIX

userProfile

addRule Method

Creates a new style rule for the **styleSheet** object, and returns the index into the **rules** collection.

Syntax

styleSheet.addRule(*sSelector*, *sStyle* [, *iIndex*])

Parameters

sSelector Required. Selector for the new rule. Single contextual selectors are valid. For example, "DIV P B" is a valid contextual selector.

sStyle Required. Style assignments for this style rule. This style takes the same form as an inline style specification. For example, "color:blue" is a valid style parameter.

iIndex Optional. Location in the **rules** collection where the new style rule is added. If an index is not provided, the rule is added to the end of the collection by default.

Return Value

The return value is reserved; do not use.

Remarks

You can apply rules to a disabled **styleSheet**, but they do not apply to the document until you enable the **styleSheet**.

Example

The following example shows how to add a rule that sets the color of all bold text appearing in a **DIV** to blue.

```
<DIV>
Internet Explorer makes <B>HTML</B> dynamic.
</DIV>

<SCRIPT>
    styleSheet[0].addRule("DIV B", "color:blue", 0);
</SCRIPT>
```

The next example shows how to add two rules to the end of the **rules** collection. The rules apply the **hover** and **link** pseudo-class attributes to all anchors that appear within an **H2**.

```
<H2>
<A HREF="http://www.microsoft.com/">
    Where Do You Want to Go Today?
</A>
</H2>

<SCRIPT>
    document.styleSheet[0].addRule("H2 A:hover", "color:gold");
    document.styleSheet[0].addRule("H2 A:link", "color:black");
</SCRIPT>
```

Applies To

 WIN16   WIN32   MAC   UNIX

styleSheet

alert Method

Displays a dialog box containing an application-defined message.

Syntax

window.alert([*sMessage*])

Parameters

sMessage   Optional. String to display in the Alert dialog box. If no value is provided, the dialog box contains no message.

Return Value

No return value.

Remarks

You cannot change the title bar of the Alert dialog box.

Applies To

 WIN16   WIN32   MAC

window

 UNIX

window

appendChild Method

Appends an element as a child to the object.

Syntax

oElement = *object*.appendChild(*oNode*)

Parameters

oNode   Required. Existing object.

Return Value

Returns a reference to the element that is appended to the object.

Remarks

The **appendChild** method appends elements to the end of the **childNodes** collection.

You must append new elements within the **BODY** element to be displayed on the page. For example, the following code shows how to add a **DIV** element to the **BODY**.

```
var oDiv=document.createElement("DIV");
document.body.appendChild(oDiv);
```

This method is accessible at run time. If elements get removed at run time before the closing tag is parsed, areas of the document might not render.

Example

The following example shows how to use the **appendChild** method to add an item to an unordered list.

```
<SCRIPT>
function fnAppend(){
    var oNewNode = document.createElement("LI");
    oList.appendChild(oNewNode);
    oNewNode.innerText="List node 5";
}
</SCRIPT>
<BODY>
<UL ID = oList>
<LI>List node 1
<LI>List node 2
<LI>List node 3
<LI>List node 4
</UL>

<INPUT
    TYPE = "button"
    VALUE = "Append Child"
    onclick = "fnAppend()"
>
</BODY>
```

Applies To

 WIN16   WIN32   MAC   UNIX

A, ACRONYM, ADDRESS, B, BDO, BIG, BLOCKQUOTE, BODY, BUTTON, CAPTION, CENTER, CITE, CODE, COL, COLGROUP, COMMENT, DD, DEL, DFN, DIR, DIV, DL, DT, EM, FIELDSET, FONT, FORM, FRAMESET, HEAD, Hn, HTML, I, IFRAME, INPUT type=button, INPUT type=checkbox, INPUT type=file, INPUT type=image, INPUT type=password, INPUT type=radio, INPUT type=reset, INPUT type=submit, INPUT type=text, INS, KBD, LABEL, LEGEND, LI, LISTING, MAP, MARQUEE, MENU, NEXTID, OL, OPTION, P, PLAINTEXT, PRE, Q, S, SAMP, SELECT, SMALL, SPAN, STRIKE, STRONG, SUB, SUP, TABLE, TBODY, TD, TEXTAREA, TFOOT, TH, THEAD, TR, TT, U, UL, VAR, XMP

applyElement Method

Makes the element a child of the element passed as a parameter.

Syntax

object.applyElement(*oNewElement* [, *sWhere*])

Parameters

oNewElement   Required. Element that becomes the parent of the object invoking the **applyElement** method.

sWhere   outside   Optional. String specifying that the element is made a parent of the object.

inside   Optional. String specifying that the element is made a child of the object, but contains all children in the object.

Return Value

No return value.

Remarks

This method is accessible at run time. If elements get removed at run time before the closing tag is parsed, areas of the document might not render.

Example

The following example shows how to use the **applyElement** method to apply the **I** element to an unordered list.

```
<SCRIPT>
function fnApply(){
    var oNewNode = document.createElement("I");
    oList.applyElement(oNewNode);
}
</SCRIPT>

<UL ID = oList>
<LI>List item 1
<LI>List item 2
<LI>List item 3
<LI>List item 4
</UL>

<INPUT
    TYPE="button"
    VALUE="Apply Element"
    onclick="fnApply()">
```

Applies To

 WIN16   WIN32   MAC   UNIX

A, ACRONYM, ADDRESS, APPLET, AREA, B, BASE, BASEFONT, BDO,
BGSOUND, BIG, BLOCKQUOTE, BODY, BR, BUTTON, CAPTION, CENTER,
CITE, CODE, COL, COLGROUP, COMMENT, DD, DEL, DFN, DIR, DIV, DL, DT,
EM, EMBED, FIELDSET, FONT, FORM, FRAME, FRAMESET, HEAD, Hn, HR,
HTML, I, IFRAME, IMG, INPUT type=button, INPUT type=checkbox, INPUT
type=file, INPUT type=hidden, INPUT type=image, INPUT type=password, INPUT
type=radio, INPUT type=reset, INPUT type=submit, INPUT type=text, INS, KBD,
LABEL, LEGEND, LI, LINK, LISTING, MAP, MARQUEE, MENU, NEXTID,
OBJECT, OL, OPTION, P, PLAINTEXT, PRE, Q, S, SAMP, SCRIPT, SELECT,
SMALL, SPAN, STRIKE, STRONG, SUB, SUP, TABLE, TBODY, TD,
TEXTAREA, TFOOT, TH, THEAD, TITLE, TR, TT, U, UL, VAR, XMP

assign Method

Loads a new HTML document.

Syntax

location.assign(*sURL*)

Parameters

sURL Required. URL of the document to load.

Return Value

No return value.

Applies To

 WIN16   WIN32   MAC   UNIX

location

attachEvent Method

Binds the specified function to an event that fires on the object when the function is called.

Syntax

bSuccess = *object*.attachEvent(*sEvent*, *fpNotify*)

Parameters

sEvent   Required. Any one of the standard DHTML events.

fpNotify   Required. Function to be called when *sEvent* fires.

Return Value

Boolean. Returns true if the function is bound successfully to the event, or false otherwise.

Remarks

When *sEvent* fires on the object, the object's *sEvent* handler is called before the specified function, *fpNotify*. If you attach multiple functions to the same event on the same object, the functions are called in a random order, immediately after the object's event handler is called.

This method enables a behavior to listen in on events that occur on the containing page. It is not limited, however, to behaviors. You can also define a function on a page that attaches to events fired on the same page.

Behaviors that attach to events using the **attachEvent** method must explicitly call the **detachEvent** method to stop receiving notifications from the page when the **ondetach** event fires. A behavior that attaches to events on the page using the HTML Component (HTC) **ATTACH** element automatically stops receiving notifications when the behavior is detached from the element. In this case, the behavior does not need to call the **detachEvent** method.

Example

The following example shows how to call the **attachEvent** method from an HTC to implement a mouseover highlighting effect.

```
<PUBLIC:ATTACH EVENT="ondetach" ONEVENT="cleanup()" />

<SCRIPT LANGUAGE="JScript">

attachEvent ('onmouseover', Hilite);

attachEvent ('onmouseout', Restore);
```

```
function cleanup()
{
   detachEvent ('onmouseover', Hilite);
   detachEvent ('onmouseout', Restore);
}

function Hilite()
{
   if (event.srcElement == element)
   {
     normalColor = style.color;
     runtimeStyle.color  = "red";
     runtimeStyle.cursor = "hand";
   }
}

function Restore()
{
   if (event.srcElement == element)
   {
      runtimeStyle.color  = normalColor;
      runtimeStyle.cursor = "";
   }
}
}
</SCRIPT>
```

To see this code in action, refer to the Web Workshop CD-ROM.

Applies To

WIN16   WIN32   MAC   UNIX

A, ACRONYM, ADDRESS, APPLET, AREA, B, BASE, BASEFONT, BGSOUND, BIG, BLOCKQUOTE, BODY, BR, BUTTON, CAPTION, CENTER, CITE, CODE, COL, COLGROUP, COMMENT, DD, DEL, DFN, DIR, DIV, DL, document, DT, EM, EMBED, FIELDSET, FONT, FORM, FRAME, FRAMESET, HEAD, Hn, HR, HTML, I, IFRAME, IMG, INPUT type=button, INPUT type=checkbox, INPUT type=file, INPUT type=hidden, INPUT type=image, INPUT type=password, INPUT type=radio, INPUT type=reset, INPUT type=submit, INPUT type=text, INS, KBD, LABEL, LEGEND, LI, LINK, LISTING, MAP, MARQUEE, MENU, NOBR, OBJECT, OL, OPTION, P, PLAINTEXT, PRE, Q, S, SAMP, SCRIPT, SELECT, SMALL, SPAN, STRIKE, STRONG, SUB, SUP, TABLE, TBODY, TD, TEXTAREA, TFOOT, TH, THEAD, TITLE, TR, TT, U, UL, VAR, window, XMP

AutoCompleteSaveForm Method

Saves the specified form in the AutoComplete data store.

Syntax

window.external.`AutoCompleteSaveForm(`*oForm*`)`

Parameters

oForm Required. Reference to a **FORM** element.

Return Value

No return value.

Remarks

The AutoComplete feature in Internet Explorer 5 saves values for **INPUT type=text** and **INPUT type=password** controls when a form is submitted to a server. Use the **AutoCompleteSaveForm** method to save these values if a form is submitted through the **submit** method, or is not submitted to a server.

You can enable the AutoComplete feature for forms by clicking Tools, Internet Options, Content, and then AutoComplete. You can disable the feature for individual form controls and entire forms by using the **AUTOCOMPLETE** attribute.

This method is not supported in HTML Applications (HTAs).

Example

The following example shows how to use the **AutoCompleteSaveForm** method to save the value of a text field without submitting the form to a server.

```
<SCRIPT>
function fnSaveForm(){
    window.external.AutoCompleteSaveForm(oForm);
    oForm.AutoCompleteTest.value="";
    oForm.AutoCompleteIgnore.value="";
}
</SCRIPT>
<FORM NAME="oForm">

This text is saved:
<INPUT TYPE="text" NAME="AutoCompleteTest">

This text is not saved:
<INPUT TYPE="text" NAME="AutoCompleteIgnore" AUTOCOMPLETE="off">

</FORM>
<INPUT TYPE=button VALUE="Save Value" onclick="fnSaveForm()">
```

To see this code in action, refer to the Web Workshop CD-ROM.

Applies To

 WIN16   WIN32   MAC   UNIX

external

AutoScan Method

Attempts to connect to a Web server by passing the specified query through completion templates.

Syntax

window.external.AutoScan(*sUserQuery* [, *sURL*, *sTarget*])

Parameters

sUserQuery Required. Domain name that has www. before it, and .com, .org, .net, or .edu after it.

sURL Optional. Web page to display if the domain address created from *sUserQuery* is invalid. The default Internet Explorer error page is displayed if a value is not provided.

sTarget Optional. Target window or frame where the results are displayed. The default value is the current window.

Return Value

No return value.

Remarks

The domain suffixes appended to the user query are located in the system registry under HKEY_LOCAL_MACHINE\software\microsoft\internet explorer\main\urltemplate. Each suffix is appended in the following order until an existing server is found: .com, .org, .net, and .edu.

If no server is found, the document specified by the *sURL* parameter is displayed.

This method is not supported in HTML Applications (HTAs).

DHTML Methods

Example

The following example shows how to use the **AutoScan** method to connect to the www.microsoft.com Web site.

```
window.external.AutoScan("microsoft","InvalidSite.htm","_main");
```

Applies To

IE 5	WIN16	WIN32	MAC	UNIX

external

back Method

Loads a URL from the History list.

Syntax

history.back([*iDistance*])

Parameters

iDistance   Optional. Number of URLs to go back. If no value is provided, the previous URL is loaded.

Return Value

No return value.

Remarks

This method performs the same action as when a user clicks the Back button in the browser. The **back** method works the same as **history.go(-1)**. An error does not occur if the user tries to go beyond the beginning of the history. Instead, the user remains at the current page.

Applies To

IE 3	WIN16	WIN32	MAC

history

IE 4	UNIX

history

blur Method

Causes an object to lose focus, and fires the **onblur** event.

Syntax

object.blur()

Return Value

No return value.

Remarks

As of Internet Explorer 5, elements that expose the **blur** method must have the **TABINDEX** attribute set.

Applies To

 WIN16   WIN32   MAC

SELECT, TEXTAREA

 WIN16   WIN32   MAC   UNIX

A, APPLET, AREA, BODY, BUTTON, DIV, EMBED, FIELDSET, FRAME, FRAMESET, IFRAME, INPUT type=button, INPUT type=checkbox, INPUT type=file, INPUT type=image, INPUT type=password, INPUT type=radio, INPUT type=reset, INPUT type=submit, INPUT type=text, ISINDEX, OBJECT, SELECT, SPAN, TABLE, TD, TEXTAREA, TR, window

IE 5 **WIN16   WIN32   MAC   UNIX**

ACRONYM, ADDRESS, B, BDO, BIG, BLOCKQUOTE, CAPTION, CENTER, CITE, DD, DEL, DFN, DIR, DL, DT, EM, FONT, FORM, Hn, HR, I, IMG, INS, KBD, LABEL, LEGEND, LI, LISTING, MARQUEE, MENU, OL, P, PLAINTEXT, PRE, Q, RT, RUBY, S, SAMP, SMALL, STRIKE, STRONG, SUB, SUP, TBODY, TFOOT, TH, THEAD, TT, U, UL, VAR, XMP

DHTML Methods

clear Method

Clears the contents of the selection.

Syntax

selection.clear( )

Return Value

No return value.

Applies To

 WIN16   WIN32   MAC   UNIX

selection

clear Method

Clears the current document.

Syntax

document.clear( )

Return Value

No return value.

Applies To

 WIN16   WIN32   MAC

document

 UNIX

document

clearAttributes Method

Removes all attributes and values from the object.

Syntax

object.clearAttributes( )

Return Value

No return value.

Remarks

The **clearAttributes** method only clears persistent HTML attributes. Events, styles, and script-only properties are not cleared. If you use the **clearAttributes** method on an event, you cannot subsequently reference the **ID** of the element.

Example

The following example shows how to use the **clearAttributes** method.

```
<SCRIPT>
function fnClear(){
    oSource.children[0].clearAttributes();
}
</SCRIPT>

<SPAN ID=oSource>
<DIV
    ID="oDiv"
    ATTRIBUTE1="true"
    ATTRIBUTE2="true"
    onclick="alert('click');"
    onmouseover="this.style.color='#0000FF';"
    onmouseout="this.style.color='#000000';"
>
This is a sample <b>DIV</b> element.
</DIV>
</SPAN>

<INPUT
    TYPE="button"
    VALUE="Clear Attributes"
    onclick="fnClear()"
>
```

To see this code in action, refer to the Web Workshop CD-ROM.

Applies To

 WIN16   WIN32   MAC   UNIX

A, ACRONYM, ADDRESS, APPLET, AREA, B, BASE, BASEFONT, BDO, BGSOUND, BIG, BLOCKQUOTE, BODY, BR, BUTTON, CAPTION, CENTER, CITE, CODE, COL, COLGROUP, COMMENT, DD, DEL, DFN, DIR, DIV, DL, document, DT, EM, EMBED, FIELDSET, FONT, FORM, FRAME, FRAMESET, HEAD, Hn, HR, HTML, I, IFRAME, IMG, INPUT type=button, INPUT type=checkbox, INPUT type=file, INPUT type=hidden, INPUT type=image,

WIN16   WIN32   MAC   UNIX

INPUT type=password, INPUT type=radio, INPUT type=reset, INPUT type=submit, INPUT type=text, INS, KBD, LABEL, LEGEND, LI, LINK, LISTING, MAP, MARQUEE, MENU, NEXTID, OBJECT, OL, OPTION, P, PLAINTEXT, PRE, Q, S, SAMP, SCRIPT, SELECT, SMALL, SPAN, STRIKE, STRONG, SUB, SUP, TABLE, TBODY, TD, TEXTAREA, TFOOT, TH, THEAD, TITLE, TR, TT, U, UL, VAR, XMP

clearData Method

Removes one or more data formats from the **dataTransfer** or **clipboardData** object.

Syntax

object.clearData([*sDataFormat*])

Parameters

sDataFormat   Optional. Data format to be removed from the clipboard using the **dataTransfer** or **clipboardData** object. All formats are cleared when no parameter is passed. This string can be one of the following values:

Text   Causes the text format to be removed.

URL   Causes the URL format to be removed.

File   Causes the file format to be removed.

HTML   Causes the HTML format to be removed.

Image   Causes the image format to be removed.

Return Value

No return value.

Remarks

For drag-and-drop operations, the **clearData** method of the **dataTransfer** object is generally used in source events, such as **ondragstart**. When overriding the default behavior of the target, use **clearData** in the **ondrop** event. It is particularly useful for selectively removing data formats when multiple formats are specified.

Example

The following example shows how to use the **clearData** method to strip the text data format from the **dataTransfer** object.

```
<HEAD>
<SCRIPT>
var sGetData;

function Source_DragStart()
{
  event.dataTransfer.setData("Text", "This text is cleared");
}

function Target_Drop()
{
  event.dataTransfer.clearData("Text");
  sGetData = event.dataTransfer.getData("Text");
  oTarget.innerText = sGetData;
}
</SCRIPT>
</HEAD>
<BODY>

<P>Drag the green text and drop it over the magenta DIV.</P>

<SPAN ID="oSource" ondragstart="Source_DragStart()">
    Drag this text.
</SPAN>

<P>Drop the text below. No new text appears in the DIV.</P>

<DIV
    ID="oTarget" ondrop="Target_Drop()">
</DIV>

</BODY>
```

To see this code in action, refer to the Web Workshop CD-ROM.

Applies To

 WIN16   WIN32   MAC   UNIX

clipboardData, dataTransfer

clearInterval Method

Cancels the interval previously started using the **setInterval** method.

Syntax

window.clearInterval(*iIntervalID*)

Parameters

iIntervalID   Required. Interval to cancel. This value must have been previously
returned by the **setInterval** method.

Return Value

No return value.

Applies To

 WIN16   WIN32   MAC   UNIX

window

clearRequest Method

Clears all requests in the read-requests queue preparing it for a new request for profile
access.

Syntax

userProfile.clearRequest()

Return Value

No return value.

Applies To

 WIN32   MAC   UNIX

userProfile

clearTimeout Method

Cancels a time-out that was set with the **setTimeout** method.

Syntax

window.clearTimeout(*iTimeoutID*)

Parameters

iTimeoutID   Required. Time-out setting that was returned by a previous call to the
setTimeout method.

Return Value

No return value.

Applies To

 WIN16   WIN32   MAC

window

 UNIX

window

click Method

Simulates a click by causing the **onclick** event to fire.

Syntax

object.click()

Return Value

No return value.

Applies To

 WIN16   WIN32   MAC

A, AREA, INPUT type=button

UNIX   WIN16   WIN32   MAC

A, ADDRESS, APPLET, AREA, B, BIG, BLOCKQUOTE, BODY, BUTTON, CAPTION, CENTER, CITE, CODE, DD, DFN, DIR, DIV, DL, DT, EM, EMBED, FIELDSET, FONT, FORM, Hn, HR, I, IMG, INPUT type=button, INPUT type=checkbox, INPUT type=file, INPUT type=image, INPUT type=password, INPUT type=radio, INPUT type=reset, INPUT type=submit, INPUT type=text, KBD, LABEL, LEGEND, LI, LISTING, MAP, MARQUEE, MENU, NOBR, OBJECT, OL, OPTION, P, PLAINTEXT, PRE, S, SAMP, SELECT, SMALL, SPAN, STRIKE, STRONG, SUB, SUP, TABLE, TBODY, TD, TEXTAREA, TFOOT, TH, THEAD, TR, TT, U, UL, VAR, XMP

cloneNode Method

Copies a reference to the object from the document hierarchy.

Syntax

oClone = *object*.cloneNode(*bCloneChildren*)

Parameters

bCloneChildren   false   Optional. Cloned objects do not include **childNodes**.

true   Optional. Cloned objects include **childNodes**.

Return Value

Returns an element object.

Remarks

The **cloneNode** method copies an object, attributes, and, if specified, the **childNodes**.

A collection is returned when referring to the **ID** of a cloned element.

Example

The following example shows how to use the **cloneNode** method to copy an unordered list and its **childNodes** collection.

```
<SCRIPT>
function fnClone(){
    /* The 'true' possible value specifies to clone
       the childNodes as well.
    */
    var oCloneNode = oList.cloneNode(true);
    /* When the cloned node is added,
```

```
    'oList' becomes a collection.
    */
    document.body.insertBefore(oCloneNode);
}
</SCRIPT>

<UL ID = oList>
<LI>List node 1
<LI>List node 2
<LI>List node 3
<LI>List node 4
</UL>

<INPUT
    TYPE="button"
    VALUE="Clone List"
    onclick="fnClone()"
>
```

Applies To

 WIN16   WIN32   MAC   UNIX

A, ACRONYM, ADDRESS, APPLET, AREA, B, BASE, BASEFONT, BDO,
BGSOUND, BIG, BLOCKQUOTE, BODY, BR, BUTTON, CAPTION, CENTER,
CITE, CODE, COL, COLGROUP, COMMENT, DD, DEL, DFN, DIR, DIV, DL, DT,
EM, EMBED, FIELDSET, FONT, FORM, FRAME, FRAMESET, HEAD, Hn, HR,
HTML, I, IFRAME, IMG, INPUT type=button, INPUT type=checkbox, INPUT
type=file, INPUT type=hidden, INPUT type=image, INPUT type=password, INPUT
type=radio, INPUT type=reset, INPUT type=submit, INPUT type=text, INS, KBD,
LABEL, LEGEND, LI, LINK, LISTING, MAP, MARQUEE, MENU, NEXTID,
OBJECT, OL, OPTION, P, PLAINTEXT, PRE, Q, S, SAMP, SCRIPT, SELECT,
SMALL, SPAN, STRIKE, STRONG, SUB, SUP, TABLE, TBODY, TD,
TEXTAREA, TFOOT, TH, THEAD, TITLE, TR, TT, U, UL, VAR, XMP

close Method

Closes the current browser window or HTML Application (HTA).

Syntax

window.close()

Return Value

No return value.

Remarks

The way that you close a window programmatically determines whether the user gets prompted. If you invoke the **close** method on a window that you did not open with script, the user sees a confirm dialog box. This also happens if you use **close** to exit the last running instance of Internet Explorer. You can only use the **close** method silently with HTML Applications (HTAs). In the case of HTAs, the application is trusted and follows a different security model.

When a function fired by an event on the **BODY** object calls the **close** method, the *window*.**close** method is implied. When an event on the **BODY** object calls the **close** method, the *document*.**close** method is implied.

Applies To

WIN16	WIN32	MAC

window

UNIX

window

close Method

Closes an output stream, and forces the sent data to display.

Syntax

document.close()

Return Value

No return value.

Remarks

When a function fired by an **event** on the **BODY** object calls the **close** method, the *window*.**close** method is implied. When an **event** on the **BODY** object calls the **close** method, the *document*.**close** method is implied.

Applies To

WIN16	WIN32	MAC	UNIX

document

collapse Method

Moves the insertion point to the beginning or the end of the current range.

Syntax

TextRange.collapse([*bStart*])

Parameters

bStart Optional. Value that indicates whether the insertion point is moved to the beginning or end of the text range. True (default) moves the insertion point to the beginning of the text range. False moves the insertion point to the end of the text range.

Return Value

No return value.

Remarks

This feature might not be available on non-Win32® platforms. For the latest information on Internet Explorer cross-platform compatibility, see article Q172976 in the Microsoft Knowledge Base.

Applies To

 WIN16   WIN32   MAC   UNIX

TextRange

compareEndPoints Method

Compares an end point of one **TextRange** object with an end point of another range.

Syntax

iResult = *TextRange*.compareEndPoints(*sType*, *oRange*)

Parameters

sType Required. Value that describes which end point on the object range and which end point on *oRange* are to be compared. This can be one of these values:

StartToEnd Compare the start of the **TextRange** object with the end of the *TextRange* parameter.

Parameters *(continued)*

StartToStart   Compare the start of the **TextRange** object with the start of the *TextRange* parameter.

EndToStart   Compare the end of the **TextRange** object with the start of the *TextRange* parameter.

EndToEnd   Compare the end of the **TextRange** object with the end of the *TextRange* parameter.

oRange   Required. **TextRange** object specifying the range to compare to the object.

Return Value

Integer. Possible return values include:

-1   The end point of the object is further to the left than the end point of *oRange*.

0   The end point of the object is at the same location as the end point of *oRange*.

1   The end point of the object is further to the right than the end point of *oRange*.

Remarks

A text range has two end points. One end point is located at the beginning of the text range, and the other is located at the end of the text range. An end point also can be characterized as the position between two characters in an HTML document.

As of Internet Explorer 4.0, an end point is relative to text only, not HTML tags.

There are four possible end point locations in the following HTML:

```
<body><p><b>abc
```

Possible end point locations include:

- Before the a
- Between the a and the b
- Between the b and the c
- After the c

As of Internet Explorer 4.0, an end point cannot be established between the **BODY** and the **P**. Such an end point is considered before the a.

This method might not be available on non-Win32 platforms. For the latest information on Internet Explorer cross-platform compatibility, see article Q172976 in the Microsoft Knowledge Base.

Applies To

 WIN16   WIN32   MAC   UNIX

TextRange

componentFromPoint Method

Returns the component located at the specified coordinates.

Syntax

sScrollComponent = *object*.componentFromPoint(*iCoordX*, *iCoordY*)

Parameters

iCoordX   Required. Client window coordinate of x.

iCoordY   Required. Client window coordinate of y.

Return Value

String. Possible return values include the following:

""	Component is inside the client area of the object.
outside	Component is outside the bounds of the object.
scrollbarDown	Down scroll arrow is at the specified location.
scrollbarHThumb	Horizontal scroll thumb or box is at the specified location.
scrollbarLeft	Left scroll arrow is at the specified location.
scrollbarPageDown	Page-down scroll bar shaft is at the specified location.
scrollbarPageLeft	Page-left scroll bar shaft is at the specified location.
scrollbarPageRight	Page-right scroll bar shaft is at the specified location.
scrollbarPageUp	Page-up scroll bar shaft is at the specified location.
scrollbarRight	Right scroll arrow is at the specified location.
scrollbarUp	Up scroll arrow is at the specified location.
scrollbarVThumb	Vertical scroll thumb or box is at the specified location.
handleBottom	Bottom sizing handle is at the specified location.
handleBottomLeft	Lower-left sizing handle is at the specified location.

Return Value *(continued)*

`handleBottomRight`	Lower-right sizing handle is at the specified location.
`handleLeft`	Left sizing handle is at the specified location.
`handleRight`	Right sizing handle is at the specified location.
`handleTop`	Top sizing handle is at the specified location.
`handleTopLeft`	Upper-left sizing handle is at the specified location.
`handleTopRight`	Upper-right sizing handle is at the specified location.

Remarks

The **componentFromPoint** method, available as of Internet Explorer 5, is applicable to any object that can be given scroll bars through cascading style sheets (CSS).

The **componentFromPoint** method does not consistently return the same object when used with the **onmouseover** event. Because a user's mouse speed and entry point can vary, different components of an element can fire the **onmouseover** event. For example, when a user moves the mouse cursor over a **TEXTAREA** object with scroll bars, the event can fire when the mouse enters the component border, the scroll bars, or the client region. Once the event has fired, the expected element may not be returned unless the scroll bars were the point of entry for the mouse. In this case, the **onmousemove** event can be used to provide more consistent results.

For the object's sizing handles to appear, **designMode** must be on and the object must be selected.

Example

The following example shows how to use the **componentFromPoint** method to determine which object the mouse is hovering over.

```
<HEAD>
<SCRIPT>
function trackElement(){
    var sElem = "";
    sElem = document.body.componentFromPoint(
        event.clientX,
        event.clientY
    );
    window.status = "mousemove " + event.clientX + ", "
        + event.clientY +
        " The mouse pointer is hovering over: " + sElem;
}
</SCRIPT>
</HEAD>
```

```
<BODY onmousemove="trackElement()">
<TEXTAREA COLS=500 ROWS=500>
This text forces scroll bars to appear in the window.
</TEXTAREA>
</BODY>
```

To see this code in action, refer to the Web Workshop CD-ROM.

Applies To

 WIN16   WIN32   MAC

Hn, ISINDEX

 WIN16   WIN32   MAC   UNIX

A, ACRONYM, ADDRESS, APPLET, AREA, B, BASE, BASEFONT, BDO, BGSOUND, BIG, BLOCKQUOTE, BODY, BR, BUTTON, CAPTION, CENTER, CITE, CODE, COL, COLGROUP, COMMENT, DD, DEL, DFN, DIR, DIV, DL, DT, EM, EMBED, FIELDSET, FONT, FORM, FRAME, FRAMESET, HEAD, Hn, HR, HTML, I, IFRAME, IMG, INPUT type=button, INPUT type=checkbox, INPUT type=file, INPUT type=hidden, INPUT type=image, INPUT type=password, INPUT type=radio, INPUT type=reset, INPUT type=submit, INPUT type=text, INS, ISINDEX, KBD, LABEL, LEGEND, LI, LINK, LISTING, MAP, MARQUEE, MENU, NEXTID, NOBR, NOFRAMES, NOSCRIPT, OBJECT, OL, OPTION, P, PLAINTEXT, PRE, Q, RT, RUBY, S, SAMP, SCRIPT, SELECT, SMALL, SPAN, STRIKE, STRONG, SUB, SUP, TABLE, TBODY, TD, TEXTAREA, TFOOT, TH, THEAD, TITLE, TR, TT, U, UL, VAR, WBR, XML, XMP

confirm Method

Displays a confirm dialog box that contains the specified *sMessage* as well as OK and Cancel buttons.

Syntax

bChoice = *window*.confirm([*sMessage*])

Parameters

sMessage Optional. String to display in the confirm dialog box. If no value is provided, the dialog box has no message.

Return Value

Boolean. Returns true if the user chooses OK, or false if the user chooses Cancel.

Remarks

The title bar of the confirm dialog box cannot be changed.

Applies To

WIN16   WIN32   MAC

window

UNIX

window

contains Method

Checks whether the given element is contained within the object.

Syntax

bFound = *object*.contains(*oElement*)

Parameters

oElement   Required. Element object specifying the element to check.

Return Value

Boolean. Returns true if the element is contained within the current element, or false otherwise.

Applies To

WIN16   WIN32   MAC   UNIX

A, ADDRESS, APPLET, AREA, B, BASE, BASEFONT, BIG, BLOCKQUOTE, BODY, BUTTON, CAPTION, CENTER, CITE, CODE, COL, COLGROUP, DD, DFN, DIR, DIV, DL, DT, EM, EMBED, FIELDSET, FONT, FORM, FRAME, FRAMESET, HEAD, Hn, HR, HTML, I, IFRAME, IMG, INPUT type=button, INPUT type=checkbox, INPUT type=file, INPUT type=image, INPUT type=password, INPUT type=radio, INPUT type=reset, INPUT type=submit, INPUT type=text, KBD, LABEL, LEGEND, LI, LINK, LISTING, MAP, MARQUEE, MENU, META, NEXTID, NOBR, OL, OPTION, P, PLAINTEXT, PRE, S, SAMP, SCRIPT, SELECT, SMALL, SPAN, STRIKE, STRONG, SUB, SUP, TABLE, TBODY, TD, TEXTAREA, TFOOT, TH, THEAD, TITLE, TR, TT, U, UL, VAR, XMP

createCaption Method

Creates an empty **CAPTION** element in the **TABLE**.

Syntax

oCaption = TABLE.createCaption()

Return Value

CAPTION object. If a **CAPTION** already exists, **createCaption** returns the existing element; otherwise, it returns a pointer to the element created. If the method fails, it returns null.

Example

The following example creates a **CAPTION**.

myCaption = document.all.myTable.createCaption()

Applies To

 WIN16   WIN32   MAC   UNIX

TABLE

createControlRange Method

Creates a **controlRange** collection of nontext elements.

Syntax

oControlRange = document.body.createControlRange()

Return Value

ControlRange collection. If a **ControlRange** already exists, **createControlRange** overwrites the existing element; otherwise, it returns a pointer to the element created.

Example

The following example shows how to create a **ControlRange**.

oControlRange = document.body.createControlRange();

Applies To

 WIN16   WIN32   MAC   UNIX

BODY

createElement Method

Creates an instance of the element object for the specified tag.

Syntax

oElement = *document*.createElement(*sTag*)

Parameters

sTag   Required. String specifying the name of an element.

Return Value

Returns an element object.

Remarks

To insert new elements into the current document, use the **insertBefore** method.

You can create all elements (except for **FRAME** and **IFRAME**) in script with the **createElement** method as of Internet Explorer 5. In addition, read-only properties of independently created elements are read/write.

You must perform a second step when using **createElement** to create the **INPUT** object. The **createElement** method generates an input text box, because that is the default **input type** property. To insert any other kind of **input** object, first invoke **createElement** for **input**, then set the **type** property to the appropriate value in the next line of code.

You cannot set the **name** property at run time on **anchor** objects created with the **createElement** method. To create an **anchor** with a **NAME** attribute, include the attribute and value when using the **createElement** method, or use the **innerHTML** property. In Internet Explorer 4.0, the only new elements you can create are **IMG**, **AREA**, and **OPTION**. Before you use new objects, you must explicitly add them to their respective collections.

Example

The following example shows how to set the **NAME** attribute on a dynamically created **anchor**.

```
var oAnchor = document.createElement("<A NAME='AnchorName'></A>");
```

Applies To

 WIN16   WIN32   MAC   UNIX

document

createRange Method

Creates a **TextRange** object from the current selection.

Syntax

selection.createRange()

Return Value

Returns a **TextRange** object.

Applies To

 WIN16   WIN32   MAC   UNIX

selection

createStyleSheet Method

Creates a style sheet for the document.

Syntax

oStylesheet = *document*.createStyleSheet([*sURL*] [, *iIndex*])

Parameters

sURL   Optional. String specifying how to add the style sheet to the document. If a file name is specified for the URL, the style information is added as a **LINK** object. If the URL contains style information, this information is added to the **STYLE** object.

iIndex   Optional. Index indicating where the new style sheet is inserted in the **styleSheets** collection. The default is to insert the new style sheet at the end of the collection.

Return Value

Returns a **styleSheet** object.

Example

The following example shows how to create a link to a style sheet.

```
document.createStyleSheet('styles.css');
```

Applies To

 WIN16   WIN32   MAC   UNIX

document

createTextNode Method

Creates a text string from the specified value.

Syntax

oTextNode = *document*.createTextNode([*sText*])

Parameters

sText   Optional. String specifying the **nodeValue** property of the text node.

Return Value

Returns a **TextNode** object.

Example

The following example shows how to use the **createTextNode** method to create a text node and replace it with an existing text node in a **SPAN** object.

```
<SCRIPT>
function fnChangeNode(){
    var oTextNode = document.createTextNode("New Text");
    var oReplaceNode = oSpan.childNodes(0);
    oReplaceNode.replaceNode(oTextNode);
}
<SCRIPT>

<SPAN ID = oSPAN onclick="fnChangeNode()">
Original Text
</SPAN>
```

Applies To

 WIN16   WIN32   MAC   UNIX

document

createTextRange Method

Creates a **TextRange** object for the given object.

Syntax

oTextRange = *object*.createTextRange()

Return Value

Returns a **TextRange** object if successful, or null otherwise.

Remarks

Use a text range to examine and modify the text within an object.

Example

The following JScript (compatible with ECMA 262 language specification) example shows how to create a text range for the document, and then use the range to display all text and HTML tags in the document.

```
var rng = document.body.createTextRange( );
if (rng!=null) {
    alert(rng.htmlText);
}
```

The following JScript example shows how to create a text range for the first **BUTTON** element in the document and then use the text range to change the text in the button.

```
var coll = document.all.tags("BUTTON");
if (coll!=null && coll.length>0) {
    var rng = coll[0].createTextRange();
    rng.text = "Clicked";
}
```

Applies To

 WIN16   WIN32   MAC   UNIX

BODY, BUTTON, INPUT TYPE=button, INPUT TYPE=hidden, INPUT TYPE=password, INPUT TYPE=reset, INPUT TYPE=submit, INPUT TYPE=text, TEXTAREA

createTFoot Method

Creates an empty table footer in the **TABLE**.

Syntax

oTFoot = *TABLE*.createTFoot()

Return Value

Returns the **TFoot** element object if successful, or null otherwise.

Remarks

If a **TFOOT** already exists for the **TABLE**, **createTFoot** returns the existing element. Otherwise, it returns a pointer to the element created.

Example

The following example shows how to create a **TFOOT**.

myTFoot = document.all.myTable.createTFoot()

Applies To

WIN16	WIN32	MAC	UNIX

TABLE

createTHead Method

Creates an empty table header in the **TABLE**.

Syntax

oTHead = *TABLE*.createTHead()

Return Value

Returns the **THEAD** element object if successful, or null otherwise.

Remarks

If a **THEAD** already exists, **createTHead** returns the existing element. Otherwise, it returns a pointer to the element created.

Example

The following example creates a **THEAD**.

myTHead = document.all.myTable.createTHead()

Applies To

 WIN16   WIN32   MAC   UNIX

TABLE

deleteCaption Method

Deletes the **CAPTION** element and its contents from the **TABLE**.

Syntax

TABLE.deleteCaption()

Return Value

No return value.

Example

The following example deletes the **CAPTION**.

document.all.myTable.deleteCaption()

Applies To

 WIN16   WIN32   MAC   UNIX

TABLE

deleteCell Method

Deletes the specified cell (**TD**) in the table row, and removes the cell from the **cells** collection.

Syntax

TR.deleteCell([*iIndex*])

Parameters

iIndex   Optional. Cell to be deleted from the table row. If no value is provided, the last cell in the **cells** collection is deleted.

Return Value

No return value.

Example

The following example shows how to delete the last cell in the first row of the table.

```
document.all.myTable.rows[0].deleteCell()
```

Applies To

WIN16	WIN32	MAC	UNIX

TR

deleteRow Method

Deletes the specified row (**TR**) in the **TABLE**, and removes the row from the **rows** collection.

Syntax

object.deleteRow([*iRowIndex*])

Parameters

iRowIndex   Optional. Row to delete. The default value is the last row in the **TABLE**.

Return Value

No return value.

Remarks

If you delete a row from a **TFOOT**, **TBODY**, or **THEAD**, you also remove the row from the **rows** collection for the **TABLE**. If you delete a row in the **TABLE**, you also remove a row from the **rows** collection for the **TBODY**. If you delete the row from a **TBODY**, **TFOOT**, or **THEAD**, *iRowIndex* must contain the **sectionRowIndex** of the **TR**. If you delete the row from the **TABLE**, *iRowIndex* can contain the **rowIndex** of the **TR**.

Example

The following example shows how to delete the specified row (**TR**) in the **TABLE**.

```
myNewRow = document.all.myTable.deleteRow()
```

Applies To

WIN16	WIN32	MAC	UNIX

TABLE

deleteTFoot Method

Deletes the table footer and its contents from the **TABLE**.

Syntax

TABLE.deleteTFoot()

Return Value

No return value.

Example

The following example shows how to delete the **TFOOT** element.

document.all.myTable.deleteTFoot()

Applies To

 WIN16   **WIN32**   **MAC**   **UNIX**

TABLE

deleteTHead Method

Deletes the table header and its contents from the **TABLE**.

Syntax

TABLE.deleteTHead()

Return Value

No return value.

Example

The following example shows how to delete the **THEAD** element.

document.all.myTable.deleteTHead()

Applies To

 WIN16   **WIN32**   **MAC**   **UNIX**

TABLE

detachEvent Method

Unbinds the specified function from the event so that the function stops receiving notifications when the event fires on the object.

Syntax

object.detachEvent (*sEvent*, *fpNotify*)

Parameters

sEvent   Required. Any one of the standard **DHTML** events.

fpNotify Required. Function previously set using the **attachEvent** method.

Return Value

No return value.

Remarks

Behaviors that attach to events using the **attachEvent** method must explicitly call the **detachEvent** method to stop receiving notifications from the page when the **ondetach** event fires. Behaviors that use the **ATTACH** element to attach to events automatically stop receiving notifications when the behavior is detached from the element, and so do not need to call the **detachEvent** method.

Example

The following example shows how to call the **detachEvent** method from an HTC when the highlighting effect is removed from the page, causing the **ondetach** event to fire.

```
<PUBLIC:ATTACH EVENT="ondetach" ONEVENT="cleanup()" />

<SCRIPT LANGUAGE="JScript">
attachEvent ('onmouseover', Hilite);
attachEvent ('onmouseout', Restore);

function cleanup()
{
   detachEvent ('onmouseover', Hilite);
   detachEvent ('onmouseout', Restore);
}
```

```
function Hilite()
{
   if (event.srcElement == element)
   {
     normalColor = style.color;
     runtimeStyle.color  = "red";
     runtimeStyle.cursor = "hand";
   }
}

function Restore()
{
   if (event.srcElement == element)
   {
      runtimeStyle.color  = normalColor;
      runtimeStyle.cursor = "";
   }
}
</SCRIPT>
```

To see this code in action, refer to the Web Workshop CD-ROM.

Applies To

 WIN16   WIN32   MAC   UNIX

A, ACRONYM, ADDRESS, APPLET, AREA, B, BASE, BASEFONT, BGSOUND, BIG, BLOCKQUOTE, BODY, BR, BUTTON, CAPTION, CENTER, CITE, CODE, COL, COLGROUP, COMMENT, DD, DEL, DFN, DIR, DIV, DL, document, DT, EM, EMBED, FIELDSET, FONT, FORM, FRAME, FRAMESET, HEAD, Hn, HR, HTML, I, IFRAME, IMG, INPUT type=button, INPUT type=checkbox, INPUT type=file, INPUT type=hidden, INPUT type=image, INPUT type=password, INPUT type=radio, INPUT type=reset, INPUT type=submit, INPUT type=text, INS, KBD, LABEL, LEGEND, LI, LINK, LISTING, MAP, MARQUEE, MENU, NOBR, OBJECT, OL, OPTION, P, PLAINTEXT, PRE, Q, S, SAMP, SCRIPT, SELECT, SMALL, SPAN, STRIKE, STRONG, SUB, SUP, TABLE, TBODY, TD, TEXTAREA, TFOOT, TH, THEAD, TITLE, TR, TT, U, UL, VAR, window, XMP

doReadRequest Method

Performs all requests located in the read-requests queue.

Syntax

```
bSuccess = userProfile.doReadRequest(vUsageCode [, vFriendlyName]
     [, vDomain] [, vPath] [, vExpiration] [, vReserved])
```

Parameters

vUsageCode Required. Code that notifies the user of the type of access requested. This usage code should be one of the following 13 codes defined by the Internet Privacy Working Group (IPWG).

 0 Used for system administration.

 1 Used for research and/or product development.

 2 Used for completion and support of the current transaction.

 3 Used to customize the content and design of a site.

 4 Used to improve the content of a site that includes advertisements.

 5 Used for notifying visitors about updates to the site.

 6 Used for contacting visitors for marketing of services or products.

 7 Used for linking other collected information.

 8 Used by a site for other purposes.

 9 Disclosed to others for customization or improvement of the content and design of the site.

 10 Disclosed to others, who may contact the user for marketing of services and/or products.

 11 Disclosed to others, who may contact the user for marketing of services and/or products. The user has the opportunity to ask a site not to do this.

 12 Disclosed to others for any other purpose.

VFriendlyName Optional. Friendly name of the party requesting access to private information. For security reasons, it is not sufficient for the user agent to display this friendly name to the user. In addition to displaying this friendly name, the user agent must display the URL that originates the script requesting profile access. If this script originates from a secure connection (for example, SSL), you can use the SSL certificate to reliably identify the party requesting access.

vDomain Optional. Pages the user's choice applies to in the future in addition to the current page. The specification follows the cookie standard (RFC-2109)

vPath Optional. Path to the domain server requesting access. When the *vExpiration* is set, the path is saved with the requested attributes.

Parameters *(continued)*

vExpiration	Optional. Amount of time for which the site has requested access to these attributes. This is currently ignored by Internet Explorer.
vReserved	Optional. This parameter is reserved.

Return Value

Boolean. Returns `true` if successful, or `false` otherwise.

Remarks

If the site does not have read access, the user is prompted with a list of requested attributes and can choose to either allow or deny access.

Applies To

 WIN32   MAC   UNIX

userProfile

doScroll Method

Simulates a click on a scroll-bar component.

Syntax

object.doScroll([*sScrollAction*])

Parameters

sScrollAction Optional. Determines how the object is scrolled. This parameter can take one of the following string values:

scrollbarDown	Default. The down scroll arrow is at the specified location.
scrollbarHThumb	The horizontal scroll thumb or box is at the specified location.
scrollbarLeft	The left scroll arrow is at the specified location.
scrollbarPageDown	The page-down scroll bar shaft is at the specified location.
scrollbarPageLeft	The page-left scroll bar shaft is at the specified location.
scrollbarPageRight	The page-right scroll bar shaft is at the specified location.

Parameters *(continued)*

scrollbarPageUp	The page-up scroll bar shaft is at the specified location.
scrollbarRight	The right scroll arrow is at the specified location.
scrollbarUp	The up scroll arrow is at the specified location.
scrollbarVThumb	The vertical scroll thumb or box is at the specified location.
down	The shortcut reference to scrollbarDown.
left	The shortcut reference to scrollbarLeft.
pageDown	The shortcut reference to scrollbarPageDown.
pageLeft	The shortcut reference to scrollbarPageLeft.
pageRight	The shortcut reference to scrollbarPageRight.
pageUp	The shortcut reference to scrollbarPageUp.
right	The shortcut reference to scrollbarRight.
up	The shortcut reference to scrollbarUp.

Return Value

No return value.

Remarks

Cascading style sheets (CSS) enable you to scroll on all objects through the **overflow** property.

When the content of an element changes and causes scroll bars to display, the **doScroll** method might not work correctly immediately following the content update. When this happens, you can use the **setTimeout** method to enable the browser to recognize the dynamic changes that affect scrolling.

Example

The following example shows how to use the **doScroll** method on the browser page.

```
<HEAD>
<SCRIPT>
function scrollBehavior()
{
document.body.doScroll("scrollbarPageRight");
}

function scrollBehavior1()
{
```

```
txtScrollMe.doScroll("scrollbarDown");
}

function scrollBehavior2()
{
txtScrollMe.doScroll("scrollbarPageDown");
}
</SCRIPT>
</HEAD>
<BODY>
<BUTTON
   onclick="scrollBehavior()"
   CLASS="colorIt"
>
Click to Scroll Page
</BUTTON>
<BR>
<HR>
<BUTTON
   onclick="scrollBehavior1()"
   ondblclick="scrollBehavior2()"
   CLASS="colorIt">
   Click to Scroll Text Area
</BUTTON><BR><BR>
<TEXTAREA ID=txtScrollMe CLASS="colorIt">
   This text area
   scrolls downward when the
   "Click to Scroll the Text Area"
   button is clicked. The doScroll method
   scrolls it as if the down arrow
   component of the scroll bar had
   been clicked. Double-click the
   button to scroll down a whole page.
</TEXTAREA>
</BODY>
```

To see this code in action, refer to the Web Workshop CD-ROM.

The following example shows how to use the **doScroll** method on a text area.

```
<HEAD>
<SCRIPT>
var iTimer;
function timeIt()
{
iTimer = setInterval("scrollIt()", 1000);
}
function scrollIt()
{
oScrollMe.doScroll("down");
}
</SCRIPT>
</HEAD>
```

```
<BODY onload="timeIt()">
<DIV ID=oScrollMe STYLE="width:200px;height:75px;overflow:scroll">

</DIV>
</BODY>
```

To see this code in action, refer to the Web Workshop CD-ROM.

Applies To

 WIN16   WIN32   MAC   UNIX

BODY, DIV, SPAN, TEXTAREA

duplicate Method

Returns a duplicate of the **TextRange**.

Syntax

oTextRange = *object*.duplicate()

Return Value

Returns a **TextRange** object.

Remarks

This feature might not be available on non-Win32 platforms. For the latest information on Internet Explorer cross-platform compatibility, see article Q172976 in the Microsoft Knowledge Base.

Applies To

 WIN16   WIN32   MAC   UNIX

TextRange

elementFromPoint Method

Returns the element for the specified coordinates.

Syntax

oElement = *document*.elementFromPoint(*iX*, *iY*)

Parameters

    iX   Required. Integer specifying the X-offset, in pixels.

    iY   Required. Integer specifying the Y-offset, in pixels.

Return Value

    Returns an element object.

Remarks

    Coordinates are supplied in client coordinates. The top left corner of the client area is (0,0). For **elementFromPoint** to exhibit expected behavior, the object or element located at position (x, y) must support and respond to mouse events.

    When using this method with the structured graphics or sprite objects, you must set **MouseEventsEnabled** to 1. For more information about structured graphics and sprite objects, see the information about Microsoft® DirectAnimation™ Multimedia Controls on the Web Workshop CD-ROM.

Applies To

 WIN16   WIN32   MAC   UNIX

document

empty Method

    Deselects the current selection, sets the selection type to none, and sets the item property to null.

Syntax

    selection.empty()

Return Value

    No return value.

Applies To

 WIN16   WIN32   MAC   UNIX

selection

execCommand Method

Executes a command over the given selection or text range.

Syntax

bSuccess = *object*.execCommand(*sCommand* [, *bUserInterface*] [, *vValue*])

Parameters

sCommand   Required. Command to execute. This can be any valid command identifier. For more information, see "Command Identifiers" in Appendix C.

bUserInterface   Optional. Value that indicates whether to display a user interface if the command supports one. This value can be true or false. The default is false.

vValue   Optional. String, number, or other value to assign. Possible values depend on *sCommand*.

Return Value

Boolean. Returns true if the command is successful, or false otherwise.

Remarks

Wait to invoke the **execCommand** method until after the page has loaded.

Applies To

WIN16	WIN32	MAC	UNIX

document, TextRange

WIN16	WIN32	MAC	UNIX

controlRange

execScript Method

Executes the specified script.

Syntax

window.execScript(*sExpression*, *sLanguage*)

Parameters

sExpression   Required. Code to be executed.

sLanguage   Required. Language in which the code is executed. The language defaults to JScript (compatible with ECMA 262 language specification).

Return Value

No return value.

Applies To

 WIN16   WIN32   MAC   UNIX

window

expand Method

Expands the range so that partial units are completely contained.

Syntax

bSuccess = *TextRange*.expand(*sUnit*)

Parameters

sUnit   Required. Units to move in the range. This parameter can be one of the following:

character   Expands a character.

word   Expands a word. A word is a collection of characters terminated by a space or another white space character, such as a tab.

sentence   Expands a sentence. A sentence is a collection of words terminated by an ending punctuation character, such as a period.

textedit   Expands to enclose the entire range.

Return Value

Boolean. Returns true if it successfully expands the range, or false otherwise.

Remarks

This feature might not be available on non-Win32 platforms. For the latest information on Internet Explorer cross-platform compatibility, see article Q172976 in the Microsoft Knowledge Base.

Example

The following example shows how to create a range from the current selection and then use **expand** to ensure that any word partially enclosed by the range becomes entirely enclosed in the range.

```
var rng = document.selection.createRange();
rng.expand("word");
```

Applies To

 WIN16   WIN32   MAC   UNIX

TextRange

findText Method

Searches for text in the document, and positions the start and end points of the range to encompass the search string.

Syntax

bFound = *TextRange*.findText(*sText* [, *iSearchScope*] [, *iFlags*])

Parameters

sText Required. Text to find.

iSearchScope Optional. Number of characters to search from the starting point of the range. A positive integer indicates a forward search; a negative integer indicates a backward search.

iFlags Optional. One or more of the following flags indicating the type of search:

2   Match whole words only.

4   Match case.

Return Value

Boolean. Returns true if the search text is found, or false otherwise.

Remarks

A range has two distinct states: degenerate and nondegenerate. A degenerate range is like a text editor caret (insertion point); it does not actually select any characters. Instead it specifies a point between two characters. A degenerate range's end points are adjacent. On the other hand, a nondegenerate range is like a text editor selection. A certain amount of text is selected, and the end points of the range are not adjacent.

The value passed for the *iSearchScope* parameter controls the part of the document, relative to the range, that is searched. The behavior of the **findText** method depends on the state (degenerate or nondegenerate).

- If the range is degenerate, passing a large positive number causes the text to the right of the range to be searched. Passing a large negative number causes the text to the left of the range to be searched.

- For a nondegenerate range, passing a large positive number causes the text to the right of the start of the range to be searched. For a nondegenerate range, passing a large negative number causes the text to the left of the end of the range to be searched. If the range is nondegenerate, passing 0 causes only the text selected by the range to be searched.

This feature might not be available on non-Win32 platforms. For the latest information on Internet Explorer cross-platform compatibility, see article Q172976 in the Microsoft Knowledge Base.

A text range is not modified if the text specified for the **findText** method is not found.

Example

The following example shows how to create a text range over the body of the document and search for text using **findText** with various flag combinations. The results are indicated in the code comments.

```
<HTML>
<BODY>
Leonardo da Vinci was one of the great masters of the High
Renaissance, especially in painting, sculpture, architecture,
engineering, and science.
</BODY>
</HTML>

<SCRIPT>
    var oRange = document.body.createTextRange();
        // record the current position in a bookmark
    var sBookMark = oRange.getBookmark();
        // true - case-insensitive and partial word match
    oRange.findText('leo');
        // reset the range using the bookmark
    oRange.moveToBookmark(sBookMark);
        // false - matches whole words only
    oRange.findText('engineer', 0, 2);
    oRange.moveToBookmark(sBookMark);
        // false - case-sensitive
    oRange.findText('high', 0, 4);
    oRange.moveToBookmark(sBookMark);
        // true - case-sensitive and matches whole words
    oRange.findText('Leonardo', 0, 6);
```

```
      // the degenerate case
   oRange.moveToBookmark(sBookMark);
      // make the range degenerate
   oRange.collapse();
      // false - must specify large character count in this case
   oRange.findText('Leonardo', 0, 6);
      // true - no third parameter passed, so no count needed
   oRange.findText('Leonardo');
      // true - a large count covers the range
   oRange.findText('Leonardo', 1000000000, 6);
</SCRIPT>
```

Applies To

 WIN16   WIN32   MAC   UNIX

TextRange

firstPage Method

Moves to the first page of records in the data set, and scrolls it into view.

Syntax

TABLE.firstPage()

Return Value

No return value.

Remarks

The number of records displayed in the table is determined by the **dataPageSize** property of the table. You must set the **DATAPAGESIZE** attribute when designing the page, or set the corresponding **dataPageSize** property at run time for this method to have any effect.

Note The page author does not need to check for boundary conditions.

Applies To

 WIN16   WIN32   MAC   UNIX

TABLE

focus Method

Causes a control to receive the focus, and executes the code specified by the **onfocus** event.

Syntax

object.focus()

Return Value

No return value.

Remarks

This method fires the **onfocus** event.

As of Internet Explorer 5, elements that expose the **focus** method must have the **TABINDEX** attribute set.

Elements cannot receive focus until the document is finished loading.

Applies To

 WIN16   WIN32   MAC

INPUT type=button, INPUT type=checkbox, INPUT type=file, INPUT type=image, INPUT type=password, INPUT type=radio, INPUT type=reset, INPUT type=submit, INPUT type=text, TEXTAREA

 WIN16   WIN32   MAC   UNIX

A, APPLET, AREA, BODY, BUTTON, EMBED, FIELDSET, FRAME, FRAMESET, IFRAME, INPUT type=button, INPUT type=checkbox, INPUT type=file, INPUT type=image, INPUT type=password, INPUT type=radio, INPUT type=reset, INPUT type=submit, INPUT type=text, ISINDEX, OBJECT, SELECT, SPAN, TABLE, TD, TEXTAREA, window

IE 5 **WIN16   WIN32   MAC   UNIX**

ACRONYM, ADDRESS, B, BDO, BIG, BLOCKQUOTE, CAPTION, CENTER, CITE, DD, DEL, DFN, DIR, DL, DT, EM, FONT, FORM, Hn, HR, I, IMG, INS, KBD, LABEL, LEGEND, LI, LISTING, MARQUEE, MENU, OL, P, PLAINTEXT, PRE, Q, RT, RUBY, S, SAMP, SMALL, STRIKE, STRONG, SUB, SUP, TBODY, TFOOT, TH, THEAD, TR, TT, U, UL, VAR, XMP

DHTML Methods

forward Method

Loads the next URL in the History list.

Syntax

history.forward()

Return Value

No return value.

Remarks

This method performs the same action as when a user clicks the Forward button in the browser. The **forward** method works the same as **history.go(1)**. An error does not occur if the user tries to go beyond the end of the history. Instead, the user remains at the current page.

Applies To

 WIN16   WIN32   MAC

history

 UNIX

history

getAdjacentText Method

Returns the adjacent text character.

Syntax

object.getAdjacentText(*sWhere*)

Parameters

sWhere   Required. Position where the text is located. This position can be one of the following:

beforeBegin   Text is returned immediately before the element.

afterBegin   Text is returned after the start of the element, but before all other content in the element.

beforeEnd   Text is returned immediately before the end of the element, but after all other content in the element.

Parameters *(continued)*

> `afterEnd`   Text is returned immediately after the end of the element.

Return Value

Returns the first adjacent text character.

Example

The following example shows how to use the **getAdjacentText** method to find specific text.

```
<SCRIPT>
function fnFind(){
    var sWhere = oSel.options[oSel.selectedIndex].text;
    alert(oPara.getAdjacentText(sWhere));
}
</SCRIPT>
This is the text before (beforeBegin).
<P ID=oPara>
This is the text after (afterBegin).
<B>A few extra words.</B>
This is the text before (beforeEnd).
</P>
This is the text after (afterEnd).

<SELECT ID=oSel>
<OPTION SELECTED>beforeBegin
<OPTION>afterBegin
<OPTION>beforeEnd
<OPTION>afterEnd
</SELECT>
<INPUT TYPE="button" VALUE="Find text" onclick="fnFind()">
```

Applies To

 WIN16   WIN32   MAC   UNIX

A, ACRONYM, ADDRESS, APPLET, AREA, B, BASE, BASEFONT, BDO, BIG, BLOCKQUOTE, BODY, BR, BUTTON, CAPTION, CENTER, CITE, CODE, COL, COLGROUP, COMMENT, DD, DEL, DFN, DIR, DIV, DL, DT, EM, EMBED, FIELDSET, FONT, FORM, FRAME, FRAMESET, HEAD, Hn, HR, HTML, I, IFRAME, IMG, INPUT type=button, INPUT type=checkbox, INPUT type=file, INPUT type=hidden, INPUT type=image, INPUT type=password, INPUT type=radio, INPUT type=reset, INPUT type=submit, INPUT type=text, INS, KBD, LABEL, LEGEND, LI, LINK, LISTING, MAP, MARQUEE, MENU, NEXTID, OBJECT, OL, OPTION, P, PLAINTEXT, PRE, Q, S, SAMP, SCRIPT, SELECT, SMALL, SPAN, STRIKE, STRONG, SUB, SUP, TABLE, TBODY, TD, TEXTAREA, TFOOT, TH, THEAD, TITLE, TR, TT, U, UL, VAR, XMP

DHTML Methods

getAttribute Method

Retrieves the value of the specified attribute.

Syntax

vAttrValue = `object.getAttribute(`*sAttrName* [, *iFlags*] `)`

Parameters

sAttrName   Required. Name of the attribute.

iFlags   Optional. One or more of the following flags can be specified:

0 Default. Performs a property search that is not case-sensitive, and returns an interpolated value if the property is found.

1 Performs a case-sensitive property search. To find a match, the uppercase and lowercase letters in *sAttrName* must exactly match those in the attribute name. If the *iFlags* parameter for **setAttribute** is set to `true` and this option is set to 0 (default), a conflict arises. The specified property name may not be found.

2 Returns the value exactly as it was set in script or in the source document.

Return Value

Variant. Returns a string, number, or Boolean value as defined by the attribute. If the attribute is not present, this method returns `null`.

Remarks

If two or more attributes have the same name (differing only in uppercase and lowercase letters) and *iFlags* is 0, this method retrieves values only for the last attribute to be created with this name. All other attributes of the same name are ignored.

Applies To

 WIN16   **WIN32**   **MAC**   **UNIX**

A, ADDRESS, APPLET, AREA, B, BASE, BASEFONT, BGSOUND, BIG, BLOCKQUOTE, BODY, BR, BUTTON, CAPTION, CENTER, CITE, CODE, COL, COLGROUP, COMMENT, DD, DFN, DIR, DIV, DL, DT, EM, EMBED, FIELDSET, FONT, FORM, FRAME, FRAMESET, HEAD, Hn, HR, HTML, I, IFRAME, IMG, INPUT type=button, INPUT type=checkbox, INPUT type=file, INPUT type=hidden,

Applies To *(continued)*

 WIN16   WIN32   MAC   UNIX

INPUT type=image, INPUT type=password, INPUT type=radio, INPUT type=reset, INPUT type=submit, INPUT type=text, KBD, LABEL, LEGEND, LI, LINK, LISTING, MAP, MARQUEE, MENU, META, NEXTID, NOBR, OBJECT, OL, OPTION, P, PLAINTEXT, PRE, S, SAMP, SCRIPT, SELECT, SMALL, SPAN, STRIKE, STRONG, SUB, SUP, TABLE, TBODY, TD, TEXTAREA, TFOOT, TH, THEAD, TITLE, TR, TT, U, UL, VAR, WBR, XMP

getAttribute Method

Returns the value of the named attribute.

Syntax

sValue = *userProfile*.getAttribute(*sAttributeName*)

Parameters

sAttributeName   Required. One of the standard vCard names listed in Remarks. If one of these names is not used, the request is ignored.

Return Value

String. If read access for this attribute is not already available, this method returns a null value.

Remarks

The following schema is used for the field names of the user data store. These names are specified when you use the **getAttribute** method on the **userProfile** object. The format has changed from vCard_xxx to vCard.xxx, and the older format is no longer supported.

vCard Names

vCard.Business.City	vCard.Business.Country	vCard.Business.Fax
vCard.Business.Phone	vCard.Business.State	vCard.Business.StreetAddress
vCard.Business.URL	vCard.Business.Zipcode	vCard.Cellular
vCard.Company	vCard.Department	vCard.DisplayName

Note An asterisk (*) denotes extensions to the vCard schema, which are referenced as X-elements as defined in the vCard schema.

DHTML Methods

Remarks *(continued)*

vCard.Email	vCard.FirstName	vCard.Gender*
vCard.Home.City	vCard.Home.Country	vCard.Home.Fax
vCard.Home.Phone	vCard.Home.State	vCard.Home.StreetAddress
vCard.Home.Zipcode	vCard.Homepage	vCard.JobTitle
vCard.LastName	vCard.MiddleName	vCard.Notes
vCard.Office	vCard.Pager	

Note An asterisk (*) denotes extensions to the vCard schema, which are referenced as X-elements as defined in the vCard schema.

Applies To

WIN16	WIN32	MAC	UNIX

userProfile

getBookmark Method

Retrieves a bookmark (opaque string) that can be used with **moveToBookmark** to return to the same range.

Syntax

sBookmark = *TextRange*.getBookmark()

Return Value

String. Returns the bookmark if successfully retrieved, or null otherwise.

Remarks

This feature might not be available on non-Win32 platforms. For the latest information on Internet Explorer cross-platform compatibility, see article Q172976 in the Microsoft Knowledge Base.

Applies To

WIN16	WIN32	MAC	UNIX

TextRange

getBoundingClientRect Method

Retrieves an object specifying the bounds of a collection of **TextRectangle** objects.

Syntax

oRect = *object*.getBoundingClientRect()

Return Value

oRect. The return value is a **TextRectangle** object having four integer properties (**top**, **left**, **right**, and **bottom**), each representing a coordinate of the rectangle, in pixels.

Remarks

The method retrieves the left, top, right, and bottom coordinates of the union of rectangles relative to the client's upper-left corner. In Internet Explorer 5, the window's upper-left is at 2,2 (pixels) with respect to the true client.

Example

The following example shows how to use the **getClientRects** and **getBoundingClientRect** methods to highlight text lines in an object.

```
<SCRIPT>
function newHighlite(obj) {
    oRcts = obj.getClientRects();
    iLength= oRcts.length;
    if (event.altKey == true) {
        keyCount=keyCount+1;
        if (keyCount > iLength-1) {
            keyCount = 0
            }
    }

    // Determine the coordinates for the yellow DIV.
    iRight = oRcts[keyCount].right + sBody.scrollLeft;   // right
    iLeft = oRcts[keyCount].left + sBody.scrollLeft;     // left
    iTop = oRcts[keyCount].top + sBody.scrollTop;        // top
    // Set the rendering properties for the yellow DIV.
    sYellow.style.top = iTop;
    sYellow.style.width = (iRight-iLeft) - 5;
    sYellow.style.display = 'inline';
    // Determine the coordinates for the beige DIV.
    iBndRight = obj.getBoundingClientRect().right + sBody.scrollLeft;
    iBndLeft = obj.getBoundingClientRect().left + sBody.scrollLeft;
    iBndTop = obj.getBoundingClientRect().top + sBody.scrollTop;
    // Set the rendering properties for the beige DIV.
    sBeige.style.top = iBndTop;
    sBeige.style.width = (iBndRight-iBndLeft) - 5;
    sBeige.style.height = iTop - iBTop;
```

DHTML Methods

```
            // Display beige area only after 1st line.
            if (event.altKey == true) {
                idBeige.style.display = 'inline';
            }
    }
    </SCRIPT>
    :
    <DIV ID=s1 STYLE="position:absolute; left:5; top:250; z-index:1"
        onclick="newHighlite(this)" onkeypress="newHighlite(this)">
    :
    </DIV>
    <DIV ID=sYellow STYLE="position:absolute; left:5; top:400; z-index:0;
    background-color:'yellow'; display:'none'"></DIV>
    <DIV ID=sBeige STYLE="position:absolute; left:5; top:400; z-index:-1;
    background-color:'beige'; display:'none'"></DIV>
```

To see this code in action, refer to the Web Workshop CD-ROM.

The next example shows how to use the **TextRectangle** collection and the **getBoundingClientRect** method to determine position within an element. In each line, the left-justified text does not extend to the right margin of the box that contains the text. Using the collection, you can determine the coordinates of the rectangle that surrounds only the content in each line. By reading these rectangles and then comparing the coordinates against the rectangle around the ball image, the example instructs the ball to move over the text only, and not to the end of the line.

```
function LoadDone()
{
    oTxtRng = document.body.createTextRange();
    // Get rectangles of the range:
    oRcts = oTxtRng.getClientRects();
    iLine = 0;
    // Get bounds of the rectangle on the DIV encasing the ball image:
    oBndRct = obj.getBoundingClientRect();
    iDivLen = oBndRct.right - oBndRct.left + 1;
    :
    iPosInLine = oRcts[iLine].left;
    :
    // Make comparison:
    if(iPosInLine >= oRcts[iLine].right - iDivLen)
    :
}
```

To see this code in action, refer to the Web Workshop CD-ROM.

Applies To

WIN16	WIN32	MAC	UNIX

A, ACRONYM, ADDRESS, APPLET, AREA, B, BASE, BASEFONT, BIG, BLOCKQUOTE, BODY, BUTTON, CAPTION, CENTER, CITE, CODE, COL, COLGROUP, COMMENT, DD, DEL, DFN, DIR, DIV, DL, DT, EM, EMBED, FIELDSET, FONT, FORM, Hn, I, IMG, INPUT type=button, INPUT type=checkbox, INPUT type=file, INPUT type=image, INPUT type=password, INPUT type=radio, INPUT type=reset, INPUT type=submit, INPUT type=text, INS, ISINDEX, KBD, LABEL, LEGEND, LI, LINK, LISTING, MAP, MARQUEE, MENU, NEXTID, NOBR, OBJECT, OL, OPTION, P, PRE, Q, S, SAMP, SELECT, SMALL, SPAN, STRIKE, STRONG, SUB, SUP, TABLE, TBODY, TD, TEXTAREA, TextRange, TFOOT, TH, THEAD, TR, TT, U, UL, VAR, XMP

getClientRects Method

Retrieves a collection of rectangles that describes the layout of the contents of an object or range within the client. Each rectangle describes a single line.

Syntax

collRect = *object*.getClientRects()

Return Value

collRect. The return value is the **TextRectangle** collection, each rectangle having four integer properties (**top**, **left**, **right**, and **bottom**). Each property represents a coordinate of the rectangle, in pixels.

Example

The following example shows how to use the **getClientRects** and **getBoundingClientRect** methods to highlight text lines in an object.

```
<SCRIPT>
function newHighlite(obj) {
    oRcts = obj.getClientRects();
    iLength= oRcts.length;
    if (event.altKey == true) {
        keyCount=keyCount+1;
        if (keyCount > iLength-1) {
            keyCount = 0
            }
        }
```

```
        // Determine the coordinates for the yellow DIV.
        iRight = oRcts[keyCount].right + sBody.scrollLeft;   // right
        iLeft = oRcts[keyCount].left + sBody.scrollLeft;     // left
        iTop = oRcts[keyCount].top + sBody.scrollTop;        // top
        // Set the rendering properties for the yellow DIV.
        sYellow.style.top = iTop;
        sYellow.style.width = (iRight-iLeft) - 5;
        sYellow.style.display = 'inline';
        // Determine the coordinates for the beige DIV.
        iBndRight = obj.getBoundingClientRect().right + sBody.scrollLeft;
        iBndLeft = obj.getBoundingClientRect().left + sBody.scrollLeft;
        iBndTop = obj.getBoundingClientRect().top + sBody.scrollTop;
        // Set the rendering properties for the beige DIV.
        sBeige.style.top = iBndTop;
        sBeige.style.width = (iBndRight-iBndLeft) - 5;
        sBeige.style.height = iTop - iBTop;
        // Display beige area only after 1st line.
        if (event.altKey == true) {
            idBeige.style.display = 'inline';
        }
    }
}
</SCRIPT>
:
<DIV ID=s1 STYLE="position:absolute; left:5; top:250; z-index:1"
    onclick="newHighlite(this)" onkeypress="newHighlite(this)">
:
</DIV>
<DIV ID=sYellow STYLE="position:absolute; left:5; top:400; z-index:0;
background-color:'yellow'; display:'none'"></DIV>
<DIV ID=sBeige STYLE="position:absolute; left:5; top:400; z-index:-1;
background-color:'beige'; display:'none'"></DIV>
```

To see this code in action, refer to the Web Workshop CD-ROM.

The next example shows how to use the **TextRectangle** collection and
getBoundingClientRect method to determine position within an element. In each
line, the left-justified text does not extend to the right margin of the box that contains
the text. Using the collection, you can determine the coordinates of the rectangle that
surround only the content in each line. By reading these rectangles and then
comparing the coordinates against the rectangle around the ball image, the example
instructs the ball to only move over the text, and not to the end of the line.

```
function LoadDone()
{
    oTxtRng = document.body.createTextRange();
    // Get rectangles of the range:
    oRcts = oTxtRng.getClientRects();
    iLine = 0;
    // Get bounds of the rectangle on the DIV encasing the ball image:
    oBndRct = obj.getBoundingClientRect();
    iDivLen = oBndRct.right - oBndRct.left + 1;
    :
```

```
iPosInLine = oRcts[iLine].left;
:
// Make comparison:
if(iPosInLine >= oRcts[iLine].right - iDivLen)
    :
}
```

To see this code in action, refer to the Web Workshop CD-ROM.

Applies To

 WIN16   WIN32   MAC   UNIX

A, ACRONYM, ADDRESS, APPLET, AREA, B, BASE, BASEFONT, BIG,
BLOCKQUOTE, BODY, BUTTON, CAPTION, CENTER, CITE, CODE, COL,
COLGROUP, COMMENT, DD, DEL, DFN, DIR, DIV, DL, DT, EM, EMBED,
FIELDSET, FONT, FORM, Hn, I, IMG, INPUT type=button, INPUT type=checkbox,
INPUT type=file, INPUT type=image, INPUT type=password, INPUT type=radio,
INPUT type=reset, INPUT type=submit, INPUT type=text, INS, ISINDEX, KBD,
LABEL, LEGEND, LI, LINK, LISTING, MAP, MARQUEE, MENU, NEXTID,
NOBR, OBJECT, OL, OPTION, P, PRE, Q, S, SAMP, SELECT, SMALL, SPAN,
STRIKE, STRONG, SUB, SUP, TABLE, TBODY, TD, TEXTAREA, TextRange,
TFOOT, TH, THEAD, TR, TT, U, UL, VAR, XMP

getData Method

Specifies which data format to retrieve from the clipboard through the **dataTransfer**
or **clipboardData** object.

Syntax

sRetrieveData = *object*.getData(*sDataFormat*)

Parameters

sDataFormat   Required. Data format that the target object reads from the clipboard
using the **dataTransfer** or **clipboardData** object. This string value
can be one of the following:

Text   Specifies that the data being transferred is text.

URL   Specifies that the data being transferred is a URL.

Return Value

String. Represents the data in the format retrieved from the **dataTransfer** or **clipboardData** object. Depending on what information the **setData** method contains, this variable can retrieve a path to an image, text, or an anchor URL.

Remarks

The **getData** method enforces cross-frame security and allows data transfers within the same domain only. Dragging a selection between different security protocols, such as HTTP to HTTPS, does not work. Dragging a selection between two instances of the browser, where the first instance has its security level set to medium and the second has it set to high, also does not work. Finally, dragging a selection into the browser from another drag-enabled application such as Microsoft® Word does not work.

To use the **getData** method to retrieve data from the clipboard within the **oncopy** or **oncut** event, specify `window.event.returnValue=false` within the event handler script.

Example

The following example shows how to use the **setData** and **getData** methods of the **dataTransfer** object to drop text in a new location and create a desktop shortcut.

```
<HEAD>
<SCRIPT>
function InitiateDrag(){
   event.dataTransfer.setData(oSource.innerText);
}

function FinishDrag(){
   window.event.returnValue=false;
   oTarget.innerText = event.dataTransfer.getData("Text");
}
function OverDrag(){
   window.event.returnValue=false;
}
</SCRIPT>
</HEAD>
<BODY>

<B ID="oSource"
   ondragstart="InitiateDrag()">
drag this text</B>

<SPAN ID="oTarget"
   ondragover="OverDrag()"
   ondragenter="FinishDrag()"">
drop text here</SPAN>

</BODY>
```

The next example shows how to use **getData** to drag text and drop it in a new location.

```
<HEAD>
<SCRIPT>
var sUseData;

function InitiateDrag()
{
  event.dataTransfer.setData(oSource.innerText);
}

function FinishDrag()
{
  sUseData = event.dataTransfer.getData("Text");
  oTarget.innerText = sUseData;
}
</SCRIPT>
</HEAD>
<BODY>

<B ID=oSource ondragstart="InitiateDrag()">drag this text</B>

<SPAN ID=oTarget ondrop="FinishDrag()">drop text here</SPAN>

</BODY>
```

To see this code in action, refer to the Web Workshop CD-ROM.

The final example shows how to create a desktop shortcut using a drag-and-drop operation.

```
<HEAD>
<SCRIPT>
var sAnchorURL;

function InitiateDrag()
/*  The setData parameters tell the source object
    to transfer data as a URL and to provide the path.  */
{
  event.dataTransfer.setData("URL", oSource.href);
}

function FinishDrag()
/*  The parameter passed to getData tells the target
    object what data format to expect.  */
{
  sAnchorURL = event.dataTransfer.getData("URL")
  oTarget.innerText = sAnchorURL;
}
</SCRIPT>
</HEAD>
<BODY>
```

DHTML Methods

```
<A ID=oSource HREF="about:Example_Complete"
   onclick="return(false)" ondragstart="InitiateDrag()">Test Anchor</A>

<SPAN ID=oTarget ondrop="FinishDrag()">Drop Here</SPAN>

</BODY>
```

To see this code in action, refer to the Web Workshop CD-ROM.

Applies To

 WIN16   WIN32   MAC   UNIX

clipboardData, dataTransfer

getElementById Method

Returns a reference to the first object with the specified value of the **ID** attribute.

Syntax

oElement = *document*.getElementById(*sIDValue*)

Parameters

sIDValue   Required. String specifying the value of an **ID** attribute.

Return Value

Returns the first object with the same **ID** attribute as the specified value.

Remarks

If the **ID** value belongs to a collection, the **getElementById** method returns the first object in the collection.

The **getElementById** method is equivalent to using the **item** method on the **all** collection. For example, the following code samples show how to retrieve the first element with the **ID** oDiv from the **document** object.

Using the DHTML Object Model:

```
var oVDiv = document.body.all.item("oDiv");
```

Using the Document Object Model (DOM):

```
var oVDiv = document.getElementById("oDiv");
```

Example

The following example shows how to use the **getElementById** method to return the first occurrence of the **ID** attribute value, oDiv.

```
<SCRIPT>
function fnGetId(){
   // Returns the first DIV element in the collection.
   var oVDiv=document.getElementById("oDiv");
}
</SCRIPT>
<DIV ID="oDiv">Div #1</DIV>
<DIV ID="oDiv">Div #2</DIV>
<DIV ID="oDiv">Div #3</DIV>
<INPUT TYPE="button" VALUE="Get Names" onclick="fnGetId()">
```

Applies To

IE 5	WIN16	WIN32	MAC	UNIX

document

getElementsByName Method

Retrieves a collection of objects based on the value of the **NAME** attribute.

Syntax

cObjects = *document*.getElementsByName(*sNameValue*)

Parameters

sNameValue   Required. String specifying the value of a **NAME** attribute.

Return Value

Returns a collection of objects with the same **NAME** attribute value.

Remarks

When you use the **getElementsByName** method, all elements in the document that have the specified **NAME** attribute value are returned.

Elements that support the **NAME** attribute are included in the collection returned by the **getElementsByName** method, but not elements with a **NAME expando**.

Example

The following example shows how to use the **getElementsByName** method to return a collection of **INPUT type=text** elements with the specified **NAME** attribute value, firstName.

```
<SCRIPT>
function fnGetNames(){
    // Returns a collection with 2 INPUT type=text elements.
    var aInput=document.getElementsByName("firstName");
}
</SCRIPT>
<INPUT TYPE="text" NAME="firstName">
<INPUT TYPE="text" NAME="firstName">
<INPUT TYPE="button" VALUE="Get Names" onclick="fnGetNames()">
```

Applies To

 WIN16   WIN32   MAC   UNIX

document

getElementsByTagName Method

Retrieves a collection of objects based on the specified element name.

Syntax

cObjects = *document*.getElementsByTagName(*sTagName*)

Parameters

sTagName   Required. String specifying the name of an element.

Return Value

Returns a collection of objects with the specified element name.

Remarks

The **getElementsByTagName** method is equivalent to using the **tags** method on the **all** collection. For example, the following code samples show how to retrieve a collection of **DIV** elements from the **BODY** element.

Using the DHTML Object Model:

```
var aDivs = document.body.all.tags("DIV");
```

Using the DOM:

```
var aDivs = document.body.getElementsByTagName("DIV");
```

When you invoke the **getElementsByTagName** method, all child elements with the specified tag name are returned.

Example

The following example shows how to use the **getElementsByTagName** method to return the children of a **UL** element based on the selected **LI** element.

```
<SCRIPT>
function fnGetTags(){
    var oWorkItem=event.srcElement;
    var aReturn=oWorkItem.parentElement.getElementsByTagName("LI");
    alert("Length: "
        + aReturn.length
        + "\nFirst Item: "
        + aReturn[0].childNodes[0].nodeValue);
}
</SCRIPT>
<UL onclick="fnGetTags()">
<LI>Item 1
    <UL>
        <LI>Sub Item 1.1
        <OL>
            <LI>Super Sub Item 1.1
            <LI>Super Sub Item 1.2
        </OL>
        <LI>Sub Item 1.2
        <LI>Sub Item 1.3
    </UL>
<LI>Item 2
    <UL>
        <LI>Sub Item 2.1
        <LI>Sub Item 2.3
    </UL>
<LI>Item 3
</UL>
```

To see this code in action, refer to the Web Workshop CD-ROM.

Applies To

  WIN16   WIN32   MAC   UNIX

A, ACRONYM, ADDRESS, APPLET, AREA, B, BASE, BASEFONT, BDO, BGSOUND, BIG, BLOCKQUOTE, BODY, BR, BUTTON, CAPTION, CENTER, CITE, CODE, COL, COLGROUP, DD, DEL, DFN, DIR, DIV, DL, document, DT, EM, EMBED, FIELDSET, FONT, FORM, FRAME, FRAMESET, HEAD, Hn, HR, HTML, I, IFRAME, IMG, INS, KBD, LABEL, LEGEND, LI, LINK, LISTING,

Applies To *(continued)*

 WIN16   WIN32   MAC   UNIX

MAP, MARQUEE, MENU, OL, P, PLAINTEXT, PRE, Q, S, SAMP, SCRIPT, SELECT, SMALL, SPAN, STRIKE, STRONG, SUB, SUP, TABLE, TBODY, TD, TEXTAREA, TFOOT, TH, THEAD, TITLE, TR, TT, U, UL, VAR, XMP

getExpression Method

Retrieves the expression for the given property.

Syntax

vExpression = *object*.getExpression(*sPropertyName*)

Parameters

sPropertyName Required. Name of the property from which to retrieve the expression.

Return Value

Variant. Returns a variant value representing the expression of the property.

Remarks

The **getExpression** method, which applies to the **style** object, can be used to return expressions set on supported cascading style sheets (CSS) attributes. This method also is available in scripting for the **innerHTML** and **value** properties.

The **getExpression** method can be used in script as follows:

```
var sExpression = object.getExpression(sProperty)
```

The **getExpression** method can be used on a style as follows:

```
var sExpression = object.style.getExpression(sProperty)
```

Example

The following example shows how to use the **getExpression** method. The para1 paragraph's width is set equal to the sum of two images' widths. The **getExpression** method returns a variant containing the expression.

```
<P ID=para1 STYLE="width:expression(Img1.width + Img2.width);
back-color:blue" onclick="getexp()">Click here to see the
expression.</P>
```

```
<SCRIPT>
var s;

function getexp()
{
    s=para1.style.getExpression("width");
    alert("Expression for the width of the paragraph is \n\n"
        + s + "\n\nThe width property has a value of "
        + oBox3.style.width);
}
</SCRIPT>
```

Applies To

 WIN16   WIN32   MAC   UNIX

A, ACRONYM, ADDRESS, AREA, B, BDO, BIG, BLOCKQUOTE, BODY, BR, BUTTON, CAPTION, CENTER, CITE, CODE, COL, COLGROUP, DD, DEL, DFN, DIR, DIV, DL, DT, EM, FIELDSET, FONT, FORM, Hn, HR, I, IFRAME, IMG, INPUT type=button, INPUT type=checkbox, INPUT type=file, INPUT type=hidden, INPUT type=image, INPUT type=password, INPUT type=radio, INPUT type=reset, INPUT type=submit, INPUT type=text, INS, KBD, LABEL, LEGEND, LI, LISTING, MARQUEE, MENU, NOBR, OL, OPTION, P, PRE, Q, RT, RUBY, S, SAMP, SELECT, SMALL, SPAN, STRIKE, STRONG, style, SUB, SUP, TABLE, TBODY, TD, TEXTAREA, TFOOT, TH, THEAD, TR, TT, U, UL, VAR

go Method

Loads a URL from the History list.

Syntax

history.go(*vLocation*)

Parameters

vLocation   Required. Integer specifying the relative position of the URL in the History list, or string specifying all or part of a URL in the browser history.

Return Value

No return value.

Remarks

An error does not occur if the user tries to go beyond the beginning or end of the history. Instead, the user remains at the current page.

Applies To

 WIN16   WIN32   MAC

history

 UNIX

history

hasChildNodes Method

Returns whether the object has children.

Syntax

bChildNodes = *object*.hasChildNodes()

Return Value

Boolean. Returns true if the object has children.

Remarks

If the object has children, they can be accessed from the **childNodes** or **children** collections.

Applies To

 WIN16   WIN32   MAC   UNIX

A, ACRONYM, ADDRESS, APPLET, AREA, B, BASE, BASEFONT, BDO, BIG, BLOCKQUOTE, BODY, BR, BUTTON, CAPTION, CENTER, CITE, CODE, COL, COLGROUP, COMMENT, DD, DEL, DFN, DIR, DIV, DL, DT, EM, EMBED, FIELDSET, FONT, FORM, FRAME, FRAMESET, HEAD, Hn, HR, HTML, I, IFRAME, IMG, INPUT type=button, INPUT type=checkbox, INPUT type=file, INPUT type=image, INPUT type=password, INPUT type=radio, INPUT type=reset, INPUT type=submit, INPUT type=text, INS, KBD, LABEL, LEGEND, LI, LINK, LISTING, MAP, MARQUEE, MENU, NEXTID, OL, OPTION, P, PLAINTEXT, PRE, Q, S, SAMP, SCRIPT, SELECT, SMALL, SPAN, STRIKE, STRONG, SUB, SUP, TABLE, TBODY, TD, TEXTAREA, TFOOT, TH, THEAD, TITLE, TR, TT, U, UL, VAR, XMP

ImportExportFavorites Method

Imports or exports Favorites information.

Syntax

*window.external.*ImportExportFavorites(*bImportExport* [, *sImportExportPath*])

Parameters

bImportExport Required. Boolean value specifying whether the user has requested an import or an export . If the Boolean is `true`, the user has requested an import. If the Boolean is `false`, the user has requested an export.

sImportExportPath Optional. String specifying the location (URL) to import or export, depending on *bImportExport*. If a value is not provided, a file dialog box is opened.

Return Value

No return value.

Remarks

Confirmation is always required before the import or export begins.

All favorites are uploaded to the server when exported, and it is recommended that the server be configured to erase previously stored favorites before accepting the updates. Favorites imported from the server merge with existing favorites on the client. Deletions on the server do not propagate to the client.

This method is not supported in HTML Applications (HTAs).

Example

The following example shows how to use the **ImportExportFavorites** method.

```
// 'true' specifies that the favorites are imported from the server.
window.external.ImportExportFavorites(
    true,"http://www.your_server.com");
// 'false' specifies that the favorites are exported to the server.
window.external.ImportExportFavorites(
    false,"http://www.your_server.com");
// If the path is not provided, a dialog box is opened.
window.external.ImportExportFavorites(false);
```

DHTML Methods

Applies To

 WIN16   WIN32   MAC   UNIX

external

inRange Method

Returns whether one range is contained within another.

Syntax

bFound = *TextRange*.inRange(*oRange*)

Parameters

oRange   Required. Reference to a **TextRange** object.

Return Value

Boolean. Returns true if the range passed as the method parameter is contained within or is equal to the range on which the method is called; otherwise, it returns false.

Remarks

This feature might not be available on non-Win32 platforms. For the latest information on Internet Explorer cross-platform compatibility, see article Q172976 in the Microsoft Knowledge Base.

Example

The following example shows how to use equal text ranges, a contained range, and a range that is outside the range on which the **inRange** method is called.

```
<HTML>
   <SCRIPT>
      var oRng1 = document.body.createTextRange();
      var oRng2 = oRng1.duplicate();
      var bInside = oRng1.inRange(oRng2); // returns true;

      oRng1.moveToElementText(div1);
      oRng2.moveToElementText(div2);
      bInside = oRng1.inRange(oRng2); // returns false;

      var oRng3 = oRng1.duplicate();
      oRng3.findText('division 1');
      bInside = oRng1.inRange(oRng3); // returns false;
   </SCRIPT>
```

```
<BODY>
   <DIV ID=div1>
   Content for division 1.
   </DIV>
   <DIV ID=div2>
   Content for division 2.
   </DIV>
   </BODY>
</HTML>
```

To see this code in action, refer to the Web Workshop CD-ROM.

Applies To

 WIN16   WIN32   MAC   UNIX

TextRange

insertAdjacentElement Method

DHTML Methods

Inserts an element at the specified location.

Syntax

oElement = *object*.insertAdjacentElement(*sWhere*, *oElement*)

Parameters

sWhere   Required. Position where the HTML text is to be inserted. This position can be one of the following:

beforeBegin   Inserts *oElement* immediately before the object.

afterBegin   Inserts *oElement* after the start of the object but before all other content in the object.

beforeEnd   Inserts *oElement* immediately before the end of the object but after all other content in the object.

afterEnd   Inserts *oElement* immediately after the end of the object.

oElement   Required. Element to be inserted adjacent to the object that invoked the **insertAdjacentElement** method.

Return Value

Returns an element object.

Remarks

This method is accessible at run time. If elements get removed at run time before the closing tag is parsed, areas of the document might not render.

Example

The following example shows how to use the **insertAdjacentElement** method to add a new list item to an **OL** object.

```
<SCRIPT>
function fnAdd(){
    var oNewItem = document.createElement("LI");
    oList.children(0).insertAdjacentElement("AfterBegin",oNewItem);
    oNewItem.innerText = "List Item 0";
}
</SCRIPT>
:
<BODY>
<OL ID = "oList">
<LI>List Item 1</LI>
<LI>List Item 2</LI>
<LI>List Item 3</LI>
</OL>

<INPUT TYPE = "button" VALUE = "Add Item" onclick="fnAdd()">

</BODY>
```

Applies To

 WIN16   WIN32   MAC   UNIX

A, ACRONYM, ADDRESS, APPLET, AREA, B, BASE, BASEFONT, BDO, BGSOUND, BIG, BLOCKQUOTE, BODY, BR, BUTTON, CAPTION, CENTER, CITE, CODE, COL, COLGROUP, COMMENT, DD, DEL, DFN, DIR, DIV, DL, DT, EM, EMBED, FIELDSET, FONT, FORM, FRAME, FRAMESET, HEAD, Hn, HR, HTML, I, IFRAME, IMG, INPUT type=button, INPUT type=checkbox, INPUT type=file, INPUT type=hidden, INPUT type=image, INPUT type=password, INPUT type=radio, INPUT type=reset, INPUT type=submit, INPUT type=text, INS, KBD, LABEL, LEGEND, LI, LINK, LISTING, MAP, MARQUEE, MENU, NEXTID, OBJECT, OL, OPTION, P, PLAINTEXT, PRE, Q, S, SAMP, SCRIPT, SELECT, SMALL, SPAN, STRIKE, STRONG, SUB, SUP, TABLE, TBODY, TD, TEXTAREA, TFOOT, TH, THEAD, TITLE, TR, TT, U, UL, VAR, XMP

insertAdjacentHTML Method

Inserts the given HTML text into the element at the specified location.

Syntax

object.insertAdjacentHTML(*sWhere*, *sText*)

Parameters

sWhere   Required. Position where the HTML text is to be inserted. This position can be one of the following:

    beforeBegin   Inserts *sText* immediately before the object.

    afterBegin   Inserts *sText* after the start of the object but before all other content in the object.

    beforeEnd   Inserts *sText* immediately before the end of the object but after all other content in the object.

    afterEnd   Inserts *sText* immediately after the end of the object.

sText   Required. HTML text to insert. The string can be a combination of text and HTML tags. This must be well-formed, valid HTML or this method fails.

Return Value

No return value.

Remarks

If the text contains HTML tags, the method parses and formats the text as it is inserted.

You cannot insert text while the document is loading. Wait for the **onload** event before attempting to call this method.

As of Internet Explorer 5, this method is accessible at run time. If elements get removed at run time before the closing tag is parsed, areas of the document might not render.

When inserting script using the **insertAdjacentHTML** method, you must include the **DEFER** attribute in the **SCRIPT** element.

DHTML Methods

Example

The following example shows how to use the **insertAdjacentHTML** method to insert script into the page.

```
var sHTML="<input type=button onclick=" +
    "go2()" + " value='Click Me'><BR>"
var sScript='<SCRIPT DEFER>'
sScript = sScript +
    'function go2(){ alert("Hello from inserted script.") }'
sScript = sScript + '</script' + '>';
ScriptDiv.insertAdjacentHTML("afterBegin",sHTML + sScript);
```

To see this code in action, refer to the Web Workshop CD-ROM.

Applies To

 WIN16   WIN32   MAC   UNIX

A, ADDRESS, AREA, B, BASEFONT, BIG, BLOCKQUOTE, BODY, BUTTON, CAPTION, CENTER, CITE, CODE, COMMENT, DD, DFN, DIR, DIV, DL, DT, EM, FIELDSET, FONT, FORM, FRAMESET, Hn, HR, I, IFRAME, IMG, INPUT type=button, INPUT type=checkbox, INPUT type=file, INPUT type=hidden, INPUT type=image, INPUT type=password, INPUT type=radio, INPUT type=reset, INPUT type=submit, INPUT type=text, KBD, LABEL, LEGEND, LI, LISTING, MAP, MARQUEE, MENU, NOBR, OL, OPTION, P, PLAINTEXT, PRE, S, SAMP, SELECT, SMALL, SPAN, STRIKE, STRONG, SUB, SUP, TD, TEXTAREA, TH, TT, U, UL, VAR, XMP

insertAdjacentText Method

Inserts the given text into the element at the given location.

Syntax

object.insertAdjacentText(*sWhere*, *sText*)

Parameters

sWhere   Required. Location to insert the text. This can be one of the following:

beforeBegin   Inserts the text immediately before the element.

afterBegin   Inserts the text after the start of the element, but before all other content in the element.

beforeEnd   Inserts the text immediately before the end of the element, but after all other content in the element.

Parameters *(continued)*

        `afterEnd`   Inserts the text immediately after the end of the element.

sText   Required. Text to insert.

Return Value

No return value.

Remarks

The text is inserted as plain text.

You cannot insert text while the document is loading. Wait for the **onload** event to fire before attempting to call this method.

Applies To

 WIN16   WIN32   MAC   UNIX

A, ADDRESS, AREA, B, BASEFONT, BIG, BLOCKQUOTE, BODY, BUTTON, CAPTION, CENTER, CITE, CODE, COMMENT, DD, DFN, DIR, DIV, DL, DT, EM, FIELDSET, FONT, FORM, FRAMESET, Hn, HR, I, IFRAME, IMG, INPUT type=button, INPUT type=checkbox, INPUT type=file, INPUT type=hidden, INPUT type=image, INPUT type=password, INPUT type=radio, INPUT type=reset, INPUT type=submit, INPUT type=text, KBD, LABEL, LEGEND, LI, LISTING, MAP, MARQUEE, MENU, NOBR, OL, OPTION, P, PRE, S, SAMP, SELECT, SMALL, SPAN, STRIKE, STRONG, SUB, SUP, TD, TEXTAREA, TH, TT, U, UL, VAR

insertBefore Method

Inserts an element into the document hierarchy.

Syntax

oElement = *object*.`insertBefore`(*oNewNode* [, *oChildNode*])

Parameters

oNewNode   Required. New element to be inserted into the hierarchy. Elements can be created with the **createElement** method.

oChildNode   Optional. New element is inserted before this child element, if specified.

Return Value

Returns a reference to the element that is inserted into the document.

Remarks

Do not specify an *oChildNode* parameter when inserting the first child node. If children already exist and you do not specify the *oChildNode* parameter, the *oNewNode* becomes the last child of the parent object.

This method is accessible at run time. If elements are removed at run time before the closing tag is parsed, areas of the document might not render.

Example

The following example shows how to insert a block of bold text into the document.

```
<HEAD>
    <SCRIPT>
    function insertElement()
    {
        var nod=document.createElement("B");
        document.body.insertBefore(nod);
        nod.innerText="A New bold object has been
                       inserted into the document."
    }
    </SCRIPT>
</HEAD>
<BODY>
<DIV ID=Div1 onclick="insertElement()">
Click here to insert a new bold element into this div.
</DIV>
```

Applies To

 WIN16   WIN32   MAC   UNIX

A, ACRONYM, ADDRESS, B, BDO, BIG, BLOCKQUOTE, BODY, BUTTON, CAPTION, CENTER, CITE, CODE, COL, COLGROUP, COMMENT, DD, DEL, DFN, DIR, DIV, DL, DT, EM, FIELDSET, FONT, FORM, FRAMESET, HEAD, Hn, HTML, I, IFRAME, INPUT type=button, INPUT type=checkbox, INPUT type=file, INPUT type=image, INPUT type=password, INPUT type=radio, INPUT type=reset, INPUT type=submit, INPUT type=text, INS, KBD, LABEL, LEGEND, LI, LISTING, MAP, MARQUEE, MENU, NEXTID, OBJECT, OL, OPTION, P, PLAINTEXT, PRE, Q, S, SAMP, SELECT, SMALL, SPAN, STRIKE, STRONG, SUB, SUP, TABLE, TBODY, TD, TEXTAREA, TFOOT, TH, THEAD, TR, TT, U, UL, VAR, XMP

insertCell Method

Creates a new cell in the table row (**TR**), and adds the cell to the **cells** collection.

Syntax

oTD = *TR*.insertCell([*iIndex*])

Parameters

iIndex   Optional. Location to insert the cell in the **TR**. The default value is -1, which appends the new cell to the end of the **cells** collection.

Return Value

Returns the **TD** element object if successful, or null otherwise.

Remarks

The preferred technique for inserting a cell is to add the cell at the end of the **cells** collection. It is faster to add a cell at the end of a row than somewhere in the middle. To add a cell at the end of the collection, specify the -1 possible value, or the length of the **cells** collection minus 1.

Example

The following example shows how to add a cell to the end of the **TR**.

```
myNewCell = document.all.myTable.rows[0].insertCell()
```

Applies To

WIN16	WIN32	MAC	UNIX

TR

insertRow Method

Creates a new row (**TR**) in the table, and adds the row to the **rows** collection.

Syntax

oTR = *object*.insertRow([*iIndex*])

Parameters

iIndex   Optional. Location to insert the row in the **rows** collection. The default value is -1, which appends the new row to the end of the **rows** collection.

Return Value

Returns the **TR** element object if successful, or `null` otherwise.

Remarks

If you insert a row in a **TFOOT, TBODY,** or **THEAD,** you also need to add the row to the **rows** collection for the **TABLE**. If you insert a row in the **TABLE**, you also need to add a row to the **rows** collection for the **TBODY**. If you specify an index, the index should be relative to the **rows** collection for the element that first contains the **TR**. For example, if you call this method for a **TBODY**, you must specify an index value relative to the **rows** collection that is on the **TBODY**, not the **TABLE**.

The preferred technique for inserting a row is to add the row at the end of the **rows** collection. It is faster to add a row at the end of a table than somewhere in the middle. To add a row at the end of the collection, specify the `-1` possible value, or the length of the **rows** collection minus 1.

Example

The following example shows how to add a row to the **TABLE**.

```
myNewRow = document.all.myTable.insertRow()
```

Applies To

WIN16	**WIN32**	**MAC**	**UNIX**

TABLE

isEqual Method

Returns whether the specified range is equal to the current range.

Syntax

bEqual = *TextRange*.isEqual(*oCompareRange*)

Parameters

oCompareRange Required. **TextRange** object to compare to the parent object.

Return Value

Boolean. Returns `true` if equal, or `false` otherwise.

Applies To

 WIN16　WIN32　MAC　UNIX

TextRange

IsSubscribed Method

Returns whether the client subscribes to the given channel.

Syntax

bSubscribed = *window.external*.IsSubscribed(*sURLToCDF*)

Parameters

sURLToCDF　Required. URL of a Channel Definition Format (CDF) file to be
checked for a subscription.

Return Value

Boolean. Returns true if the channel is subscribed to, or false if no subscription
exists for that CDF file.

Remarks

If you use this method in an HTML page that is not in the same secondary domain
specified in *sURLToCDF*, the method returns a scripting error.

This method is not supported in HTML Applications (HTAs).

Applies To

 WIN16　WIN32　MAC　UNIX

external

item Method

Retrieves an object or a collection from the given collection depending on the *vIndex*
parameter.

Syntax

vItem = *object*.item(*vIndex* [, *iSubIndex*])

Parameters

vIndex   Required. Number or string specifying the object or collection to retrieve. If this parameter is a number, the method returns the object in the collection at the given position, where the first object has value 0, the second has 1, and so on. If this parameter is a string and there is more than one object with the **name** or **id** properties equal to the string, the method returns a collection of matching objects.

iSubIndex   Optional. Position of an object to retrieve. This parameter is used when *vIndex* is a string. The method uses the string to construct a collection of all objects that have a **name** or **id** equal to the string, and then retrieves from this collection the object at the position specified by *iSubIndex*.

Return Value

Variant. Returns an object or a collection of objects if successful, or `null` otherwise.

Remarks

The **TextRectangle**, **attributes**, and **rules** collections only accept an integer value for the *vIndex* parameter.

Example

The following JScript (compatible with ECMA 262 language specification) example shows how to use the **item** method to retrieve each object from the document. In this case, the method parameter is a number, so the objects are retrieved in the order in which they appear in the document.

```
var coll = document.all;
if (coll!=null) {
    for (i=0; i<coll.length; i++)
        alert(coll.item(i).tagName);
}
```

The following JScript example shows how to use the **item** method to retrieve a collection of all objects in the document having "Sample" as an **id**. Then it uses **item** again to retrieve each object from the "Sample" collection.

```
var coll = document.all.item("Sample");
If (coll != null) {
    for (i=0; i<coll.length; i++) {
        alert(coll.item(i).tagName);
    }
}
```

The following JScript example is similar to the previous example, but uses the optional *subindex* parameter of **item** to retrieve individual objects.

```
var coll = document.all.item("Sample")
if (coll!=null) {
    for (i=0; i<coll.length; i++)
        alert(document.all.item("Sample",i).tagName);
}
```

Applies To

 WIN16   WIN32   MAC   UNIX

all, anchors, applets, areas, cells, children, elements, embeds, filters, forms, frames, images, imports, links, options, plugins, rows, rules, scripts, styleSheets, tbodies, TextRectangle

 WIN16   WIN32   MAC   UNIX

attributes, behaviorUrns, bookmarks, boundElements, childNodes, controlRange

javaEnabled Method

Returns whether Java is enabled.

Syntax

bEnabled = *navigator*.javaEnabled()

Return Value

Boolean. Returns `true` if Java is enabled, or `false` otherwise.

Applies To

 WIN16   WIN32   MAC   UNIX

navigator

lastPage Method

Moves to the last page of records in the data set, and scrolls it into view.

Syntax

TABLE.lastPage()

Return Value

No return value.

Remarks

The **dataPageSize** property of the table determines the number of records displayed in the table. You must set the **DATAPAGESIZE** attribute when designing the page, or set the corresponding **dataPageSize** property at run time for this method to have any effect.

Note You do not need to check for boundary conditions.

Applies To

 WIN16   WIN32   MAC   UNIX

TABLE

mergeAttributes Method

Copies all read/write attributes to the specified element.

Syntax

object.mergeAttributes(*oSource*)

Parameters

oSource   Required. Element containing the attributes copied to the object that invoked the **mergeAttributes** method.

Return Value

No return value.

Remarks

The **mergeAttributes** method copies persistent HTML attributes, events, and styles. Attributes that are read-only, such as **ID**, are not merged.

Example

The following example shows how to use the **mergeAttributes** method to copy attributes, events, and styles from one object to another.

```
<SCRIPT>
function fnMerge(){
    oSource.children[1].mergeAttributes(oSource.children[0]);
}
</SCRIPT>
```

```
<SPAN ID=oSource>
<DIV
    ID="oDiv"
    ATTRIBUTE1="true"
    ATTRIBUTE2="true"
    onclick="alert('click');"
    onmouseover="this.style.color='#0000FF';"
    onmouseout="this.style.color='#000000';"
>
This is a sample <B>DIV</B> element.
</DIV>
<DIV ID="oDiv2">
This is another sample <B>DIV</B> element.
</DIV>
</SPAN>

<INPUT
    TYPE="button"
    VALUE="Merge Attributes"
    onclick="fnMerge()"
>
```

To see this code in action, refer to the Web Workshop CD-ROM.

Applies To

 WIN16   WIN32   MAC   UNIX

A, ACRONYM, ADDRESS, APPLET, AREA, B, BASE, BASEFONT, BDO,
BGSOUND, BIG, BLOCKQUOTE, BODY, BR, BUTTON, CAPTION, CENTER,
CITE, CODE, COL, COLGROUP, COMMENT, DD, DEL, DFN, DIR, DIV, DL,
document, DT, EM, EMBED, FIELDSET, FONT, FORM, FRAME, FRAMESET,
HEAD, Hn, HR, HTML, I, IFRAME, IMG, INPUT type=button, INPUT
type=checkbox, INPUT type=file, INPUT type=hidden, INPUT type=image, INPUT
type=password, INPUT type=radio, INPUT type=reset, INPUT type=submit, INPUT
type=text, INS, KBD, LABEL, LEGEND, LI, LINK, LISTING, MAP, MARQUEE,
MENU, NEXTID, OBJECT, OL, OPTION, P, PLAINTEXT, PRE, Q, S, SAMP,
SCRIPT, SELECT, SMALL, SPAN, STRIKE, STRONG, SUB, SUP, TABLE,
TBODY, TD, TEXTAREA, TFOOT, TH, THEAD, TITLE, TR, TT, U, UL, VAR,
XMP

move Method

Collapses the given text range, and moves the empty range by the given number of units.

Syntax

iMoved = TextRange.move(*sUnit* [, *iCount*])

Parameters

sUnit   Required. Units to move. This can be one of the following:

character   Moves one or more characters.

word   Moves one or more words. A word is a collection of characters terminated by a space or some other white space character, such as a tab.

sentence   Moves one or more sentences. A sentence is a collection of words terminated by a punctuation character, such as a period.

textedit   Moves to the start or end of the original range.

iCount   Optional. Number of units to move. This can be positive or negative. The default is 1.

Return Value

Integer. Returns the number of units moved.

Remarks

This feature might not be available on non-Win32 platforms. For the latest information on Internet Explorer cross-platform compatibility, see article Q172976 in the Microsoft Knowledge Base.

Applies To

 WIN16   WIN32   MAC   UNIX

TextRange

moveBy Method

Moves the screen position of the window by the specified x- and y-offsets relative to its current position.

Syntax

window.moveBy(*iX*, *iY*)

Parameters

iX   Required. Horizontal scroll offset, in pixels.

iY   Required. Vertical scroll offset, in pixels.

Return Value

No return value.

Applies To

 WIN16   WIN32   MAC   UNIX

window

moveEnd Method

Changes the end position of the range.

Syntax

iMoved = *TextRange*.moveEnd(*sUnit* [, *iCount*])

Parameters

sUnit   Required. Units to move. This can be one of the following:

    character   Moves one or more characters.

    word   Moves one or more words. A word is a collection of characters terminated by a space or some other white space character, such as a tab.

    sentence   Moves one or more sentences. A sentence is a collection of words terminated by a punctuation character, such as a period.

    textedit   Moves to the start or end of the original range.

iCount   Optional. Number of units to move. This can be positive or negative. The default is 1.

DHTML Methods

Return Value

Integer. Returns the number of units moved.

Remarks

This feature might not be available on non-Win32 platforms. For the latest information on Internet Explorer cross-platform compatibility, see article Q172976 in the Microsoft Knowledge Base.

Applies To

 WIN16   WIN32   MAC   UNIX

TextRange

moveStart Method

Changes the start position of the range.

Syntax

iMoved = *TextRange*.moveStart(*sUnit* [, *iCount*])

Parameters

sUnit   Required. Units to move. This can be one of the following:

character Moves one or more characters.

word Moves one or more words. A word is a collection of characters terminated by a space or some other white space character, such as a tab.

sentence Moves one or more sentences. A sentence is a collection of words terminated by a punctuation character, such as a period.

textedit Moves to the start or end of the original range.

iCount Optional. Number of units to move. This can be positive or negative. The default is 1.

Return Value

Integer. Returns the number of units moved.

Remarks

This feature might not be available on non-Win32 platforms. For the latest information on Internet Explorer cross-platform compatibility, see article Q172976 in the Microsoft Knowledge Base.

Applies To

 WIN16   WIN32   MAC   UNIX

TextRange

moveTo Method

Moves the screen position of the upper-left corner of the window to the specified *iX* and *iY* pixel position.

Syntax

window.moveTo(*iX*, *iY*)

Parameters

iX   Required. Horizontal scroll offset, in pixels.

iY   Required. Vertical scroll offset, in pixels.

Return Value

No return value.

Applies To

 WIN16   WIN32   MAC   UNIX

window

moveToBookmark Method

Moves to a bookmark.

Syntax

bSuccess = *TextRange*.moveToBookmark(*sBookmark*)

Parameters

sBookmark   Required. Bookmark to move to.

Return Value

Boolean. Returns `true` if successful, or `false` otherwise.

Remarks

Bookmarks are opaque strings created with the **getBookmark** method.

This feature might not be available on non-Win32 platforms. For the latest information on Internet Explorer cross-platform compatibility, see article Q172976 in the Microsoft Knowledge Base.

Applies To

 WIN16   WIN32   MAC   UNIX

TextRange

moveToElementText Method

Moves the text range so that the start and end positions of the range encompass the text in the given element.

Syntax

TextRange.moveToElementText(*oElement*)

Parameters

oElement   Required. Element object to move to.

Return Value

No return value.

Remarks

This feature might not be available on non-Win32 platforms. For the latest information on Internet Explorer cross-platform compatibility, see article Q172976 in the Microsoft Knowledge Base.

Applies To

 WIN16   WIN32   MAC   UNIX

TextRange

moveToPoint Method

Moves the start and end positions of the text range to the given point.

Syntax

TextRange.moveToPoint(*iX, iY*)

Parameters

iX   Required. Horizontal offset relative to the upper-left corner of the window, in pixels.

iY   Required. Vertical offset relative to the upper-left corner of the window, in pixels.

Return Value

No return value.

Remarks

The coordinates of the point must be in pixels and be relative to the upper-left corner of the window. The resulting text range is empty, but you can expand and move the range using methods such as **expand** and **moveEnd**.

This feature might not be available on non-Win32 platforms. For the latest information on Internet Explorer cross-platform compatibility, see article Q172976 in the Microsoft Knowledge Base.

Example

The following JScript (compatible with ECMA 262 language specification) example shows how to move the text range to the point where the user clicked the mouse, expand the range, and select the text within the new range.

```
<SCRIPT FOR=document EVENT=onclick LANGUAGE="JScript"
    var rng = document.body.createTextRange();
    rng.moveToPoint(window.event.x, window.event.y);
    rng.expand("word");
    rng.select();
</SCRIPT>
```

Applies To

 WIN16   WIN32   MAC   UNIX

TextRange

namedRecordset Method

Retrieves the record set object corresponding to the named data member from a data source object.

Syntax

oRecordset = *object*.namedRecordset([*sQualifier*] [, *sSubChapter*])

Parameters

sQualifier   Required. String specifying the data member or the empty string corresponding to the default data member.

sSubChapter   Optional. String specifying the subchapter.

Return Value

Object. Returns a record set, or null if the specified data member or subchapter is unavailable.

Remarks

Valid names for a data member are specific to the data source object (DSO) implementation. Check the DOS documentation to determine if it supports named data members and to determine the valid names for those data members.

If null values or empty strings are passed to the **namedRecordset** method, the default record set is returned. This is identical to referring directly to the **recordset** property.

If the second parameter is omitted, the top-level record set is returned. If the first parameter is omitted but the second parameter is specified, the specified subchapter of the default record set is returned.

Example

The following example shows how to traverse a named record set in the handler for the **ondatasetcomplete** event of a hypothetical DSO that provides data from a spreadsheet. The name of the record set corresponds to the value of the **qualifier** property of the **event** object.

In this example, the named record set corresponds to the first seven cells of the first column of a spreadsheet.

```
<SCRIPT>
// Fired when all the data is available.
function handle_dscomplete()
{
    var oEvent = window.event;
    // Ignore the notification for the default record set.
    if (oEvent.qualifier != "")
    {
        // Get a reference to the named record set as indicated by the
        // qualifier property.
        var oNamedRS = oEvent.srcElement.namedRecordset(oEvent.qualifier);
```

```
            // Now walk the named record set.
            oNamedRS.MoveFirst();
            for (int i = 0; i < oNamedRS.RecordCount; i++)
            {
                var vValue = oNamedRS.Fields(0).value;
                oNamedRS.MoveNext();
            }
        }
    }
}
</SCRIPT>

<!-- The CLASSID below does not correspond to a valid object. -->
<OBJECT CLASSID="clsid:00000000-0000-0000-0000-000000000000" ID="dsoSpreadSheet"
    ondatasetcomplete="handle_dscomplete()">

<!-- Bind the TABLE to named record set A1:A7 provided by the spreadsheet control. -->
<TABLE DATASRC="#dsoSpreadsheet.A1:A7">
    <TR><TD><SPAN DATAFLD="A"></SPAN></TD></TR>
</TABLE>
```

Applies To

 WIN16   WIN32   MAC   UNIX

APPLET, OBJECT

navigate Method

Navigates to the URL indicated by *sURL*.

Syntax

window.navigate(*sURL*)

Parameters

sURL Required. URL to be displayed.

Return Value

No return value.

Applies To

 WIN16   WIN32   MAC

window

UNIX

window

NavigateAndFind Method

Opens a Web page, and highlights a specific string.

Syntax

window.*external*.NavigateAndFind(*sLocation*, *sQuery*, *sTargetFrame*)

Parameters

sLocation   Required. URL of a Web page.

sQuery   Required. Text to highlight on the Web page specified by *sLocation*.

sTargetFrame   Required. Name of the target frame to query.

Return Value

No return value.

Remarks

The **NavigateAndFind** method requires a full qualified path, including a location prefix (http://, c:\, and so on).

The target frame argument might be empty.

This method is not supported in HTML Applications (HTAs).

Example

The following example shows how to use the **NavigateAndFind** method to search for a word or phrase on another page.

```
<HEAD>
<SCRIPT>
function fnNAF(){
    window.external.NavigateAndFind(
        "http://www.domain.ext/path/file.htm",
        oSearchText.options[oSearchText.selectedIndex].text,"");
}
</SCRIPT>
</HEAD>
```

```
<BODY>
<SELECT id=oSearchText onchange="fnNAF()">
<OPTION>Persnickety
<OPTION>Seattle rain
<OPTION;> ...
</SELECT>
</BODY>
```

To see this code in action, refer to the Web Workshop CD-ROM.

Applies To

 WIN16   WIN32   MAC   UNIX

external

nextPage Method

Displays the next page of records in the data set to which the table is bound.

Syntax

TABLE.nextPage()

Return Value

No return value.

Remarks

The number of records displayed in the table is determined by the **dataPageSize** property of the table. You must set the **DATAPAGESIZE** attribute when designing the page, or set the corresponding **dataPageSize** property at run time for this method to have an effect.

Note You do not need to check for boundary conditions.

Applies To

 WIN16   WIN32   MAC   UNIX

TABLE

open Method

Opens a new window and loads the document given by *sURL*, or opens a blank
document if a URL is not provided.

Syntax

oNewWindow = *window*.open([*sURL*] [, *sName*] [, *sFeatures*] [, *bReplace*])

Parameters

sURL
Optional. URL of the document to display. If no URL is specified, a new
window with a blank document is displayed.

sName
Optional. Name of the window. This name is used as the value for the
TARGET attribute on a **FORM** element or an **A** element.

In Internet Explorer 5 or later, specifying the value _search opens *sURL*
in the browser's search pane.

sFeatures
Optional. Window ornaments to display. The following features are
supported.

channelmode = { yes | no | 1 | 0 }
Specifies whether to display the
window in theater mode and show the
channel band. The default is no.

directories = { yes | no | 1 | 0 }
Specifies whether to add directory
buttons. The default is yes.

fullscreen = { yes | no | 1 | 0 }
Specifies whether to display the
browser in a full-screen or normal
window. The default is no, which
displays the browser in a normal
window.

Use full-screen mode carefully.
Because this mode hides the browser's
title bar and menus, you should always
provide a button or other visual clue to
help the user close the window. The
user can press ALT+F4 to close the
new window.

height = *number*
Specifies the height of the window, in
pixels. The minimum value is 100.

Parameters *(continued)*

left = *number*	Specifies the left position, in pixels. This value is relative to the upper-left corner of the screen.
location = { yes | no | 1 | 0 }	Specifies whether to display the input field for entering URLs directly into the browser. The default is yes.
menubar = { yes | no | 1 | 0 }	Specifies whether to display the menu bar. The default is yes.
resizable = { yes | no | 1 | 0 }	Specifies whether to display resize handles at the corners of the window. The default is yes.
scrollbars = { yes | no | 1 | 0 }	Specifies whether to display horizontal and vertical scroll bars. The default is yes.
status = { yes | no | 1 | 0 }	Specifies whether to add a status bar at the bottom of the window. The default is yes.
titlebar = { yes | no | 1 | 0 }	Specifies whether to display a title bar for the window. This parameter is ignored unless the caller is an HTML Application or a trusted dialog box. The default is yes.
toolbar = { yes | no | 1 | 0 }	Specifies whether to display the browser toolbar, making buttons, such as Back, Forward, and Stop, available. The default is yes.
top = *number*	Specifies the top position, in pixels. This value is relative to the upper-left corner of the screen.
width = *number*	Sets the width of the window, in pixels. The minimum value is 100.

bReplace   Optional. Value that specifies whether the URL that is loaded into the new page should become a new entry in the window's browsing history or replace the current entry in the browsing history. If set to true, no new history entry is created.

Return Value

Returns a reference to the new window object. Use this reference when scripting properties and methods on the new window.

Remarks

By default, the **open** method creates a window that has a default width and height and the standard menu, toolbar, and other features of Internet Explorer. You can alter this set of features by using the *sFeatures* parameter. This parameter is a string consisting of one or more feature settings. When one feature is specified, any additional features that are not specified are disabled. If no features are specified, the window features maintain their default values. In addition to enabling a feature with the specified possible value, simply listing the feature name also enables that feature for the new window.

Internet Explorer 5 allows further control over windows through implementation of `title` in the *sFeatures* parameter of the **open** method. Turn off the title bar by opening the window from a trusted application, such as Visual Basic or an HTML Application (HTA). These applications are considered trusted because each uses Internet Explorer interfaces instead of the browser.

Example

The following example shows how to create a new window that contains Sample.htm. The new window is 200 pixels by 400 pixels and has a status bar, but it does not have a toolbar, menu bar, or address field.

```
window.open("sample.htm",null,
    "height=200,width=400,status=yes,toolbar=no,
        menubar=no,location=no");
```

Applies To

WIN16	WIN32	MAC

window

UNIX

window

open Method

Opens a document to collect the output of **write** or **writeln** methods.

Syntax

document.open(*sMimeType* [, *sReplace*])

Parameters

sMimeType   Required. String specifying the MIME type. Currently supports text/html only.

sReplace   Optional. String ("replace") specifying whether the new document being written is to replace the current document in the History list. Otherwise, by default, the document being created does not replace the current document in the History list.

Return Value

No return value.

Example

The following example shows how to replace the existing document with the new document.

```
document.open("text/html", "replace")
```

Applies To

 WIN16   WIN32   MAC

document

 UNIX

document

parentElement Method

Retrieves the parent element for the given text range. The parent element is the element that completely encloses the text in the range.

Syntax

oElement = *TextRange*.parentElement()

Return Value

Returns an element object if successful, or null otherwise.

Remarks

If the text range spans text in more than one element, this method returns the smallest element that encloses all the elements. When you insert text into a range that spans multiple elements, the text is placed in the parent element rather than in any of the contained elements.

This feature might not be available on non-Win32 platforms. For the latest information on Internet Explorer cross-platform compatibility, see article Q172976 in the Microsoft Knowledge Base.

Example

The following JScript (compatible with ECMA 262 language specification) example shows how to retrieve the parent element for the text range created from the current selection and display the tag name of the element.

```
var sel = document.selection;
var rng = sel.createRange();
var el = rng.parentElement();
alert(el.tagName);
```

Applies To

 WIN16   WIN32   MAC   UNIX

TextRange

pasteHTML Method

Pastes HTML text into the given text range. The text replaces any previous text and HTML elements in the range.

Syntax

TextRange.pasteHTML(*sHTMLText*)

Parameters

sHTMLText   Required. HTML text to paste. The string can contain text and any combination of the HTML tags described in HTML Elements. For more information, see the Web Workshop CD-ROM.

Return Value

No return value.

Remarks

Although this method never fails, it might alter the HTML text to make it fit the given text range. For example, pasting a table cell into a text range that does not contain a table might cause the method to insert a **TABLE** element. For predictable results, paste into the text only well-formed HTML text that fits within the given text range.

This method is accessible at run time. If elements get removed at run time before the closing tag is parsed, areas of the document might not render.

This feature might not be available on non-Win32 platforms. For the latest information on Internet Explorer cross-platform compatibility, see article Q172976 in the Microsoft Knowledge Base.

Example

The following JScript (compatible with ECMA 262 language specification) example shows how to replace the current selection with a new paragraph.

```
var sel = document.selection;
if (sel!=null) {
    var rng = sel.createRange();
    if (rng!=null)
        rng.pasteHTML("<P><B>Selection has been replaced.</B></P>");
}
```

Applies To

 WIN16   WIN32   MAC   UNIX

TextRange

previousPage Method

Scrolls into view the previous page of records in the data set.

Syntax

table.previousPage()

Return Value

No return value.

Remarks

The **dataPageSize** property of the table determines the number of records displayed in the table. You must set the **DATAPAGESIZE** attribute when designing the page, or set the corresponding **dataPageSize** property at run time for this method to have an effect.

Note You do not need to check for boundary conditions.

Applies To

 WIN16   WIN32   MAC   UNIX

TABLE

print Method

Prints the document associated with the window.

Syntax

window.print()

Return Value

No return value.

Remarks

Calling the **print** method has the same effect as choosing Print from the Internet Explorer File menu. The **print** method activates the print dialog box, prompting the user to change print settings. When the user clicks the OK button, the following sequence of events occurs.

1. The **onbeforeprint** event fires.

2. The document prints.

3. The **onafterprint** event fires.

The **onbeforeprint** and **onafterprint** events are particularly useful when not all the information on the page is visible at all times. Using the **onbeforeprint** event, you can modify the document to make all the information on the page visible for printing purposes. Using the **onafterprint** event, you can return the document to its original state.

Applies To

	WIN16	WIN32	MAC	UNIX

window

prompt Method

Displays a Prompt dialog box with a message and an input field.

Syntax

vTextData = window.prompt([*sMessage*] [, *sDefaultValue*])

Parameters

> *sMessage*   Optional. String specifying the message to display in the dialog box. By default, this parameter is set to empty.
>
> *sDefaultValue* Optional. String specifying the default value of the input field. By default, this parameter is set to `undefined`.

Return Value

> String or Integer. Returns the value typed in by the user.

Remarks

> The title of the prompt dialog box cannot be changed.

Applies To

 WIN16   WIN32   MAC

window

 UNIX

window

queryCommandEnabled Method

> Returns whether the command can be successfully executed using **execCommand**, given the current state of the document.

Syntax

> *bEnabled* = *object*.`queryCommandEnabled(`*sCmdID*`)`

Parameters

> *sCmdID* Required. String specifying a command identifier. For more information, see "Command Identifiers" in Appendix C.

Return Value

> Boolean. Returns `true` if the command is enabled, or `false` otherwise.

Remarks

> Using **queryCommandEnabled**("delete") on a **TextRange** object returns `true`, while using **queryCommandEanbled**("delete") on a **document** object returns `false`. However, **execCommand**("delete") can still be used to delete the selected text.

Applies To

 WIN16   WIN32   MAC   UNIX

document, TextRange

 WIN16   WIN32   MAC   UNIX

controlRange

queryCommandIndeterm Method

Returns whether the specified command is in the indeterminate state.

Syntax

$bIndeterminate$ = $object$.queryCommandIndeterm($sCmdID$)

Parameters

sCmdID   Required. String specifying a command identifier. For more information, see "Command Identifiers" in Appendix C.

Return Value

Boolean. Returns true if indeterminate, or false otherwise.

Applies To

 WIN16   WIN32   MAC   UNIX

document, TextRange

 WIN16   WIN32   MAC   UNIX

controlRange

queryCommandState Method

Returns the current state of the command.

Syntax

$bDone$ = $object$.queryCommandState($sCmdID$)

Parameters

sCmdID   Required. String specifying a command identifier. For more information, see "Command Identifiers" in Appendix C.

Return Value

Boolean. Returns `true` if the given command has been carried out on the object, `false` if it has not, and `null` if it is not possible to determine the command state.

Applies To

WIN16	WIN32	MAC	UNIX

document, TextRange

WIN16	WIN32	MAC	UNIX

controlRange

queryCommandSupported Method

Returns whether the current command is supported on the current range.

Syntax

bSupported = *object*.`queryCommandSupported`(*sCmdID*)

Parameters

sCmdID   Required. String specifying a command identifier. For more information, see "Command Identifiers" in Appendix C.

Return Value

Boolean. Returns `true` if the command is supported, or `false` otherwise.

Applies To

WIN16	WIN32	MAC	UNIX

document, TextRange

WIN16	WIN32	MAC	UNIX

controlRange

queryCommandValue Method

Returns the current value of the given command.

Syntax

vCmdValue = `object.queryCommandValue(sCmdID)`

Parameters

sCmdID   Required. String specifying a command identifier. For more information, see "Command Identifiers" in Appendix C.

Return Value

String or Boolean. Returns a string representing the command value if the command is supported, or `true/false` otherwise.

Remarks

If the command returns a value, such as a color, rather than a `true/false` state, this command is used to retrieve the current value of the document or range.

Applies To

WIN16	WIN32	MAC	UNIX

document, TextRange

WIN16	WIN32	MAC	UNIX

controlRange

recalc Method

Recalculates all dynamic properties in the current document.

Syntax

document.`recalc([bForceAll])`

Parameters

bForceAll   Optional. If set to `true`, this method evaluates all expressions in the document. If set to `false`, only those expressions that reference properties that have changed since the last recalculation are recalculated. The default value is `false`.

Return Value

No return value.

Remarks

Implicit dependencies refer to properties that might be altered by changes in other properties. For instance, the **height** of a **DIV** implicitly depends on the **innerHTML** of the **DIV**. However, if an expression references the **height**, a change in the **innerHTML**, which may alter the **height**, does not cause a recalculation of the expression on a subsequent call to **recalc**.

Internal property changes might not prompt recalculations of expressions referencing such properties on subsequent calls to **recalc**. For instance, resizing the main window changes **document.body.clientWidth**. Expressions that reference **clientWidth** may not be recalculated because the change may not be recognized.

Related properties are properties that access or manipulate data or behavior that is also accessed or manipulated by one or more other properties. For instance, **pixelLeft** and **posLeft** set or retrieve the left position of the element. However, if an expression that references **element.pixelLeft** and **element.posLeft** is altered, the expression may not be recalculated on subsequent calls to **recalc**.

Related properties that might result in this behavior include the following: **clientHeight**, **clientLeft**, **clientTop**, **clientWidth**, **height**, **left**, **offsetHeight**, **offsetLeft**, **offsetTop**, **offsetWidth**, **pixelHeight**, **pixelLeft**, **pixelTop**, **pixelWidth**, **posHeight**, **posLeft**, **posTop**, **posWidth**, and **top.**

You should refer to the same property name or manually call **recalc(true)** to force recalculations of all expressions.

Example

The following examples show how to use **recalc** in both HTML and scripting.

The example below shows how to use **recalc** in HTML.

```
<INPUT TYPE=text ID=oBox1 value=40>The sum of the values in
    these two text boxes determines the width
<BR><INPUT TYPE=text ID=oBox2 value=40>of the blue text
    box below.
<BR><INPUT TYPE=text ID=oBox3
    STYLE="width:expression(eval(oBox1.value) +
    eval(oBox2.value)); background-color:blue">
<BR><INPUT TYPE=button ID=Button
    value="Click to resize blue box above" onclick="recalc()">
```

To see this code in action, refer to the Web Workshop CD-ROM.

DHTML Methods

The same functionality can be implemented in script as shown in the following code.

```
<INPUT TYPE=text ID=oBox1 value=40>The sum of the values in
    these two text boxes determines the
<BR><INPUT TYPE=text ID=oBox2 value=40>width of the
    blue text box below.
<BR><INPUT TYPE=text ID=oBox3 STYLE="background-color:blue">
<BR><INPUT TYPE=button ID=Button
    value="Click to resize blue box above" onclick="update()">

<SCRIPT>
oBox3.style.setExpression("width","eval(oBox1.value) +
    eval(oBox2.value)","jscript");
function update()
{
    document.recalc();
}
</SCRIPT>
```

To see this code in action, refer to the Web Workshop CD-ROM.

The example below shows how to define a style that works in previous versions of Internet Explorer. This sample HTML positions the **DIV** at 200px, 200px on Internet Explorer 4.0, but animates over time on Internet Explorer 5.

```
<Div style="position: absolute; top: 200px; left: 200px;
left: function(time.ms / 100);" />
```

To see this code in action, refer to the Web Workshop CD-ROM.

Applies To

IE 5	WIN16	WIN32	MAC	UNIX

document

refresh Method

Refreshes the content of the table.

Syntax

table.refresh()

Return Value

No return value.

Applies To

 WIN16   WIN32   MAC   UNIX

TABLE

releaseCapture Method

Removes mouse capture from the object in the current document.

Syntax

object.releaseCapture()

Return Value

No return value.

Remarks

For **releaseCapture** to have an effect, you must set mouse capture through the **setCapture** method.

You can invoke the **releaseCapture** method off the **document** object. The **releaseCapture** method makes it unnecessary to determine which element has capture to programmatically release it. Other actions also release document capture, such as displaying a modal dialog box and switching focus to another application or browser window.

Example

The following example shows how to invoke the **releaseCapture** method on the document object.

```
<BODY onload="oOwnCapture.setCapture();"
    onclick="document.releaseCapture();">
<DIV ID=oOwnCapture
    onmousemove="oWriteLocation.value =
        event.clientX + event.clientY";
    onlosecapture="alert(event.srcElement.id +
        ' has lost mouse capture.')">
<TEXTAREA ID=oWriteLocation COLS=2></TEXTAREA>
</DIV>
<HR>
<DIV ID=oNoCapture>
<P>Click on the document to invoke the releaseCapture method.</P>
</DIV>
</BODY>
```

To see this code in action, refer to the Web Workshop CD-ROM.

DHTML Methods

Applies To

 WIN16   WIN32   MAC   UNIX

A, ADDRESS, APPLET, AREA, B, BIG, BLOCKQUOTE, BODY, BR, BUTTON, CAPTION, CENTER, CITE, CODE, DD, DFN, DIR, DIV, DL, document, DT, EM, EMBED, FIELDSET, FONT, FORM, Hn, HR, I, IMG, INPUT type=button, INPUT type=checkbox, INPUT type=file, INPUT type=hidden, INPUT type=image, INPUT type=password, INPUT type=radio, INPUT type=reset, INPUT type=submit, INPUT type=text, KBD, LABEL, LEGEND, LI, LISTING, MAP, MARQUEE, MENU, NOBR, OBJECT, OL, OPTION, P, PLAINTEXT, PRE, S, SAMP, SELECT, SMALL, SPAN, STRIKE, STRONG, SUB, SUP, TABLE, TBODY, TD, TEXTAREA, TFOOT, TH, THEAD, TR, TT, U, UL, VAR, XMP

reload Method

Reloads the current page.

Syntax

location.reload([*bReloadSource*])

Parameters

bReloadSource   Optional. Boolean value specifying whether to reload the page from the cache or server. If true, the page is reloaded from the server. By default, this parameter is false.

Return Value

No return value.

Applies To

 WIN16   WIN32   MAC   UNIX

location

remove Method

Removes an element from the collection.

Syntax

object.remove(*iIndex*)

Parameters

iIndex   Required. Integer specifying the zero-based index of the element to remove from the collection.

Return Value

No return value.

Applies To

WIN16	WIN32	MAC	UNIX

areas, options

WIN16	WIN32	MAC	UNIX

controlRange

removeAttribute Method

Removes the given attribute from the object.

Syntax

bSuccess = *object*.removeAttribute(*sName* [, *iCaseSensitive*])

Parameters

sName   Required. String specifying the attribute name.

iCaseSensitive   Optional. Integer specifying whether to use a case-sensitive search to locate the attribute. By default, this value is set to 1 to indicate that the uppercase and lowercase letters in the specified *sName* parameter must exactly match those in the attribute name. If there are multiple attributes specified with different case sensitivity, the attribute returned might vary across platforms.

Return Value

Boolean. Returns true if successful, or false otherwise.

Remarks

If two or more attributes have the same name (differing only in uppercase and lowercase letters) and *iCaseSensitive* is set to 0, this method removes only the last attribute to be created with this name. All other attributes of the same name are ignored.

Applies To

 WIN16   WIN32   MAC   UNIX

A, ADDRESS, APPLET, AREA, B, BASE, BASEFONT, BGSOUND, BIG,
BLOCKQUOTE, BODY, BR, BUTTON, CAPTION, CENTER, CITE, CODE, COL,
COLGROUP, COMMENT, DD, DFN, DIR, DIV, DL, DT, EM, EMBED, FIELDSET,
FONT, FORM, FRAME, FRAMESET, HEAD, Hn, HR, HTML, I, IFRAME, IMG,
INPUT type=button, INPUT type=checkbox, INPUT type=file, INPUT type=hidden,
INPUT type=image, INPUT type=password, INPUT type=radio, INPUT type=reset,
INPUT type=submit, INPUT type=text, KBD, LABEL, LEGEND, LI, LINK,
LISTING, MAP, MARQUEE, MENU, META, NEXTID, NOBR, OBJECT, OL,
OPTION, P, PLAINTEXT, PRE, S, SAMP, SCRIPT, SELECT, SMALL, SPAN,
STRIKE, STRONG, SUB, SUP, TABLE, TBODY, TD, TEXTAREA, TFOOT, TH,
THEAD, TITLE, TR, TT, U, UL, VAR, WBR, XMP

removeBehavior Method

Detaches a behavior from the element.

Syntax

bSuccess = object.removeBehavior(*iID*)

Parameters

iID   Required. Identifier returned from a previous **addBehavior** call.

Return Value

Boolean. Returns true if the behavior was removed successfully, or false otherwise.

Example

The following example shows how to dynamically remove a behavior that implements
a mouseover highlighting effect from all **LI** elements on a page.

```
<SCRIPT LANGUAGE="JScript">
var collBehaviorID = new Array();
var collLI = new Array ();
var countLI = 0;

    :
function detachBehavior()
{
    for (i=0; i < countLI; i++)
        collLI[i].removeBehavior (collBehaviorID [i]);
}
```

```
</SCRIPT>

:
Click <A HREF="javascript:detachBehavior()">here</A>
to remove highlighting effect.
:
```

To see this code in action, refer to the Web Workshop CD-ROM.

Applies To

 WIN16   WIN32   MAC   UNIX

A, ACRONYM, ADDRESS, APPLET, AREA, B, BASE, BASEFONT, BGSOUND, BIG, BLOCKQUOTE, BODY, BR, BUTTON, CAPTION, CENTER, CITE, CODE, COL, COLGROUP, COMMENT, DD, DEL, DFN, DIR, DIV, DL, DT, EM, EMBED, FIELDSET, FONT, FORM, FRAME, FRAMESET, HEAD, Hn, HR, HTML, I, IFRAME, IMG, INPUT type=button, INPUT type=checkbox, INPUT type=file, INPUT type=hidden, INPUT type=image, INPUT type=password, INPUT type=radio, INPUT type=reset, INPUT type=submit, INPUT type=text, INS, ISINDEX, KBD, LABEL, LEGEND, LI, LINK, LISTING, MAP, MARQUEE, MENU, NEXTID, NOBR, NOFRAMES, NOSCRIPT, OBJECT, OL, OPTION, P, PLAINTEXT, PRE, Q, RT, RUBY, S, SAMP, SCRIPT, SELECT, SMALL, SPAN, STRIKE, STRONG, STYLE, SUB, SUP, TABLE, TBODY, TD, TEXTAREA, TFOOT, TH, THEAD, TITLE, TR, TT, U, UL, VAR, WBR, XML, XMP

removeChild Method

Removes a child node from an element.

Syntax

oRemove = *object*.removeChild(*oNode*)

Parameters

oNode   Required. Element to be removed from the document.

Return Value

Returns a referencc to the object that is removed.

Remarks

The node to be removed must be an immediate child of the parent object.

This method is accessible at run time. If elements get removed at run time before the closing tag is parsed, areas of the document might not render.

Example

The following example shows how to remove a bold element from a **DIV** using the **removeChild** method.

```
<HEAD>
<SCRIPT>
function removeElement()
{
  try
  {
      //The first child of the div is the bold element.
    var oChild=Div1.children(0);
    Div1.removeChild(oChild);
  }
  catch(x)
  {
    alert("You have already removed the bold element.
      Page is refreshed when you click OK.")
    document.location.reload();
  }
}
</SCRIPT>
</HEAD>
<BODY>
<DIV ID=Div1 onclick="removeElement()">
Click anywhere in this sentence to remove this<B> Bold</B> word.
</DIV>
</BODY>
```

Applies To

 WIN16   WIN32   MAC   UNIX

A, ACRONYM, ADDRESS, B, BDO, BIG, BLOCKQUOTE, BODY, BUTTON, CAPTION, CENTER, CITE, CODE, COL, COLGROUP, COMMENT, DD, DEL, DFN, DIR, DIV, DL, DT, EM, FIELDSET, FONT, FORM, FRAMESET, HEAD, Hn, HTML, I, IFRAME, INPUT type=button, INPUT type=checkbox, INPUT type=file, INPUT type=hidden, INPUT type=image, INPUT type=password, INPUT type=radio, INPUT type=reset, INPUT type=submit, INPUT type=text, INS, KBD, LABEL, LEGEND, LI, LISTING, MAP, MARQUEE, MENU, NEXTID, OL, OPTION, P, PLAINTEXT, PRE, Q, S, SAMP, SELECT, SMALL, SPAN, STRIKE, STRONG, SUB, SUP, TABLE, TBODY, TD, TEXTAREA, TFOOT, TH, THEAD, TR, TT, U, UL, VAR, XMP

removeExpression Method

Removes an expression from the given property.

Syntax

bSuccess = *object*.removeExpression(*sPropertyName*)

Parameters

sPropertyName Required. Name of the property from which to remove an expression.

Return Value

Boolean. Returns true if the expression was successfully removed, or false otherwise.

Remarks

The value of the property after the expression has been removed is equal to the last computed value of the expression. You can remove expressions set by the **setExpression** method only by invoking **removeExpression**.

The **removeExpression** method applies to the **style** subobject and can be used to remove expressions from supported cascading style sheets (CSS) attributes. This method also is available in scripting for the **innerHTML** and **value** properties.

The following example shows how to use **removeExpression** in script.

```
object.removeExpression(sProperty, sExpression, sLanguage)
```

The following example shows how to use **removeExpression** on a style.

```
object.style.removeExpression(sProperty, sExpression, sLanguage)
```

Example

The following example shows how to use the **removeExpression** method. The width of the blue box is defined as an expression equal to the sum of the two values in the first two text boxes. The first button brings up an alert box revealing the expression for the width of the blue box. The second button removes the expression. The third button brings up another alert box revealing the expression for the width of the blue box. However, the blue box no longer has an expression for its width, so **getExpression** returns undefined. After the expression is removed, the value for the blue box's **width** property remains equal to the last calculated value of the expression.

```
<INPUT TYPE=text ID=oBox1 value=40>The sum of the values in
    these two text boxes determines the width
<BR><INPUT TYPE=text ID=oBox2 value=40>of the blue
    text box below.
<BR><INPUT TYPE=text ID=oBox3 STYLE="background-color:blue">
<BR><BR><INPUT TYPE=button ID=Button1
    value="Step 1: Get expression" onclick="getexp()">
<INPUT TYPE=button ID=Button2 value="Step 2: Remove expression"
    onclick="remexp()">
<INPUT TYPE=button ID=Button3 value="Step 3: Get expression again"
    onclick="getexp()">
<BR>
<HR>
<BR>
Right-click anywhere on this page to view the source code.

<SCRIPT>
var s;
var b;
oBox3.style.setExpression("width","eval(oBox1.value) +
    eval(oBox2.value)","jscript");

function getexp()
{
    s=oBox3.style.getExpression("width");
    alert("Expression for the width of the blue box is \n\n" + s +
    "\n\nThe width property has a value of " + oBox3.style.width);
}
function remexp()
{
    b = oBox3.style.removeExpression("width");
    alert("Expression removed successfully? \n" + b);
}
</SCRIPT>
```

To see this code in action, refer to the Web Workshop CD-ROM.

Applies To

 WIN16   WIN32   MAC   UNIX

A, ACRONYM, ADDRESS, APPLET, AREA, B, BDO, BIG, BLOCKQUOTE,
BODY, BR, BUTTON, CAPTION, CENTER, CITE, CODE, COL, COLGROUP,
DD, DEL, DFN, DIR, DIV, DL, DT, EM, EMBED, FIELDSET, FONT, FORM, Hn,
HR, I, IFRAME, IMG, INPUT type=button, INPUT type=checkbox, INPUT
type=file, INPUT type=hidden, INPUT type=image, INPUT type=password, INPUT
type=radio, INPUT type=reset, INPUT type=submit, INPUT type=text, INS, KBD,
LABEL, LEGEND, LI, LISTING, MARQUEE, MENU, NOBR, OBJECT, OL,
OPTION, P, PARAM, PRE, Q, RT, RUBY, S, SAMP, SELECT, SMALL, SPAN,
STRIKE, STRONG, style, SUB, SUP, TABLE, TBODY, TD, TEXTAREA, TFOOT,
TH, THEAD, TR, TT, U, UL, VAR

removeNode Method

Removes the object from the document hierarchy.

Syntax

oRemoved = *object*.removeNode(*bRemoveChildren*)

Parameters

bRemoveChildren   Optional. If set to `true`, the **ChildNodes** collection of the object is removed from the hierarchy; if set to false, it is not. The default value is `false`.

Return Value

Returns a reference to the object that is removed.

Remarks

This property is accessible at run time. Removing elements at run time, before the closing tag has been parsed, could prevent other areas of the document from rendering.

Example

The following example shows how to use the **removeNode** method to remove a table from the document hierarchy.

```
<SCRIPT>
function fnRemove(){
    // 'true' possible value specifies removal of childNodes also.
    oTable.removeNode(true);
}
</SCRIPT>

<TABLE ID = oTable>
<TR>
<TD>Cell 1</TD>
<TD>Cell 2</TD>
</TR>
</TABLE>

<INPUT TYPE = button VALUE = "Remove Table" onclick = "fnRemove()">
```

Applies To

 WIN16   WIN32   MAC   UNIX

A, ACRONYM, ADDRESS, B, BDO, BIG, BLOCKQUOTE, BODY, BUTTON, CAPTION, CENTER, CITE, CODE, COL, COLGROUP, COMMENT, DD, DEL, DFN, DIR, DIV, DL, DT, EM, FIELDSET, FONT, FORM, FRAMESET, HEAD, Hn, HTML, I, IFRAME, INPUT type=button, INPUT type=checkbox, INPUT type=file, INPUT type=image, INPUT type=password, INPUT type=radio, INPUT type=reset, INPUT type=submit, INPUT type=text, INS, KBD, LABEL, LEGEND, LI, LISTING, MAP, MARQUEE, MENU, NEXTID, OBJECT, OL, OPTION, P, PLAINTEXT, PRE, Q, S, SAMP, SELECT, SMALL, SPAN, STRIKE, STRONG, SUB, SUP, TABLE, TBODY, TD, TEXTAREA, TFOOT, TH, THEAD, TR, TT, U, UL, VAR, XMP

removeRule Method

Deletes an existing style rule for the **styleSheet** object, and adjusts the index of the **rules** collection accordingly.

Syntax

styleSheet.removeRule[*iIndex*]

Parameters

iIndex   Optional. Integer specifying the index value of the rule that is to be deleted from the style sheet. If an index is not provided, the last rule in the **rules** collection is removed.

Return Value

No return value.

Remarks

The page does not automatically reflow when the rule is removed. You have to reflow the page to see the change. You can reflow the objects affected using a number of methods. For example, you can reflow the style change only on affected text by setting the text equal to itself as shown in the following example. Alternatively, you can reload the entire page using the **reload** method. When you use the **refresh** method on a table, its content is reflowed.

Example

The following example shows how to delete a rule from the **rules** collection, and reflow the text according to the new rules.

```
<STYLE>
P {color:green}
</STYLE>
:
<SCRIPT>
function removeTheRule() {
    // Style sheets and rules are zero-based collections; therefore,
    // the first item is item 0 in the collection.
    var iSheets = document.styleSheets.length;
    var iRules = document.styleSheets[iSheets-1].rules.length;
    // Make sure there is a rule to delete.
    if (1 < iRules) {
        document.styleSheets[iSheets-1].removeRule(1);
        // Force the page to render the change.
        oEffectRules.innerHTML=oEffectRules.innerHTML;
    }
}
</SCRIPT>
:
<P ID=oEffectRules>This text has the new style applied to it.
</P>
:
<BUTTON onclick="removeTheRule()">Remove the new rule.</BUTTON>
```

To see this code in action, refer to the Web Workshop CD-ROM.

Applies To

WIN16	WIN32	MAC	UNIX

A, ACRONYM, ADDRESS, B, BDO, BIG, BLOCKQUOTE, BODY, BUTTON, CAPTION, CENTER, CITE, CODE, COL, COLGROUP, COMMENT, DD, DEL, DFN, DIR, DIV, DL, DT, EM, FIELDSET, FONT, FORM, FRAMESET, HEAD, Hn, HTML, I, IFRAME, INPUT type=button, INPUT type=checkbox, INPUT type=file, INPUT type=image, INPUT type=password, INPUT type=radio, INPUT type=reset, INPUT type=submit, INPUT type=text, INS, KBD, LABEL, LEGEND, LI, LISTING, MAP, MARQUEE, MENU, NEXTID, OL, OPTION, P, PLAINTEXT, PRE, Q, S, SAMP, SELECT, SMALL, SPAN, STRIKE, STRONG, SUB, SUP, TABLE, TBODY, TD, TEXTAREA, TFOOT, TH, THEAD, TR, TT, U, UL, VAR, XMP

replace Method

Replaces the current document by loading the document at the specified URL.

Syntax

location.replace(*sURL*)

Parameters

sURL   Required. String specifying the URL to insert into the session history.

Return Value

No return value.

Remarks

Replacing a document causes it to be inaccessible through the **history** object. Also, the URL is no longer accessible through the user interface navigation methods (like the Back and Forward buttons).

Applies To

 WIN16   WIN32   MAC   UNIX

location

replaceAdjacentText Method

Replaces the adjacent text character.

Syntax

object.replaceAdjacentText(*sWhere*, *sReplaceText*)

Parameters

sWhere   Required. Position where the text to be replaced is located. This position can be one of the following:

beforeBegin   Text is replaced immediately before the element.

afterBegin   Text is replaced after the start of the element, but before all other content in the element.

beforeEnd   Text is replaced immediately before the end of the element, but after all other content in the element.

Parameters *(continued)*

        `afterEnd`   Text is replaced immediately after the end of the element.

  sReplaceText   Required. Replacement text.

Return Value

No return value.

Applies To

WIN16	**WIN32**	**MAC**	**UNIX**

A, ACRONYM, ADDRESS, APPLET, AREA, B, BASE, BASEFONT, BDO, BIG, BLOCKQUOTE, BODY, BR, BUTTON, CAPTION, CENTER, CITE, CODE, COL, COLGROUP, COMMENT, DD, DEL, DFN, DIR, DIV, DL, DT, EM, EMBED, FIELDSET, FONT, FORM, FRAME, FRAMESET, HEAD, Hn, HR, HTML, I, IFRAME, IMG, INPUT type=button, INPUT type=checkbox, INPUT type=file, INPUT type=hidden, INPUT type=image, INPUT type=password, INPUT type=radio, INPUT type=reset, INPUT type=submit, INPUT type=text, INS, KBD, LABEL, LEGEND, LI, LINK, LISTING, MAP, MARQUEE, MENU, NEXTID, OBJECT, OL, OPTION, P, PLAINTEXT, PRE, Q, S, SAMP, SCRIPT, SELECT, SMALL, SPAN, STRIKE, STRONG, SUB, SUP, TABLE, TBODY, TD, TEXTAREA, TFOOT, TH, THEAD, TITLE, TR, TT, U, UL, VAR, XMP

replaceChild Method

Replaces an existing child element with a new child element.

Syntax

oReplace = *object*.`replaceChild`(*oNewNode*, *oOldNode*)

Parameters

  oNewNode   Required. New element to be inserted into the document. You can create new elements using the **createElement** method.

  oOldNode   Required. Existing element to be replaced.

Return Value

Returns a reference to the object that is replaced.

Remarks

The node to be replaced must be an immediate child of the parent object. The new node must be created using the **createElement** method.

This method is accessible at run time. If elements are removed at run time, before the closing tag is parsed, areas of the document might not render..

Example

The following example shows how to use the **replaceChild** method to replace a bold element from a **DIV** with an italic element.

```
<HEAD>
<SCRIPT>
function replaceElement()
{
        //The first child of the div is the bold element.
    var oChild=Div1.children(0);
    var sInnerHTML = oChild.innerHTML;
    if (oChild.tagName=="B")
    {
        oNewChild=document.createElement("I");
        Div1.replaceChild(oNewChild, oChild);
        oNewChild.innerHTML=sInnerHTML
    }
    else
    {
        oNewChild=document.createElement("B");
        Div1.replaceChild(oNewChild, oChild);
        oNewChild.innerHTML=sInnerHTML
    }
}
</SCRIPT>
</HEAD>
<BODY>
<DIV ID=Div1 onclick="replaceElement()">
Click anywhere in this sentence to toggle this <B>word</B>
between bold and italic.</DIV>
</BODY>
```

Applies To

 WIN16   WIN32   MAC   UNIX

A, ACRONYM, ADDRESS, B, BDO, BIG, BLOCKQUOTE, BODY, BUTTON, CAPTION, CENTER, CITE, CODE, COL, COLGROUP, COMMENT, DD, DEL, DFN, DIR, DIV, DL, DT, EM, FIELDSET, FONT, FORM, FRAMESET, HEAD, Hn, HTML, I, IFRAME, INPUT type=button, INPUT type=checkbox, INPUT type=file, INPUT type=hidden, INPUT type=image, INPUT type=password,

Applies To *(continued)*

WIN16	WIN32	MAC	UNIX

INPUT type=radio, INPUT type=reset, INPUT type=submit, INPUT type=text, INS, KBD, LABEL, LEGEND, LI, LISTING, MAP, MARQUEE, MENU, NEXTID, OL, OPTION, P, PLAINTEXT, PRE, Q, S, SAMP, SELECT, SMALL, SPAN, STRIKE, STRONG, SUB, SUP, TABLE, TBODY, TD, TEXTAREA, TFOOT, TH, THEAD, TR, TT, U, UL, VAR, XMP

replaceNode Method

Replaces the object with another element.

Syntax

oReplace = *object*.replaceNode(*oNewNode*)

Parameters

oNewNode   Required. New element to replace the object.

Return Value

Returns a reference to the object that is replaced.

Remarks

When a node is replaced, all values associated with the replaced object are removed. For example, if a **B** object is replaced with an **I** object, any attributes and text between the opening and closing tags are also replaced. To preserve these values, copy them to the new element before replacing the original object.

This method is accessible at run time. Removing elements at run time, before the closing tag has been parsed, could prevent other areas of the document from rendering.

Example

The following example shows how to use the **replaceNode** method to replace an unordered list with an ordered list.

```
<SCRIPT>
function fnReplace(){
    var sPreserve = oList.innerHTML;
    var oNewNode = document.createElement("OL");
    oList.replaceNode(oNewNode);
    oNewNode.innerHTML = sPreserve;
}
```

```
</SCRIPT>

<UL ID = oList>
<LI>List Item 1
<LI>List Item 2
<LI>List Item 3
<LI>List Item 4
</UL>
<INPUT TYPE = button VALUE = "Replace List" onclick = "fnReplace()">
```

Applies To

 WIN16   WIN32   MAC   UNIX

A, ACRONYM, ADDRESS, B, BDO, BIG, BLOCKQUOTE, BODY, BUTTON, CAPTION, CENTER, CITE, CODE, COL, COLGROUP, COMMENT, DD, DEL, DFN, DIR, DIV, DL, DT, EM, FIELDSET, FONT, FORM, FRAMESET, HEAD, Hn, HTML, I, IFRAME, INPUT type=button, INPUT type=checkbox, INPUT type=file, INPUT type=image, INPUT type=password, INPUT type=radio, INPUT type=reset, INPUT type=submit, INPUT type=text, INS, KBD, LABEL, LEGEND, LI, LISTING, MAP, MARQUEE, MENU, NEXTID, OBJECT, OL, OPTION, P, PLAINTEXT, PRE, Q, S, SAMP, SELECT, SMALL, SPAN, STRIKE, STRONG, SUB, SUP, TABLE, TBODY, TD, TEXTAREA, TFOOT, TH, THEAD, TR, TT, U, UL, VAR, XMP

reset Method

Simulates a mouse click on a reset button for the calling form.

Syntax

form.reset()

Return Value

No return value.

Applies To

 WIN16   WIN32   MAC   UNIX

form

resizeBy Method

Changes the current size of the window by the specified x- and y-offset.

Syntax

window.resizeBy(*iX*, *iY*)

Parameters

iX   Required. Integer specifying the horizontal offset, in pixels.

iY   Required. Integer specifying the vertical offset, in pixels.

Return Value

No return value.

Applies To

 WIN16   WIN32   MAC   UNIX

window

resizeTo Method

Sets the size of the window to the specified width and length values.

Syntax

window.resizeTo(*iWidth*, *iHeight*)

Parameters

iWidth   Required. Integer specifying the width of the window, in pixels.

iHeight   Required. Integer specifying the height of the window, in pixels.

Return Value

No return value.

Applies To

 WIN16   WIN32   MAC   UNIX

window

scroll Method

Causes the window to scroll to the specified x- and y-offset at the upper-left corner of the window.

Syntax

window.scroll(*iX*, *iY*)

Parameters

iX　Required. Integer specifying the horizontal scroll offset, in pixels.

iY　Required. Integer specifying the vertical scroll offset, in pixels.

Return Value

No return value.

Remarks

This method is provided for backward compatibility only. The recommended way to scroll a window is to use the **scrollTo** method.

Applies To

WIN16	WIN32	MAC	UNIX

window

scrollBy Method

Causes the window to scroll relative to the current scrolled position by the specified x- and y-pixel offsets.

Syntax

window.scrollBy(*iX*, *iY*)

Parameters

iX　Required. Integer specifying the horizontal scroll offset, in pixels. Positive values scroll the window right, and negative values scroll it left.

iY　Required. Integer specifying the vertical scroll offset, in pixels. Positive values scroll the window down, and negative values scroll it up.

Return Value

No return value.

Applies To

 WIN16   WIN32   MAC   UNIX

window

scrollIntoView Method

Causes the object to scroll into view, aligning it either at the top or bottom of the window.

Syntax

object.scrollIntoView([*bAlignToTop*])

Parameters

bAlignToTop   Optional. Boolean value specifying whether to place the object at the top or bottom of the window. If true, the method causes the object to scroll so that its top is visible at the top of the window. If false, the method causes the object to scroll so that its bottom is visible at the bottom of the window. If no value is specified, the object scrolls to the top by default.

Return Value

No return value.

Remarks

This method is useful for immediately showing the user the result of some action without requiring the user to manually scroll through the document to find the result.

Example

The following example shows how to underline the content of the document's fifth paragraph and scroll it into view at the top of the window.

```
var coll = document.all.tags("P");
if (coll.length >= 5)
{
    coll(4).style.textDecoration = "underline";
    coll(4).scrollIntoView(true);
}
```

Applies To

 WIN16   WIN32   MAC   UNIX

A, ADDRESS, APPLET, AREA, B, BIG, BLOCKQUOTE, BR, BUTTON, CAPTION, CENTER, CITE, CODE, COL, COLGROUP, COMMENT, DD, DFN, DIR, DIV, DL, DT, EM, EMBED, FIELDSET, FONT, FORM, Hn, HR, I, IFRAME, IMG, INPUT type=button, INPUT type=checkbox, INPUT type=file, INPUT type=image, INPUT type=password, INPUT type=radio, INPUT type=reset, INPUT type=submit, INPUT type=text, KBD, LABEL, LEGEND, LI, LISTING, MAP, MARQUEE, MENU, NOBR, OBJECT, OL, P, PLAINTEXT, PRE, S, SAMP, SELECT, SMALL, SPAN, STRIKE, STRONG, SUB, SUP, TABLE, TBODY, TD, TEXTAREA, TextRange, TFOOT, TH, THEAD, TR, TT, U, UL, VAR, XMP

 WIN16   WIN32   MAC   UNIX

controlRange, WBR

scrollTo Method

Scrolls the window to the specified x- and y-offsets.

Syntax

window.scrollTo(*iX, iY*)

Parameters

iX   Required. Integer specifying the horizontal scroll offset, in pixels.

iY   Required. Integer specifying the vertical scroll offset, in pixels.

Return Value

No return value.

Remarks

The specified offsets are relative to the upper-left corner of the window.

Applies To

 WIN16   WIN32   MAC   UNIX

window

select Method

Highlights the input area of a form element.

Syntax

object.select()

Return Value

No return value.

Remarks

Use this method with the **focus** method to highlight a field and position the cursor for a user response.

Applies To

 WIN16   WIN32   MAC   UNIX

INPUT type=button, INPUT type=checkbox, INPUT type=file, INPUT type=image, INPUT type=password, INPUT type=radio, INPUT type=reset, INPUT type=submit, INPUT type=text, TEXTAREA

select Method

Makes the active selection equal to the current object.

Syntax

object.select()

Return Value

No return value.

Remarks

This feature might not be available on non-Win32 platforms. For the latest information on Internet Explorer cross-platform compatibility, see article Q172976 in the Microsoft Knowledge Base.

Applies To

 WIN16   WIN32   MAC   UNIX

TextRange

WIN16   WIN32   MAC   UNIX

controlRange

setAttribute Method

Sets the value of the given attribute. If the attribute is not already present, the method adds the attribute to the object and sets the value.

Syntax

object.setAttribute(*sName*, *vValue* [, *iFlags*])

Parameters

sName   Required. String specifying the name of the attribute.

vValue   Required. String, number, or Boolean value to assign to the attribute.

iFlags   Optional. One or more of the following flags may be specified:

0   When the attribute is set, it overwrites any attributes with the same name, regardless of their case.

1   The case of the attribute that you set is respected when it is set on the object.

Return Value

No return value.

Remarks

Be careful when spelling attribute names. If you set *iFlags* to 1 and *sName* does not have the same uppercase and lowercase letters as the attribute, a new attribute is created for the object.

Applies To

 WIN16   WIN32   MAC   UNIX

A, ADDRESS, APPLET, AREA, B, BASE, BASEFONT, BGSOUND, BIG, BLOCKQUOTE, BODY, BR, BUTTON, CAPTION, CENTER, CITE, CODE, COL, COLGROUP, COMMENT, DD, DFN, DIR, DIV, DL, DT, EM, EMBED, FIELDSET, FONT, FORM, FRAME, FRAMESET, HEAD, Hn, HR, HTML, I, IFRAME, IMG, INPUT type=button, INPUT type=checkbox, INPUT type=file, INPUT type=hidden, INPUT type=image, INPUT type=password, INPUT type=radio, INPUT type=reset,

WIN16   WIN32   MAC   UNIX

INPUT type=submit, INPUT type=text, KBD, LABEL, LEGEND, LI, LINK, LISTING, MAP, MARQUEE, MENU, META, NEXTID, NOBR, OBJECT, OL, OPTION, P, PLAINTEXT, PRE, S, SAMP, SCRIPT, SELECT, SMALL, SPAN, STRIKE, STRONG, SUB, SUP, TABLE, TBODY, TD, TEXTAREA, TFOOT, TH, THEAD, TITLE, TR, TT, U, UL, VAR, WBR, XMP

setCapture Method

Sets the mouse capture to the object belonging to the current document.

Syntax

object.setCapture([*bContainerCapture*])

Parameters

bContainerCapture   Optional. Boolean value of `true` is the default. By default, the element having mouse capture fires all events, regardless of where the events originate in the document.

Return Value

No return value.

Remarks

Once mouse capture is set to an object, that object fires all mouse events for the document. Supported mouse events include **onmousedown**, **onmouseup**, **onmousemove**, **onclick**, **ondblclick**, **onmouseover**, and **onmouseout**. The **srcElement** property of the window **event** object always returns the object that is positioned under the mouse rather than the object that has mouse capture.

When a container object, such as a **DIV**, has mouse capture, events originating on objects within that container are fired by the **DIV**, unless the *bContainerCapture* parameter of the **setCapture** method is set to `false`. Passing the value `false` causes the container to no longer capture all document events. Instead, objects within that container still fire events, and those events also bubble as expected.

Drag-and-drop as well as text selection through the user interface are disabled when mouse capture is set programmatically.

Key events, such as **onkeydown**, **onkeyup**, and **onkeypress**, are unaffected by mouse capture and fire as usual.

DHTML Methods

Example

The following examples show how to use different aspects of mouse capture.

The example below shows the difference between detecting events using event bubbling and mouse capture.

```
<BODY onload="oOwnCapture.setCapture()"
    onclick="document.releaseCapture()">
<DIV ID=oOwnCapture
    onmousemove="oWriteLocation.value = event.x + event.y";
    onlosecapture="alert(event.srcElement.id +
        ' lost mouse capture.')">
<P>Mouse capture has been set to this gray division (DIV)
    at load time using the setCapture method. The text area
    tracks the mousemove event through the <B>x</B>
    and <B>y</B> properties of the event object.<BR>
<P>Event bubbling works as usual on objects within a
    container that has mouse capture. Demonstrate this concept by
    clicking the button below or changing the active window from
    this one then back. After oOwnCapture has lost mouse capture,
    the text area continues tracking the mousemove events only
    while the cursor is over objects it contains.</P>
    <BR><BR>
<TEXTAREA ID=oWriteLocation COLS=2>
    mouse location</TEXTAREA>
</DIV>
<HR>
<DIV ID=oNoCapture>
<P>This white division is here to illustrate that mousemove
    events over objects it contains are captured on the gray
    division, oOwnCapture.
<P>Click this text and check mouse coordinates captured in
    the text area within the division above.</P>
<INPUT VALUE="Move mouse over this object.">
<INPUT TYPE=button VALUE="Click to End Mouse Capture">
</DIV>
</BODY>
```

To see this code in action, refer to the Web Workshop CD-ROM.

The next example below shows how to use mouse capture to animate graphics.

```
<HEAD>
<SCRIPT>
var iRad = 25;
var iX01 = 165;
var iY01 = 170;
var iX02 = 285;
var iY02 = 170;

/* The doImgMouseMove function contains calculations to
    reposition black.bmp in response to mouse movement.   */
```

```
function doImgMouseMove()
{
  var iX1 = event.x - iX01;
  var iY1 = event.y - iY01;
  var iX2 = event.x - iX02;
  var iY2 = event.y - iY02;
  var change1 = Math.sqrt(iX1 * iX1 + iY1 * iY1);
  var change2 = Math.sqrt(iX2 * iX2 + iY2 * iY2);

  oPupilLeft.style.left = iX01 + iRad * iX1 / change1;
  oPupilLeft.style.top = iY01 + iRad * iY1 / change1;
  oPupilRight.style.left = iX02 + iRad * iX2 / change2;
  oPupilRight.style.top = iY02 + iRad * iY2 / change2;
}
</SCRIPT>
</HEAD>
<BODY onload="oEye.setCapture(false)"
    onclick="oEye.releaseCapture()"
    ondragstart="event.returnValue = false;">
<INPUT TYPE=button ID=oToggle VALUE="Switch Mouse Capture On"
    onclick="doClick()">
<IMG ID=oEye SRC="/workshop/graphics/eye.gif"
    onmousemove="doImgMouseMove()">
<IMG ID=oPupilLeft SRC="/workshop/graphics/black.gif">
<IMG ID=oPupilRight SRC="/workshop/graphics/black.gif">
<P>The eyeballs track mouse pointer movement. When mouse
    capture is on, they follow the mouse pointer no matter where it
    is positioned in the document. When mouse capture is off, they
    detect and follow mouse position only while the pointer is
    positioned over the eyeball graphic.</P>
<P>In this example, mouse capture is set when the document is
    loaded. Click anywhere on the document to remove mouse
    capture.</P>
</BODY>
```

To see this code in action, refer to the Web Workshop CD-ROM.

Applies To

 WIN16   WIN32   MAC   UNIX

A, ADDRESS, APPLET, AREA, B, BIG, BLOCKQUOTE, BODY, BR, BUTTON,
CAPTION, CENTER, CITE, CODE, DD, DFN, DIR, DIV, DL, DT, EM, EMBED,
FIELDSET, FONT, FORM, Hn, HR, I, IMG, INPUT type=button, INPUT
type=checkbox, INPUT type=file, INPUT type=hidden, INPUT type=image, INPUT
type=password, INPUT type=radio, INPUT type=reset, INPUT type=submit, INPUT
type=text, KBD, LABEL, LEGEND, LI, LISTING, MAP, MARQUEE, MENU,
NOBR, OBJECT, OL, OPTION, P, PLAINTEXT, PRE, S, SAMP, SELECT, SMALL,
SPAN, STRIKE, STRONG, SUB, SUP, TABLE, TBODY, TD, TEXTAREA,
TFOOT, TH, THEAD, TR, TT, U, UL, VAR, XMP

setData Method

Specifies what data format and information to add to the Clipboard through the **dataTransfer** or **clipboardData** object.

Syntax

object.setData([*sDataFormat*][, *vHelperData*])

Parameters

sDataFormat Optional. Data format to add to the system clipboard using the **dataTransfer** or **clipboardData** object. This string value can be one of the following:

Text   Default. Specifies that the data being transferred is text.

URL   Specifies that the data being transferred is a URL.

vHelperData Optional. Associates information with the source object. This information can be descriptive text, a source path to an image, or a URL for an anchor. When you pass URL as the *sDataFormat* parameter, you must use *vHelperData* to provide the location of the object being transferred.

Return Value

No return value.

Remarks

The **setData** parameters are not case-sensitive.

Example

The following example shows how to create a shortcut to an image using the **setData** and **getData** methods with the **dataTransfer** object.

```
<HEAD>
<SCRIPT>
var sImageURL;

function InitiateDrag()
/*  The setData parameters tell the source object
    to transfer data as a URL and provide the path.   */
{
    event.dataTransfer.setData("URL", oImage.src);
}
```

```
function FinishDrag()
/*  The parameter passed to getData tells the target
    object what data format to expect.  */
{
    sImageURL = event.dataTransfer.getData("URL")
    oTarget.innerText = sImageURL;
}
</SCRIPT>
</HEAD>
<BODY>

<P>This example shows how to use the setData and
    getData methods of the dataTransfer object to enable
    the source path of the image to be dragged.</P>

<IMAGE ID=oImage SRC="/workshop/graphics/black.gif"
       ondragstart="InitiateDrag()">

<SPAN ID=oTarget ondragenter="FinishDrag()">
    Drop the image here
</SPAN>

</BODY>
```

To see this code in action, refer to the Web Workshop CD-ROM.

Applies To

 WIN16   WIN32   MAC   UNIX

clipboardData, dataTransfer

setEndPoint Method

Sets the end point of one range based on the end point of another range.

Syntax

textRange.setEndPoint(*sType*, *oTextRange*)

Parameters

sType　　　　Required. String that describes the end point to transfer. This can be one of the following values:

StartToEnd　　Move the start of the **TextRange** object to the end of the specified *oTextRange* parameter.

StartToStart Move the start of the **TextRange** object to the start of the specified *oTextRange* parameter.

Parameters *(continued)*

	EndToStart	Move the end of the **TextRange** object to the start of the specified *oTextRange* parameter.
	EndToEnd	Move the end of the **TextRange** object to the end of the specified *oTextRange* parameter.
oTextRange		Required. **TextRange** object specifying the range from which the source end point is to be taken.

Return Value

No return value.

Remarks

A text range has two end points: one at the beginning of the text range and one at the end. An end point also can be the position between two characters in an HTML document.

In Internet Explorer 4.0, an end point is relative to text only, not HTML tags.

There are four possible end point locations in the following HTML:

```
<BODY><P><B>abc
```

The possible end point locations are:

- Before the A
- Between the a and the b
- Between the b and the c
- After the c

In Internet Explorer 4.0, an end point cannot be established between the **BODY** and the **P**. Such an end point is considered to occur before the a.

This method might not be available on non-Win32 platforms. For the latest information on Internet Explorer cross-platform compatibility, see article Q172976 in the Microsoft Knowledge Base.

Example

The following JScript (compatible with ECMA 262 language specification) example shows how to set the start point of the current range (r1) to the end point of the second range (r2).

```
r1.setEndPoint("StartToEnd", r2);
```

Applies To

 WIN16   WIN32   MAC   UNIX

TextRange

setExpression Method

Sets an expression for a given object.

Syntax

HTML   *<ELEMENT* STYLE=*"sAttributeName*:expression(*sExpression*)*">*

Scripting   *object*.setExpression(*sPropertyName*, *sExpression2*, *sLanguage*)

Parameters

sAttributeName Required. Name of the attribute to which *sExpression* is added.

sPropertyName Required. Name of the property to which *sExpression* is added.

sExpression   Required. Any valid JScript (compatible with ECMA 262 language specification) statement without quotations or semicolons. This string may include references to other properties on the current page. Array references are not allowed on object properties included in this script.

sExpression2   Required. Any valid script. This string may include references to other properties on the current page. Array references are not allowed on object properties included in this script.

sLanguage   Required. This can be one of the following values:

JScript   Specifies the language as JScript.

VBScript   Specifies the language as VBScript.

JavaScript   Specifies the language as JavaScript.

Return Value

No return value.

Remarks

The data type of the evaluated expression in the second argument must match one of the possible values allowed for the first argument. For instance, the following code sets a property that requires an integer argument.

```
numRows = 5;
oTextArea.setExpression("rows", numRows, "jscript");
```

Likewise, if the property being set requires a string, the data type of the second argument must be a string. Be sure to handle empty strings properly by passing two single-quotation characters enclosed within two double-quotation characters. For example, the following code causes an error because the second argument evaluates to a null string.

```
// This code causes an error.
picFile = "abc.gif";
document.body.setExpression("background", picFile, "jscript");
```

To fix this problem, you can pass quotation characters along with the second argument to force it to pass as a string, as the following example shows.

```
// This code executes correctly.
picFile = "abc.gif";
document.body.setExpression("background", '"' + picFile + '"',
    "jscript");
```

The **cssText** property is a unique property that is not compatible with the dynamic properties implementation. Do not use **cssText** with any dynamic property methods.

The **setExpression** method applies to the **style** subobject and can be used to add expressions to supported Cascading Style Sheet (CSS) attributes. This method is also available in scripting for the **innerHTML** and **value** attributes of objects. Only the **removeExpression** method can clear values set using **setExpression**.

The following example shows how to use **setExpression** on an object in scripting:

```
object.setExpression(sProperty, sExpression, sLanguage)
```

The following example shows how to use **setExpression** on the **style** subobject:

```
object.style.setExpression(sProperty, sExpression, sLanguage)
```

Example

The following examples show how to use **setExpression** in HTML and scripting. In each example, the width of the blue box is equal to the sum of the values of the first two text boxes. When a value in one of the text boxes is changed, the width of the blue box is recalculated.

The example below shows the HTML implementation of **setExpression**.

```
<INPUT TYPE=text ID=oBox1 value=40>The sum of the values in
    these two text boxes determines the width<BR>
<INPUT TYPE=text ID=oBox2 value=40>of the blue text box below.
<BR><INPUT TYPE=text ID=oBox3
    STYLE="width:expression(eval(oBox1.value) +
    eval(oBox2.value));background-color:blue">
<BR><INPUT TYPE=button ID=Button
    value="Click to resize blue box above"
    onclick="recalc()">
```

To see this code in action, refer to the Web Workshop CD-ROM.

The example below shows the same functionality is implemented in script:

```
<INPUT TYPE=text ID="oBox1" value=40>The sum of the values
    in these two text boxes determines the<BR>
<INPUT TYPE=text ID=oBox2 value=40>width of the blue text
    box below.<BR>
<INPUT TYPE=text ID=oBox3 STYLE="background-color:blue"><BR>
<INPUT TYPE=button ID=Button
    value="Click to resize blue box above"
    onclick="update()">

<SCRIPT>
oBox3.style.setExpression("width","eval(oBox1.value) +
eval(oBox2.value)","jscript");
function update()
{
    document.recalc();
}
</SCRIPT>
```

To see this code in action, refer to the Web Workshop CD-ROM.

Applies To

 WIN16   WIN32   MAC   UNIX

A, ACRONYM, ADDRESS, APPLET, AREA, B, BDO, BIG, BLOCKQUOTE, BODY, BR, BUTTON, CAPTION, CENTER, CITE, CODE, COL, COLGROUP, DD, DEL, DFN, DIR, DIV, DL, DT, EM, EMBED, FIELDSET, FONT, FORM, Hn, HR, I, IFRAME, IMG, INPUT type=button, INPUT type=checkbox, INPUT type=file, INPUT type=hidden, INPUT type=image, INPUT type=password, INPUT type=radio, INPUT type=reset, INPUT type=submit, INPUT type=text, INS, KBD, LABEL, LEGEND, LI, LISTING, MARQUEE, MENU, NOBR, OBJECT, OL, OPTION, P, PARAM, PRE, Q, RT, RUBY, S, SAMP, SELECT, SMALL, SPAN, STRIKE, STRONG, style, SUB, SUP, TABLE, TBODY, TD, TEXTAREA, TFOOT, TH, THEAD, TR, TT, U, UL, VAR

setInterval Method

Evaluates an expression each time a specified number of milliseconds has elapsed.

Syntax

iTimerID = *window*.setInterval(*vCode*, *iMilliSeconds* [, *sLanguage*])

Parameters

vCode	Required. Function pointer or string specifying the code to be executed when the specified interval has elapsed.
iMilliSeconds	Required. Integer specifying the number of milliseconds.
sLanguage	Optional. String specifying any one of the possible values for the **LANGUAGE** attribute.

Return Value

Integer. Returns an identifier that is used to cancel the timer with the **clearInterval** method.

Remarks

The **setInterval** method continuously evaluates the specified expression until the timer is removed with the **clearInterval** method.

Prior to Internet Explorer 5, the first argument of **setInterval** must be a string. Evaluation of the string is deferred until the specified interval elapses.

In Internet Explorer 5 or later, the first argument of **setInterval** can be passed as a string or as a function pointer.

To pass a function as a string, be sure to suffix the function name with parentheses as in the following example:

```
window.setInterval("someFunction()", 5000);
```

When passing a function pointer, do not to include the parentheses.

```
window.setInterval(someFunction, 5000);
```

Include the parentheses to have the function evaluated immediately before **setInterval** is called. The result of the function is passed to **setInterval** rather than to the function.

To get a function pointer, use the code shown in the following example.

```
function callback()
{
    alert("callback");
}

function callback2()
{
    alert("callback2");
}
```

```
function chooseCallback(iChoice)
{
    switch (iChoice)
    {
    case 0:
        return callback;
    case 1:
        return callback2;
    default:
        return "";
    }
}

// If i is 0, callback is invoked after 5 seconds.
// If i is 1, callback2 is invoked.
// Otherwise, the timer is not set.
window.setInterval(chooseCallback(i), 5000);
```

Example

The following example shows how to use the **setInterval** method to create a DHTML clock.

```
var oInterval = "";

function fnStartInterval(){
    oInterval = window.setInterval("fnRecycle()",1000);
}
function fnRecycle(){
    // Code to display hours, minutes, and seconds.
}
```

To see this code in action, refer to the Web Workshop CD-ROM.

Applies To

 WIN16   WIN32   MAC   UNIX

window

setTimeout Method

Evaluates an expression after a specified number of milliseconds has elapsed.

Syntax

iTimerID = *window*.setTimeout(*vCode*, *iMilliSeconds* [, *sLanguage*])

DHTML Methods

Parameters

vCode   Required. Function pointer or string specifying the code to be executed when the specified interval has elapsed.

iMilliSeconds Required. Integer specifying the number of milliseconds.

sLanguage   Optional. String specifying any one of the possible values for the **LANGUAGE** attribute.

Return Value

Integer. Returns an identifier that you can use to cancel the evaluation with the **clearTimeout** method.

Remarks

In versions earlier than Internet Explorer 5, the first argument of **setTimeout** must be a string. Evaluation of the string is deferred until the specified interval elapses.

As of Internet Explorer 5, the first argument of **setTimeout** can be a string or a function pointer.

The specified expression or function is evaluated once. For repeated evaluation, use the **setInterval** method.

Example

The following example shows how to use the **setTimeout** method to evaluate a simple expression after 1 second has elapsed.

```
window.setTimeout("alert('Hello, world')", 1000);
```

The example below shows how to use the **setTimeout** method to evaluate a slightly more complex expression than the one in the preceding example after 1 second has elapsed.

```
var sMsg = "Hello, world";
window.setTimeout("alert(" + sMsg + ")", 1000);
```

The next example shows how to use the **setTimeout** method to hide a **button** object after three seconds. If the user clicks the Count Down button and then counts to three, the Now You See Me button disappears.

```
<SCRIPT>
function fnHide(oToHide){
    window.setTimeout("fnHide2(" + oToHide.id + ")", 3000);
}
function fnHide2(sID){
    var o = eval(sID);
    o.style.display="none";
}
```

```
</SCRIPT>
<INPUT TYPE=button VALUE="Now you see me ..."
    ID="oHideButton" onclick="fnHide(this)">
```

In the previous example, the ID of the button is passed as a parameter to the function invoked by the **setTimeout** method. This is only possible when a string is passed as the first argument.

The following example shows how to use a function pointer to pass the data. In this case, the data is stored in a global variable because it cannot be passed directly.

```
<SCRIPT>
var g_oToHide = null;

function fnHide(oToHide){
    g_oToHide = oToHide;
    window.setTimeout(fnHide2, 3000);
}
function fnHide2(sID){
    if (g_oToHide) {
        g_oToHide.style.display="none";
    }
}
</SCRIPT>
<INPUT TYPE=button VALUE="Now you see me ..." ID="oHideButton"
    onclick="fnHide(this)">
```

To see this code in action, refer to the Web Workshop CD-ROM.

Applies To

 WIN16   WIN32   MAC

window

 UNIX

window

ShowBrowserUI Method

Opens the specified browser dialog box.

Syntax

*vReturn = window.external.*ShowBrowserUI(*sUI*, null)

Parameters

sUI   Required. String specifying a browser dialog box.

        `LanguageDialog`   Opens the Language Preference dialog box.

        `OrganizeFavorites` Opens the Organize Favorites dialog box.

`null`   Required. Null value.

Return Value

Variant. Return value is determined by the dialog box.

Example

```
<BUTTON
    onclick="window.external.ShowBrowserUI('LanguageDialog', null)"
>Show Language Dialog</BUTTON>
<BUTTON
    onclick="window.external.ShowBrowserUI('OrganizeFavorites', null)"
>Show Organize Favorites</BUTTON>
```

Applies To

 WIN16   WIN32   MAC   UNIX

external

showHelp Method

Displays a Help file. This method can be used with Microsoft HTML Help.

Syntax

window.showHelp(*sURL* [, *vContextID*])

Parameters

sURL   Required. String specifying the URL of the Help (.hlp) file to display.

vContextID   Optional. String or integer specifying a context identifier in a Help file.

Return Value

No return value.

Remarks

When implementing this method, a second Help dialog box appears if the user presses F1 or clicks Help on the menu bar. You can prevent the default Help dialog box from appearing by setting the following:

```
window.event.returnValue = false
```

Applies To

 WIN16   WIN32   MAC   UNIX

window

showModalDialog Method

Creates a modal dialog box that displays the HTML document specified in *sURL*.

Syntax

vReturnValue = *window*.showModalDialog(*sURL* [, *vArguments*][, *sFeatures*])

Parameters

sURL Required. String specifying the URL of the document to load and display.

vArguments Optional. Variant specifying the arguments to use when displaying the document. This parameter can be used to pass a value of any type, including an array of values. The dialog box can extract the values passed by the caller from the **dialogArguments** property of the **window** object.

sFeatures Optional. String specifying the window ornaments for the dialog box. It can be a combination of the following values:

dialogHeight:*iHeight*	Sets the height of the dialog window.
dialogLeft:*iXPos*	Sets the left position of the dialog window relative to the upper-left corner of the desktop.
dialogTop:*iYPos*	Sets the top position of the dialog window relative to the upper-left corner of the desktop.
dialogWidth:*iWidth*	Sets the width of the dialog window.

Parameters *(continued)*

`center:{ yes	no	1	0 }`	Specifies whether to center the dialog window within the desktop. The default is `yes`.
`help:{ yes	no	1	0 }`	Specifies whether the dialog window displays the context-sensitive Help icon. The default is `yes`.
`resizable:{ yes	no	1	0 }`	Specifies whether the dialog window is of set dimensions. The default for trusted and untrusted dialog windows is `no`.
`tustatus:{ yes	no	1	0 }`	Specifies whether the dialog window displays a status bar. The default is `yes` for untrusted dialog windows and `no` for trusted dialog windows.

Return Value

Variant. Returns the value of the **returnValue** property as set by the window of the document specified in *sURL*.

Remarks

The dialog box displayed is modal, meaning it retains the input focus until the user closes it.

Because a modal dialog box can include a URL to a resource in a different domain, do not to pass information through the *vArguments* parameter from a page that the user might consider private.

As of Internet Explorer 4.0, you can eliminate scroll bars from dialog boxes. To turn off the scroll bar, set the **SCROLL** attribute to `false` in the **BODY** element for the dialog window, or call the modal dialog box from a trusted application.

Internet Explorer 5 allows further control over modal dialog boxes through the `status` and `resizable` values in the *sFeatures* parameter of the **showModalDialog** method. Turn off the status bar by calling the dialog box from a trusted application, such as Visual Basic or an HTML Application (HTA), or from a trusted window, such as a trusted modal dialog box. These are considered trusted because they use Internet Explorer interfaces instead of the browser. Any dialog box generated from a trusted source has the status bar off by default. Resizing is off by default but you can turn it on by specifying `resizable=yes` in the *sFeatures* string of the **showModalDialog** method.

You can set the default font settings the same way that you set cascading style sheets (CSS) attributes (for example, "font:3;font-size:4"). To define multiple font values, use multiple font attributes.

The dcfault unit of measure for `dialogHeight` and `dialogWidth` in Internet Explorer 4.0 is the em; in Internet Explorer 5 it is the pixel. For consistent results, specify the `dialogHeight` and `dialogWidth` in pixels when designing modal dialog boxes.

Example

This following example shows how to use the **showModalDialog** method.

```
<SCRIPT>
function fnRandom(iModifier){
    return parseInt(Math.random()*iModifier);
}
function fnSetValues(){
    var iHeight=oForm.oHeight.options[
        oForm.oHeight.selectedIndex].text;
    if(iHeight.indexOf("Random")>-1){
        iHeight=fnRandom(document.body.clientHeight);
    }
    var sFeatures="dialogHeight: " + iHeight + "px;";
    return sFeatures;
}
function fnOpen(){
    var sFeatures=fnSetValues();
    window.showModalDialog("showModalDialog_target.htm", "",
        sFeatures)
}
</SCRIPT>

<FORM NAME=oForm>
Dialog Height <SELECT NAME="oHeight">
    <OPTION>-- Random --
    <OPTION>150
    <OPTION>200
    <OPTION>250
    <OPTION>300
</SELECT>

Create Modal Dialog Box
<INPUT TYPE="button" VALUE="Push To Create"
    onclick="fnOpen()">
</FORM>
```

To see this code in action, refer to the Web Workshop CD-ROM.

Applies To

 WIN16   WIN32   MAC   UNIX

window

showModelessDialog Method

Creates a modeless dialog box.

Syntax

vReturnValue = *window*.showModelessDialog(*sURL* [, *vArguments*][, *sFeatures*])

Parameters

sURL
: Required. String specifying the URL of the document to load and display.

vArguments
: Optional. Variant specifying the arguments to use when displaying the document. Use this parameter to pass a value of any type, including an array of values. The dialog box can extract the values passed by the caller from the **dialogArguments** property of the **window** object.

sFeatures
: Optional. String specifying the window ornaments for the dialog box. It can be a combination of the following values:

dialogHeight:*iHeight*	Sets the height, in pixels, of the dialog window.
dialogLeft:*iXPos*	Sets the left position of the dialog window relative to the upper-left corner of the desktop.
dialogTop:*iYPos*	Sets the top position of the dialog window relative to the upper-left corner of the desktop.
dialogWidth:*iWidth*	Sets the width, in pixels, of the dialog window.
center:{ yes l no l 1 l 0 }	Specifies whether to center the dialog window within the desktop. The default is yes.
help:{ yes l no l 1 l 0 }	Specifies whether the dialog box displays the context-sensitive Help icon. The default is yes.
resizable:{ yes l no l 1 l 0 }	Specifies whether the dialog window is of set dimensions. The default for trusted and untrusted dialog windows is no.

Parameters *(continued)*

status:{ yes | no | 1 | 0 }   Specifies whether the dialog window displays a status bar. The default is yes for untrusted dialog windows and no for trusted dialog windows.

Return Value

Variant. Returns a reference to the new window object. Use this reference to script properties and methods on the new window.

Remarks

The **showModelessDialog** method is useful for menus and Help systems. When you invoke the method, a dialog box appears that is layered in front of the browser window or HTML Application (HTA). The modeless dialog box displays even when the user switches input focus to the window.

By convention, modeless dialog boxes can differ from an application window in that they do not have scroll bar, status bar, or resize capabilities. To create this type of dialog box, implement the following steps:

- Turn off the scroll bar. Use the **SCROLL** attribute by including scroll="no" in the **BODY** tag for the dialog window.

- Turn off the status bar. Set the value of status to no in the *sFeatures* parameter for the **showModelessDialog** call. A second option is to call the dialog window from a trusted application, such as Visual Basic or an HTA, or from a trusted window, such as a trusted dialog box. These are considered trusted because they use Internet Explorer interfaces instead of the browser. Any dialog box generated from a trusted source has the status bar off by default.

- Do not allow resizing. Resizing is off by default.

To create a return value for **showModalDialog, you can** pass in a callback function or an object from the calling document. To accomplish this task, set the *vArguments* parameter for the **showModelessDialog** call to the callback function or object. In the modeless dialog box, you can reference this function or object through the **dialogArguments** property of the **window** object. The same arguments are valid for the **showModelessDialog** and **showModalDialog** methods.

You can set the default font settings in the same way you set cascading style sheets (CSS) attributes (for example, "font:3; font-size:4"). To define multiple font values, use multiple font attributes.

When you specify dialogLeft and/or dialogTop, center is overridden, although the default for center is yes.

Example

The following example shows how to create a return value when you invoke the **showModelessDialog** method. In addition, the example shows how to handle user actions in the modeless dialog box.

```
<HEAD>
<SCRIPT>
// Supplies a return value from modeless dialog box.
var sUserName="";

// Passes URL and file name of dialog box as a variable.
var oDialog = "myDialog.htm";

// Passing the window object allows for the creation of a
// callback to return information from the modeless dialog box.

function fnCallDialog()
{
    showModelessDialog(oDialog,window,
        "status:false;dialogWidth:300px;dialogHeight:300px");
}

</SCRIPT>
</HEAD>
```

To see this code in action, refer to the Web Workshop CD-ROM.

Applies To

 WIN16   WIN32   MAC   UNIX

window

splitText Method

Divides a text node at the specified index.

Syntax

oSplitNode = *TextNode*.splitText(*iIndex*)

Parameters

iIndex   Optional. Integer specifying the index of the string where the separation occurs. If a value is not provided, a new text node with no value is created.

Return Value

Returns a text node object.

Remarks

The text node that invokes the **splitText** method has a **nodeValue** equal to the substring of the value, from 0 to *iIndex*. The new text node has a **nodeValue** of the substring of the original value, from the specified index to the value length. Text node integrity is not preserved when the document is saved or persisted.

Example

The following example shows how to use the **splitText** method to divide a text node in half in a **UL** object. When the text node is split, a new **LI** object is created with the **createElement** method. The new **LI** element, and the split text node are appended to the **UL** object with the **appendChild** method.

```
<SCRIPT>
function fnSplitNode(){
var oNode=oList.firstChild.childNodes(0);
var oNewNode=document.createElement("LI");
var oSplitNode = oNode.splitText(oNode.nodeValue.length/2);
oList.appendChild(oNewNode);
oNewNode.appendChild(oSplitNode);
}
</SCRIPT>
<UL onclick="fnSplitNode()">
<LI>This is a list item.
</UL>
```

Applies To

 WIN16   WIN32   MAC   UNIX

TextNode

start Method

Starts scrolling the marquee.

Syntax

marquee.start()

Return Value

No return value.

Remarks

Invoking the **start** method does not fire the **onstart** event handler.

Applies To

 WIN16 WIN32 MAC UNIX

MARQUEE

stop Method

Stops the marquee from scrolling.

Syntax

marquee.stop()

Return Value

No return value.

Applies To

 WIN16 WIN32 MAC UNIX

MARQUEE

submit Method

Submits the form, and fires the **onsubmit** event.

Syntax

form.submit()

Return Value

No return value.

Applies To

 WIN16 WIN32 MAC

FORM

 UNIX

FORM

swapNode Method

Exchanges the location of two objects in the document hierarchy.

Syntax

oSwapped = *object*.swapNode(*oNode*)

Parameters

oNode   Required. Existing element.

Return Value

Returns a reference to the object that invoked the method.

Remarks

This method is accessible at run time. Removing elements at run time, before the closing tag has been parsed, could prevent other areas of the document from rendering.

Example

The following example shows how to use the **swapNode** method to exchange the location of two objects.

```
<SCRIPT>
function fnSwap(){
    oList.children(0).swapNode(oList.children(1));
}
</SCRIPT>

<UL ID = oList>
<LI>List Item 1
<LI>List Item 2
<LI>List Item 3
<LI>List Item 4
</UL>
<INPUT TYPE = button VALUE = "Swap List" onclick = "fnSwap()">
```

Applies To

 WIN16   WIN32   MAC   UNIX

A, ACRONYM, ADDRESS, APPLET, AREA, B, BASE, BASEFONT, BDO, BGSOUND, BIG, BLOCKQUOTE, BODY, BR, BUTTON, CAPTION, CENTER, CITE, CODE, COL, COLGROUP, COMMENT, DD, DEL, DFN, DIR, DIV, DL, DT, EM, EMBED, FIELDSET, FONT, FORM, FRAME, FRAMESET, HEAD, Hn, HR, HTML, I, IFRAME, IMG, INPUT type=button, INPUT type=checkbox,

Applies To *(continued)*

 WIN16   WIN32   MAC   UNIX

INPUT type=file, INPUT type=hidden, INPUT type=image, INPUT type=password, INPUT type=radio, INPUT type=reset, INPUT type=submit, INPUT type=text, INS, KBD, LABEL, LEGEND, LI, LINK, LISTING, MAP, MARQUEE, MENU, NEXTID, OBJECT, OL, OPTION, P, PLAINTEXT, PRE, Q, S, SAMP, SCRIPT, SELECT, SMALL, SPAN, STRIKE, STRONG, SUB, SUP, TABLE, TBODY, TD, TEXTAREA, TFOOT, TH, THEAD, TITLE, TR, TT, U, UL, VAR, XMP

tags Method

Retrieves a collection of objects that have the specified HTML tag name.

Syntax

collElements = *object*.tags(*sTag*)

Parameters

sTag   Required. String specifying an HTML tag. It can be any one of the **objects** exposed by the DHTML Object Model.

Return Value

Returns a collection of element objects if successful, or null otherwise.

Remarks

This method returns an empty collection if no elements having the given name are found. Use the **length** property on the collection to determine the number of elements it contains.

Example

The following example in JScript (compatible with ECMA 262 language specification) shows how to retrieve a collection of all **P** elements in the document, and then apply an underline to each element.

```
var coll = document.all.tags("P");
if (coll!=null)
{
    for (i=0; i<coll.length; i++)
      coll[i].style.textDecoration="underline";
}
```

Applies To

 WIN16   WIN32   MAC   UNIX

all, anchors, applets, areas, cells, children, elements, embeds, forms, images, links, options, plugins, rows, scripts, tbodies

 WIN16   WIN32   MAC   UNIX

boundElements

taintEnabled Method

Returns whether data tainting is enabled.

Syntax

bEnabled = *navigator*.taintEnabled()

Return Value

Boolean. Returns true if data tainting is supported, or false otherwise.

Remarks

Internet Explorer 5 and earlier do not support data tainting. The method, therefore, always returns false.

Applies To

 WIN16   WIN32   MAC   UNIX

navigator

urns Method

Retrieves a collection of all objects to which a specified behavior is attached.

Syntax

collObjects = *object*.urns(*sUrn*)

Parameters

sUrn   Required. String specifying a behavior's Uniform Resource Name (URN).

Return Value

Returns a collection of objects if successful, or `null` otherwise.

Remarks

This method returns an empty collection if no element has the specified behavior attached to it.

Use the **length** property on the collection to determine the number of elements it contains, and the **item** method to obtain a particular item in the collection.

Example

The following example in JScript (compatible with ECMA 262 language specification) shows how to retrieve a collection of all elements currently attached to the specified behavior, and displays a comma-delimited list of IDs of the elements in a message box.

```
var coll  = document.all.urns("URN1");
var sText = '';

if (coll != null)
{
    for (i=0; i<coll.length; i++)
    sText += coll.item(i).id + ', ';

    window.alert (sText);
}
```

Applies To

 WIN16   WIN32   MAC   UNIX

all, anchors, applets, areas, boundElements, cells, childNodes, children, elements, embeds, FORM, forms, images, links, options, rows, scripts, SELECT, stylesheets, tags, tbodies

write Method

Writes one or more HTML expressions to a document in the specified window.

Syntax

document.write(*sText*)

Parameters

sText   Required. String specifying the text and/or HTML tags to write.

Return Value

No return value.

Applies To

 WIN16   WIN32   MAC

document

 UNIX

document

writeln Method

Writes one or more HTML expressions, followed by a carriage return, to a document in the specified window.

Syntax

document.writeln(*sText*)

Parameters

sText   Required. String specifying the text and/or HTML tags to write.

Return Value

No return value.

Remarks

In HTML, the carriage return is ignored unless it occurs within preformatted text.

Applies To

 WIN16   WIN32   MAC

document

 UNIX

document

Events

The following section provides a complete list of events exposed by the DHTML Object Model. Entries are arranged alphabetically.

Although the event object is available to all DHTML events as a way to obtain and modify information about the event, not all of the event object's properties have meaningful values·for all events. Each event reference has an Event Object Properties section that includes only the properties of the **event** object that are relevant to that particular event.

onabort Event

Fires when the user aborts the download of an image.

Syntax

Inline HTML	*<ELEMENT* onabort = "*handler*" ... >	All platforms
Event property	*object*.onabort = *handler*	JScript (compatible with ECMA 262 language specification) only
Named script	<SCRIPT FOR = *object* EVENT = onabort>	Internet Explorer only

Remarks

Bubbles	No
Cancels	Yes
To invoke	• Click an **anchor**.
	• Click the browser Stop button.
	• Navigate to another page.
Default action	Halts downloading of the designated image.

Event Object Properties

returnValue	**srcElement**	**type**

Applies To

IE 4	WIN16	WIN32	MAC	UNIX

IMG

onafterprint Event

Fires on the object immediately after its associated document prints.

Syntax

Inline HTML	`<ELEMENT onafterprint = "handler" ... >`	All platforms
Event property	`object.onafterprint = handler`	JScript (compatible with ECMA 262 language specification) only
Named script	`<SCRIPT FOR = object EVENT = onafterprint>`	Internet Explorer only

Remarks

Bubbles	No
Cancels	No
To invoke	• Choose Print from the File menu in Internet Explorer.
	• Press CTRL + P.
	• Right-click anywhere on a page, and choose Print.
	• Right-click on a link on a page, and choose Print.
	• From Windows Explorer, select an .htm file, and then choose Print from the File menu.
	• From Windows Explorer, right-click on an .htm file, and then choose Print.
Default Action	None

This event is usually used with the **onbeforeprint** event. Use the **onbeforeprint** event gives the Web to make changes to the document just before it prints. Use the **onafterprint** event to undo those changes, reverting the document back to its pre-print state.

Event Object Properties

altKey	button	cancelBubble	clientX	clientY
ctrlKey	returnValue	screenX	screenY	shiftKey
srcElement	type	x	y	

Example

The following example shows how to use the **onafterprint** event to return the document back to its pre-print state. In this case, because the **onbeforeprint** event handler makes all currently hidden sections of the page visible for printing, the **onafterprint** event sets those sections back to hidden.

```
function window.onafterprint()
{
    // Walk through all the elements in the doc with CLASS="expanded"
    // and set it back to "collapsed" if expanded just for
    // printing purposes.
    var coll = document.all.tags("DIV");
    if (coll!=null)
    {
        for (i=0; i<coll.length; i++)
            if ((coll[i].className == "expanded") &&
                (coll[i].bExpandedForPrinting))
            {
                coll[i].className = "collapsed";
                coll[i].bExpandedForPrinting = false;
            }
    }
}

function window.onbeforeprint()
{
    // Walk through all the elements in the doc with CLASS="collapsed"
    // and set it to "expanded" just for printing.
    var coll = document.all.tags("DIV");
    if (coll!=null)
    {
        for (i=0; i<coll.length; i++)
            if (coll[i].className == "collapsed")
            {
                coll[i].className = "expanded";

        // After printing, make sure to set
        // CLASS="collapsed" only for those that were
        // expanded just for printing purposes.
                coll[i].bExpandedForPrinting = true;
            }

            else if (coll[i].className == "expanded")
                coll[i].bExpandedForPrinting = false;
    }
}
```

To see this code in action, refer to the Web Workshop CD-ROM.

Applies To

WIN16	WIN32	MAC	UNIX

window, BODY, FRAMESET

onafterupdate Event

Fires on a databound object after successfully updating the associated data in the data source object.

Syntax

Inline HTML	*<ELEMENT* onafterupdate = "*handler*" ... >	All platforms
Event property	*object*.onafterupdate = *handler*	JScript (compatible with ECMA 262 language specification) only
Named script	<SCRIPT FOR = *object* EVENT = onafterupdate>	Internet Explorer only

Remarks

Bubbles	Yes
Cancels	No
To invoke	Change the data that the object contains.
Default action	Confirms that data has been transferred.

This event only fires when the object is databound and an **onbeforeupdate** event has fired (for example, because the data has changed).

Event Object Properties

cancelBubble   srcElement   type

Applies To

WIN16	WIN32	MAC	UNIX

INPUT TYPE=text, TEXTAREA

WIN16	WIN32	MAC	UNIX

BDO, RT, RUBY

onbeforecopy Event

Fires on the source object before the selection is copied to the system clipboard.

Syntax

Inline HTML	*<ELEMENT* onbeforecopy = "*handler*" ... >	All platforms
Event property	*object*.onbeforecopy = *handler*	JScript (compatible with ECMA 262 language specification) only
Named script	<SCRIPT FOR = *object* EVENT = onbeforecopy>	Internet Explorer only

Remarks

Bubbles	Yes
Cancels	Yes
To invoke	After selecting the text:

- Right-click to display the shortcut menu and select Copy.
- Or press CTRL+C.

Default action None.

The **onbeforecopy** event fires on the source element. Use the **setData** method to specify a data format for the selection.

Event Object Properties

altKey	**cancelBubble**	**clientX**	**clientY**	**ctrlKey**
offsetX	**offsetY**	**returnValue**	**screenX**	**screenY**
shiftKey	**srcElement**	**type**	**x**	**y**

Example

The following example shows how to use the **onbeforecopy** event to customize copy behavior.

```
<HEAD>
<SCRIPT>
var sNewValue = "copy event fired";
var bFired = false;
var sSave = "";
```

```
function Source_Beforecopy()
{
  sSave = oSource.innerText;
  bFired = true;
  event.returnValue = false;
}

function Source_Copy()
{
  window.clipboardData.setData("Text", sNewValue);
}

function Target_BeforePaste()
{
  event.returnValue = false;
}

function Target_Paste()
{
  event.returnValue = false;
  oTarget.value = window.clipboardData.getData("Text");
}

</SCRIPT>
</HEAD>
<BODY>
<SPAN ID=oSource onbeforecopy="Source_Beforecopy()"
      oncopy="Source_Copy()">copy this text</SPAN>
<INPUT ID=oTarget onbeforepaste="Target_BeforePaste()"
      onpaste="Target_Paste()">
</BODY>
```

To see this code in action, refer to the Web Workshop CD-ROM.

Applies To

 WIN16   WIN32   MAC   UNIX

A, ADDRESS, AREA, B, BDO, BIG, BLOCKQUOTE, CAPTION, CENTER, CITE, CODE, DD, DFN, DIR, DIV, DL, DT, EM, FIELDSET, FORM, Hn, I, IMG, LABEL, LEGEND, LI, LISTING, MENU, NOBR, OL, P, PLAINTEXT, PRE, S, SAMP, SMALL, SPAN, STRIKE, STRONG, SUB, SUP, TD, TEXTAREA, TH, TR, TT, U, UL

onbeforecut Event

Fires on the source object before the selection is deleted from the document.

Syntax

Inline HTML	*<ELEMENT* onbeforecut = "*handler*" ... >	All platforms
Event property	*object*.onbeforecut = *handler*	JScript (compatible with ECMA 262 language specification) only
Named script	<SCRIPT FOR = *object* EVENT = onbeforecut>	Internet Explorer only

Remarks

Bubbles	Yes
Cancels	Yes
To invoke	After selecting the text:

- Right-click to display the shortcut menu and select Cut.
- Or press CTRL+X.

Default action None.

Creating custom code for cutting requires several steps:

1. Set event.returnValue=false in the **onbeforecut** event to enable the Cut shortcut menu item.
2. Specify a data format in which to transfer the selection through the **setData** method of the **clipboardData** object.
3. Invoke the **setData** method in the **oncut** event.

Event Object Properties

altKey	**cancelBubble**	**clientX**	**clientY**	**ctrlKey**
offsetX	**offsetY**	**returnValue**	**screenX**	**screenY**
shiftKey	**srcElement**	**type**	**x**	**y**

DHTML Events

Example

The following example shows how to use the **setData** and **getData** methods with the **clipboardData** object to perform a cut-and-paste operation on the shortcut menu.

```
<HEAD>
<SCRIPT>

function fnBeforeCut() {
    event.returnValue = false;
}

function fnCut() {
    window.clipboardData.setData("Text");
    oSource.innerText = "";
}

function fnBeforePaste() {
    event.returnValue = false;
}

function fnPaste() {
    event.returnValue = false;
    oTarget.innerText = window.clipboardData.getData("Text");
}

</SCRIPT>
</HEAD>

<BODY>
<SPAN ID="oSource" onbeforecut="fnBeforeCut()" oncut="fnCut()">Select and Cut this Text
</SPAN>

<BR>
<BR>
<DIV ID="oTarget" onbeforepaste="fnBeforePaste()" onpaste="fnPaste()">Paste the Text
Here
</DIV>
</BODY>
```

To see this code in action, refer to the Web Workshop CD-ROM.

Applies To

 WIN16   WIN32   MAC   UNIX

A, ADDRESS, AREA, B, BDO, BIG, BLOCKQUOTE, CAPTION, CENTER, CITE, CODE, DD, DFN, DIR, DIV, DL, DT, EM, FIELDSET, FORM, Hn, I, IMG, LABEL, LEGEND, LI, LISTING, MENU, NOBR, OL, P, PLAINTEXT, PRE, S, SAMP, SMALL, SPAN, STRIKE, STRONG, SUB, SUP, TD, TEXTAREA, TH, TR, TT, U, UL

onbeforeeditfocus Event

Fires prior to a control entering a User Interface (UI) activated state.

Syntax

Inline HTML	*<ELEMENT* onbeforeeditfocus = *"handler"* ... >	All platforms
Event property	*object*.onbeforeeditfocus = *handler*	JScript (compatible with ECMA 262 language specification) only
Named script	<SCRIPT FOR = *object* EVENT = onbeforeeditfocus>	Internet Explorer only

Remarks

Bubbles	Yes
Cancels	Yes
To invoke	• Press the ENTER key or click an object when it has focus.
	• Double-click an object.

Default action Moves the object into a UI activated state.

The **designMode** property must be set to yes for this event to fire.

When the browser is in design mode, objects enter a UI activated state when the user presses the ENTER key or clicks the object when it has focus, or when the user double-clicks the object. Objects that are UI activated have their own window within the document. To place an object in a UI activated state, you must use the **designMode** property to put the document in design mode.

The **onbeforeeditfocus** event differs from the **onfocus** event. The **onbeforeeditfocus** event fires before an object enters a UI activated state, whereas the **onfocus** event fires when an object has focus.

Event Object Properties

cancelBubble	**clientX**	**clientY**	**returnValue**	**screenX**
screenY	**srcElement**	**type**	**x**	**y**

DHTML Events

Applies To

 WIN16   WIN32   MAC   UNIX

A, APPLET, AREA, BUTTON, DIV, document, FIELDSET, INPUT type=button, INPUT type=checkbox, INPUT type=file, INPUT type=hidden, INPUT type=image, INPUT type=password, INPUT type=radio, INPUT type=reset, INPUT type=submit, INPUT type=text, MARQUEE, OBJECT, SELECT, SPAN, TABLE, TD, TEXTAREA, TR

onbeforepaste Event

Fires on the target object before the selection is pasted from the system clipboard to the document.

Syntax

Inline HTML	`<ELEMENT onbeforepaste = "handler" ... >`	All platforms
Event property	`object.onbeforepaste = handler`	JScript (compatible with ECMA 262 language specification) only
Named script	`<SCRIPT FOR = object EVENT = onbeforepaste>`	Internet Explorer only

Remarks

Bubbles	Yes
Cancels	Yes
To invoke	After copying or cutting text:

- Right-click to display the shortcut menu and select Paste.
- Or press CTRL+V.

Default action None.

Creating custom code for pasting requires several steps.

1. Set `event.returnValue=false` in the **onbeforepaste** event to enable the Paste shortcut menu item.

2. Cancel the default behavior of the browser by including `event.returnValue=false` in the **onpaste** event handler. This guideline applies only to objects, such as the text box, that have a defined default behavior.

3. Specify a data format in which to paste the selection through the **getData** method of the **clipboardData** object.

4. Invoke the **getData** method in the **onpaste** event to execute custom code for pasting.

Event Object Properties

altKey	**cancelBubble**	**clientX**	**clientY**	**ctrlKey**
offsetX	**offsetY**	**returnValue**	**screenX**	**screenY**
shiftKey	**srcElement**	**type**	**x**	**y**

Applies To

 WIN16   WIN32   MAC   UNIX

A, ADDRESS, AREA, B, BDO, BIG, BLOCKQUOTE, CAPTION, CENTER, CITE, CODE, DD, DFN, DIR, DIV, DL, DT, EM, FIELDSET, FORM, Hn, I, IMG, LABEL, LEGEND, LI, LISTING, MENU, NOBR, OL, P, PLAINTEXT, PRE, S, SAMP, SMALL, SPAN, STRIKE, STRONG, SUB, SUP, TD, TEXTAREA, TH, TR, TT, U, UL

onbeforeprint Event

Fires on the object before its associated document prints.

Syntax

Inline HTML	*<ELEMENT* onbeforeprint = *"handler"* ... >	All platforms
Event property	*object*.onbeforeprint = *handler*	JScript (compatible with ECMA 262 language specification) only
Named script	<SCRIPT FOR = *object* EVENT = onbeforeprint>	Internet Explorer only

Remarks

Bubbles	No
Cancels	No
To invoke	• Choose Print from the File menu in Internet Explorer.
	• Press CTRL + P.
	• Right-click anywhere on a page, and choose Print.

DHTML Events

Remarks *(continued)*

- Right-click on a link on a page, and choose Print.
- From Windows Explorer, select an .htm file and choose Print from the File menu.
- From Windows Explorer, right-click on an .htm file and choose Print.

Default action Prints the document associated with the object for which the event is specified.

Use this event to make all the information on the page visible just before printing.

Use this event with the **onafterprint** event to undo the changes made to the document in the **onbeforeprint** event.

Event Object Properties

altKey	button	cancelBubble	clientX	clientY
ctrlKey	returnValue	screenX	screenY	shiftKey
srcElement	type	x	y	

Example

The following example shows how to use the **onbeforeprint** event to make all hidden sections of the page visible just before the page prints. The **onafterprint** event is processed after the page prints to return the document to its original state.

```
function window.onbeforeprint()
{
    // Walk through all the elements in the document with
    // CLASS="collapsed" and set it to "expanded" just for printing.
    var coll = document.all.tags("DIV");
    if (coll!=null)
    {
        for (i=0; i<coll.length; i++)
            if (coll[i].className == "collapsed")
            {
                coll[i].className = "expanded";

            // After printing make sure to set CLASS="collapsed"
            // only for those that were expanded just for printing
            // purposes.
                coll[i].bExpandedForPrinting = true;
            }

            else if (coll[i].className == "expanded")
                coll[i].bExpandedForPrinting = false;
    }
}
```

```
function window.onafterprint()
{
   // Walk through all the elements in the doc with CLASS="expanded"
   // and set it to "collapsed" if expanded just for printing.
   var coll = document.all.tags("DIV");
   if (coll!=null)
   {
      for (i=0; i < coll.length; i++)
         if ((coll[i].className == "expanded") &&
            (coll[i].bExpandedForPrinting))
         {
           coll[i].className = "collapsed";
           coll[i].bExpandedForPrinting = false;
         }
   }
}
```

To see this code in action, refer to the Web Workshop CD-ROM.

Applies To

WIN16	WIN32	MAC	UNIX

window, BODY, FRAMESET

onbeforeunload Event

Fires prior to a page being unloaded.

Syntax

Inline HTML	*<ELEMENT* onbeforeunload = "*handler*" ... >	All platforms
Event property	*object*.onbeforeunload = *handler*	JScript (compatible with ECMA 262 language specification) only
Named script	<SCRIPT FOR = *object* EVENT = onbeforeunload>	Internet Explorer only

Remarks

Bubbles	No
Cancels	No

Remarks *(continued)*

To invoke
- Close the current browser window.
- Navigate to another location by entering a new address or selecting a Favorite.
- Click the Back, Forward, Refresh, or Home button.
- Click on an **anchor** that refers the browser to another Web page.
- Invoke the **anchor click** method.
- Invoke the **document write** method.
- Invoke the **document open** method.
- Invoke the **document close** method.
- Invoke the **window close** method.
- Invoke the **window open** method, providing the possible value _self for the window name.
- Invoke the **window navigate** or **NavigateAndFind** method.
- Invoke the **location replace** method.
- Invoke the **location reload** method.
- Specify a new value for the **location href** property.
- Submit a **FORM** to the address specified in the **ACTION** attribute via the **INPUT_submit** control, or invoke the **form submit** method.

Default action   Signals that the page is about to be unloaded.

When a string is returned to this event, a dialog box appears that gives the user the option of staying on the page. The returned string displays in a predefined area.

```
<SCRIPT>
function Window_beforeUnload()  {
    alert("Window is unloading");
    event.returnValue = "Click cancel to stay on this page.";
}
</SCRIPT>
```

Event Object Properties

altKey	clientX	clientY	ctrlKey	returnValue
shiftKey	type			

Example

The following example shows how to use the **onbeforeunload** event.

```
<HTML>
<HEAD>
<SCRIPT>
function closeIt()
  {
    event.returnValue = "Any string value here forces a dialog
                         box to appear before closing the window.";
  }
</SCRIPT>
</HEAD>
<BODY onbeforeunload="closeIt()">
<P>Navigate to another page to fire the before unload event.
</BODY>
</HTML>
```

Applies To

 WIN16   WIN32   MAC   UNIX

FRAMESET, window

onbeforeupdate Event

Fires on a databound object before updating the associated data in the data source object.

Syntax

Inline HTML	*<ELEMENT* onbeforeupdate = *"handler"* ... >	All platforms
Event property	*object*.onbeforeupdate = *handler*	JScript (compatible with ECMA 262 language specification) only
Named script	<SCRIPT FOR = *object* EVENT = onbeforeupdate>	Internet Explorer only

Remarks

Bubbles	Yes
Cancels	Yes
To invoke	Cause an object to receive, change the value of the object, and either cause the object to lose focus or force the page to unload.
Default action	Signals that the data contained in an object has changed.

DHTML Events

Because this event can be cancelled, the programmer can fail the validation and leave the content of the field as well as the cursor intact. All subsequent events are not fired when this event is canceled.

If the **onbeforeupdate** event is cancelled, the **onafterupdate** event does not fire.

Event Object Properties

cancelBubble	**clientX**	**clientY**	**offsetX**	**offsetY**
returnValue	**screenX**	**screenY**	**srcElement**	**type**
x	**y**			

Applies To

 WIN16   WIN32   MAC   UNIX

INPUT TYPE=text, TEXTAREA

 WIN16   WIN32   MAC   UNIX

BDO, RT, RUBY

onblur Event

Fires when the object loses the input focus.

Syntax

Inline HTML	`<ELEMENT onblur = "handler" ... >`	All platforms
Event property	`object.onblur = handler`	JScript (compatible with ECMA 262 language specification) and VBScript
Named script	`<SCRIPT FOR = object EVENT = onblur>`	Internet Explorer only

Remarks

Bubbles	No
Cancels	No

Remarks *(continued)*

To invoke   Cause an object to lose focus:

- Click the mouse on the document background or another control.
- Use the keyboard to navigate from one object to the next.
- Invoke the **blur** method when an object has focus.
- Switch focus to a different application or open a second browser window.

Default action   Switches focus away from the object on which the event is fired.

The **onblur** event fires on the original object before the **onfocus** or **onclick** event fires on the object that is receiving focus. Where applicable, the **onblur** event fires after the **onchange** event.

Use the focus events to determine when to prepare an object to receive or validate input from the user.

As of Microsoft Internet Explorer 5, you must set the **TABINDEX** attribute for elements that expose the **onblur** event.

Event Object Properties

clientX	**clientY**	**offsetX**	**offsetY**	**screenX**
screenY	**srcElement**	**type**	**x**	**y**

Example

The following example shows how to display the name of the object that has lost focus—that is, the object that fires the **onblur** event.

```
<HTML>
<BODY>
<INPUT TYPE=text NAME=txtFName VALUE="First Name"
    onblur="alert(event.srcElement.name)">
<INPUT TYPE=text NAME=txtLName VALUE="Last Name"
    onblur="alert(event.srcElement.name)">
<INPUT TYPE=text NAME=txtPhone VALUE="Phone"
    onblur="alert(event.srcElement.name)">
</BODY>
</HTML>
```

To see this code in action, refer to the Web Workshop CD-ROM.

DHTML Events

Applies To

 WIN16   WIN32   MAC

SELECT, TEXTAREA

 WIN16   WIN32   MAC   UNIX

A, APPLET, AREA, BUTTON, DIV, EMBED, FIELDSET, FRAME, FRAMESET, HR, IFRAME, INPUT type=button, INPUT type=checkbox, INPUT type=file, INPUT type=image, INPUT type=password, INPUT type=radio, INPUT type=reset, INPUT type=submit, INPUT type=text, ISINDEX, OBJECT, SELECT, SPAN, TABLE, TD, TEXTAREA, TR, window

 WIN16   WIN32   MAC   UNIX

ACRONYM, ADDRESS, B, BDO, BIG, BLOCKQUOTE, CAPTION, CENTER, CITE, DD, DEL, DFN, DIR, DL, DT, EM, FONT, FORM, Hn, I, IMG, INS, KBD, LABEL, LEGEND, LI, LISTING, MARQUEE, MENU, OL, P, PLAINTEXT, PRE, Q, RT, RUBY, S, SAMP, SMALL, STRIKE, STRONG, SUB, SUP, TBODY, TFOOT, TH, THEAD, TT, U, UL, VAR, XMP

onbounce Event

Fires when the **behavior** property of the **MARQUEE** object is set to "alternate" and the contents of the marquee reach the side of the window.

Syntax

Inline HTML	*<MARQUEE* onbounce *= "handler"* ... *>*	All platforms
Event property	*marquee*.onbounce *= handler*	JScript (compatible with ECMA 262 language specification) only
Named script	<SCRIPT FOR *= object* EVENT = onbounce>	Internet Explorer only

Remarks

Bubbles	No
Cancels	Yes
To invoke	Cause the **MARQUEE** contents to loop.
Default action	**MARQUEE** contents begin scrolling in the opposite direction.

Event Object Properties

clientX	**clientY**	**offsetX**	**offsetY**	**returnValue**
screenX	**screenY**	**srcElement**	**type**	**x**
y				

Example

The following example displays an alert each time the **onbounce** event occurs.

```
<BODY>
<MARQUEE ID=mqBounce BEHAVIOR=alternate
    onbounce="alert('onbounce fired')" LOOP=3
        WIDTH=200>Marquee text
</MARQUEE>
</BODY>
```

To see this code in action, refer to the Web Workshop CD-ROM.

Applies To

 WIN16   WIN32   MAC   UNIX

MARQUEE

oncellchange Event

Fires when data changes in a data provider.

Syntax

Inline HTML	*<ELEMENT* oncellchange = "*handler*" ... >	All platforms
Event property	*object*.oncellchange = *handler*	JScript (compatible with ECMA 262 language specification) only
Named script	<SCRIPT FOR = *object* EVENT = oncellchange>	Internet Explorer only

Remarks

Bubbles	Yes
Cancels	No
To invoke	Cause data in a data source to change.
Default action	Signals that the data contained in an object has changed.

Event Object Properties

bookmarks	**boundElements**	**cancelBubble**	**clientX**	**clientY**
dataFld	**offsetX**	**offsetY**	**recordset**	**screenX**
screenY	**srcElement**	**type**	**x**	**y**

Applies To

 WIN16   WIN32   MAC   UNIX

APPLET, BDO, OBJECT

onchange Event

Fires when the contents of the object or selection have changed.

Syntax

Inline HTML	*<ELEMENT* onchange = "*handler*" ... >	All platforms
Event property	*object*.onchange = *handler*	JScript (compatible with ECMA 262 language specification) only
Named script	<SCRIPT FOR = *object* EVENT = onchange>	Internet Explorer only

Remarks

Bubbles	No
Cancels	Yes
To invoke	• Choose a different **OPTION** in a **SELECT** object using mouse or keyboard navigation.
	• Alter text in the text area, and then navigate out of the object.
Default action	Changed text selection is committed.

This event is fired when the contents are committed and not while the value is changing. For example, on a text box, this event is not fired while the user is typing, but rather when the user commits the change by leaving the text box that has focus. In addition, this event is executed before the code specified by **onblur** when the control is also losing the focus.

On the **SELECT** object, this event does not fire programmatically when the **SELECTED** attribute is changed from one **OPTION** to another.

Event Object Properties

clientX	**clientY**	**offsetX**	**offsetY**	**returnValue**
screenX	**screenY**	**srcElement**	**type**	**x**
y				

Example

The example below shows how the **onchange** event works on the **SELECT** object.

```
<BODY>
<FORM>
<P>Select a different option in the
   dropdown listbox to trigger the onchange event.
  <SELECT NAME=selTest onchange="alert(event.srcElement.name +
        ' fired the onchange event')">
    <OPTION VALUE="Books">Books
    <OPTION VALUE="Clothing">Clothing
    <OPTION VALUE="Housewares">Housewares
  </SELECT>
</FORM>
</BODY>
```

To see this code in action, refer to the Web Workshop CD-ROM.

Applies To

 WIN16   WIN32   MAC

INPUT TYPE=text, SELECT, TEXTAREA

 UNIX

INPUT TYPE=text, SELECT, TEXTAREA

onclick Event

Fires when the user clicks the left mouse button on the object.

Syntax

Inline HTML	*<ELEMENT* onclick = "*handler*" ... >	All platforms
Event property	*object*.onclick = *handler*	JScript (compatible with ECMA 262 language specification) only
Named script	<SCRIPT FOR = *object* EVENT = onclick>	Internet Explorer only

Remarks

Bubbles	Yes
Cancels	Yes

To invoke
- Click the object.
- Invoke the **click** method.
- Press the ENTER key in a form.
- Press the access key for a control.
- Select an item in a combo box or list box by clicking the left mouse button, or by pressing the arrow keys and then pressing the ENTER key.

Default action   Initiates any action associated with the object. For example, if a user clicks an **A** object, the browser loads the document specified by the **href** property. To cancel the default behavior, set the **returnValue** property of the **event** object to FALSE.

If the user clicks the left mouse button, the **onclick** event for an object occurs only if the mouse pointer is over the object and an **onmousedown** event and an **onmouseup** event occur in that order. For example, if the user clicks the mouse on the object but moves the mouse pointer away from the object before releasing, no **onclick** event occurs.

The **onclick** event changes the value of a control in a group. This change initiates the event for the group, not for the individual control. For example, if the user clicks a radio button or check box in a group, the **onclick** event occurs after the **onbeforeupdate** and **onafterupdate** events for the control group.

If the user clicks an object that can receive the input focus but does not already have the focus, the **onfocus** event occurs for that object before the **onclick** event. If the user double-clicks the left mouse button in a control, an **ondblclick** event occurs immediately after the **onclick** event.

Although the **onclick** event is available on a large number of HTML elements, if a Web page is to be accessible to keyboard users, you should restrict its use to the **A**, **INPUT**, **AREA**, and **BUTTON** elements. These elements automatically allow keyboard access through the TAB key, making Web pages that use the elements accessible to keyboard users.

Event Object Properties

altKey	**cancelBubble**	**clientX**	**clientY**	**ctrlKey**
offsetX	**offsetY**	**returnValue**	**screenX**	**screenY**
shiftKey	**srcElement**	**type**	**x**	**y**

Example

The following example shows how to use the **event** object to gain information about the origin of the click and cancel the default action if the **onclick** event is fired off an anchor while the user presses the SHIFT key.

```
<SCRIPT LANGUAGE="JScript">
/* This code determines whether the click occurred in an anchor
   and then cancels the event, preventing the jump, if the SHIFT
   key is down. */
function clickIt()
{
    txtOutput.value = window.event.srcElement.tagName;
    txtOutput1.value = window.event.srcElement.type;

if ((window.event.srcElement.tagName) && ("A" + window.event.shiftKey))
   { window.event.returnValue = false; }
}
</SCRIPT>

<BODY onclick="clickIt()" TOPMARGIN="0" LEFTMARGIN="0">
```

To see this code in action, refer to the Web Workshop CD-ROM.

The next example shows how to bind the **onclick** event to grouped controls.

```
<SCRIPT LANGUAGE="JScript">

function CookieGroup()
{
txtOutput.value = window.event.srcElement.value;
}
</SCRIPT>
</HEAD>
<BODY>
<!-- Controls are grouped by giving them the same NAME but unique IDs. -->
<P>Grouped Radio Buttons<BR>
<INPUT TYPE=radio NAME=rdoTest ID=Cookies VALUE="accept_cookies" CHECKED
      onclick="CookieGroup()"><BR>
<INPUT TYPE=radio NAME=rdoTest ID=NoCookies VALUE="refuse_cookies"
      onclick="CookieGroup()"><BR>
<P>Ungrouped Radio Button<BR>
<INPUT TYPE=radio NAME=rdoTest1 VALUE="chocolate-chip_cookies"
      onclick="CookieGroup()"><BR>
<P>Value of control on which the onclick event has fired<BR>
<TEXTAREA NAME=txtOutput STYLE="width:250"></TEXTAREA>
</BODY>
```

To see this code in action, refer to the Web Workshop CD-ROM.

Applies To

 WIN16   WIN32   MAC   UNIX

A, ADDRESS, APPLET, AREA, B, BIG, BLOCKQUOTE, BODY, BUTTON, CAPTION, CENTER, CITE, CODE, DD, DFN, DIR, DIV, DL, document, DT, EM, EMBED, FIELDSET, FONT, FORM, Hn, HR, I, IMG, INPUT type=button, INPUT type=checkbox, INPUT type=file, INPUT type=image, INPUT type=password, INPUT type=radio, INPUT type=reset, INPUT type=submit, INPUT type=text, KBD, LABEL, LEGEND, LI, LISTING, MAP, MARQUEE, MENU, NEXTID, NOBR, OBJECT, OL, P, PLAINTEXT, PRE, S, SAMP, SELECT, SMALL, SPAN, STRIKE, STRONG, SUB, SUP, TABLE, TBODY, TD, TEXTAREA, TFOOT, TH, THEAD, TR, TT, U, UL, VAR, XMP

IE 5   **WIN16   WIN32   MAC   UNIX**

BDO, RT, RUBY

oncontextmenu Event

Fires when the user clicks the right mouse button in the client area, opening the context menu..

Syntax

Inline HTML	*<ELEMENT* oncontextmenu = "*handler*" ... >	All platforms
Event property	*object*.oncontextmenu = *handler*	JScript (compatible with ECMA 262 language specification) only
Named script	<SCRIPT FOR = *object* EVENT = oncontextmenu>	Internet Explorer only

Remarks

Bubbles	Yes
Cancels	Yes
To invoke	Right-click the object.
Default action	Opens the context menu. To cancel the default behavior, set the **returnValue** property of the **event** object to false.

Event Object Properties

altKey	**cancelBubble**	**clientX**	**clientY**	**ctrlKey**
offsetX	**offsetY**	**returnValue**	**screenX**	**screenY**
shiftKey	**srcElement**	**type**	**x**	**y**

Example

The example shows how to use the **oncontextmenu** event handlers for the document.

```
<SCRIPT FOR = document EVENT = oncontextmenu>
   document.oncontextmenu = fnContextMenu;
</SCRIPT>

<SCRIPT>
function fnContextMenu(){
   event.returnValue = false;
}
</SCRIPT>
```

To see this code in action, refer to the Web Workshop CD-ROM.

Applies To

WIN16	**WIN32**	**MAC**	**UNIX**

document

oncopy Event

Fires on the source element when the user duplicates the object or selection and adds the duplicated object or selection to the system clipboard.

Syntax

Inline HTML	*<ELEMENT* oncopy = "*handler*" ... > All platforms	
Event property	*object*.oncopy = *handler*	JScript (compatible with ECMA 262 language specification) only
Named script	<SCRIPT FOR = *object* EVENT = oncopy>	Internet Explorer only

Remarks

Bubbles	Yes
Cancels	Yes

DHTML Events

Remarks *(continued)*

> **To invoke**   After selecting text:
>
> - Right-click to display the shortcut menu and select Copy.
> - Or press CTRL+C.
>
> **Default action** Duplicates the selection.
>
> Use the **setData** method to specify a data format for the selection.

Event Object Properties

altKey	cancelBubble	clientX	clientY	ctrlKey
offsetX	offsetY	returnValue	screenX	screenY
shiftKey	srcElement	type	x	y

Applies To

WIN16   WIN32   MAC   UNIX

A, ADDRESS, AREA, B, BDO, BIG, BLOCKQUOTE, CAPTION, CENTER, CITE, CODE, DD, DFN, DIR, DIV, DL, DT, EM, FIELDSET, FORM, Hn, HR, I, IMG, LEGEND, LI, LISTING, MENU, NOBR, OL, P, PLAINTEXT, PRE, S, SAMP, SMALL, SPAN, STRIKE, STRONG, SUB, SUP, TD, TH, TR, TT, U, UL

oncut Event

Fires on the source element when the object or selection is removed from the document and added to the system clipboard.

Syntax

Inline HTML	*<ELEMENT* oncut = *"handler"* ... >	All platforms
Event property	*object*.oncut = *handler*	JScript (compatible with ECMA 262 language specification) only
Named script	<SCRIPT FOR = *object* EVENT = oncut>	Internet Explorer only

Remarks

Bubbles   Yes

Cancels   Yes

To invoke   After selecting text:

- Right-click to display the shortcut menu and select Cut.
- Or press CTRL+X.

Default action Removes the selection from the document and persists it in the clipboard.

Creating custom code for cutting requires several steps.

1. Set event.returnValue=false in the **onbeforecut** event to enable the Cut shortcut menu item.
2. Specify a data format in which to transfer the selection through the **setData** method of the **clipboardData** object.
3. Invoke the **setData** method in the **oncut** event.

Event Object Properties

altKey	**cancelBubble**	**clientX**	**clientY**	**ctrlKey**
offsetX	**offsetY**	**returnValue**	**screenX**	**screenY**
shiftKey	**srcElement**	**type**	**x**	**y**

Applies To

 WIN16   WIN32   MAC   UNIX

A, ADDRESS, AREA, B, BDO, BIG, BLOCKQUOTE, CAPTION, CENTER, CITE, CODE, DD, DFN, DIR, DIV, DL, DT, EM, FIELDSET, FORM, Hn, I, IMG, LEGEND, LI, LISTING, MENU, NOBR, OL, P, PLAINTEXT, PRE, S, SAMP, SMALL, SPAN, STRIKE, STRONG, SUB, SUP, TD, TH, TR, TT, U, UL

DHTML Events

ondataavailable Event

Fires periodically as data arrives from data source objects that asynchronously transmit their data.

Syntax

Inline HTML	`<ELEMENT ondataavailable = "handler" ... >`	All platforms
Event property	`object.ondataavailable = handler`	JScript (compatible with ECMA 262 language specification) only
Named script	`<SCRIPT FOR = object EVENT = ondataavailable>`	Internet Explorer only

Remarks

Bubbles	Yes
Cancels	No
To invoke	Fires when new data is received from the data source.
Default action	Signals that new data is available.

This event originates from data source objects.

Event Object Properties

bookmarks	boundElements	cancelBubble	dataFld	recordset
srcElement	type			

Applies To

IE 4   **WIN16**   **WIN32**   **MAC**   **UNIX**

APPLET, OBJECT

IE 5   **WIN16**   **WIN32**   **MAC**   **UNIX**

XML

ondatasetchanged Event

Fires when the data set exposed by a data source object changes.

Syntax

Inline HTML	*<ELEMENT* ondatasetchanged = *"handler"* ... >	All platforms
Event property	*object*.ondatasetchanged = *handler*	JScript (compatible with ECMA 262 language specification) only
Named script	<SCRIPT FOR = *object* EVENT = ondatasetchanged>	Internet Explorer only

Remarks

Bubbles	Yes
Cancels	No
To invoke	• Make initial data available from a data source object.
	• Have the data source object expose a different data set.
	• Perform a filter operation.

Default action Signals that the data set has changed.

This event originates from data source objects.

Event Object Properties

bookmarks	**boundElements**	**cancelBubble**	**dataFld**	**reason**
recordset	**srcElement**	**type**		

Applies To

 WIN16   WIN32   MAC   UNIX

APPLET, OBJECT

IE 5 **WIN16   WIN32   MAC   UNIX**

XML

DHTML Events

ondatasetcomplete Event

Fires to indicate that all data is available from the data source object.

Syntax

Inline HTML	*<ELEMENT* ondatasetcomplete = *"handler"* ... >	All platforms
Event property	*object*.ondatasetcomplete = *handler*	JScript (compatible with ECMA 262 language specification) only
Named script	<SCRIPT FOR = *object* EVENT = ondatasetcomplete>	Internet Explorer only

Remarks

Bubbles	Yes
Cancels	No
To invoke	Allow data set change to complete.
Default action	Sets the **reason** property of the **event** object to indicate the reason for completion to one of three values:

    0 Data transmitted successfully.

    1 Data transfer aborted.

    2 Data transferred in error.

This event originates from data source objects.

Event Object Properties

bookmarks	**boundElements**	**cancelBubble**	**dataFld**	**reason**
recordset	**srcElement**	**type**		

Applies To

IE 4	WIN16	WIN32	MAC	UNIX

APPLET, OBJECT

IE 5	WIN16	WIN32	MAC	UNIX

XML

ondblclick Event

Fires when the user double-clicks the object.

Syntax

Inline HTML	*<ELEMENT* ondblclick = "*handler*" ... >	All platforms
Event property	*object*.ondblclick = *handler*	JScript (compatible with ECMA 262 language specification) only
Named script	<SCRIPT FOR = *object* EVENT = ondblclick>	Internet Explorer only

Remarks

Bubbles	Yes
Cancels	Yes
To invoke	Click the left mouse button twice in rapid succession over an object. The two clicks must occur within the time limit specified by the double-click speed setting of the user's system.
Default action	Initiates any action that is associated with the event.

The order of events leading to the **ondblclick** event is **onmousedown**, **onmouseup**, **onclick**, **onmouseup**, and then **ondblclick**. Actions associated with any of these events are executed when the **ondblclick** event fires.

Event Object Properties

altKey	**cancelBubble**	**clientX**	**clientY**	**ctrlKey**
offsetX	**offsetY**	**returnValue**	**screenX**	**screenY**
shiftKey	**srcElement**	**type**	**x**	**y**

Example

The following example shows how to use the **ondblclick** event to add items to a list box by double-clicking.

```
<HEAD>
<SCRIPT>
function addItem()
{
sNewItem = new Option(txtEnter.value)
selList.add(sNewItem);
}
```

DHTML Events

```
  </SCRIPT>
  </HEAD>
  <BODY>
  <P>Enter text and then double-click in the text box to
     add text to the list box.
  <INPUT TYPE=text NAME=txtEnter VALUE="Enter_text"
     ondblclick="addItem()">
  <SELECT NAME=selList SIZE=5></SELECT>
  </BODY>
```

To see this code in action, refer to the Web Workshop CD-ROM.

Applies To

 WIN16   WIN32   MAC   UNIX

A, ADDRESS, APPLET, AREA, B, BIG, BLOCKQUOTE, BODY, BUTTON, CAPTION, CENTER, CITE, CODE, DD, DFN, DIR, DIV, DL, document, DT, EM, EMBED, FIELDSET, FONT, FORM, Hn, HR, I, IMG, INPUT type=button, INPUT type=checkbox, INPUT type=file, INPUT type=image, INPUT type=password, INPUT type=radio, INPUT type=reset, INPUT type=submit, INPUT type=text, KBD, LABEL, LEGEND, LI, LISTING, MAP, MARQUEE, MENU, NEXTID, NOBR, OBJECT, OL, P, PLAINTEXT, PRE, S, SAMP, SELECT, SMALL, SPAN, STRIKE, STRONG, SUB, SUP, TABLE, TBODY, TD, TEXTAREA, TFOOT, TH, THEAD, TR, TT, U, UL, VAR, XMP

 WIN16   WIN32   MAC   UNIX

BDO, RT, RUBY

ondrag Event

Fires on the source object continuously during a drag operation.

Syntax

Inline HTML	*<ELEMENT* ondrag = *"handler"* ... >	All platforms
Event property	*object*.ondrag = *handler*	JScript (compatible with ECMA 262 language specification) only
Named script	<SCRIPT FOR = *object* EVENT = ondrag>	Internet Explorer only

Remarks

Bubbles	Yes
Cancels	Yes

To invoke

- Drag a text selection or object within the browser.
- Drag a text selection or object to another browser.
- Drag a text selection or object to a drop target in another application.
- Drag a text selection or object to the system desktop.

Default action Calls the associated event handler if there is one.

This event fires on the source object after the **ondragstart** event. The **ondrag** event fires throughout the drag operation, whether the selection being dragged is over the drag source, a valid target, or an invalid target.

Event Object Properties

altKey	cancelBubble	clientX	clientY	ctrlKey
dataTransfer	offsetX	offsetY	returnValue	screenX
screenY	srcElement	type	x	y

Applies To

 WIN16 WIN32 MAC UNIX

A, ACRONYM, ADDRESS, AREA, B, BDO, BIG, BLOCKQUOTE, BODY, CAPTION, CENTER, CITE, CODE, DD, DEL, DFN, DIR, DIV, DL, document, DT, EM, FIELDSET, FONT, FORM, Hn, HR, I, IMG, INPUT type=button, INPUT type=checkbox, INPUT type=file, INPUT type=image, INPUT type=password, INPUT type=radio, INPUT type=reset, INPUT type=submit, INPUT type=text, KBD, LABEL, LI, LISTING, MAP, MARQUEE, MENU, NOBR, OBJECT, OL, P, PLAINTEXT, PRE, Q, S, SAMP, SMALL, SPAN, STRIKE, STRONG, SUB, SUP, TABLE, TBODY, TD, TEXTAREA, TR, TT, U, UL, VAR, XMP

DHTML Events

ondragend Event

Fires on the source object when the user releases the mouse at the close of a drag operation.

Syntax

Inline HTML	*<ELEMENT* ondragend = "*handler*" ... >	All platforms
Event property	*object*.ondragend = *handler*	JScript (compatible with ECMA 262 language specification) only
Named script	<SCRIPT FOR = *object* EVENT = ondragend>	Internet Explorer only

Remarks

Bubbles	Yes
Cancels	Yes
To invoke	Release the mouse button during a drag operation.
Default action	Calls the associated event handler.

The **ondragend** event is the final drag event to fire, following the **ondragleave** event, which fires on the target object.

Event Object Properties

altKey	cancelBubble	clientX	clientY	ctrlKey
dataTransfer	offsetX	offsetY	returnValue	screenX
screenY	srcElement	type	x	y

Applies To

 WIN16   WIN32   MAC   UNIX

A, ACRONYM, ADDRESS, AREA, B, BDO, BIG, BLOCKQUOTE, BODY, CAPTION, CENTER, CITE, CODE, DD, DEL, DFN, DIR, DIV, DL, document, DT, EM, FIELDSET, FONT, FORM, Hn, HR, I, IMG, INPUT type=button, INPUT type=checkbox, INPUT type=file, INPUT type=image, INPUT type=password, INPUT type=radio, INPUT type=reset, INPUT type=submit, INPUT type=text, KBD, LABEL, LI, LISTING, MAP, MARQUEE, MENU, NOBR, OBJECT, OL, P, PLAINTEXT, PRE, Q, S, SAMP, SMALL, SPAN, STRIKE, STRONG, SUB, SUP, TABLE, TBODY, TD, TEXTAREA, TR, TT, U, UL, VAR, XMP

ondragenter Event

Fires on the target element when the user drags the object to a valid drop target.

Syntax

Inline HTML	*<ELEMENT* ondragenter = *"handler"* ... >	All platforms
Event property	*object*.ondragenter = *handler*	JScript (compatible with ECMA 262 language specification) only
Named script	<SCRIPT FOR = *object* EVENT = ondragenter>	Internet Explorer only

Remarks

Bubbles	Yes
Cancels	Yes
To invoke	• Drag the selection over a valid drop target within the browser.
	• Drag the selection to a valid drop target within another browser window.
Default action	Calls the associated event handler. When scripting custom functionality, use the **returnValue** property to disable the default action.

You can handle the **ondragenter** event on the source or on the target object. Of the target events, it is the first to fire during a drag operation. Target events use the **getData** method to stipulate which data and data formats to retrieve. The list of drag-and-drop target events includes:

- **onbeforepaste**
- **onpaste**
- **ondragenter**
- **ondragover**
- **ondragleave**
- **ondrop**

Event Object Properties

altKey	**cancelBubble**	**clientX**	**clientY**	**ctrlKey**
dataTransfer	**offsetX**	**offsetY**	**returnValue**	**screenX**
screenY	**srcElement**	**type**	**x**	**y**

Example

The following example shows when and where each event fires during a drag-and-drop operation by listing each event and the name of the object firing it in a list box.

```
<HEAD>
<SCRIPT>
var oNewOption;

// Code for dynamically adding options to a select.

function ShowResults()
{                   // Information about the events
                    // and what object fired them.
  arg = event.type + "  fired by  " + event.srcElement.id;
  oNewOption = new Option();
  oNewOption.text = arg;
  oResults.add(oNewOption,0);
}
</SCRIPT>
</HEAD>
<BODY>
<P>Source events are wired up to this text box.</P>
<INPUT ID=txtDragOrigin VALUE="Text to Drag"
    ondragstart="ShowResults()"
    ondrag="ShowResults()"
    ondragend="ShowResults()"
>
<P>Target events are bound to this text box.</P>
<INPUT ID=txtDragDestination VALUE="Drag Destination"
    ondragenter="ShowResults()"
    ondragover="ShowResults()"
    ondragleave="ShowResults()"
    ondrop="ShowResults()"
>
<SELECT ID=oResults SIZE=30>
  <OPTION>List of Events Fired
</SELECT>
</BODY>
```

To see this code in action, refer to the Web Workshop CD-ROM.

Applies To

 WIN16   WIN32   MAC   UNIX

A, ACRONYM, ADDRESS, AREA, B, BDO, BIG, BLOCKQUOTE, BODY, BUTTON, CAPTION, CENTER, CITE, CODE, DD, DEL, DFN, DIR, DIV, DL, document, DT, EM, FIELDSET, FONT, FORM, Hn, HR, I, IMG, INPUT type=button, INPUT type=checkbox, INPUT type=file, INPUT type=image, INPUT type=password, INPUT type=radio, INPUT type=reset, INPUT type=submit,

WIN16   WIN32   MAC   UNIX

INPUT type=text, KBD, LABEL, LI, LISTING, MAP, MARQUEE, MENU, NOBR, OBJECT, OL, P, PLAINTEXT, PRE, Q, S, SAMP, SELECT, SMALL, SPAN, STRIKE, STRONG, SUB, SUP, TABLE, TBODY, TD, TEXTAREA, TFOOT, TH, THEAD, TR, TT, U, UL, VAR, XMP

ondragleave Event

Fires on the target object when the user moves the mouse out of a valid drop target during a drag operation.

Syntax

Inline HTML	*<ELEMENT* ondragleave = *"handler"* ... >	All platforms
Event property	*object*.ondragleave = *handler*	JScript (compatible with ECMA 262 language specification) only
Named script	<SCRIPT FOR = *object* EVENT = ondragleave>	Internet Explorer only

Remarks

Bubbles	Yes
Cancels	Yes
To invoke	Drag the selection over a valid drop target, and then move that selection out again without dropping it.
Default action	Calls the associated event handler.

Event Object Properties

altKey	**cancelBubble**	**clientX**	**clientY**	**ctrlKey**
dataTransfer	**offsetX**	**offsetY**	**returnValue**	**screenX**
screenY	**srcElement**	**type**	**x**	**y**

DHTML Events

Applies To

 WIN16   WIN32   MAC   UNIX

A, ACRONYM, ADDRESS, AREA, B, BDO, BIG, BLOCKQUOTE, BODY, BUTTON, CAPTION, CENTER, CITE, CODE, DD, DEL, DFN, DIR, DIV, DL, document, DT, EM, FIELDSET, FONT, FORM, Hn, HR, I, IMG, INPUT type=button, INPUT type=checkbox, INPUT type=file, INPUT type=image, INPUT type=password, INPUT type=radio, INPUT type=reset, INPUT type=submit, INPUT type=text, KBD, LABEL, LI, LISTING, MAP, MARQUEE, MENU, NOBR, OBJECT, OL, P, PLAINTEXT, PRE, Q, S, SAMP, SELECT, SMALL, SPAN, STRIKE, STRONG, SUB, SUP, TABLE, TBODY, TD, TEXTAREA, TR, TT, U, UL, VAR, XMP

ondragover Event

Fires on the target element continuously while the user drags the object over a valid drop target.

Syntax

Inline HTML	`<ELEMENT ondragover = "handler" ... >`	All platforms
Event property	`object.ondragover = handler`	JScript (compatible with ECMA 262 language specification) only
Named script	`<SCRIPT FOR = object EVENT = ondragover>`	Internet Explorer only

Remarks

Bubbles	Yes
Cancels	Yes
To invoke	• Drag the selection over a valid drop target within the browser.
	• Drag the selection to a valid drop target within another browser window.
Default action	Calls the associated event handler.

The **ondragover** event fires on the target object after the **ondragenter** event has fired.

When scripting this event, use the **returnValue** property to disable the default action.

Event Object Properties

altKey	cancelBubble	clientX	clientY	ctrlKey
dataTransfer	offsetX	offsetY	returnValue	screenX
screenY	srcElement	type	x	y

Applies To

 WIN16   WIN32   MAC   UNIX

A, ACRONYM, ADDRESS, AREA, B, BDO, BIG, BLOCKQUOTE, BODY,
BUTTON, CAPTION, CENTER, CITE, CODE, DD, DEL, DFN, DIR, DIV, DL,
document, DT, EM, FIELDSET, FONT, FORM, Hn, HR, I, IMG, INPUT
type=button, INPUT type=checkbox, INPUT type=file, INPUT type=image, INPUT
type=password, INPUT type=radio, INPUT type=reset, INPUT type=submit, INPUT
type=text, KBD, LABEL, LI, LISTING, MAP, MARQUEE, MENU, NOBR,
OBJECT, OL, P, PLAINTEXT, PRE, Q, S, SAMP, SELECT, SMALL, SPAN,
STRIKE, STRONG, SUB, SUP, TABLE, TBODY, TD, TEXTAREA, TR, TT, U, UL,
VAR, XMP

ondragstart Event

Fires on the source object when the user starts to drag a text selection or selected
object.

Syntax

Inline HTML	*<ELEMENT* ondragstart = "*handler*" ... >	All platforms
Event property	*object*.ondragstart = *handler*	JScript (compatible with ECMA 262 language specification) only
Named script	<SCRIPT FOR = *object* EVENT = ondragstart>	Internet Explorer only

Remarks

Bubbles	Yes
Cancels	Yes
To invoke	Drag the selected text or object.
Default action	Calls the associated event handler.

DHTML Events

The **ondragstart** event is the first to fire when the user starts to drag the mouse. It is essential to every drag operation, yet is just one of several source events in the data transfer object model. Source events use the **setData** method of the **dataTransfer** object to provide information about data being transferred. Source events include: **ondragstart**, **ondrag**, and **ondragend**.

Event Object Properties

altKey	**cancelBubble**	**clientX**	**clientY**	**ctrlKey**
dataTransfer	**offsetX**	**offsetY**	**returnValue**	**screenX**
screenY	**srcElement**	**type**	**x**	**y**

Example

The following example shows how to detect the **tagName** property of the object from which the **ondragstart** event has originated. The example uses event bubbling to handle the **ondragstart** event at the **BODY** level.

```
<BODY ondragstart="alert(event.srcElement.tagName)">
  <INPUT TYPE=text VALUE="Select and drag this text">
  <SPAN>Select and drag this text</SPAN>
  <TEXTAREA>Select and drag this text</TEXTAREA>
</BODY>
```

To see this code in action, refer to the Web Workshop CD-ROM.

The next example shows the order of event firing for drag-and-drop events.

```
<HEAD>
<SCRIPT>
function ShowResults()
var oNewOption;

// Code for dynamically adding options to a select.

function ShowResults()
{                  // Information about the events
                   // and what object fired them.
  arg = event.type + "  fired by  " + event.srcElement.id;

  oNewOption = new Option();
  oNewOption.text = arg;
  oResults.add(oNewOption,0);
}
</SCRIPT>
</HEAD>
<BODY>
<P>Source events are wired up to this text box.</P>
<INPUT ID=txtDragOrigin VALUE="Text to Drag"
    ondragstart="ShowResults()"
    ondrag="ShowResults()"
```

```
    ondragend="ShowResults()"
>
<P>Target events are bound to this text box.</P>
<INPUT ID=txtDragDestination VALUE="Drag Destination"
    ondragenter="ShowResults()"
    ondragover="ShowResults()"
    ondragleave="ShowResults()"
    ondrop="ShowResults()"
>
<SELECT ID=oResults SIZE=30>
  <OPTION>List of Events Fired
</SELECT>
</BODY>
```

To see this code in action, refer to the Web Workshop CD-ROM.

Applies To

 WIN16   WIN32   MAC   UNIX

A, ACRONYM, ADDRESS, AREA, B, BIG, BLOCKQUOTE, BODY, CAPTION, CENTER, CITE, CODE, DD, DEL, DFN, DIR, DIV, DL, document, DT, EM, FIELDSET, FONT, FORM, Hn, HR, I, IMG, INPUT type=button, INPUT type=checkbox, INPUT type=file, INPUT type=image, INPUT type=password, INPUT type=radio, INPUT type=reset, INPUT type=submit, INPUT type=text, KBD, LABEL, LI, LISTING, MAP, MARQUEE, MENU, NEXTID, NOBR, OBJECT, OL, P, PLAINTEXT, PRE, Q, S, SAMP, SMALL, SPAN, STRIKE, STRONG, SUB, SUP, TABLE, TBODY, TD, TEXTAREA, TFOOT, TH, THEAD, TR, TT, U, UL, VAR, XMP

 WIN16   WIN32   MAC   UNIX

BDO, RT, RUBY

ondrop Event

Fires on the target object when the mouse button is released during a drag-and-drop operation.

Syntax

| **Inline HTML** | *<ELEMENT* ondrop = *"handler"* ... > | All platforms |
| **Event property** | *object*.ondrop = *handler* | JScript (compatible with ECMA 262 language specification) only |

Syntax *(continued)*

Named	`<SCRIPT FOR = `*`object`*` EVENT` Internet Explorer only
script	`= ondrop>`

Remarks

Bubbles	Yes
Cancels	Yes
To invoke	Drag the selection over a valid drop target and release the mouse.
Default action	Calls the associated event handler.

The **ondrop** event fires before the **ondragleave** and **ondragend** events.

When scripting this event, use the **returnValue** property to disable the default action.

Event Object Properties

altKey	cancelBubble	clientX	clientY	ctrlKey
dataTransfer	offsetX	offsetY	returnValue	screenX
screenY	srcElement	type	x	y

Applies To

 WIN16   WIN32   MAC   UNIX

A, ACRONYM, ADDRESS, AREA, B, BDO, BIG, BLOCKQUOTE, BODY, BUTTON, CAPTION, CENTER, CITE, CODE, DD, DEL, DFN, DIR, DIV, DL, document, DT, EM, FIELDSET, FONT, FORM, Hn, HR, I, IMG, INPUT type=button, INPUT type=checkbox, INPUT type=file, INPUT type=image, INPUT type=password, INPUT type=radio, INPUT type=reset, INPUT type=submit, INPUT type=text, KBD, LABEL, LI, LISTING, MAP, MARQUEE, MENU, NOBR, OBJECT, OL, P, PLAINTEXT, PRE, Q, S, SAMP, SELECT, SMALL, SPAN, STRIKE, STRONG, SUB, SUP, TABLE, TBODY, TD, TEXTAREA, TR, TT, U, UL, VAR, XMP

onerror Event

Fires when an error occurs during object loading.

Syntax

Inline HTML	*<ELEMENT* onerror = *"handler"* ... >	All platforms
Event property	*object*.onerror = *handler*	JScript (compatible with ECMA 262 language specification) only
Named script	<SCRIPT FOR = *object* EVENT = onerror>	Internet Explorer only

Event Handler Parameters

When this event is bound to the **window** object, the following parameters apply. These parameters are required in Microsoft® Visual Basic® Scripting Edition (VBScript).

Parameter	Description
sMsg	Optional. Description of the error that occurred.
sUrl	Optional. URL of the page on which the error occurred.
sLine	Optional. Line number on which the error occurred.

Remarks

Bubbles	No
Cancels	Yes
To invoke	Cause an error to occur:

- Produce a run-time script error, such as an invalid object reference or security violation.
- Produce an error while downloading an object, such as an image.

Default action	• Displays the browser error message when a problem occurs.
	• Executes any error handling routine associated with the event.

To set the **returnValue** property of the **event** object to `true`, or simply return `true` in JScript, suppress the default Internet Explorer error message for the **window** event.

The **onerror** event fires for run-time errors, but not for compilation errors. In addition, error dialog boxes raised by script debuggers are not suppressed by returning true. To turn off script debuggers, disable script debugging in Internet Explorer by clicking Tools, Internet Options, and then Advanced.

Event Object Properties

returnValue   **srcElement**   **type**

Example

The following example shows how to specify an invalid script entry. The script in the text field is evaluated when the Throw Error button is clicked. The **onerror** event fires because the script is invalid. The error results are inserted at the bottom of the sample page instead of in a dialog box.

```
<SCRIPT>
window.onerror=fnErrorTrap;
function fnErrorTrap(sMsg,sUrl,sLine){
   oErrorLog.innerHTML="<b>An error was thrown and caught.</b><p>";
   oErrorLog.innerHTML+="Error: " + sMsg + "<br>";
   oErrorLog.innerHTML+="Line: " + sLine + "<br>";
   oErrorLog.innerHTML+="URL: " + sUrl + "<br>";
   return false;
}
function fnThrow(){
   eval(oErrorCode.value);
}
</SCRIPT>
<INPUT TYPE="text" ID=oErrorCode VALUE="someObject.someProperty=true;">
<INPUT TYPE="button" VALUE="Throw Error" onclick="fnThrow()">
<P>
<DIV ID="oErrorLog">
</DIV>
```

To see this code in action, refer to the Web Workshop CD-ROM.

The next example shows how to set the handler for the **onerror** event in script before an image source is specified. When the invalid source is set on the **IMG** element, the event fires.

```
<SCRIPT>
var sImg='<IMG STYLE="display: none;" ID=oStub ALT="Default Text">';
function fnLoadFirst(){
   oContainer.innerHTML=sImg;
   oStub.onerror=fnLoadFail1;
   oStub.src="";
   oStub.style.display="block";
}
function fnLoadFail1(){
   oStub.alt="Image failed to load.";
   return true;
}
</SCRIPT>
```

```
<INPUT TYPE=button VALUE="Load First Image" onclick="fnLoadFirst()">
<DIV ID=oContainer></DIV>
```

To see this code in action, refer to the Web Workshop CD-ROM.

Applies To

 WIN16   WIN32   MAC

window

 WIN16   WIN32   MAC   UNIX

IMG, LINK, OBJECT, SCRIPT, STYLE, window

onerrorupdate Event

Fires on a databound object when an error occurs while updating the associated data in the data source object.

Syntax

Inline HTML	*<ELEMENT* onerrorupdate = *"handler"* ... >	All platforms
Event property	*object*.onerrorupdate = *handler*	JScript (compatible with ECMA 262 language specification) only
Named script	<SCRIPT FOR = *object* EVENT = onerrorupdate>	Internet Explorer only

Remarks

Bubbles	Yes
Cancels	No
To invoke	Cause the **onbeforeupdate** event to fire and cancel the data transfer.
Default action	Executes any error handling you have included.

Event Object Properties

cancelBubble   srcElement   type

Applies To

IE 4 **WIN16** **WIN32** **MAC** **UNIX**
_____
INPUT TYPE=text, TEXTAREA

IE 5 **WIN16** **WIN32** **MAC** **UNIX**
_____
BDO, RT, RUBY

onfilterchange Event

Fires when a visual filter changes state or completes a transition.

Syntax

Inline HTML	*<ELEMENT* onfilterchange = "*handler*" ... >	All platforms
Event property	*object*.onfilterchange = *handler*	JScript (compatible with ECMA 262 language specification) only
Named script	<SCRIPT FOR = *object* EVENT = onfilterchange>	Internet Explorer only

Remarks

Bubbles   No

Cancels   No

To invoke   Change the filter state.

Default action Signals that the filter on an object has changed state.

Event Object Properties

cancelBubble   **srcElement**   **srcFilter**   **type**

Example

The following example shows how to use the **onfilterchange** event to trigger a filter effect. When the page loads, the block of text disappears from view using a checkerboard-down **transition**. Once the checkerboard **transition** is complete, the image gradually appears using a box-in **transition**.

```
<HTML>
<HEAD>
<TITLE>Microsoft Cascading Style Sheet Controls Samples</TITLE>
</HEAD>
```

```
<BODY>
<H2>Some text filters out (checkerboard), and at its completion
an image filters in (box-in).  Refresh repeats.</H2>
<DIV ID="TextRegion" STYLE="Position: absolute; border: solid red;
    background-color: lightblue; LEFT: 0; TOP: 100; WIDTH: 100%;
    VISIBILITY: visible; FILTER: revealTrans(Transition = 11,
    Duration = 1.25)">
Text that filters upon pageload.<br>
Text that filters upon pageload.<br>
Text that filters upon pageload.<br>
Text that filters upon pageload.<br>
Text that filters upon pageload.<br>
Text that filters upon pageload.<br>
Text that filters upon pageload.
</DIV>
<DIV ID="ImageRegion" STYLE="Position: absolute; border: solid red;
    LEFT: 0; TOP: 100; WIDTH: 30%; VISIBILITY: hidden;
    FILTER: revealTrans(Transition = 0, Duration = 1.25)">
<IMAGE id=image1 SRC="/workshop/samples/author/graphics/dhtml/blupan.gif">
</DIV>
<SCRIPT LANGUAGE=VBScript>
Sub Window_onload
    Call TextRegion.filters.revealTrans.Apply ()
    Call ImageRegion.filters.revealTrans.Apply()
    Call Start
End Sub

Sub Start
    TextRegion.style.visibility = "hidden"
    ImageRegion.style.visibility = "visible"
    Call TextRegion.filters.revealTrans.Play()
End Sub

Sub TextRegion_onfilterchange
    if TextRegion.filters.revealTrans.Status = 0 then
        Call ImageRegion.filters.revealTrans.Play(1.5)
    End If
End Sub
</SCRIPT>
</BODY>
</HTML>
```

To see this code in action, refer to the Web Workshop CD-ROM.

Applies To

 WIN16　　WIN32　　MAC　　UNIX

BODY, BUTTON, DIV, FIELDSET, IMG, INPUT type=button, INPUT
type=checkbox, INPUT type=file, INPUT type=image, INPUT type=password,
INPUT type=radio, INPUT type=reset, INPUT type=submit, INPUT type=text,
MARQUEE, NEXTID, SPAN, TABLE, TD, TEXTAREA, TH, TR

IE 5 **WIN16   WIN32   MAC   UNIX**

BDO, RT, RUBY

onfinish Event

Fires when marquee looping is complete.

Syntax

Inline HTML	*<MARQUEE* onfinish *= "handler"* ... *>*	All platforms
Event property	*marquee.*onfinish *= handler*	JScript (compatible with ECMA 262 language specification) only
Named script	<SCRIPT FOR *= marquee* EVENT *=* onfinish>	Internet Explorer only

Remarks

Bubbles	No
Cancels	Yes
To invoke	Specify a value for the **LOOP** attribute of the **MARQUEE** object.
Default action	Marquee ceases to loop.

A value greater than 1 and less than infinity must be set on the **LOOP** attribute for this event to fire.

Event Object Properties

clientX	**clientY**	**offsetX**	**offsetY**	**returnValue**
screenX	**screenY**	**srcElement**	**type**	**x**
y				

Example

The following example shows how to use the **srcElement** property of the **event** object to determine which marquee has fired the **onfinish** event.

```
<BODY>
<LABEL>mqLooper1</LABEL>
<MARQUEE ID=mqLooper1 LOOP=2
        onfinish="alert(event.srcElement.id + ' finished looping.')">
        this marquee loops twice
```

```
</MARQUEE>
<HR>
<LABEL>mqLooper2</LABEL>
<MARQUEE ID=mqLooper2 LOOP=5
         onfinish="alert(event.srcElement.id + ' finished looping.')">
         this marquee loops five times
</MARQUEE>
</BODY>
```

To see this code in action, refer to the Web Workshop CD-ROM.

Applies To

 WIN16   WIN32   MAC   UNIX

MARQUEE

onfocus Event

Fires when the object receives the focus.

Syntax

Inline HTML	*<ELEMENT* onfocus = "*handler*" ... >	All platforms
Event property	*object*.onfocus = *handler*	JScript (compatible with ECMA 262 language specification) only
Named script	<SCRIPT FOR = *object* EVENT = onfocus>	Internet Explorer only

Remarks

Bubbles	No
Cancels	No
To invoke	Give focus to an object:

- Click an object.
- Use keyboard navigation.
- Invoke the **focus** method.

Default action Sets focus to an object.

When one object loses focus and another object receives focus, the **onfocus** event fires on the object receiving focus only after the **onblur** event fires on the object losing focus.

DHTML Events

As of Microsoft Internet Explorer 5, you can force elements that do not implicitly receive focus to receive focus by adding them to the document tabbing order using the **TABINDEX** attribute.

Elements cannot receive focus until the document is finished loading.

As of Internet Explorer 5, elements retain focus within the current browser history when the user returns to a page. To avoid firing the **onfocus** event unintentionally for an element when the document loads, invoke the **focus** method on another element.

Event Object Properties

clientX	**clientY**	**offsetX**	**offsetY**	**returnValue**
screenX	**screenY**	**srcElement**	**type**	**x**
y				

Example

The following example shows how to use the **onfocus** event to make **INPUT_text** and **LABEL** objects more accessible. When the **INPUT_text** object has focus, the **onfocus** event fires and the **backgroundColor**, **fontSize**, and **fontWeight** properties are changed to give the control more prominence.

```
<STYLE>
.accessible {
    background-color: "#AAAAFF";
    font-weight: bold;
    font-size: 12pt;
}
</STYLE>

<SCRIPT>
function fnSetStyle(){
    event.srcElement.className="accessible";
    var oWorkLabel=eval(event.srcElement.id + "_label");
    oWorkLabel.className="accessible";
}
</SCRIPT>

<LABEL FOR="oInput" CLASS="normal" ID="oInput_label">
Enter some text</LABEL>

<INPUT TYPE="text"
    CLASS="normal"
    onfocus="fnSetStyle()"
    ID="oInput"
>
```

To see this code in action, refer to the Web Workshop CD-ROM.

Applies To

WIN16   WIN32   MAC

INPUT type=button, INPUT type=checkbox, INPUT type=file, INPUT type=hidden, INPUT type=image, INPUT type=password, INPUT type=radio, INPUT type=reset, INPUT type=submit, INPUT type=text, TEXTAREA

WIN16   WIN32   MAC   UNIX

A, APPLET, AREA, BUTTON, DIV, EMBED, FIELDSET, FRAME, FRAMESET, IFRAME, INPUT type=button, INPUT type=checkbox, INPUT type=file, INPUT type=hidden, INPUT type=image, INPUT type=password, INPUT type=radio, INPUT type=reset, INPUT type=submit, INPUT type=text, ISINDEX, OBJECT, SELECT, SPAN, TABLE, TD, TEXTAREA, TR, window

WIN16   WIN32   MAC   UNIX

ACRONYM, ADDRESS, B, BDO, BIG, BLOCKQUOTE, CAPTION, CENTER, CITE, DD, DEL, DFN, DIR, DL, DT, EM, FONT, FORM, Hn, HR, I, IMG, INS, KBD, LABEL, LEGEND, LI, LISTING, MARQUEE, MENU, OL, P, PLAINTEXT, PRE, Q, RT, RUBY, S, SAMP, SMALL, STRIKE, STRONG, SUB, SUP, TBODY, TFOOT, TH, THEAD, TT, U, UL, VAR, XMP

onhelp Event

Fires when the user presses the F1 key while the browser is the active window.

Syntax

Inline HTML	*<ELEMENT* onhelp *= "handler"* ... >	All platforms
Event property	*object*.onhelp *= handler*	JScript (compatible with ECMA 262 language specification) only
Named script	<SCRIPT FOR = *object* EVENT = onhelp>	Internet Explorer only

Remarks

Bubbles	Yes
Cancels	Yes
To invoke	Press the F1 key.

DHTML Events

Remarks *(continued)*

Default action Firing the **onhelp** event opens an online Help window.

Event Object Properties

cancelBubble	**clientX**	**clientY**	**ctrlKey**	**offsetX**
offsetY	**returnValue**	**screenX**	**screenY**	**shiftKey**
srcElement	**type**	**x**	**y**	

Applies To

 WIN16   WIN32   MAC   UNIX

A, ADDRESS, APPLET, AREA, B, BIG, BLOCKQUOTE, BUTTON, CAPTION, CENTER, CITE, CODE, DD, DFN, DIR, DIV, DL, document, DT, EM, EMBED, FIELDSET, FONT, FORM, Hn, HR, I, IMG, INPUT type=button, INPUT type=checkbox, INPUT type=file, INPUT type=image, INPUT type=password, INPUT type=radio, INPUT type=reset, INPUT type=submit, INPUT type=text, KBD, LABEL, LEGEND, LI, LISTING, MAP, MARQUEE, MENU, NEXTID, NOBR, OL, P, PLAINTEXT, PRE, S, SAMP, SELECT, SMALL, SPAN, STRIKE, STRONG, SUB, SUP, TABLE, TBODY, TD, TEXTAREA, TFOOT, TH, THEAD, TR, TT, U, UL, VAR, window, XMP

 WIN16   WIN32   MAC   UNIX

BDO, RT, RUBY

onkeydown Event

Fires when the user presses a key.

Syntax

Inline HTML	*<ELEMENT* onkeydown = "*handler*" ... >	All platforms
Event property	*object*.onkeydown = *handler*	JScript (compatible with ECMA 262 language specification) only
Named script	<SCRIPT FOR = *object* EVENT = onkeydown>	Internet Explorer only

Remarks

Bubbles	Yes
Cancels	Yes
To invoke	Press any keyboard key.
Default action	Returns a number specifying the **keyCode** of the key that was pressed.

In Microsoft Internet Explorer 4.0, the **onkeydown** event fires for the following keys:

- Editing: DELETE, INSERT
- Function: F1 - F12
- Letters: a - z
- Navigation: HOME, END, Left Arrow, Right Arrow, Up Arrow, Down Arrow
- Numerals: 0 - 9
- Symbols: ! @ # $ % ^ & * ( ) _ - + = < > [ ] { } , . / ? \ | ' ` " ~
- System: ESCAPE, SPACE, SHIFT, TAB

In addition, the event fires for the following keys in Internet Explorer 5:

- Editing: BACKSPACE
- Navigation: PAGE UP, PAGE DOWN
- System: SHIFT+TAB

As of Internet Explorer 5, the following keys and key combinations can be canceled by specifying `event.returnValue=false`:

- Editing: BACKSPACE, DELETE
- Letters: a - z
- Navigation: PAGE UP, PAGE DOWN, END, HOME, Left Arrow, Right Arrow, Up Arrow, Down Arrow
- Numerals: 0 - 9
- Symbols: ! @ # $ % ^ & * ( ) _ - + = < > [ ] { } , . / ? \ | ' ` " ~
- System: SPACE, ESCAPE, TAB, SHIFT+TAB

You can cancel all keys that fire the **onkeydown** event in HTML Applications (HTAs), including most accelerator keys, such as ALT+F4.

In Internet Explorer 4.0, you cannot cancel the **onkeydown** event. You can, however, use the **onkeypress** event to cancel keyboard events.

DHTML Events

Event Object Properties

altKey	**cancelBubble**	**clientX**	**clientY**	**ctrlKey**
keyCode	**offsetX**	**offsetY**	**repeat**	**returnValue**
screenX	**screenY**	**shiftKey**	**srcElement**	**type**
x	**y**			

Example

The following sample code shows how to use the **onkeydown** event to cancel input from the keyboard.

```
<SCRIPT>
function fnTrapKD(){
   if(oTrap.checked){
      oOutput.innerText+="[trap = " + event.keyCode + "]";
      event.returnValue=false;
   }
   else{
      oOutput.innerText+=String.fromCharCode(event.keyCode);
   }
}
</SCRIPT>
<INPUT TYPE="checkbox" ID="oTrap">
<INPUT ID="oExample" TYPE="text" onkeydown="fnTrapKD()">
<TEXTAREA ID="oOutput" ROWS="10" COLS="50">
</TEXTAREA>
```

To see this code in action, refer to the Web Workshop CD-ROM.

Applies To

 WIN16   WIN32   MAC   UNIX

A, ACRONYM, ADDRESS, APPLET, AREA, B, BIG, BLOCKQUOTE, BODY, BUTTON, CAPTION, CENTER, CITE, CODE, DD, DEL, DFN, DIR, DIV, document, DT, EM, FIELDSET, FONT, FORM, Hn, HR, I, INPUT type=button, INPUT type=checkbox, INPUT type=file, INPUT type=image, INPUT type=password, INPUT type=radio, INPUT type=reset, INPUT type=submit, INPUT type=text, KBD, LABEL, LEGEND, LI, LISTING, MAP, MARQUEE, MENU, NEXTID, NOBR, OBJECT, OL, P, PLAINTEXT, PRE, Q, S, SAMP, SELECT, SMALL, SPAN, STRIKE, STRONG, SUB, SUP, TABLE, TBODY, TD, TEXTAREA, TFOOT, TH, THEAD, TR, TT, U, UL, VAR, XMP

 WIN16   WIN32   MAC   UNIX

BDO, RT, RUBY

onkeypress Event

Fires when the user presses an alphanumeric key.

Syntax

Inline HTML	*<ELEMENT* onkeypress = "*handler*" ... >	All platforms
Event property	*object*.onkeypress = *handler*	JScript (compatible with ECMA 262 language specification) only
Named script	<SCRIPT FOR = *object* EVENT = onkeypress>	Internet Explorer only

Remarks

Bubbles	Yes
Cancels	Yes
To invoke	Press an alphanumeric keyboard key.
Default action	Returns a number specifying the Unicode value of the key that was pressed.

Alphanumeric keyboard keys include uppercase letters, lowercase letters, numbers, symbols, punctuation characters, and the ESC, SPACE, and ENTER keys.

As of Microsoft Internet Explorer 4.0, the **onkeypress** event fires and can be canceled for the following keys:

- Letters: a - z
- Numerals: 0 - 9
- Symbols: ! @ # $ % ^ & * ( ) _ - + = < > [ ] { } , . / ? \ | ' ` " ~
- System: ESCAPE, SPACE, SHIFT

Event Object Properties

altKey	**cancelBubble**	**clientX**	**clientY**	**ctrlKey**
keyCode	**offsetX**	**offsetY**	**returnValue**	**screenX**
screenY	**shiftKey**	**srcElement**	**type**	**x**
y				

Example

The following example shows how to retrieve information from the **shiftKey** property of the **event** object. When the user simultaneously presses the SHIFT key and types a character in the first text field, the value "true" appears in the second text field.

```
<HEAD>
<SCRIPT>
function checkKey()
{
if (window.event.shiftKey)  // checks whether the SHIFT key
                            // is pressed
   {
   txtOutput.value = "true"; // returns TRUE if SHIFT is pressed
                            // when the event fires
   }
}
</SCRIPT>
</HEAD>
<BODY>
<P>Press the SHIFT key while pressing another key.<BR>
   <INPUT TYPE=text NAME=txtEnterValue onkeypress="checkKey()">
<P>Indicates "true" if the shift key is used.<BR>
   <INPUT TYPE=text NAME=txtOutput>
</BODY>
```

To see this code in action, refer to the Web Workshop CD-ROM.

Applies To

 WIN16   WIN32   MAC   UNIX

A, ACRONYM, ADDRESS, APPLET, AREA, B, BIG, BLOCKQUOTE, BODY,
BUTTON, CAPTION, CENTER, CITE, CODE, DD, DEL, DFN, DIR, DIV,
document, DT, EM, FIELDSET, FONT, FORM, Hn, HR, I, INPUT type=button,
INPUT type=checkbox, INPUT type=file, INPUT type=image, INPUT
type=password, INPUT type=radio, INPUT type=reset, INPUT type=submit, INPUT
type=text, KBD, LABEL, LEGEND, LI, LISTING, MAP, MARQUEE, MENU,
NEXTID, NOBR, OBJECT, OL, P, PLAINTEXT, PRE, Q, S, SAMP, SELECT,
SMALL, SPAN, STRIKE, STRONG, SUB, SUP, TABLE, TBODY, TD,
TEXTAREA, TFOOT, TH, THEAD, TR, TT, U, UL, VAR, XMP

 WIN16   WIN32   MAC   UNIX

BDO, RT, RUBY

onkeyup Event

Fires when the user releases a key.

Syntax

Inline HTML	*<ELEMENT* onkeyup = "*handler*" ... >	All platforms
Event property	*object*.onkeyup = *handler*	JScript (compatible with ECMA 262 language specification) only
Named script	<SCRIPT FOR = *object* EVENT = onkeyup>	Internet Explorer only

Remarks

Bubbles	Yes
Cancels	No
To invoke	Release any keyboard key.
Default action	Returns a number specifying the **keyCode** of the key that was released.

In Microsoft Internet Explorer 4.0, the **onkeyup** event fires for the following keys:

- Editing: DELETE, INSERT
- Function: F1 - F12
- Letters: a - z
- Navigation: HOME, END, Left Arrow, Right Arrow, Up Arrow, Down Arrow
- Numerals: 0 - 9
- Symbols: ! @ # $ % ^ & * ( ) _ - + = < > [ ] { } , . / ? \ | ' ` " ~
- System: ESCAPE, SPACE, SHIFT, TAB

In addition, the event fires for the following keys in Internet Explorer 5:

- Editing: BACKSPACE
- Navigation: PAGE UP, PAGE DOWN
- System: SHIFT+TAB

DHTML Events

Event Object Properties

altKey	cancelBubble	clientX	clientY	ctrlKey
keyCode	offsetX	offsetY	returnValue	screenX
screenY	shiftKey	srcElement	type	x
y				

Applies To

 WIN16   WIN32   MAC   UNIX

A, ACRONYM, ADDRESS, APPLET, AREA, B, BIG, BLOCKQUOTE, BODY, BUTTON, CAPTION, CENTER, CITE, CODE, DD, DEL, DFN, DIR, DIV, document, DT, EM, FIELDSET, FONT, FORM, Hn, HR, I, INPUT type=button, INPUT type=checkbox, INPUT type=file, INPUT type=image, INPUT type=password, INPUT type=radio, INPUT type=reset, INPUT type=submit, INPUT type=text, KBD, LABEL, LEGEND, LI, LISTING, MAP, MARQUEE, MENU, NEXTID, NOBR, OBJECT, OL, P, PLAINTEXT, PRE, Q, S, SAMP, SELECT, SMALL, SPAN, STRIKE, STRONG, SUB, SUP, TABLE, TBODY, TD, TEXTAREA, TFOOT, TH, THEAD, TR, TT, U, UL, VAR, XMP

 WIN16   WIN32   MAC   UNIX

BDO, RT, RUBY

onload Event

Fires immediately after the browser loads the object.

Syntax

Inline HTML	`<ELEMENT onload = "handler" ... >`	All platforms
Event property	`object.onload = handler`	JScript (compatible with ECMA 262 language specification) only
Named script	`<SCRIPT FOR = object EVENT = onload>`	Internet Explorer only

Remarks

Bubbles	No
Cancels	No
To invoke	Open a page in the browser to invoke this event for the document or any object within it.
Default action	Loads the object for which the event is specified.

The browser loads applications, embedded objects, and images as soon as it encounters the **APPLET**, **EMBED**, and **IMG** objects during parsing. Consequently, the **onload** event for these objects occurs before the browser parses any subsequent objects. To ensure that an event handler receives the **onload** event for these objects, place the **SCRIPT** object that defines the event handler before the object and use the **onload** attribute in the object to set the handler.

The **onload** attribute of the **BODY** object sets an **onload** event handler for the **window**. This technique of calling the window **onload** event through the **BODY** object is overridden by any other means of invoking the window **onload** event, provided the handlers are in the same script language.

Event Object Properties

clientX	**clientY**	**offsetX**	**offsetY**	**screenX**
screenY	**type**	**x**	**y**	

Example

This example shows how to use an **onload** event handler to display a message in the window's status bar when the page has finished loading.

```
<BODY>
<SCRIPT FOR=window EVENT=onload LANGUAGE="JScript">
  window.status = "Page is loaded!";
</SCRIPT>
</BODY>
```

The following example sets an **onload** event handler for an **IMG** object. The handler uses the **event** object to retrieve the URL of the image.

```
<SCRIPT>
function imageLoaded()
{
  window.status = "Image " + event.srcElement.src + " is loaded";
}
</SCRIPT>
<BODY>
<IMG SRC="sample.gif" onload="imageLoaded()">
</BODY>
```

Applies To

 WIN16   WIN32   MAC

window

 WIN16   WIN32   MAC   UNIX

APPLET, EMBED, FRAMESET, IMG, LINK, SCRIPT, window

onlosecapture Event

Fires when the object loses the mouse capture.

Syntax

Inline HTML	*<ELEMENT* onlosecapture = "*handler*" ... >	All platforms
Event property	*object*.onlosecapture = *handler*	JScript (compatible with ECMA 262 language specification) only
Named script	<SCRIPT FOR = *object* EVENT = onlosecapture>	Internet Explorer only

Remarks

Bubbles	No
Cancels	No
To invoke	Cause the object to release mouse capture:

- Set mouse capture to a different object.
- Change the active window so that the current document using mouse capture loses focus.
- Invoke the **releaseCapture** method on the **document** or object.

Default action Sends the event notification to the object that is losing the mouse capture.

Event Object Properties

altKey	**clientX**	**clientY**	**ctrlKey**	**offsetX**
offsetY	**screenX**	**screenY**	**shiftKey**	**srcElement**
type	**x**	**y**		

Example

The following example shows how to fire the **onlosecapture** event. When the user clicks the mouse, the **releaseCapture** method is invoked and subsequently fires the **onlosecapture** event..

```
<BODY onload="divOwnCapture.setCapture()"
    onclick="divOwnCapture.releaseCapture();">
<DIV ID=divOwnCapture
    onmousemove="txtWriteLocation.value=event.clientX
        + event.clientY";
    onlosecapture="alert(event.srcElement.id
        + ' lost mouse capture.')">
<P>Mouse capture has been set to this gray division (DIV) at
    load time using the setCapture method. The text area tracks
    the mousemove event anywhere in the document.<BR><BR>
<TEXTAREA ID=txtWriteLocation COLS=2></TEXTAREA>
</DIV>
<HR>
<DIV ID=divNoCapture>
<P>Click anywhere on the document to invoke the releaseCapture
    method, whereby the onlosecapture event fires.</P>
</DIV>
</BODY>
```

To see this code in action, refer to the Web Workshop CD-ROM.

Applies To

WIN16   WIN32   MAC   UNIX

A, ADDRESS, APPLET, AREA, B, BDO, BIG, BLOCKQUOTE, BODY, BR, BUTTON, CAPTION, CENTER, CITE, CODE, DD, DFN, DIR, DIV, DL, DT, EM, EMBED, FIELDSET, FONT, FORM, Hn, HR, I, IMG, INPUT type=button, INPUT type=checkbox, INPUT type=file, INPUT type=hidden, INPUT type=image, INPUT type=password, INPUT type=radio, INPUT type=reset, INPUT type=submit, INPUT type=text, KBD, LABEL, LEGEND, LI, LISTING, MAP, MARQUEE, MENU, NOBR, OBJECT, OL, OPTION, P, PLAINTEXT, PRE, S, SAMP, SELECT, SMALL, SPAN, STRIKE, STRONG, SUB, SUP, TABLE, TBODY, TD, TEXTAREA, TFOOT, TH, THEAD, TR, TT, U, UL, VAR, XMP

DHTML Events

onmousedown Event

Fires when the user clicks the object with either mouse button.

Syntax

Inline HTML	*<ELEMENT* onmousedown = *"handler"* ... >	All platforms
Event property	*object*.onmousedown = *handler*	JScript (compatible with ECMA 262 language specification) only
Named script	<SCRIPT FOR = *object* EVENT = onmousedown>	Internet Explorer only

Remarks

Bubbles	Yes
Cancels	Yes
To invoke	Click a mouse button.
Default action	Initiates actions associated with the event and with the object being clicked.

You can use the **button** property to determine which mouse button the user has clicked.

Event Object Properties

altKey	**button**	**cancelBubble**	**clientX**	**clientY**
ctrlKey	**offsetX**	**offsetY**	**returnValue**	**screenX**
screenY	**shiftKey**	**srcElement**	**type**	**x**
y				

Example

The example shows how to determine the origin of the **onmousedown** event when event bubbling is used.

```
<BODY onmousedown="alert(event.srcElement.tagName)">
<TABLE BORDER=1>
  <TH>Click the items below with your mouse.</TH>
  <TR><TD><BUTTON>Click Me</BUTTON></TD></TR>
  <TR><TD><INPUT TYPE=text VALUE="Click Me"></TD></TR>
  <TR><TD><SPAN>Click Me</SPAN></TD></TR>
</TABLE>
```

```
<P>This code retrieves the tagName of the object on which
   the onmousedown event has fired.
</BODY>
```

To see this code in action, refer to the Web Workshop CD-ROM.

Applies To

WIN16   WIN32   MAC   UNIX

A, ADDRESS, APPLET, AREA, B, BIG, BLOCKQUOTE, BODY, BUTTON,
CAPTION, CENTER, CITE, CODE, DD, DFN, DIR, DIV, DL, document, DT, EM,
EMBED, FIELDSET, FONT, FORM, Hn, HR, I, IMG, INPUT type=button, INPUT
type=checkbox, INPUT type=file, INPUT type=image, INPUT type=password,
INPUT type=radio, INPUT type=reset, INPUT type=submit, INPUT type=text, KBD,
LABEL, LEGEND, LI, LISTING, MAP, MARQUEE, MENU, OL, P, PLAINTEXT,
PRE, S, SAMP, SELECT, SMALL, SPAN, STRIKE, STRONG, SUB, SUP, TABLE,
TBODY, TD, TEXTAREA, TFOOT, TH, THEAD, TR, TT, U, UL, VAR, XMP

WIN16   WIN32   MAC   UNIX

BDO, RT, RUBY

onmousemove Event

Fires when the user moves the mouse over the object.

Syntax

Inline HTML	*<ELEMENT* onmousemove = "*handler*" ... >	All platforms
Event property	*object*.onmousemove = *handler*	JScript (compatible with ECMA 262 language specification) only
Named script	<SCRIPT FOR = *object* EVENT = onmousemove>	Internet Explorer only

Remarks

Bubbles	Yes
Cancels	No
To invoke	Move the mouse over the document.
Default action	Initiates any action associated with this event.

You can use the **button** property to determine what mouse button the user has clicked.

Event Object Properties

altKey	**cancelBubble**	**clientX**	**clientY**	**ctrlKey**
offsetX	**offsetY**	**screenX**	**screenY**	**shiftKey**
srcElement	**type**	**x**	**y**	

Example

The following example shows how to use the **onmousemove** event to monitor the location of the mouse cursor on the screen. When the mouse cursor moves over the **DIV** object, a **SPAN** object is updated with the **clientX** and **clientY** property values. The **clientX** and **clientY** properties are exposed by the **event** object.

```
<SCRIPT>
function fnTrackMouse(){
    oNotice.innerText="Coords: (" + event.clientX + ",
        " + event.clientY + ")";
}
</SCRIPT>

<DIV ID="oScratch" onmousemove="fnTrackMouse()">
<SPAN ID="oNotice"></SPAN>

</DIV>
```

To see this code in action, refer to the Web Workshop CD-ROM.

Applies To

IE 4   **WIN16**   **WIN32**   **MAC**   **UNIX**

A, ADDRESS, APPLET, AREA, B, BIG, BLOCKQUOTE, BODY, BUTTON, CAPTION, CENTER, CITE, CODE, DD, DFN, DIR, DIV, DL, document, DT, EM, EMBED, FIELDSET, FONT, FORM, Hn, HR, I, IMG, INPUT type=button, INPUT type=checkbox, INPUT type=file, INPUT type=image, INPUT type=password, INPUT type=radio, INPUT type=reset, INPUT type=submit, INPUT type=text, KBD, LABEL, LEGEND, LI, LISTING, MAP, MARQUEE, MENU, NEXTID, NOBR, OL, P, PLAINTEXT, PRE, S, SAMP, SELECT, SMALL, SPAN, STRIKE, STRONG, SUB, SUP, TABLE, TBODY, TD, TEXTAREA, TFOOT, TH, THEAD, TR, TT, U, UL, VAR, XMP

IE 5   **WIN16**   **WIN32**   **MAC**   **UNIX**

BDO, RT, RUBY

onmouseout Event

Fires when the user moves the mouse pointer outside the boundaries of the object.

Syntax

Inline HTML	*<ELEMENT* onmouseout = *"handler"* ... >	All platforms
Event property	*object*.onmouseout = *handler*	JScript (compatible with ECMA 262 language specification) only
Named script	<SCRIPT FOR = *object* EVENT = onmouseout>	Internet Explorer only

Remarks

Bubbles	Yes
Cancels	No
To invoke	Move the mouse pointer out of an object.
Default action	Initiates any action associated with this event.

When the user moves the mouse over an object, one **onmouseover** event occurs, followed by one or more **onmousemove** events as the user moves the mouse pointer within the object. One **onmouseout** event occurs when the user moves the mouse pointer out of the object.

Event Object Properties

altKey	button	cancelBubble	clientX	clientY
ctrlKey	fromElement	offsetX	offsetY	screenX
screenY	shiftKey	srcElement	toElement	type
x	y			

Example

The following example shows how to use the **onmouseout** event to apply a new style to an object.

```
<BODY>
<P onmouseout="this.style.color='black';"
   onmouseover="this.style.color='red';">
Move the mouse pointer over this text, and then move it elsewhere
in the document. Move the mouse pointer over this text, and then
move it elsewhere in the document.
</BODY>
```

The next example shows how to swap images on mouse events.

```
<SCRIPT>
function flipImage(url)
{
    if (window.event.srcElement.tagName == "IMG" )
    {
        window.event.srcElement.src = url;
    }
}
</SCRIPT>
</HEAD>
<BODY>
<P>Move the mouse over the image to see it switch.<P>
  <IMG SRC="/workshop/graphics/prop_ro.gif"
     onmouseover="flipImage('/workshop/graphics/prop_rw.gif');"
     onmouseout="flipImage('/workshop/graphics/prop_ro.gif');"
  </BODY>
```

To see this code in action, refer to the Web Workshop CD-ROM.

Applies To

 WIN16   WIN32   MAC   UNIX

A, ADDRESS, APPLET, AREA, B, BIG, BLOCKQUOTE, BODY, BUTTON, CAPTION, CENTER, CITE, CODE, DD, DFN, DIR, DIV, DL, document, DT, EM, EMBED, FIELDSET, FONT, FORM, Hn, HR, I, IMG, INPUT type=button, INPUT type=checkbox, INPUT type=file, INPUT type=image, INPUT type=password, INPUT type=radio, INPUT type=reset, INPUT type=submit, INPUT type=text, KBD, LABEL, LEGEND, LI, LISTING, MAP, MARQUEE, MENU, OL, P, PLAINTEXT, PRE, S, SAMP, SELECT, SMALL, SPAN, STRIKE, STRONG, SUB, SUP, TABLE, TBODY, TD, TEXTAREA, TFOOT, TH, THEAD, TR, TT, U, UL, VAR, XMP

IE 5 **WIN16   WIN32   MAC   UNIX**

BDO, RT, RUBY

onmouseover Event

Fires when the user moves the mouse pointer into the object.

Syntax

Inline HTML	*<ELEMENT* onmouseover = "*handler*" ... >	All platforms
Event property	*object*.onmouseover = *handler*	JScript (compatible with ECMA 262 language specification) only
Named script	<SCRIPT FOR = *object* EVENT = onmouseover>	Internet Explorer only

Remarks

Bubbles	Yes
Cancels	Yes
To invoke	Move the mouse pointer into an object.
Default action	Initiates any action associated with this event.

The event occurs when the user first moves the mouse pointer into the object and does not repeat unless the user moves the pointer out of the object and then back into it.

Event Object Properties

altKey	**button**	**cancelBubble**	**clientX**	**clientY**
ctrlKey	**fromElement**	**offsetX**	**offsetY**	**returnValue**
screenX	**screenY**	**shiftKey**	**srcElement**	**toElement**
type	**x**	**y**		

Example

The following example shows how to use the **onmouseover** event to apply a new style to an object.

```
<DIV>
<P onmouseover="this.style.color='red'"
   onmouseout="this.style.color='black'">
Move the mouse pointer over this text, then move it elsewhere in the
document. Move the mouse pointer over this text, then move it
elsewhere in the document.
</DIV>
```

The next example shows how to change the value of a text area in response to mouse events.

```
<DIV>
<P>Move mouse pointer into the text area to fire the
   onmouseover event. Move it back out to clear the text.
<TEXTAREA NAME=txtMouseTrack
   onmouseover="this.value='onmouseover fired'"
   onmouseout="this.value=''">
</TEXTAREA>
</DIV>
```

To see this code in action, refer to the Web Workshop CD-ROM.

Applies To

WIN16	WIN32	MAC

A

UNIX	WIN16	WIN32	MAC

A, ADDRESS, APPLET, AREA, B, BIG, BLOCKQUOTE, BODY, BUTTON, CAPTION, CENTER, CITE, CODE, DD, DFN, DIR, DIV, DL, document, DT, EM, EMBED, FIELDSET, FONT, FORM, Hn, HR, I, IMG, INPUT type=button, INPUT type=checkbox, INPUT type=file, INPUT type=image, INPUT type=password, INPUT type=radio, INPUT type=reset, INPUT type=submit, INPUT type=text, KBD, LABEL, LEGEND, LI, LISTING, MAP, MARQUEE, MENU, NEXTID, NOBR, OL, P, PLAINTEXT, PRE, S, SAMP, SELECT, SMALL, SPAN, STRIKE, STRONG, SUB, SUP, TABLE, TBODY, TD, TEXTAREA, TFOOT, TH, THEAD, TR, TT, U, UL, VAR, XMP

WIN16	WIN32	MAC	UNIX

BDO, RT, RUBY

onmouseup Event

Fires when the user releases a mouse button while the mouse is over the object.

Syntax

Inline HTML	*<ELEMENT* onmouseup = "*handler*" ... >	All platforms
Event property	*object*.onmouseup = *handler*	JScript (compatible with ECMA 262 language specification) only
Named script	<SCRIPT FOR = *object* EVENT = onmouseup>	Internet Explorer only

Remarks

Bubbles	Yes
Cancels	Yes
To invoke	Press and release a mouse button.
Default action	Initiates any action associated with this event.

You can use the **button** property to determine which mouse button the user has clicked.

Event Object Properties

altKey	button	cancelBubble	clientX	clientY
ctrlKey	offsetX	offsetY	returnValue	screenX
screenY	shiftKey	srcElement	type	x
y				

Applies To

 WIN16   WIN32   MAC   UNIX

A, ADDRESS, APPLET, AREA, B, BIG, BLOCKQUOTE, BODY, BUTTON, CAPTION, CENTER, CITE, CODE, DD, DFN, DIR, DIV, DL, document, DT, EM, EMBED, FIELDSET, FONT, FORM, Hn, HR, I, IMG, INPUT type=button, INPUT type=checkbox, INPUT type=file, INPUT type=image, INPUT type=password, INPUT type=radio, INPUT type=reset, INPUT type=submit, INPUT type=text, KBD,

Applies To *(continued)*

 WIN16   WIN32   MAC   UNIX

LABEL, LEGEND, LI, LISTING, MAP, MARQUEE, MENU, NEXTID, NOBR, OL, P, PLAINTEXT, PRE, S, SAMP, SELECT, SMALL, SPAN, STRIKE, STRONG, SUB, SUP, TABLE, TBODY, TD, TEXTAREA, TFOOT, TH, THEAD, TR, TT, U, UL, VAR, XMP

 WIN16   WIN32   MAC   UNIX

BDO, RT, RUBY

onpaste Event

Fires on the target object when the user transfers data from the system clipboard to the document.

Syntax

Inline HTML	*<ELEMENT* onpaste = *"handler"* ... >	All platforms
Event property	*object*.onpaste = *handler*	JScript (compatible with ECMA 262 language specification) only
Named script	<SCRIPT FOR = *object* EVENT = onpaste>	Internet Explorer only

Remarks

Bubbles	Yes
Cancels	Yes
To invoke	After copying or cutting the text:

- Right-click to display the shortcut menu and select Paste.
- Or press CTRL+V.

Default action Inserts the data from the system clipboard into the specified location on the document.

Creating custom code for pasting requires several steps.

1. Set `event.returnValue=false` in the **onbeforepaste** event to enable the Paste shortcut menu item.

2. Cancel the default behavior of the browser by including `event.returnValue=false` in the **onpaste** event handler. Canceling applies only to objects, such as the text box, that have a default behavior defined for them.

3. Specify a data format in which to paste the selection through the **getData** method of the **clipboardData** object.

4. Invoke the method in the **onpaste** event to execute custom paste code.

Event Object Properties

altKey	**cancelBubble**	**clientX**	**clientY**	**ctrlKey**
offsetX	**offsetY**	**returnValue**	**screenX**	**screenY**
shiftKey	**srcElement**	**type**	**x**	**y**

Example

The following example shows how to customize editing functionality with the **clipboardData** object.

```
<HEAD>
<SCRIPT>

var sNewString = "new content associated with this object";
var sSave = "";


// Selects the text that is to be cut.

function fnLoad() {
    var r = document.body.createTextRange();
    r.findText(oSource.innerText);
    r.select();
}


// Stores the text of the SPAN in a variable that is set
// to an empty string in the variable declaration above.

function fnBeforeCut() {
    sSave = oSource.innerText;
    event.returnValue = false;
}
```

DHTML Events

```
// Associates the variable sNewString with the text being cut.

function fnCut() {
    window.clipboardData.setData("Text", sNewString);
}

function fnBeforePaste() {
    event.returnValue = false;
}


// The second parameter set in getData causes sNewString
// to be pasted into the text input. Passing no second
// parameter causes the SPAN text to be pasted instead.

function fnPaste() {
    event.returnValue = false;
    oTarget.value = window.clipboardData.getData("Text", sNewString);
}

</SCRIPT>
</HEAD>
<BODY onload="fnLoad()">

<SPAN ID="oSource"
      onbeforecut="fnBeforeCut()"
      oncut="fnCut()">Cut this Text</SPAN>

<INPUT ID="oTarget" TYPE="text" VALUE="Paste the Text Here"
      onbeforepaste="fnBeforePaste()"
      onpaste="fnPaste()">
</BODY>
```

To see this code in action, refer to the Web Workshop CD-ROM.

Applies To

 WIN16　　WIN32　　MAC　　UNIX

A, ADDRESS, AREA, B, BDO, BIG, BLOCKQUOTE, CAPTION, CENTER, CITE, CODE, DD, DFN, DIR, DIV, DL, DT, EM, FIELDSET, FORM, Hn, I, IMG, LEGEND, LI, LISTING, MENU, NOBR, OL, P, PLAINTEXT, PRE, S, SAMP, SMALL, SPAN, STRIKE, STRONG, SUB, SUP, TD, TH, TR, TT, U, UL

onpropertychange Event

Fires when a property changes on the object.

Syntax

Inline HTML	*<ELEMENT* onpropertychange = *"handler"* ... >	All platforms
Event property	*object*.onpropertychange = *handler*	JScript (compatible with ECMA 262 language specification) only
Named script	<SCRIPT FOR = *object* EVENT = onpropertychange>	Internet Explorer only

Remarks

Bubbles	No
Cancels	No
To invoke	Cause a property to change value.
Default action	Sends notification when a property changes.

The **onpropertychange** event fires when object, **expando**, or style subobject properties change. You can retrieve the name of the changed property by using the **event** object's **propertyName** property. This property returns a read-only string of the name of the property that has changed. In the case of style properties, the property name is prefixed with style. For example, if the CSS property **pixelLeft** is altered, the value of window.event.propertyName is style.pixelLeft. By contrast, if the non-CSS property **name** is altered, the value of window.event.propertyName is name.

When the **onpropertychange** event fires, the **srcElement** property of the **event** object is set to the object whose property has changed.

Event Object Properties

propertyName   **srcElement**   **type**

Example

The following example shows how to use **onpropertychange**, **srcElement**, and **propertyName** for an object and a **style** subobject property.

```
<HEAD>
<SCRIPT>
function changeProp()
{
  oProp.value = "This is the new VALUE";
}

function changeCSSProp()
{
  oStyleProp.style.backgroundColor = "aqua";
}
</SCRIPT>
</HEAD>
<BODY ID=bdyChange>
<INPUT TYPE=button ID=oProp onclick="changeProp()"
   VALUE="Click to change the VALUE property of this button"
   onpropertychange='alert(event.srcElement.id +
      " received a change to " + event.propertyName)'>
<INPUT TYPE=button ID=oStyleProp onclick="changeCSSProp()"
   VALUE="Click to change the CSS backgroundColor property
      of this button"
   onpropertychange='alert(event.srcElement.id +
      " received a change to " + event.propertyName)'>
</BODY>
```

To see this code in action, refer to the Web Workshop CD-ROM.

Applies To

 WIN16   WIN32   MAC   UNIX

A, ADDRESS, APPLET, AREA, B, BDO, BIG, BLOCKQUOTE, BODY, BUTTON, CAPTION, CENTER, CITE, CODE, COMMENT, DD, DFN, DIR, DIV, DL, document, DT, EM, EMBED, FIELDSET, FONT, FORM, Hn, HR, I, IMG, INPUT type=button, INPUT type=checkbox, INPUT type=file, INPUT type=hidden, INPUT type=image, INPUT type=password, INPUT type=radio, INPUT type=reset, INPUT type=submit, INPUT type=text, KBD, LABEL, LEGEND, LI, LISTING, MAP, MARQUEE, MENU, NOBR, OBJECT, OL, OPTION, P, PLAINTEXT, PRE, S, SAMP, SCRIPT, SELECT, SMALL, SPAN, STRIKE, STRONG, SUB, SUP, TABLE, TBODY, TD, TEXTAREA, TFOOT, TH, THEAD, TR, TT, U, UL, VAR, XMP

onreadystatechange Event

Fires whenever the state of the object has changed.

Syntax

Inline HTML	`<ELEMENT`
	`onreadystatechange =`
	`"handler" ... >`
		All platforms

Event property	*object*.`onreadystatechange =` *handler*	JScript (compatible with ECMA 262 language specification) only
Named script	`<SCRIPT FOR =` *object* `EVENT =` `onreadystatechange>`	Internet Explorer only

Remarks

Bubbles	No
Cancels	No
To invoke	Change the ready state.
Default action	Signals the ready state of the document.

When the **onreadystatechange** event fires, you can use the **readyState** to query the current state of the element.

All elements expose an **onreadystatechange** event. The following objects always fire the event because they load data: **APPLET**, **document**, **FRAME**, **FRAMESET**, **IFRAME**, **IMG**, **LINK**, **OBJECT**, **SCRIPT**, and **XML** elements. Other objects only fire the **onreadystatechange** event when a DHTML Behavior is attached.

When working with behaviors, wait for the **onreadystatechange** event to fire and verify that the **readyState** property of the element is set to `complete` to ensure that the behavior is completely downloaded and applied to the element. Until this event fires, attempting to use any of the behavior-defined members before the behavior is attached to the element can result in a scripting error indicating that the object does not support that particular property or method.

Event Object Properties

srcElement   **type**

DHTML Events

Example

The following sample shows how to use the **onreadystatechange** event to invoke a function when **readyState** is complete.

```
document.onreadystatechange=fnStartInit;
function fnStartInit(){
   if(event.readyState=="complete"){
      // Finish initialization.
   }
}
```

Applies To

 WIN16 WIN32 MAC

Hn

 WIN16 WIN32 MAC UNIX

document, IMG, LINK, OBJECT, SCRIPT

 WIN16 WIN32 MAC UNIX

A, ACRONYM, ADDRESS, APPLET, AREA, B, BASE, BASEFONT, BDO,
BGSOUND, BIG, BLOCKQUOTE, BODY, BR, BUTTON, CAPTION, CENTER,
CITE, CODE, COL, COLGROUP, COMMENT, DD, DEL, DFN, DIR, DIV, DL, DT,
EM, EMBED, FIELDSET, FONT, FORM, HEAD, Hn, HR, HTML, I, INPUT
type=button, INPUT type=checkbox, INPUT type=file, INPUT type=hidden, INPUT
type=image, INPUT type=password, INPUT type=radio, INPUT type=reset, INPUT
type=submit, INPUT type=text, INS, ISINDEX, KBD, LABEL, LEGEND, LI,
LISTING, MAP, MARQUEE, MENU, NEXTID, NOBR, NOFRAMES, NOSCRIPT,
OL, OPTION, P, PLAINTEXT, PRE, Q, RT, RUBY, S, SAMP, SELECT, SMALL,
SPAN, STRIKE, STRONG, SUB, SUP, TABLE, TBODY, TD, TEXTAREA,
TFOOT, TH, THEAD, TITLE, TR, TT, U, UL, VAR, XML, XMP

onreset Event

Fires when a user resets a form.

Syntax

Inline HTML	*<FORM* onreset = "*handler*" ... >	All platforms
Event property	*form*.onreset = *handler*	JScript (compatible with ECMA 262 language specification) only
Named script	<SCRIPT FOR = *form* EVENT = onreset>	Internet Explorer only

Remarks

Bubbles	No
Cancels	Yes
To invoke	• Click a **Reset** button.
	• Invoke the **reset** method of the **FORM** object.
	• Refresh the page.
Default action	Executes associated code.

Event Object Properties

returnValue   srcElement   type

Applies To

 WIN16   WIN32   MAC   UNIX

FORM

DHTML Events

onresize Event

Fires when the size of the object is about to change.

Syntax

Inline HTML	*<ELEMENT* onresize = "*handler*" ... >	All platforms
Event property	*object*.onresize = *handler*	JScript (compatible with ECMA 262 language specification) only
Named script	<SCRIPT FOR = *object* EVENT = onresize>	Internet Explorer only

Remarks

Bubbles	No
Cancels	No
To invoke	Cause the object to change height or width.
Default action	No default action.

The **onresize** event fires for block and inline objects with layout even if document or CSS (cascading style sheets) property values are changed. Objects have layout when measurements such as the **height** and **width** attributes are set, or when the **position** of the object is set. Intrinsic objects, such as **BUTTON**, and windowed objects, such as **window** and **IFRAME**, fire as expected. This event does not fire for files with embedded controls.

Resizing HTML applications also fires the **onresize** event.

Event Object Properties

altKey	clientX	clientY	ctrlKey	offsetX
offsetY	returnValue	screenX	screenY	shiftKey
srcElement	type	x	y	

Applies To

 WIN16   WIN32   MAC   UNIX

A, ADDRESS, APPLET, B, BIG, BLOCKQUOTE, BUTTON, CENTER, CITE, CODE, DD, DFN, DIR, DIV, DL, DT, EM, EMBED, FIELDSET, FORM, Hn, HR, I, IMG, INPUT type=button, INPUT type=file, INPUT type=image,

Applies To *(continued)*

 WIN16   WIN32   MAC   UNIX

INPUT type=password, INPUT type=reset, INPUT type=submit, INPUT type=text, ISINDEX, KBD, LABEL, LEGEND, LI, LISTING, MARQUEE, MENU, OBJECT, OL, P, PRE, S, SAMP, SELECT, SMALL, SPAN, STRIKE, STRONG, SUB, SUP, TABLE, TEXTAREA, TT, U, UL, VAR, window, XMP

 WIN16   WIN32   MAC   UNIX

FRAME

onrowenter Event

Fires to indicate that the current row has changed and new data values are available on the object.

Syntax

Inline HTML	`<ELEMENT onrowenter = "handler" ... >`	All platforms
Event property	`object.onrowenter = handler`	JScript (compatible with ECMA 262 language specification) only
Named script	`<SCRIPT FOR = object EVENT = onrowenter>`	Internet Explorer only

Remarks

Bubbles	No
Cancels	Yes
To invoke	Change data values in the current row.
Default action	Signals that new data is available in the current row.

The **onrowenter** event only fires on data bound objects. This event applies only to objects that identify themselves as data providers.

Event Object Properties

bookmarks	**boundElements**	**dataFld**	**recordset**
returnValue	**srcElement**	**type**	

Applies To

IE 4 | **WIN16** **WIN32** **MAC** **UNIX**
APPLET, OBJECT

IE 5 | **WIN16** **WIN32** **MAC** **UNIX**
XML

onrowexit Event

Fires just before the data source control changes the current row in the object.

Syntax

Inline HTML	*<ELEMENT* onrowexit = "*handler*" ... >	All platforms
Event property	*object*.onrowexit = *handler*	JScript (compatible with ECMA 262 language specification) only
Named script	<SCRIPT FOR = *object* EVENT = onrowexit>	Internet Explorer only

Remarks

Bubbles	No
Cancels	Yes
To invoke	Change rows in the data source.
Default action	Signals that the row in the data bound object is about to be changed.

The **onrowexit** event only fires on data bound objects. This event applies to objects that identify themselves as data providers.

Event Object Properties

bookmarks	**boundElements**	**dataFld**	**recordset**
returnValue	**srcElement**	**type**	

Applies To

 WIN16 **WIN32** **MAC** **UNIX**
APPLET, OBJECT

IE 5 **WIN16   WIN32   MAC   UNIX**

XML

onrowsdelete Event

Fires when rows are about to be deleted from the record set.

Syntax

Inline HTML	*<ELEMENT* onrowsdelete = "*handler*" ... >	All platforms
Event property	*object*.onrowsdelete = *handler*	JScript (compatible with ECMA 262 language specification) only
Named script	<SCRIPT FOR = *object* EVENT = onrowsdelete>	Internet Explorer only

Remarks

Bubbles	Yes
Cancels	No
To invoke	Fires when the **delete** method is called on the record set.
Default action	Signals that rows are about to be deleted.

Event Object Properties

bookmarks	**boundElements**	**cancelBubble**	**dataFld**
reason	**recordset**	**srcElement**	**type**

Applies To

IE 5   **WIN16   WIN32   MAC   UNIX**

APPLET, OBJECT, XML

onrowsinserted Event

Fires just after new rows are inserted in the current record set.

Syntax

Inline HTML	*<ELEMENT* onrowsinserted = "*handler*" ... >	All platforms
Event property	*object*.onrowsinserted = *handler*	JScript (compatible with ECMA 262 language specification) only
Named script	<SCRIPT FOR = *object* EVENT = onrowsinserted>	Internet Explorer only

Remarks

Bubbles	Yes
Cancels	No
To invoke	Fires when the Universal Data Access **AddNew** method is called on the current record set.
Default action	Signals that a new row has been inserted into the record set.

Event Object Properties

bookmarks	**boundElements**	**cancelBubble**	**dataFld**
reason	**recordset**	**srcElement**	**type**

Applies To

 WIN16 WIN32 MAC UNIX

APPLET, BDO, OBJECT

onscroll Event

Fires when the user repositions the scroll box in the scroll bar on the object.

Syntax

Inline HTML	*<ELEMENT* onscroll = *"handler"* ... >	All platforms
Event property	*object*.onscroll = *handler*	JScript (compatible with ECMA 262 language specification) only
Named script	<SCRIPT FOR = *object* EVENT = onscroll>	Internet Explorer only

Remarks

Bubbles	No
Cancels	No
To invoke	Begin scrolling in the object that has a scroll bar:

- Click and drag the scroll box with the mouse.
- Click the scroll arrow.
- Click the scroll bar.
- Invoke the **doScroll** method.
- Press the PAGE UP or PAGE DOWN key.
- Press the ARROW UP or ARROW DOWN key until scrolling occurs.

Default action Scrolls the contents of an object until new portions of the object become visible.

You can control the scroll bar components using the **componentFromPoint** and **doScroll** methods.

Cascading style sheets (CSS) enable scrolling on all objects through the **overflow** property. These objects are not listed in the Applies To list for this event.

Event Object Properties

clientX	**clientY**	**offsetX**	**offsetY**	**screenX**
screenY	**srcElement**	**type**	**x**	**y**

Applies To

 WIN16   WIN32   MAC   UNIX

APPLET, BODY, DIV, EMBED, MAP, MARQUEE, OBJECT, SELECT, TABLE,
TEXTAREA

 WIN16   WIN32   MAC   UNIX

BDO

onselect Event

Fires when the current selection changes.

Syntax

Inline HTML	`<ELEMENT onselect = "handler" ... >`	All platforms
Event property	`object.onselect = handler`	JScript (compatible with ECMA 262 language specification) only
Named script	`<SCRIPT FOR = object EVENT = onselect>`	Internet Explorer only

Remarks

Bubbles	No
Cancels	Yes
To invoke	Initiate text selection:

- Move the mouse from character to character during a drag selection.
- Press the SHIFT key while moving the cursor over text.

Default action Moves the selection to a given character and highlights that selection.

Event Object Properties

clientX	**clientY**	**offsetX**	**offsetY**	**returnValue**
screenX	**screenY**	**srcElement**	**type**	**x**
y				

Applies To

WIN16   WIN32   MAC

INPUT TYPE=text, TEXTAREA

UNIX

INPUT TYPE=text, TEXTAREA

onselectstart Event

Fires when the object is being selected.

Syntax

Inline HTML	*<ELEMENT* onselectstart = "*handler*" ... >	All platforms
Event property	*object*.onselectstart = *handler*	JScript (compatible with ECMA 262 language specification) only
Named script	<SCRIPT FOR = *object* EVENT = onselectstart>	Internet Explorer only

Remarks

Bubbles	Yes
Cancels	Yes
To invoke	Begin selecting of one or more objects.
Default action	Moves the selection to an object and highlights that selection.

The object at the beginning of the selection fires the event.

Event Object Properties

cancelBubble	clientX	clientY	offsetX	offsetY
returnValue	screenX	screenY	srcElement	type
x	y			

DHTML Events

Applies To

 WIN16   WIN32   MAC   UNIX

A, ACRONYM, ADDRESS, AREA, B, BIG, BLOCKQUOTE, BODY, BUTTON, CAPTION, CENTER, CITE, CODE, DD, DEL, DFN, DIR, DIV, DL, DT, EM, FIELDSET, FONT, FORM, Hn, HR, I, IMG, INPUT type=button, INPUT type=checkbox, INPUT type=file, INPUT type=image, INPUT type=password, INPUT type=radio, INPUT type=reset, INPUT type=submit, INPUT type=text, KBD, LABEL, LI, LISTING, MAP, MARQUEE, MENU, NEXTID, NOBR, OBJECT, OL, OPTION, P, PLAINTEXT, PRE, Q, S, SAMP, SELECT, SMALL, SPAN, STRIKE, STRONG, SUB, SUP, TABLE, TBODY, TD, TEXTAREA, TFOOT, TH, THEAD, TR, TT, U, UL, VAR, XMP

 WIN16   WIN32   MAC   UNIX

BDO, RT, RUBY

onstart Event

Fires at the beginning of every loop of the **MARQUEE** object.

Syntax

Inline HTML	*<MARQUEE* onstart = *"handler"* ... >	All platforms
Event property	*marquee*.onstart = *handler*	JScript (compatible with ECMA 262 language specification) only
Named script	<SCRIPT FOR = *marquee* EVENT = onstart>	Internet Explorer only

Remarks

Bubbles	No
Cancels	No
To invoke	• Set the **LOOP** attribute to 1 or higher.
	• Omit the **LOOP** attribute so that the **MARQUEE** loops indefinitely.
Default action	Initiates the next loop of the **MARQUEE** contents.

The **start** method does not cause the **onstart** event to fire.

Event Object Properties

clientX	**clientY**	**offsetX**	**offsetY**	**screenX**
screenY	**srcElement**	**type**	**x**	**y**

Example

The example shows how to use the **onstart** event on a **MARQUEE**.

```
<BODY>
<P>An alert dialog box displays each time the onstart event fires.
<MARQUEE onstart="alert('onstart fired')"
         BEHAVIOR=alernate LOOP=2>Marquee Text</MARQUEE>
</BODY>
```

To see this code in action, refer to the Web Workshop CD-ROM.

Applies To

WIN16	**WIN32**	**MAC**	**UNIX**

MARQUEE

onstop Event

Fires when the user clicks the Stop button or the document is unloaded.

Syntax

Inline HTML	*<ELEMENT* onstop = "*handler*" ... >	All platforms
Event property	*object*.onstop = *handler*	JScript (compatible with ECMA 262 language specification) only
Named script	<SCRIPT FOR = *object* EVENT = onstop>	Internet Explorer only

Remarks

Bubbles	No
Cancels	No
To invoke	• Click the Stop button.
	• Leave the Web page.

Default action Initiates any action associated with this event.

The **onstop** event fires after the **onbeforeunload** event, and before the **onunload** event.

Event Object Properties

type

Example

The following example shows how to use the **onstop** event to stop a function from executing in a continuous cycle. The **setInterval** method is used to execute script every millisecond. If the user clicks the Stop button, the **clearInterval** method removes the interval and the script is no longer executed.

```
document.onstop=fnTrapStop;
window.onload=fnInit;
var oInterval;
function fnInit(){
    oInterval=window.setInterval("fnCycle()",1);
}
function fnCycle(){
    // Do something
}
function fnTrapStop(){
    window.clearInterval(oInterval);
}
```

Applies To

WIN16	WIN32	MAC	UNIX

document

onsubmit Event

Fires when a **form** is about to be submitted.

Syntax

Inline HTML	*<FORM* onsubmit = "*handler*" ... >	All platforms
Event property	*form*.onsubmit = *handler*	JScript (compatible with ECMA 262 language specification) only
Named script	<SCRIPT FOR = *form* EVENT = onsubmit>	Internet Explorer only

Remarks

Bubbles	No
Cancels	Yes
To invoke	Submit a **form** using the **INPUT TYPE=submit, INPUT TYPE=image**, or **BUTTON TYPE=submit** object.
Default action	Causes a **form** to be sent to whatever location is stipulated in the **ACTION** attribute of the **form** object.

You can override this event by returning `false` in the event handler. You can use this capability to validate data on the client side to prevent invalid data from being submitted to the server. If you call the event handler using the **onsubmit** attribute of the **form** object, you must explicitly request the return value using the return function, and you must provide an explicit return value for each possible code path in the event handler function.

The **submit** method does not invoke the **onsubmit** event handler.

Event Object Properties

altKey	**ctrlKey**	**returnValue**	**shiftKey**	**srcElement**
type				

Example

The following example shows how to use **onsubmit** on a **form** to request the return value.

```
<BODY>
<FORM NAME="oDoSubmit" onsubmit="return(myOnSubmitEventHandler());">
</FORM>
</BODY>
```

Applies To

 WIN16   WIN32   MAC

FORM

 UNIX

FORM

onunload Event

Fires immediately before the object is unloaded.

Syntax

Inline HTML	*<ELEMENT* onunload = "*handler*" ... >	All platforms
Event property	*object*.onunload = *handler*	JScript (compatible with ECMA 262 language specification) only
Named script	<SCRIPT FOR = *object* EVENT = onunload>	Internet Explorer only

Remarks

Bubbles	No
Cancels	No

To invoke
- Close the current browser window.
- Navigate to another location by entering a new address or selecting a Favorite.
- Click the Back, Forward, Refresh, or Home button.
- Click on an **anchor** that refers the browser to another Web page.
- Invoke the **anchor click** method.
- Invoke the **document write** method.
- Invoke the **document open** method.
- Invoke the **document close** method.
- Invoke the **window close** method.
- Invoke the **window open** method, providing the value _self for the window name.
- Invoke the **window navigate** or **NavigateAndFind** method.
- Invoke the **location replace** method.
- Invoke the **location reload** method.
- Specify a new value for the **location href** property.
- Submit a **FORM** to the address specified in the **ACTION** attribute using the **INPUT_submit** control, or invoke the **form submit** method.

Default action Removes the object or document from the browser window.

Event Object Properties

> type

Example

> The following example shows how to use the **onunload** event to run script when the
> window object has been unloaded.

```
<HEAD>
<SCRIPT FOR=window EVENT=onunload>
    alert("The onunload event fired for the window object.");
</SCRIPT>
<SCRIPT>
  function fnRelocate(){
  location.href="/workshop/samples/author/dhtml/refs/onunloadEX_target.htm";
  }
</SCRIPT>
</HEAD>
<BODY>
  <INPUT TYPE=button VALUE="Go To Page 2" onclick="fnRelocate()">
  <IMG ID=imgTest SRC="/workshop/graphics/prop_rw.gif">
</BODY>
```

> To see this code in action, refer to the Web Workshop CD-ROM.

Applies To

 WIN16   WIN32   MAC

window

 WIN16   WIN32   MAC   UNIX

FRAMESET, window

Collections

The following section provides an alphabetical list of collections exposed by the DHTML Object Model. Each collection definition contains a list of properties and methods for the collection.

all Collection

Returns a reference to the collection of elements contained by the object.

Syntax

[*collAll* =] *object*.**all**

[*oObject* =] *object*.**all**(*vIndex* [, *iSubIndex*])

Possible Values

collAll   Array of elements contained by the object.

oObject   Reference to an individual item in the array of elements contained by the object.

vIndex   Required. Number or string specifying the element or collection to retrieve. If this parameter is an integer, the method returns the element in the collection at the given position, where the first element has value 0, the second has 1, and so on. If this parameter is a string and there is more than one element with the **name** or **id** property equal to the string, the method returns a collection of matching elements.

iSubIndex Optional. Position of an element to retrieve. This parameter is used when *vIndex* is a string. The method uses the string to construct a collection of all elements that have a **name** or **id** equal to the string, and then retrieves from this collection the element at the position specified by *iSubIndex*.

Properties

length

Methods

item   **tags**   **urns**

Remarks

The **all** collection includes one element object for each valid HTML tag. If a valid tag has a matching end tag, both tags are represented by the same element object.

The collection returned by the document's **all** collection always includes a reference to the **HTML**, **HEAD**, **TITLE**, and **BODY** objects regardless of whether the tags are present in the document.

If the document contains invalid or unknown tags, the collection includes one element object for each. Unlike valid end tags, unknown end tags are represented by their own element objects. The order of the element objects is the HTML source order. Although the collection indicates the order of tags, it does not indicate hierarchy.

Examples

The following example in JScript (compatible with ECMA 262 language specification) shows how to display the names of all tags in the document in the order the tags appear in the document.

```
for(i = 0; i < document.all.length; i++){
    alert(document.all(i).tagName);
}
```

The following example in JScript shows how to use the **item** method on the **all** collection to retrieve all element objects for which the **name** property or **ID** attribute is set to sample. Depending on the number of times the **name** or **ID** is defined in the document, the **item** method returns null, a single element object, or a collection of element objects. The **length** property of the collection determines whether **item** returns a collection or a single object.

```
var oObject = document.all.item("sample");
if (oObject != null){
    if (oObject.length != null){
        for (i = 0; i < oObject.length; i++){
            alert(oObject(i).tagName);
        }
    }
}
else{
    alert(oObject.tagName);
}
```

Applies To

 WIN16   WIN32   MAC   UNIX

A, ACRONYM, ADDRESS, APPLET, AREA, B, BASE, BASEFONT, BGSOUND, BIG, BLOCKQUOTE, BODY, BUTTON, CAPTION, CENTER, CITE, CODE, COL, COLGROUP, DD, DEL, DFN, DIR, DIV, DL, document, DT, EM, EMBED, FIELDSET, FONT, FORM, FRAME, FRAMESET, HEAD, Hn, HR, HTML, I, IFRAME, IMG, INS, KBD, LABEL, LEGEND, LI, LINK, LISTING, MAP, MARQUEE, MENU, OBJECT, OL, P, PLAINTEXT, PRE, Q, S, SAMP, SCRIPT, SELECT, SMALL, SPAN, STRIKE, STRONG, SUB, SUP, TABLE, TBODY, TD, TEXTAREA, TFOOT, TH, THEAD, TITLE, TR, TT, U, UL, VAR, XMP

IE 5   **WIN16   WIN32   MAC   UNIX**

BDO

anchors Collection

Retrieves a collection of all **A** objects that have a **name** and/or **id** property. Objects in this collection are in HTML source order.

Syntax

[*collAnchors* =] *document*.**anchors**

[*oObject* =] *document*.**anchors**(*vIndex* [, *iSubIndex*])

Possible Values

collAnchors Array of **A** objects.

oObject   Reference to an individual item in the array of elements contained by the object.

vIndex   Required. Number or string specifying the element or collection to retrieve. If this parameter is an integer, the method returns the element in the collection at the given position. The first element has value 0, the second has 1, and so on. If this parameter is a string and there is more than one element with the **name** or **id** property equal to the string, the method returns a collection of matching elements.

iSubIndex   Optional. Position of an element to retrieve. This parameter is used when *vIndex* is a string. The method uses the string to construct a collection of all elements that have a **name** or **id** equal to the string, and then retrieves from this collection the element at the position specified by *iSubIndex*.

Properties

length

Methods

item   **tags**   **urns**

Examples

The following example shows how to display the **name** property of the third anchor defined in the document.

```
alert(document.anchors(2).name);
```

Applies To

 WIN16   WIN32   MAC

document

 UNIX

document

applets Collection

Retrieves a collection of all **APPLET** objects in the document.

Syntax

[*collApplets* =] *document*.**applets**

[*oObject* =] *document*.**applets**(*vIndex* [, *iSubIndex*])

Possible Values

collApplets Array of **APPLET** objects.

oObject   Reference to an individual item in the array of elements contained by the object.

vIndex   Required. Number or string specifying the element or collection to retrieve. If this parameter is an integer, the method returns the element in the collection at the given position, where the first element has value 0, the second has 1, and so on. If this parameter is a string and there is more than one element with the **name** or **id** property equal to the string, the method returns a collection of matching elements.

Possible Values *(continued)*

iSubIndex Optional. Position of an element to retrieve. This parameter is used when *vIndex* is a string. The method uses the string to construct a collection of all elements that have a **name** or **id** equal to the string, and then retrieves from this collection the element at the position specified by *iSubIndex*.

Properties

length

Methods

item   **tags**   **urns**

Applies To

 WIN16   WIN32   MAC   UNIX

document

areas Collection

Retrieves a collection of the **AREA** objects defined for the given **MAP** object.

Syntax

[*collAreas* =] *map*.**areas**

[*oObject* =] *map*.**areas**(*vIndex* [, *iSubIndex*])

Possible Values

collAreas Array of **AREA** objects.

oObject Reference to an individual item in the array of elements contained by the object.

vIndex Required. Number or string specifying the element or collection to retrieve. If this parameter is an integer, the method returns the element in the collection at the given position, where the first element has value 0, the second has 1, and so on. If this parameter is a string and there is more than one element with the **name** or **id** property equal to the string, the method returns a collection of matching elements.

Possible Values *(continued)*

ISubIndex Optional. Position of an element to retrieve. This parameter is used when *vIndex* is a string. The method uses the string to construct a collection of all elements that have a **name** or **id** equal to the string, and then retrieves from this collection the element at the position specified by *iSubIndex*.

Properties

length

Methods

add   **item**   **remove**   **tags**   **urns**

Remarks

Areas can be added to or removed from the collection. If duplicate identifiers are found, a collection of those items is returned. Collections of duplicates must be referenced subsequently by ordinal position.

Applies To

 WIN16   **WIN32**   **MAC**   **UNIX**

MAP

attributes Collection

Retrieves a collection of attributes of the object.

Syntax

[*collattributes* =] *object*.**attributes**

[*oObject* =] *object*.**attributes**(*iIndex*)

Possible Values

collattributes Zero-based array of attributes applied to the object.

oObject   Reference to an individual attribute in the array of attributes assigned to the object.

iIndex   Required. Integer specifying the zero-based index of the item to be returned.

Properties

length

Methods

item

Remarks

The **attributes** collection does not include **expando** properties. To access the **expando** properties of an object, use the JScript (compatible with ECMA 262 language specification) **for**...**in** construct.

The **attributes** collection does not expose the **style** object. Use the **cssText** property of the object's **style** property to retrieve the persistent representation of the cascading styles associated with an object.

Unlike other DHTML collections, such as **all** and **children**, the **attributes** collection is static. Modifications to the properties of an object are not automatically reflected by an existing reference to the **attributes** collection of that object.

Example

The following example shows how to iterate through the collection of attributes of the specified object, displaying the name and value of the attributes as well as the language of the attribute (HTML or script).

```
<SCRIPT>
function ShowAttribs(oElem)
{
    txtAttribs.innerHTML = '';

    // Retrieve the collection of attributes for the specified object.
    var oAttribs = oElem.attributes;

    // Iterate through the collection.
    for (var i = 0; i < oAttribs.length; i++)
    {
        var oAttrib = oAttribs[i];

        // Print the name and value of the attribute.
        // Additionally, print whether or not the attribute was specified in
        // HTML or script.
        txtAttribs.innerHTML += oAttrib.nodeName + '=' +
            oAttrib.nodeValue + ' (' + oAttrib.specified + ')<BR>';
    }
}
</SCRIPT>
```

DHTML Collections

Applies To

 WIN16   WIN32   MAC   UNIX

A, ACRONYM, ADDRESS, APPLET, AREA, B, BASE, BASEFONT, BDO, BGSOUND, BIG, BLOCKQUOTE, BODY, BR, BUTTON, CAPTION, CENTER, CITE, CODE, COL, COLGROUP, COMMENT, DD, DEL, DFN, DIR, DIV, DL, DT, EM, EMBED, FIELDSET, FONT, FORM, FRAME, FRAMESET, HEAD, Hn, HR, HTML, I, IFRAME, IMG, INPUT type=button, INPUT type=checkbox, INPUT type=file, INPUT type=hidden, INPUT type=image, INPUT type=password, INPUT type=radio, INPUT type=reset, INPUT type=submit, INPUT type=text, INS, KBD, LABEL, LEGEND, LI, LINK, LISTING, MAP, MARQUEE, MENU, NEXTID, OBJECT, OL, OPTION, P, PLAINTEXT, PRE, Q, S, SAMP, SCRIPT, SELECT, SMALL, SPAN, STRIKE, STRONG, SUB, SUP, TABLE, TBODY, TD, TEXTAREA, TFOOT, TH, THEAD, TITLE, TR, TT, U, UL, VAR, XMP

behaviorUrns Collection

Returns a collection of Uniform Resource Name (URN) strings identifying the behaviors attached to the element.

Syntax

[*collUrns* =] *object*.**behaviorUrns**

[*sUrn* =] *object*.**behaviorUrns**(*iIndex*)

Possible Values

collUrns Array of URNs identifying the behaviors attached to the element.

sUrn Reference to an item in the array of behavior URNs.

iIndex Required. Integer specifying the zero-based index of the item to be returned.

Remarks

A behavior can specify a unique identifier in the form of a URN. If no URN is specified for a behavior, an empty string is specified in the collection. If no behaviors are attached to the element, an empty collection is returned.

Properties

length

Methods

item

Example

The following example shows how to display the URN of every behavior attached to a specified **DIV**.

```
<HEAD>
<STYLE>
   DIV { behavior:url(fly.htc) url (zoom.htc) url (fade.htc)}
</STYLE>

function window.onload()
{
   oColl = oDiv.behaviorUrns;
   if (oColl != null)
   {
      for (i=0; i < oColl.length; i++)
        alert (oColl(i));
   }
}
</HEAD>

<DIV ID=oDiv>I just want to fly</DIV>
```

Applies To

 WIN16   WIN32   MAC   UNIX

A, ACRONYM, ADDRESS, APPLET, AREA, B, BASE, BASEFONT, BGSOUND, BIG, BLOCKQUOTE, BODY, BR, BUTTON, CAPTION, CENTER, CITE, CODE, COL, COLGROUP, COMMENT, DD, DEL, DFN, DIR, DIV, DL, DT, EM, EMBED, FIELDSET, FONT, FORM, FRAME, FRAMESET, HEAD, Hn, HR, HTML, I, IFRAME, IMG, INPUT type=button, INPUT type=checkbox, INPUT type=file, INPUT type=hidden, INPUT type=image, INPUT type=password, INPUT type=radio, INPUT type=reset, INPUT type=submit, INPUT type=text, INS, ISINDEX, KBD, LABEL, LEGEND, LI, LINK, LISTING, MAP, MARQUEE, MENU, NEXTID, NOBR, NOFRAMES, NOSCRIPT, OBJECT, OL, OPTION, P, PLAINTEXT, PRE, Q, RT, RUBY, S, SAMP, SCRIPT, SELECT, SMALL, SPAN, STRIKE, STRONG, STYLE, SUB, SUP, TABLE, TBODY, TD, TEXTAREA, TFOOT, TH, THEAD, TITLE, TR, TT, U, UL, VAR, WBR, XML, XMP

DHTML Collections

bookmarks Collection

Returns a collection of ActiveX Data Objects (ADO) bookmarks tied to the rows affected by the current event.

Syntax

[*collBookmarks* =] *event*.**bookmarks**

[*oObject* =] *event*.**bookmarks**(*iIndex*)

Possible Values

collBookmarks	Array of ADO bookmarks.
oObject	Reference to an individual item in the array of elements contained by the object.
iIndex	Required. Integer specifying the zero-based index of the item to be returned.

Properties

length

Methods

item

Applies To

 WIN16   WIN32   MAC   UNIX

event

boundElements Collection

Returns a collection of all elements on the page bound to a data set.

Syntax

[*collBoundElements* =] *event*.**boundElements**

[*oObject* =] *event*.**boundElements**(*vIndex* [, *iSubIndex*])

Possible Values

collBoundElements	Array of elements found on a page that are bound to a data set.
oObject	Reference to an individual item in the array of elements contained by the object.
vIndex	Required. Number or string specifying the element or collection to retrieve. If this parameter is an integer, the method returns the element in the collection at the given position, where the first element has value 0, the second has 1, and so on. If this parameter is a string and there is more than one element with the **name** or **id** property equal to the string, the method returns a collection of matching elements.
iSubIndex	Optional. Position of an element to retrieve. This parameter is used when *vIndex* is a string. The method uses the string to construct a collection of all elements that have a **name** or **id** equal to the string, and then retrieves from this collection the element at the position specified by *iSubIndex*.

Remarks

This collection is only applicable to data events.

Properties

length

Methods

item   **tags**   **urns**

Applies To

  **WIN16   WIN32   MAC   UNIX**

event

cells Collection

Retrieves a collection of all cells in the table row or in the entire table.

Syntax

[*oCellColl* =] *object*.*oTR*.**cells**

[*oCellObject* =] *object*.**cells**(*vIndex* [, *iSubIndex*])

Possible Values

oCellColl Array of **TD** and **TH** elements contained by the object. If the object is a **TR**, the array contains elements only in that table row. If the object is a **TABLE**, the array contains all elements in the table.

oCellObject Reference to an individual item in the array of elements contained by the object.

vIndex Required. Number or string specifying the element or collection to retrieve. If this parameter is an integer, the method returns the element in the collection at the given position, where the first element has value 0, the second has 1, and so on. If this parameter is a string and there is more than one element with the **name** or **id** property equal to the string, the method returns a collection of matching elements. The parameter can specify a string as a range of table rows and columns by providing a spreadsheet format, such as A1:B1.

iSubIndex Optional. Position of an element to retrieve. This parameter is used when *vIndex* is a string. The method uses the string to construct a collection of all elements that have a **name** or **id** equal to the string, and then retrieves from this collection the element at the position specified by *iSubIndex*.

Properties

length

Methods

item   **tags**   **urns**

Remarks

A **cells** collection is comprised of **TH** and **TD** elements.

When a cell spans multiple rows, that cell appears only in the **cells** collection for the first of the rows that the cell spans.

If duplicate identifiers are found, a collection of those items is returned. Collections of duplicates must be referenced subsequently by ordinal position.

Individual **cells** or an array of **cells** can be specified using a spreadsheet format. By specifying a colon-delimited string of the starting and ending cells, a **cells** collection can be retrieved from anywhere in the table. Specifying a particular cell with this format returns that object. The format of this string uses letters to indicate columns, starting with A, and numbers to indicate rows, starting with 1. A **cells** collection on a table row only includes the elements within that row if the *vIndex* string specifies a range of multiple rows using the spreadsheet format.

Examples

The following example shows how to use the **rows** collection on the **TABLE** object and the **cells** collection to insert a number into each cell of the table.

```
<HTML>
<SCRIPT LANGUAGE="JScript">
function numberCells() {
    var count=0;
    for (i=0; i < document.all.oTable.rows.length; i++) {
        for (j=0; j < document.all.oTable.rows(i).cells.length; j++) {
            document.all.oTable.rows(i).cells(j).innerText = count;
            count++;
        }
    }
}
</SCRIPT>
<BODY onload="numberCells()">
<TABLE id=oTable border=1>
<TR><TH> </TH><TH> </TH><TH> </TH><TH> </TH></TR>
<TR><TD> </TD><TD> </TD><TD> </TD><TD> </TD></TR>
<TR><TD> </TD><TD> </TD><TD> </TD><TD> </TD></TR>
</TABLE>
</BODY>
</HTML>
```

Applies To

WIN16	WIN32	MAC	UNIX

TR

WIN16	WIN32	MAC	UNIX

TABLE

childNodes Collection

Retrieves a collection of children from the specified object.

Syntax

[*oNodeList* =] *object*.**childNodes**

[*oNode* =] *object*.**childNodes**(*vIndex* [, *iSubIndex*])

Possible Values

oNodeList Array containing the children of a specified object.

oNode Reference to an individual item in the array of elements contained by the object.

vIndex Required. Number or string specifying the element or collection to retrieve. If this parameter is an integer, the method returns the element in the collection at the given position, where the first element has value 0, the second has 1, and so on. If this parameter is a string and there is more than one element with the **name** or **id** property equal to the string, the method returns a collection of matching elements.

iSubIndex Optional. Position of an element to retrieve. This parameter is used when *vIndex* is a string. The method uses the string to construct a collection of all elements that have a **name** or **id** equal to the string, and then retrieves from this collection the element at the position specified by *iSubIndex*.

Properties

length

Methods

item   **urns**

Example

The following example shows how you can assign to a variable the **childNodes** collection of the **BODY** object.

```
<SCRIPT>
var aNodeList = oBody.childNodes;
</SCRIPT>
     :
<BODY ID="oBody">
<SPAN ID="oSpan">A Span</SPAN>
</BODY>
```

The next example shows how you can assign to a variable the **childNodes** collection of a node created by using the **createElement** method.

```
var oParentNode = document.createElement("DIV");
var oNode = document.createElement("B");
document.body.insertBefore(oParentNode);
oParentNode.insertBefore(oNode);
var aNodeList = oParentNode.childNodes;
```

Applies To

| IE 5 | WIN16 | WIN32 | MAC | UNIX | WIN16 |

A, ACRONYM, ADDRESS, APPLET, AREA, B, BASE, BASEFONT, BDO, BIG, BLOCKQUOTE, BODY, BUTTON, CAPTION, CENTER, CITE, CODE, COL, COLGROUP, COMMENT, DD, DEL, DFN, DIR, DIV, DL, document, DT, EM, EMBED, FIELDSET, FONT, FORM, FRAME, FRAMESET, HEAD, Hn, HR, HTML, I, IFRAME, IMG, INS, KBD, LABEL, LEGEND, LI, LINK, LISTING, MAP, MARQUEE, MENU, NEXTID, OL, OPTION, P, PLAINTEXT, PRE, Q, S, SAMP, SCRIPT, SELECT, SMALL, SPAN, STRIKE, STRONG, SUB, SUP, TABLE, TBODY, TD, TEXTAREA, TFOOT, TH, THEAD, TITLE, TR, TT, U, UL, VAR, XMP

children Collection

Retrieves a collection of the direct descendants of the object.

Syntax

[*collChildren* =] *object*.**children**

[*oObject* =] *object*.**children**(*vIndex* [, *iSubIndex*])

Possible Values

collChildren	Array containing the direct descendants of an object.
oObject	Reference to an individual item in the array of elements contained by the object.
vIndex	Required. Number or string specifying the element or collection to retrieve. If this parameter is an integer, the method returns the element in the collection at the given position, where the first element has value 0, the second has 1, and so on. If this parameter is a string and there is more than one element with the **name** or **id** property equal to the string, the method returns a collection of matching elements.
iSubIndex	Optional. Position of an element to retrieve. This parameter is used when *vIndex* is a string. The method uses the string to construct a collection of all elements that have a **name** or **id** equal to the string, and then retrieves from this collection the element at the position specified by *iSubIndex*.

DHTML Collections

children Collection

Properties

length

Methods

item   **tags**   **urns**

Remarks

Similar to the objects contained in the **all** collection, the objects contained in the **children** collection are undefined if the child elements are overlapping tags.

Examples

The following example shows how to determine the collections for two **DIV** elements, divOne and divTwo. The **children** collection for divONE includes **IMG**, **DIV**, and **BUTTON**. The **children** collection for divTWO includes **P**.

```
<DIV id=divONE>
<IMG src=mygif.gif>
<DIV id=divTWO>
<P>Some text in a paragraph
</DIV>
<BUTTON> The label for the button </BUTTON>
</DIV>
```

Applies To

 WIN16   WIN32   MAC   UNIX

A, ACRONYM, ADDRESS, APPLET, AREA, B, BASE, BASEFONT, BIG, BLOCKQUOTE, BODY, BUTTON, CAPTION, CENTER, CITE, CODE, COL, COLGROUP, DD, DEL, DFN, DIR, DIV, DL, document, DT, EM, EMBED, FIELDSET, FONT, FORM, FRAME, FRAMESET, HEAD, Hn, HR, HTML, I, IFRAME, IMG, INS, KBD, LABEL, LEGEND, LI, LINK, LISTING, MAP, MARQUEE, MENU, NEXTID, OL, OPTION, P, PLAINTEXT, PRE, Q, S, SAMP, SCRIPT, SELECT, SMALL, SPAN, STRIKE, STRONG, SUB, SUP, TABLE, TBODY, TD, TEXTAREA, TFOOT, THEAD, TITLE, TR, TT, U, UL, VAR, XMP

 WIN16   WIN32   MAC   UNIX

BDO, RT, RUBY

controlRange Collection

Returns an array of elements specified in the **createControlRange** method.

Syntax

[*collRange* =] *document.body*.**createControlRange**()

Possible Values

collRange Array of elements created by using the **createControlRange** method.

Remarks

Instead of using the collection's **item** method, you can use an index to directly access an element in the collection. For example, the element returned from the collection represented by `collRange(0)` is the same as the element returned by `collRange.item(0)`.

The **controlRange** collection is available as of Internet Explorer 5.

Properties

length

Methods

add	**execCommand**	**item**
queryCommandEnabled	**queryCommandIndeterm**	**queryCommandState**
queryCommandSupported	**queryCommandValue**	**remove**
scrollIntoView	**select**	

elements Collection

Retrieves a collection, in source order, of all objects in a given form.

Syntax

[*collElements* =] *form*.**elements**

[*oObject* =] *form*.**elements**(*vIndex* [, *iSubIndex*])

Possible Values

collElements	Array of **INPUT**, **SELECT**, and **TEXTAREA** objects.
oObject	Reference to an individual item in the array of elements contained by the object.
vIndex	Required. Number or string specifying the element or collection to retrieve. If this parameter is an integer, the method returns the element in the collection at the given position, where the first element has value 0, the second has 1, and so on. If this parameter is a string and there is more than one element with the **name** or **id** property equal to the string, the method returns a collection of matching elements.
iSubIndex	Optional. Position of an element to retrieve. This parameter is used when *vIndex* is a string. The method uses the string to construct a collection of all elements that have a **name** or **id** equal to the string, and then retrieves from this collection the element at the position specified by *iSubIndex*.

Properties

length

Methods

item   **tags**   **urns**

Remarks

This collection can contain any combination of the **INPUT**, **SELECT**, and **TEXTAREA** objects.

Applies To

 WIN16   WIN32   MAC

FORM

 UNIX

FORM

embeds Collection

Retrieves a collection of all **EMBED** objects in the document.

Syntax

[*collEmbeds* =] *document*.**embeds**

[*oObject* =] *document*.**embeds**(*vIndex* [, *iSubIndex*])

Possible Values

collEmbeds	Array of **EMBED** objects.
oObject	Reference to an individual item in the array of elements contained by the object.
vIndex	Required. Number or string specifying the element or collection to retrieve. If this parameter is an integer, the method returns the element in the collection at the given position, where the first element has value 0, the second has 1, and so on. If this parameter is a string and there is more than one element with the **name** or **id** property equal to the string, the method returns a collection of matching elements.
iSubIndex	Optional. Position of an element to retrieve. This parameter is used when *vIndex* is a string. The method uses the string to construct a collection of all elements that have a **name** or **id** equal to the string, and then retrieves from this collection the element at the position specified by *iSubIndex*.

Properties

length

Methods

item   **tags**   **urns**

Applies To

WIN16   WIN32   MAC   UNIX

document

DHTML Collections

filters Collection

Retrieves the collection of filters that have been applied to the object.

Syntax

[*collFilters* =] *object*.**filters**

[*oObject* =] *object*.**filters**(*vIndex* [, *iSubIndex*])

Possible Values

collFilters Array of filters applied to the object.

oObject Reference to an individual item in the array of elements contained by the object.

vIndex Required. Number or string specifying the element or collection to retrieve. If this parameter is an integer, the method returns the element in the collection at the given position, where the first element has value 0, the second has 1, and so on. If this parameter is a string and there is more than one element with the **name** or **id** property equal to the string, the method returns a collection of matching elements.

iSubIndex Optional. Position of an element to retrieve. This parameter is used when *vIndex* is a string. The method uses the string to construct a collection of all elements that have a **name** or **id** equal to the string, and then retrieves from this collection the element at the position specified by *iSubIndex*.

Properties

length

Methods

item

Remarks

For a filter to render, the **SPAN** and **DIV** elements must have one of the following cascading style sheets (CSS) attributes: **height**, **width**, or **position** (absolute or relative).

Applies To

 WIN32   UNIX

BODY, BUTTON, DIV, FIELDSET, IMG, INPUT type=button, INPUT
type=checkbox, INPUT type=file, INPUT type=image, INPUT type=password,
INPUT type=radio, INPUT type=reset, INPUT type=submit, INPUT type=text,
MARQUEE, NEXTID, SPAN, TABLE, TD, TEXTAREA, TH

 WIN32   UNIX

BDO, RT, RUBY

forms Collection

Retrieves a collection, in source order, of all **FORM** objects in the document.

Syntax

[*collForms* =] *document*.**forms**

[*oObject* =] *document*.**forms**(*vIndex* [, *iSubIndex*])

Possible Values

collForms   Array of **FORM** objects.

oObject   Reference to an individual item in the array of elements contained by the
object.

vIndex   Required. Number or string specifying the element or collection to
retrieve. If this parameter is an integer, the method returns the element in
the collection at the given position, where the first element has value 0,
the second has 1, and so on. If this parameter is a string and there is more
than one element with the **name** or **id** property equal to the string, the
method returns a collection of matching elements.

iSubIndex   Optional. Position of an element to retrieve. This parameter is used when
vIndex is a string. The method uses the string to construct a collection of
all elements that have a **name** or **id** equal to the string, and then retrieves
from this collection the element at the position specified by *iSubIndex*.

Properties

length

DHTML Collections

Methods

> **item** **tags** **urns**

Applies To

 WIN16 **WIN32** **MAC**

document

 UNIX

document

frames Collection

Retrieves a collection of all **window** objects defined by the given document or defined by the document associated with the given window.

Syntax

> [*collFrames* =] *object*.**frames**
>
> [*oObject* =] *object*.**frames**(*vIndex* [, *iSubIndex*])

Possible Values

> *collFrames*   Array of **window** objects.
>
> *oObject*   Reference to an individual item in the array of elements contained by the object.
>
> *vIndex*   Required. Number or string specifying the element or collection to retrieve. If this parameter is an integer, the method returns the element in the collection at the given position, where the first element has value 0, the second has 1, and so on. If this parameter is a string and there is more than one element with the **name** or **id** property equal to the string, the method returns a collection of matching elements.
>
> *iSubIndex*   Optional. Position of an element to retrieve. This parameter is used when *vIndex* is a string. The method uses the string to construct a collection of all elements that have a **name** or **id** equal to the string, and then retrieves from this collection the element at the position specified by *iSubIndex*.

Properties

> **length**

Methods

item

Remarks

If the HTML source document contains a **BODY** tag, the collection contains one window for each **IFRAME** object in the document. If the source document contains **FRAMESET** tags, the collection contains one window for each **FRAME** tag in the document. In both cases, the order is determined by the HTML source.

This collection contains only **window** objects and does not provide access to the corresponding **FRAME** and **IFRAME** objects. To access these objects, use the **all** collection for the document containing the objects.

Although you can use names with the **item** method on this collection, the method never returns a collection. Instead, it always returns the first window having the given name. To ensure that all windows are accessible, make sure that no two windows in a document have the same name.

Examples

The following example in JScript (compatible with ECMA 262 language specification) shows how to display the URLs of the HTML documents contained in windows created by the **IFRAME** objects in the document.

```
var frm = document.frames;
for (i=0; i < frm.length; i++)
    alert(frm(i).location);
```

The next example in JScript shows how to display the name of each window defined by **FRAME** tags in the parent window of the current document.

```
var frm = window.parent.frames;
for (i=0; i < frm.length; i++)
    alert(frm(i).name);
```

Applies To

 WIN16   WIN32   MAC

document, window

 UNIX

document, window

images Collection

Retrieves a collection, in source order, of **IMG** objects in the document.

Syntax

[*collImages* =] *document*.**images**

[*oObject* =] *document*.**images**(*vIndex* [, *iSubIndex*])

Possible Values

collImages	Array of **IMG** objects.
oObject	Reference to an individual item in the array of elements contained by the object.
vIndex	Required. Number or string specifying the element or collection to retrieve. If this parameter is an integer, the method returns the element in the collection at the given position, where the first element has value 0, the second has 1, and so on. If this parameter is a string and there is more than one element with the **name** or **id** property equal to the string, the method returns a collection of matching elements.
iSubIndex	Optional. Position of an element to retrieve. This parameter is used when *vIndex* is a string. The method uses the string to construct a collection of all elements that have a **name** or **id** equal to the string, and then retrieves from this collection the element at the position specified by *iSubIndex*.

Properties

length

Methods

item   **tags**   **urns**

Applies To

 WIN16   WIN32   MAC   UNIX

document

imports Collection

Retrieves a collection of all the imported style sheets defined for the **styleSheet** object. An imported style sheet is one that is brought into the document using the cascading style sheets (CSS) **@import** rule.

Syntax

[*collImports* =] *styleSheet*.**imports**

[*oObject* =] *styleSheet*.**imports**(*iIndex*)

Possible Values

collImports   Array of imported style sheets.

oObject   Reference to an individual item in the array of elements contained by the object.

iIndex   Required. Integer specifying the zero-based index of the item to be returned.

Properties

length

Methods

item

Examples

The following example shows how to display the URLs of the imported style sheets in the document.

```
for ( i = 0; i < document.styleSheets.length; i++ )
{
    if ( document.styleSheets(i).owningElement.tagName == "STYLE" )
    {
        for ( j = 0; j < document.styleSheets(i).imports.length; j++ )
            alert("Imported style sheet " + j + " is at " +
                    document.styleSheets(i).imports(j).href);
    }
}
```

DHTML Collections

links Collection

Applies To

 WIN16   WIN32   MAC   UNIX

styleSheet

links Collection

Retrieves a collection of all **A** objects that specify the **href** property and all **AREA** objects in the document.

Syntax

[*collLinks* =] *document*.**links**

[*oObject* =] *document*.**links**(*iIndex*)

Possible Values

collLinks   Array of **A** objects.

oObject   Reference to an individual item in the array of elements contained by the object.

iIndex   Required. Integer specifying the zero-based index of the item to be returned.

Properties

length

Methods

item   tags   urns

Remarks

For **A** objects to appear in the collection, they must have a **name** and/or **id** property.

Examples

The following example shows how to display the **HREF** attribute of the third link defined in the document.

```
alert(document.links(2).href);
```

Applies To

 WIN16   WIN32   MAC

document

 UNIX

document

mimeTypes Collection

Not implemented.

options Collection

Retrieves a collection of the **OPTION** objects in a **SELECT** object.

Syntax

[*collOptions* =] *select*.**options**

[*oObject* =] *select*.**options**(*vIndex* [, *iSubIndex*])

Possible Values

collOptions	Array of **OPTION** objects.
oObject	Reference to an individual item in the array of elements contained by the object.
vIndex	Required. Number or string specifying the element or collection to retrieve. If this parameter is an integer, the method returns the element in the collection at the given position, where the first element has value 0, the second has 1, and so on. If this parameter is a string and there is more than one element with the **name** or **id** property equal to the string, the method returns a collection of matching elements.
iSubIndex	Optional. Position of an element to retrieve. This parameter is used when *vIndex* is a string. The method uses the string to construct a collection of all elements that have a **name** or **id** equal to the string, and then retrieves from this collection the element at the position specified by *iSubIndex*.

Properties

length

DHTML Collections

Methods

add   **item**   **remove**   **tags**   **urns**

Remarks

To delete an **OPTION** from a **SELECT** object, assign the **OPTION** a null value. This compresses the array.

If duplicate identifiers are found, a collection of those items is returned. Collections of duplicates must be referenced subsequently by ordinal position.

Examples

The following example shows how to display the text and values of all **OPTION** objects in the first **SELECT** object in the document.

```
var coll = document.all.tags("SELECT");
if (coll.length>0) {
    for (i=0; i< coll(0).options.length; i++)
        alert("Element " + i + " is " + coll(0).options(i).text +
            " and has the value " + coll(0).options(i).value);
}
```

Applies To

 WIN16   WIN32   MAC

SELECT

 UNIX

SELECT

plugins Collection

Retrieves a collection of all **EMBED** objects within the document.

Syntax

[*collPlugins* =] *navigator*.**plugins**

[*oObject* =] *navigator*.**plugins**(*iIndex*)

Possible Values

collPlugins Array of **EMBED** objects.

oObject Reference to an individual item in the array of elements contained by the object.

iIndex Required. Integer specifying the zero-based index of the item to be returned.

Properties

length

Methods

item **tags**

Remarks

The **plugins** collection is exposed for compatibility with other browsers.

The collection is an alias for the **embeds** collection on the document.

Applies To

 WIN16 WIN32 MAC UNIX

navigator

rows Collection

Retrieves a collection of **TR** objects (rows) from a **TABLE** object.

Syntax

[*collRows* =] *object*.**rows**

[*oObject* =] *object*.**rows**(*vIndex* [, *iSubIndex*])

Possible Values

collRows Array of **TR** objects.

oObject Reference to an individual item in the array of elements contained by the object.

Possible Values *(continued)*

vIndex   Required. Number or string specifying the element or collection to retrieve. If this parameter is an integer, the method returns the element in the collection at the given position, where the first element has value 0, the second has 1, and so on. If this parameter is a string and there is more than one element with the **name** or **id** property equal to the string, the method returns a collection of matching elements.

iSubIndex Optional. Position of an element to retrieve. This parameter is used when *vIndex* is a string. The method uses the string to construct a collection of all elements that have a **name** or **id** equal to the string, and then retrieves from this collection the element at the position specified by *iSubIndex*.

Properties

> **length**

Methods

> **item**   **tags**   **urns**

Remarks

The scope of the **rows** collection is for the **THEAD**, **TBODY**, or **TFOOT** object of the table. In addition, there is a **rows** collection for the **TABLE** object, which contains all the rows for the entire table. A row that appears in one of the table sections also appears in the **rows** collection for the **TABLE**. The **TR** object has two index properties, **rowIndex** and **sectionRowIndex**, that indicate where a given row appears. The **rowIndex** property indicates where the **TR** appears with respect to the **rows** collection for the whole table. By contrast, **sectionRowIndex** returns where the **TR** appears with respect to the **rows** collection for the specific table section in which it is located.

If duplicate identifiers are found, a collection of those items is returned. Collections of duplicates must be referenced subsequently by ordinal position.

Examples

The following example shows how to use the **rows** and **cells** collections to insert a number into each cell of the table.

```
<HTML>
<SCRIPT LANGUAGE="JScript">
function numberCells() {
    var count=0;
    for (i=0; i < document.all.oTable.rows.length; i++) {
        for (j=0; j < document.all.oTable.rows(i).cells.length; j++) {
            document.all.oTable.rows(i).cells(j).innerText = count;
```

```
                    count++;
                }
            }
        }
        </SCRIPT>
        <BODY onload="numberCells()">
        <TABLE id=oTable border=1>
        <TR><TH> </TH><TH> </TH><TH> </TH><TH> </TH></TR>
        <TR><TD> </TD><TD> </TD><TD> </TD><TD> </TD></TR>
        <TR><TD> </TD><TD> </TD><TD> </TD><TD> </TD></TR>
        </TABLE>
        </BODY>
        </HTML>
```

Applies To

 WIN16   WIN32   MAC   UNIX

TABLE, TBODY, TFOOT, THEAD

rules Collection

Retrieves a collection of rules defined in the style sheet.

Syntax

[*collRules* =] *stylesheet*.**rules**

[*oObject* =] *stylesheet*.**rules**(*iIndex*)

Possible Values

collRules   Array of rules.

oObject   Reference to an individual item in the array of elements contained by the
             object.

iIndex   Required. Integer specifying the zero-based index of the item to be
             returned.

Properties

length

Methods

item

Remarks

This collection is always accessible, even if the style sheet is not enabled. Rules are added to the **rules** collection with the **addRule** method on the individual style sheet. A rule that is added to a **disabled** style sheet does not apply to the document unless the style sheet is enabled. Rules are deleted with the **removeRule** method.

The rules in this collection are in the source order of the document. As rules are added or deleted through the cascading style sheets (CSS) Object Model, a rule's absolute position in the **rules** collection might change, but its position relative to other rules remains the same. When you add rules without specifying an index, the rule gets added to the document last. If you specify an index, however, the rule is inserted before the rule currently in that ordinal position in the collection. If the specified index is greater than the number of rules in the collection, the rule is added to the end.

Example

The following example shows how to use the **rules** collection to identify the color specified in style sheet rules.

```
<HTML>
<HEAD>
<SCRIPT>
function ruleColor(ruleIndex) {
    alert("The color of rule " + ruleIndex + " is " +
        document.styleSheets[0].rules.item(ruleIndex).style.color + ".");
}
</SCRIPT>

<STYLE>
.rule0 {color:"red"}
.rule1 {color:"blue"}
</STYLE>
</HEAD>

<BODY>
<P class="rule0" id="oRule0Span">
    Rule 0 is applied to this line.
</P>
<P class="rule1" id="oRule1Span">
    Rule 1 is applied to this line.
</P>

<BUTTON onclick="ruleColor(0)">Color of Rule 0</BUTTON>
<BUTTON onclick="ruleColor(1)">Color of Rule 1</BUTTON>

</BODY>
</HTML>
```

To see this code in action, refer to the Web Workshop CD-ROM.

Applies To

 WIN16   WIN32   MAC   UNIX

styleSheet

scripts Collection

Retrieves a collection of all **SCRIPT** objects in the document.

Syntax

[*collScripts* =] *document*.**scripts**

[*oObject* =] *document*.**scripts**(*vIndex* [, *iSubIndex*])

Possible Values

collScripts   Array of **SCRIPT** objects.

oObject   Reference to an individual item in the array of elements contained by the object.

vIndex   Required. Number or string specifying the element or collection to retrieve. If this parameter is an integer, the method returns the element in the collection at the given position, where the first element has value 0, the second has 1, and so on. If this parameter is a string and there is more than one element with the **name** or **id** property equal to the string, the method returns a collection of matching elements.

iSubIndex   Optional. Position of an element to retrieve. This parameter is used when *vIndex* is a string. The method uses the string to construct a collection of all elements that have a **name** or **id** equal to the string, and then retrieves from this collection the element at the position specified by *iSubIndex*.

Properties

length

Methods

item   tags   urns

DHTML Collections

Remarks

This collection contains all the scripts in the document in source order regardless of the script's location in the document (whether in the **HEAD** or **BODY**).

If duplicate identifiers are found, a collection of those items is returned. Collections of duplicates must be referenced subsequently by ordinal position.

Applies To

 WIN16   WIN32   MAC   UNIX

document

styleSheets Collection

Retrieves a collection of **styleSheet** objects representing the style sheets that correspond to each instance of a **LINK** or **STYLE** object in the document.

Syntax

[*collStyleSheets* =] *document*.**styleSheets**

[*oObject* =] *document*.**styleSheets**(*vIndex* [, *iSubIndex*])

Possible Values

collStyleSheets	Array of **styleSheet** objects.
oObject	Reference to an individual item in the array of elements contained by the object.
vIndex	Required. Number or string specifying the element or collection to retrieve. If this parameter is an integer, the method returns the element in the collection at the given position, where the first element has value 0, the second has 1, and so on. If this parameter is a string and there is more than one element with the **name** or **id** property equal to the string, the method returns a collection of matching elements.
iSubIndex	Optional. Position of an element to retrieve. This parameter is used when *vIndex* is a string. The method uses the string to construct a collection of all elements that have a **name** or **id** equal to the string, and then retrieves from this collection the element at the position specified by *iSubIndex*.

Properties

length   styleSheet

Methods

item   urns

Remarks

Style sheets that are imported using the @**import** rule and are contained within the **STYLE** object are available through the **imports** collection.

Examples

The following example shows how to display the titles of the style sheets in the document.

```
for ( i = 0; i < document.styleSheets.length; i++ )
{
    alert("Style sheet " + i + " is titled " + document.styleSheets(i).title);
}
```

Applies To

 WIN16   WIN32   MAC   UNIX

document

tBodies Collection

Retrieves a collection of all **TBODY** objects in the table. Objects in this collection are in HTML source order.

Syntax

[*collTBodies* =] *table*.**tBodies**

[*oObject* =] *table*.**tBodies**(*vIndex* [, *iSubIndex*])

Possible Values

collTBodies Array of **TBODY** objects.

oObject   Reference to an individual item in the array of elements contained by the object.

vIndex   Required. Number or string specifying the element or collection to retrieve. If this parameter is an integer, the method returns the element in the collection at the given position, where the first element has value 0, the second has 1, and so on. If this parameter is a string and there is more than one element with the **name** or **id** property equal to the string, the method returns a collection of matching elements.

iSubIndex   Optional. Position of an element to retrieve. This parameter is used when *vIndex* is a string. The method uses the string to construct a collection of all elements that have a **name** or **id** equal to the string, and then retrieves from this collection the element at the position specified by *iSubIndex*.

Properties

length

Methods

item   **tags**   **urns**

Remarks

This collection can be indexed by name (ID). If duplicate names are found, a collection of those named items is returned. Collections of duplicate names must be referenced subsequently by ordinal position.

Examples

The following example shows how to put text in the first cell in the first row of the first **TBODY** object in the **TABLE**. For each **TABLE**, an initial **TBODY** object is synthesized in the HTML tree even if a **TBODY** element does not exist in the HTML source.

```
document.all.oTable.tBodies[0].rows[0].cells[0].innerText =
"Text for the first table cell";
```

Applies To

 WIN16   **WIN32**   **MAC**   **UNIX**

TABLE

TextRectangle Collection

Returns a collection of **TextRectangle** objects.

Properties

length

Methods

item

Remarks

The **TextRectangle** collection is returned from the **getClientRects** method.

The collection returns an empty collection for objects that do not have text.

If the window is resized, the collection is not updated. Because the collection is a snapshot of the layout, always update the collection following the **onresize** event.

The **TextRectangle** collection is available as of Internet Explorer 5.

Example

The following example shows how to use the **getClientRects** method and the **TextRectangle** collection to iterate through the lines of text in an object.

```
<SCRIPT>
function newHighlite(obj) {
  oRcts = obj.getClientRects();
  iLength = oRcts.length
  for (i = 0;i < iLength; i++)
  {
    alert("Line number " + (i + 1) + " is " +
        (oRcts(i).right - oRcts(i).left) + " pixels wide.")
  }
}
</SCRIPT>
```

 IE 5   **WIN16**   **WIN32**   **MAC**   **UNIX**

BDO

CHAPTER 4

HTML Components Reference

Components

The following section describes the elements that can be used within an HTML Component (HTC) to implement a behavior. References in this section are listed alphabetically within each of the following categories:

- Elements
- Events
- Methods
- Objects

ATTACH Element

Binds a function to an event so that the function is called whenever the event fires on the specified object.

Syntax

```
<PUBLIC:ATTACH
    EVENT = sEvent
    FOR = "document" | "element" | "window"
    ONEVENT = sEventHandler
    ID = sID
/>
```

Attributes

EVENT

Required. String that specifies the name of a Dynamic HTML (DHTML) **event**, or any of the events specific to HTCs.

FOR

Optional. String that specifies any one of the following values to identify the source of the event.

document   Refers to the **document** object.

element   Refers to the element to which the behavior is attached.

window   Refers to the **window** object.

ONEVENT

Required. String that contains inline script or a direct invocation of the event handler function.

ID

Optional. String that uniquely identifies the **ATTACH** element within the component. This attribute is analogous to the **ID** attribute in DHTML. All HTC elements can be accessed from scripting as objects using the specified **ID** of the HTC element. All attributes and methods of HTC elements can then be dynamically manipulated through scripting as properties and methods of these objects.

Element Information

Number of occurrences	Any number
Parent elements	**COMPONENT**
Child elements	None
Requires closing tag	No

Remarks

The **ATTACH** element is a declarative form of the **attachEvent** method.

When the specified event fires on the element to which the behavior is attached, the element's event handler is called first, before the behavior's. If multiple behaviors are attached to an element and multiple event handlers have been defined for the same event on the same element, the functions are called in random order, immediately after the element's event handler is called.

Example

The following example implements an expanding/collapsing table of contents using an HTC. The HTC attaches to the element's **onclick** event, and then expands or collapses the list each time the **onclick** event is received.

```
<PUBLIC:PROPERTY NAME="child" />
<PUBLIC:ATTACH EVENT="onclick" ONEVENT="ExpandCollapse()" />
```

```
<SCRIPT LANGUAGE="JScript">
function ExpandCollapse()
{
   var i;
   var sDisplay;

   // Determine current state of the list (expanded or collapsed)
   // based on the current display property of the child.
   bCollapsed = (element.document.all(child).style.display == "none");

   if (bCollapsed)
   {
      style.listStyleImage = "url('/workshop/graphics/blueminus.gif')";
      element.document.all(child).style.display = "";
   }
   else
   {
      style.listStyleImage = "url('/workshop/graphics/blueplus.gif')";
      element.document.all(child).style.display = "none";
   }
}
</SCRIPT>
```

To see this code in action, refer to the Web Workshop CD-ROM.

COMPONENT Element

Identifies the content as an HTC.

Syntax

```
<PUBLIC:COMPONENT
   NAME = sName
   URN = sURN
   ID = sID
/>
```

Attributes

NAME

Optional. String that defines the name by which the behavior is referred to in the containing document. This is especially useful when multiple behaviors are attached to an element, as it allows the Web author to invoke the properties or methods of the desired behavior from the containing document.

For example, if multiple behaviors are attached to a <SPAN ID = "mySpan"> element in a document, the **delay** property of the behavior named behaviorABC can be set using the following syntax:

```
mySpan.behaviorABC.delay = 1000;
```

URN

Required. String, in Universal Resource Name (URN) format, that uniquely identifies the component. This allows events to be uniquely identified when multiple behaviors fire events of the same name. When the event is fired, the **event** object's **srcURN** property is set to the URN of the behavior that fired the event.

ID

Optional. String that uniquely identifies the **COMPONENT** element within the component. This attribute is analogous to the **ID** attribute in DHTML. All HTC elements can be accessed from scripting as objects using the specified **ID** of the HTC element. All attributes and methods of HTC elements can then be dynamically manipulated through scripting as properties and methods of these objects.

Element Information

Number of occurrences	None or one
Parent elements	None
Child elements	**ATTACH, EVENT, METHOD, PROPERTY**
Requires closing tag	Yes

EVENT Element

Defines an event of the HTC to be exposed to the containing document.

Syntax

```
<PUBLIC:EVENT
    NAME = sName
    ID = sEventID
/>
```

Attributes

NAME

Required. String that specifies the name of the event exposed to the containing document.

ID

Optional. String that uniquely identifies the **EVENT** element within the component. This attribute is analogous to the **ID** attribute in DHTML. All HTC elements can be accessed from scripting as objects using the specified **ID** of the HTC element. All attributes and methods of HTC elements can then be dynamically manipulated through scripting as properties and methods of these objects.

Methods

eventID.**fire**([*oEvent*])

Fires the event to the containing document. This method has an optional *oEvent* parameter that specifies the **event** object containing context information.

Element Information

Number of occurrences	Any number
Parent elements	**COMPONENT**
Child elements	None
Requires closing tag	No

Remarks

By specifying a **NAME** attribute similar to a standard event already defined for the element, a behavior can override the element's default behavior.

Events defined for a behavior do not bubble and only fire on the element to which the behavior is attached.

Example

The following example is derived from a calculator behavior sample. Whenever the result changes, the HTC fires a custom onResultChange event back to the page, passing the result as an **expando** property of the **event** object.

```
<PUBLIC:EVENT NAME="onResultChange" ID="rcID" />

<SCRIPT LANGUAGE="JScript">
function doCalc()
{
    :
    oEvent = createEventObject();
    oEvent.result = sResult;
    rcID.fire (oEvent);
}
</SCRIPT>
```

The next example shows what the containing page looks like:

```
<HTML XMLNS:InetSDK>
<HEAD>
<STYLE>
@media all {
    InetSDK\:CALC     {behavior:url(engine.htc)}
}
</STYLE>
</HEAD>

<InetSDK:CALC id="myCalc" onResultChange="resultWindow.innerText=window.event.result">
```

```
<TABLE>
<TR><DIV ID="resultWindow" STYLE="border: '.025cm solid gray'"
ALIGN=RIGHT>0.</DIV></TR>
<TR><TD><INPUT TYPE=BUTTON VALUE=" 7 "></TD>
    <TD><INPUT TYPE=BUTTON VALUE=" 8 "></TD>
    <TD><INPUT TYPE=BUTTON VALUE=" 9 "></TD>
    <TD><INPUT TYPE=BUTTON VALUE=" / "></TD>
    <TD><INPUT TYPE=BUTTON VALUE=" C "></TD>
</TR>
<TR><TD><INPUT TYPE=BUTTON VALUE=" 4 "></TD>
    <TD><INPUT TYPE=BUTTON VALUE=" 5 "></TD>
    <TD><INPUT TYPE=BUTTON VALUE=" 6 "></TD>
    <TD><INPUT TYPE=BUTTON VALUE=" * "></TD>
    <TD><INPUT TYPE=BUTTON VALUE=" % " DISABLED></TD>
</TR>
<TR><TD><INPUT TYPE=BUTTON VALUE=" 1 "></TD>
    <TD><INPUT TYPE=BUTTON VALUE=" 2 "></TD>
    <TD><INPUT TYPE=BUTTON VALUE=" 3 "></TD>
    <TD><INPUT TYPE=BUTTON VALUE=" - "></TD>
    <TD><INPUT TYPE=BUTTON VALUE="1/x" DISABLED></TD>
</TR>
<TR><TD><INPUT TYPE=BUTTON VALUE=" 0 "></TD>
    <TD><INPUT TYPE=BUTTON VALUE="+/-"></TD>
    <TD><INPUT TYPE=BUTTON VALUE=" . "></TD>
    <TD><INPUT TYPE=BUTTON VALUE=" + "></TD>
    <TD><INPUT TYPE=BUTTON VALUE=" = "></TD>
</TR>

</TABLE>
</InetSDK:CALC>
</HTML>
```

To see this code in action, refer to the Web Workshop CD-ROM.

METHOD Element

Defines a method of the HTC to be exposed to the containing document.

Syntax

```
<PUBLIC:METHOD
    NAME = sName
    INTERNALNAME = sInternalName
    ID = sID
/>
```

Attributes

NAME

Required. String that defines the name by which the method is referred to in the containing document. By default, the **NAME** specified is also used to refer to the method within the component, unless an **INTERNALNAME** attribute is specified.

INTERNALNAME

Optional. String that defines the name of the method within the component. If no value is specified, the **NAME** attribute is used by default.

ID

Optional. String that uniquely identifies the **METHOD** element within the component. This attribute is analogous to the **ID** attribute in DHTML. All HTC elements can be accessed from scripting as objects using the specified **ID** of the HTC element. All attributes and methods of HTC elements can then be dynamically manipulated through scripting as properties and methods of these objects.

Element Information

Number of occurrences	Any number
Parent elements	**COMPONENT**
Child elements	None
Requires closing tag	No

Remarks

By specifying a **NAME** attribute similar to a standard method name already defined for the element, a behavior can override the element's default behavior.

Example

The following example shows how to use the **METHOD** tag to expose the `startFlying()` method from the HTC to the containing document.

```
<PUBLIC:METHOD NAME="startFlying" />

<SCRIPT LANGUAGE="JScript" >
function startFlying()
{
    // Insert flying code here.
}
</SCRIPT>
```

PROPERTY Element

Defines a property of the HTC to be exposed to the containing document.

Syntax

```
<PUBLIC:PROPERTY
    NAME = sName
    ID = sPropertyID
    INTERNALNAME = sInternalName
    GET = sGetFunction
    PUT = sPutFunction
    PERSIST = bPersist
    VALUE = vValue
/>
```

Attributes

NAME

Required. String that defines the name of the property exposed to the containing document. By default, the **NAME** specified is also used to refer to the property within the component, unless an **INTERNALNAME** attribute is specified.

ID

Optional. String that uniquely identifies the **PROPERTY** element within the component. This attribute is analogous to the **ID** attribute in DHTML. All HTC elements can be accessed from scripting as objects using the specified **ID** of the HTC element. All attributes and methods of HTC elements can then be dynamically manipulated through scripting as properties and methods of these objects.

INTERNALNAME

Optional. String that defines the property name within the component. This internal name must be declared globally before it can be referenced anywhere in the component; otherwise, a scripting error occurs indicating that the name is undefined. If no internal name is specified, the **NAME** attribute is used by default.

GET

Optional. String that specifies the function to be called when the value of the property is retrieved. A **PROPERTY** element that specifies a **GET** attribute without specifying a **PUT** attribute is a read-only property.

PUT

Optional. String that specifies the function to be called whenever the value of the property is set.

Note The function specified in this attribute must notify the element in the containing document about the property change by calling the **PROPERTY** element's **fireChange** method. Invoking this method causes the **onpropertychange** event to fire on the element in the containing page, with the **event** object's **propertyName** set to the name of the property. A **PROPERTY** element that specifies the **GET** and **PUT** attributes is a read/write property. Failure to specify a **GET** function, when a **PUT** function is specified, causes the property to be write-only, which often might not be desired.

PERSIST

Optional. Boolean value that specifies whether to persist the property as part of the page.

VALUE

Optional. Variant that specifies the default value for the property.

Methods

propertyID.**fireChange()**

Notifies the containing document that the value of the property has changed by firing the **onpropertychange** event on the element. If no **PUT** attribute is specified on the property, the **onpropertychange** event is automatically fired when the property is set in the containing document.

Element Information

Number of occurrences	Any number
Parent elements	**COMPONENT**
Child elements	None
Requires closing tag	No

Remarks

By specifying a **NAME** attribute similar to a standard property already defined for the element, a behavior can override the element's default behavior.

If either the **PUT** or **GET** attribute is specified, the **INTERNALNAME** attribute is ignored. Setting and/or retrieving the value of the property through the function(s) specified in the **PUT** and **GET** attributes takes precedence over setting and/or retrieving the value of the property through the **INTERNALNAME**.

Example

The following example shows how to create an expanding/collapsing table of contents using an HTC. The HTC exposes a "child" property to the containing document to indicate which element needs to toggle its **display** property to achieve the effect of an expanding/collapsing list.

```
<PUBLIC:PROPERTY NAME="child" />
<PUBLIC:ATTACH EVENT="onclick" ONEVENT="ExpandCollapse()" />

<SCRIPT LANGUAGE="JScript">

function ExpandCollapse()
{
    var i;
    var sDisplay;

    // Determine current state of the list (expanded or collapsed)
    // based on the current display property of the child.
    bCollapsed = (element.document.all(child).runtimeStyle.display == "none");

    if (bCollapsed)
    {
        runtimeStyle.listStyleImage = "url('/workshop/graphics/blueminus.gif')";
        element.document.all(child).runtimeStyle.display = "";
    }
    else
    {
        runtimeStyle.listStyleImage = "url('/workshop/graphics/blueplus.gif')";
        element.document.all(child).runtimeStyle.display = "none";
    }
}
</SCRIPT>
```

To see this code in action, refer to the Web Workshop CD-ROM.

The next example shows how to specify **PUT** and **GET** functions in an HTC.

```
<PUBLIC:PROPERTY ID="propID" NAME="child"
    PUT="saveChild" GET="returnChild"/>
:
<SCRIPT LANGUAGE="JScript">
var myChild=null;

function saveChild (vValue)
{
    myChild = vValue;
    propID.fireChange();
}
```

```
function returnChild()
{
    return myChild;
}
</SCRIPT>
```

oncontentready Event

Fires when the content of the element, to which the behavior is attached, has been completely parsed.

Syntax

```
<PUBLIC:ATTACH
    EVENT = "oncontentready"
    ONEVENT = sEventHandler
    FOR = "element"
    ID = sID />
```

Remarks

The **innerHTML** property of the element may not return the correct value until this event fires.

Example

The following example shows how to use the **oncontentready** event on a page.

```
<PUBLIC:ATTACH EVENT="oncontentready" ONEVENT="show_innerHTML()" />

<SCRIPT LANGUAGE="JScript">
function show_innerHTML()
{
    window.alert ('innerHTML = ' + element.innerHTML);
}
</SCRIPT>
```

ondetach Event

Fires before the behavior is detached from the element.

Syntax

```
<PUBLIC:ATTACH
    EVENT = "ondetach"
    ONEVENT = sEventHandler
    FOR = "element"
    ID = sID />
```

Remarks

A behavior can become detached from an element when one of the following occurs:

- The containing page is closed.
- The **removeBehavior** method is called on the behavior.
- The **behavior** property of the element is set to `null`, or reset to point to another behavior.
- The **className** property of the element is set to `null`, or reset to some other class other than the one defined for the behavior.

The **ondetach** event allows the behavior to perform some cleanup just before it is completely detached from the element. In cases where a behavior attaches to events on the containing page using the **attachEvent** method, this event gives the behavior the opportunity to call the **detachEvent** method to stop receiving notifications from the page.

Note A behavior that attaches to events on the page using the **ATTACH** element automatically stops receiving notifications when the behavior is detached from the element, and does not need to call the **detachEvent** method when the **ondetach** event fires.

Example

The following example shows how the **ondetach** event can be used to turn off the highlighting effect on a list of items initially attached to a highlighting behavior.

```
<PUBLIC:ATTACH EVENT="ondetach" ONEVENT="cleanup()" />

<SCRIPT LANGUAGE="JScript">
attachEvent ('onmouseover', Hilite);
attachEvent ('onmouseout', Restore);

function cleanup()
{
   detachEvent ('onmouseover', Hilite);
   detachEvent ('onmouseout', Restore);
}

function Hilite()
{
   if (event.srcElement == element)
   {
     normalColor = style.color;
     runtimeStyle.color  = "red";
     runtimeStyle.cursor = "hand";
   }
}
```

```
function Restore()
{
   if (event.srcElement == element)
   {
      runtimeStyle.color  = normalColor;
      runtimeStyle.cursor = "";
   }
}
</SCRIPT>
```

To see this code in action, refer to the Web Workshop CD-ROM.

ondocumentready Event

Fires when the behavior's containing document has been completely parsed.

Syntax

```
<PUBLIC:ATTACH
    EVENT = "ondocumentready"
    ONEVENT = sEventHandler
    FOR = "element"
    ID = sID />
```

Remarks

The **ondocumentready** event fires after all scripts, images, ActiveX controls, and all other elements on the page are completely downloaded.

A behavior that is attached to an element after the **window.onload** event fires receives both the **ondocumentready** and **oncontentready** notifications; however, the behavior cannot attach to the **window.onload** event within the HTC.

You can modify an element's **style** property, such as setting its visibility or changing its colors or fonts, by making the changes inline in the HTC's **SCRIPT** block, as shown in the following code. Otherwise, if you make the change in the **ondocumentready** event handler, flashing occurs.

```
<PUBLIC:COMPONENT>
<SCRIPT LANGUAGE="JScript">
   style.color = "green";
   style.letterSpacing = 5;
   :
</SCRIPT>
</PUBLIC:COMPONENT>
```

Example

The following example shows how to use the **ondocumentready** event on a page.

```
<PUBLIC:ATTACH EVENT="ondocumentready" ONEVENT="docready_handler()" />

<SCRIPT LANGUAGE="JScript">
function docready_handler()
{
    window.alert ("The ondocumentready event fired.");
}
</SCRIPT>
```

createEventObject Method

Creates an **event** object to be used optionally in passing event context information to the **EVENT** element's **fire** method.

Syntax

oEvent = createEventObject()

Return Value

Returns an **event** object.

Remarks

The same **event** object cannot be reused in multiple **fire** calls.

Note All properties of the **event** object created using **createEventObject** are read/write, including those that would be read-only in DHTML. This allows you to set properties on the **event** object from the HTC before firing the event.

Example

The following example is derived from a calculator behavior sample. When the result changes, the behavior fires a custom onResultChange event back to the page, passing the result as a custom property of the **event** object.

```
<PUBLIC:EVENT NAME="onResultChange" ID="rcID"  />

<SCRIPT LANGUAGE="JScript">

:
function doCalc()
{
    :
    oEvent = createEventObject();
    oEvent.result = sResult;
    rcID.fire (oEvent);
}
</SCRIPT >
```

The following example shows what the containing page looks like:

```
<HTML XMLNS:InetSDK>
<HEAD>
<STYLE>
@media all {
    InetSDK\:CALC      {behavior:url(engine.htc)}
}
</STYLE>
</HEAD>

<InetSDK:CALC id="myCalc"
    onResultChange="resultWindow.innerText=window.event.result">
<TABLE>
<TR><DIV ID="resultWindow" STYLE="border:'.025cm solid gray'"
        ALIGN=RIGHT>0.</DIV></TR>
<TR><TD><INPUT TYPE=BUTTON VALUE=" 7 "></TD>
    <TD><INPUT TYPE=BUTTON VALUE=" 8 "></TD>
    <TD><INPUT TYPE=BUTTON VALUE=" 9 "></TD>
    <TD><INPUT TYPE=BUTTON VALUE=" / "></TD>
    <TD><INPUT TYPE=BUTTON VALUE=" C "></TD>
</TR>
     :
</TABLE>
</InetSDK:CALC>
</HTML>
```

To see this code in action, refer to the Web Workshop CD-ROM.

element Object

Returns the element to which the behavior is attached.

Remarks

All properties, methods, and events of the element are accessible to an HTC through this object. Alternatively, you can access the properties, methods, and events of the element by using the property, method, or event name directly, without prefixing it with the **element** keyword. In the following example, the color of the element can be toggled through the **style** property of the element directly, instead of referring to it as **element.style**.

Example

The following example shows how to implement an expanding/collapsing table of contents using a behavior. The HTC attaches to the element's **onmouseover** event and sets the **color** property of the element to red, as well as the **cursor** property to `"hand"` to signal the user that the element can be clicked to toggle visibility of its children.

```
<PUBLIC:ATTACH EVENT="onmouseover" ONEVENT="Hilite" />

<SCRIPT LANGUAGE="JScript">
var prevColor;

function Hilite()
{
   prevColor = style.color;
   element.style.color  = "red";
   element.style.cursor = "hand";
}
</SCRIPT>
```

To see this code in action, refer to the Web Workshop CD-ROM.

CHAPTER 5

Default Behaviors References

Behaviors

The following section describes the default behaviors in the Dynamic HTML (DHTML) Object Model. References in this section are listed alphabetically within each of the following categories:

- Element | Behavior
- Event
- Method
- Attribute | Property

This section also describes technologies available as an experimental implementation of HTML+TIME within Internet Explorer 5. While you are encouraged to evaluate these features, note that they are subject to change. For further information about HTML+TIME technologies, see the Web Workshop CD included with this book.

anchor Behavior

Enables browser navigation to a folder view.

Syntax

XML	N/A
HTML	`<ELEMENT STYLE="behavior:url('#default#AnchorClick')" ID=sID>`
Scripting	`object.style.behavior = "url('#default#AnchorClick')"`
	`object.addBehavior ("#default#AnchorClick")`

Possible Values

sID   String that uniquely specifies the object.

Attributes/Properties

folder   **navType**   **target**

Remarks

You can use the **anchor** behavior to open a folder view through an anchor object using the exposed **folder** property. The folder property must be present for a folder navigation to occur. If the **folder** property is not included, the **href** on the anchor is used as normal.

For this behavior to work, the Web Folders component must be installed with Internet Explorer. If the Web Folders component is not installed and this behavior is invoked, the user is prompted to download the component. To open a Web address in folder view, the Web server must include a WebDAC server (available as of Microsoft Internet Information Server 5), or support WEC extensions (available as of Microsoft® FrontPage™ 2000).

Using the **folder** property with the **anchor** behavior is the same as invoking the **navigate** or **navigateFrame** method from the **httpFolder** behavior.

Internet Explorer 5 displays the value of the **folder** property when the mouse moves over the **anchor**. Downlevel browsers can display the value of the **href** property in the status bar or as a title, so the file name and the contents of the downlevel file are important to keep in mind.

The **TARGET** attribute can be used to specify the window or frame that loads the specified location in the **FOLDER** attribute.

Example

The following example shows how to use the anchor behavior to navigate to a folder view.

```
<STYLE>
A {behavior:url(#default#AnchorClick);}
</STYLE>

<!--
    The href points to folder.htm for downlevel browsers;
    the FOLDER attribute points to the local root.
 -->

<A HREF = "folder.htm" FOLDER = "/" >
Open Folder
</A>
```

Applies To

 WIN32

A

anim:DA Element | anim Behavior

Defines an instance of the Microsoft® DirectAnimation™ viewer in an HTML page, to render DirectAnimation objects and play DirectAnimation sounds.

Syntax

XML	*<Prefix*:DA ID="*sID*" STYLE="height:*sHeight*; width:*sWidth*" />
HTML	N/A
Scripting	N/A

Possible Values

Prefix   Prefix used to associate the element with an XML namespace. A prefix of anim must be used for the experimental implementation of HTML+TIME. Include the following line in the **HEAD** section of your HTML document when using this element:

```
<XML:NAMESPACE PREFIX="anim"/>
```

sID   String that uniquely specifies the object.

sHeight   String that specifies the height of the DirectAnimation viewer.

sWidth   String that specifies the width of the DirectAnimation viewer.

Properties

image	sound	statics

Methods

addDABehavior	removeDABehavior

Remarks

In addition to defining the `anim` XML namespace prefix, you also need to define the custom `DA` element and associate it with the default **anim** behavior by adding the following line to the **STYLE** block of your document:

```
<STYLE>
    anim\:DA{ behavior: url(#default#anim); }
</STYLE>
```

Note The height and width properties are required for the DirectAnimation viewer to display properly. Other inline style properties can be used to control the DirectAnimation viewer's position and z-index.

The **anim:DA** element is available as of Internet Explorer 5 only for the Win32 platform.

ANIMATION Element | animation Behavior

Defines a timed animation element in an HTML document.

Syntax

XML   *<Prefix*:ANIMATION ID="*sID*" STYLE="behavior:url(#default#time)" />

HTML   N/A

Scripting   N/A

Possible Values

Prefix   Prefix used to associate the element with an XML namespace. A prefix of t must be used for the experimental implementation of HTML+TIME. Include the following line in the **HEAD** section of your HTML document when using this element:

           `<XML:NAMESPACE PREFIX="t"/>`

sID   String that uniquely specifies the object.

Attributes/Properties

accelerate	autoReverse	begin	beginAfter
beginEvent	beginWith	clipBegin	clipEnd
clockSource	decelerate	dur	end
endEvent	endHold	eventRestart	img
player	playerObject [1]	repeat	repeatDur
src	syncBehavior	syncTolerance	timeAction
type			

1   This property has no corresponding attribute.

Methods

beginElement	endElement	pause	resume

Events

onbegin	onend	onmediacomplete	onmedialoadfailed
onmediaslip	onpause	onrepeat	onresume
onresync	onreverse	onscriptcommand	

Remarks

The behavior-defined members listed in the preceding list might not be accessible through scripting until the **window.onload** event fires. Waiting for this event to fire ensures that the page is completely loaded, that all behaviors have been applied to corresponding elements on the page, and that all the behavior's properties, methods, and events are available for scripting. Attempting to use any of the behavior-defined members before firing the **window.onload** event can result in a scripting error indicating that the object does not support that particular member.

Although different media-based elements exist, there is no functional difference in their current implementation. However, using the different elements, such as **ANIMATION**, **AUDIO**, **IMG**, **MEDIA**, and **VIDEO**, for document readability and enhanced future support is encouraged.

The **ANIMATION** element is available as of Internet Explorer 5 only for the Win32 platform.

AUDIO Element | audio Behavior

Defines a timed audio element in an HTML document.

Syntax

XML	*<Prefix*:AUDIO ID="*sID*" STYLE="behavior:url(#default#time)" />
HTML	N/A
Scripting	N/A

Possible Values

Prefix   Prefix used to associate the element with an XML namespace. A prefix of t must be used for the experimental implementation of HTML+TIME. Include the following line in the **HEAD** section of your HTML document when using this element:

```
<XML:NAMESPACE PREFIX="t"/>
```

sID   String that uniquely specifies the object.

Attributes/Properties

accelerate	**autoReverse**	**begin**	**beginAfter**
beginEvent	**beginWith**	**clipBegin**	**clipEnd**
clockSource	**decelerate**	**dur**	**end**
endEvent	**endHold**	**eventRestart**	**player**
playerObject [1]	**repeat**	**repeatDur**	**src**
syncBehavior	**syncTolerance**	**timeAction**	**type**

[1]   This property has no corresponding attribute.

Methods

beginElement	**endElement**	**pause**	**resume**

Events

onbegin	**onend**	**onmediacomplete**	**onmedialoadfailed**
onmediaslip	**onpause**	**onrepeat**	**onresume**
onresync	**onreverse**	**onscriptcommand**	

Remarks

The behavior-defined members listed in the preceding list might not be accessible through scripting until the **window.onload** event fires. Waiting for this event to fire ensures that the page is completely loaded, that all behaviors have been applied to corresponding elements on the page, and that all the behavior's properties, methods, and events are available for scripting. Attempting to use any of the behavior-defined members before firing the **window.onload** event can result in a scripting error indicating that the object does not support that particular member.

Although different media-based elements exist, there is no functional difference in their current implementation. However, using the different elements, such as **ANIMATION**, **AUDIO**, **IMG**, **MEDIA**, and **VIDEO**, for document readability and enhanced future support is encouraged.

The **AUDIO** element is available as of Internet Explorer 5 only for the Win32 platform.

clientCaps Behavior

Provides information about features supported by Internet Explorer, and serves as a means to install browser components on demand.

Syntax

XML   *<Prefix:CustomTag* ID=*sID*
          STYLE="behavior:url('#default#clientCaps')" />

HTML   *<ELEMENT* STYLE="behavior:url('#default#clientCaps')"
          ID=*sID*>

Scripting *object*.style.behavior = "url('#default#clientCaps')"

          object.addBehavior ("#default#clientCaps")

Possible Values

Prefix   Prefix used to associate *CustomTag* with a namespace. This prefix is set using the **XMLNS** attribute of the **HTML** tag.

CustomTag User-defined tag.

sID   String that uniquely specifies the object.

Properties

availHeight	availWidth	bufferDepth	colorDepth
connectionType	cookieEnabled	cpuClass	height
javaEnabled	platform	systemLanguage	userLanguage
width			

Methods

addComponentRequest	clearComponentRequest	compareVersions
doComponentRequest	getComponentVersion	isComponentInstalled

Remarks

The behavior-defined members listed in the preceding list might not be accessible through scripting until the **window.onload** event fires. Waiting for this event to fire ensures that the page is completely loaded, that all behaviors have been applied to corresponding elements on the page, and that all the behavior's properties, methods, and events are available for scripting. Attempting to use any of the behavior-defined members before firing the **window.onload** event can result in a scripting error indicating that the object does not support that particular member.

Example

The following example shows how to retrieve all the properties exposed by the **clientCaps** behavior.

```
<HTML XMLNS:IE>
<HEAD>
<STYLE>
@media all {
    IE\:clientCaps {behavior:url(#default#clientCaps)}
}
</STYLE>
</HEAD>

<BODY>
<IE:clientCaps ID="oClientCaps" />

<PRE id=oPre></PRE>

<SCRIPT>
<!--
function window.onload()
{
    sTempStr = "availHeight     = " + oClientCaps.availHeight    + "\n" +
               "availWidth      = " + oClientCaps.availWidth     + "\n" +
               "bufferDepth     = " + oClientCaps.bufferDepth    + "\n" +
               "colorDepth      = " + oClientCaps.colorDepth     + "\n" +
```

```
                    "connectionType = " + oClientCaps.connectionType + "\n" +
                    "cookieEnabled  = " + oClientCaps.cookieEnabled  + "\n" +
                    "cpuClass       = " + oClientCaps.cpuClass        + "\n" +
                    "height         = " + oClientCaps.height         + "\n" +
                    "javaEnabled    = " + oClientCaps.javaEnabled    + "\n" +
                    "platform       = " + oClientCaps.platform       + "\n" +
                    "systemLanguage = " + oClientCaps.systemLanguage + "\n" +
                    "userLanguage   = " + oClientCaps.userLanguage   + "\n" +
                    "width          = " + oClientCaps.width          + "\n" ;

        oPre.innerText = sTempStr;
}
-->
</SCRIPT>
</BODY>
</HTML>
```

To see this code in action, refer to the Web Workshop CD-ROM.

Using the **getComponentVersion** method of the **clientCaps** behavior, the next
example shows one way to determine the browser version.

```
<SCRIPT>
function window.onload()
{
    var sVersion = oClientCaps.getComponentVersion ("{89820200-ECBD-11CF-8B85-
00AA005B4383}","componentid");
    myText.innerHTML = "<FONT SIZE=4>You are running Internet Explorer " + sVersion +
".</FONT>";
}
</SCRIPT>


<BODY BGCOLOR="#FFFFFF" STYLE="behavior:url(#default#clientCaps)" ID="oClientCaps">
    :
<DIV ID="myText"></DIV>
```

To see this code in action, refer to the Web Workshop CD-ROM.

The next example shows how the Internet Explorer Data Binding component can be
installed if the component does not already exist in the user's system.

```
<HEAD>
<SCRIPT>
function window.onload()
{
    // Dynamically set the behavior through script.
    oClientCaps.style.behavior = "url(#default#clientCaps)";

    var bDBAvailable = false;
    var sDBVersion = '';
    var sDBID = "{9381D8F2-0288-11D0-9501-00AA00B911A5}";

    bDBAvailable = oClientCaps.isComponentInstalled(sDBID,"componentid");
```

```
      // If data binding is unavailable, install it.
      if (!bDBAvailable)
      {
         oClientCaps.addComponentRequest (sDBID, "componentid");
         bDBAvailable = oClientCaps.doComponentRequest();
      }
      :
   }
   </SCRIPT>
   </HEAD>

   <BODY BGCOLOR="#FFFFFF" ID="oClientCaps">
    :
   <PRE ID="preText"></PRE>
```

To see this code in action, refer to the Web Workshop CD-ROM.

Applies To

 WIN32   UNIX

A, ACRONYM, ADDRESS, APPLET, AREA, B, BASE, BASEFONT, BDO,
BGSOUND, BIG, BLOCKQUOTE, BODY, BR, BUTTON, CAPTION, CENTER,
CITE, CODE, COL, COLGROUP, COMMENT, DD, DEL, DFN, DIR, DIV, DL, DT,
EM, EMBED, FIELDSET, FONT, FORM, FRAME, FRAMESET, HEAD, Hn, HR,
HTML, I, IFRAME, IMG, INPUT type=button, INPUT type=checkbox, INPUT
type=file, INPUT type=hidden, INPUT type=image, INPUT type=password, INPUT
type=radio, INPUT type=reset, INPUT type=submit, INPUT type=text, INS,
ISINDEX, KBD, LABEL, LEGEND, LI, LINK, LISTING, MAP, MARQUEE,
MENU, NEXTID, NOBR, NOFRAMES, NOSCRIPT, OBJECT, OL, OPTION, P,
PLAINTEXT, PRE, Q, RT, RUBY, S, SAMP, SCRIPT, SELECT, SMALL, SPAN,
STRIKE, STRONG, SUB, SUP, TABLE, TBODY, TD, TEXTAREA, TFOOT, TH,
THEAD, TITLE, TR, TT, U, UL, VAR, WBR, XML, XMP

download Behavior

Downloads a file and notifies a specified callback function when the download is complete.

Syntax

XML	*<Prefix:CustomTag* ID=*sID* STYLE="behavior:url('#default#download')" />
HTML	*<ELEMENT* STYLE="behavior:url('#default#download')" ID=*sID>*
Scripting	*object*.style.behavior = "url('#default#download')" *object*.addBehavior ("#default#download")

Possible Values

Prefix	Prefix used to associate *CustomTag* with a namespace. This prefix is set using the **XMLNS** attribute of the **HTML** element.
CustomTag	User-defined tag.
sID	String that uniquely specifies the object.

Methods

startDownload

Remarks

The behavior-defined members listed in the preceding list might not be accessible through scripting until the **window.onload** event fires. Waiting for this event to fire ensures that the page is completely loaded, that all behaviors have been applied to corresponding elements on the page, and that all the behavior's properties, methods, and events are available for scripting. Attempting to use any of the behavior-defined members results in a scripting error indicating that the object does not support that particular member.

The **download** behavior and the files it accesses must exist on the same domain.

Example

The following example shows how to download a page using the **download** behavior.

```
<HTML XMLNS:IE>

<SCRIPT>
    function onDownloadDone(s) { alert (s); }
</SCRIPT>

<IE:Download ID="oDownload" STYLE="behavior:url(#default#download)" />
<P>Click <A HREF="javascript:oDownload.startDownload('download.htm',
onDownloadDone)">here</A> to download this page.
```

To see this code in action, refer to the Web Workshop CD-ROM.

Applies To

 WIN32   UNIX

A, ACRONYM, ADDRESS, APPLET, AREA, B, BASE, BASEFONT, BDO,
BGSOUND, BIG, BLOCKQUOTE, BODY, BR, BUTTON, CAPTION, CENTER,
CITE, CODE, COL, COLGROUP, COMMENT, DD, DEL, DFN, DIR, DIV, DL, DT,
EM, EMBED, FIELDSET, FONT, FORM, FRAME, FRAMESET, HEAD, Hn, HR,
HTML, I, IFRAME, IMG, INPUT type=button, INPUT type=checkbox, INPUT
type=file, INPUT type=hidden, INPUT type=image, INPUT type=password, INPUT
type=radio, INPUT type=reset, INPUT type=submit, INPUT type=text, INS,
ISINDEX, KBD, LABEL, LEGEND, LI, LINK, LISTING, MAP, MARQUEE,
MENU, NEXTID, NOBR, NOFRAMES, NOSCRIPT, OBJECT, OL, OPTION, P,
PLAINTEXT, PRE, Q, RT, RUBY, S, SAMP, SCRIPT, SELECT, SMALL, SPAN,
STRIKE, STRONG, SUB, SUP, TABLE, TBODY, TD, TEXTAREA, TFOOT, TH,
THEAD, TITLE, TR, TT, U, UL, VAR, WBR, XML, XMP

homePage Behavior

Contains information about a user's homepage.

Syntax

XML   *<Prefix:CustomTag* ID=*sID*
STYLE="behavior:url('#default#homepage')" />

HTML   *<ELEMENT* STYLE="behavior:url('#default#homepage')" ID=*sID>*

Scripting *object*.style.behavior = "url('#default#homepage')"

object.addBehavior ("#default#homepage")

Possible Values

Prefix   Prefix used to associate *CustomTag* with a namespace. This prefix is set using the **XMLNS** attribute of the **HTML** tag.

CustomTag User-defined tag.

sID   String that uniquely specifies the object.

Methods

isHomePage   **navigateHomePage**   **setHomePage**

Remarks

The behavior-defined members listed in the preceding list might not be accessible through scripting until the **window.onload** event fires. Waiting for this event to fire ensures that the page is completely loaded, that all behaviors have been applied to corresponding elements on the page, and that all the behavior's properties, methods, and events are available for scripting. Attempting to use any of the behavior-defined members before firing the **window.onload** event can result in a scripting error indicating that the object does not support that particular member.

Example

The following example shows how to use the **homePage** behavior.

```
<HTML XMLNS:IE>
<HEAD>
<STYLE>
@media all {
    IE\:homePage {behavior:url(#default#homepage)}
}
</STYLE>

<SCRIPT>
function fnVerify(){
    sQueryHome = oHomePage.isHomePage(oHomeHref.value);
    alert(sQueryHome);
    event.returnValue = false;
}
function fnGo(){
    oHomePage.navigateHomePage();
    event.returnValue=false;
}
function fnSet(){
    oHomePage.setHomePage(oHomeHref.value);
    event.returnValue = false;
}
</SCRIPT>
</HEAD>
<BODY>
<IE:homePage ID="oHomePage" />
<INPUT TYPE=text ID=oHomeHref VALUE="http://www.microsoft.com">
```

```
<INPUT TYPE=button VALUE="Verify" onclick="fnVerify()">
<INPUT TYPE=button VALUE="Set" onclick="fnSet()">
<INPUT TYPE=button VALUE="Navigate" onclick="fnGo()">
</BODY>
</HTML>
```

To see this code in action, refer to the Web Workshop CD-ROM.

Applies To

 WIN32   UNIX

A, ACRONYM, ADDRESS, APPLET, AREA, B, BASE, BASEFONT, BDO,
BGSOUND, BIG, BLOCKQUOTE, BODY, BR, BUTTON, CAPTION, CENTER,
CITE, CODE, COL, COLGROUP, COMMENT, DD, DEL, DFN, DIR, DIV, DL, DT,
EM, EMBED, FIELDSET, FONT, FORM, FRAME, FRAMESET, HEAD, Hn, HR,
HTML, I, IFRAME, IMG, INPUT type=button, INPUT type=checkbox, INPUT
type=file, INPUT type=hidden, INPUT type=image, INPUT type=password, INPUT
type=radio, INPUT type=reset, INPUT type=submit, INPUT type=text, INS,
ISINDEX, KBD, LABEL, LEGEND, LI, LINK, LISTING, MAP, MARQUEE,
MENU, NEXTID, NOBR, NOFRAMES, NOSCRIPT, OBJECT, OL, OPTION, P,
PLAINTEXT, PRE, Q, RT, RUBY, S, SAMP, SCRIPT, SELECT, SMALL, SPAN,
STRIKE, STRONG, SUB, SUP, TABLE, TBODY, TD, TEXTAREA, TFOOT, TH,
THEAD, TITLE, TR, TT, U, UL, VAR, WBR, XML, XMP

httpFolder Behavior

Contains scripting features that enable browser navigation to a folder view.

Syntax

XML   N/A

HTML   *<ELEMENT* STYLE="behavior:url('#default#httpFolder')" ID=*sID>*

Scripting   *object*.style.behavior = "url('#default#httpFolder')"

           object.addBehavior ("#default#httpFolder")

Possible Values

sID   String that uniquely specifies the object.

Methods

navigate   **navigateFrame**

Remarks

The **httpFolder** behavior can be defined in a **STYLE** block, or inline with the element.

Example

The following example shows how to use the **httpFolder** behavior to navigate to a folder view.

```
<STYLE>
.httpFolder{behavior:url(#default#httpFolder);}
</STYLE>

<SCRIPT>
function fnNavigate(){
    var sFolder=location.href.substring(0,location.href.lastIndexOf("/"));
    oViewFolder.navigate(sFolder);
}
</SCRIPT>

<SPAN ID=oViewFolder
      CLASS = "httpFolder"
      onclick = "fnNavigate()"
>
Display this page in folder view.
</SPAN>
```

Applies To

 WIN32   UNIX

A, ACRONYM, ADDRESS, AREA, B, BIG, BLOCKQUOTE, BODY, BUTTON, CAPTION, CENTER, CITE, CODE, DD, DEL, DFN, DIR, DIV, DL, DT, EM, FONT, FORM, Hn, HR, I, IMG, INPUT type=button, INPUT type=checkbox, INPUT type=file, INPUT type=hidden, INPUT type=image, INPUT type=password, INPUT type=radio, INPUT type=reset, INPUT type=submit, INPUT type=text, KBD, LABEL, LI, LISTING, MAP, MARQUEE, MENU, OBJECT, OL, OPTION, P, PLAINTEXT, PRE, Q, S, SAMP, SELECT, SMALL, SPAN, STRIKE, STRONG, SUB, SUP, TABLE, TEXTAREA, TT, U, UL, VAR, XMP

IMG Element | img Behavior

Defines a timed image element in an HTML document.

Syntax

XML	*<Prefix*:`IMG ID="`*sID*`" STYLE="behavior:url(#default#time)" />`
HTML	N/A
Scripting	N/A

Possible Values

Prefix   Prefix used to associate the element with an XML namespace. A prefix of t must be used for the experimental implementation of HTML+TIME. Include the following line in the **HEAD** section of your HTML document when using this element:

```
<XML:NAMESPACE PREFIX="t"/>
```

sID   String that uniquely specifies the object.

Attributes/Properties

accelerate	**autoReverse**	**begin**	**beginAfter**
beginEvent	**beginWith**	**clipBegin**	**clipEnd**
clockSource	**decelerate**	**dur**	**end**
endEvent	**endHold**	**eventRestart**	**player**
playerObject [1]	**repeat**	**repeatDur**	**src**
syncBehavior	**syncTolerance**	**timeAction**	**type**

1   This property has no corresponding attribute.

Methods

beginElement	**endElement**	**pause**	**resume**

Events

onbegin	**onend**	**onmediacomplete**	**onmedialoadfailed**
onmediaslip	**onpause**	**onrepeat**	**onresume**
onresync	**onreverse**	**onscriptcommand**	

Remarks

This element duplicates the HTML **IMG** element and provides control over media loading. Use this element instead of the HTML **IMG** element for timing images in Internet Explorer 5.

The behavior-defined members listed in the preceding list might not be accessible through scripting until the **window.onload** event fires. Waiting for this event to fire ensures that the page is completely loaded, that all behaviors have been applied to corresponding elements on the page, and that all the behavior's properties, methods, and events are available for scripting. Attempting to use any of the behavior-defined members before firing the **window.onload** event can result in a scripting error indicating that the object does not support that particular member.

Although different media-based elements exist, there is no functional difference in their current implementation. However, using the different elements, such as **ANIMATION**, **AUDIO**, **IMG**, **MEDIA**, and **VIDEO**, for document readability and enhanced future support is encouraged.

The **IMG** element is available as of Internet Explorer 5 only for the Win32 platform.

media Element | media Behavior

Defines a generic, timed media element in an HTML document.

Syntax

XML	*<Prefix*:media ID="*sID*" STYLE="behavior:url(#default#time)" />
HTML	N/A
Scripting	N/A

Possible Values

Prefix   Prefix used to associate the attribute with an XML namespace. A prefix of t must be used for the experimental implementation of HTML+TIME. Include the following line in the **HEAD** section of your HTML document when using this element:

```
<XML:NAMESPACE PREFIX="t"/>
```

sID   String that uniquely specifies the object.

Attributes/Properties

accelerate	autoReverse	begin	beginAfter
beginEvent	beginWith	clipBegin	clipEnd
clockSource	decelerate	dur	end
endEvent	endHold	eventRestart	img
player	playerObject [1]	repeat	repeatDur
src	syncBehavior	syncTolerance	timeAction
type			

1   This property has no corresponding attribute.

Methods

beginElement	endElement	pause	resume

Events

onbegin	onend	onmediacomplete	onmedialoadfailed
onmediaslip	onpause	onrepeat	onresume
onresync	onreverse	onscriptcommand	

Remarks

The behavior-defined members listed in the preceding list might not be accessible through scripting until the **window.onload** event fires. Waiting for this event to fire ensures that the page is completely loaded, that all behaviors have been applied to corresponding elements on the page, and that all the behavior's properties, methods, and events are available for scripting. Attempting to use any of the behavior-defined members before firing the **window.onload** event can result in a scripting error indicating that the object does not support that particular member.

Although different media-based behaviors exist, there is no functional difference in their current implementation. However, using the different behaviors, such as **animation**, **audio**, **img**, **media**, and **video,** for document readability and enhanced future support is encouraged.

The **MEDIA** element is available as of Internet Explorer 5 only for the Win32 platform.

PAR Element | par Behavior

Defines a new timeline container in an HTML document. All HTML descendants of this element have independent, or parallel, timing.

Syntax

XML	*Prefix*:PAR ID="*sID*" STYLE="behavior:url(#default#time)" />
HTML	N/A
Scripting	N/A

Possible Values

Prefix   Prefix used to associate the element with an XML namespace. A prefix of t must be used for the experimental implementation of HTML+TIME. Include the following line in the **HEAD** section of your HTML document when using this element:

```
<XML:NAMESPACE PREFIX="t"/>
```

sID   String that uniquely specifies the object.

Attributes/Properties

accelerate	**autoReverse**	**begin**	**beginAfter**
beginEvent	**beginWith**	**decelerate**	**dur**
end	**endEvent**	**endHold**	**eventRestart**
repeat	**repeatDur**	**syncBehavior**	**syncTolerance**

Methods

beginElement	**endElement**	**pause**	**resume**

Events

onbegin	**onend**	**onmediacomplete**	**onmedialoadfailed**
onmediaslip	**onpause**	**onrepeat**	**onresume**
onresync	**onreverse**		

Remarks

This element can be used instead of the timeline attribute to create a time container without using an HTML element. All descendant elements, or time children, of this new time container inherit the time properties of their container. Unlike the time children of the SEQ element, the PAR descendants have no implicit timing relationships to each other, and their timelines might overlap. The PAR element effectively groups elements together, so they can be easily modified as a single unit.

The **PAR** element is available as of Internet Explorer 5 only for the Win32 platform.

Example

The following example shows how to use the **PAR** element to apply a timeline to a group of HTML elements.

```
<!DOCTYPE HTML PUBLIC "-//W3C//DTD HTML 4.0 Transitional//EN">
<HTML>
<HEAD>
<XML:NAMESPACE PREFIX="t"/>

<STYLE>
.time            { behavior: url(#default#time);}
</STYLE>
</HEAD>

<BODY BGCOLOR="white">
<FONT FACE="Verdana">
<t:PAR CLASS=time t:BEGIN="0" t:DUR="10" t:TIMEACTION="display">
    <H3>Paragraph 1</H3>
    <P>This is paragraph number one. It appears for ten seconds
    immediately after the page is loaded.</P>
    <SPAN CLASS=time t:BEGIN="5">
        <H3>Paragraph 2</H3>
        <P>This is paragraph number two. It appears five seconds
        after the page is loaded, and remains displayed until its
        parent element's timeline ends at ten seconds.</P>
    </SPAN>
</t:PAR>
</FONT>
</BODY>
</HTML>
```

To see this code in action, refer to the Web Workshop CD-ROM.

saveFavorite Behavior

Enables the object to persist data in a Favorite.

Syntax

XML	N/A
HTML	*<ELEMENT* STYLE="behavior:url('#default#saveFavorite')" ID=*sID>*
Scripting	*object*.style.behavior = "url('#default#saveFavorite')"
	object.addBehavior ("#default#saveFavorite")

Possible Values

sID   String that uniquely specifies the object.

Properties

XMLDocument

Methods

getAttribute   **removeAttribute**   **setAttribute**

Events

onload   **onsave**

Remarks

The **saveFavorite** behavior allows the current state of a page to be saved when the user adds the page to Favorites. When the user returns to the page through a shortcut or the Favorites menu, the state of the page is restored.

The **saveFavorite** behavior persists data across sessions, using one UserData store for each object. If two objects try to use the same attribute, both are persisted in the UserData store for each element. The **saveFavorite** UserData store is persisted in the Favorites .ini file, which includes the URL of the page as well as the UserData store data. When the page has been loaded through a shortcut or Favorites, the data from the UserData store is loaded from the .ini file, even if Internet Explorer has been closed and reopened.

For example, a page with several dynamically updated styles can save these updates using the **onload** and **onsave** events. The style values can be saved as attributes when **onsave** fires, and restored when **onload** fires.

To use the **saveFavorite** behavior, you must use a **META** tag identifying the type of persistence.

```
<META NAME="save" CONTENT="favorite">
```

The required **STYLE** can be set inline, or in the document header, as shown below.

```
<STYLE>
    .saveFavorite {behavior:url(#default#savefavorite);}
</STYLE>
```

An **ID** is optional for **saveFavorite**, but including an **ID** increases performance.

Example

The following example shows how to use the saveFavorite behavior.

```
<HTML>
<HEAD>
<META NAME="save" CONTENT="favorite">
<STYLE>
    .saveFavorite {behavior:url(#default#savefavorite);}
</STYLE>
<SCRIPT>
    function fnSaveInput(){
        oPersistInput.setAttribute("sPersistValue",oPersistInput.value);
    }
    function fnLoadInput(){
        oPersistInput.value=oPersistInput.getAttribute("sPersistValue");
    }
</SCRIPT>
</HEAD>
<BODY>
<INPUT class=saveFavorite onsave="fnSaveInput()" onload="fnLoadInput()" type=text
id=oPersistInput>
</BODY>
</HTML>
```

To see this code in action, refer to the Web Workshop CD-ROM.

Applies To

 WIN32   UNIX

A, ACRONYM, ADDRESS, AREA, B, BIG, BLOCKQUOTE, BUTTON, CAPTION, CENTER, CITE, CODE, DD, DEL, DFN, DIR, DIV, DL, DT, EM, FONT, FORM, Hn, HR, I, IMG, INPUT type=button, INPUT type=checkbox, INPUT type=file, INPUT type=hidden, INPUT type=image, INPUT type=password, INPUT type=radio, INPUT type=reset, INPUT type=submit, INPUT type=text, KBD,

Applies To *(continued)*

 WIN32   UNIX

LABEL, LI, LISTING, MAP, MARQUEE, MENU, OBJECT, OL, OPTION, P, PLAINTEXT, PRE, Q, S, SAMP, SELECT, SMALL, SPAN, STRIKE, STRONG, SUB, SUP, TABLE, TEXTAREA, TT, U, UL, VAR, XMP

saveHistory Behavior

Enables the object to persist data in the browser history.

Syntax

XML   N/A

HTML   *<ELEMENT* STYLE="behavior:url('#default#saveHistory')"
             ID=*sID>*

Scripting *object*.style.behavior = "url('#default#saveHistory')"

             object.addBehavior ("#default#saveHistory")

Possible Values

sID   String that uniquely specifies the object.

Properties

XMLDocument

Methods

getAttribute   **removeAttribute**   **setAttribute**

Events

onload   **onsave**

Remarks

The **saveHistory** behavior saves the current state of the page when the user navigates away from the page. When the user returns to the page by pressing the back or forward button, the values are restored.

The **saveHistory** behavior persists only for the current session. When the user navigates away from the page containing the **saveHistory** behavior, the data is persisted in the UserData store. The **saveHistory** behavior uses one UserData store for the entire document. Thus, if two elements write the same attribute, the first is overwritten by the second. The UserData store is saved in an in-memory stream and is not saved to disk. Therefore, it is not available after Internet Explorer has been closed.

For example, a page with several dynamically updated styles can save these updates using the **onload** and **onsave** events. The style values can be saved as attributes when **onsave** fires, and restored when **onload** fires.

To use the **saveHistory** behavior, you must use a **META** tag identifying the type of persistence.

```
<META NAME="save" CONTENT="history">
```

The required **STYLE** can be set inline, or in the document header, as shown below.

```
<STYLE>
    .saveHistory {behavior:url(#default#savehistory);}
</STYLE>
```

An **ID** is optional for **saveHistory**, but including an **ID** increases performance.

Example

The following example shows how to use the **saveHistory** behavior.

```
<HTML>
<HEAD>
<META NAME="save" CONTENT="history">
<STYLE>
    .saveHistory {behavior:url(#default#savehistory);}
</STYLE>
</HEAD>
<BODY>
<INPUT class=saveHistory type=text id=oPersistInput>
</BODY>
</HTML>
```

To see this code in action, refer to the Web Workshop CD-ROM.

Applies To

 WIN32   UNIX

A, ACRONYM, ADDRESS, AREA, B, BIG, BLOCKQUOTE, BUTTON, CAPTION, CENTER, CITE, CODE, DD, DEL, DFN, DIR, DIV, DL, DT, EM, FONT, FORM, Hn, HR, I, IMG, INPUT type=button, INPUT type=checkbox, INPUT type=file, INPUT type=hidden, INPUT type=image, INPUT type=password,

WIN32   UNIX

INPUT type=radio, INPUT type=reset, INPUT type=submit, INPUT type=text, KBD, LABEL, LI, LISTING, MAP, MARQUEE, MENU, OBJECT, OL, OPTION, P, PLAINTEXT, PRE, Q, S, SAMP, SELECT, SMALL, SPAN, STRIKE, STRONG, SUB, SUP, TABLE, TEXTAREA, TT, U, UL, VAR, XMP

saveSnapshot Behavior

Enables the object to persist data in a snapshot.

Syntax

XML   N/A

HTML   `<ELEMENT STYLE="behavior:url('#default#saveSnapshot')" ID=sID>`

Scripting `object.style.behavior="url('#default#saveSnapshot')"`

`object.addBehavior ("#default#saveSnapshot>")`

Possible Values

sID   String that uniquely specifies the object.

Events

onsave

Remarks

The **saveSnapshot** behavior can persist form values, styles, dynamically updated content, and scripting variables when a Web page has been saved locally as Web Page, HTML Only. The **saveSnapshot** behavior persists data by including the new object values and content in the saved document.

The **BODY** element and individual table elements, such as **rows** and **cells**, cannot be persisted.

Contents of the **SCRIPT** element can persist if the element is assigned an **ID** and a **class**. Only string, Boolean, and integer variants persist. Comments, functions, and scripting objects, such as arrays, are stripped out. Persistent **SCRIPT** elements with an external source write the variables from the source into the persistent page.

To use the **saveSnapshot** behavior, you must use a **META** tag identifying the type of persistence.

```
<META NAME="save" CONTENT="snapshot">
```

The required **STYLE** can be set inline, or in the document header, as shown below.

```
<STYLE>
   .saveSnapshot {behavior:url(#default#savesnapshot);}
</STYLE>
```

To persist an object, you must use an **ID** on the object.

Example

The following examples show how to use the **saveSnapshot** behavior.

The sample below provides an elementary look at using persistence.

```
<HTML>
<HEAD>
<META NAME="save" CONTENT="history">
<STYLE>
   .saveSnapshot {behavior:url(#default#savesnapshot);}
</STYLE>
</HEAD>
<BODY>
<INPUT class=saveSnapshot type=text id=oPersistInput>
</BODY>
</HTML>
```

To see this code in action, refer to the Web Workshop CD-ROM.

The sample below persists an entire form either in HTML or in scripting.

```
<HTML>
<HEAD>
<META NAME="save" CONTENT="snapshot">
<STYLE>
   .saveSnapshot {behavior:url(#default#savesnapshot);}
</STYLE>
<SCRIPT CLASS="saveSnapshot" id=oPersistScript>
   var sData="";
</SCRIPT>
<SCRIPT>
function PersistArray(){
   var sData="";
   for(var i=0;i<oPersistForm.elements.length;i++){
      if(oPersistForm.elements[i].type == "text"){
         sData+=oPersistForm.elements[i].value + "|";
         oPersistForm.elements[i].value="";
      }
```

```
        if(oPersistForm.elements[i].tagName == "SELECT"){
                sData+="spamtype=" + oPersistForm.elements[i].selectedIndex;
                oPersistForm.oSelSpam.selected=-1;
            }
        }
    sPersistData=sData;
}
function RestoreArray(){
    if(sPersistData!="~Empty~"){
        collData=sPersistData.split("|");
        for(var i=0;i<collData.length;i++){
            if(collData[i].indexOf("spamtype=")==-1){
                oPersistForm.elements[i].value=collData[i];
            }
            if(collData[i].indexOf("spamtype=")>=0){
                oPersistForm.oSelSpam.selectedIndex=
                    collData[i].substring(
                        collData[i].indexOf("=")+1,collData[i].length
                    );
            }
        }
    }
}
</SCRIPT>
</HEAD>
<BODY>
<FORM ID="oPersistForm">
<TABLE CLASS="oSampleStyle">
<TR><TD><LABEL FOR="oFirstName">First Name:</LABEL></TD>
<TD><INPUT CLASS="saveSnapshot" TYPE="text" ID="oFirstName"
SIZE=15></TD></TR>
<TR><TD><LABEL FOR="oSelSpam">Select Method of Spam:</LABEL></TD>
<TD>
<SELECT ID="oSelSpam">
<OPTION>E-mail<OPTION>Postal Mail<OPTION>Telemarketing
</SELECT></TD></TR>
:
</TABLE>
<INPUT TYPE="button"
    VALUE="Save form data in script."
    onclick="PersistArray()"
>
<INPUT TYPE="button"
    VALUE="Restore data from script."
    onclick="RestoreArray()"
>
</FORM>
</BODY>
</HTML>
```

To see this code in action, refer to the Web Workshop CD-ROM.

Applies To

 WIN32   UNIX

A, ACRONYM, ADDRESS, AREA, B, BIG, BLOCKQUOTE, BUTTON, CENTER, CITE, CODE, DD, DEL, DFN, DIR, DIV, DL, DT, EM, FONT, FORM, Hn, HR, I, IMG, INPUT type=button, INPUT type=checkbox, INPUT type=file, INPUT type=hidden, INPUT type=image, INPUT type=password, INPUT type=radio, INPUT type=reset, INPUT type=submit, INPUT type=text, KBD, LABEL, LI, LISTING, MAP, MARQUEE, MENU, OBJECT, OL, OPTION, P, PLAINTEXT, PRE, Q, S, SAMP, SCRIPT, SELECT, SMALL, SPAN, STRIKE, STRONG, SUB, SUP, TABLE, TEXTAREA, TT, U, UL, VAR, XMP

SEQ Element | seq Behavior

Defines a new timeline container in an HTML document for sequentially timed elements.

Syntax

XML *<Prefix*:SEQ ID="*sID*" STYLE="behavior:url(#default#time)" />

HTML N/A

Scripting N/A

Possible Values

Prefix Prefix used to associate the element with an XML namespace. A prefix of t must be used for the experimental implementation of HTML+TIME. Include the following line in the **HEAD** section of your HTML document when using this element:

`<XML:NAMESPACE PREFIX="t"/>`

sID String that uniquely specifies the object.

Properties

accelerate	**autoReverse**	**begin**	**beginAfter**
beginEvent	**beginWith**	**decelerate**	**dur**
end	**endEvent**	**endHold**	**eventRestart**
repeat	**repeatDur**	**syncBehavior**	**syncTolerance**

Methods

beginElement	**endElement**	**pause**	**resume**

Events

onbegin	**onend**	**onmediacomplete**	**onmedialoadfailed**
onmediaslip	**onpause**	**onrepeat**	**onresume**
onresync	**onreverse**		

Remarks

All timed HTML descendants of this XML element have sequential timing. These sequential elements are timed as though each one has the **beginAfter** property set to the previous timed element. As with **beginAfter** timing, a duration value (**dur**) must be specified or the next element in the sequence might never be displayed. Elements without timing attributes are ignored by the timing mechanism and are statically rendered. A timed element is an HTML element with an associated time behavior.

The **SEQ** element is available as of Internet Explorer 5 only for the Win32 platform.

Example

The following example shows how to use the **SEQ** element to display a sequence of text lines without specifying begin times for each timed element in the sequence.

```
<!DOCTYPE HTML PUBLIC "-//W3C//DTD HTML 4.0 Transitional//EN">
<HTML>
<HEAD>
<XML:NAMESPACE PREFIX="t"/>
<STYLE>
.time            { behavior: url(#default#time);            }
</STYLE>
</HEAD>
<BODY BGCOLOR="white">
<FONT FACE="Verdana" COLOR="Blue">
<t:SEQ ID="parent" CLASS="time" t:BEGIN="0" t:DUR="indefinite">
    <DIV ID="div1" CLASS="time" t:DUR="2">First line of text.</DIV>
    <DIV ID="div1" CLASS="time" t:DUR="2">Second line of text.</DIV>
    <DIV ID="div1" CLASS="time" t:DUR="2">Third line of text.</DIV>
    <DIV ID="div1" CLASS="time" t:DUR="2">Fourth line of text.</DIV>
    <SPAN STYLE="color:black" ID="span1" CLASS="time"
    t:DUR="indefinite"><B>End of sequence.</B></SPAN>
</t:SEQ>
</FONT>
</BODY>
</HTML>
```

To see this code in action, refer to the Web Workshop CD-ROM.

time Behavior

Provides an active timeline for an HTML element.

Syntax

XML	N/A
HTML	*<ELEMENT* STYLE="behavior:url('#default#time')" ID=*sID>*
Scripting	*object*.style.behavior = "url('#default#time')"
	object.addBehavior ("#default#time")

Possible Values

sID	String that uniquely specifies the object.

Attributes/Properties

accelerate	**autoReverse**	**begin**	**beginAfter**
beginEvent	**beginWith**	**currTime** [1]	**decelerate**
dur	**end**	**endEvent**	**endHold**
eventRestart	**localTime** [1]	**onOffBehavior** [1]	**progressBehavior** [1]
repeat	**repeatDur**	**syncBehavior**	**syncTolerance**
timeAction	**timeline**	**timelineBehavior** [1]	**timeStartRule**

1   This property has no corresponding attribute.

Methods

beginElement	**endElement**	**pause**	**resume**

Events

onbegin	**onend**	**onrepeat**	**onreverse**

Remarks

This default behavior adds timing to HTML pages. The **time** behavior supports all time-related attributes, properties, methods, and events. The XML elements that are associated with this behavior are **ANIMATION**, **AUDIO**, **IMG**, **MEDIA**, **PAR**, **SEQ**, and **VIDEO**.

The behavior-defined members listed in the preceding list might not be accessible through scripting until the **window.onload** event fires. Waiting for this event to fire ensures that the page is completely loaded, that all behaviors have been applied to corresponding elements on the page, and that all the behavior's properties, methods, and events are available for scripting. Attempting to use any of the behavior-defined members before firing the **window.onload** event can result in a scripting error indicating that the object does not support that particular member.

Example

The following example shows how to make text appear and disappear over time.

```
<!DOCTYPE HTML PUBLIC "-//W3C//DTD HTML 4.0 Transitional//EN">
<HTML>
<HEAD>
<TITLE>Time Behavior</TITLE>
<XML:NAMESPACE PREFIX="t"/>
<STYLE>
.time              { behavior: url(#default#time);}
</STYLE>
</HEAD>
<BODY TOPMARGIN=0 LEFTMARGIN=0 BGPROPERTIES="FIXED" BGCOLOR="#FFFFFF"
LINK="#000000" VLINK="#808080" ALINK="#000000">
<BLOCKQUOTE>
<P>Images and lines of text should start appearing 2 seconds
after the page is loaded.</P>
<IMG CLASS=time t:BEGIN="2" t:DUR="7" t:TIMEACTION="display"
    SRC="/workshop/graphics/icons/author.gif" WIDTH=31 HEIGHT=32
    BORDER="0" STYLE="position:relative; left:50;">
<IMG CLASS=time t:BEGIN="11" t:DUR="indefinite" t:TIMEACTION="display"
    SRC="/workshop/graphics/icons/messaging.gif" WIDTH=31 HEIGHT=32
    BORDER="0" STYLE="position:relative; left:50;">
<UL STYLE="COLOR:Green;">
    <LI CLASS=time t:BEGIN="2" t:DUR="7" t:TIMEACTION="display">
        This line appears with the image.
    </LI>
    <LI CLASS=time t:BEGIN="4" t:DUR="5" t:TIMEACTION="display">
        This line appears two seconds after the image.
    </LI>
    <LI CLASS=time t:BEGIN="6" t:DUR="3" t:TIMEACTION="display">
        This line appears four seconds after the image.
    </LI>
</UL>
<UL STYLE="COLOR:Red;">
    <LI CLASS=time t:BEGIN="11" t:DUR="indefinite"
    t:TIMEACTION="display">
        This line appears with the image.
    </LI>
    <LI CLASS=time t:BEGIN="13" t:DUR="indefinite"
    t:TIMEACTION="display">
        This line appears two seconds after the image.
    </LI>
```

```
        <LI CLASS=time t:BEGIN="15" t:DUR="indefinite"
        t:TIMEACTION="display">
            This line appears four seconds after the image.
        </LI>
</UL>
<P CLASS=time t:BEGIN="16" t:DUR="indefinite">The page is now
finished.</P>
</BLOCKQUOTE>
</BODY>
</HTML>
```

To see this code in action, refer to the Web Workshop CD-ROM.

Applies To

 WIN32   UNIX

A, ACRONYM, ADDRESS, AREA, B, BIG, BLOCKQUOTE, BODY, BUTTON,
CAPTION, CENTER, CITE, CODE, DD, DEL, DFN, DIR, DIV, DL, DT, EM,
FIELDSET, FONT, FORM, Hn, HR, I, IFRAME, IMG, INPUT type=button, INPUT
type=checkbox, INPUT type=file, INPUT type=hidden, INPUT type=image, INPUT
type=password, INPUT type=radio, INPUT type=reset, INPUT type=submit, INPUT
type=text, INS, KBD, LABEL, LEGEND, LI, LISTING, MAP, MARQUEE, MENU,
OBJECT, OL, OPTION, P, PLAINTEXT, PRE, Q, S, SAMP, SELECT, SMALL,
SPAN, STRIKE, STRONG, SUB, SUP, TABLE, TBODY, TD, TEXTAREA,
TFOOT, TH, THEAD, TR, TT, U, UL, VAR, XMP

userData Behavior

Enables the object to persist data in user data.

Syntax

XML   N/A

HTML   *<ELEMENT* STYLE="behavior:url('#default#userData')" ID=*sID>*

Scripting *object*.style.behavior = "url('#default#userData')"

                object.addBehavior ("#default#userData")

Possible Values

sID   String that uniquely specifies the object.

Properties

expires   **XMLDocument**

Methods

getAttribute   **load**   **removeAttribute**   **save**   **setAttribute**

Remarks

The **userData** behavior persists information across sessions by writing to a UserData store. This provides a data structure that is more dynamic and has a greater capacity than cookies. The capacity of the UserData store is 64K per page, with a limit of 640K per domain.

The **userData** behavior persists data across sessions, using one UserData store for each object. The UserData store is persisted in the cache using the **save** and **load** methods. Once the UserData store has been saved, it can be reloaded even if Internet Explorer has been closed and reopened.

For security reasons, a UserData store is available only in the same directory and with the same protocol used to persist the store.

Setting the **userData** behavior (proposed) class on the **HTML**, **HEAD**, **TITLE**, or **STYLE** objects causes an error when the **save** or **load** methods are called.

The required **STYLE** can be set inline, or in the document header, as shown below.

```
<STYLE>
   .userData {behavior:url(#default#userdata);}
</STYLE>
```

An **ID** is optional for **userData**, but including one increases performance.

Example

The following example shows how to use the **userData** behavior.

```
<HTML>
<HEAD>
<STYLE>
   .userData {behavior:url(#default#userdata);}
</STYLE>
<SCRIPT>
function fnSaveInput(){
   var oPersist=oPersistForm.oPersistInput;
   oPersist.setAttribute("sPersist",oPersist.value);
   oPersist.save("oXMLBranch");
}
```

```
function fnLoadInput(){
   var oPersist=oPersistForm.oPersistInput;
   oPersist.load("oXMLBranch");
   oPersistInput.value=oPersistInput.getAttribute("sPersist");
}
</SCRIPT>
</HEAD>
<BODY>
<FORM ID="oPersistForm">
<INPUT CLASS=userData" TYPE="text" ID="oPersistInput">
<INPUT TYPE="button" VALUE="Load" onclick="fnLoadInput()">
<INPUT TYPE="button" VALUE="Save" onclick="fnSaveInput()">
</FORM>
</BODY>
</HTML>
```

To see this code in action, refer to the Web Workshop CD-ROM.

Applies To

 WIN32   UNIX

A, ACRONYM, ADDRESS, AREA, B, BIG, BLOCKQUOTE, BUTTON,
CAPTION, CENTER, CITE, CODE, DD, DEL, DFN, DIR, DIV, DL, DT, EM,
FONT, FORM, Hn, HR, I, IMG, INPUT type=button, INPUT type=checkbox,
INPUT type=file, INPUT type=hidden, INPUT type=image, INPUT type=password,
INPUT type=radio, INPUT type=reset, INPUT type=submit, INPUT type=text, KBD,
LABEL, LI, LISTING, MAP, MARQUEE, MENU, OBJECT, OL, OPTION, P,
PLAINTEXT, PRE, Q, S, SAMP, SELECT, SMALL, SPAN, STRIKE, STRONG,
SUB, SUP, TABLE, TEXTAREA, TT, U, UL, VAR, XMP

VIDEO Element | video Behavior

Defines a timed video element in an HTML document.

Syntax

XML   *<Prefix*:VIDEO ID="*sID*" STYLE="behavior:url(#default#time)" />

HTML   N/A

Scripting N/A

Possible Values

Prefix   Prefix used to associate the element with an XML namespace. A prefix of t must be used for the experimental implementation of HTML+TIME. Include the following line in the **HEAD** section of your HTML document when using this element:

```
<XML:NAMESPACE
PREFIX="t"/>
```

sID   String that uniquely specifies the object.

Attributes/Properties

accelerate	**autoReverse**	**begin**	**beginAfter**
beginEvent	**beginWith**	**clipBegin**	**clipEnd**
clockSource	**decelerate**	**dur**	**end**
endEvent	**endHold**	**eventRestart**	**img**
player	**playerObject** [1]	**repeat**	**repeatDur**
src	**syncBehavior**	**syncTolerance**	**timeAction**

1   This property has no corresponding attribute.

Methods

beginElement	**endElement**	**pause**	**resume**

Events

onbegin	**onend**	**onmediacomplete**	**onmedialoadfailed**
onmediaslip	**onpause**	**onrepeat**	**onresume**
onresync	**onreverse**	**onscriptcommand**	

Remarks

The behavior-defined members listed in the preceding list might not be accessible through scripting until the **window.onload** event fires. Waiting for this event to fire ensures that the page is completely loaded, that all behaviors have been applied to corresponding elements on the page, and that all the behavior's properties, methods, and events are available for scripting. Attempting to use any of the behavior-defined members before firing the **window.onload** event can result in a scripting error indicating that the object does not support that particular member.

Although different media-based elements exist, there is no functional difference in their current implementation. However, using the different elements, such as **ANIMATION**, **AUDIO**, **IMG**, **MEDIA**, and **VIDEO**, for document readability and enhanced future support is encouraged.

The **VIDEO** element is available as of Internet Explorer 5 only for the Win32 platform.

onbegin Event

Fires when the timeline starts on an element.

Syntax

Inline HTML	`<ELEMENT onbegin = "handler" ... >`	All platforms
Event property	*object*`.onbegin = handler`	JScript (compatible with ECMA 262 language specification) only
Named script	`<SCRIPT FOR = object EVENT = onbegin >`	Internet Explorer only

Remarks

Bubbles	No
Cancels	No
To invoke	When the event is actually fired is determined by the value of the element's begin time, which might depend on other elements.
Default action	Calls the associated event handler.

This event also fires for the element when the **beginElement** method is invoked on it, or in response to other dependencies created by the **BEGINWIDTH** or **BEGINEVENT** attribute. This event does not fire when the timeline on the element repeats. However, it fires if the parent element's timeline repeats.

Event Object Properties

Although event handlers in the DHTML Object Model do not receive parameters directly, the handler can query the event object for data. The following properties of the **event** object are relevant to an **onbegin** event:

SrcElement	Retrieves the object that fired the event.
Type	Retrieves the event name from the **event** object.

WIN32

animation, audio, img, media, par, seq, time, video

onend Event

Fires when the timeline stops on an element.

Syntax

Inline HTML	*<ELEMENT* onend = "*handler*" ... >	All platforms
Event property	*object*.onend = *handler*	JScript (compatible with ECMA 262 language specification) only
Named script	<SCRIPT FOR = *object* EVENT = onend >	Internet Explorer only

Remarks

Bubbles	No
Cancels	No
To invoke	When the event is actually fired is determined by the value of the element's end time, which might depend on other elements.
Default action	Calls the associated event handler.

This event also fires for the element when the **endElement** method is invoked on it, or in response to other dependencies created by the **ENDEVENT** attribute. If the element timeline is set to repeat, this event fires only once after all repetitions are complete. The timing of this event is not affected by the **ENDHOLD** attribute. If the **ENDHOLD** attribute is set to true for the element, this event is fired when the parent element's timeline completes.

Event Object Properties

Although event handlers in the DHTML Object Model do not receive parameters directly, the handler can query the event object for data. The following properties of the **event** object are relevant to an **onend** event:

srcElement	Retrieves the object that fired the event.
type	Retrieves the event name from the **event** object.

Applies To

 WIN32

animation, audio, img, media, par, seq, time, video

onload Event

Fires from a persistent element when the page is reloaded.

Syntax

Inline HTML	*<ELEMENT* onload *= "handler"* ... >	All platforms
Event property	*object*.onload *= handler*	JScript (compatible with ECMA 262 language specification) only
Named script	<SCRIPT FOR = *object* EVENT = onload>	Internet Explorer only

Remarks

Bubbles	No
Cancels	Yes
To invoke	Load the persistent Web page through a favorite or shortcut or through an Internet address.
Default action	Initiates any action associated with this script. The **onload** event for behaviors overrides the **onload** event for DHTML objects.

Event Object Properties

Although event handlers in the DHTML Object Model do not directly receive parameters, the handler can query the event object for data. The following property of the **event** object is relevant to an **onload** event:

srcElement   Retrieves the object that fired the event.

Example

The following example shows how to use the **onload** event for a persistence behavior.

```
<HTML>
<HEAD>
<META NAME="save" CONTENT="favorite">
<STYLE>
   .saveFavorite {behavior:url(#default#savefavorite);}
</STYLE>
```

```
<SCRIPT>
   function fnSaveInput(){
      oPersistInput.setAttribute("sPersistValue",oPersistInput.value);
   }
   function fnLoadInput(){
      alert("The onload event fired.");
      oPersistInput.value=oPersistInput.getAttribute("sPersistValue");
   }
</SCRIPT>
</HEAD>
<BODY>
<INPUT class=saveFavorite onsave="fnSaveInput()" onload="fnLoadInput()"
   type=text id=oPersistInput>
</BODY>
</HTML>
```

To see this code in action, refer to the Web Workshop CD-ROM.

Applies To

 WIN32   UNIX

saveFavorite, saveHistory

onmediacomplete Event

Fires when the element's associated media finish loading.

Syntax

Inline HTML	*<ELEMENT* onmediacomplete = *"handler"* ... >	All platforms
Event property	*object.*onmediacomplete = *handler*	JScript (compatible with ECMA 262 language specification) only
Named script	<SCRIPT FOR = *object* EVENT = onmediacomplete>	Internet Explorer only

Remarks

Bubbles	No
Cancels	No
To invoke	Open a page in the browser that contains a media file affected by HTML+TIME. This event fires when the media are finished loading.
Default action	Calls the associated event handler.

When streaming media are used, this event might occur before the media finish playing.

Event Object Properties

Although event handlers in the DHTML Object Model do not receive parameters directly, the handler can query the event object for data. The following properties of the **event** object are relevant to an **onmediacomplete** event:

srcElement   Retrieves the object that fired the event.

type   Retrieves the event name from the **event** object.

Applies To

 WIN32

animation, audio, img, media, par, seq, time, video

onmedialoadfailed Event

Fires when the media for an element cannot be loaded.

Syntax

Inline HTML	*<ELEMENT* onmedialoadfailed = *"handler"* ... >	All platforms
Event property	*object*.onmedialoadfailed = *handler*	JScript (compatible with ECMA 262 language specification) only
Named script	<SCRIPT FOR = *object* EVENT = onmedialoadfailed>	Internet Explorer only

Remarks

Bubbles   No

Cancels   No

To invoke   Open a page in the browser that contains a media file affected by HTML+TIME. This event fires when the media fails to load for any reason.

Default action   Calls the associated event handler.

Event Object Properties

Although event handlers in the DHTML Object Model do not receive parameters directly, the handler can query the event object for data. The following properties of the **event** object are relevant to an **onmedialoadfailed** event:

srcElement   Retrieves the object that fired the event.

type   Retrieves the event name from the **event** object.

Applies To

 WIN32

animation, audio, img, media, par, seq, video

onmediaslip Event

Fires when the media for an element cannot keep up with the defined timeline.

Syntax

Inline HTML	*<ELEMENT* onmediaslip = *"handler"* ... >	All platforms
Event property	*object.* onmediaslip = *handler*	JScript (compatible with ECMA 262 language specification) only
Named script	<SCRIPT FOR = *object* EVENT = onmediaslip>	Internet Explorer only

Remarks

Bubbles	No
Cancels	No
To invoke	Open a page in the browser that contains a media file affected by HTML+TIME. This event fires when the media fails to keep up with the defined timeline. This event might be fired as a result of network problems.
Default action	Calls the associated event handler.

Event Object Properties

Although event handlers in the DHTML Object Model do not receive parameters directly, the handler can query the event object for data. The following properties of the **event** object are relevant to an **onmediaslip** event:

srcElement   Retrieves the object that fired the event.

type   Retrieves the event name from the **event** object.

Applies To

 WIN32

animation, audio, img, media, par, seq, video

onpause Event

Fires when the timeline on an element is paused.

Syntax

Inline HTML	`<BODY onpause = "handler" ... >`	All platforms
Event property	*object*.onpause = *handler*	JScript (compatible with ECMA 262 language specification) only
Named script	`<SCRIPT FOR = object EVENT = onpause>`	Internet Explorer only

Remarks

Bubbles   No

Cancels   No

To invoke   Call the pause method.

Default action   Calls the associated event handler.

This event is fired only on the HTML **BODY** element.

Event Object Properties

Although event handlers in the DHTML Object Model do not receive parameters directly, the handler can query the event object for data. The following properties of the **event** object are relevant to an **onpause** event:

srcElement   Retrieves the object that fired the event.

type   Retrieves the event name from the **event** object.

Applies To

 WIN32

animation, audio, img, media, par, seq, video

onrepeat Event

Fires when the timeline repeats on an element, beginning with the second iteration.

Syntax

Inline HTML	*<ELEMENT* onrepeat = "*handler*" ... >	All platforms
Event property	*object*.onrepeat = *handler*	JScript (compatible with ECMA 262 language specification) only
Named script	<SCRIPT FOR = *object* EVENT = onrepeat>	Internet Explorer only

Remarks

Bubbles	No
Cancels	No
To invoke	Set the **repeat** property to a value greater than 1.
Default action	Calls the associated event handler.

The event fires once for each repetition of the timeline, excluding the first full cycle. Therefore, the **onrepeat** event fires repeat–1 times, unless it is stopped by other dependencies before completion. This event fires only if the **repeat** or **repeatDur** property is set directly on the element. This event does not fire on child elements that have the **repeat** or **repeatDur** property set only on their parent elements.

Event Object Properties

Although event handlers in the DHTML Object Model do not receive parameters directly, the handler can query the event object for data. The following properties of the **event** object are relevant to an **onrepeat** event:

iteration   Retrieves the current iteration of the timeline's repeat cycle.

srcElement   Retrieves the object that fired the event.

type   Retrieves the event name from the **event** object.

To access the **iteration** value, use the **getAttribute** method on the **window.event** object.

Example

The following example shows how to display a message box indicating the current repeat iteration every time the **onrepeat** event is fired on a timeline.

```
<!DOCTYPE HTML PUBLIC "-//W3C//DTD HTML 4.0 Transitional//EN">
<HTML>
<HEAD>
<STYLE>
.time           { behavior: url(#default#time);}
</STYLE>

</HEAD>

<BODY BGCOLOR="white">
<SPAN ID="parent" CLASS=time t:BEGIN="0" t:DUR="6" t:REPEAT="4"
      t:TIMELINE="par"
    t:TIMEACTION="display" onrepeat="alert('Current iteration: ' +
        window.event.getAttribute('iteration'));">
    <SPAN CLASS=time t:BEGIN="0" t:DUR="2">This text is
        displayed for two seconds.</SPAN><BR>
    <SPAN CLASS=time t:BEGIN="3" t:DUR="4">This text is
        displayed for four seconds.</SPAN>
</SPAN>
</BODY>
</HTML>
```

To see this code in action, refer to the Web Workshop CD-ROM.

Applies To

 WIN32

animation, audio, img, media, par, seq, time, video

onresume Event

Fires when an element's timeline is resuming from a paused state.

Syntax

Inline HTML	`<BODY onresume = "`*handler*`" ... >`	All platforms
Event property	*object*`.onresume = `*handler*	JScript (compatible with ECMA 262 language specification) only
Named script	`<SCRIPT FOR = `*object*` EVENT = onresume>`	Internet Explorer only

Remarks

Bubbles	No
Cancels	No
To invoke	Call the resume method.
Default action	Calls the associated event handler.

This event is fired only on the HTML **BODY** element.

Event Object Properties

Although event handlers in the DHTML Object Model do not receive parameters directly, the handler can query the event object for data. The following properties of the **event** object are relevant to an **onresume** event:

srcElement	Retrieves the object that fired the event.
type	Retrieves the event name from the **event** object.

Applies To

 WIN32

animation, audio, img, media, par, seq, video

onreverse Event

Fires when the timeline on an element begins to play backward.

Syntax

Inline HTML	*<ELEMENT* onreverse = "*handler*" ... >	All platforms
Event property	*object*.onreverse = *handler*	JScript (compatible with ECMA 262 language specification) only
Named script	<SCRIPT FOR = *object* EVENT = onreverse>	Internet Explorer only

Remarks

Bubbles	No
Cancels	No
To invoke	Set the **autoReverse** property on the element to true.
Default action	Calls the associated event handler.

If the element is also set to repeat, this event fires every time the timeline begins to play backward.

Event Object Properties

Although event handlers in the DHTML Object Model do not receive parameters directly, the handler can query the event object for data. The following properties of the **event** object are relevant to an **onreverse** event:

srcElement	Retrieves the object that fired the event.
type	Retrieves the event name from the **event** object.

Applies To

 WIN32

animation, audio, img, media, par, seq, time, video

onresync Event

Fires when the element's associated media synchronization is interrupted.

Syntax

Inline HTML	`<ELEMENT onresync = "handler" ... >`	All platforms
Event property	`object.onresync = handler`	JScript (compatible with ECMA 262 language specification) only
Named script	`<SCRIPT FOR = object EVENT = onresync>`	Internet Explorer only

Remarks

Bubbles	No
Cancels	No
To invoke	Cause the element's media synchronization to be interrupted. Setting the **syncTolerance** property to 0 on a timeline with locked **syncBehavior** increases the chances that the element needs to be resynchronized somewhere along the timeline.
Default action	Calls the associated event handler and re-establishes media synchronization.

Event Object Properties

Although event handlers in the DHTML Object Model do not receive parameters directly, the handler can query the event object for data. The following properties of the **event** object are relevant to an **onresync** event:

SrcElement	Retrieves the object that fired the event.
Type	Retrieves the event name from the **event** object.

Applies To

 WIN32

animation, audio, img, media, par, seq, time, video

onsave Event

Fires from a persisted element when the Web page is saved or bookmarked, or when the user navigates away from the page.

Syntax

Inline HTML	*<ELEMENT* onsave = "*handler*" ... >	All platforms
Event property	*object*.onsave = *handler*	JScript (compatible with ECMA 262 language specification) only
Named script	<SCRIPT FOR = *object* EVENT = onsave>	Internet Explorer only

Remarks

Bubbles	No
Cancels	Yes
To invoke	Save the Web page, bookmark the Web page, or navigate to another page.
Default action	Initiates any action associated with this script.

Event Object Properties

Although event handlers in the DHTML Object Model do not receive parameters directly, the handler can query the event object for data. The following property of the **event** object is relevant to an **onsave** event:

srcElement Retrieves the object that fired the event.

Example

The following example shows how to use the **onsave** event for a persistence behavior.

```
<HTML>
<HEAD>
<META NAME="save" CONTENT="favorite">
<STYLE>
   .saveFavorite {behavior:url(#default#savefavorite);}
</STYLE>
<SCRIPT>
   function fnSaveInput(){
      alert("The onsave event fired.");
      oPersistInput.setAttribute("sPersistValue",oPersistInput.value);
   }
```

```
    function fnLoadInput(){
        oPersistInput.value=oPersistInput.getAttribute("sPersistValue");
    }
</SCRIPT>
</HEAD>
<BODY>
<INPUT class=saveFavorite onsave="fnSaveInput()" onload="fnLoadInput()"
    type=text id=oPersistInput>
</BODY>
</HTML>
```

To see this code in action, refer to the Web Workshop CD-ROM.

Applies To

 WIN32   UNIX

saveFavorite, saveHistory, saveSnapshot

onscriptcommand Event

Fires when the Windows Media Player control receives a synchronized command or URL.

Syntax

Inline HTML	*<ELEMENT* onscriptcommand = "*handler*" ... >	All platforms
Event property	*object.*onscriptcommand = *handler*	JScript (compatible with ECMA 262 language specification) only
Named script	<SCRIPT FOR = *object* EVENT = onscriptcommand>	Internet Explorer only

Remarks

Bubbles	No
Cancels	No
To invoke	Open a document in the browser that plays a streaming media file affected by HTML+TIME. The streaming media file (.asf) must contain embedded commands, or triggers, in the stream.
Default action	Calls the associated event handler.

This event is fired when the Windows Media Player is used with one of the HTML+TIME media elements, including **ANIMATION**, **AUDIO**, **IMG**, **MEDIA**, and **VIDEO**.

Commands can be embedded among the sounds and images of an .asf file. A command consists of a pair of Unicode strings associated with a designated time in the stream. When the stream reaches the time associated with the command, the Windows Media Player control fires this event and sets two properties on the event object, the **scType** property and the **Param** property. The **scType** property specifies the type of command, and the **Param** property specifies the command value. The **scType** property determines how the Windows Media Player control processes the command parameter.

Any type of command can be embedded in an ASF stream to be handled by this event. For example, if the Windows Media Player encounters a URL trigger in the .asf file, the **scType** property would be set to URL, and the **Param** property is set to the value of the URL (http://...).

In addition to the **onscriptcommand** event, a second event is also fired in response to the .asf trigger. The event prefix on is added to the front of the string specified in the **scType** property, and that event is fired. For example, suppose a stream defines a trigger with the **scType** property set to the string mytype. In this case, the custom onmytype event is fired at that point in the stream with the **onscriptcommand**.

Event Object Properties

Although event handlers in the DHTML Object Model do not receive parameters directly, the handler can query the event object for data. The following properties of the **event** object are relevant to an **onscriptcommand** event:

Param   Retrieves a string representing the value of the trigger encountered in the streaming media file.

scType   Retrieves a string representing the type of trigger encountered in the streaming media file.

srcElement Retrieves the object that fired the event.

type   Retrieves the event name from the **event** object.

To access the **Param** and **scType** values, use the **getAttribute** method on the **window.event** object.

Applies To

 WIN32

animation, audio, img, media, video

addComponentRequest Method

Adds the specified component to the queue of components to be installed.

Syntax

oClientCaps.addComponentRequest (*sID*, *sIDType* [, *sMinVer*])

Parameters

sID Required. Any of the component identifiers listed in "Installable Components in Internet Explorer" in Appendix C.

sIDType Required. Case-insensitive type of the identifier specified in *sID*.

   componentid Active Setup ID of the component.

sMinVer Optional. Minimum version number of the component to be installed.

Return Value

No return value.

Remarks

Only Internet Explorer components can be specified with this method. Components not supported by Internet Explorer are ignored.

The **addComponentRequest** method queues a download request for the specified component. Actual download of the component does not occur until a call to the **doComponentRequest** method is made.

Example

The following example shows how to install the Internet Explorer Data Binding component if the component does not already exist in the user's system.

```
<HTML xmlns:IE>
<HEAD>
<STYLE>
@media all {
     IE\:clientCaps {behavior:url(#default#clientCaps)}
}
</STYLE>
```

```
<SCRIPT>
function window.onload()
{
    var bDBAvailable  = false;
    var sDBVersion = '';
    var sDBID = "{9381D8F2-0288-11D0-9501-00AA00B911A5}";

    bDBAvailable = oClientCaps.isComponentInstalled(sDBID,"componentid");

    // If data binding is unavailable, install it.
    if (!bDBAvailable)
    {
        oClientCaps.addComponentRequest (sDBID, "componentid");
        bDBAvailable = oClientCaps.doComponentRequest();
    }
    :
}
</SCRIPT>
</HEAD>

<BODY BGCOLOR="#FFFFFF">
    :
    <IE:clientCaps ID="oClientCaps" />

    :
</BODY>
```

To see this code in action, refer to the Web Workshop CD-ROM.

Applies To

 WIN32   UNIX

clientCaps

addDABehavior Method

Adds a behavior to the run list when the behavior is not part of the animation model. When the system starts the animation, the additional behaviors are run with the same start time as the behaviors included in the original animation.

Syntax

object.addDABehavior(*oBehavior*, *lID*)

Parameters

oBehavior   Required. DirectAnimation behavior (DABehavior) object to be added.

lID   Required. Identifier for the added behavior is returned in this output parameter. Use this identifier to remove the behavior with the **removeDABehavior** method

Return Value

No return value.

Remarks

For further information about DirectAnimation, see the DirectAnimation SDK.

Applies To

 WIN32

anim

beginElement Method

Starts the element on the timeline.

Syntax

object.beginElement()

Return Value

No return value.

Remarks

This method applies the same action as fixed timing does when the **begin** time for the element is reached on the local timeline. When the **beginElement** method is called, the element begins. All time children elements are notified and aligned correctly to the local timeline.

Applies To

 WIN32

animation, audio, img, media, par, seq, time, video

clearComponentRequest Method

Clears the queue of all component download requests.

Syntax

oClientCaps.clearComponentRequest()

Return Value

No return value.

Applies To

WIN32	UNIX

clientCaps

compareVersions Method

Compares two version numbers.

Syntax

iResult = *oClientCaps*.compareVersions(*sVersionNumber1*, *sVersionNumber2*)

Parameters

sVersionNumber1   Required. First of two version numbers to compare.

sVersionNumber2   Required. Second of two version numbers to compare.

Return Value

Returns one of the following values:

-1   *sVersionNumber1* is less than *sVersionNumber2*

0   *sVersionNumber1* is equal to *sVersionNumber2*

1   *sVersionNumber1* is greater than *sVersionNumber2*

Example

The following example compares the version of the installed Microsoft virtual machine component with a specified version.

```
<HTML xmlns:IE >
<HEAD>
<STYLE>
@media all {
        IE\:clientCaps {behavior:url(#default#clientcaps)}
}
</STYLE>
</HEAD>

<BODY >
<IE:clientCaps ID="oClientCaps" />
:
<SCRIPT>
    sMSvmVersion = oClientCaps.getComponentVersion
        ("{08B0E5C0-4FCB-11CF-AAA5-00401C608500}","ComponentID");
    if (0 == oClientCaps.compareVersions (sMSvmVersion, "5,0,18,1024"))
        window.alert ("Versions matched!");
</SCRIPT>
 :
</BODY>
```

Applies To

 WIN32   UNIX

clientCaps

doComponentRequest Method

Downloads all the components that have been queued using **addComponentRequest**.

Syntax

bSuccess = *oClientCaps*.doComponentRequest()

Return Value

Boolean. Returns `true` if the specified component/s downloaded successfully, or `false` otherwise.

Example

The following example shows how to install the Internet Explorer Data Binding component if the component does not already exist in the user's system.

```
<HTML xmlns:IE>
<HEAD>
<STYLE>
@media all {
        IE\:clientCaps {behavior:url(#default#clientcaps);}
}
</STYLE>

<SCRIPT>
function window.onload()
{
    var bDBAvailable  = false;
    var sDBVersion = '';
    var sDBID = "{9381D8F2-0288-11D0-9501-00AA00B911A5}";

    bDBAvailable = oClientCaps.isComponentInstalled(sDBID,"componentid");

    // If data binding is unavailable, install it.
    if (!bDBAvailable)
    {
        oClientCaps.addComponentRequest (sDBID, "componentid");
        bDBAvailable = oClientCaps.doComponentRequest();
    }
    :
}
</SCRIPT>
</HEAD>

<BODY BGCOLOR="#FFFFFF">
    :
    <IE:clientCaps ID="oClientCaps" />

    :
</BODY>
```

To see this code in action, refer to the Web Workshop CD-ROM.

Applies To

 WIN32   UNIX

clientCaps

endElement Method

Stops the element on the timeline.

Syntax

object.endElement()

Return Value

No return value.

Remarks

This method applies the same action as if the element's **end** time is reached on the local timeline, or the element's duration (**dur**) has expired. All time children elements are notified and aligned correctly to the local timeline. In addition, the **endElement** method fires the **onend** event.

Applies To

 WIN32

animation, audio, img, media, par, seq, time, video

getAttribute Method

Retrieves the value of the specified attribute.

Syntax

vAttribute = *oPersistObject*.getAttribute(*sAttrName*)

Parameters

sAttrName   Required. Name of the persistent attribute.

Return Value

Variant. Returns a string, number, or Boolean, defined by *sAttrName*. If an explicit attribute doesn't exist, an empty string is returned. If a custom attribute doesn't exist, null is returned.

Remarks

The **sAttrName** value is not case sensitive.

This method requires an object participating in persistence, where that object has a class name equal to the desired persistence behavior. An **ID** is required for the **userData** and **saveSnapshot** behaviors, and is recommended for the **saveHistory** and **saveFavorite** behaviors.

The **getAttribute** method for behaviors overrides the DHTML **getAttribute** method.

Example

This example uses the **getAttribute** method to get an attribute on an object participating in userData persistence.

```
<HEAD>

<STYLE>
    .userData {behavior:url(#default#userdata);}
</STYLE>

<SCRIPT>
    function fnGet(){
        oPersistInput.load("oDataStore");
        oPersistInput.value=oPersistInput.getAttribute("sPersistAttr");
    }
    function fnSet(){
        oPersistInput.setAttribute("sPersistAttr",oPersistInput.value);
        oPersistInput.save("oDataStore");
    }
    function fnRem(){
        oPersistInput.removeAttribute("sPersistAttr");
        oPersistInput.save("oDataStore");
    }
</SCRIPT>
</HEAD>

<BODY >
<INPUT type=text class=userData id=oPersistInput>
<INPUT type=button value="Get Attribute" onclick="fnGet()">
<INPUT type=button value="Set Attribute" onclick="fnSet()">
<INPUT type=button value="Remove Attribute" onclick="fnRem()">
</BODY>
```

To see this code in action, refer to the Web Workshop CD-ROM.

Applies To

 WIN32   UNIX

saveFavorite, saveHistory, userData

getComponentVersion Method

Retrieves the version of the specified component.

Syntax

sVersion = *oClientCaps*.getComponentVersion(*sID*, *sIDType*)

Parameters

sID　　　Required. Any of the component identifiers listed in "Detectable Components in Internet Explorer" in Appendix C.

sIDType　Required. Case-insensitive type of the identifier specified in *sID*.

　　　componentid　　Active Setup ID of the component.

Return Value

String. Returns the version number of the component if it is installed, or `null` otherwise.

Remarks

Only components installed by Internet Explorer components can be detected by this method. If a component identifier of a third-party component is specified, the method returns `null`.

Example

The following example detects whether the Microsoft virtual machine is installed and, if it is, indicates the currently installed version, using the **getComponentVersion** method.

```
<HTML xmlns:IE>
<HEAD>
<STYLE>
@media all {
     IE\:clientCaps {behavior:url(#default#clientcaps)}
}
</STYLE>
</HEAD>

<BODY>
<IE:clientCaps ID="oClientCaps" />

<SCRIPT>
    sMSvmVersion = oClientCaps.getComponentVersion("{08B0E5C0-4FCB-11CF-AAA5-
00401C608500}",
    "ComponentID");
</SCRIPT>
```

```
      :
</BODY>
```

To see this code in action, refer to the Web Workshop CD-ROM.

Applies To

 WIN32   UNIX

clientCaps

isComponentInstalled Method

Determines whether the specified component is available.

Syntax

bInstalled = *oClientCaps*.isComponentInstalled(*sID*, *sIDType* [, *sMinVersion*])

Parameters

sID	Required. Any of the component identifiers listed in "Detectable Components in Internet Explorer" in Appendix C.
sIDType	Required. Case-insensitive type of the identifier specified in *sID*.
	`componentid` Active Setup ID of the component.
sMinVersion	Optional. Version number of the component.

Return Value

Boolean. Returns `true` if the component is installed and its version number is greater than or equal to the specified *sMinVersion*, or `false` otherwise.

Remarks

Only Internet Explorer components can be detected by this method. If a component identifier of a third-party component is specified, the method returns `false`.

Example

The following example shows how to check whether the Microsoft virtual machine is available.

```
<HTML xmlns:IE>
<HEAD>
<STYLE>
@media all {
      IE\:clientCaps {behavior:url(#default#clientcaps)}
}
```

```
</STYLE>
</HEAD>

<BODY>
<IE:clientCaps ID="oClientCaps" />

<SCRIPT>
    bMSvmAvailable = oClientCaps.isComponentInstalled("{08B0E5C0-4FCB-11CF-AAA5-
00401C608500}",
    "ComponentID");
</SCRIPT>

 :
</BODY>
```

To see this code in action, refer to the Web Workshop CD-ROM.

Applies To

 WIN32   UNIX

clientCaps

isHomePage Method

Returns a Boolean when comparing a URL to the client's home page.

Syntax

bQueryHome = *oHomePage*.isHomePage(*sPageURL*)

Parameters

sPageURL   Required. Path and/or file name to compare against a client's specified home page.

Return Value

Boolean   Returns true if the client's Web page is the same as the provided argument or false otherwise..

Remarks

The **isHomePage** method returns false if the argument and a user's home page are the same, but the document calling the method is on a different domain than the user's home page.

Example

The following example shows how to use the **isHomePage** method to check if a user's home page is the same as a provided URL.

```
<HTML XMLNS:IE>
<HEAD>
<STYLE>
@media all {
    IE\:HOMEPAGE {behavior:url(#default#homepage)}
}
</STYLE>
<SCRIPT>
function fnVerify(){
    sQueryHome = oHomePage.isHomePage(oHomeHref.value);
    alert(sQueryHome);
    event.returnValue = false;
}
</SCRIPT>
</HEAD>
<BODY>
<IE:HOMEPAGE ID="oHomePage" />
<INPUT TYPE=text ID=oHomeHref VALUE="http://www.microsoft.com">
<INPUT TYPE=button VALUE="Verify" onclick="fnVerify()">
</BODY>
</HTML>
```

To see this code in action, refer to the Web Workshop CD-ROM.

Applies To

 WIN32   UNIX

homePage

load Method

Loads an object participating in **userData** persistence from a UserData store.

Syntax

oPersistObject.load(*sStoreName*)

Parameters

sStoreName Required. Arbitrary name assigned to a persistent object within a UserData store.

Return Value

No return value.

Remarks

The **load** method reads information from a UserData store. You can determine access to an UserData store by specifying a path within the immediate directory tree between the Web root and the current folder. For example, if the UserData store is saved in the /private/ folder, a Web page located in the /public/ folder cannot access the UserData store.

This method requires an object participating in **userData** persistence, where the object has an **ID** and a class name equal to the persistence behavior.

Example

The following example shows how to use the **load** method to read information about an object participating in **userData** persistence saved in a UserData store.

```
<HEAD>

<STYLE>
    .userData {behavior:url(#default#userdata);}
</STYLE>

<SCRIPT>
    function fnLoad(){
        oPersistInput.load("oDataStore");
        oPersistInput.value=oPersistInput.getAttribute("sPersistAttr");
    }
    function fnSave(){
        oPersistInput.setAttribute("sPersistAttr",oPersistInput.value);
        oPersistInput.save("oDataStore");
    }
</SCRIPT>
</HEAD>

<BODY >
<INPUT type=text class=userData id=oPersistInput>
<INPUT type=button value="Load Attribute" onclick="fnLoad()">
<INPUT type=button value="Save Attribute" onclick="fnSave()">
</BODY>
```

To see this code in action, refer to the Web Workshop CD-ROM.

Applies To

 WIN32   UNIX

userData

navigate Method

Navigates the window to the specified location and displays the contents in folder view.

Syntax

oDAVObject.navigate(*sHTTP*)

Parameters

sHTTP Required. Any valid HTTP address.

Return Value

No return value.

Remarks

The **navigate** method is a shortcut whose function is identical to that of the **navigateFrame** method with _self as the target value.

Applies To

 WIN32   UNIX

httpFolder

navigateFrame Method

Navigates the window or frame to the specified location and displays the contents in folder view.

Syntax

oDAVObject.navigateFrame(*sHTTP*, *sTarget*)

Parameters

sHTTP   Required. Any valid HTTP address.

sTarget   Required. Name of a frame: _self for the current window, or _top for a new window.

Return Value

No return value.

Remarks

This method requires an object with the **httpFolder** behavior.

Applies To

WIN32	UNIX

httpFolder

navigateHomePage Method

Navigates the browser to a user's home page.

Syntax

oHomePage.navigateHomePage()

Return Value

No return value.

Example

The following example uses the **navigateHomePage** method to load a user's home page. Portions of the **HEAD** block, highlighted as bold text in the example below, are necessary for the behavior to work correctly.

```
<HTML XMLNS:IE>
<HEAD>
<STYLE>
@media all {
    IE\:HOMEPAGE {behavior:url(#default#homepage)}
}
</STYLE>

<SCRIPT>
function fnGo(){
    oHomePage.navigateHomePage();
    event.returnValue=false;
}
</SCRIPT>
</HEAD>
<BODY>
<IE:HOMEPAGE ID="oHomePage" />
<INPUT TYPE=button VALUE="Navigate" onclick="fnGo()">
</BODY>
</HTML>
```

To see this code in action, refer to the Web Workshop CD-ROM.

Applies To

 WIN32   UNIX

homePage

pause Method

Pauses the timeline on the HTML document.

Syntax

body.pause()

Return Value

No return value.

Remarks

This method can be used only on behaviors associated with the HTML **BODY** element. When this method is invoked, the **onpause** event occurs.

Applies To

 WIN32

animation, audio, img, media, par, seq, time, video

removeAttribute Method

Removes the given attribute from the object.

Syntax

oPersistObject.removeAttribute(*sAttrName*)

Parameters

sAttrName   Required. Name of the persistent attribute.

Return Value

No return value.

Remarks

The *sAttrName* value is not case sensitive.

This method requires an object participating in persistence, where that object has a class name equal to the desired persistence behavior. An **ID** is required for the **userData** and **saveSnapshot** behaviors, and recommended for the **saveHistory** and **saveFavorite** behaviors.

The **removeAttribute** method for behaviors overrides the DHTML **removeAttribute** method.

Example

The following example uses the **removeAttribute** method to remove an attribute on an object participating in **userData** persistence.

```
<HEAD>

<STYLE>
   .userData {behavior:url(#default#userdata);}
</STYLE>

<SCRIPT>
   function fnGet(){
      oPersistInput.load("oDataStore");
      oPersistInput.value=oPersistInput.getAttribute("sPersistAttr");
   }
   function fnSet(){
      oPersistInput.setAttribute("sPersistAttr",oPersistInput.value);
      oPersistInput.save("oDataStore");
   }
   function fnRem(){
      oPersistInput.removeAttribute("sPersistAttr");
      oPersistInput.save("oDataStore");
   }
</SCRIPT>
</HEAD>

<BODY >
<INPUT type=text class=userData id=oPersistInput>
<INPUT type=button value="Get Attribute" onclick="fnGet()">
<INPUT type=button value="Set Attribute" onclick="fnSet()">
<INPUT type=button value="Remove Attribute" onclick="fnRem()">
</BODY>
```

To see this code in action, refer to the Web Workshop CD-ROM.

Applies To

 WIN32   UNIX

saveFavorite, saveHistory, userData

removeDABehavior Method

Removes a behavior previously added with the **addDABehavior** method.

Syntax

object.removeDABehavior(*lID*)

Parameters

lID   Required. Identifier of the DirectAnimation behavior (DABehavior) to be removed. This value is obtained from a previous **addDABehavior** call.

Return Value

No return value.

Remarks

For further information about DirectAnimation, see the DirectAnimation SDK .

Applies To

 WIN32

anim

resume Method

Resumes a paused timeline on the HTML document.

Syntax

body.resume()

Return Value

No return value.

Remarks

This method can be used only on behaviors associated with the HTML **BODY** element. When this method is invoked, the **onresume** event occurs.

Applies To

 WIN32

animation, audio, img, media, par, seq, time, video

save Method

Saves an object participating in **userData** persistence to a UserData store.

Syntax

oPersistObject.save(*sStoreName*)

Parameters

sStoreName Required. Arbitrary name assigned to a persistent object within an
UserData store.

Return Value

No return value.

Remarks

The **save** method writes information into a UserData store. You can determine access
to a UserData store by specifying a path within the immediate directory tree between
the Web root and the current folder. For example, if the UserData store is saved in the
/private/ folder, a Web page located in the /public/ folder cannot access the UserData
store.

This method requires an object participating in **userData** persistence, where that
object has an **ID** and a class name equal to the desired persistence behavior.

Example

The following example shows how to use the save method to save an object
participating in userData persistence to a UserData store.

```
<HEAD>

<STYLE>
   .userData {behavior:url(#default#userdata);}
</STYLE>

<SCRIPT>
   function fnLoad(){
      oPersistInput.load("oDataStore");
      oPersistInput.value=oPersistInput.getAttribute("sPersistAttr");
   }
   function fnSave(){
      oPersistInput.setAttribute("sPersistAttr",oPersistInput.value);
      oPersistInput.save("oDataStore");
   }
</SCRIPT>
</HEAD>
```

```
<BODY >
<INPUT type=text class=userData id=oPersistInput>
<INPUT type=button value="Load Attribute" onclick="fnLoad()">
<INPUT type=button value="Save Attribute" onclick="fnSave()">
</BODY>
```

To see this code in action, refer to the Web Workshop CD-ROM.

Applies To

 WIN32   UNIX

userData

setAttribute Method

Sets the value of the specified attribute. If the attribute is not already present, the method adds the attribute to the object and sets the value.

Syntax

oPersistObject.setAttribute(*sAttrName*, *vAttrValue*)

Parameters

sAttrName   Required. Name of the persistent attribute.

vAttrValue   Required. Value of the persistent attribute.

Return Value

No return value.

Remarks

The *sAttrName* value is not case sensitive.

This method requires an object participating in persistence, where that object has a class name equal to the desired persistence behavior. An **ID** is required for the **userData** and **saveSnapshot** behaviors, and recommended for the **saveHistory** and **saveFavorite** behaviors.

The **setAttribute** method for behaviors overrides the DHTML **setAttribute** method.

Example

The following example uses the **setAttribute** method to set an attribute on an object participating in **userData** persistence.

```html
<HEAD>

<STYLE>
    .userData {behavior:url(#default#userdata);}
</STYLE>

<SCRIPT>
    function fnGet(){
        oPersistInput.load("oDataStore");
        oPersistInput.value=oPersistInput.getAttribute("sPersistAttr");
    }
    function fnSet(){
        oPersistInput.setAttribute("sPersistAttr",oPersistInput.value);
        oPersistInput.save("oDataStore");
    }
    function fnRem(){
        oPersistInput.removeAttribute("sPersistAttr");
        oPersistInput.save("oDataStore");
    }
</SCRIPT>
</HEAD>

<BODY >
<INPUT type=text class=userData id=oPersistInput>
<INPUT type=button value="Get Attribute" onclick="fnGet()">
<INPUT type=button value="Set Attribute" onclick="fnSet()">
<INPUT type=button value="Remove Attribute" onclick="fnRem()">
</BODY>
```

To see this code in action, refer to the Web Workshop CD-ROM.

Applies To

 WIN32   UNIX

saveFavorite, saveHistory, userData

setHomePage Method

Sets a user's homepage to the specified value.

Syntax

oHomePage.setHomePage(*sPageURL*)

Parameters

sPageURL   Required. String specifying a path and/or file name.

Return Value

No return value.

Remarks

The **setHomePage** method prompts the user to confirm the new home page value before setting it on the browser.

Example

The following example shows how to use the **setHomePage** method to set a user's home page. Portions of the **HEAD** block, highlighted as bold text in the example below, are necessary for the behavior to work correctly.

```
<HTML XMLNS:IE>
<HEAD>
<STYLE>
@media all {
    IE\:HOMEPAGE {behavior:url(#default#homepage)}
}
</STYLE>

<SCRIPT>
function fnSet(){
    oHomePage.setHomePage(oHomeHref.value);
    event.returnValue = false;
}
</SCRIPT>
</HEAD>
<BODY>
<IE:HOMEPAGE ID="oHomePage" />
<INPUT TYPE=text ID=oHomeHref VALUE="http://www.microsoft.com">
<INPUT TYPE=button VALUE="Set" onclick="fnSet()">
</BODY>
</HTML>
```

To see this code in action, refer to the Web Workshop CD-ROM.

Applies To

 WIN32   UNIX

homePage

startDownload Method

Downloads the specified file.

Syntax

oDownload.startDownload (*sUrl, fpCallback*)

Parameters

sUrl   Required. Location of the file to download.

fpCallback Required. Function pointer specifying the code to be executed when download is complete.

Return Value

No return value.

Remarks

The callback function pointer takes a single parameter. When a file is downloaded successfully, the file contents are passed as the parameter and are accessible in script.

The **startDownload** method returns only the content of text documents. If a different document format is downloaded, the format is returned, but the file content is not.

The following sample code shows a callback function.

```
// The callback function accepts one parameter.
function fnCallBack(vData){
   /* vData stores the downloaded file content.
      The content can be split into an array,
      written to another file, or processed in a form.
   */
   var aData=vData.split("\n");
}
```

Example

The following example shows how to start downloading a file using the **startDownload** method when the user clicks a link, and to notify the specified callback function, onDownloadDone, when the download is complete.

```
<HTML XMLNS:MSIE >

<MSIE:DOWNLOAD ID="oDownload" STYLE="behavior:url(#default#download)" />

<SCRIPT>
    function onDownloadDone(s) { alert (s); }
</SCRIPT>

<P>Click <A HREF="javascript:oDownload.startDownload('download.htm',
onDownloadDone)">here</A> to download this page.
```

To see this code in action, refer to the Web Workshop CD-ROM.

Applies To

 WIN32   UNIX

DOWNLOAD

ACCELERATE Attribute | accelerate Property

Sets or retrieves a value that applies an acceleration to the element's timeline.

Syntax

HTML   *<ELEMENT* STYLE="behavior:url(#default#time);"
          *prefix:***ACCELERATE** = *iPercent...* >

Scripting   *object.***accelerate** [= *iPercent*]

Possible Values

iPercent   Integer between 0 and 100 that represents the percentage of the local timeline over which the acceleration is applied. The local timeline refers to the timeline associated with a particular HTML element (such as a **DIV** or **SPAN**), rather than the global timeline associated with the entire document.

prefix   Prefix used to associate the attribute with an XML namespace. A prefix of t must be used for the experimental implementation of HTML+TIME.

The property is read/write with a default value of 0. This property cannot be modified in script after the **onload** event is fired on the document body.

Remarks

If the **REPEAT** or **REPEATDUR** attribute is set on an element, the acceleration occurs each time the element repeats.

The **ACCELERATE** attribute is especially well suited to animation content and behaviors. Setting the **ACCELERATE** attribute to a nonzero value does not affect the duration of the timeline in any way, but it might change the effective play speed of the local timeline. The sum of the values for the **ACCELERATE** and **DECELERATE** attributes must not exceed 100. This attribute is also commonly known as "ease-in" in some systems.

Applies To

 WIN32

animation, audio, img, media, par, seq, time, video

AUTOREVERSE Attribute | autoReverse Property

Sets or retrieves whether the timeline on an element immediately begins playing in reverse after it finishes playing in the forward direction.

Syntax

HTML   *<ELEMENT* STYLE="behavior:url(#default#time);"
           *prefix:***AUTOREVERSE** = true | false... >

Scripting *object*.**autoReverse** [= *bReverse*]

Possible Values

true   Timeline plays in the forward direction until it completes, then immediately plays in the reverse direction.

false   Timeline does not play in the reverse direction after it finishes playing in the forward direction.

prefix   Prefix used to associate the attribute with an XML namespace. A prefix of t must be used for the experimental implementation of HTML+TIME.

The property is read/write with a default value of false. This property cannot be modified in script after the **onload** event is fired on the document body.

Remarks

On some systems, this attribute is referred to as "Play forward, then backward."

Applies To

 WIN32

animation, audio, img, media, par, seq, time, video

availHeight Property

Retrieves the height of the working area of the system's screen, excluding the Windows taskbar.

Syntax

HTML   N/A

Scripting [*iHeight* =] *oClientCaps*.**availHeight**

Possible Values

iHeight   Integer specifying the available screen height, in pixels.

The property is read-only with no default value.

Example

The following example shows how to retrieve the **availHeight** property exposed by the **clientCaps** behavior.

```
<HTML xmlns:IE>
<HEAD>
<STYLE>
@media all {
    IE\:clientCaps {behavior:url(#default#clientcaps_)}
}
</STYLE>
<SCRIPT>
    alert ("availHeight = " + oClientCaps.availHeight);
</SCRIPT>
</HEAD>

<BODY>
    <IE:clientCaps ID="oClientCaps" />
</BODY>
</HTML>
```

To see this code in action, refer to the Web Workshop CD-ROM.

Applies To

 WIN32   UNIX

clientCaps

availWidth Property

Retrieves the width of the working area of the system's screen, excluding the Windows taskbar.

Syntax

HTML   N/A

Scripting [*iWidth* =] *oClientCaps*.**availWidth**

Possible Values

iWidth   Integer specifying the available screen width, in pixels.

The property is read-only with no default value.

Example

The following example shows how to retrieve the **availWidth** property exposed by the **clientCaps** behavior.

```
<HTML xmlns:IE>
<HEAD>
<STYLE>
@media all {
    IE\:clientCaps {behavior:url(#default#clientcaps)}
}
</STYLE>
<SCRIPT>
    alert ("availWidth = " + oClientCaps.availWidth);
</SCRIPT>
</HEAD>

<BODY>
    <IE:clientCaps ID="oClientCaps" />
</BODY>
</HTML>
```

To see this code in action, refer to the Web Workshop CD-ROM.

Applies To

 WIN32   UNIX

clientCaps

BEGIN Attribute | begin Property

Sets or retrieves the delay time before the timeline begins playing on the element.

Syntax

HTML   *<ELEMENT* STYLE=`"behavior:url(#default#time);"`
*prefix:***BEGIN** = *sTime... >*

Scripting   *object.***begin** [= *sTime*]

Possible Values

sTime   String specifying the time delay before the element becomes active on
the timeline. This is an offset from the time the page is loaded. The time
must be specified as described in "Time Formats" in Appendix C.

prefix   Prefix used to associate the attribute with an XML namespace. A prefix
of t must be used for the experimental implementation of
HTML+TIME.

The property is read/write with a default value of 0. This property cannot be modified
in script after the **onload** event is fired on the document body.

Example

The following example shows how to make text appear and disappear over time.

```
<!DOCTYPE HTML PUBLIC "-//W3C//DTD W3 HTML//EN">
<HTML>
<HEAD>
<XML:NAMESPACE PREFIX="t"/>
<STYLE>
.time         { behavior: url(#default#time);}
</STYLE>
</HEAD>
<BODY BGCOLOR="white">
<SPAN CLASS=time STYLE="COLOR:Red;" t:BEGIN="0" t:DUR="3"
    t:TIMEACTION="display">
    <H3>Paragraph #1</H3>
    <P>This is paragraph number one. It appears for three seconds immediately
    after the page is loaded.</P>
</SPAN>
```

```
<SPAN CLASS=time STYLE="COLOR:Blue;" t:BEGIN="4" t:DUR="4"
    t:TIMEACTION="display">
    <H3>Paragraph 2</H3>
    <P>This is paragraph number two. It appears one second after the first
    paragraph disappears, and remains displayed for four seconds.</P>
</SPAN>
<H1 CLASS=time t:BEGIN="8" t:DUR="indefinite" t:TIMEACTION="display">
    The End.
</H1>
</BODY>
</HTML>
```

To see this code in action, refer to the Web Workshop CD-ROM.

Applies To

 WIN32

animation, audio, img, media, par, seq, time, video

BEGINAFTER Attribute | beginAfter Property

Sets or retrieves a value indicating that the timeline of an element starts when the referenced element ends.

Syntax

HTML   *<ELEMENT* STYLE="behavior:url(#default#time);"
             *prefix:***BEGINAFTER** = *sID...* >

Scripting   *object.***beginAfter** [= *sID*]

Possible Values

sID   String specifying the unique ID of another timed element within the
               current time scope. The timeline begins on the current element when the
               referenced element ends. For more information about time scope, see the
               Remarks section below.

prefix   Prefix used to associate the attribute with an XML namespace. A prefix of
               t must be used for the experimental implementation of HTML+TIME.

The property is read/write with no default value. This property cannot be modified in script after the **onload** event is fired on the document body.

Remarks

This attribute supports relative sequential timing. You can offset the start time by specifying a nonzero value for the **BEGIN** attribute on the element. This indicates that the timeline should start a specified amount of time after the timeline on the referenced element ends. If the referenced element has an indefinite duration, the timeline on the current element does not start. This attribute cannot be used on the same element as the **BEGINEVENT** or **BEGINWITH** attribute.

The current time scope is defined by the closest parent time container created with the **TIMELINE** attribute or the **PAR** or **SEQ** element. All timed elements within the same parent time container (time siblings) share the current time scope. If no time containers are explicitly declared, the document root is defined as the parent time container. In this case, all timed elements in the document share the current time scope. To create begin dependencies between elements in different time scopes, use the **BEGINEVENT** attribute instead of the **BEGINAFTER** attribute.

Example

The following example shows how to use the **BEGINAFTER** and **BEGIN** attributes to create a paragraph that appears one second after the first one is displayed.

```
<!DOCTYPE HTML PUBLIC "-//W3C//DTD W3 HTML//EN">
<HTML>
<HEAD>
<XML:NAMESPACE PREFIX="t"/>
<STYLE>
.time           { behavior: url(#default#time);}
</STYLE>
</HEAD>
<BODY BGCOLOR="white">
<SPAN ID="span1" CLASS=time STYLE="COLOR:Red;" t:BEGIN="2" t:DUR="5"
    t:TIMEACTION="display">
    <H3>Paragraph 1</H3>
    <P>This is paragraph number one. It appears 2 seconds after the
    page is loaded and remains displayed for 5 seconds.</P>
</SPAN>
<SPAN CLASS=time STYLE="COLOR:Blue;" t:BEGIN="1" t:BEGINAFTER="span1"
    t:TIMEACTION="display">
    <H3>Paragraph 2</H3>
    <P>This is paragraph number two. It appears one second after the
    first paragraph disappears, and remains displayed indefinitely.</P>
</SPAN>
</BODY>
</HTML>
```

To see this code in action, refer to the Web Workshop CD-ROM.

Applies To

 WIN32

animation, audio, img, media, par, seq, time, video

BEGINEVENT Attribute | beginEvent Property

Sets or retrieves a value that starts the timeline of an element when the referenced event occurs.

Syntax

HTML *<ELEMENT* STYLE="`behavior:url(#default#time);`"
*prefix:***BEGINEVENT** = *sEventName...* >

Scripting *object.***beginEvent** [= *sEventName*]

Possible Values

sEventName String specifying a timing event or an event supported by the DHTML Object Model. Valid values are *object.EventName* or the string "`none`". Examples of event names include `span1.onBegin` and `document.onLoad`.

prefix Prefix used to associate the attribute with an XML namespace. A prefix of t must be used for the experimental implementation of HTML+TIME.

The property is read/write with no default value. This property cannot be modified in script after the **onload** event is fired on the document body.

Remarks

This property supports interactive timing, where element timelines can begin in response to events from users, media players, or the presentation. You can offset the start time by specifying a nonzero value for the **BEGIN** attribute on the element. This indicates that the timeline should start a specified amount of time after the referenced event occurs. If the referenced event doesn't occur, the timeline on the current element does not start. This property cannot be used on the same element as the **BEGINAFTER** or **BEGINWITH** attribute.

You can specify more than one event that starts the timeline on the current element by setting the **BEGINEVENT** attribute to a string containing a list of semicolon-separated events. For example, the following example shows how to make the timeline begin on the heading when either button is pressed:

```
<BUTTON ID="btn1">Button #1</BUTTON>
<BUTTON ID="btn2">Button #2</BUTTON>
    .
    .
    .
<H1 CLASS="time" t:BEGINEVENT="btn1.onclick;btn2.onclick" t:DUR="5">
    My Heading
</H1>
```

Example

The following example shows how to use the **BEGINEVENT** and **BEGIN** attributes to make a paragraph appear one second after the button is pressed.

```
<!DOCTYPE HTML PUBLIC "-//W3C//DTD W3 HTML//EN">
<HTML>
<HEAD>
<XML:NAMESPACE PREFIX="t"/>
<STYLE>
.time            { behavior: url(#default#time);}
</STYLE>
</HEAD>
<BODY BGCOLOR="white">
<P>Click the following button to display a paragraph one second later.
The paragraph remains displayed for five seconds.</P><BR><BR>
<BUTTON ID="button1">Show Paragraph</BUTTON><BR><BR>
<SPAN ID="span1" CLASS=time STYLE="COLOR:Red;"
    t:BEGINEVENT="button1.onclick" t:BEGIN="1" t:DUR="5"
    t:TIMEACTION="display">
    <H3>Paragraph 1</H3>
    <P>This is paragraph number one. It appears one second after
    the button was pressed.</P>
</SPAN>
</BODY>
</HTML>
```

To see this code in action, refer to the Web Workshop CD-ROM.

Applies To

 WIN32

animation, audio, img, media, par, seq, time, video

BEGINWITH Attribute | beginWith Property

Sets or retrieves a value that starts the timeline of an element at the same time as the referenced element.

Syntax

HTML   *<ELEMENT* STYLE="`behavior:url(#default#time);`"
             *prefix:***BEGINWITH** = *sID...* >

Scripting   *object.***beginWith** [= *sID*]

Possible Values

sID   String specifying the unique ID of another element within the current time scope. The timeline on the current element starts when this referenced element starts. For more information about time scope, see Remarks.

prefix   Prefix used to associate the attribute with an XML namespace. A prefix of t must be used for the experimental implementation of HTML+TIME.

The property is read/write with no default value. This property cannot be modified in script after the **onload** event is fired on the document body.

Remarks

This property supports relative timing between elements. You can offset the start time by specifying a nonzero value for the **BEGINWITH** attribute on the element. The timeline should start a specified amount of time after the referenced element starts. This property cannot be used on the same element as the **BEGINAFTER** or **BEGINEVENT** attributes.

The current time scope is defined by the closest parent time container created with the **TIMELINE** attribute or the **PAR** or **SEQ** element. All timed elements within the same parent time container (time siblings) share the current time scope. If no time containers are explicitly declared, the document root is defined as the parent time container. In this case, all timed elements in the document would share the current time scope. If you need to create begin dependencies between elements in different time scopes, use the **BEGINEVENT** attribute instead.

Example

The following example shows how to use the **BEGINWITH** and **BEGIN** attributes to make a paragraph appear two seconds after the first one is displayed.

```
<!DOCTYPE HTML PUBLIC "-//W3C//DTD W3 HTML//EN">
<HTML>
<HEAD>
<XML:NAMESPACE PREFIX="t"/>
```

```
<STYLE>
.time            { behavior: url(#default#time);}
</STYLE>
</HEAD>
<BODY BGCOLOR="white">
<SPAN ID="span1" CLASS=time STYLE="COLOR:Red;" t:BEGIN="2" t:DUR="5"
    t:TIMEACTION="visibility">
    <H3>Paragraph 1</H3>
    <P>This is paragraph number one. It appears two seconds after
    the page is loaded and remains displayed for five seconds.</P>
</SPAN>
<SPAN ID="span2" CLASS=time STYLE="COLOR:Blue;" t:BEGINWITH="span1"
    t:BEGIN="2" t:TIMEACTION="display">
    <H3>Paragraph 2</H3>
    <P>This is paragraph number two. It appears two seconds after
    the first paragraph appears, and remains displayed indefinitely.</P>
</SPAN>
</BODY>
</HTML>
```

To see this code in action, refer to the Web Workshop CD-ROM.

Applies To

 WIN32

animation, audio, img, media, par, seq, time, video

bufferDepth Property

Specifies the number of bits per pixel used for colors on the off-screen bitmap buffer.

Syntax

HTML   N/A

Scripting   [*iBitsPerPixel* =] *oClientCaps*.**bufferDepth**

Possible Values

0	Integer specifying no explicit buffering. The **colorDepth** property is set to the screen depth.
-1	Integer specifying buffering at the screen depth. The **colorDepth** property is set to the screen depth.
1, 4, 8, 15, 16, 24, 32	Integer specifying the number of bits per pixel to use for the off-screen buffer. The **colorDepth** property is also set to this value. The value 15 specifies 16 bits per pixel, in which only 15 bits are used in a 5-5-5 layout of RGB values.

The property is read-only with a default value of 0.

Remarks

Nonsupported values cause **bufferDepth** to be set to -1.

When **bufferDepth** is -1 and the user changes system settings that affect the screen depth, the buffer depth is automatically updated to the new depth. This does not happen if **bufferDepth** is set to a specific value.

Example

The following example shows how to retrieve the **bufferDepth** property exposed by the **clientCaps** behavior.

```
<HTML xmlns:IE>
<HEAD>
<STYLE>
@media all {
        IE\:clientCaps {behavior:url(#default#clientcaps)}
}
</STYLE>
<SCRIPT>
    alert ("bufferDepth = " + oClientCaps.bufferDepth);
</SCRIPT>
</HEAD>

<BODY>
    <IE:clientCaps ID="oClientCaps" />
</BODY>
</HTML>
```

To see this code in action, refer to the Web Workshop CD-ROM.

Applies To

 WIN32   UNIX

clientCaps

CLIPBEGIN Attribute | clipBegin Property

Sets or retrieves the beginning of a sub-clip of a continuous media object.

Syntax

HTML   *<ELEMENT* STYLE="behavior:url(#default#time);"
*prefix:***CLIPBEGIN** = *sTime*... >

Scripting   *object*.**clipBegin** [= *sTime*]

Possible Values

sTime   String specifying the beginning point of a media object as an offset from the start time. The time must be specified as described in "Time Formats" in Appendix C.

prefix   Prefix used to associate the attribute with an XML namespace. A prefix of t must be used for the experimental implementation of HTML+TIME.

The property is read/write with no default value. This property cannot be modified in script after the **onload** event is fired on the document body.

Applies To

 WIN32

animation, audio, img, media, video

CLIPEND Attribute | clipEnd Property

Sets or retrieves the end point of a sub-clip of a continuous media object.

Syntax

HTML   *<ELEMENT* STYLE="behavior:url(#default#time);" *prefix:***CLIPEND** = *sTime...* >

Scripting *object.***clipEnd** [= *sTime*]

Possible Values

sTime   String specifying the end point of a media object as an offset from the start time. The time must be specified as described in "Time Formats" in Appendix C.

prefix   Prefix used to associate the attribute with an XML namespace. A prefix of t must be used for the experimental implementation of HTML+TIME.

The property is read/write with no default value. This property cannot be modified in script after the **onload** event is fired on the document body.

Remarks

If the **CLIPEND** attribute exceeds the duration of the media object, the value is ignored and **CLIPEND** is set equal to the end of the media object.

Applies To

 WIN32

animation, audio, img, media, video

CLOCKSOURCE Attribute | clockSource Property

Sets or retrieves whether all the elements within the local time scope are synchronized with this element's timeline.

Syntax

HTML *<ELEMENT* STYLE="`behavior:url(#default#time);`"
*prefix:***CLOCKSOURCE** = `true` | `false`... >

Scripting *object*.**clockSource** [= *bUseClock*]

Possible Values

`true`	Boolean indicating that the elements within the local time scope are synchronized with the timeline on this element. The local time scope is determined by the **SYNCBEHAVIOR** attribute on the parent element.
`false`	Boolean indicating that the elements within the local time scope are not synchronized with the timeline on this element.
prefix	Prefix used to associate the attribute with an XML namespace. A prefix of `t` must be used for the experimental implementation of HTML+TIME.

The property is read/write with a default value of `false`. This property cannot be modified in script after the **onload** event is fired on the document body.

Remarks

For this release, this property must be used with the **SYNCBEHAVIOR** attribute to ensure synchronization between a designated media object, such as a video file, and other timed elements in the document.

Applies To

 WIN32

animation, audio, img, media, video

colorDepth Property

Retrieves the number of bits per pixel used for colors on the destination device or buffer.

Syntax

HTML   N/A

Scripting   [*iBitsPerPixel* =] *oClientCaps*.**colorDepth**

Possible Values

1, 4, 8, 15, 16, 24, 32	Integer specifying the number of bits per pixel to use for the off-screen buffer. The value 15 specifies 16 bits per pixel, in which only 15 bits are used in a 5-5-5 layout of RGB values.

The property is read-only with no default value.

Remarks

To select an appropriate color to return to the browser, retrieve the property's value through script.

If **bufferDepth** is 0 or -1, **colorDepth** is equal to the bits-per-pixel value for the screen or printer. If **bufferDepth** is nonzero, **colorDepth** is equal to **bufferDepth**.

Example

The following example shows how to retrieve the **colorDepth** property exposed by the **clientCaps** behavior.

```
<HTML xmlns:IE>
<HEAD>
<STYLE>
@media all {
      IE\:clientCaps {behavior:url(#default#clientcaps)}
}
</STYLE>
<SCRIPT>
    alert ("colorDepth = " + oClientCaps.colorDepth);
</SCRIPT>
</HEAD>

<BODY>
    <IE:clientCaps ID="oClientCaps" />
</BODY>
</HTML>
```

To see this code in action, refer to the Web Workshop CD-ROM.

Applies To

 WIN32   UNIX

clientCaps

connectionType Property

Specifies the type of connection in use.

Syntax

HTML   N/A

Scripting [*sConnectionType* =] *oClientCaps*.**connectionType**

Possible Values

"lan"   User is connected through a network.

"modem"   User is connected through a modem.

"offline"   User is working offline.

The property is read-only with no default value.

Example

The following example shows how to retrieve the **connectionType** property exposed by the **clientCaps** behavior.

```
<HTML xmlns:IE>
<HEAD>
<STYLE>
@media all {
      IE\:clientCaps {behavior:url(#default#clientcaps)}
}
</STYLE>
<SCRIPT>
    alert ("connectionType = " + oClientCaps.connectionType);
</SCRIPT>
</HEAD>

<BODY>
    <IE:clientCaps ID="oClientCaps" />
</BODY>
</HTML>
```

To see this code in action, refer to the Web Workshop CD-ROM.

Applies To

 WIN32   UNIX

clientCaps

cookieEnabled Property

Returns whether client-side cookies are enabled in the browser.

Syntax

HTML   N/A

Scripting   [*bEnabled* =] *oClientCaps*.**cookieEnabled**

Possible Values

false	Browser does not support cookies.
true	Browser supports cookies.

The property is read-only with no default value.

Example

The following example shows how to retrieve the **cookieEnabled** property exposed by the **clientCaps** behavior.

```
<HTML xmlns:IE>
<HEAD>
<STYLE>
@media all {
      IE\:clientCaps {behavior:url(#default#clientcaps)}
}
</STYLE>
<SCRIPT>
    alert ("cookieEnabled = " + oClientCaps.cookieEnabled);
</SCRIPT>
</HEAD>

<BODY>
    <IE:clientCaps ID="oClientCaps" />
</BODY>
</HTML>
```

To see this code in action, refer to the Web Workshop CD-ROM.

Applies To

 WIN32   UNIX

clientCaps

cpuClass Property

Retrieves a string specifying the CPU class.

Syntax

HTML   N/A

Scripting [*sCPU* =] *oClientCaps*.**cpuClass**

Possible Values

"x86"   x86 processor.

"Alpha"   Alpha processor.

The property is read-only with no default value.

Example

The following example shows how to retrieve the **cpuClass** property exposed by the **clientCaps** behavior.

```
<HTML xmlns:IE>
<HEAD>
<STYLE>
@media all {
      IE\:clientCaps {behavior:url(#default#clientcaps)}
}
</STYLE>
<SCRIPT>
    alert ("cpuClass = " + oClientCaps.cpuClass);
</SCRIPT>
</HEAD>

<BODY>
    <IE:clientCaps ID="oClientCaps" />
</BODY>
</HTML>
```

To see this code in action, refer to the Web Workshop CD-ROM.

Applies To

 WIN32   UNIX

clientCaps

currTime Property

Retrieves a value indicating the current time along the simple duration, as defined by the element's **DUR** or **END** attribute.

Syntax

HTML   N/A

Scripting   [*sTime* =] *object*.**currTime**

Possible Values

sTime   String specifying the current time on the element's simple duration. The simple duration represents the segment of time from when the element begins playing until it completes one forward cycle of its behavior, excluding repetitions.

The property is read-only with no default value.

Remarks

If the **REPEAT** or **REPEATDUR** attribute is set on an element, the value of the **currTime** property is reset each time the element repeats.

Applies To

 WIN32

time

DECELERATE Attribute | decelerate Property

Sets or retrieves a value that applies a deceleration to the end of a simple duration.

Syntax

HTML   <ELEMENT STYLE="behavior:url(#default#time);"
            prefix:**DECELERATE** = *iPercent*... >

Scripting   *object*.**decelerate** [= *iPercent*]

Possible Values

iPercent   Integer between 0 and 100 that represents the percentage of the local timeline over which the deceleration is applied. The local timeline refers to the timeline associated with a particular HTML element (such as a **DIV** or **SPAN**), rather than the global timeline associated with the entire document.

prefix   Prefix used to associate the attribute with an XML namespace. A prefix of t must be used for the experimental implementation of HTML+TIME.

The property is read/write with a default value of 0. This property cannot be modified in script after the **onload** event is fired on the document body.

Remarks

The simple duration represents the segment of time from when the element begins playing until it completes one forward cycle of its behavior, excluding repetitions. If the **REPEAT** or **REPEATDUR** attribute is set on an element, the deceleration occurs each time the element repeats.

The **DECELERATE** attribute is especially well suited to animation content and behaviors. Setting the **DECELERATE** attribute to a nonzero value does not affect the duration of the timeline in any way, but it might change the effective play speed of the local timeline. The sum of the values for the **ACCELERATE** and **DECELERATE** attributes must not exceed 100. This attribute is also commonly known as "ease-out" in some systems.

Applies To

 WIN32

animation, audio, img, media, par, seq, time, video

DUR Attribute | dur Property

Sets or retrieves a value indicating the amount of time for which the element remains active or displayed.

Syntax

HTML   *<ELEMENT* STYLE="behavior:url(#default#time);" *prefix:***DUR =** "indefinite" | *sTime...* >

Scripting   *object.***dur** [= *sTime*]

Possible Values

indefinite	Value indicating that the timeline remains active for an indefinite amount of time.
sTime	String specifying the amount of time that the element remains active or is displayed. The time must be specified as described in "Time Formats" in Appendix C.
prefix	Prefix used to associate the attribute with an XML namespace. A prefix of t must be used for the experimental implementation of HTML+TIME.

The property is read/write with a default value of indefinite. This property cannot be modified in script after the **onload** event is fired on the document body.

Remarks

The **DUR** attribute represents a value relative to the element's begin time. By contrast, the **END** attribute represents an absolute value along the parent element's timeline starting at 0 seconds. The **DUR** attribute should not be used on the same element as the **END** attribute.

Example

The following example shows how to set lines of text with different **DUR** values.

```
<!DOCTYPE HTML PUBLIC "-//W3C//DTD W3 HTML//EN">
<HTML>
<HEAD>
<XML:NAMESPACE PREFIX="t"/>
<STYLE>
.time            { behavior: url(#default#time);}
</STYLE>
</HEAD>
<BODY BGCOLOR="white">
<SPAN CLASS=time STYLE="COLOR:Red;" t:BEGIN="0" t:DUR="5"
    t:TIMEACTION="visibility">
    <H3>Paragraph 1</H3>
    <P>This is paragraph number one. It is displayed for five
    seconds.</P>
</SPAN>
<SPAN CLASS=time STYLE="COLOR:Blue;" t:BEGIN="0" t:DUR="10"
    t:TIMEACTION="visibility">
    <H3>Paragraph 2</H3>
    <P>This is paragraph number two. It is displayed for ten
    seconds.</P>
</SPAN>
```

```
<SPAN CLASS=time STYLE="COLOR:Green;" t:BEGIN="0" t:DUR="indefinite"
    t:TIMEACTION="visibility">
    <H3>Paragraph 3</H3>
    <P>This is paragraph number three. It remains displayed
    indefinitely.</P>
</SPAN>
</BODY>
</HTML>
```

To see this code in action, refer to the Web Workshop CD-ROM.

Applies To

 WIN32

animation, audio, img, media, par, seq, time, video

END Attribute | end Property

Sets or retrieves a value indicating the end time for the element, or the end of the simple duration when the element is set to `repeat`.

Syntax

HTML   *<ELEMENT* STYLE=`"behavior:url(#default#time);"` *prefix:***END =** `"indefinite"` | *sTime... >*

Scripting *object.***end** [= *sTime*]

Possible Values

`indefinite`	Value indicating that the timeline remains active for an indefinite amount of time.
sTime	String specifying the number of seconds along the timeline at which the element becomes inactive. The time must be specified as described in "Time Formats" in Appendix C.
prefix	Prefix used to associate the attribute with an XML namespace. A prefix of `t` must be used for the experimental implementation of HTML+TIME.

The property is read/write with a default value of `indefinite`. This property cannot be modified in script after the **onload** event is fired on the document body.

Remarks

The **END** attribute represents an absolute value along the parent element's timeline starting at 0 seconds. By contrast, the **DUR** attribute represents a value relative to the element's begin time. The **END** attribute should not be used on the same element as the **DUR** attribute.

Example

The following example shows how to set lines of text with different **END** values.

```
<!DOCTYPE HTML PUBLIC "-//W3C//DTD W3 HTML//EN">
<HTML>
<HEAD>
<XML:NAMESPACE PREFIX="t"/>
<STYLE>
.time            { behavior: url(#default#time);}
</STYLE>
</HEAD>
<BODY BGCOLOR="white">
<SPAN CLASS=time STYLE="COLOR:Red;" t:BEGIN="0" t:END="10"
    t:TIMEACTION="visibility">
    <H3>Paragraph 1</H3>
    <P>This is paragraph number one. It is displayed as soon as
    the page is loaded.</P>
</SPAN>
<SPAN CLASS=time STYLE="COLOR:Blue;" t:BEGIN="3" t:END="10"
    t:TIMEACTION="visibility">
    <H3>Paragraph 2</H3>
    <P>This is paragraph number two. It is displayed three seconds
    after the page is loaded.</P>
</SPAN>
<SPAN CLASS=time STYLE="COLOR:Green;" t:BEGIN="6" t:END="10"
    t:TIMEACTION="visibility">
    <H3>Paragraph 3</H3>
    <P>This is paragraph number three. It is displayed six seconds
    after the page is loaded.</P>
</SPAN>
<P>The preceding paragraphs have different start times, but they
all have an end value of ten. Therefore, all three paragraphs
disappear when the timeline reaches ten seconds.</P>
</BODY>
</HTML>
```

To see this code in action, refer to the Web Workshop CD-ROM.

Applies To

 WIN32

animation, audio, img, media, par, seq, time, video

ENDEVENT Attribute | endEvent Property

Sets or retrieves a value indicating that the timeline of an element ends immediately when the referenced event occurs, regardless of the element's **repeat** count or **repeatDur** property.

Syntax

HTML	*<ELEMENT* STYLE="`behavior:url(#default#time);`" *prefix:***ENDEVENT** = *sEventName... >*
Scripting	*object.***endEvent** [= *sEventName*]

Possible Values

sEventName	String specifying a timing event or an event supported by the DHTML Object Model. Valid values use the format *object.EventName*, or the string "`none`". Examples of event names include `span1.onBegin` and `document.onLoad`.
prefix	Prefix used to associate the attribute with an XML namespace. A prefix of `t` must be used for the experimental implementation of HTML+TIME.

The property is read/write with no default value. This property cannot be modified in script after the **onload** event is fired on the document body.

Remarks

This property supports interactive timing, where element timelines can end in response to events from users, media players, or the presentation itself. If the referenced event doesn't occur, the timeline on the current element does not start. You can override this behavior by specifying a maximum duration for the timeline by using either the **DUR** or **END** attribute on the same element. This behavior is sometimes referred to as "lazy interactive."

Example

The following example shows how to create a paragraph that disappears when the button is clicked.

```
<!DOCTYPE HTML PUBLIC "-//W3C//DTD W3 HTML//EN">
<HTML>
<HEAD>
<XML:NAMESPACE PREFIX="t"/>
<STYLE>
.time          { behavior: url(#default#time);}
</STYLE>
</HEAD>
```

```
<BODY BGCOLOR="white">
<BUTTON ID="button1">Hide Paragraph</BUTTON><BR><BR>
<SPAN ID="span1" CLASS=time STYLE="COLOR:Red;"
    t:ENDEVENT="button1.onclick" t:TIMEACTION="display">
    <H3>Paragraph 1</H3>
    <P>This is paragraph number one. It disappears when the button
    is clicked.</P>
</SPAN>
</BODY>
</HTML>
```

To see this code in action, refer to the Web Workshop CD-ROM.

Applies To

 WIN32

animation, audio, img, media, par, seq, time, video

ENDHOLD Attribute | endHold Property

Sets or retrieves whether an element remains active if its timeline ends before the timeline on its parent element ends.

Syntax

HTML   <*ELEMENT* STYLE="behavior:url(#default#time);"
*prefix:***ENDHOLD** = true | false ... >

Scripting *object*.**endHold** [= *bHold*]

Possible Values

true	Value that indicates the element is frozen at the end of its local timeline. This last "snapshot" of the element is displayed until the end of the element's parent timeline is reached.
false	Value that indicates the element is not held until the end of the parent timeline is reached.
prefix	Prefix used to associate the attribute with an XML namespace. A prefix of t must be used for the experimental implementation of HTML+TIME.

The property is read/write with a default value of false. This property cannot be modified in script after the **onload** event is fired on the document body.

Remarks

This property does not affect the defined duration (**DUR**) of the timeline nor the timeline's defined **END** time. However, the **ENDHOLD** attribute does affect the display of the element between the end of the element's timeline and the end of the parent element's timeline. For example, suppose an element has an end value of 10 seconds and its parent element has an end value of 15 seconds. In this case, the **ENDHOLD** attribute defines whether the element is displayed during the five second interval (seconds 11 through 15) after the timeline has ended.

Applies To

 WIN32
_____

animation, audio, img, media, par, seq, time, video

EVENTRESTART Attribute | eventRestart Property

Sets or retrieves whether the element should restart if a **beginEvent** call occurs while the local timeline is already running.

Syntax

HTML   *<ELEMENT* STYLE="`behavior:url(#default#time);`"
          *prefix:***EVENTRESTART** = `true` | `false`... >

Scripting *object.***eventRestart** [*= bRestart*]

Possible Values

`true`   Value that indicates the timeline immediately restarts every time the referenced event happens.

`false`   Value that indicates the timeline can't be restarted until after it has played through once.

prefix   Prefix used to associate the attribute with an XML namespace. A prefix of `t` must be used for the experimental implementation of HTML+TIME.

The property is read/write with a default value of `true`. This property cannot be modified in script after the **onload** event is fired on the document body.

Applies To

 WIN32

animation, audio, img, media, par, seq, time, video

expires Property

Sets or retrieves the expiration date of data persisted with the **userData** behavior.

Syntax

HTML   N/A

Scripting   *oPersistObject*.**expires** [= *sUTCString*]

Possible Values

sUTCString   String in UTC format specifying when information persisted from an object participating in **userData** persistence expires.

The property is read/write with no default value.

Remarks

The **expires** property is used to designate the amount of time that persisted information is available. Internet Explorer removes the persisted information when the browser checks the date and the designated time has expired.

Example

The following example shows how to use the **expires** property to set the expiration date of persisted data to one minute after the information is persisted.

```
<STYLE>
.userData { behavior: url(#default#userdata)}
</STYLE>

<SCRIPT>
function fnSave(){
    var oTimeNow = new Date(); // Start time
    oTimeNow.setMinutes(oTimeNow.getMinutes() + 1);
    var sExpirationDate = oTimeNow.toLocaleString();

    oPersistDiv.expires = sExpirationDate;
    oPersistDiv.setAttribute("sData",oPersistText.value);
    // Save the persistence data as "sTimeout".
    oPersistDiv.save("sTimeout");
}
</SCRIPT>
```

```
:
<DIV CLASS = "userData" ID=oPersistDiv onsave = "fnSave()" >
<INPUT TYPE=text ID=oPersistText>
```

Applies To

WIN32   UNIX

userData

FOLDER Attribute | folder Property

Specifies a namespace extension, address, or path.

Syntax

HTML   <A **FOLDER** = "*sFolder*" .. >

Scripting *oAnchor*.**folder** [= *sFolder*]

Possible Values

sFolder Valid namespace extension, address, or path.

The property is read/write with no default value.

Remarks

Downlevel browsers that do not support the **FOLDER** attribute navigate to the location specified in the **HREF** attribute. Internet Explorer 5 displays the value of the **FOLDER** attribute in the browser screen instead of the value of the **HREF** attribute.

Example

The following example shows how to use the **FOLDER** attribute to specify a location to open in folder view.

```
<STYLE>
   A {behavior:url(#default#AnchorClick);}
</STYLE>

<!--
    The href points to folder.htm for downlevel browsers;
    the FOLDER attribute points to the local root.
 -->

<A HREF = "folder.htm" FOLDER = "/" >
Open Folder
</A>
```

Applies To

 WIN32   UNIX

anchor

height Property

Retrieves the vertical resolution of the screen.

Syntax

HTML   N/A

Scripting [*iHeight* =] *oClientCaps*.**height**

Possible Values

iHeight   Integer specifying the screen height, in pixels.

The property is read-only with no default value.

Example

The following example shows how to retrieve the **height** property exposed by the **clientCaps** behavior.

```
<HTML xmlns:IE>
<HEAD>
<STYLE>
@media all {
        IE\:clientCaps {behavior:url(#default#clientcaps)}
}
</STYLE>
<SCRIPT>
    alert ("height = " + oClientCaps.height);
</SCRIPT>
</HEAD>

<BODY>
    <IE:clientCaps ID="oClientCaps" />
</BODY>
</HTML>
```

To see this code in action, refer to the Web Workshop CD-ROM.

Applies To

 WIN32   UNIX

clientCaps

image Property

Sets the DirectAnimation image (DAImage) object to be displayed by the **anim:DA** element.

Syntax

Scripting   *object*.**image** [*= oImage*]

Possible Values

oImage   DAImage object to be displayed by the **anim:DA** element.

The property is read/write with no default value.

Example

The following example shows how to display a static DAImage object.

```
<HTML>
<HEAD>
<TITLE>image</TITLE>
<XML:NAMESPACE PREFIX="t"/>
<XML:NAMESPACE PREFIX="anim"/>
<STYLE>
.time       { behavior: url(#default#time); }
anim\:DA    { behavior: url(#default#anim); }
</STYLE>
</HEAD>

<BODY>
<P>The image below is specified using the image property.</P>
<SPAN ID="spanImg" CLASS="time" t:TIMEACTION="visibility" t:BEGIN="3"
t:DUR="5">
</SPAN>
<DIV ALIGN="center">
    <anim:DA ID="da1" STYLE="width:200; height:200; z-index: -1;" />
</DIV>
<BR>
```

```
<SCRIPT LANGUAGE="JScript">
<!--
   // Assign a variable to the DA statics library.
   m = da1.statics;
   // Create the DAImage.
   img1 = m.ImportImage("/workshop/graphics/sun.gif");
   // Specify the DAImage to be displayed by the ANIM:DA tag.
   da1.image = img1;
//-->
</SCRIPT>
</BODY>
</HTML>
```

To see this code in action, refer to the Web Workshop CD-ROM.

Applies To

 WIN32

anim

IMG Attribute | img Property

Sets or retrieves the URL of an alternate image to be displayed if the Multipurpose Internet Mail Extensions (MIME type) is not supported.

Syntax

HTML   *<ELEMENT* STYLE="behavior:url(#default#time);" *prefix:***IMG** = *sURL...* >

Scripting *object.***img** [= *sURL*]

Possible Values

sURL   String specifying the URL of an alternate image to be displayed for this element if the MIME type is not supported on the user's computer.

The property is read/write with no default value. This property cannot be modified in script after the **onload** event is fired on the document body.

Applies To

 WIN32

animation, media, video

javaEnabled Property

Specifies whether the Microsoft virtual machine is enabled.

Syntax

HTML   N/A

Scripting [*bEnabled* =] *oClientCaps*.**javaEnabled**

Possible Values

false   Microsoft virtual machine is not available.

true   Microsoft virtual machine is available.

The property is read-only with no default value.

Example

The following example shows how to retrieve the **javaEnabled** property exposed by the behavior.

```
<HTML xmlns:IE>
<HEAD>
<STYLE>
@media all {
      IE\:clientCaps {behavior:url(#default#clientcaps)}
}
</STYLE>
<SCRIPT>
    alert ("javaEnabled = " + oClientCaps.javaEnabled);
</SCRIPT>
</HEAD>

<BODY>
    <IE:clientCaps ID="oClientCaps" />
</BODY>
</HTML>
```

To see this code in action, refer to the Web Workshop CD-ROM.

Applies To

 WIN32   UNIX

clientCaps

localTime Property

Retrieves a value indicating the current time along the local duration, as defined by the element's **REPEAT** or **REPEATDUR** attribute.

Syntax

HTML   N/A

Scripting [*sTime* =] *object*.**localTime**

Possible Values

sTime   String specifying the current time on the element's local duration. The local duration is defined as the amount of time from when the element begins until it stops, including playing in reverse and all repetitions.

The property is read-only with no default value.

Remarks

If the **AUTOREVERSE** attribute is set to `true` on an element, the **localTime** is effectively doubled. The **localTime** property also includes the element's **REPEAT** or **REPEATDUR** value.

Applies To

 WIN32

time

onOffBehavior Property

Retrieves an object indicating whether the specified DirectAnimation behavior is currently running.

Syntax

Scripting [*oOn* =] *object*.**onOffBehavior**

Possible Values

oOn   DirectAnimation Boolean (DABoolean) object indicating whether the behavior is currently running. If the DABoolean object contains the value `true`, the behavior is currently running. A value of `false` indicates that the behavior is not running.

The property is read-only with no default value.

Remarks

This property allows you to incorporate multimedia elements, such as 2-D and 3-D animated images and sounds, into an HTML page with the **anim:DA** element. The object this property is applied to must be an HTML object with a valid HTML+TIME timeline. Use this property to create custom XML for multimedia elements that are to be synchronized with other elements in the page. This property is not part of the HTML+TIME specification.

Example

The following example shows how to attach a timeline specified with HTML+TIME to an image that is animated with DirectAnimation. The **onOffBehavior** property is used to conditionally display one image while the animation is running, and display a different image while it is stopped.

```
<HTML>
<HEAD>
<TITLE>progressBehavior</TITLE>
<XML:NAMESPACE PREFIX="t"/>
<XML:NAMESPACE PREFIX="anim"/>
<STYLE>
.time           { behavior: url(#default#time);          }
anim\:DA{ behavior: url(#default#anim);         }
</STYLE>
</HEAD>

<BODY>
<P>Initially, an image of the sun is displayed before the
DirectAnimation behavior starts. In five seconds, the image is
replaced with a new image, and it begins "fading out" until it disappears
after five seconds of animation. When the animation stops, the original
image of the sun reappears.</P>
<SPAN ID="spanImg" CLASS="time" t:TIMEACTION="visibility" t:BEGIN="5"
t:DUR="5">
</SPAN>
<DIV ALIGN="center">
    <anim:DA ID="da1" STYLE="width:504; height:126; z-index: -1;"/>
</DIV>
<BR>
<BUTTON onclick="spanImg.beginElement();">Restart</BUTTON>

<SCRIPT LANGUAGE="JScript">
<!--
   // Assign a variable to the DA statics library.
   m = da1.statics;
   // Create the DAImages.
   img1 = m.ImportImage("/workshop/graphics/solarsys.gif");
   img2 = m.ImportImage("/workshop/graphics/sun.gif");
```

```
            // Display image 1 while the behavior is running, and
            // image 2 while it is stopped.
            img3 = m.Cond(spanImg.onOffBehavior, img1, img2)
            // Animate the opacity of the image from 100% to 0%, based on the
            // progress of the time behavior. Use (1 - progress) to get the
            // proper opacity.
            img4 = img3.OpacityAnim(m.Sub(m.DANumber(1),spanImg.progressBehavior));
            // Set the image of the DA Object to be the final image behavior.
            da1.image = img4;
        //-->
        </SCRIPT>
        </BODY>
        </HTML>
```

To see this code in action, refer to the Web Workshop CD-ROM.

Applies To

 WIN32

time

platform Property

Retrieves the platform on which the browser is running.

Syntax

HTML   N/A

Scripting   [*sPlatform* =] *oClientCaps*.**platform**

Possible Values

Win32   Windows 32-bit platform.

Win16   Windows 16-bit platform.

WinCE   Windows CE platform.

The property is read-only with no default value.

Example

The following example shows how to retrieve the **platform** property exposed by the **clientCaps** behavior.

```
<HTML xmlns:IE>
<HEAD>
<STYLE>
@media all {
        IE\:clientCaps {behavior:url(#default#clientcaps)}
}
</STYLE>
<SCRIPT>
    alert ("platform = " + oClientCaps.platform);
</SCRIPT>
</HEAD>

<BODY>
    <IE:clientCaps ID="oClientCaps" />
</BODY>
</HTML>
```

To see this code in action, refer to the Web Workshop CD-ROM.

Applies To

 WIN32   UNIX

clientCaps

PLAYER Attribute | player Property

Sets or retrieves the object to be used to render the media associated with this element.

Syntax

HTML   *<ELEMENT* STYLE="behavior:url(#default#time);"
*prefix:***PLAYER** = *sID*... >

Scripting *object.***player** [= *sID*]

Possible Values

sID   String specifying the class identifier of the object to be used for rendering the element's media. The format is "clsid:*XXXXXXXX-XXXX-XXXX-XXXX-XXXXXXXXXXXX*" for registered ActiveX controls.

prefix   Prefix used to associate the attribute with an XML namespace. A prefix of t must be used for the experimental implementation of HTML+TIME.

The property is read/write with no default value. This property cannot be modified in script after the **onload** event is fired on the document body.

Remarks

This property only works for media playing objects that support HTML+TIME. To support HTML+TIME, a media player must implement the **ITIMEMediaPlayer** interface.

Applies To

 WIN32

animation, audio, img, media, video

playerObject Property

Retrieves the object that plays media files.

Syntax

HTML   N/A

Scripting   [*oPlayer =*] *object*.**playerObject**

Possible Values

oPlayer   Player object used for rendering the element's media. This property provides access to all the properties, methods, and events available on the player object.

The property is read-only with no default value.

Remarks

The object that plays media files is specified with the   attribute.

Example

The example on the Web Workshop CD plays a video clip with the Windows Media Player control. The video clip begins playing five seconds after the page is loaded, and continues playing for 20 seconds. The **playerObject** property is used to access the **mute** property and **AboutBox** method available on the Windows Media Player control.

Applies To

 WIN32

animation, audio, img, media, video

progressBehavior Property

Retrieves an object indicating the progress of the specified DirectAnimation behavior.

Syntax

Scripting [*oProgress* =] *object*.**progressBehavior**

Possible Values

oProgress DirectAnimation number (DANumber) object indicating the progress of the behavior. The DANumber object contains a long floating-point number with a value between 0.0 and 1.0 indicating how much of the behavior has been completed.

The property is read-only with no default value.

Remarks

This property allows you to incorporate multimedia elements, such as 2-D and 3-D animated images and sounds, into an HTML page with the **anim:DA** element. The object that this property is applied to must be an HTML object with a valid HTML+TIME timeline. Use this property to create custom XML for multimedia elements that are to be synchronized with other elements in the page. This property is not part of the HTML+TIME specification.

Example

The following example attaches a timeline specified with HTML+TIME to an image that is animated with DirectAnimation. The **progressBehavior** property is used to animate the opacity of the image.

```
<HTML>
<HEAD>
<TITLE>progressBehavior</TITLE>
<XML:NAMESPACE PREFIX="t"/>
<XML:NAMESPACE PREFIX="anim"/>
<STYLE>
.time            { behavior: url(#default#time); }
anim\:DA{ behavior: url(#default#anim); }
</STYLE>
</HEAD>

<BODY>
<P>In two seconds, the image begins "fading out" until
it disappears after five seconds of animation. This process
repeats three times.</P>
<SPAN ID="spanImg" CLASS="time" t:TIMEACTION="visibility" t:BEGIN="2"
t:DUR="5" t:REPEAT="3">
</SPAN>
```

```
<DIV ALIGN="center">
   <anim:DA ID="da1" STYLE="width:504; height:126; z-index: -1;"/>
</DIV>
<BR>
<BUTTON onclick="spanImg.beginElement();">Restart</BUTTON>

<SCRIPT LANGUAGE="JScript">
<!--
   // Assign a variable to the DA statics library.
   m = da1.statics;
   // Create a DAImage.
   img1 = m.ImportImage("/workshop/graphics/solarsys.gif");
   // Animate the opacity of the image from 100% to 0%, based
   // on the progress of the time behavior. Use (1 - progress)
   // to get the proper opacity.
   img2 = img1.OpacityAnim(m.Sub(m.DANumber(1),spanImg.progressBehavior));
   // Set the image do be displayed.
   da1.image = img2;
//-->
</SCRIPT>
</BODY>
</HTML>
```

To see this code in action, refer to the Web Workshop CD-ROM.

Applies To

WIN32

time

REPEAT Attribute | repeat Property

Sets or retrieves the number of times an element's timeline repeats.

Syntax

HTML	*<ELEMENT* STYLE="behavior:url(#default#time);" *prefix:***REPEAT** = "indefinite"	*fRepetitions...* >
Scripting	*object*.**repeat** [= *fRepetitions*]

Possible Values

indefinite	Timeline repeats indefinitely.
fRepetitions	Floating-point number greater than 0 that indicates how many times the timeline is repeated.
prefix	Prefix used to associate the attribute with an XML namespace. A prefix of t must be used for the experimental implementation of HTML+TIME.

The property is read/write with a default value of 1. This property cannot be modified in script after the **onload** event is fired on the document body.

Remarks

Each repeat iteration lasts for the duration defined by the **DUR** or **END** attribute. The **REPEAT** attribute has no effect if the duration is not defined or it is indefinite. This attribute should not be used on the same element as the **REPEATDUR** attribute. Typically, **REPEAT** is set only on elements that are time containers, such as the **PAR** or **SEQ** element, or elements containing the **TIMELINE** attribute. If the **REPEAT** attribute is set on an element that is not a time container, it increases the duration by multiplying the duration by the repeat count.

Example

The following example shows how to display a series of three different paragraphs over time using the **REPEAT** attribute.

```
<!DOCTYPE HTML PUBLIC "-//W3C//DTD W3 HTML//EN">
<HTML>
<HEAD>
<XML:NAMESPACE PREFIX="t"/>
<STYLE>
.time              { behavior: url(#default#time);}
</STYLE>
</HEAD>
<BODY BGCOLOR="white">
<P>Three paragraphs are shown for three seconds each, on
three-second intervals, and the entire process is repeated
three times.<P>
<SPAN ID="parent" CLASS=time t:BEGIN="0" t:DUR="9" t:TIMELINE="par"
t:REPEAT="3" t:TIMEACTION="display">
    <SPAN ID="span1" CLASS=time STYLE="COLOR:Red;" t:BEGIN="0"
    t:DUR="3" t:TIMEACTION="visibility">
        <H3>Paragraph 1</H3>
        <P>This is paragraph number one.</P>
    </SPAN>
    <SPAN ID="span2" CLASS=time STYLE="COLOR:Blue;" t:BEGIN="3"
    t:DUR="3" t:TIMEACTION="visibility">
        <H3>Paragraph 2</H3>
        <P>This is paragraph number two.</P>
    </SPAN>
    <SPAN ID="span3" CLASS=time STYLE="COLOR:Green;" t:BEGIN="6"
    t:DUR="3" t:TIMEACTION="visibility">
        <H3>Paragraph 3</H3>
        <P>This is paragraph number three.</P>
    </SPAN>
</SPAN>
</BODY>
</HTML>
```

To see this code in action, refer to the Web Workshop CD-ROM.

Applies To

 WIN32

animation, audio, img, media, par, seq, time, video

REPEATDUR Attribute | repeatDur Property

Specifies the number of seconds an element's timeline repeats.

Syntax

HTML   *<ELEMENT* STYLE="behavior:url(#default#time);"
*prefix:***REPEATDUR** = "indefinite" | *sTime* ... >

Scripting   *object.***repeatDur** [= *sTime*]

Possible Values

indefinite   Value indicating the timeline repeats for an indefinite amount of time.

sTime   String specifying the total amount of time to repeat an element's timeline. The time must be specified as described in "Time Formats" in Appendix C.

prefix   Prefix used to associate the attribute with an XML namespace. A prefix of t must be used for the experimental implementation of HTML+TIME.

The property is read/write with no default value. This property cannot be modified in script after the **onload** event is fired on the document body.

Remarks

Each repeat iteration lasts for the duration defined by the **DUR** or **END** attribute. The **REPEATDUR** attribute has no effect if the duration is not defined or it is indefinite. This attribute should not be used on the same element as the **REPEAT** attribute. Typically, **REPEATDUR** is set only on elements that are time containers, such as the **PAR** or **SEQ** element, or elements containing the **TIMELINE** attribute. If the **REPEATDUR** attribute is set on an element that is not a time container, it sets the element's duration to the **REPEATDUR** value. This property is useful for coordinating the timing of an element with a media element that has a fractional duration, such as an audio file with a length of 3.45 seconds.

Applies To

 WIN32

animation, audio, img, media, par, seq, time, video

sound Property

Sets or retrieves the DirectAnimation sound (DASound) object to be played by the **anim:DA** element.

Syntax

Scripting *object*.**sound** [= *oSound*]

Possible Values

oSound   DASound object to be played by the **anim:DA** element.

The property is read/write with no default value.

Applies To

 WIN32

anim

SRC Attribute | src Property

Sets or retrieves the source URL of the media.

Syntax

HTML   *<ELEMENT* STYLE="behavior:url(#default#time);" *prefix:***SRC** = *sURL* ... >

Scripting *object*.**src** [= *sURL*]

Possible Values

sURL   String specifying the URL of the media.

prefix   Prefix used to associate the attribute with an XML namespace. A prefix of t must be used for the experimental implementation of HTML+TIME.

The property is read/write with no default value. This property cannot be modified in script after the **onload** event is fired on the document body.

Applies To

 WIN32

animation, audio, img, media, video

statics Property

Retrieves an object containing the Direct Animation statics (DAStatics) class library.

Syntax

Scripting [*oLibrary* =] *object*.**statics**

Possible Values

oLibrary DAStatics object containing a variety of functions and properties available through DirectAnimation.

The property is read-only with no default value.

Remarks

The following example shows how to assign a scripting variable to the value of this property to enable access to all DirectAnimation functions and properties.

```
<anim:da ID="da1"/>
  .
  .
  .
<SCRIPT>
m = da1.statics;
var x = m.property
</SCRIPT>
```

Applies To

 WIN32

anim

SYNCBEHAVIOR Attribute | syncBehavior Property

Sets or retrieves the synchronization rules for the element's timeline.

Syntax

HTML   *<ELEMENT* STYLE="behavior:url(#default#time);"
         *prefix:***SYNCBEHAVIOR** = "canSlip" | "locked" ... >

Scripting   *object*.**syncBehavior** [= *sRule*]

Possible Values

canSlip String specifying that the associated element can slip on the parent
         element's timeline. This setting allows an HTML page to have enough
         flexibility to handle network problems.

locked   String specifying that this element must stay in synchronization with the
         parent element's timeline. For example, a parent element's timeline does
         not progress until the child element's media is ready to be played.

prefix   Prefix used to associate the attribute with an XML namespace. A prefix of
         t must be used for the experimental implementation of HTML+TIME.

The property is read/write with a default value of canSlip. This property cannot be
modified in script after the **onload** event is fired on the document body.

Remarks

This property must be used with the **CLOCKSOURCE** attribute to determine the
scope of which elements are to be synchronized. If a media file isn't ready when the
timeline begins, the canSlip setting enables the parent timeline to continue without
interruption. Then, the timeline on the element associated with the media begins when
the file is loaded. In contrast, if the **SYNCBEHAVIOR** attribute is locked, the parent
timeline must pause and wait for the element to catch up. If the parent element's
timeline is also locked, the scope of the synchronization behavior is extended to
include all the time children of the parent's parent element. If all timelines are locked,
the entire document pauses when an element cannot maintain its synchronization.

Applies To

 WIN32

animation, audio, img, media, par, seq, time, video

syncTolerance Property

Retrieves the time variance allowed on a timeline with locked synchronization.

Syntax

HTML   N/A

Scripting   [*sTime=*] *object*.**syncTolerance**

Possible Values

sTime   String specifying the amount of time variance, in seconds, allowed
            between synchronized elements.

The property is read-only with a default value of .2 seconds.

Remarks

This property is valid only for time containers with locked timelines, as defined using
the **SYNCBEHAVIOR** and **CLOCKSOURCE** attributes. Once the synchronization
of locked elements is off by more than the **syncTolerance** value, the elements are
resynchronized and the **onresync** event is fired.

Applies To

 WIN32

animation, audio, img, media, par, seq, time, video

systemLanguage Property

Retrieves the default language that the system is running.

Syntax

HTML   N/A

Scripting   [*sLanguage* =] *oClientCaps*.**systemLanguage**

Possible Values

sLanguage   String specifying any of the language code values. For more information about the codes, see the Web Workshop CD.

The property is read-only with a system-specific default value.

Example

The following example shows how to retrieve the **systemLanguage** property exposed by the **clientCaps** behavior.

```
<HTML xmlns:IE>
<HEAD>
<STYLE>
@media all {
        IE\:clientCaps {behavior:url(#default#clientcaps)}
}
</STYLE>
<SCRIPT>
    alert ("systemLanguage = " + oClientCaps.systemLanguage);
</SCRIPT>
</HEAD>

<BODY>
    <IE:clientCaps ID="oClientCaps" />
</BODY>
</HTML>
```

To see this code in action, refer to the Web Workshop CD-ROM.

Applies To

 WIN32   UNIX

clientCaps

TARGET Attribute | target Property

Sets or retrieves the name of a window or frame that is the target for navigation.

Syntax

HTML   *<ELEMENT* **TARGET** = ["_self" | "_top" | "*sTarget*"]... >

Scripting *object*.**target** [= "*sTarget*"]

Possible Values

sTarget   String specifying the name of the frame or window.

_self   String specifying that the linked document loads into the same window as the link.

_top   String specifying that the linked document loads into the topmost window.

The property is read/write, has no default value, and is case insensitive.

Remarks

The **TARGET** attribute is exposed to objects participating in the **anchor** behavior.

Example

The following example shows how to use the **TARGET** attribute to specify the name of a window or frame when using the **anchor** behavior.

```
<STYLE>
    SPAN {behavior:url(#default#AnchorClick);}
</STYLE>

<!--
    The href points to folder.htm for downlevel browsers,
    the FOLDER attribute points to the local root.
 -->

<SPAN TARGET="_top" "FOLDER = "/" >
Open Folder
</SPAN>
```

Applies To

 WIN32   **UNIX**
_____

anchor

TIMEACTION Attribute | timeAction Property

Sets or retrieves what action is taken on the element while the timeline is active.

Syntax

HTML   *<ELEMENT* STYLE="behavior:url(#default#time);"
*prefix:***TIMEACTION** = "display" | "none" | "onOff" | "style" |
"visibility" ... >

Scripting *object*.**timeAction** [= *sAction*]

Possible Values

display   Element displays when the timeline is active, and disappears when the timeline is inactive. As the element changes between active and inactive states, the surrounding HTML elements dynamically reflow within the page.

none   No action taken. This is useful for time grouping when the parent element should not do anything in response to timing.

onOff   Element's **on** property is toggled between `true` and `false` over time. If no **on** property exists for the element, nothing happens.

style   Element is displayed with the inline style when the timeline is active, and is displayed without the inline style when the timeline is inactive. If no inline style is defined for this element, nothing happens.

visibility Element's **style.visibility** property displays the element when the timeline is active, and makes the element disappear when the timeline is inactive. The surrounding HTML elements do not reflow as a result of the local element changing between active and inactive states.

prefix   Prefix used to associate the attribute with an XML namespace. A prefix of t must be used for the experimental implementation of HTML+TIME.

The property is read/write with a default value of `visibility`. This property cannot be modified in script after the **onload** event is fired on the document body.

Remarks

When this property is used on the HTML **BODY** element, the default value is `none`.

Example

The following example shows text with different **timeAction** values.

```
<!DOCTYPE HTML PUBLIC "-//W3C//DTD W3 HTML//EN">
<HTML>
<HEAD>
<XML:NAMESPACE PREFIX="t"/>
<STYLE>
.time          { behavior: url(#default#time);}
</STYLE>
</HEAD>
<BODY BGCOLOR="white">
```

```
<SPAN CLASS=time STYLE="Color:Red; Font-Weight:bold;" t:BEGIN="0"
t:DUR="5" t:TIMEACTION="style">
    <H3>Paragraph 1</H3>
    <P>This is paragraph number one. It is displayed in red, bold
    typeface for five seconds. After five seconds, the inline style
    is no longer applied. The timeAction property is set to
    "style."</P>
</SPAN>
<SPAN CLASS=time STYLE="COLOR:Blue;" t:BEGIN="0" t:DUR="10"
t:TIMEACTION="display">
    <H3>Paragraph 2</H3>
    <P>This is paragraph number two. It is displayed for ten
    seconds. The timeAction property is set to "display."</P>
</SPAN>
<SPAN>
    <H3>Paragraph 3</H3>
    <P>This is paragraph number three. When the second paragraph
    disappears, this paragraph moves into its place because
    the document is reflowed.</P>
</SPAN>
</BODY>
</HTML>
```

To see this code in action, refer to the Web Workshop CD-ROM.

Applies To

 WIN32

animation, audio, img, media, par, seq, time, video

TIMELINE Attribute | timeline Property

Sets or retrieves the type of timeline associated with an HTML element.

Syntax

HTML   *<ELEMENT* STYLE="behavior:url(#default#time);"
            *prefix:***TIMELINE** = "none" | "par" | "seq" ... >

Scripting *object*.**timeline** [= *sType*]

Possible Values

none   Current element does not define a local timeline, and has no affect on its
        contained time descendants.

par   New timeline container element in a document. All HTML descendants of this
        element have independent, or parallel, timing.

Possible Values *(continued)*

seq   Sequence timeline container element in a document. All HTML descendants of this element are timed as though they have a **BEGINAFTER** attribute set to the previous element.

prefix Prefix used to associate the attribute with an XML namespace. A prefix of t must be used for the experimental implementation of HTML+TIME.

The property is read/write with a default value of none. This property cannot be modified in script after the **onload** event is fired on the document body.

Example

The following example shows how the **TIMELINE** attribute is used.

```
<!DOCTYPE HTML PUBLIC "-//W3C//DTD HTML 4.0 Transitional//EN">
<HTML>
<HEAD>
<XML:NAMESPACE PREFIX="t"/>
<STYLE>
.time            { behavior: url(#default#time);}
</STYLE>
</HEAD>
<BODY BGCOLOR="white">
<SPAN ID="parent" CLASS="time" t:TIMELINE="par" t:BEGIN="0"
    t:DUR="10">
    <P>This paragraph inherits the "parallel" timeline set on its
    parent <SPAN> element. It is displayed for ten
    seconds. <BR><BR>
    </P>
    <P CLASS="time" t:BEGIN="5">This paragraph also inherits the
    "parallel" timeline set on its parent <SPAN> element, but it
    can have independent timing attributes as well.<BR><BR>
    </P>
</SPAN>
<P>This paragraph is not a child of the <SPAN> element
containing a timeline.</P>
</BODY>
</HTML>
```

To see this code in action, refer to the Web Workshop CD-ROM.

Applies To

 WIN32

time

timelineBehavior Property

Retrieves an object containing the timeline behavior associated with the specified object.

Syntax

Scripting [*oBehavior* =] *object*.**timelineBehavior**

Possible Values

oBehavior   DirectAnimation number (DANumber) object containing the behavior associated with the specified object. The object this property is applied to must have a valid HTML+TIME timeline associated with it.

The property is read-only with no default value.

Remarks

Typically, this property is used with the **SubstituteTime** function to replace the timeline of the DirectAnimation behavior with the specified HTML+TIME timeline.

This property allows you to incorporate multimedia elements, such as 2-D and 3-D animated images and sounds, into an HTML page with the **anim:DA** element. The object this property is applied to must be an HTML object with a valid HTML+TIME timeline. Use this property when you want to create custom XML for multimedia elements that are to be synchronized with other elements in the page. This property is not part of the HTML+TIME specification.

Example

The following example shows how to apply a timeline created with HTML+TIME to a simple animation that rotates an image.

```
<HTML>
<HEAD>
<TITLE>progressBehavior</TITLE>
<XML:NAMESPACE PREFIX="t"/>
<XML:NAMESPACE PREFIX="anim"/>
<STYLE>
.time          { behavior: url(#default#time);          }
anim\:DA{ behavior: url(#default#anim);          }
</STYLE>
</HEAD>
<BODY>
<P>The image begins rotating three seconds after the page is
loaded, and continues rotating for five seconds.</P>
<SPAN ID="spanImg" CLASS="time" t:TIMEACTION="visibility" t:BEGIN="3"
t:DUR="5">
</SPAN>
```

```
<DIV ALIGN="center">
    <anim:DA ID="da1" STYLE="width:200; height:200; z-index: -1;" />
</DIV>
<BR>
<SCRIPT LANGUAGE="JScript">
<!--
    // Assign a variable to the DA statics library.
    m = da1.statics;
    // Create the DAImage.
    img1 = m.ImportImage("/workshop/graphics/sun.gif");
    // Rotate the image at a rate of 60 degrees/second.
    img2 = img1.Transform(m.Rotate2RateDegrees(60));
    // Apply the HTML+TIME timeline to the DAImage.
    img3 = img2.SubstituteTime(spanImg.timelineBehavior);
    da1.image = img3;
//-->
</SCRIPT>
</BODY>
</HTML>
```

To see this code in action, refer to the Web Workshop CD-ROM.

Applies To

 WIN32

time

TIMESTARTRULE Attribute | timeStartRule Property

Sets or retrieves the point at which the document's timeline begins.

Syntax

HTML   `<BODY STYLE="behavior:url(#default#time);"`
*prefix:***TIMESTARTRULE** = "onDocLoad" ... >

Scripting   *body*.**timeStartRule** [= *sAction*]

Possible Values

`onDocLoad`   Document timeline should start when the document is fully loaded, but without waiting for any document-associated media. This ties the start of the document timeline to the **window.onload** event.

prefix   Prefix used to associate the attribute with an XML namespace. A prefix of t must be used for the experimental implementation of HTML+TIME.

The property is read/write with a default value of `onDocLoad`. This property cannot be modified in script after the **onload** event is fired on the document body.

Remarks

This property is available for use only with the HTML **BODY** element. Other possible values might be available in future versions.

Applies To

 WIN32

time

TYPE Attribute | type Property

Specifies the MIME type of the media object referenced by the **SRC** attribute.

Syntax

HTML   *<ELEMENT* STYLE="`behavior:url(#default#time);`" *prefix:***TYPE** = *sType ... >*

Scripting   *object*.**type** [= *sType*]

Possible Values

sType   String specifying the MIME type of the media associated with the element.

prefix   Prefix used to associate the attribute with an XML namespace. A prefix of t must be used for the experimental implementation of HTML+TIME.

The property is read/write with no default value. This property cannot be modified in script after the **onload** event is fired on the document body.

Remarks

By default, the server should send the MIME type to the user agent. If that mechanism fails, the MIME type is obtained from this property.

Applies To

 WIN32

animation, audio, img, media, video

userLanguage Property

Indicates the current user language.

Syntax

HTML   N/A

Scripting [*sLanguage* =] *oClientCaps*.**userLanguage**

Possible Values

sLanguage String specifying any of the language code values. For more information about the codes, see the Web Workshop CD.

The property is read-only with a browser-specific default value.

Example

The following example shows how to retrieve the **userLanguage** property exposed by the **clientCaps** behavior.

```
<HTML xmlns:IE>
<HEAD>
<STYLE>
@media all {
      IE\:clientCaps {behavior:url(#default#clientcaps)}
}
</STYLE>
<SCRIPT>
    alert ("userLanguage = " + oClientCaps.userLanguage);
</SCRIPT>
</HEAD>

<BODY>
    <IE:clientCaps ID="oClientCaps" />
</BODY>
</HTML>
```

To see this code in action, refer to the Web Workshop CD-ROM.

Applies To

 WIN32   UNIX

clientCaps

width Property

Retrieves the horizontal resolution of the screen.

Syntax

HTML   N/A

Scripting   [*iWidth* =] *oClientCaps*.**width**

Possible Values

iWidth   Integer specifying the width, in pixels.

The property is read-only with no default value.

Example

The following example shows how to retrieve the **width** property exposed by the
clientCaps behavior.

```
<HTML xmlns:IE>
<HEAD>
<STYLE>
@media all {
        IE\:clientCaps {behavior:url(#default#clientcaps)}
}
</STYLE>
<SCRIPT>
    alert ("width = " + oClientCaps.width);
</SCRIPT>
</HEAD>

<BODY>
    <IE:clientCaps ID="oClientCaps" />
</BODY>
</HTML>
```

To see this code in action, refer to the Web Workshop CD-ROM.

Applies To

 WIN32   UNIX

clientCaps

XMLDocument Property

Returns a reference to the XML Document Object Model (DOM) exposed by the object.

Syntax

HTML   N/A

Scripting   [*oXMLObject* =] *oObject*.**XMLDocument**

Possible Values

oXMLObject   Reference to the XML DOM exposed by the object.

The property is read-only with no default value.

Remarks

For a complete description of the DOM for XML that is exposed by the **XMLDocument** property, see the XML DOM Reference on the Web Workshop CD.

When persistence is applied to an element, a root node is automatically created within the exposed XML document. This node is accessed through the **documentElement** property. You can use **setAttribute** to add attributes to the root node, and you can use **appendChild** to add child nodes to the root node.

The **XMLDocument** property is available only to the **saveFavorite** and **saveHistory** behaviors when the **onload** and **onsave** events are fired.

Example

The following example shows how to use a persistent object to access the XML DOM through the **XMLDocument** property. The **setAttribute** method is exposed through the XML DOM. The **setAttribute** method is not the same as the DHTML and persistence methods of the same name.

```
<HTML>
<HEAD>
<META NAME="save" CONTENT="history">
<STYLE>
   .saveHistory {behavior:url(#default#savehistory);}
</STYLE>
```

```
<SCRIPT>
function fnSave(){
    var oXMLDoc=oPersistObject.XMLDocument;
    var oNode=oXMLDoc.createNode(1,"Trunk", "");
    oNode.text="A tree trunk.";
    oNode.setAttribute("desc",oPersistObject.innerHTML);
    oXMLDoc.documentElement.insertBefore(oNode, null);
}
function fnLoad(){
    var oXMLDoc=oPersistObject.XMLDocument;
    var oItem=oXMLDoc.documentElement.childNodes.item(1);
    oPersistObject.innerHTML=oItem.getAttribute("desc");
}
function fnInsTxt(){
    oPersistObject.innerHTML="I am an Ash.  I am an Ash sapling."
        + "Well, I am the trunk of an Ash sapling.";
}
</SCRIPT>
</HEAD>
<BODY>
<INPUT TYPE="button" VALUE="Insert Text" ONCLICK="fnInsTxt()">
<A HREF="/workshop/samples/author/persistence/saveTarget_1.htm">
    Leave The Page
</A>
<DIV
    ID="oPersistObject"
    CLASS="saveHistory"
    ONSAVE="fnSave()"
    ONLOAD="fnLoad()">
</DIV>
</BODY>
</HTML>
```

To see this code in action, refer to the Web Workshop CD-ROM.

Applies To

 WIN32   UNIX

saveFavorite, saveHistory, userData

Appendixes

This section includes the following appendixes:

A: HTA References

This appendix describes the extensions to the Dynamic HTML (DHTML) Object Model that allow you to customize the user interface of an HTML Application (HTA).

B: Visual Filters and Transition Reference

This appendix lists reference pages for filters and transitions, which can be used to create visually engaging and interactive documents.

C: Tables and Charts

This appendix contains reference information applicable to Internet Explorer 5, including supported colors, character sets, cascading style sheets (CSS) attributes, installable components, and command identifiers.

D: Web Resources

This appendix lists Web sites that provide information about Internet Explorer, DHTML, and other Internet technologies.

HTML Applications

The following section describes the extensions to the Dynamic HTML (DHTML) Object Model that allow you to customize the user interface of an HTML Application (HTA). References in this section are listed alphabetically within each of the following categories:

- Element | Object
- Attribute | Property

HTA:APPLICATION Element | HTA:APPLICATION Object

Enables an extended object model for building HTAs.

Attributes/Properties

applicationName	border	borderStyle	caption
commandLine[1]	icon	maximizeButton	minimizeButton
showInTaskBar	singleInstance	sysMenu	version
windowState			

1   This property has no corresponding attribute.

Remarks

An HTA can be created simply by saving an HTML page with the .hta file extension. However, inclusion of the **HTA:APPLICATION** tag enables the applications-oriented functionality listed in this reference. This tag must be positioned within the paired **HEAD** tag to take effect.

Including `SCROLL="no"` in the **BODY** tag turns off scroll bars for the application window.

Example

The following example shows how to retrieve all the properties exposed by **HTA:APPLICATION**.

```
<HTML>
<HEAD>
  <TITLE>HTA Demo</TITLE>
    <HTA:APPLICATION ID="oHTA"
    APPLICATIONNAME="myApp"
    BORDER="thin"
    BORDERSTYLE="normal"
    CAPTION="yes"
    ICON=""
    MAXIMIZEBUTTON="yes"
    MINIMIZEBUTTON="yes"
    SHOWINTASKBAR="no"
    SINGLEINSTANCE="no"
    SYSMENU="yes"
    VERSION="1.0"
    WINDOWSTATE="maximize"
    >

<SCRIPT>

/* This function also gets the value of commandLine,
   which cannot be set as an attribute.  */

function window.onload()
{
    sTempStr = "applicationName = " + oHTA.applicationName + "\n" +
               "border          = " + oHTA.border          + "\n" +
               "borderStyle     = " + oHTA.borderStyle      + "\n" +
               "caption         = " + oHTA.caption          + "\n" +
               "commandLine     = " + oHTA.commandLine      + "\n" +
               "icon            = " + oHTA.icon             + "\n" +
               "maximizeButton  = " + oHTA.maximizeButton   + "\n" +
               "minimizeButton  = " + oHTA.minimizeButton   + "\n" +
               "showInTaskBar   = " + oHTA.showInTaskbar    + "\n" +
               "singleInstance  = " + oHTA.singleInstance   + "\n" +
               "sysMenu         = " + oHTA.sysMenu          + "\n" +
               "version         = " + oHTA.version          + "\n" +
               "windowState     = " + oHTA.windowState      + "\n" ;

    oPre.innerText = sTempStr;
}
</SCRIPT>
</HEAD>
```

```
<BODY SCROLL="no">
  <PRE ID=oPre> </PRE>
</BODY>
</HTML>
```

To see this code in action, refer to the Web Workshop CD-ROM.

APPLICATION Attribute

Indicates whether the content of the **FRAME** or **IFRAME** is an HTA and, therefore, exempt from the browser security model.

Syntax

HTML   *<ELEMENT* **APPLICATION** = "yes" | "no" ... >

Scripting N/A

Possible Values

yes   Treats all content of the **FRAME** or **IFRAME** element as an HTA, in which case the content is trusted.

no   Treats all content of the **FRAME** or **IFRAME** element as part of an HTML document by applying the browser security rules for unsafe content.

The attribute has a default value of no.

Remarks

Limited to use in HTAs, the **APPLICATION** attribute gives the applications developer the choice of how to treat content. An HTA can contain one **FRAME** that allows browsing to unsafe content, such as Internet URLs, and another **FRAME** that accesses content known to be safe. Cross-domain scripting between HTA-enabled frames works.

Nested **FRAME** or **IFRAME** elements require that all of the container **FRAME** elements be HTA-enabled (for example, APPLICATION="yes") for the innermost **FRAME** or **IFRAME** to honor a value of APPLICATION="yes". Take, for instance, an **IFRAME** that contains **FRAMESET**. The **FRAME** elements within the **FRAMESET** qualify as nested. For the innermost **FRAME** to be considered safe, it must be declared as APPLICATION="yes", as must all parent **FRAME** elements.

HTAs are designed so that untrusted HTML **FRAME** and **IFRAME** elements have no script access to the HTA containing them. In the case of non-HTA-enabled **FRAME** elements, the highest level frame comprises the top window for all **FRAME** elements it contains. For that **FRAME**, **window.top** and **window.self** are the same. In addition, unsafe **FRAME** and **IFFRAME** elements receive neither a **referrer** nor an **opener** URL from the parent HTA. The result is that they are unaware that the containing HTA is the parent window.

Applies To

 WIN32

FRAME, IFRAME

APPLICATIONNAME Attribute | applicationName Property

Retrieves the name of the HTA.

Syntax

HTML   *<HTA:APPLICATION* **APPLICATIONNAME**=*sAppName>*

Scripting   [*sAppName* =] *oHTA*.**applicationName**

Possible Values

sAppName   String that identifies the application.

The property is read-only with no default value.

Remarks

When set to true, the **singleInstance** property checks the **applicationName** value before launching an instance of the application. For this check to be valid, the **applicationName** property must have a unique value assigned to it. The **applicationName** property enables a single application to be recognized, regardless of the URL used to access it.

Example

The following example shows how to retrieve the **applicationName** property.

```
<HTML>
<HEAD>
   <HTA:APPLICATION ID="oHTA"
    APPLICATIONNAME="myApp"
   >
   <SCRIPT>
      alert("applicationName    = " + oHTA.applicationName);
   </SCRIPT>
</HEAD>
<BODY SCROLL="no">

</BODY>
</HTML>
```

To see this code in action, refer to the Web Workshop CD-ROM.

Applies To

 WIN32

HTA:APPLICATION

BORDER Attribute | border Property

Retrieves the type of window border for the HTA.

Syntax

HTML	*<HTA:APPLICATION* **BORDER**=*sType>*
Scripting	[*sType* =] *oHTA*.**border**

Possible Values

sType		
	thick	String specifying a window with a thick border, plus a size grip and sizing border for resizing the window.
	dialog window	String specifying a border for a dialog window.
	none	String specifying a borderless window.
	thin	String specifying a window with a thin border.

The property is read-only with a default value of thick.

Remarks

The **border** property affects the window border and is only valid for HTA windows that contain a title bar or caption. Setting **border** to none eliminates the title bar, the program icon, and Minimize/Maximize buttons. This property can be used with the **borderStyle** property, which controls the content border within the window.

Example

The following example shows how to retrieve the **border** property exposed by the HTA.

```
<HTML>
<HEAD>
    <TITLE>Hello, World!</TITLE>
    <HTA:APPLICATION ID="oHTA"
     APPLICATIONAME="myApp"
     BORDER="thin"
    >
    <SCRIPT>
        alert("border    = " + oHTA.border);
    </SCRIPT>
</HEAD>
<BODY SCROLL="no">

</BODY>
</HTML>
```

To see this code in action, refer to the Web Workshop CD-ROM.

Applies To

 WIN32

HTA:APPLICATION

BORDERSTYLE Attribute | borderStyle Property

Retrieves the style set for the content border within the HTA window.

Syntax

HTML   *<HTA:APPLICATION **BORDERSTYLE**=sStyle>*

Scripting   [*sStyle* =] *oHTA*.**borderStyle**

Possible Values

sStyle   normal   Normal border style.

       complex   Border that is a combination of the raised and sunken styles.

       raised   Raised 3-D border.

       static   3-D border style. This style is typically used for windows that do not take user input.

       sunken   Sunken 3-D border.

The property is read-only with a default value of normal.

Remarks

In any HTA, there are two adjacent borders: the border around all of the content and the border for the application window. The **borderStyle** property controls only the content border and does not affect the application window border surrounding it. Use the **border** property to set the actual application window border.

Example

The following example shows how to retrieve the **borderStyle** property exposed by the HTA.

```
<HTML>
<HEAD>
   <TITLE>Hello, World!</TITLE>
   <HTA:APPLICATION ID="oHTA"
    APPLICATIONNAME="sampleApp"
    CAPTION="yes"
    BORDER="thin"
    BORDERSTYLE="normal"
   >
   <SCRIPT>
      alert("borderStyle    = " + oHTA.borderStyle);
   </SCRIPT>
</HEAD>
<BODY SCROLL="no">

</BODY>
</HTML>
```

To see this code in action, refer to the Web Workshop CD-ROM.

Applies To

 WIN32

HTA:APPLICATION

CAPTION Attribute | caption Property

Retrieves whether the window is set to display a title bar or caption for the HTA.

Syntax

HTML	*<HTA:APPLICATION* **CAPTION**=*bTitleBar>*
Scripting	[*bTitleBar* =] *oHTA*.**caption**

Possible Values

bTitleBar   Boolean value that specifies whether the HTA displays a title bar or caption. The title bar displays by default.

The property is read-only with a default value of yes.

Remarks

The application **title** does not appear unless the **caption** property is set to yes. Turning off the caption also disables the program icon and the Minimize and Maximize buttons. In this case, be sure to provide an alternate way for the user to quit the HTA, such as a button that invokes the **close** method of the **window** object.

Example

The following example shows how to retrieve the **caption** property.

```
<HTML>
<HEAD>
   <HTA:APPLICATION ID="oHTA"
    CAPTION="yes">
   <SCRIPT>
      alert ("caption    = " + oHTA.caption);
   </SCRIPT>
</HEAD>
<BODY SCROLL="no">

</BODY>
</HTML>
```

To see this code in action, refer to the Web Workshop CD-ROM.

Applies To

 WIN32

HTA:APPLICATION

commandLine Property

Retrieves the argument used to launch the HTA.

Syntax

HTML   N/A

Scripting   [*sPath* =] *oHTA*.**commandLine**

Possible Values

sPath   Returns the path and arguments that were used to launch the HTA.

The property is read-only with no default value.

Remarks

The **commandLine** property returns an empty string when the HTA is launched over the HTTP protocol.

Example

The following example shows how to retrieve the **commandLine** property value.

```
<HTML>
<HEAD>
   <HTA:APPLICATION ID="oHTA"
    APPLICATIONNAME="myApp">
   <SCRIPT>
      alert("commandLine    = " + oHTA.commandLine);
   </SCRIPT>
</HEAD>
<BODY SCROLL="no">

</BODY>
</HTML>
```

To see this code in action, refer to the Web Workshop CD-ROM.

Applies To

 WIN32

HTA:APPLICATION

ICON Attribute | icon Property

Retrieves the name and location of the icon specified in the HTA.

Syntax

HTML   *<HTA:APPLICATION* **ICON=***sIcon>*

Scripting [*sIcon* =] *oHTA*.**icon**

Possible Values

sIcon   String specifying an icon for the application.

The property is read-only with a default value of the system application icon.

Remarks

The **icon** attribute recognizes the standard 32x32 pixel Windows format for icon (.ico) image files.

Example

The following example shows how to retrieve the **icon** property.

```
<HTML>
<HEAD>
   <HTA:APPLICATION ID="oHTA"
    APPLICATIONAME="myApp"
    ICON="graphics/face01.ico" >
   <SCRIPT>
      alert ("icon    = " + oHTA.icon);
   </SCRIPT>
</HEAD>
<BODY SCROLL="no">

</BODY>
</HTML>
```

To see this code in action, refer to the Web Workshop CD-ROM.

Applies To

 WIN32

HTA:APPLICATION

MAXIMIZEBUTTON Attribute | maximizeButton Property

Retrieves whether a Maximize button is displayed in the title bar of the HTA window.

Syntax

HTML	*<HTA:APPLICATION* **MAXIMIZEBUTTON**=*bShowButton>*
Scripting	[*bShowButton* =] *oHTA*.**maximizeButton**

Possible Values

bShowButton   Boolean value specifying whether the HTA window displays a Maximize button in the title bar. By default, the Maximize button appears.

The property is read-only with a default value of yes.

Remarks

The window must have a title bar, or caption, for the Minimize and Maximize buttons to display.

Example

The following example shows how to retrieve the **maximizeButton** property.

```
<HTML>
<HEAD>
  <TITLE>Hello, World!</TITLE>
  <HTA:APPLICATION ID="oHTA"
   APPLICATIONNAME="myApp"
   CAPTION="yes"
   MAXIMIZEBUTTON="yes"
  >
  <SCRIPT>
     alert("maximizeButton    = " + oHTA.maximizeButton);
  </SCRIPT>
</HEAD>
<BODY SCROLL="no">

</BODY>
</HTML>
```

To see this code in action, refer to the Web Workshop CD-ROM.

Applies To

 WIN32

HTA:APPLICATION

MINIMIZEBUTTON Attribute | minimizeButton Property

Retrieves whether a Minimize button is displayed in the title bar of the HTA window.

Syntax

HTML	*<HTA:APPLICATION* **MINIMIZEBUTTON**=*bShowButton>*
Scripting	[*bShowButton* =] *oHTA*.**minimizeButton**

Possible Values

bShowButton   Boolean value specifying whether the HTA window displays a Minimize button in the title bar. By default, the Minimize button appears.

The property is read-only with a default value of yes.

Remarks

The window must have a title bar, or caption, for the Minimize and Maximize buttons to display.

Example

The following example shows how to retrieve the **minimizeButton** property.

```
<HTML>
<HEAD>
   <TITLE>Hello, World!</TITLE>
   <HTA:APPLICATION ID="oHTA"
    APPLICATIONNAME="myApp"
    CAPTION="yes"
    MINIMIZEBUTTON="yes"
   >
   <SCRIPT>
      alert ("minimizeButton    = " + oHTA.minimizeButton);
   </SCRIPT>
</HEAD>
```

```
<BODY SCROLL="no">

</BODY>
</HTML>
```

To see this code in action, refer to the Web Workshop CD-ROM.

Applies To

 WIN32

HTA:APPLICATION

SHOWINTASKBAR Attribute | showInTaskBar Property

Retrieves whether the HTA appears in the Windows taskbar.

Syntax

HTML   *<HTA:APPLICATION* **SHOWINTASKBAR**=*bShow>*

Scripting [*bShow* =] *oHTA*.**showInTaskBar**

Possible Values

bShow   Boolean value specifying whether the application appears in the Windows taskbar. By default, the application name displays in the taskbar.

The property is read-only with a default value of yes.

Remarks

The **showInTaskBar** property does not affect whether the application appears in the list of applications that the user obtains by pressing ALT+TAB.

Example

The following example shows how to use the **showInTaskBar** property.

```
<HTML>
<HEAD>
   <HTA:APPLICATION ID="oHTA"
    APPLICATIONNAME="myApp"
    SHOWINTASKBAR="no" >
```

```
    <SCRIPT>
      alert ("showInTaskBar    = " + oHTA.showInTaskBar);
    </SCRIPT>
</HEAD>
<BODY SCROLL="no">

</BODY>
</HTML>
```

To see this code in action, refer to the Web Workshop CD-ROM.

Applies To

 WIN32

HTA:APPLICATION

SINGLEINSTANCE Attribute | singleInstance Property

Retrieves whether only one instance of the HTA can run at a time.

Syntax

HTML   *<HTA:APPLICATION* **SINGLEINSTANCE**=*bOpen>*

Scripting   [*bOpen* =] *oHTA*.**singleInstance**

Possible Values

bOpen   Boolean value specifying whether only one instance of the application can run at a time. The default value of no allows multiple instances of a given application to be launched.

The property is read-only with a default value of no.

Remarks

When set to true, the **singleInstance** property checks the **applicationName** value before launching an instance of the application. For this check to be valid, the **applicationName** property must have a unique value assigned to it. The **applicationName** property enables a single application to be recognized, regardless of the URL used to access it.

Example

The following example shows how to retrieve the **singleInstance** property.

```
<HTML>
<HEAD>
   <HTA:APPLICATION ID="oHTA"
    APPLICATIONAME="myApp"
    SINGLEINSTANCE="yes"
   >
   <SCRIPT>
      alert("singleInstance    = " + oHTA.singleInstance);
   </SCRIPT>
</HEAD>
<BODY SCROLL="no">

</BODY>
</HTML>
```

To see this code in action, refer to the Web Workshop CD-ROM.

Applies To

 WIN32

HTA:APPLICATION

SYSMENU Attribute | sysMenu Property

Retrieves whether a system menu is set to display in the HTA.

Syntax

HTML   *<HTA:APPLICATION* **SYSMENU**=*bMenu>*

Scripting   [*bMenu* =] *oHTA*.**sysMenu**

Possible Values

bMenu   Boolean value specifying whether a program icon displays in the
              application title bar. By default, the program icon displays.

The property is read-only with a default value of yes.

Remarks

The HTA program icon displays all of the commands included in the standard
Windows program icon. The user can move, resize, or close a window by using the
program icon, which appears in the upper-left corner of the window.

Many of the properties that affect the user interface of the window are interdependent. When **sysMenu** is set to no, the program icon and the Minimize and Maximize buttons are disabled. Similarly, when border is set to none, neither program icon, title bar, nor Minimize and Maximize buttons can display.

Example

The following example shows how to use the **sysMenu** property.

```
<HTML>
<HEAD>
   <HTA:APPLICATION ID="oHTA"
    APPLICATIONAME="myApp"
    SYSMENU="yes"
   >
   <SCRIPT>
      alert("sysMenu    = " + oHTA.sysMenu);
   </SCRIPT>
</HEAD>
<BODY SCROLL="no">

</BODY>
</HTML>
```

To see this code in action, refer to the Web Workshop CD-ROM.

Applies To

 WIN32

HTA:APPLICATION

VERSION Attribute | version Property

Retrieves the iteration, or version, of the HTA.

Syntax

HTML   *<HTA:APPLICATION* **VERSION**=*sVersion>*

Scripting   [*sVersion* =] *oHTA*.**version**

Possible Values

sVersion   String specifying the application iteration, or version.

The property is read-only with a default value of an empty string.

Remarks

The version number set through this property can be found under the application's properties. This value is for display only. The script parser does not attempt to interpret the version string.

Example

The following example shows how to use the **version** property.

```
<HTML>
<HEAD>
   <HTA:APPLICATION ID="oHTA"
    VERSION="1.0">
   <SCRIPT>
      alert("version  = " + oHTA.version);
   </SCRIPT>
</HEAD>
<BODY SCROLL="no">

</BODY>
</HTML>
```

To see this code in action, refer to the Web Workshop CD-ROM.

Applies To

 WIN32

HTA:APPLICATION

WINDOWSTATE Attribute | windowState Property

Sets or retrieves the initial size of the HTA window.

Syntax

HTML	*<HTA:APPLICATION* **WINDOWSTATE**=*sWindowSize>*
Scripting	*oHTA*.**windowState**[= *sWindowSize*]

Possible Values

sWindowSize	normal	The HTA window is the default size for Internet Explorer.
	minimize	The HTA window does not display on launch. The **title** of the minimized application appears in the taskbar.
	maximize	The HTA is sized to fill the screen.

The property is read/write with a default value of normal.

Example

The following example shows how to use the **windowState** property.

```
<HTML>
<HEAD>
   <HTA:APPLICATION ID="oHTA"
    APPLICATIONAME="myApp"
    WINDOWSTATE="maximize">
   <SCRIPT>
      alert("windowState   = " + oHTA.windowState);
   </SCRIPT>
</HEAD>
<BODY SCROLL="no">

</BODY>
</HTML>
```

To see this code in action, refer to the Web Workshop CD-ROM.

Applies To

 WIN32

HTA:APPLICATION

Visual Filters and
Transition References

First available in Internet Explorer 4.0, filters and transitions allow you to create visually engaging and interactive documents. The following section describes the filters and transitions available in Dynamic HTML (DHTML).

alpha Filter

Sets the level of opacity for the visual object.

Syntax

HTML   *<ELEMENT* STYLE="filter: alpha(*sProperties*)" ...>

Scripting *object*.style.filter = "alpha(*sProperties*)"

Possible Values

sProperties String specifying one or more properties exposed by the filter.

Remarks

The opacity can be set as uniform or graded, in a linear or radial fashion.

Attributes/Properties

enabled [1]	finishOpacity	finishX	finishY	opacity
startX	startY	style		

1 This property has no corresponding attribute.

Example

The following example shows how to use the **alpha** filter and the **opacity** property to change the appearance of a button.

```
<STYLE>
    INPUT.aFilter {filter: alpha(opacity=50);}
</STYLE>

<INPUT TYPE=button VALUE="Button" CLASS="aFilter">
```

Applies To

 WIN32   UNIX   WIN16

BODY, BUTTON, DIV, IMG, INPUT type=button, INPUT type=checkbox, INPUT type=file, INPUT type=image, INPUT type=password, INPUT type=radio, INPUT type=reset, INPUT type=submit, INPUT type=text, MARQUEE, SPAN, style, TABLE, TD, TEXTAREA, TH

 WIN16   WIN32   MAC   UNIX

runtimeStyle

blendTrans Filter

Fades the visual object in or out.

Syntax

HTML   *<ELEMENT* STYLE="filter: blendTrans(*sProperties*)" ...>

Scripting *object*.style.filter = "blendTrans(*sProperties*)"

Possible Values

sProperties   String specifying one or more properties exposed by the filter.

Remarks

This attribute is not inherited.

Attributes/Properties

duration   **enabled** [1]   **status** [1]

1   This attribute has no corresponding property

Methods

apply   **play**   **stop**

Example

The following example shows how to use the **blendTrans** filter.

```
<HEAD>
<SCRIPT>
function fadeOut() {
    oDiv.style.filter="blendTrans(duration=2)";
    // Make sure filter is not already playing.
    if (oDiv.filters.blendTrans.status != 2) {
        oDiv.filters.blendTrans.apply();
        oDiv.style.visibility="hidden";
        oDiv.filters.blendTrans.play();
    }
}
function fadeIn() {
    oDiv.style.filter="blendTrans(duration=2)";
    // Make sure that the filter is not already playing.
    if (oDiv.filters.blendTrans.status != 2) {
        oDiv.filters.blendTrans.apply();
        oDiv.style.visibility="visible";
        oDiv.filters.blendTrans.play();
    }
}
</SCRIPT>
</HEAD>

<BODY>
<!-- DIV must be assigned a width to give it layout. -->
<DIV ID="oDiv" STYLE="width: 200">
This text can be faded in and out.
</DIV>
<P>
<BUTTON onclick="fadeOut()">Fade Text Out</BUTTON>
<BUTTON onclick="fadeIn()">Fade Text In</BUTTON>
</P>
</BODY>
```

Applies To

 WIN32   UNIX   WIN16

BODY, BUTTON, DIV, IMG, INPUT type=button, INPUT type=checkbox, INPUT type=file, INPUT type=image, INPUT type=password, INPUT type=radio, INPUT type=reset, INPUT type=submit, INPUT type=text, MARQUEE, SPAN, style, TABLE, TD, TEXTAREA, TH

IE 5   **WIN16   WIN32   MAC   UNIX**

runtimeStyle

blur Filter

Causes the object to appear to be in motion.

Syntax

HTML   <*ELEMENT* STYLE="filter: blur(*sProperties*)" ...>

Scripting   *object*.style.filter = "blur(*sProperties*)"

Possible Values

sProperties   String specifying one or more properties exposed by the filter.

Attributes/Properties

add   **direction**   **enabled** [1]   **strength**

[1]   This attribute has no corresponding property.

Example

The following example uses the **blur** filter to make the text appear out of focus, as if it were moving.

```
<STYLE>
    DIV.aFilter {filter: blur(Strength=5,Direction=90);}
</STYLE>

<DIV CLASS="aFilter" STYLE="width:200">
Blurred Text
</DIV>
```

Applies To

 IE 4   **WIN32   UNIX   WIN16**

BODY, BUTTON, DIV, IMG, INPUT type=button, INPUT type=checkbox, INPUT type=file, INPUT type=image, INPUT type=password, INPUT type=radio, INPUT type=reset, INPUT type=submit, INPUT type=text, MARQUEE, SPAN, style, TABLE, TD, TEXTAREA, TH

 IE 5   **WIN16   WIN32   MAC   UNIX**

runtimeStyle

chroma Filter

Selectively renders a specific color transparent for the selected visual object.

Syntax

HTML   *<ELEMENT* STYLE="filter: chroma(*sProperties*)" ...>

Scripting *object*.style.filter = "chroma(*sProperties*)"

Possible Values

sProperties String specifying one or more properties exposed by the filter.

Remarks

This effect is not recommended for use with files that have been dithered from 24- to 8-bit. In particular, JPEG files, which are dithered and compressed, do not produce an entirely solid chromakey color, resulting in uneven effects. Chromakey doesn't work well on anti-aliased sources, in which sharp lines are smoothed by blending the colors of surrounding pixels. Choosing a specific chromakey color causes some colors to be fully opaque.

Attributes/Properties

color   **enabled** [1]

1 This attribute has no corresponding property.

Applies To

 WIN32   UNIX   WIN16

BODY, BUTTON, DIV, IMG, INPUT type=button, INPUT type=checkbox, INPUT type=file, INPUT type=image, INPUT type=password, INPUT type=radio, INPUT type=reset, INPUT type=submit, INPUT type=text, MARQUEE, SPAN, style, TABLE, TD, TEXTAREA, TH

 WIN16   WIN32   MAC   UNIX

runtimeStyle

dropShadow Filter

Paints a solid silhouette of the selected visual object, offset in the specified direction, thus creating the illusion that the visual object is floating above the page and is casting a shadow onto the page.

Syntax

HTML   *<ELEMENT* STYLE="filter: dropShadow(*sProperties*)" ...>

Scripting *object*.style.filter = "dropShadow(*sProperties*)"

Possible Values

sProperties   String specifying one or more properties exposed by the filter.

Remarks

If you want to retain the usual shadow effect on a transparent object, set the positive property to 0. The transparent object has a drop shadow outside the transparent region, rather than inside the transparent region.

Attributes/Properties

color	enabled[1]	offX	offY	positive

1   This property has no corresponding attribute.

Applies To

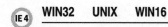

WIN32   UNIX   WIN16

DIV, MARQUEE, SPAN, style, TABLE, TD, TH

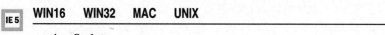

WIN16   WIN32   MAC   UNIX

runtimeStyle

flipH Filter

Renders the visual object as a mirror image of itself along the horizontal plane.

Syntax

HTML   *<ELEMENT* STYLE="filter: flipH" ...>

Scripting *object*.style.filter = "flipH"

Attributes/Properties

enabled[1]

1 This property has no corresponding attribute.

Applies To

 WIN32   UNIX   WIN16

BODY, BUTTON, DIV, IMG, INPUT type=button, INPUT type=checkbox, INPUT type=file, INPUT type=image, INPUT type=password, INPUT type=radio, INPUT type=reset, INPUT type=submit, INPUT type=text, MARQUEE, SPAN, style, TABLE, TD, TEXTAREA, TH

 WIN16   WIN32   MAC   UNIX

runtimeStyle

flipV Filter

Renders the visual object as a mirror image of itself along the vertical plane.

Syntax

HTML   *<ELEMENT* STYLE="filter: flipV" ...>

Scripting *object*.style.filter = "flipV"

Attributes/Properties

enabled[1]

1 This property has no corresponding attribute.

Applies To

 WIN32   UNIX   WIN16

BODY, BUTTON, DIV, IMG, INPUT type=button, INPUT type=checkbox, INPUT type=file, INPUT type=image, INPUT type=password, INPUT type=radio, INPUT type=reset, INPUT type=submit, INPUT type=text, MARQUEE, SPAN, style, TABLE, TD, TEXTAREA, TH

 WIN16   WIN32   MAC   UNIX

runtimeStyle

glow Filter

Adds radiance around the outside edges of the object, giving it the appearance of a glow.

Syntax

HTML   *<ELEMENT* STYLE="filter: glow(*sProperties*)" ...>

Scripting *object*.style.filter = "glow(*sProperties*)"

Possible Values

sProperties String specifying one or more properties exposed by the filter.

Attributes/Properties

color   **enabled**[1]   **strength**

1   This property has no corresponding attribute.

Example

The following example shows how to use the **glow** filter to add a blue-colored glow to text within a **DIV** element.

```
<STYLE>
    DIV.aFilter {filter: glow(Color=blue,Strength=5); width: 150;}
</STYLE>

<DIV CLASS="aFilter">
Glowing Text
</DIV>
```

Applies To

 WIN32   UNIX   WIN16

BODY, BUTTON, DIV, IMG, INPUT type=button, INPUT type=checkbox, INPUT type=file, INPUT type=image, INPUT type=password, INPUT type=radio, INPUT type=reset, INPUT type=submit, INPUT type=text, MARQUEE, SPAN, style, TABLE, TD, TEXTAREA, TH

 WIN16   WIN32   MAC   UNIX

runtimeStyle

gray Filter

Drops the color information from the visual object's color palette, rendering the object in grayscale.

Syntax

HTML   *<ELEMENT* STYLE="filter: gray" ...>

Scripting *object*.style.filter = "gray"

Attributes/Properties

enabled[1]

1   This property has no corresponding attribute.

Applies To

 WIN32   UNIX   WIN16

BODY, BUTTON, DIV, IMG, INPUT type=button, INPUT type=checkbox, INPUT type=file, INPUT type=image, INPUT type=password, INPUT type=radio, INPUT type=reset, INPUT type=submit, INPUT type=text, MARQUEE, SPAN, style, TABLE, TD, TEXTAREA, TH

 WIN16   WIN32   MAC   UNIX

runtimeStyle

invert Filter

Reverses the hue, saturation, and brightness values of the visual object.

Syntax

HTML   *<ELEMENT* STYLE="filter: invert" ...>

Scripting *object*.style.filter = "invert"

Attributes/Properties

enabled[1]

1   This property has no corresponding attribute.

Applies To

 WIN32   UNIX   WIN16

BODY, BUTTON, DIV, IMG, INPUT type=button, INPUT type=checkbox, INPUT type=file, INPUT type=image, INPUT type=password, INPUT type=radio, INPUT type=reset, INPUT type=submit, INPUT type=text, MARQUEE, SPAN, style, TABLE, TD, TEXTAREA, TH

 WIN16   WIN32   MAC   UNIX

runtimeStyle

light Filter

Simulates the projection of a light source onto the selected visual object.

Syntax

HTML   *<ELEMENT* STYLE="filter: light(*sProperties*)" ...>

Scripting *object*.style.filter = "light(*sProperties*)"

Possible Values

sProperties   String specifying one or more properties exposed by the filter.

Remarks

Once you have defined the light filter effect collection for an object, you can use the methods exposed by the filter to set or change its properties.

You can control the virtual position of the light source, the x- and y-coordinates of the focus of the light, the type of light (point or cone) and whether the light has hard or diffuse edges, the color of the light, and its intensity. The maximum number of lights available to each visual filter control is 10. To add more than 10 lights to your page, you need multiple visual filter controls.

When a light effect is created, it has a default ambient light associated with it. The first light you add to the object replaces this default ambient light.

You can associate only one object per light effect. To light several different objects (for example, a text phrase and a bitmap image), you need a separate instance of the light filter effect for each object. However, if you combine several objects into a single object by using a **DIV** element, you can use one light object to light the combined object.

Attributes/Properties

enabled[1]

1   This property has no corresponding attribute.

Methods

addAmbient	**addCone**	**addPoint**	**changeColor**
changeStrength	**clear**	**moveLight**	

Example

The following example shows how to use the **light** filter and the **addCone** method.

```
<STYLE>
    .aFilter {background-color: #FFFFFF; filter: light();
             color: #000000;
             width: 150;}
</STYLE>
<SCRIPT>
window.onload=fnInit;
function fnInit(){
   var iX2=oDiv.offsetWidth/2;
   var iY2=oDiv.offsetHeight;
   oDiv.filters[0].addCone(0,0,1,iX2,iY2,255,0,0,20,60);
}
<SCRIPT>
<DIV CLASS="aFilter" ID="oDiv">
This text is highlighted by a red cone light.
</DIV>
```

Applies To

 WIN32   UNIX   WIN16

BODY, BUTTON, DIV, IMG, INPUT type=button, INPUT type=checkbox, INPUT type=file, INPUT type=image, INPUT type=password, INPUT type=radio, INPUT type=reset, INPUT type=submit, INPUT type=text, MARQUEE, SPAN, style, TABLE, TD, TEXTAREA, TH

 WIN16   WIN32   MAC   UNIX

runtimeStyle

mask Filter

Takes the selected visual object, paints the transparent pixels a specific color, and makes a transparent mask from its nontransparent pixels.

Syntax

HTML   *<ELEMENT* STYLE="filter: mask(*sProperties*)" ...>

Scripting   *object*.style.filter = "mask(*sProperties*)"

Possible Values

sProperties   String specifying one or more properties exposed by the filter.

Attributes/Properties

color   **enabled**[1]

1   This property has no corresponding attribute.

Example

The following example shows how to use the **mask** filter and the **color** property to make a magenta mask of the **DIV**; that is, all transparent pixels are colored magenta and all nontransparent pixels are made transparent.

```
<STYLE>
   DIV.aFilter {filter: mask(color=#FF00FF); width: 150;}
</STYLE>

<DIV CLASS="aFilter">
This text is masked.
</DIV>
```

Applies To

 WIN32   UNIX   WIN16

BODY, BUTTON, DIV, IMG, INPUT type=button, INPUT type=checkbox, INPUT type=file, INPUT type=image, INPUT type=password, INPUT type=radio, INPUT type=reset, INPUT type=submit, INPUT type=text, MARQUEE, SPAN, style, TABLE, TD, TEXTAREA, TH

 WIN16   WIN32   MAC   UNIX

runtimeStyle

redirect Filter

Converts the object into a DAImage object—that is, an image that can be manipulated using DirectAnimation.

Syntax

HTML   *<ELEMENT* STYLE="filter: redirect(*sProperties*)" ...>

Scripting *object*.style.filter = "redirect(*sProperties*)"

Possible Values

sProperties   String specifying one or more properties exposed by the filter.

Remarks

Any changes made to the specified object are reflected in the DirectAnimation version as well.

Attributes/Properties

enabled[1]

[1]   This property has no corresponding attribute.

Methods

elementImage

Example

Note This example requires the DirectAnimation browser component.

The following example shows how to convert a **DIV** object containing text and an image into a DirectAnimation image that rotates continuously using a 2-D transformation.

```
<BODY>
<OBJECT ID="DAControl"
    STYLE="position:absolute; left:200; top:125; width:350; height:300;
        z-index: -1"
    CLASSID="CLSID:B6FFC24C-7E13-11D0-9B47-00C04FC2F51D">
</OBJECT>

<DIV ID="oDiv" STYLE="WIDTH:250; FILTER:redirect">
    <H2>This is the DIV after being converted into an image.</H2>
    <P><IMG SRC="sphere.jpg"></P>
</DIV>
```

```
<SCRIPT LANGUAGE="JScript">

    // The DirectAnimation library
    oLib = DAControl.MeterLibrary;

    // Get the filter.
    oFilter = oDiv.filters[0];

    // Grab the image converted by the filter.
    oImage = oFilter.elementImage();

    // Perform the image transformation.
    DAControl.Image = oImage.Transform(oLib.Rotate2RateDegrees(30)) ;
    DAControl.Start();

</SCRIPT>
</BODY>
```

To see this code in action, refer to the Web Workshop CD-ROM.

Applies To

 WIN32   UNIX   WIN16

BODY, BUTTON, DIV, IMG, INPUT type=button, INPUT type=checkbox, INPUT type=file, INPUT type=image, INPUT type=password, INPUT type=radio, INPUT type=reset, INPUT type=submit, INPUT type=text, MARQUEE, SPAN, style, TABLE, TD, TEXTAREA, TH

 WIN16   WIN32   MAC   UNIX

runtimeStyle

revealTrans Filter

Shows or hides visual objects, using any of the 23 predefined transition effects.

Syntax

HTML   *<ELEMENT* STYLE="filter: revealTrans(*sProperties*)" ...>

Scripting *object*.style.filter = "revealTrans(*sProperties*)"

Possible Values

sProperties   String specifying one or more properties exposed by the filter.

Remarks

For a list of the 23 predefined transitions that can be used with the **revealTrans** filter, see the **transition** property.

Attributes/Properties

duration **enabled**[1] **status**[1] **transition**

1 This property has no corresponding attribute.

Methods

apply **play** **stop**

Example

The following example shows how to use the **revealTrans** filter.

```
<SCRIPT>
function go() {
    C1.filters[0].Apply();

if (C1.style.visibility == "visible") {
        C1.style.visibility = "hidden";
    C1.filters.revealTrans.transition=2;
    }
    else {
        C1.style.visibility = "visible";
    C1.filters[0].transition=3;
    }
    C1.filters[0].Play();
}
</SCRIPT>
<INPUT TYPE=BUTTON VALUE="Play Transition" onClick="go();"></INPUT>
<SPAN ID=C1 Style="position:absolute;Visibility:visible;Filter:revealTrans(duration=2,
    transition=3);width:300;height:300;background-color: lightgreen">
<CENTER>
<DIV style="background-color=red;height=100;width:100;position:relative;top:100"></DIV>
</CENTER>
</SPAN>
```

Applies To

 WIN32   UNIX   WIN16

BODY, BUTTON, DIV, IMG, INPUT type=button, INPUT type=checkbox, INPUT type=file, INPUT type=image, INPUT type=password, INPUT type=radio, INPUT type=reset, INPUT type=submit, INPUT type=text, MARQUEE, SPAN, style, TABLE, TD, TEXTAREA, TH

WIN16   WIN32   MAC   UNIX

runtimeStyle

shadow Filter

Paints a solid silhouette of the selected visual object along one of its edges, in the specified direction, creating the illusion of a shadow around the visual object.

Syntax

HTML   *<ELEMENT* STYLE="filter: shadow(*sProperties*)" ...>

Scripting *object*.style.filter = "shadow(*sProperties*)"

Possible Values

sProperties   String specifying one or more properties exposed by the filter.

Attributes/Properties

color   **direction**   **enabled**[1]

1   This property has no corresponding attribute.

Example

The following example shows how to use the **shadow** filter to add a shadow effect to the text.

```
<STYLE>
   DIV.aFilter {filter: shadow(color=#0000FF,direction=45); width: 150; color: FF0000;}
</STYLE>

<DIV CLASS="aFilter">
This red text is displayed with a 45 degree blue shadow.
</DIV>
```

Applies To

 WIN32   UNIX   WIN16

BODY, BUTTON, DIV, IMG, INPUT type=button, INPUT type=checkbox, INPUT type=file, INPUT type=image, INPUT type=password, INPUT type=radio, INPUT type=reset, INPUT type=submit, INPUT type=text, MARQUEE, SPAN, style, TABLE, TD, TEXTAREA, TH

wave Filter

Performs a sine wave distortion of the visual display of the object along the vertical axis.

Syntax

HTML   *<ELEMENT* STYLE="filter: wave(*sProperties*)" ...>

Scripting *object*.style.filter = "wave(*sProperties*)"

Possible Values

sProperties String specifying one or more properties exposed by the filter.

Attributes/Properties

add	**enabled**[1]	**freq**	**lightStrength**
phase	**strength**		

1   This property has no corresponding attribute.

Example

The following example shows how to use the **wave** filter to render text along a sine wave.

```
<STYLE>
   DIV.aFilter {filter: wave(
      strength=8,
      freq=3,
      lightstrength=20,
      add=0,
      phase=90);
      width: 150; color: #FF0000;}
</STYLE>

<DIV CLASS="aFilter">
This red text is displayed along a sine wave.
</DIV>
```

Applies To

 WIN32 UNIX WIN16

BODY, BUTTON, DIV, IMG, INPUT type=button, INPUT type=checkbox, INPUT type=file, INPUT type=image, INPUT type=password, INPUT type=radio, INPUT type=reset, INPUT type=submit, INPUT type=text, MARQUEE, SPAN, style, TABLE, TD, TEXTAREA, TH

 WIN16 WIN32 MAC UNIX

runtimeStyle

xray Filter

Changes the color depth of the visual object and renders the object in black and white, making the visual display look like a black and white x-ray.

Syntax

HTML   *<ELEMENT* STYLE="filter: xray" ...>

Scripting *object*.style.filter = "xray"

Attributes/Properties

enabled[1]

1   This property has no corresponding attribute.

Example

The following example shows how to use the **xray** filter to render colored text in grayscale.

```
<STYLE>
    DIV.aFilter {filter: xray; width: 150; color: #FF0000;}
</STYLE>

<DIV CLASS="aFilter">
This red text is displayed in grayscale.
</DIV>
```

Applies To

WIN32   UNIX   WIN16

BODY, BUTTON, DIV, IMG, INPUT type=button, INPUT type=checkbox, INPUT type=file, INPUT type=image, INPUT type=password, INPUT type=radio, INPUT type=reset, INPUT type=submit, INPUT type=text, MARQUEE, SPAN, style, TABLE, TD, TEXTAREA, TH

WIN16   WIN32   MAC   UNIX

runtimeStyle

addAmbient Method

Adds an ambient light to the light filter effect object.

Syntax

*object.*filters.light.addAmbient(*iRed, iGreen, iBlue, iStrength*)

Parameters

iRed   Required. Red value. This is an integer from 0 to 255, with 0 the lowest saturation and 255 the highest.

iGreen   Required. Green value. This is an integer from 0 to 255, with 0 the lowest saturation and 255 the highest.

iBlue   Required. Blue value. This is an integer from 0 to 255, with 0 the lowest saturation and 255 the highest.

iStrength Required. Integer specifying the intensity setting.

Return Value

No return value.

Remarks

Ambient light is nondirectional light that sheds parallel beams perpendicular to the surface of the page. Ambient light has color and strength values and can be used to add more color to the page; it is often used with other lights.

The following example shows how to create a blue ambient light with a fairly low intensity.

```
<STYLE>
    .aFilter {background-color: #FFFFFF; filter: light();
             color: #000000;
             width: 150;}
</STYLE>
<SCRIPT>
function init()
{
    :
    oDiv.filters.light.addAmbient(0,0,255,10);
    :
}
</SCRIPT>
<DIV CLASS="aFilter" ID="oDiv" onload="init()">
  This text is applied with a low intensity light filter.
</DIV>
```

Applies To

 WIN32   UNIX

light

addCone Method

Adds a cone light to the light filter effect object to cast a directional light on the page.

Syntax

object.filters.light.addCone(*iX1, iY1, iZ1, iX2, iY2, iRed, iGreen, iBlue, iStrength, iSpread*)

Parameters

iX1   Required. Integer specifying the left coordinate of the light source.

iY1   Required. Integer specifying the top coordinate of the light source.

iZ1   Required. Integer specifying the z-axis level of the light source.

iX2   Required. Integer specifying the left coordinate of the target light focus.

iY2   Required. Integer specifying the top coordinate of the target light focus.

iRed   Required. Red value. This is an integer from 0 to 255, with 0 the lowest saturation and 255 the highest.

iGreen   Required. Green value. This is an integer from 0 to 255, with 0 the lowest saturation and 255 the highest.

iBlue   Required. Blue value. This is an integer from 0 to 255, with 0 the lowest saturation and 255 the highest.

Parameters *(continued)*

iStrength Required. Integer specifying the intensity setting. The strength specified pertains to the target coordinates. When the light is moved, the strength is rescaled to pertain to the new target.

iSpread Required. Integer specifying the angle of light spread in the relationship between the vertical position of the light source and the surface of the visual object. This can be from 0 to 90 degrees. A lower spread, defined by lower integer values, produces a smaller shaped cone of light. A high angle of spread produces an oblique oval or circle of light.

Return Value

No return value.

Remarks

The cone light fades with distance from the target x,y position. It displays a hard edge at the near edge of the cone light's focus and fades gradually as it reaches the cone light's distance threshold.

Applies To

 WIN32   UNIX

light

addPoint Method

Adds a point light source, like a light bulb.

Syntax

object.filters.light.addPoint(*iX, iY, iZ, iRed, iGreen, iBlue, iStrength*)

Parameters

iX   Required. Integer specifying the left coordinate of the light source.

iY   Required. Integer specifying the top coordinate of the light source.

iZ   Required. Integer specifying the z-axis level of the light source.

Parameters *(continued)*

    iRed   Required. Red value. This is an integer from 0 to 255, with 0 the lowest saturation and 255 the highest.

    iGreen   Required. Green value. This is an integer from 0 to 255, with 0 the lowest saturation and 255 the highest.

    iBlue   Required. Blue value. This is an integer from 0 to 255, with 0 the lowest saturation and 255 the highest.

    iStrength Required. Integer specifying the intensity setting.

Return Value

No return value.

Remarks

Intensity on the page is controlled by the angle of light on the surface.

Applies To

 WIN32   UNIX

light

apply Method

Applies a transition to the designated object.

Syntax

object.`filters`.*filterName*.`apply()`

Return Value

No return value.

Applies To

 WIN32   UNIX

blendTrans, revealTrans

changeColor Method

Changes the light color for any light on the page.

Syntax

    object.filters.light.changeColor(*iLightNumber, iRed, iGreen, iBlue, vAbsolute*)

Parameters

iLightNumber Required. Integer specifying the identifying number for the light, for use in scripting.

iRed Required. Red value. This is an integer from 0 to 255, with 0 the lowest saturation and 255 the highest.

iGreen Required. Green value. This is an integer from 0 to 255, with 0 the lowest saturation and 255 the highest.

iBlue Required. Blue value. This is an integer from 0 to 255, with 0 the lowest saturation and 255 the highest.

vAbsolute Required. If this flag is `true`, **changeColor** sets the value to be that new value. If this flag is `false`, **changeColor** increments or decrements the color value by that amount.

Return Value

No return value.

Applies To

 WIN32   UNIX

light

changeStrength Method

Changes the intensity of the light.

Syntax

    object.filters.light.changeStrength(*iLightNumber, iStrength, vAbsolute*)

Parameters

iLightNumber   Required. Integer specifying the identifying number for the light, for use in scripting.

iStrength   Required. Integer specifying the light intensity.

vAbsolute   Required. If this flag is true (nonzero), **changeStrength** sets the strength value to be the new value. If this flag is false (zero), **changeStrength** increments or decrements the strength value by that amount.

Return Value

No return value.

Applies To

 WIN32   UNIX

light

clear Method

Deletes all lights associated with the specified light filter.

Syntax

object.filters.light.clear()

Return Value

No return value.

Remarks

This method clears all light sources on the object.

Applies To

 WIN32   UNIX

light

elementImage Method

Returns a DirectAnimation image (DAImage) object.

Syntax

oImage = *object*`.filters.redirect.elementImage()`

Return Value

Returns a DAImage object.

Example

Note This example requires the DirectAnimation browser component.

The following example shows how to make a **DIV** object containing text and an image into a DAImage that rotates continuously using a 2-D transformation.

```
<BODY>
<OBJECT ID="DAControl"
    STYLE="position:absolute; left:200; top:125; width:350; height:300;
        z-index: -1"
    CLASSID="CLSID:B6FFC24C-7E13-11D0-9B47-00C04FC2F51D">
</OBJECT>

<DIV ID="oDiv" STYLE="WIDTH:250; FILTER:Redirect">
    <H2>This is the DIV after being converted into an image.</H2>
    <P><IMG SRC="sphere.jpg"></P>
</DIV>

<SCRIPT LANGUAGE="JScript">

    // The DirectAnimation library
    oLib = DAControl.MeterLibrary;

    // Get the filter.
    oFilter = oDiv.filters[0];

    // Grab the image converted by the filter.
    oImage = oFilter.elementImage();

    // Perform the image transformation.
    DAControl.Image = oImage.Transform(oLib.Rotate2RateDegrees(30)) ;
    DAControl.Start();

</SCRIPT>
</BODY>
```

To see this code in action, refer to the Web Workshop CD-ROM.

Applies To

 WIN32 **UNIX**

redirect

moveLight Method

Moves the light effect on the page.

Syntax

object.filters.light.moveLight(*iLightNumber, iX, iY, iZ, bAbsolute*)

Parameters

iLightNumber	Required. Integer specifying the identifying number for the light, for use in scripting.
iX	Required. Integer specifying the left coordinate of the light source.
iY	Required. Integer specifying the top coordinate of the light source.
iZ	Required. Integer specifying the z-axis level of the light source.
bAbsolute	Required. Boolean specifying whether the move is absolute or relative.

Return Value

No return value.

Remarks

For cone lights, this method changes the target x,y values to move the light's focus. For point lights, this method changes the source x,y,z values to move the source location. This method has no effect on ambient lights.

Applies To

 WIN32 **UNIX**

light

play Method

Plays the transition.

Syntax

object.filters.*filterName*.play([*iDuration*])

Parameters

iDuration Optional. Floating-point value specifying the amount of time to play the filter. Valid values are 0.0-N.n.

Return Value

No return value.

Remarks

If a playback duration is explicitly specified as a parameter of this method, it overrides the **duration** property assigned to the transition for that instance of the transition's playback.

Applies To

 WIN32   UNIX

blendTrans, revealTrans

stop Method

Stops transition playback.

Syntax

object.filters.*filterName*.stop()

Return Value

No return value.

Remarks

This method fires the **onfilterchange** event.

Applies To

 WIN32   UNIX

blendTrans, revealTrans

ADD Attribute | add Property

Sets or retrieves whether to add the original image to the image applied with the filter.

Syntax

HTML   { **filter**:*filterName* (**ADD** = "true" | "false"...) }

Scripting *object*.**filters**.*filterName*.**add** [= *bAddImage*]

Possible Values

true   Image is added.

false   Image is not added.

The property is read/write with a default value of true.

Applies To

 WIN32   UNIX

blur, wave

COLOR Attribute | color Property

Sets or retrieves the value of the color applied with the filter.

Syntax

HTML   { **filter**:*filterName* (**COLOR** = *sColor* ...) }

Scripting *object*.**filters**.*filterName*.**color** [= *sColor*]

Possible Values

sColor String specifying the color value. Color is expressed in #RRGGBB format, where RR is the red hexadecimal value, GG is the green hexadecimal value, and BB is the blue hexadecimal value. For more information about the range of color values supported by Microsoft Internet Explorer version 4.0 and later, see "Color Table" in Appendix C.

The property is read/write with no default value.

Remarks

For the chroma filter, the **color** property specifies the value of the color to be subjected to chromakey transparency as follows:

dropShadow filter	Specifies the color for the drop shadow effect.
glow filter	Specifies the color of the radiance applied to the object.
mask filter	Specifies the color that the transparent regions are painted.
shadow filter	Specifies the color for the shadow effect.

Applies To

 WIN32   UNIX

chroma, dropShadow, glow, mask, shadow

DIRECTION Attribute | direction Property

Sets or retrieves the directional offset for the filter, expressed in 45-degree increments, clockwise from the vertical orientation of the object.

Syntax

HTML   { **filter**:*filterName* (**DIRECTION** = 0 | 45 | 90 | 135 | 180 | 225 | 270 | 315 ...) }

Scripting *object*.**filters**.*filterName*.**direction** [= *iOffset*]

Possible Values

0	Top.
45	Top right.
90	Bottom.
135	Bottom right.
180	Bottom.
225	Bottom left.
270	Left.
315	Top left.

The property is read/write with a default value of 270.

Remarks

Negative values or values greater than 360 degrees wrap around to their equivalent angle. For example, a -45 degree orientation is equivalent to a 315-degree orientation. This allows you to code mathematical manipulations easily.

Example

The following example shows how to set a **blur** filter with an initial strength of 1 on an image. When the page loads, the **onfilterchange** event of the image is fired. The **strength** and **direction** properties on the **blur** filter cause the **onfilterchange** event to fire repeatedly until the **strength** reaches 100.

```
<SCRIPT>
function HandleChange()
{
   with (window.event.srcElement.filters[0])
   {
      if (strength < 100)
      {
         strength += 1;
         direction += 45;
      }
   }
}</SCRIPT>
<IMG ID="img1" SRC="joker2.jpg" onfilterchange="HandleChange()"
   STYLE="filter:blur (STRENGTH=1 DIRECTION=0)" />
```

To see this code in action, refer to the Web Workshop CD-ROM.

Applies To

 WIN32   UNIX

blur, shadow

DURATION Attribute | duration Property

Sets or retrieves the length of time the transition takes to complete.

Syntax

HTML   { **filter:**_filterName_ (**DURATION** = _fDuration..._) }

Scripting _object_.**filters.**_filterName_.**duration** [= _fDuration_]

Possible Values

fDuration Floating-point value specifying the length of time it takes to complete the transition. The value is specified in seconds.milliseconds format (0.0000).

The property is read/write with no default value. However, once the transition is applied, or starts playing, the property becomes read-only.

Remarks

You can set a transition's playback duration as a parameter of the **play** method.

Example

The following example shows how to set the **DURATION** attribute for the **revealTrans** filter.

```
<SCRIPT>
function go() {
    C1.filters[0].Apply();

if (C1.style.visibility == "visible") {
        C1.style.visibility = "hidden";
    C1.filters.revealTrans.transition=2;
    }
    else {
        C1.style.visibility = "visible";
    C1.filters[0].transition=3;
    }
    C1.filters[0].Play();
}
</SCRIPT>
<INPUT TYPE=BUTTON VALUE="Play Transition" onClick="go();"></INPUT>
<SPAN ID=C1 STYLE="position:absolute;visibility:visible;
    filter:revealTrans(DURATION=2, TRANSITION=3);
    width:300; height:300; background-color: lightgreen">
<CENTER>
    <DIV STYLE="background-color=red;height=100;width:100;
        position:relative;top:100"></DIV>
</CENTER>
</SPAN>
```

To see this code in action, refer to the Web Workshop CD-ROM.

Applies To

 WIN32   UNIX

blendTrans, revealTrans

enabled Property

Sets or retrieves whether the filter is currently enabled.

Syntax

HTML   { **filter:***filterName* (**ENABLED** = "true" | "false"...) }

Scripting *object*.**filters**.*filterName*.**enabled** [= *bEnabled*]

Possible Values

true   Filter is enabled.

false   Filter is disabled.

The property is read/write with a default value of true.

Example

The following example shows how to toggle the **enabled** property of a filter as the user moves the mouse in and out of the image.

```
<IMG ID="image1" SRC="sample.jpg"
    onmouseover="image1.filters.flipv.enabled = false;"
    onmouseout ="image1.filters.flipv.enabled = true;"
    STYLE="filter:blur(STRENGTH=50) flipv()">
```

Applies To

 WIN32   UNIX

alpha, blur, blendTrans, chroma, dropShadow, flipH, flipV, glow, gray, invert, light, mask, redirect, revealTrans, shadow, wave, xray

FINISHOPACITY Attribute | finishOpacity Property

Sets or retrieves the opacity level.

Syntax

HTML   { **filter:alpha** (**FINISHOPACITY** = *iOpacity*...) }

Scripting *object*.**filters**.alpha.**finishOpacity** [= *iOpacity*]

Possible Values

> *iOpacity* Integer specifying the opacity level. Values can range from 0 (fully transparent) to 100 (fully opaque).

> The property is read/write with a default value of 0.

Remarks

> This property only applies to objects that have an opacity gradient specified—that is, the **style** set to 1, 2, or 3.

Applies To

 WIN32   UNIX

> alpha

FINISHX Attribute | finishX Property

> Sets or retrieves the x-coordinate of the point at which the opacity gradient ends.

Syntax

> **HTML**   { **filter:alpha** (**FINISHX** = *iXCoord*...) }
>
> **Scripting** *object*.**filters**.alpha.**finishX** [= *iXCoord*]

Possible Values

> *iXCoord* Integer specifying the x-coordinate of the point at which the opacity gradient ends.

> The property is read/write with no default value.

Remarks

> This property only applies to objects that have an opacity gradient specified—that is, the **style** set to 1, 2, or 3.

Applies To

 WIN32   UNIX

> alpha

FINISHY Attribute | finishY Property

Sets or retrieves the y-coordinate of the point at which the opacity gradient ends.

Syntax

HTML   { **filter:alpha (FINISHY** = *iYCoord*...) }

Scripting *object*.**filters**.alpha.**finishY** [= *iYCoord*]

Possible Values

iYCoord Integer specifying the y-coordinate of the point at which the opacity gradient ends.

The property is read/write with no default value.

Remarks

This property only applies to objects that have an opacity gradient specified—that is, the **style** set to 1, 2, or 3.

Applies To

 WIN32   **UNIX**
_____

alpha

FREQ Attribute | freq Property

Sets or retrieves the number of waves to appear in the visual distortion.

Syntax

HTML   { **filter:wave (FREQ** = *iWaveCount*...) }

Scripting *object*.**filters**.wave.**freq** [= *iWaveCount*]

Possible Values

iWaveCount Integer specifying the number of waves.

The property is read/write with no default value.

Applies To

 WIN32   UNIX

wave

LIGHTSTRENGTH Attribute | lightStrength Property

Sets or retrieves the intensity of light applied by the filter.

Syntax

HTML   { **filter:wave** (**LIGHTSTRENGTH** = *iPercentage*...) }

Scripting *object*.**filters**.wave.**lightStrength** [= *iPercentage*]

Possible Values

iPercentage Integer specifying the intensity of light, as a percentage, ranging from 0 to 100.

The property is read/write with no default value.

Applies To

 WIN32   UNIX

wave

OFFX Attribute | offX Property

Sets or retrieves the offset of the drop shadow from the object, along the x-axis.

Syntax

HTML   { **filter:dropShadow** (**OFFX** = *iOffsetX*...) }

Scripting *object*.**filters**.dropShadow.**offX** [= *iOffsetX*]

Possible Values

> *iOffsetX* Integer specifying the offset value, in pixels. Positive values move the drop
> shadow to the right. Negative values move the drop shadow to the left.

> The property is read/write with no default value.

Applies To

 WIN32   UNIX

> dropShadow

OFFY Attribute | offY Property

> Sets or retrieves the offset of the drop shadow from the object, along the y-axis.

Syntax

> **HTML**   { **filter:dropShadow** (**OFFY** = *iOffsetY*...) }
>
> **Scripting** *object*.**filters**.dropShadow.**offY** [= *iOffsetY*]

Possible Values

> *iOffsetY* Integer specifying the offset value, in pixels. Positive values move the drop
> shadow down. Negative values move the drop shadow up.

> The property is read/write with no default value.

Applies To

 WIN32   UNIX

> dropShadow

OPACITY Attribute | opacity Property

> Sets or retrieves the opacity level.

Syntax

> **HTML**   { **filter:alpha** (**OPACITY** = *iOpacity*...) }
>
> **Scripting** *object*.**filters**.alpha.**opacity** [= *iOpacity*]

Possible Values

    iOpacity Integer specifying the opacity level. Values can range from 0 (fully transparent) to 100 (fully opaque).

    The property is read/write with a default value of 100.

Applies To

 WIN32   **UNIX**

alpha

PHASE Attribute | phase Property

    Sets or retrieves the phase offset at which the sine wave starts.

Syntax

    HTML   { **filter**:**wave** (**PHASE** = *iPercentage*...) }

    Scripting *object*.**filters**.wave.**phase** [= *iPercentage*]

Possible Values

    iPercentage Integer specifying the offset value, as a percentage, ranging from 0 to 100. A value of 25 starts the sine wave effect at 90 degrees. A value of 360 is equivalent to 0 degrees.

    The property is read/write with a default value of 0.

Applies To

 WIN32   **UNIX**

wave

POSITIVE Attribute | positive Property

    Sets or retrieves whether the filter creates a drop shadow from the nontransparent pixels of the object.

Syntax

    HTML   { **filter**:**dropShadow** (**POSITIVE** = "true" | "false"...) }

    Scripting *object*.**filters**.dropShadow.**positive** [= *bPositive*]

Possible Values

`true`   Drop shadow is created from the nontransparent pixels of the object.

`false` Drop shadow is created from the transparent pixels of the object.

The property is read/write with a default value of `true`.

Remarks

If you have a transparent object but still want the usual drop shadow effect, set the **positive** property to `false`. This causes the transparent object to have a drop shadow outside the transparent region, rather than a drop shadow inside the transparent region.

Applies To

 WIN32   **UNIX**

dropShadow

STARTX Attribute | startX Property

Sets or retrieves the x-coordinate of the point at which the opacity gradient starts.

Syntax

HTML   { **filter:alpha** (**STARTX** = *iXCoord*...) }

Scripting *object*.**filters**.`alpha`.**startX** [= *iXCoord*]

Possible Values

iXCoord Integer specifying the x-coordinate of the point at which the opacity gradient starts.

The property is read/write with no default value.

Remarks

This property only applies to objects that have an opacity gradient specified—that is, the **style** set to 1, 2, or 3.

Applies To

 WIN32   **UNIX**

alpha

STARTY Attribute | startY Property

Sets or retrieves the y-coordinate of the point at which the opacity gradient starts.

Syntax

HTML   { **filter:alpha** (**STARTY** = *iYCoord...*) }

Scripting *object*.**filters**.alpha.**startY** [= *iYCoord*]

Possible Values

iYCoord   Integer specifying the y-coordinate of the point at which the opacity
            gradient starts.

The property is read/write with no default value.

Remarks

This property only applies to objects that have an opacity gradient specified—that is,
the **style** set to 1, 2, or 3.

Applies To

 WIN32   **UNIX**
_____

alpha

status Property

Retrieves the current state of the transition.

Syntax

HTML   N/A

Scripting [*iStatus*] = *object*.**filters**.*filterName*.**status**

Possible Values

0   Transition has stopped.

1   Transition has been applied.

2   Transition is playing.

The property is read-only with no default value.

Applies To

 WIN32   UNIX

blendTrans, revealTrans

STRENGTH Attribute | strength Property

Sets or retrieves the intensity of the filter.

Syntax

HTML   { **filter**:*filterName* (**STRENGTH** = *iIntensity*...) }

Scripting *object*.**filters**.*filterName*.**strength** [= *iIntensity*]

Possible Values

iIntensity   Integer specifying the intensity of the filter. Values can range from 1 to 255.

The property is read/write with no default value.

Example

The following example shows how to set a **blur** filter with an initial **strength** of 1 on an image. When the page loads, the **onfilterchange** event of the image is fired. Setting the **strength** and **direction** properties on the **blur** filter causes the **onfilterchange** event to fire repeatedly until the **strength** reaches 100.

```
<SCRIPT>
function HandleChange()
{
   with (window.event.srcElement.filters[0])
   {
      if (strength < 100)
      {
         strength += 1;
         direction += 45;
      }
   }
}</SCRIPT>
<IMG ID="img1" SRC="joker2.jpg" onfilterchange="HandleChange()"
   STYLE="filter:blur (STRENGTH=1 DIRECTION=0)" />
```

To see this code in action, refer to the Web Workshop CD-ROM.

Applies To

 WIN32   UNIX

blur, glow, wave

STYLE Attribute | style Property

Sets or retrieves the shape characteristics of the opacity gradient.

Syntax

HTML   { **filter:alpha** (**STYLE** = 0 | 1 | 2 | 3 ...) }

Scripting   *object*.**filters**.alpha.**style** [= *iStyle*]

Possible Values

0   Uniform opacity gradient.

1   Linear opacity gradient.

2   Radial opacity gradient.

3   Rectangular opacity gradient.

The property is read/write with a default value of 0.

Applies To

 WIN32   UNIX

alpha

TRANSITION Attribute | transition Property

Sets or retrieves the type of transition.

Syntax

HTML   { **filter**:**revealTrans** (**TRANSITION** = *iTransitionType* ...) }

Scripting   *object*.**filters**.revealTrans.**transition** [= *iTransitionType*]

Possible Values

0	Box in.	12	Random dissolve.
1	Box out.	13	Split vertical in.
2	Circle in.	14	Split vertical out.
3	Circle out.	15	Split horizontal in.
4	Wipe up.	16	Split horizontal out.
5	Wipe down.	17	Strips left down.
6	Wipe right.	18	Strips left up.
7	Wipe left.	19	Strips right down.
8	Vertical blinds.	20	Strips right up.
9	Horizontal blinds.	21	Random bars horizontal.
10	Checkerboard across.	22	Random bars vertical.
11	Checkerboard down.	23	Random.

The property is read/write with no default value.

Example

The following example shows how to set the **TRANSITION** attribute for the **revealTrans** filter.

```
<SCRIPT>
function go() {
    C1.filters[0].Apply();

if (C1.style.visibility == "visible") {
        C1.style.visibility = "hidden";
    C1.filters.revealTrans.transition=2;
    }
    else {
        C1.style.visibility = "visible";
    C1.filters[0].transition=3;
    }
    C1.filters[0].Play();
}
</SCRIPT>
<INPUT TYPE=BUTTON VALUE="Play Transition" onClick="go();"></INPUT>
<SPAN ID=C1 STYLE="position:absolute;visibility:visible;
    filter:revealTrans(DURATION=2, TRANSITION=3);
    width:300; height:300; background-color: lightgreen">
<CENTER>
    <DIV STYLE="background-color=red;height=100;width:100;
        position:relative;top:100"></DIV>
</CENTER>
</SPAN>
```

To see this code in action, refer to the Web Workshop CD-ROM.

Applies To

 WIN32   UNIX

revealTrans

Tables

Color Table

Colors can be specified in HTML pages in two ways—by using a color name, or by using numbers to denote a red-green-blue (RGB) color value. An RGB color value consists of three two-digit hexadecimal numbers specifying the intensity of the corresponding color.

For example, the color value #FF0000 is rendered red because the red number is set to its highest value, FF (or 255 in decimal form).

Note While these color names might not be recognized by other browsers, the RGB color values should display accurately across browsers. When specifying color values for Web pages targeted to work across different browsers, use the RGB color values.

The following table lists the colors supported as of Microsoft Internet Explorer 4.0.

Color Name	Value	Color Name	Value
aliceblue	#F0F8FF	antiquewhite	#FAEBD7
aqua	#00FFFF	aquamarine	#7FFFD4
azure	#F0FFFF	beige	#F5F5DC
bisque	#FFE4C4	black	#000000
blanchedalmond	#FFEBCD	blue	#0000FF
blueviolet	#8A2BE2	brown	#A52A2A
burlywood	#DEB887	cadetblue	#5F9EA0
chartreuse	#7FFF00	chocolate	#D2691E
coral	#FF7F50	cornflower	#6495ED
cornsilk	#FFF8DC	crimson	#DC143C
cyan	#00FFFF	darkblue	#00008B

Color Name	Value	Color Name	Value
darkcyan	#008B8B	darkgoldenrod	#B8860B
darkgray	#A9A9A9	darkgreen	#006400
darkkhaki	#BDB76B	darkmagenta	#8B008B
darkolivegreen	#556B2F	darkorange	#FF8C00
darkorchid	#9932CC	darkred	#8B0000
darksalmon	#E9967A	darkseagreen	#8FBC8B
darkslateblue	#483D8B	darkslategray	#2F4F4F
darkturquoise	#00CED1	darkviolet	#9400D3
deeppink	#FF1493	deepskyblue	#00BFFF
dimgray	#696969	dodgerblue	#1E90FF
firebrick	#B22222	floralwhite	#FFFAF0
forestgreen	#228B22	fuchsia	#FF00FF
gainsboro	#DCDCDC	ghostwhite	#F8F8FF
gold	#FFD700	goldenrod	#DAA520
gray	#808080	green	#008000
greenyellow	#ADFF2F	honeydew	#F0FFF0
hotpink	#FF69B4	indianred	#CD5C5C
indigo	#4B0082	ivory	#FFFFF0
khaki	#F0E68C	lavender	#E6E6FA
lavenderblush	#FFF0F5	lawngreen	#7CFC00
lemonchiffon	#FFFACD	lightblue	#ADD8E6
lightcoral	#F08080	lightcyan	#E0FFFF
lightgoldenrodyellow	#FAFAD2	lightgreen	#90EE90
lightgray	#D3D3D3	lightpink	#FFB6C1
lightsalmon	#FFA07A	lightseagreen	#20B2AA
lightskyblue	#87CEFA	lightslategray	#778899
lightsteelblue	#B0C4DE	lightyellow	#FFFFE0
lime	#00FF00	limegreen	#32CD32
linen	#FAF0E6	magenta	#FF00FF
maroon	#800000	mediumaquamarine	#66CDAA
mediumblue	#0000CD	mediumorchid	#BA55D3
mediumpurple	#9370DB	mediumseagreen	#3CB371
mediumslateblue	#7B68EE	mediumspringgreen	#00FA9A
mediumturquoise	#48D1CC	mediumvioletred	#C71585
midnightblue	#191970	mintcream	#F5FFFA
mistyrose	#FFE4E1	moccasin	#FFE4B5
navajowhite	#FFDEAD	navy	#000080

Color Name	Value	Color Name	Value
oldlace	#FDF5E6	olive	#808000
olivedrab	#6B8E23	orange	#FFA500
orangered	#FF4500	orchid	#DA70D6
palegoldenrod	#EEE8AA	palegreen	#98FB98
paleturquoise	#AFEEEE	palevioletred	#DB7093
papayawhip	#FFEFD5	peachpuff	#FFDAB9
peru	#CD853F	pink	#FFC0CB
plum	#DDA0DD	powderblue	#B0E0E6
purple	#800080	red	#FF0000
rosybrown	#BC8F8F	royalblue	#4169E1
saddlebrown	#8B4513	salmon	#FA8072
sandybrown	#F4A460	seagreen	#2E8B57
seashell	#FFF5EE	sienna	#A0522D
silver	#C0C0C0	skyblue	#87CEEB
slateblue	#6A5ACD	slategray	#708090
snow	#FFFAFA	springgreen	#00FF7F
steelblue	#4682B4	tan	#D2B48C
teal	#008080	thistle	#D8BFD8
tomato	#FF6347	turquoise	#40E0D0
violet	#EE82EE	wheat	#F5DEB3
white	#FFFFFF	whitesmoke	#F5F5F5
yellow	#FFFF00	yellowgreen	#9ACD32

User-Defined System Colors

Windows maintains a set of system colors for painting various parts of the display. In addition to the colors defined in the color table, as of Internet Explorer 4.0 these system colors may also be specified as color values in Web pages.

Users can set system colors for future Windows sessions using the Windows Control Panel. The following table illustrates the correspondence of these color names with the colors defined in the Windows Control Panel.

Note The colors that do not correspond to any Control Panel colors can only be set programmatically using Windows APIs and cannot be defined by the user.

Color Name	Control Panel Text	Color Name	Control Panel Text
activeborder	Active Window Border	activecaption	Active Title Bar
appworkspace		background	Desktop
buttonface		buttonhighlight	
buttonshadow		buttontext	

Color Name	Control Panel Text	Color Name	Control Panel Text
captiontext	Active Title Bar Text	graytext	
highlight	Selected Items	highlighttext	Selected Items Text
inactiveborder	Inactive Window Border	inactivecaption	Inactive Title Bar
inactivecaptiontext	Inactive Title Bar Text	infobackground	Tooltip
infotext	Tooltip Text	menu	Menu
menutext	Menu Text	scrollbar	Scrollbar
threedface	3D Objects	threedhighlight	
threedshadow		threeddarkshadow	
threedlightshadow		window	Window
windowframe		windowtext	Window Text

CSS Attributes Reference

This section defines the supported cascading style sheets (CSS) attributes and DHTML properties. An asterisk (*) indicates the attribute or property was introduced with Internet Explorer 5. A dagger (†) indicates the attribute or property has been proposed to the World Wide Web Consortium (W3C) but not yet made standard as of March 1999.

Behavior properties

Attribute	DHTML Property
behavior †*	behavior †*

Font and text properties

Attribute	DHTML Property
direction*	direction*
font	font
@font-face	
font-family	fontFamily
font-size	fontSize
font-style	fontStyle
font-variant	fontVariant
font-weight	fontWeight

Attribute	DHTML Property
ime-mode [†*]	imeMode [†*]
layout-grid [†]	layoutGrid [†]
layout-grid-char [†]	layoutGridChar [†]
layout-grid-char-spacing [†]	layoutGridCharSpacing [†]
layout-grid-line [†]	layoutGridLine [†]
layout-grid-mode [†]	layoutGridMode [†]
layout-grid-type [†]	layoutGridType [†]
line-break [†*]	lineBreak [†*]
line-height	lineHeight
letter-spacing	letterSpacing
ruby-align [†*]	rubyAlign [†*]
ruby-overhang [†*]	rubyOverhang [†*]
ruby-position [†*]	rubyPosition [†*]
text-align	textAlign
text-decoration	textDecoration
text-justify [†*]	textJustify [†*]
text-indent	textIndent
text-transform	textTransform
unicode-bidi	unicodeBidi
vertical-align	verticalAlign
word-break [†*]	wordBreak [†*]
word-spacing (Macintosh only)	wordSpacing (Macintosh only)

Color and background properties

Attribute	DHTML Property
background	background
background-attachment	backgroundAttachment
background-color	backgroundColor
background-image	backgroundImage

Attribute	DHTML Property
background-position	backgroundPosition
background-repeat	backgroundRepeat
color	color

Layout properties

Attribute	DHTML Property
border	border
border-bottom	borderBottom
border-bottom-color	borderBottomColor
border-bottom-style	borderBottomStyle
border-bottom-width	borderBottomWidth
border-collapse[*]	borderCollapse[*]
border-color	borderColor
border-left	borderLeft
border-left-color	borderLeftColor
border-left-style	borderLeftStyle
border-left-width	borderLeftWidth
border-right	borderRight
border-right-color	borderRightColor
border-right-style	borderRightStyle
border-right-width	borderRightWidth
border-style	borderStyle
border-top	borderTop
border-top-color	borderTopColor
border-top-style	borderTopStyle
border-top-width	borderTopWidth
border-width	borderWidth
clear	clear
float	styleFloat

Attribute	DHTML Property
margin	margin
margin-bottom	marginBottom
margin-left	marginLeft
margin-right	marginRight
margin-top	marginTop
padding	padding
padding-bottom	paddingBottom
padding-left	paddingLeft
padding-right	paddingRight
padding-top	paddingTop
table-layout[*]	tableLayout[*]

Classification properties

Attribute	DHTML Property
display	display
list-style	listStyle
list-style-image	listStyleImage
list-style-position	listStylePosition
list-style-type	listStyleType

Positioning properties

Attribute	DHTML Property
bottom	bottom
clip	clip
height	height
left	left
overflow	overflow
overflow-x [†]	overflowX [†]
overflow-y [†]	overflowY [†]

Attribute	DHTML Property
position	position
right	right
top	top
visibility	visibility
width	width
z-index	zIndex

Printing properties

Attribute	DHTML Property
page-break-after	pageBreakAfter
page-break-before	pageBreakBefore

Filter properties

Attribute	DHTML Property
filter [†]	filter [†]

Pseudo-classes and other properties

Attribute	DHTML Property
active	
cursor	cursor
hover	
@import	
!important	
link	link
visited	

Unsupported CSS attributes

Attribute	DHTML Property
first-letter pseudo	
first-line pseudo	
white-space	

CSS Length Units

This section defines the supported length units for CSS attributes. Unless otherwise specified, the length units are supported as of Internet Explorer 3.0 or later. An asterisk (*) indicates the length unit is available as of Internet Explorer 4.0 or later.

Relative length units

em *	The height of the element's font.
ex *	The height of the letter "x".
px	Pixels.
%	Percentage.

Absolute length units

in	Inches (*1 inch = 2.54 centimeters*).
cm	Centimeters.
mm	Millimeters.
pt	Points (*1 point = 1/72 inches*).
pc	Picas (*1 pica = 12 points*).

Measurements and positions in CSS properties are indicated in length units. Internet Explorer supports two types of length units: relative and absolute.

A relative length unit specifies a length in relation to another length property. Relative length units scale better from one output device to another, such as from a monitor to a printer. Percentages and keywords perform similarly.

An absolute length unit specifies an absolute measurement, such as inches or centimeters. Absolute length units are useful when the physical properties of the output device are known.

Command Identifiers

Command identifiers specify an action to take on the given object. Use them with the following methods:

- **execCommand**
- **queryCommandEnabled**
- **queryCommandIndeterm**
- **queryCommandState**
- **queryCommandSupported**
- **queryCommandValue**

The following command identifiers are currently available:

BackColor Command	**Bold Command**	**Copy Command**
CreateBookmark Command	**CreateLink Command**	**Cut Command**
Delete Command	**Find Command**	**FontName Command**
FontSize Command	**ForeColor Command**	**FormatBlock Command**
Indent Command	**InsertButton Command**	**InsertFieldset Command**
InsertHorizontalRule Command	**InsertIFrame Command**	**InsertImage Command**
InsertInputButton Command	**InsertInputCheckbox Command**	**InsertInputFileUpload Command**
InsertInputHidden Command	**InsertInputPassword Command**	**InsertInputRadio Command**
InsertInputReset Command	**InsertInputSubmit Command**	**InsertInputText Command**
InsertMarquee Command	**InsertOrderedList Command**	**InsertParagraph Command**
InsertSelectDropdown Command	**InsertSelectListbox Command**	**InsertTextArea Command**
InsertUnorderedList Command	**Italic Command**	**JustifyCenter Command**
JustifyLeft Command	**JustifyRight Command**	**Outdent Command**
OverWrite Command	**Paste Command**	**Refresh Command**

RemoveFormat Command	SelectAll Command	UnBookmark Command
Underline Command	Unlink Command	Unselect Command

HTML Character Sets

Character sets determine how the bytes that represent the text of your HTML document are translated to readable characters. Internet Explorer interprets the bytes in your document according to the applied character set translations. It interprets numeric or hex character references ("〹" or "ሴ") as ISO10646 code points, consistent with the Unicode Standard, version 2.0, and independent of the chosen character set. Named entities ("&") are displayed independently of the chosen character set as well. The display of an arbitrary numeric character reference requires the existence of a font that is able to display that particular character on the user's system. Accordingly, the content in the first column of the following tables may not render as expected on all systems.

1. ISO Latin-1 Character Set
2. Additional Named Entities for HTML
3. Character Entities for Special Symbols and BIDI Text
4. Character Set Recognition

ISO Latin-1 Character Set

The following table contains the complete ISO Latin-1 character set, corresponding to the first 256 entries of the Unicode character repertoire in Internet Explorer version 4.0 and later. The table provides each character, its decimal code, its named entity reference for HTML, and also a brief description.

Character	Decimal code	Named entity	Description
—	&#00;	—	Unused
—	&#01;	—	Unused
—	&#02;	—	Unused
—	&#03;	—	Unused
—	&#04;	—	Unused
—	&#05;	—	Unused
—	&#06;	—	Unused
—	&#07;	—	Unused
—	&#08;	—	Unused
—	&#09;	—	Horizontal tab

Character	Decimal code	Named entity	Description
—	&#10;	—	Line feed
—	&#11;	—	Unused
—	&#12;	—	Unused
—	&#13;	—	Carriage Return
—	&#14;	—	Unused
—	&#15;	—	Unused
—	&#16;	—	Unused
—	&#17;	—	Unused
—	&#18;	—	Unused
—	&#19;	—	Unused
—	&#20;	—	Unused
—	&#21;	—	Unused
—	&#22;	—	Unused
—	&#23;	—	Unused
—	&#24;	—	Unused
—	&#25;	—	Unused
—	&#26;	—	Unused
—	&#27;	—	Unused
—	&#28;	—	Unused
—	&#29;	—	Unused
—	&#30;	—	Unused
—	&#31;	—	Unused
	&#32;	—	Space
!	&#33;	—	Exclamation mark
"	&#34;	&quot;	Quotation mark
#	&#35;	—	Number sign
$	&#36;	—	Dollar sign
%	&#37;	—	Percent sign
&	&#38;	&amp;	Ampersand
'	&#39;	—	Apostrophe
(	&#40;	—	Left parenthesis
)	&#41;	—	Right parenthesis
*	&#42;	—	Asterisk
+	&#43;	—	Plus sign
,	&#44;	—	Comma
-	&#45;	—	Hyphen
.	&#46;	—	Period (fullstop)

Character	Decimal code	Named entity	Description
/	/	—	Solidus (slash)
0	0	—	Digit 0
1	1	—	Digit 1
2	2	—	Digit 2
3	3	—	Digit 3
4	4	—	Digit 4
5	5	—	Digit 5
6	6	—	Digit 6
7	7	—	Digit 7
8	8	—	Digit 8
9	9	—	Digit 9
:	:	—	Colon
;	;	—	Semicolon
<	<	<	Less than
=	=	—	Equals sign
>	>	>	Greater than
?	?	—	Question mark
@	@	—	Commercial at
A	A	—	Capital A
B	B	—	Capital B
C	C	—	Capital C
D	D	—	Capital D
E	E	—	Capital E
F	F	—	Capital F
G	G	—	Capital G
H	H	—	Capital H
I	I	—	Capital I
J	J	—	Capital J
K	K	—	Capital K
L	L	—	Capital L
M	M	—	Capital M
N	N	—	Capital N
O	O	—	Capital O
P	P	—	Capital P
Q	Q	—	Capital Q
R	R	—	Capital R
S	S	—	Capital S

Character	Decimal code	Named entity	Description
T	&#84;	—	Capital T
U	&#85;	—	Capital U
V	&#86;	—	Capital V
W	&#87;	—	Capital W
X	&#88;	—	Capital X
Y	&#89;	—	Capital Y
Z	&#90;	—	Capital Z
[	&#91;	—	Left square bracket
\	&#92;	—	Reverse solidus (backslash)
]	&#93;	—	Right square bracket
^	&#94;	—	Caret
_	&#95;	—	Horizontal bar (underscore)
`	&#96;	—	Acute accent
a	&#97;	—	Small a
b	&#98;	—	Small b
c	&#99;	—	Small c
d	&#100;	—	Small d
e	&#101;	—	Small e
f	&#102;	—	Small f
g	&#103;	—	Small g
h	&#104;	—	Small h
i	&#105;	—	Small i
j	&#106;	—	Small j
k	&#107;	—	Small k
l	&#108;	—	Small l
m	&#109;	—	Small m
n	&#110;	—	Small n
o	&#111;	—	Small o
p	&#112;	—	Small p
q	&#113;	—	Small q
r	&#114;	—	Small r
s	&#115;	—	Small s
t	&#116;	—	Small t
u	&#117;	—	Small u
v	&#118;	—	Small v
w	&#119;	—	Small w
x	&#120;	—	Small x

Character	Decimal code	Named entity	Description
y	&#121;	—	Small y
z	&#122;	—	Small z
{	&#123;	—	Left curly brace
|	|	—	Vertical bar
}	&#125;	—	Right curly brace
~	&#126;	—	Tilde
—	&#127;	—	Unused
			Nonbreaking space
¡	&#161;	&iexcl;	Inverted exclamation
¢	&#162;	&cent;	Cent sign
£	&#163;	&pound;	Pound sterling
¤	&#164;	&curren;	General currency sign
¥	&#165;	&yen;	Yen sign
¦	&#166;	¦ or &brkbar;	Broken vertical bar
§	&#167;	&sect;	Section sign
¨	&#168;	¨ or ¨	Dieresis / umlaut
©	&#169;	&copy;	Copyright
a	&#170;	&ordf;	Feminine ordinal
«	&#171;	&laquo;	Left angle quote, guillemot left
¬	&#172;	&not	Not sign
	&#173;	&shy;	Soft hyphen
®	&#174;	&reg;	Registered trademark
¯	&#175;	¯ or &hibar;	Macron accent
°	&#176;	&deg;	Degree sign
±	&#177;	&plusmn;	Plus or minus
2	&#178;	&sup2;	Superscript two
3	&#179;	&sup3;	Superscript three
´	&#180;	&acute;	Acute accent
µ	&#181;	&micro;	Micro sign
¶	&#182;	&para;	Paragraph sign
·	&#183;	&middot;	Middle dot
¸	&#184;	&cedil;	Cedilla
1	&#185;	&sup1;	Superscript one
o	&#186;	&ordm;	Masculine ordinal
»	&#187;	&raquo;	Right angle quote, guillemot right
¼	&#188;	&frac14;	Fraction one-fourth
½	&#189;	&frac12;	Fraction one-half

Character	Decimal code	Named entity	Description
¾	&#190;	&frac34;	Fraction three-fourths
¿	&#191;	&iquest;	Inverted question mark
À	&#192;	&Agrave;	Capital A, grave accent
Á	&#193;	&Aacute;	Capital A, acute accent
Â	&#194;	&Acirc;	Capital A, circumflex
Ã	&#195;	&Atilde;	Capital A, tilde
Ä	&#196;	&Auml;	Capital A, dieresis / umlaut
Å	&#197;	&Aring;	Capital A, ring
Æ	&#198;	&AElig;	Capital AE ligature
Ç	&#199;	&Ccedil;	Capital C, cedilla
È	&#200;	&Egrave;	Capital E, grave accent
É	&#201;	&Eacute;	Capital E, acute accent
Ê	&#202;	&Ecirc;	Capital E, circumflex
Ë	&#203;	&Euml;	Capital E, dieresis / umlaut
Ì	&#204;	&Igrave;	Capital I, grave accent
Í	&#205;	&Iacute;	Capital I, acute accent
Î	&#206;	&Icirc;	Capital I, circumflex
Ï	&#207;	&Iuml;	Capital I, dieresis / umlaut
Ð	&#208;	&ETH;	Capital Eth, Icelandic
Ñ	&#209;	&Ntilde;	Capital N, tilde
Ò	&#210;	&Ograve;	Capital O, grave accent
Ó	&#211;	&Oacute;	Capital O, acute accent
Ô	&#212;	&Ocirc;	Capital O, circumflex
Õ	&#213;	&Otilde;	Capital O, tilde
Ö	&#214;	&Ouml;	Capital O, dieresis / umlaut
×	&#215;	&times;	Multiply sign
Ø	&#216;	&Oslash;	Capital O, slash
Ù	&#217;	&Ugrave;	Capital U, grave accent
Ú	&#218;	&Uacute;	Capital U, acute accent
Û	&#219;	&Ucirc;	Capital U, circumflex
Ü	&#220;	&Uuml;	Capital U, dieresis / umlaut
Ý	&#221;	&Yacute;	Capital Y, acute accent
Þ	&#222;	&THORN;	Capital Thorn, Icelandic
ß	&#223;	&szlig;	Small sharp s, German sz
à	&#224;	&agrave;	Small a, grave accent
á	&#225;	&aacute;	Small a, acute accent
â	&#226;	&acirc;	Small a, circumflex

Character	Decimal code	Named entity	Description
ã	&#227;	&atilde;	Small a, tilde
ä	&#228;	&auml;	Small a, dieresis / umlaut
å	&#229;	&aring;	Small a, ring
æ	&#230;	&aelig;	Small ae ligature
ç	&#231;	&ccedil;	Small c, cedilla
è	&#232;	&egrave;	Small e, grave accent
é	&#233;	&eacute;	Small e, acute accent
ê	&#234;	&ecirc;	Small e, circumflex
ë	&#235;	&euml;	Small e, dieresis / umlaut
ì	&#236;	&igrave;	Small i, grave accent
í	&#237;	&iacute;	Small i, acute accent
î	&#238;	&icirc;	Small i, circumflex
ï	&#239;	&iuml;	Small i, dieresis / umlaut
ð	&#240;	&eth;	Small eth, Icelandic
ñ	&#241;	&ntilde;	Small n, tilde
ò	&#242;	&ograve;	Small o, grave accent
ó	&#243;	&oacute;	Small o, acute accent
ô	&#244;	&ocirc;	Small o, circumflex
õ	&#245;	&otilde;	Small o, tilde
ö	&#246;	&ouml;	Small o, dieresis / umlaut
÷	&#247;	&divide;	Division sign
ø	&#248;	&oslash;	Small o, slash
ù	&#249;	&ugrave;	Small u, grave accent
ú	&#250;	&uacute;	Small u, acute accent
û	&#251;	&ucirc;	Small u, circumflex
ü	&#252;	&uuml;	Small u, dieresis / umlaut
ý	&#253;	&yacute;	Small y, acute accent
þ	&#254;	&thorn;	Small thorn, Icelandic
ÿ	&#255;	&yuml;	Small y, dieresis / umlaut

Character Set Recognition

Internet Explorer uses the character set specified for a document to determine how to translate the bytes in the document into characters on the screen or paper. By default, Internet Explorer uses the character set specified in the HTTP content type returned by the server to determine this translation. If this parameter is not given, Internet Explorer uses the character set specified by the **META** element in the document. It uses the user's preferences if no **META** element is given.

You can use the **META** element to explicitly set the character set for a document. In this case, you set the **HTTP-EQUIV=** attribute to "Content-Type" and specify a character set identifier in the **CONTENT=** attribute. For example, the following **META** element identifies windows-1251 as the character set for the document.

```
<META HTTP-EQUIV="Content-Type"
  CONTENT="text/html; CHARSET=windows-1251">
```

As long as you place the **META** element before the **BODY** element, it affects the whole document, including the **TITLE** element. For clarity, it should appear as the first element after **HEAD** so that all readers know the encoding before the first displayable element is parsed. Note that the **META** element applies to the document containing it. This means, for example, that a compound document (a document consisting of two or more documents in a set of frames) can use different character sets in different frames.

The following table contains information concerning the character sets supported by Internet Explorer 5. The information provided is:

1. Display Name - the name used to refer to the character set.
2. Preferred Charset ID - the most common identifier used to set character sets in Internet Explorer. For example, in the code sample above windows-1251 is the Charset ID.
3. Additional Aliases - other identifiers that may be used to set character sets.
4. MLang Code Pages - numeric value of the code pages used by the Internet Explorer MLang API.
5. Supported by Version - the versions of Internet Explorer that support the listed character sets. Note that CS indicates that the version of Internet Explorer must support complex scripts such as Arabic, Hebrew, or Thai.

Charsets in Microsoft Internet Explorer 5

Display Name	Preferred Charset ID	Additional Aliases	MLang Code Page	Supported by Versions
Arabic ASMO-708	ASMO-708		708	4CS, 5
Arabic (DOS)	DOS-720		720	4CS, 5
Arabic (ISO)	iso-8859-6	ISO_8859-6:1987, iso-ir-127, ISO_8859-6, ECMA-114, arabic, csISOLatinArabic	28596	4CS, 5
Arabic (Windows)	windows-1256		1256	4CS, 5
Baltic (ISO)	iso-8859-4	csISOLatin4, iso-ir-110, ISO_8859-4, ISO_8859-4:1988, l4, latin4	28594	4, 5

Display Name	Preferred Charset ID	Additional Aliases	MLang Code Page	Supported by Versions
Baltic (Windows)	windows 1257		1257	4, 5
Central European (DOS)	ibm852	cp852	852	4, 5
Central European (ISO)	iso-8859-2	csISOLatin2, iso-ir-101, iso8859-2, iso_8859-2, iso_8859-2:1987, l2, latin2	28592	3, 4, 5
Central European (Windows)	windows-1250	x-cp1250	1250	3, 4, 5
Chinese Simplified (GB2312)	gb2312	chinese, csGB2312, csISO58GB23128, GB2312, GBK, GB_2312-80, iso-ir-58	936	3, 4, 5
Chinese Simplified (HZ)	hz-gb-2312		52936	4, 5
Chinese Traditional	big5	csbig5, x-x-big5	950	3, 4, 5
Cyrillic (DOS)	cp866	ibm866	866	4, 5
Cyrillic (ISO)	iso-8859-5	csISOLatinCyrillic, cyrillic, iso-ir-144, ISO_8859-5, ISO_8859-5:1988	28595	4, 5
Cyrillic (KOI8-R)	koi8-r	csKOI8R, koi	20866	3, 4, 5
Cyrillic (Windows)	windows-1251	x-cp1251	1251	3, 4, 5
Greek (ISO)	iso-8859-7	csISOLatinGreek, ECMA-118, ELOT_928, greek, greek8, iso-ir-126, ISO_8859-7, ISO_8859-7:1987	28597	3, 4, 5
Greek (Windows)	Windows-1253	windows-1253	1253	5
Hebrew (DOS)	DOS-862		862	4CS, 5
Hebrew (ISO)	iso-8859-8	csISOLatinHebrew, hebrew, iso-ir-138, ISO_8859-8, visual, ISO-8859-8 Visual	28598	4CS, 5
Hebrew (Windows)	windows-1255	logical, ISO_8859-8:1988, iso-ir-138	1255	3CS, 4CS, 5
Japanese (JIS)	iso-2022-jp	csISO2022JP	50220	4, 5
Japanese (JIS-Allow 1-byte Kana)	csISO2022JP	iso-2022-jp	50221	4, 5
Japanese (JIS-Allow 1-byte Kana - SO/SI)	iso-2022-jp	csISO2022JP	50222	3, 4, 5

Display Name	Preferred Charset ID	Additional Aliases	MLang Code Page	Supported by Versions
Japanese (EUC)	euc-jp	csEUCPkdFmtJapanese, Extended_UNIX_Code_Packed_ Format_for_Japanese, x-euc, x-euc-jp	51932	3, 4, 5
Japanese (Shift-JIS)	shift_jis	csShiftJIS, csWindows31J, ms_Kanji, shift-jis, x-ms-cp932, x-sjis	932	3, 4, 5
Korean	ks_c_5601-1987	csKSC56011987, euc-kr, korean, ks_c_5601	949	3, 4, 5
Korean (ISO)	iso-2022-kr	csISO2022KR	50225	3, 4, 5
Latin 3 (ISO)	iso-8859-3		28593	4, 5
Thai (Windows)	iso-8859-11	windows-874	874	3, 4, 5
Turkish (Windows)	Windows-1254	windows-1254	1254	3, 4, 5
Turkish (ISO)	iso-8859-9	28599	28599	3, 4, 5
Ukrainian (KOI8-RU)	koi8-ru		21866	4, 5
Unicode (UTF-7)	utf-7	csUnicode11UTF7, unicode-1-1-utf-7, x-unicode-2-0-utf-7	65000	4, 5
Unicode (UFT-8)	utf-8	unicode-1-1-utf-8, unicode-2-0-utf-8, x-unicode-2-0-utf-8	65001	4, 5
Vietnamese (Windows)	windows-1258		1258	3, 4, 5
Western European (Windows)	1252	Windows-1252	1252	5
Western European (ISO)	iso-8859-1	ANSI_X3.4-1968, ANSI_X3.4-1986, ascii, cp367, cp819, csASCII, IBM367, ibm819, iso-ir-100, iso-ir-6, ISO646-US, iso8859-1, ISO_646.irv:1991, iso_8859-1, iso_8859-1:1987, latin1, us, us-ascii, x-ansi	1252	3, 4, 5

Note The following nonstandard character sets have special meaning inside Internet Explorer and MLang. These character sets are not to be used for labeling documents.

Display Name	Preferred Charset ID	Additional Aliases	MLang Code Page	Supported by Versions
Unicode	unicode		1200	4, 5
Unicode (BigEndian)	unicodeFEFF		1201	4, 5
User Defined	x-user-defined		50000	4, 5
Korean (Auto Select)	_autodetect_kr		50949	4, 5

Display Name	Preferred Charset ID	Additional Aliases	MLang Code Page	Supported by Versions
Japanese (Auto Select)	_autodetect		50932	3, 4, 5

Installable Components in Internet Explorer

The following table lists the component identifiers that can be installed with Internet Explorer 5. These identifiers are used with the **addComponentRequest** method.

Note The following components do not install on demand in Windows 2000.

Component	Component ID
Address Book	{7790769C-0471-11D2-AF11-00C04FA35D02}
AOL ART Image Format Support	{47F67D00-9E55-11D1-BAEF-00C04FC2D130}
Arabic Text Display Support	{76C19B38-F0C8-11CF-87CC-0020AFEECF20}
Chinese (Simplified) Text Display Support	{76C19B34-F0C8-11CF-87CC-0020AFEECF20}
Chinese (Traditional) Text Display Support	{76C19B33-F0C8-11CF-87CC-0020AFEECF20}
Dynamic HTML Data Binding	{9381D8F2-0288-11D0-9501-00AA00B911A5}
DirectAnimation	{283807B5-2C60-11D0-A31D-00AA00B92C03}
Hebrew Text Display Support	{76C19B36-F0C8-11CF-87CC-0020AFEECF20}
Internet Connection Wizard	{5A8D6EE0-3E18-11D0-821E-444553540000}
Internet Explorer Browsing Enhancements*	{630B1DA0-B465-11D1-9948-00C04F98BBC9}
Internet Explorer Help	{45EA75A0-A269-11D1-B5BF-0000F8051515}
Japanese Text Display Support	{76C19B30-F0C8-11CF-87CC-0020AFEECF20}
Korean Text Display Support	{76C19B31-F0C8-11CF-87CC-0020AFEECF20}
Language Auto-Selection	{76C19B50-F0C8-11CF-87CC-0020AFEECF20}
Macromedia Flash	{D27CDB6E-AE6D-11CF-96B8-444553540000}
Macromedia Shockwave Director	{2A202491-F00D-11CF-87CC-0020AFEECF20}
Windows Media Player	{22D6F312-B0F6-11D0-94AB-0080C74C7E95}
Windows Media Player RealNetwork Support	{23064720-C4F8-11D1-994D-00C04F98BBC9}
Offline Browsing Pack	{3AF36230-A269-11D1-B5BF-0000F8051515}
Pan-European Text Display Support	{76C19B32-F0C8-11CF-87CC-0020AFEECF20}
Thai Text Display Support	{76C19B35-F0C8-11CF-87CC-0020AFEECF20}
Uniscribe	{3BF42070-B3B1-11D1-B5C5-0000F8051515}
Vector Graphics Rendering (VML)	{10072CEC-8CC1-11D1-986E-00A0C955B42F}
Vietnamese Text Display Support	{76C19B37-F0C8-11CF-87CC-0020AFEECF20}
Microsoft virtual machine	{08B0E5C0-4FCB-11CF-AAA5-00401C608500}

Component	Component ID
Visual Basic Scripting Support	{4F645220-306D-11D2-995D-00C04F98BBC9}
VRML 2.0 Viewer	{90A7533D-88FE-11D0-9DBE-0000C0411FC3}
Wallet	{1CDEE860-E95B-11CF-B1B0-00AA00BBAD66}
Web Folders	{73FA19D0-2D75-11D2-995D-00C04F98BBC9}

*Includes FTP Folders and Font Embedding

Detectable Components in Internet Explorer

The following table lists the component identifiers that can be detected with Internet Explorer 5. These identifiers are used with the following methods:

- **getComponentVersion**
- **isComponentInstalled**

Component	Component ID
Address Book	{7790769C-0471-11D2-AF11-00C04FA35D02}
Windows Desktop Update NT	{89820200-ECBD-11CF-8B85-00AA005B4340}
DirectAnimation	{283807B5-2C60-11D0-A31D-00AA00B92C03}
DirectAnimation Java Classes	{4F216970-C90C-11D1-B5C7-0000F8051515}
DirectShow	{44BBA848-CC51-11CF-AAFA-00AA00B6015C}
Dynamic HTML Data Binding	{9381D8F2-0288-11D0-9501-00AA00B911A5}
Dynamic HTML Data Binding for Java	{4F216970-C90C-11D1-B5C7-0000F8051515}
Internet Connection Wizard	{5A8D6EE0-3E18-11D0-821E-444553540000}
Internet Explorer 5 Web Browser	{89820200-ECBD-11CF-8B85-00AA005B4383}
Internet Explorer Classes for Java	{08B0E5C0-4FCB-11CF-AAA5-00401C608555}
Internet Explorer Help	{45EA75A0-A269-11D1-B5BF-0000F8051515}
Internet Explorer Help Engine	{DE5AED00-A4BF-11D1-9948-00C04F98BBC9}
Windows Media Player	{22D6F312-B0F6-11D0-94AB-0080C74C7E95}
NetMeeting® NT	{44BBA842-CC51-11CF-AAFA-00AA00B6015B}
Offline Browsing Pack	{3AF36230-A269-11D1-B5BF-0000F8051515}
Outlook Express	{44BBA840-CC51-11CF-AAFA-00AA00B6015C}
Task Scheduler	{CC2A9BA0-3BDD-11D0-821E-444553540000}
Microsoft virtual machine	{08B0E5C0-4FCB-11CF-AAA5-00401C608500}
VRML 2.0 Viewer	{90A7533D-88FE-11D0-9DBE-0000C0411FC3}
Wallet	{1CDEE860-E95B-11CF-B1B0-00AA00BBAD66}

Additional Named Entities for HTML

The following table contains additional named entities, their numeric character references, and a description of each. The Symbol font contains all these characters.

Character	Named entity	Numeric character reference	Description
Latin Extended-B			
ƒ	&fnof;	&#402;	Latin small f with hook, =function, =florin, U0192 ISOtech
Greek			
A	&Alpha;	&#913;	Greek capital letter alpha, U0391
B	&Beta;	&#914;	Greek capital letter beta, U0392
Γ	&Gamma;	&#915;	Greek capital letter gamma, U0393 ISOgrk3
Δ	&Delta;	&#916;	Greek capital letter delta, U0394 ISOgrk3
E	&Epsilon;	&#917;	Greek capital letter epsilon, U0395
Z	&Zeta;	&#918;	Greek capital letter zeta, U0396
H	&Eta;	&#919;	Greek capital letter eta, U0397
Θ	&Theta;	&#920;	Greek capital letter theta, U0398 ISOgrk3
I	&Iota;	&#921;	Greek capital letter iota, U0399
K	&Kappa;	&#922;	Greek capital letter kappa, U039A
Λ	&Lambda;	&#923;	Greek capital letter lambda, U039B ISOgrk3
M	&Mu;	&#924;	Greek capital letter mu, U039C
N	&Nu;	&#925;	Greek capital letter nu, U039D
Ξ	&Xi;	&#926;	Greek capital letter xi, U039E ISOgrk3
O	&Omicron;	&#927;	Greek capital letter omicron, U039F
Π	&Pi;	&#928;	Greek capital letter pi, U03A0 ISOgrk3
P	&Rho;	&#929;	Greek capital letter rho, U03A1
Σ	&Sigma;	&#931;	Greek capital letter sigma, U03A3 ISOgrk3
T	&Tau;	&#932;	Greek capital letter tau, U03A4
Y	&Upsilon;	&#933;	Greek capital letter upsilon, U03A5 ISOgrk3
Φ	&Phi;	&#934;	Greek capital letter phi, U03A6 ISOgrk3
X	&Chi;	&#935;	Greek capital letter chi, U03A7
Ψ	&Psi;	&#936;	Greek capital letter psi, U03A8 ISOgrk3
Ω	&Omega;	&#937;	Greek capital letter omega, U03A9 ISOgrk3
α	&alpha;	&#945;	Greek small letter alpha, U03B1 ISOgrk3
β	&beta;	&#946;	Greek small letter beta, U03B2 ISOgrk3

Character	Named entity	Numeric character reference	Description
γ	&gamma;	&#947;	Greek small letter gamma, U03B3 ISOgrk3
δ	&delta;	&#948;	Greek small letter delta, U03B4 ISOgrk3
ε	&epsilon;	&#949;	Greek small letter epsilon, U03B5 ISOgrk3
ζ	&zeta;	&#950;	Greek small letter zeta, U03B6 ISOgrk3
η	&eta;	&#951;	Greek small letter eta, U03B7 ISOgrk3
θ	&theta;	&#952;	Greek small letter theta, U03B8 ISOgrk3
ι	&iota;	&#953;	Greek small letter iota, U03B9 ISOgrk3
κ	&kappa;	&#954;	Greek small letter kappa, U03BA ISOgrk3
λ	&lambda;	&#955;	Greek small letter lambda, U03BB ISOgrk3
μ	&mu;	&#956;	Greek small letter mu, U03BC ISOgrk3
ν	&nu;	&#957;	Greek small letter nu, U03BD ISOgrk3
ξ	&xi;	&#958;	Greek small letter xi, U03BE ISOgrk3
o	&omicron;	&#959;	Greek small letter omicron, U03BF NEW
π	&pi;	&#960;	Greek small letter pi, U03C0 ISOgrk3
ρ	&rho;	&#961;	Greek small letter rho, U03C1 ISOgrk3
ς	&sigmaf;	&#962;	Greek small letter final sigma, U03C2 ISOgrk3
σ	&sigma;	&#963;	Greek small letter sigma, U03C3 ISOgrk3
τ	&tau;	&#964;	Greek small letter tau, U03C4 ISOgrk3
υ	&upsilon;	&#965;	Greek small letter upsilon, U03C5 ISOgrk3
φ	&phi;	&#966;	Greek small letter phi, U03C6 ISOgrk3
χ	&chi;	&#967;	Greek small letter chi, U03C7 ISOgrk3
ψ	&psi;	&#968;	Greek small letter psi, U03C8 ISOgrk3
ω	&omega;	&#969;	Greek small letter omega, U03C9 ISOgrk3
ϑ	&thetasym	&#977;	Greek small letter theta symbol, U03D1 NEW
ϒ	&upsih;	&#978;	Greek upsilon with hook symbol, U03D2 NEW
ϖ	&piv;	&#982;	Greek pi symbol, U03D6 ISOgrk3

General Punctuation

Character	Named entity	Numeric character reference	Description
•	&bull;	&#8226;	bullet, =black small circle, U2022 ISOpub
…	&hellip;	&#8230;	horizontal ellipsis, =three dot leader, U2026 ISOpub
′	&prime;	&#8242;	prime, =minutes, =feet, U2032 ISOtech
″	&Prime;	&#8243;	double prime, =seconds, =inches, U2033 ISOtech
‾	&oline;	&#8254;	overline, =spacing overscore, U203E NEW
/	&frasl;	&#8260;	fraction slash, U2044 NEW

Character	Named entity	Numeric character reference	Description
Letterlike Symbols			
℘	&weierp;	&#8472;	script capital P, =power set, =Weierstrass p, U2118 ISOamso
ℑ	&image;	&#8465;	blackletter capital I, =imaginary part, U2111 ISOamso
ℜ	&real;	&#8476;	blackletter capital R, =real part symbol, U211C ISOamso
™	&trade;	&#8482;	trademark sign, U2122 ISOnum
ℵ	&alefsym;	&#8501;	alef symbol, =first transfinite cardinal, U2135 NEW
Arrows			
←	&larr;	&#8592;	leftward arrow, U2190 ISOnum
↑	&uarr;	&#8593;	upward arrow, U2191 ISOnum
→	&rarr;	&#8594;	rightward arrow, U2192 ISOnum
↓	&darr;	&#8595;	downward arrow, U2193 ISOnum
↔	&harr;	&#8596;	left right arrow, U2194 ISOamsa
↵	&crarr;	&#8629;	downward arrow with corner leftward, =carriage return, U21B5 NEW
⇐	&lArr;	&#8656;	leftward double arrow, U21D0 ISOtech
⇑	&uArr;	&#8657;	upward double arrow, U21D1 ISOamsa
⇒	&rArr;	&#8658;	rightward double arrow, U21D2 ISOtech
⇓	&dArr;	&#8659;	downward double arrow, U21D3 ISOamsa
⇔	&hArr;	&#8660;	left right double arrow, U21D4 ISOamsa
Mathematical Operators			
∀	&forall;	&#8704;	for all, U2200 ISOtech
∂	&part;	&#8706;	partial differential, U2202 ISOtech
∃	&exist;	&#8707;	there exists, U2203 ISOtech
∅	&empty;	&#8709;	empty set, =null set, =diameter, U2205 ISOamso
∇	&nabla;	&#8711;	nabla, =backward difference, U2207 ISOtech
∈	&isin;	&#8712;	element of, U2208 ISOtech
∉	&notin;	&#8713;	not an element of, U2209 ISOtech
∋	&ni;	&#8715;	contains as member, U220B ISOtech
∏	&prod;	&#8719;	n-ary product, =product sign, U220F ISOamsb
∑	&sum;	&#8722;	n-ary summation, U2211 ISOamsb
−	&minus;	&#8722;	minus sign, U2212 ISOtech
∗	&lowast;	&#8727;	asterisk operator, U2217 ISOtech

Character	Named entity	Numeric character reference	Description
√	&radic;	&#8730;	square root, =radical sign, U221A ISOtech
∝	&prop;	&#8733;	proportional to, U221D ISOtech
∞	&infin;	&#8734;	infinity, U221E ISOtech
∠	&ang;	&#8736;	angle, U2220 ISOamso
∧	&and;	&#8869;	logical and, =wedge, U2227 ISOtech
∨	&or;	&#8870;	logical or, =vee, U2228 ISOtech
∩	&cap;	&#8745;	intersection, =cap, U2229 ISOtech
∪	&cup;	&#8746;	union, =cup, U222A ISOtech
∫	&int;	&#8747;	integral, U222B ISOtech
∴	&there4;	&#8756;	therefore, U2234 ISOtech
~	&sim;	&#8764;	tilde operator, =varies with, =similar to, U223C ISOtech
≅	&cong;	&#8773;	approximately equal to, U2245 ISOtech
≈	&asymp;	&#8773;	almost equal to, =asymptotic to, U2248 ISOamsr
≠	&ne;	&#8800;	not equal to, U2260 ISOtech
≡	&equiv;	&#8801;	identical to, U2261 ISOtech
≤	&le;	&#8804;	less-than or equal to, U2264 ISOtech
≥	&ge;	&#8805;	greater-than or equal to, U2265 ISOtech
⊂	&sub;	&#8834;	subset of, U2282 ISOtech
⊃	&sup;	&#8835;	superset of, U2283 ISOtech
⊄	&nsub;	&#8836;	not a subset of, U2284 ISOamsn
⊆	&sube;	&#8838;	subset of or equal to, U2286 ISOtech
⊇	&supe;	&#8839;	superset of or equal to, U2287 ISOtech
⊕	&oplus;	&#8853;	circled plus, =direct sum, U2295 ISOamsb
⊗	&otimes;	&#8855;	circled times, =vector product, U2297 ISOamsb
⊥	&perp;	&#8869;	up tack, =orthogonal to, =perpendicular, U22A5 ISOtech
·	&sdot;	&#8901;	dot operator, U22C5 ISOamsb

Miscellaneous Technical

Character	Named entity	Numeric character reference	Description
⌈	&lceil;	&#8968;	left ceiling, =apl upstile, U2308, ISOamsc
⌉	&rceil;	&#8969;	right ceiling, U2309, ISOamsc
⌊	&lfloor;	&#8970;	left floor, =apl downstile, U230A, ISOamsc
⌋	&rfloor;	&#8971;	right floor, U230B, ISOamsc
⟨	&lang;	&#9001;	left-pointing angle bracket, =bra, U2329 ISOtech
⟩	&rang;	&#9002;	right-pointing angle bracket, =ket, U232A ISOtech

Character	Named entity	Numeric character reference	Description
Geometric Shapes			
◊	&loz;	&#9674;	lozenge, U25CA ISOpub
Miscellaneous Symbols			
♠	&spades;	&#9824;	black spade suit, U2660 ISOpub
♣	&clubs;	&#9827;	black club suit, =shamrock, U2663 ISOpub
♥	&hearts;	&#9829;	black heart suit, =valentine, U2665 ISOpub
♦	&diams;	&#9830;	black diamond suit, U2666 ISOpub

Character Entities for Special Symbols and BIDI Text

Character	Named entity	Numeric character reference	Description
C0 Controls and Basic Latin			
"	&quot;	&#34;	quotation mark, =apl quote, U0022 ISOnum
&	&amp;	&#38;	ampersand, U0026 ISOnum
<	&lt;	&#60;	less-than sign, U003C ISOnum
>	&gt;	&#62;	greater-than sign, U003E ISOnum
Latin Extended-A			
Œ	&OElig;	&#338;	Latin capital ligature oe, U0152 ISOlat2
œ	&oelig;	&#339;	Latin small ligature oe, U0153 ISOlat2
Š	&Scaron;	&#352;	Latin capital letter s with caron, U0160 ISOlat2
š	&scaron;	&#353;	Latin small letter s with caron, U0161 ISOlat2
Ÿ	&Yuml;	&#376;	Latin capital letter y with dieresis, U0178 ISOlat2
Spacing Modifier Letters			
ˆ	&circ;	&#710;	modifier letter circumflex accent, U02C6 ISOpub
˜	&tilde;	&#732;	small tilde, U02DC ISOdia
General Punctuation			
n/a			en space, U2002 ISOpub
n/a			em space, U2003 ISOpub
n/a			thin space, U2009 ISOpub
n/a	&zwnj;	&#8204;	zero width non-joiner, U200C NEW RFC 2070
n/a	&zwj;	&#8205;	zero width joiner, U200D NEW RFC 2070

Character	Named entity	Numeric character reference	Description
⌈	&lrm;	&#8206;	left-to-right mark, U200E NEW RFC 2070
⌉	&rlm;	&#8207;	right-to-left mark, U200F NEW RFC 2070
–	&ndash;	&#8211;	en dash, U2013 ISOpub
—	&mdash;	&#151;	em dash, U2014 ISOpub
'	&lsquo;	&#8216;	left single quotation mark, U2018 ISOnum
'	&rsquo;	&#8217;	right single quotation mark, U2019 ISOnum
‚	&sbquo;	&#8218;	single low-9 quotation mark, U201A NEW
"	&ldquo;	&#8220;	left double quotation mark, U201C ISOnum
"	&rdquo;	&#8221;	right double quotation mark, U201D ISOnum
„	&bdquo;	&#8222;	double low-9 quotation mark, U201E NEW
†	&dagger;	&#8224;	dagger, U2020 ISOpub
‡	&Dagger;	&#8225;	double dagger, U2021 ISOpub
‰	&permil;	&#8240;	per mille sign, U2030 ISOtech
‹	&lsaquo;	&#8249;	single left-pointing angle quotation mark, U2039 ISO proposed
›	&rsaquo;	&#8250;	single right-pointing angle quotation mark, U203A ISO proposed

Web Resources

This appendix lists Web sites that provide information about Internet Explorer, Dynamic HTML (DHTML), and other Internet technologies.

Microsoft Developer Network (MSDN) Online Web Workshop

http://msdn.microsoft.com/workshop

This site contains comprehensive information about how to develop Web-based content using the latest Internet Explorer features, such as DHTML, HTML Applications, HTML Components, HTML forms and Intelliforms, and other Internet technologies. The *Microsoft Internet Client Software Development Kit*, which was posted separately for earlier versions of Internet Explorer, is now a part of this site.

Note A snapshot of the Workshop content is on the Web Workshop CD-ROM that accompanies this book. However, you should periodically check the Web Workshop site to keep abreast of the latest Web authoring developments.

World Wide Web Consortium (W3C)

http://www.w3.org

This site is a definitive source for working drafts and technical recommendations relating to browser interoperability on the Internet. In consultation with others in the industry, including Microsoft, the W3C is working to establish standards for CSS1, CSS2, CSS - Positioning, and the Document Object Model.

Microsoft Press Web Site

http://mspress.microsoft.com

This site provides online information about Microsoft publications. Books about DHTML and other Internet technologies include *Programming Microsoft Internet Explorer 5* and *Inside Dynamic HTML*.

MSDN Web Site

http://msdn.microsoft.com/developer

This site features product and technology information for developers using Microsoft tools and applications. This site also provides links to many Microsoft Software Development Kits.

Microsoft Windows Web Site

http://microsoft.com/windows

This site is the source for the latest news and information about the Windows family of products, including product add-ons, updates, service packs, and accessories. Also included is information about Internet Explorer and other related Internet technologies available from Microsoft.

Microsoft Support Online Web Site

http://support.microsoft.com

This site contains Knowledge Base topics with solutions to common support issues for Microsoft products. It also provides access to product newsgroups and Microsoft Technical Support engineers.

Microsoft Windows NT Server Web Site

http://microsoft.com/ntserver

This site contains information relating to Microsoft Internet Information Server (IIS), which is a part of the Windows NT Server family of products. It provides developer news and samples relating to IIS, and describes how to develop Web applications that make the most of Internet technologies and server-side scripting.

Visual Interdev Web Site

http://msdn.microsoft.com/vinterdev

This site provides the latest information about how to use Microsoft® Visual Interdev™ to build database-driven Web applications using Internet Explorer and IIS.

Index

C

P

U

MICROSOFT LICENSE AGREEMENT

Book Companion CD

IMPORTANT—READ CAREFULLY: This Microsoft End-User License Agreement ("EULA") is a legal agreement between you (either an individual or an entity) and Microsoft Corporation for the Microsoft product identified above, which includes computer software and may include associated media, printed materials, and "online" or electronic documentation ("SOFTWARE PRODUCT"). Any component included within the SOFTWARE PRODUCT that is accompanied by a separate End-User License Agreement shall be governed by such agreement and not the terms set forth below. By installing, copying, or otherwise using the SOFTWARE PRODUCT, you agree to be bound by the terms of this EULA. If you do not agree to the terms of this EULA, you are not authorized to install, copy, or otherwise use the SOFTWARE PRODUCT; you may, however, return the SOFTWARE PRODUCT, along with all printed materials and other items that form a part of the Microsoft product that includes the SOFTWARE PRODUCT, to the place you obtained them for a full refund.

SOFTWARE PRODUCT LICENSE

The SOFTWARE PRODUCT is protected by United States copyright laws and international copyright treaties, as well as other intellectual property laws and treaties. The SOFTWARE PRODUCT is licensed, not sold.

1. **GRANT OF LICENSE.** This EULA grants you the following rights:

   a. **Software Product.** You may install and use one copy of the SOFTWARE PRODUCT on a single computer. The primary user of the computer on which the SOFTWARE PRODUCT is installed may make a second copy for his or her exclusive use on a portable computer.

   b. **Storage/Network Use.** You may also store or install a copy of the SOFTWARE PRODUCT on a storage device, such as a network server, used only to install or run the SOFTWARE PRODUCT on your other computers over an internal network; however, you must acquire and dedicate a license for each separate computer on which the SOFTWARE PRODUCT is installed or run from the storage device. A license for the SOFTWARE PRODUCT may not be shared or used concurrently on different computers.

   c. **License Pak.** If you have acquired this EULA in a Microsoft License Pak, you may make the number of additional copies of the computer software portion of the SOFTWARE PRODUCT authorized on the printed copy of this EULA, and you may use each copy in the manner specified above. You are also entitled to make a corresponding number of secondary copies for portable computer use as specified above.

   d. **Sample Code.** Solely with respect to portions, if any, of the SOFTWARE PRODUCT that are identified within the SOFTWARE PRODUCT as sample code (the "SAMPLE CODE"):

      i. **Use and Modification.** Microsoft grants you the right to use and modify the source code version of the SAMPLE CODE, *provided* you comply with subsection (d)(iii) below. You may not distribute the SAMPLE CODE, or any modified version of the SAMPLE CODE, in source code form.

      ii. **Redistributable Files.** Provided you comply with subsection (d)(iii) below, Microsoft grants you a nonexclusive, royalty-free right to reproduce and distribute the object code version of the SAMPLE CODE and of any modified SAMPLE CODE, other than SAMPLE CODE, or any modified version thereof, designated as not redistributable in the Readme file that forms a part of the SOFTWARE PRODUCT (the "Non-Redistributable Sample Code"). All SAMPLE CODE other than the Non-Redistributable Sample Code is collectively referred to as the "REDISTRIBUTABLES."

      iii. **Redistribution Requirements.** If you redistribute the REDISTRIBUTABLES, you agree to: (i) distribute the REDISTRIBUTABLES in object code form only in conjunction with and as a part of your software application product; (ii) not use Microsoft's name, logo, or trademarks to market your software application product; (iii) include a valid copyright notice on your software application product; (iv) indemnify, hold harmless, and defend Microsoft from and against any claims or lawsuits, including attorney's fees, that arise or result from the use or distribution of your software application product; and (v) not permit further distribution of the REDISTRIBUTABLES by your end user. Contact Microsoft for the applicable royalties due and other licensing terms for all other uses and/or distribution of the REDISTRIBUTABLES.

2. **DESCRIPTION OF OTHER RIGHTS AND LIMITATIONS.**

   - **Limitations on Reverse Engineering, Decompilation, and Disassembly.** You may not reverse engineer, decompile, or disassemble the SOFTWARE PRODUCT, except and only to the extent that such activity is expressly permitted by applicable law notwithstanding this limitation.

   - **Separation of Components.** The SOFTWARE PRODUCT is licensed as a single product. Its component parts may not be separated for use on more than one computer.

   - **Rental.** You may not rent, lease, or lend the SOFTWARE PRODUCT.

- **Support Services.** Microsoft may, but is not obligated to, provide you with support services related to the SOFTWARE PRODUCT ("Support Services"). Use of Support Services is governed by the Microsoft policies and programs described in the user manual, in "online" documentation, and/or in other Microsoft-provided materials. Any supplemental software code provided to you as part of the Support Services shall be considered part of the SOFTWARE PRODUCT and subject to the terms and conditions of this EULA. With respect to technical information you provide to Microsoft as part of the Support Services, Microsoft may use such information for its business purposes, including for product support and development. Microsoft will not utilize such technical information in a form that personally identifies you.

- **Software Transfer.** You may permanently transfer all of your rights under this EULA, provided you retain no copies, you transfer all of the SOFTWARE PRODUCT (including all component parts, the media and printed materials, any upgrades, this EULA, and, if applicable, the Certificate of Authenticity), **and** the recipient agrees to the terms of this EULA.

- **Termination.** Without prejudice to any other rights, Microsoft may terminate this EULA if you fail to comply with the terms and conditions of this EULA. In such event, you must destroy all copies of the SOFTWARE PRODUCT and all of its component parts.

3. **COPYRIGHT.** All title and copyrights in and to the SOFTWARE PRODUCT (including but not limited to any images, photographs, animations, video, audio, music, text, SAMPLE CODE, REDISTRIBUTABLES, and "applets" incorporated into the SOFTWARE PRODUCT) and any copies of the SOFTWARE PRODUCT are owned by Microsoft or its suppliers. The SOFT-WARE PRODUCT is protected by copyright laws and international treaty provisions. Therefore, you must treat the SOFTWARE PRODUCT like any other copyrighted material **except** that you may install the SOFTWARE PRODUCT on a single computer provided you keep the original solely for backup or archival purposes. You may not copy the printed materials accompanying the SOFTWARE PRODUCT.

4. **U.S. GOVERNMENT RESTRICTED RIGHTS.** The SOFTWARE PRODUCT and documentation are provided with RESTRICTED RIGHTS. Use, duplication, or disclosure by the Government is subject to restrictions as set forth in subparagraph (c)(1)(ii) of the Rights in Technical Data and Computer Software clause at DFARS 252.227-7013 or subparagraphs (c)(1) and (2) of the Commercial Computer Software—Restricted Rights at 48 CFR 52.227-19, as applicable. Manufacturer is Microsoft Corporation/One Microsoft Way/Redmond, WA 98052-6399.

5. **EXPORT RESTRICTIONS.** You agree that you will not export or re-export the SOFTWARE PRODUCT, any part thereof, or any process or service that is the direct product of the SOFTWARE PRODUCT (the foregoing collectively referred to as the "Restricted Components"), to any country, person, entity, or end user subject to U.S. export restrictions. You specifically agree not to export or re-export any of the Restricted Components (i) to any country to which the U.S. has embargoed or restricted the export of goods or services, which currently include, but are not necessarily limited to, Cuba, Iran, Iraq, Libya, North Korea, Sudan, and Syria, or to any national of any such country, wherever located, who intends to transmit or transport the Restricted Components back to such country; (ii) to any end user who you know or have reason to know will utilize the Restricted Components in the design, development, or production of nuclear, chemical, or biological weapons; or (iii) to any end user who has been prohibited from participating in U.S. export transactions by any federal agency of the U.S. government. You warrant and represent that neither the BXA nor any other U.S. federal agency has suspended, revoked, or denied your export privileges.

DISCLAIMER OF WARRANTY

NO WARRANTIES OR CONDITIONS. MICROSOFT EXPRESSLY DISCLAIMS ANY WARRANTY OR CONDITION FOR THE SOFTWARE PRODUCT. THE SOFTWARE PRODUCT AND ANY RELATED DOCUMENTATION ARE PROVIDED "AS IS" WITHOUT WARRANTY OR CONDITION OF ANY KIND, EITHER EXPRESS OR IMPLIED, INCLUDING, WITHOUT LIMITA-TION, THE IMPLIED WARRANTIES OF MERCHANTABILITY, FITNESS FOR A PARTICULAR PURPOSE, OR NONINFRINGEMENT. THE ENTIRE RISK ARISING OUT OF USE OR PERFORMANCE OF THE SOFTWARE PRODUCT REMAINS WITH YOU.

LIMITATION OF LIABILITY. TO THE MAXIMUM EXTENT PERMITTED BY APPLICABLE LAW, IN NO EVENT SHALL MICROSOFT OR ITS SUPPLIERS BE LIABLE FOR ANY SPECIAL, INCIDENTAL, INDIRECT, OR CONSEQUENTIAL DAM-AGES WHATSOEVER (INCLUDING, WITHOUT LIMITATION, DAMAGES FOR LOSS OF BUSINESS PROFITS, BUSINESS INTERRUPTION, LOSS OF BUSINESS INFORMATION, OR ANY OTHER PECUNIARY LOSS) ARISING OUT OF THE USE OF OR INABILITY TO USE THE SOFTWARE PRODUCT OR THE PROVISION OF OR FAILURE TO PROVIDE SUPPORT SERVICES, EVEN IF MICROSOFT HAS BEEN ADVISED OF THE POSSIBILITY OF SUCH DAMAGES. IN ANY CASE, MICROSOFT'S ENTIRE LIABILITY UNDER ANY PROVISION OF THIS EULA SHALL BE LIMITED TO THE GREATER OF THE AMOUNT ACTUALLY PAID BY YOU FOR THE SOFTWARE PRODUCT OR US$5.00; PROVIDED, HOWEVER, IF YOU HAVE ENTERED INTO A MICROSOFT SUPPORT SERVICES AGREEMENT, MICROSOFT'S ENTIRE LIABILITY REGARDING SUPPORT SERVICES SHALL BE GOVERNED BY THE TERMS OF THAT AGREEMENT. BECAUSE SOME STATES AND JURISDICTIONS DO NOT ALLOW THE EXCLUSION OR LIMITATION OF LIABILITY, THE ABOVE LIMITATION MAY NOT APPLY TO YOU.

MISCELLANEOUS

This EULA is governed by the laws of the State of Washington USA, except and only to the extent that applicable law mandates govern-ing law of a different jurisdiction.

Should you have any questions concerning this EULA, or if you desire to contact Microsoft for any reason, please contact the Microsoft subsidiary serving your country, or write: Microsoft Sales Information Center/One Microsoft Way/Redmond, WA 98052-6399.

Register Today!

Return this
Dynamic HTML Reference and Software Development Kit
registration card today

Microsoft Press
mspress.microsoft.com

Dynamic HTML Reference and Software Development Kit

FIRST NAME   MIDDLE INITIAL   LAST NAME

INSTITUTION OR COMPANY NAME

ADDRESS

CITY   STATE   ZIP

(   )

E-MAIL ADDRESS   PHONE NUMBER

U.S. and Canada addresses only. Fill in information above and mail postage-free.
Please mail only the bottom half of this page.

For information about Microsoft Press®
products, visit our Web site at
mspress.microsoft.com

Microsoft Press